MANAGERIAL ACCOUNTING

NINTH CANADIAN EDITION

MANAGERIAL ACCOUNTING

NINTH CANADIAN EDITION

Ray H. Garrison, D.B.A., CPA
Professor Emeritus
Brigham Young University

Eric W. Noreen, Ph.D., CMA
Professor Emeritus
University of Washington

Peter C. Brewer, Ph.D., CPA
Miami University—Oxford, Ohio

G. Richard Chesley, Ph.D.
Professor Emeritus
Saint Mary's University

Ray F. Carroll, Ph.D., FCGA
Dalhousie University

Alan Webb, Ph.D., FCA
University of Waterloo

Theresa Libby, Ph.D., CA
University of Waterloo

McGraw-Hill
Ryerson
Connect. Learn. Succeed.

MANAGERIAL ACCOUNTING
Ninth Canadian Edition

ISBN-13: 978-0-07-040189-1
ISBN-10: 0-07-040189-6

3 4 5 6 7 8 9 QG 1 9 8 7 6 5 4 3

Printed and bound in the United States of America.

Care has been taken to trace ownership of copyright material contained in this text; however, the publisher will welcome any information that enables it to rectify any reference or credit for subsequent editions.

Executive Sponsoring Editor: Rhondda McNabb
Executive Marketing Manager: Joy Armitage Taylor
Developmental Editor: Lindsay MacDonald
Senior Editorial Associate: Christine Lomas
Supervising Editor: Jessica Barnoski
Photo/Permissions Research: Indu Arora
Copy Editor: June Trusty
Production Coordinator: Sheryl MacAdam
Cover Design: Katherine Strain
Cover Image: Richard T. Nowitz/Getty Images
Interior Design: Katherine Strain
Page Layout: Aptara®, Inc.
Printer: Quad/Graphics Versailles

Library and Archives Canada Cataloguing in Publication

Managerial accounting / Ray H. Garrison . . . [et al.]. — 9th Canadian ed.

Includes bibliographical references and index.
ISBN 978-0-07-040189-1

1. Managerial accounting—Textbooks. I. Garrison, Ray H.

HF5657.4.M38 2012   658.15'11   C2011-904393-9

Dedication

This book builds on the foundation created by Dick Chesley and Raymond Carroll. Their long-standing dedication to making managerial accounting understandable inspired our efforts in this ninth edition.

About the Authors

Ray H. Garrison is Emeritus Professor of Accounting at Brigham Young University, Provo, Utah. He received his B.S. and M.S. degrees from Brigham Young University and his D.B.A. degree from Indiana University. As a certified public accountant, Professor Garrison has been involved in management consulting work with both national and regional accounting firms. He has published articles in *The Accounting Review, Management Accounting*, and other professional journals. Innovation in the classroom has earned Professor Garrison the Karl G. Maeser Distinguished Teaching Award from Brigham Young University.

Eric W. Noreen is Professor Emeritus of Accounting at the University of Washington and was Visiting Price Waterhouse Professor of Management Information & Control at INSEAD, an international graduate school of business located in France, and a professor at the Hong Kong University of Science and Technology. He received his B.A. degree from the University of Washington and M.B.A. and Ph.D. degrees from Stanford University. A Certified Management Accountant, he was awarded a Certificate of Distinguished Performance by the Institute of Certified Management Accountants. Professor Noreen has served as Associate Editor of *The Accounting Review* and the *Journal of Accounting and Economics*. He has published numerous articles in academic journals, and has won a number of awards for his teaching.

Peter C. Brewer is an Associate Professor in the Department of Accountancy at Miami University, Oxford, Ohio. He holds a B.S. degree in accounting from Penn State University, an M.S. degree in accounting from the University of Virginia, and a Ph.D. from the University of Tennessee. He has published numerous articles in a variety of journals. Professor Brewer has received Miami University's Richard T. Farmer School of Business Teaching Excellence Award and has been recognized on two occasions by the Miami University Associated Student Government for "making a remarkable commitment to students and their educational development." He is a leader in undergraduate management accounting curriculum innovation and the use of the case method for teaching undergraduate management accounting courses. He is a frequent presenter at various professional and academic conferences and meetings.

G. Richard Chesley is Professor Emeritus of Accounting at Saint Mary's University in Halifax, Nova Scotia. He is a graduate of Mount Allison University and Ohio State University, with B. Comm., M.A., and Ph.D. degrees. He has held appointments at Dalhousie University, the University of Pennsylvania, Hong Kong's Lingnan University, Hong Kong Baptist University, and the University of Iowa. Professor Chesley has also conducted lectures and presentations throughout Canada, the United States, and abroad, both east and west. His publications appear in *The Accounting Review,* the *Journal of Accounting Research, CA Magazine, CMA Management* magazine, and numerous books and proceedings. Research interests include Web-based reporting, non-monetary reporting, accounting regulation, and management accounting practices. In 1996, his efforts were recognized by his peers with the L. S. Rosen Outstanding Educator Award by the Canadian Academic Accounting Association. In 2005, Saint Mary's University recognized his university efforts with its inaugural Exemplary Service Award. The honourary position of Professor Emeritus was awarded by Saint Mary's University in 2007.

Ray F. Carroll was Associate Professor of Accounting at Dalhousie University in Halifax, Nova Scotia. He was a graduate of Saint Francis Xavier University, where he completed his B.B.A. and B.Ed. degrees, and Dalhousie University, from which he obtained M.B.A. and Ph.D. degrees. Professor Carroll taught at Hong Kong Baptist University and lectured in various international MBA programs throughout Hong Kong and Mainland China. His publications in recent years appeared in the *Journal of International Business, Teaching Business Ethics,* and the *Journal of Intellectual Capital.* He was a Fellow of Certified General Accountants–Canada and a member of the Institute of Management Accountants of Australia. He served as chairperson of the Canadian Certified General Accountants' National Education Committee and as a member of the American Accounting Association's Globalization Initiatives Committee. Professor Carroll passed away in February 2008 after a lengthy illness.

R. Alan Webb is an Associate Professor in the School of Accounting and Finance at the University of Waterloo. He is a graduate of Mount Allison University and the University of Alberta, with B. Comm. and Ph.D. degrees. His primary research interests are in the areas of goal-setting, incentives and performance measurement. Professor Webb has presented his work throughout North America and he is an Associate Editor of *Contemporary Accounting Research.* His recent publications appear in *The Accounting Review, Journal of Accounting Research, Journal of Management Accounting Research, Contemporary Accounting Research, Issues in Accounting Education, CA Magazine,* and *CMA Management* magazine. He is a fellow of the Chartered Institute of Accountants of Ontario and has volunteered in numerous professional activities both in Canada and abroad. In 2011, Professor Webb was awarded the L. S. Rosen Outstanding Educator Award by the Canadian Academic Accounting Association.

Theresa Libby is a Professor of Accounting in the School of Accounting and Finance, University of Waterloo. She received her Ph.D. from the University of Waterloo and a B. Comm. from the University of Windsor. Professor Libby is also a chartered accountant. Her research interests include the manager's use of accounting information for decision making, the effects of budgeting processes on performance, and accounting ethics. She has published articles in *CA Magazine* and *CMA Management,* as well as in leading research journals including *The Accounting Review, Contemporary Accounting Research, Business Ethics Quarterly,* and the *Journal of Management Accounting Research.* Professor Libby sits on the editorial boards of *Contemporary Accounting Research* and *Management Accounting Research* and has served as the editor of *Behavioral Research in Accounting.*

Brief Contents

SECTION 1   Overview and Foundation   1

Chapter One   Managerial Accounting and the Business Environment   2

Chapter Two   Cost Terms, Concepts, and Classifications   30

SECTION 2   Costing   68

Chapter Three   Systems Design: Job-Order Costing   69

Chapter Four   Systems Design: Process Costing   128

Chapter Five   Activity-Based Costing: A Tool to Aid Decision Making   171

Chapter Six   Cost Behaviour: Analysis and Use   229

Chapter Seven   Cost–Volume–Profit Relationships   269

Chapter Eight   Variable Costing: A Tool for Management   314

SECTION 3   Planning and Control   348

Chapter Nine   Budgeting   349

Chapter Ten   Standard Costs and Overhead Analysis   403

Chapter Eleven   Reporting for Control   473

SECTION 4   Short-Term and Long-Term Decisions   553

Chapter Twelve   Relevant Costs for Decision Making   554

Chapter Thirteen   Capital Budgeting Decisions   609

SECTION 5   External Reporting and Analysis   675

Online Chapter Fourteen   Financial Statement Analysis   1

Endnotes   677

Photo Credits   681

Company/Name Index   I–1

Subject Index   I–3

Contents

SECTION 1

Overview and Foundation   1

Chapter One

Managerial Accounting and the Business Environment   2

THE WORK OF MANAGERS AND THEIR NEED FOR MANAGERIAL ACCOUNTING INFORMATION   3

Planning   4

Directing and Motivating   5

Controlling   5

The Results of Managers' Activities   5

The Planning and Control Cycle   5

The Business Plan   6

COMPARISON OF FINANCIAL AND MANAGERIAL ACCOUNTING   8

Emphasis on the Future   8

Relevance of Data   9

Less Emphasis on Precision   9

Segments of an Organization   9

Generally Accepted Accounting Principles   9

Managerial Accounting—Not Mandatory   10

ORGANIZATIONAL STRUCTURE   10

Decentralization   10

Line and Staff Relationships   11

The Controller   11

THE PROFESSIONAL MANAGEMENT ACCOUNTANT   12

PROFESSIONAL ETHICS   12

Corporate Governance   13

Corporate Social Responsibility   16

PROCESS MANAGEMENT   17

Lean Production   18

The Lean Thinking Model   18

Six Sigma   20

Enterprise Systems   21

Enterprise Risk Management   21

Identifying and Controlling Business Risks   22

Summary   23

Questions   23

Exercises   24

Problems   25

Research   29

Chapter Two

Cost Terms, Concepts, and Classifications   30

GENERAL COST CLASSIFICATIONS   31

Manufacturing Costs   31

Direct Materials   31

Direct Labour   32

Manufacturing Overhead   32

Classification of Labour Costs of Manufacturing   32

Non-Manufacturing Costs   33

PRODUCT COSTS VERSUS PERIOD COSTS   34

Product Costs   35

Period Costs   35

COST CLASSIFICATIONS ON FINANCIAL STATEMENTS   35

The Balance Sheet   35

The Income Statement   37

SCHEDULE OF COST OF GOODS MANUFACTURED   40

Product Costs—A Closer Look   41

Inventoriable Costs   42

An Example of Cost Flows   42

COST CLASSIFICATIONS FOR PREDICTING
COST BEHAVIOUR   43
   Variable Cost   44
   Fixed Cost   45

COST CLASSIFICATIONS FOR ASSIGNING
COSTS TO COST OBJECTS   46
   Direct Cost   46
   Indirect Cost   46

COST CLASSIFICATIONS FOR DECISION
MAKING   46
   Differential Cost and Revenue   46
   Opportunity Cost   48
   Sunk Cost   48

Summary   49
Review Problem 1: Cost Terms   49
Review Problem 2: Schedule of Cost of Goods Manufactured and
   Income Statement   51
Questions   52
Exercises   53
Problems   57
Cases   65
Research   67

SECTION 2
Costing   68

Chapter Three
Systems Design: Job-Order Costing   69

PROCESS AND JOB-ORDER COSTING   71
   Process Costing   71
   Job-Order Costing   71

JOB-ORDER COSTING—AN OVERVIEW   72
   Measuring Direct Materials Cost   72
   Job Cost Sheet   73
   Measuring Direct Labour Cost   73

CALCULATING PREDETERMINED
MANUFACTURING OVERHEAD RATES   76
   Using the Predetermined Overhead Rate   76
   The Need for a Predetermined Rate   78
   Choice of an Allocation Base for Overhead
      Cost   78

   Computation of Unit Costs   79
   Summary of Document Flows   79

JOB-ORDER COSTING—THE FLOW
OF COSTS   80
   The Purchase and Issue of Materials   80
      Issue of Direct and Indirect Materials   80
      Issue of Direct Materials Only   81
   Labour Cost   81
   Manufacturing Overhead Costs   81

THE APPLICATION OF MANUFACTURING
OVERHEAD   82
      The Concept of a Clearing Account   83
   Non-Manufacturing Costs   84

COST OF GOODS MANUFACTURED   85
   Cost of Goods Sold   86
   Summary of Cost Flows   86

COMPLICATIONS OF OVERHEAD
APPLICATION   89
   Underapplied and Overapplied Overhead   89
   Disposition of Underapplied or Overapplied
      Overhead Balances   91
      Close Out to Cost of Goods Sold   91
      Allocate among Accounts   91
      Carry the Balance Forward   92
   A General Model of Product Cost Flows   93
   Variations from the General Model of
      Product Cost Flow   94
   Multiple Predetermined Overhead
      Rates   94

USE OF INFORMATION TECHNOLOGY   95

INTERNATIONAL JOB COSTING   96

Summary   97
Review Problem: Job-Order Costing   97
Questions   100
Exercises   101
Problems   108
Cases   119
Research and Application   121

APPENDIX 3A: THE PREDETERMINED OVERHEAD
RATE AND CAPACITY   122

Chapter Four

Systems Design: Process Costing   128

COMPARISON OF JOB-ORDER AND PROCESS COSTING   129

PROCESS COST FLOWS   130

Processing Departments   130

The Flow of Materials, Labour, and Overhead Costs   131

Materials, Labour, and Overhead Cost Entries   132

Materials Costs   132

Labour Costs   133

Overhead Costs   133

Completing the Cost Flows   133

EQUIVALENT UNITS OF PRODUCTION   134

Weighted-Average Method   135

COMPUTE AND APPLY COSTS   137

Cost per Equivalent Unit—Weighted-Average Method   137

APPLYING COSTS—WEIGHTED-AVERAGE METHOD   138

Summary of Double Diamond Skis Costing   139

OPERATION COSTING   140

FLEXIBLE MANUFACTURING SYSTEMS   141

Summary   141

Review Problem 1: Process Cost Flows and Reports   142

Review Problem 2: Units and Cost Assignment   144

Questions   145

Exercises   145

Problems   148

Cases   152

Research and Application   154

APPENDIX 4A: FIFO METHOD   154

Equivalent Units—FIFO Method   155

Comparison of Equivalent Units of Production under the Weighted-Average and FIFO Methods   155

PRODUCTION REPORT—FIFO METHOD   157

A Comparison of Costing Methods   159

APPENDIX 4B: SERVICE DEPARTMENT ALLOCATIONS   163

Interdepartmental Services   163

DIRECT METHOD   164

STEP-DOWN METHOD   165

RECIPROCAL METHOD   166

Revenue-Producing Department   167

ONLINE APPENDIX 4C: SHRINKAGE AND LOST UNITS

Chapter Five

Activity-Based Costing: A Tool to Aid Decision Making   171

THE TREATMENT OF COSTS UNDER THE ACTIVITY-BASED COSTING MODEL   172

Non-Manufacturing Costs and Activity-Based Costing   172

Manufacturing Costs and Activity-Based Costing   173

Cost Pools, Allocation Bases, and Activity-Based Costing   173

The Costs of Idle Capacity in Activity-Based Costing   174

Designing an Activity-Based Costing System   174

Step 1: Identify and Define Activities, Activity Cost Pools, and Activity Measures   176

THE MECHANICS OF ACTIVITY-BASED COSTING   178

Step 2: Assign Overhead Costs to Activity Cost Pools   178

Step 3: Calculate Activity Rates   180

SECOND-STAGE ALLOCATION OF OVERHEAD COSTS   182

Step 4: Assign Overhead Costs to Cost Objects   182

PRODUCT AND CUSTOMER MARGINS   184

Step 5: Prepare Management Reports   184

Targeting Process Improvements   186

COMPARISON OF TRADITIONAL AND ABC
PRODUCT COSTS   186

*Product Margins Computed Using the Traditional
Cost System   187*

*The Differences between ABC and Traditional
Product Costs   188*

Activity-Based Costing and External Reports   189

THE LIMITATIONS OF ACTIVITY-BASED
COSTING   191

Summary   193
Review Problem: Activity-Based Costing   193
Questions   195
Exercises   195
Problems   203
Cases   207
Research and Application   210

APPENDIX 5A: ABC ACTION ANALYSIS   211

Activity Rates—Action Analysis Report   211

*Assignment of Overhead Costs to Products—Action
Analysis Report   211*

Ease of Adjustment Codes   214

The Action Analysis View of the ABC Data   214

Wrap-Up   215

*APPENDIX 5B: USING A MODIFIED FORM OF
ACTIVITY-BASED COSTING TO DETERMINE
PRODUCT COSTS FOR EXTERNAL REPORTS   221*

Chapter Six
Cost Behaviour: Analysis and Use   229

TYPES OF COST BEHAVIOUR PATTERNS   230

Variable Costs   230
The Activity Base   231
Extent of Variable Costs   232
True Variable versus Step-Variable Costs   232
True Variable Costs   233
Step-Variable Costs   233
*The Linearity Assumption and the Relevant
Range   234*
Fixed Costs   234
Types of Fixed Costs   235
Committed Fixed Costs   236
Discretionary Fixed Costs   236

The Trend toward Fixed Costs   236
Is Labour a Variable or a Fixed Cost?   237
Fixed Costs and the Relevant Range   238
Mixed Costs   239

THE ANALYSIS OF MIXED COSTS   240

*Diagnosing Cost Behaviour with a Scattergram
Plot   241*
The High–Low Method   244

THE CONTRIBUTION FORMAT   247

Why a New Income Statement Format?   247
The Contribution Approach   247

Summary   248
Review Problem 1: Cost Behaviour   249
Review Problem 2: High–Low Method   249
Questions   250
Exercises   251
Problems   254
Cases   259
Research and Application   262

*APPENDIX 6A: LEAST-SQUARES REGRESSION
CALCULATIONS   262*

Economic Plausibility   264
Multiple Regression Analysis   265

Chapter Seven
Cost–Volume–Profit Relationships   269

THE BASICS OF COST–VOLUME–PROFIT
ANALYSIS   270

Contribution Margin   271

CVP RELATIONSHIPS IN GRAPHIC FORM   273

Preparing the CVP Graph   273

CONTRIBUTION MARGIN RATIO   275

SOME APPLICATIONS OF CVP CONCEPTS   276

Change in Fixed Cost and Sales Volume   277

Change in Variable Costs and Sales Volume   278

*Change in Fixed Costs, Selling Price, and Sales
Volume   278*

*Change in Variable Cost, Fixed Cost, and Sales
Volume   279*

Change in Regular Selling Price 280

Importance of the Contribution Margin 280

BREAK-EVEN ANALYSIS 281

Break-Even Computations 281

The Equation Method 281

The Contribution Margin Method 282

TARGET OPERATING PROFIT ANALYSIS 283

The CVP Equation 283

The Contribution Margin Approach 283

After-Tax Analysis 284

THE MARGIN OF SAFETY 285

CVP CONSIDERATIONS IN CHOOSING A COST
STRUCTURE 285

Cost Structure and Profit Stability 285

Operating Leverage 287

*Automation: Risks and Rewards from a CVP
Perspective 289*

Indifference Analysis 289

THE CONCEPT OF SALES MIX 290

The Definition of Sales Mix 290

Sales Mix and Break-Even Analysis 291

ASSUMPTIONS OF CVP ANALYSIS 293

Summary 293

Review Problem: CVP Relationships 294

Questions 296

Exercises 297

Problems 302

Cases 311

Research and Application 313

*ONLINE APPENDIX 7A: COST–VOLUME–PROFIT
WITH UNCERTAINTY*

Chapter Eight
Variable Costing: A Tool for Management 314

OVERVIEW OF ABSORPTION AND VARIABLE
COST 315

Absorption Costing 315

Variable Costing 315

Selling and Administrative Expense 316

Unit Cost Computations 316

INCOME COMPARISON OF ABSORPTION AND
VARIABLE COSTING 317

EXTENDED COMPARISON OF INCOME
DATA 319

*Effect of Changes in Production on Operating
Income 323*

Variable Costing 323

Absorption Costing 323

CHOOSING A COSTING METHOD 325

The Impact on the Manager 325

CVP Analysis and Absorption Costing 326

Decision Making 327

*External Reporting, Income Taxes, and Management
Performance Evaluation 327*

*Advantages of Variable Costing and the Contribution
Approach 327*

IMPACT OF LEAN PRODUCTION 329

Summary 330

*Review Problem: Contrasting Variable and Absorption
Costing 330*

Questions 332

Exercises 333

Problems 337

Cases 343

Research and Application 347

SECTION 3
Planning and Control 348

Chapter Nine
Budgeting 349

THE BASIC FRAMEWORK OF
BUDGETING 350

Definition of Budgeting 350

*Budgets' Dual Role: Planning and
Control 350*

Advantages of Budgeting 350

Responsibility Accounting 351

Choosing a Budget Period 351

The Participative Budget 352

Behavioural Factors in Budgeting 353

Zero-Base Budgeting 355

THE MASTER BUDGET: AN OVERVIEW 355
    The Sales Budget 355
    The Cash Budget 355
   Sales Forecasting—A Critical Step 355
   Preparing the Master Budget 356
   The Sales Budget 357
   The Production Budget 357
   Inventory Purchases—Merchandising Firm 359
   The Direct Materials Purchases Budget 359
   The Direct Labour Budget 360
   The Manufacturing Overhead Budget 361
   The Ending Finished Goods Inventory Budget 362
   The Selling and Administrative Expense Budget 363
   The Cash Budget 364
   The Budgeted Income Statement 366
   The Budgeted Balance Sheet 367

FLEXIBLE BUDGET 369
   How a Flexible Budget Works 369

USING THE FLEXIBLE BUDGETING CONCEPT IN PERFORMANCE EVALUATION 370

BUDGETING FOR NOT-FOR-PROFIT ENTITIES 374
   Activity-Based Budgeting 375

INTERNATIONAL ASPECTS OF BUDGETING 375

Summary 376
Review Problem: Completing a Master Budget 376
Questions 380
Exercises 381
Problems 385
Cases 396
Research and Application 402

ONLINE APPENDIX 9A: INVENTORY DECISIONS

Chapter Ten
Standard Costs and Overhead Analysis 403

STANDARD COSTS—MANAGEMENT BY EXCEPTION 405

SETTING STANDARD COSTS 406
   Who Uses Standard Costs? 406
   Ideal versus Practical Standards 406

Setting Direct Materials Standards 407
Setting Direct Labour Standards 408
Setting Variable Manufacturing Overhead Standards 409
Are Standards the Same as Budgets? 410
A General Model for Variance Analysis 410

USING STANDARD COSTS—DIRECT MATERIALS VARIANCES 411
   Materials Price Variance—A Closer Look 413
     Isolation of Variances 414
     Responsibility for the Variance 414
   Materials Quantity Variance—A Closer Look 415

USING STANDARD COSTS—DIRECT LABOUR VARIANCES 416
   Labour Rate Variance—A Closer Look 416
   Labour Efficiency Variance—A Closer Look 417

USING STANDARD COSTS—VARIABLE MANUFACTURING OVERHEAD VARIANCES 418
   Variable Manufacturing Overhead Variances—A Closer Look 419
     Interpreting the Spending Variance 419
     Interpreting the Efficiency Variance 420
     Control of the Efficiency Variance 421

OVERHEAD RATES AND FIXED OVERHEAD ANALYSIS 421
   Flexible Budgets and Overhead Rates 422
     Denominator Activity 422
     Computing the Overhead Rate 423

OVERHEAD APPLICATION AND FIXED OVERHEAD VARIANCES 424
   Overhead Application in a Standard Cost System 424
   Budget Variance 425
   Volume Variance 425
   Graphic Analysis of Fixed Overhead Variances 426
   Cautions in Fixed Overhead Analysis 427
   Overhead Variances and Under- or Overapplied Overhead Cost 427

OVERHEAD REPORTING, VARIANCE
INVESTIGATIONS, AND CAPACITY
ANALYSIS   428

   Variance Investigation Decisions   430

   Capacity Analysis   432

INTERNATIONAL USES OF STANDARD
COSTS   433

EVALUATION OF CONTROLS BASED ON
STANDARD COSTS   433

   Advantages of Standard Costs   433

   *Potential Problems with the Use of Standard
      Costs   433*

Summary   435

Review Problem: Standard Costs   436

Questions   438

Exercises   438

Problems   444

Cases   456

Research and Application   461

*APPENDIX 10A: FURTHER ANALYSIS OF
MATERIALS VARIANCES   462*

*APPENDIX 10B: GENERAL LEDGER ENTRIES TO
RECORD VARIANCES   467*

   Direct Materials Variances   467

   Direct Labour Variances   468

   *Variable and Fixed Manufacturing Overhead
      Variances   468*

   Cost Flows in a Standard Cost System   468

*ONLINE APPENDIX 10C: PREDICTION OF LABOUR
TIME—LEARNING CURVE*

Chapter Eleven

Reporting for Control   473

DECENTRALIZATION IN ORGANIZATIONS   474

   Decentralization and Segment Reporting   475

SEGMENT REPORTING   475

   Differing Levels of Segmented Statements   475

   Assigning Costs to Segments   477

   Sales and Contribution Margin   477

The Importance of Fixed Costs   478

Traceable and Common Fixed Costs   478

Identifying Traceable Fixed Costs   479

Breakdown of Traceable Fixed Costs   479

   Activity-Based Costing   480

Traceable Costs Can Become Common   480

Segment Margin   481

Segment Reporting for Financial Accounting   482

Hindrances to Proper Cost Assignment   482

   Omission of Costs   482

   Inappropriate Methods for Assigning Traceable
      Costs among Segments   482

   Failure to Trace Costs Directly   482

   Inappropriate Allocation Base   483

   Arbitrarily Dividing Common Costs among
      Segments   483

RESPONSIBILITY CENTRES   484

   Cost Centre   484

   Profit Centre   484

   Investment Centre   484

TRANSFER PRICING   485

   Negotiated Transfer Prices   486

   The Selling Division's Lowest Acceptable
      Transfer Price   487

   The Purchasing Division's Highest Acceptable
      Transfer Price   487

   Selling Division with Idle Capacity   488

   Selling Division with No Idle Capacity   488

   Selling Division with Some Idle Capacity   489

   No Outside Supplier   489

   Evaluation of Negotiated Transfer Prices   490

   Transfers to the Selling Division at Cost   490

   Transfers at Market Price   490

   Divisional Autonomy and Suboptimization   491

   International Aspects of Transfer Pricing   491

EVALUATING INVESTMENT CENTRE
PERFORMANCE—RETURN ON
INVESTMENT   492

   The Return on Investment (ROI) Formula   492

   *Operating Income and Operating Assets
      Defined   492*

Understanding ROI 493

    Example 1: Increased Sales without Any Increase in Operating Assets 495

    Example 2: Decreased Operating Expenses with No Change in Sales or Operating Assets 496

    Example 3: Invest in Operating Assets to Increase Sales 496

Criticisms of ROI 497

RESIDUAL INCOME 497

Motivation and Residual Income 498

Divisional Comparison and Residual Income 499

Criticisms of Residual Income 500

BALANCED SCORECARD 500

Common Characteristics of Balanced Scorecards 501

A Company's Strategy and the Balanced Scorecard 503

Tying Compensation to the Balanced Scorecard 504

Advantages of Timely Feedback 504

Some Measures of Internal Business Process Performance 505

    Delivery Cycle Time 505

    Throughput (Manufacturing Cycle) Time 505

    Manufacturing Cycle Efficiency (MCE) 505

    Some Final Observations Concerning the Balanced Scorecard 507

COST OF QUALITY 507

Quality of Conformance 508

Prevention Costs 508

Appraisal Costs 509

Internal Failure Costs 510

External Failure Costs 510

Distribution of Quality Costs 510

Quality Cost Reports 511

Quality Cost Reports in Graphic Form 512

Uses of Quality Cost Information 512

International Aspects of Quality 513

Summary 514

Review Problem 1: Segmented Statements 515

Review Problem 2: Transfer Pricing 516

Review Problem 3: Return on Investment (ROI) and Residual Income 517

Questions 518

Exercises 519

Problems 525

Cases 539

Research and Application 544

APPENDIX 11A: PROFITABILITY ANALYSIS 544

Sales Variance Analysis 544

APPENDIX 11B: MARKETING EXPENSE 548

SECTION 4

Short-Term and Long-Term Decisions 553

Chapter Twelve

Relevant Costs for Decision Making 554

COST CONCEPTS FOR DECISION MAKING 555

Identifying Relevant Costs and Benefits 555

Different Costs for Different Purposes 556

An Example of Identifying Relevant Costs and Benefits 556

Reconciling the Total and Differential Approaches 558

Why Isolate Relevant Costs? 560

ANALYSIS OF VARIOUS DECISION SITUATIONS 561

Adding and Dropping Product Lines and Other Segments 561

A Comparative Format 563

Beware of Allocated Fixed Costs 563

The Make or Buy Decision 565

Strategic Aspects of the Make or Buy Decision 566

An Example of Make or Buy 566

Opportunity Cost 567

Special Orders 569

Joint Product Costs and the Sell or Process Further Decision 571

The Pitfalls of Allocation 572

Sell or Process Further Decisions 572

UTILIZATION OF A CONSTRAINED RESOURCE 573

Contribution Margin in Relation to a Constrained Resource 574

Managing Constraints 575

The Problem of Multiple Constraints 576

Summary 576

Review Problem: Relevant Costs 576

Questions 578

Exercises 578

Problems 585

Cases 592

Research and Application 598

APPENDIX 12A: PRICING PRODUCTS AND
SERVICES 598

Cost-Plus Pricing 599

Setting a Target Selling Price Using the Absorption
Costing Approach 599

Determining the Markup Percentage 600

Problems with the Absorption Costing
Approach 601

Setting a Target Selling Price Using the Variable
Costing Approach 601

Setting a Target Selling Price for Service Companies
Using Time and Materials Pricing 602

Time Component 602

Materials Component 603

An Example of Time and Materials Pricing 603

TARGET COSTING 604

Reasons for Using Target Costing 604

An Example of Target Costing 605

Chapter Thirteen
Capital Budgeting Decisions 609

CAPITAL BUDGETING—PLANNING
INVESTMENTS 610

Typical Capital Budgeting Decisions 610

The Time Value of Money 610

DISCOUNTED CASH FLOWS—THE NET PRESENT
VALUE METHOD 611

The Net Present Value Method Illustrated 611

Emphasis on Cash Flows 612

Typical Cash Outflows 612

Typical Cash Inflows 613

Recovery of the Original Investment 613

Simplifying Assumptions 614

Choosing a Discount Rate 615

An Extended Example of the Net Present Value
Method 615

The Total-Cost Approach 616

The Incremental-Cost Approach 617

Least-Cost Decisions 618

DISCOUNTED CASH FLOWS—THE INTERNAL
RATE OF RETURN METHOD 619

The Internal Rate of Return Method
Illustrated 619

Salvage Value and Other Cash Flows 620

Using the Internal Rate of Return 621

The Cost of Capital as a Screening
Tool 621

Comparison of the Net Present Value and the Internal
Rate of Return Methods 621

Real Options 622

UNCERTAIN CASH FLOWS 623

An Example of Uncertain Cash Flows 623

PREFERENCE DECISIONS—THE RANKING OF
INVESTMENT PROJECTS 624

Internal Rate of Return Method 624

Net Present Value Method 624

Comparing the Preference Rules 625

Post-Audit of Investment Projects 626

OTHER APPROACHES TO CAPITAL BUDGETING
DECISIONS 627

The Payback Method 627

Evaluation of the Payback Method 627

An Extended Example of Payback 628

Payback and Uneven Cash Flows 630

THE SIMPLE RATE OF RETURN METHOD 630

Criticisms of the Simple Rate of Return 631

BEHAVIOURAL CONSIDERATIONS 632

Summary 633

Review Problem: Comparison of Capital Budgeting Methods 634

Questions 635

Exercises 636

Problems 639

Cases 646

Research and Application 649

APPENDIX 13A: THE CONCEPT OF PRESENT VALUE 649

The Theory of Interest 649

Compound Interest 650

Present Value and Future Value 650

Present Value of a Series of Cash Flows (Annuity) 652

Present Value of an Annuity Due 653

Deferred Annuities 655

Future Value of an Annuity 655

Using Microsoft Excel 657

APPENDIX 13B: INCOME TAXES IN CAPITAL BUDGETING DECISIONS 664

The Concept of After-Tax Cost 664

Capital Cost Allowance (CCA) Tax Shield 665

Capital Cost Allowance Instead of Depreciation 666

Example of Income Taxes and Capital Budgeting 668

ENDNOTES 677

PHOTO CREDITS 681

COMPANY/NAME INDEX I–1

SUBJECT INDEX I–3

SECTION 5
External Reporting and Analysis 675

Chapter Fourteen ▓ connect
Financial Statement Analysis 1

LIMITATIONS OF FINANCIAL STATEMENT ANALYSIS 2

Comparison of Financial Data 2

The Need to Look beyond Ratios 2

STATEMENTS IN COMPARATIVE AND COMMON-SIZE FORM 2

Dollar and Percentage Changes on Statements 2

Common-Size Statements 5

RATIO ANALYSIS—THE COMMON SHAREHOLDER (PROFITABILITY RATIOS) 7

Earnings per Share 7

Price–Earnings Ratio 7

Dividend Payout and Yield Ratios 8

The Dividend Payout Ratio 8

The Dividend Yield Ratio 8

Return on Total Assets 9

Return on Common Shareholders' Equity 9

Financial Leverage 9

Book Value per Share 10

RATIO ANALYSIS—THE SHORT-TERM CREDITOR (LIQUIDITY RATIOS) 10

Working Capital 10

Current Ratio 11

Acid-Test (Quick) Ratio 11

Accounts Receivable Turnover 12

Inventory Turnover 13

RATIO ANALYSIS—THE LONG-TERM CREDITOR (SOLVENCY RATIOS) 13

Times Interest Earned Ratio 13

Debt-to-Equity Ratio 14

SUMMARY OF RATIOS AND SOURCES OF COMPARATIVE INFORMATION 14

Summary 16

Questions 17

Exercises 17

Problems 21

Garrison/Chesley/Carroll/Webb/Libby:

For centuries, the lighthouse has stood as a beacon of guidance for mariners at sea. More than an aid to navigation, the lighthouse symbolizes safety, permanence, reliability, and the comforts of the familiar.

For this reason, we have chosen to illustrate the ninth Canadian edition of our "flagship" accounting publication, *Managerial Accounting* by Garrison, Chesley, Carroll, Webb, and Libby, with an image that we feel encapsulates the greatest strengths of this market-leading text.

Garrison is your guide through the challenging waters of managerial accounting. It identifies the three functions that managers must perform within their organizations—plan operations, control activities, and make decisions—and explains what accounting information is necessary for these functions, how to collect it, and how to interpret it. To achieve this, the ninth Canadian edition of *Managerial Accounting* focuses, now as in the past, on three qualities:

Your guide through the challenging waters of managerial accounting

Relevance. Every effort is made to help students relate the concepts in this book to the decisions made by working managers. With the insightful chapter openers, scenarios and examples that reflect or discuss real-world examples, and stimulating end-of-chapter exercises, a student reading Garrison should never have to ask, "Why am I learning this?"

Balance. Garrison mixes its coverage to include a variety of business types, including not-for-profit, retail, service, and wholesale organizations, as well as manufacturing. In the ninth Canadian edition, green accounting and the shift to International Financial Reporting Standards (IFRS) are highlighted with icons in the margins of the text.

Clarity. Generations of students have praised Garrison for the friendliness and readability of its writing, but that's just the beginning. Technical discussions have been simplified, material has been reordered, and the entire book has been carefully retuned to make teaching—and learning—from Garrison as easy as it can be. Key term definitions and icons signifying ethics, writing, and Excel assignments continue to add clarity for both students and professors. In addition, students and professors will work with clear, well-written supplements that employ consistent terminology.

The authors' steady focus on these three core elements has led to tremendous results.

What makes Garrison such a powerful learning tool?

Managerial Accounting is full of pedagogy designed to make studying productive and hassle-free. On the following pages, you will see the kind of engaging, helpful pedagogical features that make Garrison a favourite among both teachers and students.

Section Overviews
The ninth Canadian edition is divided into five sections. One-page overviews map the chapters included and how they are related.

Opening Vignettes
These opening pieces, based on real-world scenarios, introduce the chapter and bring forward the issues, concepts, and practices to be discussed in the ensuing pages.

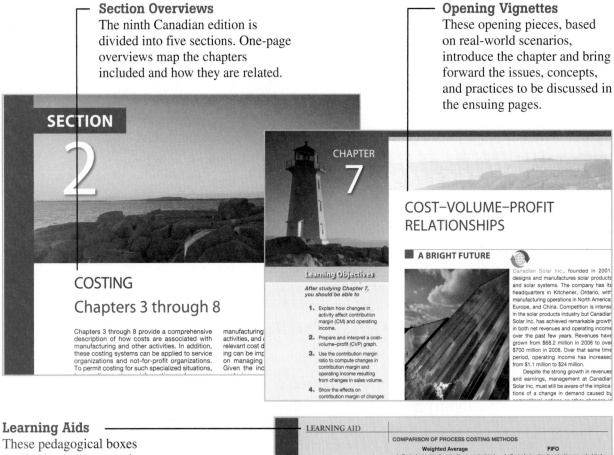

SECTION 2

COSTING

Chapters 3 through 8

Chapters 3 through 8 provide a comprehensive description of how costs are associated with manufacturing and other activities. In addition, these costing systems can be applied to service organizations and not-for-profit organizations. To permit costing for such specialized situations,

manufacturing activities, and relevant cost ing can be imp on managing Given the inc

CHAPTER 7

COST–VOLUME–PROFIT RELATIONSHIPS

Learning Objectives

After studying Chapter 7, you should be able to

1. Explain how changes in activity affect contribution margin (CM) and operating income.
2. Prepare and interpret a cost–volume–profit (CVP) graph.
3. Use the contribution margin ratio to compute changes in contribution margin and operating income resulting from changes in sales volume.
4. Show the effects on contribution margin of changes

A BRIGHT FUTURE

Canadian Solar Inc., founded in 2001, designs and manufactures solar products and solar systems. The company has its headquarters in Kitchener, Ontario, with manufacturing operations in North America, Europe, and China. Competition is intense in the solar products industry but Canadian Solar Inc. has achieved remarkable growth in both net revenues and operating income over the past few years. Revenues have grown from $68.2 million in 2006 to over $700 million in 2008. Over that same time period, operating income has increased from $1.1 million to $24 million.

Despite the strong growth in revenues and earnings, management at Canadian Solar Inc. must still be aware of the implications of a change in demand caused by

Learning Aids
These pedagogical boxes emphasize and summarize key content for students.

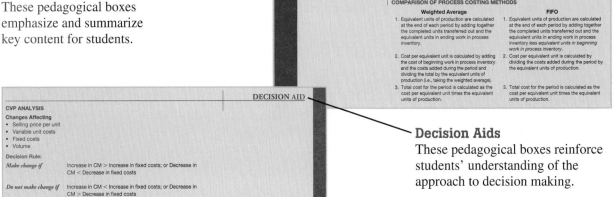

LEARNING AID

COMPARISON OF PROCESS COSTING METHODS

Weighted Average	FIFO
1. Equivalent units of production are calculated at the end of each period by adding together the completed units transferred out and the equivalent units in ending work in process inventory.	1. Equivalent units of production are calculated at the end of each period by adding together the completed units transferred out and the equivalent units in ending work in process inventory less equivalent units in beginning work in process inventory.
2. Cost per equivalent unit is calculated by adding the cost of beginning work in process inventory and the costs added during the period and dividing the total by the equivalent units of production (i.e., taking the weighted average).	2. Cost per equivalent unit is calculated by dividing the costs added during the period by the equivalent units of production.
3. Total cost for the period is calculated as the cost per equivalent unit times the equivalent units of production.	3. Total cost for the period is calculated as the cost per equivalent unit times the equivalent units of production.

DECISION AID

CVP ANALYSIS

Changes Affecting
- Selling price per unit
- Variable unit costs
- Fixed costs
- Volume

Decision Rule:

Make change if	Increase in CM > Increase in fixed costs; or Decrease in CM < Decrease in fixed costs
Do not make change if	Increase in CM < Increase in fixed costs; or Decrease in CM > Decrease in fixed costs

Decision Aids
These pedagogical boxes reinforce students' understanding of the approach to decision making.

IN BUSINESS

Industry Canada, a department of the Canadian federal government, has a Web site containing a wealth of cost data and other statistics for Canadian industries. The data are collected by Statistics Canada from a variety of sources, including annual surveys of manufacturing, retail, and wholesale companies. The information is organized according to whether the industry is in the "goods-producing" sector or the "service-producing" sector, and within each of these categories are more refined subcategories. For example, categories of goods-producing industries include manufacturing, utilities, construction, and agriculture. Manufacturing is then further broken down into categories such as food, textile, machinery, and so on. Service-producing industries include transportation, finance, real estate, and retail, and subcategories are provided for each industry. Subcategories for retailers include motor vehicles, electronics and appliances, food and beverage, etc. The site also includes separate information for small and medium-sized enterprises (SMEs), which is useful comparative data for managers of smaller organizations. A small sampling of the 2008 SME cost information available on the site is shown below.

"In Business"
These helpful boxed features offer a glimpse into how real companies use the managerial accounting concepts discussed in the chapter. Every chapter contains these current examples.

IN BUSINESS

AbitibiBowater produces newsprint, commercial printing papers, and pulp and wood products. AbitibiBowater owns or operates 23 pulp and paper facilities and 30 wood products facilities located in Canada, the United States, the United Kingdom, and South Korea. In 2009, the company installed an $84-million biomass boiler at the Fort Frances, Ontario, mill. This boiler produces 46 megawatts of carbon-neutral energy from biomass such as bark, a by-product of the paper production process. Going forward, this new green energy source will enable the facility to reduce direct greenhouse gas emissions by more than 300,000 metric tonnes of CO_2 equivalents per year—down 90% from previous levels when the mill relied on natural gas. In addition, the plant will significantly reduce conversion costs when converting wood pulp to paper since the new boiler, fired by waste from the production process, will generate enough energy to supply the equivalent of 30,000 homes.

Source: *AbitibiBowater Sustainability Report* and www.abitibibowater.com.

Green Accounting Examples
Owing to the growing number of environmentally conscious companies in business today, the ninth Canadian edition uses a helpful icon to distinguish "green" examples in the text.

SCHEDULE 3

HARRIGAN FREEZE, INC.
Direct Materials Purchases Budget
For the Year Ended December 31, 2012

	Quarter				
	1	2	3	4	Year
Units to be produced (Schedule 2)	14,000	32,000	36,000	19,000	101,000
Raw materials needed per unit (kilograms)	5	5	5	5	5
Production needs (kilograms)	70,000	160,000	180,000	95,000	505,000
Add desired ending inventory of raw materials (kilograms)*	16,000	18,000	9,500	7,500	7,500
Total needs (kilograms)	86,000	178,000	189,500	102,500	512,500
Less beginning inventory of raw materials (kilograms)	7,000	16,000	18,000	9,500	7,000
Raw materials to be purchased (kilograms)	79,000	162,000	171,500	93,000	505,500
Cost of raw materials to be purchased at $0.60 per kilogram	$ 47,400	$ 97,200	$ 102,900	$ 55,800	$ 303,300

*10% of the next quarter's production needs. For example, the second-quarter production needs are 160,000 kilograms. Therefore, the desired ending inventory for the first quarter would be 10% × 160,000 kilograms = 16,000 kilograms. The ending inventory of 7,500 kilograms for the fourth quarter is estimated.

Schedule of Expected Cash Disbursements for Materials

	1	2	3	4	Year
Accounts payable 12/31/11	$ 25,800				$ 25,800
First-quarter purchases ($47,400 × 50%, 50%)	23,700	$ 23,700			47,400
Second-quarter purchases ($97,200 × 50%, 50%)		48,600	$ 48,600		97,200
Third-quarter purchases ($102,900 × 50%, 50%)			51,450	$ 51,450	102,900
Fourth-quarter purchases ($55,800 × 50%)				27,900	27,900
Total cash disbursements	$ 49,500	$ 72,300	$ 100,050	$ 79,350	$ 301,200

Spreadsheets
These have become an increasingly common budgeting tool for managerial accountants; therefore, to assist students in understanding how budgets look in a spreadsheet, we've included Microsoft Excel® screen captures pertaining to budgeting.

Generally Accepted Accounting Principles

Financial accounting statements prepared for external users must be prepared in accordance with generally accepted accounting principles (GAAP). External users must have some assurance that the reports have been prepared in accordance with some common set of ground rules. Beginning January 1, 2011, Canada joined more than 100 other countries, including Australia, New Zealand, and European Union member countries, in adopting International Financial Reporting Standards (IFRS) for publicly accountable enterprises. As of that date, in Canada, IFRS became GAAP for public companies. The purpose of IFRS is simple: to enhance the comparability and clarity of financial information on a global basis. Given the increasing degree of globalization of the economy and the interconnectedness of capital markets, accounting standard setters in Canada concluded that it was crucial to adopt IFRS.[2] Private companies and not-for-profit organizations are not

IFRS Icon
A new IFRS icon has been added in this edition to identify where changes as a result of IFRS are impacting managerial accounting.

Managerial Accounting has earned a reputation for the best end-of-chapter review and discussion material of any text on the market. Most of the exercises, problems, and cases have been revised for the ninth Canadian edition. Features include:

Review Problems & Solutions

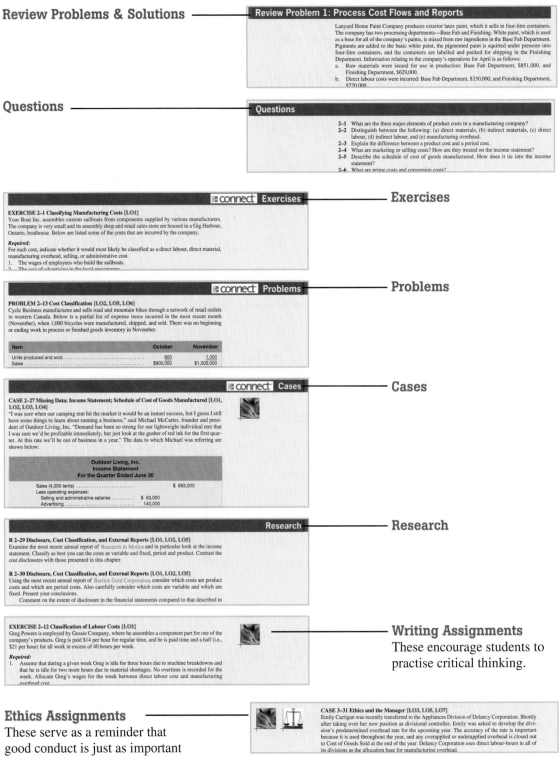

Review Problem 1: Process Cost Flows and Reports

Lanyard Home Paint Company produces exterior latex paint, which it sells in four-litre containers. The company has two processing departments—Base Fab and Finishing. White paint, which is used as a base for all of the company's paints, is mixed from raw ingredients in the Base Fab Department. Pigments are added to the basic white paint, the pigmented paint is squirted under pressure into four-litre containers, and the containers are labelled and packed for shipping in the Finishing Department. Information relating to the company's operations for April is as follows:
a. Raw materials were issued for use in production: Base Fab Department, $851,000, and Finishing Department, $629,000.
b. Direct labour costs were incurred: Base Fab Department, $330,000, and Finishing Department, $270,000.

Questions

Questions

2–1 What are the three major elements of product costs in a manufacturing company?
2–2 Distinguish between the following: (a) direct materials, (b) indirect materials, (c) direct labour, (d) indirect labour, and (e) manufacturing overhead.
2–3 Explain the difference between a product cost and a period cost.
2–4 What are marketing or selling costs? How are they treated on the income statement?
2–5 Describe the schedule of cost of goods manufactured. How does it tie into the income statement?
2–6 What are prime costs and conversion costs?

Exercises

connect Exercises

EXERCISE 2–1 Classifying Manufacturing Costs [LO1]
Your Boat Inc. assembles custom sailboats from components supplied by various manufacturers. The company is very small and its assembly shop and retail sales store are housed in a Gig Harbour, Ontario, boathouse. Below are listed some of the costs that are incurred by the company.

Required:
For each cost, indicate whether it would most likely be classified as a direct labour, direct material, manufacturing overhead, selling, or administrative cost.
1. The wages of employees who build the sailboats.
2. The cost of advertising in the local newspaper.

Problems

connect Problems

PROBLEM 2–13 Cost Classification [LO2, LO5, LO6]
Cycle Business manufactures and sells road and mountain bikes through a network of retail outlets in western Canada. Below is a partial list of expense items incurred in the most recent month (November), when 1,000 bicycles were manufactured, shipped, and sold. There was no beginning or ending work in process or finished goods inventory in November.

Item	October	November
Units produced and sold	900	1,000
Sales	$900,000	$1,000,000

Cases

connect Cases

CASE 2–27 Missing Data; Income Statement; Schedule of Cost of Goods Manufactured [LO1, LO2, LO3, LO4]
"I was sure when our camping tent hit the market it would be an instant success, but I guess I still have some things to learn about running a business," said Michael McCarter, founder and president of Outdoor Living, Inc. "Demand has been so strong for our lightweight individual tent that I was sure we'd be profitable immediately, but just look at the gusher of red ink for the first quarter. At this rate we'll be out of business in a year." The data to which Michael was referring are shown below:

| Outdoor Living, Inc.
Income Statement
For the Quarter Ended June 30		
Sales (4,000 tents)		$ 683,000
Less operating expenses:		
Selling and administrative salaries	$ 63,000	
Advertising	140,000	

Research

Research

R 2–29 Disclosure, Cost Classification, and External Reports [LO1, LO2, LO5]
Examine the most recent annual report of Research in Motion and in particular look at the income statement. Classify as best you can the costs as variable and fixed, period and product. Contrast the cost disclosures with those presented in this chapter.

R 2–30 Disclosure, Cost Classification, and External Reports [LO1, LO2, LO5]
Using the most recent annual report of Barrick Gold Corporation, consider which costs are product costs and which are period costs. Also carefully consider which costs are variable and which are fixed. Present your conclusions.
Comment on the extent of disclosure in the financial statements compared to that described in

EXERCISE 2–12 Classification of Labour Costs [LO1]
Greg Powers is employed by Gussie Company, where he assembles a component part for one of the company's products. Greg is paid $14 per hour for regular time, and he is paid time and a half (i.e., $21 per hour) for all work in excess of 40 hours per week.

Required:
1. Assume that during a given week Greg is idle for three hours due to machine breakdowns and that he is idle for two more hours due to material shortages. No overtime is recorded for the week. Allocate Greg's wages for the week between direct labour cost and manufacturing overhead cost.

Writing Assignments
These encourage students to practise critical thinking.

Ethics Assignments
These serve as a reminder that good conduct is just as important as profits in business.

CASE 3–31 Ethics and the Manager [LO3, LO5, LO7]
Emily Carrigan was recently transferred to the Appliances Division of Delancy Corporation. Shortly after taking over her new position as divisional controller, Emily was asked to develop the division's predetermined overhead rate for the upcoming year. The accuracy of the rate is important because it is used throughout the year, and any overapplied or underapplied overhead is closed out to Cost of Goods Sold at the end of the year. Delancy Corporation uses direct labour-hours in all of its divisions as the allocation base for manufacturing overhead.

Focus on the Canadian Ninth Edition

Book Philosophy and Structure

Developing a textbook on a topic as broad and varied as managerial accounting is a challenge that requires a guiding philosophy.

The authors of the ninth Canadian edition believe in the strong framework established by Garrison, Noreen, and Brewer in their fourteenth U.S. edition. While we rely on this framework in guiding our approach, we have developed a text that reflects the Canadian business and education setting. Our overarching objectives are to make readers comfortable with the subject matter while providing the flexibility necessitated by the varied requirements of our Canadian users. We have strived to develop a text that can be covered in a single term course, but that also provides users with a useful reference for subsequent courses in their academic programs.

We begin the book by describing the key responsibilities of managers, their needs for managerial accounting information, and the role of professional ethics for management accountants. We also address the major differences between financial and managerial accounting. Next, we cover two major topic areas that support the information needs of managerial accounting: the costing of products and services, and cost behaviour and analysis. This foundation material forms the basis for Chapters 3 through 8, which focus on the major types of costing systems used by organizations, cost behaviour patterns and cost prediction models, and the basics of cost–volume–profit analysis.

In Chapters 9 through 11, we build on this foundation in our coverage of planning and control topics. Chapters 9 and 10 explore how managers can use predetermined costs in the form of budgets and standard costs both in planning for the future and evaluating past performance. Chapter 11 covers a variety of management control techniques, including responsibility centre reporting and evaluation, performance measurement, and the cost of quality.

The second major use of the foundation material on costing and cost behaviour is presented in Chapters 12 and 13. In Chapter 12, we examine relevant costs used for short-term decisions, and in Chapter 13, we present the approaches used to analyze long-term capital budgeting decisions. Because the analysis required for short- and long-term decisions typically involves estimates of future costs, a thorough understanding of cost behaviour concepts covered in the foundation chapters is required. We wrap up with online Chapter 14 on financial statement analysis, which we view as an extension both of the control topics covered in earlier chapters and the decision analysis material presented in Chapters 12 and 13.

Each of the chapters provides an extensive set of exercises, problems, and cases that cover manufacturing, service, and not-for-profit organizations, as well as international businesses. This material has been developed to give users a feel for the types of situations faced in today's business environment. Feedback from our users indicates that while there is variety in the breadth of topics covered in any single course, the structure and flexibility afforded by our text makes it well suited to meet their needs.

Overall, we believe our text is written in a way that facilitates understanding and provides a solid foundation for later application.

What's New in the Ninth Edition

The ninth Canadian edition has been reviewed extensively to identify improvements over previous editions. The results of peer reviews and the authors' efforts are reflected in the revisions and reorganization presented in nearly every chapter. Many exercises, problems, cases, and research questions have been revised and new ones created, and several new "hot" topics such as green accounting, corporate social responsibility, and time-driven activity-based costing have been added. Additionally, in several chapters, we have created new Learning Aids to emphasize key materials and Decision Aids to reinforce students' understanding of the approach to decision making in certain areas. We believe these changes have improved an already user-friendly text and should enhance readers' understanding and application of key managerial accounting topics.

The specific changes in each of the individual chapters of the ninth edition are summarized below:

- **Chapter 1** now begins with a segment on the expanded role of management accountants in today's organizations. The section on generally accepted accounting principles has been updated to reflect Canada's adoption of IFRS. The discussion of professional ethics has been revised and now includes the code of ethics of CMA Ontario, one example of the codes of conduct adopted by CMAs in different provinces across Canada.

Finally, a new section has been added on corporate social responsibility.

- **Chapter 2** has been updated to include a clearer linkage to subsequent chapters that build on the cost classification and cost behaviour concepts. The In Business segments have been updated extensively to include more current material.

- In **Chapter 3,** the opening vignette has been revised to describe a simple small business setting that students can relate to where job-order costing would be useful. Finally, several of the In Business features have been updated to reflect more current material.

- **Chapter 4** now includes a Learning Aid that summarizes in one place the differences between weighted-average and FIFO methods for calculating equivalent units of production. In addition, all In Business boxes have been updated to reflect more current material and the in-chapter example of weighted-average versus FIFO methods has been clarified.

- **Chapter 5** now includes a Learning Aid to help students understand the key differences between activity-based costing and the traditional costing methods covered in earlier chapters. The section on designing activity-based costing systems has been rewritten to improve clarity. Time-driven activity-based costing (TDABC), a recent concept being employed by many organizations, is introduced through an In Business segment.

- **Chapters 6 and 7** continue to focus on cost behaviour and cost–volume–profit analysis. In Chapter 6, the regression analysis material has been moved to an appendix to allow instructors more flexibility regarding the extent of coverage for this material. A new In Business segment has been developed for Chapter 6 that provides an example of the effects of going green on cost management. Chapter 7 includes a new Decision Aid on the basics of CVP analysis and new Learning Aids for single and multi-product CVP analysis. A new exhibit on profit graphs has also been added to Chapter 7.

- **Chapter 8** now includes a Learning Aid to help students understand the effect on inventory of using absorption versus variable costing. In addition, the In Business boxes have been updated with more current material.

- **Chapter 9** has been updated to provide a clearer discussion of the advantages of budgeting. The discussion of participative budgeting has been expanded to include coverage of dysfunctional consequences such as budget slack. Stretch budgets are now defined and discussed. Several sections of the master budget example have been rewritten to improve clarity. New end-of-chapter material has been developed for activity-based budgeting.

- **Chapter 10** now includes a Learning Aid on variance analysis. The section on capacity analysis has been revised to improve understandability and emphasize the link to capital budgeting analysis covered in Chapter 13. The material on international uses of standard costs has been updated. The appendix on mix and yield variances has been revised to enhance clarity. The online appendix on learning curves has been expanded to cover the incremental unit time model.

- **Chapter 11** now includes a section on segment reporting moved from an earlier chapter. The section on segment reporting focuses on its use for

evaluation and control, which provides a good fit with the theme of this chapter. Other changes include a Learning Aid that provides students with a quick reference to key decisions in transfer pricing and a more extensive and detailed example of the use of the balanced scorecard and strategy mapping for a regional airline.

- **Chapter 12** now has an opening segment that relates relevant cost concepts to the recent struggles of North American automobile manufacturers. Chapter examples have been updated and revised to improve clarity.

- **Chapter 13** has undergone significant changes to the ordering of topics. The conceptually superior net present value and internal rate of return methods are now covered first, with the payback method and simple rate of return approaches moved to the end of the main chapter. A new Decision Aid has been created for the net present value and internal rate of return methods. The material on income taxes in capital budgeting has been moved to an appendix.

- **Chapter 14,** an online chapter, has been extensively rewritten to clarify and simplify the presentation of financial statement analysis topics.

Teaching and Learning with Technology

Managerial Accounting's technology learning solutions complement the textbook every step of the way, giving students the extra help they need while providing instructors with tools for teaching a stimulating and rewarding class.

Connect

McGraw-Hill Connect™ is a web-based assignment and assessment platform that gives students the means to better connect with their coursework, with their instructors, and with the important concepts that they will need to know for success now and in the future.

With Connect, instructors can deliver assignments, quizzes and tests online. Nearly all the questions from the text are presented in an auto-gradeable format and tied to the text's learning objectives. Instructors can edit existing questions and author entirely new problems, track individual student performance—by question, assignment or in relation to the class overall—with detailed grade reports, and integrate grade reports easily with Learning Management Systems (LMS) such as WebCT and Blackboard. And much more.

By choosing Connect, instructors are providing their students with a powerful tool for improving academic performance and truly mastering course material. Connect allows students to practise important skills at their own pace and on their own schedule.

Importantly, students' assessment results and instructors' feedback are all saved online—so students can continually review their progress and plot their course to success.

Connect also provides 24/7 online access to an eBook—an online edition of the text—to aid them in successfully completing their work, wherever and whenever they choose.

Key Features

Simple Assignment Management

With Connect, creating assignments is easier than ever, so you can spend more time teaching and less time managing.

- Create and deliver assignments easily with selectable end-of-chapter questions and test bank material to assign online
- Streamline lesson planning, student progress reporting, and assignment grading to make classroom management more efficient than ever
- Go paperless with the eBook and online submission and grading of student assignments

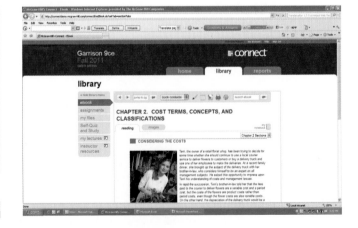

Smart Grading

When it comes to studying, time is precious. Connect helps students learn more efficiently by providing feedback and practice material when they need it, where they need it.

- Automatically score assignments, giving students immediate feedback on their work and side-by-side comparisons with correct answers
- Access and review each response; manually change grades or leave comments for students to review
- Reinforce classroom concepts with practice tests and instant quizzes

Instructor Library

The Connect Instructor Library is your course creation hub. It provides all the critical resources you'll need to build your course, just how you want to teach it.

- Assign eBook readings and draw from a rich collection of textbook-specific assignments
- Access instructor resources, including ready-made PowerPoint presentations and media to use in your lectures

- View assignments and resources created for past sections
- Post your own resources for students to use

eBook

Connect reinvents the textbook learning experience for the modern student. Every Connect subject area is seamlessly integrated with Connect eBooks, which are designed to keep students focused on the concepts key to their success.

- Provide students with a Connect eBook, allowing for anytime, anywhere access to the textbook
- Merge media, animation, and assessments with the text's narrative to engage students and improve learning and retention
- Pinpoint and connect key concepts in a snap using the powerful eBook search engine
- Manage notes, highlights and bookmarks in one place for simple, comprehensive review

Lyryx

lyryx *Lyryx Assessment Managerial Accounting* is an online assessment system designed to support both students and instructors. The assessment takes the form of a homework assignment called a Lab. The Labs are algorithmically generated and automatically graded. Students get unlimited opportunities to practise, and after they submit a Lab for marking, students receive extensive feedback on their work, thus promoting their learning experience. Recent research shows that when Labs are tied to assessment, even if they are worth only a small percentage of the total grade for the course, students will do their homework—and the result is improved student success.

Services and Support

Instructor Support

The following instructor resources are available online on Connect:

Instructor's Manual   The *Instructor's Manual* includes chapter overviews, assignment grids featuring levels of difficulty, and chapter-by-chapter lists of service examples.

Solutions Manual   This supplement contains completely worked-out solutions to all assignment material and a general discussion of the use of group exercises. In addition, the manual contains suggested course outlines and a listing of exercises, problems, and cases scaled according to difficulty.

Computerized Test Bank   Nearly 2,000 questions are organized by chapter and include true/false, multiple-choice, and essay questions, plus computational problems. Use it to make different versions of the same test, change the answer order, edit and add questions, and conduct online testing. Technical support for this software is available. The files are also available in RTF format for printing.

Microsoft® PowerPoint® Slides   Available on Connect, these slides offer a great visual complement for your lectures. A complete set of slides covers each chapter.

Microsoft® Excel® Templates   These are the solutions to the Excel templates offered online.

Other Services and Support

Blackboard   McGraw-Hill Higher Education and Blackboard have teamed up.

Blackboard, the Web-based course-management system, has partnered with McGraw-Hill to better allow students and faculty to use online materials and activities to complement face-to-face teaching. Blackboard features exciting social learning and teaching tools that foster more logical, visually impactful, and active learning opportunities for students. You'll transform your closed-door classrooms into communities where students remain connected to their educational experience 24 hours a day.

This partnership allows you and your students access to McGraw-Hill's Connect™ and Create™ right from within your Blackboard course—all with one single sign-on.

Not only do you get single sign-on with Connect™ and Create™, you also get deep integration of McGraw-Hill content and content engines right in Blackboard. Whether you're choosing a book for your course or building Connect™ assignments, all the tools you need are right where you want them—inside of Blackboard.

Gradebooks are now seamless. When a student completes an integrated Connect™ assignment, the grade for that assignment automatically (and instantly) feeds into your Blackboard grade centre.

McGraw-Hill and Blackboard can now offer you easy access to industry-leading technology and content, whether your campus hosts it or we do. Be sure to ask your local McGraw-Hill representative for details.

Tegrity   Tegrity Campus is a service that makes class time available all the time by automatically capturing every lecture in a searchable format for students to review when they study and complete assignments. With a simple one-click start-and-stop process, you capture all computer screens and corresponding audio. Students replay any part of any class with easy-to-use browser-based viewing on a PC or Mac. Educators know that the more students can see, hear, and experience class resources, the better they learn. With Tegrity Campus, students quickly recall key moments by using Tegrity Campus's unique search feature. This search helps students efficiently find what they need, when they need it across an entire semester of class recordings. Help turn all your students' study time into learning moments immediately supported by your lecture. To learn more about Tegrity watch a 2-minute Flash demo at http://tegritycampus.mhhe.com.

CourseSmart CourseSmart brings together thousands of textbooks across hundreds of courses in an eTextbook format, providing unique benefits to students and faculty. By purchasing an eTextbook, students can save up to 50% of the cost of a print textbook, reduce their impact on the environment, and gain access to powerful Web tools for learning, including full-text search, notes and highlighting, and e-mail tools for sharing notes between classmates. For faculty, CourseSmart provides instant access for reviewing and comparing textbooks and course materials in their discipline area without the time, cost, and environmental impact of mailing print examination copies. For further details, contact your *i*Learning Sales Specialist or go to www.coursesmart.com.

Create McGraw-Hill's Create Online gives you access to the most abundant resource at your fingertips—literally. With a few mouse clicks, you can create customized learning tools simply and affordably. McGraw-Hill Ryerson has included many of our market-leading textbooks within Create Online for eBook and print customization as well as many licensed readings and cases. For more information, go to www.mcgrawhillcreate.com.

_i_Learning Services At McGraw-Hill Ryerson, we take great pride in developing high-quality learning resources while working hard to provide you with the tools necessary to utilize them. We want to bring your teaching to life, and we do this by integrating technology, events, conferences, training, and other services. We call it *i*Services. For more information, contact your *i*Learning Sales Specialist.

Reviewers

The efforts of many people are needed to develop and improve a text. Among these people are the reviewers and consultants who point out areas of concern, cite areas of strength, and make recommendations for change. In this regard, the professors named on this page provided feedback that was enormously helpful in preparing the Canadian ninth edition of *Managerial Accounting*.

Suggestions have been received from many of our colleagues across Canada and throughout the world who have used the prior editions of *Managerial Accounting*. This is vital feedback that we rely on in each edition. Each of those who have offered comments and suggestions has our thanks.

Keith J. Barrett, *Humber College Institute of Technology and Advanced Learning*

Heather Cornish, *NAIT JR Shaw School of Business*

Tammy Crowell, *Dalhousie University*

Elliot Currie, *University of Guelph*

Rob Ducharme, *University of Waterloo*

Andrew Dykstra, *Georgian College*

Kathy Falk, *University of Toronto, Mississauga*

Barbara Katz, *Kwantlen Polytechnic University*

Dave Kennedy, *Lethbridge College*

Howard Leaman, *University of Guelph–Humber*

Cynthia Lone, *Red River College*

Darlene Lowe, *Grant MacEwan University*

Bonnie Martel, *Niagara College*

Jaime A. Morales Burgos, *Trent University*

Jamal Nazari, *Mount Royal University*

Patti Proulx, *Carleton University*

Pamela Quon, *Athabasca University*

Frank Saccucci, *Grant MacEwan University*

John Siambanopoulos, *University of Western Ontario*

Bill Waterman, *Mount Allison University*

Shu-Lun Wong, *Memorial University of Newfoundland*

Acknowledgements

The ninth Canadian edition of *Managerial Accounting* has benefited from the assistance of numerous individuals and groups. This assistance was invaluable in providing us with materials, review comments and suggestions, and technical assistance. Commissioned reviewers across Canada assisted with suggestions and clarifications that reflect their views of the materials they examined.

Materials were provided by the American Accounting Association, CGA–Canada, SAP Canada, and CMA–Canada. In each case, an acknowledgement is included when the material is used in the textbook. The U.S. authors acknowledge materials provided by the AICPA, the Institute of Certified Management Accountants, and the Chartered Institute of Management Accountants (United Kingdom).

Assistance was provided by the editorial, technical, and administrative staff of McGraw-Hill Ryerson Limited. Our book would have been impossible to produce without such help.

We also received invaluable input and support through the years from present and former colleagues and students. We are indebted to the following individuals who helped adapt, critique, and shape the ancillary package for the Canadian market: Robert Ducharme, University of Waterloo; Kathy Falk, University of Toronto, Mississauga; Bonnie Martel, Niagara College; and Ian Feltmate, Acadia University.

The extraordinary efforts of a talented group of individuals at McGraw-Hill Ryerson made all of this come together. We especially thank Rhondda McNabb, for her guidance throughout this project; Lindsay MacDonald, for initiating the developmental work for this edition and for tirelessly following the whole process through until the final printing; Jessica Barnoski, who managed the final production of this book; and all the marketing and sales people who helped bring this book to both instructors and students. We also thank all those who worked behind the scenes to ensure the successful completion of this book. Special thanks to June Trusty for her careful editing and proofreading of the entire textbook.

Despite the assistance we received, we acknowledge our responsibility for the contents of this book. We appreciate suggestions and questions from our audience.

OVERVIEW AND FOUNDATION
Chapters 1 and 2

Chapters 1 and 2 present an overview of matters that are background for subsequent chapters and also provide information on technical topics that appear in later chapters. Thus, it is important to study these chapters carefully in order to be prepared.

Chapter 1 provides a description of what managers do and how managerial accounting can serve these needs. The chapter highlights the key differences between financial and managerial accounting. The importance of ethics for accountants is also covered, and several basic managerial concepts important in today's organizations are discussed.

Chapter 2 commences with a description of how costs are classified and explains the distinction between product and period costs. Next,

the steps involved in calculating the cost of goods sold and the cost of goods manufactured are presented. These calculations provide a structure for the costing methods covered in subsequent chapters.

Chapter 2 also presents a basic discussion of cost behaviour, which is important to numerous topics presented in later chapters. The chapter concludes with two topics important to cost control and decision analysis. First, direct costs are distinguished from indirect costs, which will be important when special-purpose performance reports are discussed later in the book. Second, different types of "decision-focused costs" are presented: differential costs, opportunity costs, and sunk costs. Understanding these concepts is critical to decision-making analysis, which is covered in Chapter 12.

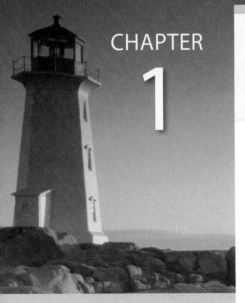

MANAGERIAL ACCOUNTING AND THE BUSINESS ENVIRONMENT

Learning Objectives

After studying Chapter 1, you should be able to

1. Describe the functions performed by managers.

2. Identify the major differences and similarities between financial and managerial accounting.

3. Describe the role of management accountants in an organization.

4. Explain the nature and importance of ethics for accountants.

5. Explain the basic concepts of lean production, Six Sigma, computer technology, and risk management.

THE ROLE OF THE MANAGEMENT ACCOUNTANT IN VALUE CREATION

The role of management accountants has evolved considerably over the past few decades. No longer considered to be just "bean-counters" who compile and report information internally in organizations, today's management accountant can play a vital leadership role on the management team. According to the national body responsible for granting the certified management accountant (CMA) designation in Canada, CMA Canada:

> Certified management accountants (CMAs) do more than just measure value, they create it. As the leaders in management accounting, CMAs actively apply a unique mix of financial expertise, strategic insight, innovative thinking and a collaborative approach to help grow successful businesses.

Today's management accountants are required to have competencies in cost management, performance measurement (financial and non-financial), process management, and risk management, and as a result, play a key role in decision making across the various functional areas of an organization. From operational-level decisions related to quality control to strategic planning decisions about the products to offer and the markets in which the company will compete, management accountants can add value. Moreover, given the growing emphasis on corporate social responsibility and "green" initiatives, management accountants also have to be aware of the needs and concerns of a broader set of stakeholders than ever before. Identifying, understanding, and addressing the needs of suppliers, customers, employees, and the communities in which the organization operates are now central to the role of management accountants.

In fulfilling their complex and challenging responsibilities, management accountants are expected to adhere strictly to a high standard of professional ethics. Indeed, the ethical behaviour of accountants in organizations has come under increasing scrutiny in recent years with the spate of corporate scandals in Canada and the United States. Codes of professional ethics for management accountants typically contain standards related to competence, confidentiality, integrity, and credibility. Serious breaches of one or more of these standards can result in severe consequences, including expulsion from the professional body that granted the professional accountant's designation.

Given the breadth of responsibilities, the expertise requirements, and the challenge of working in an increasingly global marketplace, management accounting offers the potential for a very rewarding career.

Source: Certified Management Accountants, *What Is a CMA?* www.cma-canada.org/index.cfm?ci_id=4442&la_id=1; and Giuseppe Valiante, "Data Tracker Makes Tracks," *Financial Post,* November 2, 2009.

Managerial accounting is concerned with providing information to managers—that is, people inside an organization who direct and control its operations. In contrast, **financial accounting** is concerned with providing information to shareholders, creditors, and others who are outside an organization. Managerial accounting provides data that help organizations run more efficiently. Financial accounting provides the scorecard by which a company's past performance is judged.

Managerial accounting is concerned with determining and developing internal accounting information as a tool for helping managers make business decisions that satisfy customers while continuously monitoring costs and improving efficiencies. This requires managerial accountants to prepare a variety of reports. Some reports compare actual results to plans and to benchmarks focusing on how well managers or business units have performed. Other reports provide timely updates on key indicators, such as orders received, order backlog, capacity utilization, and sales. Reports may also be prepared as needed to help investigate specific problems such as a decline in profitability of a product line or help with the decision of whether to outsource some of the business operations. Reports can also provide an analysis of a developing opportunity such as business acquisition. In contrast, financial accounting is focused on producing a limited set of specific quarterly and annual financial statements in accordance with generally accepted accounting principles (GAAP) and government regulations.

Because it is manager-oriented, any study of managerial accounting must be preceded by some understanding of what managers do, the information managers need, and the general business environment. Accordingly, the purpose of this chapter is to briefly examine these subjects.

Managerial accounting
The form of accounting concerned with providing information to managers for use in planning and controlling operations and for decision making.

Financial accounting
The form of accounting concerned with providing information to shareholders, creditors, and others outside the organization.

THE WORK OF MANAGERS AND THEIR NEED FOR MANAGERIAL ACCOUNTING INFORMATION

Every organization—large and small—has managers. Someone must be responsible for making plans, organizing resources, directing personnel, and controlling operations. This is true of the United Way, the University of Waterloo, the City of Burnaby, Petro-Canada, and the local Mac's convenience store. In this chapter, we will use a fictional organization—Metro Coffee, Inc.—to illustrate the work of management. What we have to say about the management of Metro Coffee, Inc., however, can be generalized to almost any type of organization.

Metro Coffee operates a chain of outlets that sell a full range of coffee and fast foods. The outlets are concentrated in the city of Bromley. The company has found that the best way to generate sales is to create a clean and pleasant environment. Consequently, the company puts a great deal of effort into planning the layout, decor, and location of its outlets. Management knows that different types of clientele are attracted to different kinds of products and layouts. Some clients like to sit to eat or drink while others prefer to use drive-through services.

Managers at Metro Coffee, Inc., like managers everywhere, carry out three major activities—*planning, directing and motivating,* and *controlling.* **Planning** involves selecting a course of action and specifying how the action will be implemented. **Directing and motivating** involve mobilizing people to carry out plans and run routine operations. **Controlling** involves ensuring that the plan is actually carried out and is appropriately modified as circumstances change. Management accounting information plays a vital role in these basic management activities—but most particularly in the planning and control functions.

As a fundamental element of the planning process, more than ever, companies that now face global competition must have a viable *strategy* for succeeding in the marketplace. A **strategy** is a "game plan" that enables a company to attract and retain customers by distinguishing itself from competitors. The focal point of a company's strategy should be its target customers. A company can succeed only if it creates a reason for customers to

LEARNING OBJECTIVE 1
Describe the functions performed by managers.

Planning
Developing objectives and preparing budgets to achieve these objectives.

Directing and motivating
Mobilizing people to carry out plans and run routine operations.

Controlling
Ensuring that the plan is actually carried out and is appropriately modified as circumstances change.

Strategy
A game plan that enables a company to attract and retain customers by distinguishing itself from competitors.

choose it over a competitor. These reasons, or what are more formally called *customer value propositions,* are the essence of strategy.

Customer value propositions tend to fall into three broad categories—*customer intimacy, operational excellence,* and *product leadership.* Companies that adopt a *customer intimacy* strategy are in essence saying to their target customers, "The reason that you should choose us is because we understand and respond to your individual needs better than our competitors." Cisco Systems, The Keg Steakhouse & Bar, and Dell Computer Corporation rely primarily on a customer intimacy value proposition for their success. Companies that pursue the second customer value proposition, called *operational excellence*, are saying to their target customers, "The reason that you should choose us is because we can deliver products and services faster, more conveniently, and at a lower price than our competitors." WestJet, Walmart, and Canadian National Railways are examples of companies that succeed first and foremost because of their operational excellence. Companies pursuing the third customer value proposition, called *product leadership*, are saying to their target customers, "The reason that you should choose us is because we offer higher quality products than our competitors." BMW, SABIAN Cymbals, and Research in Motion (RIM, the creator of the BlackBerry) are examples of companies that succeed because of their product leadership. Although one company may offer its customers a combination of these three customer value propositions, one usually outweighs the others in terms of importance.[1]

Planning

An important part of planning is to identify alternatives and then to select from among the alternatives the one that best meets the organization's objectives. The basic objective of Metro Coffee is to earn profits for the owners of the company by providing superior service at competitive prices in as many markets as possible. To further this objective, every year, top management carefully considers a range of options, or alternatives, for expanding into new geographic markets. This year, management is considering opening new outlets in three suburban areas: Chelton, Harold, and Binham.

When making this and other choices, management must balance the expansion opportunities against the demands made on the company's resources. Management knows from bitter experience that opening an outlet in a new market is a big step that cannot be taken lightly. It requires enormous amounts of time and energy from the company's most experienced, talented, and busy professionals. When the company attempted to open outlets in two locations in the same year, resources were stretched too thinly. The result was that neither outlet opened on schedule, and operations in the rest of the company suffered. Therefore, entering new markets is planned very carefully before proceeding.

Among other data, top management looks at the sales volumes, profit margins, and costs of the company's established outlets in similar markets. These data, supplied by the management accountant, are combined with projected sales volume data at the proposed new locations to estimate the profits that would be generated by the new outlets. In general, virtually all important alternatives considered by management in the planning process have some effect on revenues or costs, and management accounting data are essential in estimating those effects.

After considering all of the alternatives, Metro Coffee's top management decided to open an outlet in the burgeoning Chelton market in the third quarter of the year, but to defer opening any other new outlets to another year. As soon as this decision was made, detailed plans were drawn up for all parts of the company that would be involved in the Chelton opening. For example, the Personnel Department's travel budget was increased, since it would be providing extensive on-site training to the new personnel hired in Chelton.

As in the Personnel Department example, the plans of management are often expressed formally in **budgets**, and the term *budgeting* is generally used to describe this part of the planning process. Budgets are usually prepared under the direction of the

Budget
A quantitative plan for the acquisition and use of financial and other resources over a specified future time period.

controller, who is the manager in charge of the Accounting Department. Typically, budgets are prepared annually and represent management's plans in specific, quantitative terms. In addition to a travel budget, the Personnel Department will be given goals in terms of new hires, courses taught, and detailed breakdowns of expected expenses. Similarly, the manager of each outlet will be given a target for sales volume, income, expenses, inventory losses, and employee training. These data will be collected, analyzed, and summarized for management use in the form of budgets prepared by Metro Coffee's management accountants.

Directing and Motivating

In addition to planning for the future, managers must oversee day-to-day activities and keep the organization functioning smoothly. This requires motivating and directing people. Managers assign tasks to employees, arbitrate disputes, answer questions, solve on-the-spot problems, and make many small decisions that affect customers and employees. In effect, directing is the part of managers' activities that deals with the routine and the here and now. Managerial accounting data, such as daily sales reports, are often used in this type of day-to-day decision making.

Controlling

In carrying out the **control** function, managers seek to ensure that the plan is being followed. **Feedback**, which signals whether operations are on track, is the key to effective control. In sophisticated organizations, this feedback is provided by detailed reports of various types. One of these reports, which compares budgeted to actual results, is called a **performance report**. Performance reports suggest where operations are not proceeding as planned and where some parts of the organization may require additional attention. For example, before the opening of the new Chelton outlet in the third quarter of the year, the store's manager will be given sales volume, income, and expense targets for the fourth quarter of the year. As the fourth quarter progresses, periodic reports will be made in which the actual sales volume, income, and expenses are compared to the targets. If the actual results fall below the targets, top management is alerted that the Chelton outlet requires more attention. Experienced personnel can be sent in to help the new manager, or top management may come to the conclusion that plans will have to be revised. As we will see in following chapters, providing this kind of feedback to managers is one of the central purposes of managerial accounting.

The Results of Managers' Activities

As a customer enters one of the Metro Coffee's outlets, the results of management's planning, directing and motivating, and control activities will be evident in the many details that make the difference between a pleasant and an unsatisfactory experience. The outlet will be clean, fashionably decorated, and logically laid out. Clerks will be alert, friendly, and efficient. In short, what the customer experiences doesn't simply happen: It is the result of the efforts of managers who must visualize and fit together the processes that are needed to get the job done. A role of managerial accounting is to inform and facilitate management decisions throughout these processes so that managers' efforts result in the efficient achievement of company goals.

The Planning and Control Cycle

The work of management can be summarized in a model such as the one in Exhibit 1–1. The model, which depicts the **planning and control cycle**, illustrates the smooth flow of management activities from planning through directing and motivating, controlling, and then back to planning again. All of these activities involve decision making, so it is depicted as the hub around which the other activities revolve.

Controller
The manager in charge of the accounting department in an organization.

Control
Those steps taken by management that attempt to increase the likelihood that the objectives developed at the planning stage are attained and to ensure that all parts of the organization function in a manner consistent with organizational policies.

Feedback
Accounting and other reports that help managers monitor performance and focus on problems and/or opportunities that might otherwise go unnoticed.

Performance report
A detailed report comparing budgeted data to actual data.

Planning and control cycle
The flow of management activities through planning, directing and motivating, and controlling, and then back to planning again.

EXHIBIT 1–1   The Planning and Control Cycle

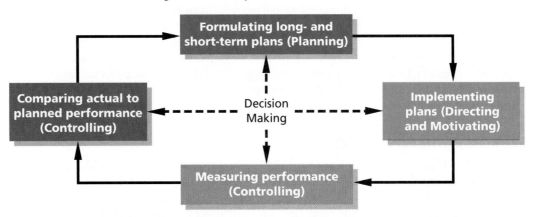

Management accounting can help serve the information needs of managers in all phases of the planning and control cycle. The management accountant can prepare detailed reports that managers need to make both day-to-day and long-term decisions, and also prepare budgets to help direct resources toward the organization's goals. Later, actual costs and revenues are compared with the budgeted figures, and reports are prepared to inform management about any significant variances from budget. Management information needs vary from business to business but as you work your way through this book, you will be introduced to many of the tools that management accountants use to meet these needs. For example, managerial accountants typically provide reports that help answer questions such as:

How much does it cost to provide a particular good or service?
How do costs behave when the company operates at different levels of activity?
How can a company reduce costs to help improve profitability?
How many units must be sold to break even?
What will the company's budgets look like at different forecasted levels of activity?
Should the company add or drop a product line?
Should the company outsource some of its operations?
How should management choose when selecting among competing investment proposals?
In what new projects should the company invest and what projects should be abandoned?

The Business Plan

New businesses typically formalize their strategic planning in the form of a business plan. A business plan consists of information about the company's basic product or service and about the steps it will take to reach its potential market. The plan includes information about production methods, the competition, the management team, and details on how the business will be financed. It is a key document for the organization's internal management. It is also valuable for external use in attracting resources from potential creditors and investors. The answers to many of the questions raised by prospective providers of funds can be found in the business plan.

Exhibit 1–2 shows a flow chart of the steps taken in developing a typical business plan. The 16-week time span is for illustrative purposes only. The actual length of the business plan process varies with the nature and complexity of the venture and could span anywhere from a few weeks to several months or more. Note from the flow chart that it is essential for certain steps to be completed before others begin. It makes no sense, for example, to talk about forecasting sales revenues (step 5) until a product or service has been picked (step 3) and the market has been researched (step 4). Although some steps clearly precede others, the process is not entirely linear. Development of the business plan

EXHIBIT 1–2   Flow Chart of the Steps in Developing a Business Plan

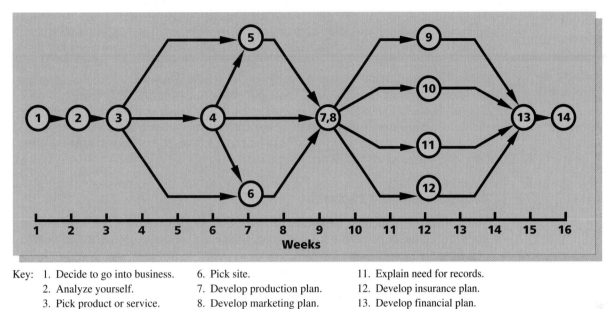

Key: 1. Decide to go into business.   6. Pick site.   11. Explain need for records.
      2. Analyze yourself.   7. Develop production plan.   12. Develop insurance plan.
      3. Pick product or service.   8. Develop marketing plan.   13. Develop financial plan.
      4. Research market.   9. Develop personnel plan.   14. Write summary overview.
      5. Forecast sales revenues.   10. Decide whether to incorporate.

Source: From SIROPOLIS. *Small Business Management*, 6e. © 1997 South-Western, a part of Cengage
Learning Inc. Reproduced by permission, www.cengage.com/permissions.

is an interactive process. In today's dynamic and complex business environment, the
business plan must be flexible enough to adapt in response to market changes that require
new estimates and forecasts. To be effective, the business plan should encourage a shared
vision with clear targets and well-defined performance measures such as those discussed
in later chapters of this text.

A business plan requires a knowledgeable person to write the report. Since most entrepreneurs are doers rather than report writers, the preparation of the plan required to start,
expand, or downsize a company will usually be done by someone with capabilities in both
financial and business affairs, using a variety of expertise from others. To help in this
regard, all of the major Canadian banks as well as several industrial development organizations such as the Community Business Development Corporations provide templates to
assist entrepreneurs in developing their business plans. These templates are usually available online, free of charge. A typical plan will include a description of the proposed or
existing company, its products or services, and the marketing plan. Operational plans will
provide details of the financial resources required and forecasted revenues and expenses.

IN BUSINESS

Ultra Electronics Maritime Systems, located in the Halifax Regional Municipality, is an international leader in the design, development, and production of advanced electronic, electro-
mechanical and hydro-acoustic sensor systems. Strategically, it operates in various countries,
including the United Kingdom, Japan, and France. To obtain financing for its international
operations, it listed its shares on the London Stock Exchange in 1996. To provide appropriate
management accounting information, it uses an enterprise information system and a broad-
based scorecard reporting of performance. Its vice-president of finance and administration is
a certified management accountant who is extensively involved in strategic planning, planning,
controlling, and directing operations.

Source: Robert Colman, "Navigating Strategic Change," *CMA Management*, October 2006, pp. 40–42.

COMPARISON OF FINANCIAL AND MANAGERIAL ACCOUNTING

LEARNING OBJECTIVE 2
Identify the major differences
and similarities between financial
and managerial accounting.

Financial accounting reports are prepared for the use of external parties such as shareholders and creditors, whereas managerial accounting reports are prepared for managers inside the organization. This contrast results in a number of major differences between financial and managerial accounting, even though both financial and managerial accounting rely on the same underlying financial data. These differences are summarized in Exhibit 1–3.

As shown in Exhibit 1–3, in addition to the reports being prepared for different people, financial and managerial accounting also differ in their emphasis between the past and the future, in the type of data provided to users, and in several other ways. These differences are discussed in the following sections.

Emphasis on the Future

Since *planning* is such an important part of the manager's job, managerial accounting has a strong future orientation. In contrast, financial accounting primarily summarizes past financial transactions. These summaries may be useful in planning, but only to a point. The future is not simply a reflection of what has happened in the past. Changes

EXHIBIT 1–3 Comparison
of Financial and Management
Accounting

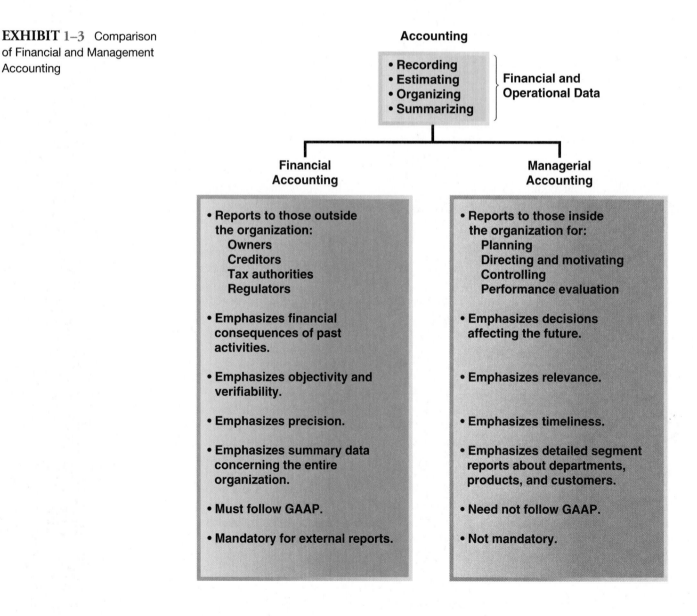

Accounting

- **Recording**
- **Estimating**
- **Organizing**
- **Summarizing**

Financial and Operational Data

Financial Accounting

- Reports to those outside the organization:
    Owners
    Creditors
    Tax authorities
    Regulators

- Emphasizes financial consequences of past activities.

- Emphasizes objectivity and verifiability.

- Emphasizes precision.

- Emphasizes summary data concerning the entire organization.

- Must follow GAAP.

- Mandatory for external reports.

Managerial Accounting

- Reports to those inside the organization for:
    Planning
    Directing and motivating
    Controlling
    Performance evaluation

- Emphasizes decisions affecting the future.

- Emphasizes relevance.

- Emphasizes timeliness.

- Emphasizes detailed segment reports about departments, products, and customers.

- Need not follow GAAP.

- Not mandatory.

are constantly taking place in economic conditions, customer needs and desires, competitive conditions, and so on. All of these changes demand that managers' planning be based in large part on estimates of what will happen rather than on summaries of what has already happened.

Relevance of Data

Financial accounting data are expected to be objective and verifiable. However, for internal uses the manager wants information that is relevant even if it is not completely objective or verifiable. By relevant, we mean *appropriate for the problem at hand.* For example, it is difficult to verify estimated sales volumes for a proposed new outlet of Metro Coffee, Inc., but this is exactly the type of information that is most useful to managers in their decision making. Managerial accounting should be flexible enough to provide whatever data are relevant for a particular decision.

Less Emphasis on Precision

Making sure that amounts are accurate down to the last dollar or penny takes time and effort. While that kind of accuracy is desirable for external reports, most managers would rather have an immediate estimate than wait for a more precise answer. For this reason, managerial accountants often place less emphasis on precision than do financial accountants. For example, in a decision involving hundreds of millions of dollars, estimates that are rounded off to the nearest million dollars are probably good enough. In addition to placing less emphasis on precision than financial accounting, managerial accounting places more weight on non-monetary data. For example, data about customer satisfaction may be routinely used in managerial accounting reports.

Segments of an Organization

Financial accounting is primarily concerned with reporting for the company as a whole. By contrast, managerial accounting focuses much more on the parts, or **segments**, of a company. These segments can be evaluated independently from other parts of the organization and may be product lines, customers, sales territories, divisions, departments, or any other categorization of the company's activities for which management finds it useful to have financial data. Financial accounting does require some breakdowns of revenues and costs by major segments in external reports, but this is a secondary emphasis. In managerial accounting, segment reporting is the primary emphasis.

Segment
Any part of an organization that can be evaluated independently of other parts and about which the manager seeks financial data.

Generally Accepted Accounting Principles

Financial accounting statements prepared for external users must be prepared in accordance with generally accepted accounting principles (GAAP). External users must have some assurance that the reports have been prepared in accordance with some common set of ground rules. Beginning January 1, 2011, Canada joined more than 100 other countries, including Australia, New Zealand, and European Union member countries, in adopting International Financial Reporting Standards (IFRS) for publicly accountable enterprises. As of that date, in Canada, IFRS became GAAP for public companies. The purpose of IFRS is simple: to enhance the comparability and clarity of financial information on a global basis. Given the increasing degree of globalization of the economy and the interconnectedness of capital markets, accounting standard setters in Canada concluded that it was crucial to adopt IFRS.[2] Private companies and not-for-profit organizations are not obligated to adopt IFRS but instead can continue to use Canadian-based GAAP. While the common ground rules established by IFRS will enhance comparability across external reporting jurisdictions, they do not necessarily lead to the type of reports that would be most useful in internal decision making since they are still based on historical information.

Managerial accounting is not bound by GAAP. Managers set their own ground rules concerning the content and form of internal reports. The only constraint is that the expected benefits from using the information should outweigh the costs of collecting, analyzing, and summarizing the data. Nevertheless, as we will see in subsequent chapters, it is undeniable that financial reporting requirements have heavily influenced management accounting practice.

Managerial Accounting—Not Mandatory

Financial accounting is mandatory; that is, it must be done. Various outside parties such as the provincial and territorial securities regulators and the tax authorities require periodic financial statements. Managerial accounting, on the other hand, is not mandatory. A company is completely free to do as much or as little as it wishes. No regulatory bodies or other outside agencies specify what is to be done or, for that matter, whether anything is to be done at all. Since managerial accounting is completely optional, the important question is always "Is the information useful?" rather than "Is the information required?"

ORGANIZATIONAL STRUCTURE

LEARNING OBJECTIVE 3
Describe the role of management accountants in an organization.

Management must accomplish its objectives by working *with* employees. Presidents of companies like Metro Coffee, Inc., could not possibly execute all of their companies' strategies alone; they must rely on other people. This is done by creating an organizational structure that permits effective *decentralization* of management decisions.

Decentralization

Decentralization
The delegation of decision making throughout an organization by providing managers at various operating levels with the authority to make key decisions relating to their areas of responsibility.

Decentralization is the delegation of decision making throughout an organization by providing managers at various operating levels with the authority to make key decisions relating to their areas of responsibility. Some organizations are more decentralized than others. Because of Metro Coffee's geographic dispersion and the peculiarities of local markets, the company is highly decentralized.

Metro Coffee's president (often synonymous with the term *chief executive officer* or *CEO*) sets the broad strategy for the company and makes major strategic decisions (such as those related to opening stores in new markets), but much of the remaining decision-making authority is delegated to managers on various levels throughout the organization. Metro Coffee has a number of outlets, each of which has a store manager as well as a separate manager for each major aspect of the store's operations, such as beverages, food, and preparation. In addition, the company has support departments, such as a central Purchasing Department and a Personnel Department that provide services for all outlets. The organizational structure of the company is depicted in Exhibit 1–4.

Organization chart
A diagram of a firm's organizational structure that depicts formal lines of reporting, communication, and responsibility between managers.

The arrangement of boxes shown in Exhibit 1–4 is called an **organization chart**. The purpose of an organization chart is to show how responsibility has been divided among managers and to show formal lines of reporting and communication, or *chain of command*. Each box depicts an area of management responsibility, and the lines between the boxes show the lines of formal authority between managers. The chart tells us, for example, that the store managers are responsible to the operations vice-president. In turn, the latter is responsible to the company president, who in turn is responsible to the board of directors. Following the lines of authority and communication on the organization chart, we can see that the manager of the Chelton outlet would ordinarily report to the operations vice-president rather than directly to the president of the company.

Informal relationships and channels of communication often develop outside the formal reporting relationships on the organization chart as a result of personal contacts between managers. The informal structure does not appear on the organization chart, but it is often vital to effective operations.

EXHIBIT 1–4   Organization Chart: Metro Coffee, Inc.

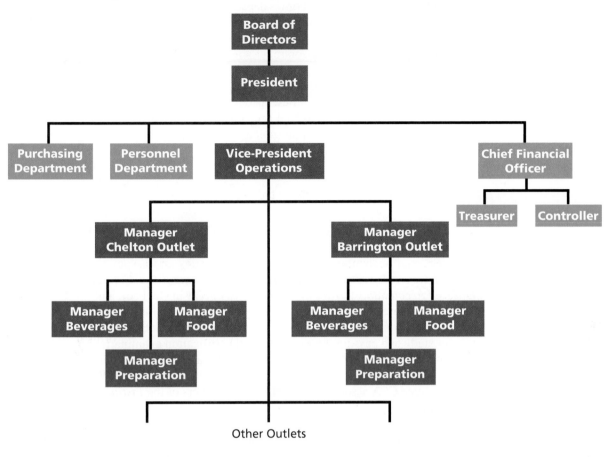

Line and Staff Relationships

An organization chart also depicts *line* and *staff* positions in an organization. A person in a **line position** is *directly* involved in achieving the basic objectives of the organization. A person in a **staff position**, by contrast, is only *indirectly* involved in achieving those basic objectives. Staff positions *support* or provide assistance to line positions or other parts of the organization, but they do not have direct authority over line positions. Refer again to the organization chart in Exhibit 1–4. Since the basic objective of Metro Coffee is to sell food and beverages at a profit, those managers whose areas of responsibility are directly related to the sales effort occupy line positions. These positions, which are shown in a darker colour in the exhibit, include the managers of the various departments in each outlet, the outlet managers, the operations vice-president, and members of top management.

By contrast, the manager of the central Purchasing Department occupies a staff position, since the only function of the Purchasing Department is to support and serve the line departments by doing their purchasing for them. However, both line and staff managers have authority over the employees in their own departments.

Line position
A job position that is directly related to the achievement of the organization's basic objectives.

Staff position
A job position that is only indirectly related to the achievement of the organization's basic objectives. Such positions are supportive in nature in that they provide service or assistance to line positions or to other staff positions.

The Controller

In Canada, the manager in charge of the Accounting Department is usually known as the *controller*. The controller, in turn, reports to the *chief financial officer* (CFO). Both the controller and CFO are staff positions. The CFO is the member of the top-management team who is given the responsibility of providing relevant and timely data to support planning and control activities and of preparing financial statements for external users. The controller is responsible for the technical details of accounting and finance, provides leadership to other professionals in her or his department, and analyzes new and evolving situations. An effective controller is able to work well with top managers from other disciplines and can communicate technical information in a simple and clear manner.

Much of the work under the controller's responsibility involves consulting and business analysis. Many managerial accountants engaged in such activities actually identify themselves as working in finance since very few, if any, of their activities are about debits and credits or preparing journal entries. As described in the opening *Business Focus* segment of this chapter, these managerial accountants are typically key members of cross-functional teams throughout the organization.

THE PROFESSIONAL MANAGEMENT ACCOUNTANT

Three professional accounting organizations in Canada have members who make up the ranks of management accountants. *CGA*, *CA*, and *CMA* are the designations used by professional accountants who belong to societies and associations such as the *Certified General Accountants Association of Canada*, the *Canadian Institute of Chartered Accountants* (*Ordre des comptables agréés* in Quebec), and *CMA Canada*.[3] Members of these three associations work in various fields—industry, commerce, government, education, and public practice—after completing their particular programs of study and passing their professional certification examinations. In the United States, both CPAs and CMAs are professional management accountants. The CPA designation is used by members of the *American Institute of Certified Public Accountants* or various state CPA associations. CMAs are members of the *Institute of Management Accountants*.

Management accounting is not subject to the type of regulation that is evident for financial accounting. However, CMA Canada issues *management accounting guidelines and management accounting practice statements* on fundamental areas of practice. Adherence to the guidelines is voluntary, but wide acceptance is expected because of the relevance and expertise used in their preparation. Currently, CMA Canada has issued 78 guidelines and 49 management accounting practice statements on topics such as strategic management, risk management and governance, performance management and measurement, and financial reporting. The difference between practice statements and guidelines is that practice statements are more prescriptive in nature and contain less background discussion and research than the guidelines. New topics are continually being presented to the accounting community.

PROFESSIONAL ETHICS

LEARNING OBJECTIVE 4
Explain the nature and importance of ethics for accountants.

A series of high-profile financial scandals in the public and private sectors have raised deep concerns about ethics in business and government.[4] Ethics are important because they help keep economies operating efficiently. As James Surowiecki wrote:

> Flourishing economies require a healthy level of trust in the reliability and fairness of everyday transactions. If you assumed every potential deal was a rip-off or that the products you were buying were probably going to be lemons, then very little business would get done. More important, the cost of the transactions that did take place would be exorbitant, since you'd have to do enormous work to investigate each deal and you'd have to rely on the threat of legal action to enforce every contract. For an economy to prosper, what's needed is not a Pollyannish faith that everyone else has your best interests at heart—"caveat emptor" (buyer beware) remains an important truth—but a basic confidence in the promises and commitments that people make about their products and services.[5]

There are good reasons for companies to be concerned about their ethical reputation. A company that is not trusted by its customers, employees, and suppliers will eventually suffer. In the short run, virtue is sometimes its own reward but in the long run, business ethics should be taken seriously because the very survival of the company may depend on the level of trust held by its stakeholders.

Professional accounting groups are given the right of association and certain rights of self-government by provincial and territorial governments in Canada. One inherent requirement of such rights is an expression of public service in the form of a code of ethics. Each accounting group is then permitted to operate according to the laws of the country, using its code of ethics as an operating guideline.[6]

Typically, these codes contain details of how members should conduct themselves in their dealings with the public, their association, and other members. For example, accountants must maintain a level of competence appropriate to their designation. Confidentiality is essential because of the importance of the information they analyze. Integrity is maintained by avoiding conflicts of interest with their employers or clients, by communicating the limits of professional competence, and by not accepting favours that would compromise their judgment. Objectivity must be present in communications, so that recipients can receive both favourable and unfavourable information.

Professional accountants must study the full text of their code of ethics because the rules for competence, confidentiality, integrity, and objectivity are complex in real situations. In addition, procedures for resolving complex situations should be known.

Some codes of ethics give more extensive guidance than others. For example, the code developed by CMA Ontario provides clear guidance concerning what professional ethical standards to follow, as shown in the excerpts provided in Exhibit 1–5. Notice how the details of this code address the concepts of confidentiality, integrity, and objectivity discussed above.

Businesses are organizations composed of people pursuing objectives (sometimes termed *missions*). These organizations have formal relationships among their members, as illustrated by the organization chart earlier in this chapter. However, informal relationships and activities are also present that must be focused on the achievement of the objectives of a wide group of people known as *stakeholders*. Stakeholders are people within and outside the organization who have an interest in the activities of the organization. Employees, shareholders, and creditors have an obvious interest in what the organization does, but so do the customers, the suppliers, the competitors, and the communities in which the organization operates. All of these stakeholders can benefit from the organization's undertakings but they also can be harmed by these activities.

A code of ethics is prepared by an organization to reflect its values and moral system. The document specifies what is expected of its employees in their dealings with the various stakeholders. Thus, the code reflects what the organization stands for when it interacts through its employees with other stakeholders. For example, the organization may wish to pursue environmental standards in excess of those specified in local laws and regulations. The organization may wish to use the standards of conduct present in its home country rather than those of its host country in its cross-border activities. Through its code of ethics, a business can express what it stands for in its activities as well as provide its members with a guide as to how their activities should be conducted to reflect the values needed to achieve the objectives of the organization.

Corporate Governance

Effective *corporate governance* enhances shareholders' confidence that a company is being run in their best interests rather than in the interests of top managers. Recent financial scandals have also increased the emphasis being placed on the development of good governance practices. **Corporate governance** is the system by which a company is directed and controlled. If properly implemented, the corporate governance system should provide incentives for the board of directors and top management to pursue objectives that are in the interests of the company's owners and it should provide for effective monitoring

Corporate governance
A system by which a company is directed and controlled.

EXHIBIT 1–5   Certified Management Accountants of Ontario: Excerpts from the Code of Professional Ethics

All Members, Students and Firms will adhere to the following Code of Professional Ethics of CMA Ontario:

(1) A Member, Student or Firm will act at all times with:
(a) responsibility for and fidelity to public needs;
(b) fairness and loyalty to such Member's, Student's or Firm's associates, clients and employers; and
(c) competence through devotion to high ideals of personal honour and professional integrity.

(2) A Member, Student or Firm will:
(a) maintain at all times independence of thought and action;
(b) not express an opinion on financial reports or statements without first assessing her or his relationship with her or his client to determine whether such Member, Student or Firm might expect her or his opinion to be considered independent, objective and unbiased by one who has knowledge of all the facts; and
(c) when preparing financial reports or statements or expressing an opinion on financial reports or statements, disclose all material facts known to such Member, Student or Firm in order not to make such financial reports or statements misleading, acquire sufficient information to warrant an expression of opinion and report all material misstatements or departures from generally accepted accounting principles.

(3) A Member, Student or Firm will:
(a) not disclose or use any confidential information concerning the affairs of such Member's, Student's or Firm's employer or client unless acting in the course of his or her duties or except when such information is required to be disclosed in the course of any defence of himself or herself or any associate or employee in any lawsuit or other legal proceeding or against alleged professional misconduct by order of lawful authority of the Board or any committee of CMA Ontario in the proper exercise of their duties but only to the extent necessary for such purpose;
(b) inform his or her employer or client of any business connections or interests of which such Member's, Student's or Firm's employer or client would reasonably expect to be informed;
(c) not, in the course of exercising his or her duties on behalf of such Member's, Student's or Firm's employer or client, hold, receive, bargain for or acquire any fee, remuneration or benefit without such employer's or client's knowledge and consent.

(4) A Member, Student or Firm will:
(a) conduct himself or herself toward other Members, Students and Firms with courtesy and good faith;
(b) not commit an act discreditable to the profession;
(c) not engage in or counsel any business or occupation which, in the opinion of CMA Ontario, is incompatible with the professional ethics of a management accountant.

(5) A Member, Student or Firm will:
(a) at all times maintain the standards of competence expressed by the Board from time to time;
(b) disseminate the knowledge upon which the profession of management accounting is based to others within the profession and generally promote the advancement of the profession;
(c) undertake only such work as he or she is competent to perform by virtue of his or her training and experience and will, where it would be in the best interests of an employer or client, engage, or advise the employer or client to engage, other specialists.

Source: Certified Management Accountants of Ontario, *Professional Misconduct and Code of Professional Ethics Regulation*, updated June 21, 2010. Reprinted by permission of Certified Management Accountants of Ontario.

of performance.[7] Many would argue that, in addition to protecting the interests of shareholders, an effective corporate governance system also should protect the interests of the company's other *stakeholders*—its customers, creditors, employees, suppliers, and the communities within which it operates.

Unfortunately, history has repeatedly shown that unscrupulous top managers, if unchecked, will sometimes exploit their power to defraud stakeholders. This unpleasant reality became all too clear in 2001 when the fall of Enron kicked off a wave of corporate scandals. These scandals were characterized by financial reporting fraud and misuse of corporate funds at the very highest levels—including CEOs and CFOs. Collectively, these scandals are estimated to have cost shareholders billions of dollars. While this was disturbing in itself, it also indicated that the institutions intended to prevent such abuses weren't working, thus raising fundamental questions about the adequacy of the existing corporate governance system. In an attempt to respond to these concerns, the U.S. Congress passed the most important reform of corporate governance in many decades—*The Sarbanes-Oxley Act of 2002*. The Act applies to all publicly traded companies in the United States, including Canadian companies such as RIM, whose shares trade on a U.S. stock exchange. Some of the key aspects of the legislation include:

- Requires the CEO and CFO to certify in writing that the financial statements fairly represent the results of operations. Certifying financial statements known to contain misrepresentations can lead to jail time for the CEO or CFO.
- Places the power to hire, compensate, and terminate the public accounting firm that audits a company's financial reports in the hands of the audit committee of the board of directors.
- Restricts the nature and extent of non-auditing services that can be provided by public accounting firms to companies that are their audit clients. Provision of non-audit services such as consulting can impair a public accounting firm's ability to act objectively when auditing the financial statements.
- Requires a company's annual report to contain an internal control report. Internal controls are established by management to provide assurance to shareholders and prospective investors that the financial statements are reliable. The report must contain a statement by management about the effectiveness of the internal controls.

The hope is that the provisions of the *Sarbanes-Oxley Act of 2002* will reduce the incidence of fraudulent financial reporting that has so seriously shaken the public's confidence in securities markets worldwide over the past decade.

IN BUSINESS

Unfortunately, Canada has not escaped its share of corporate scandals in recent years, including the ones involving Hollinger, Bre-X, Cinar, and Livent. After a lengthy legal battle, Garth Drabinsky and Myron Gottlieb, co-founders of Livent Inc., were sentenced in August 2009 to jail for seven and six years, respectively, for their role in an accounting fraud that cost investors an estimated $500 million. The fraud, which involved misrepresentation of revenues and expenses in Livent Inc.'s financial statements was perpetrated over several years, from 1993–1998. The fraud came to light beginning in August 1998 after Drabinsky and Gottlieb lost control of the financially troubled theatre company and the new management team began conducting an internal investigation. Despite having what appeared to be a strong board of directors and the fact that its financial statements were audited annually by a reputable accounting firm, Drabinsky and Gottlieb, both directly, and indirectly through their influence on company employees, were still able to conceal their wrongdoing for an extended period. As Ontario Superior Court Justice Mary Lou Benotto noted during the sentencing hearing, "Mr. Drabinsky and Mr. Gottlieb presided over a corporation whose corporate culture was one of dishonesty."

Source: Theresa Tedesco, "The Final Act? Garth Drabinsky Faces the Music in Canada's First Major Prosecution of Alleged Accounting Fraud," May 3, 2008, *Financial Post*; Barbara Schecter, "Drabinsky Gets 7 Years, Gottlieb 6 for Fraud," August 5, 2009, *Financial Post*; Michel Magnan, Denis Cormier, and Pascale Lapointe-Antunes, "Corporate Fraud's Red Flag: Arrogance," December 1, 2009, *Financial Post*.

Corporate Social Responsibility

Corporate social responsibility
A concept whereby organizations consider the needs of all stakeholders when making decisions.

As discussed above, companies are responsible for producing financial results that satisfy shareholders, but this must be balanced against the need to conduct operations and dealings in an ethical and morally responsible fashion. Organizations have a corporate social responsibility to serve other stakeholders—such as customers, employees, suppliers, communities, and environmental and human rights advocates—whose interests are tied to the company's performance. **Corporate social responsibility** (CSR) is a concept whereby organizations consider the needs of all stakeholders when making decisions. CSR extends beyond legal compliance to include voluntary actions that satisfy stakeholder expectations. Numerous companies, such as the Royal Bank of Canada, Unilever Canada, and Tim Hortons prominently describe issues related to corporate social responsibility initiatives on their Web sites.

Exhibit 1–6 presents examples of corporate social responsibilities that are of interest to six stakeholder groups. Many companies are paying increasing attention to these types of broadly defined responsibilities for four reasons. First, socially responsible investors control more than $2.3 trillion of investment capital. Companies that want access to this capital must excel in terms of their social performance. Second, a growing number of employees want to work for a company that recognizes and responds to its social responsibilities. If companies hope to recruit and retain these highly skilled employees, then they must offer fulfilling careers that serve the needs of broadly defined stakeholders. Third, many customers seek to purchase products and services from socially responsible companies. The Internet enables these customers to readily locate competing products, thereby making it even easier to avoid doing business with undesirable companies. Fourth, non-government organizations (NGOs) and activists are more capable than ever of tarnishing a company's reputation by publicizing its environmental or human rights missteps. The Internet has enabled these environmental and human rights advocacy groups to better organize their resources, spread negative information, and take coordinated actions against offending companies.[8]

It is important to understand that a company's social performance can impact its financial performance. For example, if a company's poor social performance alienates

EXHIBIT 1–6 Examples of Corporate Social Responsibilities

Companies should provide *customers* with
- Safe, high-quality products that are fairly priced.
- Competent, courteous, and rapid delivery of products and services.
- Full disclosure of product-related risks.
- Easy-to-use information systems for shopping and tracking orders.

Companies should provide *suppliers* with
- Fair contract terms and prompt payments.
- Reasonable time to prepare orders.
- Hassle-free acceptance of timely and complete deliveries.
- Cooperative rather than unilateral actions.

Companies should provide *shareholders* with
- Competent management.
- Easy access to complete and accurate financial information.
- Full disclosure of enterprise risks.
- Honest answers to knowledgeable questions.

Companies and their suppliers should provide *employees* with
- Safe and humane working conditions.
- Non-discriminatory treatment and the right to organize and file grievances.
- Fair compensation.
- Opportunities for training, promotion, and personal development.

Companies should provide *communities* with
- Payment of fair taxes.
- Honest information about plans such as plant closings.
- Resources that support charities, schools, and civic activities.
- Reasonable access to media sources.

Companies should provide *environmental and human rights advocates* with
- Greenhouse gas emissions data.
- Recycling and resource conservation data.
- Child labour transparency.
- Full disclosure of suppliers located in developing countries.

customers, then its revenues and profits will suffer. This reality explains why companies use enterprise risk management, as described later in this chapter, to meet the needs of all stakeholders.

IN BUSINESS

A recent survey conducted by Hewitt Associates, a human resources consulting and out-sourcing company, shows that employees who believe their employer has a good record for corporate social responsibility (CSR) are more engaged in their work and more committed to their employer. Employers are also aware of this, as results from the same survey indicate that they believe the top three benefits for undertaking CSR initiatives are a positive organizational reputation, higher employee engagement, and a positive impact on the environment. A similar view of the importance of an organization's reputation for CSR to prospective employees is echoed by Mario Paron, chief human resources officer for KPMG LLG in Canada. He notes that "When [young recruits] are assessing their choices as to what type of organization they want to be associated with, the entire (CSR) and green aspects are definitely things they ask us about."

Sources: Hewitt Associates, "Research from Best Employers in Canada Study Builds Business Case for Investment in Corporate Social Responsibility," *Canada News Wire,* Ottawa, January 25, 2010; and Derek Sankey, "Jobs Blooming from Companies' Growing Green Focus," *National Post,* April 22, 2009.

PROCESS MANAGEMENT

The past two decades have been a period of tremendous turmoil and change in the business environment. Competition in many industries has become worldwide in scope, and the pace of innovation in products and services has accelerated. This has been good news for consumers, since intensified competition has generally led to lower prices, higher quality, and more choices. However, for businesses, intensified global competition has presented serious challenges. More than ever companies are realizing that they must complement the functional view of their operations with a cross-functional orientation that seeks to improve the *business processes* that deliver customer value.

A **business process** is a series of steps that are followed in order to carry out some task in a business. It is quite common for the linked set of steps comprising a business process to span departmental boundaries. The term *value chain* is often used when we look at how the functional departments of an organization interact with one another to form business processes. A **value chain**, as shown in Exhibit 1–7, consists of the major business functions that add value to a company's products and services. The customer's needs are most effectively met by coordinating the business processes that span these functions.

This section discusses four different approaches to managing and improving business processes—lean production, Six Sigma, enterprise systems, and risk management. Although each is unique in certain respects, they all share the common theme of focusing on managing and improving business processes.

LEARNING OBJECTIVE 5
Explain the basic concepts of lean production, Six Sigma, enterprise systems, and risk management.

Business process
A series of steps that are followed in order to carry out some task in a business.

Value chain
Consists of the major business functions that add value to a company's products and services.

EXHIBIT 1–7 Business Functions Making Up the Value Chain

Research and Development | Product Design | Manufacturing | Marketing | Distribution | Customer Service

Lean Production

Traditionally, managers in manufacturing companies have sought to maximize production so as to spread the costs of investments in equipment and other assets over as many units as possible. In addition, managers have traditionally felt that an important part of their jobs was to keep everyone busy, based on the theory that idleness wastes money. These traditional views, often aided and abetted by traditional management accounting practices, resulted in a number of practices that have come under criticism in recent years.

In a traditional manufacturing company, work is *pushed* through the system in order to produce as much as possible and to keep everyone busy—even if products cannot be immediately sold. This almost inevitably results in large inventories of *raw materials, work in process,* and *finished goods.* **Raw materials** are the materials that are used to make a product. **Work in process** inventories consist of units of product that are only partially complete and will require further work before they are ready for sale to a customer. **Finished goods** inventories consist of units of product that have been completed but have not yet been sold to customers.

The *push* process in traditional manufacturing starts by accumulating large amounts of raw material inventories from suppliers so that operations can proceed smoothly even if unanticipated disruptions occur. Next, enough materials are released to workstations to keep everyone busy. When a workstation completes its tasks, the partially completed goods (i.e., work in process) are "pushed" forward to the next workstation, regardless of whether that workstation is ready to receive them. The result is that partially completed goods stack up, waiting for the next workstation to become available. They may not be completed for days, weeks, or even months. Additionally, when the units are finally completed, customers may or may not want them. If finished goods are produced faster than the market will absorb them, the result is high levels of finished goods inventories.

Although some may argue that maintaining large amounts of inventory has its benefits, it clearly has its costs. According to experts, in addition to tying up money, maintaining inventories encourages inefficient and sloppy work, results in too many product defects, and dramatically increases the amount of time required to complete a product. For example, when partially completed goods are stored for long periods of time before being processed by the next workstation, defects introduced by the preceding workstation go unnoticed. If a machine is out of calibration or incorrect procedures are being followed, many defective units will be produced before the problem is discovered. And when the defects are finally discovered, it may be very difficult to track down the source of the problem. In addition, units may be obsolete or out of fashion by the time they are finally completed.

Large inventories of partially completed goods create many other problems that are best discussed in more advanced courses. These problems are not obvious—if they were, companies would have long ago reduced their inventories. Managers at Toyota are credited with the insight that large inventories often create many more problems than they solve. Toyota pioneered what is known today as *lean production.*

The Lean Thinking Model

The Lean Thinking Model   The **lean thinking model** is a five-step management approach that organizes resources such as people and machines around the flow of business processes and that pulls units through these processes in response to customer orders. The result is lower inventories, fewer defects, less wasted effort, and quicker customer response times. Exhibit 1–8 depicts the five stages of the lean thinking model.

The first step is to identify the value to customers from specific products and services. The second step is to identify the *business process* that delivers this value to customers.[9] As discussed earlier, the linked set of steps comprising a business process typically span the departmental boundaries that are specified in an organization chart.

Raw materials
Materials that are used to make a product.

Work in process
Inventories consisting of units of product that are only partially complete and will require further work before they are ready for sale to a customer.

Finished goods
Inventories consisting of units of product that have been completed but have not yet been sold to customers.

Lean thinking model
A five-step management approach that organizes resources around the flow of business processes and pulls units through in response to customer orders.

EXHIBIT 1–8   The Lean Thinking Model

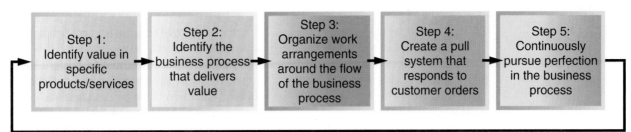

Source: This exhibit is adapted from James P. Womack and Daniel T. Jones, *Lean Thinking: Banish Waste and Create Wealth in Your Corporation.* Revised and updated (New York, NY: Simon & Schuster, 2003).

The third step is to organize work around the flow of the business process. This is often accomplished by creating what is known as a *manufacturing cell*. The cellular approach takes employees and equipment from departments that were previously separated from one another and places them side by side in a work space called a *cell*. The equipment within the cell is aligned in a sequential manner that follows the steps of the business process. Each employee is trained to perform all the steps within his or her own manufacturing cell.

The fourth step in the lean thinking model is to create a pull system where production is not initiated until a customer has ordered a product. Inventories are reduced to a minimum by purchasing raw materials and producing units only as needed to meet customer demand. Under ideal conditions, a company operating under a pull system would purchase only enough materials each day to meet that day's needs. Moreover, the company would have no goods still in process at the end of the day, and all goods completed during the day would be shipped immediately to customers. As this sequence suggests, work takes place "just in time" in the sense that raw materials are received by each manufacturing cell just in time to go into production, manufactured parts are completed just in time to be assembled into products, and products are completed just in time to be shipped to customers. Not surprisingly, this facet of the lean thinking model is often called **just-in-time production**, or **JIT** for short.

The change from *push* to *pull* production is more profound than it may appear. Among other things, producing only in response to a customer order means that workers will be idle whenever demand falls below the company's production capacity. This can be an extremely difficult cultural change for an organization. It challenges the core beliefs of many managers and raises anxieties in workers who have become accustomed to being kept busy all of the time.

The fifth step of the lean thinking model is to continuously pursue perfection in the business process. In a traditional company, parts and materials are inspected for defects when they are received from suppliers, and assembled units are inspected as they progress along the production line. In a lean production system, the company's suppliers are responsible for the quality of incoming parts and materials. And instead of using quality inspectors, the company's production workers are directly responsible for spotting defective units. A worker who discovers a defect immediately stops the flow of production. Supervisors go to the cell to determine the cause of the problem and correct it before any further defective units are produced. This procedure ensures that problems are quickly identified and corrected.

The lean thinking model can also be used to improve the business processes that link companies together. The term **supply chain management** is commonly used to refer to the coordination of business processes across companies to better serve end consumers. For example Canadian Tire Corporation and Costco coordinate their business processes with those of key suppliers to ensure that tires, cleaning supplies, and garden supplies are on shelves when customers want them.

Just-in-time (JIT) production
A pull system in the lean thinking model where production is not initiated until a customer has ordered a product.

Supply chain management
The coordination of business processes across companies to better serve end consumers.

IN BUSINESS

Tesco, a grocery retailer in Britain, used lean thinking to improve its replenishment process for cola products. Tesco and Britvic (its cola supplier) traced the cola delivery process from "the checkout counter of the grocery store through Tesco's regional distribution center (RDC), Britvic's RDC, the warehouse at the Britvic bottling plant, the filling lines for cola destined for Tesco, and the warehouse of Britvic's can supplier." Each step of the process revealed enormous waste. Tesco implemented numerous changes such as electronically linking its point-of-sale data from its grocery stores to its RDC. This change let customers pace the replenishment process and it helped increase store delivery frequency to every few hours around the clock. Britvic also began delivering cola to Tesco's RDC in wheeled dollies that could be rolled directly into delivery trucks and then to point-of-sale locations in grocery stores.

These changes reduced the total product "touches" from 150 to 50, thereby cutting labour costs. The elapsed time from the supplier's filling line to the customer's cola purchase dropped from 20 days to 5 days. The number of inventory stocking locations declined from five to two, and the supplier's distribution centre was eliminated.

Source: Ghostwriter, "Teaching the Big Box New Tricks," *Fortune*, November 14, 2005, pp. 208B–208F.

Six Sigma

Six Sigma
A process improvement method that relies on customer feedback and fact-based data gathering and analysis techniques to drive process improvement.

Six Sigma is a process improvement method that relies on customer feedback and fact-based data gathering and analysis techniques to drive process improvement. Motorola and General Electric are closely identified with the emergence of the Six Sigma movement. Technically, the term *Six Sigma* refers to a process that generates no more than 3.4 defects per million opportunities. Because this rate of defects is so low, Six Sigma is sometimes associated with the term *zero defects*.

The most common framework used to guide Six Sigma process improvement efforts is known as DMAIC (pronounced: du-may-ik), which stands for Define, Measure, Analyze, Improve, and Control. As summarized in Exhibit 1–9, the Define stage of the process focuses on defining the scope and purpose of the project, the flow of the current process, and the customer's requirements. The Measure stage is used to gather baseline performance data concerning the existing process and to narrow the scope of the project to the most important problems. The Analyze stage focuses on identifying the root causes of the problems that were identified during the Measure stage. The Analyze stage often reveals that the process includes many *activities that do not add value to the product or service*. Activities that customers are not willing to pay for because they add no value are

EXHIBIT 1–9 The Six Sigma DMAIC Framework

Stage	Goals
Define	Establish the scope and purpose of the project. Diagram the flow of the current process. Establish the customer's requirements for the process.
Measure	Gather baseline performance data related to the existing process. Narrow the scope of the project to the most important problems.
Analyze	Identify the root cause(s) of the problems identified in the Measure stage.
Improve	Develop, evaluate, and implement solutions to the problems.
Control	Ensure that problems remain fixed. Seek to improve the new methods over time.

Source: Peter C. Brewer and Nancy A. Bagranoff, "Near Zero-Defect Accounting with Six Sigma," *Journal of Corporate Accounting and Finance,* January–February 2004, pp. 67–72.

known as **non-value-added activities** and such activities should be eliminated wherever possible. During the Improve stage, potential solutions are developed, evaluated, and implemented to eliminate non-value-added activities and any other problems uncovered in the Analyze stage. Finally, the objective in the Control stage is to ensure that the problems remain fixed and that the new methods are improved over time.[10]

Managers must be very careful when attempting to translate Six Sigma improvements into financial benefits. There are only two ways to increase profits—decrease costs or increase sales. Cutting costs may seem easy—lay off workers who are no longer needed because of improvements such as eliminating non-value-added activities. However, if this approach is taken, employees quickly get the message that process improvements lead to job losses and they will understandably resist further improvement efforts. If improvement is to continue, employees must be convinced that the end result will be more-secure rather than less-secure jobs. This can happen only if management uses tools such as Six Sigma to generate more business rather than to cut the workforce.

Non-value-added activities
Activities that customers are not willing to pay for because they add no value.

Enterprise Systems

Historically, most companies implemented specific software programs to support specific business functions. The accounting department would select its own software applications to meet its needs, while manufacturing would select different software programs to support its needs. The separate systems were not integrated and could not easily pass data back and forth. The end result was data duplication and data inconsistencies coupled with lengthy customer response times and high costs.

An **enterprise system**[11] is designed to overcome these problems by integrating data across an organization into a single software system that enables all employees to have simultaneous access to a common set of data. There are two keys to the data integration inherent in an enterprise system. First, all data are recorded only once in the company's centralized digital data repository known as a *database*. When data are added to the database or are changed, the new information is simultaneously and immediately available to everyone across the organization. Second, the unique data elements contained within the database can be linked together. For example, one data element, such as a customer identification number, can be related to other data elements, such as that customer's address, billing history, shipping history, merchandise returns history, and so on. The ability to forge such relationships among data elements explains why this type of database is called a *relational database*.

Data integration helps employees communicate with one another and it also helps them communicate with their suppliers and customers. For example, consider how the *customer relationship management* process is improved when enterprise-wide information resides in one location. Whether meeting the customer's needs requires accessing information related to billing (an accounting function), delivery status (a distribution function), price quotes (a marketing function), or merchandise returns (a customer service function) the required information is readily available to the employee interacting with the customer. Although expensive and risky to install, the benefits of data integration have led many companies to invest in enterprise systems.

Enterprise system
A software system designed to overcome problems in data inconsistency and duplication by integrating data across an organization into a single software system.

Enterprise Risk Management

Businesses face risks every day. Some risks are foreseeable. For example, a company could reasonably be expected to foresee the possibility of a natural disaster or a fire destroying its centralized data storage facility. Companies respond to this type of risk by maintaining off-site backup data storage facilities. Other risks are unforeseeable. As an example, in March 2010, Bauer Hockey Corp. announced a recall of 13 different models of its junior and youth hockey sticks, most of which were manufactured in China prior to 2008. The reason for the recall was that the yellow paint used on the sticks contains lead in excess of allowable limits. Lead can cause adverse health consequences if ingested by children. Estimates indicate that worldwide, as many as 100,000 of these sticks were sold between 2006 and 2010, including nearly 70,000 in Canada.[12] The financial consequences of such recalls can be significant and would include Bauer's cost of replacing the sticks returned by customers, potential lost sales due to consumer concerns about the safety of the product, and lawsuits arising from health issues related to product use.

Every business strategy or decision involves risks. **Enterprise risk management** is a process used by a company to proactively identify and manage those risks.

Enterprise risk management
A process used by a company to proactively identify and manage foreseeable risks.

Identifying and Controlling Business Risks   Companies should identify foreseeable risks before they occur rather than react to unfortunate events that have already happened. The left-hand column of Exhibit 1–10 provides 12 examples of business risks. This list is not exhaustive; rather its purpose is to illustrate the diverse nature of business risks that companies face. Whether the risks relate to the weather, computer hackers, complying with the law, employee theft, financial reporting, or strategic decision making, they all have one thing in common: If the risks are not managed effectively, they can impair a company's ability to meet its goals.

Once a company identifies its risks, it can respond to them in various ways such as accepting, avoiding, sharing, or reducing the risk. Perhaps the most common risk management tactic is to reduce risks by implementing specific controls. The right-hand column of Exhibit 1–10 provides an example of a control that could be implemented to help reduce each of the risks mentioned in the left-hand column of the exhibit.

In conclusion, a sophisticated enterprise risk management system cannot guarantee that all risks are eliminated. Nonetheless, many companies understand that managing risks is a superior alternative to reacting, perhaps too late, to unfortunate events.

EXHIBIT 1–10   Identifying and Controlling Business Risks

Examples of Business Risks	Examples of Controls to Reduce Business Risks
• Intellectual assets being stolen from computer files	• Create firewalls that prohibit computer hackers from corrupting or stealing intellectual property
• Products harming customers	• Develop a formal and rigorous new product testing program
• Losing market share due to the unforeseen actions of competitors	• Develop an approach for legally gathering information about competitors' plans and practices
• Poor weather conditions shutting down operations	• Develop contingency plans for overcoming weather-related disruptions
• A Web site malfunctioning	• Thoroughly test the Web site before going "live" on the Internet
• A supplier strike halting the flow of raw materials	• Establish a relationship with two companies capable of providing needed raw materials
• A poorly designed incentive compensation system causing employees to make bad decisions	• Create a balanced set of performance measures that motivates the desired behaviour
• Financial statements inaccurately reporting the value of inventory	• Count the physical inventory on hand to make sure that it agrees with the accounting records
• An employee stealing assets	• Segregate duties so that the same employee does not have physical custody of an asset and the responsibility of accounting for it
• An employee accessing unauthorized information	• Create password-protected barriers that prohibit employees from obtaining information not needed to do their jobs
• Inaccurate budget estimates causing excessive or insufficient production	• Implement a rigorous budget review process
• Failing to comply with equal employment opportunity laws	• Create a report that tracks key metrics related to compliance with the laws

Summary

- Managerial accounting assists managers in carrying out their responsibilities, which include planning, directing and motivating, and controlling. **[LO1]**
- Managerial accounting differs substantially from financial accounting in that it is oriented more toward the future; places less emphasis on precision; emphasizes segments of an organization (rather than the organization as a whole); is not governed by generally accepted accounting principles; and is not mandatory. **[LO2]**
- Most organizations are decentralized to some degree. An organization chart depicts who works for whom in the organization, and which units perform the various staff and line functions. Accountants perform a staff function—they support and provide assistance to others inside the organization. **[LO3]**
- Ethical standards serve a very important practical function in an advanced market economy. Many organizations prepare a code of ethics to reflect their values and the moral system under which they operate. Professional accounting groups, such as CMA Canada, also have their own code of professional ethics to provide operating guidelines for their members. As an extension of the concept of organizational ethics, many companies have embraced corporate social responsibility whereby the needs of numerous stakeholders are considered when making decisions. **[LO4]**
- Lean production organizes resources around business processes and pulls units through those processes in response to customer orders. The result is lower inventories, fewer defects, less wasted effort, and quicker customer response times. **[LO5]**
- Six Sigma uses the DMAIC (Define, Measure, Analyze, Improve, and Control) framework to eliminate non-value-added activities and to improve processes. **[LO5]**
- An enterprise system integrates data across the organization in a single software system that makes the same data available to all managers. Enterprise risk management involves proactively identifying and managing key risks faced by an organization. **[LO5]**

Glossary

Review key terms and definitions on Connect.

Mc Graw Hill **connect**

Questions

1–1   What are the major differences between financial and managerial accounting?
1–2   What is a business plan and by whom is it used?
1–3   Describe the three broad categories of customer value propositions.
1–4   Describe the three major activities of a manager.
1–5   What are the four steps in the planning and control cycle?
1–6   Describe the responsibilities of the controller.
1–7   Distinguish between line and staff positions in an organization.
1–8   What is decentralization?
1–9   What are the three main categories of inventories in a manufacturing company?
1–10 What are the five steps in the lean thinking model?
1–11 What are the major benefits from successful implementation of the lean thinking model?
1–12 Describe what is meant by a "pull" production system.
1–13 Briefly describe Six Sigma.
1–14 Why is corporate social responsibility becoming increasingly important to organizations?
1–15 What is an enterprise system supposed to accomplish?
1–16 Why do companies prepare a code of ethics?
1–17 What are the four key aspects of the *Sarbanes-Oxley Act of 2002*?
1–18 Briefly describe what is meant by *enterprise risk management*.

Exercises ☒ connect™

EXERCISE 1–1 The Roles of Managers and Management Accountants [LO1, LO3]
A number of terms that relate to organizations, the work of management, and the role of managerial accounting are listed below:

budgets	controller
decentralization	directing and motivating
feedback	financial accounting
line	managerial accounting
non-monetary data	planning
performance report	staff
precision	chief financial officer

Choose the term or terms above that most appropriately complete the following statements.

1. _____ is concerned with providing information for the use of people inside the organization, whereas _____ is concerned with providing information for the use of people outside the organization.
2. _____ consists of identifying alternatives, selecting from among the alternatives the one that is best for the organization, and specifying what actions will be taken to implement the chosen alternative.
3. When _____, managers oversee day-to-day activities and keep the organization functioning smoothly.
4. The accounting and other reports coming to management that are used in controlling the organization are called _____.
5. The delegation of decision-making authority throughout an organization by allowing managers at various operating levels to make key decisions relating to their area of responsibility is called _____.
6. A position on the organization chart that is directly related to achieving the basic objectives of an organization is called a _____ position.
7. A _____ position provides service or assistance to other parts of the organization and does not directly achieve the basic objectives of the organization.
8. The manager in charge of the accounting department is generally known as the _____.
9. The plans of management are expressed formally in _____.
10. A detailed report to management comparing budgeted data to actual data for a specific time period is called a _____.
11. The _____ is the member of the top management team who is responsible for providing timely and relevant data to support planning and control activities and for preparing financial statements for external users.
12. Managerial accounting places less emphasis on _____ and more emphasis on _____ than financial accounting.

EXERCISE 1–2 Professional Ethics and the Business Environment [LO4, LO5]
A number of terms are listed below:

value chain	work in process	enterprise risk management
Sarbanes-Oxley Act	Six Sigma	business risks
lean thinking model	code of professional ethics	corporate social responsibility
customer value proposition	business process	enterprise system
corporate governance	non-value-added activity	just-in-time

Required:
Choose the term or terms from the above list that most appropriately completes each of the following statements:

1. Inventory consisting of units of product that are only partially complete at the end of a period is known as _____.
2. _____ is a method that relies on customer feedback and objective data gathering and analysis techniques to drive process improvement.
3. A(n) _____ is a series of steps that are followed to carry out some task in a business.

4. The system by which a company is directed and controlled is called _____.
5. The process used by a company to help identify the risks that it faces and to develop responses to those risks so that the company is reasonably assured of meeting its goals is known as _____.
6. A production and inventory control system in which materials are purchased and units are produced only as needed to meet actual customer demand is known as _____.
7. Poorly designed products that cause health problems for customers and financial statements that overstate the amount of revenue generated by the organization are examples of _____.
8. Increasing the rate of output of a(n) _____ as the result of an improvement effort is unlikely to have much effect on profits.
9. A(n) _____ consists of business functions that add value to a company's products and services, such as research and development, product design, manufacturing, marketing, distribution, and customer service.
10. A(n) _____ integrates data from across an organization into a single centralized database that enables all employees to access a common set of data.
11. Professional accounting groups such as CMA Canada have a(n) _____ that contains details of how its members should conduct themselves in their dealings with the public.
12. The _____ is a five-step management approach that organizes resources around the flow of business processes and that pulls units through those processes in response to customer orders.
13. A company can succeed only if it creates a reason for customers to choose it over a competitor; in short, a _____.
14. The _____ represents an important reform of corporate governance practices and among other things requires the CEO and CFO to certify in writing that financial statements fairly represent the results of operations.
15. The concept of organizations considering the needs of all stakeholders when making decisions is known as _____.

EXERCISE 1–3 Ethics in Business [LO4]

Tony Gallo was hired by a popular fast-food restaurant as an order-taker and cashier. Shortly after taking the job, he was shocked to overhear an employee bragging to a friend about shortchanging customers. He confronted the employee who then snapped back: "Mind your own business. Besides, everyone does it and the customers never miss the money." Tony didn't know how to respond to this aggressive stance.

Required:
What would be the practical consequences on the fast-food industry and on consumers if cashiers generally shortchanged customers at every opportunity?

McGraw Hill connect Problems

PROBLEM 1–4 Ethics in Business [LO4]

John Brigley, CMA, is the controller of Baden Foods, a large privately owned food processing company located in southern Ontario. John received his designation as a certified management accountant several years ago and has been working his way up the corporate ladder at Baden Foods. As controller, John is responsible for coordinating the preparation of the annual operating budget that includes projections of revenues and expenses for the coming year. Once the budget is approved by James Davis, the president of Baden Foods, it is used in the monthly performance report, which compares actual results to the budget projections.

To provide an incentive for the senior management team to make decisions that benefit the company as a whole, last year James Davis established a bonus plan. In any month that the company's actual operating income (revenues minus expenses) is better than the budgeted amount, all members of the senior management team, including the CFO, the controller, the vice-president of Production, and the vice-president of Marketing receive a bonus. Last year was the first year the new bonus plan was used, and bonuses were paid out in five of the twelve months of the fiscal year.

Late Friday afternoon, as John was working on finalizing the operating budget for the upcoming fiscal year, he received a call from Jan Robson, the CFO at Baden Foods. The conversation went as follows:

Jan: Hi John, how goes the budgeting process? We have the review with Davis next week so I just want to be sure we're good to go.

John: Really well, Jan, I'm just putting the final touches on the budget projections and will have a draft version for your review first thing Monday morning.

Jan: Great, glad to hear it. How do the operating income numbers look compared to last year's actual results?

John: They look great. With the success of some of our new products last year, our new marketing campaign, and the tainted food scandal that has plagued one of our key competitors, I'm budgeting significant increases in operating income each month compared to last year.

Jan: Significant increases every month? Are you sure about this?

John: Well, as sure as one can ever be when projecting what revenues and expenses will be in the future. But I'm confident that the budget is based on reasonable expectations. I've talked to all the key managers in production and marketing, and they agree that my estimates are very reasonable.

Jan: Sounds like you've done your homework, as usual. I'm thinking though that maybe being a bit more conservative in *our* budget estimates might be a better way to go.

John: I don't quite follow. It's not that the estimates are aggressive. As I said, all the key managers think the budget is reasonable, and attainable if we work hard.

Jan: Right, I understand that. I'm just saying that given the new bonus plan that Davis introduced last year, maybe we should be developing monthly budgets that we are sure we can beat. Do you follow?

John: Wait a minute—are you suggesting that we intentionally lowball the budget numbers just so we can get our bonuses each month?

Jan: I prefer to think of it as conservative budgeting as opposed to lowballing. Plus, it's not like I'm asking you to misstate the actual revenues and expenses that get reported each month. That would be unethical since the actual numbers get used by our creditors and by the tax authorities.

John: I don't know, Jan. Intentionally developing budgets that we know we can beat just to get our bonuses seems just as unethical as misstating the actual results.

Jan: I disagree. The budgets are used only for internal purposes. What's the harm in being a little conservative? Besides, we all work hard and we deserve the monthly bonuses. Davis will never know because he's so busy with his charitable foundations these days that he really doesn't have a good idea of what's realistic when it comes to the budget each year. As you know he basically approves whatever we recommend without much discussion.

John: But won't he get suspicious when actual results are better than the budget every month?

Jan: Heck no, he'll just be delighted that we're doing better than expected! It's a win–win situation, John. We'll get our bonuses and Davis will be happy the company is doing so well. I've got to run but, I look forward to seeing those conservative budget projections first thing Monday morning.

Required:
1. In deciding whether to comply with Jan's request for a "conservative budget," what aspects of the code of professional ethics featured in Exhibit 1–5 should guide John's behaviour?
2. What would you recommend that John do, and why?

PROBLEM 1–5 Preparing an Organization Chart [LO1]

Mainland University is a large university located in British Columbia. The university is headed by a president who has five vice-presidents reporting to him. These vice-presidents are responsible for auxiliary services, admissions and records, academics, financial services (controller), and the physical plant.

In addition, the university has managers who report to these vice-presidents. These include managers for central purchasing, the university press, and the university bookstore, all of whom report to the vice-president for auxiliary services; managers for computer services and for accounting and finance, who report to the vice-president for financial services; and managers for grounds and custodial services and for plant and maintenance, who report to the vice-president for the physical plant.

The university has five faculties—business, humanities, fine arts, engineering and quantitative methods, and a law school. Each of these units has a dean who is responsible to the academic vice-president. Each faculty has several departments.

Required:
1.   Prepare an organization chart for Mainland University.
2.   Which of the positions on your chart would be line positions? Why would they be line positions? Which would be staff positions? Why?
3.   Which of the positions on your chart would have a need for accounting information? Explain.

PROBLEM 1–6 Ethics in Business [LO4]

Adam Williams, CMA, was recently hired as assistant controller of GroChem Inc., which processes chemicals for use in fertilizers. Williams was selected for this position because of his past experience in chemical processing. During his first month on the job, Williams made a point of getting to know the people responsible for the plant operations and learning how things are done at GroChem.

During a conversation with the plant supervisor, Williams asked about the company procedures for handling toxic waste materials. The plant supervisor replied that he was not involved with the disposal of wastes and suggested that Williams might be wise to ignore this issue. This response strengthened Williams' determination to probe this area further to be sure that the company was not vulnerable to litigation.

On further investigation, Williams discovered evidence that GroChem was using a nearby residential landfill to dump toxic wastes—an illegal activity. It appeared that some members of GroChem's management team were aware of this situation and may have been involved in arranging for this dumping; however, Williams was unable to determine whether his superior, the controller, was involved.

Uncertain how he should proceed, Williams began to consider his options by outlining the following two alternative courses of action:
•   Seek the advice of his superior, the controller.
•   Anonymously release the information to the local newspaper.

Required:
1.   Discuss why Adam Williams has an ethical responsibility to take some action in the matter of GroChem Inc. and the dumping of toxic wastes. Refer to the code of professional ethics established by CMA Ontario to support your answer.
2.   For each of the two alternative courses of action that Williams has outlined, explain whether or not the action is appropriate according to the guidelines presented in Exhibit 1–5.
3.   Assume that Adam Williams sought the advice of his superior, the controller, and discovered that the controller was involved in the dumping of toxic wastes. Describe the steps that Williams should take to resolve this situation.

(CMA, adapted)

PROBLEM 1–7 Corporate Governance and Corporate Social Responsibility [LO4]

The recent problems experienced by Toyota Motor Corporation illustrate how important it is to identify and control business risks, even for highly reputable companies. There has been considerable speculation in the business press as to whether Toyota acted quickly enough in recalling vehicles, which some estimates place at 8 million worldwide. Also, reports suggest that Toyota did not tell federal regulators in Canada about a possible problem with the accelerator pedal when the company first learned of the issue. Instead Toyota waited until after the recall notice had been issued to tell regulators about the problem. Other analysts have suggested that Toyota's rapid growth in worldwide production and sales compromised its focus on maintaining high standards of quality. In response to the crisis, Toyota has temporarily closed some plants in Britain and France as a result of lower demand because of the recalls. The company has also offered significant discounts to win back lost customers in North America.

Required:
1.   Identify stakeholders that probably were negatively affected by the problems experienced by Toyota.
2.   What role does effective corporate governance play in reducing the likelihood that companies will experience the types of problems faced by Toyota?

PROBLEM 1–8 Line and Staff Positions; Organization Chart [LO1]

The Association of Medical Personnel (AMP) is a membership-education organization that serves a wide range of individuals who work for medical institutions including hospitals, clinics, and medical practices. The membership is composed of doctors, nurses, medical assistants, and professional administrators. The purpose of the organization is to provide individuals in the medical field with a professional organization that offers educational and training opportunities through local chapters, a monthly magazine (*AMP Review*), continuing-education programs, seminars, self-study courses, and research publications.

AMP is governed by a board of directors who are members elected to these positions by the membership. The chairperson of the board is the highest-ranking volunteer member and presides over the board; the board establishes policy for the organization. The policies are administered and carried out by AMP's paid professional staff. The president's chief responsibility is to manage the operations of the professional staff. Like any organization, the professional staff of AMP is composed of line and staff positions. A partial organization chart of the AMP professional staff is shown in Exhibit 1–A.

EXHIBIT 1–A   Partial Organization Chart for the Association of Medical Personnel

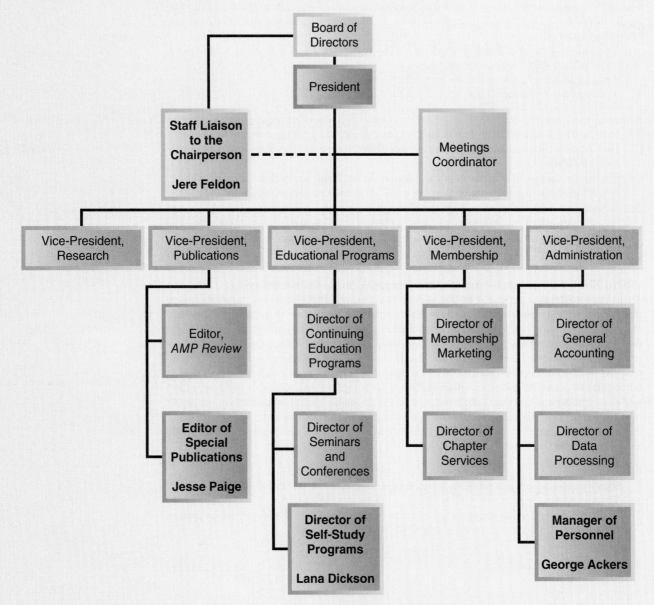

Four of the positions appearing in the organization chart are described below.

Jere Feldon, Staff Liaison to the Chairperson

Feldon is assigned to work with the chairperson of AMP by serving as an intermediary between the chairperson and the professional staff. All correspondence to the chairperson is funnelled through Feldon. Feldon also works very closely with the president of AMP, especially on any matters that have to be brought to the attention of the chairperson and the board.

Lana Dickson, Director of Self-Study Programs

Dickson is responsible for developing and marketing the self-study programs offered by AMP. Self-study courses consist of DVDs and a workbook. Most of the courses are developed by outside contractors who work under her direction. Dickson relies on the director of membership marketing to assist her in marketing these courses.

Jesse Paige, Editor of Special Publications

Paige is primarily responsible for the publication and sale of any research monographs that are generated by the research department. In addition, he coordinates the publication of any special projects that may be prepared by any other AMP committees or departments. Paige also works with AMP's Publication Committee, which sets policy on the types of publications that AMP should publish.

George Ackers, Manager of Personnel

Ackers works with all of the departments of AMP in hiring professional and clerical staff. The individual departments screen and interview prospective employees for professional positions, but Ackers is responsible for advertising open positions. Ackers plays a more active role in the hiring of clerical personnel by screening individuals before they are sent to the departments for interviews. In addition, Ackers coordinates the employee performance evaluation program and administers AMP's salary schedule and fringe benefit program.

Required:
1. Distinguish between line positions and staff positions in an organization by defining each. Include in your discussion the role, purpose, and importance of each.
2. Many times, conflicts will arise between line and staff managers in organizations. Discuss the characteristics of line and staff managers that may cause conflicts between the two.
3. For each of the four individuals identified by name in the text,
    a. Identify whether the individual's position is a line or staff position and explain why.
    b. Identify potential problems that could arise in each individual's position, either due to the type of position (i.e., line or staff) or to the location of the individual's position within the organization.

(CMA, adapted)

Research

R 1–9 Ethics and Corporate Governance [LO4]

Go to the Web site of the Canadian Imperial Bank of Commerce (www.cibc.com/ca/about.html) and find the bank's statement of corporate governance practices. Describe the nature and extent of the governance practices it uses. Locate its code of ethics for directors and code of conduct for employees. Discuss the content of these codes. Why do companies make their codes of conduct/ ethics publically available?

R 1–10 Strategies [LO1]

Using the annual report of a major company such as Canadian Tire Corporation or Canadian National Railway, describe their strategies as presented in their Management Discussion and Analysis. Discuss whether you believe their strategies are effective against major competitors.

R 1–11 Corporate Social Responsibility [LO5]

Go to the Web site for Unilever (www.unilever.ca) and use the "Sustainability" link to examine how the company is attempting to educate consumers about water conservation. Locate and download its "Sustainable Development Report" for 2010. Discuss the content of the report with respect to the types of "sustainability" measures they use. Do you think Unilever is doing a good job of balancing its growth objectives with its desire to be socially responsible? Why or why not?

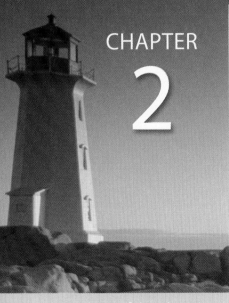

COST TERMS, CONCEPTS, AND CLASSIFICATIONS

Learning Objectives

After studying Chapter 2, you should be able to

1. Identify and give examples of each of the three basic manufacturing cost categories.

2. Distinguish between product costs and period costs and give examples of each.

3. Prepare an income statement, including the calculation of cost of goods sold.

4. Prepare a schedule of cost of goods manufactured.

5. Explain the differences between variable and fixed costs.

6. Identify the differences between direct and indirect costs.

7. Describe the cost classifications used in making decisions: differential costs, opportunity costs, and sunk costs.

■ CONSIDERING THE COSTS

Terri, the owner of a retail florist shop, has been trying to decide for some time whether she should continue to use a local courier service to deliver flowers to customers or buy a delivery truck and use one of her employees to make the deliveries. At a recent family dinner, she brought up the subject of the delivery truck with her brother-in-law, who considers himself to be an expert on all management subjects. He seized this opportunity to impress upon Terri his understanding of costs and management issues.

In rapid-fire succession, Terri's brother-in-law told her that the fees paid to the courier to deliver flowers are a variable cost and a period cost, but the costs of the flowers are product costs rather than period costs, even though the flower costs are also variable costs. On the other hand, the depreciation of the delivery truck would be a fixed cost and a period cost. And while the fuel for the truck would be a variable cost and a differential cost, the wages of the person making the deliveries would be a fixed cost, not a differential cost, and would involve an opportunity cost. At this point, Terri excused herself—pleading that she had to help in the kitchen.

Terri felt that her brother-in-law's comments were more confusing than helpful, but she knew that she could no longer put off the decision about the delivery truck. She would have to think carefully about her costs and determine what costs should be considered in this decision.

What are the different ways of classifying costs? What are these different classifications used for? What are the differences in the financial statements for merchandising versus manufacturing companies? These are some of the major topics covered in this chapter.

A s explained in Chapter 1, the work of management focuses on (1) planning, which includes setting objectives and outlining how to attain these objectives; (2) directing and motivating; and (3) controlling, which includes the steps taken to ensure that objectives are realized. To carry out these responsibilities, managers need *information* about the organization. From an accounting point of view, this information often relates to the costs of the organization.

In managerial accounting, the term *cost* is used in many different ways. The reason is that there are many types of costs, and these costs are classified differently according to the immediate needs of management. For example, managers may require cost data to prepare external financial reports, to prepare planning budgets, or to make decisions. Each different use of cost data requires a different classification and definition of costs. For example, the preparation of external financial reports requires the use of historical cost data, whereas decision making may require predictions about future costs. The idea of different costs for different purposes is a very important aspect of managerial accounting.

■ GENERAL COST CLASSIFICATIONS

All types of organizations incur costs—business, non-business, manufacturing, merchandising, and service. Generally, the kinds of costs that are incurred and the way in which these costs are classified depend on the type of organization involved. However, managerial accounting is applicable to all types of organizations. For this reason, our discussion of cost characteristics considers a variety of organizations—manufacturing, merchandising, and service.

Our initial focus in this chapter is on manufacturing companies, since their basic activities include most of the activities found in other types of business organizations. Manufacturing companies such as MEGA Brands, Bombardier, and CCM acquire raw materials, produce finished goods, market, distribute, bill, and incur costs. Therefore, an understanding of costs in a manufacturing company can be very helpful in understanding costs in other types of organizations. Categories that are not applicable to a certain type of organization can be omitted. For example, Terri's Flower Shop buys flowers so it has a product cost for flower purchases, but it does not grow flowers so it does not have production costs. The Flower Shop has delivery costs for its courier service, which is a distribution cost. Although not discussed in the opening vignette, it would likely have marketing costs and perhaps billing costs.

> **LEARNING OBJECTIVE 1**
> Identify and give examples of each of the three basic manufacturing cost categories.

Manufacturing Costs

Most manufacturing companies divide manufacturing costs into three broad categories: direct materials, direct labour, and manufacturing overhead. A discussion of each of these categories follows.

Direct Materials   The materials that go into the final product are called *raw materials*. This term is somewhat misleading, since it seems to imply unprocessed natural resources like wood pulp or iron ore. Actually, *raw materials* refer to any materials that are used in the final product, and the finished product of one company can become the raw materials of another company. For example, car batteries produced by Magna International are a raw material used by BMW in some of its automobiles.

Raw materials may include both direct and indirect materials. **Direct materials** are those materials that become an integral part of the finished product and that can be physically and conveniently traced to it. This would include, for example, the seats Bombardier purchases from subcontractors to install in its passenger trains. Also included is the tiny electric motor Panasonic uses in its DVD players to make the DVD spin.

Sometimes it is not worth the effort to trace the costs of relatively insignificant materials to the end products. Such minor items would include the solder used to make electrical connections in a Sony TV or the glue used in a pair of Saucony running shoes.

> **Direct materials**
> Those materials that become an integral part of a finished product and can be conveniently traced to it.

Indirect materials
Small items of material such as glue and nails that may become an integral part of a finished product but the costs of tracing them exceed the benefits.

Direct labour
Those factory labour costs that can be traced easily to individual units of product. Also called *touch labour.*

Indirect labour
The labour costs of janitors, supervisors, materials handlers, and other factory workers that cannot be conveniently traced directly to particular products.

Materials such as solder and glue are called **indirect materials** and are included as part of manufacturing overhead, which is discussed later in this section. Indirect materials can still be thought of as raw materials but they are not treated as direct materials because the costs of directly tracing them to the finished products exceed the benefits of doing so.

Direct Labour   **Direct labour** consists of labour costs that can be easily (i.e., physically and conveniently) traced to individual units of product. Direct labour is sometimes called *touch labour,* since direct labour workers typically touch the product while it is being made. The labour costs of assembly-line workers at Bauer Hockey, for example, would be direct labour costs, as would the labour costs of welders at Irving Shipbuilding and equipment operators at Cervélo.

Labour costs that cannot be physically traced to the creation of products, or that can be traced only at great cost and inconvenience, are termed **indirect labour** and treated as part of manufacturing overhead, along with indirect materials. Indirect labour includes the labour costs of janitors, supervisors, materials handlers, and security personnel. Although the efforts of these workers are essential to production, it would be either impractical or impossible to accurately trace their costs to specific units of product. Hence, such labour costs are treated as indirect labour.

In some industries, major shifts are taking place in the structure of labour costs. Sophisticated automated equipment, operated and maintained by skilled indirect workers, is increasingly replacing direct labour. In fact, direct labour averages only about 10% of sales revenues in many manufacturing industries. In a few companies, direct labour has become such a minor element of cost that it is no longer treated as a separate cost category. More is said in later chapters about this trend and the impact it is having on cost systems. However, the vast majority of manufacturing and service companies throughout the world continue to recognize direct labour as a separate cost category.

Manufacturing overhead
All costs associated with manufacturing except direct materials and direct labour.

Manufacturing Overhead   **Manufacturing overhead**, the third element of manufacturing costs, includes all costs of manufacturing except direct materials and direct labour. Manufacturing overhead includes items such as indirect materials, indirect labour, maintenance and repairs on production equipment, heat and light, property taxes, depreciation, and insurance on manufacturing facilities. A company also incurs costs associated with its selling and administrative functions (for heat and light, property taxes, insurance, depreciation, and so forth), but these costs are not included as part of manufacturing overhead. Only those costs associated with *operating the production facility (factory)* are included in the manufacturing overhead category. Studies show that manufacturing overhead averages about 16% of sales revenues.[1]

Various terms are used to describe manufacturing overhead, such as *indirect manufacturing cost*, *factory overhead*, and *factory burden*. All of these terms are synonymous with *manufacturing overhead.*

Conversion cost
Direct labour cost plus manufacturing overhead cost.

Prime cost
Direct materials cost plus direct labour cost.

Manufacturing overhead combined with direct labour is called **conversion cost**. This term stems from the fact that direct labour costs and overhead costs are incurred to convert materials into finished products. Direct labour combined with direct materials is called **prime cost**, which, following from the discussion above about direct and indirect costs, groups the two types of direct costs into one category.

The proportion of labour to overhead varies from company to company and even across companies within the same industry. Some automated companies have a large proportion of overhead compared to direct labour costs. Some even classify all labour as overhead. Others, such as those engaged in meat packing, have a large proportion of direct labour. How organizations determine their relative proportions of materials, direct labour, and overhead is a significant component of strategic cost management.

Classification of Labour Costs of Manufacturing

The classification of direct labour and indirect labour costs is relatively straightforward. Janitorial wages are usually classified as overhead because they represent an indirect cost, as would payroll costs for supervisors, security personnel, and maintenance workers.

However, the appropriate classification of idle time and overtime premiums of production workers is less obvious. For example, if three hours of a production worker's time are idle (i.e., not spent on production activities) and each hour costs $20, then $60 of idle time cost usually would be charged to overhead if management felt that the cost was a general cost of all production. However, if a specific job results in idle time, such as waiting for materials because of a product design change demanded by the customer, then the idle time could be charged to the direct labour costs of that job. Whether the customer will pay for the charge depends on the prevailing market conditions (e.g., degree of competition) or the details of the contract with the customer.

Overtime premiums represent the extra hourly wage rate paid to production workers who must work above their normal time requirements. For example, a worker might be paid time and a half for five overtime hours. Thus, if $20 was the base rate, the five hours would have an overtime premium of $10 × 5 hours, or $50. Classification of the overtime as direct labour or overhead depends on the cause of the overtime. A job-specific reason (e.g., a rush order) would dictate a direct job cost, whereas a normal overtime cost resulting from general conditions, such as peak production needs, would dictate an overhead (indirect) charge to all jobs completed during that peak period.

Employee benefits such as employment taxes, medical plans, and pension costs paid by the employer can be 30% to 40% of the base pay. Employee benefit costs for indirect labour would obviously be classified as indirect overhead. However, the employee benefit costs for direct labour are typically added to the base direct labour rate in calculating a total direct labour cost, including benefits.

Overtime premium
The extra hourly wage rate paid to workers who must work above their normal time requirements.

Non-Manufacturing Costs

Generally, non-manufacturing costs are divided into two categories: (1) marketing or selling costs and (2) administrative costs.

Marketing or selling costs include all costs necessary to secure customer orders and get the finished product or service to the customer. These costs are often called *order-getting and order-filling costs.* Examples of marketing costs include order-getting costs such as those for advertising, sales travel, and sales salaries. Order-filling costs would include shipping, sales commissions, and the costs of finished goods warehouses.

Administrative costs include all executive, organizational, and clerical costs associated with the *general management* of an organization rather than with manufacturing, marketing, or selling. Examples of administrative costs include executive compensation, accounting, secretarial, public relations, and similar costs involved in the overall, general administration of the organization *as a whole.*

Managerial accounting concepts and techniques apply to both non-manufacturing and manufacturing activities. Service organizations, for example, are making increased use of cost concepts in analyzing and costing their services. Banks now use cost analysis to determine the cost of offering such services as chequing accounts, consumer loans, and credit cards, and insurance companies determine costs of servicing customers by geographic location, age, marital status, and occupation. This type of cost analysis provides data for controlling selling and administrative functions in the same way that manufacturing cost analysis provides data for controlling manufacturing functions.

Refer back to the flower shop described in the opening vignette of this chapter. Consider the wage cost of the employee who prepares flower arrangements. This employee may also wait on customers, unpack purchases, prepare the payroll, and so on. How would Terri deal with such costs? She could require detailed time reports for the various activities that would permit the classification of employee wage costs as product costs for flower arrangements, selling costs for customer service, and administrative costs for payroll or bookkeeping. However, cost–benefit considerations would likely dictate that such a detailed classification is unnecessary for Terri's operation. It would be simpler to treat the employee's wages as selling costs, or Terri may not even separate selling from administrative but rather use an overall classification: operating costs. Terri will have to decide whether the benefits of having a more detailed breakdown of wages exceed the costs of collecting that data.

Marketing or selling costs
All costs necessary to secure customer orders and get the finished product or service to the customer.

Administrative costs
All executive, organizational, and clerical costs associated with the general management of an organization rather than with manufacturing, marketing, or selling.

IN BUSINESS

Industry Canada, a department of the Canadian federal government, has a Web site containing a wealth of cost data and other statistics for Canadian industries. The data are collected by Statistics Canada from a variety of sources, including annual surveys of manufacturing, retail, and wholesale companies. The information is organized according to whether the industry is in the "goods-producing" sector or the "service-producing" sector, and within each of these categories are more refined subcategories. For example, categories of goods-producing industries include manufacturing, utilities, construction, and agriculture. Manufacturing is then further broken down into categories such as food, textile, machinery, and so on. Service-producing industries include transportation, finance, real estate, and retail, and subcategories are provided for each industry. Subcategories for retailers include motor vehicles, electronics and appliances, food and beverage, etc. The site also includes separate information for small and medium-sized enterprises (SMEs), which is useful comparative data for managers of smaller organizations. A small sampling of the 2008 SME cost information available on the site is shown below.

Industry	Category	Cost of Sales	Labour as % of Cost of Sales
Transportation	Trucking	74.0%	21.1%
Retail	Accommodation and Food Service	42.3%	18.4%
Manufacturing	Food	62.0%	17.0%
Manufacturing	Furniture	66.2%	28.8%

The above data show that the cost of sales percentage differs both across industries and within industries. Accommodation and food service has the lowest cost of goods sold (42.3%), while trucking has the highest (74.0%). The amount of labour as a percentage of cost of sales also differs considerably, even within industries. Food manufacturers, which employ highly automated production processes, have direct labour costs that represent 17% of cost of goods sold, while more labour-intensive furniture manufacturers have labour that totals nearly 29% of cost of sales.

Source: Industry Canada, *Canadian Industry Statistics*, www.ic.gc.ca/eic/site/cis-sic.nsf/eng/Home.

■ PRODUCT COSTS VERSUS PERIOD COSTS

LEARNING OBJECTIVE 2
Distinguish between product costs and period costs and give examples of each.

In addition to the distinction between manufacturing and non-manufacturing costs, there are other ways to look at costs. For instance, they can also be classified as either *product costs* or *period costs*. To understand the difference between product costs and period costs, we must first discuss the matching principle from financial accounting.

Generally, costs are recognized as expenses on the income statement in the period that benefits from the cost. For example, if a company pays for liability insurance in advance for two years, the entire amount is not considered an expense of the year in which the payment is made. Instead, one-half of the cost would be recognized as an expense each year. The reason is that both years—not just the first year—benefit from the insurance payment. The unexpensed portion of the insurance payment is carried on the balance sheet as an asset called *prepaid insurance*. The *matching principle* is based on the accrual concept and states that *costs incurred to generate a particular revenue should be recognized as expenses in the same period that the revenue is recognized*. This means that if a cost is incurred to acquire or make something that will eventually be sold, then the cost should be recognized as an expense only when the sale takes place—that is, when the benefit occurs. Such costs are called *product costs*.

Product Costs

For financial accounting purposes, **product costs** include all costs involved in acquiring or making a product. In the case of manufactured goods, these costs consist of direct materials, direct labour, and manufacturing overhead. Product costs "attach" to units of product as the goods are purchased or manufactured and they remain attached as the goods go into inventory awaiting sale. Product costs are initially assigned to an inventory account on the balance sheet. When the goods are sold, the costs are released from inventory as expenses (typically called *cost of goods sold*) and matched against sales revenue. Since product costs are initially assigned to inventories, they are also known as **inventoriable costs**.

We want to emphasize that product costs are not necessarily treated as expenses in the period in which they are incurred. Rather, as explained above, they are treated as expenses in the period in which the related products *are sold*. This means that a product cost such as direct materials or direct labour might be incurred during one period but not treated as an expense until a following period when the completed product is sold. Thus, product costs will be present in inventories and cost of goods sold.

Product costs
All costs that are involved in the purchase or manufacture of goods. In the case of manufactured goods, these costs consist of direct materials, direct labour, and manufacturing overhead. Also called inventoriable costs.

Inventoriable costs
Same as product costs.

Period Costs

Period costs are all of the costs that are not included in product costs. These costs are expensed on the income statement in the period in which they are incurred, using the usual rules of accrual accounting. Period costs are not included as part of the cost of either purchased or manufactured goods. Sales commissions and advertising are good examples of these kinds of costs. Neither commissions nor advertising are included as part of the cost of purchased or manufactured goods. Rather, both items are treated as expenses on the income statement in the period in which they are incurred. Thus, they are said to be period costs.

As suggested above, *all selling and administrative expenses are considered to be period costs.* Therefore, advertising, executive salaries, sales commissions, public relations, and other non-manufacturing costs discussed earlier would all be period costs. They will appear on the income statement as expenses in the period in which they are incurred. Careful analysis of the purpose of costs is necessary to separate product from period costs. For example if Terri decided to purchase a delivery truck, the depreciation of the cost of the truck would be a selling cost. If the truck was also used for picking up flowers from a supplier, then the depreciation could be separated between the product cost of flowers (freight in) and the selling costs of delivery (freight out).

Exhibit 2–1 contains a summary of the cost terms that we have introduced so far.

Period costs
Those costs that are taken directly to the income statement as expenses in the period in which they are incurred or accrued; such costs consist of selling (marketing) and administrative expenses.

■ COST CLASSIFICATIONS ON FINANCIAL STATEMENTS

In this section, we examine the cost classifications used on the financial statements of manufacturing and merchandising companies. Financial statements prepared by a *manufacturing* company are more complex than the statements prepared by a merchandising company because the manufacturing company must account for the production of its goods as well as for the marketing of them. Conversely, merchandising companies, such as retail stores, simply purchase goods from suppliers for resale to customers. The production process gives rise to many costs that do not exist in a merchandising company, and somehow these costs must be accounted for on the manufacturing company's financial statements. In this section, we focus our attention on how this accounting is carried out in the balance sheet and income statement.

The Balance Sheet

The balance sheet, or statement of financial position, of a manufacturing company is similar to that of a merchandising company. However, there are differences in the inventory accounts. A merchandising company has only one class of inventory—goods purchased

EXHIBIT 2–1
Summary of Cost Terms

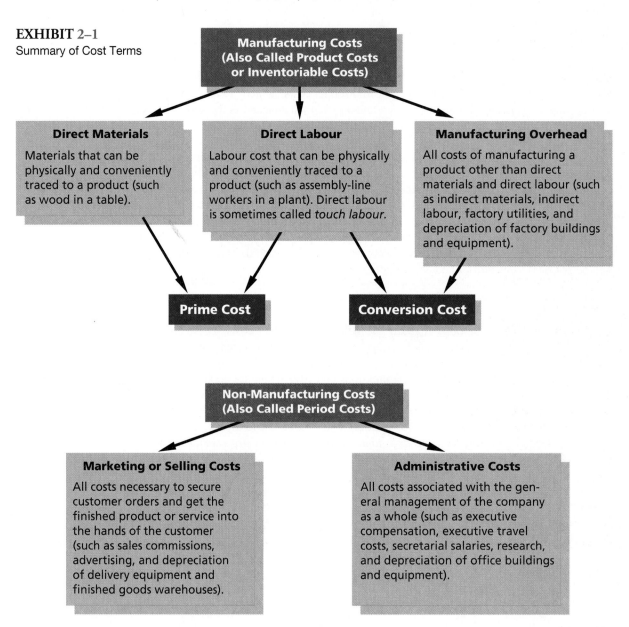

from suppliers that are awaiting resale to customers. By contrast, manufacturing companies have three classes of inventories—raw (direct) materials, work in process, and finished goods. Raw materials are the materials used to make a product, but which have not yet been placed into production. Work in process consists of units of product that are partially complete and require additional work before they will be ready to sell to a customer. Finished goods consist of complete units of product that have not yet been sold to customers. Typically, only the sum of these three categories of inventory is shown on the balance sheet of external reports. However, the footnotes to the financial statements often provide more detail about the amounts in each category.

We will use two hypothetical companies—Graham Manufacturing and Reston Bookstore—to illustrate the concepts discussed in this section. Graham Manufacturing is located in Victoria, British Columbia, and makes precision brass fittings for yachts. Reston Bookstore is a small bookstore in Moncton, New Brunswick, specializing in selling books about Maritime Canada.

The footnotes to Graham Manufacturing's annual report reveal the following information concerning its inventories:

Graham Manufacturing Corporation Inventory Accounts	Beginning Balance	Ending Balance
Raw Materials.....................	$ 60,000	$ 50,000
Work in Process..................	90,000	60,000
Finished Goods...................	125,000	175,000
Total inventory accounts	$275,000	$285,000

Graham Manufacturing's raw materials inventory consists largely of brass rods and brass blocks. The work in process inventory consists of partially completed brass fittings. The finished goods inventory consists of brass fittings that are ready to be sold to customers.

In contrast, the inventory account at Reston Bookstore consists entirely of the costs of books the company has purchased from publishers for resale to the public. In merchandising companies like Reston, these inventories may be called *merchandise inventories*. The beginning and ending balances in this account appear as follows:

Reston Bookstore Inventory Account	Beginning Balance	Ending Balance
Merchandise inventory	$100,000	$150,000

The Income Statement

Exhibit 2–2 compares the income statements of Reston Bookstore and Graham Manufacturing. For purposes of illustration, these statements contain more detail about cost of goods sold than you will generally find in published financial statements.

At first glance, the income statements of merchandising and manufacturing firms like Reston Bookstore and Graham Manufacturing are very similar. The only apparent difference is in the labels of some of the entries that go into the computation of the cost of goods sold figure. In Exhibit 2–2, the computation of cost of goods sold relies on the following basic equation for inventory accounts:

LEARNING OBJECTIVE 3
Prepare an income statement, including the calculation of cost of goods sold.

Basic Equation for Inventory Accounts

$$\text{Beginning balance} + \text{Additions to inventory} = \text{Ending balance} + \text{Withdrawals from inventory}$$

The logic underlying this equation, which applies to any inventory account, is illustrated in Exhibit 2–3. At the beginning of the period, the inventory contains a beginning balance. During the period, additions are made to the inventory through purchases or other means. The sum of the beginning balance and the additions to the account is the total amount of inventory available for sale. During the period, withdrawals are made from inventory. Whatever is left at the end of the period after these withdrawals is the ending balance. At the end of the period, all of the inventory that was available for sale must either still be in ending inventory or must have been withdrawn from the inventory account.

These concepts are applied to determine the cost of goods sold for a merchandising company like Reston Bookstore as follows:

Cost of Goods Sold in a Merchandising Company

$$\text{Beginning balance inventory} + \text{Purchases} = \text{Ending merchandise inventory} + \text{Cost of goods sold}$$

EXHIBIT 2–2   Comparative Income Statements: Merchandising and Manufacturing Companies

MERCHANDISING COMPANY
Reston Bookstore

Sales		$1,000,000
Cost of goods sold:		
Beginning merchandise inventory	$100,000	
Add: Purchases	650,000	
Goods available for sale	750,000	
Deduct: Ending merchandise inventory	150,000	600,000
Gross margin		400,000
Less operating expenses:		
Selling expense	100,000	
Administrative expense	200,000	300,000
Operating income		$ 100,000

The cost of merchandise inventory purchased from outside suppliers during the period. → (points to Cost of goods sold section)

MANUFACTURING COMPANY
Graham Manufacturing

Sales		$1,500,000
Cost of goods sold:		
Beginning finished goods inventory	$125,000	
Add: Cost of goods manufactured	850,000	
Goods available for sale	975,000	
Deduct: Ending finished goods inventory	175,000	800,000
Gross margin		700,000
Less operating expenses:		
Selling expense	250,000	
Administrative expense	300,000	550,000
Operating income		$ 150,000

The manufacturing costs associated with the goods that were finished during the period. (See Exhibit 2–4 for details.) → (points to Cost of goods sold section)

Note: Operating income is income before interest and taxes. Interest and income taxes are ignored here.

or

$$\text{Cost of goods sold} = \begin{array}{c}\text{Beginning}\\\text{merchandise}\\\text{inventory}\end{array} + \text{Purchases} - \begin{array}{c}\text{Ending}\\\text{merchandise}\\\text{inventory}\end{array}$$

The cost of goods sold for a manufacturing company like Graham Manufacturing is determined as follows:

Cost of Goods Sold in a Manufacturing Company

$$\begin{array}{c}\text{Beginning finished}\\\text{goods inventory}\end{array} + \begin{array}{c}\text{Cost of goods}\\\text{manufactured}\end{array} = \begin{array}{c}\text{Ending finished}\\\text{goods inventory}\end{array} + \begin{array}{c}\text{Cost of}\\\text{goods sold}\end{array}$$

or

$$\text{Cost of goods sold} = \begin{array}{c}\text{Beginning}\\\text{finished goods}\\\text{inventory}\end{array} + \begin{array}{c}\text{Cost}\\\text{of goods}\\\text{manufactured}\end{array} - \begin{array}{c}\text{Ending}\\\text{finished goods}\\\text{inventory}\end{array}$$

To determine the cost of goods sold in a merchandising company like Reston Bookstore, we need to know only the beginning and ending balances in the merchandise inventory account and the purchases. Total purchases can be determined easily in a merchandising company by simply adding together all purchases from suppliers.

EXHIBIT 2–3   Inventory Flow

Beginning balance + Additions = Total available – Withdrawals = Ending balance

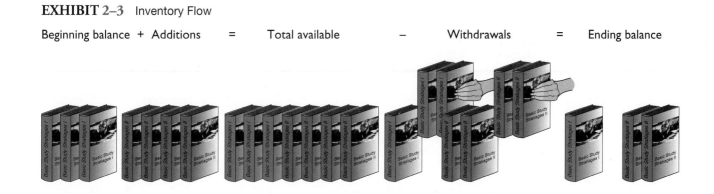

To determine the cost of goods sold in a manufacturing company like Graham Manufacturing, we need to know the *cost of goods manufactured* and the beginning and ending balances in the finished goods inventory account. The **cost of goods manufactured** consists of the manufacturing costs associated with goods that were *finished* during the period. The cost of goods manufactured figure for Graham Manufacturing is derived in Exhibit 2–4, which contains a *schedule of cost of goods manufactured*.

Cost of goods manufactured
Costs that include the direct materials, direct labour, and manufacturing overhead used for the products finished during the period.

EXHIBIT 2–4   Graham Manufacturing Schedule of Cost of Goods Manufactured

Direct materials:		
Beginning raw materials inventory*. . . . . . . $ 60,000		Direct Materials
Add: Purchases of raw materials 400,000		
Raw materials available for use 460,000		
Deduct: Ending raw materials inventory 50,000		
Raw materials used in production	$410,000	
Direct labour	60,000	Direct Labour
Manufacturing overhead:**		
Insurance, factory 6,000		
Indirect labour 100,000		
Machine rental 50,000		Manufacturing Overhead
Utilities, factory. 75,000		
Supplies 21,000		
Depreciation, factory 90,000		
Property taxes, factory 8,000		
Total overhead costs	350,000	
Total manufacturing costs:	820,000	
Add: Beginning work in process inventory	90,000	
	910,000	
Deduct: Ending work in process inventory	60,000	Cost of Goods Manufactured
Cost of goods manufactured (see Exhibit 2–2) . .	$850,000	

*We assume in this example that the Raw Materials inventory account contains only direct materials and that indirect materials are carried in a separate Supplies account. Using a Supplies account for indirect materials is a common practice among companies. In Chapter 3, we discuss the procedure to be followed if *both* direct and indirect materials are carried in a single account.

**In Chapter 3 we will see that the manufacturing overhead section of the schedule of cost of goods manufactured can be simplified considerably by using what is called a *predetermined overhead rate*.

IN BUSINESS

An example of a common supplementary income statement disclosure made by public companies such as Research in Motion (RIM), the manufacturer of BlackBerry smartphones, is shown below.

	Fiscal Year-End		
	2009	**2008**	**2007**
Revenue	100.0%	100.0%	100.0%
Cost of sales	53.9	48.7	45.4
Gross margin	46.1%	51.3%	54.6%
Expenses			
Research and development	6.2%	6.0%	7.8%
Selling and administration	13.5	14.7	17.7
Amortization	1.8	1.8	2.5
Total expenses	21.5%	22.5%	28.0%
Income from operations	24.6%	28.8%	26.6%

This income statement format expresses all product and period costs as a percentage of revenue, allowing financial statement users to readily evaluate performance trends over time. In the case of RIM, the cost of sales has been steadily increasing since 2007, resulting in a gross margin of 46.1% in 2009 compared to 54.6% in 2007. Conversely, period expenses such as research and development, and selling and administration, are both lower (as a percentage of revenue) in 2009 than they were in 2007. Managers at RIM and other financial statement users would want to know the underlying reasons for any significant trends. For example, is the declining gross margin percentage due to downward pressure on prices because of increased competition from other smartphone manufacturers? Or are production costs increasing? Are the lower selling and administrative costs due to improvements in operating efficiency, or are they a result of reductions in discretionary spending?

Source: Research in Motion, *2009 Annual Report*. Reprinted with permission.

SCHEDULE OF COST OF GOODS MANUFACTURED

LEARNING OBJECTIVE 4
Prepare a schedule of cost of goods manufactured.

Schedule of costs of goods manufactured
A schedule showing the direct materials, direct labour, and manufacturing overhead costs incurred for a period and assigned to work in process and completed goods.

At first glance, the **schedule of cost of goods manufactured** in Exhibit 2–4 appears complex. However, it is all quite logical. The schedule of cost of goods manufactured contains the three elements of product costs that we discussed earlier—direct materials, direct labour, and manufacturing overhead.

The direct material cost is not simply the cost of materials purchased during the period—rather it is the cost of materials *used* during the period. The purchases of raw materials are added to the beginning balance to determine the cost of materials available for use. The ending raw materials inventory is deducted from this amount to arrive at the cost of raw materials used in production. The sum of the three cost elements—materials, direct labour, and manufacturing overhead—is the **total manufacturing cost** of $820,000. However, this is *not* the same thing as the cost of goods manufactured for the period of $850,000. The subtle distinction between the *total manufacturing cost* and the *cost of goods manufactured* is very easy to miss. Some of the materials, direct labour, and manufacturing overhead costs incurred during the period relate to goods that are not yet completed. As stated above, the cost of goods manufactured consists of the manufacturing cost associated with the goods that were *finished* during the period. Consequently, adjustments need to be made to the total manufacturing costs of the period for the partially completed goods that were in process at the beginning and at the end of the period. The costs that relate to goods that are not yet completed are shown in the work in process inventory figures at the bottom of the schedule. Note that the beginning work in process inventory must be added to the manufacturing costs of the period, and the ending work in process inventory must be deducted, to arrive at the cost of goods manufactured. The $30,000 decline in the work in process account during the year ($90,000 − $60,000) explains the $30,000 difference between the total manufacturing cost and the cost of goods manufactured.

 Because the financial statements included in the annual report of a public company are intended for users external to the organization, accounts are often summarized so that the detail shown in Exhibits 2–2 and 2–4 would not be provided. However, financial statements generated for internal use by management would typically provide the detail shown in these exhibits. In particular, the details shown in Exhibit 2–4 for direct materials and manufacturing overhead would not be disclosed for external reporting purposes. External users do not need this level of reporting detail to evaluate a company's profitability, and it is not required by GAAP.

> **Total manufacturing costs**
> Costs that represent the direct materials, direct labour, and manufacturing overhead used to perform the production work for finished or unfinished products for the period.

Product Costs—A Closer Look

Earlier in the chapter, we defined product costs as consisting of those costs incurred to either purchase or manufacture goods. For manufactured goods, these costs consist of direct materials, direct labour, and manufacturing overhead. To understand product costs more fully, it will be helpful at this point to look briefly at the flow of costs in a manufacturing company. This will help us understand how product costs move through the various accounts and how they affect the balance sheet and the income statement.

 Exhibit 2–5 illustrates the flow of costs in a manufacturing company. Raw materials purchases are recorded in the raw materials inventory account. When raw materials are used in production, their costs are transferred to the work in process inventory account as direct materials. Notice that direct labour cost and manufacturing overhead cost are added directly to work in process. Work in process can be viewed as products on an assembly line. The direct materials, direct labour, and manufacturing overhead costs added to work in process in Exhibit 2–5 are the costs needed to complete these products as they move along this assembly line.

EXHIBIT 2–5 Cost Flows and Classifications in a Manufacturing Company

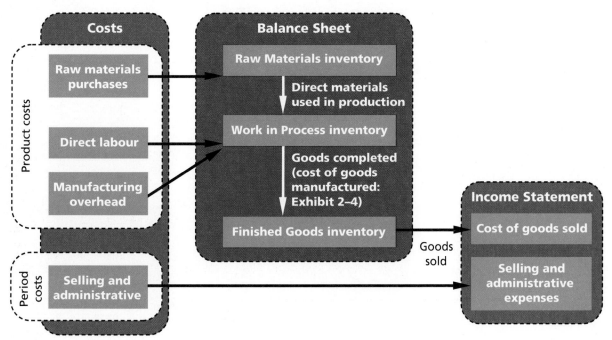

Notice from the exhibit that as goods are completed, their cost is transferred from work in process to finished goods. Here the goods await sale to a customer. As goods are sold, their cost is then transferred from finished goods to cost of goods sold. At this point, the various costs required to make the product are finally recorded as an expense.

Inventoriable Costs

As stated earlier, product costs are often called *inventoriable costs*. The reason is that these costs go directly into inventory accounts as they are incurred (first into work in process and then into finished goods), rather than going into expense accounts; hence the term *inventoriable costs. This is a key concept, since such costs can end up on the balance sheet as assets if goods are only partially completed or are unsold at the end of a period.* To illustrate this point, refer again to the data in Exhibit 2–5. At the end of the period, the materials, labour, and overhead costs that are associated with the units in the work in process and finished goods inventory accounts will appear on the balance sheet as part of the company's assets. These costs will not become expenses until the goods are completed and sold.

Selling and administrative expenses are not involved in making a product. For this reason, they are not treated as product costs but rather as period costs that are expensed as they are incurred, as shown in Exhibit 2–5.

An Example of Cost Flows

To provide an example of cost flows in a manufacturing company, assume that a company's direct labour cost is $500,000 and its administrative salaries cost is $200,000. As illustrated in Exhibit 2–6, the direct labour cost is added to work in process. As shown in the exhibit, the direct labour cost will not become an expense until the goods that are produced during the year are sold—which may not happen until the following year or even later.

EXHIBIT 2–6   An Example of Cost Flows in a Manufacturing Company

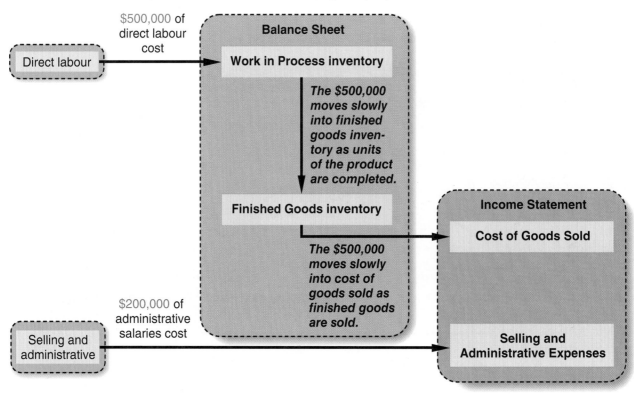

Until the goods are sold, the $500,000 will be part of inventories—either work in process or finished goods—along with the other costs of producing the goods. By contrast, $200,000 of administrative salaries cost will be expensed immediately.

Thus far, we have been mainly concerned with classifications of manufacturing costs for the purpose of determining inventory valuations on the balance sheet and cost of goods sold on the income statement of external financial reports. However, costs are used for many purposes, and each purpose requires a different classification of costs. We will consider several different purposes for cost classifications in the remaining sections of this chapter. To help keep the big picture in mind, we suggest that you refer back to Exhibit 2–7 as you progress through the rest of this chapter.

EXHIBIT 2–7   Summary of Cost Classifications

Purpose of Cost Classification	Cost Classifications

Preparing external financial statements	• Product costs (inventoriable)
	  • Direct materials
	  • Direct labour
	  • Manufacturing overhead
	• Period costs (expensed)
	  • Non-manufacturing costs
	    • Marketing or selling costs
	    • Administrative costs

Predicting cost behaviour in response to changes in activity	• Variable cost (proportional to activity) • Fixed cost (constant in total)
Assigning costs to cost objects such as departments or products	• Direct cost (can easily be traced) • Indirect cost (cannot easily be traced; must be allocated)
Making decisions	• Differential cost (differs between alternatives) • Sunk cost (past cost not affected by a decision) • Opportunity cost (forgone benefit)

■ COST CLASSIFICATIONS FOR PREDICTING COST BEHAVIOUR

Quite frequently, it is necessary to predict how a certain cost will behave in response to a change in activity. For example, Terri (in the opening vignette) needs to know how her delivery costs would change with increases and decreases in the sales of flowers. **Cost behaviour** refers to how a cost reacts or responds to changes in the level of activity. As the activity level rises and falls, a particular cost may rise and fall as well—or it may remain constant. For planning purposes, a manager must be able to anticipate which of these will happen, and if a cost can be expected to change, the manager must know by how much it will change. To help make such distinctions, costs are often categorized as *variable* or *fixed*. As you will see throughout the textbook, understanding cost behaviour is critical for management accountants when preparing reports (Chapter 6), analyzing profits (Chapter 7), developing budgets (Chapter 9), and making short-term (Chapter 12) and long-term decisions (Chapter 13). We introduce the topic of cost behaviour in this chapter and return to it in greater detail in Chapter 6.

LEARNING OBJECTIVE 5
Explain the differences between variable and fixed costs.

Cost behaviour
The way in which a cost reacts or responds to changes in the level of activity.

Variable Cost

Variable cost
A cost that varies, in total, in direct proportion to changes in the level of activity. A variable cost is constant per unit.

A **variable cost** is a cost that varies, in total, in direct proportion to changes in the level of activity. The activity can be expressed in many ways, such as units produced, units sold, kilometres driven, beds occupied, lines of print, hours worked, and so forth. A good example of a variable cost is direct materials. The cost of direct materials used during a period will vary, in total, in direct proportion to the number of units that are produced. To illustrate this idea, consider the Nova Bus Corporation. Each bus requires one battery. As the output of buses increases and decreases, the number of batteries used will increase and decrease proportionately. If bus production goes up 10%, then the number of batteries used will also go up 10%. The concept of a variable cost is shown graphically in Exhibit 2–8.

The graph on the left-hand side of Exhibit 2–8 illustrates that the *total variable* cost rises and falls as the activity level rises and falls. This idea is presented below, assuming that a battery costs $50:

Number of Buses Produced	Cost per Battery	Total Variable Cost— Batteries
1	$50	$ 50
500	50	25,000
1,000	50	50,000

Although total variable costs change as the activity level changes, it is important to note that a variable cost is constant if expressed on a *per unit* basis. Observe from the tabulation above that the per unit cost of batteries remains constant at $50 even though the total cost of the batteries increases and decreases with activity.

There are many examples of costs that are variable with respect to the products and services provided by a company. In a manufacturing company, variable costs include items such as direct materials, shipping costs, sales commissions, and some elements of manufacturing overhead, such as indirect materials. For now, we will also assume that direct labour is a variable cost, although as we will see in Chapter 7, direct labour may act more like a fixed cost in many situations. In a merchandising company, variable costs include items such as cost of goods sold, commissions to salespersons, and billing costs. In a hospital, the variable costs of providing health care services to patients would include the costs of the supplies, drugs, meals, and perhaps nursing services.

When we say that a cost is variable, we ordinarily mean that it is variable with respect to the products and services the organization produces. However, costs can be variable

EXHIBIT 2–8   Variable and Fixed Cost Behaviour

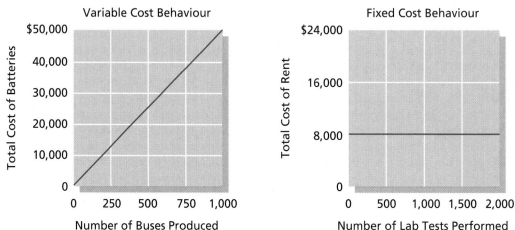

with respect to other activities. For example, the wages paid to employees at a Rogers Video outlet will depend on the number of hours the store is open and not strictly on the number of videos rented. In this case, we would say that wage costs are variable with respect to the hours of operation. Nevertheless, when we say that a cost is variable, we ordinarily mean it is variable with respect to the volume of revenue-generating output—in other words, how many Cervélo bicycles are produced, how many videos are rented, how many patients are treated, and so on.

Fixed Cost

A **fixed cost** is a cost that remains constant, in total, regardless of changes in the level of activity. Unlike variable costs, fixed costs are not affected by changes in activity. Consequently, as the activity level rises and falls, the fixed costs remain constant in total amount unless influenced by some outside force, such as price changes. Rent is a good example of a fixed cost. Suppose the Saskatchewan Clinic rents a machine for $8,000 per month that tests blood samples for the presence of leukemia cells. The $8,000 monthly rental cost will be incurred regardless of the number of tests that may be performed during the month. The concept of a fixed cost is shown graphically on the right-hand side of Exhibit 2–8.

> **Fixed cost**
> A cost that remains constant, in total, regardless of changes in the level of activity within the relevant range. If a fixed cost is expressed on a per unit basis, it varies inversely with the level of activity.

Very few costs are completely fixed. Most will change if there is a large enough change in activity. For example, suppose that the capacity of the leukemia diagnostic machine at the Saskatchewan Clinic is 2,000 tests per month. If the clinic wishes to perform more than 2,000 tests in a month, it would be necessary to rent an additional machine, which would cause a jump in the fixed costs. When we say a cost is fixed, we mean it is fixed within some *relevant range*. The **relevant range** is the range of activity within which the assumptions about variable and fixed costs are valid. For example, the assumption that the rent for diagnostic machines is $8,000 per month is valid within the relevant range of 0 to 2,000 tests per month.

> **Relevant range**
> The range of activity within which assumptions about variable and fixed cost behaviour are valid.

Fixed costs can create confusion if they are expressed on a per unit basis because the average fixed cost per unit increases and decreases *inversely* with changes in activity. In the Saskatchewan Clinic, for example, the average cost per test will fall as the number of tests performed increases. This is because the $8,000 rental cost will be spread over more tests. Conversely, as the number of tests performed in the clinic declines, the average cost per test will rise as the $8,000 rental cost is spread over fewer tests. This concept is illustrated in the table below:

Monthly Rental Cost	Number of Tests Performed	Average Cost per Test
$8,000	10	$800
8,000	500	16
8,000	2,000	4

Note that if the Saskatchewan Clinic performs only 10 tests each month, the rental cost of the equipment will average $800 per test. But if 2,000 tests are performed each month, the average cost will drop to only $4 per test. More will be said later about the problems created for both the accountant and the manager by this variation in unit costs.

Examples of fixed costs include straight-line depreciation, insurance, property taxes, rent, supervisory salaries, administrative salaries, and advertising.

Some costs contain variable and fixed cost elements; these are called **mixed costs**. An example is the total wages paid to sales staff. A portion of these wages is usually fixed and does not vary from one month to the next. However there is also usually a variable portion (sales commissions) that is based on the sales generated by the salesperson. We defer further discussion of mixed cost behaviour and analysis until Chapter 6.

> **Mixed cost**
> A cost that contains both variable and fixed cost elements.

A summary of both variable and fixed cost behaviour is presented in Exhibit 2–9.

EXHIBIT 2–9   Summary of Variable and Fixed Cost Behaviour

Cost	Behaviour of the Cost (within the relevant range)	
	In Total	**Per Unit**
Variable cost	Total variable cost increases and decreases in proportion to changes in the activity level.	Variable costs remain constant per unit.
Fixed cost	Total fixed cost is not affected by changes in the activity level within the relevant range.	Fixed costs decrease per unit as the activity level rises and increase per unit as the activity level falls.

COST CLASSIFICATIONS FOR ASSIGNING COSTS TO COST OBJECTS

LEARNING OBJECTIVE 6
Identify the differences between direct and indirect costs.

Costs are assigned to objects for a variety of purposes including pricing, preparing profitability studies, and controlling spending. A **cost object** is anything for which cost data are desired—including products, customers, jobs, and organizational subunits. For purposes of assigning costs to cost objects, costs are classified as either *direct* or *indirect*.

Cost object
Anything for which cost data are desired.

Direct Cost

A **direct cost** is a cost that can be easily and conveniently traced to the particular cost object under consideration. The concept of direct cost extends beyond just direct materials and direct labour. For example, if Roots is assigning costs to its various regional and national sales offices, then the salary of the sales manager in its Alberta office would be a direct cost of that office.

Direct cost
A cost that can be easily and conveniently traced to the particular cost object under consideration.

Indirect cost
A cost that cannot be easily and conveniently traced to the particular cost object under consideration.

Indirect Cost

An **indirect cost** is a cost that cannot be easily and conveniently traced to the particular cost object under consideration. For example, a Moosehead Breweries factory may produce many varieties of beer. The factory manager's salary would be an indirect cost of a particular variety, such as Premium Dry. The reason is that the factory manager's salary is not caused by any one variety of beer but rather is incurred as a consequence of running the entire factory. *To be traced to a cost object such as a particular product, the cost must be caused by the cost object.* The factory manager's salary is called a *common cost* of producing the various products of the factory. A **common cost** is a cost that is incurred to support a number of cost objects but cannot be traced to them individually. A common cost is a type of indirect cost.

Common cost
A common cost is a cost that is incurred to support a number of cost objects but cannot be traced to them individually.

A particular cost may be direct or indirect, depending on the cost object. While the Moosehead Breweries factory manager's salary is an *indirect* cost of manufacturing Premium Dry beer, it is a *direct* cost of the manufacturing division. In the first case, the cost object is the brand of beer. In the second case, the cost object is the entire manufacturing division.

COST CLASSIFICATIONS FOR DECISION MAKING

LEARNING OBJECTIVE 7
Describe the cost classifications used in making decisions: differential costs, opportunity costs, and sunk costs.

Costs are an important feature of many business decisions. In making decisions, it is essential to have a firm grasp of the concepts *differential cost*, *opportunity cost*, and *sunk cost*.

Differential Cost and Revenue

Decisions involve choosing among alternatives. In business decisions, each alternative will have certain costs and benefits that must be compared to the costs and benefits of the other available alternatives. A difference in costs between any two alternatives is known as a **differential cost**. A difference in revenues between any two alternatives is known as **differential revenue**.

A differential cost is also known as an **incremental cost**, although technically an incremental cost should refer only to an increase in cost from one alternative to another; decreases in cost should be referred to as *decremental costs*. Differential cost is a broader term, encompassing both cost increases (incremental costs) and cost decreases (decremental costs) between alternatives.

The accountant's differential cost concept can be compared to the economist's marginal cost concept. In speaking of changes in cost and revenue, the economist employs the terms *marginal cost* and *marginal revenue*. The revenue that can be obtained from selling one more unit of product is called *marginal revenue,* and the cost involved in producing one more unit of product is called *marginal cost*. The economist's marginal concept is basically the same as the accountant's differential concept applied to a single unit of output.

Differential costs can be either fixed or variable. To illustrate, assume that Nature Way Cosmetics Inc. is thinking about changing its marketing method from distribution through retailers to distribution by a network of neighbourhood sales representatives. Present costs and revenues are compared to projected costs and revenues in the following table:

	Retailer Distribution (present)	Sales Representatives (proposed)	Differential Costs and Revenues
Revenues	$700,000	$800,000	$100,000
Cost of goods sold (V)	350,000	400,000	50,000
Advertising (F)	80,000	45,000	(35,000)
Commissions (V)	–0–	40,000	40,000
Warehouse depreciation (F)	50,000	80,000	30,000
Other expenses (F)	60,000	60,000	–0–
Total.	540,000	625,000	85,000
Operating income	$160,000	$175,000	$ 15,000

V = Variable; F = Fixed.

According to the preceding analysis, the differential revenue is $100,000 and the differential costs total $85,000, leaving a positive differential operating income of $15,000 under the proposed marketing plan.

The decision of whether Nature Way Cosmetics should stay with the present retail distribution or switch to sales representatives could be made on the basis of the operating incomes of the two alternatives. As we see in the above analysis, the operating income under the present distribution method is $160,000, whereas the operating income under sales representatives is estimated to be $175,000. Therefore, using sales representatives is preferred, since it would result in $15,000 higher operating income. Note that we would have arrived at exactly the same conclusion by simply focusing on the differential revenues, differential costs, and differential operating income, which also show a $15,000 advantage for sales representatives.

In general, only the differences between alternatives are relevant in decisions. Those items that are the same under all alternatives and that are not affected by the decision can be ignored. For example, in the Nature Way Cosmetics example, the Other Expenses category, which is $60,000 under both alternatives, can be ignored, since it has no effect on the decision. If it was removed from the calculations, the sales representatives would still be preferred by $15,000. This is an extremely important principle in management accounting that we will return to in later chapters. Referring back to Terri's Flower Shop, the differential costs for the delivery decision would compare the courier costs with the cost of owning and using the delivery truck. The cost of Terri's wages or the store rental would not be differential because either of these costs would not likely change for either alternative in the decision.

Differential cost
A difference in cost between any two alternatives.

Differential revenue
A difference in revenue between any two alternatives.

Incremental cost
An increase in cost between two alternatives.

2. The cost of goods sold would be computed as follows:

Finished goods inventory, January 1	$ 260,000
Add: Cost of goods manufactured.	1,650,000
Goods available for sale.	1,910,000
Deduct: Finished goods inventory, December 31	210,000
Cost of goods sold.	$1,700,000

3.

KLEAR-SEAL COMPANY
Income Statement
For the Year Ended December 31

Sales.		$2,500,000
Less cost of goods sold (above)		1,700,000
Gross margin		800,000
Less selling and administrative expenses:		
Selling expenses.	$140,000	
Administrative expenses.	270,000	
Total expenses		410,000
Operating income.		$ 390,000

4. Ending finished good inventory:

Direct materials ($780,000/412,500 = $1.8909) $1.8909 × 55,176	$104,332
Direct labour ($150,000/412,500 = $0.3636) $0.3636 × 55,176.	20,062*
Manufacturing overhead ($640,000/412,500 = $1.5515) $1.5515 × 55,176	85,606
Total cost	$210,000

*Rounding down is undertaken to account for unit cost rounding.

Glossary

Review key terms and definitions on Connect.

Questions

2–1   What are the three major elements of product costs in a manufacturing company?

2–2   Distinguish between the following: (a) direct materials, (b) indirect materials, (c) direct labour, (d) indirect labour, and (e) manufacturing overhead.

2–3   Explain the difference between a product cost and a period cost.

2–4   What are marketing or selling costs? How are they treated on the income statement?

2–5   Describe the schedule of cost of goods manufactured. How does it tie into the income statement?

2–6   What are prime costs and conversion costs?

2–7   What is the difference between total manufacturing costs incurred and the cost of goods manufactured?

2–8   Is it possible for costs such as salaries or depreciation to end up as assets on the balance sheet? Explain.

2–9   What is meant by the term *cost behaviour*?

2–10   "A variable cost is a cost that varies per unit of product, whereas a fixed cost is constant per unit of product." Do you agree? Explain.

2–11   What is the relevant range and why is it important to understand this when predicting costs?

2–12   Why is manufacturing overhead considered an indirect cost of a unit of product?

2–13   Define the following terms: differential cost, opportunity cost, and sunk cost.

2–14   Only variable costs can be differential costs. Do you agree? Explain.

2–15   Rick Johnstone is employed by Westin Company. Last week he worked 46 hours assembling one of the company's products. Westin's employees work a standard 40-hour week and Johnstone is paid $18 per hour. Employees are paid time and a half for any hours worked in excess of the standard 40 hours. Assuming the overtime is the result of an overall spike in demand for all products, allocate Johnstone's earnings for the week between direct labour cost and manufacturing overhead cost.

2–16 Pat Campbell operates a moulding press at Barrie Fabrication Company. Last week Pat worked 35 hours and was idle 5 hours due to scheduled maintenance on the equipment. Her basic wage rate is $26 per hour. Allocate Pat's wages for the week between direct labour cost and manufacturing overhead cost.

connect Exercises

EXERCISE 2–1 Classifying Manufacturing Costs [LO1]
Your Boat Inc. assembles custom sailboats from components supplied by various manufacturers. The company is very small and its assembly shop and retail sales store are housed in a Gig Harbour, Ontario, boathouse. Below are listed some of the costs that are incurred by the company.

Required:
For each cost, indicate whether it would most likely be classified as a direct labour, direct material, manufacturing overhead, selling, or administrative cost.
1. The wages of employees who build the sailboats.
2. The cost of advertising in the local newspapers.
3. The cost of an aluminum mast installed in a sailboat.
4. The wages of the assembly shop's supervisor.
5. Rent on the boathouse.
6. The wages of the company's bookkeeper.
7. Sales commissions paid to the company's salespeople.
8. Depreciation on power tools.

EXERCISE 2–2 Classification of Costs as Period or Product Costs [LO2]
Suppose that you have been given a summer job as an intern at Remotely Speaking, a company that manufactures sophisticated portable two-way radio transceivers for remote-controlled military reconnaissance missions. The company, which is privately owned, has approached a bank for a loan to help finance its tremendous growth. The bank requires financial statements before approving such a loan. You have been asked to help prepare the financial statements and were given the following list of costs:
1. Depreciation on salespersons' cars.
2. Rent on equipment used in the factory.
3. Lubricants used for machine maintenance.
4. Salaries of personnel who work in the finished goods warehouse.
5. Soap and paper towels used by factory workers at the end of a shift.
6. Factory supervisors' salaries.
7. Heat, water, and power consumed in the factory.
8. Materials used for boxing company products for shipment overseas. (Units are not normally boxed.)
9. Advertising costs.
10. Workers' Compensation Insurance for factory employees.
11. Depreciation on chairs and tables in the factory lunchroom.
12. The wages of the receptionist in the administrative offices.
13. Cost of leasing the corporate jet used by the company's executives.
14. The cost of renting rooms at a British Columbia resort for the annual sales conference.
15. The cost of packaging the company's product.

Required:
Classify the above costs as either product (inventoriable) costs or period (non-inventoriable) costs for purposes of preparing the financial statements for the bank.

EXERCISE 2–3 Constructing an Income Statement [LO3]
Last month Mountain High, a mountain sporting goods retailer, had total sales of $3,200,000, selling expenses of $110,000, and administrative expenses of $470,000. The company had beginning merchandise inventory of $140,000, purchased additional merchandise inventory for $2,550,000, and had ending merchandise inventory of $180,000.

Required:
Prepare an income statement for the company for the month.

EXERCISE 2–4 Prepare a Schedule of Cost of Goods Manufactured [LO4]
Acromould Fabrication manufactures a variety of products in its factory. Data for the most recent month's operations appear below.

Beginning raw materials inventory	$ 66,000
Purchases of raw materials	528,000
Ending raw materials inventory	78,000
Direct labour	258,000
Manufacturing overhead	456,000
Beginning work in process inventory	228,000
Ending work in process inventory	264,000

Required:
Prepare a schedule of cost of goods manufactured for the company for the month.

EXERCISE 2–5 Fixed and Variable Costs [LO5]
Urban Auto Glass specializes in the repair and replacement of windshields for passenger vehicles. Variable and fixed costs related to installation activities for the most recent month (July) are listed below.

Item	
Number of windshields installed	1,000
Variable expenses:	Amount
Direct materials	$200,000
Direct labour (1 hour per installation)	30,000
Indirect materials	10,000
Fixed expenses:	
Installation supervisor's wages	$4,000
Installation scheduler's wages	2,000
Warehouse expenses	5,000

Required:
1. Calculate the per unit amounts for each of the variable expense and fixed expense items in July.
2. Management expects that 1,200 windshields will be installed in August and that this level of activity is within the relevant range for all variable and fixed expenses. Calculate:
   a. The total expense for each of the variable and fixed cost items above.
   b. The per unit amounts for each of the variable and fixed cost items above. Explain any differences in the per unit amounts between July and August.
3. Identify some factors that might cause variable costs per unit to change if the actual level of activity in a given month falls above or below the relevant range.

EXERCISE 2–6 Identifying Examples of Direct and Indirect Costs [LO6]
The Royal Hotel is located in central Alberta and has, among others, the following cost objects:
1. Hotel guests.
2. Hotel restaurant.
3. Hotel fitness centre and pool.
4. Hotel business centre (computers, printer, fax machine).

Required:
For each of the above cost objects, identify two examples of a direct cost and two examples of an indirect cost.

EXERCISE 2–7 Differential, Opportunity, and Sunk Costs [LO7]
The Sorrento Hotel is a four-star hotel located in downtown Montreal. The hotel's operations vice-president would like to replace the hotel's antiquated computer terminals at the registration desk with attractive state-of-the-art flat-panel displays. The new displays would take less space, consume less power than the old computer terminals, and provide additional security, since they can be viewed only from a restrictive angle. The new computer displays would not require any new wiring. The hotel's chef believes the funds would be better spent on a new bulk freezer for the kitchen.

Required:

For each of the items below, indicate by placing an X in the appropriate column whether it should be considered a differential cost, an opportunity cost, or a sunk cost in the decision to replace the old computer terminals with new flat-panel displays. If none of the categories apply for a particular item, leave all columns blank. The first item has been completed as an example.

Item	Differential Cost	Opportunity Cost	Sunk Cost
Ex. Cost of electricity to run the terminals	X		
1. Cost of the new flat-panel displays			
2. Cost of the old computer terminals			
3. Rent on the space occupied by the registration desk			
4. Wages of registration desk personnel			
5. Benefits from a new freezer			
6. Costs of maintaining the old computer terminals. . . .			
7. Cost of removing the old computer terminals			
8. Cost of existing registration desk wiring			

EXERCISE 2–8 Classification of Overtime Cost [LO1]

Several weeks ago, you called Jiffy Plumbing Company to have some routine repair work done on the plumbing system in your home. The plumber came about two weeks later, at four o'clock in the afternoon, and spent two hours completing your repair work. When you received your bill from the company, it contained a $75 charge for labour—$30 for the first hour and $45 for the second.

When questioned about the difference in hourly rates, the company's service manager explained that the higher rate for the second hour contained a charge for an "overtime premium," since the union required that plumbers be paid time and a half for any work in excess of eight hours per day. The service manager further explained that the company was working overtime to "catch up a little" on its backlog of work orders, but still needed to maintain a "decent" profit margin on the plumbers' time.

Required:

1. Do you agree with the company's computation of the labour charge on your job?
2. The company pays its plumbers $20 per hour for the first eight hours worked in a day and $30 per hour for any additional time worked. Show how the cost of the plumber's time for the day (nine hours) should be allocated between direct labour cost and general overhead cost on the company's books.
3. Under what circumstances might the company be justified in charging an overtime premium for repair work on your home?

EXERCISE 2–9 Product Cost Flows; Product versus Period Costs [LO2, LO3]

Gelinas Computer Company was organized on May 1. On that date, the company purchased 22,000 USB flash drives to be sold with personal computers, each pre-loaded with the company's product information brochures. The front of the USB flash drives displays the company's name and an attractive corporate logo. Each USB flash drive cost Gelinas $6.

During May, 19,500 USB flash drives were drawn from the raw materials inventory account. Of these, 500 were taken by the sales manager to an important sales meeting with prospective customers and handed out as advertising. The remaining USB flash drives drawn from inventory were sold by bundling them with units of the company's product that were being manufactured during May. Of the units of product that were bundled with the USB flash drive during May, 95% were completed and transferred from work in process to finished goods. Of the units completed during the month, 80% were sold and shipped to customers.

Required:

1. Determine the cost of flash drives that would be in each of the following accounts at May 31:
   a. Raw materials.
   b. Work in process.
   c. Finished goods.
   d. Cost of goods sold.
   e. Advertising expense.

2. Specify whether each of the above accounts would appear on the balance sheet or on the income statement at May 31.

EXERCISE 2–10 Preparation of a Schedule of Cost of Goods Manufactured and Cost of Goods Sold [LO1, LO3, LO4]

The following cost and inventory data for the year just completed are taken from the accounting records of Eccles Company:

Costs incurred:

Advertising expense	$100,000
Direct labour cost	$90,000
Purchases of raw materials	$132,000
Rent, factory building	$80,000
Indirect labour	$56,300
Sales commissions	$35,000
Utilities, factory	$9,000
Maintenance, factory equipment	$24,000
Supplies, factory	$700
Depreciation, office equipment	$8,000
Depreciation, factory equipment	$40,000

	Beginning of Year	End of Year
Inventories:		
Raw materials	$8,000	$10,000
Work in process	$5,000	$20,000
Finished goods	$70,000	$25,000

Required:
1. Prepare a schedule of cost of goods manufactured.
2. Prepare the cost of goods sold section of Eccles Company's income statement for the year.

EXERCISE 2–11 Classification of Costs as Variable or Fixed, and as Selling and Administrative or Product [LO2, LO5]

Below are listed various costs that are found in organizations.
1. The costs of turn signal switches used at a General Motors plant. These are one of the parts installed in the steering columns assembled at the plant.
2. The salary of the manager in charge of production at Research in Motion.
3. Salespersons' commissions at Avon Products, a company that sells cosmetics door to door.
4. Insurance on one of Bombardier's factory buildings.
5. The costs of shipping brass fittings from Graham Manufacturing's plant in British Columbia to customers in California.
6. Depreciation on the bookshelves at Reston Bookstore.
7. The costs of X-ray film at the Toronto General Hospital's radiology lab.
8. The cost of leasing a toll-free telephone number at Staples Canada. The monthly charge for the toll-free number is independent of the number of calls taken.
9. The depreciation on the playground equipment at a McDonald's outlet.
10. The cost of mozzarella cheese used at a Pizza Hut outlet.

Required:
Classify each cost as either variable or fixed with respect to the volume of goods or services produced and sold by the organization. Also classify each cost as a selling and administrative cost or as a product cost. Prepare your answer sheet as shown below. Place an X in the appropriate columns to show the proper classifications of each cost.

	Cost Behaviour		Selling and	Product
Cost Item	Variable	Fixed	Administrative Cost	Cost

EXERCISE 2–12 Classification of Labour Costs [LO1]

Greg Powers is employed by Gussie Company, where he assembles a component part for one of the company's products. Greg is paid $14 per hour for regular time, and he is paid time and a half (i.e., $21 per hour) for all work in excess of 40 hours per week.

Required:

1. Assume that during a given week Greg is idle for three hours due to machine breakdowns and that he is idle for two more hours due to material shortages. No overtime is recorded for the week. Allocate Greg's wages for the week between direct labour cost and manufacturing overhead cost.

2. Assume that during a following week Greg works a total of 49 hours. He has no idle time for the week. Allocate Greg's wages for the week between direct labour cost and manufacturing overhead cost.

3. Greg's company provides an attractive package of benefits for its employees. This package includes a retirement program and a health insurance program. Explain two ways that the company could handle the costs of its direct labourers' employee benefits in its cost records.

connect Problems

PROBLEM 2–13 Cost Classification [LO2, LO5, LO6]

Cycle Business manufactures and sells road and mountain bikes through a network of retail outlets in western Canada. Below is a partial list of expense items incurred in the most recent month (November), when 1,000 bicycles were manufactured, shipped, and sold. There was no beginning or ending work in process or finished goods inventory in November.

Item	October	November
Units produced and sold.................................	900	1,000
Sales	$900,000	$1,000,000
Leather used for the bicycle seats........................	$27,000	$30,000
Production manager's salary..............................	$6,000	$6,000
Life insurance for the company president..................	$200	$200
Electricity used in the production facilities*.................	$1,000	$1,100
Sales commissions	$45,000	$50,000
Internet advertising	$1,000	$1,000
Employee benefits for the production workers†	$36,000	$40,000
Property taxes on the production facilities	$1,000	$1,000
Shipping costs...	$45,000	$50,000
Salary of the chief financial officer.......................	$10,000	$10,000

*Each month, regardless of how much electricity is used, Cycle Business pays a $100 base charge to the utilities company.

†Employee benefits total 20% of the wages paid to production workers, who on average earn $20 per hour. Each bicycle requires 5 hours of direct labour.

Required:

1. With respect to the partial list of November expenses, answer the following:
   a. Which items represent variable manufacturing costs?
   b. Which items represent fixed manufacturing costs?
   c. If the bicycle is the cost object, which items from (*a*) and (*b*) above are direct costs and which are indirect costs?
   d. Which items would be classified as selling expenses?
   e. Which items would be classified as administrative expenses?

2. Assume that 1,200 bicycles will be manufactured and sold in the month of December. For the items you classified as manufacturing costs in question 1, estimate the cost for December. Assume that there will be no change in unit costs for any direct materials, hourly wages will remain the same, and employee benefits will continue at 20% of wages.

PROBLEM 2–14 Classification of Labour Costs [LO1]

Lynn Bjorland is employed by Northern Laboratories and is directly involved in preparing the company's leading antibiotic drug. Lynn's basic wage rate is $24 per hour. The company pays its employees time and a half (i.e., $36 per hour) for any work in excess of 40 hours per week.

Required:

1. Suppose that in a given week Lynn works 45 hours. Compute Lynn's total wages for the week. How much of this cost would the company allocate to direct labour cost? To manufacturing overhead cost?

2. Suppose in another week that Lynn works 50 hours but is idle for 4 hours during the week due to equipment breakdowns. Compute Lynn's total wages for the week. How much of this amount would be allocated to direct labour cost? To manufacturing overhead cost?

3. Northern Laboratories has an attractive package of fringe benefits that costs the company $8 for each hour of employee time (either regular time or overtime). During a particular week, Lynn works 48 hours but is idle for 3 hours due to material shortages. Compute Lynn's total wages and fringe benefits for the week. If the company treats all fringe benefits as part of manufacturing overhead cost, how much of Lynn's wages and fringe benefits for the week would be allocated to direct labour cost? To manufacturing overhead cost?

4. Refer to the data in (3) above. If the company treats that part of fringe benefits relating to direct labour as added direct labour cost, how much of Lynn's wages and fringe benefits for the week will be allocated to direct labour cost? To manufacturing overhead cost?

PROBLEM 2–15 Cost Classification [LO1, LO2, LO5, LO7]

Several years ago, Wallace Company purchased a small building adjacent to its manufacturing plant in order to have room for expansion when needed. Since the company had no immediate need for the extra space, the building was rented out to another company for a rental revenue of $35,000 per year. The renter's lease will expire soon, and rather than renewing the lease, Wallace Company has decided to use the building itself to manufacture a new product.

Direct materials cost for the new product will total $50 per unit. It will be necessary to hire a supervisor to oversee production. Her salary will be $3,000 per month. Workers will be hired to manufacture the new product, with direct labour cost amounting to $22 per unit. Manufacturing operations will occupy all of the building space, so it will be necessary to rent space in a warehouse nearby in order to store finished units of product. The rental cost will be $1,500 per month. In addition, the company will need to rent equipment for use in producing the new product; the rental cost will be $2,200 per month. The company will continue to depreciate the building on a straight-line basis, as in past years. Depreciation on the building is $7,000 per year.

Advertising costs for the new product will total $28,000 per year. Costs of shipping the new product to customers will be $7 per unit. Electrical costs of operating machines will be $4 per unit.

To have funds to purchase materials, meet payrolls, and so forth, the company will have to liquidate some temporary investments. These investments are presently yielding a return of $5,000 per year.

Required:

Prepare an answer sheet with the following column headings:

Name of the Cost	Variable Cost	Fixed Cost	Product Cost			Period (Selling and Administrative) Cost	Opportunity Cost	Sunk Cost
			Direct Materials	Direct Labour	Manufacturing Overhead			

List the different costs associated with the new product decision down the extreme left column (under Name of the Cost). Then place an X under each heading that helps to describe the type of cost involved. There may be Xs under several column headings for a single cost. (For example, a cost may be a fixed cost, a period cost, and a sunk cost; you would place an X under each of these column headings opposite the cost.)

PROBLEM 2–16 Classification of Costs as Variable or Fixed and Direct or Indirect [LO5, LO6]

Various costs associated with manufacturing operations are given below:

1. Plastic washers used to assemble autos.
2. Production superintendent's salary.
3. Wages of workers who assemble a product.
4. Electricity to run production equipment.
5. Janitorial salaries.
6. Clay used to make bricks.
7. Rent on a factory building.

8. Wood used to make skis.
9. Screws used to make furniture.
10. A supervisor's salary.
11. Cloth used to make shirts.
12. Depreciation of cafeteria equipment.
13. Glue used to make textbooks.
14. Lubricants for production equipment.
15. Paper used to make textbooks.

Required:
Classify each cost as being either variable or fixed with respect to the number of units produced and sold. Also indicate whether each cost would typically be treated as a direct cost or an indirect cost with respect to units of product. Prepare your answer sheet as shown below:

	Cost Behaviour		To Units of Product	
Cost Item	Variable	Fixed	Direct	Indirect
Example: Factory insurance		X		X

**PROBLEM 2–17 Schedule of Cost of Goods Manufactured; Income Statement; Cost Behaviour
[LO1, LO2, LO3, LO4, LO5]**
Various cost and sales data for Medco, Inc., are given for the just-completed year:

	A	B	C
1	Purchases of raw materials	$90,000	
2	Raw materials inventory, beginning	$10,000	
3	Raw materials inventory, ending	$17,000	
4	Depreciation, factory	$42,000	
5	Insurance, factory	$5,000	
6	Direct labour	$60,000	
7	Maintenance, factory	$30,000	
8	Administrative expenses	$70,000	
9	Sales	$450,000	
10	Utilities, factory	$27,000	
11	Supplies, factory	$1,000	
12	Selling expenses	$80,000	
13	Indirect labour	$65,000	
14	Work in process inventory, beginning	$7,000	
15	Work in process inventory, ending	$30,000	
16	Finished goods inventory, beginning	$10,000	
17	Finished goods inventory, ending	$40,000	
18			

◄ ◄ ► ►|\ **Sheet1** / Sheet2 / Sheet3 / | ◄ |

Ready   NUM

Required:
1. Prepare a schedule of cost of goods manufactured.
2. Prepare an income statement.
3. Assume that the company produced the equivalent of 10,000 units of product during the year. What was the average cost per unit for direct materials? What was the average cost per unit for factory depreciation?
4. Assume that the company expects to produce 15,000 units of product during the coming year. What average cost per unit and what total cost would you expect the company to incur for direct materials at this level of activity? For factory depreciation? (In preparing your answer, assume that direct materials is a variable cost and that depreciation is a fixed cost; also assume that depreciation is computed on a straight-line basis.)

5. As the manager responsible for production costs, explain to the president any difference in the average costs per unit between (3) and (4) above.

6. Assuming the company produced 20,000 fully and partially finished units during the year, determine the cost components of the finished goods inventory, which is composed of 4,000 finished units.

PROBLEM 2–18 Classification of Salary Cost as a Period or Product Cost [LO2]

You have just been hired by EduRom Company, which was organized on January 2 of the current year. The company manufactures and sells a variety of educational DVDs for personal computers. It is your responsibility to supervise the employees who take orders from customers over the phone and to arrange for shipping orders via Federal Express, Canada Post, and other freight carriers.

The company is unsure how to classify your annual salary in its cost records. The company's cost analyst says that your salary should be classified as a manufacturing (product) cost; the controller says that it should be classified as a selling expense; and the president says that it doesn't matter which way your salary cost is classified.

Required:
1. Which viewpoint is correct? Why?
2. From the point of view of the reported operating income for the year, is the president correct in saying that it doesn't matter which way your salary cost is classified? Explain.

PROBLEM 2–19 Classification of Various Costs [LO1, LO2, LO5, LO7]

Todd Radford has invented a new type of low-friction broom. After giving the matter much thought, Todd is pretty sure he will quit his $2,000 per month job with a janitorial service and produce and sell the brooms full time. Todd will rent a small building that will be used as a production plant. The rent will be $1,500 per month. Todd will rent production equipment at a cost of $550 per month.

The cost of materials for each broom will be $11.50. Todd will hire workers to produce the brooms. They will be paid $4.25 for each completed unit. Todd will rent a room in the house next door for use as his sales office. The rent will be $250 per month. He has arranged for the telephone company to add voicemail to his home phone to get off-hours messages from customers. The addition of voicemail will increase his monthly phone bill by $5.

Todd has some money in savings that is earning interest of $1,100 per year. These savings will be withdrawn and used for about a year to get the business going. To sell his brooms, Todd will advertise heavily in the local area. Advertising costs will be $450 per month. In addition, Todd will pay a sales commission of $0.80 for each broom sold. For the time being, Todd does not intend to draw any salary from the new company. Todd has already paid the legal and filing fees to incorporate his business. These fees amounted to $1,500.

Required:
1. Prepare an answer sheet with the following column headings:

Name of the Cost	Variable Cost	Fixed Cost	Product Cost			Period (Selling and Administrative) Cost	Opportunity Cost	Sunk Cost
			Direct Materials	Direct Labour	Manufacturing Overhead			

List the different costs associated with the new company down the extreme left column (under Name of Cost). Then place an *X* under each heading that helps to describe the type of cost involved. There may be *X*s under several column headings for a single cost. (That is, a cost may be a fixed cost, a period cost, and a sunk cost; you would place an *X* under each of these column headings opposite the cost.) Under the variable cost column, list only those costs that would be variable with respect to the number of low-friction brooms that are produced and sold.

2. All of the costs you have listed above, except one, would be differential costs between the alternatives of Todd producing brooms or staying with the janitorial service. Which cost is *not* differential? Explain.

PROBLEM 2–20 Cost Classification and Cost Behaviour [LO2, LO5, LO6]

Heritage Company manufactures a beautiful bookcase that enjoys widespread popularity. The company has a backlog of orders that is large enough to keep production going indefinitely at the plant's full capacity of 4,000 bookcases per year. Annual cost data at full capacity follow:

Direct materials used (wood and glass)...............	$430,000
General office salaries	$110,000
Factory supervision	$70,000
Sales commissions.................................	$60,000
Depreciation, factory building	$105,000
Depreciation, office equipment	$2,000
Indirect materials, factory........................	$18,000
Factory labour (cutting and assembly)...............	$90,000
Advertising	$100,000
Insurance, factory................................	$6,000
General office supplies (billing)....................	$4,000
Property taxes, factory............................	$20,000
Utilities, factory..................................	$45,000

Required:

1. Prepare an answer sheet with the column headings shown below. Enter each cost item on your answer sheet, placing the dollar amount under the appropriate headings. As examples, this has been done already for the first two items in the list above. Note that each cost item is classified in two ways: first, as either variable or fixed with respect to the number of units produced and sold; and second, as either a selling and administrative cost or a product cost. (If the item is a product cost, it should also be classified as either direct or indirect as shown.)

	Cost Behaviour		Selling or Administrative	Product Cost	
Cost Item	Variable	Fixed	Cost	Direct	Indirect*
Direct materials used...........	$430,000			$430,000	
General office salaries..........		$110,000	$110,000		

*To units of product.

2. Total the dollar amounts in each of the columns in (1) above. Compute the average product cost per bookcase.
3. Due to a recession, assume that production drops to only 2,000 bookcases per year. Would you expect the average product cost per bookcase to increase, decrease, or remain unchanged? Explain. No computations are necessary.
4. Refer to the original data. The president's next-door neighbour has considered making himself a bookcase and has priced the necessary materials at a building supply store. He has asked the president whether he could purchase a bookcase from the Heritage Company "at cost," and the president has agreed to let him do so.
    a. Would you expect any disagreement between the two men over the price the neighbour should pay? Explain. What price does the president probably have in mind? The neighbour?
    b. Since the company is operating at full capacity, what cost term used in the chapter might be justification for the president to charge the full regular price to the neighbour and still be selling "at cost"? Explain.

PROBLEM 2–21 Variable and Fixed Costs; Subtleties of Direct and Indirect Costs [LO5, LO6]

The Central Area Well-Baby Clinic provides a variety of health services to newborn babies and their parents. The clinic is organized into a number of departments, one of which is the Immunization Centre. A number of costs of the clinic and the Immunization Centre are listed below.

Example: The cost of polio immunization tablets.
a. The salary of the head nurse in the Immunization Centre.
b. Costs of incidental supplies consumed in the Immunization Centre, such as paper towels.
c. The cost of lighting and heating the Immunization Centre.
d. The cost of disposable syringes used in the Immunization Centre.
e. The salary of the Central Area Well-Baby Clinic's information systems manager.
f. The costs of mailing letters soliciting donations to the Central Area Well-Baby Clinic.
g. The wages of nurses who work in the Immunization Centre.

h. The cost of medical malpractice insurance for the Central Area Well-Baby Clinic.
i. Depreciation on the fixtures and equipment in the Immunization Centre.

Required:

For each cost listed above, indicate whether it is a direct or indirect cost of the Immunization Centre, whether it is a direct or indirect cost of immunizing particular patients, and whether it is variable or fixed with respect to the number of immunizations administered. Use the form shown below for your answer.

Item Description	Direct or Indirect Cost of the Immunization Centre		Direct or Indirect Cost of Particular Patients		Variable or Fixed with Respect to the Number of Immunizations Administered	
	Direct	Indirect	Direct	Indirect	Variable	Fixed
Example: The cost of polio immunization tablets	X		X		X	

PROBLEM 2–22 Schedule of Cost of Goods Manufactured; Income Statement [LO1, LO2, LO3, LO4]

Veekay Company was organized on November 1 of the previous year. After seven months of startup losses, management had expected to earn a profit during June, the most recent month. Management was disappointed, however, when the income statement for June also showed a loss. June's income statement follows.

VEEKAY COMPANY
Income Statement
For the Month Ended June 30

Sales.		$660,000
Less operating expenses:		
Selling and administrative salaries	$ 39,000	
Rent on facilities	40,000	
Purchases of raw materials.	209,000	
Insurance.	10,000	
Depreciation, sales equipment	11,000	
Utilities costs.	55,000	
Indirect labour.	119,000	
Direct labour	99,000	
Depreciation, factory equipment.	13,000	
Maintenance, factory.	8,000	
Advertising	88,000	691,000
Operating loss.		$(31,000)

After seeing the $31,000 loss for June, Veekay's president stated, "I was sure we'd be profitable within six months, but after eight months we're still spilling red ink. Maybe it's time for us to throw in the towel. To make matters worse, I just heard that Debbie won't be back from her surgery for at least six more weeks."

Debbie is the company's controller; in her absence, the statement above was prepared by a new assistant who has had little experience in manufacturing operations. Additional information about the company follows:

a. Only 85% of the rent on facilities applies to factory operations; the remainder applies to selling and administrative activities.

b. Inventory balances at the beginning and end of June were as follows:

	June 1	June 30
Raw materials	$19,000	$46,000
Work in process.	$77,000	$94,000
Finished goods.	$22,000	$66,000

c.   Some 90% of the insurance and 80% of the utilities cost apply to factory operations; the remaining amounts apply to selling and administrative activities.

The president has asked you to check over the above income statement and make a recommendation as to whether the company should continue operations.

Required:
1.   As one step in gathering data for a recommendation to the president, prepare a schedule of cost of goods manufactured for June.
2.   As a second step, prepare a new income statement for the month.
3.   Based on your statements prepared in (1) and (2) above, would you recommend that the company continue operations?

PROBLEM 2–23 Ethics and the Manager [LO2]

The top management of General Electronics Inc. is well known for "managing by the numbers." With an eye on the company's desired growth in overall net profit, the company's CEO sets target profits at the beginning of the year for each of the company's divisions. The CEO has stated her policy as follows: "I won't interfere with operations in the divisions. I am available for advice, but the division vice-presidents are free to do anything they want as long as they hit the target profits for the year."

In November, Stan Richart, the vice-president in charge of the Cellular Telephone Technologies Division, saw that making the current year's target profit for his division was going to be very difficult. Among other actions, he directed that discretionary expenditures be delayed until the beginning of the new year. On December 30, he was angered to discover that a warehouse clerk had ordered $350,000 of cellular telephone parts earlier in December, even though the parts weren't really needed by the assembly department until January or February. Contrary to common accounting practice, the General Electronics Inc. *Accounting Policy Manual* states that such parts are to be recorded as an expense when delivered. To avoid recording the expense, Richart asked that the order be cancelled, but the Purchasing Department reported that the parts had already been delivered and the supplier would not accept returns. Since the bill had not yet been paid, Richart asked the Accounting Department to correct the clerk's mistake by delaying recognition of the delivery until the bill is paid in January.

Required:
1.   Are Richart's actions ethical? Explain why they are or are not ethical.
2.   Do the general management philosophy and accounting policies at General Electronics encourage or discourage ethical behaviour? Explain.

PROBLEM 2–24 Schedule of Cost of Goods Manufactured; Income Statement; Cost Behaviour [LO1, LO2, LO3, LO4, LO5]

The following selected account balances for the year ended December 31 are provided for Valenko Company:

Advertising expense.	$215,000
Insurance, factory equipment	$8,000
Depreciation, sales equipment	$40,000
Rent, factory building.	$90,000
Utilities, factory	$52,000
Sales commissions	$35,000
Cleaning supplies, factory	$6,000
Depreciation, factory equipment	$110,000
Selling and administrative salaries.	$85,000
Maintenance, factory	$74,000
Direct labour.	?
Purchases of raw materials	$260,000

Inventory balances at the beginning and end of the year were as follows:

	Beginning of Year	End of Year
Raw materials	$50,000	$40,000
Work in process	?	$33,000
Finished goods	$30,000	?

The total manufacturing costs for the year were $675,000; the goods available for sale totalled $720,000; and the cost of goods sold totalled $635,000.

Required:

1. Prepare a schedule of cost of goods manufactured and the cost of goods sold section of the company's income statement for the year.
2. Assume that the dollar amounts given above are for the equivalent of 30,000 units produced during the year. Compute the average cost per unit for direct materials used, and compute the average cost per unit for rent on the factory building.
3. Assume that in the following year the company expects to produce 50,000 units. What average cost per unit and total cost would you expect to be incurred for direct materials? For rent on the factory building? (Assume that direct materials is a variable cost and that rent is a fixed cost.)
4. As the manager in charge of production costs, explain to the president the reason for any difference in the average costs per unit between (2) and (3) above.

PROBLEM 2–25 Working with Incomplete Data from the Income Statement and Schedule of Cost of Goods Manufactured [LO3, LO4]

Supply the missing data in the four cases that follow. Each case is independent of the others.

	Case			
	1	**2**	**3**	**4**
Schedule of Cost of Goods Manufactured				
Direct materials	$ 5,600	$10,400	$ 6,600	$ 7,600
Direct labour	$ 1,600	$ 4,600	?	$ 2,900
Manufacturing overhead	$ 8,000	?	$ 7,700	$20,000
Total manufacturing costs	?	$28,800	$19,800	?
Beginning work in process inventory	?	$ 1,200	$ 2,200	?
Ending work in process inventory	$ 3,200	$ 4,000	?	$ 1,900
Cost of goods manufactured	$14,400	$?	$17,600	$29,900
Income Statement				
Sales	$20,000	$46,000	$33,000	$47,500
Beginning finished goods inventory	$ 4,800	?	$ 7,700	$ 8,600
Cost of goods manufactured	$14,400	?	$17,600	$29,900
Goods available for sale	?	?	?	?
Ending finished goods inventory	$ 7,200	$ 4,600	?	$ 6,700
Cost of goods sold	?	$30,500	$19,800	?
Gross margin	?	?	?	?
Selling and administrative expenses	$ 4,800	?	?	$ 9,500
Operating income	$?	$ 6,300	$ 3,300	$?

PROBLEM 2–26 Income Statement; Schedule of Cost of Goods Manufactured [LO1, LO2, LO3, LO4]

Hickey Corporation is a manufacturer that produces a single product. The following information has been taken from the company's production, sales, and cost records for the just completed year:

Production in units	30,000
Sales in units.	?
Ending finished goods inventory in units	?
Sales in dollars	$650,000
Costs:	
Advertising	$50,000
Direct labour.	$80,000
Indirect labour	$60,000
Raw materials purchased	$160,000
Building rent (production uses 80% of the space; administrative and sales offices use the rest)	$50,000
Utilities, factory	$35,000
Royalty paid for use of production patent, $1 per unit produced	?
Maintenance, factory	$25,000
Rent for special production equipment, $6,000 per year plus $0.10 per unit produced	?
Selling and administrative salaries	$140,000
Other factory overhead costs	$11,000
Other selling and administrative expenses.	$20,000

	Beginning of Year	End of Year
Inventories:		
Raw materials....................	$20,000	$10,000
Work in process..................	$30,000	$40,000
Finished goods...................	$0	?

The finished goods inventory is being carried at the average unit production cost for the year. The selling price of the product is $25 per unit.

Required:
1.   Prepare a schedule of cost of goods manufactured for the year.
2.   Compute the following:
     a.   The number of units in the finished goods inventory at the end of the year.
     b.   The cost of the units in the finished goods inventory at the end of the year.
3.   Prepare an income statement for the year.

connect Cases

CASE 2–27 Missing Data; Income Statement; Schedule of Cost of Goods Manufactured [LO1, LO2, LO3, LO4]

"I was sure when our camping tent hit the market it would be an instant success, but I guess I still have some things to learn about running a business," said Michael McCarter, founder and president of Outdoor Living, Inc. "Demand has been so strong for our lightweight individual tent that I was sure we'd be profitable immediately, but just look at the gusher of red ink for the first quarter. At this rate we'll be out of business in a year." The data to which Michael was referring are shown below:

Outdoor Living, Inc. Income Statement For the Quarter Ended June 30		
Sales (4,000 tents)		$ 683,000
Less operating expenses:		
Selling and administrative salaries	$ 63,000	
Advertising	140,000	
Cleaning supplies, factory...............	4,000	
Indirect labour cost.....................	91,000	
Depreciation, office equipment............	13,000	
Direct labour cost	56,000	
Raw materials purchased	217,000	
Maintenance, factory...................	33,000	
Rental cost, facilities...................	50,000	
Insurance, factory	6,000	
Utilities...............................	30,000	
Depreciation, production equipment	53,000	
Travel, salespersons...................	42,000	798,000
Operating loss..........................		$ (115,000)

Outdoor Living was organized on April 1 of the current year to produce and market a revolutionary new lightweight one-person camping tent. The company's accounting system was set up by Michael's brother-in-law, who had taken an accounting course about 10 years ago.

"We may not last a year if the insurance company doesn't pay the $159,600 it owes us for the 1,000 tents lost in the warehouse fire last week," said Michael. "The agent says our claim is inflated, but that's a lot of baloney."

Just after the end of the quarter, the company's finished goods storage warehouse was destroyed by a fire and all 1,000 tents were destroyed. The tents were part of the 5,000 units completed during the quarter ended June 30. The company's insurance policy states that the company will be reimbursed for the "cost" of the goods destroyed or stolen. Michael's brother-in-law has determined this cost as follows:

$$\frac{\text{Total costs for the quarter}}{\text{Tents produced during the quarter}} = \$798{,}000/5{,}000 \text{ units} = \$159.60 \text{ per unit}$$

$$1{,}000 \text{ units} \times \$159.60 \text{ per unit} = \$159{,}600$$

The following additional information is available on the company's activities during the quarter ended June 30:

a.   Inventories at the beginning and end of the quarter were as follows:

	Beginning of the Quarter	End of the Quarter
Raw materials	$0	$28,000
Work in process	$0	$21,000
Finished goods	$0	?

b.   Ninety percent of the rental cost for facilities and 80% of the utilities cost relate to manufacturing operations. The remaining amounts relate to selling and administrative activities.

Required:

1.   What conceptual errors, if any, were made in preparing Outdoor Living's income statement above?
2.   Prepare a schedule of cost of goods manufactured for the quarter.
3.   Prepare a corrected income statement for the quarter. Your statement should show in detail how the cost of goods sold is computed. (*Note:* you will need to calculate the cost of the ending finished goods inventory on June 30 that was destroyed by fire, based on your answer to (2) above.)
4.   Do you agree that the insurance company owes Outdoor Living $159,600? Explain your answer.

CASE 2–28 Differential Revenues and Costs, Opportunity Costs and Sunk Costs [LO7]

Performance Edge (PE) is a consulting company with offices in all major Canadian cities; its corporate headquarters are in Hamilton, Ontario. The company specializes in developing employee reward and recognition programs for its clients, which range from manufacturing companies to reservation centres for hotel chains. One of the most popular programs developed by PE involves working with its clients' management teams to establish performance goals for employees. Once the performance goals are established, PE develops a reward program whereby employees receive "points" instead of cash for attaining the goals set by management. The more difficult the goal, the higher the number of points received by the employee for goal attainment. The points can be redeemed for prizes such as bicycles, barbeques, computers, cameras, vacations, and gift certificates to restaurants, clothing and jewellery stores, and so on. PE has developed a catalogue of prizes that is distributed to employees so that they can see what they will be able to redeem their points for should they attain their performance goals for the period.

As part of the service offered to its clients, PE maintains an inventory of the various prizes that can be purchased by their clients' employees with their points. PE purchases the prizes directly from manufacturers and wholesalers but maintains a reasonably large inventory of most items offered in their catalogue to ensure that they are available to clients on a timely basis. The inventory is kept in a warehouse at Stoney Creek, a small city that is just outside Hamilton. The warehouse was purchased several years ago and PE has grown considerably since then. Indeed, in recent months, delays have occurred in getting prizes to some clients because the warehouse is no longer large enough to maintain sufficient quantities of all items.

About a month ago, Reg White, the facilities manager at PE became aware of a larger warehouse in nearby Burlington that is available for a long-term lease. The lease will qualify as an operating lease so the monthly lease payments will be expensed. Although the warehouse in Burlington is larger than the current facility in Stoney Creek, Reg estimates that the utility costs will be lower because it is more modern and energy-efficient. Another benefit of moving to the new warehouse will be that PE won't have to pay property taxes or building insurance since it won't own the building. Also, because the new warehouse is larger than PE currently requires to maintain an adequate inventory of prizes, it will be able to sublet about 15% of the total space to another tenant, at least for the next few years until such time as it needs to take over the entire facility.

Reg also believes that it shouldn't be too hard to sell the existing warehouse in Stoney Creek based on conversations he has had with a commercial property real estate agent who already has clients interested in making an offer. Because the existing warehouse isn't yet fully depreciated, Reg also thinks that selling it will help PE's bottom line because the company will no longer have to charge the depreciation expense to the income statement. Another benefit of selling the existing warehouse is that PE will no longer incur the maintenance and repair costs, or the salary of the building maintenance manager who will be let go if the company decides to rent the new facility. Maintenance costs of the new warehouse will be paid by the building's owner, unless the repairs are the result of damage caused by PE, in which case PE will be responsible for the costs. Reg thinks that insurance on the inventory of prizes and the costs of security personnel on-site 24/7 will not change if PE decides to move to the new warehouse.

One drawback in selling the existing warehouse is that PE will no longer earn the operating income associated with the small parking lot it had on one corner of the property. PE rented parking spaces to employees of a business on an adjacent property that did not have its own parking. Net of the annual costs of maintaining the parking lot (e.g., snow removal, repairs, security cameras, etc.), PE made a small operating profit each year.

Required:
1. Identify the differential revenues and costs related to keeping the existing warehouse in Stoney Creek versus renting the new facility in Burlington.
2. Are there any opportunity costs associated with selling the old warehouse?
3. What kind of cost is the depreciation expense on the old warehouse? Should it be considered in deciding whether to stay in the existing location or rent the new facility? Why or why not?

Research

R 2–29 Disclosure, Cost Classification, and External Reports [LO1, LO2, LO5]
Examine the most recent annual report of Research in Motion and in particular look at the income statement. Classify as best you can the costs as variable and fixed, period and product. Contrast the cost disclosures with those presented in this chapter.

R 2–30 Disclosure, Cost Classification, and External Reports [LO1, LO2, LO5]
Using the most recent annual report of Barrick Gold Corporation, consider which costs are product costs and which are period costs. Also carefully consider which costs are variable and which are fixed. Present your conclusions.

Comment on the extent of disclosure in the financial statements compared to that described in this chapter. Determine the nature of the direct materials cost, the direct labour cost, and the overhead costs. Amounts are not required.

What difficulties, if any, were encountered in classifying costs?

COSTING

Chapters 3 through 8

Chapters 3 through 8 provide a comprehensive description of how costs are associated with manufacturing and other activities. In addition, these costing systems can be applied to service organizations and not-for-profit organizations. To permit costing for such specialized situations, two costing systems, job costing and process costing, can be mixed and matched.

Chapter 3 begins with the most basic and widely used costing system, *job-order costing.* Job-order costing permits costs to be assigned to specific outcomes, termed *jobs,* so that costs can be accumulated for what a company produces. In addition, manufacturing overhead—a term often shortened to just *overhead*—is assigned by a process of averaging to estimate its amount before actual overhead costs are known.

Chapter 4 introduces an averaging calculation used for costing similar units of product, termed *process costing*. The ordering of costs learned in financial accounting (namely, average and FIFO) can be applied. The idea of equivalent units is explained, so that partially finished work in progress can be valued in inventory. Chapter 4 also presents an elaboration of overhead methods so that overhead can be disaggregated to departments (the cost object in this case) to permit better management control of overhead and more accurate costing.

Chapter 5 introduces activity-based costing, another way to disaggregate overhead and non-

manufacturing costs. Cost objects are defined as activities, and activities are costed by identifying a relevant cost driver. By doing this, overhead costing can be improved and management can focus on managing activities rather than outcomes. Given the increasing importance of overhead costs incurred in some types of organizations, methods to improve the management of overhead costs are important contributions.

Chapter 6 describes the details of cost behaviour and how costs that contain a mixture of behaviours can be analyzed.

Chapter 7 takes the idea of cost behaviour and incorporates revenues to provide commonly used tools for analysis and short-term decisions including cost–volume–profit analysis and break-even analysis.

Chapter 8 completes the costing segment by describing variable costing. Variable costing assigns only variable manufacturing costs to production as opposed to all manufacturing costs as was described in earlier chapters under the term *absorption costing.*

On the completion of Chapter 8, the costing approaches are twofold: job costing and process costing. Added to these are two definitions of costs: absorption and variable. This two-by-two combination can be extended using departmental and activity overhead approaches to disaggregate overhead, as desired by management.

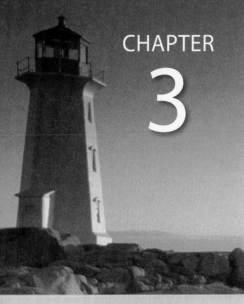

After studying Chapter 3, you should be able to

1. Distinguish between process costing and job-order costing and identify the types of companies that would use each costing method.

2. Identify the documents used in a job-order costing system.

3. Compute predetermined overhead rates and explain why estimated overhead costs (rather than actual overhead costs) are used in the costing process.

4. Record the journal entries that reflect the flow of costs in a job-order costing system.

5. Apply overhead cost to work in process using a predetermined overhead rate.

6. Prepare schedules of cost of goods manufactured and cost of goods sold.

7. Compute underapplied or overapplied overhead cost and prepare the journal entry to close the balance in manufacturing overhead to the appropriate accounts.

8. (Appendix 3A) Explain the implications of basing the predetermined overhead rate on activity at full capacity rather than on estimated activity for the period.

SYSTEMS DESIGN: JOB-ORDER COSTING

■ CUSTOM DESIGN AT ICEJERSEYS.COM

In the fall of 1989, a small retail store called Sport BUFF opened across the street from the Montreal Forum. The store was dedicated to offering the best selection of officially licensed sports merchandise and apparel in Montreal. Customers knew that no matter what team they supported, Sport BUFF would have a jersey in stock. As the Internet and online shopping became more popular, the store owners launched the Web site www.NHLHockeyJerseys.com (now just www.icejerseys.com) and began offering custom team outfitting services to hockey teams at all skill levels. Customers use an online tool called "JerseyBuilder" to choose colours and styles, and either provide a team logo or the IceJerseys.com staff will design a logo for them. Individual team members' names, numbers, and the team logo are printed or stitched on each jersey to meet customer specifications.

Accurately pricing custom-designed jerseys depends critically on the quality of costing information available to managers at companies like IceJerseys.com, as well as on the prices charged by competitors. The price quoted by IceJerseys.com for a custom batch of hockey jerseys must adequately cover costs to design and produce each customized order, leaving an adequate profit margin while remaining price-competitive. Costs might include items such as the labour devoted to designing custom logos and other artwork, the cost of materials and labour involved in manufacturing the custom batches of jerseys (or the cost of purchasing them from outside suppliers), and the costs of the manufacturing, printing, and stitching equipment used to produce the jerseys to customer specifications (called *manufacturing overhead*). Since this equipment will be used to produce several different batches of custom jerseys in any one year, we must find a way to divide up these costs between batches so that we can then estimate the total cost per unit of jerseys in each batch. In this chapter, we will examine methods of making accurate estimates of the total cost per unit and we will explore why this information is key to setting prices and to identifying opportunities for cost control for many firms.

Source: IceJerseys.com Team Outfitting: team.icejerseys.com. Reprinted with permission.

Absorption costing
A costing method that includes all manufacturing costs—direct materials, direct labour, and both variable and fixed overhead—as part of the cost of a finished unit of product; synonymous with *full costing.*

Full costing
Another name for *absorption costing.*

A s discussed in Chapter 2, product costing is the process of assigning costs to the products and services provided by a company. An understanding of this costing process is vital to managers because the way in which a product or service is costed can have a substantial impact on reported net income, as well as on key management decisions such as pricing and outsourcing.

The essential purpose of any managerial costing system should be to provide cost data to help managers plan, control, direct, and make decisions. Nevertheless, external financial reporting and tax reporting requirements often heavily influence how costs are accumulated and summarized in managerial reports. This is also true of product costing.

In this chapter and in Chapter 4, we use an *absorption costing* approach to determine product costs. This was also the method that was used in Chapter 2. In **absorption costing**, *all* manufacturing costs, fixed and variable, are assigned to units of product—units are said to *fully absorb manufacturing costs.* The absorption costing approach is also known as **full costing**. Later, in Chapter 8, we look at product costing from a different point of view called *variable costing,* which is often advocated as an alternative to absorption costing. Chapter 8 also discusses the strengths and weaknesses of the two approaches.

Most companies around the world use some form of absorption costing for both external financial reporting and for tax reporting. In addition, most of these same companies also use absorption costing for managerial accounting purposes. Since absorption costing is the most common approach to product costing, we discuss it first and then deal with alternatives in subsequent chapters.

While studying product costing, we must keep in mind that the essential purpose of any costing system is to accumulate costs for managerial use. A costing system is not an end in itself. Rather, it is a managerial tool that exists to provide managers with the cost data needed to direct the affairs of organizations.

The design of the costing system depends on cost–benefit trade-offs as assessed by managers. The level of detail and sophistication in a cost accounting system will influence its costs of development and operation. Relevance to management and external regulatory requirements will be the benefit. Usually, more sophistication yields more benefit by providing more relevant information. But when the additional cost of providing added sophistication equals the benefits from the added relevance, the system's designer is at an optimal point in the cost–benefit trade-off, so the added sophistication should stop.

The nature of systems design is also influenced by the nature of what is to be costed. The explanation provided in the pages that follow will focus on the nature of what is costed rather than the cost–benefit trade-offs. This will enable a description of what physically needs to be considered when the cost–benefit decision must be made. In other words, physical characteristics represent a fundamental consideration to the higher level and more subjective cost–benefit trade-off.

Absorption costing is a popular approach for determining the cost of goods sold and the cost of inventories for financial accounting and income taxes. These regulatory requirements influence how management determines costs because it may be easier and less expensive for the organization to use a single method of costing for both external and internal purposes.

Costing of products or services represents an approach that focuses on the costing of the efforts that make up the goods or services that are sold by the organization. This emphasis on costing products or services is one of the three common approaches used in managerial accounting. The discussion of costing begins with this focus because of its long tradition and its continued popularity for many types of organizations. After this approach to costing is thoroughly explored in the next few chapters, the alternatives—control and decision—will be studied so that a more complete picture will be available for your study of managerial accounting.

PROCESS AND JOB-ORDER COSTING

In computing the cost of a product or a service, managers are faced with a difficult problem. Many costs (such as rent) do not change much from month to month, whereas production may change frequently, with production going up in one month and then down in another. In addition to variations in the level of production, several different products or services may be produced in a given period in the same facility. Under these conditions, how is it possible to accurately determine the cost of a product or service? In practice, assigning costs to products and services involves an averaging of some type across time periods and across products. The way in which this averaging is carried out will depend heavily on the type of production process involved.

LEARNING OBJECTIVE 1
Distinguish between process costing and job-order costing and identify the types of companies that would use each costing method.

Process Costing

A **process costing system** is used in situations where the company produces many units of a single product (such as frozen orange juice concentrate) for long periods at a time. Examples include mixing cement at St. Mary's Cement, refining oil at Petro-Canada, mixing and bottling beverages at Coca-Cola, and making wieners at J. M. Schneider Inc. (owned by Maple Leaf Foods Inc.). All of these industries are characterized by an essentially homogeneous product that flows evenly through the production process on a continuous basis.

Process costing systems accumulate costs in a particular operation or department for an entire period (month, quarter, and year) and then divide this total cost by the number of units produced during the period. The basic formula for process costing is as follows:

$$\frac{\text{Unit product cost}}{\text{(per litre, kilogram, bottles)}} = \frac{\text{Total manufacturing cost}}{\text{Total units produced (litres, kilograms, bottles)}}$$

Since one unit of product (litre, kilogram, bottle) is indistinguishable from any other unit of product, each unit is assigned the same average cost. This costing technique results in a broad average unit cost figure that applies to homogeneous units flowing in a continuous stream out of the production process.

Process costing system
A costing system used in those manufacturing situations where a single, homogeneous product (such as cement or oil) flows in a continuous stream out of the production process.

Job-Order Costing

A **job-order costing system** is used in situations where many *different* products are produced each period. For example, a Levi Strauss clothing factory would typically make many different types of jeans for both men and women during a month. A particular order might consist of 1,000 stonewashed men's blue denim jeans, style number A312, with a 32-inch waist and a 30-inch inseam. This order of 1,000 jeans is called a *batch* or a *job*. In a job-order costing system, costs are traced and allocated to jobs and then the costs of the job are divided by the number of units in the job to arrive at an average cost per unit.

Other examples of situations where job-order costing would be used include large-scale construction projects managed by Bechtel Corporation, commercial aircraft produced by Bombardier, greeting cards designed and printed by Hallmark, and airline meals prepared by Cara. All of these examples are characterized by diverse outputs. Each Bechtel project is unique and different from every other—the company could be simultaneously constructing a dam in Zaire and a bridge in Indonesia. Likewise, each airline orders a different type of meal from Cara's catering service.

Job-order costing is also used extensively in service industries and not-for-profit organizations. Hospitals, social service agencies, law firms, movie studios, accounting firms, and advertising agencies all use a variation of job-order costing to accumulate costs for accounting, billing, and performance evaluation purposes. For example, the production of the British Open golf broadcast by TSN and the accumulation of treatment-related costs for each patient admitted to hospital would both be suitable as job costing projects.

Job-order costing system
A costing system used in situations where many different products, jobs, or services are produced each period.

Although the detailed example of job-order costing provided in the following section deals with a manufacturing firm, the same basic concepts and procedures are used by many service organizations. The essential difference for service organizations is the lack of raw materials in the cost of their services. For example, a public accounting firm would have cost elements involving direct labour and overhead but not raw materials, because the firm does not make a physical item. However, to avoid duplicating the discussion that follows, the more comprehensive manufacturing environment will be presented, with the service application addressed in exercises and problems.

The record-keeping and cost assignment problems are more complex when a company sells many different products and services than when it has only a single product. Since the products are different, the costs are typically different. Consequently, cost records must be maintained for each distinct product or job. For example, a lawyer in a large criminal law practice would ordinarily keep separate records of the costs of advising and defending each of her clients. The Levi Strauss factory mentioned earlier would keep the costs of filling orders for particular styles, sizes, and colours of jeans separately. Thus, a job-order costing system requires more effort than a process costing system. Nevertheless, job-order costing is used by more than half the manufacturers in North America.

In this chapter, we focus on the design of a job-order costing system. In the following chapter, we focus on process costing and also look more closely at the similarities and differences between the two costing methods.

JOB-ORDER COSTING—AN OVERVIEW

> **LEARNING OBJECTIVE 2**
> Identify the documents used in a job-order costing system.

To introduce job-order costing, we will follow a specific job as it progresses through the manufacturing process. This job consists of two experimental couplings that ABY Precision Machining has agreed to produce for Loops Unlimited, a manufacturer of roller coasters. Couplings connect the cars on the roller coaster and are a critical component in the performance and safety of the ride. Before we begin our discussion, recall from Chapter 2 that companies generally classify manufacturing costs into three broad categories: (1) direct materials, (2) direct labour, and (3) manufacturing overhead. As we study the operation of a job-order costing system, we will see how each of these three types of costs is recorded and accumulated. You may wish to refer to the summary of document flows presented in Exhibit 3–5 on page 79 as you work through the example below.

Measuring Direct Materials Cost

Bill of materials
A record that lists the type and quantity of each major item of the materials required to make a product.

ABY Precision Machining will require four G7 connectors and two M46 housings to make the two experimental couplings for Loops Unlimited. If this were a standard product, there would be a *bill of materials* for the product. A **bill of materials** is a record that lists the type and quantity of each item of the materials needed to complete a unit of product. In this case, there is no established bill of materials, so ABY's production staff determined the materials requirements from the blueprints submitted by the customer. Each coupling requires two connectors and one housing; therefore, to make two couplings, four connectors and two housings are required.

Materials requisition form
A detailed source document that specifies the type and quantity of materials that are to be drawn from the storeroom and identifies the job to which the costs of materials are to be charged.

A *production order* is issued when an agreement has been reached with the customer concerning the quantities, prices, and shipment date for the order. The Production Department then prepares a *materials requisition form* similar to the form in Exhibit 3–1. The **materials requisition form** is a detailed source document that (1) specifies the type and quantity of materials to be drawn from the storeroom, and (2) identifies the job to which the costs of the materials are to be charged. The form serves as a means for controlling the flow of materials into production and also for making entries in the accounting records.

The ABY Precision Machining materials requisition form in Exhibit 3–1 shows that the company's Milling Department has requisitioned two M46 housings and four G7 connectors for Job 2B47. A production worker presents the completed form to the storeroom clerk, who

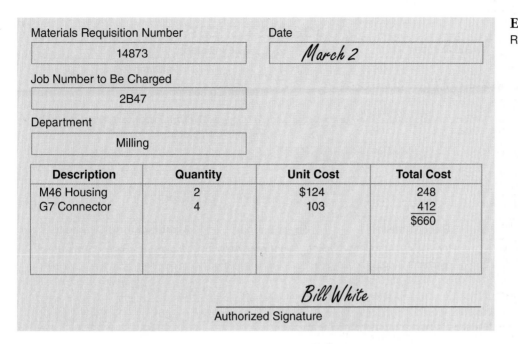

Materials Requisition Number		Date	
14873		*March 2*	

Job Number to Be Charged

2B47

Department

Milling

Description	Quantity	Unit Cost	Total Cost
M46 Housing	2	$124	248
G7 Connector	4	103	412
			$660

Bill White

Authorized Signature

EXHIBIT 3–1   Materials Requisition Form

then issues the necessary raw materials. The storeroom clerk is not allowed to release materials without a completed and properly authorized materials requisition form.

Previously, we used the terms *direct materials* and *raw materials*. This distinction should be clarified. Direct materials represent materials that are directly traced to the product or service. Raw materials are ingredients that are converted into a finished product. Semifinished materials, or supplies for a service job, could be considered direct materials if they were important enough to be directly traced to the job, but they will not be raw materials. In summary, because raw materials can be direct materials but all direct materials are not necessarily raw materials, the terms often appear interchangeably in business terminology.

Job Cost Sheet

After being notified that the production order has been issued, the Accounting Department prepares a *job cost sheet* similar to the one presented in Exhibit 3–2. A **job cost sheet** is a form prepared for each separate job that records the materials, labour, and overhead costs charged to the job.

After direct materials are issued, the Accounting Department records their costs directly on the job cost sheet. Note from Exhibit 3–2, for example, that the $660 cost for direct materials shown earlier on the materials requisition form has been charged to Job 2B47 on its job cost sheet. The requisition number 14873 is also recorded on the job cost sheet to make it easier to identify the source document for the direct materials charge.

In addition to serving as a means for charging costs to jobs, the job cost sheet also serves as a key part of a firm's accounting records. Job cost sheets serve as a subsidiary ledger to the work in process account because the detailed records that they provide for the jobs in process add up to the balance in work in process.

Job cost sheet
A form prepared for each job that records the materials, labour, and overhead costs charged to the job.

Measuring Direct Labour Cost

Direct labour cost is handled in much the same way as direct materials cost. Direct labour consists of labour charges that are easily traced to a particular job. Labour charges that cannot be easily traced directly to any job are treated as part of manufacturing overhead. As discussed in Chapter 2, this latter category of labour costs is termed *indirect labour* and includes tasks such as maintenance, supervision, and cleanup.

Workers use *time tickets* to record the time they spend on each job and task. A completed **time ticket** is an hour-by-hour summary of the employee's activities throughout

Time ticket
A detailed source document that is used to record an employee's hour-by-hour activities during a day.

EXHIBIT 3–2   Job Cost Sheet

JOB COST SHEET

Job Number	Date Initiated
2B47	March 2

Department	Date Completed
Milling	

Item	Units Completed

For Inventory

Direct Materials		Direct Labour			Manufacturing Overhead		
Req. No.	Amount	Ticket	Hours	Amount	Hours	Rate	Amount
14873	$660	843	5	$75			

Cost Summary		Units Shipped		
Direct Materials	$	Date	Number	Balance
Direct Labour	$			
Manufacturing Overhead	$			
Total Cost	$			
Unit Cost	$			

the day. An example of an employee time ticket is shown in Exhibit 3–3. When working on a specific job, the employee enters the job number on the time ticket and notes the amount of time spent on that job. When not assigned to a particular job, the employee records the nature of the indirect labour task (such as cleanup and maintenance) and the amount of time spent on the task.

EXHIBIT 3–3   Employee Time Ticket

Time Ticket No.	Date
843	March 3

Employee	Station
Mary Holden	4

Started	Ended	Time Completed	Rate	Amount	Job Number
7:00	12:00	5.0	$15	$75	2B47
12:30	2:30	2.0	15	30	2B50
2:30	3:30	1.0	15	15	Maintenance
Totals		8.0		$120	

R.W. Pace
_____
Supervisor

At the end of the day, the time tickets are sent to the Accounting Department, where the direct labour-hours and costs are recorded on individual job cost sheets. (See Exhibit 3–2 for an example of how direct labour costs are entered on the job cost sheet.) The daily time tickets are source documents that are used as the basis for labour cost entries into the accounting records.

IN BUSINESS

The 2010 *Prime Advantage Group Outlook (GO) Survey* found that managing costs of raw materials (such as metals and plastics) was among industrial manufacturers' top sourcing concerns for the first half of 2010. Results of the survey also revealed that price pressure and inflation were significant concerns for the small and mid-sized manufacturers surveyed. In addition, respondents indicated a significant focus on cost savings and efficiency measures to deal with the threat of increasing costs and inflation.

Source: http://www.primeadvantage.com/companynews/pressreleases/2009-09-02-groupoutlooksurvey.html. Accessed January 11, 2010.

The system we have just described is a manual method for recording and posting labour costs. Many companies now rely on computerized systems and no longer record labour time by hand on sheets of paper. One computerized approach uses bar codes to enter the basic data into the computer. Each employee and each job has a unique bar code. When an employee begins work on a job, he or she scans three bar codes, using a hand-held device much like the bar code readers at grocery store checkouts. The first bar code indicates that a job is being started; the second is the unique bar code on the employee's identity badge; and the third is the unique bar code of the job itself. This information is fed automatically via an electronic network to a computer that notes the time and then records all of the data. When the employee completes the task, he or she scans a bar code indicating the task is complete,

IN BUSINESS

The design was straightforward—59 black and white bars used to speed up the grocery checkout line and give supermarkets a new tool to track their stock. But the Universal Product Code has become much more than that since it was first used to read the price on a pack of gum in 1974. Today, bar codes are scanned more than 10 billion times a day around the world for many different purposes, including tracking grocery sales and inventory, loading aircraft, and tracking packages.

Although more expensive to implement, radio-frequency identification devices (RFID) are beginning to replace old bar code scanning systems. According to Phil Lempert, an industry analyst known as The Supermarket Guru, RFID tags would not only make checkout lines obsolete—you'd simply roll through a sensor station that assessed your cart's contents—but would also turn your cellphone into a personal cashier. Your phone would be equipped with a chip allowing it to talk directly to your bank account and automatically deduct the money owed to the grocery store for the items in your cart. Automatic collection of data about purchasing patterns could be linked to the stores back-office ordering and distribution systems, allowing for more integrated ordering and improved waste and cost control. In addition, revenues could be managed better, using information about purchasing patterns and the effectiveness of particular advertising campaigns in various markets.

Source: Adapted from "A Grocery Store Icon Turns 35: Bar Code Birthday," *National Post,* June 29, 2009, p. FP4; and Misty Harris, "Bar Codes Morphing So You Can Skip Checkout Lines," *CanWest News,* June 8, 2009.

the bar code on the employee's identity badge, and the bar code attached to the job. This information is relayed to the computer that again notes the time, and a time ticket is automatically prepared. Since the source data is already in computer files, the labour costs can automatically be posted to job cost sheets (or their electronic equivalents). Computers, coupled with technology such as bar codes, can eliminate much of the drudgery involved in routine bookkeeping activities while at the same time increasing timeliness and accuracy.

■ CALCULATING PREDETERMINED MANUFACTURING OVERHEAD RATES

LEARNING OBJECTIVE 3
Compute predetermined overhead rates and explain why estimated overhead costs (rather than actual overhead costs) are used in the costing process.

Manufacturing overhead must be included with direct materials and direct labour on the job cost sheet, since manufacturing overhead is also a product cost. However, assigning manufacturing overhead to units of product can be a difficult task. There are four reasons for this:

1. Manufacturing overhead is an indirect cost. This means that it is either impossible or difficult to trace these costs directly to a particular product or job.
2. Manufacturing overhead consists of many different items, ranging from the grease used in machines to the annual salary of the production manager.
3. Even though output may fluctuate due to seasonal or other factors, manufacturing overhead costs tend to remain relatively constant due to the presence of fixed costs.
4. The timing of payment of manufacturing overhead costs often varies. Some items such as property taxes for the land on which the factory is built may be paid once per year, while other items are paid for quarterly, monthly, or as acquired. But we produce finished items continuously and rather uniformly all year long.

Allocation base
A measure of activity such as direct labour-hours or machine-hours that is used to assign costs to cost objects.

Given these problems, about the only way to assign overhead costs to products is to use an allocation process. This allocation of overhead costs is accomplished by selecting an *allocation base* that is common to all of the company's products and services. An **allocation base** is a measure such as direct labour-hours (DLH) or machine-hours (MH) that is used to assign overhead costs to products and services.

The most widely used allocation bases are direct labour-hours and direct labour cost, with machine-hours and even units of product (where a company has only a single product) also used to some extent.

Predetermined overhead rate
A rate used to charge overhead costs to jobs; the rate is established in advance for each period by use of estimates of total manufacturing overhead cost and of the total allocation base for the period.

Manufacturing overhead is commonly applied to products using a *predetermined overhead rate*. The **predetermined overhead rate** is computed by dividing the total estimated manufacturing overhead cost for the period by the estimated total amount of the allocation base as follows:

$$\text{Predetermined overhead rate} = \frac{\text{Estimated total manufacturing overhead cost}}{\text{Estimated total units in the allocation base}}$$

Note that the predetermined overhead rate is based on *estimated* rather than actual results. This is because the *predetermined* overhead rate is computed *before* the period begins and is used to *apply* overhead cost to jobs throughout the period. The process of assigning overhead cost to jobs is called **overhead application**. The formula for determining the amount of overhead cost to apply to a particular job is

Overhead application
The process of charging manufacturing overhead cost to job cost sheets and to the work in process account.

$$\begin{array}{c}\text{Overhead applied to} \\ \text{a particular job}\end{array} = \begin{array}{c}\text{Predetermined} \\ \text{overhead rate}\end{array} \times \begin{array}{c}\text{Amount of the allocation} \\ \text{base incurred by the job}\end{array}$$

For example, if the predetermined overhead rate is $8 per direct labour-hour, then $8 of overhead is *applied* to a job for each direct labour-hour incurred by the job. When the allocation base is direct labour-hours, the formula becomes

$$\begin{array}{c}\text{Overhead applied to} \\ \text{a particular job}\end{array} = \begin{array}{c}\text{Predetermined} \\ \text{overhead rate}\end{array} \times \begin{array}{c}\text{Actual direct labour-hours} \\ \text{charged to the job}\end{array}$$

Using the Predetermined Overhead Rate   To illustrate the steps involved in computing and using a predetermined overhead rate, let's return to ABY Precision Machining.

The company has estimated its total manufacturing overhead costs will be $320,000 for the year and its total direct labour-hours will be 40,000. Its predetermined overhead rate for the year would be $8 per direct labour-hour, shown as follows:

$$\text{Predetermined overhead rate} = \frac{\text{Estimated total manufacturing overhead cost}}{\text{Estimated total units in the allocation base}}$$

$$\frac{\$320,000}{40,000 \text{ direct labour-hours}} = \$8 \text{ per direct labour-hour}$$

The job cost sheet in Exhibit 3–4 indicates that 27 direct labour-hours were charged to Job 2B47. Therefore, a total of $216 of overhead cost would be applied to the job:

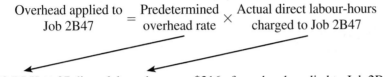

$$\text{Overhead applied to Job 2B47} = \frac{\text{Predetermined}}{\text{overhead rate}} \times \frac{\text{Actual direct labour-hours}}{\text{charged to Job 2B47}}$$

$$\$8/\text{DLH} \times 27 \text{ direct labour-hours} = \$216 \text{ of overhead applied to Job 2B47}$$

This amount of overhead has been entered on the job cost sheet in Exhibit 3–4. Note that this is *not* the actual amount of overhead caused by the job. There is no attempt to trace actual overhead costs to jobs—if that could be done, the costs would be direct costs, not

EXHIBIT 3–4   A Completed Job Cost Sheet

JOB COST SHEET

Job Number	Date Initiated
2B47	March 2

Department	Date Completed
Milling	March 8

Item	Units Completed
Special order coupling	2

For Inventory

Direct Materials		Direct Labour			Manufacturing Overhead		
Req. No.	Amount	Ticket	Hours	Amount	Hours	Rate	Amount
14873	$ 660	843	5	$ 75	27	$8/DLH	$216
14875	506	846	8	80			
14912	238	850	4	45			
	$1,404	851	10	120			
			27	$320			

Cost Summary		Units Shipped		
Direct Materials	$1,404	Date	Number	Balance
Direct Labour	$ 320	March 8	—	2
Manufacturing Overhead	$ 216			
Total Cost	$1,940			
Unit Cost	$ 970*			

* $1,940 ÷ 2 units = $970 per unit

Normal cost system
A costing system in which overhead costs are applied to jobs by multiplying a predetermined overhead rate by the actual amount of the allocation base incurred by the job.

overhead. The overhead assigned to the job is simply a share of the total overhead that was estimated at the beginning of the year. When a company applies overhead cost to jobs as we have done—that is, by multiplying actual activity by the predetermined overhead rate—it is called a **normal cost system**.

The overhead may be applied when direct labour-hours are charged to jobs, or all of the overhead can be applied at once when the job is completed. The choice is up to the company. If a job is not completed at year-end, however, overhead should be applied to jobs so as to value the work in process inventory.

The Need for a Predetermined Rate   Instead of using a predetermined rate, a company could wait until the end of the accounting period to compute an actual overhead rate based on the actual total manufacturing costs and the actual total units in the allocation base for the period. However, managers cite several reasons for using predetermined overhead rates instead of actual overhead rates:

1. Managers would like to know the accounting system's valuation of completed jobs *before* the end of the accounting period. Suppose, for example, that ABY Precision Machining waits until the end of the year to compute its overhead rate. Then the cost of goods sold for Job 2B47 would not be known until the close of the year, even though the job was completed and shipped to the customer in March. This problem can be reduced by computing the actual overhead more frequently, but that immediately leads to another problem, as discussed below.
2. If actual overhead rates were computed frequently, seasonal factors in overhead costs or in the allocation base could produce fluctuations in the overhead rates. For example, the costs of heating and cooling a production facility in Halifax will be highest in the winter and summer months and lowest in the spring and fall. If an overhead rate was computed each month or each quarter, the predetermined overhead rate would go up in the winter and summer and down in the spring and fall. Two identical jobs, one completed in the winter and one completed in the spring, would be assigned different costs if the overhead rate was computed on a monthly or quarterly basis. Managers generally feel that such fluctuations in overhead rates and costs serve no useful purpose and are misleading.
3. The use of a predetermined overhead rate simplifies record-keeping. To determine the overhead cost to apply to a job, the accounting staff at ABY Precision Machining simply multiplies the direct labour-hours recorded for the job by the predetermined overhead rate of $8 per direct labour-hour.

For these reasons, most companies use predetermined overhead rates rather than actual overhead rates in their cost accounting systems.

Choice of an Allocation Base for Overhead Cost

Cost driver
A factor that causes overhead costs, such as machine-hours, beds occupied, computer time, or flight-hours.

Ideally, the allocation base used in the predetermined overhead rate should *drive* the overhead cost. A **cost driver** is a factor that causes overhead costs, such as machine-hours, beds occupied, computer time, or flight-hours. If a base is used to compute overhead rates that does not "drive" overhead costs, then the result will be inaccurate overhead rates and distorted product costs. For example, if direct labour-hours are used to allocate overhead, but in reality, overhead has little to do with direct labour-hours, then products with high direct labour-hour requirements will be allocated too much overhead and will be overcosted.

Most companies use direct labour-hours or direct labour cost as the allocation base for manufacturing overhead. However, as discussed in earlier chapters, major shifts are taking place in the structure of costs in many industries. In the past, direct labour accounted for up to 60% of the cost of many products, with overhead cost making up only a portion of the remainder. This situation has been changing for two reasons. First, sophisticated automated equipment has taken over functions that used to be performed by direct labour workers. Since the costs of acquiring and maintaining such equipment are classified as overhead, this increases overhead while decreasing direct labour. Second, products are themselves becoming more sophisticated and complex and change more frequently. This increases the need for highly skilled indirect workers such as engineers. As a result of these two trends, direct labour cost is decreasing relative to overhead as a component of product costs.

In companies where direct labour and overhead costs have been moving in opposite directions, it would be difficult to argue that direct labour "drives" overhead costs. Accordingly, in recent years, managers in some companies have used *activity-based costing* principles to redesign their cost accounting systems. Activity-based costing is a costing technique that is designed to reflect more accurately the demands that products, customers, and other cost objects make on overhead resources. The activity-based approach is discussed in more detail in Chapter 5.

We hasten to add that although direct labour may not be an appropriate allocation basis in some industries, in others it continues to be a significant driver of manufacturing overhead. Indeed, most manufacturing companies in North America continue to use direct labour as the primary or secondary allocation base for manufacturing overhead. The key point is that the allocation base used by the company should really drive, or cause, overhead costs, and direct labour is not always an appropriate allocation base.

Computation of Unit Costs

With the application of ABY Precision Machining's $216 manufacturing overhead to the job cost sheet in Exhibit 3–4, the job cost sheet is almost complete. There are two final steps. First, the totals for direct materials, direct labour, and manufacturing overhead are transferred to the Cost Summary section of the job cost sheet and added together to obtain the total cost for the job. Then the total cost ($1,940) is divided by the number of units (2) to obtain the unit cost ($970). As indicated earlier, *this unit cost is an average cost and should not be interpreted as the cost that would actually be incurred if another unit was produced.* Much of the actual overhead would not change at all if another unit was produced, so the incremental cost of an additional unit is something less than the average unit cost of $970.

The completed job cost sheet will serve as the basis for valuing unsold units in ending inventory and determining cost of goods sold.

Summary of Document Flows

The sequence of events discussed above is summarized in Exhibit 3–5. A careful study of the flow of documents in this exhibit provides a good overview of the overall operation of a job-order costing system.

EXHIBIT 3–5   The Flow of Documents in a Job-Order Costing System

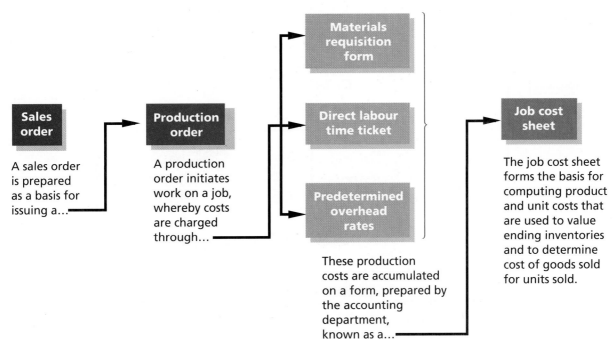

■ JOB-ORDER COSTING—THE FLOW OF COSTS

We are now ready to take a more detailed look at the flow of costs through the company's formal accounting system. To illustrate, we will consider a single month's activity for Rand Company, a producer of gold and silver commemorative medallions. We will work through the example step by step and then summarize our work in Exhibits 3–9, 3–10, and 3–11.

Rand Company has two jobs in process during April, the first month of its fiscal year. Job A, a special minting of 1,000 gold medallions commemorating the recent world hockey championships held in Canada, was started during March and had $30,000 in manufacturing costs already accumulated on April 1. Job B, an order for 10,000 silver medallions commemorating the same event, was started in April.

The Purchase and Issue of Materials

On April 1, Rand Company had $7,000 in raw materials on hand. During the month, the company purchased an additional $60,000 in raw materials. The purchase is recorded in journal entry (1) below:

(1)

Raw Materials Inventory	60,000	
Accounts Payable		60,000

As explained in Chapter 2, Raw Materials Inventory is an asset account. Thus, when raw materials are purchased, they are initially recorded as an asset—not as an expense.

Issue of Direct and Indirect Materials   During April, $52,000 in raw materials were requisitioned from the storeroom for use in production. These raw materials include $50,000 of direct materials and $2,000 of indirect materials. Entry (2) records the issue of the materials to the production departments:

(2)

Work in Process Inventory	50,000	
Manufacturing Overhead	2,000	
Raw Materials Inventory		52,000

The materials charged to Work in Process Inventory represent direct materials for specific jobs. As these materials are entered into the Work in Process account, they are also recorded on the appropriate job cost sheets. This point is illustrated in Exhibit 3–6,

EXHIBIT 3–6   Raw Materials Cost Flows

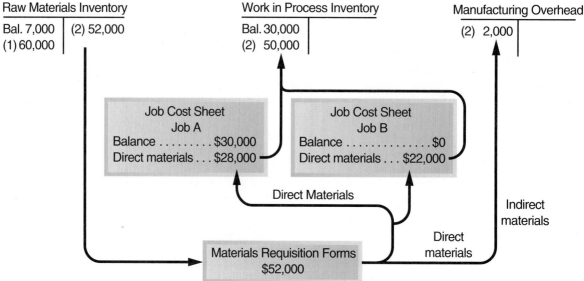

where $28,000 of the $50,000 in direct materials is charged to Job A's cost sheet and the remaining $22,000 is charged to Job B's cost sheet. (In this example, all data are presented in summary form and the job cost sheet is abbreviated.)

The $2,000 charged to Manufacturing Overhead in entry (2) represents indirect materials used in production during April. Observe that the Manufacturing Overhead account is separate from the Work in Process account. The purpose of the Manufacturing Overhead account is to accumulate all manufacturing overhead costs as they are incurred during a period.

Before leaving Exhibit 3–6, note that the job cost sheet for Job A contains a beginning balance of $30,000. We stated earlier that this balance represents the cost of work done during March that has been carried forward to April. Also note that the Work in Process account contains the same $30,000 balance. *The reason the $30,000 appears in both places is that the Work in Process account is a control account and the job cost sheets form a subsidiary ledger. Thus, the Work in Process account contains a summarized total of all costs appearing on the individual job cost sheets for all jobs in process at any given point in time.* (Since Rand Company had only Job A in process at the beginning of April, Job A's $30,000 balance on that date is equal to the balance in the Work in Process account.)

Issue of Direct Materials Only   Sometimes the materials drawn from the Raw Materials Inventory account are all direct materials. In this case, the entry to record the issue of the materials into production would be as follows:

Work in Process Inventory	XXX	
Raw Materials Inventory		XXX

Labour Cost

As work is performed in various departments of Rand Company from day to day, employee time tickets are filled out by workers, collected, and forwarded to the Accounting Department. In the Accounting Department, the tickets are costed according to the various employee wage rates, and the resulting costs are classified as either direct or indirect labour. In April, $60,000 was recorded for direct labour and $15,000 for indirect labour resulting in the following summary entry:

(3)

Work in Process Inventory	60,000	
Manufacturing Overhead	15,000	
Salaries and Wages Payable		75,000

Only direct labour is added to the Work in Process account. For Rand Company, this amounted to $60,000 for April.

At the same time that direct labour costs are added to Work in Process, they are also added to the individual job cost sheets, as shown in Exhibit 3–7. During April, $40,000 of direct labour cost was charged to Job A and the remaining $20,000 was charged to Job B.

The labour costs charged to Manufacturing Overhead represent the indirect labour costs of the period, such as supervision, janitorial work, and maintenance.

Manufacturing Overhead Costs

Recall that all costs of operating the factory other than direct materials and direct labour are classified as manufacturing overhead costs. These costs are entered directly into the Manufacturing Overhead account as they are incurred. To illustrate, assume that Rand Company incurred the following general factory costs during April:

Utilities (heat, water, and power)	$21,000
Rent on factory equipment	16,000
Miscellaneous factory costs	3,000
Total	$40,000

EXHIBIT 3–7   Labour Cost Flows

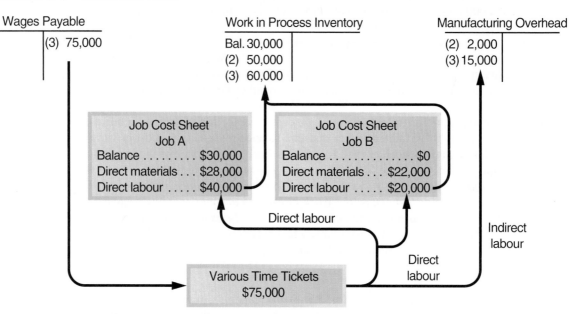

The following entry records the incurrence of these costs:

(4)

Manufacturing Overhead..	40,000	
Accounts Payable..		40,000

In addition, let us assume that during April, Rand Company recognized $13,000 in accrued property taxes and that $7,000 in prepaid insurance expired on factory buildings and equipment. The following entry records these items:

(5)

Manufacturing Overhead..	20,000	
Property Taxes Payable....................................		13,000
Prepaid Insurance..		7,000

Finally, assume that the company recognized $18,000 in depreciation on factory equipment during April. The following entry records the accrual of this depreciation:

(6)

Manufacturing Overhead..	18,000	
Accumulated Depreciation		18,000

In short, *all* manufacturing overhead costs are recorded directly into the Manufacturing Overhead account as they are incurred day by day throughout a period. It is important to understand that Manufacturing Overhead is a control account for many—perhaps thousands—of subsidiary accounts such as Indirect Materials, Indirect Labour, Factory Utilities, and so forth. As the Manufacturing Overhead account is debited for costs during a period, the various subsidiary accounts are also debited. In the example above and also in the assignment material for this chapter, we omit the entries to the subsidiary accounts for the sake of brevity.

THE APPLICATION OF MANUFACTURING OVERHEAD

LEARNING OBJECTIVE 5
Apply overhead cost to Work in Process using a predetermined overhead rate.

Since actual manufacturing overhead costs are charged to the Manufacturing Overhead control account rather than to Work in Process, how are manufacturing overhead costs assigned to Work in Process? The answer is, by means of the predetermined overhead rate. Recall from our discussion earlier in the chapter that a predetermined overhead rate is established at the beginning of each year. The rate is calculated by dividing the estimated total manufacturing overhead cost for the year by the estimated total units in the allocation base (measured in machine-hours, direct labour-hours, or some other base). The predetermined overhead rate is then used to apply overhead costs to jobs. For example, if direct labour-hours is the allocation base, overhead cost is applied to each job by multiplying the number of direct labour-hours charged to the job by the predetermined overhead rate.

To illustrate, assume that Rand Company has used machine-hours in computing its predetermined overhead rate and that this rate is $6 per machine-hour. Also assume that during April, 10,000 machine-hours were worked on Job A and 5,000 machine-hours were worked on Job B (a total of 15,000 machine-hours). Thus, $90,000 in overhead cost (15,000 machine-hours × $6 = $90,000) would be applied to Work in Process. The following entry records the application of Manufacturing Overhead to Work in Process:

(7)

Work in Process..	90,000	
Manufacturing Overhead..................................		90,000

The flow of costs through the Manufacturing Overhead account is detailed in Exhibit 3–8.

The "actual overhead costs" in the Manufacturing Overhead account shown in Exhibit 3–8 are the costs that were added to the account in entries (2)–(6). Observe that the incurrence of these actual overhead costs [entries (2)–(6)] and the application of overhead to Work in Process [entry (7)] represent two separate and entirely distinct processes.

The Concept of a Clearing Account

The Manufacturing Overhead account operates as a clearing account. As we have noted, actual factory overhead costs are debited to the accounts as they are incurred day by day throughout the year. At certain intervals during the year, usually when a job is completed, overhead cost is released from the Manufacturing Overhead account and is applied to the Work in Process account by means

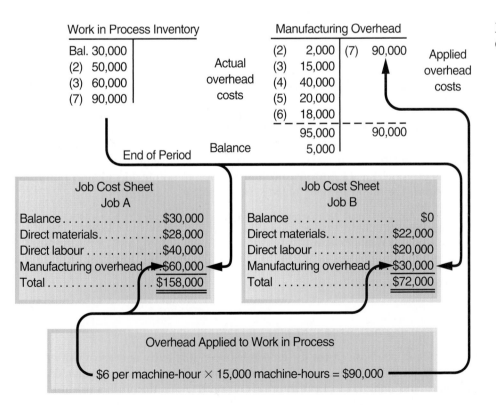

EXHIBIT 3–8 The Flow of Costs in Overhead Application

of the predetermined overhead rate. Work in Process is debited and Manufacturing Overhead is credited. This sequence of events is illustrated as follows:

**Manufacturing Overhead
(a clearing account)**

| Actual overhead costs are charged to the account as these costs are incurred day by day throughout the period. → | → Overhead is applied to Work in Process using the predetermined overhead rate. |

The actual overhead costs incurred and shown as debits in the Manufacturing Overhead account are a result of many different types of overhead costs. A brief list of some of the different types is presented in the journal entries, numbers 4, 5 and 6, or in the schedule of cost of goods manufactured, shown in Exhibit 3–11 or previously in Exhibit 2–4. The clearing account concept actually represents a general ledger control account for a subsidiary ledger that contains the detailed information on each type of overhead cost.

As we emphasized earlier, the predetermined overhead rate is based entirely on estimates of what overhead costs are *expected* to be, and it is established before the year begins. As a result, the overhead cost applied during a year will almost certainly turn out to be more or less than the overhead cost that is actually incurred. For example, notice from Exhibit 3–8 that Rand Company's actual overhead costs for the period are $5,000 greater than the overhead cost that has been applied to Work in Process, resulting in a $5,000 debit balance in the Manufacturing Overhead account. We will reserve discussion of what to do with this $5,000 balance until a later section in this chapter, Complications of Overhead Application.

For the moment, we can conclude by noting from Exhibit 3–8 that the cost of a completed job consists of the actual materials cost of the job, the actual labour cost of the job, and the overhead cost *applied* to the job. Pay particular attention to the following subtle but important point: *Actual overhead costs are not charged to jobs; actual overhead costs do not appear on the job cost sheet nor do they appear in the Work in Process account. Only the applied overhead cost, based on the predetermined overhead rate, appears on the job cost sheet and in the Work in Process account.* Study this point carefully.

Non-Manufacturing Costs

In addition to manufacturing costs, companies also incur marketing and selling costs. As explained in Chapter 2, these costs should be treated as period expenses and charged directly to the income statement. *Non-manufacturing costs should not go into the Manufacturing Overhead account.* To illustrate the correct treatment of non-manufacturing costs, assume that Rand Company incurred $30,000 of selling and administrative costs during April. The following entry records these salaries:

(8)

Salaries Expense..	30,000	
Salaries and Wages Payable................................		30,000

Assume that depreciation on office equipment during April was $7,000. The entry is as follows:

(9)

Depreciation Expense..	7,000	
Accumulated Depreciation		7,000

Pay particular attention to the difference between this entry and entry (6) where we recorded depreciation on factory equipment. In journal entry (6), depreciation on factory equipment was debited to Manufacturing Overhead and is therefore a product cost. In journal entry (9) above, depreciation on office equipment was debited to Depreciation Expense. Depreciation on office equipment is considered to be a period expense rather than a product cost.

Finally, assume that advertising was $42,000 and that other selling and administrative expenses in April totalled $8,000. The following entry records these items:

(10)

Advertising Expense.	42,000	
Other Selling and Administrative Expense..	8,000	
Accounts Payable*.		50,000

*Other accounts such as Cash may be credited.

Because the amounts in entries (8) through (10) all go directly into expense accounts, they will have no effect on product costs. The same will be true of any other selling and administrative expenses incurred during April, including sales commissions, depreciation on sales equipment, rent on office facilities, insurance on office facilities, and related costs.

The distinction between manufacturing overhead costs and non-manufacturing costs such as selling and administrative expenses is sometimes difficult because of the type of cost. For example, depreciation or salaries should be classified as product costs if related to manufacturing but are classified as period costs and expensed if related to non-manufacturing activities. In practice, the classification has to be based on what the firm does to incur the costs. If it sells or markets, then this is not production and the distinction is clear. If it involves administration, then the distinction depends on what is administered and how important it is to decision making to separate production administration from overall administration. For example, if all the company does is produce the Hibernia oil platform, then administration is production (manufacturing) overhead. However, if the company is administering many jobs and marketing new jobs at the same time, it may not be able to distinguish overhead from administrative time on the part of the senior management. Thus, unless costs are needed for a cost-recovery billing, administration salaries expense may be the expeditious way to treat the salaries.

COST OF GOODS MANUFACTURED

When a job has been completed, the finished output is transferred from the production departments to the finished goods warehouse. By this time, the Accounting Department will have charged the job with direct materials and direct labour cost, and manufacturing overhead will have been applied using the predetermined rate. A transfer of these costs must be made within the costing system that *parallels* the physical transfer of the goods to the finished goods warehouse. The costs of the completed job are transferred out of the Work in Process account and into the Finished Goods account. The sum of all amounts transferred between these two accounts represents the cost of goods manufactured for the period.

LEARNING OBJECTIVE 6
Prepare schedules of cost of goods manufactured and cost of goods sold.

In the case of Rand Company, let us assume that Job A was completed during April. The following entry transfers the cost of Job A from Work in Process to Finished Goods:

(11)

Finished Goods Inventory.	158,000	
Work in Process Inventory.		158,000

The $158,000 represents the completed cost of Job A, as shown on the job cost sheet in Exhibit 3–8. Since Job A was the only job completed during April, the $158,000 also represents the cost of goods manufactured for the month.

Job B was not completed by month-end, so its cost will remain in the Work in Process account and carry over to the next month. If a balance sheet is prepared at the end of April, the cost accumulated thus far on Job B will appear as "Work in Process Inventory" in the assets section.

Cost of Goods Sold

As units in finished goods are shipped to customers, their cost is transferred from the Finished Goods account into the Cost of Goods Sold account. If a complete job is shipped, as in the case where a job has been done to a customer's specifications, then it is a simple matter to transfer the entire cost appearing on the job cost sheet into the Cost of Goods Sold account. In most cases, however, only a portion of the units involved in a particular job will be immediately sold. In these situations, the unit cost must be used to determine how much product cost should be removed from Finished Goods and charged to Cost of Goods Sold.

For Rand Company, we will assume that 750 of the 1,000 gold medallions in Job A were shipped to customers by the end of the month, for total sales revenue of $225,000. Since 1,000 units were produced and the total cost of the job from the job cost sheet was $158,000, the unit product cost was $158. The following journal entries would record the sale (all sales are on account):

(12)

Accounts Receivable..	225,000	
Sales..		225,000

(13)

Cost of Goods Sold..	118,500	
Finished Goods Inventory..................................		118,500
($158 per unit × 750 units = $118,500)		

With entry (13), the flow of costs through our job-order costing system is completed.

Summary of Cost Flows

To pull the entire Rand Company example together, journal entries (1) through (13) are summarized in Exhibit 3–9. The flow of costs through the accounts is presented in T-account form in Exhibit 3–10.

Exhibit 3–11 presents a schedule of cost of goods manufactured and a schedule of cost of goods sold for Rand Company. Note particularly from Exhibit 3–11 that the manufacturing overhead cost on the schedule of cost of goods manufactured is the overhead applied to jobs during the month—not the actual manufacturing overhead costs incurred. The reason for this can be traced back to journal entry (7) and the T-account for Work in Process that appears in Exhibit 3–10. Under a normal costing system as illustrated in this chapter, applied—not actual—overhead costs are assigned to jobs and thus to Work in Process Inventory. In contrast, in Chapter 2, actual overhead costs were assigned to Work in Process and included in the schedule of cost of goods manufactured. This is because we had not introduced the concept of normal costing in that chapter. Note also that the cost of goods manufactured for the month ($158,000) agrees with the amount transferred from Work in Process to Finished Goods for the month, as recorded earlier in entry (11). Also note that this $158,000 figure is used in computing the cost of goods sold for the month.

An income statement for April is presented in Exhibit 3–12. Observe that the cost of goods sold figure on this statement ($123,500) is carried down from Exhibit 3–11.

EXHIBIT 3–9   Summary of Rand Company Journal Entries

(1)

Raw Materials.	60,000	
Accounts Payable		60,000

(2)

Work in Process	50,000	
Manufacturing Overhead	2,000	
Raw Materials..		52,000

(3)

Work in Process	60,000	
Manufacturing Overhead	15,000	
Salaries and Wages Payable.		75,000

(4)

Manufacturing Overhead	40,000	
Accounts Payable		40,000

(5)

Manufacturing Overhead	20,000	
Property Taxes Payable		13,000
Prepaid Insurance.		7,000

(6)

Manufacturing Overhead	18,000	
Accumulated Depreciation..		18,000

(7)

Work in Process	90,000	
Manufacturing Overhead.		90,000

(8)

Salaries Expense	30,000	
Salaries and Wages Payable.		30,000

(9)

Depreciation Expense	7,000	
Accumulated Depreciation		7,000

(10)

Advertising Expense.	42,000	
Other Selling and Administrative Expense.	8,000	
Accounts Payable		50,000

(11)

Finished Goods	158,000	
Work in Process		158,000

(12)

Accounts Receivable	225,000	
Sales		225,000

(13)

Cost of Goods Sold	118,500	
Finished Goods.		118,500

EXHIBIT 3–10   Summary of Cost Flows—Rand Company

Raw Materials			
Bal.	7,000	(2)	52,000
(1)	60,000		
Bal.	15,000		

Work in Process			
Bal.	30,000	(11)	158,000
(2)	50,000		
(3)	60,000		
(7)	90,000		
Bal.	72,000		

Finished Goods			
Bal..	10,000	(13)	118,500
(11)	158,000		
Bal.	49,500		

Manufacturing Overhead			
(2)	2,000	(7)	90,000
(3)	15,000		
(4)	40,000		
(5)	20,000		
(6)	18,000		
Bal.	5,000		

Accumulated Depreciation			
		XX	
		(6)	18,000
		(9)	7,000

Cost of Goods Sold			
(13)	118,500		

Accounts Payable			
		XX	
		(1)	60,000
		(4)	40,000
		(10)	50,000

Salaries and Wages Payable			
		XX	
		(3)	75,000
		(8)	30,000

Property Taxes Payable			
		XX	
		(5)	13,000

Accounts Receivable			
XX*			
(12)	225,000		

Prepaid Insurance			
XX			
		(5)	7,000

Capital Stock			
		XX	

Retained Earnings			
		XX	

Sales			
		(12)	225,000

Salaries Expense			
(8)	30,000		

Depreciation Expense			
(9)	7,000		

Advertising Expense			
(10)	42,000		

Other Selling and Administrative Expense			
(10)	8,000		

Explanation of entries:
(1) Raw materials purchased.
(2) Direct and indirect materials issued into production.
(3) Direct and indirect factory labour cost incurred.
(4) Utilities and other factory costs incurred.
(5) Property taxes and insurance incurred on the factory.
(6) Depreciation recorded on factory assets.
(7) Overhead cost applied to Work in Process.
(8) Administrative salaries expense incurred.
(9) Depreciation recorded on office equipment.
(10) Advertising and other expense incurred.
(11) Cost of goods manufactured transferred into finished goods.
(12) Sale of job A recorded.
(13) Cost of goods sold recorded for job A.

*XX = Normal balance in the account (for example, Accounts Receivable normally carries a debit balance).

EXHIBIT 3–11   Schedules of Cost of Goods Manufactured and Cost of Goods Sold

Cost of Goods Manufactured
Direct materials:

Raw materials inventory, beginning	$ 7,000	
Add: Purchases of raw materials	60,000	
Total raw materials available	67,000	
Deduct: Raw materials inventory, ending.	15,000	
Raw materials used in production	52,000	
Less indirect materials included in manufacturing overhead.	2,000	$ 50,000
Direct labour.		60,000
Manufacturing overhead applied to work in process.		90,000
Total manufacturing costs		200,000
Add: Beginning work in process inventory.		30,000
		230,000
Deduct: Ending work in process inventory		72,000
Cost of goods manufactured		$158,000

Cost of Goods Sold

Finished goods inventory, beginning	$ 10,000	
Add: Cost of goods manufactured.	158,000	
Goods available for sale.	168,000	
Deduct: Finished goods inventory, ending.	49,500	
Unadjusted cost of goods sold	118,500	
Add: Underapplied overhead*	5,000	
Adjusted cost of goods sold	$123,500	

*Note that the underapplied overhead is added to cost of goods sold. If overhead was overapplied, it would be deducted from costs of goods sold.

EXHIBIT 3–12   Income Statement

RAND COMPANY
Income Statement
For the Month Ending April 30

Sales.		$225,000
Less cost of goods sold ($118,500 + $5,000).		123,500
Gross margin		101,500
Less selling and administrative expenses:		
Salaries expense	$30,000	
Depreciation expense.	7,000	
Advertising expense.	42,000	
Other expense	8,000	87,000
Net income.		$ 14,500

COMPLICATIONS OF OVERHEAD APPLICATION

We need to consider two complications relating to overhead application. These are (1) the computation of underapplied and overapplied overhead and (2) the disposition of any balance remaining in the Manufacturing Overhead account at the end of a period.

Underapplied and Overapplied Overhead

Since the predetermined overhead rate is established before a period begins and is based entirely on estimated data, there generally will be a difference between the amount of overhead cost applied to Work in Process and the amount of overhead cost actually incurred during a period. In the case of Rand Company, for example, the predetermined overhead rate of $6 per hour resulted in $90,000 of overhead cost being applied to Work in Process, whereas actual overhead costs for April proved to be $95,000 (as shown in Exhibit 3–8). The difference between the overhead cost applied to Work in Process and

LEARNING OBJECTIVE 7
Compute underapplied or overapplied overhead cost and prepare the journal entry to close the balance in Manufacturing Overhead to the appropriate accounts.

Underapplied overhead
A debit balance in the Manufacturing Overhead account that arises when the amount of overhead cost actually incurred is greater than the amount of overhead cost applied to Work in Process during a period.

Overapplied overhead
A credit balance in the Manufacturing Overhead account that arises when the amount of overhead cost applied to Work in Process is greater than the amount of overhead cost actually incurred during a period.

the actual overhead costs of a period is termed either **underapplied** or **overapplied overhead**. For Rand Company, overhead was underapplied because the applied cost ($90,000) was $5,000 less than the actual cost ($95,000). If the tables had been reversed and the company had applied $95,000 in overhead cost to Work in Process while incurring actual overhead costs of only $90,000, then the overhead would have been overapplied.

What is the cause of underapplied or overapplied overhead? The causes can be complex, and a full explanation will have to wait for Chapter 10. Nevertheless, the basic problem is that the method of applying overhead to jobs using a predetermined overhead rate assumes that actual overhead costs will be proportional to the actual amount of the allocation base incurred during the period. If, for example, the predetermined overhead rate is $6 per machine-hour, then it is assumed that actual overhead costs incurred will be $6 for every machine-hour that is actually worked. There are at least two reasons why this may not be true. First, much of the overhead often consists of fixed costs that do not change as the number of machine-hours incurred goes up or down. Second, spending on overhead items may or may not be under control. A fuller explanation of the causes of underapplied and overapplied overhead will have to wait for later chapters.

To illustrate what can happen, suppose that two companies—Turbo Crafters and Black & Howell—have prepared the following estimated data for the coming year:

	Company	
	Turbo Crafters	**Black & Howell**
Predetermined overhead rate based on	Machine-hours	Direct materials cost
Estimated manufacturing overhead (a).	$300,000 (a)	$120,000 (a)
Estimated amount of allocation base (b)	75,000	80,000
Predetermined overhead rate, (a) ÷ (b)	$4 per machine-hour	150% of direct materials cost

Note that when the allocation base is dollars—such as direct material cost in the case of Black & Howell—the predetermined overhead rate is a *percentage* of the allocation base. When dollars are divided by dollars, the result is a *percentage*.

Now assume that because of unexpected changes in overhead spending and changes in demand for the companies' products, the *actual* overhead cost and the *actual* activity recorded during the year in each company are as follows:

	Company	
	Turbo Crafters	**Black & Howell**
Actual manufacturing overhead costs	$290,000	$130,000
Actual amount of allocation base	68,000	$ 90,000

For each company, note that the actual data for both cost and the allocation base differ from the estimates used in computing the predetermined overhead rate. This results in underapplied and overapplied overhead as follows:

	Company	
	Turbo Crafters	**Black & Howell**
Actual manufacturing overhead cost	$290,000	$130,000
Manufactured overhead cost applied to Work in Process during the year:		
Predetermined overhead rate (a)	$4 per machine-hour	150% of direct material cost
Actual total amount of allocation base (b) . .	68,000 machine-hours	$90,000 direct material cost
Manufacturing overhead applied (a) × (b)	$272,000	$135,000
Underapplied (overapplied) manufacturing overhead	$ 18,000	$ (5,000)

For Turbo Crafters, notice that the amount of overhead cost that has been applied to Work in Process ($272,000) is less than the actual overhead cost for the year ($290,000). Therefore, overhead is underapplied. Also notice that the original estimate of overhead in Turbo Crafters ($300,000) is not directly involved in this computation. Its impact is felt only through the $4 predetermined overhead rate that is used.

For Black & Howell, the amount of overhead cost that has been applied to Work in Process ($135,000) is greater than the actual overhead cost for the year ($130,000), so overhead is overapplied.

Disposition of Underapplied or Overapplied Overhead Balances

What disposition should be made of any underapplied or overapplied balance remaining in the Manufacturing Overhead account at the end of a period? Generally, any balance in the account is treated in one of three ways:

1. Close out to Cost of Goods Sold.
2. Allocate among Work in Process, Finished Goods, and Cost of Goods Sold in proportion to the overhead applied during the current period in the ending balances of these accounts.[1]
3. Carry forward to the next period.

The second method, which allocates the under- or overapplied overhead among ending inventories and Cost of Goods Sold, is equivalent to using an "actual" overhead rate and is for that reason considered by many to be more accurate than the first method. Consequently, if the amount of underapplied or overapplied overhead is material, many accountants would insist that the second method be used. In problem assignments, we will always indicate which method you are to use for disposing of under- or overapplied overhead.

Close Out to Cost of Goods Sold   As mentioned above, closing out the balance in Manufacturing Overhead to Cost of Goods Sold is simpler than the allocation method. Returning to the example of Rand Company, the entry to close the $5,000 of underapplied overhead to Cost of Goods Sold would be as follows:

(14)

Cost of Goods Sold	5,000	
Manufacturing Overhead		5,000

Note that since there is a debit balance in the Manufacturing Overhead account, Manufacturing Overhead must be credited to close out the account. This has the effect of increasing Cost of Goods Sold for April to $123,500:

Unadjusted cost of goods sold [from entry (13)]	$118,500
Add underapplied overhead [entry (14) above]...............	5,000
Adjusted cost of goods sold...........................	$123,500

After this adjustment has been made, Rand Company's income statement for April will appear as was shown earlier in Exhibit 3–12.

Allocate among Accounts   Allocation of underapplied or overapplied overhead among Work in Process, Finished Goods, and Cost of Goods Sold is more accurate than closing the entire balance into Cost of Goods Sold. This allocation assigns overhead costs to where they would have gone in the first place had it not been for the errors in the estimates going into the predetermined overhead rate.

Had Rand Company chosen to allocate the underapplied overhead among the inventory accounts and Cost of Goods Sold, it would first be necessary to determine the amount of overhead that had been applied during April in each of the accounts. The computations would have been as follows:

Overhead applied in work in process inventory, April 30	$30,000	33.33%
Overhead applied in finished goods inventory, April 30		
($60,000/1,000 units = $60 per unit) × 250 units	15,000	16.67%
Overhead applied in cost of goods sold, April		
($60,000/1,000 units = $60 per unit) × 750 units	45,000	50.00%
Total overhead applied	$90,000	100.00%

Based on the above percentages, the underapplied overhead (i.e., the debit balance in Manufacturing Overhead) would be allocated as in the following journal entry:

Work in Process (33.33% × $5,000)	1,666.50	
Finished Goods (16.67% × $5,000)	833.50	
Cost of Goods Sold (50.00% × $5,000)	2,500.00	
Manufacturing Overhead		5,000.00

Note that the first step in the allocation was to determine the amount of overhead applied in each of the accounts. For Finished Goods, for example, the total amount of overhead applied to Job A, $60,000, was divided by the total number of units in Job A, 1,000 units, to arrive at the average overhead applied of $60 per unit. Since 250 units from Job A were still in ending finished goods inventory, the amount of overhead applied in the Finished Goods Inventory account was $60 per unit multiplied by 250 units, or $15,000 in total.

If overhead had been overapplied, the entry above would have been just the reverse, since a credit balance would have existed in the Manufacturing Overhead account.

An alternative but less accurate way to allocate under- or overapplied overhead among Work in Process, Finished Goods, and Cost of Goods Sold is to use the entire cost of manufacturing in each account.

Had we chosen to allocate the underapplied overhead in the Rand Company example, the computations and entry would have been:

Work in process inventory, April 30			$ 72,000	36.00%
Finished goods inventory, April 30			49,500	24.75%
Cost of goods sold		$118,500		
Less: Work in process inventory, April 1		30,000		
Less: Finished goods inventory, April 1		10,000	78,500	39.25%
Total			$200,000	100.00%
Work in Process (36.0% × $5,000)		1,800		
Finished Goods (24.75% × $5,000)		1,237		
Cost of Goods Sold (39.25% × $5,000)		1,963		
Manufacturing Overhead			5,000	

A comparison of the percentages above with those using only overhead suggests that total manufacturing costs and overhead were not in the same proportions in each account. This difference is the inaccuracy in the problem resulting from using total manufacturing costs to conduct the allocation.

The rationale for deducting the beginning work in process and finished goods inventories from the cost of goods sold is to permit the allocation to be based on costs from the current period. By doing so, the 39.25% in the Rand Company example reflects only total manufacturing costs from April and thus corresponds to the period in which the underapplied overhead occurred. Without this adjustment, cost of goods sold would be assigned the overhead difference based on costs carried over from March and thus bear a disproportionate amount of the under- or overapplied overhead.

Carry the Balance Forward   Recall the section earlier in this chapter entitled The Application of Manufacturing Overhead. Notice that some firms have large seasonal variations in output while being faced with relatively constant overhead costs. Predetermined overhead was used to even out fluctuations in the cost of overhead caused by seasonal variations in output and seasonal variations in costs (e.g., heating costs). The predetermined overhead rate is computed using estimated total manufacturing costs for a year divided by estimated total units in the base. The result is an average rate. When the average predetermined rate is applied to actual production for the period, the applied overhead is determined. The under- or overapplied overhead is a result of two factors: an actual base that is different from one-twelfth of the annual estimated base and actual overhead costs that do not equal one-twelfth of the total estimated overhead costs. Therefore, for any given month, an under- or overapplied overhead amount would be expected. In some months, it would be positive; in other months, it would be negative. Over the year, these amounts may largely cancel out. If this is the situation, then significant debits and credits could be carried forward to the year-end so that a final disposition can be made either by adjusting Cost of Goods Sold or allocating (sometimes termed *prorating*) the amount to the inventories and Cost of Goods Sold.

The Rand Company example would be treated as follows:

```
Underapplied Overhead
   [a deferred debit balance on the balance sheet] . . . . . . . . . . . . . . . . . . . . .   5,000
   Manufacturing Overhead . . . . . . . . . . . . . . . . . . . . . . . . . . . . . . . . . . . .          5,000
```

A summary of the concepts discussed in this section is presented in Exhibit 3–13.

A General Model of Product Cost Flows

The flow of costs in a product costing system is presented in the form of a T-account model in Exhibit 3–14. This model applies as much to a process costing system as it does to a job-order costing system. Examination of this model can be very helpful in gaining a perspective as to how costs enter a system, flow through it, and finally end up as Cost of Goods Sold on the income statement.

At the beginning of the period:

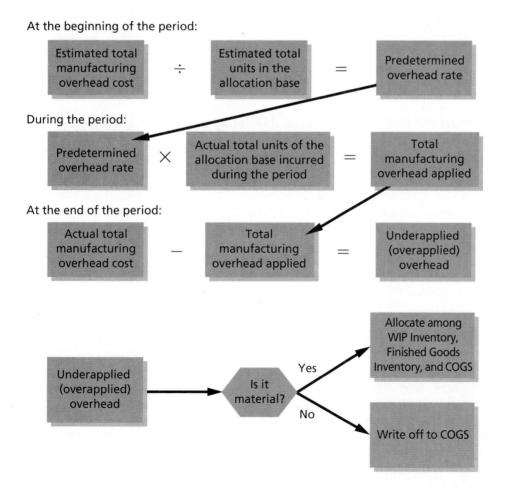

EXHIBIT 3–13 Learning Aid: Summary of Overhead Concepts

EXHIBIT 3–14   A General Model of Cost Flows

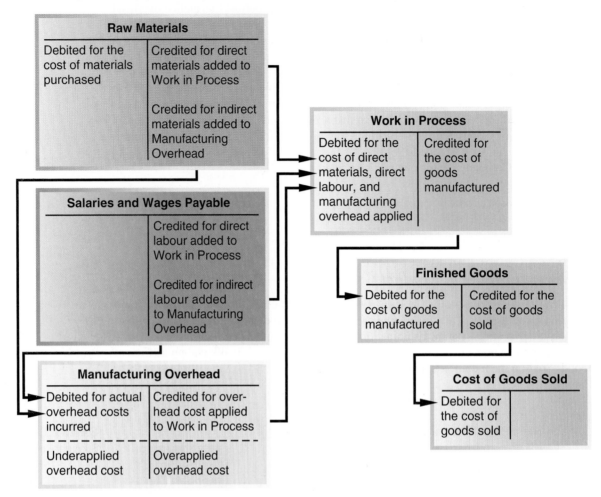

Variations from the General Model of Product Cost Flow

Costing systems can vary from what is reflected by the general model. While the general model is the most complete description, circumstances may make such a complete system too costly. For example, a system variation known as *backflush costing* can permit labour charges to be made directly to manufacturing overhead. Then, overhead is applied to the cost of completed jobs along with raw materials, so that the need to keep work in process records can be avoided. Such a minimal treatment of work in process is justified in a mechanized lean manufacturing (JIT) environment. Cost of completed jobs still reflects the material and overhead (including labour), but the record-keeping system reflects the simplified needs of the production environment.

Multiple Predetermined Overhead Rates

Our discussion of overhead in this chapter has assumed that there is a single predetermined overhead rate for an entire factory called a **plantwide overhead rate**. This is, in fact, a common practice—particularly in smaller companies. But in larger companies, *multiple predetermined overhead rates* are often used. In a **multiple predetermined overhead rate** system there is usually a different overhead rate for each production department. Such a system, while more complex, is considered to be more accurate, because it can reflect differences across departments in how overhead costs are incurred. For example, overhead might be allocated based on direct labour-hours in departments that are relatively labour-intensive and based on machine-hours in departments that are

Plantwide overhead rate
A single predetermined overhead rate that is used throughout a plant.

Multiple predetermined overhead rates
A costing system in which there are multiple overhead cost pools with a different predetermined rate for each cost pool, rather than a single predetermined overhead rate for the entire company. Frequently, each production department is treated as a separate overhead cost pool.

relatively machine-intensive. When multiple predetermined overhead rates are used, overhead is applied in each department according to its own overhead rate as a job proceeds through the department.

To illustrate, refer to the data in the following table, where Cook Company has two departments (A and B) and several jobs in process. Data is provided for two of these jobs (X and Y). If the company uses a plantwide overhead rate of $12 ($336,000 ÷ 28,000 DLH) then the overhead costs applied to Job X and Job Y will be $8,400 ($12 × 700 hours + $12 × 0) and $12 ($12 × 0 hours + $12 × 1 hour), respectively. However, if overhead is applied using department overhead rates, then Job X will be assigned $2,800 ($4 × 700 direct labour-hours) and Job Y will be assigned $8,400 ($12 × 700 machine-hours).

Cook Company	Department A	Department B	Total
Overhead cost	$84,000	$252,000	$336,000
Direct labour-hours	21,000	7,000	28,000 DLH
Machine-hours	7,000	21,000	28,000 MH
Overhead cost driver	21,000 DLH	21,000 MH	
Overhead rate: Plantwide			$12 per DLH
By department	$4/DLH	$12/MH	
Direct labour-hours—Job X	700	0	
Direct labour-hours—Job Y	0	1	
Machine-hours—Job X	1	0	
Machine-hours—Job Y	0	700	

The decision to use a plantwide rate versus separate rates for each department comes down to costs versus benefits. It is cheaper to use a plantwide rate since the costs of gathering and analyzing information are lower, but separate rates are more informative when the activities that drive overhead costs differ among departments. Improved decision making resulting from more accurate overhead data can justify the added costs of gathering separate departmental overhead data.

USE OF INFORMATION TECHNOLOGY

Earlier in the chapter, we discussed how bar code technology can be used to record labour time—reducing the drudgery in that task and increasing accuracy. Bar codes have many other uses.

In a company with a well-developed bar code system, the manufacturing cycle begins with the receipt of a customer's order in electronic form. Until very recently, the order would have been received via electronic data interchange (EDI), which involves a network of computers linking organizations. An EDI network allows companies to electronically exchange business documents and other information that extend into all areas of business activity, from ordering raw materials to shipping completed goods. EDI was developed in the 1980s and requires significant investment in programming and networking hardware. Recently, EDI has been challenged by a far cheaper Internet-based alternative—XML (Extensible Markup Language), an extension of HTML (Hypertext Markup Language). HTML uses codes to tell your Web browser how to display information on your screen, but the computer doesn't know what the information is—it just displays it. XML provides additional tags that identify the kind of information that is being exchanged. For example, price data might be coded as <price> 14.95 <price>. When your computer reads this data and sees the tag <price> surrounding 14.95, your computer immediately knows that this is a price. XML tags can designate many different kinds of information—customer orders, medical records, bank statements, and so on—and the tags will indicate to your computer how to display, store, and retrieve the information. Office Depot was an early adopter of XML, which it is using to facilitate e-commerce with its big customers.

Canadian National Railway (CN Rail) is best known as the leading Class 1 railway in North America. Spanning all of Canada and the United States, CN Rail has the largest footprint of any railway in the world and, as such, requires a reliable and effective enterprise resource planning (ERP) system to integrate its business systems and optimize its resources. To this end, CN Rail partnered with SAP AG, a market leader in enterprise resource planning software, to develop an ERP system to help manage all back-office activities including financial, human resources, "mobile assets" (i.e., trains), and corporate services. The unique ability of such a system to integrate information for use across all aspects of the company has helped CN Rail to rebuild its core rail operating systems. In addition, CN Rail is working with SAP to develop industry standards for ERP solutions in order to improve its own efficiency and the efficiency of the North American rail industry as a whole.

Source: *SAP ERP: Customer Testimonials:* www.sap.com/solutions/business-suite/erp/customers/videos/index.epx.

Once an order has been received via EDI or over the Internet in the form of an XML file, the computer draws up a list of required raw materials and sends out electronic purchase orders to suppliers. When materials arrive at the company's plant from the suppliers, bar codes that have been applied by the suppliers are scanned to update inventory records and to trigger payment for the materials.

Goods ready to be shipped are packed into containers, which are bar-coded with information that includes the customer number, the type and quantity of goods being shipped, and the order number. This bar code is then used for preparing billing information and for tracking the packed goods until they are placed on a carrier for shipment to the customer. Some customers require that the packed goods be bar-coded with point-of-sale labels that can be scanned at retail checkout counters. These scans allow the retailer to update inventory records, verify price, and generate a customer receipt.

In short, bar code technology is being integrated into all areas of business activity. When combined with EDI or XML, it eliminates a lot of clerical drudgery and allows companies to capture and exchange more data and to analyze and report information much more quickly and completely and with less error than with manual systems.

The integration of XML and the internal computer system for management reporting is called an *enterprise resource planning system* (ERP system). An ERP system represents a real-time computer system using a single uniform database that is coupled with modules for accounting, logistics, and human resources. Full use of these modules permits an integrated system response for Internet-based orders in XML, supplier purchases and payables, inventory management, production, sales and receivables, treasury, and capital (fixed) assets management. Major suppliers of such ERP systems include Oracle, SAP, and Epicor. Other companies provide certified software that is compatible with these systems.

INTERNATIONAL JOB COSTING

Studies of the international accounting scene suggest that the general principles of product costing are universally applicable. Nevertheless, differences do exist from country to country in how specific costs are classified. For example, a study of Russian operational accounting and statistical record-keeping, the equivalent of product costing, suggests that the required reporting structure in Russia would assign some cost elements to inventory that we might classify as selling or administrative. Other costs such as the rent on plant facilities would be classified outside of the usual overhead category. In Germany, many companies classify only materials as variable costs since labour laws in Germany make it very difficult to downsize. Consequently, labour costs are treated as fixed costs by these firms. If a company was executing a contract with a foreign government, the differences in what is or is not permitted as contract costs would be particularly important. Similarly, what Public Works and Government Services Canada will allow as contract costs is described by the word "prudent" and elaborated in a specific list of costs excluded from product costs. For example, these requirements would permit certain general and selling costs to be included if a prudent person would incur such costs as part of the contract. Thus, while the general principles may be similar, the specifics can vary as a result of government regulations.

Summary

- Job-order costing and process costing are widely used to track costs. Job-order costing is used in situations where the organization offers many different products or services, such as in furniture manufacturers, hospitals, and legal firms. **[LO1]**
- Process costing is used where units of product are homogeneous, such as in flour milling or cement production. **[LO1]**
- Materials requisition forms and labour time tickets are used to assign direct materials and direct labour costs to jobs in a job costing system. Manufacturing overhead costs are assigned to jobs through use of a predetermined overhead rate. **[LO2, LO3]**
- The predetermined overhead rate is determined before the period begins by dividing the estimated total manufacturing overhead cost for the period by the estimated total allocation base for the period. The most frequently used allocation bases are direct labour-hours and machine-hours. Overhead is applied to jobs by multiplying the predetermined overhead rate by the actual amount of the allocation base used by the job. **[LO3, LO5]**
- Since the predetermined overhead rate is based on estimates, the actual overhead cost incurred during a period may be more or less than the amount of overhead cost applied to production. Such a difference is referred to as *underapplied* or *overapplied overhead*. **[LO7]**
- The under- or overapplied overhead for a period can be (1) closed out to Cost of Goods Sold or (2) allocated among Work in Process, Finished Goods, and Cost of Goods Sold, or (3) carried forward to the end of the year. **[LO7]**
- When overhead is underapplied, manufacturing overhead costs have been understated and therefore inventories and/or expenses must be adjusted upward. When overhead is overapplied, manufacturing overhead costs have been overstated and therefore inventories and/or expenses must be adjusted downward. **[LO7]**

Review Problem: Job-Order Costing

Hogle Company is a manufacturing firm that uses job-order costing. On January 1, the beginning of its fiscal year, the company's inventory balances were as follows:

Raw materials.	$20,000
Work in process.	15,000
Finished goods.	30,000

The company applies overhead cost to jobs on the basis of machine-hours worked. For the current year, the company estimated that it would work 75,000 machine-hours and incur $450,000 in manufacturing overhead cost. The following transactions were recorded for the year:

a. Raw materials were purchased on account: $410,000.
b. Raw materials were requisitioned for use in production: $380,000 ($360,000 direct materials and $20,000 indirect materials).

c.   The following costs were incurred for employee services: direct labour, $75,000; indirect labour, $110,000; sales commissions, $90,000; and administrative salaries, $200,000.
d.   Sales travel costs were incurred: $17,000.
e.   Utility costs were incurred in the factory: $43,000.
f.   Advertising costs were incurred: $180,000.
g.   Depreciation was recorded for the year: $350,000 (80% relates to factory operations, and 20% relates to selling and administrative activities).
h.   Insurance expired during the year: $10,000 (70% relates to factory operations, and the remaining 30% relates to selling and administrative activities).
i.   Manufacturing overhead was applied to production. Due to greater than expected demand for its products, the company worked 80,000 machine-hours during the year.
j.   Goods costing $900,000 to manufacture according to their job cost sheets were completed during the year.
k.   Goods were sold on account to customers during the year at a total selling price of $1,500,000. The goods cost $870,000 to manufacture according to their job cost sheets.

Required:
1.   Prepare journal entries to record the preceding transactions.
2.   Post the entries in (1) above to T-accounts (do not forget to enter the opening balances in the inventory accounts).
3.   Is Manufacturing Overhead underapplied or overapplied for the year? Prepare a journal entry to close any balance in the Manufacturing Overhead account to Cost of Goods Sold. Do not allocate the balance between ending inventories and Cost of Goods Sold.
4.   Prepare an income statement for the year.

Solution to Review Problem

1.   *a.* Raw Materials.   410,000
         Accounts Payable   410,000
     b. Work in Process.   360,000
         Manufacturing Overhead   20,000
             Raw Materials.   380,000
     c. Work in Process.   75,000
         Manufacturing Overhead   110,000
         Sales Commissions Expense.   90,000
         Administrative Salaries Expense   200,000
             Salaries and Wages Payable   475,000
     d. Sales Travel Expense, ...   17,000
             Accounts Payable, ...   17,000
     e. Manufacturing Overhead   43,000
             Accounts Payable   43,000
     f. Advertising Expense.   180,000
             Accounts Payable   180,000
     g. Manufacturing Overhead   280,000
         Depreciation Expense   70,000
             Accumulated Depreciation.   350,000
     h. Manufacturing Overhead   7,000
         Insurance Expense.   3,000
             Prepaid Insurance.   10,000
     i. The predetermined overhead rate for the year would be computed as follows:

$$\frac{\text{Estimated manufacturing overhead, } \$450,000}{\text{Estimated machine-hours, } 75,000} = \$6 \text{ per machine-hour}$$

Based on the 80,000 machine-hours actually worked during the year, the company would have applied $480,000 in overhead cost to production: 80,000 machine-hours × $6 = $480,000. The following entry records this application of overhead cost:

             Work in Process   480,000
                 Manufacturing Overhead.   480,000

j. Finished Goods	900,000	
Work in Process......................		900,000
k. Accounts Receivable	1,500,000	
Sales.................................		1,500,000
Cost of Goods Sold	870,000	
Finished Goods		870,000

2.

Raw Materials

Bal.	20,000	(b)	380,000
(a)	410,000		
Bal.	50,000		

Work in Process

Bal.	15,000	(j)	900,000
(b)	360,000		
(c)	75,000		
(i)	480,000		
Bal.	30,000		

Finished Goods

Bal.	30,000	(k)	870,000
(j)	900,000		
Bal.	60,000		

Cost of Goods Sold

(k)	870,000	

Manufacturing Overhead

(b)	20,000	(i)	480,000
(c)	110,000		
(e)	43,000		
(g)	280,000		
(h)	7,000		
	460,000		480,000
		Bal.	20,000

Prepaid Insurance

		(h)	10,000

Commissions Expense

(c)	90,000	

Accumulated Depreciation

		(g)	350,000

Accounts Receivable

(k)	1,500,000	

Administrative Salary Expense

(c)	200,000	

Sales Travel Expense

(d)	17,000	

Accounts Payable

		(a)	410,000
		(d)	17,000
		(e)	43,000
		(f)	180,000

Sales

		(k)	1,500,000

Advertising Expense

(f)	180,000	

Depreciation Expense

(g)	70,000	

Salaries and Wages Payable

		(c)	475,000

Insurance Expense

(h)	3,000	

3.   Manufacturing overhead is overapplied for the year. The entry to close it out to Cost of Goods
    Sold is as follows:

Manufacturing Overhead	20,000	
Cost of Goods Sold		20,000

4.

HOGLE COMPANY
Income Statement
For the Year Ended December 31

Sales.		$1,500,000
Less cost of goods sold.		850,000
Gross margin		650,000
Less selling and administrative expenses:		
Commissions expense	$ 90,000	
Administrative salaries expense	200,000	
Sales travel expense.	17,000	
Advertising expense	180,000	
Depreciation expense.	70,000	
Insurance expense..	3,000	560,000
Operating income.		$ 90,000

HOGLE COMPANY
Schedule of Cost of Goods Manufactured and
Cost of Goods Sold

Cost of Goods Manufactured
Direct Materials:

Raw materials inventory, January 1.	$ 20,000	
Add: Purchases of raw materials	410,000	
Total raw materials available	430,000	
Deduct: Raw materials inventory, December 31	50,000	
Raw materials used in production	380,000	
Less: Indirect materials,	20,000	
Direct materials used in production		$360,000
Direct labour.		75,000
Manufacturing overhead applied to work-in-process		480,000
Total manufacturing costs		915,000
Add: Beginning work in process inventory		15,000
		930,000
Deduct: Ending work in process inventory		(30,000)
Cost of goods manufactured		$900,000

Cost of Goods Sold

Finished goods inventory, January 1		$ 30,000
Add: Cost of goods manufactured.		900,000
Goods available for sale.		930,000
Deduct: Finished goods inventory, December 31		(60,000)
Unadjusted cost of goods sold		870,000
Deduct: Overapplied overhead		(20,000)
Adjusted cost of goods sold.		$850,000

Glossary

Review key terms and definitions on Connect.

Questions

3–1 Why aren't actual overhead costs traced to jobs just as direct materials and direct labour costs are traced to jobs?

3–2 When would job-order costing be used instead of process costing?

3–3 What is the purpose of the job cost sheet in a job-order costing system?

3–4   What is a predetermined overhead rate, and how is it computed?

3–5   Explain how a sales order, a production order, a materials requisition form, and a labour time ticket are involved in producing and costing products.

3–6   Explain why some production costs must be assigned to products through an allocation process.

3–7   Why do companies use predetermined overhead rates rather than actual manufacturing overhead costs to apply overhead to jobs?

3–8   Define the term *cost driver* and indicate how it is used in job-order costing.

3–9   If a company fully allocates all of its overhead costs to jobs, does this guarantee that a profit will be earned for the period?

3–10   What account is credited when overhead cost is applied to work in process? Would you expect the amount applied for a period to equal the actual overhead costs of the period? Why or why not?

3–11   What is underapplied overhead? Overapplied overhead? What disposition is made of these amounts at the end of the period?

3–12   Provide two reasons why overhead might be underapplied in a given year.

3–13   What adjustment is made for underapplied overhead on the schedule of cost of goods sold? What adjustment is made for overapplied overhead?

3–14   Gorman Company applies overhead cost to jobs on the basis of direct labour cost. Job A, which was started and completed during the current period, shows charges of $6,000 for direct materials, $15,000 for direct labour, and $7,500 for overhead on its job cost sheet. Job B, which is still in process at year-end, shows charges of $2,500 for direct materials and $4,000 for direct labour. Should any overhead cost be added to Job B at year-end? Explain and calculate the amount.

3–15   A company assigns overhead cost to completed jobs on the basis of 150% of direct labour cost. The job cost sheet for Job 313 shows that $12,000 in direct materials has been used on the job and that $16,000 in direct labour cost has been incurred. If 750 units were produced in Job 313, what is the unit product cost?

3–16   What is a plantwide overhead rate? Why are multiple overhead rates, rather than a plantwide overhead rate, used in some companies?

3–17   Under what conditions would direct labour be a poor allocation base to use in allocating manufacturing overhead?

3–18   "Predetermined overhead rates smooth product costs." Do you agree? Why?

3–19   Explain clearly the rationale for why under- and overapplied overhead for an interim period should be carried to the balance sheet. What conceptual factor is assumed in the argument?

3–20   Why does the calculation of the percentages for prorating the under- or overapplied overhead reduce the costs of goods sold by the opening inventories? What would happen if such a deduction were not made?

connect Exercises

EXERCISE 3–1 Process Costing and Job-Order Costing [LO1]
Which would be more appropriate in each of the following situations—job-order costing or process costing?
a.   A custom home builder.
b.   A golf course designer.
c.   A textbook publisher.
d.   A business consultant.
e.   An oil refinery.
f.   A soft-drink bottler.
g.   A film studio.
h.   A firm that supervises bridge construction projects.
i.   A manufacturer of fine custom jewellery.
j.   A paint factory
k.   An auto repair shop.
l.   A factory making frozen orange juice concentrate.

EXERCISE 3–2 Job-Order Costing Documents [LO2]

Ontario Machine Tool Company has incurred the following costs on Job ES34, an order for eight specialized cutting tools to be delivered at the end of next month.

Direct materials:
   On March 5, requisition number 870 was issued for 8 titanium blanks to be used in the special order. The blanks cost $25.00 each.
   On March 8, requisition number 873 was issued for 8 hardened cutting nibs, also to be used in the special order. The nibs cost $9.20 each.

Direct labour:
   On March 9, Harry Turner worked from 9:00 A.M. until 12:15 P.M. on Job ES34. He is paid $18.00 per hour.
   On March 21, Mary Gonzales worked from 2:15 P.M. until 4:30 P.M. on Job ES34. She is paid $19.00 per hour.

Required:
1.   On what documents would these costs be recorded?
2.   How much cost should have been recorded on each of the documents for Job ES34?

EXERCISE 3–3 Compute the Predetermined Overhead Rate [LO3]

Logan Products computes its predetermined overhead rate annually on the basis of direct labour-hours. At the beginning of the year, it estimated that its total manufacturing overhead would be $586,000 and the total direct labour would be 40,000 hours. Its actual total manufacturing overhead for the year was $713,400 and its actual total direct labour was 41,000 hours.

Required:
Compute the company's predetermined overhead rate for the year, calculate the total overhead applied, and determine the amount of under- or overapplied overhead in the year.

EXERCISE 3–4 Prepare Journal Entries [LO4]

Lancaster Company recorded the following transactions for the just-completed month.
a. $45,000 in raw materials were purchased on account.
b. $125,000 in raw materials were requisitioned for use in production. Of this amount, $70,000 was for direct materials and the remainder was for indirect materials.
c.   Total labour wages of $212,000 were incurred. Of this amount, $183,000 was for direct labour and the remainder was for indirect labour.
d.   Additional manufacturing overhead costs of $189,000 were incurred.

Required:
Record the above transactions in journal entries.

EXERCISE 3–5 Apply Overhead [LO5]

Carera Corporation uses a predetermined overhead rate of $23.10 per direct labour-hour. This predetermined rate was based on 12,000 estimated direct labour-hours and $277,200 of estimated total manufacturing overhead.

The company incurred actual total manufacturing overhead costs of $266,000 and 12,600 total direct labour-hours during the period.

Required:
Determine the amount of manufacturing overhead that would have been applied to units of product during the period as well as the amount of over- or underapplied overhead for the period.

EXERCISE 3–6 Applying Overhead; Cost of Goods Manufactured [LO5, LO6, LO7]

The following cost data relate to the manufacturing activities of Black Company during the just-completed year:

Manufacturing overhead costs:	
Property taxes, factory............................	$ 3,000
Utilities, factory	5,000
Indirect labour	10,000
Depreciation, factory	24,000
Insurance, factory	6,000
Total actual manufacturing overhead costs	$48,000
Other costs incurred:	
Purchases of raw materials.	$32,000
Direct labour cost	$40,000
Inventories:	
Raw materials, beginning	$ 8,000
Raw materials, ending	$ 7,000
Work in process, beginning.......................	$ 6,000
Work in process, ending	$ 7,500

The company uses a predetermined overhead rate to apply overhead cost to production. The rate for the year was $5 per machine-hour; a total of 10,000 machine-hours were recorded for the year. All raw materials ultimately become direct materials—none are classified as indirect materials.

Required:
1. Compute the amount of underapplied or overapplied overhead cost for the year.
2. Prepare a schedule of cost of goods manufactured for the year.

EXERCISE 3–7 Prepare T-Accounts [LO4, LO6]

Granger Products recorded the following transactions for the just-completed month. The company had no beginning inventories.
a. $75,000 in raw materials were purchased for cash.
b. $73,000 in raw materials were requisitioned for use in production. Of this amount, $67,000 was for direct materials and the remainder was for indirect materials.
c. Total labour wages of $152,000 were incurred and paid. Of this amount, $134,000 was for direct labour and the remainder was for indirect labour.
d. Additional manufacturing overhead costs of $126,000 were incurred and paid.
e. Manufacturing overhead costs of $178,000 were applied to jobs using the company's predetermined overhead rate.
f. All of the jobs in progress at the end of the month were completed and shipped to customers.
g. The underapplied or overapplied overhead for the period was closed out to cost of goods sold.

Required:
1. Post the above transactions to T-accounts.
2. Determine the cost of goods sold for the period.

EXERCISE 3–8 Underapplied and Overapplied Overhead [LO7]

Cretin Enterprises uses a predetermined overhead rate of $21.40 per direct labour-hour. This predetermined rate was based on 16,000 estimated direct labour-hours and $171,200 of estimated total manufacturing overhead.

The company incurred actual total manufacturing overhead costs of $345,000 and 16,500 total direct labour-hours during the period.

Required:
1. Determine the amount of underapplied or overapplied manufacturing overhead for the period.
2. Assuming that the entire amount of the underapplied or overapplied overhead is closed out to cost of goods sold, what would be the effect of the underapplied or overapplied overhead on the company's gross margin for the period?

EXERCISE 3–9 Applying Overhead in a Service Company [LO2, LO3, LO5]
Drew Architectural Design began operations on January 2. The following activity was recorded in the company's Work in Process account for the first month of operations:

Work in Process

Costs of subcontracted work	90,000	To completed projects	570,000
Direct staff costs	200,000		
Studio overhead	320,000		

Drew Architectural Design is a service firm, so the names of the accounts it uses are different from the names used in manufacturing companies. Costs of Subcontracted Work is comparable to Direct Materials; Direct Staff Costs is the same as Direct Labour; Studio Overhead is the same as Manufacturing Overhead; and Completed Projects is the same as Finished Goods. Apart from the difference in terms, the accounting methods used by the company are identical to the methods used by manufacturing companies.

Drew Architectural Design uses a job-order costing system and applies studio overhead to Work in Process on the basis of direct staff costs. At the end of January, only one job was still in process. This job (the Kareen Corporation Headquarters project) had been charged with $13,500 in direct staff costs.

Required:
1. Compute the predetermined overhead rate that was in use during January.
2. Complete the following job cost sheet for the partially completed Kareen Corporation Headquarters project.

Job Cost Sheet
Kareen Corporation Headquarters Project
as of January 31

Costs of subcontracted work	$?
Direct staff costs	?
Studio overhead	?
Total cost to January 31	$?

EXERCISE 3–10 Schedules of Cost of Goods Manufactured and Cost of Goods Sold [LO6]
Anthony Co. manufactures office furniture at its plant in central Ontario. In August, the plant accountant collected the following data concerning operations during the month of July:

Purchases of raw materials	$45,000
Direct labour.	68,000
Manufacturing overhead applied to work in process.	96,000
Overapplied overhead	6,500

Inventory:	Beginning	Ending
Raw materials.	$15,000	$23,000
Work in process	52,000	71,000
Finished goods.	27,000	32,000

Required:
Prepare a schedule of cost of goods manufactured and cost of goods sold for the month of July.

EXERCISE 3–11 Applying Overhead in a Service Company; Journal Entries [LO4, LO5, LO7]
Local Landscaping uses a job-order costing system to track the costs of its landscaping projects. The company provides complete garden design and landscaping services. The following table provides

data concerning the three landscaping projects that were in progress during May. There was no work in process at the beginning of May.

	Project		
	Williams	**Chandler**	**Nguyen**
Designer-hours	200	80	120
Direct materials cost	$4,800	$1,800	$3,600
Direct labour cost.	$2,400	$1,000	$1,500

Actual overhead costs were $16,000 for May. Overhead costs are applied to projects on the basis of designer-hours since most of the overhead is related to the costs of the garden design studio. The predetermined overhead rate is $45 per designer-hour. The Williams and Chandler projects were completed in May; the Nguyen project was not completed by the end of the month. No other jobs were in process during May.

Required:
1. Compute the amount of overhead cost that would have been charged to each project during May.
2. Prepare a journal entry showing the completion of the Williams and Chandler projects and the transfer of costs to the Completed Projects (i.e., Finished Goods) account.
3. What is the balance in the Work in Process account at the end of the month?
4. What is the balance in the Overhead account at the end of the month? What is this balance called?

EXERCISE 3–12 Varying Predetermined Overhead Rates [LO3, LO5]

Jacarda Company makes a composting bin that is subject to wide seasonal variations in demand. Unit product costs are computed on a quarterly basis by dividing each quarter's manufacturing costs (materials, labour, and overhead) by the quarter's production in units. The company's estimated costs, by quarter, for the coming year are given below:

	Quarter			
	First	**Second**	**Third**	**Fourth**
Direct materials	$240,000	$120,000	$ 60,000	$180,000
Direct labour	96,000	48,000	24,000	72,000
Manufacturing overhead	228,000	204,000	192,000	216,000
Total manufacturing costs	$564,000	$372,000	$276,000	$468,000
Number of units to be produced . .	80,000	40,000	20,000	60,000
Estimated unit product cost	$7.05	$9.30	$13.80	$7.80

Management finds the variation in unit product costs to be confusing and difficult to work with. It has been suggested that the problem lies with manufacturing overhead, since it is the largest element of cost. Accordingly, you have been asked to find a more appropriate way of assigning manufacturing overhead cost to units of product. After some analysis, you have determined that the company's overhead costs are mostly fixed and therefore show little sensitivity to changes in the level of production.

Required:
1. The company uses a job-order costing system. How would you recommend that manufacturing overhead cost be assigned to production? Be specific, and show computations.
2. Recompute the company's unit product costs in accordance with your recommendations in (1) above.

EXERCISE 3–13 Applying Overhead; Journal Entries; Disposition of Underapplied or Overapplied Overhead [LO4, LO7]

The following information is taken from the accounts of Foster Corp. The entries in the T-accounts are summaries of the transactions that affected those accounts during the year.

Manufacturing Overhead			
(a)	380,000	(b)	410,000
		Bal.	30,000

Work in Progress			
Bal.	105,000	(c)	760,000
	210,000		
	115,000		
(b)	410,000		
Bal.	80,000		

Finished Goods			
Bal.	160,000	(d)	820,000
(c)	760,000		
Bal.	100,000		

Cost of Goods Sold			
(d)	820,000		

The overhead that had been applied to production during the year is distributed among the ending balances in the accounts as follows:

Work in Process, ending	$ 32,800
Finished Goods, ending.	41,000
Cost of Goods Sold.	336,200
Overhead applied.	$410,000

For example, of the $80,000 ending balance in Work in Process, $32,800 was overhead that had been applied during the year.

Required:
1. Identify the reasons for entries (a) through (d).
2. Assume that the company closes any balance in the Manufacturing Overhead account directly to Cost of Goods Sold. Prepare the necessary journal entry.
3. Assume instead that the company allocates any balance in the Manufacturing Overhead account to the other accounts in proportion to the overhead applied during the year that is in the ending balance in each account. Prepare the necessary journal entry, with supporting computations.

EXERCISE 3–14 Departmental Overhead Rates [LO3, LO5]

Grange Company has two departments, Stamping and Assembly. The company uses a job-order cost system and computes a predetermined overhead rate in each department. The Stamping Department bases its rate on machine-hours, and the Assembly Department bases its rate on direct labour cost. At the beginning of the year, the company made the following estimates:

	Department	
	Stamping	Assembly
Direct labour-hours	40,000	125,000
Machine-hours.	300,000	15,000
Manufacturing overhead cost.	$2,550,000	$4,000,000
Direct labour cost	$360,000	$3,200,000

Required:
1. Compute the predetermined overhead rate to be used in each department.
2. Assume that the overhead rates you computed in (1) above are in effect. The job cost sheet for Job 407, which was started and completed during the year, showed the following:

	Department	
	Stamping	**Assembly**
Direct labour-hours	25	100
Machine-hours	450	20
Materials requisitioned.	$400	$1,850
Direct labour cost.	$225	$800

Compute the total overhead cost applied to Job 407.

3.   Would you expect substantially different amounts of overhead cost to be charged to some jobs if the company used a plantwide overhead rate based on direct labour cost instead of using departmental rates? Explain. No computations are necessary.

EXERCISE 3–15 Applying Overhead; T-Accounts; Journal Entries [LO3, LO4, LO5, LO7]

Medusa Products uses a job-order costing system. Overhead costs are applied to jobs on the basis of machine-hours. At the beginning of the year, management estimated that the company would incur $170,000 in manufacturing overhead costs for the year and work 85,000 machine-hours.

Required:
1.   Compute the company's predetermined overhead rate.
2.   Assume that during the year the company actually works only 80,000 machine-hours and incurs the following costs in the Manufacturing Overhead and Work in Process accounts:

Manufacturing Overhead			Work in Process	
(Utilities)	14,000	?	(Direct materials)	530,000
(Insurance)	9,000		(Direct labour)	85,000
(Maintenance)	33,000		(Overhead)	?
(Indirect materials)	7,000			
(Indirect labour)	65,000			
(Depreciation)	40,000			

Copy the data in the T-accounts above onto your answer sheet. Compute the amount of overhead cost that would be applied to Work in Process for the year, and make the entry in your T-accounts.
3.   Compute the amount of underapplied or overapplied overhead for the year, and show the balance in your Manufacturing Overhead T-account. Prepare a journal entry to close out the balance in this account to Cost of Goods Sold.
4.   Explain why the manufacturing overhead was underapplied or overapplied for the year.

EXERCISE 3–16 Overhead Application [LO3]

Sportway Inc. produces high-quality tennis racquets and golf clubs using a patented forming process and high-quality hand-finishing. Products move through two production departments: Forming and Finishing. The company uses departmental overhead rates to allocate overhead costs. Overhead is allocated based on machine-hours in Forming and direct labour cost in Finishing. Information related to costs for last year is provided below:

	Tennis Racquets	Golf Clubs
Annual production and sales	5,000	8,000
Direct materials per unit	$4.50	$3.50
Direct labour cost per unit:		
Forming Department	$8.00	$3.50
Finishing Department	$3.50	$4.00
Machine hours per unit:		
Forming Department	0.75	0.25
Finishing Department	0.25	0.50

In addition, the firm budgets manufacturing overhead in the Forming Department at $52,000 and at $45,000 in Finishing.

Required:
1.   Determine the overhead application rate for each department.
2.   Determine the total cost per unit of tennis racquets and golf clubs.

Problems connect

PROBLEM 3–17 Comprehensive Problem [LO3, LO4, LO5, LO7]

Regal Millwork, Ltd., produces reproductions of antique residential mouldings at a plant located in Manchester, England. Since there are hundreds of products, some of which are made only to order, the company uses a job-order costing system. On July 1, the start of the company's fiscal year, inventory account balances were as follows:

Raw Materials..........................	£10,000
Work in Process.......................	£4,000
Finished Goods........................	£8,000

The company applies overhead cost to jobs on the basis of machine-hours. For the fiscal year starting July 1, it was estimated that the plant would operate 45,000 machine-hours and incur £99,000 in manufacturing overhead cost. During the year, the following transactions were completed:

a. Raw materials purchased on account, £160,000.
b. Raw materials requisitioned for use in production, £140,000 (materials costing £120,000 were chargeable directly to jobs; the remaining materials were indirect).
c. Costs for employee services were incurred as follows:

Direct labour...........................	£90,000
Indirect labour.........................	£60,000
Sales commissions.....................	£20,000
Administrative salaries..................	£50,000

d. Prepaid insurance expired during the year: £18,000 (£13,000 of this amount related to factory operations, and the remainder related to selling and administrative activities).
e. Utility costs incurred in the factory: £10,000.
f. Advertising costs incurred: £15,000.
g. Depreciation recorded on equipment: £25,000. (£20,000 of this amount was on equipment used in factory operations; the remaining £5,000 was on equipment used in selling and administrative activities.)
h. Manufacturing overhead cost was applied to jobs: £ ?. (The company recorded 50,000 machine-hours of operating time during the year.)
i. Goods that had cost £310,000 to manufacture according to their job cost sheets were completed.
j. Sales (all on account) to customers during the year totalled £498,000. These goods had cost £308,000 to manufacture according to their job cost sheets.

Required:

1. Prepare journal entries to record the transactions for the year.
2. Prepare T-accounts for inventories, Manufacturing Overhead, and Cost of Goods Sold. Post relevant data from your journal entries to these T-accounts (don't forget to enter the opening balances in your inventory accounts). Compute an ending balance in each account.
3. Is Manufacturing Overhead underapplied or overapplied for the year? Prepare a journal entry to close any balance in the Manufacturing Overhead account to Cost of Goods Sold.
4. Prepare an income statement for the year. (Do not prepare a schedule of cost of goods manufactured; all of the information needed for the income statement is available in the journal entries and T-accounts you have prepared.)

PROBLEM 3–18 Journal Entries; T-Accounts; Cost Flows [LO4, LO5, LO7]

Ravsten Company uses a job-order costing system. On January 1, the beginning of the current year, the company's inventory balances were as follows:

Raw materials..........................	$16,000
Work in process.......................	$10,000
Finished goods........................	$30,000

The company applies overhead cost to jobs on the basis of machine-hours. For the current year, the company estimated that it would work 36,000 machine-hours and incur $153,000 in manufacturing overhead cost. The following transactions were recorded for the year:

a. Raw materials purchased on account, $200,000.
b. Raw materials requisitioned for use in production, $190,000 (80% direct and 20% indirect).

c.   The following costs were incurred for employee services:

Direct labour	$160,000
Indirect labour	$27,000
Sales commissions	$36,000
Administrative salaries	$80,000

d.   Heat, power, and water costs incurred in the factory, $42,000.

e.   Prepaid insurance expired during the year, $10,000 (90% relates to factory operations, and 10% relates to selling and administrative activities).

f.   Advertising costs incurred, $50,000.

g.   Depreciation recorded for the year, $60,000 (85% relates to factory operations, and 15% relates to selling and administrative activities).

h.   Manufacturing overhead cost was applied to production. The company recorded 40,000 machine-hours for the year.

i.   Goods that cost $480,000 to manufacture according to their job cost sheets were transferred to the finished goods warehouse.

j.   Sales for the year totalled $700,000 and were all on account. The total cost to manufacture these goods according to their job cost sheets was $475,000.

Required:
1.   Prepare journal entries to record the transactions given above.
2.   Prepare T-accounts for inventories, Manufacturing Overhead, and Cost of Goods Sold. Post relevant data from your journal entries to these T-accounts (don't forget to enter the opening balances in your inventory accounts). Compute an ending balance in each account.
3.   Is Manufacturing Overhead underapplied or overapplied for the year? Prepare a journal entry to close any balance in the Manufacturing Overhead account to Cost of Goods Sold.
4.   Prepare an income statement for the year. (Do not prepare a schedule of cost of goods manufactured; all of the information needed for the income statement is available in the journal entries and T-accounts you have prepared.)

PROBLEM 3–19 T-Accounts; Applying Overhead [LO3, LO5, LO7]

Durham Company's trial balance as of January 1, the beginning of the current year, is shown below.

Cash	$ 8,000	
Accounts Receivable	13,000	
Raw Materials	7,000	
Work in Process	18,000	
Finished Goods	20,000	
Prepaid Insurance	4,000	
Plant and Equipment	230,000	
Accumulated Depreciation		$ 42,000
Accounts Payable		30,000
Capital Stock		150,000
Retained Earnings		78,000
Total	$300,000	$300,000

Durham Company uses a job-order costing system. During the year, the following transactions took place:

a.   Raw materials purchased on account: $45,000.

b.   Raw materials requisitioned for use in production: $40,000 (80% direct and 20% indirect).

c.   Factory utility costs incurred: $14,600.

d.   Depreciation recorded on plant and equipment: $28,000. Three-fourths of the depreciation relates to factory equipment, and the remainder relates to selling and administrative equipment.

e.   Costs for salaries and wages were incurred as follows:

Direct labour	$40,000
Indirect labour	$18,000
Sales commissions	$10,400
Administrative salaries	$25,000

f.   Prepaid insurance expired during the year: $3,000 (80% relates to factory operations, and 20% relates to selling and administrative activities).

g.   Miscellaneous selling and administrative expenses incurred: $18,000.
h.   Manufacturing overhead was applied to production. The company applies overhead on the basis of 150% of direct labour cost.
i.   Goods that cost $130,000 to manufacture according to their job cost sheets were transferred to the finished goods warehouse.
j.   Goods that had cost $120,000 to manufacture according to their job cost sheets were sold on account for $200,000.
k.   Collections from customers during the year totalled $197,000.
l.   Payments to suppliers on account during the year: $100,000; payments to employees for salaries and wages: $90,000.

Required:

1.   Prepare a T-account for each account in the company's trial balance, and enter the opening balances shown above.
2.   Record the transactions above directly into the T-accounts. Prepare new T-accounts as needed. Key your entries to the letters (a) through (l) above. Find the ending balance in each account.
3.   Is manufacturing overhead underapplied or overapplied for the year? Make an entry in the T-accounts to close any balance in the Manufacturing Overhead account to Cost of Goods Sold.
4.   Prepare an income statement for the year. (Do not prepare a schedule of cost of goods manufactured; all of the information needed for the income statement is available in the T-accounts you have prepared.)

PROBLEM 3–20 Cost Flows; T-Accounts; Income Statement [LO3, LO5, LO7]
PQB, Inc., designs and fabricates movie props such as mockups of starfighters and cybernetic robots. The company's balance sheet as of January 1, the beginning of the current year, appears below.

PQB, Inc.
Balance Sheet
January 1

Assets

Current assets:		
Cash.		$ 15,000
Accounts receivable.		40,000
Inventories:		
Raw materials.	$ 25,000	
Work in process	30,000	
Finished goods (props awaiting shipment)	45,000	100,000
Prepaid insurance		5,000
Total current assets.		160,000
Buildings and equipment.	500,000	
Less accumulated depreciation.	210,000	290,000
Total assets.		$450,000

Liabilities and Shareholders' Equity

Accounts payable		$ 75,000
Capital stock.	$250,000	
Retained earnings.	125,000	375,000
Total liabilities and shareholders' equity		$450,000

Since each prop is a unique design and may require anything from a few hours to a month or more to complete, PQB uses a job-order costing system. Overhead in the fabrication shop is charged to props on the basis of direct labour cost. The company estimated that it would incur $80,000 in manufacturing overhead and $100,000 in direct labour cost during the year. The following transactions were recorded during the year:

a.   Raw materials, such as wood, paints, and metal sheeting, were purchased on account: $80,000.
b.   Raw materials were issued to production: $90,000; $5,000 of this amount was for indirect materials.
c.   Payroll costs incurred and paid: direct labour, $120,000; indirect labour, $30,000; and selling and administrative salaries, $75,000.
d.   Fabrication shop utilities costs incurred: $12,000.

e.   Depreciation recorded for the year: $30,000 ($5,000 on selling and administrative assets; $25,000 on fabrication shop assets).

f.   Prepaid insurance expired: $4,800 ($4,000 related to fabrication shop operations, and $800 related to selling and administrative activities).

g.   Shipping expenses incurred: $40,000.

h.   Other manufacturing overhead costs incurred: $17,000 (credit Accounts Payable).

i.   Manufacturing overhead was applied to production. Overhead is applied on the basis of direct labour cost.

j.   Movie props that cost $310,000 to produce according to their job cost sheets were completed.

k.   Sales for the year totalled $450,000 and were all on account. The total cost to produce these movie props was $300,000 according to their job cost sheets.

l.   Collections on account from customers: $445,000.

m.   Payments on account to suppliers: $150,000.

Required:

1.   Prepare a T-account for each account on the company's balance sheet, and enter the beginning balances.

2.   Make entries directly into the T-accounts for the transactions given above. Create new T-accounts as needed. Determine an ending balance for each T-account.

3.   Was manufacturing overhead underapplied or overapplied for the year? Assume that the company allocates any overhead balance between the Work in Process, Finished Goods, and Cost of Goods Sold accounts, using the overall balances in each account. Prepare a journal entry to show the allocation. (Round allocation percentages to one decimal place.)

4.   Prepare an income statement for the year. (Do not prepare a schedule of cost of goods manufactured; all of the information needed for the income statement is available in the T- accounts.)

PROBLEM 3–21 T-Accounts; Overhead Rates; Journal Entries [LO3, LO4, LO5, LO7]

Kenworth Company uses a job-order costing system. Only three jobs—Job 105, Job 106, and Job 107—were worked on during November and December. Job 105 was completed on December 10; the other two jobs were still in production on December 31, the end of the company's operating year. Data from the job cost sheets of the three jobs follow:

	Job Cost Sheet		
	Job 105	**Job 106**	**Job 107**
November costs incurred:			
Direct materials	$16,500	$9,300	$0
Direct labour	$13,000	$7,000	$0
Manufacturing overhead	$20,800	$11,200	$0
December costs incurred:			
Direct materials	$0	$8,200	$21,300
Direct labour	$4,000	$6,000	$10,000
Manufacturing overhead	?	?	?

The following additional information is available:

a.   Manufacturing overhead is applied to jobs on the basis of direct labour cost.

b.   Balances in the inventory accounts at November 30 were as follows:

Raw Materials	$40,000
Work in Process.	?
Finished Goods	$85,000

Required:

1.   Prepare T-accounts for Raw Materials, Work in Process, Finished Goods, and Manufacturing Overhead. Enter the November 30 inventory balances given above; in the case of Work in Process, compute the November 30 balance and enter it into the Work in Process T-account.

2.   Prepare journal entries for *December* as follows:

a.   Prepare an entry to record the issue of materials into production and post the entry to appropriate T-accounts. (In the case of direct materials, it is not necessary to make a separate entry for each job.) Indirect materials used during December totalled $4,000.

b. Prepare an entry to record the incurrence of labour cost and post the entry to appropriate T-accounts. (In the case of direct labour cost, it is not necessary to make a separate entry for each job.) Indirect labour cost totalled $8,000 for December.

c. Prepare an entry to record the incurrence of $19,000 in various actual manufacturing overhead costs for December (credit Accounts Payable). Post this entry to the appropriate T-accounts.

3. What apparent predetermined overhead rate does the company use to assign overhead cost to jobs? Using this rate, prepare a journal entry to record the application of overhead cost to jobs for December (it is not necessary to make a separate entry for each job). Post this entry to the appropriate T-accounts.

4. As stated earlier, Job 105 was completed during December. Prepare a journal entry to show the transfer of this job off the production line and into the finished goods warehouse. Post the entry to the appropriate T-accounts.

5. Determine the balance at December 31 in the Work in Process inventory account. How much of this balance consists of costs charged to Job 106? Job 107?

PROBLEM 3–22 Multiple Departments; Overhead Rates; Underapplied or Overapplied Overhead [LO3, LO5, LO7]

Winder, Knotter, and Nale is a small law firm that has 10 partners and 10 support people. The firm employs a job-order costing system to accumulate costs chargeable to each client, and it is organized into two departments—the Research and Documents Department and the Litigation Department. The firm uses predetermined overhead rates to charge the costs of these departments to its clients. At the beginning of the current year, the firm's management made the following estimates for the year:

	Department	
	Research and Documents	**Litigation**
Research-hours	20,000	—
Direct lawyer-hours..................	9,000	16,000
Materials and supplies.................	$18,000	$5,000
Direct lawyer cost...................	$430,000	$800,000
Departmental overhead cost	$700,000	$320,000

The predetermined overhead rate in the Research and Documents Department is based on research-hours, and the rate in the Litigation Department is based on direct lawyer cost.

The costs charged to each client are made up of three elements: materials and supplies used, direct lawyer costs incurred, and an applied amount of overhead from each department in which work is performed on the case.

Case 618-3 was initiated on February 10 and completed on June 30. During this period, the following costs and time were recorded on the case:

	Department	
	Research and Documents	**Litigation**
Research-hours	18	—
Direct lawyer-hours..................	9	42
Materials and supplies.................	$50	$30
Direct lawyer cost...................	$410	$2,100

Required:
1. Compute the predetermined overhead rate used during the year in the Research and Documents Department. Compute the rate used in the Litigation Department.
2. Using the rates you computed in (1) above, compute the total overhead cost applied to Case 618-3.
3. What would be the total cost charged to Case 618-3? Show computations by department and in total for the case.

4. At the end of the year, the firm's records revealed the following *actual* cost and operating data for all cases handled during the year:

	Department	
	Research and Documents	Litigation
Research-hours	23,000	—
Direct lawyer-hours....................	8,000	15,000
Materials and supplies..................	$19,000	$6,000
Direct lawyer cost.	$400,000	$725,000
Departmental overhead cost	$770,000	$300,000

Determine the amount of underapplied or overapplied overhead cost in each department for the year.

PROBLEM 3–23 Journal Entries; T-Accounts; Disposition of Underapplied or Overapplied Overhead; Income Statement [LO3, LO4, LO5, LO7]

Heavenly Displays Inc. puts together large-scale fireworks displays—primarily for Canada Day celebrations sponsored by corporations and municipalities. The company assembles and orchestrates complex displays using pyrotechnic components purchased from suppliers throughout the world. The company has built a reputation for safety and for the awesome power and brilliance of its computer-controlled shows. Heavenly Displays builds its own launch platforms and its own electronic controls. Because of the company's reputation, customers order shows up to a year in advance. Since each show is different in terms of duration and components used, Heavenly Displays uses a job-order costing system.

Heavenly Displays' trial balance as of January 1, the beginning of the current year, is given below.

Cash	$ 9,000	
Accounts Receivable	30,000	
Raw Materials............................	16,000	
Work in Process	21,000	
Finished Goods..........................	38,000	
Prepaid Insurance........................	7,000	
Buildings and Equipment..................	300,000	
Accumulated Depreciation		$128,000
Accounts Payable........................		60,000
Salaries and Wages Payable..............		3,000
Capital Stock.............................		200,000
Retained Earnings........................		30,000
Total	$421,000	$421,000

The company charges manufacturing overhead costs to jobs on the basis of direct labour-hours. (Each customer order for a complete fireworks display is a separate job.) Management estimated that the company would incur $135,000 in manufacturing overhead costs in the fabrication and electronics shops and would work 18,000 direct labour-hours during the year. The following transactions occurred during the year:

a. Raw materials, consisting mostly of skyrockets, mortar bombs, flares, wiring, and electronic components, were purchased on account: $820,000.

b. Raw materials were issued to production: $830,000 ($13,000 of this amount was for indirect materials, and the remainder was for direct materials).

c. Fabrication and electronics shop payrolls were accrued: $200,000 (70% direct labour and 30% indirect labour). A total of 20,800 direct labour-hours were worked during the year.

d. Sales and administrative salaries were accrued: $150,000.

e. The company prepaid additional insurance premiums of $38,000 during the year. Prepaid insurance expiring during the year was $40,000 (only $600 relates to selling and administrative; the other $39,400 relates to the fabrication and electronics shops because of the safety hazards involved in handling fireworks).

f. Marketing cost incurred: $100,000.

g. Depreciation charges for the year: $40,000 (70% relates to fabrication and electronics shop assets, and 30% relates to selling and administrative assets).

h.   Property taxes accrued on the shop buildings: $12,600 (credit Accounts Payable).
i.   Manufacturing overhead cost was applied to jobs.
j.   Jobs completed during the year had a total production cost of $1,106,000 according to their job cost sheets.
k.   Revenue (all on account): $1,420,000. Cost of Goods Sold (before any adjustment for underapplied or overapplied overhead): $1,120,000.
l.   Cash collections on account from customers: $1,415,000.
m.   Cash payments on accounts payable: $970,000. Cash payments to employees for salaries and wages: $348,000.

Required:
1.   Prepare journal entries for the year's transactions.
2.   Prepare a T-account for each account in the company's trial balance, and enter the opening balances given above. Post your journal entries to the T-accounts. Prepare new T-accounts as needed. Compute the ending balance in each account.
3.   Is manufacturing overhead underapplied or overapplied for the year? Prepare the necessary journal entry to close the balance in the Manufacturing Overhead account to Cost of Goods Sold.
4.   Prepare an income statement for the year. (Do not prepare a statement of cost of goods manufactured; all of the information needed for the income statement is available in the T-accounts.)

PROBLEM 3–24 Multiple Departments; Applying Overhead [LO3, LO5, LO7]
WoodGrain Technology makes home office furniture from fine hardwoods. The company uses a job-order costing system and predetermined overhead rates to apply manufacturing overhead cost to jobs. The predetermined overhead rate in the Preparation Department is based on machine-hours, and the rate in the Fabrication Department is based on direct materials cost. At the beginning of the year, the company's management made the following estimates for the year:

	Department	
	Preparation	**Fabrication**
Machine-hours	80,000	21,000
Direct labour-hours.	35,000	65,000
Direct materials cost.	$190,000	$400,000
Direct labour cost.	$280,000	$530,000
Manufacturing overhead cost.	$416,000	$720,000

Job 127 was started on April 1 and completed on May 12. The company's cost records show the following information concerning the job:

	Department	
	Preparation	**Fabrication**
Machine-hours	350	70
Direct labour-hours.	80	130
Direct materials cost.	$940	$1,200
Direct labour cost.	$710	$980

Required:
1.   Compute the predetermined overhead rate used during the year in the Preparation Department. Compute the rate used in the Fabrication Department.
2.   Compute the total overhead cost applied to Job 127.
3.   What would be the total cost recorded for Job 127? If the job contained 25 units, what would be the unit product cost?
4.   At the end of the year, the records of WoodGrain Technology revealed the following *actual* cost and operating data for all jobs worked on during the year:

	Department	
	Preparation	Fabrication
Machine-hours	73,000	24,000
Direct labour-hours.	30,000	68,000
Direct materials cost.	$165,000	$420,000
Manufacturing overhead cost.	$390,000	$740,000

What was the amount of underapplied or overapplied overhead in each department at the end of the year?

PROBLEM 3–25 T-Account Analysis of Cost Flows [LO3, LO6, LO7]

Selected ledger accounts for Realm Company are given below for the just completed year:

Raw Materials

Bal. 1/1	30,000	Credits	?
Debits	420,000		
Bal. 12/31	60,000		

Manufacturing Overhead

Debits	385,000	Credits	?

Work in Progress

Bal. 1/1	70,000	Credits	810,000
Direct materials	320,000		
Direct labour	110,000		
Overhead	400,000		
Bal. 12/31	?		

Factory Wages Payable

Debits	179,000	Bal. 1/1	10,000
		Credits	175,000
		Bal. 12/31	6,000

Finished Goods

Bal. 1/1	40,000	Credits	?
Debits	?		
Bal. 12/31	130,000		

Cost of Goods Sold

Debits	?		

Required:
1. What was the cost of raw materials put into production during the year?
2. How much of the materials in (1) consisted of indirect materials?
3. How much of the factory labour cost for the year consisted of indirect labour?
4. What was the cost of goods manufactured for the year?
5. What was the cost of goods sold for the year (before considering underapplied or overapplied overhead)?
6. If overhead is applied to production on the basis of direct materials cost, what rate was in effect during the year?
7. Was manufacturing overhead underapplied or overapplied? By how much?
8. Compute the ending balance in the Work in Process inventory account. Assume that this balance consists entirely of goods started during the year. If $32,000 of this balance is direct materials cost, how much of it is direct labour cost? Manufacturing overhead cost?

PROBLEM 3–26 Schedule of Cost of Goods Manufactured; Overhead Analysis [LO3, LO5, LO6, LO7]

The Pacific Manufacturing Company operates a job-order costing system and applies overhead cost to jobs on the basis of direct labour cost. In computing an overhead rate for the year, the company's estimates were: manufacturing overhead cost, $126,000; and direct labour cost, $84,000. The company has provided the following data in the form of an Excel worksheet:

	A	B	C	D
1		*Beginning*	*Ending*	
2	Raw Materials	$21,000	$16,000	
3	Work in Process	$44,000	$40,000	
4	Finished Goods	$68,000	$60,000	
5				
6	*The following actual costs were incurred during the year:*			
7	Purchase of raw materials (all direct)		$133,000	
8	Direct labour cost		$80,000	
9	Manufacturing overhead costs:			
10	Insurance, factory		$7,000	
11	Depreciation of equipment		$18,000	
12	Indirect labour		$42,000	
13	Property taxes		$9,000	
14	Maintenance		$11,000	
15	Rent, building		$36,000	
16				
17				

◄ ◄ ► ►◄ \ **Sheet1** ⟋ Sheet2 ⟋ Sheet3 ⟋

Required:
1. *a.* Compute the predetermined overhead rate for the year.
    b. Compute the amount of underapplied or overapplied overhead for the year.
2. Prepare a schedule of cost of goods manufactured for the year.
3. Compute the cost of goods sold for the year. (Do not include any underapplied or overapplied overhead in your cost of goods sold figure.) What options are available for disposing of under applied or overapplied overhead?
4. Job 137 was started and completed during the year. What price would have been charged to the customer if the job required $3,200 in materials and $4,200 in direct labour cost, and the company priced its jobs at 40% above the job's cost according to the accounting system?
5. Direct labour made up $8,000 of the $40,000 ending Work in Process inventory balance. Supply the information missing below:

Direct materials.	$?
Direct labour.	8,000
Manufacturing overhead.	?
Work in process inventory.	$40,000

PROBLEM 3–27 Predetermined Overhead Rate; Disposition of Underapplied or Overapplied Overhead [LO3, LO7]
Savallas Company is highly automated and uses computers to control manufacturing operations. The company uses a job-order costing system and applies manufacturing overhead cost to products on the basis of computer-hours. The following estimates were used in preparing the predetermined overhead rate at the beginning of the year:

Computer-hours.	85,000
Manufacturing overhead cost.	$1,530,000

During the year, a severe economic recession resulted in cutting back production and a buildup of inventory in the company's warehouse. The company's cost records revealed the following actual cost and operating data for the year:

Computer-hours.....................	60,000
Manufacturing overhead cost...........	$1,350,000
Inventories at year-end:	
Raw materials.....................	$400,000
Work in process....................	$160,000
Finished goods....................	$1,040,000
Cost of goods sold..................	$2,800,000

Required:
1. Compute the company's predetermined overhead rate for the year.
2. Compute the underapplied or overapplied overhead for the year.
3. Assume the company closes any underapplied or overapplied overhead directly to Cost of Goods Sold. Prepare the appropriate entry.
4. Assume that the company allocates any underapplied or overapplied overhead to Work in Process, Finished Goods, and Cost of Goods Sold on the basis of the amount of overhead applied during the year that remains in each account at the end of the year. These amounts are $43,200 for Work in Process, $280,800 for Finished Goods, and $756,000 for Cost of Goods Sold. Prepare the journal entry to show the allocation.
5. How much higher or lower will operating income be for the year if the underapplied or overapplied overhead is allocated rather than closed directly to Cost of Goods Sold?

PROBLEM 3–28 Comprehensive Problem: Journal Entries; T-Accounts; Financial Statements [LO3, LO4, LO5, LO6, LO7]
Southworth Company uses a job-order costing system and applies manufacturing overhead cost to jobs on the basis of the cost of direct materials used in production. At the beginning of the current year, the following estimates were made for the purpose of computing the predetermined overhead rate: manufacturing overhead cost, $248,000; and direct materials cost, $155,000. The following transactions took place during the year (all purchases and services were acquired on account):
a. Raw materials purchased: $142,000.
b. Raw materials requisitioned for use in production (all direct materials): $150,000.
c. Utility bills incurred in the factory: $21,000.
d. Costs for salaries and wages were incurred as follows:

Direct labour.	$216,000
Indirect labour.	$90,000
Selling and administrative salaries	$145,000

e. Maintenance costs incurred in the factory: $15,000.
f. Advertising costs incurred: $130,000.
g. Depreciation recorded for the year: $50,000 (90% relates to factory assets, and the remainder relates to selling and administrative assets).
h. Rental cost incurred on buildings: $90,000 (80% of the space is occupied by the factory, and 20% is occupied by sales and administration).
i. Miscellaneous selling and administrative costs incurred: $17,000.
j. Manufacturing overhead cost was applied to jobs: $\underline{\ \ ?\ \ }$.
k. Cost of goods manufactured for the year: $590,000.
l. Sales for the year (all on account) totalled $1,000,000. These goods cost $600,000 according to their job cost sheets.

The balances in the inventory accounts at the beginning of the year were as follows:

Raw Materials..........................	$18,000
Work in Process	$24,000
Finished Goods........................	$35,000

Required:
1. Prepare journal entries to record the above data.
2. Post your entries to T-accounts. (Don't forget to enter the opening inventory balances above.) Determine the ending balances in the inventory accounts and in the Manufacturing Overhead account.

3. Prepare a schedule of cost of goods manufactured.
4. Prepare a journal entry to close any balance in the Manufacturing Overhead account to Cost of Goods Sold. Prepare a schedule of cost of goods sold.
5. Prepare an income statement for the year.
6. Job 218 was one of the many jobs started and completed during the year. The job required $3,600 in direct materials and 400 hours of direct labour time at a rate of $11 per hour. If the job contained 500 units and the company billed at 75% above the unit product cost on the job cost sheet, what price per unit would have been charged to the customer?

PROBLEM 3–29 Plantwide versus Departmental Overhead Rates; Underapplied or Overapplied Overhead [LO3, LO5, LO7]

"Don't tell me we've lost another bid!" exclaimed Janice Hudson, president of Prime Products, Inc. "I'm afraid so," replied Doug Martin, the operations vice-president. "One of our competitors underbid us by about $10,000 on the Hastings job." "I just can't figure it out," said Hudson. "It seems we're either too high to get the job or too low to make any money on half the jobs we bid. What's happened?"

Prime Products manufactures specialized goods to customers' specifications and operates a job-order costing system. Manufacturing overhead cost is applied to jobs on the basis of direct labour cost. The following estimates were made at the beginning of the year:

	Department			
	Cutting	Machining	Assembly	Total Plant
Direct labour...............	$300,000	$200,000	$400,000	$900,000
Manufacturing overhead......	$540,000	$800,000	$100,000	$1,440,000

Jobs require varying amounts of work in the three departments. The Hastings job, for example, would have required manufacturing costs in the three departments as follows:

	Department			
	Cutting	Machining	Assembly	Total Plant
Direct material	$12,000	$900	$5,600	$18,500
Direct labour...............	$6,500	$1,700	$13,000	$21,200
Manufacturing overhead	?	?	?	?

The company uses a plantwide overhead rate to apply manufacturing overhead cost to jobs.

Required:
1. Assuming the use of a plantwide overhead rate:
    a. Compute the rate for the current year.
    b. Determine the amount of manufacturing overhead cost that would have been applied to the Hastings job.
2. Suppose that instead of using a plantwide overhead rate, the company had used a separate predetermined overhead rate in each department. Under these conditions:
    a. Compute the rate for each department for the current year.
    b. Determine the amount of manufacturing overhead cost that would have been applied to the Hastings job.
3. Explain the difference between the manufacturing overhead that would have been applied to the Hastings job using the plantwide rate in question 1(b) above and using the departmental rates in question 2(b).
4. Assume that it is customary in the industry to bid jobs at 150% of total manufacturing cost (direct materials, direct labour, and applied overhead). What was the company's bid price on the Hastings job? What would the bid price have been if departmental overhead rates had been used to apply overhead cost?
5. At the end of the year, the company assembled the following *actual* cost data relating to all jobs worked on during the year:

	Department			
	Cutting	Machining	Assembly	Total Plant
Direct materials.............	$760,000	$90,000	$410,000	$1,260,000
Direct labour..............	$320,000	$210,000	$340,000	$870,000
Manufacturing overhead	$560,000	$830,000	$92,000	$1,482,000

Compute the underapplied or overapplied overhead for the year (a) assuming that a plantwide overhead rate is used, and (b) assuming that departmental overhead rates are used.

 Cases

CASE 3–30 Critical Thinking; Interpretation of Manufacturing Overhead Rates [LO3, LO5]
Sharpton Fabricators Corporation manufactures a variety of parts for the automotive industry. The company uses a job-order costing system with a plantwide predetermined overhead rate based on direct labour-hours. On December 10, 2008, the company's controller made a preliminary estimate of the predetermined overhead rate for 2009. The new rate was based on the estimated total manufacturing overhead cost of $3,402,000 and the estimated 63,000 total direct labour-hours for 2009:

$$\text{Predetermined overhead rate} = \frac{\$3,402,000}{63,000 \text{ hours}}$$

$$= \$54 \text{ per direct labour-hour}$$

This new predetermined overhead rate was communicated to top managers in a meeting on December 11. The rate did not cause any comment because it was within a few pennies of the overhead rate that had been used during 2008. One of the subjects discussed at the meeting was a proposal by the production manager to purchase an automated milling machine centre built by Central Robotics. The president of Sharpton Fabricators, Kevin Reynolds, agreed to meet with the regional sales representative from Central Robotics to discuss the proposal.

On the day following the meeting, Reynolds met with Jay Warner, Central Robotics' sales representative. The following discussion took place:

Reynolds: Larry Winter, our production manager, asked me to meet with you since he's interested in installing an automated milling machine centre. Frankly, I'm skeptical. You're going to have to show me this isn't just another expensive toy for Larry's people to play with.

Warner: That shouldn't be too difficult, Mr. Reynolds. The automated milling machine centre has three major advantages. First, it's much faster than the manual methods you're using. It can process about twice as many parts per hour as your present milling machines. Second, it's much more flexible. There are some up-front programming costs, but once those have been incurred, almost no setup is required on the machines for standard operations. You just punch in the code of the standard operation, load the machine's hopper with raw material, and the machine does the rest.

Reynolds: Yeah, but what about cost? Having twice the capacity in the milling machine area won't do us much good. That centre is idle much of the time, anyway.

Warner: I was getting there. The third advantage of the automated milling machine centre is lower cost. Larry Winters and I looked over your present operations, and we estimated that the automated equipment would eliminate the need for about 6,000 direct labour-hours a year. What is your direct labour cost per hour?

Reynolds: The wage rate in the milling area averages about $32 per hour. Fringe benefits raise that figure to about $41 per hour.

Warner: Don't forget your overhead.

Reynolds: Next year the overhead rate will be about $54 per direct labour-hour.

Warner: So including fringe benefits and overhead, the cost per direct labour-hour is about $95.

Reynolds: That's right.

Warner: Since you can save 6,000 direct labour-hours per year, the cost savings would amount to about $457,000 a year and our 60-month lease plan would require payments of only $348,000 per year.

Reynolds: Sold! When can you install the equipment?

Shortly after this meeting, Reynolds informed the company's controller of the decision to lease the new equipment, which would be installed over the Christmas vacation period. The controller realized that this decision would require a recomputation of the predetermined overhead rate for the year 2009, since the decision would affect both the manufacturing overhead and the direct labour-hours for the year. After talking with both the production manager and the sales representative from Central Robotics, the controller discovered that in addition to the annual lease cost of $348,000, the new machine would also require a skilled technician/programmer who would have to be hired at a cost of $50,000 per year to maintain and program the equipment. Both of these costs would be included in factory overhead. There would be no other changes in total manufacturing overhead cost, which is almost entirely fixed. The controller assumed that the new machine would result in a reduction of 6,000 direct labour-hours for the year from the levels that had initially been planned.

When the revised predetermined overhead rate for the year 2009 was circulated among the company's top managers, there was considerable dismay.

Required:

1. Recompute the predetermined rate assuming that the new machine will be installed. Explain why the new predetermined overhead rate is higher (or lower) than the rate that was originally estimated for the year 2009.
2. What effect (if any) would this new rate have on the cost of jobs that do not use the new automated milling machine?
3. Why would managers be concerned about the new overhead rate?
4. After seeing the new predetermined overhead rate, the production manager admitted that he probably wouldn't be able to eliminate all of the 6,000 direct labour-hours. He had been hoping to accomplish the reduction by not replacing workers who retire or quit, but that would not be possible. As a result, the real labour savings would be only about 2,000 hours—one worker. In the light of this additional information, evaluate the original decision to acquire the automated milling machine from Central Robotics.

CASE 3–31 Ethics and the Manager [LO3, LO5, LO7]

Emily Carrigan was recently transferred to the Appliances Division of Delancy Corporation. Shortly after taking over her new position as divisional controller, Emily was asked to develop the division's predetermined overhead rate for the upcoming year. The accuracy of the rate is important because it is used throughout the year, and any overapplied or underapplied overhead is closed out to Cost of Goods Sold at the end of the year. Delancy Corporation uses direct labour-hours in all of its divisions as the allocation base for manufacturing overhead.

To compute the predetermined overhead rate, Emily divided her estimate of the total manufacturing overhead for the coming year by the production manager's estimate of the total direct labour-hours for the coming year. She took her computations to the division's general manager for approval but was quite surprised when he suggested a modification in the base. Her conversation with the general manager of the Appliances Division, Harry Dafoe, went like this:

Carrigan: Here are my calculations for next year's predetermined overhead rate. If you approve, we can enter the rate into the computer on January 1 and be up and running in the job-order costing system right away for this year.

Dafoe: Thanks for coming up with the calculations so quickly. They look just fine. There is, however, one slight modification I'd like to see. Your estimate of the total direct labour-hours for the year is 110,000 hours. How about cutting that to about 105,000 hours?

Carrigan: I don't know if I can do that. The production manager says she will need about 110,000 direct labour-hours to meet the sales projections for next year. Besides, there are going to be over 108,000 direct labour-hours during the current year and sales are projected to be higher next year.

Dafoe: Emily, I know all of that. I would still like to reduce the direct labour-hours in the base to something like 105,000 hours. You probably don't know that I had an agreement with your predecessor as divisional controller to shave 5% or so off the estimated direct labour-hours every year. That way, we kept a reserve that usually resulted in a big boost to operating income at the end of the fiscal year in December. We called it our Christmas bonus. Corporate headquarters always seemed as pleased as punch that we could pull off such a miracle at the end of the year. This system has worked well for many years, and I don't want to change it now.

Required:

1. Explain how shaving 5% off the estimated direct labour-hours in the base for the predetermined overhead rate usually results in a big boost in operating income at the end of the fiscal year.
2. Should Emily Carrigan go along with the general manager's request to reduce the direct labour-hours in the predetermined overhead rate computation to 105,000 direct labour-hours?

CASE 3–32 Single versus Multiple Overhead Application Rates [LO3, LO5]

Foster Appliance Repair has developed a reputation over many years of providing high-quality, reliable repair services at a fair price. The company has grown from a two-person operation (run by Victor Foster and his wife Sally) to a much larger company employing Victor and Sally as well as four skilled repair personnel and two service technicians. Sally manages the front office and prepares all accounting-related records for the company. Recently, Sally has noticed a decline in profits generated by the repair business. Victor has also noticed some decline in the number of repairs completed over the past few months. He believes this reduction may be due to increased competition from a new repair shop in the area. Since pricing is based to a large degree on the cost of repairs, Victor asked Sally to spend some time analyzing the way in which repair costs were charged to jobs, to better understand the problem. He was quick to remind Sally that he was committed to keeping all personnel on fixed salaries since he believes this allows him to keep good employees and encourages loyalty to the company.

Sally collected the following information about the costing system:

- Direct materials used in repairs are charged directly to the job.
- The four repair personnel are paid a fixed salary of $50,000 per year and the two technicians are paid a fixed salary of $38,000 per year. Sally estimates that each of the six repair personnel work 1,750 hours per year on customer jobs.
- Other budgeted indirect support costs for the year (e.g., rent, insurance, utilities, supplies, repair van maintenance, repair van depreciation) total $178,450, including Victor's and Sally's salaries.
- The price for each job is calculated on a cost-plus basis. Customers pay the total cost to complete the job multiplied by a markup of 10%.
- The total cost for each job is calculated as follows: total direct material cost plus the "shop rate" × number of repair hours to complete the job. The shopwide rate is applied to all types of repair jobs. The shop rate is calculated as the sum of the repair personnel salaries plus budgeted indirect support costs for the year divided by the estimated total hours to be worked on customer jobs for the year.
- Sally noted that about 65% of total indirect costs related to complex repairs over the last couple of years, while the other 35% of total indirect costs related to simpler repairs. Even so, about half of the total time worked on customer jobs by repair personnel and technicians was related to complex repairs, while the other half was related to simple repairs. While Sally believed this was important information, she realized it was not taken into account when calculating the overall shop rate for the year.

Required:
1. Calculate the shopwide rate for the year based on the above information gathered by Sally.
2. Use the information gathered by Sally about the proportion of complex and simple repairs each year to calculate different shop rates that could be applied to complex and simple repair work.
3. Consider Job 1246 completed by Foster Appliance Repair last month. The job cost sheet indicates $115 cost of direct materials plus 6 hours of labour time × the shopwide rate.
   a. Calculate the total price charged to the customer, assuming a 10% markup on cost.
   b. By doing a little more digging, Sally was able to determine that 2 of the 6 hours spent on Job 1246 were related to complex repairs, while 4 of the 6 hours spent on the job were related to simple repairs. Use this information and the two shop rates calculated in (2) above to estimate the price that would have been charged for Job 1246 under this new system.
4. Using all of the information gathered to this point, explain why Foster Appliance Repair may be selling fewer repairs, resulting in lower profitability.

Research and Application

R 3–33 Job Costing Systems and Risks [LO1, LO2, LO3]

The questions in this exercise are based on Bombardier Inc., a Canadian company in the transportation business. To answer the questions, you will need to download Bombardier's 2009 annual report and related *Management Discussion and Analysis* (MD&A). Go to www.sedar. com, click on "Company Profiles," then click on "B" in the "Public Companies" rectangle, and then select "Bombardier Inc." You do not need to print any documents to answer the following questions.

Required

1. What are the key drivers for success of Bombardier Inc.?
2. What business risks does Bombardier face that may threaten the company's ability to satisfy shareholders' expectations? What are some examples of control activities that the company could use to reduce these risks?
3. Would Bombardier Inc. be more likely to use process costing or job-order costing? Why?
4. Bombardier has two main business segments, Aerospace and Rail Transportation. Choose one of these segments and provide some examples of direct material costs in this segment. Would you expect the bill of materials for each of Bombardier's aerospace and rail systems to be the same or different? Why?
5. Describe the type of direct labour costs incurred by Bombardier Inc. when constructing an aircraft or rail system.
6. What are some examples of overhead costs that are incurred by Bombardier Inc. in its aerospace or rail transportation segments?
7. Assume that Bombardier is engaged in building rail cars for subway systems in several different cities. Suggest how overhead costs related to these different rail car projects may be assigned. From a financial reporting standpoint, why does the entity need to assign manufacturing overhead costs to cost objects?

R 3–34 Enterprise Systems and Job Costing [LO1, LO2, LO4, LO6]

Use the Web site of Oracle or SAP to locate applications of ERP and XML to company costing operations. Make a list of five companies and determine if job costing is appropriate for them or whether any is a merchandiser.

R 3–35 Costing Systems and Overhead [LO1, LO3, LO7, LO8]

Wind power is a popular environmentally friendly electrical power-generating system. In 2007, 1,588 megawatts of capacity (1,588,000 kilowatts) were reportedly installed in Canada and much more capacity is in the planning stages.

The Natural Resources Canada Web site (www.nrcan.gc.ca) and the Canadian Wind Energy Association (CWEA) Web site (www.canwea.ca) provide historical, technical, and operational descriptions of activities in Canada.. The CWEA site even provides brief case studies of some Canadian projects.

Required

1. Describe how you believe the operations of wind farms would be costed. List as many cost elements as you deem appropriate.
2. Would the use of different definitions of activity amounts be useful in providing cost information?

◼ APPENDIX 3A: THE PREDETERMINED OVERHEAD RATE AND CAPACITY

LEARNING OBJECTIVE 8

Explain the implications of basing the predetermined overhead rate on activity at full capacity rather than on estimated activity for the period.

Companies typically base their predetermined overhead rates on the estimated, or budgeted, amount of the allocation base for the upcoming period. This is the method that is used in the chapter, but it is a practice that has recently come under severe criticism. An example will be very helpful in understanding why. Harmony Corporation manufactures music CDs for local recording studios. The company has a CD duplicating machine that is capable of producing a new CD every 10 seconds from a master CD. The company leases the CD duplicating machine for $180,000 per year, and this is the company's only manufacturing overhead. With allowances for setups and maintenance, the machine is theoretically capable of producing up to 900,000 CDs per year. However, due to weak retail sales of CDs, the company's commercial customers are unlikely to order more than 600,000

CDs next year. The company uses machine time as the allocation base for applying manu-facturing overhead. These data are summarized below:

Harmony Corporation Data	
Total manufacturing overhead cost......................	$180,000 per year
Allocation base: Machine time per CD	10 seconds per CD
Capacity	900,000 CDs per year
Budgeted output for next year	600,000 CDs

If Harmony follows common practice and computes its predetermined overhead rate using estimated, or budgeted, figures, then its predetermined overhead rate for next year would be $0.03 per second of machine time, computed as follows:

$$\frac{\text{Estimated total manufacturing overhead cost, \$180,000}}{\text{Estimated total units in the allocation base, 600,000 CDs} \times \text{10 seconds per CD}} = \$0.03 \text{ per second}$$

Since each CD requires 10 seconds of machine time, each CD will be charged $0.30 of overhead cost.

Critics charge that there are two problems with this procedure. First, if predetermined overhead rates are based on budgeted activity, then the unit product costs will fluctuate, depending on the budgeted level of activity for the period. For example, if the budgeted output for the year was only 300,000 CDs, the predetermined overhead rate would be $0.06 per second of machine time or $0.60 per CD rather than $0.30 per CD. In general, if budgeted output falls, the overhead cost per unit will increase; it will appear that the CDs cost more to make. Managers may then be tempted to increase prices at the worst possible time—just as demand is falling.

Second, critics charge that under the traditional approach, products are charged for resources that they do not use. When the fixed costs of capacity are spread over estimated activity, the units that are produced must shoulder the costs of unused capacity. That is why the applied overhead cost per unit increases as the level of activity falls. The critics argue that products should be charged only for the capacity that they use; they should not be charged for the capacity they do not use. This can be accomplished by basing the pre-determined overhead rate on capacity as follows:

$$\frac{\text{Total manufacturing overhead cost at capacity, \$180,000}}{\text{Total units in the allocation base at capacity, 900,000 CDs} \times \text{10 seconds per CD}} = \$0.02 \text{ per second}$$

Since the predetermined overhead rate is $0.02 per second, the overhead cost applied to each CD would be $0.20. This charge is constant and would not be affected by the level of activity during a period. If output falls, the charge would still be $0.20 per CD.

The use of capacity will almost certainly result in underapplied overhead. If actual output at Harmony Corporation is 600,000 CDs, then only $120,000 of overhead cost would be applied to products ($0.20 per CD × 600,000 CDs). Since the actual overhead cost is $180,000, there would be underapplied overhead of $60,000. In another departure from tradition, the critics suggest that the underapplied overhead that results from idle capacity should be separately disclosed on the income statement as the Cost of Unused Capacity—a period expense. Disclosing this cost as a lump sum on the income statement, rather than burying it in Cost of Goods Sold or ending inventories, makes it much more visible to managers.

Official pronouncements do not prohibit basing predetermined overhead rates on capac-ity for external reports. Nevertheless, basing the predetermined overhead rate on estimated, or budgeted, activity is a long-established practice in industry, and some managers and accountants may object to the large amounts of underapplied overhead that would often result from using capacity to determine predetermined overhead rates. And some may insist that the underapplied overhead be allocated among Cost of Goods Sold and ending inventories—which would defeat the purpose of basing the predetermined overhead rate on capacity.

Appendix 3A Summary

- In this chapter, we have calculated the overhead application rate using a denominator equal to budgeted or estimated amount of the allocation base for the period. **(LO8)**
- Critics argue that this means the application rate for manufacturing overhead will fluctuate as the budgeted amount of the allocation base fluctuates from period to period. **(LO8)**
- Instead, it is suggested that the predetermined overhead rate should be based on total units of the allocation base at capacity. **(LO8)**
- The result will almost always be underapplied overhead since most firms do not operate at full capacity all of the time. **(LO8)**
- Managers may wish to separate out underapplied overhead resulting from idle capacity in the Income Statement as the Cost of Unused Capacity, making it much more visible to managers and reminding them that unused capacity could be managed better in the next period. **(LO8)**

Appendix 3A Questions, Exercises, Problems, and Cases **connect**

3A–1 If the plant is operated at less than capacity and the predetermined overhead rate is based on the estimated total units in the allocation base at capacity, will overhead ordinarily be overapplied or underapplied?

3A–2 Define the Cost of Unused Capacity and discuss why it might be calculated.

EXERCISE 3A–1 Overhead Rates and Capacity Issues [LO3, LO5, LO7, LO8]
Estate Pension Services helps clients to set up and administer pension plans that are in compliance with tax laws and regulatory requirements. The firm uses a job-order costing system in which overhead is applied to clients' accounts on the basis of professional staff-hours charged to the accounts. Data concerning two previous years appear below:

	2008	2009
Estimated professional staff-hours to be charged to clients' accounts..............	2,400	2,250
Estimated overhead cost........................	$144,000	$144,000
Professional staff-hours available	3,000	3,000

"Professional staff-hours available" is a measure of the capacity of the firm. Any hours available that are not charged to clients' accounts represent unused capacity.

Required:
1. Jennifer Miyami is an established client whose pension plan was set up many years ago. In both 2008 and 2009, only five hours of professional staff time were charged to Miyami's account. If the company bases its predetermined overhead rate on the estimated overhead cost and the estimated professional staff-hours to be charged to clients, how much overhead cost would have been applied to Miyami's account in 2008? In 2009?
2. Suppose that the company bases its predetermined overhead rate on the estimated overhead cost and the estimated professional staff-hours to be charged to clients as in (1) above. Also suppose that the actual professional staff-hours charged to clients' accounts and the actual overhead costs turn out to be exactly as estimated in both years. By how much would the overhead be underapplied or overapplied in 2008? In 2009?
3. Refer back to the data concerning Miyami in (1) above. If the company bases its predetermined overhead rate on the estimated overhead cost and the professional staff-hours available, how much overhead cost would have been applied to Miyami's account in 2008? In 2009?
4. Suppose that the company bases its predetermined overhead rate on the estimated overhead cost and the professional staff-hours available as in (3) above. Also suppose that the actual professional staff-hours charged to clients' accounts and the actual overhead costs turn out to be exactly as estimated in both years. By how much would the overhead be underapplied or overapplied in 2008? In 2009?

PROBLEM 3A–2 Predetermined Overhead Rate and Capacity [LO3, LO5, LO7, LO8]
Alderberry Recording Inc. is a small audio recording studio. The company handles work for
advertising agencies—primarily for radio ads—and has a few singers and bands as clients.
Alderberry Recording handles all aspects of recording, from editing to making a digital master
from which CDs can be copied. The competition in the audio recording industry has always
been tough, but it has been getting even tougher over the last several years. The studio has been
losing customers to newer studios that are equipped with more up-to-date equipment and are
able to offer very attractive prices and excellent service. Summary data concerning the last two
years of operations follow:

	2008	2009
Estimated hours of studio service	1,000	750
Estimated studio overhead cost	$90,000	$90,000
Actual hours of studio service provided	900	600
Actual studio overhead cost incurred	$90,000	$90,000
Hours of studio service at capacity	1,800	1,800

The company applies studio overhead to recording jobs on the basis of the hours of studio service provided. For example, 30 hours of studio time were required to record, edit, and master the
Fire music CD for a local band. All of the studio overhead is fixed, and the actual overhead cost
incurred was exactly as estimated at the beginning of the year in both 2008 and 2009.

Required:
1. Alderberry Recording computes its predetermined overhead rate at the beginning of each year
    based on the estimated studio overhead and the estimated hours of studio service for the year.
    How much overhead would have been applied to the *Fire* job if it had been done in 2008? In
    2009? By how much would overhead have been underapplied or overapplied in 2008? In 2009?
2. The president of Alderberry Recording has heard that some companies in the industry have
    changed to a system of computing the predetermined overhead rate at the beginning of each
    year based on the estimated studio overhead for the year and the hours of studio service that
    could be provided at capacity. He would like to know what effect this method would have on
    job costs. How much overhead would have been applied using this method to the *Fire* job if it
    had been done in 2008? In 2009? By how much would overhead have been underapplied or
    overapplied in 2008 using this method? In 2009?
3. How would you interpret the underapplied or overapplied overhead that results from using
    studio-hours at capacity to compute the predetermined overhead rate?
4. What fundamental business problem is Alderberry Recording facing? Which method of com-
    puting the predetermined overhead rate is likely to be more helpful in facing this problem?
    Explain.

CASE 3A–3 Ethics; Predetermined Overhead Rate and Capacity [LO5, LO8]
Melissa Loester, the new controller of PowerDrives Inc. has just returned from a seminar on the
choice of the activity level in the predetermined overhead rate. Even though the subject did not
sound exciting at first, she found that there were some important ideas presented that should get a
hearing at her company. After returning from the seminar, she arranged a meeting with the production manager, Jan Laird, and the assistant production manager, Lonny Lee.

Melissa: I ran across an idea that I wanted to check out with both of you. It's about the way we
compute predetermined overhead rates.
Jan: We're all ears.
Melissa: We compute the predetermined overhead rate by dividing the estimated total factory overhead for the coming year by the estimated total units produced for the coming year.
Lonny: We've been doing that as long as I've been with the company.
Jan: And it has been done that way at every other company I've worked at, except at most places
they divide by direct labour-hours.
Melissa: We use units because it is simpler and we basically make one product with minor variations. But, there's another way to do it. Instead of dividing the estimated total factory overhead
by the estimated total units produced for the coming year, we could divide by the total units
produced at capacity.

Lonny: Oh, the Marketing Department will love that. It will drop the costs on all of our products. They'll go wild over there cutting prices.

Melissa: That is a worry, but I wanted to talk to both of you first before going over to Marketing.

Jan: Aren't you always going to have a lot of underapplied overhead?

Melissa: That's correct, but let me show you how we would handle it. Here's an example based on our budget for next year.

Budgeted (estimated) production	80,000 units
Budgeted sales	80,000 units
Capacity..	100,000 units
Selling price...	$70 per unit
Variable manufacturing cost	$18 per unit
Total manufacturing overhead cost (all fixed)	$2,000,000
Selling and administrative expenses (all fixed)	$1,950,000
Beginning inventories	$0

Traditional approach to computation of the predetermined overhead rate:

$$\text{Predetermined overhead rate} = \frac{\text{Estimated total manufacturing overhead cost}}{\text{Estimated total amount of the allocation base}}$$

$$= \frac{\$2,000,000}{80,000 \text{ units}} = \$25 \text{ per unit}$$

Budgeted Income Statement		
Revenue (80,000 units × $70 per unit)		$5,600,000
Cost of goods sold:		
Variable manufacturing (80,000 units × $18 per unit).	$1,440,000	
Manufacturing overhead applied		
(80,000 units × $25 per unit)................................	2,000,000	3,440,000
Gross margin...		2,160,000
Selling and administrative expenses...........................		1,950,000
Operating income		$ 210,000

New approach to computation of the predetermined overhead rate using capacity in the denominator:

$$\text{Predetermined overhead rate} = \frac{\text{Estimated total manufacturing overhead cost at capacity}}{\text{Estimated total amount of the allocation base at capacity}}$$

$$= \frac{\$2,000,000}{100,000 \text{ units}} = \$20 \text{ per unit}$$

Budgeted Income Statement		
Revenue (80,000 units × $70 per unit).........................		$5,600,000
Cost of goods sold:		
Variable manufacturing (80,000 units × $18 per unit)	$1,440,000	
Manufacturing overhead applied		
(80,000 units × $20 per unit)	1,600,000	3,040,000
Gross margin...		2,560,000
Cost of unused capacity [(100,000 units − 80,000 units)		
× $20 per unit]...		400,000
Selling and administrative expenses.		1,950,000
Operating income		$ 210,000

Jan: Whoa!! I don't think I like the looks of that "Cost of unused capacity." If that thing shows up on the income statement, someone from headquarters is likely to come down here looking for some people to lay off.

Lonny: I'm worried about something else, too. What happens when sales are not up to expectations? Can we pull the "hat trick"?

Melissa: I'm sorry, I don't understand.

Jan: Lonny's talking about something that happens fairly regularly. When sales are down and profits look like they are going to be lower than the president told the owners they were going to be, the president comes down here and asks us to deliver some more profits.

Lonny: And we pull them out of our hat.

Jan: Yeah, we just increase production until we get the profits we want.

Melissa: I still don't understand. You mean you increase sales?

Jan: Nope, we increase production. We're the production managers, not the sales managers.

Melissa: I get it. Since you have produced more, the sales force has more units it can sell.

Jan: Nope, the marketing people don't do a thing. We just build inventories and that does the trick.

Required:

In all of the questions below, assume that the predetermined overhead rate under the traditional method is $25 per unit, and under the new method it is $20 per unit. Also assume that under the traditional method, any underapplied or overapplied overhead is taken directly to the income statement as an adjustment to Cost of Goods Sold.

1. Suppose actual production is 80,000 units. Compute the operating incomes that would be realized under the traditional and new methods if actual sales are 75,000 units and everything else turns out as expected.

2. How many units would have to be produced under each of the methods in order to realize the budgeted operating income of $210,000 if actual sales are 75,000 units and everything else turns out as expected?

3. What effect does the new method based on capacity have on the volatility of operating income?

4. Will the "hat trick" be easier or harder to perform if the new method based on capacity is used?

5. Do you think the "hat trick" is ethical?

SYSTEMS DESIGN: PROCESS COSTING

■ COSTING GIRL GUIDE COOKIES

Dare Foods Limited is a 115-year-old family-owned business based in Kitchener, Ontario. It manufactures cookies, candies, and breads at seven plants in Ontario, Quebec, and South Carolina. Dare is probably best known for operating "peanut-free" facilities and as the exclusive supplier of Girl Guide cookies to the Girl Guides of Canada.

It would be difficult for Dare to use job-order costing to determine the cost to produce boxes of cookies, since raw ingredients are constantly being mixed and finished products are always coming off the end of the baking lines. Since all boxes of cookies of the same flavour are alike, it would be easier to calculate the total costs incurred to produce each type of cookie each reporting period and divide that by the number of boxes produced. This method, called *process costing*, spreads the total production cost uniformly across all boxes of cookies produced. Dare can apply this methodology to determine the cost of boxes of candy, loaves of bread, or any other relatively homogeneous product that is produced in large, continuous batches.

Source: Dare Foods Limited Web site: www.darefoods.com, and Girl Guides of Canada "Cookie FAQ": www.girlguides.ca/cookie_faq.

Learning Objectives

After studying Chapter 4, you should be able to

1. Record the flow of materials, labour, and overhead through a process costing system.

2. Compute the equivalent units of production using the weighted-average method.

3. Compute the cost per equivalent unit using the weighted-average method.

4. Assign cost to units using the weighted-average method.

5. Prepare a cost reconciliation report accounting for the costs transferred out and the costs in work in process inventory at the end of the period using the weighted-average method.

6. (Appendix 4A) Compute the equivalent units of production using the FIFO method.

7. (Appendix 4A) Compute the cost per equivalent unit using the FIFO method.

8. (Appendix 4A) Prepare a cost reconciliation report accounting for the costs transferred out and the costs in work in process inventory at the end of the period using the FIFO method.

9. (Appendix 4B) Allocate service department costs to operating department costs using the direct method.

10. (Appendix 4B) Allocate service department costs to operating department costs using the step-down method.

11. (Appendix 4B) Identify the differences between the reciprocal allocation method and the direct and step-down methods.

12. (Online Appendix 4C) Compute the cost of lost units or shrinkage.

A s explained in Chapter 3, there are two basic costing systems in use: job-order costing and process costing. A job-order costing system is used in situations where many different jobs or products are worked on each period. Examples of industries that would typically use job-order costing include furniture manufacturers, special-order printers, shipbuilders, and many types of service organizations, such as repair shops and professional accounting services.

By contrast, process costing is most commonly used in industries that produce essentially homogeneous (i.e., uniform) products on a continuous basis, such as bricks, corn flakes, pop, or paper. Process costing is particularly used in companies that convert basic raw materials into homogeneous products, such as Alcan (aluminum ingots), Kimberly-Clark (toilet paper), Dover Industries (flour), Imperial Oil (gasoline and lubricating oils), and Christie (crackers). In addition, process costing is often employed in companies that use an assembly operation, such as Panasonic (video monitors), Hewlett-Packard (personal computers), General Electric (refrigerators), Toyota (automobiles), Maytag (washing machines), and Sony (DVD players). A form of process costing may also be used by utilities that produce gas, water, and electricity. As suggested by the length of this list, process costing is in very wide use.

Our purpose in this chapter is to extend the discussion of product costing to include a process costing system.

■ COMPARISON OF JOB-ORDER AND PROCESS COSTING

Much of what was learned in the preceding chapter about costing and cost flows applies equally well to process costing in this chapter. We are not throwing out all that we have learned about costing and starting from scratch with a whole new system. The similarities that exist between job-order and process costing can be summarized as follows:

1. Both systems have the same basic purposes—to assign materials, labour, and overhead costs to products and to provide a mechanism for computing unit costs.
2. Both systems use the same basic manufacturing accounts, including Manufacturing Overhead, Raw Materials, Work in Process, and Finished Goods.
3. The flow of costs through the manufacturing accounts is basically the same in both systems.

The differences between job-order and process costing arise from two factors. The first is that the flow of units in a process costing system is more or less continuous, and the second is that these units are indistinguishable from one another. Under process costing, it makes no sense to try to identify materials, labour, and overhead costs with a particular order from a customer (as we did with job-order costing), since each order is just one of many that are filled from a continuous flow of virtually identical units from the production line. Under process costing, we accumulate costs *by department,* rather than by order, and assign these costs equally to all units that pass through the department during a period.

A further difference between the two costing systems is that the job cost sheet is not used in process costing, since the focal point of that method is departments. Instead of using job cost sheets, a document known as a **production report** is prepared for each department in which work is done on products. The production report serves several functions: It provides a summary of the number of units moving through a department during a period, and it also provides a computation of unit costs. In addition, it shows what costs were charged to the department and what disposition was made of these costs. The department production report is the key document in a process costing system.

The major differences between job-order and process costing are summarized in Exhibit 4–1.

Production report
A report that summarizes all activity in a department's Work in Process account during a period and that contains three parts: a quantity schedule and a computation of equivalent units, a computation of total and unit costs, and a cost reconciliation.

EXHIBIT 4–1 Differences between Job-Order and Process Costing

Job-Order Costing	Process Costing
1. Many different jobs are worked on during each period, with each job having different production requirements.	1. A single product is produced either on a continuous basis or for long periods of time. All units of product are identical.
2. Costs are accumulated by individual job, regardless of the accounting period during which the work is done.	2. Costs are accumulated by department, during an accounting period.
3. The *job cost sheet* is the key document controlling the accumulation of costs by a job.	3. The *department production report* is the key document showing the accumulation and disposition of costs by a department.
4. Unit costs are computed *by job on* the job cost sheet.	4. Unit costs are computed *by department* on the department production report.

IN BUSINESS

In 2009, Coca-Cola Company sold more than $30 billion of products in over 200 countries. Some of the key processing steps in its bottling process include washing and rinsing bottles, mixing and blending ingredients, filling and capping bottles, and labelling and packaging bottles. Raw material costs are added at various stages during this process. For example, sugar, filtered water, carbon dioxide, and syrup are added during the filling and capping step, and labels are added during the labelling and packaging stage.

Coca-Cola's manufacturing process is well suited for process costing because it produces a continuous stream of identical bottles of soda. The material costs and conversion costs that are incurred at the various stages of the production process can be assigned to products by spreading them evenly over the total production volume.

Source: The Coca-Cola Company *2009 Annual Report* and www.thecoca-colacompany.com.

PROCESS COST FLOWS

Before presenting a detailed example of process costing, it will be helpful to see how manufacturing costs flow through a process costing system.

Processing Departments

Processing department
Any location in an organization where work is performed on a product and where materials, labour, or overhead costs are added to the product.

A **processing department** is part of an organization where work is performed on a product and where materials, labour, or overhead costs are added to the product. For example, a potato chip factory operated by Frito-Lay might have three processing departments—one for preparing potatoes, one for cooking, and one for inspecting and packaging. A brick factory might have two processing departments—one for mixing and moulding clay into brick form and one for firing the moulded brick. A company can have as many or as few processing departments as are needed to complete a product or service. Some products and services may go through several processing departments, while others may go through only one or two. Regardless of the number of departments involved, all processing departments have two essential features: First, the activity performed in the processing department must be performed uniformly on all of the units passing through it. Second, the output of the processing department must be identical.

Products in a process costing environment, such as bricks or potato chips, typically flow in a sequence from one department to another, as shown in Exhibit 4–2.

EXHIBIT 4–2 Sequential Processing Departments

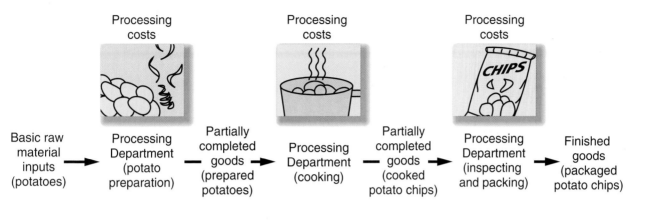

The Flow of Materials, Labour, and Overhead Costs

Cost accumulation is simpler in a process costing system than in a job-order costing system. In a process costing system, instead of having to trace costs to hundreds of different jobs, costs are traced to only a few processing departments. In a process costing system, production costs are not identified with specific units or batches of product. Instead, an average unit cost is computed by dividing total production costs for the period by the number of units produced during the same period. This is discussed in more detail later in this chapter.

A T-account model of materials, labour, and overhead cost flows in a process costing system is given in Exhibit 4–3. Several key points should be noted from this exhibit. First, note that a separate Work in Process account is maintained for *each processing department.* In contrast, in a job-order costing system there may be only a single Work in Process account for the entire company. Second, note that the completed production of the first processing department (Department A in the exhibit) is transferred into the Work in Process account of the second processing department (Department B), where it undergoes further work. After this further work, the completed units are then transferred into Finished Goods. (In Exhibit 4–3, we show only two processing departments, but a company may have many processing departments.)

Finally, note that materials, labour, and overhead costs can be added in *any* processing department—not just the first. Costs in Department B's Work in Process account would consist of the materials, labour, and overhead costs incurred in Department B plus the costs attached to partially completed units transferred in from Department A (called **transferred-in costs**).

IN BUSINESS

AbitibiBowater produces newsprint, commercial printing papers, and pulp and wood products. AbitibiBowater owns or operates 23 pulp and paper facilities and 30 wood products facilities located in Canada, the United States, the United Kingdom, and South Korea. In 2009, the company installed an $84-million biomass boiler at the Fort Frances, Ontario, mill. This boiler produces 46 megawatts of carbon-neutral energy from biomass such as bark, a by-product of the paper production process. Going forward, this new green energy source will enable the facility to reduce direct greenhouse gas emissions by more than 300,000 metric tonnes of CO_2 equivalents per year—down 90% from previous levels when the mill relied on natural gas. In addition, the plant will significantly reduce conversion costs when converting wood pulp to paper since the new boiler, fired by waste from the production process, will generate enough energy to supply the equivalent of 30,000 homes.

Source: *AbitibiBowater Sustainability Report* and www.abitibibowater.com.

LEARNING OBJECTIVE 1
Record the flow of materials, labour, and overhead through a process costing system.

Transferred-in cost
The cost attached to products that have been received from a prior processing department.

EXHIBIT 4-3   T-Account Model of Process Costing Flows

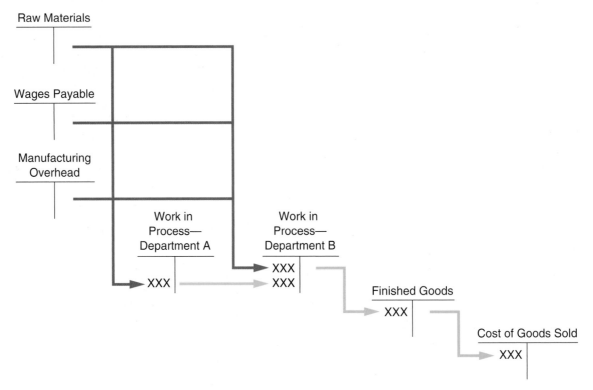

Materials, Labour, and Overhead Cost Entries

To complete our discussion of cost flows in a process costing system, in this section we show journal entries relating to materials, labour, and overhead costs at Standard Products Co., a producer of Green Clean, a multi-purpose household cleaner. The company has two processing departments—Mixing and Filling. In the Mixing Department, the various ingredients are checked for quality and then mixed to create bulk liquid cleaner. In the Filling Department, bottles are checked for defects, filled with cleaner, capped, and labelled, and then the bottles are packed for shipping.

Materials Costs   As in job-order costing, materials are drawn from the storeroom using a materials requisition form. Materials can be added in any processing department, although it is not unusual for materials to be added only in the first processing department, with subsequent departments adding only labour and overhead costs as the partially completed units move along toward completion.

At Standard Products Co., some materials (water, cleaning agents, and fragrances) are added in the Mixing Department, and other materials (bottles, caps, labels, and packing materials) are added in the Filling Department. The journal entry for placing materials into process in the first department is as follows:

Work in Process—Mixing.	XXX	
Raw Materials		XXX

The journal entry to record the material used in the second processing department, the Filling Department, is as follows:

Work in Process—Filling	XXX	
Raw Materials		XXX

Labour Costs   In process costing, labour costs are traced to departments, not to individual jobs. The following entry records the labour costs in the Mixing Department at Standard Products Co.:

Work in Process—Mixing.	XXX	
Salaries and Wages Payable.		XXX

Overhead Costs   If production is stable from period to period and if overhead costs are incurred uniformly over the year, actual overhead costs can be charged to departments. However, if production levels fluctuate or if overhead costs are not incurred uniformly, charging products with actual overhead costs will result in unit product costs that vary randomly from one period to the next. In such a situation, predetermined overhead rates should be used to charge overhead cost to products, the same as in job-order costing. When predetermined overhead rates are used, each department has its own separate rate, with the rates being computed as discussed in Chapter 3. Overhead cost is then applied to units of product as the units move through the various departments. Since predetermined overhead rates are widely used in process costing, we will assume their use throughout the remainder of this chapter.

The following journal entry is used to apply overhead costs to units of product for the Mixing Department:

Work in Process—Mixing.	XXX	
Manufacturing Overhead		XXX

Completing the Cost Flows   Once processing has been completed in a department, the product units are transferred to the next department for further processing, as illustrated earlier in the T-accounts in Exhibit 4–3. The following journal entry is used to transfer the costs of partially completed units from the Mixing Department to the Filling Department:

Work in Process—Filling	XXX	
Work in Process—Mixing		XXX

After processing has been completed in the final department, the costs of the completed units are then transferred to the Finished Goods inventory account:

Finished Goods	XXX	
Work in Process—Filling.		XXX

Finally, when a customer's order is filled and units are sold, the cost of the units is transferred to Cost of Goods Sold:

Cost of Goods Sold	XXX	
Finished Goods.		XXX

To summarize, the cost flows between accounts are basically the same in a process costing system as they are in a job-order costing system. The only noticeable difference at this point is that a process costing system has a separate Work in Process account for each department.

We now turn our attention to Double Diamond Skis, a company that manufactures a high-performance deep-powder ski, and that uses process costing to determine its unit product costs. The company's production process is illustrated in Exhibit 4–4. Skis go through a sequence of five processing departments, starting with the Shaping and Milling Department and ending with the Finishing and Pairing Department. The basic idea in process costing is to add together all of the costs incurred in a department during a period and then spread those costs uniformly across the units processed in that department during that period. As we will see, applying this simple idea involves a few complications.

EXHIBIT 4-4   The Production Process at Double Diamond Skis*

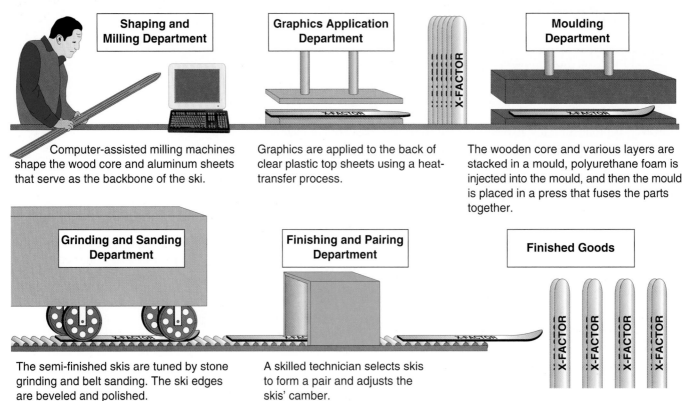

| Shaping and Milling Department | Graphics Application Department | Moulding Department |

Computer-assisted milling machines shape the wood core and aluminum sheets that serve as the backbone of the ski.

Graphics are applied to the back of clear plastic top sheets using a heat-transfer process.

The wooden core and various layers are stacked in a mould, polyurethane foam is injected into the mould, and then the mould is placed in a press that fuses the parts together.

| Grinding and Sanding Department | Finishing and Pairing Department | Finished Goods |

The semi-finished skis are tuned by stone grinding and belt sanding. The ski edges are beveled and polished.

A skilled technician selects skis to form a pair and adjusts the skis' camber.

*Adapted from Bill Gout, Jesse James Duquilo, and Studio MD, "Capped Crusaders," *Skiing*, October 1993, pp. 138–144. Go to www.dynastar.com and click on "Corporate" and then on "Factory Tour" for a close look at the ski production process.

EQUIVALENT UNITS OF PRODUCTION

> **LEARNING OBJECTIVE 2**
> Compute the equivalent units of production using the weighted-average method.

After materials, labour, and overhead costs have been accumulated in a department, the department's output must be determined so that unit costs can be computed. In the simplest case, average unit cost can be computed by dividing total manufacturing costs by the number of units produced during a given time period. The difficulty is that a department usually has some partially completed units in its ending inventory. It does not seem reasonable to count these partially completed units as equivalent to fully completed units when counting the department's output. Therefore, Double Diamond Skis will mathematically convert those partially completed units into an *equivalent* number of fully completed units. In process costing, this is done using the following formula:

Equivalent units = Number of partially completed units × Percentage completion

Equivalent units
The product of the number of partially completed units and their percentage of completion with respect to a particular cost. Equivalent units are the number of complete whole units one could obtain from the materials and effort contained in partially completed units.

As the formula states, **equivalent units** are defined as the product of the number of partially completed units and the percentage completion of those units. Equivalent units are the number of complete units that could have been obtained from the materials and effort that went into the partially complete units.

For example, suppose the Moulding Department at Double Diamond has 500 units in its ending work in process inventory that are 60% complete. These 500 partially complete units are equivalent to 300 fully complete units (500 × 60% = 300). Therefore, the ending work in process inventory would be said to contain 300 equivalent units. These equivalent units would be added to any fully completed units to determine the period's output for the department—called the *equivalent units of production*.

Equivalent units of production for a period can be computed in two different ways. In this chapter, we discuss the *weighted-average method*. In Appendix 4A, the *FIFO ("first in, first out) method* is discussed. The **FIFO method** of process costing is a method in which equivalent units and unit costs relate only to work done during the current period. In contrast, the **weighted-average method** blends together units and costs from the current period with units and costs from the prior period. In the weighted-average method, the **equivalent units of production** for a department are the number of units transferred to the next department (or to finished goods) plus the equivalent units in the department's ending work in process inventory.

Weighted-Average Method

Under the weighted-average method, a department's equivalent units are computed as follows:

Weighted-Average Method
(a separate calculation is made for each cost category in
each processing department)

$$\text{Equivalent units of production} = \text{Units transferred to the next department or to finished goods} + \text{Equivalent units in ending work in process inventory}$$

Note that computation of the equivalent units of production involves adding the number of units transferred out of the department to the equivalent units in the department's ending inventory. There is no need to compute the equivalent units for the units transferred out of the department—they are 100% complete with respect to the work done in that department or they would not be transferred out. In other words, each unit transferred out of the department is counted as one equivalent unit.

Consider the Shaping and Milling Department at Double Diamond. This department uses computerized milling machines to precisely shape the wooden core and metal sheets that will be used to form the backbone of the ski (see Exhibit 4–4 for an overview of the production process at Double Diamond). The following activity took place in the department in May, several months into the production of the new model of The Ultimate ski:

		Percentage Completed	
	Units	Materials	Conversion
Work in process, May 1	200	55%	30%
Units started into production during May	5,000		
Units completed during May and transferred to the next department	4,800	100%*	100%*
Work in process, May 31	400	40%	25%

*It is always assumed that units transferred out of a department are 100% complete with respect to the processing done in that department.

Note the use of the term *conversion* in the above table. Conversion cost, as defined in Chapter 2, is direct labour cost plus manufacturing overhead cost. In process costing, conversion cost is often—but not always—treated as a single element of product cost.

Note that the May 1 beginning work in process was 55% complete with respect to materials costs and 30% complete with respect to conversion costs. This means that 55% of the materials costs required to complete the units had already been incurred. Likewise, 30% of the conversion costs required to complete the units had already been incurred.

Two equivalent unit figures must be computed—one for materials and one for conversion. These computations are shown in Exhibit 4–5.

Note that the computations in Exhibit 4–5 ignore the fact that the units in the beginning work in process inventory were partially complete. For example, the 200 units in beginning inventory were already 30% complete with respect to conversion costs. The 4,800 units transferred to the next department consist of 200 units in the beginning

FIFO method
A method of accounting for cost flows in a process costing system in which equivalent units and unit costs relate only to work done during the current period.

Weighted-average method
A method of process costing that blends together units and costs from both the current and prior periods.

Equivalent units of production (weighted-average method)
The units transferred to the next department (or to finished goods) during the period plus the equivalent units in the department's ending work in process inventory.

EXHIBIT 4–5   Equivalent Units of Production: Weighted-Average Method

	Materials	Conversion
Units transferred to the next department.................	4,800	4,800
Work in process, May 31:		
400 units × 40% complete with respect to materials	160	
400 units × 25% complete with respect to conversion		100
Equivalent units of production	4,960	4,900

inventory plus 4,600 units started and completed during the current period. The weighted-average method is concerned only with the equivalent units that are in the ending inventories and in units transferred to the next department: It is not concerned with the fact that the beginning inventory was already partially complete. In other words, the equivalent units computed using the weighted-average method includes work that was accomplished in prior periods.

The weighted-average method blends together the work that was accomplished in prior periods with the work that was accomplished in the current period. In the FIFO method, the units and costs of prior periods are cleanly separated from the units and costs of the current period. Some managers believe the FIFO method is more accurate for this reason. However, the FIFO method is more complex than the weighted-average method and for that reason is covered in Appendix 4A.

Averages, in general, hide the details of the elements that make up the average. For example, the average of 2 + 4 is 3. The average of 1 + 5 is 3. If the manager is not interested in the details of the elements, then the average provides all of the information needed. If costs from one period to the next are approximately equal (for example, 3 + 3) the average is also a reasonable representation of the results. A third explanation for the use of the average approach is the relative size of the beginning inventory of work in process compared to the current production. For example, if the beginning inventory is only one-tenth of the current production, the average (weighted) of $\frac{1}{10}$ (1) + $\frac{9}{10}$ (5) = 4.60 is very accurate and very close to a FIFO result. In addition to the advantage of ease of computation, another advantage of the weighted-average method is that it generates very accurate results when costs are relatively stable from one period to the next or when the size of current production dominates the beginning inventory. All of these factors are commonly a characteristic of process cost environments!

Exhibit 4–6 provides an alternative way of looking at the computation of equivalent units of production. Study this exhibit carefully before going on.

EXHIBIT 4–6   Visual Perspective of Equivalent Units of Production

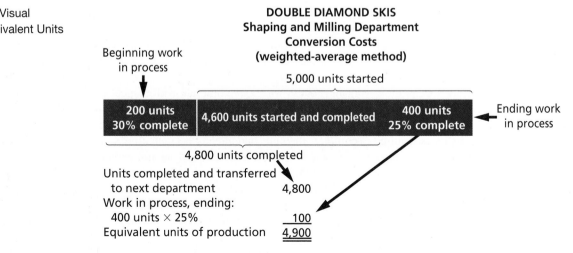

COMPUTE AND APPLY COSTS

In the last section we computed the equivalent units of production for materials and for conversion at Double Diamond Skis. In this section, we will compute the cost per equivalent unit for materials and for conversion. We will then use these costs to value ending work in process and finished goods inventories. Exhibit 4–7 displays all of the data concerning May's operations in the Shaping and Milling Department that we will need to complete these tasks.

LEARNING OBJECTIVE 3
Compute the cost per equivalent unit using the weighted-average method.

EXHIBIT 4–7   Shaping and Milling Department Data for May Operations

Work in process, beginning:	
Units in process	200
Stage of completion with respect to materials	55%
Stage of completion with respect to conversion.	30%
Costs in the beginning inventory:	
Materials cost	$ 9,600
Conversion cost	5,575
Total cost in the beginning inventory	$ 15,175
Units started into production during the period	5,000
Units completed and transferred out	4,800
Costs added to production during the period:	
Materials cost	$368,600
Conversion cost	350,900
Total cost added in the department	$719,500
Work in process, ending:	
Units in process	400
Stage of completion with respect to materials	40%
Stage of completion with respect to conversion.	25%

Cost per Equivalent Unit—Weighted-Average Method

In the weighted-average method, the cost per equivalent unit is computed as follows:

Weighted-Average Method
(a separate calculation is made for each cost category in each processing department)

$$\text{Cost per equivalent unit} = \frac{\text{Cost of beginning work in process inventory} + \text{Cost added during the period}}{\text{Equivalent units of production}}$$

Note that the numerator is the sum of the cost of beginning work in process inventory and of the cost added during the period. Thus, the weighted-average method blends together costs from the prior and current periods. That is why it is called the weighted-average method: It averages together units and costs from both the prior and current periods.

The costs per equivalent unit for materials and for conversion are computed below for the Shaping and Milling Department for May:

Shaping and Milling Department Costs per Equivalent Unit		
	Materials	**Conversion**
Cost of beginning work in process inventory	$ 9,600	$ 5,575
Costs added during the period	368,600	350,900
Total cost (a)	$378,200	$356,475
Equivalent units of production (see the computations in Exhibit 4–5) (b)	4,960	4,900
Cost per equivalent unit (a) ÷ (b)	$76.25	$72.75

equivalent unit summarizes the production costs for the month of May plus the beginning work in process for May. These costs are used together with the equivalent units from the quantity schedule to compute the weighted unit costs. Finally, the production report is completed by computing the cost reconciliation. The sum of the input costs, work in process May 1 and the May production costs are tested with the cost of units transferred to the next department and the work in process costs at May 31.

It is worth noting at this point the relationship of the costs reflected in the production report to the schedules of cost of goods manufactured presented in Chapters 2 and 3 and the work in process general ledger account. Exhibit 3–11 will help to picture the relationships.

Exhibit 4–9 provides an example calculation of the cost of goods manufactured for Double Diamond Skis. The cost of the beginning work in process inventory, $15,175, is the beginning general ledger balance for work in process. The total manufacturing costs of $719,500 represent the cost of raw material used, the cost of direct labour used, and the manufacturing overhead applied during May. These three types of costs, $719,500, increase the work in process account for May. The cost of goods manufactured is $715,200, which represents what is transferred out of work in process for May, leaving the ending work in process balance in the general ledger of $19,475. A careful tracing of the description of these costs to the schedule of costs of goods manufactured as shown in Exhibit 3–11 will assist in visualizing how the costs from the production report for process costs link to the general ledger.

EXHIBIT 4–9   Schedule of Cost of Goods Manufactured

DOUBLE DIAMOND SKIS Schedule of Cost of Goods Manufactured	
Cost of goods manufactured:	
Total manufacturing costs..	$719,500
Add: Beginning work in process inventory	15,175
	734,675
Deduct: Ending work in process inventory	19,475
Cost of goods manufactured..	$715,200

OPERATION COSTING

The costing systems discussed in Chapter 3 and in this chapter represent the two ends of a continuum. On one end, we have job-order costing, which is used by companies that produce many different items—generally to customers' specifications. On the other end, we have process costing, which is used by companies that produce basically homogeneous products in large quantities. Between these two extremes, there are many hybrid systems that include characteristics of both job-order and process costing. One of these hybrids is called *operation costing*.

Operation costing
A hybrid costing system used when products are manufactured in batches and when the products have some common characteristics and some individual characteristics. This system handles materials the same as in job-order costing, and labour and overhead the same as in process costing.

Operation costing is used in situations where products have some common characteristics and also some individual characteristics. Shoes, for example, have common characteristics in that all styles involve cutting and sewing that can be done on a repetitive basis, using the same equipment and following the same basic procedures. Shoes also have individual characteristics—some are made of expensive leathers and others may be made using inexpensive synthetic materials. In a situation such as this, where products have some common characteristics but also must be handled individually, operation costing may be used to determine product costs.

As mentioned above, operation costing is a hybrid system that employs aspects of both job-order and process costing. Products are typically handled in batches when operation costing is in use, with each batch charged for its own specific materials. In this sense, operation costing is similar to job-order costing. However, labour and overhead costs are accumulated by operation or by department, and these costs are assigned to units as in process costing. If shoes are being produced, for example, each shoe is charged the same per unit conversion cost, regardless of the style involved, but it is charged with its specific materials cost. Thus, the company is able to distinguish between styles in terms of materials, but it is able to employ the simplicity of a process costing system for labour and overhead costs.

Examples of other products for which operation costing may be used include electronic equipment (such as semiconductors), textiles, clothing, and jewellery (such as rings, bracelets, and medallions). Products of this type are typically produced in batches, but they can vary considerably from model to model or from style to style in terms of the cost of raw material inputs. Therefore, an operation costing system is well suited for providing cost data.

FLEXIBLE MANUFACTURING SYSTEMS

A plant that uses a flexible manufacturing system (FMS) is heavily automated and its activities are organized around cells, or islands, of automated equipment. The FMS concept is having a major impact on costing in several ways. One of these is through allowing companies to switch their systems from the more costly job-order approach to a less costly process or operation approach. This switching is made possible because FMS is proving to be highly efficient in reducing the setup time required between products and jobs. With setup time only a small fraction of previous levels, companies are able to move between products and jobs with about the same speed as if they were working in a continuous, process-type environment. The result is that these companies are able to employ process costing techniques in situations that previously required job-order costing. As the use of FMS grows (and becomes even more efficient), some managers predict that job-order costing will slowly disappear except in a few selected industries.

A further impact of FMS is through its focus on cells rather than on departments. Although production reports are still prepared in FMS settings, these reports are either much broader to include the entire production process (many cells) or much narrower to include only a single cell or workstation. If JIT is practised, then the production report becomes greatly simplified, regardless of the level at which it is prepared.

Summary

- Process costing is used in situations where homogeneous products or services are produced on a continuous basis. Costs flow through the manufacturing accounts in basically the same way in a process costing system as in a job-order costing system. However, costs are accumulated by department rather than by job in process costing. **[LO1]**
- In process costing, the equivalent units of production must be determined for each cost category in each department. Under the weighted-average method, the equivalent units of production equals the number of units transferred out to the next department or to finished goods plus the equivalent units in ending work in process inventory. The equivalent units in ending inventory equal the product of the number of partially completed units in ending work in process inventory and their percentage of completion with respect to the specific cost category. **[LO2]**
- Under the weighted-average method, the cost per equivalent unit for a specific cost category is computed by adding the cost of beginning work in process inventory and the cost added during the period and then dividing the result by the equivalent units of production (i.e., calculating the average). **[LO3]**
- The cost per equivalent unit is then used to value the ending work in process inventory and the units transferred out to the next department or to finished goods. **[LO4]**
- Costs are transferred from one department to the next until the last processing department. At that point, the cost of completed units is transferred to finished goods. At the end of the period, a cost reconciliation is prepared to account for the costs transferred out and costs in work in process inventory at the end of the period. **[LO5]**

Review Problem 1: Process Cost Flows and Reports

Lanyard Home Paint Company produces exterior latex paint, which it sells in four-litre containers. The company has two processing departments—Base Fab and Finishing. White paint, which is used as a base for all of the company's paints, is mixed from raw ingredients in the Base Fab Department. Pigments are added to the basic white paint, the pigmented paint is squirted under pressure into four-litre containers, and the containers are labelled and packed for shipping in the Finishing Department. Information relating to the company's operations for April is as follows:

a.   Raw materials were issued for use in production: Base Fab Department, $851,000, and Finishing Department, $629,000.

b.   Direct labour costs were incurred: Base Fab Department, $330,000, and Finishing Department, $270,000.

c.   Manufacturing overhead cost was applied: Base Fab Department, $665,000, and Finishing Department, $405,000.

d.   Basic white paint was transferred from the Base Fab Department to the Finishing Department, $1,850,000.

e.   Paint that had been prepared for shipping was transferred from the Finishing Department to Finished Goods, $3,200,000.

Required:

1.   Prepare journal entries to record items (a) through (e) above.

2.   Post the journal entries from (1) above to T-accounts. The balance in the Base Fab Department's Work in Process account on April 1 was $150,000; the balance in the Finishing Department's Work in Process account was $70,000. After posting entries to the T-accounts, find the ending balance in each department's Work in Process account.

3.   Prepare a production report for the Base Fab Department for April. The following additional information is available regarding production in the Base Fab Department during April:

Production data for four-litre containers of paint:
Units (containers) in process, April 1: 100% complete as to materials, 60% complete as to labour and overhead	30,000
Units (containers) started into production during April.	420,000
Units (containers) completed and transferred to the Finishing Department.	370,000
Units (containers) in process, April 30: 50% complete as to materials, 25% complete as to labour and overhead	80,000

Cost data:
Work in process inventory, April 1:	
Materials	$ 92,000
Labour.	21,000
Overhead.	37,000
Total cost.	$150,000

Cost added during April:
Materials.	$851,000
Labour.	330,000
Overhead	665,000

Solution to Review Problem 1

1.	a.	Work in Process—Base Fab Department.	851,000	
		Work in Process—Finishing Department	629,000	
		Raw Materials		1,480,000
	b.	Work in Process—Base Fab Department.	330,000	
		Work in Process—Finishing Department	270,000	
		Salaries and Wages Payable.		600,000
	c.	Work in Process—Base Fab Department.	665,000	
		Work in Process—Finishing Department	405,000	
		Manufacturing Overhead.		1,070,000
	d.	Work in Process—Finishing Department	1,850,000	
		Work in Process—Base Fab Department		1,850,000
	e.	Finished Goods.	3,200,000	
		Work in Process—Finishing Department.		3,200,000

2.

Raw Materials			
Bal.	XXX	(a)	1,480,000

Salaries and Wages Payable			
		(b)	600,000

Work in Process— Base Fab Department			
Bal.	150,000	(d)	1,850,000
(a)	851,000		
(b)	330,000		
(c)	665,000		
Bal.	146,000		

Manufacturing Overhead			
(Various actual costs)		(c)	1,070,000

Work in Process— Finishing Department			
Bal.	70,000	(e)	3,200,000
(a)	629,000		
(b)	270,000		
(c)	405,000		
(d)	1,850,000		
Bal.	24,000		

Finished Goods			
Bal.	XXX		
(e)	3,200,000		

LANYARD HOME PAINT COMPANY
Production Report—Base Fab Department
For the Month Ended April 30

Quantity Schedule and Equivalent Units

Quantity Schedule

Units (four-litre containers) to be accounted for:
- Work in process, April 1 (all materials, 60% labour and overhead added last month)   30,000
- Started into production   420,000
-      Total units   450,000

	Equivalent Units (EU)		
	Materials	**Labour**	**Overhead**
Units (four-litre containers) accounted for as follows:			
Transferred to Finishing Department 370,000	370,000	370,000	370,000
Work in process, April 30 (materials 50% complete; labour and overhead 25% complete) 80,000	40,000*	20,000*	20,000*
Total units and equivalent units of production 450,000	410,000	390,000	390,000

*Materials: 80,000 units × 50% = 40,000 equivalent units; labour and overhead: 80,000 units × 25% = 20,000 equivalent units.

Costs per Equivalent Unit (EU)

	Total Cost	Materials	Labour	Overhead	Whole Unit
Cost to be accounted for:					
Work in process, April 1	$ 150,000	$ 92,000	$ 21,000	$ 37,000	
Cost added by the Base Fab Department	1,846,000	851,000	330,000	665,000	
Total cost (a)	$1,996,000	$943,000	$351,000	$702,000	
Equivalent units of production (b).	—	410,000	390,000	390,000	
Cost per EU, (a) ÷ (b)	—	$2.30 +	$0.90 +	$1.80 =	$5.00

Cost Reconciliation

	Total Cost	Materials	Labour	Overhead
Cost accounted for as follows:				
Transferred to				
Finishing Department:				
370,000 units × $5.00 each . .	$1,850,000	370,000	370,000	370,000
Work in process, April 30:				
Materials, at $2.30 per EU. . . .	92,000	40,000		
Labour, at $0.90 per EU.	18,000		20,000	
Overhead, at $1.80 per EU . . .	36,000			20,000
Total work in process	146,000			
Total cost.	$1,996,000			

Review Problem 2: Units and Cost Assignment

Power Company passes its product through several departments, the last of which is the finishing department. Conversion costs are added evenly throughout the process in this department. One-fourth of direct materials is added at the beginning of the process and the remaining three-fourths are added when the process is 50% complete with respect to conversion costs.

During June, 475,000 units of product were transferred to finished goods. Of these units, 100,000 units were 40% complete with respect to conversion costs at the beginning of the period and 375,000 were started and completed during the period. At the end of June, the work in process inventory comprised 225,000 units that were 30% complete with respect to conversion costs. Total costs to account for include $949,375 for conversion costs and $616,250 for direct materials.

Required:
1. Determine equivalent units of production with respect to conversion costs and with respect to direct materials for the finishing department.
2. Compute the conversion cost and the direct materials cost per equivalent unit.
3. Compute the amount of conversion cost and the amount of the direct materials cost assigned to the units completed and to the ending goods in process inventory.

Solution to Review Problem 2

1. Equivalent unit calculations:

		Equivalent Units (EU)	
		Materials	Conversion
Units accounted for as follows:			
Transferred to the next department.	475,000	475,000	475,000
Work in process, June 30:			
Material, 25% complete; conversion, 30% complete . .	225,000	56,250	67,500
Total units accounted for	700,000	531,250	542,500

2. Unit cost calculations:
Conversion cost per equivalent unit   = $949,375/542,500 units = $1.75
Direct materials cost per equivalent unit   = $616,250/531,250 units = $1.16

3. Allocation of materials and conversion cost to products:

	Equivalent Units	Per Unit Cost	Allocated Cost
Transferred out:			
Materials.	475,000	$1.16	$ 551,000
Conversion costs	475,000	1.75	831,250
			$1,382,250 (a)
Work in Process			
Materials (225,000 × 0.25).	56,250	$1.16	$ 65,250
Conversion (225,000 × 0.3)	67,500	1.75	118,125
			183,375 (b)
Total cost accounted for: (a) + (b)			$1,565,625

Review key terms and definitions on Connect.

4–1 Under what conditions would it be appropriate to use a process costing system?

4–2 In what ways are job-order and process costing different?

4–3 Why is cost accumulation easier in a process costing system than it is in a job-order costing system?

4–4 How many Work in Process accounts are maintained in a company that uses process costing?

4–5 Assume that a company has two processing departments—Mixing and Firing. Prepare a journal entry to show a transfer of partially completed units from the Mixing Department to the Firing Department.

4–6 Assume that a company has two processing departments—Mixing followed by Firing. Explain what costs might be added to the Firing Department's Work in Process account during a period.

4–7 What is meant by the term *equivalent units of production* when the weighted-average method is used?

4–8 Wellington Trophies, Inc., produces thousands of medallions made of bronze, silver, and gold. The medallions are identical except for the materials used in their manufacture. What costing system would you advise the company to use?

4–9 "The increasing use of flexible manufacturing systems will result in a reduction in the importance of process costing over time." Do you agree or disagree and why?

4–10 Suppose there are 5,000 full-time students and 1,250 part-time students (taking approximately half of the regular class load) in the faculty of Management at Westly University. Using the concept of equivalent units, how many "full-time equivalent" students are enrolled in the faculty of Management?

EXERCISE 4–1 Process Costing Journal Entries [LO1]
Arizona Brick Corporation produces bricks in two processing departments—Moulding and Firing. Information relating to the company's operations in March follows:

a. Raw materials were issued for use in production: Moulding Department, $28,000; Firing Department, $5,000.

b. Direct labour costs were incurred: Moulding Department, $18,000; Firing Department, $5,000.

c. Manufacturing overhead was applied: Moulding Department, $24,000; Firing Department, $37,000.

d. Unfired, moulded bricks were transferred from the Moulding Department to the Firing Department. According to the company's process costing system, the cost of the unfired, moulded bricks was $67,000.

e. Finished bricks were transferred from the Firing Department to the finished goods warehouse. According to the company's process costing system, the cost of the finished bricks was $108,000.

f. Finished bricks were sold to customers. According to the company's process costing system, the cost of the finished bricks sold was $106,000.

Required:
Prepare journal entries to record items (a) through (f) above.

EXERCISE 4–2 Computation of Equivalent Units—Weighted-Average Method [LO2]
Lindex Company manufactures a product that goes through three processing departments. Information relating to activity in the first department during October is given below:

		Percentage Completed	
	Units	Materials	Conversion
Work in process, October 1	25,000	90%	60%
Work in process, October 31 . . .	15,000	70%	50%

The department started 195,000 units into production during the month and transferred 205,000 completed units to the next department.

Required:

Compute the equivalent units of production for the first department for October, assuming that the company uses the weighted-average method of accounting for units and costs.

EXERCISE 4–3 Cost per Equivalent Unit—Weighted-Average Method [LO3]

Ainsley Industries uses the weighted-average method in its process costing system. Data for the Assembly Department for May appear below:

	Materials	Labour	Overhead
Work in process, May 1	$14,550	$23,620	$118,100
Cost added during May	$88,350	$14,330	$71,650
Equivalent units of production	1,200	1,100	1,100

Required:

Compute the cost per equivalent unit for materials, for labour, for overhead, and in total.

EXERCISE 4–4 Applying Costs to Units—Weighted-Average Method [LO4]

Data concerning a recent period's activity in the Prep Department, the first processing department in a company that uses process costing, appear below:

	Materials	Conversion
Equivalent units of production in ending work in process.	300	100
Cost per equivalent unit.	$31.56	$9.32

A total of 1,300 units were completed and transferred to the next processing department during the period.

Required:

Compute the cost of the units transferred to the next department during the period and the cost of ending work in process inventory.

EXERCISE 4–5 Process Costing Journal Entries [LO1]

Faber Brot is a bread-baking company located in Aachen, Germany, near the Dutch border. The company uses a process costing system for its single product—a popular pumpernickel bread. Faber Brot has two processing departments—Mixing and Baking. The T-accounts below show the flow of costs through the two departments in April (all amounts are in euros: €):

Work in Process—Mixing

Balance 4/1	10,000	Transferred out	760,000
Direct materials	330,000		
Direct labour	260,000		
Overhead	190,000		

Work in Process—Baking

Balance 4/1	20,000	Transferred out	980,000
Transferred in	760,000		
Direct labour	120,000		
Overhead	90,000		

Required:

Prepare journal entries showing the flow of costs through the two processing departments during April.

EXERCISE 4–6 Equivalent Units and Cost per Equivalent Unit—Weighted-Average Method [LO2, LO3]

Lockery Corp. manufactures an antacid product that passes through two departments. Data for May for the first department follow:

	Litres	Materials	Labour	Overhead
Work in process, May 1	80,000	$68,600	$30,000	$48,000
Litres started in process.	760,000			
Litres transferred out	790,000			
Work in process, May 31	50,000			
Cost added during May		$907,200	$370,000	$592,000

The beginning work in process inventory was 80% complete with respect to materials and 75% complete with respect to labour and overhead. The ending work in process inventory was 60% complete with respect to materials and 20% complete with respect to labour and overhead.

Required:
Assume that the company uses the weighted-average method of accounting for units and costs.
1. Compute the equivalent units for May's activity for the first department.
2. Determine the costs per equivalent unit for May.

EXERCISE 4–7 Equivalent Units—Weighted-Average Method [LO2]
Gulf Fisheries, Inc., processes tuna for various distributors. Two departments are involved— Cleaning and Packing. Data relating to kilograms of tuna processed in the Cleaning Department during May are given below:

	Kilograms of Tuna	Percentage Completed*
Work in process, May 1	15,000	55%
Work in process, May 31	10,000	90%

*Labour and overhead only.

A total of 240,000 kilograms of tuna were started into processing during May. All materials are added at the beginning of processing in the Cleaning Department.

Required:
Compute the equivalent units for May for the Cleaning Department, assuming that the company uses the weighted-average method of accounting for units.

EXERCISE 4–8 Equivalent Units and Cost per Equivalent Unit—Weighted-Average Method [LO2, LO3, LO4, LO5]
Grand River Company produces a high-quality insulation material that passes through two production processes. Data for November for the first process follow:

	Units	Completion with Respect to Materials	Completion with Respect to Conversion
Work in process inventory, November 1	80,000	50%	25%
Work in process inventory, November 30	60,000	45%	20%
Materials cost in work in process inventory, June 1	$76,600		
Conversion cost in work in process inventory, June 1	$34,900		
Units started into production	300,000		
Units transferred to the next process.	320,000		
Materials cost added during June	$410,000		
Conversion cost added during June	$234,500		

Required:
1. Assume that the company uses the weighted-average method of accounting for units and costs. Determine the equivalent units for November for the first process.
2. Compute the costs per equivalent unit for November for the first process.
3. Determine the total cost of ending work in process inventory and the total cost of units transferred to the next process in November.

Required:
1. How many units were started and completed during May?
2. What were the equivalent units for May for materials and conversion costs?
3. What were the costs per equivalent unit for May? The following additional data are available concerning the department's costs:

	Materials	Conversion	Total
Work in process, May 1	£9,000	£4,400	£13,400
Costs added during May	£57,000	£30,800	£87,800

4. Verify the accountant's ending work in process inventory figure (£8,200) given in the report.
5. The new manager of the CPU Assembly Department was asked to estimate the incremental cost of processing an additional 1,000 units through the department. He took the unit cost for an equivalent whole unit that you computed in (3) above and multiplied this figure by 1,000. Will this method yield a valid estimate of incremental cost? Explain.

eXcel

PROBLEM 4–13 Analysis of Work in Process T-Account—Weighted-Average Method [LO1, LO2, LO3, LO4, LO5]
Brady Products manufactures a silicone paste wax that goes through three processing departments—Cracking, Blending, and Packing. All of the raw materials are introduced at the start of work in the Cracking Department. The Work in Process T-account for the Cracking Department for May follows:

Work in Process—Cracking Department

Inventory, May 1 (35,000 kilograms,		Completed and transferred to	
conversion 4/5 complete)	63,700	Blending (____?____ kilograms)	____?____
May costs added:			
Raw materials (280,000 kilograms)	397,600		
Conversion costs	189,700		
Inventory, May 31 (45,000 kilograms,			
conversion 2/3 complete)	?		

The May 1 work in process inventory consists of $43,400 in materials cost and $20,300 in conversion cost. The company uses the weighted-average method.

Required:
1. Determine the equivalent units of production for May.
2. Determine the costs per equivalent unit for May.
3. Determine the cost of the units completed and transferred to Blending during May and the cost of ending work in process inventory.
4. What criticism can be made of the unit costs that you have computed if they are used to evaluate how well costs have been controlled?

PROBLEM 4–14 Equivalent Units; Costing of Inventories; Journal Entries—Weighted-Average Method [LO1, LO2, LO3, LO4]
Zap Rap, Inc., is a manufacturer of audio CDs. The company's chief financial officer is trying to verify the accuracy of the December 31 work in process and finished goods inventories prior to closing the books for the year. He strongly suspects that the year-end dollar balances are incorrect, but he believes that all the other data are accurate. The year-end balances shown on Zap Rap's books are as follows:

	Units	Costs
Work in process, Dec. 31 (materials 100% complete; conversion 50% complete).	30,000	$95,000
Finished goods, Dec. 31.	50,000	$201,000

There were no finished goods inventories at the beginning of the year. The company uses the weighted-average method of process costing. There is only one processing department.

A review of the company's inventory and cost records has disclosed the following data:

		Costs	
	Units	Materials	Conversion
Work in process, Jan. 1 (materials 100% complete; conversion 80% complete)	20,000	$22,000	$48,000
Started into production	800,000		
Costs added during the year		$880,000	$2,367,000
Units completed during the year	790,000		

Required:
1. Determine the equivalent units and the costs per equivalent unit for materials and conversion for the year.
2. Determine the amount of cost that should be assigned to the ending work in process and finished goods inventories.
3. Prepare the necessary correcting journal entry to adjust the work in process and finished goods inventories to the correct balances as of December 31.
4. Determine the cost of goods sold for the year, assuming that there is no underapplied or overapplied overhead.

(CPA, adapted)

PROBLEM 4–15 Comprehensive Process Costing Problem [LO1, LO2, LO3, LO4, LO5]
Fryer's Choice produces a specially blended vegetable oil widely used in restaurant deep fryers. The blending process creates a cooking oil that can be heated to a high temperature, but does not smoke or smell. The oil is produced in two departments: Blending and Bottling. Raw materials are introduced at various points in the Blending Department.

The following incomplete Work in Process T-account is available for the Blending Department for March:

Work in Process—Blending

March 1 balance (20,000 litres; materials 100% complete; labour and overhead 90% complete)	$38,000	Completed and transferred to Bottling (? litres)	$???
March costs added:			
Oils (390,000 litres)	495,000		
Direct labour	72,000		
Overhead	181,000		
March 31 inventory (40,000 litres; materials 75% complete, labour and overhead 25% complete)	$???		

The March 1 beginning inventory in the Blending Department consists of the following cost elements: raw materials, $25,000; direct labour, $4,000: and overhead, $9,000.

Costs incurred during March in the Bottling department were: materials used, $115,000; direct labour, $18,000; and overhead cost applied to production, $42,000. The company uses the weighted-average method in its process costing.

Required:
1. Prepare journal entries to record the cost incurred in both the Blending Department and the Bottling Department during March. Key your entries to the items (a) through (g) below:
   a. Raw materials were issued for use in production
   b. Direct labour costs were incurred.
   c. Manufacturing overhead costs for the entire factory were incurred, $225,000. (*Hint*: Credit Accounts Payable.)
   d. Manufacturing overhead cost was applied to production using a predetermined overhead rate.
   e. Units that were completed with respect to processing in the Blending Department were transferred to the Bottling Department, $740,000.

    f. Units that were complete with respect to processing in the Bottling Department were trans-
ferred to Finished Goods, $950,000.

    g. Completed units were sold on account, $1,500,000. The cost of goods sold was $890,000.

2. Post the journal entries from (1) above to T-accounts. The following account balances existed
at the beginning of March. (*Note*: The beginning balance in the Blending Department's Work
in Process account is given above).

Raw materials.....................................	$681,000
Work in Process—Bottling Department................	$65,000
Finished Goods	$20,000

After posting the entries to the T-accounts, find the ending balance in the inventory accounts
and the manufacturing overhead accounts.

3. Prepare a production report for the Blending Department for March.

Cases  connect

CASE 4–16 Ethics and the Manager; Understanding the Impact of Percentage Completion on
Profit [LO2, LO3, LO4]
Jason Bieler and Nancy Delirion are production managers in the Appliances Division of Meester
Corporation, which has several dozen plants scattered in locations throughout the world. Nancy
manages the plant located in Toronto, while Jason manages the plant in Vancouver. Production
managers are paid a salary and get an additional bonus equal to 10% of their base salary if the entire
division meets or exceeds its target profits for the year. The bonus is determined in March after the
company's annual report has been prepared and issued to shareholders.

Late in February, Nancy received a phone call from Jason that went like this:

Jason: How's it going, Nancy?
Nancy: Fine, Jason. How's it going with you?
Jason: Great! I just got the preliminary profit figures for the division for last year and we are within
$62,500 of making the year's target profits. All we have to do is to pull a few strings, and we'll
be over the top!
Nancy: What do you mean?
Jason: Well, one thing that would be easy to change is your estimate of the percentage completion
of your ending work in process inventories.
Nancy: I don't know if I should do that, Jason. Those percentage completion numbers are supplied by Marita Janovski, my lead supervisor. I have always trusted her to provide us with
good estimates. Besides, I have already sent the percentage completion figures to corporate
headquarters.
Jason: You can always tell them there was a mistake. Think about it, Nancy. All of us managers
are doing as much as we can to pull this bonus out of the hat. You may not want the bonus
cheque, but the rest of us sure could use it.

The final processing department in Nancy's production facility began the year with no work in
process inventories. During the year, 270,000 units were transferred in from the prior processing
department and 250,000 units were completed and sold. Costs transferred in from the prior department totalled $49,221,000. No materials are added in the final processing department. A total of
$16,320,000 of conversion cost was incurred in the final processing department during the year.

Required:
1. Marita Janovski estimated that the units in ending inventory in the final processing department were 25% complete with respect to the conversion costs of the final processing department. If this estimate of the percentage completion is used, what would be the cost of goods
sold for the year?
2. Does Jason Bieler want the estimated percentage completion to be increased or decreased?
Explain why.
3. What percentage completion figure would result in increasing the reported operating income
by $62,500 over the operating income that would be reported if the 25% figure was used?
4. Do you think Nancy Delirion should go along with the request to alter estimates of the percentage completion? Why or why not?

CASE 4–17 Effect of Incorrect Costing across Departments—Weighted-Average Method [LO2, LO3, LO4, LO5]

Tavia Limited manufactures a plastic gasket that is used in automobile engines. The gaskets go through three processing departments: Mixing, Forming, and Stamping. The company's accountant (who is very inexperienced) has prepared a summary of production and costs for the Forming Department for October, as follows:

Work in process inventory, October 1, 8,000 units; materials 100% complete; conversion $7/8$ complete	$ 22,420*
Costs transferred in from the Mixing Department	81,480
Material added during October (added when processing is 50% complete in the Forming Department)	27,600
Conversion costs added during October	96,900
Total departmental costs	$228,400

Forming Department costs assigned to:
  Units completed and transferred to the Stamping
    Department, 100,000 units at $2.284 each. . . . .
	$228,400

Work in process inventory, October 31, 5,000 units, conversion $2/5$ complete	—
Total departmental costs assigned	$228,400

*Consists of cost transferred in, $8,820; materials cost, $3,400; and conversion costs, $10,200.

After mulling over the data above, Tavia's president commented, "I can't understand what's happening here. Despite a concentrated effort at cost reduction, our unit cost actually went up in the Forming Department last month. With that kind of performance, year-end bonuses are out of the question for the people in that department."

The company uses the weighted-average method in its process costing.

Required:
1. Prepare a report for the Forming Department for October showing how much cost should have been assigned to the units completed and transferred to the Stamping Department and to the ending work in process inventory.
2. Explain to the president why the unit cost appearing on the report prepared by the accountant is so high.

CASE 4–18 Inventory Valuation under Process Costing—Weighted-Average Method [LO2, LO3, LO4. LO5]

Using an old family recipe, Rachel Archer started a company that produced root beer. Rachel opened the doors of Rachel's Real Root Beer on January 1. The company struggled for the first few months, but by the end of September, the customer list was expanding rapidly. Rachel realized that bottling by hand was becoming more and more difficult as the orders continued to come in. To purchase the automated equipment needed to expand further, Rachel realized it would be necessary to borrow money.

Rachel was disappointed to find that few banks were willing to make a loan to such a small company, but she finally found a bank that would consider her loan application. However, Rachel was informed that she would have to supply up-to-date financial statements with her loan application.

Rachel had not bothered with formal financial statements so far—she felt that as long as the balance in the company's chequebook kept increasing, the company was doing fine. She wondered how she was going to determine the value of the root beer in the work in process and finished goods inventories to put on her company's balance sheet.

Rachel approached Ed Switzer, an old friend currently working for a local accounting firm. After talking with Rachel and touring her production facility, Ed suggested a process costing system (using the weighted-average method) since Rachel's company produces only one standard product in a continuous production process. During the plant tour, Ed noted that Rachel ran the operation as one department. At the beginning of the process, the various ingredients were checked for quality and then mixed and injected with carbon dioxide to create bulk root beer. Then bottles were checked for defects, filled with root beer, capped, visually inspected again for defects, and then packed into cases (12 bottles per case) for shipping. At this point, completed cases were transferred to finished goods.

Rachel asked Ed to help her calculate the work in process and finished goods inventory cost to put on the company balance sheet at the end of August. To get started, John asked Rachel to collect several pieces of information. Details collected by Rachel are listed below:

a. Approximately 75% of raw materials cost is added at the beginning of the process and 25% is added when the product is 85% complete. Conversion costs are added evenly throughout the process.

b. Rachel estimated there were 550 units of product that were 75% complete for raw materials and 60% complete for conversion on August 1. From her bank records, she calculated that the raw materials cost added to the opening inventory was about $650 and conversion cost was about $430.

c. During August, 3,000 units of product were started into production and 2,400 of these were completed and transferred to finished goods. Costs added to production during August were $3,840 for materials and $3,480 for conversion.

d. At the end of August, the work in process inventory was made up of 1,150 units that were 75% complete for materials and 50% complete for conversion costs.

Using this information, Ed agreed to prepare a report indicating the cost of both work in process and finished goods inventory that Rachel would need to report on her balance sheet as at August 30.

Required:

Take on the role of Ed Switzer and prepare the report for Rachel. Be sure to provide all details, including a full production report, to help Rachel understand how costs were calculated.

Research and Application

R 4–19 Process Costing at BIC Group [LO1]

The questions in this exercise are based on BIC Group, a manufacturer of stationery and office supplies, cigarette lighters, and shavers. The BIC Group had approximately $1.5 billion in net sales worldwide in 2009. Although the company derives revenue from various sources, we are going to focus on one of the company's core manufacturing process—the production of ballpoint pens. To answer the questions, you will need to take an online tour of the company's ballpoint pen production process at www.bicworld.com. Click on "North America" and then "United States." Then click on "Our Products," then on "How It Is Manufactured," and then on "In the Making" to take the tour. Roll your mouse over each photo to view the production process. Click on the "View More Information" button to learn more about each stage of the production process.

Required:

1. List each of the processing departments in the ballpoint pen production process. For each department, identify any raw materials that are added to production in that department.
2. Would you expect BIC's production process to require fairly large amounts of manufacturing overhead costs? Why or why not?
3. Prepare a T-account model of the process costing flows for the BIC Group that is similar to the one shown in Exhibit 4–3. You need not take the diagram beyond the first two processes: Ball and Point Production and Moulding.
4. Why might BIC Group use a form of operation costing as described on page 140?

APPENDIX 4A: FIFO METHOD

The FIFO method of process costing differs from the weighted-average method in two ways: (1) the computation of equivalent units, and (2) the way in which costs of beginning inventory are treated. The FIFO method is generally considered to be more accurate than the weighted-average method, but it is more complex. The complexity is not a problem for computers, but the FIFO method is a little more difficult to understand and to learn than the weighted-average method.

Equivalent Units—FIFO Method

The computation of equivalent units under the FIFO (or "first in, first out") method differs in two ways from computation under the weighted-average method.

First, the "units transferred out" is divided into two parts. One part consists of the units from the beginning inventory that were completed and transferred out, and the other part consists of the units that were both *started* and *completed* during the current period.

Second, full consideration is given to the amount of work expended during the current period on units in the *beginning* work in process inventory as well as on units in the ending inventory. Thus, under the FIFO method, both beginning and ending inventories are converted to an equivalent units basis. For the beginning inventory, the equivalent units represent the work done to *complete* the units; for the ending inventory, the equivalent units represent the work done to bring the units to a stage of partial completion at the end of the period (the same as with the weighted-average method).

The formula for computing the equivalent units of production under the FIFO method is more complex than under the weighted-average method:

FIFO Method
(a separate calculation is made for each cost category
in each processing department)

Equivalent units of production = Equivalent units to complete beginning work in process inventory*

+ Units started and completed during the period

+ Equivalent units in ending work in process inventory

$$\text{*Equivalent units to complete beginning work in process inventory} = \text{Units in beginning work in process inventory} \times \left(100\% - \text{Percentage completion of beginning work in process inventory}\right)$$

Or, the equivalent units of production can also be determined as follows:

Equivalent units of production = Units transferred out

+ Equivalent units in ending work in process inventory

− Equivalent units in beginning work in process inventory

To illustrate the FIFO method, refer again to the data for the Shaping and Milling Department at Double Diamond Skis (see page 135). The department completed and transferred 4,800 units to the Graphics Application Department during May. Since 200 of these units came from the beginning inventory, the Shaping and Milling Department must have started and completed 4,600 units during May. The 200 units in the beginning inventory were 55% complete with respect to materials and only 30% complete with respect to conversion costs when the month started. Thus, to complete these units the department must have added another 45% of materials costs (100% − 55% = 45%) and another 70% of conversion costs (100% − 30% = 70%). Following this line of reasoning, the equivalent units for the department for May would be computed as shown in Exhibit 4A–1.

Comparison of Equivalent Units of Production under the Weighted-Average and FIFO Methods

Stop at this point and compare the data in Exhibit 4A–1 with the data in Exhibit 4–5 in the chapter, which shows the computation of equivalent units under the weighted-average method. Also refer to Exhibit 4A–2, which compares the two methods.

EXHIBIT 4A–1   Equivalent
Units of Production: FIFO Method

	Materials	Conversion
To complete beginning work in process:		
Materials: 200 units × (100% − 55%*)	90	
Conversion: 200 units × (100% − 30%*)		140
Units started and completed during the period.	4,600†	4,600†
Ending work in process:		
Materials: 400 units × 40% complete	160	
Conversion: 400 units × 25% complete		100
Equivalent units of production.	4,850	4,840

*This is the work needed to complete the units in beginning inventory.
†5,000 units started − 400 units in ending work in process = 4,600 units started and completed. This
can also be computed as 4,800 units completed and transferred to the next department − 200 units in
beginning work in process inventory. The FIFO method assumes that the units in beginning inventory
are finished first.

EXHIBIT 4A–2
Visual Perspective
of Equivalent Units
of Production—
Conversion

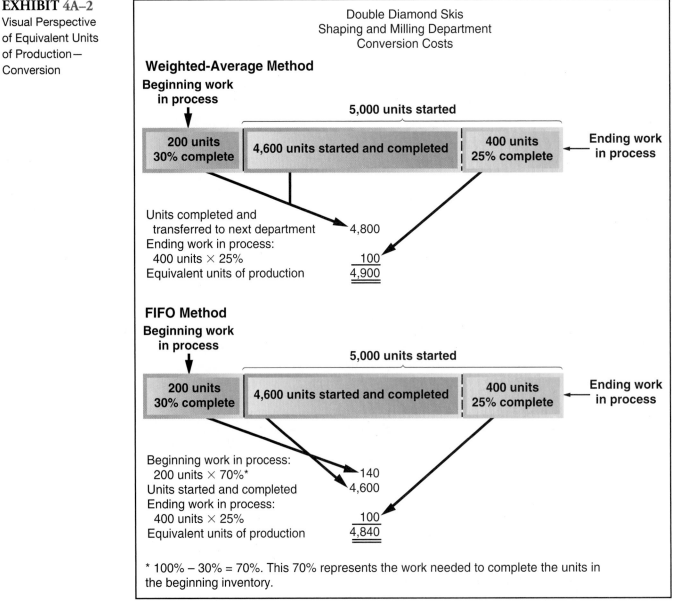

The essential difference between the two methods is that the weighted-average method blends work and costs from the prior period with work and costs in the current period, whereas the FIFO method separates the two periods. To see this more clearly, consider the following reconciliation of the two calculations of equivalent units:

Shaping and Milling Department	Materials	Conversion
Equivalent units—weighted-average method.....................	4,960	4,900
Less equivalent units in beginning inventory:		
200 units × 55%...	110	
200 units × 30%...		60
Equivalent units of production—FIFO method	4,850	4,840

From the above, it is evident that the FIFO method removes the equivalent units that were already in beginning inventory from the equivalent units as defined using the weighted-average method. Thus, the FIFO method isolates the equivalent units due to work performed during the current period. The weighted-average method, on the other hand, blends together the equivalent units already in beginning inventory with the equivalent units due to work performed in the current period.

■ PRODUCTION REPORT—FIFO METHOD

The steps followed to prepare a production report under the FIFO method are the same as those discussed earlier for the weighted-average method. However, since the FIFO method makes a distinction between units in the beginning inventory and units started during the year, the cost reconciliation portion of the report is more complex under the FIFO method. To illustrate the FIFO method, we will again use the data for Double Diamond Skis on page 135.

Step 1: Prepare a quantity schedule and compute the equivalent units. There is only one difference between a quantity schedule prepared under the FIFO method and one prepared under the weighted-average method. This difference relates to units transferred out. As explained earlier in our discussion of equivalent units, the FIFO method divides units transferred out into two parts. One part consists of the units in the beginning inventory, and the other part consists of the units started and completed during the current period.

A quantity schedule showing this format for units transferred out is presented in Exhibit 4A-3, along with a computation of equivalent units for the month. We explained earlier that in computing equivalent units under the FIFO method, we must first show the amount of work required *to complete* the units in the beginning inventory. We then show the number of units started and completed during the period, and finally we show the amount of work *completed* on the units still in process at the end of the period. Carefully trace through these computations in Exhibit 4A–3.

Step 2: Compute the cost per equivalent unit. In computing unit costs under the FIFO method, we use only those costs that were incurred during the current period, and we ignore any costs in the beginning work in process inventory. Under the FIFO method, *unit costs relate only to work done during the current period* as follows:

LEARNING OBJECTIVE 7
Compute the cost per equivalent unit using the FIFO method.

FIFO Method
(a separate calculation is made for each cost category in each processing department)

$$\text{Cost per equivalent unit} = \frac{\text{Cost added during the period}}{\text{Equivalent units of production}}$$

The costs per equivalent unit computed in Exhibit 4A–3 are used to cost units of product transferred to the next department; in addition, they are used to show the cost attached to partially completed units in the ending work in process inventory.

EXHIBIT 4A–3 Production Report—FIFO Method

DOUBLE DIAMOND SKIS
Shaping and Milling Department Production Report
(FIFO method)

Quantity Schedule and Equivalent Units

	Quantity Schedule		
Units to be accounted for:			
Work in process, May 1 (materials 55% complete; conversion 30% complete)	200		
Started into production	5,000		
Total units	5,200		

	Quantity Schedule	Equivalent Units (EU)	
		Materials	**Conversion**
Units accounted for as follows:			
Transferred to the next department			
From beginning inventory*	200	90	140
Started and completed in the month†	4,600	4,600	4,600
Work in process, May 31 (materials 40% complete; conversion 25% complete)	400	160	100
Total units and equivalent units of production	5,200	4,850	4,840

Costs per Equivalent Unit

	Total Cost	Materials	Conversion	Whole Unit
Cost to be accounted for:				
Work in process, May 1	$ 15,175			
Cost added in the department (a)	719,500	$368,600	$350,900	
Total cost	$734,675			
Equivalent units of production (above) (b) (see above)		4,850	4,840	
Cost per EU, (a) ÷ (b)		$ 76.00 +	$ 72.50 =	$148.50

Cost Reconciliation

	Total Cost	Equivalent Units	
		Materials	**Conversion**
Cost accounted for as follows:			
Transferred to next department:			
From beginning inventory:			
Cost in beginning inventory	$ 15,175		
Cost to complete these units			
Materials at $76.00 per EU	6,840	90	
Conversion at $72.50 per EU	10,150		140
Total cost from beginning inventory	$ 32,165		
Units started and completed this month at $148.50 per EU	$683,100	4,600	4,600
Total cost transferred out	$715,265		
Work in process, May 31:			
Materials, at $76.00 per EU	$ 12,160	160	
Conversion, at $72.50 per EU	7,250		100
Total work in process, May 31	19,410		
Total cost	$734,675		

---

*Materials: 200 × (100% − 55%) = 90 EU. Conversion: 200 × (100% − 30%) = 140 EU.
†5,000 units started − 400 units in ending inventory = 4,600 units started and completed.

The costs per equivalent unit are used to value units in ending inventory and units that are transferred to the next department. For example, each unit transferred out of the Shaping and Milling Department to the Graphics Application Department will carry with it a cost of $148.50—$76.00 for materials cost and $72.50 for conversion cost for work done in the current period. Since 4,600 units were started and transferred out in May to the next department, the total cost assigned to those units would be $683,100 (4,600 units × $148.50 per unit).

Step 3: Prepare a cost reconciliation. The purpose of the cost reconciliation is to show how the costs charged to a department during a period are accounted for. With the FIFO method, two cost elements are associated with the units in the beginning work in process inventory. The first element is the cost carried over from the prior period ($15,175 from Exhibit 4A–3). The second element is the cost needed to complete these units ($6,840 of materials plus $10,150 of conversion costs in Exhibit 4A–3).

For units started and completed in the month, we simply multiply the number of units started and completed by the total cost per unit to determine the amount transferred out. This would be $683,100 for the department (see Exhibit 4A–3).

Finally the amount of cost attached to the ending work in process inventory is computed by multiplying the cost per equivalent unit figures for the month by the number of equivalent units for materials and conversion costs in ending inventory.

Note that the $715,265 cost of the units transferred to the next department, Graphics Application, will be accounted for in that department as "costs transferred in." As in the weighted-average method, this cost will be treated in the process costing system as just another category of costs, like materials or conversion costs. The only difference is that the costs transferred in will always be 100% complete with respect to the work done in the Graphics Application Department. Costs are passed on from one department to the next in this fashion, until they reach the last processing department, Finishing and Pairing. When the products are completed in this last department, their costs are transferred to finished goods.

> **LEARNING OBJECTIVE 8**
> Prepare a cost reconciliation report accounting for the costs transferred out and the costs in work in process inventory at the end of the period using the FIFO method.

A Comparison of Costing Methods

In most situations, the weighted-average and FIFO methods will produce very similar unit costs. If there never are any ending inventories, as in an ideal lean production (JIT) environment, the two methods will produce identical results. The reason for this is that without any ending inventories, no costs can be carried forward into the next period and the weighted-average method will base the unit costs on just the current period's costs—just as in the FIFO method. If there *are* ending inventories, either erratic input prices or erratic production levels would also be required to generate much of a difference in unit costs under the two methods. This is because the weighted-average method will blend the unit costs from the prior period with the unit costs of the current period. Unless these unit costs differ greatly, the blending will not make much difference.

Nevertheless, from the standpoint of cost control, the FIFO method is superior to the weighted-average method. Current performance should be measured in relation to costs of the current period only, and the weighted-average method mixes costs of the current period with costs of the prior period. Thus, under the weighted-average method, the manager's apparent performance in the current period is influenced by what happened in the prior period. This problem does not arise under the FIFO method because the FIFO method makes a clear distinction between costs of prior periods and costs incurred during the current period. For the same reason, the FIFO method also provides more up-to-date cost data for decision-making purposes.

On the other hand, the weighted-average method is simpler to apply than the FIFO method, but computers can handle the additional calculations with ease once they have been appropriately programmed. A detailed comparison of the weighted-average and FIFO methods is provided in the Learning Aid that follows.

LEARNING AID

COMPARISON OF PROCESS COSTING METHODS

Weighted Average	FIFO
1. Equivalent units of production are calculated at the end of each period by adding together the completed units transferred out and the equivalent units in ending work in process inventory.	1. Equivalent units of production are calculated at the end of each period by adding together the completed units transferred out and the equivalent units in ending work in process inventory *less equivalent units in beginning work in process inventory*.
2. Cost per equivalent unit is calculated by adding the cost of beginning work in process inventory and the costs added during the period and dividing the total by the equivalent units of production (i.e., taking the weighted average).	2. Cost per equivalent unit is calculated by dividing the costs added during the period by the equivalent units of production.
3. Total cost for the period is calculated as the cost per equivalent unit times the equivalent units of production.	3. Total cost for the period is calculated as the cost per equivalent unit times the equivalent units of production.

Appendix 4A Summary

- Under the FIFO method of process costing, both beginning and ending inventories are converted to an equivalent units basis. For the beginning inventory, the equivalent units represent the work done to *complete* the units; for the ending inventory, the equivalent units represent the work done to bring the units to a stage of partial completion at the end of the period (the same as with the weighted-average method). **[LO6]**
- Under the FIFO method, the cost per equivalent unit, we use only those costs that were incurred during the current period, and we ignore any costs in the beginning work in process inventory. Under the FIFO method, *unit costs relate only to work done during the current period.* **[LO7]**
- The cost per equivalent unit is then used to value the ending work in process inventory and the units transferred out to the next department or to finished goods. Costs are transferred from one department to the next until the last processing department. At that point, the cost of completed units is transferred to finished goods. At the end of the period, a cost reconciliation is prepared to account for the costs transferred out and costs in work in process inventory at the end of the period. **[LO8]**

Appendix 4A Questions, Exercises, Problems, and Cases connect

4A–1 How does the computation of equivalent units under the FIFO method differ from the computation of equivalent units under the weighted-average method?

4A–2 From the standpoint of cost control, why is the FIFO method superior to the weighted-average method?

EXERCISE 4A–1 Computation of Equivalent Units—FIFO Method [LO6]

QualityCo produces wine bottles for vintners in a process that starts in the Melt and Mould Department. Data concerning that department's operations in the most recent period appear below:

Beginning work in process:	
Units in process	400
Stage of completion with respect to materials.	75%
Stage of completion with respect to conversion	25%
Units started into production during the month.	42,600
Units completed and transferred out	42,500
Ending work in process:	
Units in process	500
Stage of completion with respect to materials.	80%
Stage of completion with respect to conversion	30%

CHAPTER 5

Learning Objectives

After studying Chapter 5, you should be able to

1. Explain the activity-based costing model and how it differs from a traditional costing system.

2. Assign costs to cost pools using a first-stage allocation, and compute activity rates.

3. Assign costs to a cost object using a second-stage allocation.

4. Use activity-based costing to compute product and customer margins.

5. Compare product costs computed using traditional and activity-based costing methods.

6. (Appendix 5A) Prepare an action analysis report using activity-based costing data, and interpret the report.

7. (Appendix 5B) Use activity-based costing techniques to compute unit product costs for external reports.

ACTIVITY-BASED COSTING: A TOOL TO AID DECISION MAKING

■ HELP FOR AN AILING REPORTING SYSTEM

Toronto's Hospital for Sick Children is the largest children's hospital in Canada and has a worldwide reputation for conducting leading-edge medical research. The annual volume of activity is impressive, with 15,000 inpatients and 237,000 emergency patients and outpatients. Prior to adopting an activity-based costing (ABC) system, financial analysis was often prepared on an ad hoc basis because the standard monthly reports were not providing managers with information useful for decision-making purposes. To address this problem, an ABC system was developed on a pilot test basis in five different operating departments, which combined had over 600 employees and an annual operating expense budget of $80 million.

As is typical in ABC implementations, considerable effort was required to identify activity cost pools and activity measures in the various departments. For example, in the Health Records Department, 14 different activity cost pools (e.g., emergency patient registration) and activity measures (e.g., number of patients registered) were identified. The key benefit of the new system is that operational managers now have significantly improved information with which to run their departments. In particular, the ABC system allows managers to track the actual cost per unit of an activity (e.g., cost per emergency patient registered), compare these amounts with budget, and take action as necessary. Moreover, having accurate information on a per activity measure basis allows managers to develop more accurate forecasts of costs, given anticipated changes in overall activity levels.

What are the different types of activity cost pools? How are costs allocated to the various pools? How do companies decide which activity measures to use? How are activity costs assigned to cost objects? These are the key questions addressed in this chapter.

Source: Brian Mackie, "Merging GPK and ABC on the Road to RCA," *Strategic Finance*, November 2006, pp. 32–39.

Activity-based costing (ABC)
A costing method based on activities that is designed to provide managers with cost information for strategic and other decisions that potentially affect capacity and therefore fixed costs.

This chapter introduces the concept of *activity-based costing,* which has been embraced by manufacturing, service, and not-for-profit organizations worldwide. **Activity-based costing (ABC)** is a costing method that is designed to provide managers with cost information for strategic and other decisions that potentially affect capacity and therefore "fixed" as well as variable costs. Activity-based costing is typically used as a supplement to, rather than as a replacement for, a company's usual costing system. Most organizations that use activity-based costing have two costing systems—the official costing system that is used for preparing external financial reports and the activity-based costing system that is used for internal decision making and for managing activities.

This chapter focuses primarily on ABC applications in manufacturing to provide a contrast with the material presented in earlier chapters. More specifically, Chapters 2, 3, and 4 focused on traditional absorption costing systems used by manufacturing companies to calculate unit product costs for the purpose of valuing inventories and determining cost of goods sold for external financial reports. In contrast, this chapter explains how manufacturing companies can use activity-based costing rather than traditional methods to calculate unit product costs for the purposes of managing overhead and making decisions. Because of the broad role that activity-based costing can play in facilitating decisions related to product pricing, cost management, capacity utilization, and customer profitability, it is important that both accountants and non-accountants understand its purpose and application.

THE TREATMENT OF COSTS UNDER THE ACTIVITY-BASED COSTING MODEL

LEARNING OBJECTIVE 1
Explain the activity-based costing model and how it differs from a traditional costing system.

Overhead cost pool
A group of overhead cost elements.

As noted above, traditional absorption costing is designed to provide data for external financial reports. In contrast, activity-based costing is designed for use in internal decision making. As a consequence, activity-based costing differs from traditional cost accounting in several ways. In activity-based costing:

1. Non-manufacturing as well as manufacturing costs may be assigned to products, but only on a cause-and-effect basis.
2. Some manufacturing costs may be excluded from product costs.
3. Numerous **overhead cost pools** are used, each of which is allocated to products and other cost objects using its own unique measure of activity.
4. Overhead rates, or activity rates, may be based on the level of activity at capacity rather than on the budgeted level of activity.

Each of these departures from traditional costing accounting practices will be discussed in turn.

Non-Manufacturing Costs and Activity-Based Costing

In traditional cost accounting, only manufacturing costs are assigned to products. Selling, general, and administrative expenses are treated as period expenses and are not assigned to products. However, many of these non-manufacturing costs are also part of the costs of producing, selling, distributing, and servicing products. For example, commissions paid to salespeople, shipping costs, and warranty repair costs can easily be traced to individual products. In this chapter, we will use the term *overhead* to refer to non-manufacturing costs as well as to indirect manufacturing costs. In activity-based costing, products are assigned all of the overhead costs—non-manufacturing as well as manufacturing—that they can reasonably be estimated to have caused. In essence, we will be determining the entire cost of a product rather than just its manufacturing cost. The focus in Chapters 2, 3, and 4 was on determining just the manufacturing cost of a product.

Manufacturing Costs and Activity-Based Costing

In traditional cost accounting, *all* manufacturing costs are assigned to products—even manufacturing costs that are not caused by the products. For example, a portion of the factory security guard's wages would be allocated to each product even though the guard's wages are totally unaffected by which products are made or not made during a period. In activity-based costing, a cost is assigned to a product only if there is good reason to believe that the cost would be affected by decisions concerning the product. In activity-based costing, costs that are unaffected by product-related decisions are treated as period expenses instead of product costs. As will be seen in the example presented in this chapter, this departure from traditional costing approaches (see Chapter 3) represents one of the key benefits of activity-based costing as it results in better information for decision-making purposes.

Cost Pools, Allocation Bases, and Activity-Based Costing

Historically, cost system designs were simple and satisfactory. Typically, either one plantwide overhead cost pool or a number of departmental overhead cost pools was used to assign overhead costs to products. The plantwide and departmental approaches always had one thing in common—they relied on allocation bases such as direct labour-hours and machine-hours for allocating overhead costs to products. In labour-intensive production processes, direct labour was the most common choice for an overhead allocation base because it represented a large component of product costs, direct labour-hours were closely tracked, and many managers believed that direct labour-hours, the total volume of units produced, and overhead costs were highly correlated. Given that most companies at the time were producing a very limited variety of products that required similar resources to produce, allocation bases such as direct labour-hours, or even machine-hours, worked fine because in fact there was probably little difference in the overhead costs attributable to different products.

Then conditions began to change. Many tasks previously done by direct labourers were being performed by automated equipment—a component of overhead. Companies began creating new products and services at an ever-accelerating rate that differed in volume, batch size, and complexity. Managing and sustaining this product diversity required investing in many more overhead resources, such as product design engineers, that had no obvious connection to direct labour-hours or machine-hours. In this new environment, continuing to rely exclusively on a limited number of overhead cost pools and traditional allocation bases posed the risk that reported unit product costs would be distorted and, therefore, misleading when used for decision-making purposes. The activity-based approach has appeal in today's business environment because it uses more cost pools and unique measures of activity to better understand the costs of managing and sustaining product diversity.

In activity-based costing, an **activity** is any event that causes the consumption of overhead resources. An **activity cost pool** is a "bucket" in which costs are accumulated that relate to a single activity measure in the ABC system. An **activity measure** is an allocation base in an activity-based costing system. The term *cost driver* is also used to refer to an activity measure because the activity measure should "drive" the cost being allocated. The two most common types of activity measures are *transaction drivers* and *duration drivers*. **Transaction drivers** are simple counts of the number of times an activity occurs such as the number of bills sent out to customers. **Duration drivers** measure the amount of time required to perform an activity such as the time spent preparing individual bills for customers. In general, duration drivers are more accurate measures of resource consumption than transaction drivers, but they take more effort to record. For that reason, transaction drivers are often used in practice.

Many companies throughout the world continue to base overhead allocations on direct labour-hours or machine-hours. In situations where overhead costs and direct labour-hours are highly correlated or in situations where the goal of the overhead allocation process is to prepare external financial reports, this practice makes sense. However, if plantwide overhead costs do not move in tandem with plantwide direct labour-hours or machine-hours, product costs will be distorted. Activity-based costing addresses this issue by

Activity
Any event that causes the consumption of overhead resources.

Activity cost pool
A "bucket" in which costs are accumulated that relate to a single activity measure in the activity-based costing system.

Activity measure
An allocation base in an activity-based costing system; ideally, a measure of the amount of activity that drives the costs in an activity cost pool; also called a *cost driver*.

Transaction driver
A simple count of the number of times an activity occurs.

Duration driver
A measure of the amount of time required to perform an activity.

defining five levels of activity—unit-level, batch-level, product-level, customer-level, and organization-sustaining—of which only the costs and corresponding activity measures for unit-level activities relate to the volume of units produced. The remaining categories do not. These levels are described as follows:[1]

1. **Unit-level activities** are performed each time a unit is produced. The costs of unit-level activities should be proportional to the number of units produced. For example, providing power to run processing equipment would be a unit-level activity since power tends to be consumed in proportion to the number of units produced.

2. **Batch-level activities** are performed each time a batch is handled or processed, regardless of how many units are in the batch. For example, tasks such as placing purchase orders, setting up equipment, and arranging for shipments to customers are batch-level activities. They are incurred once for each batch (or customer order). Costs at the batch level depend on the number of batches processed rather than on the number of units produced, the number of units sold, or other measures of volume. For example, the cost of setting up a machine for batch processing is the same regardless of whether the batch contains 100 or 10,000 items.

3. **Product-level activities** relate to specific products and typically must be carried out regardless of how many batches are run or units of product are produced or sold. For example, activities such as designing a product, advertising a product, and maintaining a product manager and staff are all product-level activities.

4. **Customer-level activities** relate to specific customers and include activities such as sales calls, catalogue mailings, and general technical support that are not tied to any specific product.

5. **Organization-sustaining activities** are carried out regardless of which customers are served, which products are produced, how many batches are run, or how many units are made. This category includes activities such as heating the factory, cleaning executive offices, providing a computer network, arranging for loans, preparing annual reports to shareholders, and so on.

Unit-level activities
Activities that arise as a result of the total volume of goods and services that are produced and that are performed each time a unit is produced.

Batch-level activities
Activities that are performed each time a batch of goods is handled or processed, regardless of how many units are in a batch. The amount of resources consumed depends on the number of batches run rather than on the number of units in the batch.

Product-level activities
Activities that relate to specific products that must be carried out regardless of how many units are produced and sold or batches run.

Customer-level activities
Activities that are carried out to support customers but that are not related to any specific product.

Organization-sustaining activities
Activities that are carried out regardless of which customers are serviced, which products are produced, how many batches are run, or how many units are made.

The Costs of Idle Capacity in Activity-Based Costing

In a traditional absorption costing system, predetermined overhead rates are computed by dividing budgeted overhead costs by a measure of budgeted activity such as budgeted direct labour-hours. This practice results in applying the costs of unused, or idle, capacity to products, and it results in unstable unit product costs. If budgeted activity falls, the overhead rate increases because the fixed components of overhead are spread over a smaller base, resulting in increased unit product costs.

In activity-based costing, products are charged for the costs of capacity they use—not for the costs of capacity they do not use. In other words, the costs of idle capacity are not charged to products. This results in more stable unit costs and is consistent with the objective of assigning only those costs to products that are actually caused by the products. Instead of assigning the costs of idle capacity to products, in activity-based costing, these costs are considered to be period costs that flow through to the income statement as an expense of the current period. This treatment highlights the cost of idle capacity rather than burying it in inventory and cost of goods sold.

Designing an Activity-Based Costing System

There are three essential characteristics of a successful activity-based costing implementation. First, top managers must strongly support the implementation because their leadership is instrumental in properly motivating all employees to accept the need for change. Second, top managers should ensure that ABC data is linked to how people are evaluated and rewarded. If employees continue to be evaluated and rewarded using traditional (non-ABC) cost data, they will quickly get the message that ABC is not important and will ignore the information provided by the system. Third, a cross-functional team should be created to design and implement the ABC system. The team should include representatives from each area that will use ABC data such as marketing, production, engineering, and accounting departments. These cross-functional employees possess detailed knowledge of many parts of an organization's operations that is crucial for designing an effective ABC system. Moreover, utilizing the knowledge of cross-functional managers reduces their resistance to change because they feel involved in the ABC implementation process. Time after time, when accountants have attempted to implement an ABC system on their own without top-management support and cross-functional involvement, the results have been ignored.

To illustrate the design and use of an activity-based costing system, we use Classic Brass Inc., a company that makes two main product lines for luxury yachts—standard stanchions and custom compass housings. Based on the company's disappointing financial result for the most recent year-end (see Exhibit 5–1) senior management at Classic Brass decided that more accurate costing information was needed for making decisions such as product pricing. After studying the existing cost accounting system at Classic Brass and reviewing articles in professional and trade journals, they decided to implement an activity-based costing system. A cross-functional team was put together to design and implement the system. Like most other ABC implementations, the new ABC system would supplement, rather than replace, the existing cost accounting system, which would continue to be used for external financial reports. The new ABC system would be used to prepare special reports for management decisions such as bidding on new business.

The accounting manager drew the chart appearing in Exhibit 5–2 to explain the general structure of the ABC model. Cost objects such as products give rise to activities. For

Classic Brass Income Statement Year Ended December 31, 2010		
Sales		$3,200,000
Cost of goods sold:		
Direct materials	$ 975,000	
Direct labour	351,250	
Manufacturing overhead*	1,000,000	2,326,250
Gross margin		873,750
Selling and administrative expenses:		
Shipping expenses	65,000	
Marketing expenses	300,000	
General administrative expenses	510,000	875,000
Operating income		($ 1,250)

*The company's traditional cost system allocates manufacturing overhead to products using a plantwide overhead rate and machine-hours as the allocation base. Inventory levels did not change during the year.

EXHIBIT 5–1   Classic Brass Income Statement

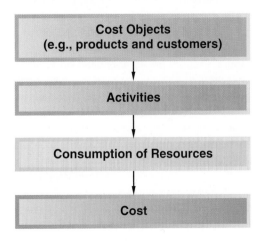

EXHIBIT 5–2   The Activity-Based Costing Model

example, a customer order for a compass housing requires the activity of preparing a production order. Such an activity consumes resources. A production order uses a sheet of paper and takes time to fill out and the consumption of resources causes costs. The greater the number of sheets used to fill out production orders and the greater the amount of time devoted to filling out such orders, the greater the cost. Activity-based costing involves analysis of these types of relationships to identify how products and customers affect costs.

As in most companies, the ABC team at Classic Brass felt that the company's traditional cost accounting system adequately measured the direct material and direct labour costs of products since these costs are directly traced to products. Therefore, the ABC system would be concerned solely with manufacturing overhead, selling, general, and administrative costs.

The implementation process was broken down into the following five basic steps:

1. Identify and define activities, activity cost pools, and activity measures.
2. Assign overhead costs to activity cost pools.
3. Calculate activity rates.
4. Assign overhead costs to cost objects using the activity rates and activity measures.
5. Prepare management reports.

Step 1: Identify and Define Activities, Activity Cost Pools, and Activity Measures

The first major step is to identify the activities that will form the foundation for the system. This can be difficult and time-consuming, and involves a great deal of judgment. A common procedure is for the individuals on the ABC implementation team to interview people who work in overhead departments and ask them to describe their major activities. Ordinarily, this results in a very long list of activities, which can pose a problem. On one hand, the greater the number of activities tracked in the ABC system, the more accurate the costs are likely to be. On the other hand, it is costly to design, implement, maintain, and use a complex system involving large numbers of activities. Consequently, the original lengthy list of activities is usually reduced to a small number by combining similar activities. For example, several actions may be involved in handling and moving raw materials—from receiving raw materials on the loading dock to sorting them into the appropriate bins in the storeroom. All of these activities might be combined into a single activity called *materials handling*.

IN BUSINESS

Xi Agricultural Machine Company (XAMC), a state-owned manufacturer of farming equipment in China, provides a good international example of the potential benefits of activity-based costing. XAMC adopted ABC because of declining profit margins, high overhead costs, and considerable production volume and complexity differences across products. Prior to adopting ABC, the company used a traditional approach to allocating overhead costs to products based on direct labour-hours. Product prices are based on total costs (including overhead) plus a markup for a desired profit margin. In recent years, management became increasingly concerned as demand for one of its high-volume products, a four-wheel-drive tractor, began to decrease as competitors consistently underbid XAMC. Conversely, demand for one of its seeders, a low-volume, high-complexity product, was rapidly increasing as the price charged by XAMC was significantly below its competitors. Management began to suspect that its costing system was responsible for these shifts in demand.

An extensive ABC implementation process was conducted and resulted in the identification of 14 main activities. Employing the standard two-stage allocation process, the total cost of each activity was determined by management in stage one. In stage two, activity costs were assigned to products based on the amount of the activity measure consumed by each product.

Activity measures were selected based on the extent to which they were correlated with the incurrence of the activity costs. The results have been dramatic. Revised product costs based on the ABC system indicated that the overhead costs of the four-wheel-drive tractor had been overestimated by 46% while the overhead costs of the seeder were underestimated by 43%. Within months of implementing the ABC system, XAMC began to see the benefits of more accurate product costs as it lowered the price on its tractors and demand began to increase.

Source: Pingxin Wang, Qinglu Jin, and Thomas Lin, "How an ABC Study Helped a China State-Owned Company Stay Competitive," *Cost Management,* November–December 2005, pp. 39–47.

When combining activities in an ABC system, activities should be grouped together at the appropriate level. Batch-level activities should not be combined with unit-level activities, or product-level activities with batch-level activities, and so on. In general, it is best to combine only those activities that are highly correlated with each other within a level. For example, the number of customer orders received is likely to be highly correlated with the number of completed customer orders shipped, so these two batch-level activities (receiving and shipping orders) can usually be combined with little loss of accuracy.

At Classic Brass, the ABC team, in consultation with top managers, selected the following *activity cost pools* and *activity measures*:

Activity Cost Pools at Classic Brass

Activity Cost Pool	Activity Measure
Customer Orders	Number of customer orders
Product Design	Number of product designs
Order Size	Machine-hours
Customer Relations	Number of active customers
Other	Not applicable

The Customer Orders cost pool will be assigned all costs of resources that are consumed by taking and processing customer orders, including costs of processing paperwork and any costs involved in setting up machines for specific orders. The activity measure for this cost pool is simply the number of customer orders received. This is a *batch-level activity*, since each order generates work that occurs regardless of whether the order is for 1 unit or 1,000 units.

The Product Design cost pool will be assigned all costs of resources consumed in designing products. The activity measure for this cost pool is the number of products designed. This is a *product-level activity,* since the amount of design work on a new product does not depend on the number of units ultimately ordered or batches ultimately run.

The Order Size cost pool will be assigned all costs of resources consumed as a consequence of the number of units produced, including the costs of miscellaneous factory supplies, power to run machines, and some equipment depreciation. This is a *unit-level activity* since each unit requires some of these resources. The activity measure for this cost pool is machine-hours.

The Customer Relations cost pool will be assigned all costs associated with maintaining relations with customers, including the costs of sales calls and the costs of entertaining customers. The activity measure for this cost pool is the number of customers the company has on its active customer list. The Customer Relations cost pool represents a customer-level activity.

The Other cost pool will be assigned all overhead costs that are not associated with customer orders, product design, production units, or customer relations. These costs mainly consist of organization-sustaining costs and the costs of unused, idle capacity. These costs will *not* be assigned to products since they represent resources that are *not* consumed by products.

■ THE MECHANICS OF ACTIVITY-BASED COSTING

After the ABC system had been designed, the team was ready to begin the process of actually computing the costs of products, customers, and other objects of interest. As shown in Exhibit 5–3, assigning costs to cost objects under activity-based costing is a two-stage process. In the first stage, manufacturing and non-manufacturing overhead is allocated to the activity costs pools. In the second stage, the costs for the activities are allocated to the various cost objects. As with the traditional cost systems discussed in Chapters 3 and 4, direct costs are traced directly to cost objects. We begin our discussion of the mechanics of activity-based costing with the first-stage allocations.

EXHIBIT 5–3   ABC Two-Stage Cost Allocation Process

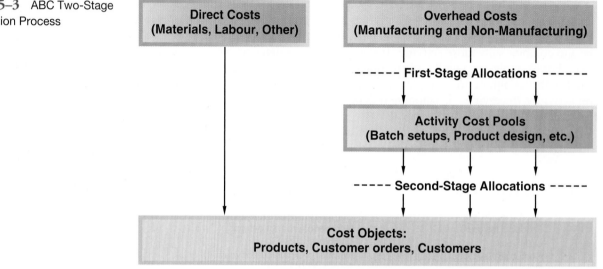

Step 2: Assign Overhead Costs to Activity Cost Pools

Exhibit 5–4 shows the annual overhead costs (both manufacturing and non-manufacturing) that Classic Brass intends to assign to its activity cost pools. Notice that the data in the exhibit are organized by department (e.g., Production, General Administrative, and Marketing). This is because the data have been extracted from the company's general ledger. General ledgers usually classify costs within the departments where the costs are incurred. For example, salaries, supplies, rent, and so forth incurred in the marketing department are charged to that department. The functional orientation of the general ledger mirrors the presentation of costs in the absorption income statement in Exhibit 5–1. In fact, you'll notice the total costs for the Production Department in Exhibit 5–4 ($1,000,000) equal the total manufacturing overhead costs from the income statement in Exhibit 5–1. Similarly, the total costs for the General

EXHIBIT 5–4   Annual Overhead Costs (Both Manufacturing and Non-Manufacturing) at Classic Brass

Production Department:		
Indirect factory wages	$500,000	
Factory equipment depreciation	300,000	
Factory utilities	120,000	
Factory building lease	80,000	$1,000,000
General Administrative Department:		
Administrative wages and salaries	400,000	
Office equipment depreciation	50,000	
Administrative building lease	60,000	510,000
Marketing Department:		
Marketing wages and salaries	250,000	
Selling expenses	50,000	300,000
Total overhead cost		$1,810,000

Administrative and Marketing Departments in Exhibit 5–4 ($510,000 and $300,000) equal the marketing and general and administrative expenses shown in Exhibit 5–1.

Three costs included in the income statement in Exhibit 5–1—direct materials, direct labour, and shipping—are excluded from the costs shown in Exhibit 5–4. The ABC team purposely excluded these costs from Exhibit 5–4 because the existing cost system can accurately trace direct materials, direct labour, and shipping costs to products.

Classic Brass's activity-based costing system will divide the nine types of overhead costs in Exhibit 5–4 among its activity cost pools via an allocation process called *first-stage allocation*. The **first-stage allocation** in an ABC system is the process of assigning functionally organized overhead costs derived from a company's general ledger to the activity cost pools.

First-stage allocation
The process by which overhead costs are assigned to activity cost pools in an activity-based costing system.

First-stage allocations are usually based on the results of interviews with employees who have first-hand knowledge of the activities. For example, Classic Brass needs to allocate $500,000 of indirect factory wages to its five activity cost pools. These allocations will be more accurate if the employees who are classified as indirect factory workers (e.g., supervisors, engineers, and quality inspectors) are asked to estimate what percentage of their time is spent dealing with customer orders, with product design, with processing units of product (i.e., order size), and with customer relations. Departmental managers are typically interviewed to determine how the non-personnel costs should be distributed across the activity cost pools. For example, the Classic Brass production manager would be interviewed to determine how the $300,000 of factory equipment depreciation (shown in Exhibit 5–4) should be allocated to the activity cost pools. The key question that the production manager would need to answer is "What percentage of the available machine capacity is consumed by each activity such as the number of customer orders or the number of units processed (i.e., size of orders)?"

The results of the interviews at Classic Brass are displayed in Exhibit 5–5. For example, factory equipment depreciation is distributed 20% to Customer Orders, 60% to Order Size, and 20% to the Other cost pool. The resource in this instance is machine time. According to the estimates made by the production manager, 60% of the total available machine time was used to actually process units to fill orders. This percentage is entered in the Order Size column. Each customer order requires setting up, which also requires machine time. This activity consumes 20% of the total available machine time and is entered under the Customer Orders column. The remaining 20% of available machine time represents idle time and is entered under the Other column.

Exhibit 5–5 and many of the other exhibits in this chapter are presented in the form of Excel spreadsheets. Setting up an activity-based costing system on a spreadsheet or using special ABC software can save a lot of work—particularly in situations involving many activity cost pools and in organizations that periodically update their ABC systems.

We will not go into the details of how all of the percentages in Exhibit 5–5 were determined. However, note that 100% of the factory building lease has been assigned to the Other cost pool. Classic Brass has a single production facility. It has no plans to expand or to sublease any excess space. The cost of this production facility is treated as an organization-sustaining cost because there is no way to avoid even a portion of this cost if a particular product or customer were to be dropped. (Remember that organization-sustaining costs are assigned to the Other cost pool and are not allocated to products.) In contrast, some companies have separate facilities for manufacturing specific products. The costs of these separate facilities could be directly traced to the specific products.

Once the percentage distributions in Exhibit 5–5 have been established, it is easy to allocate costs to the activity cost pools. The results of this first-stage allocation are displayed in Exhibit 5–6. Each cost is allocated across the activity cost pools by multiplying it by the percentages in Exhibit 5–5. For example, the indirect factory wages of $500,000 are multiplied by the 25% entry under Customer Orders in Exhibit 5–5 to arrive at the $125,000 entry under Customer Orders in Exhibit 5–6. Similarly, the indirect factory wages of $500,000 are multiplied by the 40% entry under Product Design in Exhibit 5–5 to arrive at the $200,000 entry under Product Design in Exhibit 5–6. All of the entries in Exhibit 5–6 are computed in this way.

Now that the first-stage allocations to the activity cost pools have been completed, the next step is to compute the activity rates.

EXHIBIT 5–5   Results of Interviews: Distribution of Resource Consumption across Activity Cost Pools

	A	B	C	D	E	F	G
1				Activity Cost Pools			
2		Customer Orders	Product Design	Order Size	Customer Relations	Other	Totals
4	Production Department:						
5	Indirect factory wages	25%	40%	20%	10%	5%	100%
6	Factory equipment depreciation	20%	0%	60%	0%	20%	100%
7	Factory utilities	0%	10%	50%	0%	40%	100%
8	Factory building lease	0%	0%	0%	0%	100%	100%
10							
12	General Administrative Department:						
13	Administrative wages and salaries	15%	5%	10%	30%	40%	100%
14	Office equipment depreciation	30%	0%	0%	25%	45%	100%
15	Administrative building lease	0%	0%	0%	0%	100%	100%
17	Marketing Department:						
18	Marketing wages and salaries	22%	8%	0%	60%	10%	100%
19	Selling expenses	10%	0%	0%	70%	20%	100%

Exhibit 5-5 \ Exhibit 5-6 / Exhibit 5-7 / Exhibit 5-9 / Exhibit 5-10   Ready   NUM

EXHIBIT 5–6   First-Stage Allocations to Activity Cost Pools

	A	B	C	D	E	F	G
1				Activity Cost Pools			
2		Customer Orders	Product Design	Order Size	Customer Relations	Other	Totals
4	Production Department:						
5	Indirect factory wages	$ 125,000	$ 200,000	$ 100,000	$ 50,000	$ 25,000	$ 500,000
6	Factory equipment depreciation	60,000	0	180,000	0	60,000	300,000
7	Factory utilities	0	12,000	60,000	0	48,000	120,000
8	Factory building lease	0	0	0	0	80,000	80,000
10	General Administrative Department:						
11	Administrative wages and salaries	60,000	20,000	40,000	120,000	160,000	400,000
12	Office equipment depreciation	15,000	0	0	12,500	22,500	50,000
13	Administrative building lease	0	0	0	0	60,000	60,000
15	Marketing Department:						
16	Marketing wages and salaries	55,000	20,000	0	150,000	25,000	250,000
17	Selling expenses	5,000	0	0	35,000	10,000	50,000
19	Total	$ 320,000	$ 252,000	$ 380,000	$ 367,500	$ 490,500	$ 1,810,000

Exhibit 5-5 \ Exhibit 5-6 / Exhibit 5-7 / Exhibit 5-9 / Exhibit 5-10   Ready   NUM

> Exhibit 5–5 shows that Customer Orders consume 25% of the resources represented by the $500,000 of indirect factory wages.
>
> 25% × $500,000 = $125,000
>
> Other entries in the spreadsheet are computed in a similar fashion.

Step 3: Calculate Activity Rates

The activity rates that will be used for assigning overhead costs to products and customers are computed in Exhibit 5–7. The ABC team determined the total activity for each cost pool that would be required to produce the company's present product mix and to serve its present customers. These numbers are listed in Exhibit 5–7. For example, the ABC team found that 400 new product designs are required each year to serve the company's present customers. The activity rates are computed by dividing the *total* cost for each activity by its *total* activity. For example, the $320,000 total annual cost for the Customer Orders cost pool is divided by the total of 1,000 customer orders per year to arrive at the activity rate of $320 per customer order. Similarly, the $252,000 *total* cost for the Product Design cost pool is divided by the *total* number of designs (i.e., 400 product designs) to determine the activity rate of $630 per design. Note that activity rates are not computed for the Other

EXHIBIT 5-7   Computation of Activity Rates

	A	B	C	D	E	F
1	*Activity Cost Pools*	*(a)* *Total Cost**	*(b)* *Total Activity*		*(a) ÷ (b)* *Activity Rate*	
2	Customer orders	$320,000	1,000	orders	$320	per order
3	Product design	$252,000	400	designs	$630	per design
4	Order size	$380,000	20,000	MHs	$19	per MH
5	Customer relations	$367,500	250	customers	$1,470	per customer
6	Other	$490,500	Not applicable		Not applicable	
8	*From Exhibit 5-6.					
9						

Exhibit 5-5   Exhibit 5-6   Exhibit 5-7   Exhibit 5-9

category of costs. This is because the Other cost pool consists of organization-sustaining costs and costs of idle capacity that are not allocated to products and customers.

The entries in Exhibit 5–7 indicate that on average a customer order consumes resources that cost $320; a product design consumes resources that cost $630; an order consumes resources that cost $19 per machine-hour; and maintaining relations with a customer consumes resources that cost $1,470. Note that these are *average* figures. Some members of the ABC design team at Classic Brass argued that it would be unfair to charge all new products the same $630 product design cost regardless of how much design time they actually require. After discussing the pros and cons, the team concluded that it would not be worth the effort at the present time to keep track of actual design time spent on each new product. They felt that the benefits of increased accuracy would not be great enough to justify the higher cost of implementing and maintaining the more detailed costing system. Similarly, some team members were uncomfortable assigning the same $1,470 cost to each customer because different customers place different demands on the resources of the company. However, while everyone agreed with this concern, the data that would be required to measure individual customers' demands on resources were not currently available. Rather than delay implementation of the ABC system, the team decided to defer such refinements to a later date.

Before proceeding, it would be helpful to review the overall process of assigning costs to products and other cost objects in an ABC system. Exhibit 5–8 provides a summary of

EXHIBIT 5-8   The Activity-Based Costing Model at Classic Brass

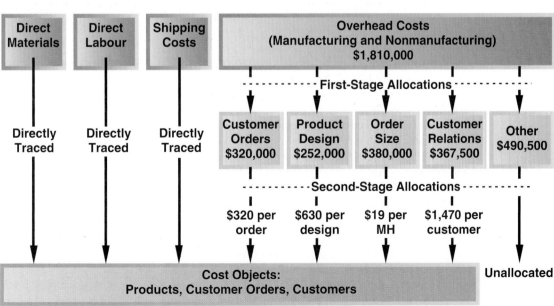

the ABC system at Classic Brass. We recommend that you carefully go over this exhibit. In particular, two things about Exhibit 5–8 are important to keep in mind. First, direct materials, direct labour, and shipping costs are included because they are all direct costs of the cost objects and must be considered when analyzing total costs related to products, customer orders, and customers. These costs were not included in the first-stage allocations because that process deals with assigning overhead costs to activity cost pools. Second, the Other category, which contains organization-sustaining costs and costs of idle capacity, is not allocated to products or customers.

SECOND-STAGE ALLOCATION OF OVERHEAD COSTS

LEARNING OBJECTIVE 3
Assign costs to a cost object using a second-stage allocation.

Second-stage allocation
The process by which activity rates are used to apply costs to products and customers in activity-based costing.

The fourth step in the implementation of activity-based costing is called *second-stage allocation*. In the **second-stage allocation**, activity rates are used to apply overhead costs to products and customers.

Step 4: Assign Overhead Costs to Cost Objects

First, we will illustrate how to assign costs to products, followed by an example of how to assign costs to customers. The data needed by the ABC team to assign overhead costs to Classic Brass's two products—standard stanchions and custom compass housings—are as follows:

> **Standard Stanchions**
>
> 1. This product line does not require any new design resources.
> 2. 30,000 units were ordered during the year, comprising 600 separate orders.
> 3. Each stanchion requires 35 minutes of machine time for a total of 17,500 machine-hours.
>
> **Custom Compass Housings**
>
> 1. This is a custom product that requires new design resources.
> 2. There were 400 orders for custom compass housings. Orders for this product are placed separately from orders for standard stanchions.
> 3. There were 400 custom designs prepared. One custom design was prepared for each order.
> 4. Since some orders were for more than one unit, a total of 1,250 custom compass housings were produced during the year. A custom compass housing requires an average of 2 machine-hours for a total of 2,500 machine-hours.

Notice that 600 customer orders were placed for standard stanchions and 400 customer orders were placed for custom compass housings, for a total of 1,000 customer orders. All 400 product designs related to custom compass housings; none related to standard stanchions. Producing 30,000 standard stanchions required 17,500 machine-hours and producing 1,250 custom compass housings required 2,500 machine-hours, for a total of 20,000 machine-hours.

Exhibit 5–9 illustrates how overhead costs are assigned to the standard stanchions and custom compass housings. For example, the exhibit shows that $192,000 of overhead costs are assigned from the Customer Orders activity cost pool to the standard stanchions ($320 per order × 600 orders). Similarly, $128,000 of overhead costs are assigned from the Customer Orders activity cost pool to the custom compass housings ($320 per order × 400 orders). The Customer Orders cost pool contained a total of $320,000 (see Exhibit 5–6 or 5–7) and this total amount has been assigned to the two products ($192,000 + $128,000 = $320,000).

Exhibit 5–9 shows that a total of $952,000 of overhead costs is assigned to Classic Brass's two product lines—$524,500 to standard stanchions and $427,500 to custom compass housings. This amount is less than the $1,810,000 of overhead costs included in the

EXHIBIT 5–9   Assigning
Overhead Costs to Products

	A	B	C	D	E	F	G
1	**Overhead Cost for the Standard Stanchions**						
2							
3	*Activity Cost Pools*	*(a)* *Activity Rate**		*(b)* *Activity*		*(a) × (b)* *ABC Cost*	
4	Customer orders	$320	per order	600	orders	$192,000	
5	Product design	$630	per design	0	designs	0	
6	Order size	$19	per MH	17,500	MHs	332,500	
7	Total					$524,500	
8							
9							
10	**Overhead Cost for the Custom Compass Housing**						
11							
12	*Activity Cost Pools*	*(a)* *Activity Rate**		*(b)* *Activity*		*(a) × (b)* *ABC Cost*	
13	Customer orders	$320	per order	400	orders	$128,000	
14	Product design	$630	per design	400	designs	252,000	
15	Order size	$19	per MH	2,500	MHs	47,500	
16	Total					$427,500	
17							
18	*From Exhibit 5–7.						
19							
20							

Exhibit 5-6 / Exhibit 5-7 / Exhibit 5-9 \ Exhibit 5-9

Ready   NUM

EXHIBIT 5–9   Assigning
Overhead Costs to Products

ABC system. Why? The total amount of overhead assigned to products does not match the total amount of overhead cost in the ABC system, because the ABC team purposely did not assign the $367,500 of Customer Relations and $490,500 of Other costs to products. The Customer Relations activity is a customer-level activity and the Other activity is an organization-sustaining activity—neither activity is caused by products. As shown below, when the Customer Relations and Other activity costs are added to the $952,000 of overhead costs assigned to products, the total is $1,810,000.

	Standard Stanchions	Custom Compass Housings	Total
Overhead Costs Assigned to Products			
Customer orders	$192,000	$128,000	$ 320,000
Product design	0	252,000	252,000
Order size	332,500	47,500	380,000
Subtotal	$524,500	$427,500	952,000
Overhead Costs Not Assigned to Products			
Customer relations			367,500
Other			490,500
Subtotal			858,000
Total overhead cost			$1,810,000

Next, we describe another aspect of second-stage allocations—assigning activity costs to customers. The data needed by the design team to assign overhead costs to one of its company's customers—Windward Yachts—are as follows:

Windward Yachts

1. The company placed a total of three orders.
   a. Two orders were for 150 standard stanchions per order.
   b. One order was for a single custom compass housing unit.
2. A total of 177 machine-hours were used to fulfill the three customer orders.
   a. The 300 standard stanchions required 175 machine-hours.
   b. The custom compass housing required 2 machine-hours.
3. Windward Yachts is one of 250 customers served by Classic Brass.

As shown in Exhibit 5–10, the ABC team calculated that $6,423 of overhead costs should be assigned to Windward Yachts. The exhibit shows that Windward Yachts is assigned $960 ($320 per order × 3 orders) of overhead costs from the Customer Orders activity cost pool; $630 ($630 per design × 1 design) from the Product Design cost pool; $3,363 ($19 per machine-hour × 177 machine-hours) from the Order Size cost pool; and $1,470 ($1,470 per customer × 1 customer) from the Customer Relations cost pool.

With second-stage allocations complete, the ABC design team was ready to turn its attention to creating reports that would help explain the company's first-ever operating loss.

EXHIBIT 5–10   Assigning Overhead Costs to Customers

	A	B	C	D	E	F	
1	**Overhead Cost for Windward Yachts**						
2							
3	*Activity Cost Pools*	*(a)* *Activity Rate**		*(b)* *Activity*		*(c)* *ABC Cost*	
4	Customer orders	$320	per order	3	orders	$ 960	
5	Product design	$630	per design	1	design	630	
6	Order size	$19	per MH	177	MHs	3,363	
7	Customer relations	$1,470	per customer	1	customer	1,470	
8	Total overhead cost assigned to customer					$6,423	
9							
10	*From Exhibit 5–7						
11							

Exhibit 5-10 / Exhibit 5-11 / Exhibit 5-12 / Exhibit 5 ◀

PRODUCT AND CUSTOMER MARGINS

The most common management reports prepared with ABC data are product and customer profitability reports. These reports help companies channel their resources to their most profitable growth opportunities, while at the same time highlighting products and customers that drain profits. We begin by illustrating a product profitability report followed by a customer profitability report.

Step 5: Prepare Management Reports

The Classic Brass ABC team realized that the profit from a product, also called the *product margin,* is a function of the product's sales and the direct and indirect costs that the product incurs. The ABC cost allocations shown in Exhibit 5–9 summarize only each product's indirect (i.e., overhead) costs. Therefore, to compute a product's profit (i.e., product margin), the design team needed to gather each product's sales and direct costs in addition to the overhead costs previously computed. The pertinent sales and direct cost data for each product are shown below. Notice the numbers in the total column agree with the income statement in Exhibit 5–1.

	Standard Stanchions	Custom Compass Housings	Total
Sales	$2,660,000	$540,000	$3,200,000
Direct costs:			
Direct materials	905,500	69,500	975,000
Direct labour.............	263,750	87,500	351,250
Shipping................	60,000	5,000	65,000

Having gathered the above data, the design team created the product profitability report shown in Exhibit 5–11. The report reveals that standard stanchions are profitable, with a positive product margin of $906,250, whereas the custom compass housings are

	A	B	C	D	E	F	
1	**Product Margins—Activity-Based Costing**						
2			*Standard Stanchions*		*Custom Compass Housing*		
3	Sales		$ 2,660,000			$ 540,000	
4	Costs:						
5	Direct materials	$ 905,500			$ 69,500		
6	Direct labour	263,750			87,500		
7	Shipping costs	60,000			5,000		
8	Customer orders (from Exhibit 5-9)	192,000			128,000		
9	Product design (from Exhibit 5-9)				252,000		
10	Order size (from Exhibit 5-9)	332,500			47,500		
11	Total cost		1,753,750			589,500	
12	Product margin		$ 906,250			$ (49,500)	

Ready   NUM

EXHIBIT 5–11   Product Margins—Activity-Based Costing

unprofitable, with a negative product margin of $49,500. Keep in mind that the product profitability report purposely does not include the costs in the Customer Relations and Other activity cost pools. These costs, which total $858,000, are excluded from the report because they are not caused by the products. Customer Relations costs are caused by customers, not products. The Other costs are organization-sustaining costs that are not caused by any particular product or customer.

The product margins can be reconciled with the company's operating income as follows:

	Standard Stanchions	Custom Compass Housings	Total
Sales (see Exhibit 5–11).	$2,660,000	$540,000	$3,200,000
Total costs (see Exhibit 5–11)	1,753,750	589,500	2,343,250
Product margins (see Exhibit 5–11).	$ 906,250	$ (49,500)	856,750
Overhead costs not assigned to products:			
Customer relations (see Exhibit 5–7)			367,500
Other (see Exhibit 5–7).			490,500
Total.			858,000
Operating income			$ (1,250)

Next, the design team created a customer profitability report for Windward Yachts. Similar to the product profitability report, the design team needed to gather data concerning sales to Windward Yachts and the direct material, direct labour, and shipping costs associated with those sales. Those data are presented below:

	Windward Yachts
Sales	$11,350
Direct costs:	
Direct material costs	2,123
Direct labour costs.	1,900
Shipping costs	205

Using these data and the data from Exhibit 5–10, the design team created the customer profitability report shown in Exhibit 5–12. The report revealed that the customer margin for Windward Yachts is $699. A similar report could be prepared for each of Classic Brass's 250 customers, thereby enabling the company to cultivate relationships with its most profitable customers, while taking steps to reduce the negative impact of unprofitable customers.

EXHIBIT 5–12   Customer Margin—Activity-Based Costing

	A	B	C	
1	**Customer Margin—Activity-Based Costing**			
2			*Windward Yachts*	
3	Sales		$11,350	
4	Costs:			
5	Direct materials	$2,123		
6	Direct labour	1,900		
7	Shipping	205		
8	Customer orders (from Exhibit 5–10)	960		
9	Product design (from Exhibit 5–10)	630		
10	Order size (from Exhibit 5–10)	3,363		
11	Customer relations (from Exhibit 5–10)	1,470	10,651	
12	Customer margin		$ 699	
13				

Exhibit 5-12   Exhibit 5-13   Ext

Targeting Process Improvements

The activity-based costing model illustrated in the preceding sections can readily be used to identify areas that would benefit from process improvements. Indeed, managers often cite this as the major benefit of activity-based costing.[2] **Activity-based management (ABM)** is used in conjunction with activity-based costing to improve processes and reduce costs. Activity-based management is used in organizations as diverse as manufacturing companies, hospitals, and the Canadian Coast Guard.[3] When "forty percent of the cost of running a hospital involves storing, collecting and moving information," there is obviously a great deal of room for eliminating waste and for improvement.[4]

Activity-based management (ABM)
A management approach that, in conjunction with ABC, improves processes and reduces costs.

The first step in any improvement program is to decide what to improve. The theory of constraints approach, which is discussed in Chapter 12, is a powerful tool for targeting the area in an organization where improvement will yield the greatest benefit. Activity-based management provides another approach. The activity rates computed in activity-based costing can provide valuable clues concerning where there is waste and scope for improvement in an organization. For example, managers at Classic Brass were surprised at the high cost of customer orders. Some customer orders are for less than $100 worth of products, and yet it costs, on average, $320 to process an order according to the activity rates calculated in Exhibit 5–7. This seemed very expensive for an activity that adds no value to the product. As a consequence, the customer order processing activity was targeted for improvement.

Benchmarking is another way to utilize the information in activity rates. **Benchmarking** is a systematic approach to identifying the activities with the greatest room for improvement. It is based on comparing the performance of some aspect of an organization's operations (e.g., quality control) with the performance of other, similar organizations known for their outstanding performance. Using outside organizations as the basis for comparison is known as *external benchmarking*. Some companies also use *internal benchmarking* where performance on one division's operations (e.g., customer order processing) is compared to other divisions that are performing well on that activity. If a particular part of the organization performs well below the external or internal benchmark, managers will likely target that area for improvement.

Benchmarking
A systematic approach of comparing the performance of some aspect of an organization's operations to that of outstanding external companies or to other divisions within the same organization.

◼ COMPARISON OF TRADITIONAL AND ABC PRODUCT COSTS

The ABC team used a two-step process to compare its traditional and ABC product costs. First, the team reviewed the product margins reported by the traditional cost system. Then, they contrasted the differences between the traditional and ABC product margins.

Product Margins Computed Using the Traditional Cost System

Classic Brass's traditional cost system assigns only manufacturing costs to products—this includes direct materials, direct labour, and manufacturing overhead. Selling and administrative costs are not assigned to products. Exhibit 5–13 shows the product margins reported by Classic Brass's traditional cost system. We will explain how these margins were calculated in three steps. First, the sales and direct materials and direct labour cost data are the same numbers used by the ABC team to prepare Exhibit 5–11. In other words, the traditional cost system and the ABC system treat these three pieces of revenue and cost data identically.

Second, the traditional cost system uses a plantwide overhead rate to assign manufacturing overhead costs to products. The numerator for the plantwide overhead rate is $1,000,000, which is the total amount of manufacturing overhead shown on the income statement in Exhibit 5–1. The footnote in Exhibit 5–1 mentions that the traditional cost system uses machine-hours to assign manufacturing overhead costs to products. The Order Size activity in Exhibit 5–7 used 20,000 machine-hours as its level of activity. These same 20,000 machine-hours would be used in the denominator of the plantwide overhead rate, which is computed as follows:

$$\text{Plantwide overhead rate} = \frac{\text{Total estimated manufacturing overhead}}{\text{Total estimated machine-hours}}$$

$$= \frac{\$1,000,000}{20,000 \text{ machine-hours}}$$

$$= \$50 \text{ per machine-hour}$$

Since 17,500 machine-hours were worked on standard stanchions, this product line is assigned $875,000 (17,500 machine-hours × $50 per machine-hour) of manufacturing overhead cost. Similarly, the custom compass housings required 2,500 machine-hours, so this product line is assigned $125,000 (2,500 machine-hours × $50 per machine-hour) of manufacturing overhead cost. The sales of each product minus its cost of goods sold equals the product margin of $615,750 for standard stanchions and $258,000 for custom compass housings.

Notice that the operating loss of $1,250 shown in Exhibit 5–13 agrees with the loss reported in the income statement in Exhibit 5–1 and with the loss shown in the table in the middle of page 185. The company's *total* sales, *total* costs, and its resulting operating loss are the same regardless of whether you are looking at the absorption income statement in Exhibit 5–1, the ABC product profitability analysis depicted on page 185, or the traditional product profitability analysis in Exhibit 5–13. Although the "total pie" remains constant across the traditional and ABC systems, what differs is how the pie is divided between the two product lines. The traditional product margin calculations suggest

LEARNING OBJECTIVE 5
Compare product costs computed using traditional and activity-based costing methods.

EXHIBIT 5–13 Product Margins—Traditional Costing System

	A	B	C	D	E	F	G	H	I	
1	**Product Margins—Traditional Cost System**									
2			*Standard Stanchions*			*Custom Compass Housings*			*Total*	
3	Sales		$2,660,000			$540,000			$3,200,000	
4	Cost of goods sold:									
5	Direct materials	$905,500			$ 69,500			$ 975,000		
6	Direct labour	263,750			87,500			351,250		
7	Manufacturing overhead	875,000	2,044,250		125,000	282,000		1,000,000	2,326,250	
8	Product margin		$ 615,750			$258,000			873,750	
9	Selling and administrative								875,000	
10	Operating income								$ (1,250)	
11										

I◀ ◀ ▶ ▶I ⟋ Exhibit 5-12 ⟍ Exhibit 5-13 ⟋ Exhibit 5-14 ⟋ Exhibit 5-15 ⟋ Exhibit 5- │◀│

that standard stanchions are generating a product margin of $615,750 and the custom compass housings a product margin of $258,000. However, these product margins differ from the ABC product margins reported in Exhibit 5–11. Indeed, the traditional cost system is sending misleading signals to Classic Brass's managers about each product's profitability. We explain why in the next section.

Caution should be exercised before taking action based on an ABC analysis such as that shown in Exhibits 5–11 and 5–12. The product and customer margins computed in those exhibits are a useful starting point for further analysis, but managers need to know what costs are really affected before taking any action such as dropping a product or customer or changing the prices of products or services. Appendix 5A to this chapter shows how an action analysis report can be constructed to help managers make such decisions. An **action analysis report** shows what costs have been assigned to a cost object such as a product or customer, and how difficult it would be to adjust the cost given a change in activity. As such, it is considerably more detailed than the ABC analysis presented in Exhibits 5–11 and 5–12.

Action analysis report
A report showing what costs have been assigned to a cost object, such as a product or customer, and how difficult it would be to adjust the cost if there is a change in activity.

The Differences between ABC and Traditional Product Costs

The changes in product margins caused by switching from the traditional cost system to the activity-based costing system are shown below:

	Standard Stanchions	Custom Compass Housings
Product margins—traditional (from Exhibit 5–13)	$615,750	$258,000
Product margins—ABC (from Exhibit 5–11)	906,250	(49,500)
Change in reported product margins	$290,500	($307,500)

The traditional cost system overcosts the standard stanchions and consequently reports an artificially low product margin for this product. The switch to an activity-based view of product profitability increases the product margin on standard stanchions by $290,500. In contrast, the traditional cost system undercosts the custom compass housings and reports an artificially high product margin for this product. The switch to activity-based costing decreases the product margin on custom compass housings by $307,500.

The reasons for the change in reported product margins between the two costing methods are revealed in Exhibit 5–14. The top portion of the exhibit shows each product's direct and indirect cost assignments as reported by the traditional cost system in Exhibit 5–13. For example, Exhibit 5–14 includes the following costs for standard stanchions: direct materials, $905,500; direct labour, $263,750; and manufacturing overhead, $875,000. Each of these costs corresponds with those reported in Exhibit 5–13. Notice that the selling and administrative costs of $875,000 are purposely not allocated to products because these costs are considered to be period costs. Similarly, the bottom portion of Exhibit 5–14 summarizes the direct and indirect cost assignments as reported by the activity-based costing system in Exhibit 5–11. The only new information in Exhibit 5–14 is shown in the two columns of percentages. The first column of percentages shows the percentage of each cost assigned to standard stanchions. For example, the $905,500 of direct materials cost traced to standard stanchions is 92.9% of the company's total direct materials cost of $975,000. The second column of percentages does the same thing for custom compass housings.

There are three reasons why the traditional and activity-based costing systems report different product margins:

1. The traditional cost system allocates *all* manufacturing costs to products regardless of whether they consumed those costs. The ABC system does not assign manufacturing overhead costs to products for either Customer Relations activities or Other (organization-sustaining) activities because they are not caused by any particular product.

EXHIBIT 5–14   A Comparison of Traditional and Activity-Based Cost Assignments

	Standard Stanchions		Custom Compass Housings		Total
	(a) Amount	(a) ÷ (c) %	(b) Amount	(b) ÷ (c) %	(c) Amount
Traditional Cost System					
Direct materials	$ 905,500	92.9%	$ 69,500	7.1%	$ 975,000
Direct labour	263,750	75.1%	87,500	24.9%	351,250
Manufacturing overhead	875,000	87.5%	125,000	12.5%	1,000,000
Total cost assigned to products	$2,044,250		$282,000		2,326,250
Selling and administrative					875,000
Total cost.					$3,201,250
Activity-Based Costing System					
Direct costs:					
Direct materials	$ 905,500	92.9%	$ 69,500	7.1%	$ 975,000
Direct labour.	263,750	75.1%	87,500	24.9%	351,250
Shipping.	60,000	92.3%	5,000	7.7%	65,000
Indirect costs:					
Customer orders	192,000	60.0%	128,000	40.0%	320,000
Product design.	0	0.0%	252,000	100.0%	252,000
Order size.	332,500	87.5%	47,500	12.5%	380,000
Total cost assigned to products	$1,753,750		$589,500		2,343,250
Costs not assigned to products:					
Customer relations.					367,500
Other					490,500
Total cost.					$3,201,250

2. The traditional cost system allocates *all* manufacturing overhead costs using machine-hours, a volume-related allocation base. The ABC system uses unique activity measures (most of which are *not* volume-related) to allocate the cost of each activity cost pool selected on the basis of management's assessment of the driver of overhead costs for that activity. For example, the traditional cost system assigns 87.5% of the Product Design activity to standard stanchions even though that product caused none of these costs. Conversely, all of the Product Design activity costs should be assigned to custom compass housings, not just the 12.5% under the traditional system. The overall effect is that traditional cost systems overcost high-volume products (such as custom compass housings) and undercost low-volume products (such as standard stanchions) because they assign batch-level and product-level costs using volume-related allocation bases (such as machine hours).

3. The ABC system assigns non-manufacturing overhead costs such as shipping to products on a cause-and-effect basis. The traditional cost system excludes these costs because they are classified as period costs.

Activity-Based Costing and External Reports

Although activity-based costing generally provides more accurate product costs than traditional costing methods, it is infrequently used for external reports for a number of reasons. First, external reports are less detailed than internal reports prepared for decision making. On the external reports, individual product costs are not reported. Cost of goods sold and inventory valuations are disclosed, but there is no breakdown of these accounts by product. If some products are undercosted and some are overcosted, the errors tend to offset each other when the product costs are added together.

Second, it is often very difficult to make changes in a company's accounting system. The official cost accounting systems in most large companies are usually embedded in complex computer applications that have been modified in-house over the course of many years. It is extremely difficult to make changes in such applications without causing numerous bugs, which can lead to errors in the resultant information.

Third, an ABC system such as the one described in this chapter does not conform to generally accepted accounting principles (GAAP). As discussed in Chapter 2, product costs computed for external reports must include all of the manufacturing costs and only manufacturing costs; however, in an ABC system as described in this chapter, product costs exclude some manufacturing costs and include some non-manufacturing costs. It is possible to adjust the ABC data at the end of the period to conform to GAAP, but that requires more work. Appendix 5B presents an approach for using a modified form of ABC for external reporting purposes.

Fourth, auditors are likely to be uncomfortable with allocations that are based on interviews with the company's personnel. Such subjective data can easily be manipulated by management to make earnings and other key variables look more favourable.

For all of these reasons, most companies confine their ABC efforts to special studies for management, and do not attempt to integrate activity-based costing into their formal cost accounting systems.

LEARNING AID

ABC VERSUS TRADITIONAL PRODUCT COSTING

Item	ABC	Traditional
1. Number of cost pools.	1. Numerous, based on key activities involved in product/service.	1. Small number, based on key production/service departments.
2. Treatment of manufacturing overhead (MOH).	2. Allocated to products only if *caused* by products.	2. All MOH allocated to products.
3. Activity measures used for applying overhead.	3. Mix of unit-level (e.g., labour-hours) and non-unit-level (e.g., batches). Vary by activity.	3. Typically unit-level (e.g., labour-hours). Vary by department.
4. Treatment of non-manufacturing overhead (e.g., shipping costs).	4. Allocated to products or customers if *caused* by products or customers.	4. Expensed as period costs.
5. Treatment of direct materials and labour.	5. Directly traced to cost objects.	5. Directly traced to cost objects
6. Use for external financial reporting.	6. Usually requires modification because of items 2 and 4 (see Appendix 5B).	6. Typically no modifications required as it conforms to GAAP.

IN BUSINESS

Implementing and maintaining an activity-based costing system can be expensive and time-consuming, particularly for companies with complex operations involving a multitude of activities. To overcome some of the obstacles that have deterred many companies from adopting ABC, a revised approach called *time-driven activity-based costing* (TDABC) has emerged over the past few years. Importantly, TDABC bypasses one of the more time-consuming aspects of the traditional ABC approach—the identification of activities and the assignment of costs to those activities.

TDABC starts by taking the total cost of each department involved with the company's products or services (e.g., Customer Service Department) and dividing it by the total time spent by employees in that department actually performing their various activities (e.g., processing orders, handling complaints, or providing technical support). Time spent by employees on vacation, breaks, training, etc., is *not* included in the calculation of the departmental cost rate. The result is the total cost per hour (or minute, if appropriate) of actual service provision in each department. So, if the total cost of the Customer Service Department is $600,000 per month (for all activities) and the total time spent by employees on all customer service-related activities is 600,000 minutes, the departmental cost rate will be $1 per minute. The next step is to estimate the time required to perform each activity in the department (e.g., the average number of minutes needed to handle a customer complaint), which is often tracked by the ERP systems used by many companies. Continuing our example, if it takes, on average, 15 minutes to handle a customer complaint, the expected cost is $15 per complaint (15 minutes × $1 per minute).

TDABC can then easily be used to develop budgeted activity costs each month by multiplying the time per activity by the expected quantity for the activity in the upcoming month. If 500 customer complaints are expected in a month, 7,500 minutes will be required to process them (500 × 15 minutes per complaint) and the budgeted activity cost will be $7,500 (7,500 minutes × $1 per minute). Tracking the standard cost of actual services provided to customers can also easily be tracked in any period in total and by individual customer. A customer that requires two hours of technical support in a month would be "charged" $120 by the TDABC system. If 7,000 minutes is required in total to handle all complaints in a month, the cost will be $7,000 (7,000 minutes × $1/minute). Similarly, the total standard cost of providing all activities in a department for a given period can be estimated, as can the cost of unused capacity. If Customer Service Department employees spent 550,000 minutes across all activities in a month, the standard cost for the month would be $550,000 and the cost of unused capacity would be $50,000 ($600,000 − $550,000).

The TDABC approach has several benefits. First, it avoids the time-consuming interview and cost assignment process summarized in Exhibits 5–5 and 5–6 by calculating a departmental cost rate that can readily be used to determine the total cost of individual activities. Second, it can easily handle the addition of new activities to a department through a simple recalculation of the departmental cost rate by adding the cost of the new activity to the numerator (total cost) and the time it will require to the denominator. Third, the TDABC approach can provide more accurate cost information in settings where customers (or products) place different demands on the resources of an activity. In the above example, the cost of handling a complaint for Customer A that took 15 minutes to resolve would be $15, while the cost of resolving one complaint for Customer B that took 30 minutes to resolve would be $30. Differences such as this are easily accommodated by the TDABC approach.

Source: Robert Kaplan and Steven Anderson, "The Innovation of Time-Driven Activity-Based Costing," *Cost Management,* March/April 2007, pp. 5–15.

THE LIMITATIONS OF ACTIVITY-BASED COSTING

Implementing an activity-based costing system is a major undertaking, requiring substantial resources. And once implemented, an activity-based costing system is more costly to maintain than a traditional costing system—data concerning numerous activity measures must be collected, checked, and entered into the system. The benefits of increased accuracy may not outweigh these costs.

IN BUSINESS

Marconi is a Portuguese telecommunications company that encountered problems with its ABC system. The company's production managers felt that 23% of the costs included in the system were common costs that should not be allocated to products and that allocating these costs to products was not only inaccurate, but also irrelevant to their operational cost-reduction efforts. Furthermore, Marconi's front-line workers resisted the ABC system because they felt it might be used to weaken their autonomy and to justify downsizing, outsourcing, and work intensification. They believed that ABC created a "turkeys queuing for Christmas syndrome" because they were expected to volunteer information to help create a cost system that could eventually lead to their demise. These two complications created a third problem—the data necessary to build the ABC cost model were provided by disgruntled and distrustful employees. Consequently, the accuracy of the data was questionable at best. In short, Marconi's experiences illustrate some of the challenges that complicate real-world ABC implementations.

Source: Maria Major and Trevor Hopper, "Managers Divided: Implementing ABC in a Portuguese Telecommunications Company," *Management Accounting Research,* June 2005, pp. 205–229.

Activity-based costing produces numbers, such as product margins, that may be at odds with the numbers produced by traditional costing systems. But managers are accustomed to using traditional costing systems to run their operations and traditional costing systems are often used in performance evaluations. Essentially, activity-based costing changes the rules of the game. It is well-established that changes in organizations—particularly those that alter the rules of the game—inevitably face resistance. This underscores the importance of top-management support and the full participation of line managers, as well as the accounting staff, in any activity-based costing initiative. If activity-based costing is viewed as an accounting initiative that does not have the full support of top management, it is doomed to failure.

In practice, most managers insist on fully allocating all costs to products, customers, and other cost objects in an activity-based costing system—including the costs of idle capacity and organization-sustaining costs. This results in overstated costs and understated margins and mistakes in pricing and other critical decisions.[5]

IN BUSINESS

In a survey of large manufacturing companies in Canada, nearly 66% of the respondents indicated they believed an activity-based costing system could potentially add value to their organization. However, despite acknowledging its perceived usefulness, only 39% of the responding companies had actually implemented an ABC system across all business units in the organization. Kaplan and Anderson (2007) provide some possible reasons for this relatively low adoption rate:

- High implementation and maintenance costs of ABC systems.
- Inaccuracies in activity costs due to the need for subjective estimates of the amount of time spent on various activities.
- Inability of ABC systems to completely capture the complexity of actual operations.
- Difficulties integrating ABC data from multiple business units across the organization.

Although ABC offers the potential for more accurate product costs, managers must carefully consider all costs of implementing, maintaining, and using the system. Further, some of the reasons cited by Kaplan and Anderson (2007) suggest that implementing a more complex costing system will not automatically result in more accurate costs. Only if estimated benefits exceed all estimated costs should the ABC implementation proceed.

Sources: Alnoor Bhimani, Maurice Gosselin, Mthuli Ncube, and Hiroshi Okano, "Activity-Based Costing: How Far Have We Come Internationally?" *Cost Management*, May–June 2007, pp. 12–17; and Robert Kaplan and Steven Anderson, "The Innovation of Time-Driven Activity-Based Costing," *Cost Management*, March–April 2007, pp. 5–15.

Activity-based costing data can easily be misinterpreted and must be used with care in making decisions. Costs assigned to products, customers, and other cost objects are only *potentially* relevant. Before making any significant decisions using activity-based costing data, managers must identify which costs are really relevant for the decision at hand. See Appendix 5A for more details.

As discussed in the previous section, reports generated by the best activity-based costing systems do not conform to generally accepted accounting principles. Consequently, an organization involved in activity-based costing should have two cost systems—one for internal use and one for preparing external reports. This is costlier than maintaining just one system and may cause confusion about which system is to be believed and relied on.

Summary

- Under traditional cost accounting methods all manufacturing costs—even those not caused by specific products—are allocated to products. Non-manufacturing costs that are caused by products are not assigned to products. Traditional costing methods also allocate the costs of idle capacity to products, which in effect, charges them for resources not used. **[LO1]**
- Traditional costing methods rely on unit-level allocation bases such as direct labour and machine-hours. This results in overcosting high-volume products and undercosting low-volume products and can lead to mistakes when making decisions. **[LO1]**
- Activity-based costing estimates the costs of the resources consumed by cost objects such as products and customers. The approach taken in ABC recognizes that cost objects generate the need for activities that in turn consume costly resources. Activities form the link between costs and cost objects. **[LO1, LO2]**
- Activity-based costing is concerned with overhead—both manufacturing overhead and selling, general, and administrative overhead. The accounting for direct labour and direct materials is usually unaffected by the use of ABC. **[LO1, LO2]**
- To develop an ABC system, companies typically choose a small set of activities that summarize much of the work performed in overhead departments. Associated with each activity is an activity cost pool. Where possible, overhead costs are directly traced to these activity cost pools. Remaining overhead costs are assigned to the activity cost pools in the first-stage allocation. **[LO2]**
- An activity rate is computed for each cost pool by dividing the costs assigned to the cost pool by the measure of activity for the cost pool. In the second-stage allocation, activity rates are used to apply costs to cost objects such as products and customers. **[LO3, LO4]**
- Activity-based management utilizes information from the ABC system to target activities in need of process improvements. Benchmarking performance against world-class organizations or other high-performing divisions within the same organization can help identify activities most in need of improvement. **[LO4]**
- Product costs computed under activity-based costing are often quite different from the costs generated by a company's traditional cost accounting system because ABC assigns only costs caused by products, uses activity-measures that are not necessarily volume-related, and assigns non-manufacturing costs such as shipping on a cause-and-effect basis. **[LO5]**
- To help identify which exhibits to refer to when working on the exercises, problems, cases, use the following guide: (a) First-stage allocations to activity cost pools: Exhibit 5–6; (b) computation of activity rates: Exhibit 5–7; (c) assigning overhead costs to products: Exhibit 5–9; (d) assigning overhead costs to customers: Exhibit 5–10; (e) product margins: Exhibit 5–11; and (f) customer margins: Exhibit 5–12.

Review Problem: Activity-Based Costing

Advanced Products Corporation has supplied the following data from its activity-based costing system:

Overhead Costs

Wages and salaries	$300,000
Other overhead costs.	100,000
Total overhead costs	$400,000

Activity Cost Pool	Activity Measure	Total Activity for the Year
Volume-related	Number of direct labour-hours	20,000 DLHs
Order-related.	Number of customer orders	400 orders
Customer support . . .	Number of customers	200 customers
Other	These costs are not allocated to products or customers	Not applicable

Distribution of Resource Consumption across Activities

	Volume-Related	Order-Related	Customer Support	Other	Total
Wages and salaries	40%	30%	20%	10%	100%
Other overhead costs	30%	10%	20%	40%	100%

During the year, Advanced Products completed one order for a new customer, Shenzhen Enterprises. This customer did not order any other products during the year. Data concerning that order follow:

Data concerning the Shenzhen Enterprises Order

Units ordered.	10 units
Direct labour-hours	2 DLHs per unit
Selling price.	$300 per unit
Direct materials	$180 per unit
Direct labour	$50 per unit

Required:

1. Prepare a report showing the first-stage allocations of overhead costs to the activity cost pools. (Use Exhibit 5–6 as a guide.)
2. Compute the activity rates for the activity cost pools. (Use Exhibit 5–7 as a guide.)
3. Prepare a report showing the overhead costs for the order from Shenzhen Enterprises. (Use Exhibit 5–10 as a guide. Do not include the customer support costs at this point in the analysis.)
4. Prepare a report showing the product margin for the order and the customer margin for Shenzhen Enterprises. (Use Exhibit 5–12 as a guide.)

Solution to Review Problem

1. The first-stage allocation is as follows:

	Volume-Related	Order-Related	Customer Support	Other	Totals
Wages and salaries	$120,000	$ 90,000	$60,000	$30,000	$300,000
Other overhead costs	30,000	10,000	20,000	40,000	100,000
Total overhead costs	$150,000	$100,000	$80,000	$70,000	$400,000

Example: According to the distribution of resources across activities, 40% of the $300,000 wages and salaries cost is attributable to volume-related activities.

$$\$300,000 \times 40\% = \$120,000$$

Other entries in the table are determined in a similar manner.

2. Computation of activity rates:

Activity Cost Pools	(a) Total Cost	(b) Total Activity	(a) ÷ (b) Activity Rate
Volume-related	$150,000	20,000 DLHs	$7.50 per DLH
Order-related.	$100,000	400 orders	$250 per order
Customer support	$80,000	200 customers	$400 per customer

3. Computation of the overhead costs for the Shenzhen Enterprises order:

Activity Cost Pool	(a) Activity Rate	(b) Activity	(a) × (b) ABC Cost
Volume-related	$7.50 per DLH	20 DLHs*	$150
Order-related.	$250 per order	1 order	250
Total.			$400

*2 DLHs per unit × 10 units = 20 DLHs

4. The margins for the order and for the customer follow:

Product Profitability Analysis

Sales (10 units × $300 per unit)		$3,000
Costs:		
Direct materials (10 units × $180 per unit)	$1,800	
Direct labour (10 units × $50 per unit)	500	
Volume overhead ($7.50 × 20 DLH)	150	
Order-related overhead	250	2,700
Product margin		$ 300

Customer Profitability Analysis

Product margin (above)	$ 300
Less: Customer support overhead	
(1 customer @ $400 per customer)	400
Customer margin	$ (100)

Glossary

Review key terms and definitions on Connect.

Mc Graw Hill connect

Questions

5–1   How are non-manufacturing costs related to selling, shipping, and distribution activities treated under the activity-based costing approach?

5–2   Why is direct labour a poor base for allocating overhead in many companies?

5–3   Why are overhead rates in activity-based costing based on the level of activity at capacity rather than on the budgeted level of activity?

5–4   What is an activity cost pool?

5–5   What are unit-level, batch-level, product-level, customer-level, and organization-sustaining activities?

5–6   What types of costs should not be assigned to products in an activity-based costing system?

5–7   Why are transaction drivers typically used more often in practice than duration drivers?

5–8   Why is the first stage of the allocation process in activity-based costing often based on interviews?

5–9   What is benchmarking?

5–10 When activity-based costing is used, why are manufacturing overhead costs often shifted from high-volume products to low-volume products?

5–11 What is the second-stage allocation in activity-based costing?

5–12 What are the two chief limitations of activity-based costing?

5–13 Can activity-based costing be used in service organizations?

Mc Graw Hill connect Exercises

EXERCISE 5–1 ABC Cost Hierarchy [LO1]

The following activities occur at Greenwich Corporation, a company that manufactures a variety of products.

a.   Various individuals manage the parts inventories.

b.   A clerk in the factory issues purchase orders for a job.

c.   The Personnel Department trains new production workers.

d.   The factory's general manager meets with other department heads, such as marketing, to coordinate plans.

e.   Direct labour workers assemble products.

f.   Engineers design new products.

g.   The materials storekeeper issues raw materials to be used in jobs.

h.   The Maintenance Department performs periodic preventive maintenance on general-use equipment.

Required:

Classify each of the activities above as either a unit-level, batch-level, product-level, or organization-sustaining activity.

EXERCISE 5–2 First-Stage Allocation [LO2]

MobileCash Corporation operates a fleet of armoured cars that make scheduled pickups and deliveries for its customers. The company is implementing an activity-based costing system that has four activity cost pools: Travel, Pickup and Delivery, Customer Service, and Other. The activity measures are kilometres for the Travel cost pool, number of pickups and deliveries for the Pickup and Delivery cost pool, and number of customers for the Customer Service cost pool. The Other cost pool has no activity measure. The following costs will be assigned using the activity-based costing system:

Driver and guard wages..................................	$ 840,000
Vehicle operating expense..............................	270,000
Vehicle depreciation......................................	150,000
Customer representative salaries and expenses.............	180,000
Office expenses...	40,000
Administrative expenses	340,000
Total cost..	$1,820,000

The distribution of resource consumption across the activity cost pools is as follows:

	Travel	Pickup and Delivery	Customer Service	Other	Totals
Driver and guard wages.................	40%	45%	10%	5%	100%
Vehicle operating expense...............	75%	5%	0%	20%	100%
Vehicle depreciation....................	70%	10%	0%	20%	100%
Customer representative salaries and expenses........................	0%	0%	85%	15%	100%
Office expenses........................	0%	25%	35%	40%	100%
Administrative expenses	0%	5%	55%	40%	100%

Required:

Carry out the first-stage allocations of costs to activity cost pools as illustrated in Exhibit 5–6.

EXERCISE 5–3 Compute Activity Rates [LO2]

Brookside Property Management is a property management service company for small shopping malls and uses activity-based costing to estimate costs for pricing and other purposes. The proprietor of the company believes that costs are driven primarily by the area of outdoor maintenance (parking lots, sidewalks, and gardens), the area of indoor tenant space in the shopping mall, the distance to travel to the shopping mall, and the number of shopping malls managed. In addition, the costs of managing the indoor tenant space depend on whether the tenants are located on the main level or other levels of the mall. Accordingly, the company uses the five activity cost pools listed below:

Activity Cost Pool	Activity Measure
Management of outdoor areas	Square metres of outdoor areas
Management of indoor mall space—main level	Square metres of main level mall space
Management of indoor mall space—other levels	Square metres of non-main level mall space
Travel to jobs	Kilometres
Customer billing and service	Number of shopping malls

The company has already carried out its first-stage allocations of costs. The company's annual costs and activities are summarized as follows:

Activity Cost Pool	Estimated Overhead Cost	Expected Activity
Management of outdoor areas	$69,850	127,000 square metres of outdoor areas
Management of indoor mall space—main level	$114,400	104,000 square metres of main level mall space
Management of indoor mall space—other levels	$307,500	246,000 square metres of non-main level mall space
Travel to jobs.	$6,600	22,000 kilometres
Customer billing and service	$13,800	8 shopping malls

Required:
Compute the activity rate for each of the activity cost pools.

EXERCISE 5–4 Second-Stage Allocation [LO3]

Larner Corporation is a diversified manufacturer of industrial goods. The company's activity-based costing system contains the following six activity cost pools and activity rates:

Activity Cost Pool	Activity Rates
Supporting direct labour	$7.00 per direct labour-hour
Machine processing	$3.00 per machine-hour
Machine setups.	$40.00 per setup
Production orders	$160.00 per order
Shipments	$120.00 per shipment
Product sustaining.	$800.00 per product

Activity data have been supplied for the following products:

	Total Expected Activity	
	J78	W52
Direct labour-hours	1,000	40
Machine-hours.	3,200	30
Machine setups	5	1
Production orders	5	1
Shipments	10	1
Product sustaining	1	1

Required:
Determine the total overhead cost that would be assigned to each of the products listed above in the activity-based costing system.

EXERCISE 5–5 Product and Customer Profitability Analysis [LO3, LO4]

PWC Systems, Inc., makes jet skis and other personal watercraft for sale through specialty sporting goods stores. The company has a standard jet ski model, but also makes custom-designed models. Management has designed an activity-based costing system with the following activity cost pools and activity rates:

Activity Cost Pool	Activity Rates
Supporting manufacturing.	$22 per direct labour-hour
Order processing.	$212 per order
Custom design processing	$243 per custom design
Customer service.	$307 per customer

Management would like an analysis of the profitability of a particular customer, WaveRider, which has ordered the following products over the last 12 months:

	Standard Model	Custom Design
Number of jet skis	16	3
Number of orders	2	3
Number of custom designs	0	3
Direct labour-hours per jet ski	24.5	28.0
Selling price per jet ski	$10,600	$13,200
Direct materials cost per jet ski	$7,950	$9,240

The company's direct labour rate is $24 per hour.

Required:
Using the company's activity-based costing system, compute the customer margin of WaveRider.

EXERCISE 5–6 Activity Measures [LO1]
Various activities at Husang Corporation, a manufacturing company, are listed below. Each activity has been classified as unit-level, batch-level, product-level, customer-level, or organization-sustaining.

Required:
Complete the table by listing an example of an activity measure for each activity.

	Activity	Activity Classification	Examples of Activity Measures
a.	Direct labour workers assemble a product	Unit-level	
b.	Products are designed by engineers	Product-level	
c.	Equipment is set up to process a batch	Batch-level	
d.	Machines are used to shape and cut materials	Unit-level	
e.	Monthly bills are sent out to regular customers	Customer-level	
f.	Materials are moved from the receiving dock to production lines	Batch-level	
g.	All completed units are inspected for defects	Unit-level	
h.	Diversity training is provided to all employees in the company	Organization-sustaining	

EXERCISE 5–7 Computing ABC Product Costs [LO2, LO3]
High-Calibre Products Corporation makes two products: titanium rims and posts. Data regarding the two products follow:

	Direct Labour-Hours per Unit	Annual Production
Rims	0.40	20,000 units
Posts	0.20	80,000 units

Additional information about the company follows:
a.   Rims require $17 in direct materials per unit, and posts require $10.
b.   The direct labour wage rate is $16 per hour.
c.   Rims are more complex to manufacture than posts, and they require special equipment.

d.   The ABC system has the following activity cost pools:

Activity Cost Pool	Activity Measure	Estimated Overhead Cost	Rims	Posts	Total
Machine setups	Number of setups	$21,600	100	80	180
Special processing.	Machine-hours	$180,000	4,000	0	4,000
General factory	Direct labour-hours	$288,000	8,000	16,000	24,000

Required:
1.   Compute the activity rate for each activity cost pool.
2.   Determine the unit cost of each product according to the ABC system, including direct materials and direct labour.

EXERCISE 5–8 First-Stage Allocations [LO2]

The operations vice-president of the Regal Bank of Canada, Kristin Wu, has been interested in investigating the efficiency of the bank's operations. She has been particularly concerned about the costs of handling routine transactions at the bank and would like to compare these costs at the bank's various branches. If the branches with the most efficient operations can be identified, their methods can be studied and then replicated elsewhere. While the bank maintains meticulous records of wages and other costs, there has been no attempt thus far to show how those costs are related to the various services provided by the bank. Wu has asked for your help in conducting an activity-based costing study of bank operations. In particular, she would like to know the cost of opening an account, the cost of processing deposits and withdrawals, and the cost of processing other customer transactions.

The Windsor branch of the Regal Bank of Canada submitted the following cost data for last year:

Teller wages.	$150,000
Assistant branch manager salary	70,000
Branch manager salary	85,000
Total.	$305,000

Virtually all of the other costs of the branch—rent, depreciation, utilities, and so on—are organization-sustaining costs that cannot be meaningfully assigned to individual customer transactions such as depositing cheques.

In addition to the cost data above, the employees of the Windsor branch have been interviewed concerning how their time was distributed last year across the activities included in the activity-based costing study. The results of those interviews appear below.

	Distribution of Resource Consumption across Activities				
	Opening Accounts	Processing Deposits and Withdrawals	Processing Other Customer Transactions	Other Activities	Totals
Teller wages.	0%	75%	15%	10%	100%
Assistant branch manager salary.	10%	15%	25%	50%	100%
Branch manager salary	0%	0%	20%	80%	100%

Required:
Prepare the first-stage allocation for Wu as illustrated in Exhibit 5–6.

EXERCISE 5–9 Computing and Interpreting Activity Rates [LO2]
(This exercise is a continuation of Exercise 5–8; it should be assigned *only* if Exercise 5–8 is also assigned.) The manager of the Windsor branch of the Regal Bank of Canada has provided the following data concerning the transactions of the branch during the past year.

Activity	Total Activity at the Windsor Branch
Opening accounts	200 accounts opened
Processing deposits and withdrawals	50,000 deposits and withdrawals
Processing other customer transactions	1,000 other customer transactions

The lowest costs reported by other branches for these activities are displayed below.

Activity	Lowest Cost among All Regal Bank of Canada Branches
Opening accounts	$24.35 per account opened
Processing deposits and withdrawals	$2.72 per deposit or withdrawal
Processing other customer transactions	$48.90 per other customer transaction

Required:
1. Using the first-stage allocation from Exercise 5–8 and the above data, compute the activity rates for the activity-based costing system. (Use Exhibit 5–7 as a guide.) Round all computations to the nearest whole cent.
2. What do these results suggest to you concerning operations at the Windsor branch?

EXERCISE 5–10 Second-Stage Allocation to an Order [LO3]
Transvaal Mining Tools Ltd. of South Africa makes specialty tools used in the mining industry. The company uses an activity-based costing system for internal decision-making purposes. The company has four activity cost pools as listed below. The currency in South Africa is the rand, denoted here by R.

Activity Cost Pool	Activity Measure	Activity Rate
Order size	Number of direct labour-hours	R17.60 per direct labour-hour
Customer orders	Number of customer orders	R360 per customer order
Product testing	Number of testing hours	R79 per testing hour
Selling	Number of sales calls	R1,494 per sales call

The managing director of the company would like information concerning the cost of a recently completed order for hard-rock drills. The order required 150 direct labour-hours, 18 hours of product testing, and three sales calls.

Required:
Prepare a report showing the overhead cost of the order for hard-rock drills according to the activity-based costing system. What is the total overhead cost assigned to the order?

EXERCISE 5–11 Cost Hierarchy [LO1]
Green Glider Corporation makes golf carts that it sells directly to golf courses throughout the world. Several basic models are available, which are modified to suit the needs of each particular golf course. A golf course located in British Columbia, for example, would typically specify that its golf carts come equipped with retractable rain-proof covers. In addition, each customer (i.e., golf course) customizes its golf carts with its own colour scheme and logo. The company typically makes all of the golf carts for a customer before starting work on the next customer's golf carts.

Below are listed a number of activities and costs at Green Glider Corporation:
a. The purchasing department orders the specific colour of paint specified by the customer from the company's supplier.
b. A steering wheel is installed in a golf cart.
c. An outside lawyer draws up a new generic sales contract for the company, limiting Green Glider's liability in case of accidents that involve its golf carts.
d. The company's paint shop makes a stencil for a customer's logo.
e. A sales representative visits a previous customer to check on how the company's golf carts are working out and to try to make a new sale.
f. The accounts receivable department prepares the bill for a completed order.
g. Electricity is used to heat and light the factory and the administrative offices.
h. A golf cart is painted.

i.   The company's engineer modifies the design of a model to eliminate a potential safety problem.
j.   The marketing department has a catalogue printed and then mails copies to golf course managers.
k.   Completed golf carts are individually tested on the company's test track.
l.   A new model golf cart is shipped to the leading golfing trade magazine to be evaluated for the magazine's annual rating of golf carts.

Required:
Classify each of the costs or activities above as unit-level, batch-level, product-level, customer-level, or organization-sustaining. In this case, customers are golf courses, products are the various models of the golf cart, a batch is a specific order from a customer, and units are individual golf carts.

EXERCISE 5–12 Second-Stage Allocation and Margin Calculations [LO3, LO4]
Roll Board Inc. manufactures several models of high-quality skateboards. The company's activity-based costing system has four activity cost pools, which are listed below along with their activity measures and activity rates:

Activity Cost Pool	Activity Measure	Activity Rate
Supporting direct labour	Number of direct labour-hours	$14 per direct labour-hour
Batch processing.	Number of batches	$98 per batch
Order processing.	Number of orders	$173 per order
Customer service.	Number of customers	$1,320 per customer

The company just completed a single order from SkateCo for 3,200 entry-level skateboards. The order was produced in 27 batches. Each skateboard required 0.7 direct labour-hours. The selling price was $125 per skateboard, the direct materials cost was $77.50 per skateboard, and the direct labour cost was $17.50 per skateboard. This was the only order from SkateCo for the year.

Required:
Using Exhibit 5–12 as a guide, prepare a report showing the customer margin on sales to SkateCo for the year.

EXERCISE 5–13 Cost Hierarchy and Activity Measures [LO1]
Various activities at Companhia de Textils, S.A., a manufacturing company located in Brazil, are listed below. The company makes a variety of products.
a.   Preventive maintenance is performed on general-purpose production equipment.
b.   Products are assembled by hand.
c.   Reminder notices are sent to customers who are late in making payments.
d.   Purchase orders are issued for materials to be used in production.
e.   Modifications are made to product designs.
f.   New employees are hired by the personnel office.
g.   Machine settings are changed between batches of different products.
h.   Parts inventories are maintained in the storeroom. (Each product requires its own unique parts.)
i.   Insurance costs are incurred on the company's facilities.

Required:
1.   Classify each of the activities as either unit-level, batch-level, product-level, customer-level, or organization-sustaining.
2.   Where possible, name one or more activity measures that could be used to assign costs generated by the activity to products or customers.

EXERCISE 5–14 Comprehensive Activity-Based Costing Exercise [LO2, LO3, LO4]
Cancico Communications has supplied the following data for use in its activity-based costing system:

Overhead Costs	
Wages and salaries	$262,500
Other overhead costs	150,000
Total overhead costs.	$412,500

Activity Cost Pool	Activity Measure	Total Activity
Direct labour support...........	Number of direct labour-hours	7,500 DLHs
Order processing..............	Number of orders	600 orders
Customer support	Number of customers	120 customers
Other	These costs are not allocated to products or customers	Not applicable

	Distribution of Resource Consumption across Activity Cost Pools				
	Direct Labour Support	Order Processing	Customer Support	Other	Total
Wages and salaries	20%	40%	30%	10%	100%
Other overhead costs	15%	25%	25%	35%	100%

During the year, Cancico Communications completed an order for special telephone equipment for a new customer, HurnTel. This customer did not order any other products during the year. Data concerning that order follow:

Selling price...............	$220 per unit
Units ordered..............	115 units
Direct materials	$195 per unit
Direct labour-hours	0.6 DLH per unit
Direct labour rate...........	$22 per DLH

Required:
1. Using Exhibit 5–6 as a guide, prepare a report showing the first-stage allocations of overhead costs to the activity cost pools.
2. Using Exhibit 5–7 as a guide, compute the activity rates for the activity cost pools.
3. Prepare a report showing the overhead costs for the order from HurnTel, including customer support costs.
4. Using Exhibit 5–12 as a guide, prepare a report showing the customer margin for HurnTel.

EXERCISE 5–15 Calculating and Interpreting Activity-Based Costing Data [LO2, LO3]
Jane's Cookhouse is a popular restaurant located in a scenic setting. The owner of the restaurant has been trying to better understand costs at the restaurant and has hired a student intern to conduct an activity-based costing study. The intern, in consultation with the owner, identified three major activities. The intern then completed the first-stage allocations of costs to the activity cost pools, using data from last month's operations. The results appear below:

Activity Cost Pool	Activity Measure	Total Cost	Total Activity
Serving a party of diners	Number of parties served	$12,000	5,000 parties
Serving a diner....................	Number of diners served	$90,000	12,000 diners
Serving a drink....................	Number of drinks ordered	$26,000	10,000 drinks

The above costs include all of the costs of the restaurant except for organization-sustaining costs such as rent, property taxes, and top-management salaries. A group of diners who ask to sit at the same table are counted as a party. Some costs, such as the costs of cleaning linen, are the same whether one person is at a table or the table is full. Other costs, such as washing dishes, depend on the number of diners served.

Prior to the activity-based costing study, the owner knew very little about the costs of the restaurant. She knew that the total cost for the month (including organization-sustaining costs) was $180,000 and that 12,000 diners had been served. Therefore, the average cost per diner was $15.

Required:
1. According to the activity-based costing system, what is the total cost of serving each of the following parties of diners?
   a. A party of four diners who order three drinks in total.
   b. A party of two diners who do not order any drinks.
   c. A lone diner who orders two drinks.
2. Convert the total costs you computed in (1) above to costs per diner. In other words, what is the average cost per diner for serving each of the following parties?
   a. A party of four diners who order three drinks in total.
   b. A party of two diners who do not order any drinks.
   c. A lone diner who orders two drinks.
3. Why do the costs per diner for the three different parties differ from each other and from the overall average cost of $15.00 per diner?

EXERCISE 5–16 Benefits of Activity-Based Costing [LO1]

Implementing an activity-based costing system should proceed only if management believes the benefits of doing so will exceed the costs. The costs of an ABC system are not difficult to quantify. They would include identifying the key activities, developing an information system to record and report information, collecting data for activity measures, and maintaining the system.

Required:
1. Identify, qualitatively, some potential benefits of adopting an ABC system.
2. How could these benefits be quantified?
3. How could management deal with the uncertainty related to any potential benefits of adopting an ABC system?

connect **Problems**

PROBLEM 5–17 Evaluating the Profitability of Services [LO2, LO3, LO4]

Kenosha Winter Services is a small family-owned snow removal business. For its services, the company has always charged a flat fee per hundred square metres of snow removal. The current fee is $12.75 per hundred square metres. However, there is some question about whether the company is actually making any money on jobs for some customers—particularly those located on more remote properties that require considerable travel time. The owner's daughter, home for the summer from college, has suggested investigating this question using activity-based costing. After some discussion, a simple system consisting of four activity cost pools seemed to be adequate. The activity cost pools and their activity measures appear below:

eXcel

Activity Cost Pool	Activity Measure	Activity for the Year
Snow removal	Square metres cleaned (00s)	32,000 hundred square metres
Travel to jobs	Kilometres driven	15,000 kilometres
Job support	Number of jobs	400 jobs
Other (costs of idle capacity and organization-sustaining costs)	None	Not applicable

The total cost of operating the company for the year is $390,000, which includes the following costs:

Wages	$150,000
Supplies	40,000
Snow removal equipment depreciation	20,000
Vehicle expenses	40,000
Office expenses	60,000
President's compensation	80,000
Total cost	$390,000

Resource consumption is distributed across the activities as follows:

	Distribution of Resource Consumption across Activity Cost Pools				
	Snow Removal	Travel to Jobs	Job Support	Other	Total
Wages	80%	10%	0%	10%	100%
Supplies.	100%	0%	0%	0%	100%
Snow removal equipment depreciation.	80%	0%	0%	20%	100%
Vehicle expenses.	0%	60%	0%	40%	100%
Office expenses.	0%	0%	45%	55%	100%
President's compensation.	0%	0%	40%	60%	100%

Job support consists of receiving calls from potential customers at the home office, scheduling jobs, billing, resolving issues, and so on.

Required:

1. Using Exhibit 5–6 as a guide, prepare the first-stage allocation of costs to the activity cost pools.
2. Using Exhibit 5–7 as a guide, compute the activity rates for the activity cost pools.
3. The company recently completed a 3,500 square-metre snow removal job at the Hometown Hardware—a 75-kilometre round-trip journey from Kenosha's offices. Compute the cost of this job using the activity-based costing system.
4. The revenue from the Hometown Hardware job was $446.25 (3,500 square metres at $12.75 per hundred square metres). Using Exhibit 5–12 as a guide, prepare a report showing the margin from this job.
5. What do you conclude concerning the profitability of the Hometown Hardware job? Explain.
6. What advice would you give the president concerning pricing jobs in the future?

PROBLEM 5–18 Activity-Based Costing and Bidding on Jobs [LO2, LO3]

Vance Asbestos Removal Company removes potentially toxic asbestos insulation and related products from buildings. The company's estimator has been involved in a long-simmering dispute with the on-site work supervisors. The on-site supervisors claim that the estimator does not adequately distinguish between routine work such as removal of asbestos insulation around heating pipes in older homes and non-routine work such as removing asbestos-contaminated ceiling plaster in industrial buildings. The on-site supervisors believe that non-routine work is far more expensive than routine work and should bear higher customer charges. The estimator sums up his position in this way: "My job is to measure the area to be cleared of asbestos. As directed by top management, I simply multiply the square metres by $4,000 per thousand square metres to determine the bid price. Since our average cost is only $3,000 per thousand square metres, that leaves enough cushion to take care of the additional costs of non-routine work that shows up. Besides, it is difficult to know what is routine or not routine until you actually start tearing things apart."

To shed light on this controversy, the company initiated an activity-based costing study of all of its costs. Data from the activity-based costing system follow:

Activity Cost Pool	Activity Measure	Total Activity
Removing asbestos.	Thousands of square metres	500,000 m²
Estimating and job setup	Number of jobs	200 jobs*
Working on non-routine jobs.	Number of non-routine jobs	25 non-routine jobs
Other (costs of idle capacity and organization-sustaining costs).	Not applicable; these costs are not allocated to jobs	

*The total number of jobs includes non-routine jobs as well as routine jobs. Non-routine jobs as well as routine jobs require estimating and setup work.

Wages and salaries	$ 200,000
Disposal fees	600,000
Equipment depreciation	80,000
On-site supplies	60,000
Office expenses	190,000
Licensing and insurance	370,000
Total cost	$1,500,000

| | Distribution of Resource Consumption across Activity Cost Pools | | | | |
	Removing Asbestos	Estimating and Job Setup	Working on Non-routine Jobs	Other	Total
Wages and salaries	40%	10%	35%	15%	100%
Disposal fees	70%	0%	30%	0%	100%
Equipment depreciation	50%	0%	40%	10%	100%
On-site supplies	55%	15%	20%	10%	100%
Office expenses	10%	40%	30%	20%	100%
Licensing and insurance	50%	0%	40%	10%	100%

Required:
1. Using Exhibit 5–6 as a guide, perform the first-stage allocation of costs to the activity cost pools.
2. Using Exhibit 5–7 as a guide, compute the activity rates for the activity cost pools.
3. Using the activity rates you have computed, determine the total cost and the average cost per thousand square metres of each of the following jobs according to the activity-based costing system.
   a. A routine 2,000-square-metre asbestos removal job.
   b. A routine 4,000-square-metre asbestos removal job.
   c. A non-routine 2,000-square-metre asbestos removal job.
4. Given the results you obtained in (3) above, do you agree with the estimator that the company's present policy for bidding on jobs is adequate?

PROBLEM 5–19 Second-Stage Allocations and Product Margins [LO3, LO4]
AnimPix, Inc., is a small company that creates computer-generated animations for films and television. Much of the company's work consists of short commercials for television, but the company also does realistic computer animations for special effects in movies.

The young founders of the company have become increasingly concerned with the economics of the business—particularly since many competitors have sprung up recently in the local area. To help understand the company's cost structure, an activity-based costing system has been designed. Three major activities are carried out in the company: animation concept, animation production, and contract administration. The animation concept activity is carried out at the contract proposal stage when the company bids on projects. This is an intensive activity that involves individuals from all parts of the company in creating storyboards and prototype stills to be shown to the prospective client. After the client has accepted a project, the animation goes into production and contract administration begins. Technical staff do almost all of the work involved in animation production, whereas the administrative staff is largely responsible for contract administration. The activity cost pools and their activity measures and rates are listed below:

Activity Cost Pool	Activity Measure	Activity Rate
Animation concept	Number of proposals	$6,000 per proposal
Animation production	Minutes of animation	$7,700 per minute of animation
Contract administration	Number of contracts	$6,600 per contract

These activity rates include all of the costs of the company, except for the costs of idle capacity and organization-sustaining costs. There are no direct labour or direct materials costs.

Preliminary analysis using these activity rates has indicated that the local commercials segment of the market may be unprofitable. This segment is highly competitive. Producers of local commercials may ask several companies like AnimPix to bid, which results in an unusually low ratio of accepted contracts to bids. Furthermore, the animation sequences tend to be much shorter for local commercials than for other work. Since animation work is billed at standard rates according to the running time of the completed animation, the revenues from these short projects tend to be below average. Data concerning activity in the local commercials market appear below:

Activity Measure	Local Commercials
Number of proposals	20
Minutes of animation	12
Number of contracts	8

The total sales for local commercials amounted to $240,000.

Required:
1. Determine the cost of the local commercials market. (Think of the local commercials market as a product.)
2. Prepare a report showing the product margin of the local commercials market. (Remember, this company has no direct materials or direct labour costs.)
3. What would you recommend to management concerning the local commercials market?

PROBLEM 5–20 Activity Rates and Activity-Based Management [LO2, LO3]
Onassis Catering is a Greek company that provides passenger and crew meals to airlines operating out of two international airports in Athens and Corfu. The operations at the two airports are managed separately, and top management believes that there may be benefits to greater sharing of information between the two operations.

To better compare the two operations, an activity-based costing system has been designed with the active participation of the managers at both airports. The activity-based costing system is based on the following activity cost pools and activity measures.

Activity Cost Pool	Activity Measure
Meal preparation.	Number of meals
Flight-related activities	Number of flights
Customer service	Number of customers
Other (costs of idle capacity and organization-sustaining costs)	Not applicable

The operation at Athens International Airport (AIA) serves 1 million meals annually on 5,000 flights for 10 different airlines. (Each airline is considered one customer.) The annual cost of running the AIA airport operation, excluding only the costs of raw materials for meals, totals €3,675,000. *Note*: The currency in Greece is the euro, denoted by €.

Annual Cost of the AIA Operation	
Cooks and delivery personnel wages	€3,000,000
Kitchen supplies	37,500
Chef salaries	225,000
Equipment depreciation	75,000
Administrative wages and salaries	187,500
Building costs	150,000
Total cost.	€3,675,000

To help determine the activity rates, employees were interviewed and asked how they divided their time among the four major activities. The results of employee interviews at AIA are displayed below:

Distribution of Resource Consumption across Activities at the AIA Operation					
	Meal Preparation	Flight-Related	Customer Service	Other	Total
Cooks and delivery personnel wages	75%	20%	0%	5%	100%
Kitchen supplies	100%	0%	0%	0%	100%
Chef salaries	30%	20%	40%	10%	100%
Equipment depreciation	60%	0%	0%	40%	100%
Administrative wages and salaries	0%	20%	60%	20%	100%
Building costs	0%	0%	0%	100%	100%

Required:
1. Perform the first-stage allocation of costs to the activity cost pools. (Use Exhibit 5–6 as a guide.)
2. Compute the activity rates for the activity cost pools. (Use Exhibit 5–7 as a guide.) Do not round off.
3. The Corfu operation has already concluded its activity-based costing study and has reported the following activity rates: €2.48 per meal for meal preparation; €144.50 per flight for flight-related activities; and €12,000 for customer service. Comparing the activity rates for the AIA operation you computed in (2) above to the activity rates for Corfu, do you have any suggestions for the top management of Onassis Catering?

---

connect Cases

CASE 5–21 Comprehensive Activity-Based Costing [LO2, LO3, LO5]

Kolbec Community College (KCC) has 4,000 full-time students and offers a variety of academic programs in three areas: professional studies, arts, and technology. The professional studies programs prepare students for administrative and clerical jobs in a variety of professional settings, including accounting, medicine, and law. The arts programs offerings are wide-ranging and include graphic design, digital animation, culinary arts, cosmetology, and music arts. The technology programs are also varied, including information technology, medical laboratory technology, electrical engineering technology, pharmacy technology, and natural resources technology.

The chief financial officer of KCC, Lynn Jones, has consistently emphasized to other members of the senior management team the importance of understanding the costs of delivering the various academic programs. To that end, the costing system used at KCC tracks the direct costs of each program, which are shown below on an annual basis, along with the number of full-time students.

Item	Professional Studies	Arts	Technology	Total
Full-time students	2,000	1,000	1,000	4,000
Professors' salaries	$1,260,000	$ 650,000	$ 780,000	$2,690,000
Administrative salaries.	105,000	70,000	70,000	245,000
Supplies.	40,000	150,000	50,000	240,000
Teaching support.	160,000	100,000	80,000	340,000
Facilities.	275,000	150,000	175,000	600,000
Total direct cost	$1,840,000	$1,120,000	$1,155,000	$4,115,000

It is very important to understand the overhead costs consumed by each academic program at KCC in determining the full cost of operating the programs. Central administration at KCC allocates financial resources to academic programs based on the estimated full cost per student of delivering the program. The overhead costs at KCC are significant, totalling over 60% of direct costs. Total annual overhead costs at KCC are as follows:

	Cost
Administrative salaries........................	$900,000
Facility costs	1,300,000
Office expenses...............................	300,000
Total overhead costs.........................	$2,500,000

Traditionally, KCC has allocated overhead costs to academic programs on the basis of the number of full-time students in each program. This approach was deemed appropriate since CFO Jones reasoned that increasing the number of students at KCC would result in higher overhead costs (e.g., more facilities would be needed, more indirect support costs would be incurred, etc.). However, Jones was beginning to question the accuracy of the traditional approach since it results in a similar full-cost per student amount for the arts and technology programs, which she did not feel made sense. Based on her knowledge of the programs, Jones felt that the technology program was probably more expensive to deliver than the arts program, but this did not come through in the traditional costing approach.

Jones recently attended a seminar on management techniques being used by leading educational institutions that, among other topics, covered the basics of the activity-based costing approach. She liked the idea of being able to assign indirect costs to academic programs on the basis of how much of the support activity resources are consumed by each program. If Jones's instincts are correct in that some programs consume more resources of certain activities than others, this could have a significant impact on the overhead costs assigned to each under the activity-based costing approach.

Upon returning to KCC, Jones decided to undertake an implementation of ABC. She, along with Assistant CFO James West, began by identifying the key activities used to support the teaching programs. Rather than getting too detailed with respect to identifying activities in the initial implementation, Jones decided to keep the process manageable and came up with six key activities. Next, based on a series of interviews with various KCC employees who work in the departments covered by the identified activities, Jones and West estimated the percentage of the total administrative, facility, and office expense resources consumed by each activity. Again, to keep the process efficient, Jones rounded all percentages to the nearest 5%, figuring that a "close enough" approach would suffice for this initial implementation and recognizing that the estimates are subjective to begin with. The results are shown below.

	Resource Distribution across Activities		
Activity	Administrative	Facilities	Office
Central administration	20%	5%	15%
Information systems technology	20%	15%	15%
Student counselling services..............	5%	5%	10%
Human resources	10%	5%	10%
Library operations	20%	60%	30%
Registrar's office	25%	10%	20%
Total................................	100%	100%	100%

Working with key personnel from each of the six activities shown above, Jones and West then identified the activity measure and the quantity of that measure used for each teaching program. Fortunately, KCC had implemented an ERP system a few years ago, which was already tracking much of the information needed regarding the activity measures and the specific quantities for each academic program.

Activity	Measure	Professional	Arts	Technology
Central administration	Hours spent on program	6,000	7,000	7,000
Information systems technology ..	Processing hours	6,000	3,000	12,000
Student counselling services.....	Number of students counselled	180	115	205
Human resources	Number of admin. staff and faculty members	21	15	14
Library operations	Number of library circulations	6,000	3,000	3,000
Registrar's office	Full-time students	2,000	1,000	1,000

Required:

1. Using the traditional approach to assigning overhead costs to academic programs:
    a. Calculate the predetermined overhead rate.
    b. Assign the overhead costs to each academic program using the predetermined rate.
    c. Calculate the total cost per student (direct costs plus overhead) of operating each academic program.

2. Using activity-based costing, complete the following requirements:
    a. Using Exhibit 5–6 as a guide, complete the first-stage allocation of overhead costs to academic programs.
    b. Using Exhibit 5–7 as a guide, calculate the activity rates for each of the activity cost pools.
    c. Using the activity rates calculated in (b), complete the second-stage allocation of overhead to academic programs.

3. Based on the results of (2), calculate the total cost per student (direct costs plus overhead) of operating each academic program.

4. Draft a memo to CFO Jones explaining the key reasons for differences in the total cost per student of operating each academic program that arise between the traditional costing approach and activity-based costing.

CASE 5–22 Activity-Based Costing and Pricing [LO2, LO3, LO4, LO5]

Oxford Concrete, Inc., (OCI) is a processor and distributor of various types of cement. The company buys quarried local rock, limestone, and clay from around the world and mixes, blends, and packages the processed cement for resale. OCI offers a large variety of different cement types that it sells in one-kilogram bags to local retailers for small do-it-yourself jobs. The major cost of the cement is raw materials. However, the company's predominantly automated mixing, blending, and packaging processes require a substantial amount of manufacturing overhead. The company uses relatively little direct labour.

Some of OCI's cement mixtures are very popular and sell in large volumes, while a few of the recently introduced cement mixtures sell in very low volumes. OCI prices its cements at manufacturing cost plus a 25% markup, with some adjustments made to keep the company's prices competitive.

For the coming year, OCI's budget includes estimated manufacturing overhead cost of $4,400,000. OCI assigns manufacturing overhead to products on the basis of direct labour-hours. The expected direct labour cost totals $1,200,000, which represents 100,000 hours of direct labour time. Based on the sales budget and expected raw materials costs, the company will purchase and use $10,000,000 of raw materials (mostly quarried rock, limestone, and clay) during the year.

The expected costs for direct materials and direct labour for one-kilogram bags of two of the company's cement products appear below.

	Normal Portland	High Sulphate Resistance
Direct materials	$9.00	$5.80
Direct labour (0.02 hours per bag)	$0.24	$0.24

OCI's controller believes that the company's traditional costing system may be providing misleading cost information. To determine whether this is the case, the controller has prepared an analysis of the year's expected manufacturing overhead costs, as shown in the following table:

Activity Cost Pool	Activity Measure	Expected Activity for the Year	Expected Cost for the Year
Purchasing.	Purchase orders	4,000 orders	$1,120,000
Materials handling	Number of setups	2,000 setups	386,000
Quality control	Number of batches	1,000 batches	180,000
Mixing	Mixing hours	190,000 mixing hours	2,090,000
Blending.	Blending hours	64,000 blending hours	384,000
Packaging	Packaging hours	48,000 packaging hours	240,000
Total manufacturing overhead cost			$4,400,000

Data regarding the expected production of Normal Portland and High Sulphate Resistance cement mixes are presented below.

	Normal Portland	High Sulphate Resistance
Expected sales	160,000 kilograms	8,000 kilograms
Batch size	10,000 kilograms	500 kilograms
Setups	4 per batch	4 per batch
Purchase order size.	20,000 kilograms	500 kilograms
Mixing time per 100 kilograms	3 mixing hours	3 mixing hours
Blending time per 100 kilograms.	1 blending hour	1 blending hour
Packaging time per 100 kilograms	0.6 packaging hours	0.6 packaging hours

Required:
1. Using direct labour-hours as the base for assigning manufacturing overhead cost to products, do the following:
    a. Determine the predetermined overhead rate that will be used during the year.
    b. Determine the unit product cost of one kilogram of the Normal Portland cement and one kilogram of the High Sulphate Resistance cement.
2. Using activity-based costing as the basis for assigning manufacturing overhead cost to products, do the following:
    a. Determine the total amount of manufacturing overhead cost assigned to the Normal Portland cement and to the High Sulphate Resistance cement for the year.
    b. Using the data developed in 2(a) above, compute the amount of manufacturing overhead cost per kilogram of the Normal Portland cement and the High Sulphate Resistance cement. Round all computations to the nearest whole cent.
    c. Determine the unit product cost of one kilogram of the Normal Portland cement and one kilogram of the High Sulphate Resistance cement.
3. Write a brief memo to the president of OCI explaining what you have found in (1) and (2) above and discuss the implications to the company of using direct labour as the base for assigning manufacturing overhead cost to products.

(CMA, adapted)

Research and Application

R 5–23 Activity-Based Costing Applied [LO1, LO2, LO3]
Activity-based costing can be applied in not-for-profit organizations such as colleges and universities (see Case 5–21). Arrange a meeting with an administrative officer in the business faculty of your college or university to discuss the cost allocation process currently employed and the implications of adopting an activity-based costing system.

Required:
1. Identify the key cost objects (e.g., teaching departments) currently used in the business faculty's management control system.
2. Determine how costs are currently assigned to these cost objects.
3. Determine the key activities required to support the teaching departments of the business faculty.
4. Identify an activity measure for each activity identified in (1).
5. Qualitatively evaluate how use of an ABC system [based on the data gathered in (3) and (4) above] would affect the assignment of costs to the cost objects in the business faculty.

■ APPENDIX 5A: ABC ACTION ANALYSIS

A conventional ABC analysis, such as the one presented in Exhibit 5–11, has several important limitations. Referring back to Exhibit 5–11, recall that the custom compass housing shows a negative product margin of $49,500. Because of this apparent loss, managers were considering dropping this product. However, it is unlikely that all of the $589,500 cost of the product would be avoided if the product was dropped. Some of these costs would continue even if the product was totally eliminated. *Before* taking action, it is vital to identify which costs would be avoided and which costs would continue. Only those costs that can be avoided are relevant in the decision. Moreover, many of the costs would require explicit management action to eliminate. If the custom compass housing product was eliminated, the direct materials cost would be avoided without any explicit management action—the materials simply would not be ordered. On the other hand, explicit management action *would* be required to eliminate the salaries of overhead workers that have been assigned to the custom compass housing product.

Simply shifting these managed costs to other products would not solve anything. These costs would have to be eliminated or the resources shifted to a work centre that is currently a *constraint*. As will be more fully described in Chapter 12, a constraint is a resource limitation, such as machine time or raw material supply, that prevents a company from fully meeting demand for its products or services. While eliminating the cost is obviously beneficial, redeploying a resource is beneficial only if the resource is shifted to the constraint in the process. If resources are redeployed to a work centre that is not a constraint, it would have the effect of increasing the excess capacity in that work centre— which has no direct benefit to the company.

Additionally, if some overhead costs need to be eliminated as a result of dropping a product, specific managers must be held responsible for eliminating those costs or the savings are unlikely to occur. If no one is specifically held responsible for eliminating the costs, they will almost certainly continue to be incurred. Without external pressure, managers usually avoid cutting costs in their areas of responsibility. The action analysis report developed in this appendix is intended to help top managers identify which costs are relevant in a decision and to place responsibility for the elimination of the costs on the appropriate managers.

LEARNING OBJECTIVE 6
Prepare an action analysis report using activity-based costing data, and interpret the report.

Activity Rates—Action Analysis Report

Constructing an action analysis report begins with the results of the first-stage allocation, which is reproduced as Exhibit 5A–1. In contrast to the conventional ABC analysis covered in the chapter, the calculation of the activity rates for an action analysis report is a bit more detailed. In addition to computing an overall activity rate for each activity cost pool, an activity rate is computed for each cell in Exhibit 5A–1. The computations of activity rates for the action analysis are carried out in Exhibit 5A–2. For example, the $125,000 cost of indirect factory wages for the Customer Orders cost pool is divided by the total activity for that cost pool—1,000 orders—to arrive at the activity rate of $125 per customer order for indirect factory wages. Similarly, the $200,000 cost of indirect factory wages for the Product Design cost pool is divided by the total activity for that cost pool—400 designs—to arrive at the activity rate of $500 per design for indirect factory wages. Note that the totals at the bottom of Exhibit 5A–2 agree with the overall activity rates in Exhibit 5–7 in the chapter. Exhibit 5A–2, which shows the activity rates for the action analysis report, contains more detail than Exhibit 5–7, which contains the activity rates for the conventional ABC analysis.

Assignment of Overhead Costs to Products— Action Analysis Report

Similarly, computing the overhead costs to be assigned to products for an action analysis report involves more detail than a conventional ABC analysis. The computations for Classic Brass are carried out in Exhibit 5A–3. For example, the activity rate of $125 per customer

EXHIBIT 5A–1   First-Stage Allocations to Activity Cost Pools

	A	B	C	D	E	F	G
1				Activity Cost Pools			
2		Customer Orders	Product Design	Order Size	Customer Relations	Other	Total
4	Production Department:						
5	Indirect factory wages	$ 125,000	$ 200,000	$ 100,000	$ 50,000	$ 25,000	$ 500,000
6	Factory equipment depreciation	60,000	0	180,000	0	60,000	300,000
7	Factory utilities	0	12,000	60,000	0	48,000	120,000
8	Factory building lease	0	0	0	0	80,000	80,000
10	General Administrative Department:						
11	Administrative wages and salaries	60,000	20,000	40,000	120,000	160,000	400,000
12	Office equipment depreciation	15,000	0	0	12,500	22,500	50,000
13	Administrative building lease	0	0	0	0	60,000	60,000
15	Marketing Department:						
16	Marketing wages and salaries	55,000	20,000	0	150,000	25,000	250,000
17	Selling expenses	5,000	0	0	35,000	10,000	50,000
19	Total cost	$ 320,000	$ 252,000	$ 380,000	$ 367,500	$ 490,500	$ 1,810,000
20							

Exhibit 5A–1 / Exhibit 5A–2 / Exhibit 5-

Ready   NUM

EXHIBIT 5A–2   Computation of the Activity Rates for the Action Analysis Report

	A	B	C	D	E	F
1			Activity Cost Pools			
2		Customer Orders	Product Design	Order Size	Customer Relations	Other
4	Total activity	1,000 orders	400 product designs	20,000 machine-hours	250 active customers	Not applicable*
7	Production Department:					
8	Indirect factory wages	$ 125	$ 500	$ 5	$ 200	
9	Factory equipment depreciation	60	0	9	0	
10	Factory utilities	0	30	3	0	
11	Factory building lease	0	0	0	0	
13	General Administrative Department:					
14	Administrative wages and salaries	60	50	2	480	
15	Office equipment depreciation	15	0	0	50	
16	Administrative building lease	0	0	0	0	
18	Marketing Department:					
19	Marketing wages and salaries	55	50	0	600	
20	Selling expenses	5	0	0	140	
22	Total (conventional ABC analysis)	$ 320	$ 630	$ 19	$ 1,470	
24	*Activity rates are not computed for the Other cost pool since these costs will not be allocated further.					

Exhibit 5A–1 / Exhibit 5A–2

Ready   NUM

$125,000 ÷ 1,000 orders = $125 per order.

Other entries in the spreadsheet are computed similarly.

order for indirect factory wages is multiplied by 600 orders for the standard stanchions to arrive at the cost of $75,000 for indirect factory wages in Exhibit 5A–3. Instead of just a single cost number for each cost pool as in the conventional ABC analysis, we now have an entire cost matrix showing much more detail. Note that the column totals for the cost matrix in Exhibit 5A–3 agree with the ABC costs for stanchions in Exhibit 5–9. Indeed, the conventional ABC analysis of Exhibit 5–11 can be easily constructed using the column totals at the bottom of the cost matrices in Exhibit 5A–3. In contrast, the action analysis report will be based on the row totals at the right of the cost matrices in Exhibit 5A–3. In addition, the action analysis report will include a simple colour-coding scheme that will help managers identify how easily the various costs can be adjusted.

EXHIBIT 5A–3   Action Analysis Cost Matrices

	Customer Orders	Product Design	Order Size	Customer Relations	Total
Action Analysis Cost Matrix for Standard Stanchions					
	Activity Cost Pools				
Total activity for stanchions	600 orders	0 product designs	17,500 machine-hours	Not applicable	
Production Department:					
Indirect factory wages	$ 75,000	$ 0	$87,500		$162,500
Factory equipment depreciation	36,000	0	157,500		193,500
Factory utilities	0	0	52,500		52,500
Factory building lease	0	0	0		0
General Administrative Department:					
Administrative wages and salaries	36,000	0	35,000		71,000
Office equipment depreciation	9,000	0	0		9,000
Administrative building lease	0	0	0		0
Marketing Department:					
Marketing wages and salaries	33,000	0	0		33,000
Selling expenses	3,000	0	0		3,000
Total (conventional ABC analysis)	$192,000	$ 0	$332,500		$524,500

From Exhibit 5A–2 the activity rate for indirect factory wages for the Customer Orders cost pool is $125 per order.

$125 per order × 600 orders = $75,000

Other entries in the table are computed in a similar way.

	Customer Orders	Product Design	Order Size	Customer Relations	Total
Action Analysis Cost Matrix for the Custom Compass Housing					
	Activity Cost Pools				
Total activity for custom compass housings	400 order	400 product design	2,500 machine-hours	Not applicable	
Production Department:					
Indirect factory wages	$ 50,000	$200,000	$ 12,500		$262,500
Factory equipment depreciation	24,000	0	22,500		46,500
Factory utilities	0	12,000	7,500		19,500
Factory building lease	0	0	0		0
General Administrative Department:					
Administrative wages and salaries	24,000	20,000	5,000		49,000
Office equipment depreciation	6,000	0	0		6,000
Administrative building lease	0	0	0		0
Marketing Department:					
Marketing wages and salaries	22,000	20,000	0		42,000
Selling expenses	2,000	0	0		2,000
Total (conventional ABC analysis)	$128,000	$252,000	$ 47,500		$427,500

From Exhibit 5A–2 the activity rate for indirect factory wages for the Customer Orders cost pool is $125 per order.

$125 per order × 400 orders = $50,000

Other entries in the table are computed in a similar way.

EXHIBIT 5A–4   Ease of Adjustment Codes

Green: Costs that adjust automatically to changes in activity without management action.

Direct materials
Shipping costs

Yellow: Costs that could, in principle, be adjusted to changes in activity, but management action would be required.

Direct labour
Indirect factory wages
Factory utilities
Administrative wages and salaries
Office equipment depreciation
Marketing wages and salaries
Selling expenses

Red: Costs that would be very difficult to adjust to changes in activity and management action would be required.

Factory equipment depreciation
Factory building lease
Administrative building lease

Ease of Adjustment Codes

The ABC team constructed Exhibit 5A–4 to aid managers in the use of the ABC data. In this exhibit, each cost has been assigned an *ease of adjustment code*—Green, Yellow, or Red. The ease of adjustment code reflects how easily the cost could be adjusted to changes in activity.[6] Green costs are those that would adjust more or less automatically to changes in activity without any action by managers. For example, direct materials costs would adjust to increases or decreases in orders without any action being taken by managers. If a customer does not order stanchions, the direct materials for the stanchions would not be required and would not be ordered. Yellow costs are those that could be adjusted in response to changes in activity, but such adjustments require management action; the adjustment is not automatic. The ABC team believes, for example, that direct labour costs should be included in the Yellow category. Managers must make difficult decisions and take explicit action to increase or decrease, in aggregate, direct labour costs—particularly since the company has a no layoff policy. Red costs are costs that could be adjusted to changes in activity only with a great deal of difficulty, and the adjustment would require management action. The building lease falls into this category, since breaking the lease contract would likely be very difficult and expensive.

The Action Analysis View of the ABC Data

Looking at Exhibit 5A–3, the totals on the right-hand side of the table indicate that the $427,500 of overhead cost for the custom compass housing consists of $262,500 of indirect factory wages, $46,500 of factory equipment depreciation, and so on. These data are displayed in Exhibit 5A–5, which shows an action analysis of the custom compass housing product. An action analysis report is a report showing what costs have been assigned to the cost object, such as a product or customer, and how difficult it would be to adjust the cost if there is a change in activity. Note that the Red Margin at the bottom of Exhibit 5A–5, ($49,500), is the same as the Product Margin for the custom compass housing shown in Exhibit 5–11.

The cost data in the Exhibit 5A–5 action analysis are arranged by the colour-coded ease of adjustment. All of the Green costs—those that adjust more or less automatically to changes in activity—appear together at the top of the list. These costs total $74,500 and are subtracted from the sales of $540,000 to yield a Green margin of $465,500. The same procedure is followed for the Yellow and Red costs. This action analysis approach indicates what costs would have to be cut and how difficult it would be to cut them if the custom compass housing product was dropped. Prior to making any decision about dropping products, the managers responsible for the costs must agree to either eliminate the resources represented by those costs or to transfer the resources to an area in the

	A	B	C	D
1	**Custom Compass Housing**			
2	Sales (from Exhibit 5–11)		$540,000	
4	Green costs:			
5	Direct materials (from Exhibit 5–11)	$ 69,500		
6	Shipping (from Exhibit 5–11)	5,000	74,500	
7	Green margin		465,500	
9	Yellow costs:			
10	Direct labour (from Exhibit 5–11)	87,500		
11	Indirect factory wages (from Exhibit 5A–3)	262,500		
12	Factory utilities (from Exhibit 5A–3)	19,500		
13	Administrative wages and salaries (from Exhibit 5A–3)	49,000		
14	Office equipment depreciation (from Exhibit 5A–3)	6,000		
15	Marketing wages and salaries (from Exhibit 5A–3)	42,000		
16	Selling expenses (from Exhibit 5A–3)	2,000	468,500	
17	Yellow margin		(3,000)	
19	Red costs:			
20	Factory equipment depreciation (from Exhibit 5A–3)	46,500		
21	Factory building lease (from Exhibit 5A–3)	0		
22	Administrative building lease (from Exhibit 5A–3)	0	46,500	
23	Red margin		$ (49,500)	
24				

Exhibit 5A–2 \ Exhibit 5A–3 \ Exhibit 5A–5

Ready / NUM

EXHIBIT 5A–5   Action Analysis of Custom Compass Housings: Activity-Based Costing System

organization that really needs the resources—namely, a constraint. If managers do not make such a commitment, it is likely that the costs would continue to be incurred. As a result, the company would lose the sales from the products without fully eliminating the related costs, particularly those in the Yellow and Red categories.

Wrap-Up

To be of value in the decision-making process, managers must properly interpret the results of action analysis. For example it is highly unlikely that a decision to eliminate the custom compass housings product line will allow Classic Brass to avoid an operating loss of $49,500. The reason is that the Red cost (factory equipment depreciation) in Exhibit 5A–5 is very difficult (if not impossible) to avoid in the short-term. Similarly, the Yellow margin loss of $3,000 is also unlikely to represent the actual loss avoided by dropping the custom compass housings line. The largest Yellow cost in Exhibit 5A–5 is indirect factory wages of $262,500, which, given the company's no layoff policy, will not be avoided if the product is discontinued. Thus, while the Yellow costs are adjustable if management decides to take action, eliminating the entire $468,500 is very unlikely. Instead of thinking about Yellow or Red costs as avoidable if the product is discontinued, management is likely better served by thinking about how to reduce (not eliminate) costs such as indirect factory wages that primarily relate to the product design activity. For example, total quality management techniques could be used to identify opportunities to reduce product design costs or Classic Brass could get benchmark data from industry leaders to identify potential efficiency gains. By measuring the resources consumed by products (and other cost objects), a "best practice" ABC system provides a much better basis for decision making than a traditional cost accounting system that allocates overhead costs with little regard for what might be causing the overhead.

A well-designed ABC system provides managers with estimates of potentially relevant costs that can be a very useful starting point for management analysis. Exhibit 5A–6 summarizes all of the steps required to create both an action analysis report as illustrated in this appendix and an activity analysis as shown in the chapter.

EXHIBIT 5A–6 Summary of the Steps to Produce an Action Analysis Report

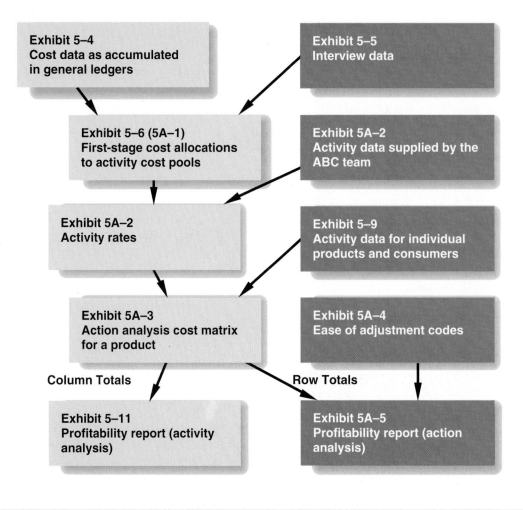

Appendix 5A Summary

- An action analysis report provides more information for decision making than a conventional ABC analysis. The action analysis report makes it clear where costs would have to be adjusted in the organization as a result of an action. **[LO6]**
- In a conventional ABC analysis, a cost such as $320 for processing an order represents costs from many parts of the organization. If an order is dropped, there will be little pressure to actually eliminate the $320 cost unless it is clear where the costs are incurred and which managers would be responsible for reducing the cost. **[LO6]**
- An action analysis report traces the costs to where they are incurred in the organization and makes it much easier to assign responsibility to managers for reducing costs. **[LO6]**
- An action analysis report uses ease of adjustment codes to provide information on how easily a cost can be adjusted to changes in activity. Green costs will adjust automatically to changes in activity, Yellow costs will change but only if management takes action, and Red costs would be very difficult to adjust and will also require management action. **[LO6]**

Appendix 5A Review Problem: Activity Analysis Report

Refer to the data for Advanced Products Corporation in the Review Problem at the end of the main body of the chapter, beginning on page 193.

Required:

1. Compute activity rates for Advanced Products Corporation as in Exhibit 5A–2.
2. Using Exhibit 5A–3 as a guide, prepare a report showing the overhead costs for the Shenzhen order described in requirement 3 on page 194.

3. The management of Advanced Products Corporation has assigned ease of adjustment codes to costs as follows:

Cost	Ease of Adjustment Code
Direct materials	Green
Direct labour	Yellow
Wages and salaries.	Yellow
Other overhead costs	Red

Using Exhibit 5A–5 as a guide, prepare an action analysis of the Shenzhen order.

Solution to Appendix 5A Review Problem

1. The activity rates are computed by dividing the costs in the cells of the first-stage allocation above by the total activity from the top of the column:

Activity Cost Pools	Volume-Related	Order-Related	Customer Support
Total activity	20,000 DLHs	400 orders	200 customers
Wages and salaries.	$6.00	$225.00	$300.00
Other overhead costs	1.50	25.00	100.00
Total cost	$7.50	$250.00	$400.00

Example: $120,000 ÷ 20,000 DLHs = $6.00 per DLH

Volume-related wages and salaries from the first-stage allocation in (1) of the end-of-chapter review problem.

2. The overhead cost for the order is computed as follows:

Activity Cost Pools	Volume-Related	Order-Related	Customer Support	Total
Total activity	20 DLHs	1 order	1 customer	
Wages and salaries.	$120.00	$225.00	$300.00	$645.00
Other overhead costs	30.00	25.00	100.00	155.00
Total cost	$150.00	$250.00	$400.00	$800.00

Example: 20 DLHs × $6.00 per DLH = $120.00

Activity rate for volume-related wages and salaries from (1) above.

3. The action analysis report is constructed as follows:

Sales (10 units × $300 per unit)		$3,000
Green Costs:		
Direct materials (10 units × $180 per unit)	$1,800	1,800
Green margin.		1,200
Yellow Costs:		
Direct labour (10 units × $50 per unit).	500	
Wages and salaries (see above)	645	1,145
Yellow margin		55
Red Costs:		
Other overhead costs (see above).	155	155
Red margin		$ (100)

Appendix 5A Exercises and Problems ■ connect™

EXERCISE 5A–1 Preparing an Action Analysis Report [LO6]

Pro Golf Corporation produces private-label golf clubs for pro shops throughout North America. The company uses activity-based costing to evaluate the profitability of serving its customers. This analysis is based on categorizing the company's costs as follows, using the ease of adjustment colour-coding scheme described in this appendix:

	Ease of Adjustment Code
Direct materials	Green
Direct labour	Yellow
Indirect labour	Yellow
Factory equipment depreciation	Red
Factory administration	Red
Selling and administrative wages and salaries	Red
Selling and administrative depreciation	Red
Marketing expenses	Yellow

Management would like to evaluate the profitability of a particular customer—the Castleview Golf Club. Over the past 12 months, this customer submitted one order for 80 golf clubs that had to be produced in two batches due to differences in product labelling requested by the customer. Summary data concerning the order appear below:

Number of clubs	80
Number of orders	1
Number of batches	2
Direct labour-hours per club	0.3
Selling price per club	$48.00
Direct materials cost per club	$25.40
Direct labour rate per hour	$21.50

A cost analyst working in the controller's office at the company has already produced the following action analysis cost matrix for Castleview Golf Club:

Action Analysis Cost Matrix for Castleview Golf Club

	Activity Cost Pools				
Activity	Volume (24 direct labour-hours)	Batch Processing (2 batches)	Order Processing (1 order)	Customer Service (1 customer)	Total
Manufacturing overhead:					
Indirect labour	$ 33.60	$51.60	$ 4.80	$ 0.00	$ 90.00
Factory equipment depreciation	105.60	0.80	0.00	0.00	106.40
Factory administration	16.80	0.60	14.00	231.00	262.40
Selling and administrative overhead:					
Wages and salaries	12.00	0.00	38.00	386.00	436.00
Depreciation	0.00	0.00	5.00	25.00	30.00
Marketing expenses	115.20	0.00	57.00	368.00	540.20
Total	$283.20	$53.00	$118.80	$1,010.00	$1,465.00

Required:

Prepare an action analysis report showing the profitability of the Castleview Golf Club. Include direct materials and direct labour costs in the report. Use Exhibit 5A–5 as a guide for organizing the report.

EXERCISE 5A–2 Second-Stage Allocation to an Order Using the Action Analysis Approach [LO3, LO6]

This exercise should be assigned in conjunction with Exercise 5–10.

The results of the first-stage allocation of the activity-based costing system at Transvaal Mining Tools Ltd., in which the activity rates were computed, appear at the top of the next page.

	Order Size	Customer Orders	Product Testing	Selling
Manufacturing overhead:				
Indirect labour	R 9.60	R 231.00	R 36.00	R 0.00
Factory depreciation...............	7.00	0.00	18.00	0.00
Factory utilities....................	0.20	0.00	1.00	0.00
Factory administration	0.00	46.00	24.00	12.00
Selling and administrative:				
Wages and salaries	0.80	72.00	0.00	965.00
Depreciation.....................	0.00	11.00	0.00	36.00
Taxes and insurance	0.00	0.00	0.00	49.00
Selling expenses	0.00	0.00	0.00	432.00
Total overhead cost................	R17.60	R 360.00	R 79.00	R 1,494.00

Required:

1. Using Exhibit 5A–3 as a guide, prepare a report showing the overhead cost of the order for hard-rock drills discussed in Exercise 5–10. What is the total overhead cost of the order?

2. Explain the two different perspectives this report gives to managers concerning the nature of the overhead costs involved in the order. (*Hint*: Look at the row and column totals of the report you have prepared.)

EXERCISE 5A–3 Second-Stage Allocations and Margin Calculations Using the Action Analysis Approach [LO3, LO6]

Refer to the data for Roll Board Inc. in Exercise 5–12 and the following additional details concerning the activity rates:

	Activity Rates			
	Supporting Direct Labour	Batch Processing	Processing	Customer Service
Manufacturing overhead:				
Indirect labour	$ 3.60	$55.00	$ 21.00	$ 0.00
Factory equipment depreciation ..	4.00	17.00	0.00	0.00
Factory administration	2.05	7.00	35.00	180.00
Selling and administrative:				
Wages and salaries	2.90	16.00	61.00	538.00
Depreciation...................	0.00	3.00	10.00	27.00
Marketing expenses............	1.45	0.00	46.00	575.00
Total activity rate	$14.00	$98.00	$173.00	$1,320.00

Management has provided their ease of adjustment codes for the purpose of preparing action analyses.

	Ease of Adjustment Codes
Direct materials	Green
Direct labour	Yellow
Manufacturing overhead:	
Indirect labour	Yellow
Factory equipment depreciation	Red
Factory administration................	Red
Selling and administrative:	
Wages and salaries	Red
Depreciation.......................	Red
Marketing expenses..................	Yellow

Required:

Using Exhibit 5A–5 as a guide, prepare an action analysis report for SkateCo. similar to those prepared for products.

EXERCISE 5A–4 Comprehensive Activity-Based Costing Exercise [LO2, LO3, LO6]
Refer to the data for Cancico Communications in Exercise 5–14.

Required:
1. Using Exhibit 5A–1 as a guide, prepare a report showing the first-stage allocations of overhead costs to the activity cost pools.
2. Using Exhibit 5A–2 as a guide, compute the activity rates for the activity cost pools.
3. Using Exhibit 5–12 as a guide, prepare a report showing the overhead costs for the order from HurnTel including customer support costs.
4. Using Exhibit 5–12 as a guide, prepare a report showing the customer margin for HurnTel.
5. Using Exhibit 5A–5 as a guide, prepare an action analysis report showing the customer margin for HurnTel. Direct materials should be coded as a Green cost, direct labour and wages and salaries as Yellow costs, and other overhead costs as Red costs.
6. What action, if any, do you recommend as a result of the above analyses?

PROBLEM 5A–5 Evaluating the Profitability of Services Using an Action Analysis [LO2, LO3, LO6]
Refer to the data for Kenosha Winter Services in Problem 5–17.

Required:
1. Using Exhibit 5A–1 as a guide, prepare the first-stage allocation of costs to the activity cost pools.
2. Using Exhibit 5A–2 as a guide, compute the activity rates for the activity cost pools.
3. The company recently completed a 3,500-square metre snow removal job at Hometown Hardware—a 75-kilometre round-trip journey from the Kenosha's offices. Compute the cost of this job using the activity-based costing system.
4. The revenue from the Hometown Hardware job was $446.25 (3,500 square metres at $12.75 per hundred square metres). Using Exhibit 5A–5 as a guide, prepare an action analysis report of the Hometown Hardware job. The president of Kenosha Winter Services considers all of the company's costs to be Green costs except for office expenses, which are coded Yellow, and his own compensation, which is coded Red. The people who do the actual snow removal are all trained part-time workers who are paid only for work actually done.
5. What do you conclude concerning the profitability of the Hometown Hardware job? Explain.
6. What advice would you give the president concerning pricing jobs in the future?

PROBLEM 5A–6 Second-Stage Allocations and Product Margins [LO3, LO6]
Refer to the data for AnimPix, Inc., in Problem 5–19. In addition, the company has provided the following details concerning its activity rates:

	Activity Rates		
	Animation Concept	Animation Production	Contract Administration
Technical staff salaries.	$3,500	$5,000	$1,800
Animation equipment depreciation.	600	1,500	0
Administrative wages and salaries	1,400	200	4,600
Supplies costs	300	600	100
Facility costs	200	400	100
Total	$6,000	$7,700	$6,600

Management has provided the following ease of adjustment codes for the various costs:

	Ease of Adjustment Code
Technical staff salaries.	Red
Animation equipment depreciation.	Red
Administrative wages and salaries	Yellow
Supplies costs.	Green
Facility costs	Red

These codes created some controversy. In particular, some administrators objected to coding their own salaries Yellow, while the technical staff salaries were coded Red. However, the founders of the firm overruled these objections by pointing out that "our technical staff is our most valuable asset. Good animators are extremely difficult to find, and they would be the last to go if we had to cut back."

Required:
1. Using Exhibit 5A–3 as a guide, determine the cost of the local commercials market. (Think of the local commercials market as a product.)
2. Using Exhibit 5A–5 as a guide, prepare an action analysis report concerning the local commercials market. (This company has no direct materials or direct labour costs.)
3. What would you recommend to management concerning the local commercials market?

APPENDIX 5B: USING A MODIFIED FORM OF ACTIVITY-BASED COSTING TO DETERMINE PRODUCT COSTS FOR EXTERNAL REPORTS

This chapter has emphasized using activity-based costing information in internal decisions. However, a modified form of activity-based costing can also be used to develop product costs for external financial reports. For this purpose, product costs include *all* manufacturing overhead costs—including organization-sustaining costs and the costs of idle capacity—and exclude all non-manufacturing costs, even costs that are clearly caused by the products.

> **LEARNING OBJECTIVE 7**
> Use activity-based costing techniques to compute unit product costs for external reports.

The simplest absorption costing systems as described in Chapter 3 assign manufacturing overhead costs to products using a single factorywide predetermined overhead rate based on direct labour-hours or machine-hours. When activity-based costing is used to assign manufacturing overhead costs to products, a predetermined overhead rate is computed for each activity cost pool. An example will make this difference clear.

Maxtar Industries manufactures high-quality smoker/barbecue units. The company has two product lines—Premium and Standard. The company has traditionally applied manufacturing overhead costs to these products using a plantwide predetermined overhead rate based on direct labour-hours. Exhibit 5B–1 details how the unit product costs of the

EXHIBIT 5B–1   Maxtar Industries' Traditional Costing System

Basic Data		
Total estimated manufacturing overhead cost	$1,520,000	
Total estimated direct labour-hours	400,000 DLHs	

	Premium	Standard
Direct materials per unit.	$40.00	$30.00
Direct labour per unit.	$24.00	$18.00
Direct labour-hours per unit.	2.0 DLHs	1.5 DLHs
Units produced	50,000 units	200,000 units

Computation of the Predetermined Overhead Rate

$$\text{Predetermined overhead rate} = \frac{\text{Total estimated manufacturing overhead}}{\text{Total estimated amount of the allocation base}}$$

$$= \frac{\$1,520,000}{400,000} = \$3.80 \text{ per DLH}$$

Traditional Unit Product Costs

	Premium	Standard
Direct materials	$40.00	$30.00
Direct labour	24.00	18.00
Manufacturing overhead (2.0 DLHs × $3.80 per DLH;		
1.5 DLHs × $3.80 per DLH).	7.60	5.70
Unit product cost.	$71.60	$53.70

two product lines are computed using the company's traditional costing system. The unit product cost of the Premium product line is $71.60 and the unit product cost of the Standard product line is $53.70 according to this traditional costing system.

Maxtar Industries has recently experimented with an activity-based costing approach to determine its unit product costs for external reporting purposes. The company's activity-based costing system has three activity cost pools: (1) supporting direct labour; (2) setting up machines; and (3) parts administration. The top of Exhibit 5B–2 displays basic data concerning these activity cost pools. Note that the total estimated overhead cost in these three costs pools, $1,520,000, agrees with the total estimated overhead cost in the company's traditional costing system. The company's activity-based costing system simply provides an alternative way to allocate the company's manufacturing overhead across the two products.

EXHIBIT 5B–2   Maxtar Industries' Activity-Based Costing System

Basic Data

1. Activities and Activity Measures	Estimated Overhead Cost	Premium	Standard	Total
		Expected Activity		
Supporting direct labour (DLHs)	$ 800,000	100,000	300,000	400,000
Setting up machines (setups)	480,000	600	200	800
Parts administration (part types)	240,000	140	60	200
Total manufacturing overhead cost.	$1,520,000			

2. Computation of Activity Rates

Activities	(a) Estimated Overhead Cost	(b) Total Expected Activity	(a) ÷ (b) Activity Rate
Supporting direct labour	$800,000	400,000 DLHs	$2 per DLH
Setting up machines	$480,000	800 setups	$600 per setup
Parts administration.	$240,000	200 part types	$1,200 per part type

3. Assigning Overhead Costs to Products

Overhead Cost for the Premium Product

Activity Cost Pools	(a) Activity Rate	(b) Activity	(a) × (b) ABC Cost
Supporting direct labour	$2 per DLH	100,000 DLHs	$200,000
Setting up machines	$600 per setup	600 setups	360,000
Parts administration.	$1,200 per part type	140 part types	168,000
Total.			$728,000

Overhead Cost for the Standard Product

Activity Cost Pools	(a) Activity Rate	(b) Activity	(a) × (b) ABC Cost
Supporting direct labour	$2 per DLH	300,000 DLHs	$600,000
Setting up machines	$600 per setup	200 setups	120,000
Parts administration.	$1,200 per part type	60 part types	72,000
Total.			$792,000

4. Activity-Based Costing Product Costs

	Premium	Standard
Direct materials	$40.00	$30.00
Direct labour	24.00	18.00
Manufacturing overhead ($728,000 ÷ 50,000 units; $792,000 ÷ 200,000 units)	14.56	3.96
Unit product cost.	$78.56	$51.96

The activity rates for the three activity cost pools are computed in the second table in Exhibit 5B–2. For example, the total cost in the "Setting up machines" activity cost pool, $480,000, is divided by the total activity associated with that cost pool, 800 setups, to determine the activity rate of $600 per setup.

The activity rates are used to allocate overhead costs to the two products in the third table in Exhibit 5B–2. For example, the activity rate for the "Setting up machines" activity cost pool, $600 per setup, is multiplied by the Premium product line's 600 setups to determine the $360,000 machine setup cost allocated to the Premium product line. The overhead cost per unit is determined at the bottom of this table by dividing the total overhead cost by the number of units produced. For example, the Premium product line's total overhead cost of $728,000 is divided by 50,000 units to determine the $14.56 overhead cost per unit.

The table at the bottom of Exhibit 5B–2 displays the activity-based costing unit product costs. Note that these unit product costs differ from those computed using the company's traditional costing system in Exhibit 5B–1. Because the activity-based costing system contains both a batch-level (setting up machines) and a product-level (parts administration) activity cost pool, the unit product costs under activity-based costing follow the usual pattern in which overhead costs are shifted from the high-volume to the low-volume product. The unit product cost of the Standard product line, the high-volume product, has gone down from $53.70 under the traditional costing system to $51.96 under activity-based costing. In contrast, the unit product cost of the Premium product line, the low-volume product, has increased from $71.60 under the traditional costing system to $78.56 under activity-based costing. Instead of arbitrarily assigning most of the costs of setting up machines and of parts administration to the high-volume product, the activity-based costing system more accurately assigns these costs to the two products.

Appendix 5B Summary

- A modified form of activity-based costing can be used for external financial reporting. However, when used for external reports, product costs include only manufacturing costs and exclude all non-manufacturing costs. **[LO7]**

▦ connect™ Appendix 5B Exercises, Problems, and Cases

EXERCISE 5B–1 Activity-Based Costing Product Costs for External Reports [LO7]
Data concerning Cranur Architects Corporation's two major business lines are given below:

	Commercial	Residential
Direct materials per square metre......	$6.00	$4.50
Direct labour per square metre........	$48	$36
Direct labour-hours per square metre...	0.1 DLHs	0.075 DLHs
Estimated annual output.............	40,000 m²	280,000 m²

The company has a traditional costing system in which architecture department overhead is applied to units (square metres of architectural drawings) based on direct labour-hours. Data concerning architecture department overhead and direct labour-hours for the upcoming year appear below:

Estimated total architecture department overhead.....	$670,000
Estimated total direct labour-hours................	25,000 DLHs

Required:
1. Determine the unit costs of the Commercial and Residential products under the company's traditional costing system.

2. The company is considering replacing its traditional costing system for determining unit product costs for external reports with an activity-based costing system. The activity-based costing system would have the following three activity cost pools:

Activities and Activity Measures	Estimated Overhead Cost	Expected Activity Commercial	Residential	Total
Supporting direct labour (direct labour-hours)	$600,000	4,000	21,000	25,000
Drawing software modifications (changes)	60,000	100	25	125
Quality review and technical checks (tests)........	10,000	80	20	100
Total service department overhead cost	$670,000			

Determine the unit costs (cost per square metre of architectural drawings) of the Commercial and Residential lines of business under the activity-based costing system.

EXERCISE 5B–2 Activity-Based Costing Product Costs for External Reports [LO7]
Krunkel Company makes two products and uses a traditional costing system in which a single plant-wide predetermined overhead rate is computed based on direct labour-hours. Data for the two products for the upcoming year follow:

	Mercon	Wurcon
Direct materials cost per unit............	$10.00	$8.00
Direct labour cost per unit..............	$3.00	$3.75
Direct labour-hours per unit.............	0.20	0.25
Number of units produced..............	10,000	40,000

These products are customized to some degree for specific customers.

Required:
1. The company's manufacturing overhead costs for the year are expected to be $336,000. Using the company's traditional costing system, compute the unit product costs for the two products.
2. Management is considering an activity-based costing system in which half of the overhead would continue to be allocated on the basis of direct labour-hours and half would be allocated on the basis of engineering design time. The Mercon product is expected to need 4,000 engineering design hours and the Wurcon product is also expected to need 4,000 engineering design hours. Compute the unit product costs for the two products using the proposed ABC system.
3. Explain why the unit product costs differ between the two systems.

PROBLEM 5B–3 Activity-Based Costing as an Alternative to Traditional Product Costing [LO7]
Rehm Company manufactures a product that is available in both a deluxe model and a regular model. The company has manufactured the regular model for years. The deluxe model was introduced several years ago to tap a new segment of the market. Since introduction of the deluxe model, the company's profits have steadily declined, and management has become increasingly concerned about the accuracy of its costing system. Sales of the deluxe model have been increasing rapidly.

Manufacturing overhead is assigned to products on the basis of direct labour-hours. For the current year, the company has estimated that it will incur $6,000,000 in manufacturing overhead cost and produce 15,000 units of the deluxe model and 120,000 units of the regular model. The deluxe model requires 1.6 hours of direct labour time per unit, and the regular model requires 0.8 hours. Material and labour costs per unit are as follows:

	Model	
	Deluxe	Regular
Direct materials	$154	$112
Direct labour	$16	$8

Required:
1. Using direct labour-hours as the base for assigning manufacturing overhead cost to products, compute the predetermined overhead rate. Using this rate and other data from the problem, determine the unit product cost of each model.
2. Management is considering using activity-based costing to apply manufacturing overhead costs to products for external financial reports. The activity-based costing system would have the following four activity cost pools:

Activity Cost Pool	Estimated Activity Measure	Overhead Costs
Purchase orders	Number of purchase orders	$ 252,000
Scrap/rework orders	Number of scrap/rework orders	648,000
Product testing	Number of tests	1,350,000
Machine-related	Machine-hours	3,750,000
Total overhead cost.		$6,000,000

Activity Measure	Expected Activity		
	Deluxe	Regular	Total
Number of purchase orders.	400	800	1,200
Number of scrap/rework orders.	500	400	900
Number of tests.	6,000	9,000	15,000
Machine-hours.	20,000	30,000	50,000

Using Exhibit 5–7 as a guide, compute the predetermined overhead rates (i.e., activity rates) for each of the four activity cost pools.
3. Using the predetermined overhead rates computed in (2) above, do the following:
   a. Compute the total amount of manufacturing overhead cost that would be applied to each model using the activity-based costing system. After these totals have been computed, determine the amount of manufacturing overhead cost per unit for each model.
   b. Compute the unit product cost of each model (materials, labour, and manufacturing overhead).
4. From the data you have developed in (1) through (3) above, identify factors that may account for the company's declining profits.

PROBLEM 5B–4 Activity-Based Costing as an Alternative to Traditional Product Costing [LO7]

For many years, Sinclair Graphic Design has provided design and digital-printing services for indoor banners. The nylon banners, which come in a standard size, are used for a variety of purposes, including trade shows, sporting events, and other promotional activities. Three years ago, the company introduced a second printing and production service for outdoor banners that have become increasingly popular. The outdoor banners are a more complex product than the indoor banners, requiring weatherproof vinyl materials and a different printing process to improve the visibility of the text and graphics content. Moreover, outdoor banners are printed in smaller production runs because of less frequent orders, the setup of the printing equipment takes longer, and because of the need for higher durability to withstand the elements, more quality inspections are needed. Under the traditional costing approach, overhead costs are assigned to the products on the basis of direct labour-hours.

Despite the introduction of the new outdoor banners, profits have declined steadily over the past three years. Management is beginning to believe that the company's costing system may be at fault. Unit costs for materials and labour for the two products follow:

	Indoor banners	Outdoor banners
Direct materials	$9	$26
Direct labour ($20 per hour).	$20	$60

Management estimates that the company will incur $600,000 in overhead costs during the current year and that 10,000 indoor banners and 2,000 outdoor banners will be produced and sold.

Required:

1. Compute the predetermined overhead rate assuming that the company continues to apply overhead cost to products on the basis of direct labour-hours. Using this rate and other data from the problem, determine the unit product cost of each product.
2. Management is considering using activity-based costing to apply overhead cost to products for external financial reports. Some preliminary work has been done and the data that have been collected are displayed below in the form of an Excel spreadsheet. Determine the predetermined overhead rate (i.e., activity rate) for each of the four activity cost pools.

	A	B	C	D	E	F	G
1					Activity Measure		
2			Estimated	Indoor	Outdoor		
3	Activity Cost Pool (and Activity Measure)		Overhead Cost	Banners	Banners	Total	
4	Order processing (orders received)		$150,000	500	500	1,000	
5	Print set-up (number of batches)		50,000	800	200	1,000	
6	Artwork/graphic design (labour hours)		350,000	7000	7000	14,000	
7	Quality control (number of inspections)		50,000	400	400	800	
8	Total overhead cost		$600,000				
9							

Sheet1 / Sheet2 / Sheet3 / +

3. Using the predetermined manufacturing overhead rates that you computed in (2) above, do the following:
   a. Determine the total amount of manufacturing overhead cost that would be applied to each product using the activity-based costing system. After these totals have been computed, determine the amount of overhead cost per unit of each product.
   b. Compute the unit product cost of each product.
4. Based on your calculations in (1) through (3) above, in terms of overhead cost, what factors make the outdoor banners more costly to produce than the indoor banners? Are the outdoor banners as profitable as the company thinks they are? Explain.

PROBLEM 5B–5 Activity-Based Costing as an Alternative to Traditional Product Costing [LO7]
Erte Inc. manufactures two models of high-pressure steam valves, the XR7 model and the ZD5 model. Data regarding the two products follow:

Product	Direct Labour-Hours	Annual Production	Total Direct Labour-Hours
XR7	0.2 DLHs per unit	20,000 units	4,000 DLHs
ZD5	0.4 DLHs per unit	40,000 units	16,000 DLHs
			20,000 DLHs

Additional information about the company follows:
a. Product XR7 requires $35 in direct materials per unit, and product ZD5 requires $25.
b. The direct labour rate is $20 per hour.
c. The company has always used direct labour-hours as the base for applying manufacturing overhead cost to products. Manufacturing overhead totals $1,480,000 per year.
d. Product XR7 is more complex to manufacture than product ZD5 and requires the use of a special milling machine.
e. Because of the special work required in (d) above, the company is considering the use of activity-based costing to apply overhead cost to products. Three activity cost pools have been identified and the first-stage allocations have been completed. Data concerning these activity cost pools appear below:

Activity Cost Pool	Activity Measure	Estimated Total Cost	Estimated Total Activity XR7	ZD5	Total
Machine setups	Number of setups	$ 180,000	150	100	250
Special milling	Machine-hours	300,000	1,000	0	1,000
General factory	Direct labour-hours	1,000,000	4,000	16,000	20,000
		$1,480,000			

Required:

1. Assume that the company continues to use direct labour-hours as the base for applying overhead cost to products.
    a. Compute the predetermined overhead rate.
    b. Determine the unit product cost of each product.
2. Assume that the company decides to use activity-based costing to apply overhead cost to products.
    a. Compute the activity rate for each activity cost pool. Also compute the amount of overhead cost that would be applied to each product.
    b. Determine the unit product cost of each product.
3. Explain why overhead cost shifted from the high-volume product to the low-volume product under activity-based costing.

CASE 5B–6 Contrasting Activity-Based Costing and Traditional Costing [LO2, LO3, LO4, LO7]
"Wow! Is that R-92 model ever a loser! It's time to cut back its production and shift our resources toward the new T-95 model," said Graham Thomas, executive vice-president of Thomas Products, Inc. "Just look at this income statement I've received from accounting. The T-95 is generating over eight times as much profit as the R-92 on one-sixth of the unit sales. I'm convinced that our future depends on the T-95." The year-end statement to which Thomas was referring is shown below.

	Total	Model R-92	T-95
Sales	$11,125,000	$9,000,000	$2,125,000
Cost of goods sold	6,900,000	5,490,000	1,410,000
Gross margin	4,225,000	3,510,000	715,000
Less selling and administrative expenses	3,675,000	3,450,000	225,000
Operating income	$ 550,000	$ 60,000	$ 490,000
Number of units produced and sold		30,000	5,000

"The numbers sure look that way," replied Julie Williams, the company's sales manager. "But why isn't the competition more excited about the T-95? I know we've been producing the model for only three years, but I'm surprised that more of our competitors haven't recognized what a cash cow it is."

"I think it's our new automated plant," replied Thomas. "Now it takes only two direct labour-hours to produce a unit of the R-92 and three direct labour-hours to produce a unit of the T-95. That's considerably less than it used to take us."

"I agree that automation is wonderful," replied Williams. "I suppose that's how we're able to hold down the price of the T-95. Taylor Company in England tried to bring out a T-95 but discovered they couldn't touch our price. But Taylor is killing us on the R-92 by undercutting our price with some of our best customers. I suppose they'll pick up all of our R-92 business if we move out of that market. But who cares? We don't even have to advertise the T-95; it just seems to sell itself."

"My only concern about automation is how our manufacturing overhead rate has shot up," said Thomas. "Our total manufacturing overhead cost is $2,700,000. That comes out to be a hefty amount per direct labour-hour, but Dianne down in accounting has been using direct labour-hours as the base for computing overhead rates for years and doesn't want to change. I don't suppose it matters as long as costs get assigned to products."

"I've never understood that debit and credit stuff," replied Williams. "But I think you've got a problem in production. I had lunch with Janet yesterday and she complained about how complex the

T-95 is to produce. Apparently they have to do a lot of setups, special soldering, and other work on the T-95 just to keep production moving. And they have to inspect every single unit."

"It'll have to wait," said Thomas. "I'm writing a proposal to the board of directors to phase out the R-92. We've got to increase our bottom line or we'll all be looking for jobs."

Required:

1. Compute the predetermined overhead rate based on direct labour-hours that the company used during the year. (There was no underapplied or overapplied overhead for the year.)
2. Direct materials and direct labour costs per unit for the two products are as follows:

	R-92	T-95
Direct materials.	$75	$120
Direct labour.	$36	$ 54

Using these data and the rate computed in (1) above, determine the unit product cost of each product under the company's traditional costing system.

3. Assume that the company's $2,700,000 in manufacturing overhead cost can be assigned to six activity cost pools, as follows:

Activity Cost Pool (and Activity Measure)	Estimated Overhead Costs	Total	Expected Activity R-92	T-95
Machine setups (number of setups)	$ 312,000	$ 1,600	1,000	600
Quality control (number of inspections).	540,000	9,000	4,000	5,000
Purchase orders (number of orders)	135,000	1,200	840	360
Soldering (number of solder joints)	675,000	200,000	60,000	140,000
Shipments (number of shipments).	198,000	600	400	200
Machine-related (machine-hours)	840,000	70,000	30,000	40,000
	$2,700,000			

Given these data, would you support a recommendation to expand sales of the T-95? Explain your position.

4. From the data you prepared in (3) above, why do you suppose the T-95 "just seems to sell itself"?
5. If you were president of Thomas Products, Inc., what strategy would you follow from this point forward to improve the company's overall profits?

 Practise and learn online with Connect.

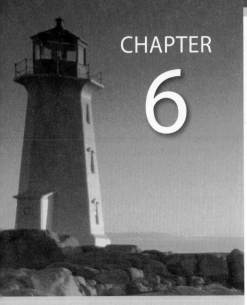

CHAPTER

6

Learning Objectives

After studying Chapter 6, you should be able to

1. Describe how fixed and variable costs behave and how to use them to predict costs.

2. Analyze mixed costs using various approaches.

3. Prepare an income statement using the contribution format.

4. (Appendix 6A) Analyze a mixed cost using the least-squares regression method.

COST BEHAVIOUR: ANALYSIS AND USE

■ COSTLY BEHAVIOUR REQUIRED

Cervélo Cycles manufactures racing bike frames and has its headquarters in Toronto, Ontario. Founded in 1996, the company is now the world's largest manufacturer of triathlon and time-trial bikes. Before deciding to introduce a new model to its current lineup of bikes, Cervélo's management must estimate the profits that will be generated. Developing profit estimates will require management to forecast unit sales for the new model, set the selling price, and estimate the incremental costs that will be incurred. Predicting some of the incremental costs such as raw materials will be relatively straightforward, since they tend to vary in direct proportion with the estimated number of units to be produced. However, other costs such as direct labour will be more challenging to predict, since management will have to consider whether additional production employees will have to be hired or whether the production needs for the new model can be fully or partially met with the existing workforce. Still other costs may be even more difficult to predict. For example, if introducing a new model requires Cervélo to expand its production facilities, a portion of the costs related to maintaining the new plant (e.g., indirect materials) will vary with production volume. However, other components of maintenance costs, such as the salary of the maintenance supervisor, will remain constant across a fairly wide range of production volumes. Thus it may be necessary to break down some categories of costs such as maintenance into fixed and variable components in order to estimate how they will behave in total.

To develop a reasonable estimate of the profits that may be realized through the introduction of a new model, it is clear from the discussion above that Cervélo's management must have a thorough understanding of how a wide variety of costs behave. Moreover, they must use this understanding of cost behaviour to predict the total costs that will be incurred under different assumptions about the demand for the new model. Analyzing the profit implications of new product development is just one of many examples of how a detailed knowledge of cost behaviour can help management make sound decisions.

What are the different cost behaviour patterns that management should understand? What approaches can be used to develop cost-prediction models? These are key topics covered in this chapter.

Source: www.cervelo.com.

I n Chapter 2, we stated that costs can be classified by behaviour. *Cost behaviour* refers to how a cost will react or change as changes take place in the level of business activity. An understanding of cost behaviour is the key to many decisions in an organization. Managers who understand how costs behave are better able to predict what costs will be under various operating circumstances. Attempts at decision making without a thorough understanding of cost behaviour patterns can lead to disaster. For example, a decision to drop a particular product line might result in far lower cost savings than managers had assumed—leading to a drop in profits. To avoid such problems, a manager must be able to accurately predict what costs will be at various activity levels.

This chapter briefly reviews the definitions of variable costs and fixed costs and then discusses the behaviour of these costs in greater depth than in Chapter 2. The chapter also introduces the concept of a mixed cost, which is a cost that has both variable and fixed cost elements. We conclude the chapter by introducing a new income statement format—called the *contribution format*—in which costs are organized by behaviour rather than by the traditional functions of production, sales, and administration.

Cost behaviour, as presented in this chapter, introduces the description and analytical techniques needed for all areas of managerial accounting, including costing, planning and control, and decision making. The descriptions and techniques presented here are simplified so that they are easily understandable but the ideas are appropriate for analysis of more complex situations that will appear in later chapters. Thus, careful study of the concepts introduced in Chapter 2 is important because they form the foundation for numerous topics that follow.

In Chapter 2, we mentioned only variable and fixed costs. There is a third behaviour pattern, generally known as a *mixed* or *semivariable* cost. All three cost behaviour patterns—variable, fixed, and mixed—are found in most organizations. The relative proportion of each type of cost present in a firm is known as the firm's **cost structure**. For example an organization might have many fixed costs but few variable or mixed costs. Alternatively, it might have many variable costs but few fixed or mixed costs. A firm's cost structure can have a significant effect on decisions. In this chapter, we will concentrate on gaining a fuller understanding of the behaviour of each type of cost. In the next chapter, we will more fully discuss how cost structure affects decisions.

Cost structure
The relative proportion of fixed, variable, and mixed costs found in an organization.

TYPES OF COST BEHAVIOUR PATTERNS

LEARNING OBJECTIVE 1
Describe how fixed and variable costs behave and how to use them to predict costs.

Variable Costs

We explained in Chapter 2 that a variable cost is a cost whose *total dollar* amount varies in direct proportion to changes in the activity level. *Direct proportion* signifies that if the activity level doubles, the total dollar amount of the variable costs also doubles. If the activity level increases by only 10%, then the total dollar amount of the variable costs increases by 10% as well.

We also found in Chapter 2 that a variable cost remains constant if expressed on a *per unit* basis. To provide an example, consider Adventure Rafting, a small company that provides daylong white-water rafting excursions on rivers in the Yukon. The company provides all of the necessary equipment and experienced guides, and it serves gourmet meals to its guests. The meals are purchased from an exclusive caterer for $30 per person for a daylong excursion. If we look at the cost of the meals on a *per person* basis, the cost remains constant at $30. This $30 cost per person will not change, regardless of how many people participate in a daylong excursion. The behaviour of this variable cost, on both a per unit and a total basis, is tabulated as follows:

Number of Guests	Cost of Meals per Guest	Total Cost of Meals
250	$30	$ 7,500
500	30	15,000
750	30	22,500
1,000	30	30,000

The idea that a variable cost is constant per unit but varies in total with the activity level is crucial to an understanding of cost behaviour patterns. We will rely on this concept again and again in this chapter and in chapters ahead. Note however that it is possible for the variable cost per unit to change once activity levels are outside the relevant range. In the above example, if Adventure Rafting was to need 2,000 meals, the unit cost per meal might drop below $30 if a quantity discount was provided by the caterer. Similarly, if fewer than 250 meals were required, the unit cost per meal might be more than $30.

Exhibit 6–1 provides a graphic illustration of variable cost behaviour. Note that the graph of the total cost of the meals slopes upward to the right. This is because the total cost of the meals is directly proportional to the number of guests. In contrast, the graph of the per unit cost of meals is flat because the cost of the meals per guest is constant at $30.

The Activity Base   For a cost to be variable, it must be variable *with respect to some-thing*. That "something" is its *activity base*. An **activity base** is a measure of whatever causes the incurrence of a variable cost. As we learned in Chapter 5, an activity base is sometimes referred to as a *cost driver*. Some of the most common activity bases are direct labour-hours, machine-hours, units produced, and units sold. Other activity bases (cost drivers) might include the number of kilometres driven by salespeople, the number of kilograms of laundry processed by a hotel, the number of calls handled by a customer service department, and the number of occupied beds in a hospital.

To plan and control variable costs, a manager must be well acquainted with the various activity bases within the firm. People sometimes think that if a cost doesn't vary with production or with sales, then it is not really a variable cost. This is incorrect. As suggested by the range of bases or drivers listed above, costs are caused by many different activities within an organization. Whether a cost is considered to be variable depends on whether it is caused by the activity under consideration. For example, if a manager is analyzing the cost of service calls for a product warranty, the relevant activity measure will be the

Activity base
A measure of whatever causes the incurrence of a variable cost. For example, the total cost of X-ray film in a hospital will increase as the number of X-rays taken increases. Therefore, the number of X-rays is an activity base for explaining the total cost of X-ray film.

EXHIBIT 6–1   Variable Cost Behaviour

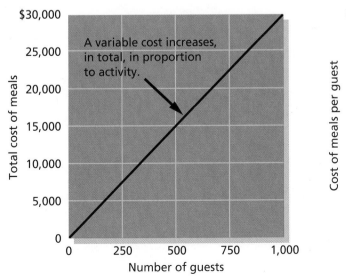

Total Cost of Meals

A variable cost increases, in total, in proportion to activity.

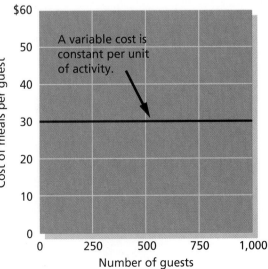

Per Unit Cost of Meals

A variable cost is constant per unit of activity.

number of service calls made. Those costs that vary in total with the number of service calls made are the variable costs of making service calls.

Nevertheless, unless stated otherwise, you can assume that the activity base under consideration is the total volume of goods and services produced or sold by the organization. So, for example, if we ask whether the cost of direct materials at Ford Canada is a variable cost, the answer is yes, since the cost of direct materials is variable with respect to Ford's total volume of production. We will specify the activity base only when it is something other than total production or sales.

Extent of Variable Costs   The number and type of variable costs present in an organization will depend in large part on the organization's structure and purpose. A public utility like New Brunswick Power, with large investments in equipment, will tend to have few variable costs. Most of the costs are associated with its plant, and these costs tend to be insensitive to changes in levels of service provided. A manufacturing company like Cervélo, by contrast, will often have many variable costs; these costs will be associated with both manufacturing and distributing its products to customers.

A merchandising company like Canadian Tire or Atlantic Superstore will usually have a high proportion of variable costs in its cost structure. In most merchandising companies, the cost of merchandise purchased for resale, a variable cost, constitutes a very large component of total cost. Service companies, by contrast, have diverse cost structures. Some service companies, such as the restaurant chain Tim Hortons, have fairly large variable costs because of their raw material costs. On the other hand, service companies involved in consulting, auditing, engineering, dental, medical, and architectural activities have very large fixed costs in the form of expensive facilities and highly trained salaried employees.

Some of the more frequently encountered variable costs are listed in Exhibit 6–2. This exhibit is not a complete listing of all costs that can be considered variable. Moreover, some of the costs listed in the exhibit may behave more like fixed than variable costs in some organizations and in some circumstances. We will see some examples of this later in the chapter. Nevertheless, Exhibit 6–2 provides a useful listing of many of the costs that normally would be considered variable with respect to the volume of output.

True Variable versus Step-Variable Costs

Not all variable costs have exactly the same behaviour pattern. Some variable costs behave in a *true variable* or *proportionately variable* pattern. Other variable costs behave in a *step-variable* pattern.

EXHIBIT 6–2   Examples of Variable Costs

Type of Organization	Costs That Are Normally Variable with Respect to Volume of Output
Merchandising company	Cost of goods (merchandise) sold
Manufacturing company	Manufacturing costs: Direct materials Direct labour*
	Variable portion of manufacturing overhead: Indirect materials, such as lubricants or supplies Power
Both merchandising and manufacturing companies	Selling, general, and administrative costs: Commissions Clerical costs, such as invoicing Shipping costs
Service organizations	Supplies, travel, clerical

*Direct labour may or may not be variable in practice. See the discussion later in this chapter.

Majestic Ocean Kayaking, of Ucluelet, British Columbia, is owned and operated by Tracy Morben-Eeftink. The company offers a number of guided kayaking excursions ranging from three-hour tours of the Ucluelet harbor to six-day kayaking and camping trips in Clayoquot Sound. One of the company's excursions is a four-day kayaking and camping trip to The Broken Group Islands in the Pacific Rim National Park. Special regulations apply to trips in the park—including a requirement that one certified guide must be assigned for every five guests or fraction thereof. For example, a trip with 12 guests must have at least three certified guides. Guides are not salaried and are paid on a per day basis. Therefore, the cost to the company of the guides for a trip is a step-variable cost rather than a fixed cost or a strictly variable cost. One guide is needed for 1 to 5 guests, two guides for 6 to 10 guests, three guides for 11 to 15 guests, and so on.

Sources: Tracy Morben-Eeftink, owner, Majestic Ocean Kayaking. For more information about the company, see www.oceankayaking.com.

True Variable Costs   Direct materials is a true or proportionately variable cost because the amount used during a period will vary in direct proportion to the level of production activity. Moreover, any amounts purchased but not used can be stored and carried forward to the next period as inventory.

Step-Variable Costs   The cost of a resource that is obtainable only in large chunks (such as maintenance workers) and that increases or decreases only in response to fairly wide changes in activity is known as a **step-variable cost**. For example, the wages of maintenance workers are often considered to be a variable cost, but this labour cost doesn't behave in quite the same way as the cost of direct materials. Unlike direct materials, the time of maintenance workers is obtainable only in large chunks. Moreover, any maintenance time not utilized cannot be stored as inventory and carried forward to the next period. If the time is not used effectively, it is gone forever. Furthermore, a maintenance crew can work at a fairly leisurely pace if pressures are light but intensify its efforts if pressures build up. For this reason, small changes in the level of production may have no effect on the number of maintenance workers employed by the company.

> **Step-variable cost**
> A cost (such as the cost of a maintenance worker) that is obtainable only in large chunks and that increases and decreases only in response to fairly wide changes in the activity level.

The behaviour of a step-variable cost is contrasted with the behaviour of a true variable cost in Exhibit 6–3. Notice that the need for maintenance help changes only with fairly wide changes in volume and that when additional maintenance time is obtained, it comes in large, indivisible chunks. The strategy of management in dealing with step-variable costs must be to obtain the fullest use of services possible for each separate step. Great care must be taken in working with these kinds of costs to prevent "fat" from building up in an organization. There may be a tendency to employ additional help more quickly than needed, and there is a natural reluctance to lay off people when volume declines.

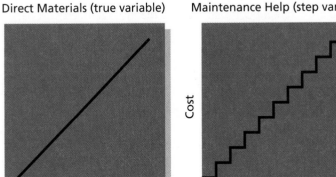

Direct Materials (true variable)   Maintenance Help (step variable)

EXHIBIT 6–3   True Variable versus Step-Variable Costs

The Linearity Assumption and the Relevant Range

In dealing with variable costs, we have assumed a strictly linear relationship between cost and volume, except in the case of step-variable costs. Economists correctly point out that many costs classified by accountants as variable actually behave in a *curvilinear* fashion. The behaviour of a **curvilinear cost** is shown in Exhibit 6–4.

Although many costs are not strictly linear, a curvilinear cost can be satisfactorily approximated with a straight line within a narrow band of activity known as the *relevant range*. The relevant range is that range of activity within which the assumptions made about cost behaviour are valid. For example, note that the dashed line in Exhibit 6–4 can be used as an approximation to the curvilinear cost with very little loss of accuracy within the shaded relevant range. However, outside of the relevant range, this particular straight line is a poor approximation to the curvilinear cost relationship. Managers should always keep in mind that a particular assumption made about cost behaviour may be invalid if activity falls outside of the relevant range.

Curvilinear costs
A relationship between cost and activity that is a curve rather than a straight line.

EXHIBIT 6–4 Curvilinear Costs and the Relevant Range

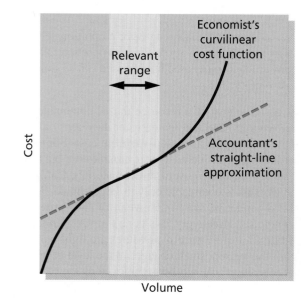

Fixed Costs

In our discussion of cost behaviour patterns in Chapter 2, we stated that total fixed costs remain constant within the relevant range of activity. To continue the Adventure Rafting example, assume the company decides to rent a building for $500 per month to store its equipment. The *total* amount of rent paid is the same regardless of the number of guests the company takes on its expeditions during any given month. This cost behaviour pattern is shown graphically in Exhibit 6–5.

Since fixed costs remain constant in total, the average fixed cost *per unit* becomes progressively smaller as the level of activity increases. If Adventure Rafting has only 250 guests in a month, the $500 fixed rental cost would amount to an average of $2 per guest. If there are 1,000 guests, the fixed rental cost would average only 50 cents per guest. This aspect of the behaviour of fixed costs is also displayed in Exhibit 6–5. Note that as the number of guests increases, the average unit cost drops, but it drops at a decreasing rate. The first guests have the greatest impact on the average fixed costs per unit.

It is necessary in some contexts to express fixed costs on an average per unit basis. For example, in Chapter 2 we showed how unit product costs computed for use in external financial statements contain both variable and fixed costs. As a general rule, however, we caution against expressing fixed costs on an average per unit basis in internal reports because it creates the false impression that fixed costs are like variable costs and that total fixed costs actually change as the level of activity changes. To avoid confusion in internal

EXHIBIT 6–5   Fixed Cost Behaviour

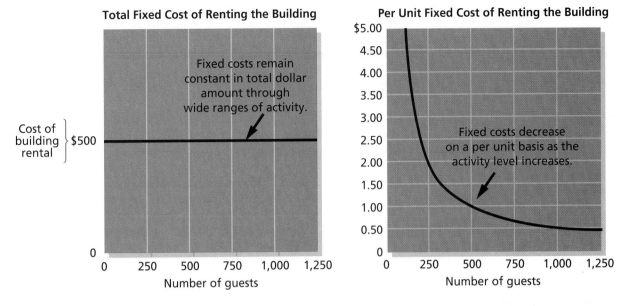

reporting and decision-making situations, fixed costs should be expressed in total rather than on a per unit basis.

Types of Fixed Costs

Fixed costs are sometimes referred to as *capacity costs*, since they result from outlays made for buildings, equipment, skilled professional employees, and other items needed to provide the basic capacity for sustained operations. For planning purposes, fixed costs can be viewed as being either *committed* or *discretionary*.

Committed fixed costs
Those fixed costs that are difficult to adjust and that relate to the investment in facilities, equipment, and the basic organizational structure of a firm.

Committed Fixed Costs   **Committed fixed costs** are those investments in facilities, equipment, and the basic organizational structure that cannot be significantly reduced, even for short time periods, without making fundamental changes that would impair a firm's long-run goals or profitability. Examples include depreciation of buildings and equipment, property taxes, insurance expenses, and salaries of top management and operating personnel. Even if operations are interrupted or cut back, committed fixed costs remain largely unchanged in the short term. During a recession, for example, a company won't usually eliminate key executive positions or sell off key facilities—the basic organizational structure and facilities ordinarily are kept intact. The costs of restoring them later are likely to be far greater than any short-run savings that might be realized.

Once a decision is made to acquire committed fixed resources, the company may be locked into that decision for many years to come. Consequently, such commitments should be made only after careful analysis of the available alternatives. Long-term investment decisions involving committed fixed costs will be examined in Chapter 13.

Discretionary fixed costs
Those fixed costs that arise from annual decisions by management to spend in certain fixed cost areas, such as advertising and research.

Discretionary Fixed Costs   **Discretionary fixed costs**, often called *managed fixed costs*, are those costs that arise from annual decisions by management to spend in certain fixed cost areas. Examples of discretionary fixed costs include advertising, research and development, and management training programs.

Two key differences exist between discretionary and committed fixed costs. First, the planning horizon for a discretionary fixed cost is short term—usually a single year. By contrast, committed fixed costs have a planning horizon that encompasses many years. Second, unlike committed costs, discretionary fixed costs can be cut for short time periods with minimal damage to the long-run organizational goals. For example, spending on management training programs can be reduced because of poor economic conditions. Although some unfavourable consequences may result from the cutback, it is doubtful that these consequences would be as great as those that would result if the company decided to reduce committed fixed costs by laying off key personnel.

Caution should be taken not to confuse discretionary costs with unnecessary costs. For example, if a high-tech company such as Research in Motion were to cut its research and development budget, serious harm could be done to its ability to compete in the future. Similarly, cutting training costs can lead to lower employee morale and a resulting drop in productivity.

Whether a particular cost is regarded as committed or discretionary may depend on management's strategy. For example, during recessions when the level of home building is down, many construction companies lay off most of their workers and virtually disband operations. Other construction companies retain large numbers of employees on the payroll, even though the workers have little or no work to do. While these latter companies may be faced with short-term cash flow problems, it will be easier for them to respond quickly when economic conditions improve. Also the higher morale and loyalty of their employees may give these companies a significant competitive advantage.

The most important characteristic of discretionary fixed costs is that management is not locked into its decisions regarding such costs. Discretionary costs can be adjusted from year to year or even perhaps during the course of a year if necessary.

The Trend toward Fixed Costs   The trend in many companies is toward greater fixed costs relative to variable costs. Tasks that used to be performed by hand have been taken over by machines. For example, grocery clerks at Loblaws and Sobeys used to key in prices by hand on cash registers. Now, most stores are equipped with bar code readers that enter price and other product information automatically. In general, competition has created pressure to give customers more value for their money—a demand that often can be satisfied only by automating business processes. For example, H&R Block used to fill out tax returns for customers mainly by hand and the advice given to a customer largely depended on the knowledge of that particular employee. Now, sophisticated computer software based on the accumulated knowledge of many experts is used to complete tax returns, and the software provides the customer with tax planning and other advice tailored to their needs.

As the extent of automation increases, the demand for "knowledge workers"—those who work primarily with their minds rather than their muscles—has grown tremendously. Knowledge workers tend to be salaried, highly trained, and difficult to replace; the costs of compensating knowledge workers are often relatively fixed and are committed rather than discretionary costs.

Is Labour a Variable or a Fixed Cost?   As the preceding discussion suggests, wages and salaries may be fixed or variable. The behaviour of wage and salary costs will differ from one country to another, depending on labour regulations, labour contracts, and custom. In some countries, such as France, Germany, and Japan, management has little flexibility in adjusting the labour force to changes in business activity. In countries such as Canada and the United States, management typically has much greater latitude. However, even in these less restrictive environments, managers may choose to treat employee compensation as a fixed cost for several reasons.

First, many managers are reluctant to decrease the workforce in response to short-term declines in sales. Most companies realize that their employees are a very valuable asset. More and more, highly skilled and trained employees are required to run a successful business, and these workers are not easy to replace. Trained workers who are laid off may never return, and layoffs undermine the morale of those workers who remain.

Second, managers do not want to be caught with a bloated payroll in an economic downturn. Therefore, there is a reluctance to add workers in response to short-term sales increases. Many companies are turning to temporary and part-time workers to take up the slack when their permanent, full-time employees are unable to handle all of the demand for the company's products and services. In such companies, labour costs are a complex mixture of fixed and variable costs.

Many major companies have undergone waves of downsizing in recent years, particularly during the recession in which large numbers of employees—particularly managers—lost their jobs. It may seem that this downsizing proves that even management salaries should be regarded as variable costs, but this would not be a valid conclusion. Downsizing has been the result of attempts to re-engineer business processes and cut costs rather than simply a response to a decline in sales activity. This underscores an important, but subtle, point: Fixed costs can change—they just do not change in response to small changes in activity.

In summary, we cannot provide a clear-cut answer to the question "Is labour a variable or fixed cost?" It depends on how much flexibility management has to adjust the workforce and the organization's strategy. Nevertheless, we will assume in this text that, unless otherwise stated, direct labour is a variable cost. This assumption is more likely to be valid for companies in Canada than in countries where employment laws permit much less flexibility.

IN BUSINESS

Companies in white-collar industries such as media, public relations, and technology frequently hire contingent employees from staffing agencies to reduce the risk of being saddled with a bloated payroll during a business downturn. Contingent employees earn an hourly wage from their staffing agency, but they do not receive any employee benefits. Companies employing contingent workers like the flexibility of being able to lay off these people with one telephone call to the staffing agency. Brad Karsh, president of a Chicago employment-coaching service called Job Bound recommends a similar lack of commitment to his clients who accept contingent employment positions. "It's exactly like dating," he says. "You don't want to be loyal if they're not going to be loyal to you."

Source: Daniel Nasaw, "Companies Are Hedging Their Bets by Hiring Contingent Employees," *The Wall Street Journal*, September 14, 2004, p. B10.

Fixed Costs and the Relevant Range

The concept of the relevant range, which was introduced in the discussion of variable costs, is also important in understanding fixed costs—particularly discretionary fixed costs. The levels of discretionary fixed costs are typically decided at the beginning of the year and depend on the support needs of the planned programs such as advertising and training. The scope of these programs will depend, in turn, on the overall anticipated level of activity for the year. At very high levels of activity, programs are usually broadened or expanded. For example, if the company hopes to increase sales by 25%, it would probably plan for much larger advertising costs than if no sales increase was planned. So the *planned* level of activity may affect total discretionary fixed costs. However, once the total discretionary fixed costs have been budgeted, they are unaffected by the *actual* level of activity. For example, once the advertising budget has been decided on and has been spent, it will not be affected by how many units are actually sold. Therefore, the cost is fixed with respect to the *actual* number of units sold.

Discretionary fixed costs are easier to adjust than committed fixed costs. They also tend to be less "lumpy." Committed fixed costs tend to consist of costs of buildings, equipment, and the salaries of key personnel. It is difficult to buy half of a piece of equipment or to hire a quarter of a product-line manager, so the step pattern depicted in Exhibit 6–6 is typical for such costs. The relevant range of activity for a fixed cost is the range of activity over which the graph of the cost is flat, as in Exhibit 6–6. As a company expands its level of activity, it may outgrow its present facilities, or the key management team may need to be expanded. The result, of course, will be increased committed fixed costs as larger facilities are built and as new management positions are created.

One reaction to the step pattern depicted in Exhibit 6–6 is to say that discretionary and committed fixed costs are really just step-variable costs. To some extent this is true, since almost *all* costs can be adjusted in the long run. There are two major differences, however, between the step-variable costs depicted earlier in Exhibit 6–3 and the fixed costs depicted in Exhibit 6–6.

The first difference is that the step-variable costs can often be adjusted quickly as conditions change, whereas once fixed costs have been set, they often cannot be changed easily. A step-variable cost such as maintenance labour, for example, can be adjusted upward or downward by hiring and laying off maintenance workers. By contrast, once a company has signed a lease for a building, it is locked into that level of lease cost for the life of the contract.

EXHIBIT 6–6   Fixed Costs
and the Relevant Range

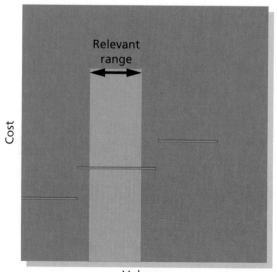

The second difference is that the *width of the steps* depicted for step-variable costs is much narrower than the width of the steps depicted for the fixed costs in Exhibit 6–6. The width of the steps relates to the volume or level of activity. For step-variable costs, the width of a step may be 40 hours of activity or less if one is dealing, for example, with maintenance labour cost. For fixed costs, however, the width of a step may be *thousands* or even *tens of thousands* of hours of activity. In essence, the width of the steps for step-variable costs is generally so narrow that these costs can be treated essentially as variable costs for most purposes. The width of the steps for fixed costs, on the other hand, is so wide that these costs must generally be treated as being entirely fixed within the relevant range.

Mixed Costs

A mixed cost contains both variable and fixed cost elements. Mixed costs are also known as *semivariable costs*. To continue the Adventure Rafting example, the company must pay a licence fee of $25,000 per year plus $3 per rafting party to Environment Yukon. If the company runs 1,000 rafting parties this year, then the total fees paid to Environment Yukon would be $28,000, made up of $25,000 in fixed cost plus $3,000 in variable cost. Exhibit 6–7 shows the behaviour of this mixed cost.

Even if Adventure Rafting fails to attract any customers and there are no rafting parties, the company will still have to pay the licence fee of $25,000. This is why the cost line in Exhibit 6–7 intersects the vertical cost axis at the $25,000 point. For each rafting party that the company organizes, the total cost of the government fees will increase by $3. Therefore, the total cost line slopes upward as the variable cost element is added to the fixed cost element.

Since the mixed cost in Exhibit 6–7 is represented by a straight line, the following equation for a straight line can be used to express the relationship between mixed cost and the level of activity:

$$Y = a + bX$$

In this equation,

Y = The total mixed cost
a = The total fixed cost (the vertical intercept of the line)
b = The variable cost per unit of activity (the slope of the line)
X = The level of activity

Because the variable cost per unit equals the slope of the straight line, the steeper the slope, the higher the variable cost per unit.

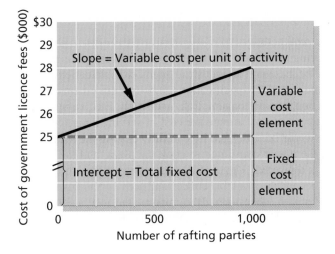

EXHIBIT 6–7   Mixed Cost Behaviour

In the case of the licensing fees paid by Adventure Rafting to Environment Yukon, the equation is written as follows:

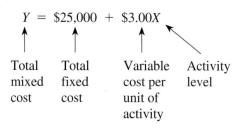

$$Y = \$25,000 + \$3.00X$$

| Total mixed cost | Total fixed cost | Variable cost per unit of activity | Activity level |

This equation makes it very easy to calculate what the total mixed cost would be for any level of activity within the relevant range. For example, suppose that the company expects to organize 800 rafting parties in the next year. Then the total licensing fees would be $27,400, calculated as follows:

$$Y = \$25,000 + (\$3.00 \text{ per rafting party} \times 800 \text{ rafting parties})$$
$$= \$27,400$$

THE ANALYSIS OF MIXED COSTS

LEARNING OBJECTIVE 2
Analyze mixed costs using various approaches.

Account analysis
A method for analyzing cost behaviour in which each account under consideration is classified as either variable or fixed based on the analyst's prior knowledge of how the cost in the account behaves.

Engineering approach
A detailed analysis of cost behaviour based on an industrial engineer's evaluation of the inputs that are required to carry out a particular activity and of the prices of those inputs.

Mixed costs are very common. For example, the cost of providing X-ray services to patients at southwestern Ontario's Grand River Hospital is a mixed cost. The costs of equipment depreciation, and radiologists' and technicians' salaries are fixed, but the costs of X-ray film, power, and supplies are variable. At Air Canada facilities across Canada, maintenance costs are a mixed cost. The company must incur fixed costs for renting maintenance facilities and for keeping skilled mechanics on the payroll, but the costs of replacement parts, lubricating oils, tires, and so forth, are variable with respect to how often and how far the company's aircraft are flown.

The fixed portion of a mixed cost represents the basic minimum cost of just having a service *ready and available* for use. The variable portion represents the cost incurred for *actual consumption* of the service. The variable element varies in proportion to the amount of service that is consumed.

How does management go about actually estimating the fixed and variable components of a mixed cost? The most common methods used in practice are *account analysis* and the *engineering approach*.

In **account analysis**, each account under consideration is classified as either variable or fixed, based on the analyst's prior knowledge of how the cost in the account behaves. For example, direct materials would be classified as variable and a building lease cost would be classified as fixed because of the nature of those costs. The total fixed cost is the sum of the costs for the accounts that have been classified as fixed. The variable cost per unit is estimated by dividing the sum of the costs for the accounts that have been classified as variable by the total activity.

The **engineering approach** to cost analysis involves a detailed analysis of what cost behaviour should be, based on an industrial engineer's evaluation of the production methods to be used, the materials specifications, labour requirements, equipment usage, efficiency of production, power consumption, and so on. For example, Pizza Hut might use the engineering approach to estimate the cost of serving a particular take-out pizza. The cost of the pizza would be estimated by carefully costing the specific ingredients used to make the pizza, the power consumed to cook the pizza, and the cost of the container in which the pizza is delivered. The engineering approach must be used in those situations where no past experience is available concerning activity and costs. In addition, it is sometimes used together with other methods to improve the accuracy of cost analysis.

Account analysis works best when analyzing costs at a fairly aggregated level, such as the cost of caring for patients in the emergency room (ER) of Grand River Hospital. The costs of drugs, supplies, forms, wages, equipment, and so on, can be roughly classified as variable or fixed and a mixed cost formula for the overall cost of the emergency room can be estimated fairly quickly. However, this method does not recognize that some of the accounts may have elements of both fixed and variable costs. For example, the cost of electricity for the ER is a mixed cost. Most of the electricity used for heating and lighting is a fixed cost. However, the consumption of electricity increases with activity in the ER, since diagnostic equipment, defibrillators, and so on all consume electricity. The most effective way to estimate the fixed and variable elements of such a mixed cost may be to analyze past records of cost and activity data. These records should reveal whether electrical costs vary significantly with the number of patients, and if so, by how much. The remainder of this section will be concerned with how to conduct such an analysis of past cost and activity data.

White Grizzly Adventures is a snowcat skiing and snowboarding company in Meadow Creek, British Columbia, that is owned and operated by Brad and Carole Karafil. The company shuttles 12 guests to the top of the company's steep and tree-covered terrain in a single snowcat. Guests stay as a group at the company's lodge for a fixed number of days and are provided with healthy gourmet meals.

Brad and Carole must decide each year when snowcat operations will begin in December, when they will end in early spring, and how many non-operating days to schedule between groups of guests for maintenance and rest. These decisions affect a variety of costs. Examples of costs that are fixed and variable with respect to the number of days of operation at White Grizzly include the following:

Costs	Cost Behaviour—Fixed or Variable with Respect to Days of Operations
Property taxes	Fixed
Summer road maintenance and tree-clearing	Fixed
Lodge depreciation	Fixed
Snowcat operator and guides	Variable
Cooks and lodge help	Variable
Snowcat depreciation	Variable
Snowcat fuel	Variable
Food	Variable

Diagnosing Cost Behaviour with a Scattergram Plot

Kinh Nguyen, the chief financial officer of Brentline Hospital, began his analysis of maintenance costs by collecting cost and activity data for a number of recent months. Those data are as follows:

Month	Activity Level: Patient-Days	Maintenance Cost Incurred
January	5,600	$7,900
February	7,100	8,500
March	5,000	7,400
April	6,500	8,200
May	7,300	9,100
June	8,000	9,800
July	6,200	7,800

The first step in analyzing the cost and activity data should be to plot the data on a scattergram. This plot immediately reveals any non-linearities or other problems with the data.

Dependent variable
A variable that responds to some causal factor; total cost is the dependent variable, as represented by the letter Y in the equation $Y = a + bX$.

Independent variable
A variable that acts as a causal factor; activity is the independent variable, as represented by the letter X in the equation $Y = a + bX$.

The scattergram of maintenance costs versus patient-days at Brentline Hospital is reproduced in the first panel of Exhibit 6–8. Two things should be noted about this scattergram:

1. The total maintenance cost, Y, is plotted on the vertical axis. Cost is known as the **dependent variable**, since the amount of cost incurred during a period depends on the level of activity for the period. That is, as the level of activity increases, total cost will also ordinarily increase.
2. The activity, X (patient-days in this case), is plotted on the horizontal axis. Activity is known as the **independent variable**, since it causes variations in the cost.

From the scattergram, it is evident that maintenance costs do increase with the number of patient-days. In addition, the scattergram reveals that the relationship between maintenance

EXHIBIT 6–8 Scattergram Method of Cost Analysis

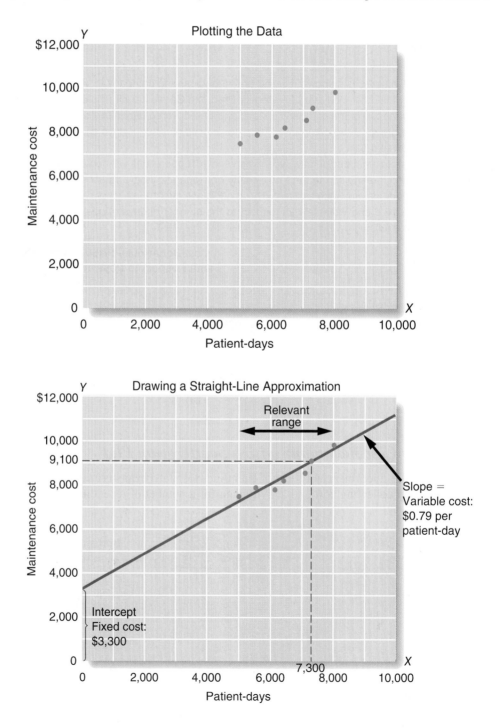

costs and patient-days is approximately *linear*. In other words, the points lie more or less along a straight line. Such a straight line has been drawn using a ruler in the second panel of Exhibit 6–8. Cost behaviour is said to be **linear** whenever a straight line is a reasonable approximation for the relationship between cost and activity. Note that the data points do not fall exactly on the straight line. This will almost always happen in practice; the relationship is seldom perfectly linear.

Note that the straight line in Exhibit 6–8 has been drawn through the point representing 7,300 patient-days and a total maintenance cost of $9,100. Drawing the straight line through one of the data points allows the analyst to make a quick estimate of variable and fixed costs. The vertical intercept where the straight line crosses the *Y*-axis—in this case, about $3,300—is the rough estimate of the fixed cost. The variable cost can quickly be estimated by subtracting the estimated fixed cost from the total cost at the point lying on the straight line:

Total maintenance cost for 7,300 patient-days
   (a point falling on the straight line) $9,100
Less estimated fixed cost (the vertical intercept). 3,300
Estimated total variable cost for 7,300 patient-days $5,800

The average variable cost per unit at 7,300 patient-days is computed as follows:

$$\text{Variable cost per unit} = \$5,800 \div 7,300 \text{ patient-days}$$
$$= \$0.79 \text{ per patient-day (rounded)}$$

Combining the estimate of the fixed cost and the estimate of the variable cost per patient-day, we can write the relationship between cost and activity as follows:

$$Y = \$3,300 + \$0.79X$$

where *X* is the number of patient-days.

We emphasize that this is a quick method of estimating the fixed and variable cost elements of a mixed cost; it is seldom used in practice when the financial implications of a decision based on the data are significant. However, setting aside the estimates of the fixed and variable cost elements, plotting the data on a scattergram is an essential diagnostic step that is too often overlooked. Suppose, for example, we had been interested in the relationship between total nursing wages and the number of patient-days at the hospital. The permanent, full-time nursing staff can handle up to 7,000 patient-days in a month. Beyond that level of activity, part-time nurses must be utilized. The cost and activity data for nurses are plotted on the scattergram in Exhibit 6–9. Looking at that scattergram, it is evident that two straight lines would do a much better job of fitting the data than a single straight line. Up to 7,000 patient-days, total nursing wages are essentially a fixed cost. Above 7,000 patient-days, total nursing wages are a mixed cost. This happens because, as stated above, the permanent full-time nursing staff can handle up to 7,000 patient-days in a month. Above that level, part-time nurses are called in to help, which adds to the cost. Consequently, two straight lines (and two equations) would be used to represent total nursing wages—one for the relevant range of 5,600 to 7,000 patient-days and one for the relevant range of 7,000 to 8,000 patient-days.

As another example, suppose that Brentline Hospital management is interested in the relationship between the hospital's telephone costs and patient-days. Patients are billed directly for their use of telephones, so those costs do not appear on the hospital's cost records. The telephone costs of concern to management are the charges for the staff's use of telephones. The data for this cost are plotted in Exhibit 6–10. It is evident from that plot that while the telephone costs do vary from month to month, they are not related to patient-days. Something other than patient-days is driving the telephone bills. Therefore, it would not make sense to analyze this cost any further by attempting to estimate a variable cost per patient-day for telephone costs. Plotting the data helps diagnose such situations.

Linear cost behaviour
Cost behaviour is linear when a straight line is a reasonable approximation for the relationship between cost and activity.

Having determined that the variable rate for maintenance cost is 80 cents per patient-day, we can now determine the amount of fixed cost. This is done by taking total cost at *either* the high or the low activity level and deducting the variable cost element. In the computation below, total cost at the high activity level is used in computing the fixed cost element:

$$\text{Fixed cost element} = \text{Total cost} - \text{Variable cost element}$$
$$= \$9,800 - (\$0.80 \text{ per patient-day} \times 8,000 \text{ patient-days})$$
$$= \$3,400$$

Both the variable and fixed cost elements have now been isolated. The cost of maintenance can be expressed as $3,400 per month plus 80 cents per patient-day.

The total cost of maintenance can also be expressed in terms of the equation for a straight line as follows:

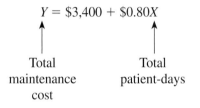

$$Y = \$3,400 + \$0.80X$$

Total maintenance cost   Total patient-days

The data used in this illustration are shown graphically in Exhibit 6–11. Notice that a straight line has been drawn through the points corresponding to the low and high levels of activity. In essence, that is what the high–low method does—it draws a straight line through those two points.

Sometimes the high and low levels of activity don't coincide with the high and low amounts of cost. For example, the period that has the highest level of activity may not have the highest amount of cost. Nevertheless, the highest and lowest levels of *activity* are always used to analyze a mixed cost under the high–low method. The reason is that the analyst would like to use data that reflect the greatest possible variation in activity.

EXHIBIT 6–11   High–Low Method of Cost Analysis

Activity Level	Patient-Days	Maintenance Cost
High	8,000	$9,800
Low	5,000	$7,400

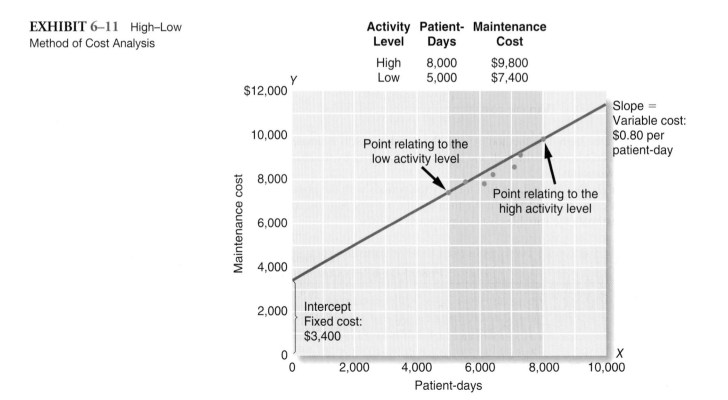

The high–low method is very simple to apply, but it suffers from a major (and some-times critical) defect—it utilizes only two data points. Generally, two points are not enough to produce accurate results. Additionally, the periods with the highest and lowest activity tend to be unusual in that they represent the two extremes. A cost formula that is estimated solely using data from these unusual periods may seriously misrepresent the true cost relationship that holds during normal periods. Such a distortion is evident in Exhibit 6–11. The straight line should probably be shifted down somewhat so that it is closer to more of the data points. For these reasons, other methods of cost analysis that utilize a greater number of points, such as *least-squares regression*, will generally be more accurate than the high–low method. If managers choose to use the high–low method, they should do so with a full awareness of its limitations.

Fortunately, computer software makes it very easy to use sophisticated statistical cost estimation methods that use all of the data and are capable of providing much more infor-mation than just the estimates of variable and fixed costs. The details of these statistical methods are beyond the scope of this text, but the least-squares regression method is dis-cussed in the appendix to this chapter. Regardless of the cost estimation approach used, it is always a good idea to first plot the data in a scattergram. By simply looking at the scat-tergram, you can quickly verify whether it makes sense to fit a straight line to the data using least-squares regression or some other method.

■ THE CONTRIBUTION FORMAT

Separating costs into fixed and variable elements helps to predict costs and provide bench-marks. As we will see in later chapters, separating costs into fixed and variable elements is often crucial in making decisions. This crucial distinction between fixed and variable costs is at the heart of the **contribution approach** to constructing income statements. The unique thing about the contribution approach is that it provides managers with an income statement that clearly distinguishes between fixed and variable costs and therefore facili-tates planning, control, and decision making.

> **LEARNING OBJECTIVE 3**
> Prepare an income statement using the contribution format.

Contribution approach
An income statement format that is geared to cost behaviour in that costs are separated into variable and fixed categories.

Why a New Income Statement Format?

An income statement prepared using the *traditional approach*, as illustrated in Chapter 2, is organized in a "functional" format—emphasizing the functions of production, adminis-tration, and sales. No attempt is made to distinguish between fixed or variable costs. Under the heading Administrative Expense, for example, both variable and fixed costs are lumped together.

Although an income statement prepared in the functional format may be useful for external reporting purposes, it has serious limitations when used for internal purposes. Internally, the manager needs cost data organized in a format that will facilitate planning, control, and decision making. As we will see in later chapters, these tasks are much easier when cost data are available in a fixed and variable format. The contribution approach to the income statement was developed in response to this need.

The Contribution Approach

Exhibit 6–12 illustrates the contribution approach to the income statement with a simple example based on assumed data, along with the traditional approach discussed in Chapter 2.

Notice that the contribution approach separates costs into fixed and variable categories, first deducting variable expenses from sales to obtain what is known as the *contribution margin*. The **contribution margin** is the amount remaining from sales revenues after vari-able expenses have been deducted. This amount *contributes* toward covering fixed expenses and then toward profits for the period.

Contribution margin
The amount remaining from sales revenues after all variable expenses have been deducted.

EXHIBIT 6–12   Comparison of the Contribution Income Statement with the Traditional Income Statement

Traditional Approach (costs organized by function)			Contribution Approach (costs organized by behaviour)		
Sales		$12,000	Sales		$12,000
Less cost of goods sold		6,000*	Less variable expenses:		
Gross margin.........................		6,000	Variable production	$2,000	
Less operating expenses:			Variable selling....................	600	
Selling..........................	$3,100*		Variable administrative..............	400	3,000
Administrative	1,900*	5,000	Contribution margin..................		9,000
Operating income		$ 1,000	Less fixed expenses:		
			Fixed production	4,000	
			Fixed selling.......................	2,500	
			Fixed administrative................	1,500	8,000
			Operating income		$ 1,000

*Contains both variable and fixed expenses. This is the income statement for a manufacturing company; thus, when the income statement is placed in the contribution format, the cost of goods sold figure is divided between variable production costs and fixed production costs. If this was the income statement for a *merchandising* company (which simply purchases completed goods from a supplier), then the cost of goods sold would be *all* variable.

The simplified contribution approach income statement makes a common assumption that can cause confusion. The variable production expenses assume production equals sales in terms of units. Thus, these expenses for production, like those for selling and administrative costs, use sales volume as the driver. A more complete income statement would need to show inventory levels so that variable production costs can use production volume activity as the cost driver.

The contribution-format income statement is used as an internal planning and decision-making tool. Its emphasis on cost behaviour facilitates cost–volume–profit analysis (such as we will be doing in the next chapter), management performance appraisals, and budgeting. Moreover, the contribution approach helps managers organize data pertinent to numerous decisions such as product-line analysis, pricing, use of scarce resources, and make or buy analysis. All of these topics are covered in later chapters.

Summary

- Three major classifications of costs were discussed in this chapter: variable, fixed, and mixed. **[LO1]**
- Mixed costs are a combination of variable and fixed elements and can be expressed in equation form as $Y = a + bX$, where Y is the cost, a is the fixed cost element, b is the variable cost per unit of activity, and X is the activity. **[LO1]**
- The first step in analyzing a mixed cost is to prepare a scattergram to permit a visual inspection of the relationship between the cost and activity. Costs are plotted on the vertical axis and activity levels on the horizontal axis of the scattergram. **[LO2]**
- If the scattergram indicates that the relationship between cost and activity is linear, the variable and fixed components of the mixed cost can be estimated using the quick method, the high–low method, or the least-squares regression method. **[LO2]**
- The quick method is based on drawing a straight line on the scatter plot of the data and then using the slope and intercept of the line to estimate the variable and fixed cost components **[LO2]**
- The high–low method estimates the variable and fixed cost components by analyzing the change in cost between the high and low levels of activity. The method is based on the rise-over-run formula for the slope of a straight line. **[LO2]**
- To facilitate decision making, the income statement can be prepared in a contribution format. The contribution format classifies costs on the income statement by cost behaviour (i.e., variable versus fixed) rather than by functional areas such as production, administration, and sales. **[LO3]**

Review Problem 1: Cost Behaviour

Indie Scooters operates a scooter rental service. Consider the following costs of the company over the relevant range of 6,000 to 9,000 hours of operating time for its scooters:

	Hours of Operating Time			
	6,000	7,000	8,000	9,000
Total costs:				
Variable costs	$ 27,000	$?	$?	$?
Fixed costs	252,000	?	?	?
Total costs	$279,000	$?	$?	$?
Cost per hour:				
Variable cost	$?	$?	$?	$?
Fixed cost	?	?	?	?
Total cost per hour	$?	$?	$?	$?

Required:
Compute the missing amounts, assuming that cost behaviour patterns remain unchanged within the relevant range of 6,000 to 9,000 hours.

Solution to Review Problem 1

The variable cost per hour can be computed as follows:

$$\$27,000 \div 6,000 \text{ hours} = \$4.50 \text{ per hour}$$

Therefore, the missing amounts are as follows:

	Hours of Operating Time			
	6,000	7,000	8,000	9,000
Total costs:				
Variable costs				
(@ $4.50 per hour)	$ 27,000	$ 31,500	$ 36,000	$ 40,500
Fixed costs	252,000	252,000	252,000	252,000
Total costs	$279,000	$283,500	$288,000	$292,500
Cost per hour:				
Variable cost	$ 4.50	$ 4.50	$ 4.50	$ 4.50
Fixed cost	42.00	36.00	31.50	28.00
Total cost per hour	$ 46.50	$ 40.50	$ 36.00	$ 32.50

Observe that the total variable costs increase in proportion to the number of hours of operating time, but that these costs remain constant at $4.50 if expressed on a per hour basis.

In contrast, the total fixed costs do not change with changes in the level of activity. They remain constant at $252,000 within the relevant range. With increases in activity, however, the fixed cost per hour decreases, dropping from $42.00 per hour when the scooters are operated 6,000 hours a period to only $28.00 per hour when they are operated 9,000 hours a period. *Because of this troublesome aspect of fixed costs, they are most easily (and most safely) dealt with on a total basis, rather than on a unit basis, in cost analysis work.*

Review Problem 2: High–Low Method

The administrator of Sarconia Hills Hospital would like a cost formula linking the administrative costs involved in admitting patients to the number of patients admitted during a month. The admitting department's costs and the number of patients admitted during the immediately preceding eight months are given in the following table:

Month	Number of Patients Admitted	Admitting Department Costs
May	1,800	$14,700
June	1,900	$15,200
July.	1,700	$13,700
August	1,600	$14,000
September	1,500	$14,300
October	1,300	$13,100
November.	1,100	$12,800
December.	1,500	$14,600

Required:
1. Use the high–low method to establish the fixed and variable components of admitting costs.
2. Express the fixed and variable components of admitting costs as a cost formula in the form $Y = a + bX$.

Solution to Review Problem 2

1. The first step in the high–low method is to identify the periods of the lowest and highest activity. Those periods are November (1,100 patients admitted) and June (1,900 patients admitted). The second step is to compute the variable cost per unit using those two data points:

Month	Number of Patients Admitted	Admitting Department Costs
High activity level (June).	1,900	$15,200
Low activity level (November) . . .	1,100	12,800
Change.	800	$ 2,400

$$\text{Variable cost} = \frac{\text{Change in cost}}{\text{Change in activity}} = \frac{\$2,400}{800 \text{ patients admitted}} = \$3 \text{ per patient admitted}$$

The third step is to compute the fixed cost element by deducting the variable cost element from the total cost at either the high or low activity. In the computation below, the high point of activity is used:

$$\text{Fixed cost element} = \text{Total cost} - \text{Variable cost element}$$
$$= \$15,200 - (\$3 \text{ per patient admitted} \times 1,900 \text{ patients admitted})$$
$$= \$9,500$$

2. The cost formula is $Y = \$9,500 + \$3X$.

Glossary

Mc Graw Hill connect   Review key terms and definitions on Connect.

Questions

6–1   What is an activity base?
6–2   What effect does a decrease in volume have on
    a.   Unit fixed costs?
    b.   Unit variable costs?
    c.   Total fixed costs?
    d.   Total variable costs?
6–3   Define the following terms: (a) cost behaviour and (b) relevant range.

6–4 What are curvilinear costs? What are some examples of costs that might behave in a curvi-linear fashion?

6–5 Distinguish between (*a*) a variable cost, (*b*) a mixed cost, and (*c*) a step-variable cost. Plot the three costs on a graph, with activity plotted horizontally and cost plotted vertically.

6–6 Managers often assume a strictly linear relationship between cost and volume. How can this practice be defended in light of the fact that many costs are curvilinear?

6–7 Distinguish between discretionary fixed costs and committed fixed costs.

6–8 Classify the following fixed costs as normally being either committed or discretionary:
a. Insurance on buildings.
b. Advertising.
c. Travel.
d. Long-term equipment leases.
e. Pension payments to a company's retirees.
f. Training.

6–9 Does the concept of the relevant range apply to fixed costs? Explain.

6–10 What is the engineering approach to cost analysis? In what situations might this approach be used?

6–11 What is the major disadvantage of the high–low method?

6–12 Why does the high–low method use the high–low activity levels instead of the high–low cost levels?

6–13 Give the general formula for a mixed cost. Which term represents the variable cost? The fixed cost?

6–14 What is the difference between a contribution approach income statement and a traditional approach income statement?

☰ connect Exercises

EXERCISE 6–1 Fixed and Variable Cost Behaviour [LO1]

Goes-Down-Smooth operates a number of smoothie bars in busy suburban malls. The fixed weekly expense of a smoothie bar is $2,500 and the variable cost per smoothie served is $0.75.

Required:
1. Fill in the following table with your estimates of total costs and cost per smoothie at the indicated levels of activity for a smoothie bar. Round off the cost of a smoothie to the nearest tenth of a cent.

	Smoothies Served in a Week		
	2,100	2,800	3,500
Fixed cost	?	?	?
Variable cost	?	?	?
Total cost.	?	?	?
Cost per smoothie served	?	?	?

2. Does the cost per smoothie increase, decrease, or remain the same as the number of smoothies served in a week increases? Explain.

EXERCISE 6–2 Scattergram Analysis [LO2]

The data below have been taken from the cost records of the Barrie Processing Company. The data relate to the cost of operating one of the company's processing facilities at various levels of activity.

Month	Units Processed	Total Cost
January	8,000	$14,000
February	4,500	$10,000
March	7,000	$12,500
April.	9,000	$15,500
May.	3,750	$10,000
June	6,000	$12,500
July	3,000	$ 8,500
August	5,000	$11,500

Required:

1. Prepare a scattergram using the above data. Plot cost on the vertical axis and activity on the horizontal axis. Fit a line to your plotted points using a ruler.
2. Using the scattergram method, what is the approximate monthly fixed cost? The approximate variable cost per unit processed? Show your computations.

EXERCISE 6–3 High–Low Method [LO2]

The Edelweiss Hotel has accumulated records of the total electrical costs of the hotel and the number of occupancy-days over the past year. An occupancy-day represents a room rented out for one day. The hotel's business is highly seasonal, with peaks occurring during the ski season and in the summer.

Month	Occupancy-Days	Electrical Costs
January..............	2,604	$6,257
February.............	2,856	$6,550
March...............	3,534	$7,986
April................	1,440	$4,022
May.................	540	$2,289
June	1,116	$3,591
July.................	3,162	$7,264
August	3,608	$8,111
September	1,260	$3,707
October.............	186	$1,712
November............	1,080	$3,321
December............	2,046	$5,196

Required:

1. Using the high–low method, estimate the fixed cost of electricity per month and the variable cost of electricity per occupancy-day. Round off the fixed cost to the nearest whole dollar and the variable cost to the nearest whole cent.
2. What other factors other than occupancy-days are likely to affect the variation in electrical costs from month to month?

EXERCISE 6–4 Contribution-Format Income Statement [LO3]

The Rhythm Shop is a large retailer of acoustic, electric, and bass guitars. An income statement for the company's acoustic guitar department for a recent quarter is presented below:

The Rhythm Shop Income Statement—Acoustic Guitar Department For the Quarter Ended March 31		
Sales		$1,600,000
Cost of goods sold		800,000
Gross margin........................		800,000
Selling and administrative expenses:		
Selling expenses	$400,000	
Administrative expenses	200,000	600,000
Operating income		$ 200,000

The guitars sell, on average, for $800 each. The department's variable selling expenses are $75 per guitar sold. The remaining selling expenses are fixed. The administrative expenses are 25% variable and 75% fixed. The company purchases its guitars from several suppliers at an average cost of $400 per guitar.

Required:

1. Prepare an income statement for the quarter using the contribution approach.
2. What was the contribution toward fixed expenses and profits from each guitar sold during the quarter? (State this figure in a single dollar amount per guitar.)
3. If The Rhythm Shop sells 100 more guitars in the quarter ending June 30 than they did in the quarter ending March 31, and fixed costs remain the same, by how much will operating income increase?

EXERCISE 6–5 Cost Behaviour; Contribution-Format Income Statement [LO1, LO3]
Parker Company manufactures and sells a single product. A partially completed schedule of the company's total and per unit costs over a relevant range of 60,000 to 100,000 units produced and sold each year is given below:

	Units Produced and Sold		
	60,000	80,000	100,000
Total costs:			
Variable costs	$150,000	?	?
Fixed costs	360,000	?	?
Total costs	$510,000	?	?
Cost per unit:			
Variable cost	?	?	?
Fixed cost	?	?	?
Total cost per hour	?	?	?

Required:
1. Complete the schedule of the company's total and unit costs above.
2. Assume that the company produces and sells 90,000 units during the year at the selling price of $7.50 per unit. Prepare a contribution-format income statement for the year.

EXERCISE 6–6 High–Low Method; Scattergram Analysis [LO2]
Zerbel Company, a wholesaler of large, custom-built air-conditioning units for commercial buildings, has noticed considerable fluctuation in its shipping expense from month to month, as shown below:

Month	Units Shipped	Total Shipping Expense
January	4	$2,200
February	7	$3,100
March	5	$2,600
April	2	$1,500
May	3	$2,200
June	6	$3,000
July	8	$3,600

Required:
1. Using the high–low method, estimate the cost formula for shipping expense.
2. The president has no confidence in the high–low method and would like you to check your results using the scattergram method. Do the following:
   a. Prepare a scattergram using the data given above. Plot cost on the vertical axis and activity on the horizontal axis. Use a ruler to fit a straight line to your plotted points.
   b. Using your scattergram, estimate the approximate variable cost per unit shipped and the approximate fixed cost per month with the scattergram method.
3. What factors, other than the number of units shipped, are likely to affect the company's shipping expense? Explain.

EXERCISE 6–7 Cost Behaviour; High–Low Method [LO2]
Prompt Parcel Service operates a fleet of delivery trucks in a large metropolitan area. A careful study by the company's cost analyst has determined that if a truck is driven 120,000 kilometres during a year, the average operating cost is 11.6 cents ($0.116) per kilometre. If a truck is driven only 80,000 kilometres during a year, the average operating cost increases to 13.6 cents ($0.136) per kilometre.

Required:
1. Using the high–low method, estimate the variable and fixed cost elements of the annual cost of truck operation.
2. Express the variable and fixed costs in the form $Y = a + bX$.
3. If a truck was driven 100,000 kilometres during a year, what total cost would you expect to be incurred?

EXERCISE 6–8 High–Low Method; Predicting Cost [LO2]

The number of blood tests performed and the related costs over the last nine months in Brentline Hospital are given below:

Month	Blood Tests Performed	Blood Test Costs
January	3,125	$14,000
February	3,500	$14,500
March	2,500	$11,500
April.	2,125	$10,000
May.	2,250	$11,000
June	1,500	$ 8,500
July.	1,875	$ 9,000
August	2,750	$12,000
September	2,875	$13,000

Required:
1. Using the high–low method, estimate the cost formula for blood tests.
2. Using the cost formula you derived above, what blood test costs would you expect to be incurred during a month in which 2,300 blood tests are performed?

EXERCISE 6–9 Scattergram Analysis; High–Low Method [LO2]

Refer to the data in Exercise 6–8 for Brentline Hospital.

Required:
1. Prepare a scattergram using the data from Exercise 6–8. Plot cost on the vertical axis and activity on the horizontal axis. Using a ruler, fit a line to your plotted points.
2. Using the scattergram method, what is the approximate monthly fixed cost for blood tests? The approximate variable cost per blood test performed?
3. Scrutinize the points on your graph, and explain why the high–low method would or would not yield an accurate cost formula in this situation.

EXERCISE 6–10 High–Low Method; Predicting Cost [LO2]

Northern Lights Inns has a total of 2,000 rooms in its nationwide chain of motels. On average, 70% of the rooms are occupied each day. The company's operating costs are $21 per occupied room per day at this occupancy level, assuming a 30-day month. This $21 figure contains both variable and fixed cost elements. During October, the occupancy rate dropped to only 45%. A total of $792,000 in operating cost was incurred during October.

Required:
1. Estimate the variable cost per occupied room per day.
2. Estimate the total fixed operating costs per month.
3. Assume that the occupancy rate increases to 60% during November. What total operating costs would you expect the company to incur during November?

Problems   Mc Graw Hill connect™

PROBLEM 6–11 Contribution Format versus Traditional Income Statement [LO3]

Home Entertainment is a small, family-owned business that purchases LCD televisions from a reputable manufacturer and sells them at the retail level. The televisions sell, on average, for $1,500 each. The average cost of a television from the manufacturer is $900.

Home Entertainment has always kept careful accounting records and the costs that it incurs in a typical month are as follows:

Costs	Cost Formula
Selling:	
Advertising	$950 per month
Delivery of televisions	$40 per television sold
Sales salaries and commissions	$2,900 per month, plus 4% of sales
Utilities	$400 per month
Depreciation of sales facilities	$3,000 per month
Administrative:	
Executive salaries	$8,000 per month
Depreciation of office equipment	$500 per month
Clerical	$1,500 per month, plus $40 per television sold
Insurance	$400 per month

During April, the company sold and delivered 150 televisions.

Required:
1. Prepare an income statement for April using the traditional format with costs organized by function.
2. Redo (1) above, this time using the contribution format with costs organized by behaviour. Show costs and revenues on both a total and a per unit basis down through contribution margin.
3. Refer to the income statement you prepared in (2) above. Why might it be misleading to show the fixed costs on a per unit basis?

PROBLEM 6–12 Cost Behaviour; High–Low Method; Contribution-Format Income Statement [LO1, LO2, LO3]
Frankel Ltd., a British merchandising company, is the exclusive distributor of a product that is gaining rapid market acceptance. The company's revenues and expenses (in British pounds: £) for the last three months are given below:

Frankel Ltd. Comparative Income Statements For the Three Months Ended June 30			
	April	May	June
Sales in units	3,000	3,750	4,500
Sales revenue	£420,000	£525,000	£630,000
Cost of goods sold	168,000	210,000	252,000
Gross margin	252,000	315,000	378,000
Selling and administrative expenses:			
Shipping expense	44,000	50,000	56,000
Advertising expense	70,000	70,000	70,000
Salaries and commissions	107,000	125,000	143,000
Insurance expense	9,000	9,000	9,000
Depreciation expense	42,000	42,000	42,000
Total selling and administrative expenses	272,000	296,000	320,000
Operating income (loss)	£ (20,000)	£ 19,000	£ 58,000

(*Note:* Frankel Ltd.'s income statement has been recast in the functional format common in North America.)

Required:
1. Identify each of the company's expenses (including cost of goods sold) as variable, fixed, or mixed.
2. Using the high–low method, separate each mixed expense into variable and fixed elements. State the cost formula for each mixed expense.
3. Redo the company's income statement at the 4,500-unit level of activity using the contribution format.

PROBLEM 6–13 Identifying Cost Behaviour Patterns [LO1]

A number of graphs displaying cost behaviour patterns are shown below. The vertical axis on each graph represents total cost and the horizontal axis represents the level of activity (volume).

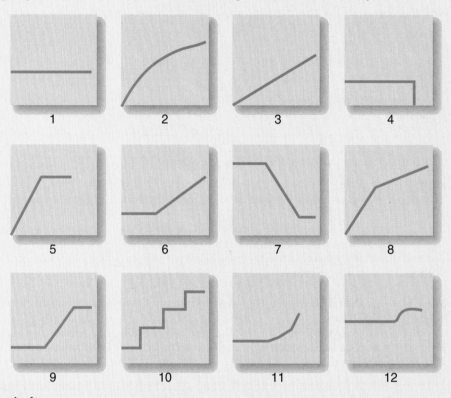

Required:

1. For each of the following situations, identify the graph that illustrates the cost behaviour pattern involved. Any graph may be used more than once.

    a. Electricity bill—a flat fixed charge, plus a variable cost after a certain number of kilowatt-hours are used.

    b. City water bill, which is computed as follows:

First 1,000,000 m³ or less	$1,000 flat fee
Next 10,000 m³	$0.003 per m³ used
Next 10,000 m³	$0.006 per m³ used
Next 10,000 m³	$0.009 per m³ used
Etc	Etc.

    c. Depreciation of equipment, where the amount is computed by the straight-line method. When the depreciation rate was established, it was anticipated that the obsolescence factor would be greater than the wear and tear factor.

    d. Rent on a factory building donated by the city, where the agreement calls for a fixed fee payment unless 200,000 labour-hours or more are worked, in which case no rent need be paid.

    e. Cost of raw materials, where the cost starts at $7.50 per unit and then decreases by 5 cents per unit for each of the first 100 units purchased, after which it remains constant at $2.50 per unit.

    f. Salaries of maintenance workers, where one maintenance worker is needed for every 1,000 hours of machine-hours or less (that is, 0 to 1,000 hours requires one maintenance worker, 1,001 to 2,000 hours requires two maintenance workers, etc.).

    g. Cost of raw material used.

    h. Rent on a factory building donated by the county, where the agreement calls for rent of $100,000 less $1 for each direct labour-hour worked in excess of 200,000 hours, but a minimum rental payment of $20,000 must be paid.

    i. Use of a machine under a lease, where a minimum charge of $1,000 is paid for up to 400 hours of machine time. After 400 hours of machine time, an additional charge of $2 per hour is paid up to a maximum charge of $2,000 per period.

2.   How would a knowledge of cost behaviour patterns such as those above be of help to a manager in analyzing the cost structure of his or her company?

(CPA, adapted)

PROBLEM 6–14 High–Low and Scattergram Analysis [LO2]

Davidson Engine Repairs provides maintenance and repair services for small engines such as those found in lawnmowers, power saws, snowthrowers, etc. The repair shop costs include the salaries for the mechanics, insurance and depreciation on the repair equipment, materials and parts used for the jobs, and utilities. The repair shop manager would like to develop a model for predicting repair costs and over the past 10 months has carefully recorded the total repair costs incurred, along with the number of maintenance and repair jobs completed each month. The data are shown below:

Month	Jobs	Repair Costs
January...............	220	$22,000
February..............	180	$18,000
March................	160	$17,600
April.................	200	$20,000
May..................	260	$24,000
June.................	240	$22,400
July.................	140	$16,000
August	120	$12,800
September	100	$13,600
October..............	80	$ 9,600

Required:

1.   Using the high–low method, estimate a cost formula for repair costs. Express the formula in the form $Y = a + bX$.

2.   Prepare a scattergram by plotting jobs performed and repair costs on a graph. Fit a straight line to the plotted points using a ruler, and estimate a cost formula for repair costs using the scattergram method.

3.   Using the cost formula developed in (1) above, predict total repair costs in a month where 200 jobs will be completed.

4.   Now assume the manager wants to predict costs for a month where 600 jobs will be completed. Should you use either of the formulas developed above to predict costs for a 600-job month? Why or why not?

PROBLEM 6–15 High–Low Method; Predicting Cost [LO1, LO2]

Prince Company's total overhead costs at various levels of activity are presented below:

Month	Direct Labour- Hours	Total Overhead Cost
September	100,000	$388,000
October..............	80,000	$340,400
November............	135,000	$485,600
December............	140,000	$483,200

Assume that the overhead cost above consists of utilities, supervisory salaries, depreciation, and maintenance. The breakdown of these costs at the 80,000 machine-hour level of activity in October is as follows:

Utilities (variable)..................	$104,000
Supervisory salaries and depreciation (fixed)..........	120,000
Maintenance (mixed)..............	116,400
Total overhead cost	$340,400

The company wants to break down the maintenance cost into its variable and fixed cost elements.

Required:
1. Estimate how much of the $483,200 of overhead cost in December was maintenance cost. (*Hint*: To do this, it may be helpful to first determine how much of the $483,200 consisted of utilities and supervisory salaries. Think about the behaviour of variable and fixed costs within the relevant range.)
2. Using the high–low method, estimate a cost formula for maintenance.
3. Express the company's total overhead cost in the form $Y = a + bX$.
4. What total overhead cost would you expect to be incurred at an activity level of 90,000 machine-hours?

PROBLEM 6–16 High–Low Method; Cost of Goods Manufactured [LO1, LO2]

Nurally, Inc., manufactures a single product. Selected data from the company's cost records for two recent months are given below:

	Level of Activity	
	July—Low	October—High
Number of units produced	9,000	12,000
Cost of goods manufactured...................	$285,000	$390,000
Work in process inventory, beginning...........	$14,000	$22,000
Work in process inventory, ending	$25,000	$15,000
Direct materials cost per unit.................	$15	$15
Direct labour cost per unit....................	$6	$6
Manufacturing overhead cost, total............	?	?

The company's manufacturing overhead cost consists of both variable and fixed cost elements. To have data available for planning, management wants to determine how much of the overhead cost is variable with units produced and how much of it is fixed per year.

Required:
1. For both July and October, estimate the amount of manufacturing overhead cost added to production. The company had no underapplied or overapplied overhead in either month. (*Hint*: A useful way to proceed might be to construct a schedule of cost of goods manufactured.)
2. Using the high–low method, estimate a cost formula for manufacturing overhead. Express the variable portion of the formula in terms of a variable rate per unit of product.
3. If 9,500 units are produced during a month, what would be the cost of goods manufactured? (Assume that the company's beginning work in process inventory for the month is $16,000 and that its ending work in process inventory is $19,000. Also assume that there is no underapplied or overapplied overhead cost for the month.)

PROBLEM 6–17 High–Low Method; Predicting Cost [LO1, LO2]

Echeverria, S.A. is an Argentinian manufacturing company whose total factory overhead costs fluctuate somewhat from year to year, according to the number of machine-hours worked in its production facility. These costs (in Argentinian pesos) at high and low levels of activity over recent years are given below:

	Level of Activity	
	Low	High
Machine-hours........................	60,000	80,000
Total factory overhead costs	274,000 pesos	312,000 pesos

The factory overhead costs above consist of indirect materials, rent, and maintenance. The company has analyzed these costs at the 60,000 machine-hours level of activity as follows:

Indirect materials (variable)	90,000 pesos
Rent (fixed)	130,000
Maintenance (mixed).........................	54,000
Total factory overhead costs..................	274,000 pesos

For planning purposes, the company wants to break down the maintenance cost into its variable and fixed cost elements.

Required:
1. Estimate how much of the factory overhead cost of 312,000 pesos at the high level of activity consists of maintenance cost. (*Hint*: To do this, it may be helpful to first determine how much of the 312,000 pesos cost consists of indirect materials and rent. Think about the behaviour of variable and fixed costs.)
2. Using the high–low method, estimate a cost formula for maintenance.
3. What *total* overhead costs would you expect the company to incur at an operating level of 65,000 machine-hours?

connect **Cases**

CASE 6–18 Scattergram Analysis; Selection of an Activity Base; High–Low Method [LO2]

Waverley Welding Company provides welding services for a variety of industrial customers in the manufacturing, aerospace, and electronics industries. The number of jobs completed from one month to the next varies considerably and jobs differ in terms of the complexity of the welding requirements. More complex jobs can take significantly longer to complete. Management knows that overhead costs have a fixed and variable component but, until now, has not attempted to determine which measure of activity should be used for planning and forecasting purposes.

The table below shows data for the most recent fiscal year. Management believes that either the number of jobs completed each month or the number of direct labour-hours incurred each month could be used as the activity base. However, they are not sure which would be more appropriate.

Month	Overhead	Direct Labour-Hours	Jobs
January.	$75,045	4,781	500
February.	$69,491	3,548	350
March.	$71,993	3,990	400
April	$81,217	5,466	550
May	$60,162	1,914	200
June	$68,364	3,157	250
July.	$78,351	5,000	500
August	$81,582	6,114	600
September	$77,691	5,108	500
October	$68,355	3,624	350
November.	$69,886	3,900	400
December.	$83,434	5,700	510

Overhead includes costs such as the maintenance supervisor's salary, depreciation on the welding equipment, and indirect materials used on each job. Electricity costs are also included in overhead and are significant since welding equipment consumes a relatively high amount of energy. Waverley Welding also employs a mix of experienced and inexperienced welders. Experienced welders are paid a higher hourly wage but are more efficient and tend to incur less wastage of indirect materials. Inexperienced welders are of course paid less on a per hour basis but work more slowly and use more indirect materials.

Required:
1. Prepare a scattergram with overhead costs on the vertical axis and direct labour-hours on the horizontal axis.
2. Prepare a scattergram with overhead costs on the vertical axis and number of jobs on the horizontal axis.
3. Which activity measure should be used as the activity base for predicting overhead costs?
4. For the activity measure you recommended in (3) above, use the high–low method to estimate a cost formula for maintenance.

CASE 6–19 Analysis of Mixed Costs, Job-Order Costing, and Activity-Based Costing [LO1, LO2]

Arburg Bärlach PLC, a company located in Switzerland, manufactures custom-designed high-precision industrial tools. The company has a traditional job-order costing system in which direct labour and direct materials costs are assigned directly to jobs, but factory overhead is applied to jobs using a predetermined overhead rate based on direct labour-hours. Management uses this job cost data for valuing cost of goods sold and inventories for external reports. For internal decision making, management has largely ignored this cost data since direct labour costs are basically fixed and management believes overhead costs actually have little to do with direct labour-hours. Recently, management has become interested in activity-based costing (ABC) as a way of estimating job costs and other costs for decision-making purposes.

Management assembled a cross-functional team to design a prototype ABC system. Electrical costs were among the first factory overhead costs investigated by the team. Electricity is used to provide light, to power equipment, and to heat the building in the winter. The ABC team proposed allocating electrical costs to jobs based on machine-hours since running the machines consumes significant amounts of electricity. Data assembled by the team concerning actual direct labour-hours, machine-hours, and electrical costs over a recent eight-week period have been entered into the spreadsheet that appears below. (The Swiss currency is the Swiss franc, which is denoted by SFr.)

◇	A	B	C	D	E
1		Direct Labour-Hours	Machine-Hours	Electrical Costs	
2	Week 1	8,910	7,700	SFr 84,600	
3	Week 2	8,920	8,620	82,270	
4	Week 3	8,870	8,600	81,000	
5	Week 4	8,840	8,500	80,800	
6	Week 5	8,990	7,600	79,400	
7	Week 6	8,940	7,100	82,800	
8	Week 7	8,870	6,000	73,100	
9	Week 8	8,910	6,800	80,800	
10		71,250	60,920	SFr 644,770	
11					
12					
13					
14					

Sheet1 Sheet2 Sheet3

To help assess the effect of the proposed change to machine-hours as the allocation base, the above eight-week totals were converted to approximate annual figures by multiplying them by six.

	Direct Labour-Hours	Machine-Hours	Electrical Costs (SFr)
Estimated annual total (Eight-week total above × 6) ...	427,500	365,520	3,868,620

Required:
1. Assume that the estimated annual totals shown above are used to compute the company's predetermined overhead rate. What would be the predetermined overhead rate for electrical costs if the allocation base is direct labour-hours? Machine-hours?
2. Management intends to bid on a job for a set of custom tools for a watchmaker that would require 30 direct labour-hours and 25 machine-hours. How much electrical cost would be charged to this job, using the predetermined overhead rate computed in (1) above if the allocation base is direct labour-hours? Machine-hours?
3. Prepare a scattergram in which you plot direct labour-hours on the horizontal axis and electrical costs on the vertical axis. Prepare another scattergram in which you plot machine-hours on the horizontal axis and electrical costs on the vertical axis. Do you agree with the ABC team that machine-hours constitute a better allocation base for electrical costs than direct labour-hours? Why?

4. Using machine-hours as the measure of activity and the high–low method, estimate the fixed and variable components of electrical costs.
5. How much electrical cost do you think would actually be caused by the custom tool job for the toolmaker in (2) above? Explain.
6. What factors, apart from direct labour-hours and machine-hours, are likely to affect consumption of electrical power in the company?

CASE 6–20 Analysis of Mixed Costs in a Pricing Decision [LO1, LO2, LO3]

Christine Dandra owns a catering company that serves food and beverages at exclusive parties and business functions. Dandra's business is seasonal, with a heavy schedule during the summer months and holidays and a lighter schedule at other times.

One of the major events that Dandra's customers request is a cocktail party. She offers a standard cocktail party and has estimated the cost per guest for this type of party as follows:

Food and beverages	$19.00
Labour (0.5 hour @ $15.00 per hour).	7.50
Overhead (0.5 hour @ $20.50 per hour)	10.25
Total cost per guest	$36.75

This standard cocktail party lasts three hours and Dandra hires one worker for every six guests, which is one-half hour of labour per guest. These workers are hired only as needed and are paid only for the hours they actually work.

Dandra ordinarily charges $50 per guest. She is confident about her estimates of the costs of food and beverages and labour, but is not as comfortable with the estimate of overhead cost. The $20.50 overhead cost per labour-hour was determined by dividing total overhead expenses for the past 12 months by total labour-hours for the same period. Monthly data concerning overhead costs and labour-hours appear below:

Month	Labour-Hours	Overhead Expenses
January.	1,500	$ 48,400
February	1,680	51,920
March	1,800	52,800
April.	2,520	56,320
May.	2,700	58,960
June	3,300	62,480
July	3,900	65,120
August	4,500	67,750
September	4,200	66,000
October.	2,700	59,840
November.	1,860	54,560
December.	3,900	64,240
Total	34,560	$708,390

Dandra has received a request to bid on a 200-guest fundraising cocktail party to be given next month by an important local charity. (The party would last the usual three hours.) She would like to win this contract because the guest list for this charity event includes many prominent individuals that she would like to land as future clients. Dandra is confident that these potential customers would be favourably impressed by her company's services at the charity event.

Required:
1. Estimate the contribution to profit of a standard 200-guest cocktail party if Dandra charges her usual price of $50 per guest. (In other words, by how much would her overall profit increase?)
2. How low could Dandra bid for the charity event, in terms of a price per guest, and still not lose money on the event itself?
3. The individual who is organizing the charity's fundraising event has indicated that he has already received a bid under $45 from another catering company. Do you think Dandra should bid below her normal $50 per guest price for the charity event? Why or why not?

(CMA, adapted)

Research and Application

R 6–21 Variable and Fixed Costs in Practice [LO1, LO2, LO3]
Form a team to investigate how an organization in your area handles variable and fixed costs. It may be in any industry and can be a business, a not-for-profit organization, or part of the government. Research the organization on the Web and in business magazines to learn what the organization does and how it has performed financially. Make an appointment to meet with the controller, chief financial officer, or with another top manager who is familiar with the financial side of the organization. After meeting with that individual, write a memo in which you discuss the following issues:

Required:
1. Does the organization distinguish between variable and fixed costs in planning and controlling operations? If not, why not?
2. If the organization does distinguish between variable and fixed costs, how are variable and fixed costs estimated? What activity bases are used? How are these activity bases selected? How often are these estimates made? Does the company prepare scattergrams of past cost and activity data?
3. If the organization does distinguish between variable and fixed costs, how does this help managers in planning and controlling operations?

APPENDIX 6A: LEAST-SQUARES REGRESSION CALCULATIONS

LEARNING OBJECTIVE 4
Analyze a mixed cost using the least-squares regression method.

Least-squares regression method
A method of separating a mixed cost into its fixed and variable elements by fitting a regression line that minimizes the sum of the squared errors.

The **least-squares regression method**, unlike the high-low method discussed earlier in the chapter, uses all the data to separate a mixed cost into its fixed and variable components. A *regression line* of the form $Y = a + bX$ is fitted to the data, where *a* represents the total fixed cost and *b* represents the variable cost per unit of activity. The basic idea underlying the least-squares regression method is illustrated in Exhibit 6A–1 using hypothetical data points. Notice from the exhibit that the deviations from the plotted points to the regression line are measured vertically on the graph. These vertical deviations are called the *regression errors* and represent the difference between the estimated cost and actual cost at a given level of activity. A regression line that perfectly explains the relationship between *X* and *Y* would have all the points on the line. The least-squares regression method computes the regression line that minimizes the sum of these squared errors and the formulas that accomplish this are shown below.[1]

$$b = \frac{n(\Sigma XY) - (\Sigma X)(\Sigma Y)}{n(\Sigma X^2) - (\Sigma X)^2}$$

$$a = \frac{(\Sigma Y) - b(\Sigma X)}{n}$$

where

X = The level of activity (independent variable)
Y = The total mixed cost (dependent variable)
a = The total fixed cost (the vertical intercept of the line)
b = The variable cost per unit of activity (the slope of the line)
n = Number of observations
Σ = Sum across all *n* observations

Manually performing the calculations required by the formulas is tedious and prone to possible errors. Fortunately, statistical software packages such as SPSS and SAS are widely available that quickly and accurately perform the calculations automatically. Spreadsheet software, such as Microsoft Excel, can also be used to do least-squares regression as can some hand-held calculators. In addition to estimates

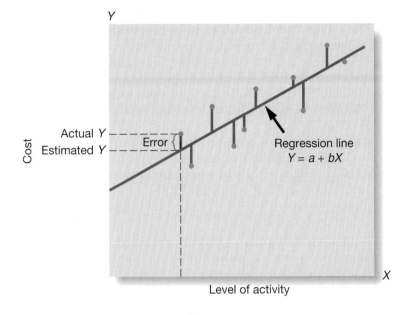

EXHIBIT 6A–1   The Concept of Least-Squares Regression

of the intercept (fixed cost) and slope (variable cost per unit), least-squares regression software ordinarily provides a number of other very useful statistics. One of these statistics is the R^2, which is a measure of "goodness of fit." The R^2 tells us the percentage of the variation in the dependent variable (cost) that is explained by variation in the independent variable (activity). The R^2 varies from 0% to 100%, and the higher the percentage, the better. A regression line that fits the data perfectly would have an R^2 of 1 (100%), but R^2 would be 0 in a situation where no fit was achieved by the regression line.

To illustrate how Excel can be used to calculate the intercept a, the slope b, and the R^2, we will use the Brentline Hospital data for maintenance costs on page 241. The worksheet in Exhibit 6A–2 contains the data and the calculations.

	A	B	C	D	E
1		Patient-	Maintenance		
2		Days	Costs		
3	Month	X	Y		
4	January	5,600	$7,900		
5	February	7,100	8,500		
6	March	5,000	7,400		
7	April	6,500	8,200		
8	May	7,300	9,100		
9	June	8,000	9,800		
10	July	6,200	7,800		
11					
12	Intercept	$3,431			
13	Slope	$0.759			
14	RSQ	0.90			
15					

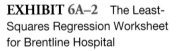

EXHIBIT 6A–2   The Least-Squares Regression Worksheet for Brentline Hospital

Ready   NUM

As you can see, the X values (the independent variable) have been entered in cells B4 through B10. The Y values (the dependent variable) have been entered in cells C4 through C10. The slope, intercept, and R^2 are computed using the Excel functions INTERCEPT, SLOPE, and RSQ. In each case, you must specify the range of cells for the Y values and for the X values. In the Exhibit 6A–2 worksheet, the value shown in cell B12 results from the formula = INTERCEPT(C4:C10,B4:B10); the value shown in cell B13 results from the formula = SLOPE(C4:C10,B4:B10); and the value in B14 results from the formula = RSQ(C4:C10,B4:B10).[2]

According to the calculations carried out by Excel, the fixed maintenance cost (the intercept) is \$3,431 per month (cell B12) and the variable cost (the slope) is \$0.759 per patient-day (cell B13). Therefore, the cost formula for maintenance cost is

$$Y = a + bX$$
$$Y = \$3,431 + \$0.759X$$

Note that the R^2 (RSQ) is 0.90 (cell B14), which is very high, indicating that 90% of the variation in maintenance costs is explained by the variation in patient-days. This is an excellent fit of the regression line to the actual data. On the other hand, a low R^2 would be an indication of a poor fit.

Even when using the regression method you should still always plot the data in a scattergram, but it is particularly important to check the data visually when the R^2 is low. A quick look at the scattergram can reveal the strength of the relationship between the cost and the activity, or that the relationship is something other than a simple straight line. In such cases, additional analysis would be required. Plotting the data to create a scattergram is easy in Excel, the results of which appear in Exhibit 6A–3. Consistent with the high R^2 value of 0.90, the relationship between cost and activity is approximately linear, so it is reasonable to fit a straight line to the data as we have done with the least-squares regression.

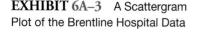

Economic plausibility
A qualitative assessment of whether the relationship between the independent and dependent variable in a cost estimation model makes sense from an economic perspective.

Economic Plausibility

Statistical software packages and spreadsheets such as Excel can readily perform the calculations required for the least-squares regression method and provide fit statistics such as R^2 that permit evaluation of the model fit. But managers must also carefully consider the **economic plausibility** of the relationship between the activity chosen as the independent

EXHIBIT 6A–3   A Scattergram Plot of the Brentline Hospital Data

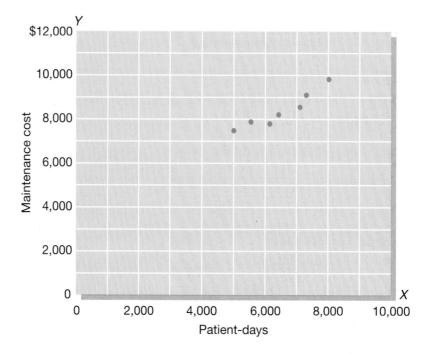

variable and the cost being predicted. The question that managers must think about in assessing economic plausibility is whether it makes *economic* sense that a change in the activity level of the independent variable would cause a change in the dependent variable. In our example above, it is economically plausible that an increase in patient-days would cause an increase in maintenance costs at Brentline Hospital. More patient-days would lead to increased use of resources, which in turn would increase maintenance activities. However, using the number of full-time nurses employed at the hospital as the independent variable would have lower economic plausibility. One would not expect a strong association between maintenance costs and the number of full-time nurses. That said, the R^2 of a regression model using the number of full-time nurses as the independent variable instead of the number of patient-days might still be reasonably good, although likely lower than the 0.90 found above. Why? Because as the number of patient-days increases, more nurses will probably be hired, making it appear that the number of full-time nurses causes an increase in maintenance costs. However, the real driver of maintenance costs in this example is patient-days.

Because it is easy to generate cost estimation models with tools such as Excel, managers might be tempted to use a "see what works" approach when selecting activities to use as independent variables. Therefore, applying the economic plausibility criterion, in addition to statistical criteria such as R^2, is always a good idea.

Multiple Regression Analysis

In the discussion thus far, we have assumed that a single factor such as patient-days drives the variable cost component of a mixed cost. This assumption is acceptable for many mixed costs, but in some situations there may be more than one causal factor driving the variable cost element. For example, shipping costs may depend on both the number of units shipped *and* the weight of the units. In a situation such as this, *multiple regression* is more appropriate to use. **Multiple regression** is an analytical method that is used when the dependent variable (i.e., cost) is caused by more than one activity. Although adding more activities, or independent variables, makes the computations more complex, the principles involved are the same as in the simple least-squares regressions discussed above. The R^2 for multiple regression analysis represents the amount of variation in the dependent variable explained by the *set* of independent variables included in the model and, as with simple regression, ranges from 0 to 1. Managers should also consider the economic plausibility of each independent variable included in the cost estimation model.

Multiple regression
An analytical method required in those situations where variations in a dependent variable are caused by more than one activity.

Appendix 6A Summary

- The least-squares method is a superior approach for cost estimation because it incorporates all data points in the analysis. Computer software such as SPSS and SAS can perform the calculations required by the least-squares regression method. Regression analysis software also calculates other useful statistics such as R^2, which quantifies the goodness of fit. Spreadsheet packages such as Excel can also be used to perform least-squares regression calculations. **[LO4]**
- In addition to examining fit statistics such as R^2 and preparing a scattergram to visually assess the relationship between the independent and dependent variables, managers should also consider the economic plausibility of the relationship. This involves qualitatively assessing whether it makes economic sense for the independent and dependent variables to be related. **[LO4]**
- Multiple regression analysis involves the use of more than one independent variable in predicting the behaviour of a dependent variable. Fit statistics such as R^2 can be computed for multiple regression analysis and economic plausibility is still important to evaluate. **[LO4]**

Appendix 6A Exercises, Problems, and Cases connect™

EXERCISE 6A–1 Least-Squares Regression [LO4]
Spentz Company offers rental cars in several off-airport locations. Management would like to better understand the behaviour of the company's costs. One of those costs is the cost of cleaning cars. The company operates its own car wash and cleaning facilities in which each rental car that is returned is thoroughly cleaned before being released for rental to another customer. Management believes that the costs of operating the cleaning facilities should be related to the number of rental returns. Accordingly, the following data have been compiled:

Month	Rental Returns	Cleaning Costs
January.	4,620	$15,170
February	4,906	$19,036
March	5,282	$16,358
April.	5,748	$19,423
May.	7,080	$23,001
June	9,722	$32,182
July	10,864	$31,905
August	10,536	$29,895
September	9,256	$32,790
October.	7,480	$27,574
November.	4,212	$14,745
December.	4,990	$16,621

Required:
Using least-squares regression, estimate the fixed cost and variable cost elements of monthly car wash costs. The fixed cost element should be estimated to the nearest dollar and the variable cost element to the nearest cent.

EXERCISE 6A–2 Least-Squares Regression [LO4]
Refer to the data for Zerbel Company in Exercise 6–6.

Required:
1. Using the least-squares regression method, estimate the cost formula for shipping expense.
2. If you also completed Exercise 6–6, prepare a simple table comparing the variable and fixed cost elements of shipping expense as computed under the scattergram method, the high–low method, and the least-squares regression method.

EXERCISE 6A–3 Least-Squares Regression [LO4]
Serenity Living manufactures gas fireplaces for home use. Each unit produced goes through a complex quality control process. The company has observed quality control costs as follows over the past six weeks:

Week	Units Produced	Total Quality Control Costs
1	24	$540
2	15	$400
3	30	$620
4	12	$380
5	18	$480
6	27	$580

For planning purposes, the company's management wants to know the amount of variable quality control costs per unit and the total fixed quality control costs per week.

Required:
1. Using the least-squares regression method, estimate the variable and fixed elements of the quality control cost.
2. Express the cost data in (1) above in the form $Y = a + bX$.
3. If the company produces 20 gas fireplaces next week, what would be the expected total quality control costs?
4. Evaluate the economic plausibility of using units produced to predict total quality control costs.

PROBLEM 6A–4 Scattergram; Cost Behaviour; Least-Squares Regression Method [LO4]

Melody Baker has just been appointed director of recreation programs for Highland Park. In the past, the city has sponsored a number of softball leagues in the summer months. From the city's cost records, Amanda has found the following total costs associated with the softball leagues over the last five years:

	A	B	C	D
1	Number of Leagues	Total Cost		
2	5	$13,000		
3	2	$ 7,000		
4	4	$10,500		
5	6	$14,000		
6	3	$10,000		
7				

Sheet1 / Sheet2 / Sheet3

Each league requires its own paid supervisor and paid umpires as well as printed schedules and other copy work. Therefore, Amanda knows that some variable costs are associated with the leagues. She would like to know the amount of variable cost per league and the total fixed cost per year associated with the softball program. This information would help her for planning purposes.

Required:
1. Using the least-squares regression method, estimate the variable cost per league and the total fixed cost per year for the softball program.
2. Express the cost data derived in (1) above in the form $Y = a + bX$.
3. Assume that Melody would like to expand the softball program during the coming year to involve a total of seven leagues. Compute the expected total cost for the softball program. Can you see any problem with using the cost formula from (2) above to derive this total cost figure? Explain.
4. Prepare a scattergram and fit a line to the plotted points using the cost formula expressed in (2) above.

PROBLEM 6A–5 Least-Squares Regression Analysis; Contribution-Format Income Statement [LO3, LO4]

Mayer Company has decided to use a contribution approach income statement for internal planning purposes. The company has analyzed its expenses and has developed the following cost formulas:

Cost	Cost Formula
Cost of goods sold	$20 per unit sold
Advertising expense	$170,000 per quarter
Sales commissions	5% of sales
Administrative salaries.	$80,000 per quarter
Shipping expense	?
Depreciation expense	$50,000 per quarter

Management has concluded that shipping expense is a mixed cost, containing both variable and fixed cost elements. Units sold and the related shipping expenses for the past eight quarters are given below:

Quarter	Units Sold (000)	Shipping Expense
Year 1:		
First	16	$160,000
Second	18	$175,000
Third	23	$210,000
Fourth	19	$180,000
Year 2:		
First	17	$170,000
Second	20	$190,000
Third	25	$230,000
Fourth	22	$205,000

Management would like a cost formula derived for shipping expense so that a budgeted income statement using the contribution approach can be prepared for the next quarter.

Required:
1. Using the least-squares regression method, estimate a cost formula for shipping expense. (Since the Units Sold above are in thousands of units, the variable cost you compute will also be in thousands of units. It can be left in this form, or you can convert your variable cost to a per unit basis by dividing it by 1,000.)
2. In the first quarter of year 3, the company plans to sell 21,000 units at a selling price of $50 per unit. Prepare a contribution-format income statement for the quarter.

CASE 6A–6 Least-Squares Regression; Scattergram; Comparison of Activity Bases [LO2, LO4]
Green Care Limited (GCL) manufactures environment-friendly electric lawnmowers, and demand has been growing rapidly. Management would like to develop cost formulas for planning and decision-making purposes. The company's cost analyst has concluded that utilities cost is a mixed cost, and she is attempting to find an activity base with which the cost might be closely related. The controller has suggested that units produced might be a good base to use in developing a cost formula. The production superintendent disagrees; he thinks that direct labour-hours would be a better base since different lawnmower models have different production requirements. The cost analyst has decided to try both bases and has assembled the following information for the past eight months:

Month	Units Produced	Direct Labour-Hours	Utilities Cost
January	60,000	15,000	$200,000
February	44,000	9,000	$180,000
March	84,000	12,000	$240,000
April	48,000	18,000	$300,000
May	72,000	30,000	$400,000
June	100,000	27,000	$420,000
July	120,000	24,000	$340,000
August	112,000	33,000	$480,000

Required:
1. Using units produced as the independent (X) variable:
   a. Determine a cost formula for utilities cost using the least-squares regression method.
   b. Prepare a scattergram and plot the units produced and utilities cost. (Place cost on the vertical axis and units produced on the horizontal axis.) Fit a straight line to the plotted points using the cost formula determined in (a) above.
2. Using direct labour-hours as the independent (X) variable, repeat 1(a) and (b) above.
3. Would you recommend that the company use units produced or direct labour-hours as a base for planning utilities cost?
4. Evaluate the economic plausibility of using units produced or direct labour-hours to predict utilities cost.

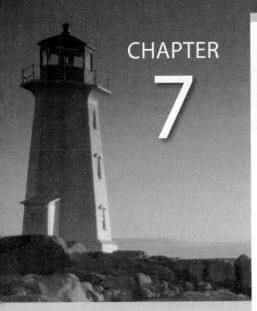

CHAPTER

7

Learning Objectives

After studying Chapter 7, you should be able to

1. Explain how changes in activity affect contribution margin (CM) and operating income.

2. Prepare and interpret a cost–volume–profit (CVP) graph.

3. Use the contribution margin ratio to compute changes in contribution margin and operating income resulting from changes in sales volume.

4. Show the effects on contribution margin of changes in variable costs, fixed costs, selling price, and volume.

5. Compute the break-even point in unit sales and sales dollars.

6. Determine the level of sales needed to achieve a desired target profit.

7. Compute the margin of safety and explain its significance.

8. Explain cost structure and compute the degree of operating leverage at a particular level of sales and explain how it can be used to predict changes in operating income.

9. Compute the break-even point for a multi-product company and explain the effects of shifts in the sales mix on the contribution margin and the break-even point.

10. (Online Appendix 7A) Conduct a cost–volume–profit analysis with uncertainty.

COST–VOLUME–PROFIT RELATIONSHIPS

■ A BRIGHT FUTURE

Canadian Solar Inc., founded in 2001, designs and manufactures solar products and solar systems. The company has its headquarters in Kitchener, Ontario, with manufacturing operations in North America, Europe, and China. Competition is intense in the solar products industry but Canadian Solar Inc. has achieved remarkable growth in both net revenues and operating income over the past few years. Revenues have grown from $68.2 million in 2006 to over $700 million in 2008. Over that same time period, operating income has increased from $1.1 million to $24 million.

Despite the strong growth in revenues and earnings, management at Canadian Solar Inc. must still be aware of the implications of a change in demand caused by competitors' actions or other changes in the operating environment. A key metric tracked by both management and external stakeholders is the volume of total product sales expressed in total megawatts (MW). Management estimates that total demand for Canadian Solar Inc. products in 2009 will be about 300 MW, with the expectation for 2010 in the range of 600 MW to 700 MW. Importantly, financial analysts estimate that Canadian Solar Inc. has a break-even level of sales of around 260 MW. At the break-even level of activity, operating income will be $0. So, as long as Canadian Solar Inc. has sales in excess of 260 MW, its operating income will be positive.

Knowing what the break-even level of activity is helps management and other stakeholders such as investors and lenders to evaluate the cushion (if any) between a company's expected level of sales and the level required just to earn a $0 profit. For Canadian Solar Inc., sales could drop from expected levels by around 15% in 2009 and over 50% in 2010 and the company would still break even. The larger the cushion, the less likely it is that the company will fail to generate positive operating income.

How is the break-even level of activity calculated? What information is required? What assumptions are necessary in performing the analysis? These and other issues related to understanding key relationships among cost, volume, and profit are the focus of this chapter.

Sources: Adapted from Thomson Reuters, "Barclays Raises Canadian Solar to Equal Weight," *National Post,* November 17, 2009; and the Canadian Solar Inc. Web site at www.canadiansolar.com.

C ost–volume–profit (CVP) analysis is a powerful tool that helps managers to understand the relationships among cost, volume, and profit. CVP focuses on how profits are affected by the following five elements:

1. Prices of products.
2. Volume or level of activity.
3. Per unit variable costs.
4. Total fixed costs.
5. Mix of products sold.

Because CVP analysis helps managers understand how profits are affected by these key factors, it is a vital tool in many business decisions. These decisions include what products to manufacture and services to offer, what prices to charge, what marketing strategy to adopt, and what cost structures to implement. Careful study of the elements and assumptions, however, is needed to avoid mistakes and to know when to extend the ideas presented in this chapter to more complex situations. One additional area of potential confusion is the use of the terms *profit* and *income* interchangeably. This confused terminology has not been corrected because the older term *profit* is often used to mean *income* by both managers and accountants.

To help understand the role of CVP analysis in business decisions, consider the hypothetical case of Acoustic Concepts, Inc., a company founded by Prem Narayan. Prem, a graduate engineering student at the time, started Acoustic Concepts to market a radical new speaker that he had designed for automobile sound systems. The speaker, called the Sonic Blaster, uses an advanced microprocessor chip to boost amplification to awesome levels. Prem contracted with a Taiwanese electronics manufacturer to produce the speaker. With start-up money provided by his family, Prem placed an order with the manufacturer for completed units and ran advertisements in auto magazines.

The Sonic Blaster was an almost immediate success, and sales grew to the point that Prem moved the company's headquarters out of his apartment and into rented quarters in a neighbouring industrial park. He also hired a receptionist, an accountant, a sales manager, and a small sales staff to sell the speakers to retail stores. The accountant, Bob Luchinni, had worked for several small companies where he had acted as a business advisor as well as accountant and bookkeeper.

THE BASICS OF COST–VOLUME–PROFIT ANALYSIS

LEARNING OBJECTIVE 1
Explain how changes in activity affect contribution margin (CM) and operating income.

Prem has asked Bob to analyze several things he has been thinking about, including the profit effect of a drop in sales volume or a change in variable cost per unit, the incremental sales necessary to justify a new advertising campaign under consideration, and the profit impact of dropping the selling price. As the first step in preparing the analyses, Bob begins with the contribution income statement. The contribution income statement emphasizes the behaviour of costs and therefore is extremely helpful to a manager in judging the impact on profits of changes in selling price, cost, or volume. Bob will base his analysis on the following contribution income statement he prepared last month:

ACOUSTIC CONCEPTS, INC.
Contribution Income Statement
For the Month of June

	Total	Per Unit
Sales (400 speakers)	$100,000	$250
Less variable expenses	60,000	150
Contribution margin	40,000	$100
Less fixed expenses	35,000	
Operating income*	$ 5,000	

*Operating income less interest expense less income tax expense equals net income.

This contribution-format income statement was prepared for management's use inside the company and would not ordinarily be made available to those outside the company. Note that this statement reports sales, variable expenses, and contribution margin on both a per unit basis and a total basis. These per unit figures will be very helpful for performing the cost–volume–profit analysis that we will be studying over the next several pages. Also, note that we use operating income as our measure of profit. We ignore income taxes throughout most of this chapter so that we can more easily focus on the central issues of cost–volume–profit analysis.

Contribution Margin

As explained in Chapter 6, contribution margin (CM) is the amount remaining from sales revenue after variable expenses have been deducted. Thus, it is the amount available to cover fixed expenses and then to provide profits for the period. Notice the sequence here— contribution margin is used *first* to cover the fixed expenses, and then whatever remains goes toward profits. If the contribution margin is not sufficient to cover the fixed expenses, then a loss occurs for the period. To illustrate with an extreme example, assume that by the middle of a particular month Acoustic Concepts has been able to sell only one speaker. At that point, the company's income statement will appear as follows:

	Total	Per Unit	Percentage of Sales
Sales (1 speaker)	$ 250	$250	100%
Less variable expenses	150	150	60%
Contribution margin	100	$100	40%
Less fixed expenses	35,000		
Operating loss	$(34,900)		

For each additional speaker that the company is able to sell during the month, $100 more in contribution margin will become available to help cover the fixed expenses. If a second speaker is sold, for example, then the total contribution margin will increase by $100 (to a total of $200) and the company's operating loss will decrease by $100, to $34,800:

	Total	Per Unit	Percentage of Sales
Sales (2 speakers)	$ 500	$250	100%
Less variable expenses	300	150	60%
Contribution margin	200	$100	40%
Less fixed expenses	35,000		
Operating loss	$(34,800)		

If enough speakers can be sold to generate $35,000 in contribution margin, then all of the fixed costs will be covered and the company will have managed to at least *break even* for the month—that is, to show neither profit nor loss but just cover all of its expenses. To reach the break-even point, the company will have to sell 350 speakers in a month, since each speaker sold yields $100 in contribution margin:

	Total	Per Unit	Percentage of Sales
Sales (350 speakers)	$87,500	$250	100%
Less variable expenses	52,500	150	60%
Contribution margin	35,000	$100	40%
Less fixed expenses	35,000		
Operating income	$ –0–		

Break-even point
The level of sales at which profit is zero. The break-even point can also be defined as the point where total sales equals total expenses, or as the point where total contribution margin equals total fixed expenses. Sales – variable expenses – fixed expenses = $0.

Computation of the break-even point is discussed in detail later in the chapter; for the moment, note that the **break-even point** is the level of sales at which profit is zero.

Once the break-even point has been reached, operating income will increase by the unit contribution margin for each additional unit sold. If 351 speakers are sold in a month, for example, then we can expect that the operating income for the month will be $100, since the company will have sold 1 speaker more than the number required to break even:

	Total	Per Unit	Percentage of Sales
Sales (351 speakers)	$87,750	$250	100%
Less variable expenses	52,650	150	60%
Contribution margin.	35,100	$100	40%
Less fixed expenses	35,000		
Operating income	$ 100		

If 352 speakers are sold (2 speakers above the break-even point), then the operating income for the month will be $200, and so forth. To estimate profit at any sales level above the break-even point, simply multiply the number of units sold in excess of the break-even point by the unit contribution margin. The result represents the anticipated operating income for the period. Or, to estimate the effect of a planned increase in sales on profits, the manager can simply multiply the increase in units sold by the unit contribution margin. The result will be the expected increase in operating income. To illustrate, if Acoustic Concepts is currently selling 400 speakers per month and plans to increase sales to 425 speakers per month, the anticipated effect on operating profits can be computed as follows:

Increased number of speakers to be sold.	25
Contribution margin per speaker.	×$100
Increase in operating income.	$2,500

These calculations can be verified as follows:

	Sales Volume			
	400 speakers	425 speakers	Difference 25 speakers	Per Unit
Sales	$100,000	$106,250	$6,250	$250
Less variable expenses	60,000	63,750	3,750	150
Contribution margin.	40,000	42,500	2,500	$100
Less fixed expenses	35,000	35,000	–0–	
Operating income	$ 5,000	$ 7,500	$2,500	

To summarize, if sales are zero, the company's operating loss would equal its fixed expenses. Each unit that is sold reduces the loss by the amount of the unit contribution margin. Once the break-even point has been reached, each additional unit sold increases the company's operating profit by the amount of the unit contribution margin.

The income statements shown above for Acoustic Concepts illustrate the fundamentals of cost–volume–profit analysis but are based on some simplifying assumptions. For example, we assumed that selling price per unit, variable expenses per unit, and total fixed expenses remained constant even for large changes in sales volumes. Simplifications such as these make the analysis easier to prepare and permit a preliminary examination of the profit effects of alternative scenarios (e.g., increased sales volume, decreased selling price per unit, etc.). However, a more complex examination of cost–volume–profit relationships that relaxes the simplifying assumptions can be easily handled by computer spreadsheet programs that permit more sophisticated forms of "what if" analysis.

When Airbus launched the A380 555-seat jetliner in 2000 the company said it would need to sell 250 units to break even on the project. By 2006, Airbus was admitting that more than $3 billion of cost overruns had raised the project's break-even point to 420 airplanes. Although Airbus has fewer than 170 orders for the A380, the company remains optimistic that it will sell 751 units over the next 20 years. Given that Airbus rival Boeing predicts the total market size for all airplanes with more than 400 seats will not exceed 990 units, it remains unclear if Airbus will ever break even on its investment in the A380 aircraft.

Source: Daniel Michaels, "Embattled Airbus Lifts Sales Target fo A380 to Profit," *The Wall Street Journal,* October 20, 2006, p. A6.

CVP RELATIONSHIPS IN GRAPHIC FORM

Relationships among revenue, cost, profit, and volume can be expressed graphically by preparing a **cost–volume–profit graph**. A CVP graph highlights CVP relationships over wide ranges of activity. To help explain his analysis to Prem Narayan, Bob Luchinni decided to prepare a CVP graph for Acoustic Concepts.

Preparing the CVP Graph

In a CVP graph (sometimes called a *break-even chart*), unit volume is commonly represented on the horizontal *x*-axis and dollars on the vertical *y*-axis. Preparing a CVP graph involves three steps, as depicted in Exhibit 7–1.

Cost–volume–profit (CVP) graph
The relationships among revenues, costs, and level of activity presented in graphic form.

1. Draw a line parallel to the volume axis to represent total fixed expenses. For Acoustic Concepts, total fixed expenses are $35,000.
2. Choose some volume of sales and plot the point representing total expenses (fixed plus variable) at the activity level you have selected. In Exhibit 7–1, Bob chose a volume of 600 speakers. Total expenses at that activity level would be as follows:

Fixed expenses	$ 35,000
Variable expenses (600 speakers × $150)	90,000
Total expenses.	$125,000

After the point has been plotted, draw a line through it back to the point where the fixed expenses line intersects the dollars axis.

3. Again choose some sales volume and plot the point representing total sales dollars at the activity level you have selected. In Exhibit 7–1, Bob again chose a volume of 600 speakers. Sales at that activity level total $150,000 (600 speakers × $250 per speaker). Draw a line through this point back to the origin.

The interpretation of the completed CVP graph is given in Exhibit 7–2. The anticipated profit or loss at any given level of sales is measured by the vertical distance between the total revenue line (sales) and the total expenses line (variable expenses plus fixed expenses).

The break-even point is where the total revenue and total expenses lines intersect. The break-even point of 350 speakers in Exhibit 7–2 agrees with the break-even point computed earlier.

EXHIBIT 7–1   Preparing the
CVP Graph

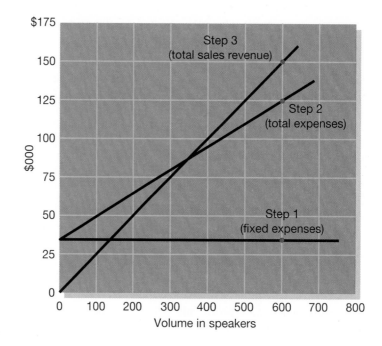

As discussed earlier, when sales are below the break-even point, in this case, 350 units, the company incurs a loss. Note that the loss (represented by the vertical distance between the total expense and total revenue lines) becomes larger as sales decline. When sales are above the break-even point, the company earns a profit and the amount of the profit (represented by the vertical distance between the total revenue and total expense lines) increases as sales increase.

EXHIBIT 7–2   The Completed
CVP Graph

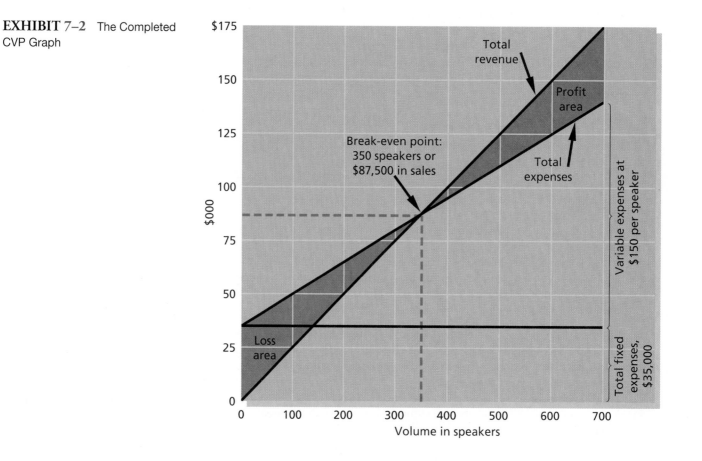

A simpler form of the CVP graph, which we call a *profit graph*, is presented in Exhibit 7–3. That graph is based on the following equation:

$$\text{Profit} = \text{Unit CM} \times Q - \text{Fixed expenses}$$

In the case of Acoustic Concepts, the equation can be expressed as

$$\text{Profit} = \$100 \times Q - \$35,000$$

Because this is a linear equation, it plots profit as a single straight line. To plot the line, compute the profit at two different sales volumes, plot the points, and then connect them with a straight line. For example, when the sales volume is zero (i.e., $Q = 0$), the profit is $-\$35,000$ (= $\$100 \times 0 - \$35,000$). When Q is 600, the profit is $\$25,000$ (= $\$100 \times 600 - \$35,000$). These two points are plotted in Exhibit 7–3 and a straight line has been drawn through them.

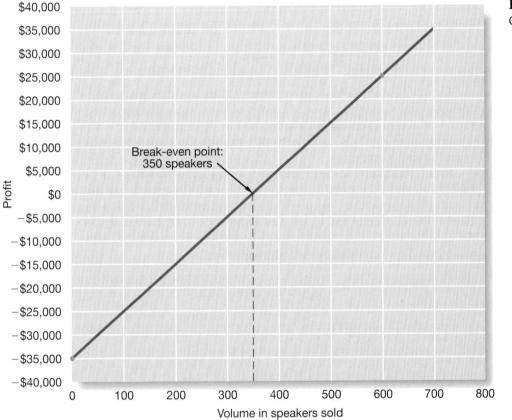

EXHIBIT 7–3   The Profit Graph

The break-even point on the profit graph is the volume of sales at which profit is zero and is indicated by the dashed line on the graph. Note that the profit steadily increases to the right of the break-even point as the sales volume increases and that the loss becomes steadily worse to the left of the break-even point as the sales volume decreases.

CONTRIBUTION MARGIN RATIO

In the previous section, we explored how cost–volume–profit relationships can be visualized by using a CVP graph. In this section, we show how the contribution margin ratio can be used in cost–volume–profit calculations. As the first step, we have added a column to Acoustic Concepts' contribution income statement, in which sales revenues, variable expenses, and contribution margin are expressed as a percentage of sales:

	Total	Per Unit	Percentage of Sales
Sales (400 speakers)	$100,000	$250	100%
Less variable expenses	60,000	150	60%
Contribution margin.	40,000	$100	40%
Less fixed expenses	35,000		
Operating income	$ 5,000		

Contribution margin (CM) ratio
The contribution margin as a percentage of total sales.

The contribution margin expressed as a percentage of total sales is referred to as the **contribution margin (CM) ratio.** This ratio is computed as follows:

$$\text{CM ratio} = \frac{\text{Contribution margin}}{\text{Sales}}$$

For Acoustic Concepts, the computations are

$$\frac{\text{Total contribution margin, \$40,000}}{\text{Total sales, \$100,000}} = 40\% \text{ or } \frac{\text{Per unit contribution margin, \$100}}{\text{Per unit sales, \$250}} = 40\%$$

The CM ratio shows how the contribution margin will be affected by a change in total sales. Acoustic Concepts has a CM ratio of 40%, meaning that for each dollar increase in sales, total contribution margin will increase by 40 cents ($1 sales $\times$ CM ratio of 40%). Operating income will also increase by 40 cents, assuming that fixed costs are not affected by the increase in sales.

As this illustration suggests, *the effect on operating income of any dollar change in total sales can be computed by simply applying the CM ratio to the dollar change.* For example, if Acoustic Concepts plans a $30,000 increase in sales during the coming month, the contribution margin will increase by $12,000 ($30,000 increased sales $\times$ CM ratio of 40%). As we noted above, operating income will also increase by $12,000 if fixed costs do not change. This is verified by the following table:

	Sales Volume			Percentage of Sales
	Present	**Expected**	**Increase**	
Sales.	$100,000	$130,000	$30,000	100%
Less variable expenses	60,000	78,000*	18,000	60%
Contribution margin	40,000	52,000	12,000	40%
Less fixed expenses.	35,000	35,000	–0–	
Operating income.	$ 5,000	$ 17,000	$12,000	

*$130,000 expected sales $\div$ $250 per unit = 520 units. 520 units $\times$ $150 per unit = $78,000. Alternatively, (1 − 0.40) $\times$ $130,000 = $78,000.

Some managers prefer to work with the CM ratio rather than the unit contribution margin. The CM ratio is particularly valuable when trade-offs must be made between more dollar sales of one product versus more dollar sales of another. Generally speaking, when trying to increase sales, products that yield the greatest amount of contribution margin per dollar of sales should be emphasized.

SOME APPLICATIONS OF CVP CONCEPTS

Bob Luchinni, the accountant at Acoustic Concepts, wants to demonstrate how the concepts developed on the preceding pages of this text can be used to analyze some of the issues that the company's president, Prem Narayan, is worried about. Bob gathered the following basic data:

Recall that fixed expenses are $35,000 per month. Bob will use these data to show the effects of changes in variable costs, fixed costs, sales price, and sales volume on the company's profitability.

LEARNING OBJECTIVE 4
Show the effects on contribution margin of changes in variable costs, fixed costs, selling price, and volume.

	Per Unit	Percentage of Sales
Sales price.....................................	$250	100%
Less variable expenses..........................	150	60%
Contribution margin	$100	40%

Change in Fixed Cost and Sales Volume

Acoustic Concepts is currently selling 400 speakers per month at $250 per speaker for total monthly sales of $100,000. The sales manager feels that a $10,000 increase in the monthly advertising budget would increase monthly sales by $30,000 to a total of $130,000. Should the advertising budget be increased? The following table shows the effect of the proposed change in monthly advertising budget:

	Sales Volume			
	Current Sales	Sales with Additional Advertising Budget	Difference	Percentage of Sales
Sales	$100,000	$130,000*	$30,000	100%
Less variable expenses	60,000	78,000†	18,000	60%
Contribution margin	40,000	52,000	12,000	40%
Less fixed expenses	35,000	45,000‡	10,000	
Operating income	$ 5,000	$ 7,000	$ 2,000	

*New unit sales: $130,000 ÷ $250 per unit = 520 units
†520 units × $150 per unit = $78,000
‡$35,000 plus additional $10,000 monthly advertising budget = $45,000

Assuming no other factors need to be considered, the increase in the advertising budget should be approved since it would lead to an increase in operating income of $2,000. There are two shorter ways to present this solution. The first alternative solution follows:

Alternative Solution 1

Expected total contribution margin:	
$130,000 × 40% CM ratio	$52,000
Present total contribution margin:	
$100,000 × 40% CM ratio	40,000
Incremental contribution margin.......................................	12,000
Change in fixed costs:	
Less incremental advertising expense	10,000
Increased operating income	$ 2,000

Since in this case only the fixed costs and the sales volume change, the solution can be presented in an even shorter format, as follows:

Alternative Solution 2

Incremental contribution margin:	
$30,000 × 40% CM ratio	$12,000
Less incremental advertising expense	10,000
Increased operating income	$ 2,000

Notice that this approach does not require a knowledge of previous sales. Also notice that it is unnecessary under either alternative approach to prepare an income statement. Both approaches involve an **incremental analysis**—they consider only those items of revenue, cost, and volume that will change if the new program is implemented.[1] Although in each case a new income statement could have been prepared, the incremental approach is more direct and focuses attention on the specific items involved in the decision.

Incremental analysis
An analytical approach that focuses only on those items of revenue, cost, and volume that will change as a result of a decision.

Change in Variable Costs and Sales Volume

Refer to the original data. Recall that Acoustic Concepts is currently selling 400 speakers per month. Management is contemplating the use of higher-quality components, which would increase variable costs (and thereby reduce the contribution margin) by $10 per speaker. However, the sales manager predicts that the higher overall quality would increase sales to 480 speakers per month. Should the higher-quality components be used? The $10 increase in variable costs will decrease the unit contribution margin by $10—from $100 to $90.

Solution

Expected total contribution margin with higher-quality components:	
480 speakers × $90 per speaker	$43,200
Present total contribution margin:	
400 speakers × $100 per speaker	40,000
Increase in total contribution margin	$ 3,200

According to this analysis, the higher-quality components should be used. Since fixed costs will not change, the $3,200 increase in contribution margin shown above should result in a $3,200 increase in operating income.

Change in Fixed Costs, Selling Price, and Sales Volume

Refer to the original data and recall again that the company is currently selling 400 speakers per month. To increase sales, the sales manager would like to cut the selling price by $20 per speaker and increase the advertising budget by $15,000 per month. The sales manager argues that if these two steps are taken, unit sales will increase by 50% to 600 speakers per month. Should the changes be made? A decrease of $20 per speaker in the selling price will cause the unit contribution margin to decrease from $100 to $80.

Solution

Expected total contribution margin with lower selling price:	
600 speakers × $80 per speaker	$48,000
Present total contribution margin:	
400 speakers × $100 per speaker	40,000
Incremental contribution margin	8,000
Change in fixed costs:	
Less incremental advertising expense	15,000
Reduction in operating income	$ (7,000)

According to this analysis, the changes should not be made. The $7,000 reduction in operating income that is shown above can be verified by preparing comparative income statements as follows:

	Present 400 Speakers per Month		Expected 600 Speakers per Month		
	Total	Per Unit	Total	Per Unit	Difference
Sales	$100,000	$250	$138,000	$230	$38,000
Less variable expenses	60,000	150	90,000	150	30,000
Contribution margin.	40,000	$100	48,000	$ 80	8,000
Less fixed expenses	35,000		50,000*		15,000
Operating income (loss).	$ 5,000		$ (2,000)		$ (7,000)

*35,000 + Additional monthly advertising budget of $15,000 = $50,000.

Change in Variable Cost, Fixed Cost, and Sales Volume

Refer to the original data. As before, the company is currently selling 400 speakers per month. The sales manager would like to pay the salespeople a commission of $15 per speaker sold, rather than the flat salaries that now total $6,000 per month. The sales manager is confident that the change will increase monthly sales by 15% to 460 speakers per month. Should the change be made?

Solution

Changing the sales staff from a salaried basis to a commission basis will affect both fixed and variable costs. Fixed costs will decrease by $6,000, from $35,000 to $29,000. Variable costs will increase by $15, from $150 to $165, and the unit contribution margin will decrease from $100 to $85.

Expected total contribution margin with sales staff on commission:	
460 speakers × $85 per speaker.	$39,100
Present total contribution margin:	
400 speakers × $100 per speaker.	40,000
Decrease in total contribution margin	(900)
Change in fixed costs:	
Add salaries avoided if a commission is paid	6,000
Increase in operating income.	$ 5,100

According to this analysis, the change should be made. Again, the same answer can be obtained by preparing comparative income statements:

	Present 400 Speakers per Month		Expected 460 Speakers per Month		Difference: Increase or (Decrease) in Net income
	Total	Per Unit	Total	Per Unit	
Sales	$100,000	$250	$115,000	$250	$15,000
Less variable expenses	60,000	150	75,900	165	(15,900)
Contribution margin.	40,000	$100	39,100	$ 85	(900)
Less fixed expenses	35,000		29,000		6,000
Operating income	$ 5,000		$ 10,100		$ 5,100

Change in Regular Selling Price

Refer to the original data where Acoustic Concepts is currently selling 400 speakers per month. The company has an opportunity to make a bulk sale of 150 speakers to a wholesaler if an acceptable price can be worked out. This sale would not affect the company's regular sales and would not impact total fixed expenses. What price per speaker should be quoted to the wholesaler if Acoustic Concepts wants to increase its monthly profits by $3,000?

Variable cost per speaker	$150
Desired profit per speaker:	
$3,000 ÷ 150 speakers	20
Quoted price per speaker	$170

Notice that no fixed expenses are included in the computation. This is because fixed expenses are not affected by the bulk sale, so all of the additional revenue that is in excess of variable costs goes to increasing the profits of the company.

If Acoustic Concepts had been operating at a loss rather than at a profit, some managers might look at the situation somewhat differently. Instead of a modest profit of $3,000, these managers might attempt to reverse all or part of the company's overall loss by quoting a higher price. To illustrate this point, assume that Acoustic Concepts presently has a loss of $6,000 this month and that the company would like to make enough money on the bulk sale of speakers to turn this loss into a profit of $3,000. Under these circumstances, the quoted price on the 150 new speakers would be computed as shown below:

Variable cost per speaker	$150
Present net loss:	
$6,000 ÷ 150 speakers	40
Desired profit:	
$3,000 ÷ 150 speakers	20
Quoted price per speaker	$210

The $210 price still represents a substantial discount from the $250 regular selling price per speaker. Thus, both the wholesaler and the company would benefit from the bulk order at this price. However, this may not always be the case. By attempting to offset losses through a special order, a manager may quote such a high price that the order will be lost. A manager must always keep such market considerations in mind when deciding on prices. Moreover, we assume that the bulk order will not affect sales to regular customers. There may be serious strategic implications to accepting this bulk order if this assumption does not hold. For example, existing customers may find out about this order and demand the same low price, or they may simply buy from competitors. Also, the bulk sale could lead to more orders from this new customer so accepting a lower price in the short-run may produce longer-term benefits through repeat sales. In summary, managers should consider both the short-term and long-term strategic consequences of their decision before accepting or rejecting such opportunities. We will return to this topic in more detail in Chapter 12.

Importance of the Contribution Margin

As stated in the introduction to this chapter, CVP analysis seeks the most profitable combination of variable costs, fixed costs, selling price, and sales volume. The above examples show that the effect on the contribution margin is a major consideration in deciding on the most profitable combination of these factors. We have seen that profits can sometimes be improved by reducing the contribution margin if fixed costs can be reduced by a greater amount. More commonly, however, we have seen that the way to improve profits is to increase the total contribution margin. Sometimes this can be done by reducing the selling price and thereby increasing volume; sometimes it can be done by increasing the fixed costs (such as advertising) and thereby increasing volume; and sometimes it can be done by trading off variable and fixed costs with appropriate changes in volume. Many other combinations of factors are possible.

The amount of the unit contribution margin figure (and the size of the CM ratio) will have a significant influence on the steps a company is willing to take to improve profits. For example, the greater the unit contribution margin, the greater the amount the company may be willing to spend in order to increase unit sales. This explains in part why companies with high unit contribution margins (such as auto manufacturers) advertise so heavily, while companies with low unit contribution margins (such as dishware manufacturers) tend to spend much less for advertising.

In short, the effect on the contribution margin is critical to many operating decisions.

DECISION AID

CVP ANALYSIS

Changes Affecting
- Selling price per unit
- Variable unit costs
- Fixed costs
- Volume

Decision Rule:

Make change if   Increase in CM > Increase in fixed costs; or Decrease in
                            CM < Decrease in fixed costs

Do not make change if   Increase in CM < Increase in fixed costs; or Decrease in
                            CM > Decrease in fixed costs

■ BREAK-EVEN ANALYSIS

Break-even analysis is an aspect of CVP analysis that is designed to answer questions such as how far sales could drop before the company begins to lose money.

LEARNING OBJECTIVE 5
Compute the break-even point in unit sales and sales dollars.

Break-Even Computations

Earlier in the chapter, we defined the break-even point to be the level of sales at which the company's profit (operating income) is zero. The break-even point can be computed using either the *equation method* or the *contribution margin method*—the two methods are equivalent.

The Equation Method   The **equation method** translates the contribution-format income statement illustrated earlier in the chapter into an equation form, as follows:

$$\text{Profits} = (\text{Sales} - \text{Variable expenses}) - \text{Fixed expenses}$$

Rearranging this equation slightly yields the following equation, which is widely used in CVP analysis:

$$\text{Sales} = \text{Variable expenses} + \text{Fixed expenses} + \text{Profits}$$

At the break-even point, profits are zero. Therefore, the break-even point can be computed by finding that point where sales just equal the total of the variable expenses plus the fixed

Equation method
A method of computing break-even sales using the contribution-format income statement.

expenses. For Acoustic Concepts, the break-even point in unit sales, Q, can be computed as follows:

$$\text{Sales} = \text{Variable expenses} + \text{Fixed expenses} + \text{Profits}$$

$$\$250Q = \$150Q + \$35,000 + \$0$$
$$\$100Q = \$35,000$$
$$Q = \$35,000 \div 100$$
$$Q = 350 \text{ speakers}$$

where

$$Q = \text{Number (quantity) of speakers sold}$$
$$\$250 = \text{Unit sales price}$$
$$\$150 = \text{Unit variable expenses}$$
$$\$35,000 = \text{Total fixed expenses}$$

The break-even point in sales dollars can be computed by multiplying the break-even level of unit sales by the selling price per unit:

$$350 \text{ speakers} \times \$250 = \$87,500$$

The break-even in total sales dollars, X, can also be directly computed as follows:

$$\text{Sales} = \text{Variable expenses} + \text{Fixed expenses} + \text{Profits}$$

$$X = 0.60X + \$35,000 + \$0$$
$$0.40X = \$35,000$$
$$X = \$35,000 \div 0.40$$
$$X = \$87,500$$

where

$$X = \text{Total sales dollars}$$
$$0.60 = \text{Variable expenses as a percentage of sales}$$
$$\$35,000 = \text{Total fixed expenses}$$

Variable expense ratio
The ratio of variable expenses to sales dollars.

Note that in the above analysis the *variable expense ratio* is used. The **variable expense ratio** is the ratio of variable expenses to sales dollars. It can be computed by dividing the total variable expenses by the total sales dollars, or in a single product analysis, it can be computed by dividing the variable cost per unit by the unit selling price.

Also note that the use of the ratios in the above analysis yields a break-even point expressed in sales dollars rather than in units sold. If desired, the break-even point in units sold can be computed as follows:

$$\$87,500 \div \$250 = 350 \text{ speakers}$$

Contribution margin method
A method of computing the break-even point where the fixed expenses are divided by the contribution margin per unit.

The Contribution Margin Method   The **contribution margin method** is a short-cut version of the equation method already described. The approach centres on the idea discussed earlier that each unit sold provides a certain amount of contribution margin that goes toward covering fixed costs. To find how many units must be sold to break even, we simply rearrange the profit equation to divide total fixed costs by the unit contribution margin:[2]

$$\text{Break-even point in units sold} = \frac{\text{Fixed expenses}}{\text{Unit contribution margin}}$$

Each speaker generates a contribution margin of $100 ($250 selling price, less $150 variable expenses). Since the total fixed expenses are $35,000, the break-even point is as follows:

$$\frac{\text{Fixed expenses}}{\text{Unit contribution margin}} = \frac{\$35,000}{\$100 \text{ per speaker}} = 350 \text{ speakers}$$

A variation of this method uses the CM ratio instead of the unit contribution margin. The result is the break-even in total sales dollars rather than in total units sold.

$$\text{Break-even point in total sales dollars} = \frac{\text{Fixed expenses}}{\text{CM ratio}}$$

In the Acoustic Concepts example, the calculations are as follows:

$$\frac{\text{Fixed expenses}}{\text{CM ratio}} = \frac{\$35,000}{40\%} = \$87,500$$

This approach, based on the CM ratio, is particularly useful when a company has multiple product lines and wishes to compute a single break-even point for the company as a whole. We will return to this concept later in the chapter.

TARGET OPERATING PROFIT ANALYSIS

CVP formulas can be used to determine the sales volume needed to achieve a target operating profit. Suppose that Prem Narayan of Acoustic Concepts would like to earn a target operating profit of $40,000 per month. How many speakers would have to be sold?

> **LEARNING OBJECTIVE 6**
> Determine the level of sales needed to achieve a desired target profit.

The CVP Equation

One approach is to use the equation method. Instead of solving for the unit sales where operating profits are zero, you instead solve for the unit sales where operating profits are $40,000:

$$\text{Sales} = \text{Variable expenses} + \text{Fixed expenses} + \text{Profits}$$

$$\$250Q = \$150Q + \$35,000 + \$40,000$$
$$\$100Q = \$75,000$$
$$Q = \$75,000 \div 100$$
$$Q = 750 \text{ speakers}$$

where

$$Q = \text{Number of speakers sold}$$
$$\$250 = \text{Unit sales price}$$
$$\$150 = \text{Unit variable expenses}$$
$$\$35,000 = \text{Total fixed expenses}$$
$$\$40,000 = \text{Target operating profit}$$

Thus, the target operating profit can be achieved by selling 750 speakers per month, which represents $187,500 in total sales ($250 × 750 speakers).

The Contribution Margin Approach

A second approach involves expanding the contribution margin formula to include the target operating profit:

$$\text{Units sold to attain the target profit} = \frac{\text{Fixed expenses} + \text{Target operating profit}}{\text{Unit contribution margin}}$$

$$\frac{\$35,000 \text{ fixed expenses} + \$40,000 \text{ target operating profit}}{\$100 \text{ contribution margin per speaker}} = 750 \text{ speakers}$$

This approach gives the same answer as the equation method since it is simply a shortcut version of the equation method. Similarly, the dollar sales needed to attain the target operating profit can be computed as follows:

$$\text{Dollar sales to attain target profit} = \frac{\text{Fixed expenses} + \text{Target operating profit}}{\text{CM ratio}}$$

$$= \frac{\$35,000 + \$40,000}{0.40}$$

$$= \$187,500$$

The problem of computing a desired dollar sales level is very similar to the problem of finding a break-even point. In the case of finding a break-even point, the target operating profit is zero. For any targeted amount of sales above zero, we simply add the desired profit to fixed expenses because the target profit is another fixed amount that must be covered.

After-Tax Analysis

Operating profit in the preceding analysis has ignored income taxes, but for-profit organizations are required to pay corporate income tax. In general, operating profit after tax can be computed as a fixed percentage of income before taxes. To calculate the income taxes, we simply multiply the tax rate (t) by the operating income before taxes (B). Therefore, after-tax profit is equal to profit before taxes × (1 − tax rate), and is derived as follows:

$$\text{Profit after taxes} = \text{Before-tax profit} - \text{Taxes}$$
$$= B - t(B)$$
$$= B(1 - t)$$

Dividing both sides by (1 − t), income before taxes is equal to profit after taxes divided by 1 minus the tax rate (1 − t):

$$B = \frac{\text{Profit after taxes}}{(1 - t)}$$

LEARNING AID

SINGLE PRODUCT CVP ANALYSIS

Break-Even (Shortcut Formula)
- **Units:**

$$\text{Break-even point in units sold} = \frac{\text{Fixed expenses}}{\text{Unit contribution margin}}$$

- **Sales Dollars:**

$$\text{Break-even point in total sales dollars} = \frac{\text{Fixed expenses}}{\text{CM ratio}}$$

Target Operating Profit (Shortcut Formula)
- **Units:**

$$\text{Units sold to attain target profit} = \frac{\text{Fixed expenses} + \left[\dfrac{\text{Target after-tax profit}}{1 - \text{Tax rate}}\right]}{\text{Unit contribution margin}}$$

- **Sales Dollars:**

$$\text{Dollar sales to attain target profit} = \frac{\text{Fixed expenses} + \left[\dfrac{\text{Target after-tax profit}}{1 - \text{Tax rate}}\right]}{\text{CM ratio}}$$

Using the previous example, assume that the tax rate is 30% and the target operating profit is $48,000 *after* taxes. The target profit can be achieved by selling 1,036 speakers. The appropriate formula to use would be

$$\frac{\text{Fixed expenses} + [(\text{Target after-tax profit})/(1 - \text{tax rate})]}{\text{Contribution margin per unit}}$$

$$\frac{\$35,000 + [\$48,000/(1 - 0.3)]}{\$100} = 1,036 \text{ speakers (rounded)}$$

Thus, whenever target operating profit is expressed on an after-tax basis, the equation method can be used as described earlier, except that target operating profit must be restated to a pre-tax basis.

THE MARGIN OF SAFETY

The **margin of safety** is the excess of budgeted (or actual) sales over the break-even volume of sales. It states the amount by which sales can drop before losses begin to be incurred. The higher the margin of safety, the lower the risk of not breaking even. The formula for its calculation is as follows:

> **LEARNING OBJECTIVE 7**
> Compute the margin of safety and explain its significance.

Margin of safety = Total budgeted (or actual) sales − Break-even sales

The margin of safety can also be expressed in percentage form. This percentage is obtained by dividing the margin of safety in dollar terms by total sales:

Margin of safety
The excess of budgeted (or actual) sales over the break-even volume of sales.

$$\text{Margin of safety percentage} = \frac{\text{Margin of safety in dollars}}{\text{Total budgeted (or actual) sales}}$$

The calculations for the margin of safety for Acoustic Concepts are as follows:

Sales (at the current volume of 400 speakers) (a)	$100,000
Break-even sales (at 350 speakers)	87,500
Margin of safety (in dollars) (b)	$ 12,500
Margin of safety as a percentage of sales, (b) ÷ (a)	12.5%

This margin of safety means that with the company's current prices and costs, a reduction in sales of $12,500, or 12.5% from the current level, would result in just breaking even.

In a single-product firm like Acoustic Concepts, the margin of safety can also be expressed in terms of the number of units sold by dividing the margin of safety in dollars by the selling price per unit. In this case, the margin of safety is 50 speakers ($12,500 ÷ $250 per speaker = 50 speakers).

CVP CONSIDERATIONS IN CHOOSING A COST STRUCTURE

Cost structure refers to the relative proportion of fixed and variable costs in an organization. An organization often has some latitude in trading off between fixed and variable costs. For example, fixed investments in automated equipment can reduce variable labour costs. In this section, we discuss the choice of a cost structure, focusing on the effect of cost structure on profit stability, in which *operating leverage* plays a key role.

> **LEARNING OBJECTIVE 8**
> Explain cost structure and compute the degree of operating leverage at a particular level of sales and explain how it can be used to predict changes in operating income.

Cost Structure and Profit Stability

Which cost structure is better—high variable costs and low fixed costs, or the opposite? No single answer to this question is possible: Either structure has its advantages. To show what we mean, refer to the contribution-format income statements given below for two blueberry farms. Bogside Farm depends on migrant workers to pick its berries by hand, whereas Sterling Farm has invested in expensive berry-picking machines. Consequently, Bogside Farm has higher variable costs, but Sterling Farm has higher fixed costs:

| | Bogside Farm | | Sterling Farm | |
	Total	Percentage	Total	Percentage
Sales	$100,000	100%	$100,000	100%
Less variable expenses	60,000	60%	30,000	30%
Contribution margin	40,000	40%	70,000	70%
Less fixed expenses	30,000		60,000	
Operating income	$ 10,000		$ 10,000	

Which farm has the better cost structure? The answer depends on many factors, including the long-run trend in sales, year-to-year fluctuations in the level of sales, and the attitude of the owners toward risk. If sales are expected to be above $100,000 in the future, then Sterling Farm probably has the better cost structure. The reason is that its CM ratio is higher, and its operating income will therefore increase more rapidly as sales increase. To illustrate, assume that each farm experiences a 10% increase in sales without any increase in fixed costs. The new income statements would be as follows:

| | Bogside Farm | | Sterling Farm | |
	Total	Percentage	Total	Percentage
Sales	$110,000	100%	$110,000	100%
Less variable expenses	66,000	60%	33,000	30%
Contribution margin	44,000	40%	77,000	70%
Less fixed expenses	30,000		60,000	
Operating income	$ 14,000		$ 17,000	

Sterling Farm has experienced a greater increase in operating income due to its higher CM ratio, even though the increase in sales was the same for both farms.

What if sales drop below $100,000? What are the break-even points of the two farms? What are their margins of safety? The computations needed to answer these questions are carried out as follows, using the contribution margin method:

	Bogside Farm	Sterling Farm
Fixed expenses	$ 30,000	$ 60,000
Contribution margin ratio	÷40%	÷70%
Break-even in total sales dollars	$ 75,000	$ 85,714
Total current sales (a)	$100,000	$100,000
Break-even sales	75,000	85,714
Margin of safety in sales dollars (b)	$ 25,000	$ 14,286
Margin of safety as a percentage of sales, (b) ÷ (a)	25.0%	14.3%

Bogside Farm is less vulnerable to downturns than Sterling Farm, and we can identify two reasons for this. First, due to its lower fixed expenses, Bogside Farm has a lower break-even point and a higher margin of safety, as shown by the computations above. Therefore, it will not incur losses as quickly as Sterling Farm in periods of sharply declining sales. Second, due to its lower CM ratio, Bogside Farm will not lose contribution margin as rapidly as Sterling Farm when sales fall off. Thus, Bogside Farm's income will be less volatile. We saw earlier that this is a drawback when sales increase, but it provides more protection when sales drop.

To summarize, without knowing the future, it is not obvious which cost structure is better. Both have advantages and disadvantages. Sterling Farm, with its higher fixed costs and lower variable costs, will experience wider swings in operating income as changes take place in sales, with greater profits in good years and greater losses in bad years. Bogside Farm, with its lower fixed costs and higher variable costs, will enjoy greater stability in operating income and will be more protected from losses during bad years, but at the cost of lower operating income in good years.

Operating Leverage

A lever is a tool for multiplying force. Using a lever, a massive object can be moved with only a modest amount of force. In business, *operating leverage* serves a similar purpose. **Operating leverage** is a measure of how sensitive operating income is to percentage changes in sales. Operating leverage acts as a multiplier. If operating leverage is high, a small percentage increase in sales can produce a much larger percentage increase in operating income.

Operating leverage can be illustrated by returning to the data given above for the two blueberry farms. We previously showed that a 10% increase in sales (from $100,000 to $110,000 for each farm) results in a 70% increase in the operating income of Sterling Farm (from $10,000 to $17,000) and only a 40% increase in the operating income of Bogside Farm (from $10,000 to $14,000). Thus, for a 10% increase in sales, Sterling Farm experiences a much greater percentage increase in profits than does Bogside Farm. Therefore, Sterling Farm has greater operating leverage than Bogside Farm.

The **degree of operating leverage** is a measure, at a given level of sales, of how a percentage change in sales volume will affect profits. It is computed by the following formula:

$$\text{Degree of operating leverage} = \frac{\text{Contribution margin}}{\text{Operating income}}$$

To illustrate, the degree of operating leverage for the two farms at a $100,000 sales level would be as follows:

$$\text{Bogside Farm} = \frac{\$40,000}{\$10,000} = 4 \text{ times}$$

$$\text{Sterling Farm} = \frac{\$70,000}{\$10,000} = 7 \text{ times}$$

Since the degree of operating leverage for Bogside Farm is 4, the farm's operating income grows four times as fast as its sales. Similarly, Sterling Farm's operating income grows seven times as fast as its sales. Thus, if sales increase by 10%, then we can expect the operating income of Bogside Farm to increase by four times this amount, or by 40%, and the operating income of Sterling Farm to increase by seven times this amount, or by 70%.

Operating leverage
A measure of how sensitive operating income is to a given percentage change in sales. It is computed by dividing the contribution margin by operating income.

Degree of operating leverage
A measure, at a given level of sales, of how a percentage change in sales volume will affect profits. The degree of operating leverage is computed by dividing contribution margin by operating income.

	(1) Percentage Increase in Sales	(2) Degree of Operating Leverage	(3) Percentage Increase in Operating Income (1) × (2)
Bogside Farm	10%	4 times	40%
Sterling Farm	10%	7 times	70%

What is responsible for the higher operating leverage at Sterling Farm? The only difference between the two farms is their cost structure. If two companies have the same total revenue and same total expense but different cost structures, then the company with the higher proportion of fixed costs in its cost structure will have higher operating leverage.

Referring back to the original example on page 286, when both farms have sales of $100,000 and total expenses of $90,000, one-third of Bogside Farm's costs are fixed but two-thirds of Sterling Farm's costs are fixed. As a consequence, Sterling's degree of operating leverage is higher than Bogside's.

The degree of operating leverage is greatest at sales levels near the break-even point and decreases as sales and profits rise. This can be seen from the tabulation below, which shows the degree of operating leverage for Bogside Farm at various sales levels. (Data used earlier for Bogside Farm are shown in colour.)

Sales	$75,000	$80,000	$100,000	$150,000	$225,000
Less variable expenses	45,000	48,000	60,000	90,000	135,000
Contribution margin (a)	30,000	32,000	40,000	60,000	90,000
Less fixed expenses	30,000	30,000	30,000	30,000	30,000
Operating income (b)	$ –0–	$ 2,000	$ 10,000	$ 30,000	$ 60,000
Degree of operating leverage, (a) ÷ (b)	∞	16	4	2	1.5

Thus, a 10% increase in sales would increase operating profits by only 15% (10% × 1.5) if the company was operating at a $225,000 sales level, as compared to the 40% increase we computed earlier at the $100,000 sales level. The degree of operating leverage will continue to decrease the farther the company moves from its break-even point. At the break-even point, the degree of operating leverage will be infinitely large ($30,000 contribution margin ÷ $0 operating income = ∞).

A manager can use the degree of operating leverage to quickly estimate what effect various percentage changes in sales will have on profits, without needing to prepare detailed income statements. As shown by our examples, the effects of operating leverage can be dramatic. If a company is near its break-even point, then even small percentage increases in sales can yield large percentage increases in profits. *This explains why management will often work very hard for only a small increase in sales volume.* If the degree of operating leverage is 5, then a 6% increase in sales would translate into a 30% increase in profits.

In summary, we can predict the percentage change in operating income before taxes (OIBT) resulting from a given percentage change in sales. The following equation does this by multiplying the percentage change in sales by the degree of operating leverage:

$$\%\Delta \text{ OIBT} = \%\Delta \text{ Sales} \times \text{Degree of operating leverage}$$

IN BUSINESS

The effects of the recent recession have been widespread, hitting manufacturing and service companies alike. In the United States, an estimated 22,000 legal jobs have been lost as a result of layoffs and firm closures. However, Canadian law firms operating in the United States have not fared nearly as badly with respect to job losses, in part due to their considerably lower operating leverage. According to one senior executive of a Canadian law firm with headquarters in Montreal and offices in the United States, the degree of operating leverage averages 1.5 to 2 for Canadian firms, compared to 5 for many U.S. law firms. The larger degree of operating leverage for U.S. firms is in part due to much higher fixed overhead costs relative to Canadian firms. The higher overhead costs relate to a larger number of administrative and support staff typically employed at U.S. firms. When tough economic times hit, firms with a high degree of operating leverage (and high fixed costs) are sometimes forced to cut costs through a reduction in the size of their workforce.

Source: Julius Melnitzer, "Canadian Firms in U.S. Avoiding Big Layoff Hits," *Financial Post*, April 29, 2009, p. 3.

Automation: Risks and Rewards from a CVP Perspective

We have noted in preceding chapters that several factors, including the move toward flexible manufacturing systems and other uses of automation, have resulted in a shift toward greater fixed costs and smaller variable costs in organizations. In turn, this shift in cost structure has had an impact on the CM ratio, the break-even point, and the degree of operating leverage.

Many benefits can accrue from automation, but certain risks are introduced when a company moves toward greater amounts of fixed costs. These risks suggest that management must be careful as it automates to ensure that investment decisions are made in accordance with a carefully devised long-term strategy. This issue is discussed further in Chapter 13, where we deal with investment decisions in an automated environment.

Indifference Analysis

We have seen that cost–volume–profit analysis can be used as input for decisions about the profitability of individual products. CVP analysis is also useful for aiding decisions about the comparative profitability of alternative products or methods of production. The analysis focuses on cost behaviour in relation to changes in activity level. Relative profitability depends on activity level. A product with a high level of fixed costs will require a higher sales activity level to generate a profit than will a product with low fixed costs and comparatively high variable costs. Cost–volume–profit analyses facilitate the comparison of alternatives with different fixed and variable cost structures.

To illustrate, assume that Goodwin Company has decided to introduce a new product that can be manufactured by either a labour-intensive production (LIP) system or a capital-intensive production (CIP) system. The manufacturing method will not affect the quality of the product. The estimated manufacturing costs of a labour-intensive production system and a capital-intensive production system are as follows:

	Labour-Intensive Production System		Capital-Intensive Production System	
Selling price per unit sold		$40.00		$40.00
Direct material*		6.00		5.00
Direct labour-hours (DLH)	0.8 DLH @ $15	12.00	0.5 DLH @ $20	10.00
Variable overhead	0.8 DLH @ $10	8.00	0.5 DLH @ $10	5.00
Variable selling expense		2.00		2.00
Total variable costs		28.00		22.00
Contribution margin.		$12.00		$18.00
Fixed overhead†		$1,200,000.00		$3,000,000.00
Fixed selling expenses		$ 600,000.00		$ 600,000.00
Break-even sales		$6,000,000.00		$8,000,000.00
Break-even units		150,000		200,000

*The labour-intensive system results in higher direct material costs per unit because of more wastage of materials.
†These costs are directly traceable to the new product line. They would not be incurred if the new product was not produced.

We can calculate the point at which Goodwin will be indifferent about using a labour-intensive production system versus a capital-intensive production system as follows:

1. Determine the unit CM times the number of units (Q) minus total fixed costs of each alternative.
2. Set up an equation with each alternative on opposite sides of the equals sign.
3. Solve for Q, the indifference point.

$$\$12Q - \$1,800,000 = \$18Q - \$3,600,000$$

$$\$6Q = \$1,800,000$$

$$Q = 300,000 \text{ units}$$

Note from line 2 of the equation that the $6 difference in contribution margin is on the left-hand side of the equation, and the $1,800,000 on the right-hand side of the equation is the difference in fixed costs. The indifference point can therefore be found quickly by dividing the difference in fixed costs by the difference in contribution margins between the two alternatives:

$$\frac{\text{Fixed cost of CIP} - \text{Fixed cost of LIP}}{\text{CM of CIP} - \text{CM of LIP}} = \frac{\$3,600,000 - \$1,800,000}{\$18 - \$12} = 300,000 \text{ units}$$

At sales below the indifference point of 300,000 units, profitability will be higher for LIP. Sales above the indifference point will generate higher profitability for CIP, because CIP generates a higher contribution margin per unit than LIP does.

THE CONCEPT OF SALES MIX

Sales mix
The relative proportions in which a company's products are sold. Sales mix is computed by expressing the sales of each product as a percentage of total sales.

Before concluding our discussion of CVP concepts, we consider the effect of changes in sales mix on a firm's profits.

The Definition of Sales Mix

The term **sales mix** refers to the relative proportions in which a company's products are sold. Managers try to achieve the combination, or mix, that will yield the greatest amount of profits. Most companies have several products, and often these products are not equally profitable; therefore, profits will depend to some extent on the company's sales mix. Profits will be greater if high-margin rather than low-margin items make up a relatively large proportion of total sales.

Changes in the sales mix can cause perplexing variations in a company's profits. A shift in the sales mix from high-margin items to low-margin items can cause total profits to decrease even though total sales may increase. Conversely, a shift in the sales mix from low-margin items to high-margin items can cause the reverse effect—total profits may increase even though total sales decrease. It is one thing to achieve a particular sales volume, but it is quite another to sell the most profitable mix of products.

IN BUSINESS

For companies such as Research in Motion (RIM), the manufacturer of the BlackBerry line of smartphones, managing profits in an extremely competitive operating environment is a constant challenge. With over 15 different smartphone models available as of early 2010, RIM managers need a detailed understanding of how introducing a new model will impact profits. For example, when a new model is introduced, determining the net effect on total contribution margin is not simply a matter of estimating the demand for the new product and the per unit contribution margin. Companies that offer multiple product choices for consumers must also estimate the extent to which sales of a new model will "cannibalize" sales of existing models. So, as sales increase for a new model, declines are to be expected for older models, which must be taken into account when evaluating the incremental effects on profit from new product introductions.

Moreover, in light of increasing competition in the smartphone market, RIM and other manufacturers have responded by offering new models with lower selling prices and lower contribution margins. This ever-evolving product mix must be monitored continuously to ensure that the company generates a return on investment that is acceptable to its shareholders. Adding to this complexity are the different market segments and geographic regions served by RIM. For example, the functionality demanded by business users of their smartphones differs from that of personal users, as does their willingness and ability to pay for those features. Understanding the fundamentals of cost–volume–profit relationships is essential in such a dynamic multi-product environment.

Sources: Eric Lam, "Mixed Results Expected for RIM," *Financial Post*, December 4, 2009. Also, go to RIM's Web page "Compare BlackBerry Smartphones" at http://ca.blackberry.com/smartphones/compare.

Sales Mix and Break-Even Analysis

If a company sells more than one product, break-even analysis is somewhat more complex than has been discussed to this point. The reason is that different products will have different selling prices, different costs, and different contribution margins. Consequently, the break-even point will depend on the mix in which the various products are sold. To illustrate, consider Sound Unlimited, a small company that imports DVDs from France for use in personal computers. At present, the company distributes the following to retail computer stores: the Le Louvre DVD, a multimedia free-form tour of the famous art museum in Paris, and the Le Vin DVD, which features the wines and wine-growing regions of France. Both multimedia products have sound, photos, video clips, and sophisticated software. The company's September sales, expenses, and break-even point are shown in Exhibit 7–4.

As shown in the exhibit, the break-even point is $60,000 in sales, which was computed by dividing the fixed costs by the company's *overall* CM ratio of 45%. But $60,000 in sales represents the break-even point for the company only as long as the sales mix does not change. *If the sales mix changes, then the break-even point will also change.* This is illustrated by the results for October, in which the sales mix shifted away from the more profitable Le Vin DVD (which has a 50% CM ratio) toward the less profitable Le Louvre DVD (which has only a 25% CM ratio). These results appear in Exhibit 7–5.

EXHIBIT 7–4   Multiple-Product Break-Even Analysis

SOUND UNLIMITED
Contribution Income Statement
For the Month of September

	Le Louvre DVD		Le Vin DVD		Total	
	Amount	Percent	Amount	Percent	Amount	Percent
Sales	$20,000	100%	$80,000	100%	$100,000	100%
Variable expenses	15,000	75%	40,000	50%	55,000	55%
Contribution margin	$ 5,000	25%	$40,000	50%	45,000	45%
Fixed expenses					27,000	
Operating income					$ 18,000	

Computation of the break-even point:

$$\frac{\text{Fixed expenses}}{\text{Overall CM ratio}} = \frac{\$27,000}{0.45} = \$60,000$$

Verification of the break-even point:

	Le Louvre DVD	Le Vin DVD	Total
Current dollar sales	$20,000	$80,000	$100,000
Percentage of total dollar sales	20%	80%	100%
Sales at the break-even point	$12,000	$48,000	$60,000

	Le Louvre DVD		Le Vin DVD		Total	
	Amount	Percent	Amount	Percent	Amount	Percent
Sales	$12,000	100%	$48,000	100%	$ 60,000	100%
Variable expenses	9,000	75%	24,000	50%	33,000	55%
Contribution margin	$ 3,000	25%	$24,000	50%	27,000	45%
Fixed expenses					27,000	
Operating income					$ 0	

EXHIBIT 7–5 Multiple-Product Break-Even Analysis: A Shift in Sales Mix (see Exhibit 7–4)

SOUND UNLIMITED
Contribution Income Statement
For the Month of October

	Le Louvre DVD		Le Vin DVD		Total	
	Amount	Percent	Amount	Percent	Amount	Percent
Sales	$80,000	100%	$20,000	100%	$100,000	100%
Less variable expenses	60,000	75%	10,000	50%	70,000	70%
Contribution margin	$20,000	25%	$10,000	50%	30,000	30%
Less Fixed expenses					27,000	
Operating income					$ 3,000	

Computation of the break-even point:

$$\frac{\text{Fixed expenses}}{\text{Overall CM ratio}} = \frac{\$27,000}{0.30} = \$90,000$$

In Exhibit 7–5, although sales have remained unchanged at $100,000, the sales mix is exactly the reverse of what it was in Exhibit 7–4, with the bulk of the sales now coming from the less profitable Le Louvre DVD. Notice that this shift in the sales mix has caused both the overall CM ratio and total profits to drop sharply from the prior month—the overall CM ratio has dropped from 45% in September to only 30% in October, and operating income has dropped from $18,000 to only $3,000. In addition, with the drop in the overall CM ratio, the company's break-even point is no longer $60,000 in sales. Since the company is now realizing a lower average contribution margin per dollar of sales, it takes more sales to cover the same amount of fixed costs. Thus, the break-even point has increased from $60,000 to $90,000 in sales per year.

In preparing a break-even analysis, some assumptions must be made concerning the sales mix. Usually the assumption is that it will not change. However, if the manager knows that shifts in various factors (consumer tastes, market share, and so forth) are causing shifts in the sales mix, then these factors must be explicitly considered in any CVP computations. Otherwise, the manager may make decisions on the basis of outdated or faulty data.

LEARNING AID

MULTI-PRODUCT CVP ANALYSIS

Overall Contribution Margin Ratio

$$\text{Overall CM ratio} = \frac{\text{Total contribution margin, all products}}{\text{Total sales, all products}}$$

Break-Even (Shortcut Formula)
Sales Dollars

$$\text{Total sales dollars to break even} = \frac{\text{Fixed expenses}}{\text{Overall CM ratio}}$$

Target Operating Profit (Shortcut Formula)
Sales Dollars

$$\text{Dollar sales to attain target profit} = \frac{\text{Fixed expenses} + \left[\dfrac{\text{Target after-tax profit}}{1 - \text{Tax rate}}\right]}{\text{Overall CM ratio}}$$

■ ASSUMPTIONS OF CVP ANALYSIS

A number of assumptions typically underlie CVP analysis:

1. Selling price is constant throughout the entire relevant range. The price of a product or service will not change as volume changes.
2. Costs are linear throughout the entire relevant range, and they can accurately be divided into variable and fixed elements. The variable element is constant per unit, and the fixed element is constant in total over the entire relevant range.
3. In multi-product companies, the sales mix is constant.
4. In manufacturing companies, inventories do not change. The number of units produced equals the number of units sold (this assumption is considered further in the next chapter).

While some of these assumptions may be violated in practice, the results of CVP analysis are often "good enough" to be quite useful. For example, in most multi-product companies, the sales mix is constant enough that the results of CVP analysis are reasonably valid. Perhaps the greatest danger lies in relying on simple CVP analysis when a manager is contemplating a large change in volume that lies outside of the relevant range. For example, a manager might consider increasing the level of sales far beyond what the company has previously experienced. However, even in these situations, a manager can adjust the model as we have done in this chapter to take into account anticipated changes in selling prices, fixed costs, and the sales mix that would otherwise violate the assumptions. For example, in a decision that would affect fixed costs, the change in fixed costs can explicitly be taken into account, as illustrated earlier in this chapter in the Acoustic Concepts example on page 277.

Summary

- CVP analysis is based on a simple model of how contribution margin and operating income respond to changes in selling prices, costs, and volume. The analysis is based on the contribution income statement approach and requires a detailed understanding of cost behaviour. **[LO1]**
- A CVP graph depicts the relationships between sales volume in units and fixed expenses, variable expenses, total expenses, total sales, and profits. The CVP graph is useful for developing intuition about how costs and profits respond to changes in sales volume. **[LO2]**
- The contribution margin ratio is the ratio of the total contribution margin to total sales. This ratio can be used to quickly estimate the effect of a change in total sales on operating income. **[LO3]**
- The techniques of CVP analysis can be used to estimate the effects on contribution margin and operating profit of changes to sales volume, fixed costs, variable costs per unit, and selling prices. A useful aspect of the analysis is that managers can evaluate the profit impact of the trade-offs inherent to many operating decisions such as increasing advertising costs to boost sales volumes. **[LO4]**
- The break-even point is the level of sales (in units or in dollars) at which the company generates zero profits. The break-even point can be computed using several different techniques that are all based on the simple profit equation. **[LO5]**
- The profit equation can also be used to compute the level of sales required to attain a target profit. **[LO6]**
- The margin of safety is the amount by which the company's current sales exceed break-even sales. **[LO7]**
- The degree of operating leverage measures the effect of a percentage change in sales on the company's operating income. The higher the degree of operating leverage, the more sensitive operating income will be to a change in sales. The degree of operating leverage is not constant—it depends on the company's current level of sales. **[LO8]**
- The profits of a multi-product company are affected by its sales mix. Changes in the sales mix can affect the break-even point, margin of safety, and other critical measures. **[LO9]**

Review Problem: CVP Relationships

Networks Company manufactures wireless routers. The company's contribution-format income statement for the most recent year is given below:

	Total	Per Unit	Percentage of Sales
Sales (25,000 units)	$2,500,000	$100	100%
Less variable expenses	1,500,000	60	? %
Contribution margin.	1,000,000	$ 40	? %
Less fixed expenses	800,000		
Operating income	$ 200,000		

Management believes operating income can be further improved and would like you to prepare the following analysis.

Required:
1. Compute the company's CM ratio and variable expense ratio.
2. Compute the company's break-even point in both units and sales dollars. Use the equation method.
3. Assume that sales increase by $600,000 next year. If cost behaviour patterns remain unchanged, by how much will the company's operating income increase? Use the CM ratio to determine your answer.
4. Refer to the original data. Assume that next year, management wants the company to earn a minimum profit of $500,000. How many units will have to be sold to meet this target profit figure?
5. Refer to the original data. Compute the company's margin of safety in both dollar and percentage form.
6. *a.* Compute the company's degree of operating leverage at the present level of sales.
   b. Assume that, through a more intense effort by the sales staff, the company's sales increase by 12% next year. By what percentage would you expect operating income to increase? Use the operating leverage concept to obtain your answer.
   c. Verify your answer to (*b*) by preparing a new income statement showing a 12% increase in sales.
7. In an effort to increase sales and profits, management is considering the use of a higher-quality microprocessor in the router. The higher-quality microprocessor would increase variable costs by $8 per unit, but management could eliminate one quality inspector who is paid a salary of $40,000 per year. The sales manager estimates that the higher-quality speaker would increase annual sales by at least 10%.
   a. Assuming that changes are made as described above, prepare a projected income statement for next year. Show data on a total, per unit, and percentage basis.
   b. Compute the company's new break-even point in both units and dollars of sales. Use the contribution margin method.
   c. Would you recommend that the changes be made? Why or why not?

Solution to Review Problem

1. Contribution margin ratio: Variable expense ratio:

$$\frac{\text{Contribution margin}}{\text{Selling price}} = \frac{\$40}{\$100} = 40\% \qquad \frac{\text{Variable expenses}}{\text{Selling price}} = \frac{\$60}{\$100} = 60\%$$

2.   Sales = Variable expenses + Fixed expenses + Profits

$$\$100Q = \$60Q + \$800,000 + \$0$$
$$\$40Q = \$800,000$$
$$Q = 20,000 \text{ units; or at } \$100 \text{ per unit, } \$2,000,000$$

Alternative solution where X equals the break-even level of sales in dollars:

$$X = 0.60X + \$800,000$$
$$0.40X = \$800,000$$
$$X = \$2,000,000; \text{ or at } \$100 \text{ per unit, } 20,000 \text{ units}$$

3.

Increase in sales	$600,000
Multiply by the CM ratio	× 40%
Expected increase in contribution margin	$240,000

Since the fixed expenses are not expected to change, operating income will increase by the entire $240,000 increase in contribution margin computed above.

4. Equation method:

$$Sales = Variable\ expenses + Fixed\ expenses + Profits$$
$$\$100Q = \$60Q + \$800,000 + \$500,000$$
$$\$40Q = \$1,300,000$$
$$Q = 32,500\ units$$

Contribution margin method:

$$\frac{Fixed\ expenses\ +\ Target\ profit}{Contribution\ margin\ per\ unit} = \frac{\$800,000\ +\ \$500,000}{\$40} = 32,500\ units$$

5.

$$Total\ sales - Break\text{-}even\ sales = Margin\ of\ safety\ in\ dollars$$
$$\$2,500,000 - \$2,000,000 = \$500,000$$

$$\frac{Margin\ of\ safety\ in\ dollars}{Total\ sales} = \frac{\$500,000}{\$2,500,000} = 20\%$$

6. *a.* $\dfrac{Contribution\ margin}{Operating\ income} = \dfrac{\$1,000,000}{\$200,000} = 5\ times$

b.

Expected increase in sales	12%
Degree of operating leverage	× 5
Expected increase in operating income	60%

c.   If sales increase by 12%, then 28,000 units (25,000 × 1.12) will be sold next year. The new income statement will be as follows:

	Total	Per Unit	Percentage of Sales
Sales (28,000 units)	$2,800,000	$100	100%
Less variable expenses	1,680,000	60	60%
Contribution margin	1,120,000	$40	40%
Less fixed expenses	800,000		
Operating income	$ 320,000		

The $320,000 expected operating income for next year represents a 60% increase over the $200,000 operating income earned during the current year:

$$\frac{\$320,000 - \$200,000}{\$200,000} = 60\%$$

Note from the income statement above that the increase in sales from 25,000 to 28,000 units has resulted in increases in *both* total sales and total variable expenses. It is a common error to overlook the increase in variable expenses when preparing a projected income statement.

7. *a.*   A 10% increase in sales would result in 27,500 units being sold next year: 25,000 units × 1.10 = 27,500 units.

	Total	Per Unit	Percentage of Sales
Sales (27,500 units)	$2,750,000	$100	100%
Less variable expenses	1,870,000	68*	68%
Contribution margin	880,000	$32	32%
Less fixed expenses	760,000†		
Operating income	$ 120,000		

*$60 + $8 = $68; $68 ÷ $100 = 68%.
†$800,000 − $40,000 = $760,000.

Note that the change in per unit variable expenses results in a change in both the per unit contribution margin and the CM ratio.

b.   Break even in units:

$$\frac{\text{Fixed expenses}}{\text{Contribution margin per unit}} = \frac{\$760,000}{\$32} = 23{,}750 \text{ units}$$

Break even in sales dollars:

$$\frac{\text{Fixed expenses}}{\text{Contribution margin ratio}} = \frac{\$760,000}{0.32} = \$2{,}375{,}000$$

c.   No, based on these data the changes should not be made. The company's operating income will decrease from the present $200,000 to $120,000 per year. Also, the changes will result in a higher break-even point (23,750 units compared to the present 20,000 units). Finally, the margin of safety will be reduced from $500,000 as calculated in (5) above to

$$\text{Margin of safety in dollars} = \text{Total sales} - \text{Break-even sales}$$
$$\$2{,}750{,}000 - \$2{,}375{,}000 = \$375{,}000$$

Overall, this change would not be good for the company.

Glossary

Review key terms and definitions on Connect.

Questions

7–1   What is meant by a product's contribution margin ratio? How is this ratio useful in planning business operations?

7–2   Where is the break-even point in a CVP graph?

7–3   Company A's costs are mostly variable, whereas Company B's costs are mostly fixed. When sales increase, which company will tend to realize the greatest increase in profits? Explain.

7–4   What is meant by the term *operating leverage?*

7–5   What is meant by the term *break-even point?*

7–6   If a company experiences a decrease in its contribution margin ratio, what will be the impact on its break-even level of sales?

7–7   Name three approaches to break-even analysis. Briefly explain how each approach works.

7–8   In response to a request from your immediate supervisor, you have prepared a CVP graph portraying the cost and revenue characteristics of your company's product and operations. Explain how the lines on the graph and the break-even point would change if (*a*) the selling price per unit increased, (*b*) fixed cost decreased throughout the entire range of activity portrayed on the graph, and (*c*) variable cost per unit decreased.

7–9   What effect would a 30% income tax rate have on the CVP formula?

7–10   What is meant by the term *cost structure?*

7–11   Companies X and Y are in the same industry. Company X is highly automated, whereas Company Y relies primarily on labour to make its products. If sales and total expenses in the two companies are about the same, which company would you expect to have the lower margin of safety? Why?

7–12   What is meant by the term *sales mix?* What assumption is usually made concerning sales mix in CVP analysis?

7–13   Assume that Company Z, which sells two products, has changed its sales mix so that it sells a higher proportion of the product with the higher contribution margin. What will be the impact on the break-even level of sales? Explain your answer.

EXERCISE 7–1 Preparing a Contribution-Format Income Statement [LO1]

White Limited's most recent income statement is shown below.

	Total	Per Unit
Sales (6,000 units)	$312,000	$52.00
Variable expenses	216,000	36.00
Contribution margin	96,000	$16.00
Fixed expenses	84,000	
Operating income.	$12,000	

Required:

Prepare a new contribution-format income statement under each of the following conditions (consider each case independently):

1. The sales volume increases by 200 units.
2. The sales volume declines by 200 units.
3. The sales volume is 5,250 units.

EXERCISE 7–2 Prepare a Cost–Volume–Profit (CVP) Graph [LO2]

Kotara Enterprises distributes a single product; its selling price is $36 per unit and its variable cost is $24 per unit. The company's monthly fixed expense is $12,000.

Required:

1. Prepare a cost–volume–profit graph for the company up to a sales level of 2,000 units.
2. Estimate the company's break-even point in unit sales using your cost–volume–profit graph.

EXERCISE 7–3 Computing and Using the CM Ratio [LO3]

Last month when Harrison, Inc., sold 40,000 units, total sales were $300,000, total variable expenses were $240,000, and total fixed expenses were $45,000.

Required:

1. What is the company's contribution margin (CM) ratio?
2. Estimate the change in the company's operating income if it were to increase its total sales by $1,500.

EXERCISE 7–4 Changes in Variable Costs, Fixed Costs, Selling Price, and Volume [LO4]

Data for Moorefield Corporation are shown below:

	Per Unit	Percentage of Sales
Selling price	$90	100%
Variable expenses	63	70%
Contribution margin.	$27	30%

Fixed expenses are $65,000 per month and the company is selling 2,750 units per month.

Required:

1. The marketing manager argues that a $5,000 increase in the monthly advertising budget would increase monthly sales by $12,000. Should the advertising budget be increased?
2. Refer to the original data. Management is considering using higher-quality components that would increase the variable cost by $4 per unit. The marketing manager believes the higher-quality product would increase sales by 20% per month. Should the higher-quality components be used?

EXERCISE 7–5 Compute the Break-Even Point [LO5]

Mackson Products distributes a single product, a woven basket; its selling price is $8 and its variable cost is $6 per unit. The company's monthly fixed expense is $5,500.

Required:
1. Solve for the company's break-even point in unit sales using the equation method.
2. Solve for the company's break-even point in sales dollars using the equation method and the CM ratio.
3. Solve for the company's break-even point in unit sales using the contribution margin method.
4. Solve for the company's break-even point in sales dollars using the contribution margin method and the CM ratio.

EXERCISE 7–6 Compute the Level of Sales Required to Attain a Target Profit [LO6]

Simin Corporation has a single product; its selling price is $140 and its variable cost is $60 per unit. The company's monthly fixed expense is $40,000.

Required:
1. Using the equation method, solve for the unit sales that are required to earn a target profit before tax of $6,000.
2. Using the contribution margin approach, solve for the dollar sales that are required to earn a target profit before tax of $8,000.
3. Calculate the number of units that need to be sold to earn an after-tax income of $7,700, assuming a tax rate of 30%.

EXERCISE 7–7 Compute the Margin of Safety [LO7]

Mohan Corporation is a distributor of a sun umbrella used at resort hotels. Data concerning the next month's budget appear below:

Selling price	$25 per unit
Variable expense	$15 per unit
Fixed expense	$8,500 per month
Unit sales	1,000 units per month

Required:
1. Compute the company's margin of safety.
2. Compute the company's margin of safety as a percentage of its sales.

EXERCISE 7–8 Compute and Use the Degree of Operating Leverage [LO8]

Entergo Company installs home theatre systems. The company's most recent monthly contribution-format income statement appears below:

	Amount	Percentage of Sales
Sales	$120,000	100%
Variable expenses	84,000	70%
Contribution margin	36,000	30%
Fixed expenses	24,000	
Operating income	$ 12,000	

Required:
1. Compute the company's degree of operating leverage.
2. Using the degree of operating leverage, estimate the impact on operating income of a 10% increase in sales.
3. Verify your estimate from (2) above by constructing a new contribution-format income statement for the company, assuming a 10% increase in sales.

EXERCISE 7–9 Compute the Break-Even Point for a Multi-Service Company [LO9]
Lakeside Lawn & Garden Maintenance provides two general outdoor services: lawn maintenance and garden maintenance. A contribution-format income statement for a recent month for the two services appears below:

	Lawn Maintenance	Garden Maintenance	Total
Sales	$80,000	$40,000	$120,000
Variable expenses	20,000	4,000	24,000
Contribution margin	$60,000	$36,000	96,000
Fixed expenses			75,000
Operating income			$ 21,000

Required:
1. Compute the overall contribution margin ratio for the company.
2. Compute the overall break-even point for the company in sales dollars.
3. Verify the overall break-even point for the company by constructing a contribution-format income statement showing the appropriate levels of sales for the two services.

EXERCISE 7–10 Break-Even Analysis; Target Profit; Margin of Safety; CM Ratio [LO1, LO3, LO5, LO6, LO7]
Crabke Company distributes a single product. The company's sales and expenses for a recent month follow:

	Total	Per Unit
Sales.	$600,000	$40
Variable expenses	420,000	28
Contribution margin	180,000	$12
Fixed expenses	150,000	
Operating income.	$ 30,000	

Required:
1. What is the monthly break-even point in units sold and in sales dollars?
2. Without performing computations, what is the total contribution margin at the break-even point?
3. How many units would have to be sold each month to earn a target profit of $18,000? Use the contribution margin method. Verify your answer by preparing a contribution-format income statement at the target level of sales.
4. Refer to the original data. Compute the company's margin of safety in both dollar and percentage terms.
5. What is the company's CM ratio? If monthly sales increase by $80,000 and there is no change in fixed expenses, by how much would you expect monthly operating income to increase?

EXERCISE 7–11 Break-Even Analysis and CVP Graphing [LO2, LO4, LO5]
Horace Society is planning its annual Western Fair Raceway Gala. The Gala committee has assembled the following expected costs for the event:

Dinner (per person)	$10
Gaming tokens and program (per person).	$2
Prize payouts.	$4,300
Tickets and advertising	$800
Private box suite rental	$1,700
Lottery licences	$200

The committee members would like to charge $40 per person for the evening's activities.

Required:
1. Compute the break-even point for the Gala (in terms of the number of persons that must attend).
2. Assume only 200 persons attended the Gala last year. If the same number attend this year, what price per ticket must be charged to break even?
3. Using the $40 ticket price per person amount, prepare a CVP graph for the Gala from zero tickets up to 600 tickets sold.

EXERCISE 7–12 Using a Contribution-Format Income Statement [LO1, LO4]
Septor Enterprises' most recent contribution-format income statement is shown below:

	Total	Per Unit
Sales (30,000 units)	$150,000	$5
Variable expenses	90,000	3
Contribution margin	60,000	$2
Fixed expenses	50,000	
Operating income	$ 10,000	

Required:
Prepare a new contribution-format income statement under each of the following conditions (consider each case independently):
1. The number of units sold increases by 15%.
2. The selling price decreases by 50 cents per unit, and the number of units sold increases by 20%.
3. The selling price increases by 50 cents per unit, fixed expenses increase by $10,000, and the number of units sold decreases by 5%.
4. Variable expenses increase by 20 cents per unit, the selling price increases by 12%, and the number of units sold decreases by 10%.

EXERCISE 7–13 Missing Data; Basic CVP Concepts [LO1]
Fill in the missing amounts in each of the eight case situations below. Each case is independent of the others. (*Hint*: One way to find the missing amounts would be to prepare a contribution-format income statement for each case, enter the known data, and then compute the missing items.)
a. Assume that only one product is being sold in each of the following four case situations:

Case	Units Sold	Sales	Variable Expenses	Contribution Margin Per Unit	Fixed Expenses	Operating Income (Loss)
1	9,000	$270,000	$162,000	$?	$90,000	$?
2	?	$350,000	?	$15	$170,000	$40,000
3	20,000	?	$280,000	$6	?	$35,000
4	5,000	$160,000	?	?	$82,000	($12,000)

b. Assume that more than one product is being sold in each of the following four case situations:

Case	Sales	Variable Expenses	Average Contribution Margin (percent)	Fixed Expenses	Operating Income (loss)
1	$450,000	$?	40%	$?	$65,000
2	$200,000	$130,000	?	$60,000	?
3	?	?	80%	$470,000	$90,000
4	$300,000	$90,000	?	?	($15,000)

EXERCISE 7–14 Break-Even and Target Profit Analysis [LO3, LO4, LO5, LO6]
Memtech Company is the exclusive distributor of a high-speed computer memory chip. The product sells for $50 per unit and has a CM ratio of 30%. The company's fixed expenses are $240,000 per year.

Required:
1. What are the variable expenses per unit?
2. Using the equation method:
   a. What is the break-even point in units and in sales dollars?
   b. What sales level in units and in sales dollars is required to earn an operating income of $75,000?
   c. Assume that through negotiation with the manufacturer, the Memtech Company is able to reduce its variable expenses by $5 per unit. What is the company's new break-even point in units and in sales dollars?
3. Repeat (2) above using the contribution margin method.
4. Referring to the original data, what sales level in dollars is required to earn an annual profit of $75,000 after taxes if the company's tax rate is 20%?

EXERCISE 7–15 Operating Leverage [LO4, LO8]

Supreme Door Company sells prehung doors to home builders. The doors are sold for $60 each. Variable costs are $42 per door, and fixed costs total $450,000 per year. The company is currently selling 30,000 doors per year.

Required:
1. Prepare a contribution-format income statement for the company at the present level of sales and compute the degree of operating leverage.
2. Management is confident that the company can sell 37,500 doors next year (an increase of 7,500 doors, or 25%, over current sales). Compute the following:
   a. The expected percentage increase in operating income for next year.
   b. The expected operating income for next year. (Do not prepare an income statement; use the degree of operating leverage to compute your answer.)

EXERCISE 7–16 Break-Even and Target Profit Analysis [LO4, LO5, LO6]

Bait-N-Tackle sells fishing equipment. One of the company's products, a basic tackle box, sells for $48 per unit. Variable expenses are $36 per tackle box, and fixed expenses associated with the tackle box total $18,000 per month.

Required:
1. Compute the company's break-even point in number of tackle boxes and in total sales dollars.
2. If the variable expenses per tackle box increase as a percentage of the selling price, will it result in a higher or a lower break-even point? Why? (Assume that the fixed expenses remain unchanged.)
3. At present, the company is selling 2,600 tackle boxes per month. The sales manager is convinced that a 12.5% reduction in the selling price will result in a 20% increase in the number of tackle boxes sold each month. Prepare two contribution income statements, one under present operating conditions, and one as operations would appear after the proposed changes. Show both total and per unit data on your statements.
4. Refer to the data in (3) above. How many tackle boxes would have to be sold at the new selling price to yield a minimum operating income of $14,400 per month?

EXERCISE 7–17 Multi-Product Break-Even Analysis [LO9]

Rastacan Enterprises distributes two products: Model X300 and Model Z900. Monthly sales and the contribution margin ratios for the two products follow:

	Product		
	Model X300	Model Z900	Total
Sales	$700,000	$300,000	$1,000,000
Contribution margin ratio	60%	70%	?

The company's fixed expenses total $598,500 per month.

Required:
1. Prepare a contribution-format income statement for the company as a whole.
2. Compute the break-even point for the company based on the current sales mix.
3. If sales increase by $50,000 per month, by how much would you expect operating income to increase? What are your assumptions?

Problems ⓂＣＣ connect™

eXcel

PROBLEM 7–18 Basic CVP Analysis [LO1, LO3, LO4, LO5, LO8]
Klein Company distributes a high-quality bird feeder that sells for $30 per unit. Variable costs are $12 per unit, and fixed costs total $270,000 annually.

Required:
Answer the following independent questions:
1.   What is the product's CM ratio?
2.   Use the CM ratio to determine the break-even point in sales dollars.
3.   The company estimates that sales will increase by $60,000 during the coming year due to increased demand. By how much should operating income increase?
4.   Assume that the operating results for last year were as follows:

Sales	$600,000
Variable expenses	240,000
Contribution margin	360,000
Fixed expenses	270,000
Operating income	$ 90,000

  a.   Compute the degree of operating leverage at the current level of sales.
  b.   The president expects sales to increase by 16% next year. By how much should operating income increase?
5.   Refer to the original data. Assume that the company sold 23,000 units last year. The sales manager is convinced that a 12% reduction in the selling price, combined with a $40,000 increase in advertising expenditures, would cause annual sales in units to increase by 30%. Prepare two contribution-format income statements, one showing the results of last year's operations and one showing what the results of operations would be if these changes were made. Would you recommend that the company do as the sales manager suggests?
6.   Refer to the original data. Assume again that the company sold 23,000 units last year. The president feels that it would be unwise to change the selling price. Instead, he wants to increase the sales commission by $4 per unit. He thinks that this move, combined with some increase in advertising, would increase annual unit sales by 50%. By how much could advertising be increased with profits remaining unchanged? Do not prepare an income statement; use the incremental analysis approach.

PROBLEM 7–19 Basics of CVP Analysis; Cost Structure [LO1, LO3, LO4, LO5, LO6]
Hebrides Inc. produces memory enhancement kits for fax machines. Sales have been very erratic, with some months showing a profit and some months showing a loss. The company's contribution-format income statement for the most recent month is given below:

Sales (13,500 units at $20 per unit)	$270,000
Variable expenses	189,000
Contribution margin	81,000
Fixed expenses	90,000
Operating loss	$ (9,000)

Required:
1.   Compute the company's CM ratio and its break-even point in both units and dollars.
2.   The sales manager feels that an $8,000 increase in the monthly advertising budget, combined with an intensified effort by the sales staff, will result in a $70,000 increase in monthly sales. If the sales manager is right, what will be the effect on the company's

monthly operating income or loss? (Use the incremental approach in preparing your answer.)

3. Refer to the original data. The president is convinced that a 10% reduction in the selling price, combined with an increase of $35,000 in the monthly advertising budget, will cause unit sales to double. What will the new contribution-format income statement look like if these changes are adopted?

4. Refer to the original data. The company's advertising agency thinks that a new package would help sales. The new package being proposed would increase packaging costs by $0.60 per unit. Assuming no other changes, how many units would have to be sold each month to earn a profit of $4,500?

5. Refer to the original data. By automating certain operations, the company could slash its variable expenses in half. However, fixed costs would increase by $118,000 per month.

   a. Compute the new CM ratio and the new break-even point in both units and dollars.

   b. Assume that the company expects to sell 20,000 units next month. Prepare two contribution-format income statements, one assuming that operations are not automated and one assuming that they are.

   c. Would you recommend that the company automate its operations? Explain.

PROBLEM 7–20 Sales Mix; Multi-Product Break-Even Analysis [LO9]

Smithen Company, a wholesale distributor, has been operating for only a few months. The company sells three products—sinks, mirrors, and vanities. Budgeted sales by product and in total for the coming month are shown below:

	Product							
	Sinks		Mirrors		Vanities		Total	
Percentage of total sales....................	48%		20%		32%		100%	
Sales	$240,000	100%	$100,000	100%	$160,000	100%	$500,000	100%
Variable expenses	72,000	30%	80,000	80%	88,000	55%	240,000	48%
Contribution margin........................	$168,000	70%	$ 20,000	20%	$ 72,000	45%	260,000	52%
Fixed expenses							223,600	
Operating income							$ 36,400	

$$\text{Break-even point in sales dollars} = \frac{\text{Fixed expenses}}{\text{CM ratio}} = \frac{\$223,600}{0.52} = \$430,000$$

As shown by these data, operating income is budgeted at $36,400 for the month, and break-even sales at $430,000.

Assume that actual sales for the month total $500,000 as planned. Actual sales by product are: sinks, $160,000; mirrors, $200,000; and vanities, $140,000.

Required:

1. Prepare a contribution-format income statement for the month based on actual sales data. Present the income statement in the format shown above.

2. Compute the break-even point in sales dollars for the month, based on your actual data.

3. Considering the fact that the company met its $500,000 sales budget for the month, the president is shocked at the results shown on your income statement in (1) above. Prepare a brief memo for the president explaining why both the operating results and the break-even point in sales dollars are different from what was budgeted.

PROBLEM 7–21 Basic CVP Analysis; Graphing [LO1, LO2, LO4, LO5]

TipTops' national chain of shirt stores carry many styles of shirts that are all sold at the same price. To encourage sales personnel to step up their sales efforts, the company pays a generous sales commission on each shirt sold. Sales personnel also receive a small basic salary.

The following worksheet contains cost and revenue data for the Bradbury store. These data are typical of the company's many outlets:

	A	B	C
1		*Per Shirt*	
2	Selling price	$ 40.00	
3			
4	Variable expenses:		
5	Invoice cost	$ 18.00	
6	Sales commission	7.00	
7	Total variable expenses	$ 25.00	
8			
9		*Annual*	
10	Fixed expenses:		
11	Advertising	$ 80,000	
12	Rent	150,000	
13	Salaries	70,000	
14	Total fixed expenses	$300,000	
15			

`Sheet1 / Sheet2 / Sheet3`

TipTops is a fairly new organization. The company has asked you, as a member of its planning group, to assist in some basic analysis of its stores and company policies.

Required:
1. Calculate the annual break-even point in dollar sales and in unit sales for the Bradbury store.
2. Prepare a CVP graph showing cost and revenue data for the Bradbury store from zero shirts up to 30,000 shirts sold each year. Clearly indicate the break-even point on the graph.
3. If 19,000 shirts are sold in a year, what would be the Bradbury store's operating income or loss?
4. The company is considering paying the store manager of the Bradbury store an incentive commission of $3 per shirt (in addition to the salesperson's commissions). If this change is made, what will be the new break-even point in dollar sales and in unit sales?
5. Refer to the original data. As an alternative to (4) above, the company is considering paying the store manager a $3 commission on each shirt sold in excess of the break-even point. If this change is made, what will be the store's operating income or loss if 23,500 shirts are sold in a year?
6. Refer to the original data. The company is considering eliminating sales commissions entirely in its stores and increasing fixed salaries by $107,000 annually.
   a. If this change is made, what will be the new break-even point in dollar sales and in unit sales in the Bradbury store?
   b. Would you recommend that the change be made? Explain.

PROBLEM 7–22 Break-Even Analysis; Pricing [LO1, LO4, LO5]
Whitney Sewing and Alterations has just introduced a new line of alteration services for men's suits for which the company is trying to determine an optimal selling price. Marketing studies suggest that the company can increase sales by 2,000 units for each $2 per unit reduction in the selling price. The company's present selling price is $45 per unit, and variable expenses are $27 per unit. Fixed expenses are $111,600 per year. The present annual sales volume (at the $45 selling price) is 6,000 units.

Required:
1. What is the present yearly operating income or loss?
2. What is the present break-even point in units and in dollar sales?
3. Assuming that the marketing studies are correct, what is the *maximum* profit that the company can earn yearly? At how many units and at what selling price per unit would the company generate this profit?
4. What would be the break-even point in units and in dollar sales using the selling price you determined in (3) above (i.e., the selling price at the level of maximum profits)? Why is this break-even point different from the break-even point you computed in (2) above?

PROBLEM 7–23 Graphing; Incremental Analysis; Operating Leverage [LO2, LO4, LO5, LO6, LO8]

Teri Hall recently opened Sheer Elegance, Inc., a store specializing in fashionable stockings. Hall has just completed a course in managerial accounting, and she believes that she can apply certain aspects of the course to her business. She is particularly interested in adopting the cost–volume–profit (CVP) approach to decision making. Thus, she has prepared the following analysis:

Sales price per pair of stockings	$10.00
Variable expense per pair of stockings	4.00
Contribution margin per pair of stockings	$ 6.00
Fixed expense per year:	
Building rental	$ 48,000
Equipment depreciation	12,000
Selling	120,000
Administrative	60,000
Total fixed expense	$240,000

Required:
1. How many pairs of stockings must be sold to break even? What does this represent in total dollar sales?
2. Prepare a CVP graph for the store from zero pairs up to 60,000 pairs of stockings sold each year. Indicate the break-even point on the graph.
3. How many pairs of stockings must be sold to earn a $15,000 target profit for the first year?
4. Hall now has one full-time and one part-time salesperson working in the store. It will cost her an additional $20,000 per year to convert the part-time position to a full-time position. Hall believes that the change would bring in an additional $40,000 in sales each year. Should she convert the position? Use the incremental approach. (Do not prepare an income statement.)
5. Refer to the original data. Actual operating results for the first year are as follows:

Sales	$600,000
Variable expenses	240,000
Contribution margin	360,000
Fixed expenses	240,000
Operating income	$120,000

a. What is the store's degree of operating leverage?
b. Hall is confident that with some effort she can increase sales by 20% next year. What would be the expected percentage increase in operating income? Use the degree of operating leverage concept to compute your answer.

PROBLEM 7–24 Break-Even and Target Profit Analysis [LO5, LO6]

The Marbury Stein Shop sells steins from all parts of the world. The owner of the shop, Clint Marbury, is thinking of expanding his operations by hiring local college and university students, on a commission basis, to sell steins at the local post-secondary schools. The steins will bear the school emblem.

These steins must be ordered from the manufacturer three months in advance, and because of the unique emblem of each school, they cannot be returned. The steins would cost Marbury $15 each, with a minimum order of 200 steins. Any additional steins would have to be ordered in increments of 50.

Since Marbury's plan would not require any additional facilities, the only costs associated with the project would be the cost of the steins and the cost of sales commissions. The selling price of the steins would be $30 each. Marbury would pay the students a commission of $6 for each stein sold.

Required:
1. To make the project worthwhile in terms of his own time, Marbury would require a $7,200 operating income for the first six months of the venture. What level of sales in units and dollars would be required to attain this target operating income? Show all computations.
2. Assume that the venture is undertaken and an order is placed for 200 steins. What would be Marbury's break-even point in units and in sales dollars? Show all computations, and explain the reasoning behind your answer.

PROBLEM 7–25 Sales Mix; Break-Even Analysis; Margin of Safety [LO7, LO9]
Bultaco, a company located in Spain, manufactures and sells two models of luxuriously finished cutlery—Alvaro and Bazan. Present revenue, cost, and unit sales data for the two products appear below. All currency amounts are stated in euros, which are indicated by the symbol €.

	Alvaro	Bazan
Selling price per unit	€4.00	€6.00
Variable expenses per unit	€2.40	€1.20
Number of units sold monthly	200 units	80 units

Fixed expenses are €660 per month.

Required:
1. Assuming the sales mix above, do the following:
   a. Prepare a contribution-format income statement showing both euro and percentage columns for each product and for the company as a whole.
   b. Compute the break-even point in euros for the company as a whole and the margin of safety in both euros and percentage of sales.
2. The company has developed another product, Cano, that the company plans to sell for €8 each. At this price, the company expects to sell 40 units per month of the product. The variable expense would be €6 per unit. The company's fixed expenses would not change.
   a. Prepare another contribution-format income statement, including sales of Cano (sales of the other two products would not change).
   b. Compute the company's new break-even point in euros for the company as a whole and the new margin of safety in both euros and percentage of sales.
3. The president of the company was puzzled by your analysis. He did not understand why the break-even point has gone up even though there has been no increase in fixed expenses and the addition of the new product has increased the total contribution margin. Explain to the president what has happened.

PROBLEM 7–26 Sales Mix; Multi-Product Break-Even Analysis [LO9]
MediaSol Inc. produces affordable, high-quality personal multimedia entertainment devices. The company's Video Division manufactures three portable video players—the Standard, the Deluxe, and the Pro—that are widely used by the younger generation. Selected information on the portable video players is given below:

	Standard	Deluxe	Pro
Selling price per video player	$80.00	$120.00	$180.00
Variable expenses per video player:			
Production	$44.00	$54.00	$63.00
Selling (10% of selling price)	$8.00	$12.00	$18.00

All sales are made through the company's own retail outlets. The Video Division has the following fixed costs:

	Per Month
Fixed production costs	$ 90,000
Advertising expense	75,000
Administrative salaries	37,500
Total	$202,500

Sales, in units, over the past two months have been as follows:

	Standard	Deluxe	Pro	Total
April	1,000	500	2,500	4,000
May	3,750	750	1,500	6,000

Required:

1. Using the contribution approach, prepare an income statement for April and an income statement for May, with the following headings:

	Standard		Deluxe		Pro		Total	
	Amount	%	Amount	%	Amount	%	Amount	%
Sales								
Etc.								

Place the fixed expenses only in the Total column. Do not show percentages for the fixed expenses.

2. On seeing the income statements in (1) above, the president stated, "I can't believe this! We sold 50% more portable video players in May than in April, yet profits went down. It's obvious that costs are out of control in that division." What other explanation can you give for the drop in operating income?
3. Compute the Video Division's break-even point in dollar sales for April.
4. Has May's break-even point in dollar sales gone up or down from April's break-even point? Explain without computing a break-even point for May.
5. Assume that sales of the Standard video player increase by $35,000. What would be the effect on operating income? What would be the effect if Pro video player sales increased by $35,000? Do not prepare income statements; use the incremental analysis approach in determining your answer.

PROBLEM 7–27 Various CVP Questions: Break-Even Point; Cost Structure; Target Sales [LO1, LO3, LO4, LO5, LO6, LO8]

Fannell Products manufactures recreational equipment. One of the company's products, a skateboard, sells for $37.50. The skateboards are manufactured in an antiquated plant that relies heavily on direct labour workers. Therefore, variable costs are high, totalling $22.50 per skateboard.

Over the past year, the company sold 40,000 skateboards, with the following operating results:

Sales (40,000 skateboards)	$1,500,000
Variable expenses	900,000
Contribution margin	600,000
Fixed expenses	480,000
Operating income	$ 120,000

Management is anxious to maintain, and perhaps even improve, its present level of income from the skateboards.

Required:

1. Compute (*a*) the CM ratio and the break-even point in skateboards, and (*b*) the degree of operating leverage at last year's level of sales.
2. Due to an increase in labour rates, the company estimates that variable costs will increase by $3 per skateboard next year. If this change takes place and the selling price per skateboard remains constant at $37.50, what will be the new CM ratio and the new break-even point in skateboards?
3. Refer to the data in (2) above. If the expected change in variable costs takes place, how many skateboards will have to be sold next year to earn the same operating income ($120,000) as last year?
4. Refer again to the data in (2) above. The president has decided that the company may have to raise the selling price of its skateboards. If Fannell Products wants to maintain *the same CM ratio as last year*, what selling price per skateboard must it charge next year to cover the increased labour costs?
5. Refer to the original data. The company is considering the construction of a new, automated plant. The new plant would slash variable costs by 40%, but it would cause fixed costs to increase by 90%. If the new plant is built, what would be the company's new CM ratio and new break-even point in skateboards?

6. Refer to the data in (5) above.
    a. If the new plant is built, how many skateboards will have to be sold next year to earn the same operating income, $120,000, as last year?
    b. Assume that the new plant is constructed and that next year the company manufactures and sells 40,000 skateboards (the same number as sold last year). Prepare a contribution-format income statement, and compute the degree of operating leverage.
    c. If you were a member of top management, would you have been in favour of constructing the new plant? Explain.
7. Refer to the data in part (a) of item 6 above. If the new plant is built, how many skateboards will have to be sold next year to earn an after-tax net income of $120,000 assuming that the company tax rate is 30%?

PROBLEM 7–28 Interpretive Questions on the CVP Graph [LO2, LO5]
A CVP graph, as illustrated below, is a useful tool for showing relationships between an organization's costs, volume, and profits.

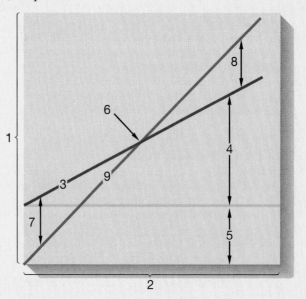

Required:
1. Identify the numbered components in the CVP graph.
2. State the effect of each of the following actions on line 3, line 9, and the break-even point. For line 3 and line 9, state whether the action will cause the line to
    *   Remain unchanged.
    *   Shift upward.
    *   Shift downward.
    *   Have a steeper slope (i.e., rotate upward).
    *   Have a flatter slope (i.e., rotate downward).
    *   Shift upward *and* have a steeper slope.
    *   Shift upward *and* have a flatter slope.
    *   Shift downward *and* have a steeper slope.
    *   Shift downward *and* have a flatter slope.

    In the case of the break-even point, state whether the action will cause the break-even point to
    *   Remain unchanged.
    *   Increase.
    *   Decrease.
    *   Probably change, but the direction is uncertain.

    Treat each case independently.
        Example: Fixed costs are increased by $20,000 each period.
        Answer (see choices above):   Line 3: Shift upward.
                                          Line 9: Remain unchanged.
                                          Break-even point: Increase.
    a. The unit selling price is decreased from $30 to $27.
    b. The per unit variable costs are increased from $12 to $15.

   c. The total fixed costs are reduced by $40,000.

   d. Five thousand fewer units are sold during the period than were budgeted.

   e. Due to purchasing a robot to perform a task that was previously done by workers, fixed costs are increased by $25,000 per period, and variable costs are reduced by $8 per unit.

   f. As a result of a decrease in the cost of materials, both unit variable costs and the selling price are decreased by $3.

   g. Advertising costs are increased by $50,000 per period, resulting in a 10% increase in the number of units sold.

   h. Due to paying salespeople a commission rather than a flat salary, fixed costs are reduced by $21,000 per period, and unit variable costs are increased by $6.

PROBLEM 7–29 Changes in Fixed and Variable Costs; Break-Even and Target Profit Analysis [LO4, LO5, LO6]

Novelties Inc. produces and sells highly faddish products directed toward the preteen market. A new product has come onto the market that the company is anxious to produce and sell. Enough capacity exists in the company's plant to produce 30,000 units each month. Variable costs to manufacture and sell one unit would be $1.60, and fixed costs would total $40,000 per month.

    The Marketing Department predicts that demand for the product will exceed the 30,000 units that the company is able to produce. Additional production capacity can be rented from another company at a fixed cost of $2,000 per month. Variable costs in the rented facility would total $1.75 per unit, due to somewhat less efficient operations than in the main plant. The product would sell for $2.50 per unit.

Required:

1. Compute the monthly break-even point for the new product in units and in total dollar sales. Show all computations in good form.

2. How many units must be sold each month to make a monthly operating income of $9,000?

3. If the sales manager receives a bonus of 15 cents for each unit sold in excess of the break-even point, how many units must be sold each month to earn a return of 25% on the monthly investment in fixed costs?

PROBLEM 7–30 Changes in Cost Structure; Break-Even Analysis; Operating Leverage; Margin of Safety [LO4, LO5, LO7, LO8]

Duchamp Company's contribution-format income statement for the most recent month is given below:

Sales (30,000 units)...............	$900,000
Variable expenses................	630,000
Contribution margin	270,000
Fixed expenses..................	180,000
Operating income	$ 90,000

    The industry in which Duchamp Company operates is quite sensitive to cyclical movements in the economy. Thus, profits vary considerably from year to year according to general economic conditions. The company has a large amount of unused capacity and is studying ways of improving profits.

Required:

1. New equipment has come on the market that would allow Duchamp Company to automate a portion of its operations. Variable costs would be reduced by $9 per unit. However, fixed costs would increase to a total of $450,000 each month. Prepare two contribution-format income statements, one showing present operations and one showing how operations would appear if the new equipment is purchased. Show an Amount column, a Per Unit column, and a Percentage column on each statement. Do not show percentages for the fixed costs.

2. Refer to the income statements in (1) above. For both present operations and the proposed new operations, compute (*a*) the degree of operating leverage, (*b*) the break-even point in dollars, and (*c*) the margin of safety in both dollar and percentage terms.

3. Refer again to the data in (1) above. As a manager, what factor would be paramount in your mind in deciding whether to purchase the new equipment? (You may assume that ample funds are available to make the purchase.)

4. Refer to the original data. Rather than purchase new equipment, the marketing manager argues that the company's marketing strategy should be changed. Instead of paying sales commissions,

which are included in variable expenses, the marketing manager suggests that salespeople be paid fixed salaries and that the company invest heavily in advertising. The marketing manager claims that this new approach would increase unit sales by 60% without any change in selling price; the company's new monthly fixed expenses would be $247,500; and its operating income would increase by 25%. Compute the break-even point in dollar sales for the company under the new marketing strategy. Do you agree with the marketing manager's proposal?

PROBLEM 7–31 Changes in Cost Structure, Break-Even Analysis: Indifference [LO4, LO5, LO6]

Lockhart Manufacturing Co. is presently manufacturing a new product for the following costs:

Direct materials per unit	$9
Direct labour per unit	1.2 DLH @ $14/DLH
Variable overhead per unit	0.75 of direct labour costs
Fixed manufacturing costs	$1,108,000
Fixed selling and administration costs	$1,685,000
Selling price per unit	$60
Variable selling costs per unit	$4

The production manager feels that savings could be achieved by automating the plant. If the plant was automated, the costs would shift as follows:

Direct materials cost per unit	$7.50
Direct labour per unit	0.75 DLH @ $18/DLH
Variable overhead per unit	0.6 of direct labour costs
Fixed manufacturing costs	$1,494,000

There would be no change to any other costs or to the selling price.

Required
1. Calculate the break-even point in annual unit sales for the new product if Lockhart Manufacturing uses the
    a. Present method of production.
    b. Automated method of production.
2. Calculate the annual number of unit sales at which Lockhart Manufacturing would be indifferent about which manufacturing method is used. If demand exceeds this amount, which method of production should be used?
3. Identify four factors that Lockhart Manufacturing might consider before selecting either the present method of production or the automated method of production.

(CGA–Canada adapted)

PROBLEM 7–32 Changes in Cost Structure, Break-Even Analysis, Target Profit [LO5, LO6, LO8]

Warton Ltd. is considering replacing an existing machine with a new and faster machine that will produce a more reliable product (that is, fewer defects). The switch to a new machine resulting in a superior product is expected to allow Warton to increase its sales price for the product. The switch will increase fixed costs, but not the variable costs. Cost and revenue estimates are as follows:

Cost Item	Old Machine	New Machine
Monthly fixed costs	$120,000	$250,000
Variable cost per unit	14	14
Sales price per unit	18	20

Required
1. Determine the break-even point in units for the two machines.
2. Determine the sales level in units at which the new machine will achieve a 10% target profit-to-sales ratio (ignore taxes).
3. Determine the sales level at which profits will be the same for either the old or new machine.
4. Which machine represents a lower risk if demand is uncertain? Explain.

(CGA–Canada adapted)

connect Cases

CASE 7–33 Multi-Product CVP Analysis [LO9]

Karges Coffee Inc. manufactures a line of single-cup brewing machines for home and office use that brew a cup of coffee, tea, or hot chocolate in less than a minute. The machines use specially packaged portions of coffee, tea, or hot chocolate that can be purchased online directly from Karges or at specialty coffee shops licensed to distribute the company's products. The appeal of the brewing machines is twofold. First, they offer a high level of convenience. The use of prepackaged coffee servings means no grinding of coffee beans and no mess. Also, the brewing machines have a water reservoir that for some models is large enough to make up to 20 cups of coffee. Second, the taste of each cup of coffee, tea, and hot chocolate is very consistent. The brewers' pressurized system uses the same amount of water for each cup and the airtight seal used in the individual portions keeps the product fresh.

The company has three models of brewers that offer different features, such as the size of the water reservoir, the number of brewing sizes, and the types of filtering devices used in the machine. Data from the most recent fiscal year for the three models is shown below.

| | Model | | |
	Home Brewer	Office Basic	Office Deluxe
Sales volume (units)	12,000	30,000	6,000
Unit selling price	$150	$200	$300
Variable cost per unit	120	140	180
Contribution margin per unit	$ 30	$ 60	$120

Fixed costs are $1,500,000 per year. The company has no work in process or finished goods inventories. The company is facing increased levels of competition from manufacturers using similar brewing technologies and believes there is no room for any increases in unit selling prices.

Required:

1. Calculate the company's overall break-even point in sales dollars.
2. Calculate the sales dollars required for each product at the overall break-even level of sales calculated in (1) above.
3. Calculate the company's overall break-even point in total units.
4. What impact would doubling the number of Office Basic units sold next year have on the overall break-even point in sales dollars? Assume that there will be no changes to the Home Brewer or Office Deluxe unit sales, that unit selling prices and variable costs will remain the same for each model, and that total fixed costs will be unchanged.
5. The company is considering a new advertising campaign to raise overall consumer awareness of the product offerings. The total cost of the year-long campaign would be $150,000. By how much would sales need to increase overall for the company to be able to justify the new campaign? Assume no change to the current product mix.
6. Suppose that instead of being designed to increase total sales volume, the new $150,000 advertising campaign will focus on getting customers who would have purchased the Office Basic model to buy the Office Deluxe model instead. To justify the cost of the new advertising, how many customers must purchase the Deluxe model instead of the Basic model? Assume that the new advertising campaign will have no impact on sales of the Home Brewer model.
7. The company is considering adding a new product to its line of brewers targeted at the office-use market. The new brewer, the Office Plus, would sell for $250 per unit and would have variable unit costs of $160. Introducing the new model would increase fixed costs by $102,000 annually and would reduce annual unit sales of the Office Basic and Office Deluxe models by 10% each. Assuming no change to the sales of the Home Brewer model, how many units of the Office Plus would need to be sold to justify its addition to the product line next year?

CASE 7–34 Cost Structure; Break-Even Point; Target Profits [LO4, LO5, LO6]

Crescent Corporation manufactures multi-function photocopiers that are sold to businesses through a network of independent sales agents located in the United States and Canada. These sales agents sell a variety of products to businesses in addition to Crescent's multi-function photocopiers. The sales agents are currently paid a 19% commission on sales, and this commission rate was used when Crescent's management prepared the following budgeted income statement for the upcoming year.

Sales		$15,000,000
Cost of goods sold:		
Variable	$8,400,000	
Fixed	1,400,000	9,800,000
Gross margin		5,200,000
Selling and administrative expenses:		
Commissions	2,850,000	
Fixed advertising expense	400,000	
Fixed administrative expense	1,600,000	4,850,000
Operating income		$ 350,000

Since the completion of the above statement, Crescent's management has learned that the independent sales agents are demanding an increase in the commission rate to 22% of sales for the upcoming year. This would be the third increase in commissions demanded by the independent sales agents in five years. As a result, Crescent's management has decided to investigate the possibility of hiring its own sales staff to replace the independent sales agents.

Crescent's controller estimates that the company will have to hire six salespeople to cover the current market area, and the total annual payroll cost of these employees will be about $350,000, including benefits. The salespeople will also be paid commissions of 12% of sales. Travel and entertainment expenses are expected to total about $200,000 for the year. The company will also have to hire a sales manager and support staff whose salaries and benefits will total $100,000 per year. To make up for the promotions that the independent sales agents had been running on behalf of Crescent, management believes that the company's budget for fixed advertising expenses should be increased by $250,000.

Required:

1. Assuming sales of $15,000,000, construct a budgeted contribution-format income statement for the upcoming year for each of the following alternatives:
   a. The independent sales agents' commission rate remains unchanged at 19%.
   b. The independent sales agents' commission rate increases to 22%.
   c. The company employs its own sales force.
2. Calculate Crescent Corporation's break-even point in sales dollars for the upcoming year assuming the following:
   a. The independent sales agents' commission rate remains unchanged at 19%.
   b. The independent sales agents' commission rate increases to 22%.
   c. The company employs its own sales force.
3. Refer to your answer to 1(b) above. If the company employs its own sales force, what volume of sales would be necessary to generate the operating income the company would realize if sales are $15,000,000 and the company continues to sell through agents (at a 22% commission rate)?
4. Determine the volume of sales at which operating income would be equal regardless of whether Crescent Corporation sells through agents (at a 22% commission rate) or employs its own sales force.
5. Prepare a profit graph on which you plot the profits for both of the following alternatives.
   a. The independent sales agents' commission rate increases to 22%.
   b. The company employs its own sales force.
   On the graph, use total sales revenue as the measure of activity.
6. Write a memo to the president of Crescent Corporation in which you make a recommendation as to whether the company should continue to use independent sales agents (at a 22% commission rate) or employ its own sales force. Fully explain the reasons for your recommendation in the memo.

(CMA, adapted)

CASE 7–35 Break-Even Analysis with Step-Fixed Costs [LO5, LO6]

The Cardiac Care Department at St. Andrew's General Clinics has a capacity of 70 beds and operates 24 hours a day, year-round. The measure of activity in the department is patient-days, where one patient-day represents one patient occupying a bed for one day. The average revenue per patient-day is $480 and the average variable cost per patient-day is $180. The fixed cost of the department (not including personnel costs) is $2,740,000.

The only personnel directly employed by the Cardiac Care Department are aides, nurses, and supervising nurses. The clinic has minimum staffing requirements for the department, based on total annual patient-days in the Cardiac Care Department. Clinic requirements, beginning at the minimum expected level of activity, follow:

Annual Patient-Days	Aides	Nurses	Supervising Nurses
10,000–12,000	7	15	3
12,001–13,750	8	15	3
13,751–16,500	9	16	4
16,501–18,250	10	16	4
18,251–20,750	10	17	5
20,751–23,000	11	18	5

These staffing levels represent full-time equivalents, and it should be assumed that the Cardiac Care Department always employs only the minimum number of required full-time equivalent personnel.

Average annual salaries for each class of employee are: aides, $36,000; nurses, $58,000; and supervising nurses, $76,000.

Required:
1. Compute the total fixed costs (including the salaries of aides, nurses, and supervising nurses) in the Cardiac Care Department for each level of activity shown above (i.e., total fixed costs at the 10,000–12,000 patient-day level of activity, total fixed costs at the 12,001–13,750 patient-day level of activity, etc.).
2. Compute the minimum number of patient-days required for the Cardiac Care Department to break even.
3. Determine the minimum number of patient-days required for the Cardiac Care Department to earn an annual "profit" of $720,000.

(CPA, adapted)

Research and Application

R 7–36 Cost–Volume–Profit Disclosures [LO4, LO5, LO6, LO7, LO8]

The questions in this exercise are based on the Benetton Group, a company headquartered in Italy and known in North America primarily for one of its brands of fashion apparel—United Colors of Benetton. To answer the questions, you will need to download the Benetton Group's 2009 annual report at http://interactive2009en.benettongroup.com. You do not need to print this document to answer the questions.

Refer to page 24 of the annual report, "Consolidated Group results."

Required:
1. Explain the distinction between "Gross operating profit" and "Contribution margin."
2. Does it appear that Benetton has properly classified its expenses as variable and fixed? Explain. Ignore all items below the "Operating profit" line.
3. Calculate Benetton's break-even point in sales amounts (euros) in 2009. What was the margin of safety?
4. Approximately what sales would Benetton have to generate to achieve a target operating profit of €240 million? Assume the contribution margin ratio will continue at the 2009 level.
5. What was Benetton's degree of operating leverage in 2008? Use this value to predict operating income (euros) in 2009, assuming sales drop by 3.7%. Compare the operating income you predicted using the degree of operating leverage with actual operating income in 2009. Why might the two amounts be different?

APPENDIX 7A: COST–VOLUME–PROFIT WITH UNCERTAINTY

Appendix available on Connect.

 Practise and learn online with Connect.

CHAPTER

8

VARIABLE COSTING: A TOOL FOR MANAGEMENT

IBM'S $2.5 BILLION INVESTMENT IN TECHNOLOGY

When it comes to state of the art in automation, IBM's $2.5 billion semiconductor manufacturing facility in East Fishkill, New York, is tough to beat. The plant uses wireless networks, 600 miles of cable, and more than 420 servers to equip itself with what IBM claims is more computing power than NASA uses to launch a space shuttle.

Each batch of 25 wafers (one wafer can be processed into 1,000 computer chips) travels through the East Fishkill plant's manufacturing process without ever being touched by human hands. A computer system "looks at orders and schedules production runs . . . adjusts schedules to allow for planned maintenance and . . . feeds vast reams of production data into enterprise-wide management and financial-reporting systems." The plant can literally run itself, as was the case a few years ago when a snowstorm hit and everyone went home while the automated system continued to manufacture computer chips until it ran out of work.

In a manufacturing environment such as this, labour costs are insignificant and fixed overhead costs are huge. There is a strong temptation to build inventories and increase profits without increasing sales. How can this be done? you ask. It would seem logical that producing more units would have no impact on profits unless the units were sold, right? Wrong! As we will discover in this chapter, absorption costing—the most widely used method of determining product costs—can artificially increase profits by increasing the quantity of units produced.

Source: Ghostwriter, "Big Blue's $2.5 Billion Sales Tool," *Fortune*, September 19, 2005, pp. 316F–316J.

Two general approaches are used in manufacturing companies for costing products for the purposes of valuing inventories and cost of goods sold. One approach, called *absorption costing,* was discussed in Chapters 2 and 3. Absorption costing is generally used for external financial reports. The other approach, called *variable costing,* is preferred by some managers for internal decision making and must be used when an income statement is prepared in the contribution format. Ordinarily, absorption costing and variable costing produce different figures for operating income, and the difference can be quite large. In addition to showing how these two methods differ, we will consider the arguments for and against each costing method and we will show how management decisions can be affected by the costing method chosen.

In Chapters 6 and 7, the presentations generally assumed inventories were insignificant or that production equals sales. This assumption is reasonable in some situations, as will be shown later in this chapter. However, inventories can be important to income results in other situations. The explanations to follow will show what is involved when production does not equal sales and thus production is a cost driver rather than sales. Also, the analysis will include the elements of production costs rather than using only the total production costs.

OVERVIEW OF ABSORPTION AND VARIABLE COST

In the last two chapters, we learned that the contribution-format income statement and cost–volume–profit (CVP) analysis are valuable management tools. Both of these tools emphasize cost behaviour and require that managers carefully distinguish between variable and fixed costs. Absorption costing, which was discussed in Chapters 2 and 3, assigns both variable and fixed costs to products—mingling them in a way that makes it difficult for managers to distinguish between them. In contrast, variable costing focuses on *cost behaviour,* clearly separating fixed from variable costs. One of the strengths of variable costing is that it harmonizes with both the contribution approach and the CVP concepts discussed in the preceding chapters.

> **LEARNING OBJECTIVE 1**
> Identify how variable costing differs from absorption costing and compute unit product costs under each method.

Absorption Costing

In Chapter 3, we learned that absorption costing treats *all* manufacturing costs as product costs, regardless of whether they are variable or fixed. The cost of a unit of product under the absorption costing method therefore consists of direct materials, direct labour, and *both* variable and fixed manufacturing overhead. Thus, absorption costing allocates a portion of fixed manufacturing overhead cost to each unit of product, along with the variable manufacturing costs. Because absorption costing includes all manufacturing costs as product costs, it is frequently referred to as full costing.

Variable Costing

Under **variable costing**, only those manufacturing costs that vary with output are treated as product costs. This would generally include direct materials, direct labour, and the variable portion of manufacturing overhead. Fixed manufacturing overhead is not treated as a product cost under this method. Rather, fixed manufacturing overhead is treated as a period cost and, like selling and administrative expenses, it is expensed in its entirety against revenue each period. Consequently, the cost of a unit of product in inventory or in cost of goods sold under the variable costing method does not contain any fixed overhead cost.

Variable costing is sometimes referred to as **direct costing** or **marginal costing**. The term *direct costing* was popular for many years, but it is slowly disappearing from day-to-day use. The term *variable costing* is more descriptive of the way in which product costs are computed when a contribution income statement is prepared.

Variable costing
A costing method that includes only variable manufacturing costs—direct materials, direct labour, and variable manufacturing overhead—in the cost of a unit of product.

Direct costing
Another name for *variable costing.*

Marginal costing
Another name for *variable costing.*

Selling and Administrative Expense

To complete this summary comparison of absorption and variable costing, we need to consider briefly the handling of selling and administrative expenses. These expenses are rarely treated as product costs, regardless of the costing method in use. Thus, under either absorption or variable costing, selling and administrative expenses are always treated as period costs (expenses) and deducted from revenues as incurred.

Exhibit 8–1 summarizes the classification of costs under both absorption and variable costing.

EXHIBIT 8–1 Cost Classifications: Absorption versus Variable Costing

Unit Cost Computations

To illustrate the computation of unit product costs under both absorption and variable costing, consider Boley Company, a small company that produces a single product and has the following cost structure:

Number of units produced each year	6,000
Variable costs per unit:	
Direct materials	$ 2
Direct labour	4
Variable manufacturing overhead	1
Variable selling and administrative expenses	3
Fixed costs per year:	
Fixed manufacturing overhead	30,000
Fixed selling and administrative expenses	10,000

Under the absorption costing method, *all* manufacturing costs, variable and fixed, are included when determining the unit product cost. Thus, if the company sells a unit of product and absorption costing is being used, then $12 (consisting of $7 variable cost and $5 fixed cost) will be deducted on the income statement as cost of goods sold. Similarly, any unsold units will be carried as inventory on the balance sheet at $12 each.

Absorption Costing	
Direct materials	$ 2
Direct labour	4
Variable manufacturing overhead	1
Total variable production cost	7
Fixed manufacturing overhead ($30,000 ÷ 6,000 units of product)	5
Unit product cost	$ 12

Under the variable costing method, only the variable manufacturing costs are included in product costs. Therefore, if the company sells a unit of product, only $7 will be deducted as cost of goods sold, and unsold units will be carried in the balance sheet inventory account at only $7 each.

Variable Costing

Direct materials	$ 2
Direct labour	4
Variable manufacturing overhead	1
Unit product cost	$ 7

(The $30,000 fixed manufacturing overhead in variable costing will be expensed in total against income as a period expense, along with the selling and administrative expenses.)

INCOME COMPARISON OF ABSORPTION AND VARIABLE COSTING

Income statements prepared under the absorption and variable costing approaches are shown in Exhibit 8–2. In preparing these statements, we use the data for Boley Company presented earlier, along with other information about the company, as given below:

LEARNING OBJECTIVE 2
Prepare income statements using both variable and absorption costing.

Units in beginning inventory.	–0–
Units produced	6,000
Units sold.	5,000
Units in ending inventory	1,000
Selling price per unit	$ 20
Selling and administrative expenses:	
Variable per unit	$ 3
Fixed per year.	$10,000

	Absorption Costing	Variable Costing
Unit product cost:		
Direct materials	$ 2	$ 2
Direct labour	4	4
Variable manufacturing over head	1	1
Fixed manufacturing over head ($30,000 ÷ 6,000 units) . . .	5	—
Unit product cost	$12	$ 7

Several points can be made about the financial statements in Exhibit 8–2:

1. Under the absorption costing method, if there is an ending inventory, the fixed manufacturing costs associated with the inventory will be carried forward as a balance sheet account, inventory, rather than being treated as a period cost. Such a deferral of costs is known as **fixed manufacturing overhead cost deferred in inventory**. The process involved can be explained by referring to the data for Boley Company. During the current period, Boley Company produced 6,000 units but sold only 5,000 units, thus leaving 1,000 unsold units in the ending inventory. Under the absorption costing method, each unit produced was assigned $5 in fixed overhead cost (see the unit cost computations above). Therefore, each of the 1,000 units going into inventory at the end of the period has $5 in fixed manufacturing overhead cost attached to it, or a total of $5,000 for the 1,000 units. *This fixed manufacturing overhead cost of the current period is deferred in inventory to the next period, when, hopefully, these units will*

Fixed manufacturing overhead cost deferred in inventory
The portion of the fixed manufacturing overhead cost of a period that goes into inventory under the absorption costing method as a result of production exceeding sales.

EXHIBIT 8–2   Comparison of Absorption and Variable Costing—Boley Company

Absorption Costing

Sales (5,000 units × $20 per unit)		$100,000
Less cost of goods sold:		
Beginning inventory	$ –0–	
Add cost of goods manufactured		
(6,000 units × $12 per unit)	72,000	
Goods available for sale	72,000	
Less ending inventory		
(1,000 units × $12 per unit)	12,000	
Cost of goods sold		60,000
Gross margin		40,000
Less selling and administrative expenses		
(5,000 units × $3 variable		
per unit + $10,000 fixed)		25,000
Operating income		$ 15,000

Note the difference in ending inventories. Fixed manufacturing overhead cost at $5 per unit is included under the absorption approach. This explains the difference in ending inventory and in operating income (1,000 units × $5 per unit = $5,000).

Variable Costing

Sales (5,000 units × $20 per unit)		$100,000
Less variable expenses:		
Variable cost of goods sold:		
Beginning inventory	$ –0–	
Add variable manufacturing costs		
(6,000 units × $7 per unit)	42,000	
Goods available for sale	42,000	
Less ending inventory		
(1,000 units × $7 per unit)	7,000	
Variable cost of goods sold	35,000	
Variable selling and administrative		
expenses (5,000 units		
× $3 per unit)	15,000	50,000
Contribution margin		50,000
Less fixed expenses:		
Fixed manufacturing overhead	30,000	
Fixed selling and administrative expenses	10,000	40,000
Operating income		$ 10,000

be taken out of inventory and sold. The deferral of $5,000 of fixed manufacturing overhead costs can be seen clearly by analyzing the ending inventory under the absorption costing method:

Variable manufacturing costs: 1,000 units × $7	$ 7,000
Fixed manufacturing overhead costs: 1,000 units × $5	5,000
Total inventory value	$12,000

In summary, under absorption costing, of the $30,000 in fixed manufacturing overhead costs incurred during the period, only $25,000 (5,000 units sold × $5) has been included in cost of goods sold. The remaining $5,000 (1,000 units *not* sold × $5) has been deferred in inventory to the next period.

2. Under the variable costing method, the entire $30,000 in fixed manufacturing overhead costs has been treated as an expense of the current period (see the bottom portion of the variable costing income statement).

3. The ending inventory figure under the variable costing method is $5,000 lower than it is under the absorption costing method. The reason is that under variable costing, only the variable manufacturing costs are assigned to units of product and therefore included in inventory:

Variable manufacturing costs: 1,000 units × $7	$7,000

Under the variable costing method, only the variable manufacturing costs are included in product costs. Therefore, if the company sells a unit of product, only $7 will be deducted as cost of goods sold, and unsold units will be carried in the balance sheet inventory account at only $7 each.

Variable Costing

Direct materials	$ 2
Direct labour	4
Variable manufacturing overhead	1
Unit product cost	$ 7

(The $30,000 fixed manufacturing overhead in variable costing will be expensed in total against income as a period expense, along with the selling and administrative expenses.)

INCOME COMPARISON OF ABSORPTION AND VARIABLE COSTING

Income statements prepared under the absorption and variable costing approaches are shown in Exhibit 8–2. In preparing these statements, we use the data for Boley Company presented earlier, along with other information about the company, as given below:

> **LEARNING OBJECTIVE 2**
> Prepare income statements using both variable and absorption costing.

Units in beginning inventory.	–0–
Units produced	6,000
Units sold.	5,000
Units in ending inventory	1,000
Selling price per unit	$ 20
Selling and administrative expenses:	
Variable per unit	$ 3
Fixed per year.	$10,000

Unit product cost:	Absorption Costing	Variable Costing
Direct materials	$ 2	$ 2
Direct labour	4	4
Variable manufacturing over head	1	1
Fixed manufacturing over head ($30,000 ÷ 6,000 units) . . .	5	—
Unit product cost	$12	$ 7

Several points can be made about the financial statements in Exhibit 8–2:

1. Under the absorption costing method, if there is an ending inventory, the fixed manufacturing costs associated with the inventory will be carried forward as a balance sheet account, inventory, rather than being treated as a period cost. Such a deferral of costs is known as **fixed manufacturing overhead cost deferred in inventory**. The process involved can be explained by referring to the data for Boley Company. During the current period, Boley Company produced 6,000 units but sold only 5,000 units, thus leaving 1,000 unsold units in the ending inventory. Under the absorption costing method, each unit produced was assigned $5 in fixed overhead cost (see the unit cost computations above). Therefore, each of the 1,000 units going into inventory at the end of the period has $5 in fixed manufacturing overhead cost attached to it, or a total of $5,000 for the 1,000 units. *This fixed manufacturing overhead cost of the current period is deferred in inventory to the next period, when, hopefully, these units will*

> **Fixed manufacturing overhead cost deferred in inventory**
> The portion of the fixed manufacturing overhead cost of a period that goes into inventory under the absorption costing method as a result of production exceeding sales.

EXHIBIT 8–2 Comparison of Absorption and Variable Costing—Boley Company

Absorption Costing

Sales (5,000 units × $20 per unit)			$100,000
Less cost of goods sold:			
Beginning inventory		$ –0–	
Add cost of goods manufactured (6,000 units × $12 per unit)		72,000	
Goods available for sale		72,000	
Less ending inventory (1,000 units × $12 per unit)		12,000	
Cost of goods sold			60,000
Gross margin			40,000
Less selling and administrative expenses (5,000 units × $3 variable per unit + $10,000 fixed)			25,000
Operating income			$ 15,000

Note the difference in ending inventories. Fixed manufacturing overhead cost at $5 per unit is included under the absorption approach. This explains the difference in ending inventory and in operating income (1,000 units × $5 per unit = $5,000).

Variable Costing

Sales (5,000 units × $20 per unit)			$100,000
Less variable expenses:			
Variable cost of goods sold:			
Beginning inventory		$ –0–	
Add variable manufacturing costs (6,000 units × $7 per unit)		42,000	
Goods available for sale		42,000	
Less ending inventory (1,000 units × $7 per unit)		7,000	
Variable cost of goods sold		35,000	
Variable selling and administrative expenses (5,000 units × $3 per unit)		15,000	50,000
Contribution margin			50,000
Less fixed expenses:			
Fixed manufacturing overhead		30,000	
Fixed selling and administrative expenses		10,000	40,000
Operating income			$ 10,000

be taken out of inventory and sold. The deferral of $5,000 of fixed manufacturing overhead costs can be seen clearly by analyzing the ending inventory under the absorption costing method:

Variable manufacturing costs: 1,000 units × $7	$ 7,000
Fixed manufacturing overhead costs: 1,000 units × $5	5,000
Total inventory value	$12,000

In summary, under absorption costing, of the $30,000 in fixed manufacturing overhead costs incurred during the period, only $25,000 (5,000 units sold × $5) has been included in cost of goods sold. The remaining $5,000 (1,000 units *not* sold × $5) has been deferred in inventory to the next period.

2. Under the variable costing method, the entire $30,000 in fixed manufacturing overhead costs has been treated as an expense of the current period (see the bottom portion of the variable costing income statement).

3. The ending inventory figure under the variable costing method is $5,000 lower than it is under the absorption costing method. The reason is that under variable costing, only the variable manufacturing costs are assigned to units of product and therefore included in inventory:

Variable manufacturing costs: 1,000 units × $7 . . . . $7,000

Learning Objectives

After studying Chapter 9, you should be able to

1. Explain why organizations budget and describe the processes they use to create budgets.

2. Prepare the supporting components of a master budget and the budgeted financial statements.

3. Prepare a flexible budget and explain the need for the flexible budget approach.

4. Prepare a performance report using the flexible budget approach.

5. Describe variations in the master budget process when applying it to not-for-profit and activity-based situations.

6. (Online Appendix 9A) Compute the optimal inventory level and order size.

BUDGETING

◼ BIG LEAGUE BUDGETING

In 2005, the National Hockey League (NHL) and its players signed a new collective bargaining agreement (CBA). One of the key features of the new CBA is that it effectively establishes a budget (salary cap) for each team's spending on player salaries. Estimates indicated that for the 2010–2011 season, each team in the league would not be able to spend more than $58.8 million. The objective of having each team assigned the same maximum budget for player salaries is to create greater parity in the league by allowing teams in smaller markets, such as Calgary, to compete with teams in larger markets, such as Chicago.

Having a set budget limit has forced teams to plan very carefully in deciding which players to sign and for how long. Deciding how to allocate the salary budget is very important, as it can have a dramatic impact on a team's on-ice success. Moreover, unlike most organizations, decisions made by NHL teams in allocating their salary budgets are subjected to intense scrutiny by the press, other teams, hockey analysts, and, of course, the fans. For example, in 2010, the day after the Chicago Blackhawks were crowned league champions for the first time in 49 years, analysts began speculating about how they would manage to stay within the salary cap for the next season. The Blackhawks had already signed 14 players through the 2010–2011 season, using up $58 million of their available budget under the cap of $58.8 million. Inevitably, some of the players who were instrumental to Chicago's success in 2009–2010 will not be re-signed as the result of budget constraints. Indeed, in the era of the new CBA, teams such as the Blackhawks find it difficult to repeat their success given the challenges of re-signing key players whose market values often go up in the season following a championship year. As evidence of this, six different teams have won the Stanley Cup since 2005.

The salary budget for NHL teams is established by the details of the CBA. However, most organizations determine the budgeted amounts for revenues and expenses on their own. Who participates in setting the budgets? How are the budget estimates determined? How is actual performance evaluated in comparison to the budget? These are all important issues covered in this chapter.

Sources: Wayne Scanlan, "Players Get What Market Will Bear; NHL Salary Cap Can Hurt or Reward, Depending on Need," *National Post*, July 6, 2007, p. B9; Michael Traikos, "Chicago's Niemi a Costly Problem," *National Post*, June 12, 2010.

Budgets are an important tool used by management to communicate financial objectives for the coming year (or years), allocate resources, and coordinate activities across the different functional areas within the organization. Budgets can also be an important tool used by managers to periodically compare actual performance of revenues, expenses, and profits to the plan. When actual results are significantly better than those in the budget, management will seek explanations as to the causes and attempt to identify whether the favourable trend will continue. If actual results are significantly worse than those in the budget, management will also seek to understand the causes and take corrective action when necessary. In this chapter, we focus on both the steps involved in preparing budgets as well as some of the issues that influence how managers use and respond to budgets.

◼ THE BASIC FRAMEWORK OF BUDGETING

Definition of Budgeting

LEARNING OBJECTIVE 1
Explain why organizations budget and describe the processes they use to create budgets

A budget is a quantitative plan for the acquisition and use of financial and other resources over a specified future time period. The act of preparing a budget is called *budgeting*. The use of budgets to control a firm's activities is known as *budgetary control*.

The **master budget** is a summary of a company's plans that sets specific targets for sales, production, distribution, and financing activities. It generally culminates in a cash budget, a budgeted income statement, and a budgeted balance sheet. In short, it represents a comprehensive financial expression of management's plans for the future and how these plans are to be accomplished.

Master budget
A summary of a company's plans in which specific targets are set for sales, production, distribution, and financing activities; it generally culminates in a cash budget, a budgeted income statement, and a budgeted balance sheet.

Budgets' Dual Role: Planning and Control

Budgets serve as both a planning tool and a control tool in organizations. However, the terms *planning* and *control* are often confused, and occasionally these terms are used in such a way as to suggest that they mean the same thing. Actually, planning and control are two quite distinct concepts. Planning involves developing objectives and preparing various budgets to achieve these objectives. Control involves the steps taken by management to increase the likelihood that the objectives developed at the planning stage are attained and to ensure that all parts of the organization function in a manner consistent with organizational policies. An effective budgeting system provides for *both* planning and control. Good planning without effective control is time wasted. On the other hand, unless plans are laid down in advance, there are no objectives toward which control can be directed.

Advantages of Budgeting

Some managers claim that while budgeting may work well in *some* situations, it would never work well in their companies because the operations are too complex or because there are too many uncertainties. Actually these complexities and uncertainties provide one of the important justifications for budgeting: to analyze alternatives being considered before consuming the resources necessary to actually implement them. Managers usually will have informal plans even before they become involved in developing their budgets. The budget process provides a mechanism for quantifying the financial consequences of these plans.

Companies realize many benefits from a budgeting program, including the following:

1. Budgets communicate management's plans throughout the organization, leading to a better understanding by all employees of the organization's goals and objectives.
2. Budgets force managers to *think about* and *plan for* the future. In the absence of the necessity to prepare a budget, many managers would spend considerable time dealing with daily emergencies.
3. The budgeting process provides a means of *allocating resources* to those parts of the organization where they can be used most effectively and are most needed. In essence,

the budgets prepared by managers are requests for the resources needed to run their operations.

4. The budgeting process can uncover potential **bottlenecks** before they occur, by identifying the demands that will be placed on all key activities and processes. If necessary, changes can be made to any activity or process that does not currently have the capability or capacity to meet the budgeted level of activity on a timely basis.

5. Budgets *coordinate* the activities of the entire organization by *integrating* the plans of the various areas. Budgeting helps to ensure that everyone in the organization is pulling in the same direction. For example, if new products are going to be manufactured and sold in the coming year, the marketing department needs to be aware of this and include the necessary advertising and promotion expenses in the total marketing budget.

6. Budgets define goals and objectives that can serve as *benchmarks* for evaluating subsequent actual performance. Periodic comparison of actual results to budgeted amounts allows management to determine whether the organization's goals are being met and to take corrective action as necessary.

> **Bottleneck**
> A machine, activity, or process that limits total output because it is operating at capacity.

Responsibility Accounting

Most of what we say in this chapter and in the next two chapters is concerned with *responsibility accounting*. The basic idea behind **responsibility accounting** is that managers should be held responsible for those items—and *only* those items—that they can actually influence to a significant extent. Each line item (i.e., revenue or cost) in the budget is made the responsibility of a manager, and that manager is held responsible for subsequent deviations between budgeted goals and actual results. This concept is central to any effective profit planning and control system. Someone must be held responsible for each cost or else no one will be responsible, and the cost will inevitably grow out of control.

Being held responsible for costs does not mean that the manager is penalized if the actual results do not measure up to the budgeted goals. However, the manager should take the initiative to correct any unfavourable discrepancies, should understand the source of significant favourable or unfavourable discrepancies, and should be prepared to explain the reasons for discrepancies to top management. The point of an effective responsibility system is to make sure that nothing "falls through the cracks," that the organization reacts quickly and appropriately to deviations from its plans, and that the organization learns from the feedback it gets by comparing budgeted goals to actual results.

> **Responsibility accounting**
> A system of accountability in which managers are held responsible for those items of revenue and cost over which they can exert significant influence—and only those items. Managers are held responsible for differences between budgeted and actual results.

Choosing a Budget Period

Operating budgets ordinarily cover a one-year period corresponding to the company's fiscal year. Many companies divide their budget year into four quarters. The first quarter is then subdivided into months, and monthly budget figures are established. The last three quarters are carried in the budget at quarterly totals only. As the year progresses, the figures for the second quarter are broken down into monthly amounts, then the third-quarter figures are broken down, and so forth. This approach has the advantage of requiring periodic review and reappraisal of budget data throughout the year.

Continuous or *perpetual budgets* are used by many organizations. A **continuous** or **perpetual budget** is a 12-month budget that rolls forward one month (or quarter) as the current month (or quarter) is completed. In other words, one month (or quarter) is added to the end of the budget as each month (or quarter) comes to a close. This approach always keeps managers focused at least one year ahead so that they do not become too narrowly fixated on short-term results.

> **Continuous or perpetual budget**
> A 12-month budget that rolls forward one month (or quarter) as the current month (or quarter) is completed.

In this chapter, we will focus on one-year operating budgets. However, using basically the same techniques, operating budgets can be prepared for periods that extend over many years. It may be difficult to accurately forecast sales and expenses much beyond a year, but even rough estimates can be invaluable in uncovering potential problems and identifying opportunities that would otherwise be overlooked.

The Participative Budget

The success of a budget program will be determined in large part by the way in which the budget is developed. The most successful budget programs involve managers with cost control responsibilities in preparing their own budget estimates—rather than having a budget imposed from above. This **participative budget** approach to preparing budget data is particularly important if the budget is to be used to control and evaluate a manager's activities. If a budget is imposed on a manager from above, it may generate resentment rather than cooperation and increased productivity. Exhibit 9–1 illustrates this approach to budget preparation.

Participative budgets have a number of advantages:

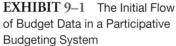

Participative budget
A method of preparing budgets in which managers prepare their own budget estimates. These budget estimates are then reviewed by the manager's supervisor, and any issues are resolved by mutual agreement, leading to a completed budget.

1. Individuals at all levels of the organization are recognized as members of the team whose views and judgments are valued by top management.
2. Budget estimates prepared by front-line managers are often more accurate and reliable than estimates prepared by top managers who have less detailed knowledge of market factors and day-to-day operations.
3. Motivation is generally higher when individuals participate in setting their own goals than when the goals are imposed from above. Participative budgets create commitment to attaining the goal.
4. A manager who is not able to meet a budget that has been imposed from above can always say that the budget was unrealistic and impossible to meet. With a participative budget, this excuse is not available.

Budgetary slack
The difference between the revenues and expenses a manager believes can be achieved and the amounts included in the budget. Slack will exist when revenue budgets are intentionally set below expected levels and expense budgets are set above expected levels.

Budget estimates prepared by lower-level managers cannot necessarily be accepted without question by higher levels of management. If no system of checks and balances is present, participative budgets may be too loose and allow too much **budgetary slack**—the difference between the revenues and expenses a manager really believes can be achieved and the amounts included in the budget. Revenue budgets that are intentionally set at lower than expected levels and expense budgets that are set higher than expected levels are said to contain slack.[1] Managers may attempt to create slack in an attempt to increase the likelihood of obtaining rewards that are contingent on meeting or beating the budget or to reduce how hard they have to work during the period to attain their budgets.

EXHIBIT 9–1   The Initial Flow of Budget Data in a Participative Budgeting System

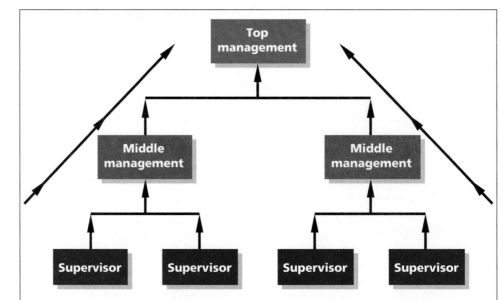

The initial flow of budget data in a participative system is from lower levels of responsibility to higher levels of responsibility. Each person with responsibility for cost control will prepare his or her own budget estimates and submit them to the next higher level of management. These estimates are reviewed and consolidated as they move upward in the organization.

Slack can result in the misallocation of resources, inefficiencies, waste, and less effort by managers. Therefore, before budgets are accepted, they must be carefully reviewed by immediate superiors. If changes from the original budget seem desirable, the items in question are discussed and modified as necessary by the mutual consent of the managers and their superiors.

All levels of an organization should work together to produce the budget. Since top management is generally unfamiliar with detailed day-to-day operations, it should rely on subordinates to provide detailed budget information. On the other hand, top management has a broader perspective on the goals for the company as a whole that is vital to budget preparation. Each level of responsibility in an organization should contribute in a *cooperative* effort to develop an integrated and realistic budget.

In an effort to ensure an effective budgeting process, many companies use a **budget committee**. This committee is typically responsible for overall policy matters related to the budget program and for coordinating the preparation of the budget itself. Committee membership usually consists of the president or CEO, heads of functional areas (e.g., sales, production, purchasing), and the controller. The budget committee handles any disagreements or problems that arise during the budgeting process, such as those between lower-level managers and their supervisors when budget reviews are being conducted. Importantly, the budget committee also approves the final budget and receives periodic progress reports regarding the company's success in meeting its targets.

Despite the advantages of participative budgets, some companies still assign budgets to their employees. The process of assigning (or imposing) budgets is often more efficient since it typically does not involve negotiations between managers and subordinates, which can take a considerable amount of time and effort. Moreover, in some circumstances, management may assign tough budgets to employees in the belief that attaining the budgets is necessary for the company's survival. Since employees are often unwilling to set highly challenging goals for themselves, imposing budgets may be deemed necessary for the sake of the long-term viability of the company.

> **Budget committee**
> A group of key management personnel responsible for overall policy matters related to the budget program, coordinating the preparation of the budget, handling disputes related to the budget, and approving the final budget.

IN BUSINESS

A survey of 720 members of the Institute of Management Accountants yielded some interesting insights into corporate budgeting practices. About 70% of the respondents indicated that budget development occurs via a participative process, whereby the final budget is the result of negotiations between higher-level and lower-level managers. The majority of respondents also indicated that positive behavioural consequences of the budget development process include the support of continuous improvement processes; the provision of information that allows managers to react to changes in the operating environment; and better information sharing among business units. Also, contrary to some common criticisms of budgeting, most respondents did not believe that budgets cause managers to focus on short-term results or create undue pressure for employees to achieve performance targets. The survey results also showed that budgeting is not a stand-alone process but instead is often integrated with other management practices. For example, of the respondents using activity-based costing, 75% integrate it with the annual budgeting process.

Source: Reproduced with permission of INSTITUTE OF MANAGEMENT ACCOUNTANTS, from Karen Shastri and David Stout, "Budgeting: Perspectives from the Real World," *Management Accounting Quarterly*, Fall 2008, pp. 18–25; permission conveyed through Copyright Clearance Center, Inc.

Behavioural Factors in Budgeting

Whether or not a budget program is accepted by lower management personnel will be reflective of (1) the degree to which top management accepts the budget program as a vital part of the company's activities, and (2) the way in which top management uses budgeted data. If a budget program is to be successful, it must have the complete acceptance and support of the persons who occupy key management positions. If lower- or middle-management personnel sense that top management simply tolerates budgeting as a necessary evil, then their own attitudes will reflect a similar lack of enthusiasm. If top management is not enthusiastic about and committed to the budget program, then it is unlikely that anyone else in the organization will be either.

It is easy to become preoccupied with the technical aspects of the budget to the exclusion of the behavioural aspects. Management should remember that the purposes of the budget are to motivate employees and to coordinate their efforts. Preoccupation with cost reductions in the budget or being rigid and inflexible is usually counterproductive and can lead to poor morale because people feel undervalued. An overemphasis on cost reduction rather than value creation can lead to budget games by which managers skillfully time revenues, expenditures, and investments in the short term, sometimes to the detriment of long-term performance. An important objective is that the budget be designed as a positive aid in achieving both individual and company goals.

An important issue in developing a budget is the difficulty of the targets. If the targets are too difficult, employees will quickly recognize that they are unattainable and motivation will suffer. If the targets are too easy, inefficiencies or less effort will result. Some experts argue that budget targets should be highly challenging and should require managers to stretch to meet them. A **stretch budget** is one that is highly difficult to attain and doing so often requires significant changes to the way the related task activities are performed. Even the most capable managers may have to scramble to meet stretch budget and they may not always succeed. However, in practice, most companies set their budget targets at a "challenging but attainable" level.[2] Such targets can usually be met by competent managers exerting reasonable effort, and are therefore motivating.

The difficulty level of budget targets becomes even more important when managers' bonuses are based on meeting or exceeding the budget. Under these commonly employed compensation schemes, a bonus is paid only if the budget is met. The bonus often increases when the budget target is exceeded, but is usually capped at some maximum level. For obvious reasons, managers who work under such a bonus plan, or whose performance is evaluated based on meeting budget targets, usually prefer to have challenging but attainable budgets rather than stretch budgets. Attainable budgets usually generate greater commitment to the budget and result in less undesirable behaviour by managers intent on earning their bonuses.

Stretch budget
A budget that is highly difficult to achieve. Attainment of stretch budgets often requires considerable changes to the way task activities are performed.

IN BUSINESS

Some leading companies such as Motorola, 3M, and General Electric have begun using stretch budgets as a means of motivating managers to come up with innovative and creative ways of improving performance. A stretch budget is by definition one that an individual has a low likelihood of attaining unless dramatic changes are made to current business activities and processes. For example, while a challenging but attainable revenue growth target might be 10% for the coming year, a stretch budget would involve a considerably more aggressive budget, such as 30% growth. Experts suggest that the keys to successfully using stretch budgets include (1) giving managers the autonomy and decision-making authority to make changes necessary to attain the budgets; (2) establishing an expedient review process whereby proposed changes, deemed necessary to attain the budgets, are quickly evaluated and approved by senior management; and (3) using an incentive system that rewards partial attainment of stretch budgets but does not punish failure. In the increasingly competitive operating environment faced by many companies, some are using stretch budgets to gain advantage.

Source: Reproduced with permission of INSTITUTE OF MANAGEMENT ACCOUNTANTS, from Clement Chen and Keith Jones, "Are Companies Really Ready for Stretch Targets?" *Management Accounting Quarterly*, Summer 2005, pp. 10–18; permission conveyed through Copyright Clearance Center, Inc.

Zero-Based Budgeting

In the traditional approach to budgeting, the manager starts with last year's budget and adds to it (or subtracts from it) according to anticipated needs. This is an incremental approach to budgeting in which the previous year's budget is taken for granted as a baseline.

Zero-base budgeting is an alternative approach that is sometimes used—particularly in the government and not-for-profit sectors of the economy. Under a **zero-base budget**, managers are required to justify *all* budgeted expenditures, not just changes in the budget from the previous year. The baseline is zero rather than last year's budget.

A zero-base budget requires considerable documentation. The manager must prepare a series of "decision packages" in which all of the activities of the department are ranked according to their relative importance and the cost of each activity is identified. Higher-level managers then review the decision packages and reduce those areas that appear to be less critical or whose costs do not appear to be justified.

A key issue for companies that use this approach is the frequency of the zero-base review. Critics argue that properly executed zero-base budgeting is too time-consuming and costly to justify on an annual basis. In addition, critics argue that annual reviews can become mechanical, limiting the benefits of zero-based budgeting. Whether a company should use an annual review is a matter of judgment. However, most managers agree that on occasion, zero-based reviews can be very helpful.

Zero-base budget
A method of budgeting in which managers are required to justify all costs as if the programs involved were being proposed for the first time.

■ THE MASTER BUDGET: AN OVERVIEW

The master budget consists of a number of separate but interdependent budgets. Exhibit 9–2 provides an overview of the various parts of the master budget and how they are related.

LEARNING OBJECTIVE 2
Prepare the supporting components of a master budget and the budgeted financial statements.

The Sales Budget A **sales budget** is a detailed schedule showing the expected sales for the budget period; typically, it is expressed in both dollars and units of product. An accurate sales budget is the key to the entire budgeting process. All of the other parts of the master budget are dependent on the sales budget in some way, as illustrated in Exhibit 9–2. So, if the sales budget is inaccurate, the rest of the budget will be inaccurate.

The sales budget will help determine how many units will have to be produced. For this reason, the production budget is prepared after the sales budget. The production budget in turn is used to determine the budgets for manufacturing costs, including the direct materials purchases budget, the direct labour budget, and the manufacturing overhead budget. These budgets are then combined with data from the sales budget and the selling and administrative expense budget to determine the cash budget. As shown in Exhibit 9–2, the selling and administrative expense budget is both dependent on and a determinant of the sales budget. This reciprocal relationship arises because sales will in part be determined by the funds committed for advertising and sales promotion.

Sales budget
A detailed schedule showing the expected sales for coming periods; these sales are typically expressed in both dollars and units.

The Cash Budget Once the operating budgets (sales, production, etc.) have been established, the cash budget and other financial budgets can be prepared. A **cash budget** is a detailed plan that shows how cash resources will be acquired and used over some specified time period. Observe from Exhibit 9–2 that all of the operating budgets have an impact on the cash budget. In the case of the sales budget, the impact comes from the planned cash receipts to be received from sales. In the case of the other budgets, the impact comes from the planned cash expenditures within the budgets themselves.

Cash budget
A detailed plan showing how cash resources will be acquired and used over a specified time period.

Sales Forecasting—A Critical Step

The sales budget is usually based on the company's *sales forecast.* Sales from prior years are often used as a starting point in preparing the sales forecast. In addition, the managers will examine the company's unfilled orders, the company's pricing policy and marketing

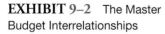
EXHIBIT 9–2   The Master Budget Interrelationships

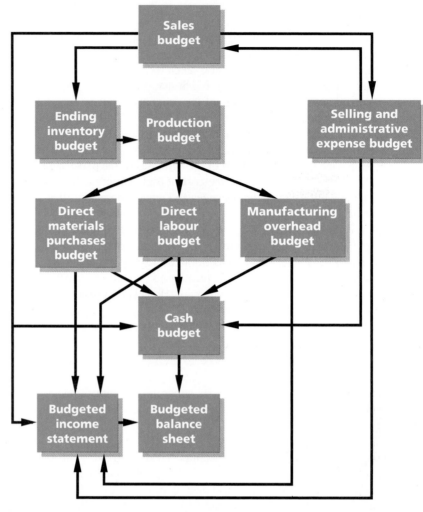

Note: For merchandising companies the production budget is replaced by a merchandise purchases budget and there would not be a manufacturing overhead budget.

Source: From SIROPOLIS. *SIROPOLIS SMALL BUS MGMT 5ED, 5E.* © 1994 South-Western, a part of Cengage Learning, Inc. Reproduced by permission. www.cengage.com/permissions.

plans, trends in the industry, and general economic conditions. Some companies utilize complex statistical tools to analyze the data and build models that predict the company's sales in the coming year. We will not go into the details of how these tools are used, as this is a topic more appropriately covered in marketing courses.

Preparing the Master Budget

Tom Wills is the majority shareholder and chief executive officer of Harrigan Freeze, Inc., a company he started in 2010.[3] The company makes premium popsicles using only natural ingredients and featuring exotic flavours such as tangy tangerine and minty mango. The company's business is highly seasonal, with most of the sales occurring in spring and summer.

In 2011, the company's second year of operations, there was a major cash crunch in the first and second quarters that almost forced the company into bankruptcy. In spite of this, 2011 turned out to be a very successful year overall in terms of both cash flow and net income. Toward the end of 2011, Tom decided to hire a professional financial manager. Tom interviewed several promising candidates for the job and settled on Larry Giano, who had considerable experience in the packaged foods industry.

Larry convinced Tom that to help avoid the problems experienced in 2011, a master budget should be prepared for 2012. In his planning for the budgeting process, Larry drew up the following list of documents that would be a part of the master budget:

1. A sales budget, including a schedule of expected cash collections.
2. A production budget.
3. A direct materials purchases budget, including a schedule of expected cash disbursements for raw materials.
4. A direct labour budget.
5. A manufacturing overhead budget.
6. An ending finished goods inventory budget.
7. A selling and administrative expense budget.
8. A cash budget.
9. A budgeted income statement.
10. A budgeted balance sheet.

Larry felt it was important to get everyone's cooperation in the budgeting process, so he asked Tom to call a companywide meeting at which the budgeting process would be explained. At the meeting, there was initially some grumbling, but Tom was able to convince nearly everyone of the necessity for planning and getting better control over spending. It helped that the cash crisis earlier in the year was still fresh in everyone's minds.

In the weeks that followed, Larry worked closely with all of the managers involved in the master budget, gathering data from them and making sure that they understood and fully supported the parts of the master budget that would affect them. In subsequent years, Larry hoped to turn the whole budgeting process over to the managers and to take a more advisory role.

The interdependent documents that Larry Giano prepared for Harrigan Freeze are Schedules 1 through 10 of his company's master budget. In the following sections, we will study these schedules.

The Sales Budget

The sales budget is the starting point in preparing the master budget. As shown earlier in Exhibit 9–2, all other items in the master budget, including production, purchases, inventories, and expenses, depend on it in some way.

The sales budget is constructed by multiplying the budgeted sales in units by the selling price. Schedule 1 contains the sales budget for Harrigan Freeze for the year 2012, by quarters. Notice from the schedule that the company plans to sell 100,000 cases of popsicles during the year, with sales peaking in the third quarter.

A schedule of expected cash collections, such as the one that appears in Schedule 1 for Harrigan Freeze, is prepared after the sales budget. This schedule will be needed later to prepare the cash budget. Cash collections consist of collections on sales made to customers in prior periods plus collections on sales made in the current budget period. At Harrigan Freeze, experience has shown that 70% of sales is collected in the quarter in which the sale is made and the remaining 30% is collected in the following quarter. So, for example, 70% of the first quarter sales of $200,000 (or $140,000) is collected during the first quarter and 30% (or $60,000) is collected during the second quarter.

The Production Budget

The **production budget** is prepared after the sales budget. The production budget lists the number of units that must be produced during each budget period to meet expected

Production budget
A detailed plan showing the number of units that must be produced during a period to meet both sales and inventory needs.

SCHEDULE 1

	A	B	C	D	E	F	G
	HARRIGAN FREEZE, INC.						
	Sales Budget						
1	**For the Year Ended December 31, 2012**						
2				**Quarter**			
3		**1**	**2**	**3**	**4**	**Year**	
4	Budgeted sales in units (cases of popsicles)	10,000	30,000	40,000	20,000	100,000	
5	Selling price per unit	$20	$20	$20	$20	$20	
6	Total sales	$200,000	$600,000	$800,000	$400,000	$2,000,000	
7			**Schedule of Expected Cash Collections**				
8	Accounts receivable, beginning balance*	$ 90,000				$ 90,000	
9	First-quarter sales ($200,000 × 70%, 30%)†	140,000	$ 60,000			200,000	
10	Second-quarter sales ($600,000 × 70%, 30%)		420,000	$180,000		600,000	
11	Third-quarter sales ($800,000 × 70%, 30%)			560,000	$240,000	800,000	
12	Fourth-quarter sales ($400,000 × 70%)‡				280,000	280,000	
13	Total cash collections	$230,000	$480,000	$740,000	$520,000	$1,970,000	
14							

Sheet1 / Sheet2 / Sheet3 /

*Cash collections from last year's fourth-quarter sales. See the December 31, 2011, balance sheet on page 368.

†Cash collections from sales are as follows: 70% collected in the quarter of sale, and the remaining 30% collected in the following quarter.

‡Uncollected fourth-quarter sales appear as accounts receivable on the company's end-of-year balance sheet (see Schedule 10 on page 367).

sales and to provide for the desired ending inventory. Production needs can be determined as follows:

Budgeted sales in units	XXXX
Add desired ending inventory	XXXX
Total needs	XXXX
Less beginning inventory	XXXX
Required production	XXXX

Schedule 2 contains the production budget for Harrigan Freeze.

Note that production requirements for a quarter are influenced by the desired level of the ending inventory. Inventories should be carefully planned. Excessive inventories tie up working capital and create storage problems. On the other hand, insufficient inventories can lead to lost sales or last-minute, high-cost production efforts. At Harrigan Freeze, management believes that an ending inventory equal to 20% of the next quarter's sales strikes the appropriate balance.

SCHEDULE 2

	A	B	C	D	E	F	G
	HARRIGAN FREEZE, INC.						
	Production Budget						
	For the Year Ended December 31, 2012						
1	**(in cases)**						
2				**Quarter**			
3		**1**	**2**	**3**	**4**	**Year**	
4	Budgeted sales (Schedule 1)	10,000	30,000	40,000	20,000	100,000	
5	Add desired ending inventory of finished goods*	6,000	8,000	4,000	3,000†	3,000	
6	Total needs	16,000	38,000	44,000	23,000	103,000	
7	Less beginning inventory of finished goods‡	2,000	6,000	8,000	4,000	2,000	
8	Required production	14,000	32,000	36,000	19,000	101,000	
9							

*Twenty percent of the next quarter's sales.

†Estimated.

‡The same as the prior quarter's ending inventory.

Inventory Purchases—Merchandising Firm

Harrigan Freeze prepares a production budget, since it is a *manufacturing* firm. If it was a *merchandising* firm, then instead of a production budget, it would prepare a merchandise purchases budget showing the amount of goods to be purchased from its suppliers during the period. The merchandise purchases budget is in the same basic format as the production budget, except that it shows goods to be purchased rather than goods to be produced, as shown below:

Budgeted sales	XXXX
Add desired ending merchandise inventory	XXXX
Total needs	XXXX
Less beginning merchandise inventory	XXXX
Required purchases	XXXX

The merchandising firm would prepare a merchandise purchases budget such as the one above for each item carried in inventory. The merchandise purchases budget can be expressed in terms of either units or the purchase cost of those units. So, for example, the budgeted sales shown in the table above can be expressed in terms of either the number of units sold or the purchase cost of the units sold. Some large retail organizations make such computations on a frequent basis (particularly at peak seasons) to ensure that adequate quantities are on hand to meet customer needs.

The Direct Materials Purchases Budget

After the production requirements have been computed, a **direct materials purchases budget** can be prepared. The direct materials purchases budget details the raw materials that must be purchased to meet the production budget and to provide for adequate inventories. The required purchases of raw materials are computed as follows:

Raw materials needed to meet the production schedule	XXXX
Add desired ending inventory of raw materials	XXXX
Total raw materials needs	XXXX
Less beginning inventory of raw materials	XXXX
Raw materials to be purchased	XXXX

Direct materials purchases budget
A detailed plan showing the amount of raw materials that must be purchased during a period to meet both production and inventory needs.

Schedule 3 contains the direct materials purchases budget for Harrigan Freeze. The only raw material included in that budget is high fructose sugar, which is the major ingredient in popsicles other than water. The remaining raw materials are relatively insignificant and are included in variable manufacturing overhead. Notice that materials requirements are first determined in units (kilograms, litres, and so on) and then translated into dollars by multiplying by the appropriate unit cost. Also note that the management of Harrigan Freeze wants to maintain ending inventories of sugar equal to 10% of the following quarter's production needs.

The first line in the direct materials purchases budget contains the required production for each quarter, which is taken directly from the production budget (Schedule 2). Looking at the first quarter, the key elements of the budget are as follows:

- Total production needs: 14,000 cases × 5 kilograms per case = 70,000 kilograms
- Desired ending inventory: 10% × 160,000 kilograms (the following quarter's needs) = 16,000 kilograms
- Total needs: 70,000 kilograms (production) + 16,000 (inventory) = 86,000 kilograms
- Total purchases: 86,000 kilograms (total needed) − 7,000 (opening inventory) = 79,000 kilograms
- Total purchase cost: 79,000 kilograms × $0.60 per kilogram = $47,400

SCHEDULE 3

	A	B	C	D	E	F	G
	HARRIGAN FREEZE, INC.						
1	Direct Materials Purchases Budget For the Year Ended December 31, 2012						
2				Quarter			
3		1	2	3	4	Year	
4	Units to be produced (Schedule 2)	14,000	32,000	36,000	19,000	101,000	
5	Raw materials needed per unit (kilograms)	5	5	5	5	5	
6	Production needs (kilograms)	70,000	160,000	180,000	95,000	505,000	
7	Add desired ending inventory of raw materials (kilograms)*	16,000	18,000	9,500	7,500	7,500	
8	Total needs (kilograms)	86,000	178,000	189,500	102,500	512,500	
9	Less beginning inventory of raw materials (kilograms)	7,000	16,000	18,000	9,500	7,000	
10	Raw materials to be purchased (kilograms)	79,000	162,000	171,500	93,000	505,500	
11	Cost of raw materials to be purchased at $0.60 per kilogram	$ 47,400	$ 97,200	$ 102,900	$ 55,800	$ 303,300	
12	*10% of the next quarter's production needs. For example, the second-quarter production needs are 160,000 kilograms. Therefore, the desired ending inventory for the first quarter would be 10%×160,000 kilograms = 16,000 kilograms. The ending inventory of 7,500 kilograms for the fourth quarter is estimated.						
13	Schedule of Expected Cash Disbursements for Materials						
14	Accounts payable 12/31/11	$ 25,800				$ 25,800	
15	First-quarter purchases ($47,400 x 50%, 50%)	23,700	$ 23,700			47,400	
16	Second-quarter purchases ($97,200 x 50%, 50%)		48,600	$ 48,600		97,200	
17	Third-quarter purchases ($102,900 x 50%, 50%)			51,450	$ 51,450	102,900	
18	Fourth-quarter purchases ($55,800 x 50%)				27,900	27,900	
19	Total cash disbursements	$ 49,500	$ 72,300	$ 100,050	$ 79,350	$ 301,200	
20							

As with the production budget, the amounts listed under the Year column are not always the sum of the quarterly amounts. The desired ending inventory of raw materials for the year is the same as the desired ending inventory of raw materials for the fourth quarter. Likewise, the beginning inventory of raw materials for the year is the same as the beginning inventory of raw materials for the first quarter.

The direct materials purchases budget is usually accompanied by a schedule of expected cash disbursements for raw materials. This schedule is needed to prepare the overall cash budget. Disbursements for raw materials consist of payments for purchases on account in prior periods plus any payments for purchases in the current budget period. Schedule 3 contains such a schedule of cash disbursements.

Ordinarily, companies do not immediately pay their suppliers. At Harrigan Freeze, the policy is to pay for 50% of purchases in the quarter in which the purchase is made and 50% in the following quarter. So, while the company intends to purchase $47,400 worth of sugar in the first quarter, the company will pay for only half, $23,700, in the first quarter and the other half will be paid in the second quarter. The company will also pay $25,800 in the first quarter for sugar that was purchased on account in the previous quarter, but not yet paid for. This is the beginning balance in the accounts payable. Therefore, the total cash disbursements for sugar in the first quarter are $49,500 minus the $25,800 payment for sugar acquired in the previous quarter plus the $23,700 payment for sugar acquired during the first quarter.

The Direct Labour Budget

Direct labour budget
A detailed plan showing labour requirements over a specified time period.

The **direct labour budget** is also developed from the production budget. By knowing in advance what will be needed in terms of labour time throughout the budget year, the company can develop plans to adjust the labour force as required. Firms that neglect to budget face the risk of labour shortages or having to hire and lay off employees at awkward times. Erratic labour policies can lead to insecurity and inefficiency on the part of employees.

To compute direct labour requirements, the number of units of finished product to be produced each period (month, quarter, and so on) is multiplied by the number of direct labour hours required to produce a single unit. For example, 14,000 cases are to be produced in the first quarter and each case requires 0.40 direct labour-hours, so a total of 5,600 direct labour-hours (14,000 cases × 0.40 direct labour-hours per case) will be required. The direct labour requirements can then be translated into expected direct labour costs. How this is done will depend on the labour policy of the firm. In Schedule 4, the management of Harrigan Freeze has assumed that the direct labour force will be adjusted as the work requirements change from quarter to quarter. In that case, the total direct labour cost is computed simply by multiplying the direct labour-hour requirements by the direct labour rate per hour. For example, the direct labour cost in the first quarter is $84,000 (5,600 direct labour-hours × $15 per direct labour-hour).

SCHEDULE 4

HARRIGAN FREEZE, INC.
Direct Labour Purchasing Budget
For the Year Ended December 31, 2012

	Quarter				
	1	2	3	4	Year
Units (cases) to be produced (Schedule 2)	14,000	32,000	36,000	19,000	101,000
Direct labour time per unit (hours)	0.4	0.4	0.4	0.4	0.4
Total hours of direct labour time needed	5,600	12,800	14,400	7,600	40,400
Direct labour cost per hour	$ 15.00	$ 15.00	$ 15.00	$ 15.00	$ 15.00
Total direct labour cost*	$ 84,000	$ 192,000	$ 216,000	$ 114,000	$ 606,000

*This schedule assumes that the direct labour workforce will be fully adjusted to the workload (i.e., "Total hours of direct labour time needed") each quarter.

However, many companies have employment policies or contracts that prevent them from laying off and rehiring workers as needed. Suppose, for example, that Harrigan Freeze has 25 workers who are classified as direct labour and each of them is guaranteed at least 480 hours of pay each quarter at a rate of $15 per hour. In that case, the minimum direct labour cost for a quarter would be as follows:

$$25 \text{ workers} \times 480 \text{ hours} \times \$15 = \$180,000$$

Note that in this case, the direct labour costs for the first and fourth quarters would have to be increased to $180,000.

The Manufacturing Overhead Budget

The **manufacturing overhead budget** provides a schedule of all costs of production other than direct materials and direct labour. Schedule 5 shows the manufacturing overhead budget for Harrigan Freeze. Note how the production costs are separated into variable and fixed components. The variable component is $4 per direct labour-hour. The fixed component is $60,600 per quarter. Because the variable component of the manufacturing overhead depends on direct labour, the first line in the manufacturing overhead budget consists of the budgeted direct labour-hours from the direct labour budget (Schedule 4). The budgeted direct labour-hours in each quarter are multiplied by the variable overhead rate to determine the variable component of manufacturing overhead. For example, the variable manufacturing overhead for the first quarter is

$$\$22,400 = 5,600 \text{ (direct labour-hours)} \times \$4.00 \text{ per direct labour-hour}$$

This is added to the fixed manufacturing overhead for the quarter to determine the total manufacturing overhead for the quarter as follows: $83,000 = $22,400 (variable) + $60,600 (fixed).

In most cases, fixed costs are the costs of supplying capacity to do things like make products, process purchase orders, handle customer calls, and so on. The amount of capacity that will be utilized depends on the expected level of activity for the period. If the expected

Manufacturing overhead budget
A detailed plan showing the indirect production costs that will be incurred over a specified time period.

SCHEDULE 5

	A	B	C	D	E	F	G
1			HARRIGAN FREEZE, INC.				
2			Manufacturing Overhead Budget				
3			For the Year Ended December 31, 2012				
4							
5				Quarter			
6			1	2	3	4	Year
7	Budgeted direct labour-hours (Schedule 4)		5,600	12,800	14,400	7,600	40,400
8	Variable overhead rate	$ 4.00	$ 4.00	$ 4.00	$ 4.00	$ 4.00	
9	Variable manufacturing overhead	$ 22,400	$ 51,200	$ 57,600	$ 30,400	$ 161,600	
10	Fixed manufacturing overhead	60,600	60,600	60,600	60,600	242,400	
11	Total manufacturing overhead	83,000	111,800	118,200	91,000	404,000	
12	Less depreciation	(15,000)	(15,000)	(15,000)	(15,000)	(60,000)	
13	Cash disbursements for manufacturing overhead	$ 68,000	$ 96,800	$ 103,200	$ 76,000	$ 344,000	
14							
15	Total manufacturing overhead (a)					$ 404,000	
16	Budgeted direct labour-hours (b)					40,400	
17	Predetermined overhead rate for the year (a)÷(b)					$ 10,00	
18							
19							

Schedule 1 / Schedule 2 / Schedule 3 / Schedule 4 \ **Schedule 5** / Schedule

level of activity is greater than the company's current capacity, then fixed costs may have to be increased. Or, if the expected level is appreciably below the company's current capacity, then it may be desirable to decrease fixed costs if that is possible. However, once the level of fixed costs has been determined in the budget, the costs really are fixed. Therefore, the time to adjust fixed costs is during the budgeting process. To determine the appropriate level of fixed costs at budget time, an activity-based costing system, as described in Chapter 5, can be very helpful. It can help answer questions like "How many clerks will we need to hire to process the anticipated number of purchase orders next year?" For simplicity, we assume in all of the budgeting examples in this book that the appropriate levels of fixed costs have already been determined for the budget with the aid of activity-based costing or some other method.

The last line of Schedule 5 for Harrigan Freeze shows its budgeted cash disbursements for manufacturing overhead. Since some of the overhead costs are not cash outflows, the total budgeted manufacturing overhead costs must be adjusted to determine the cash disbursements for manufacturing overhead. At Harrigan Freeze, the only significant non-cash manufacturing overhead cost is depreciation, which is $15,000 per quarter. These non-cash depreciation charges are deducted from the total budgeted manufacturing overhead to determine the expected cash disbursements. Harrigan Freeze pays all overhead costs involving cash disbursements in the quarter incurred. Note that the company's predetermined overhead rate for the year will be $10 per direct labour-hour, which is determined by dividing the total budgeted manufacturing overhead for the year by the total budgeted direct labour-hours for the year.

The Ending Finished Goods Inventory Budget

After completing Schedules 1 through 5, Larry Giano had all of the data he needed to compute unit product costs. This computation was needed for two reasons: first, to determine cost of goods sold on the budgeted income statement and second, to identify the amount to put on the balance sheet inventory account for unsold units. The carrying cost of the unsold units is computed on the **ending finished goods inventory budget**.

Ending finished goods inventory budget
A budget showing the dollar amount of cost expected to appear on the balance sheet for unsold units at the end of a period.

Larry Giano considered using variable costing (see Chapter 8) in preparing Harrigan Freeze's budget statements, but he decided to use absorption costing instead since the bank would very likely require that absorption costing be used. He also knew that it would be easy to convert the absorption costing financial statements to a variable costing basis later. At this point, the primary concern was to determine what financing, if any, would be required in the year 2012 and then to arrange for that financing from the bank.

The unit product cost computations are shown in Schedule 6. For Harrigan Freeze, the absorption costing unit product cost is $13 per case of popsicles—consisting of $3 of direct materials, $6 of direct labour, and $4 of manufacturing overhead. For convenience, the manufacturing overhead is applied to units of product on the basis of direct labour-hours. The budgeted carrying cost of the expected ending inventory is $39,000.

SCHEDULE 6

	A	B	C	D	F	G
	HARRIGAN FREEZE, INC.					
	Ending Finished Goods Inventory Budget					
	(absorption costing basis)					
1	**For the Year Ended December 31, 2012**					
2						
3	Item	Quantity	Cost	Total		
4	Production cost per unit (case):					
5	Direct materials	5.0 kilograms	$0.60 per kilogram	$ 3		
6	Direct labour	0.4 hours	$15.00 per hour	6		
7	Manufacturing overhead	0.4 hours	$10.00 per hour	4		
8	Unit product cost			$13		
9						
10	Budgeted finished goods inventory:					
11	Ending finished goods inventory in units (Schedule 2)			3,000		
12	Unit product cost (see above)			× $13		
13	Ending finished goods inventory in dollars			$39,000		
14						

Ready   NUM

The Selling and Administrative Expense Budget

The **selling and administrative expense budget** lists the budgeted expenses for areas other than manufacturing. In large organizations, this budget would be a compilation of many smaller, individual budgets submitted by department heads and other persons responsible for selling and administrative expenses. For example, the marketing manager in a large organization would submit a budget detailing the advertising expenses for each budget period.

Schedule 7 contains the selling and administrative expense budget for Harrigan Freeze. Like the manufacturing overhead budget, the selling and administrative expense budget is divided into variable and fixed cost components. For Harrigan Freeze, the variable selling and administrative expense is $1.80 per case. Consequently, budgeted sales in cases for each quarter are entered at the top of the schedule. These data are taken from the sales budget (Schedule 1). The budgeted variable selling and administrative expenses are

Selling and administrative expense budget
A detailed schedule of planned expenses that will be incurred in areas other than manufacturing during a budget period.

SCHEDULE 7

	A	B	C	D	E	F
	HARRIGAN FREEZE, INC.					
	Selling and Administrative Expense Budget					
1	**For the Year Ended December 31, 2012**					
2				Quarter		
3		1	2	3	4	Year
4	Budgeted sales in cases (Schedule 1)	10,000	30,000	40,000	20,000	100,000
5	Variable selling and administrative expenses per case*	$1.80	$1.80	$1.80	$1.80	$1.80
6	Budgeted variable expense	$18,000	$ 54,000	$ 72,000	$ 36,000	$180,000
7	Budgeted fixed selling and administrative expenses					
8	Advertising	40,000	40,000	40,000	40,000	160,000
9	Executive salaries	35,000	35,000	35,000	35,000	140,000
10	Insurance	9,912	9,912	9,912	9,912	39,648
11	Property taxes	4,538	4,538	4,538	4,538	18,152
12	Depreciation	2,000	2,000	2,000	2,000	8,000
13	Total budgeted fixed selling and administrative expenses	91,450	91,450	91,450	91,450	365,800
14	Total budgeted selling and administrative expenses	109,450	145,450	163,450	127,450	545,800
15	Less depreciation expense	(2,000)	(2,000)	(2,000)	(2,000)	(8,000)
16	Less insurance expense	(9,912)	(9,912)	(9,912)	(9,912)	(39,648)
17	Add insurance premium payment		1,900	37,750		39,650
18	Less property tax expense	(4,538)	(4,538)	(4,538)	(4,538)	(18,152)
19	Add property tax paid				18,150	18,150
20	Cash disbursements for selling and administrative expenses	$93,000	$130,900	$184,750	$129,150	$537,800
21						

Ready   NUM

*Commissions, clerical, and shipping.

determined by multiplying the budgeted cases sold by the variable selling and administrative expense per case. For example, the budgeted variable selling and administrative expense for the first quarter is $18,000 (10,000 cases × $1.80 per case). The fixed selling and administrative expenses (all given data) are then added to the variable selling and administrative expenses to arrive at the total budgeted selling and administrative expenses.

Finally, to determine the cash disbursements for selling and administrative expenses, the total budgeted expenses are adjusted by subtracting any non-cash items included in the budget, and adding any cash expenditures not reflected in the budgeted amounts. As shown in Schedule 7, three items must be subtracted: depreciation of $2,000 per quarter because this is a non-cash expense; insurance of $9,912 per quarter because although this is an expense under accrual accounting, it does not represent an actual outflow of cash each quarter; and property taxes of $4,538 because this too is an expense under accrual accounting, but not a cash outflow each quarter. Two cash disbursements are added: the insurance premium payments of $1,900 and $37,750 in the second and third quarters, respectively, and the property tax payment of $18,150 made in the fourth quarter. Each of these additions is necessary to reflect the actual timing of the cash outflows for insurance premiums and property taxes.

The Cash Budget

As illustrated in Exhibit 9–2 on page 356, the cash budget integrates much of the data developed in the preceding steps. It is a good idea to review Exhibit 9–2 to get the big picture firmly in mind before moving on.

The cash budget is composed of four major sections:

1. Receipts section.
2. Disbursements section.
3. Cash excess or deficiency section.
4. Financing section.

The receipts section consists of a listing of all of the cash inflows (except for financing) expected during the budget period. Generally, the major source of receipts will be from sales.

The disbursements section consists of all cash payments that are planned for the budget period. These payments will include raw materials purchases, direct labour payments, manufacturing overhead costs, and so on, as contained in their respective budgets. In addition, other cash disbursements, such as equipment purchases, dividends, and other cash withdrawals by owners, are included.

The cash excess or deficiency section is computed as follows:

Cash balance, beginning	XXXX
Add receipts	XXXX
Total cash available before financing	XXXX
Less disbursements	XXXX
Excess (deficiency) of cash available over disbursements	XXXX

If there is a cash deficiency during any budget period, the company will need to borrow funds. If there is a cash excess during any budget period, funds borrowed in previous periods can be repaid or the excess funds can be invested.

The financing section provides a detailed account of the borrowings and repayments projected to take place during the budget period. It also includes the details of interest payments that will be due on money borrowed. A well-coordinated budgeting program eliminates uncertainty as to what the cash situation will be in two months, six months, or a year from now.

The cash budget should be broken down into time periods that are short enough to capture major fluctuations in cash balances. While a monthly cash budget is most common, many firms budget cash on a weekly or even daily basis. Larry Giano has prepared a quarterly cash budget for Harrigan Freeze that can be further refined as necessary. This budget appears in Schedule 8. The cash budget builds on the earlier schedules and on additional data that are provided as follows:

- The beginning cash balance is $42,500.
- Management plans to spend $50,000 during the year on equipment purchases: $30,000 in the first quarter and $20,000 in the second quarter.
- The board of directors has approved cash dividends of $17,500 per quarter.
- Management would like to have a cash balance of at least $40,000 at the beginning of each quarter for contingencies.
- Harrigan Freeze has an open line of credit with a bank that enables the company to borrow funds as needed at a 5% annual interest rate to a maximum total loan balance of $250,000. To simplify the calculations in the example: (1) all borrowing and repayments are in round $500 amounts and (2) all borrowing occurs at the beginning of quarters and all repayments are made at the end of quarters. To simplify our example, we assume that interest is due when repayments are made and only on the amount of principal that is repaid. However, in practice, banks and other creditors typically require interest payments each month based on the average loan balance outstanding for that period.

SCHEDULE 8

HARRIGAN FREEZE, INC.
Cash Budget
For the Year Ended December 31, 2012

	Schedule	Quarter 1	2	3	4	Year
Cash balance, beginning		$42,500	$40,000	$40,000	$40,100	$42,500
Add receipts:						
Collections from customers	1	230,000	480,000	740,000	520,000	1,970,000
Total cash available before current financing		272,500	520,000	780,000	560,100	2,012,500
Less disbursements:						
Direct materials	3	49,500	72,300	100,050	79,350	301,200
Direct labour	4	84,000	192,000	216,000	114,000	606,000
Manufacturing overhead	5	68,000	96,800	103,200	76,000	344,000
Selling and administrative	7	93,000	130,900	184,750	129,150	537,800
Income taxes	9	11,000	11,000	11,000	11,000	44,000
Equipment purchases		30,000	20,000	—	—	50,000
Dividends		17,500	17,500	17,500	17,500	70,000
Total disbursements		353,000	540,500	632,500	427,000	1,953,000
Excess (deficiency) of cash available over disbursements		(80,500)	(20,500)	147,500	133,100	59,500
Financing:						
Borrowings (at beginning)		120,500	60,500	—	—	181,000
Repayments (at end)		—	—	(103,500)	(77,500)	(181,000)
Interest (at 5% per annum)*		—	—	(3,900)	(3,120)	(7,020)
Total financing		120,500	60,500	(107,400)	(80,620)	(7,020)
Cash balance, ending		$40,000	$40,000	$40,100	$52,480	$52,480

*The interest payments relate only to the principal being repaid at the time it is repaid. For example, the interest in quarter 3 relates only to the interest due on the $103,500 principal being repaid from quarter 1 borrowing, as follows: $103,500 × 5% × 3/4 = $3,900 (rounded up from $3,881). The interest paid in quarter 4 is computed as follows:

$17,000 × 5% × 1 year . . . . $ 850
$60,500 × 5% × 3/4 2,270
Total interest paid $3,120

The cash budget is prepared one quarter at a time, starting with the first quarter. Larry began the cash budget by entering the beginning cash balance of $42,500 for the first quarter. Receipts—in this case, just the $230,000 in cash collections from customers—are added to the beginning balance to arrive at the total cash available of $272,500. Since the total disbursements are $353,000 and the total cash available is only $272,500, there is a shortfall of $80,500. Since management would like to have a beginning cash balance of at least $40,000 for the second quarter, the company will need to borrow $120,500.

Required Borrowings at the End of the First Quarter	
Desired ending cash balance.	$ 40,000
Plus deficiency of cash available over disbursements.	80,500
Required borrowings	$120,500

The second quarter of the cash budget is handled similarly. Note that the ending cash balance for the first quarter is brought forward as the beginning cash balance for the second quarter. Also note that additional borrowing is required in the second quarter because of the continuing cash shortfall.

Required Borrowings at the End of the Second Quarter	
Desired ending cash balance.	$40,000
Plus deficiency of cash available over disbursements.	20,500
Required borrowings	$60,500

In the third quarter, the cash flow situation improves dramatically and the excess of cash available over disbursements is $147,500. This makes it possible for the company to repay part of its loan from the bank, which now totals $181,000. How much can be repaid?

The total amount of the principal and interest that can be repaid is determined as follows:

Total Maximum Feasible Loan Payments at the End of the Third Quarter	
Excess of cash available over disbursements	$147,500
Less desired ending cash balance.	40,000
Maximum feasible principal and interest payment	$107,500

The next step—figuring out the exact amount of the loan payment—is tricky since interest must be paid on the principal amount that is repaid. In this case, the principal amount that is repaid must be less than $107,500, so we know that we would be paying off part of the loan that was taken out at the beginning of the first quarter. Since the repayment would be made at the end of the third quarter, interest would have accrued for three quarters. So the interest owed would be $3/4$ of 5%, or 3.75%. For simplicity, we use a simple rather than compound interest rate. An algebraic approach will lead to the conclusion that the maximum principal repayment that can be made is $103,500 (rounded). The interest payment would be 3.75% of this amount, or $3,900 (rounded up from $3,881)—making the total payment $107,400.[4]

In the case of Harrigan Freeze, all loans have been repaid by year-end. If all loans are not repaid and a budgeted income statement or balance sheet is being prepared, then interest must be accrued on the unpaid loans. This interest will *not* appear on the cash budget (since it has not yet been paid), but it will appear as part of interest expense on the budgeted income statement and as a liability on the budgeted balance sheet.

As with the production and raw materials budgets, the amounts under the Year column in the cash budget are not always the sum of the amounts for the four quarters. In particular, the beginning cash balance for the year is the same as the beginning cash balance for the first quarter and the ending cash balance is the same as the ending cash balance for the fourth quarter. Also, note that the beginning cash balance for any quarter is the same as the ending cash balance for the previous quarter.

The Budgeted Income Statement

A budgeted income statement can be prepared from the data developed in Schedules 1–8. *The budgeted income statement is one of the key schedules in the budget process.* It shows the company's planned profit for the upcoming budget period, and it stands as a benchmark against which actual company performance can be measured. Schedule 9 contains the budgeted income statement for Harrigan Freeze.

SCHEDULE 9

	A	B	C	D	E	F	G
1	**HARRIGAN FREEZE, INC.** **Budgeted Income Statement** **For the Year Ended December 31, 2012**	Schedule					
2							
3	Sales (100,000 units at $20)	1	$ 2,000,000				
4	Less cost of goods sold (100,000 units at $13)	6	1,300,000				
5	Gross margin		700,000				
6	Less selling and administrative expenses	7	545,800				
7	Operating income		154,200				
8	Less interest expense	8	7,020				
9	Net income before income taxes		147,180				
10	Income taxes (30% × $147,180)		44,000*				
11	Net income		$ 103,180				

*Difference of $154 due to rounding (0.3 × $147,180 = $44,154).

The Budgeted Balance Sheet

The budgeted balance sheet is developed by beginning with the balance sheet for the fiscal period just ended, and adjusting it for the data contained in the other budgets. Harrigan Freeze's budgeted balance sheet is presented in Schedule 10.

SCHEDULE 10

	A	B	C	D	E	F	G
1	**HARRIGAN FREEZE, INC.** **Budgeted Balance Sheet** **December 31, 2012**						
2	**Assets**						
3	Current assets:						
4	Cash	$ 52,480	(a)				
5	Accounts receivable	120,000	(b)				
6	Raw materials inventory	4,500	(c)				
7	Finished goods inventory	39,000	(d)				
8	Total current assets			$ 215,980			
9	Plant and equipment:						
10	Land	80,000	(e)				
11	Buildings and equipment	750,000	(f)				
12	Accumulated depreciation	(360,000)	(g)				
13	Plant and equipment, net			470,000			
14	Total assets			$ 685,980			
15	**Liabilities and Shareholders' Equity**						
16	Current liabilities:						
17	Accounts payable (raw materials)			$ 27,900	(h)		
18	Shareholders' equity:						
19	Common shares	$ 175,000	(i)				
20	Retained earnings	483,080	(j)				
21	Total shareholders' equity			658,080			
22	Total liabilities and shareholders' equity			$ 685,980			
23							

Explanation of December 31, 2012, balance sheet figures:

a. The ending cash balance, as projected by the cash budget in Schedule 8.
b. Thirty percent of fourth-quarter sales, from Schedule 1 ($400,000 × 30% = $120,000).
c. From Schedule 3, the ending raw materials inventory will be 7,500 kilograms. This material costs $0.60 per kilogram. Therefore, the ending inventory in dollars will be 7,500 kilograms × $0.60 = $4,500.
d. From Schedule 6.
e. From the December 31, 2011, balance sheet (no change).
f. The December 31, 2011, balance sheet indicated a balance of $700,000. During 2012, $50,000 additional equipment will be purchased (see Schedule 8), bringing the December 31, 2012, balance to $750,000.
g. The December 31, 2011, balance sheet indicated a balance of $292,000. During 2012, $68,000 of depreciation will be taken ($60,000 on Schedule 5 and $8,000 on Schedule 7), bringing the December 31, 2012, balance to $360,000.
h. One-half of the fourth-quarter raw materials purchases, from Schedule 3.
i. From the December 31, 2011, balance sheet (no change).
j. December 31, 2011, balance $449,900
   Add net income, from Schedule 9   103,180
                                                      553,080
   Deduct dividends paid, from Schedule 8 . . .   70,000
   December 31, 2012, balance $483,080

Some of the data on the budgeted balance sheet have been taken from the company's end-of-year balance sheet for 2011, which appears below:

HARRIGAN FREEZE, INC.
Balance Sheet
December 31, 2011

Assets

Current assets:

Cash	$ 42,500	
Accounts receivable	90,000	
Raw materials inventory (7,000 kilograms)	4,200	
Finished goods inventory (2,000 cases)	26,000	
Total current assets		$162,700

Plant and equipment:

Land	80,000	
Buildings and equipment	700,000	
Accumulated depreciation	(292,000)	
Plant and equipment, net		488,000
Total assets		$650,700

Liabilities and Shareholders' Equity

Current liabilities:

Accounts payable (raw materials)		$ 25,800

Shareholders' equity:

Common shares	$175,000	
Retained earnings	449,900	
Total shareholders' equity		624,900
Total liabilities and shareholders' equity		$650,700

It is worth pointing out that we have simplified the treatment of income taxes on the income statement (Schedule 9) by assuming an effective rate of 30%. Most for-profit corporations in Canada are required to pay income taxes on taxable income but the calculation of the effective rate is a complex matter, which is typically covered in introductory courses on taxation. However, companies who budget positive operating income will calculate a budgeted effective tax rate and include income tax expense as an additional item on the budgeted income statement, as we have done in our example.

IN BUSINESS

The example presented in this chapter on preparing a master budget illustrates how much time and effort goes into the process. Imagine how much more effort would be required to prepare a master budget for a company with multiple divisions operating in different countries. Given the increasing complexity of organizations over the past few decades, many have questioned whether the benefits of preparing detailed operating budgets exceed the costs. A survey of 212 managers directly involved in the budgeting process at U.S. companies gathered evidence on their perceptions of both the benefits and limitations of budgets.

Over 70% of the respondents agreed that budgets are indispensable as a management tool. When asked to give the budgeting process an overall score with respect to the value added to the organization, the average grade assigned was 70 out of 100. Further, over 33% of the managers gave the budgeting process a grade of 80 or above. Importantly, managers were asked to assign this grade after taking into account the cost of preparing budgets (time and effort) and the dysfunctional consequences (e.g., budget slack) that might occur when budgets are used as a control tool.

Many of the key criticisms of the budgeting process identified by managers relate to how quickly it can become out of date if significant changes occur in the organization's operating environment. Nearly 50% of the respondents indicated that to combat this problem, they either prepare rolling budgets or use a form of flexible budget (discussed later in this chapter) in an effort to retain the control benefits of the budget process. Overall, while the budgeting process is not without its problems, this study showed that many managers continue to believe the benefits exceed the costs.

Source: Theresa Libby and Murray Lindsay, "Beyond Budgeting or Better Budgeting," *Strategic Finance*, August 2007, pp. 47–51.

FLEXIBLE BUDGET

The budgets presented in Schedules 1–10 are static budgets. A **static budget** is prepared only for the planned or budgeted level of activity. In our example, that level of activity was the forecast sales volume of 100,000 units. While this approach is suitable for planning purposes, it can be inadequate for control purposes if the actual level of activity during a period differs significantly from the budgeted level. Specifically, the problem that arises when a significant difference exists between actual and budgeted levels of activity is that it becomes very difficult to evaluate how well a manager did in generating revenues and controlling costs. For example, if actual activity levels are higher than expected, actual revenues and variable costs will be higher than static budget amounts. Should we conclude that the manager did a good job in generating revenues, but not so well in controlling costs? Clearly this would not be a fair evaluation since the reason that costs are above budget is that the volume of actual activity exceeded the static budget amount. Thus, an alternative approach is needed to restore the usefulness of budgets as a control tool.

Flexible budgets take into account changes in revenues and costs that should occur as a consequence of changes in activity. A **flexible budget** provides estimates of what revenues and costs should be for any level of activity within a specified range. When a flexible budget is used in performance evaluation, actual revenues and costs are compared to what the *revenues and costs should have been for the actual level of activity during the period* rather than to the planned budgeted revenues and costs from the static budget. This is a very important distinction—particularly for variable costs. If adjustments for the level of activity are not made it is very difficult to interpret differences between actual and budgeted revenues and costs.

> **LEARNING OBJECTIVE 3**
> Prepare a flexible budget and explain the need for the flexible budget approach
>
> **Static budget**
> A budget designed for only the planned level of activity.
>
> **Flexible budget**
> A budget that provides estimates of what revenues and costs should be for any level of activity within a specified range.

How a Flexible Budget Works

The basic idea of the flexible budget approach is that the budget is adjusted to show what revenues and costs *should be* for a specific level of activity. To illustrate how a flexible budget works, we use the data from the Harrigan Freeze, Inc., example to develop income statements for different levels of activity within a range of annual sales of 90,000 units to 110,000 units. To simplify the example, we have omitted interest expense and income tax expense, although both could easily be included using the steps presented in preparing the static budget. Note that although Exhibit 9–3 presents an annual flexible budget, the same approach can be used in developing flexible budgets for shorter reporting periods such as quarters or months. Also note that the flexible budget income statements in Exhibit 9–3 have been prepared using the variable costing approach covered in Chapter 8. As a result, the operating income shown in Exhibit 9–3 for sales of 100,000 units is $151,800 while the operating income shown in Schedule 9 on page 367 is $154,200. This difference of $2,400 arises because operating income in Schedule 9 was calculated using absorption costing and an additional 1,000 units of finished goods inventory were added in 2012 (Schedule 2). The additional manufacturing overhead deferred in finished goods inventory using absorption costing is $2,400: 1,000 units $\times$ $2.40 per unit of fixed overhead ($6 per hour $\times$ 0.4 hours per unit). The rate of $6 per hour for fixed overhead is based on the total

EXHIBIT 9–3   Flexible Budget Income Statement

HARRIGAN FREEZE, INC.
Flexible Budget
For the Year Ended December 31, 2012

	Budgeted Amount Per Unit	Sales in Units		
		90,000	100,000	110,000
Sales	$20.00	$1,800,000	$2,000,000	$2,200,000
Less variable expenses				
Direct materials*	3.00	270,000	300,000	330,000
Direct labour*	6.00	540,000	600,000	660,000
Variable manufacturing overhead#	1.60	144,000	160,000	176,000
Selling and administrative+	1.80	162,000	180,000	198,000
Total variable expenses	12.40	1,116,000	1,240,000	1,364,000
Contribution margin	$ 7.60	684,000	760,000	836,000
Less fixed expenses				
Manufacturing overhead**		242,400	242,400	242,400
Selling and administrative##		365,800	365,800	365,800
Total fixed expenses		608,200	608,200	608,200
Operating income		$ 75,800	$ 151,800	$ 227,800

*Per unit amount as per Schedule 6
#Variable overhead cost per hour (Schedule 5) multiplied by hours per unit (Schedule 6): $4 × 0.4 = $1.60
+Per unit amount as per Schedule 7
**Total budgeted fixed overhead expense as per Schedule 5
##Total budgeted fixed selling and administrative expenses as per Schedule 7

rate of $10 per hour (Schedule 6) less $4 per hour for variable overhead (Schedule 5). We use variable costing to emphasize the revenue and cost behaviour patterns expected over this relevant range of activity. Specifically, the selling price and variable costs per unit are expected to remain constant, while total fixed costs are not expected to change over the relevant range.

The calculation of the revenues and expenses in Exhibit 9–3 is straightforward. The amounts *per unit* for sales and variable expenses are multiplied by the activity level (units) to arrive at the totals for the year. For example, for an activity level of 90,000 units, total sales are calculated as $20.00 × 90,000 = $1,800,000. Each of the variable expense line items is calculated in a similar fashion. Fixed costs are not expected to change over the relevant range of activity so they stay the same for each activity level shown in Exhibit 9–3. The flexible budget provides a useful tool in estimating operating income at different levels of activity. As illustrated in Exhibit 9–3, a 10,000 unit change in sales volume, above or below the budgeted level of 100,000 units, causes a $76,000 change in operating income, which can be calculated as 10,000 units × $7.60 per unit contribution margin. Importantly, a flexible budget can be developed for any level of activity within the relevant range of activity. Thus, if actual sales volume for the year is 95,000 units, a flexible budget can be prepared showing what revenues and costs should have been for that level of activity.

USING THE FLEXIBLE BUDGETING CONCEPT IN PERFORMANCE EVALUATION

LEARNING OBJECTIVE 4
Prepare a performance report using the flexible budget approach

To demonstrate the benefits of using the flexible budgeting approach to evaluate performance, we continue with our example of Harrigan Freeze, Inc. The flexible budget performance report shown in Exhibit 9–4 has three main components. First, it presents actual revenues and expenses for the year, given an actual sales volume of 110,000 units. Second, it contains a flexible budget based on actual sales of 110,000 units, using

EXHIBIT 9–4   Flexible Budget Performance Report

	Budgeted Amount Per Unit	Actual (110,000 units)	Flexible Budget (110,000 units)	Flexible Budget Variance++
Sales	$20.00	$2,145,000	$2,200,000	$55,000 u
Less variable expenses				
Direct materials*.	3.00	335,500	330,000	5,500 u
Direct labour*.	6.00	671,000	660,000	11,000 u
Variable manufacturing overhead#.	1.60	165,000	176,000	11,000 f
Selling and administrative+	1.80	203,500	198,000	5,500 u
Total variable expenses	12.40	1,375,000	1,364,000	11,000 u
Contribution margin.	$ 7.60	770,000	836,000	66,000 u
Less fixed expenses				
Manufacturing overhead**		241,000	242,400	1,400 f
Selling and administrative##		367,500	365,800	1,700 u
Total fixed expenses		608,500	608,200	300 u
Operating income		$ 161,500	$ 227,800	$66,300 u

*Per unit amount as per Schedule 6
#Variable overhead cost per hour (Schedule 5) multiplied by hours per unit (Schedule 6): $4 × 0.4 = $1.60
+Per unit amount as per Schedule 7
**Total budgeted fixed overhead expense as per Schedule 5
##Total budgeted fixed selling and administrative expenses as per Schedule 7
++u = unfavourable variance; f = favourable variance

the revenues and expenses from Exhibit 9–3. Third, it shows the **flexible budget variance**, the difference between actual results and the flexible budget with unfavourable and favourable variances labelled "u" and "f," respectively. As shown in Exhibit 9–4, actual operating income for 2012 was $161,500, while the flexible budget indicates that at an actual volume of 110,000 unit sales, $227,800 should have been earned. The flexible budget variances for the individual line items tell the story as to why the unfavourable operating income variance of $66,300 occurred. The largest contributing factor was the unfavourable sales variance of $55,000, so management will want to determine why the actual selling price of $19.50 per unit ($2,145,000 ÷ 110,000) differed from the budget of $20 per unit. Cost control also appears to have been a problem for many of the variable expenses at Harrigan Freeze, Inc., which in total were $11,000 above budget. As will be further explored in Chapter 10, the flexible budget variances for manufacturing costs (direct materials, direct labour, variable overhead) could have been caused by actual unit prices for production inputs differing from budget, or the actual quantities used in producing the 110,000 units differing from budget. Management will want to know of the extent to which these two factors contributed to the variances shown in Exhibit 9–4.

The value of the flexible budget performance report can be further illustrated by examining Exhibit 9–5, which presents a static budget performance report. The **static budget variances** in Exhibit 9–5 represent the differences between actual results (activity level of 110,000 units) and the static budget amounts (activity level of 100,000 units). The operating income variance is $9,700 favourable, suggesting that overall, Harrigan Freeze, Inc., had a good year. However this is very misleading as it is largely attributable to the favourable sales variance of $145,000, which relates to selling 10,000 more units than planned in the static budget. While selling more units than planned is a good thing from a revenue perspective, the static budget variances for the variable expense items are not useful in evaluating how well managers did in controlling costs at actual levels of activity.

Flexible budget variance
The difference between actual and flexible budget amounts for revenues and expenses.

Static budget variance
The difference between actual and static budget amounts for revenues and expenses.

EXHIBIT 9–5 Static Budget Performance Report

HARRIGAN FREEZE, INC.
Static Budget Performance Report
For the Year Ended December 31, 2012

	Budgeted Amount Per Unit	Actual (110,000 units)	Static Budget (100,000 units)	Static Budget Variance++
Sales	$20.00	$2,145,000	$2,000,000	$145,000 f
Less variable expenses				
Direct materials*	3.00	335,500	300,000	35,500 u
Direct labour*	6.00	671,000	600,000	71,000 u
Variable manufacturing overhead#	1.60	165,000	160,000	5,000 u
Selling and administrative+	1.80	203,500	180,000	23,500 u
Total variable expenses	12.40	1,375,000	1,240,000	135,000 u
Contribution margin	$ 7.60	770,000	760,000	10,000 f
Less fixed expenses				
Manufacturing overhead**		241,000	242,400	1,400 f
Selling and administrative##		367,500	365,800	1,700 u
Total fixed expenses		608,500	608,200	300 u
Operating income		$ 161,500	$ 151,800	$ 9,700 f

*Per unit amount as per Schedule 6
#Variable overhead cost per hour (Schedule 5) multiplied by hours per unit (Schedule 6): $4 × 0.4 = $1.60
+Per unit amount as per Schedule 7
**Total budgeted fixed overhead expense as per Schedule 5
##Total budgeted fixed selling and administrative expenses as per Schedule 7
++u = unfavourable variance; f = favourable variance

As shown in Exhibit 9–5, total actual variable expenses were $135,000 above the static budget, but much of this increase relates to the 10,000 unit difference in the volume of activity. Hence, the key benefit of the flexible budget performance report shown in Exhibit 9–4 is that it removes the effects of any volume differences between actual results and the static budget. This allows for a much more meaningful analysis of how well managers did in generating revenue and controlling costs.

Finally, some companies integrate the information contained in Exhibits 9–4 and 9–5 in preparing a comprehensive performance report that includes actual results along with both flexible and static budget amounts. An example of this type of report is shown in Exhibit 9–6. Note that the total favourable static budget variance of $9,700 is the same as calculated in Exhibit 9–5, but Exhibit 9–6 shows that it consists of two components: (1) an unfavourable flexible budget variance of $66,300 from Exhibit 9–4, and (2) a favourable $76,000 *sales volume variance*. The **sales volume variance** represents the difference between the flexible and static budget amounts for revenues and expenses. Because both the flexible and static budgets are prepared using budgeted amounts per unit, the only difference that can arise between them relates to the actual level of activity differing from the static budget level. For example, the favourable sales volume variance of $200,000 for sales is calculated as follows: (110,000 units – 100,000 units) × $20 per unit. The sales volume variances for variable expenses are calculated in a similar fashion. Because total budgeted fixed expenses are constant within the relevant range of activity, no differences between the flexible and static budgets arise for these items. The advantage of preparing a comprehensive report such as that shown in Exhibit 9–6 is that it helps managers isolate the part of the static budget variance caused solely by volume differences from that caused by other factors such as actual unit prices differing from budget. In Chapter 11, we will further explore the factors that can cause sales volume variances.

Sales volume variance
The difference between flexible and static budget amounts for revenues and expenses.

EXHIBIT 9–6   Comprehensive Performance Report

	Actual (110,000 units)	Flexible Budget Variance*	Flexible Budget (110,000 units)	Sales Volume Variance*	Static Budget (100,000 units)
HARRIGAN FREEZE, INC. Comprehensive Performance Report[+] For the Year Ended December 31, 2012					
Sales	$2,145,000	$55,000 u	$2,200,000	$200,000 f	$2,000,000
Less variable expenses					
Direct materials	335,500	5,500 u	330,000	30,000 u	300,000
Direct labour.	671,000	11,000 u	660,000	60,000 u	600,000
Variable manufacturing overhead	165,000	11,000 f	176,000	16,000 u	160,000
Selling and administrative[+]	203,500	5,500 u	198,000	18,000 u	180,000
Total variable expenses	1,375,000	11,000 u	1,364,000	124,000 u	1,240,000
Contribution margin.	770,000	66,000 u	836,000	76,000 f	760,000
Less fixed expenses					
Manufacturing overhead	241,000	1,400 f	242,400	0 –	242,400
Selling and administrative	367,500	1,700 u	365,800	0 –	365,800
Total fixed expenses	608,500	300 u	608,200	0 –	608,200
Operating income	$ 161,500	$66,300 u	$ 227,800	$ 76,000 f	$ 151,800

$9,700 f

Total static-budget variance

*u = unfavourable variance; f = favourable variance
[+]All actual and flexible budget amounts as per Exhibit 9–4; all static budget amounts as per Exhibit 9–5.

IN BUSINESS

The use of flexible budgets is one way of addressing the problem of actual activity levels differing significantly from those included in the static budget. However, proponents of the beyond budgeting (BB) approach claim that flexible budgets do not go far enough in addressing the deficiencies of the static budget approach. The BB approach still involves the use of budgets for planning purposes but does not use them for control purposes. Under the BB approach, performance targets can be based either on the results of other divisions in the same organization or on those of leading competitors. This approach to setting targets can avoid some of the potential problems associated with participative budgeting where managers may be able to negotiate relatively easy performance targets.

Another key feature of the BB approach is the use of hindsight to subjectively adjust the budget at the end of a reporting period. These subjective adjustments go beyond the simple volume adjustment used in the flexible budgeting approach and can incorporate other major events that occurred during the year affecting selling prices or the costs associated with the products or services offered by the organization. Importantly, the BB approach also requires an evaluation of whether the actual volume of activity achieved (e.g., unit sales) was the desired level. For example, if actual unit sales were 100,000 while the static budget was based on 120,000 units, the flexible budget approach would restate all budget figures using 100,000 units as the new basis. Conversely, the BB approach would assess whether the sale of 100,000 units was the best the company could have done, given the circumstances. This assessment could result in a restatement of the budget using a level of activity greater than 100,000 units.

The appeal of the BB approach is that it provides much greater flexibility in evaluating the performance of a manager by incorporating subjectivity in the process. However, this greater use of subjectivity can also lead to concerns about the consistency and fairness of the evaluation process. Even if the process is well intentioned, if managers do not believe they are being evaluated fairly, motivation and performance may suffer.

Source: Stephen Hansen, David Otley, and Wim Van der Stede, "Practice Developments in Budgeting: An Overview and Research Perspective," *Journal of Management Accounting Research,* 2003, pp. 95–115. Reprinted with permission from the American Accounting Association.

■ BUDGETING FOR NOT-FOR-PROFIT ENTITIES

LEARNING OBJECTIVE 5
Describe variations in the master budget process when applying it to not-for-profit and activity-based situations

Up to this point, we have discussed budgeting in the context of profit-seeking enterprises where the sales estimate is the critical factor on which the rest of the master budget depends. Inaccurate sales estimates can create additional inaccuracies in many of the other budgets, given the intricate relationship between expenses and revenues in profit-oriented organizations. However, with not-for-profit (NFP) entities, there is often no relationship between expected revenues and expected expenditures. Examples of NFP entities include municipal, provincial, territorial, and federal governmental units as well as hospitals, universities, volunteer associations, professional associations, and many others. The profit motive is replaced with a service orientation in NFP organizations. Budget information is gathered to assist in making decisions regarding what programs and expenditures the entity will undertake. The programs undertaken by a NFP are determined by its mission statement and can be very diverse in nature. For example, the United Way sponsors programs related to seniors' care, women's shelters, independent living, community centres, and so on. Having made decisions about the programs it will offer or support, the NFP then estimates the revenues needed to support these programs and the anticipated expenditures for each. Revenue sources may be in the form of grants, donations, special taxes, or membership fees. The viability of NFP organizations depends critically on their ability to generate revenues through their donors.

Accountability is of critical importance to most NFP entities. To ensure continued support from donors, it is advantageous to have a budgeting process in place to assist in planning how resources will be used effectively and efficiently. Budgets of NFP entities should be formally approved by the entity's governing body. A formally approved budget signals to employees and volunteers alike that the organization is committed to meeting its revenue and expenditure goals.

A budget can be prepared either on an expenditure basis or on a program basis. An expenditure-based budget simply lists the total expected costs of items such as rent, insurance, salaries, and depreciation without detailing how these various expenses relate to particular programs. However, many NFP organizations report budget information on the basis of programs rather than line-item expenses. Preparation of the budget on the basis of programs facilitates performance evaluation and allows for the comparison of the budgeted revenues and expenses of each program with the actual amounts on a periodic basis. This approach facilitates decision making about resource allocation among the various programs. Budgeting by program also facilitates the stewardship objective by providing information in a format permitting determination of whether funds designated by donors for specific purposes are being spent as intended.

IN BUSINESS

Given the importance of government budgets, the Canadian Institute of Chartered Accountants' Public Sector Accounting Board (PSAB) commissioned a research report to survey current practice. The survey looked at the basis of accounting and accounting policies used by Canadian federal, provincial, and territorial governments in their budgets and estimates (appropriations) as compared with those adopted in their summary financial statements. Planning, budgeting, and reporting are elements of a government's performance management and accountability framework. The report discusses each of these elements. Traditionally, the approach begins with priority setting and planning, followed by the budgeting process, and ending with reporting and auditing. The survey findings indicate a clear trend for senior governments in Canada to (1) move to accrual-based accounting, (2) prepare a summary budget, and (3) change certain significant accounting policies to be in line with the recommendations set out in the *Public Sector Accounting Handbook*.

Source: Excerpted from J. Paul-Emile, "Accounting Bases Used in Canadian Government Budgeting," *CA Magazine*, Toronto, January/February 2005, 138:1, p. 18. Reproduced by permission from *CA Magazine* produced by the Canadian Institute of Chartered Accountants, Toronto, Canada.

Activity-Based Budgeting

In Chapter 5, we saw that activity-based costing can provide the manager with more accurate product or service costs. More accurate costs should translate into better decision making and tighter control over costs. Activity-based costing principles can also be applied to budgeting. With **activity-based budgeting**, the emphasis is on budgeting the costs of the activities needed to produce and market the firm's goods and/or services.

Activity-based budgeting
A type of budgeting in which emphasis is placed on budgeting the costs of the activities needed to produce and market the firm's goods and/or services.

Activity-based budgeting involves several stages. First, the budgeted cost of accomplishing each unit of activity is determined. Recall that an activity is a cost driver, such as machine setup, a purchase order, a quality inspection, or a maintenance request. Next, sales and production targets for the products or services offered by the organization are used to estimate the demand for these activities. The unit cost of each activity is then multiplied by the expected demand to determine the total cost of each activity. The result is a budget based on the activities that drive costs rather than the traditional budget based on business functions and expense classifications.

For activity-based budgeting, costs within the responsibility centre are classified by activity, and activity drivers other than simple quantities produced or sold are identified. Activities such as quality inspections, materials handling, assembly, shipping, purchasing, and so on are identified, measured, and costed. The costs across all activities are then compiled to determine the total budgeted costs of the product or services expected to be sold as per the sales forecast. The total budgeted costs would include unit and batch-level activities as well as the product-level, customer-level, and organization-sustaining activities. Activity-based budgeting offers two advantages. First, by focusing on the resources required by activities to meet the expected demand for products and services, it can help identify the need for additional production capacity. Second, it can lead to more accurate budgets.

◼ INTERNATIONAL ASPECTS OF BUDGETING

A multinational company (MNC) faces special problems when preparing a budget. These problems arise because of fluctuations in foreign currency exchange rates, high inflation rates found in some countries, and local economic conditions and government policies that affect everything from labour costs to marketing practices.

Fluctuations in foreign currency exchange rates create unique budgeting problems. Canadian companies that export goods and services may be able to predict with some accuracy their sales in the local foreign currency such as yen or euros. However, the amounts they eventually receive in Canadian dollars will depend on the currency exchange rates that prevail at the time the foreign currency is converted. If, for example, the currency exchange rates are less favourable than expected, the company will ultimately receive fewer Canadian dollars than it had anticipated.

Companies that have significant exports often hedge their exposure to exchange rate fluctuations by buying and selling sophisticated financial contracts that effectively lock in the conversion rate for the foreign currency. These contracts ensure that if the company loses money in its exporting operations because of exchange rate fluctuations, it will make up that loss with gains on its financial contracts. The details of foreign currency hedging are covered in finance textbooks. However, the costs of the financial contracts used to hedge foreign currency exposure, if material, should be budgeted, along with the other types of administrative expenses discussed earlier in the chapter.

Some MNCs have operations in countries with very high inflation rates—sometimes exceeding 100% a year. Such high inflation rates—called *hyperinflation*—can render a budget obsolete very quickly. A common budgeting tactic in such countries is to reduce the lead time for preparing the budget and to revise the budget frequently throughout the year in light of the actual inflation experienced to date.

In addition to problems with exchange rates and inflation, MNCs must be sensitive to government policies in the countries in which they operate that might affect labour costs, raw materials costs, equipment purchases, cash management, or other budget items.

Summary

- Budgets play a dual role in organizations (planning and control) and offer several advantages. These include the communication of management's plans, allocation of resources, coordination of activities, and establishment of goals and objectives that can be used to evaluate subsequent performance. [LO1]

- Budgets represent a key element of responsibility accounting systems, whereby managers are held responsible for revenue and cost items over which they have significant influence. The comparison of actual and budgeted results is a common feature of such systems. [LO1]

- Many companies employ a participative budgeting approach, whereby managers are allowed to participate in setting their own budgets. This approach can result in higher managerial commitment to attaining the budget goals but is subject to potential problems if managers try to set easy budgets through the creation of budget slack. [LO1]

- The preparation of a master budget involves numerous interrelated schedules and begins with the development of the sales budget, which is based on the sales forecast. Once the sales budget has been set, the production budget can be prepared since it depends on how many units are to be sold. The production budget determines how many units are to be produced, so after it is prepared, the various manufacturing cost budgets and selling and administrative budgets can be developed. [LO2]

- After the detailed budget schedules have been completed, the cash budget, budgeted income statement, and budgeted balance sheet can be prepared, which collectively provide an overall financial summary of the budget. [LO2]

- Some companies use flexible budgets to address the limitations that arise with static budgets when actual activity levels differ significantly from budgeted levels. Preparing flexible budgets involves restating the budget at the end of a reporting period using actual activity levels and budgeted per unit amounts for revenues and variable expenses. A flexible budget provides a better tool for evaluating managers' performance in generating revenue and controlling costs, given the actual volume of activity. [LO3]

- The preparation of flexible budgets also permits companies to prepare performance reports that decompose the difference between actual results and the static budget into flexible budget variances and sales volume variances. This approach is helpful in isolating the cause of variances and forms the basis for further investigation. [LO4]

- Budgeting for not-for-profit (NFP) entities begins with a determination of the costs of undertaking the planned programs and activities. Then, the revenues needed to support the programs and related expenditures are determined and budgeted. This approach is necessitated by the fact that in NFP entities there is often little relationship between revenues and expenditures because revenues often come from donors or other granting agencies. [LO5]

- Activity-based budgeting involves determining the amount of each activity required to meet the total budgeted sales level for products or services. The amount of the activity required is then combined with the estimated cost per unit of providing that activity (e.g., a batch setup) to create accurate cost budgets. [LO5]

Review Problem: Completing a Master Budget

The following data relate to the operations of Soper Company, a wholesale distributor of consumer goods:

Current assets as of March 31:	
Cash	$ 8,000
Accounts receivable	$ 20,000
Inventory	$ 36,000
Building and equipment, net	$120,000
Accounts payable	$ 21,750
Common shares	$150,000
Retained earnings	$ 12,250

a. The gross margin is 25% of sales.
b. Actual and budgeted sales data:

March (actual)..........	$50,000
April	$60,000
May.................	$72,000
June	$90,000
July.................	$48,000

c. Sales are 60% for cash and 40% on credit. Credit sales are collected in the month following sale. The accounts receivable at March 31 are a result of March credit sales.
d. Each month's ending inventory should equal 80% of the following month's budgeted cost of goods sold.
e. One-half of a month's inventory purchases is paid for in the month of purchase; the other half is paid for in the following month. The accounts payable at March 31 are the result of March purchases of inventory.
f. Monthly expenses are as follows: commissions, 12% of sales; rent, $2,500 per month; other expenses (excluding depreciation), 6% of sales. Assume that these expenses are paid monthly. Depreciation is $900 per month (includes depreciation on new assets).
g. Equipment costing $1,500 will be purchased for cash in April.
h. The company must maintain a minimum cash balance of $4,000. An open line of credit is available at a local bank. All borrowing is done at the beginning of a month, and all repayments are made at the end of a month; borrowing must be in multiples of $1,000. The annual interest rate is 12%. Interest is paid only at the time of repayment of principal; calculate interest on whole months ($\frac{1}{12}$, $\frac{2}{12}$, and so forth).

Required:
Using the preceding data:
1. Complete the following:

Schedule of Expected Cash Collections

	April	May	June	Quarter
Cash sales.........................	$36,000			
Credit sales*	20,000			
Total collections....................	$56,000			

*40% of prior month's sales

2. Complete the following:

Merchandise Purchases Budget

	April	May	June	Quarter
Budgeted cost of goods sold	$45,000*	$54,000		
Add desired ending inventory	43,200†			
Total needs	88,200			
Less beginning inventory............	36,000			
Required purchases................	$52,200			

*For April sales: $60,000 sales × 75% cost ratio = $45,000.
†$54,000 × 80% = $43,200

Schedule of Expected Cash Disbursements—Merchandise Purchases

	April	May	June	Quarter
March purchases.....................	$21,750			$21,750
April purchases	26,100	$26,100		52,200
May purchases				
June purchases......................				
Total disbursements	$47,850			

3. Complete the following:

Schedule of Expected Cash Disbursements—Operating Expenses				
	April	May	June	Quarter
Commissions.	$ 7,200			
Rent.	2,500			
Other expenses	3,600			
Total disbursements	$13,300			

4. Complete the following cash budget:

Cash Budget				
	April	May	June	Quarter
Cash balance, beginning.	$ 8,000			
Add cash collections	56,000			
Total cash available.	$64,000			
Less cash disbursements				
For inventory	$47,850			
For expenses	13,300			
For equipment	1,500			
Total cash disbursements	62,650			
Excess (deficiency) of cash	$ 1,350			
Financing:				
Etc.				

5. Prepare an absorption costing income statement, similar to the one shown in Schedule 9 on page 367, for the quarter ended June 30.
6. Prepare a balance sheet as of June 30.

Solution to Review Problem

1.

Schedule of Expected Cash Collections				
	April	May	June	Quarter
Cash sales.	$36,000	$43,200	$54,000	$133,200
Credit sales*	20,000†	24,000	28,800	72,800
Total collections.	$56,000	$67,200	$82,800	$206,000

*40% of the preceding month's sales.
†Given.

2.

Inventory Purchases Budget				
	April	May	June	Quarter
Budgeted cost of goods sold*.	$45,000†	$54,000†	$67,500	$166,500
Add desired ending inventory‡	43,200†	54,000	28,800	28,800
Total needs	88,200†	108,000	96,300	195,300
Less beginning inventory.	36,000†	43,200	54,000	36,000
Required purchases	$52,200†	$64,800	$42,300	$159,300

*For April sales: $60,000 sales × 75% cost ratio = $45,000.
†Given.
‡At April 30: $54,000 × 80% = $43,200.
  At June 30: July sales $48,000 × 75% cost ratio × 80% = $28,800.

Schedule of Expected Cash Disbursements—Purchases

	April	May	June	Quarter
March purchases.....................	$21,750*			$ 21,750*
April purchases	26,100*	$26,100*		52,200*
May purchases		32,400	$32,400	64,800
June purchases.....................			21,150	21,150
Total disbursements	$47,850*	$58,500	$53,550	$159,900

*Given.

3.

Schedule of Expected Cash Disbursements—Operating Expenses

	April	May	June	Quarter
Commissions......................	$ 7,200*	$ 8,640	$10,800	$26,640
Rent..............................	2,500*	2,500	2,500	7,500
Other expenses	3,600*	4,320	5,400	13,320
Total disbursements	$13,300*	$15,460	$18,700	$47,460

*Given.

4.

Cash Budget

	April	May	June	Quarter
Cash balance, beginning..............	$ 8,000*	$ 4,350	$ 4,590	$ 8,000
Add cash collections	56,000*	67,200	82,800	206,000
Total cash available..................	64,000*	71,550	87,390	214,000
Less disbursement				
For inventory	47,850*	58,500	53,550	159,900
For expenses	13,300*	15,460	18,700	47,460
For equipment	1,500*			1,500
Total disbursements	62,650*	73,960	72,250	208,860
Excess (deficiency) of cash	1,350*	(2,410)	15,140	5,140
Financing:				
Borrowings.......................	3,000	7,000		10,000
Repayments......................			(10,000)	(10,000)
Interest..........................			(230)†	(230)
Total financing.....................	3,000	7,000	(10,230)	(230)
Cash balance, ending	$ 4,350	$ 4,590	$ 4,910	$ 4,910

*Given.

†$3,000 × 12% × 3/12 = $ 90

  7,000 × 12% × 2/12 = 140

Total interest $230

5.

SOPER COMPANY		
Income Statement		
For the Quarter Ended June 30		
Sales ($60,000 + $72,000 + $90,000)		$222,000
Less cost of goods sold:		
Beginning inventory (Given)	$ 36,000	
Add purchases (Solution 2)	159,300	
Goods available for sale.	195,300	
Ending inventory (Solution 2)	28,800	166,500*
Gross margin		55,500
Less operating expenses:		
Commissions (Solution 3)	26,640	
Rent (Solution 3).	7,500	
Depreciation ($900 × 3)	2,700	
Other expenses (Solution 3).	13,320	50,160
Operating income		5,340
Less interest expense (Solution 4).		230
Net income		$ 5,110

*A simpler computation would be $222,000 × 75% = $166,500.

6.

SOPER COMPANY		
Balance Sheet		
June 30		
Assets		
Current assets:		
Cash (Solution 4)		$ 4,910
Accounts receivable ($90,000 × 40%)		36,000
Inventory (Solution 2)		28,800
Total current assets.		69,710
Building and equipment—net ($120,000 + $1,500 − $2,700)		118,800
Total assets		$188,510
Liabilities and Shareholders' Equity		
Accounts payable (Solution 2: $42,300 × 50%)		$ 21,150
Shareholders' equity:		
Common shares (Given).	$150,000	
Retained earnings*.	17,360	167,360
Total liabilities and shareholders' equity		$188,510
*Retained earnings, beginning.	$ 12,250	
Add net income	5,110	
Retained earnings, ending.	$ 17,360	

Glossary

Mc Graw Hill **connect**   Review key terms and definitions on Connect.

Questions

9–1   What is a budget? What is budgetary control?

9–2   Discuss some of the major benefits to be gained from budgeting.

9–3   What is meant by the term *responsibility accounting*?

9–4   What is a master budget? Briefly describe its contents.

9–5   Why is the sales forecast the starting point in budgeting?

9–6   What is a budget committee? Why is it used by some companies?

9–7   What is a perpetual budget?

9–8   What is a participative budget? What are the major advantages of participative budgets?

9–9   What is budget slack? Why might managers be tempted to build slack into their budgets?

9–10   How does zero-based budgeting differ from traditional budgeting?

9–11   "The principal purpose of the cash budget is to see how much cash the company will have in the bank at the end of the year." Do you agree? Explain.

9–12   Which budget schedule replaces the production budget for merchandising companies?

9–13   What are the advantages of activity-based budgeting?

9–14   What are some of the unique budgeting problems faced by multinational companies?

9–15   "With profit, not-for-profit, and government entities, there is generally a direct relationship between revenues and expenditures." Do you agree with this statement? Why or why not?

9–16   Describe the difference between a static budget and a flexible budget.

9–17   What is a flexible budget variance? What is it caused by?

---

connect **Exercises**

EXERCISE 9–1 Schedule of Expected Cash Collections [LO2]

Peak sales for Northern Lift, a wholesale distributor of snow shovels, occur in November. The company's sales budget for the fourth quarter showing these peak sales is given below:

	October	November	December	Total
Budgeted sales (all on account)	$400,000	$800,000	$700,000	$1,900,000

From past experience, the company has learned that 25% of a month's sales are collected in the month of sale, another 70% are collected in the month following sale, and the remaining 5% are collected in the second month following sale. Bad debts are negligible and can be ignored. August sales totalled $70,000, and September sales totalled $180,000.

Required:

1.   Prepare a schedule of expected cash collections from sales, by month and in total, for the third quarter.

2   Assume that the company will prepare a budgeted balance sheet as of September 30. Compute the accounts receivable as of that date.

EXERCISE 9–2 Production Budget [LO2]

Sound Communications has budgeted sales of its innovative smartphone over the next four months as follows:

	Sales in Units
July.	30,000
August	45,000
September.	60,000
October	50,000

The company is now in the process of preparing a production budget for the third quarter. Past experience has shown that end-of-month inventories of finished goods must equal 10% of the next month's sales. The inventory at the end of June was 3,000 units.

Required:

Prepare a production budget for the third quarter showing the number of units to be produced each month and for the quarter in total.

EXERCISE 9–3 Direct Materials Purchases Budget [LO2]

Office Wizards, Inc., has developed a very powerful electronic calculator. Each calculator requires three small "chips" that cost $2 each and are purchased from an overseas supplier. Office Wizards has prepared a production budget for the calculator by quarters for year 2 and for the first quarter of year 3, as shown below:

	Year 2				Year 3
	First	Second	Third	Fourth	First
Budgeted production, in calculators	120,000	190,000	300,000	200,000	160,000

The chip used in production of the calculator is sometimes hard to get, so it is necessary to carry large inventories as a precaution against stock-outs. For this reason, the inventory of chips at the end of a quarter must be equal to 20% of the following quarter's production needs. Some 72,000 chips will be on hand to start the first quarter of year 2.

Required:
Prepare a direct materials purchases budget for chips, by quarter and in total, for year 2. At the bottom of your budget, show the dollar amount of purchases for each quarter and for the year in total.

EXERCISE 9–4 Direct Labour Budget [LO2]
The Production Department of the Overview Plant of Roth Corporation has submitted the following forecast of units to be produced at the plant for each quarter of the upcoming fiscal year. The plant produces high-end outdoor barbecue grills.

	1st Quarter	2nd Quarter	3rd Quarter	4th Quarter
Units to be produced.	5,000	4,400	4,500	4,900

Each unit requires 0.40 direct labour-hours and direct labour-hour workers are paid $11 per hour.

Required:
1. Prepare the company's direct labour budget for the upcoming fiscal year, assuming that the direct labour workforce is adjusted each quarter to match the number of hours required to produce the forecasted number of units produced.
2. Prepare the company's direct labour budget for the upcoming fiscal year, assuming that the direct labour workforce is *not* adjusted each quarter. Instead, assume that the company's direct labour workforce consists of permanent employees who are guaranteed to be paid for at least 1,800 hours of work each quarter. If the number of required direct labour-hours is less than this number, the workers are paid for 1,800 hours anyway. Any hours worked in excess of 1,800 hours in a quarter are paid at the rate of 1.5 times the normal hourly rate for direct labour.

EXERCISE 9–5 Manufacturing Overhead Budget [LO2]
The direct labour budget of Small Corporation for the upcoming fiscal year contains the following details concerning budgeted direct labour-hours.

	1st Quarter	2nd Quarter	3rd Quarter	4th Quarter
Budgeted direct labour-hours . . .	5,000	4,800	5,200	5,400

The company's variable manufacturing overhead rate is $1.75 per direct labour-hour and the company's fixed manufacturing overhead is $35,000 per quarter. The only non-cash item included in the fixed manufacturing overhead is depreciation, which is $15,000 per quarter.

Required:
1. Prepare the company's manufacturing overhead budget for the upcoming fiscal year.
2. Compute the company's manufacturing overhead rate (including both variable and fixed manufacturing overhead) for the upcoming fiscal year. Round off to the nearest whole cent.

EXERCISE 9–6 Selling and Administrative Expense Budget [LO2]
The budgeted unit sales of Hirst Company for the upcoming fiscal year are provided below:

	1st Quarter	2nd Quarter	3rd Quarter	4th Quarter
Budgeted unit sales.	12,000	14,000	11,000	10,000

The company's variable selling and administrative expenses per unit are $2.75. Fixed selling and administrative expenses include advertising expenses of $12,000 per quarter, executive salaries of $40,000 per quarter, and depreciation of $16,000 per quarter. In addition, the company will make insurance payments of $6,000 in the 2nd quarter and $6,000 in the 4th quarter. Finally, property taxes of $6,000 will be paid in the 3rd quarter.

Required:
Prepare the company's selling and administrative expense budget for the upcoming fiscal year.

EXERCISE 9–7 Cash Budget Analysis [LO2]
A cash budget, by quarter, is given below for a retail company (000 omitted). The company requires a minimum cash balance of $5,000 to start each quarter.

Required:
Fill in the missing amounts in the table that follows.

| | Quarter | | | | |
	1	2	3	4	Year
Cash balance, beginning.	$ 6	$?	$?	$?	$?
Add collections from customers	?	?	96	?	323
Total cash available.	71	?	?	?	?
Less disbursements:					
Purchases of inventory	35	45	?	35	?
Operating expenses.	?	30	30	?	113
Equipment purchases	8	8	10	?	36
Dividends	2	2	2	2	?
Total disbursements	?	85	?	?	?
Excess (deficiency) of cash available over disbursements	(2)	?	11	?	?
Financing:					
Borrowings.	?	15	–	–	?
Repayments (including interest)*	–	–	(?)	(17)	(?)
Total financing	?	?	?	?	?
Cash balance, ending	$?	$?	$?	$?	$?

*Interest will total $4,000 for the year.

EXERCISE 9–8 Preparing a Flexible Budget [LO3]
An incomplete monthly flexible budget is given below for AutoLav Inc., a company that owns and operates a large automatic car wash facility.

| AUTOLAV INC. Flexible Budget | | | | |
| | | Monthly Activity (cars washed) | | |
	Per Car	7,000	8,000	9,000
Sales	?	?	$80,000	?
Variable expenses:				
Cleaning supplies.	?	?	6,000	?
Utilities	?	?	4,800	?
Maintenance.	?	?	1,200	?
Total variable expenses.	?	?	?	?
Contribution margin.	?	?	?	?
Fixed expenses:				
Operator wages		?	10,000	?
Depreciation.		?	20,000	?
Rent		?	8,000	?
Insurance		?	1,000	?
Selling and administrative		?	4,000	?
Total fixed expenses		?	43,000	?
Operating income		?	?	?

Required:
1. Prepare the following, by quarter and in total, for year 2:
   a. A schedule of expected cash collections on sales.
   b. A schedule of expected cash disbursements for merchandise purchases.
2. Compute the expected cash disbursements for operating expenses, by quarter and in total, for year 2.
3. Prepare a cash budget by quarter and in total for year 2.

PROBLEM 9–22 Cash Budget with Supporting Schedules [LO2]
Scott Products Inc. is a merchandising company that sells binders, paper, and other school supplies. The company is planning its cash needs for the third quarter. In the past, Scott Products has had to borrow money during the third quarter to support peak sales of back-to-school materials, which occur during August. The following information has been assembled to assist in preparing a cash budget for the quarter:

a. Budgeted monthly absorption costing income statements for July–October are as follows:

	July	August	September	October
Sales	$40,000	$70,000	$50,000	$45,000
Cost of goods sold	24,000	42,000	30,000	27,000
Gross margin	16,000	28,000	20,000	18,000
Selling and administrative expenses:				
Selling expense	7,200	11,700	8,500	7,300
Administrative expense*	5,600	7,200	6,100	5,900
Total expenses	12,800	18,900	14,600	13,200
Operating income	$ 3,200	$ 9,100	$ 5,400	$ 4,800

*Includes $2,000 depreciation each month.

b. Sales are 20% for cash and 80% on credit.
c. Credit sales are collected over a three-month period, with 10% collected in the month of sale, 70% in the month following sale, and 20% in the second month following sale. May sales totalled $30,000, and June sales totalled $36,000.
d. Inventory purchases are paid for within 15 days. Therefore, 50% of a month's inventory purchases are paid for in the month of purchase. The remaining 50% is paid in the following month. Accounts payable for inventory purchases at June 30 total $11,700.
e. The company maintains its ending inventory levels at 75% of the cost of the merchandise to be sold in the following month. The merchandise inventory at June 30 is $18,000.
f. Land costing $4,500 will be purchased in July.
g. Dividends of $1,000 will be declared and paid in September.
h. The cash balance on June 30 is $8,000; the company must maintain a cash balance of at least this amount at the end of each month.
i. The company has an agreement with a local bank that allows the company to borrow in increments of $1,000 at the beginning of each month, up to a total loan balance of $40,000. The interest rate on these loans is 1% per month, and for simplicity, we will assume that interest is not compounded. The company would, as far as it is able, repay the loan plus accumulated interest at the end of the quarter. There are no loans outstanding as at June 30.

Required:
1. Prepare a schedule of expected cash collections for July, August, and September and for the quarter in total.
2. Prepare the following for merchandise inventory:
   a. A merchandise purchases budget for July, August, and September.
   b. A schedule of expected cash disbursements for merchandise purchases for July, August, and September and for the quarter in total.
3. Prepare a cash budget for July, August, and September and for the quarter in total.

PROBLEM 9–23 Integrated Operating Budgets [LO2]
The Western Division of Keltic Company manufactures a vital component that is used in one of Keltic's major product lines. The Western Division has been experiencing some difficulty in coordinating activities among its various departments, which has resulted in some shortages of the

component at critical times. To overcome the shortages, the manager of Western Division has decided to initiate a monthly budgeting system that is integrated among departments.

The first budget is to be for the second quarter of the current year. To assist in creating the budget, the divisional controller has accumulated the following information:

Sales.   Sales through the first three months of the current year were 48,000 units. Actual sales in units for January, February, and March, and planned sales in units over the next five months, are given below:

January (actual)	9,000
February (actual)	15,000
March (actual)	24,000
April (planned)	30,000
May (planned)	53,000
June (planned)	75,000
July (planned).	68,000
August (planned)	45,000

In total, the Western Division expects to produce and sell 380,000 units during the current year.

Direct Materials.   Two different materials are used in the production of the component. Data regarding these materials are given below:

Direct Materials	Units of Direct Materials per Finished Component	Cost Per Unit	Inventory at March 31
No. 226	2 kilograms	$4.00	23,000 kilograms
No. 301	5 metres	$1.50	35,000 metres

Material No. 226 is sometimes in short supply. Therefore, the Western Division requires that enough of the material be on hand at the end of each month to provide for 60% of the following month's production needs. Material No. 301 is easier to obtain, so only 30% of the following month's production needs must be on hand at the end of each month.

Direct Labour.   The Western Division has three departments through which the components must pass before they are completed. Information relating to direct labour in these departments is given below:

Department	Direct Labour-Hours per Finished Component	Cost per Direct Labour-Hour
Cutting.	0.15	$16.00
Assembly.	0.60	$14.00
Finishing	0.10	$18.00

Direct labour is adjusted to the workload each month.

Manufacturing Overhead.   Western Division manufactured 48,000 components during the first three months of the current year. The actual variable overhead costs incurred during this three-month period are shown below. Western Division's controller believes that the variable overhead costs incurred during the last nine months of the year will be at the same rate per component as experienced during the first three months.

Utilities	$ 63,000
Indirect labour	34,000
Supplies	18,000
Other	9,800
Total variable overhead	$124,800

The actual fixed manufacturing overhead costs incurred during the first three months totalled $1,287,000. The Western Division has budgeted fixed manufacturing overhead costs for the entire year as follows:

Supervision	$ 785,000
Property taxes	129,000
Depreciation.	2,619,000
Insurance	568,000
Other	65,000
Total fixed manufacturing overhead	$4,166,000

Finished Goods Inventory.   The desired monthly ending finished goods inventory is 20% of the next month's estimated sales. The Western Division has 6,000 units in finished goods inventory on March 31.

Required:

1. Prepare a production budget for the Western Division for the second quarter ending June 30. Show computations by month and in total for the quarter.
2. Prepare a direct materials purchases budget for each type of material for the second quarter ending June 30. Again show computations by month and in total for the quarter.
3. Prepare a direct labour budget for the second quarter ending June 30. This time it is *not* necessary to show monthly figures; show quarterly totals only. Assume that the workforce is adjusted as work requirements change.
4. Assume that the company plans to produce a total of 380,000 units for the year. Prepare a manufacturing overhead budget for the nine-month period ending December 31. (Do not compute a predetermined overhead rate.) Again, it is *not* necessary to show monthly figures.

(CMA, adapted)

PROBLEM 9–24 Completing a Master Budget [LO2]

The following data relate to the operations of Lim Corporation, a wholesale distributor of consumer goods:

Current assets as of December 31:	
Cash	$6,000
Accounts receivable	$36,000
Inventory	$9,800
Buildings and equipment, net	$110,885
Accounts payable	$32,550
Common shares.	$100,000
Retained earnings	30,135

a. The gross margin is 30% of sales.
b. Actual and budgeted sales data are as follows:

December (actual)	$60,000
January	$70,000
February.	$80,000
March.	$85,000
April	$55,000

c. Sales are 40% for cash and 60% on credit. Credit sales are collected in the month following sale. The accounts receivable at December 31 are the result of December credit sales.
d. Each month's ending inventory should equal 20% of the following month's budgeted cost of goods sold.
e. One-quarter of a month's inventory purchases is paid for in the month of purchase; the other three-quarters is paid for in the following month. The accounts payable at December 31 are the result of December purchases of inventory.
f. Monthly expenses are as follows: commissions, $12,000; rent, $1,800; other expenses (excluding depreciation), 8% of sales. Assume that these expenses are paid monthly. Depreciation is $2,400 for the quarter and includes depreciation on new assets acquired during the quarter.
g. Equipment will be acquired for cash: $3,000 in January and $8,000 in February.
h. Management would like to maintain a minimum cash balance of $5,000 at the end of each month. The company has an agreement with a local bank that allows the company to borrow in increments of $1,000 at the beginning of each month, up to a total loan balance of $50,000.

The interest rate on these loans is 1% per month, and for simplicity, we will assume that interest is not compounded. The company would, as far as it is able, repay the loan plus accumulated interest at the end of the quarter.

Required:

Using the data above:

1. Complete the following schedule:

Schedule of Expected Cash Collections				
	January	February	March	Quarter
Cash sales............................	$28,000			
Credit sales	36,000	___	___	___
Total collections.....................	$64,000	___	___	___

2. Complete the following:

Merchandise Purchases Budget				
	January	February	March	Quarter
Budgeted cost of goods sold	$49,000*			
Add desired ending inventory	11,200†	___	___	___
Total needs	60,200			
Less beginning inventory..............	9,800	___	___	___
Required purchases	$50,400	___	___	___

*$70,000 sales × 70% = $49,000.
†$80,000 × 70% × 20% = $11,200.

Schedule of Expected Cash Disbursements—Merchandise Purchases				
	January	February	March	Quarter
December purchases	$32,550*			$32,550
January purchases	12,600	$37,800		50,400
February purchases..................				
March purchases.....................		___	___	___
Total disbursements	$45,150	___	___	___

*Beginning balance of the accounts payable.

3. Complete the following schedule:

Schedule of Expected Cash Disbursements—Selling and Administrative Expenses				
	January	February	March	Quarter
Commissions........................	$12,000			
Rent...............................	1,800			
Other expenses	5,600	___	___	___
Total disbursements	$19,400	___	___	___

4. Complete the following cash budget:

	January	February	March	Quarter
Cash balance, beginning..............	$ 6,000			
Add cash collections..................	64,000	___	___	___
Total cash available..................	70,000	___	___	___
For inventory	45,150			
For operating expenses.............	19,400			
For equipment	3,000	___	___	___
Total cash disbursements	67,550			
Excess (deficiency) of cash...........	$ 2,450			
Financing				
Etc.				

5. Prepare an absorption costing income statement, similar to the one shown in Schedule 9 on page 367, for the quarter ended March 31.
6. Prepare a balance sheet as of March 31.

PROBLEM 9–25 Applying the Flexible Budget Approach [LO3, LO4]

The Centrico Medical Laboratory, a government-sponsored charity, is located on the island of Ste. Lucretia. The laboratory has just finished its operations for September, which was a particularly busy month due to a chemical spill that affected a few neighbouring small islands, causing many illnesses. The chemical spill and contamination largely bypassed Ste. Lucretia's water supply, but residents of Ste. Lucretia willingly donated supplies and the laboratory assisted in the medical testing to help people on other islands. As a consequence, the medical laboratory collected and processed over 25% more laboratory samples from potentially ill residents than had been originally planned for the month.

A report prepared by a government official comparing actual costs to costs included in the static budget for the medical laboratory appears below. (The currency in Ste. Lucretia is the East Caribbean dollar.) Continued support from the government depends on the lab's ability to demonstrate control over its costs.

CENTRICO MEDICAL LABORATORY Cost Control Report For the Month Ended September 30			
	Actual	Static Budget	Static Budget Variance
Laboratory samples collected	920	700	220
Variable costs:			
Medical supplies	$14,878	$10,640	$4,238
Lab tests	16,173	12,915	3,258
Refreshments for staff and volunteers	1,779	1,435	344
Administrative supplies	284	490	(206)
Total variable cost	33,114	25,480	7,634
Fixed costs:			
Staff salaries	19,800	19,800	0
Equipment depreciation	3,150	2,850	300
Rent	2,250	2,250	0
Utilities	486	450	36
Total fixed cost	25,686	25,350	336
Total cost	$58,800	$50,830	$7,970

The managing director of the medical laboratory was very unhappy with this report, claiming that his costs were higher than expected due to the emergency on the neighbouring islands. He also pointed out that the additional costs had been fully covered by payments from grateful recipients on the other islands. The government official who prepared the report countered that all of the figures had been submitted by the medical laboratory to the government; he was just pointing out that actual costs were considerably higher than promised in the budget.

Required:
1. Prepare a new performance report for September using the flexible budget approach. (*Note*: Even though there are no revenues in this setting, the flexible budget approach can still be used to prepare a flexible budget performance report. Use Exhibit 9–4 as your guide)
2. Do you think any of the variances in the report you prepared should be investigated? Why?

Cases

CASE 9–26 The Challenges of Participative Budgeting [LO1]

Dave Ludwig, the chief financial officer (CFO) of a major sporting goods manufacturer, Playco, had recently returned from an executive education course on budgeting. Playco manufactures four major product lines: golf equipment, hockey equipment, baseball equipment, and sporting apparel.

All products are sold through an extensive network of independent retailers, some of whom are major sporting goods outlets. Each product line is considered to be a separate division, headed up by a senior product manager who is responsible for all major day-to-day operating decisions, including pricing, product mix, production, and managing and expanding dealer relationships. All of Playco's senior product managers have been with the company for at least 5 years, with experience ranging from 6 to 15 years.

In the past, Playco has always used a top–down approach to developing the master budget, whereby a senior management team including the CEO, CFO, and the vice-presidents of manufacturing and marketing set the revenue and expense budgets each year for the four major product lines. These budgets have been based on the company's strategic plans, the team's analysis of the operating environment (including the key competitors), and other factors that could affect demand for sporting goods, such as expected inflation rates, interest rates, changing demographics, and so on. Some input was sought from the senior product manager of each of the major product lines when developing the budget. However, this was limited to a one-on-one meeting between the manager and the CFO at the beginning of the budgeting process each year. These meetings typically lasted about an hour, during which the product managers were invited to provide input on the competitive environment, anticipated pricing issues, production plans (including any design changes), and so on. After these meetings had been completed, the senior management team typically met several times over a one-month period and finalized the budget. Each production manager was then assigned a detailed budget for all revenue and expense items under his or her control. The budget assignment was done during a meeting attended by all of the senior product managers and the senior management team. Each product manager's budget was presented by the CFO using a PowerPoint presentation, so all managers were aware of each other's budgets. The product managers were free to comment or react to their assigned budget at the meeting but no negotiations took place. Typically, the managers said little other than to acknowledge their assigned budgets and perhaps discuss the challenges it presented.

Dave and the other members of the senior management team had always believed that their top–down approach was appropriate for several reasons. First, it was efficient since it didn't require extensive input from the senior product managers, other than the one-hour meetings with the CFO. Typically, the entire process took about a month. Second, it resulted in what Dave believed were consistently challenging and fair budgets across the four product lines. With some small variations, the revenue growth budgets and unit cost reduction targets were very consistent across the product lines each year. Dave believed this was important because the product managers' bonuses were influenced by how well they did compared to budget, and the top–down approach eliminated the problem of budget slack. Finally, since all of the members of the senior management team had been with the company for at least 10 years, and some input was solicited from the senior product managers, Dave felt that the budget was based on good information and thus was reasonably accurate.

Despite the perceived benefits of the top–down approach, Dave had begun to hear some grumblings from the senior product managers that the process wasn't fair and wasn't resulting in accurate budgets. Dave wasn't convinced that the process was unfair but did acknowledge that there appeared to be accuracy problems. Over the past five years, it was common to see the revenues and expenses of the different product lines coming in considerably better or worse than budget. Some product lines would do well in a given year and beat their budgets while others would fail to meet their budgets. Moreover, some product lines would do well one year and then poorly the next year compared to budget. There didn't seem to be a predictable pattern to these results. Given this, Dave decided to attend an executive seminar on the use of participative budgeting to see if Playco might benefit from the approach.

After completing the seminar, Dave was convinced that the potential benefits arising from participative budgets, including more accurate budget estimates and greater commitment to the budgets by the senior product managers, justified trying the approach. He persuaded the other members of the senior management team that Playco should try the participative approach in developing budgets for 2012. The process they agreed on was as follows:

- Senior management would communicate the key strategic goals to the senior product managers (e.g., overall profit targets for the company) as well as key planning assumptions about inflation rates, unemployment rates, interest rates, etc.
- Based on the strategic goals and planning assumptions, the senior product managers would develop their own detailed revenue and expense budgets for 2012, providing written justification for any major assumptions and other key factors influencing their budgets (e.g., anticipated actions such as price cuts or new product introductions by key competitors).
- Senior management would review the budgets submitted by the senior managers and meet with them individually to discuss and negotiate the final amounts.

Richard Wood, senior product manager for the golf equipment line, was the first to have his budget review meeting with the senior management team. The attendees, included Dave Ludwig (CFO), Lois Davis (CEO), Bill Stevens (VP Marketing), and Marita Delano (VP Production). Below are excerpts from the discussion at the meeting:

Richard: I just want to start off by saying how much I appreciate being given the chance to participate in setting my own budgets this year. My team has worked very hard in putting these estimates together. We have done extensive market research, talked to our distributors at length, and identified opportunities for improvements over last year. Overall I think that our revenue budget that shows a 10% increase over last year and our gross margin percentage, which is budgeted to improve by 3% despite higher costs on some raw materials, represent aggressive but attainable targets.

Dave: Well, Richard, we're glad to hear that you appreciate being permitted more involvement with the budget this year. We too think this is the right approach to use for many reasons and value your input in developing the budgets.

Lois: I echo Dave's sentiments about your participation but I must say, Richard, that overall we think your budget estimates for both revenues and expenses are a bit soft. We think you can do better.

Richard: I don't understand, as I stated earlier, my budget represents solid growth in revenues and effective cost management. If I achieve my budgets, the performance of the golf equipment product line in 2012 will be the best it's been in five years.

Bill: There is no doubt that 10% revenue growth is a good starting point but my sense of the golf equipment market for 2012 is that 15% growth is achievable. People are more health-conscious than ever and with longer golf seasons across the country because of global warming, we should see a nice spike in sales next year.

Marita: As for your expense budget, I commend you for budgeting a 3% improvement in gross margin percentage, but I think more can be done. I've crunched the numbers and talked to some of your production people, and I don't see why you can't budget a 5% improvement. You need to lean harder on suppliers for price reductions, use less overtime on the production line, and find other ways to cut costs next year.

Richard: This doesn't make any sense, if you guys think you know better than me what my budget should be, why did you ask me to participate in the first place? I've pushed my suppliers to the limit and I'm not willing to sacrifice quality to get lower unit costs. Overtime is unavoidable given scheduled shutdowns in the plant and the rush orders that inevitably occur. And, we're already running as lean as we can in production, so there isn't room to reduce costs more than I've budgeted without severely cutting corners.

Dave: Now hold on Richard, don't get defensive. Remember, as part of our new participative approach, we are here to negotiate the final budget with you to arrive at figures we're all comfortable with.

Richard: But this doesn't feel like a negotiation, it feels like I'm being told what my budget should be, despite the fact that I've assured you my numbers are solid. I've been with Playco 10 years—surely that gives me some credibility when it comes to developing a budget!

Lois: We didn't say the negotiations would be easy or that we don't trust you, Richard. But, you have to understand that from a companywide perspective, your budgets aren't good enough. We need more from you. And don't forget, because annual bonuses are linked to actual performance against budget, it's fair for us to demand that your budgets be very challenging.

Richard: I'm at a loss here; this isn't at all what I expected the process would be like. In some ways, I liked our old top–down approach better.

Dave: I think we've thrashed this out as much as we can. Richard, your mandate is clear. Do some fine-tuning of your estimates to come in with a revenue budget that is up 15% from 2011 and a gross margin budget that shows 5% improvement over last year. Because of our new participative approach, you are free to do whatever you need to make that happen in your budget.

Lois: Dave's right, take your time with these changes, Richard, and send us each a copy of your new budget within the next couple of weeks. I don't think we need to meet again since we all know what needs to be done. Thanks everyone, this has been a very efficient process.

The budget review meetings with the other senior product managers followed a similar pattern.

Required:
1. Why might the top–down approach have led to inaccurate budgets in prior years?
2. Identify the problems with the participative budgeting approach being used at Playco? What are some consequences that may result from their approach?
3. What changes would you recommend be made to the participative budgeting approach at Playco?

CASE 9–27 Master Budget with Supporting Schedules [LO2]

Knockoffs Unlimited, a nationwide distributor of low-cost imitation designer necklaces, has an exclusive franchise on the distribution of the necklaces, and sales have grown so rapidly over the last few years that it has become necessary to add new members to the management team. To date, the company's budgeting practices have been inferior, and at times, the company has experienced a cash shortage. You have been given responsibility for all planning and budgeting. Your first assignment is to prepare a master budget for the next three months, starting April 1. You are anxious to make a favourable impression on the president and have assembled the information below.

The necklaces are sold to retailers for $10 each. Recent and forecasted sales in units are as follows:

January (actual)	20,000	June	50,000
February (actual)	26,000	July	30,000
March (actual)	40,000	August	28,000
April	65,000	September	25,000
May	100,000		

The large buildup in sales before and during May is due to Mother's Day. Ending inventories should be equal to 40% of the next month's sales in units.

The necklaces cost the company $4 each. Purchases are paid for as follows: 50% in the month of purchase and the remaining 50% in the following month. All sales are on credit, with no discount, and payable within 15 days. The company has found, however, that only 20% of a month's sales are collected by month-end. An additional 70% is collected in the following month, and the remaining 10% is collected in the second month following sale. Bad debts have been negligible.

The company's monthly operating expenses are given below:

Variable:	
Sales commissions	4% of sales
Fixed:	
Advertising	$200,000
Rent	$18,000
Wages and salaries	$106,000
Utilities	$7,000
Insurance	$3,000
Depreciation	$14,000

All operating expenses are paid during the month, in cash, with the exception of depreciation and insurance. Insurance is paid on an annual basis, in November of each year. The company plans to purchase $16,000 in new equipment during May and $40,000 in new equipment during June; both purchases will be paid in cash. The company declares dividends of $15,000 each quarter, payable in the first month of the following quarter. The company's balance sheet at March 31 is given below:

Assets	
Cash	$ 74,000
Accounts receivable ($26,000 February sales;	
$320,000 March sales)	346,000
Inventory	104,000
Prepaid insurance	21,000
Fixed assets, net of depreciation	950,000
Total assets	$1,495,000

Liabilities and Shareholders' Equity	
Accounts payable	$ 100,000
Dividends payable	15,000
Common shares	800,000
Retained earnings	580,000
Total liabilities and shareholders' equity	$1,495,000

The company wants a minimum ending cash balance each month of $50,000. All borrowing is done at the beginning of the month; any repayments are made at the end of the month. The company has an agreement with a bank that allows it to borrow in increments of $1,000 at the beginning of each month. The interest rate on these loans is 1% per month, and for simplicity, assume that interest is not compounded. At the end of the quarter, the company would pay the bank all of the accumulated interest on the loan and as much of the loan as possible (in increments of $1,000), while still retaining at least $50,000 in cash.

Required:

Prepare a master budget for the three-month period ending June 30. Include the following detailed budgets:

1. *a.* A sales budget by month and in total.
   b. A schedule of expected cash collections from sales, by month and in total.
   c. A merchandise purchases budget in units and in dollars. Show the budget by month and in total.
   d. A schedule of expected cash disbursements for merchandise purchases, by month and in total.
2. A cash budget. Show the budget by month and in total.
3. A budgeted income statement for the three-month period ending June 30. Use the variable costing approach.
4. A budgeted balance sheet as of June 30.

CASE 9–28 Selling Expense Flexible Budget [LO3, LO4]

Harriet Snowden, president of EdDEV Inc., was anticipating positive performance reports for November because she knew the company's sales for the month had exceeded budget by a considerable margin. EdDEV, a distributor of educational software packages, had been growing steadily for approximately two years. Snowden's biggest challenge at this point was to ensure that the company maintained control of expenses during this growth period. When Snowden received the November reports, her hopes were dashed by the large unfavourable variance in the company's monthly selling expense report that is presented below:

		November		
EdDEV INC. Monthly Selling Expense Report November	**Annual Budget**	**Static Budget**	**Actual**	**Static Budget Variance**
Unit sales..................	2,000,000	280,000	310,000	30,000 f
Dollar sales	$80,000,000	$11,200,000	$12,400,000	$1,200,000 f
Orders processed	54,000	6,500	5,800	700 u
Salespeople per month	90	90	96	6 u
Expenses:				
Advertising...............	$19,800,000	$ 1,650,000	$ 1,660,000	$ 10,000 u
Staff salaries..............	1,500,000	125,000	125,000	0
Sales salaries	1,296,000	108,000	115,400	7,400 u
Commissions.............	3,200,000	448,000	496,000	48,000 u
Per diem expense	1,782,000	148,500	162,600	14,100 u
Office expense............	4,080,000	340,000	358,400	18,400 u
Shipping expense	6,750,000	902,500	976,500	74,000 u
Total expense............	$38,408,000	$ 3,722,000	$ 3,893,900	$ 171,900 u

Snowden called in the company's new controller, Anne Gibson, to discuss the implications of the variances reported for November and to plan a strategy for improving performance. Gibson suggested that the reporting format the company had been using might not be giving Snowden a true picture of the company's operations and proposed that EdDEV implement flexible budgeting for reporting purposes. Gibson offered to redo the monthly selling expense report for November using flexible budgeting so that Snowden could compare the two reports and see the advantages of flexible budgeting.

After some analysis, Gibson derived the following data about the company's selling expenses:

a. Sales force total compensation is composed of a monthly base salary and commissions. The commissions vary with sales revenue.
b. Sales office expense is a mixed cost, with the variable portion pertaining to the number of orders processed. The fixed portion is $3,000,000 annually, incurred evenly throughout the year.
c. After the adoption of the annual budget for the current year, EdDEV decided to form a new sales territory, and approval was given to hire six additional salespeople effective November 1. Gibson decided that these additional six people should be included in her revised report.

d.   Sales force per diem reimbursement, while a fixed amount per day, is variable with the number of salespeople and the number of days spent travelling. EdDEV's original budget was based on an average sales force of 90 persons throughout the year, with each salesperson travelling 15 days per month.

e.   Shipping expense is a mixed cost, with the variable portion, $3 per unit, dependent on the number of units sold. The fixed portion is incurred evenly throughout the year.

Using the data above, Gibson believed she would be able to revise the November report and present it to Snowden for her review.

Required:

1.   Describe the benefits of flexible budgeting, and explain why Anne Gibson would propose that EdDev use flexible budgeting in this situation.

2.   Prepare a revised comprehensive performance report for November that would permit Harriet Snowden to more clearly evaluate EdDEV's control over selling expenses. Use Exhibit 9–6 as your guide.

3.   How much of the total unfavourable static budget variance of $171,900 relates to actual activity levels differing from the static budget?

(CMA, adapted)

CASE 9–29 Master Budget for a Manufacturer [LO3, LO4]

Garneau Manufacturing Ltd. produces and distributes a special type of chemical compound called Compound WX. The information below about Garneau's operations has been assembled to assist budget preparation. The company is preparing its master budget for the first quarter of 2012. The budget will detail each month's activity and the activity for the quarter in total. The master budget will be based on the following information:

a.   Selling price is $60 per unit in 2011 and will not change for the first two quarters of 2012. Actual and estimated sales are as follows:

Actual 2011	Estimated 2012
November: 10,000 units	January: 11,000 units
December: 12,000 units	February: 10,000 units
	March: 13,000 units
	April: 11,000 units
	May: 10,000 units

b.   The company produces enough units each month to meet that month's sales plus a desired inventory level equal to 20% of next month's estimated sales. Finished Goods inventory at the end of 2011 consisted of 2,200 units at a variable cost of $33 each.

c.   The company purchases enough raw materials each month for the current month's production requirement and 25% of next month's production requirements. Each unit of product requires 5 kilograms of raw material at $0.60 per kilogram. There were 13,500 kilograms of raw materials in inventory at the end of 2011. Garneau pays 40% of raw material purchases in the month of purchase and pays the remaining 60% in the following month.

d.   Each unit of finished product requires 1.25 labour-hours. The average wage rate is $16 per hour.

e.   Variable manufacturing overhead is 50% of the direct labour cost.

f.   Credit sales are 60% of total sales. The company collects 50% of the credit sales during the first month following the month of sale and 50% during the second month.

g.   Fixed overhead cost (per month):

Factory supervisor's salary................	$75,000
Factory insurance.......................	1,400
Factory rent	8,000
Depreciation of factory equipment..........	1,200

h.   Total fixed selling and administrative expenses are as follows:

Advertising	$ 300
Depreciation...........................	9,000
Insurance	250
Salaries...............................	4,000
Other.................................	14,550

i. Variable selling and administrative expenses consist of $4 for shipping and sales commissions of 10% of sales.
j. The company is going to acquire assets for use in the sales office at a cost of $300,000, which will be paid at the end of January 2012. The monthly depreciation expense on the additional capital assets will be $6,000.
k. The balance sheet as of December 31, 2011, is as follows:

Assets

Cash		$ 80,000
Accounts receivable		612,000
Inventory: Raw materials	$ 8,100	
Finished goods	72,600	80,700
Plant and equipment	1,000,000	
Less: accumulated depreciation	(100,000)	900,000
Total assets		$1,672,700

Liabilities and Equity

Accounts payable	$ 24,000
6% Long-term notes payable	900,000
Common shares	735,000
Retained earnings	13,700
Total liabilities and equity	$1,672,700

Additional information:
- All cash payments except purchases of raw materials are made monthly as incurred.
- All loan repayments and borrowings, when appropriate, occur at the end of each month.
- All interest on borrowed funds is paid at the end of each month at the rate of 6% per year.
- Loan repayments and borrowings, when appropriate, may be made in any amount.
- A minimum cash balance of $30,000 is required at the end of each month.

Required:
1. Prepare the following budgets for the first three months of 2012:
    a. Sales budget
    b. Production budget
    c. Raw materials purchases budget
    d. Direct labour and manufacturing overhead budget.
    e. Selling and administrative budget
    f. Budgeted income statement (using variable costing). Ignore income taxes.
    g. Cash budget
2. Prepare a budgeted balance sheet as at March 31, 2012

Research and Application

R 9–30 Budgeting at Not-for-Profit Organizations [LO5]
Form a team to examine how a not-for-profit organization in your area develops and uses its operating budgets. Make an appointment to meet with the individual responsible for the budgeting process and discuss the following issues.

Required:
1. How are budgets set each year? Is a zero-based budgeting approach used or are budgets based on prior year amounts adjusted for anticipated changes in the coming year?
2. How challenging are the budget targets?
3. How long does the budget process take and who is involved?
4. Is the budget prepared on an expenditure basis or a program basis?
5. How often are actual results compared to the budget?
6. Is any follow-up done if actual amounts differ significantly from the budget?
7. Are flexible budgets used?
8. What are the major strengths and weaknesses of the budgeting process used by the organization?

APPENDIX 9A: INVENTORY DECISIONS

connect   Appendix available on Connect.

STANDARD COSTS AND OVERHEAD ANALYSIS

■ MANAGING DISTRIBUTION COSTS

Rising fuel costs in recent years have created pressure for many organizations to find ways to improve the management of the distribution function. For many manufacturing companies, the cost of shipping products to wholesalers, retailers, and the final customer represents a significant portion of their overall cost structure. To address these issues, Catalyst Paper Corporation, a pulp and paper manufacturer based in British Columbia, has developed a comprehensive approach for managing its distribution costs.

At Catalyst Paper, shipping products to customers involves a complex network of manufacturing plants, warehouses, transportation modes (e.g., rail versus truck), and carriers within modes of transportation. To improve control over shipping expenses, analysts at Catalyst Paper have developed a model that they use to budget the cost of each shipment made to a customer throughout the year. The model is very elaborate and requires estimates of the mode of transportation to be used for each shipment (e.g., rail, truck, container ship); the specific carrier that will be used within a transportation mode (e.g., ABC Trucking); the rates charged by that carrier; and the warehouse(s) that will be used to fill the order. Combining all of these estimates allows Catalyst to calculate the budgeted or "standard" cost for each shipment made to a customer. At the end of each month, company analysts compare the actual shipping costs to the standard amounts estimated by their model.

Variances between the actual and standard costs can be caused by several factors, including using different transportation modes (rail instead of truck), different carriers (DEF Trucking instead of ABC Trucking) or using different warehouses to source the order, compared to the plan. The model developed by Catalyst allows analysts to determine the portion of the total variance between actual and standard shipping expenses attributable to each of these factors. Once the causes of the variance have been identified, managers can identify follow-up actions aimed at eliminating or reducing unfavourable variances in future periods (e.g., switch to a less expensive transportation mode or carrier).

Prior to developing their analytical model, managers at Catalyst could not pinpoint the cause of unfavourable variances in any given month. Thanks to the new approach, management believes they have a better understanding of the drivers of distribution costs. They also believe it has improved their ability to both plan and control distribution costs.

How are standards, such as those used by Catalyst Paper Corporation, set? How are the variances calculated and how do managers decide which ones to investigate? These are among the many topics examined in this chapter.

Source: Kevin Gaffney, Valeri Gladkikh, and Alan Webb, "A Case Study of a Variance Analysis Framework for Managing Distribution Costs," *Accounting Perspectives, 6*, 2007, pp. 167–190. Reprinted by permission of John Wiley and Sons via Rightslink.

C hapter 10 continues our three-chapter study of planning, control, and performance measurement. Quite often, these terms carry with them negative connotations. Indeed, performance measurements can be used counterproductively to create fear, to cast blame, and to punish. However, if used properly, as explained in the following examples, performance measurement serves a vital function in both daily life and in organizations:

> Imagine you want to improve your basketball shooting skill. You know that practice will help, so you go to the basketball court and start shooting toward the hoop. However, as soon as the ball gets close to the rim your vision goes blurry for a second, so that you cannot observe where the ball ended up in relation to the target (left, right, in front, too far back, inside the hoop?). It would be pretty difficult to improve under those conditions and eventually you would likely lose interest in continuing to practice.
>
> Alternatively, imagine someone beginning a weight loss program. A normal step in such programs is to purchase a scale to be able to track one's progress: Is this program working? Am I losing weight? A positive answer would be encouraging and would motivate me to keep up the effort, while a negative answer might lead me to reflect on the process: Am I working on the right diet and exercise program? Am I doing everything I am supposed to? But, suppose you don't want to set up a sophisticated measurement system and decide to forgo the scale. You would still have some idea of how well you are doing from simple cues such as clothes feeling looser, a belt that fastens at a different hole, or simply via observation in a mirror! Now, imagine trying to sustain a weight loss program without any feedback on how well you are doing.
>
> In these examples, availability of quantitative measures of performance can yield two types of benefits: First, performance feedback can help improve the "production process" through a better understanding of what works and what doesn't; e.g., shooting this way works better than shooting that way. Second, feedback on performance can sustain motivation and effort, because it is encouraging and/or because it suggests that more effort is required for the goal to be met.[1]

In the same way, performance measurement can be helpful in an organization. It can provide feedback concerning what works and what does not work, and it can help motivate people to sustain their efforts.

Our study of performance measurement begins with the production function. In this chapter we see how various measures are used to control operations and to evaluate performance in this key operating area. Even though we are starting with an operational area, keep in mind that performance measures should be derived from the organization's overall strategy. For example, a company like Cervélo that bases its strategy on designing and producing world-class racing bicycles should use different performance measures than a company like Purolator Courier, where on-time delivery, customer convenience, and low cost are key competitive advantages. Cervélo may want to keep close track of the percentage of revenues from new models introduced within the last year, whereas Purolator may want to closely monitor the percentage of packages delivered on time. In Chapter 11, we will have more to say concerning the role of strategy in the selection of performance measures when we discuss the balanced scorecard. But first we will examine how *standard costs* are used by managers to help control costs.

Companies in highly competitive industries like Research in Motion, WestJet, MDG Computers Canada, and Graf Canada must be able to provide high-quality goods and services at low cost. If they do not, their customers will buy from more efficient competitors. Operationally, managers must obtain inputs such as raw materials and electricity at the lowest possible prices and use them as effectively as possible—while maintaining or increasing the quality of what they sell. If inputs are purchased at prices that are too high or greater quantities are used than is really necessary, higher costs will result.

How do managers control the prices that are paid for inputs and the quantities that are used? They could examine every transaction in detail, but this obviously would be an inefficient use of management time. For many companies, the answer to this control problem lies at least partially in *standard costs*. Standards represent specific elements of budgets

(Chapter 9) such as direct materials or direct labour requirements as well as overhead projections. As such, standards serve both a planning function and a control function. Whether or not organizations employ standard costs to formally cost jobs (Chapter 3) or processes (Chapter 4) is one of the decisions managers must make. If they decide to use actual costs for jobs or processes, they can still use standard costs for budgeting and operational planning purposes.

Controlling overhead costs is also a major concern for managers in business, government, and not-for-profit organizations. Indeed, overhead is a major cost—if not *the* major cost—in many large organizations. Control of overhead costs poses special problems in part because they are more difficult to understand than direct materials and direct labour. Overhead is made up of numerous individual items, some of which are small in dollar amounts. Further, some overhead costs are variable and others are fixed. In this chapter we extend the concept of flexible budgets introduced in Chapter 9 to their use in controlling overhead costs. We also address the analysis and reporting of overhead costs within a standard cost system.

STANDARD COSTS—MANAGEMENT BY EXCEPTION

A *standard* is a benchmark or "norm" for measuring performance. Standards are found everywhere. Your doctor evaluates your weight using standards that have been set for individuals of your age, height, and gender. The food we eat in restaurants must be prepared under specified standards of cleanliness. The buildings we live in must conform to standards set in building codes. Standards are also widely used in managerial accounting, where they relate to the *quantity* and *cost* of inputs used in manufacturing goods or providing services.

Quantity and cost standards are set for each major input such as raw materials and labour time. *Quantity standards* specify how much of an input should be used to make a unit of product or provide a unit of service. *Cost (price) standards* specify how much should be paid for each unit of the input. Actual quantities and actual costs of inputs are periodically compared to these standards. If either the quantity or the cost of inputs departs significantly from the standards, managers investigate the discrepancy to find and eliminate the cause of the problem. This process is called **management by exception**.

In our daily lives, we operate in a management by exception mode most of the time. Consider what happens when you sit down in the driver's seat of your car. You put the key in the ignition, you turn the key, and your car starts. Your expectation (standard) that the car will start is met; you do not have to open the car hood and check the battery, the connecting cables, the fuel lines, and so on. If you turn the key and the car does not start, then you have a discrepancy (variance). Your expectations are not met, and you need to investigate why. Note that even if the car starts after a second try, it would be wise to investigate anyway. The fact that the expectation was not initially met should be viewed as an opportunity to uncover the cause of the problem rather than as simply an annoyance. If the underlying cause is not discovered and corrected, the problem may recur and become much worse.

This basic approach to identifying and solving problems is used in the *variance analysis cycle*, which is illustrated in Exhibit 10–1. The cycle begins with the preparation of standard cost performance reports in the accounting department. These reports highlight the variances, which are the differences between actual results and what should have occurred according to the standards. The variances can raise numerous questions. Why did the variance occur? Why is this variance larger than it was last period? The significant variances are investigated to discover their root causes. Corrective actions are taken, and then the next period's operations are carried out. The cycle then begins again with the preparation of a new standard cost performance for the most recent period. The emphasis should be on highlighting problems, finding their root causes, and taking corrective action. The goal is to improve operations—not to assign blame.

Management by exception
A system of management in which standards are set for various operating activities that are then periodically compared to actual results. Any differences that are deemed significant are brought to the attention of management as "exceptions."

EXHIBIT 10–1 The Variance Analysis Cycle

Variance Analysis Cycle

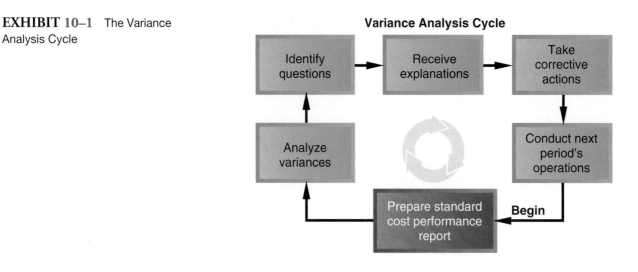

SETTING STANDARD COSTS

Setting price and quantity standards ideally combines the expertise of everyone who has responsibility for purchasing and using inputs. In a manufacturing setting, this might include accountants, purchasing managers, engineers, production supervisors, line managers, and production workers. Past records of purchase prices and of input usage can be helpful in setting standards. However, the standards should be designed to encourage efficient *future* operations, not a repetition of *past* operations that may or may not have been efficient.

Who Uses Standard Costs?

Manufacturing, service, food, and not-for-profit organizations all make use of standards to some extent. Auto service centres like Canadian Tire, for example, often set specific labour time standards for the completion of certain work tasks, such as installing a water pump or changing a tire, and then measure actual performance against these standards. Fast-food outlets such as Harvey's have exacting standards as to the quantity of meat put into a sandwich, as well as standards for the cost of the meat. Hospitals have standard costs (for food, laundry, and other items) for each occupied bed per day, as well as standard time allowances for certain routine activities, such as laboratory tests. In short, you are likely to run into standard costs in virtually any line of business.

Manufacturing companies often have highly developed standard costing systems in which standards relating to materials, labour, and overhead are developed in detail for each separate product. A **standard cost record** shows the standard quantities and costs of the inputs required to produce a unit of a specific product. The cost is calculated by multiplying the standard quantity of each input required to produce one unit of output by the price or rate for that input. These records, which used to be recorded on file cards, are now electronically created and maintained as part of the company's accounting information system. In this section, we provide a detailed example of how standard costs are set in preparing the standard cost record.

Standard cost record
A detailed listing of the standard amounts of materials, labour, and overhead that should go into a unit of product, multiplied by the standard price or rate that has been set for each cost element.

Ideal versus Practical Standards

Should standards be attainable all of the time, part of the time, or almost none of the time? Opinions vary, but standards tend to fall into one of two categories—either ideal or practical.

Ideal standards are those that can be attained only under the best circumstances. They allow for no machine breakdowns or other work interruptions, and they call for a

Ideal standards
Standards that allow for no machine breakdowns or other work interruptions and that require peak efficiency at all times.

level of effort that can be attained only by the most skilled and efficient employees working at peak effort 100% of the time. Some managers feel that such standards have motivational value. They argue that even though employees know they will rarely meet the standard, it is a constant reminder of the need for ever-increasing efficiency and effort. However, few firms use ideal standards because most managers feel they are discouraging for even the most diligent workers. Moreover, when ideal standards are used, variances from the standards have little meaning. Large variances from the ideal are normal and it is difficult to "manage by exception."

Practical standards are defined as standards that are "tight but attainable." They allow for normal machine downtime and employee rest periods, and they can be attained through reasonable, although highly efficient, efforts by the average employee. Variances from practical standards typically signal a need for management attention because they represent deviations that fall outside normal operating conditions. In addition to signalling abnormal conditions, they can also be used in forecasting cash flows and in planning inventory. By contrast, ideal standards cannot be used in normal budgets or plans; they do not allow for normal inefficiencies, and therefore they result in unrealistic planning and forecasting figures.

Throughout the remainder of this chapter, we will assume the use of practical rather than ideal standards.

Practical standards
Standards that allow for normal machine downtime and other work interruptions and can be attained through reasonable, although highly efficient, efforts by the average employee.

Setting Direct Materials Standards

We will use the hypothetical Heirloom Pewter Company to illustrate the development and application of a standard cost system. The company was organized a year ago and its only product at present is a reproduction of an eighteenth-century pewter bookend. The bookend is made largely by hand, using traditional metal-working tools. Consequently, the manufacturing process is very labour-intensive and requires a high level of skill.

Heirloom Pewter has recently expanded its workforce to take advantage of unexpected demand for the bookends as gifts. The company started with a small group of experienced pewter workers but has had to hire less experienced workers as a result of the expansion. George Hanlon is the controller of the company. He has been asked by Heirloom Pewter's president to develop a system that would allow the company to periodically evaluate the productivity of its employees, the efficiency of raw material usage and the prices paid for labour and materials.

Hanlon's first task was to prepare price and quantity standards for the company's only significant raw material, pewter ingots. The **standard price per unit** for direct materials should reflect the final, delivered cost of the materials including shipping, receiving, and other such costs, net of any discounts taken. After consulting with the purchasing manager, Hanlon prepared the following documentation for the standard price of a kilogram of pewter in ingot form:

Standard price per unit
The price that should be paid for a single unit of materials, including shipping, receiving, and other such costs, net of any discounts allowed.

Purchase price, top-grade pewter	$ 3.60
Freight, by truck, from the supplier's warehouse	0.44
Receiving and handling	0.05
Less purchase discount	(0.09)
Standard price per kilogram	$ 4.00

Notice that the standard price reflects a particular grade of material (top quality) delivered by a particular type of carrier (truck). Allowances have also been made for handling and discounts. If everything proceeds according to these expectations, the net standard price of a kilogram of pewter should therefore be $4.

The **standard quantity per unit** for direct materials should reflect the amount of material required for each unit of finished product, as well as an allowance for unavoidable waste, spoilage, and other normal inefficiencies. After consulting with the production

Standard quantity per unit
The amount of materials that should be required to complete a single unit of product, including allowances for normal waste, spoilage, and other inefficiencies.

manager, Hanlon prepared the following documentation for the standard quantity of pewter required for a pair of bookends:

Materials requirements as specified in the bill of materials for a pair of bookends, in kilograms	2.7
Allowance for waste and spoilage, in kilograms.	0.2
Allowance for rejects, in kilograms.	0.1
Standard quantity per pair of bookends, in kilograms	3.0

A bill of materials details the type and quantity of each item of material that should be used in a product. As shown above, it should be adjusted for waste and other factors when determining the standard quantity per unit of product. "Waste and spoilage" refers to materials that are wasted as a normal part of the production process or that spoil before they are used. "Rejects" refers to the direct materials contained in units that are defective and must be scrapped.

Although it is common to recognize allowances for waste, spoilage, and rejects when setting standard costs, this practice is often criticized because it contradicts the zero defects goal associated with improvement programs such as Six Sigma (Chapter 1). If allowances for waste, spoilage, and rejects are built into the standard cost, the levels of those allowances should be periodically reviewed and reduced over time to reflect improved processes, better training, and better equipment.

Once the price and quantity standards have been set, the standard cost of materials per unit of finished product can be computed as follows:

3.0 kilograms per unit $\times$ $4 per kilogram = $12 per unit

This $12 cost figure will appear as one item on the standard cost record of the product.

IN BUSINESS

Direct materials price standards should reflect the final delivered cost of the materials. Given increases in the costs of shipping raw materials across oceans, many companies have increased their price standards. For example, the average cost to rent a ship to transport raw materials from Brazil to China has increased from $65,000 to $180,000. In some instances, shipping costs now exceed the cost of the cargo itself. It costs about $88 to ship a tonne of iron ore from Brazil to Asia; however, the iron ore itself costs only $60 per tonne.

Source: Robert Guy Matthews, "Ship Shortage Pushes Up Prices of Raw Materials," *The Wall Street Journal*, October 22, 2007, pp. A1 and A12.

Setting Direct Labour Standards

Standard rate per hour
The labour rate that should be incurred per hour of labour time, including Employment Insurance, employee benefits, and other labour costs.

Direct labour price and quantity standards are usually expressed in terms of a labour rate and labour-hours. The **standard rate per hour** for direct labour would include not only wages earned but also employee benefits (e.g., Employment Insurance, extended medical insurance, etc.) and other labour costs. Using wage records and in consultation with the production manager, Hanlon determined the standard rate per hour at the Heirloom Pewter Company as follows:

Basic average wage rate per hour	$15.00
Employment taxes at 10% of the basic rate	1.50
Employee benefits at 30% of the basic rate.	4.50
Standard rate per direct labour-hour	$21.00

Many companies prepare a single standard rate for all employees in a department. This standard rate reflects the expected "mix" of workers, even though the actual wage rates may vary somewhat from individual to individual due to differing skills or seniority. According to the standard computed above, the direct labour rate for Heirloom Pewter should average $21 per hour.

The standard direct labour time required to complete a unit of product (generally called the **standard hours per unit**) is perhaps the single most difficult standard to determine. One approach for physical tasks is to break down each task into elemental body movements (such as reaching, pushing, and turning over). Published tables of standard times for such movements are available. Another approach is for an industrial engineer to do a time and motion study, which involves recording the time required for certain tasks. As stated earlier, the standard time should include allowances for breaks and personal needs of employees, cleanup, rejects, and machine downtime. After consulting with the production manager, Hanlon prepared the following documentation for the standard hours per unit:

Standard hours per unit
The amount of labour time that should be required to complete a single unit of product, including allowances for breaks, machine downtime, cleanup, rejects, and other normal inefficiencies.

Basic labour time per unit, in hours	1.9
Allowance for breaks and personal needs	0.1
Allowance for cleanup and machine downtime	0.3
Allowance for rejects	0.2
Standard labour-hours per unit of product	2.5

Once the rate and time standards have been set, the standard labour cost per unit of product can be computed as follows:

2.5 hours per unit × $21 per hour = $52.50 per unit

This $52.50 cost figure appears along with direct materials as one item on the standard cost record of the product.

Standard labour-hours have declined in relative importance for some organizations. This is particularly true in highly automated manufacturing firms. However, for many service organizations and numerous other construction and processing organizations, labour remains an important input to the production and service activities. For these organizations, standard labour-hours inform workers and managers what is expected and how labour should be used. More specifically, standards and the resulting comparisons to actual labour-hours may serve to motivate workers and managers. Labour standards can influence individuals in setting their own goals.

Setting Variable Manufacturing Overhead Standards

As with direct labour, the price and quantity standards for variable manufacturing overhead are generally expressed in terms of rate and hours. The rate represents *the variable portion of the predetermined overhead rate* first discussed in Chapter 3. Developing the rate requires an estimate of both the unit cost of the variable overhead items used in production (indirect supplies, indirect labour, etc.) as well as the quantity required for the planned level of production. The unit costs are relatively straightforward to estimate and can be based on prior year amounts or existing contractual agreements with suppliers that lock in prices. The quantities for variable overhead items can be estimated using actual results from prior periods. The hours relate to whatever activity base is used to apply overhead to units of product (usually machine-hours or direct labour-hours). At Heirloom Pewter, the variable portion of the predetermined overhead rate is $3 per direct labour-hour. Therefore, the standard variable manufacturing overhead cost per unit is computed as follows:

2.5 hours per unit × $3 per hour = $7.50 per unit

Standard cost per unit
The standard cost of a unit of product as shown on the standard cost card; it is computed by multiplying the standard quantity or hours by the standard price or rate for each cost element.

This $7.50 cost figure appears along with direct materials and direct labour as one item on the standard cost record for variable production costs in Exhibit 10–2. Observe that the **standard cost per unit** is computed by multiplying the standard quantity or hours by the standard price or rate. We expand our discussion of standard costs to include fixed manufacturing overhead later in this chapter.

EXHIBIT 10–2 Standard Cost Record—Variable Production Cost

Inputs	(1) Standard Quantity or Hours	(2) Standard Price or Rate	(3) Standard Cost (1) × (2)
Direct materials	3.0 kilograms	$ 4.00	$12.00
Direct labour	2.5 hours	21.00	52.50
Variable manufacturing overhead	2.5 hours	3.00	7.50
Total standard variable cost per unit			$72.00

Are Standards the Same as Budgets?

Standards and budgets are very similar. The major distinction between the two terms is that a standard is a *unit* amount, whereas a budget is a *total* amount. The standard cost for materials at Heirloom Pewter is $12 per pair of bookends. If 1,000 pairs of bookends are to be manufactured during a budgeting period, then the budgeted cost of materials would be $12,000. In effect, *a standard can be viewed as the budgeted cost for one unit of product.*

A General Model for Variance Analysis

An important reason for separating standards into two categories—price and quantity—is that different managers are usually responsible for buying and for using inputs and these two activities occur at different points in time. In the case of raw materials, for example, the purchasing manager is responsible for the price, and this responsibility is exercised at the time of purchase. In contrast, the production manager is responsible for the amount of the raw materials used, and this responsibility is exercised when the materials are used in production, which may be many weeks or months after the purchase date. It is important, therefore, that we separate discrepancies due to deviations from price standards from those due to deviations from quantity standards. Differences between *standard* prices and *actual* prices and *standard* quantities and *actual* quantities are called **variances**. The act of computing and interpreting variances is called *variance analysis.*

A general model for computing standard cost variances for variable costs is presented in Exhibit 10–3. This model isolates price variances from quantity variances and shows how each of these variances is computed. We will use this model to compute variances for

Variance
The difference between standard prices and quantities and actual prices and quantities.

EXHIBIT 10–3 A General Model for Variance Analysis— Variable Production Costs

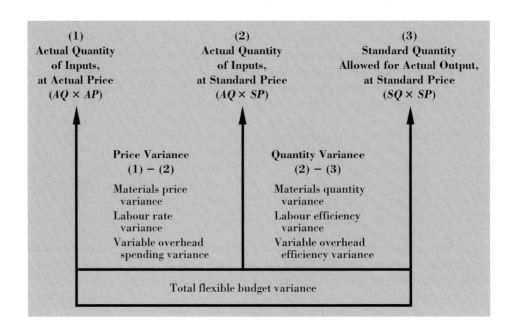

direct materials, direct labour, and variable manufacturing overhead. We will discuss the model for calculating and interpreting fixed overhead variances later in this chapter.

Four things should be noted from Exhibit 10–3. First, a price variance and a quantity variance can be computed for all three variable cost elements—direct materials, direct labour, and variable manufacturing overhead—even though the variance is not called by the same name in all cases. For example, a price variance is called a *materials price variance* in the case of direct materials but a *labour rate variance* in the case of direct labour and an *overhead spending variance* in the case of variable manufacturing overhead.

Second, although the price variance may be called different names, it is computed in exactly the same way, regardless of whether one is dealing with direct materials, direct labour, or variable manufacturing overhead. The same is true with the quantity variance.

Third, the inputs represent the actual quantity of direct materials, direct labour, and variable manufacturing overhead used; the output represents the good production of the period, expressed in terms of the *standard quantity (or the standard hours) allowed for the actual output* (see column 3 in Exhibit 10–3). The **standard quantity allowed** or **standard hours allowed**, means the amount of direct materials, direct labour, or variable manufacturing overhead *that should have been used* to produce the actual output of the period. This could be more or less than the materials, labour, or overhead that was *actually* used, depending on the efficiency or inefficiency of operations. The standard quantity allowed is computed by multiplying the actual output in units by the standard input allowed per unit.

Fourth, note that the amount in column 3 ($SQ \times SP$) of Exhibit 10–3 represents the flexible budget for the period. In Chapter 9 we prepared a simplified version of a flexible budget based on the *actual* quantity of units produced for the period multiplied by the total *budgeted* cost per unit. When a standard cost system is being used, the flexible budget is based on the *standard quantity allowed* for the *actual* output achieved multiplied by the *standard price* per unit. As will be illustrated in the sections that follow, this revised approach to calculating the flexible budget permits the flexible budget variance introduced in Chapter 9 (Exhibit 9–4) for a period to be broken down into its price and quantity components.

With this general model as a foundation, we will now examine the price and quantity variances in more detail.

Standard quantity allowed
The amount of materials that should have been used to complete the period's output, as computed by multiplying the actual number of units produced by the standard quantity per unit.

Standard hours allowed
The time that should have been taken to complete the period's output, as computed by multiplying the actual number of units produced by the standard hours per unit.

■ USING STANDARD COSTS—DIRECT MATERIALS VARIANCES

After determining Heirloom Pewter Company's standard costs for direct materials, direct labour, and variable manufacturing overhead, George Hanlon's next step was to compute the company's variances for June, the most recent month. As discussed in the preceding section, variances are computed by comparing standard costs to actual costs. To facilitate this comparison, Hanlon referred to the standard cost data contained in Exhibit 10–2. This exhibit shows that the standard cost of direct materials per unit of product is as follows:

LEARNING OBJECTIVE 2
Compute the direct materials price and quantity variances and explain their significance.

3.0 kilograms per unit × $4 per kilogram = $12 per unit

Heirloom Pewter's purchasing records for June showed that 6,500 kilograms of pewter were purchased at a cost of $3.80 per kilogram. This cost figure included freight and handling and was net of the quantity discount. All of the materials purchased were used during June to manufacture 2,000 pairs of pewter bookends. Using these data and the standard costs from Exhibit 10–2, Hanlon computed the price and quantity variances shown in Exhibit 10–4.

The three arrows in Exhibit 10–4 point to three different total cost figures. The first, $24,700, refers to the actual total cost of the pewter that was purchased during June. The second, $26,000, refers to what the actual quantity of pewter would have cost if it had been purchased at the standard price of $4.00 per kilogram rather than the actual price of $3.80 per kilogram. The difference between these two figures, $1,300 ($26,000 – $24,700), is the price variance. It exists because the actual purchase price was $0.20 per kilogram less

The formula can be factored into simpler form as follows:

$$\text{Materials price variance} = AQ(AP - SP)$$

This simpler formula permits variance computations to be made very quickly. Using the data from Exhibits 10–4 and 10–5 in this formula, we have the following:

$$6{,}500 \text{ kilograms} \; (\$3.80 \text{ per kilogram} - \$4.00 \text{ per kilogram}) = -\$1{,}300 \text{ F}$$

Notice that the answer is the same as that yielded in Exhibit 10–4. Also note that a negative variance because of the order of the calculation is always labelled as *favourable* (F) and a positive variance is always labelled as *unfavourable* (U) when the formula approach is used. This will be true of all variance formulas in this and later chapters.

Variance reports are often issued in a tabular format that shows the details and explanation of particular variances. Following is an example of such a report that has been provided by the purchasing manager:

HEIRLOOM PEWTER COMPANY
Performance Report—Purchasing Department

Item Purchased	(1) Quantity Purchased	(2) Actual Price	(3) Standard Price	(4) Difference in Price (2) − (3)	(5) Total Price Variance (1) × (4)	Explanation
Pewter	6,500 kilograms	$3.80	$4.00	−$0.20	−$1,300 F	Negotiated for an especially favourable price.

F = Favourable

Isolation of Variances   Variances should be isolated and brought to the attention of management as quickly as possible so that problems can be identified and corrected on a timely basis. The most significant variances should be viewed as "red flags"; an exception has occurred that requires explanation by the responsible manager and perhaps follow-up effort. The performance report itself may contain explanations for the variances, as illustrated above. In the case of Heirloom Pewter Company, the purchasing manager said that the favourable price variance resulted from negotiating an especially good price.

Responsibility for the Variance   Who is responsible for the materials price variance? Generally speaking, the purchasing manager has control over the price paid for goods and is therefore responsible for any price variances. Many factors influence the prices paid for goods, including how many units are ordered in a lot, how the order is delivered, whether the order is a rush order, and the quality of materials purchased. A deviation in any of these factors from what was assumed when the standards were set can result in a price variance. For example, purchase of second-grade materials rather than top-grade materials may result in a favourable price variance, since the lower-grade materials would generally be less costly (but perhaps less suitable for production).

However, someone other than the purchasing manager could be responsible for a materials price variance. Production may be scheduled in such a way, for example, that the purchasing manager must request delivery by air freight, rather than by truck. In these cases, the production manager would bear responsibility for the resulting price variances.

A word of caution is in order. Variance analysis should not be used as a means of assigning blame. The emphasis must be on the control function in the sense of *supporting* the line managers and *assisting* them in meeting the goals that they have participated in setting for the company. In short, the emphasis should be positive rather than negative. Excessive focus on what has already happened, particularly in terms of trying to assign blame, can be destructive to the functioning of an organization.

Materials Quantity Variance—A Closer Look

A **materials quantity variance** measures the difference between the quantity of materials used in production and the quantity that should have been used, according to the standard that has been set. Although the variance is concerned with the physical usage of materials, it is generally stated in dollar terms, as shown in Exhibit 10–4. The formula for the materials quantity variance is as follows:

$$\text{Materials quantity variance} = (AQ \times SP) - (SQ \times SP)$$

Actual Standard   Standard
Quantity   Price   Quantity
Used   Allowed for
                   Actual Output

> **Materials quantity variance**
> A measure of the difference between the actual quantity of materials used in production and the standard quantity allowed, multiplied by the standard price per unit of materials.

Again, the formula can be factored into simpler terms:

$$\text{Materials quantity variance} = SP(AQ - SQ)$$

Using the data from Exhibit 10–4 in the formula, we have the following:

$$\$4.00 \text{ per kilogram } (6,500 \text{ kilograms} - 6,000 \text{ kilograms*}) = \$2,000 \text{ U}$$

---
*2,000 units × 3.0 kilograms per unit = 6,000 kilograms.

The answer, of course, is the same as that yielded in Exhibit 10–4. The data might appear as follows if a formal performance report was prepared:

HEIRLOOM PEWTER COMPANY
Performance Report—Production Department

Type of Materials	(1) Standard Price	(2) Actual Quantity	(3) Standard Quantity Allowed	(4) Difference in Quantity (2) − (3)	(5) Total Quantity Variance (1) × (4)	Explanation
Pewter..................	$4.00	6,500 kg	6,000 kg	500 kg	$2,000 U	Low-quality materials unsuitable for production

U = Unfavourable.

The materials quantity variance is best isolated at the time that materials are placed into production. Materials are requisitioned for the number of units to be produced, according to the standard bill of materials for each unit. Any additional materials are usually drawn with an excess materials requisition, which is different from the normal requisition. This procedure calls attention to the excessive usage of materials *while production is still in process* and provides an opportunity for early identification and correction of any developing problem.

Excessive usage of materials can result from many factors, including faulty machines, inferior quality of materials, untrained workers, and poor supervision. Generally speaking, it is the responsibility of the production department to see that materials usage is kept in line with standards. There may be times, however, when the *purchasing* department is responsible for an unfavourable materials quantity variance. If the purchasing department obtains inferior-quality materials in an effort to reduce costs, the materials may be unsuitable for use and may result in excessive waste. Thus, purchasing rather than production would be responsible for the quantity variance. Indeed, at Heirloom Pewter, the production manager said that low-quality materials were the cause of the unfavourable materials quantity variance for June.

USING STANDARD COSTS—DIRECT LABOUR VARIANCES

LEARNING OBJECTIVE 3
Compute the direct labour rate and efficiency variances and explain their significance.

George Hanlon's next step in determining Heirloom Pewter's variances for June was to compute the direct labour variances for the month. Recall from Exhibit 10–2 that the standard direct labour cost per unit of product is $52.50, computed as follows:

2.5 hours per unit × $21 per hour = $52.50 per unit

During June, the company paid its direct labour workers $108,000, including employment taxes and benefits, for 5,400 hours of work. This was an average of $20 per hour. Using these data and the standard costs from Exhibit 10–2, Hanlon computed the direct labour rate and efficiency variances that appear in Exhibit 10–6.

Notice that the column headings in Exhibit 10–6 are the same as those used in the prior two exhibits, except that in Exhibit 10–6 the terms *hours* and *rate* are used in place of the terms *quantity* and *price*.

Labour rate variance
A measure of the difference between the actual hourly labour rate and the standard rate, multiplied by the number of hours worked during the period.

Labour Rate Variance—A Closer Look

As explained earlier, the price variance for direct labour is commonly termed a **labour rate variance**. This variance measures any deviation from standard in the average

EXHIBIT 10–6   Variance Analysis—Direct Labour

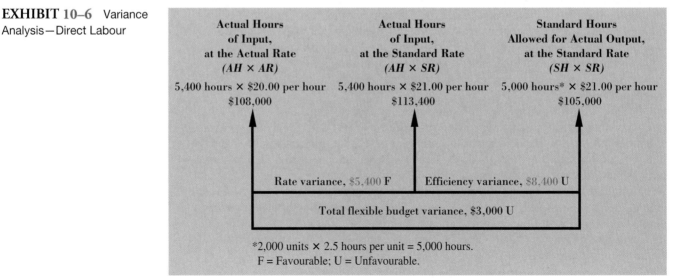

Actual Hours of Input, at the Actual Rate (AH × AR)	Actual Hours of Input, at the Standard Rate (AH × SR)	Standard Hours Allowed for Actual Output, at the Standard Rate (SH × SR)
5,400 hours × $20.00 per hour	5,400 hours × $21.00 per hour	5,000 hours* × $21.00 per hour
$108,000	$113,400	$105,000

Rate variance, $5,400 F   Efficiency variance, $8,400 U

Total flexible budget variance, $3,000 U

*2,000 units × 2.5 hours per unit = 5,000 hours.
F = Favourable; U = Unfavourable.

hourly rate paid to direct labour workers. The formula for the labour rate variance is expressed as follows:

$$\text{Labour rate variance} = (AH \times AR) - (AH \times SR)$$

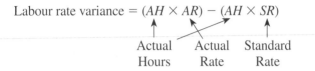

Actual	Actual	Standard
Hours	Rate	Rate

The formula can be factored into simpler form as follows:

$$\text{Labour rate variance} = AH(AR - SR)$$

Using the data from Exhibit 10–6 in the formula, we have the following:

$$5{,}400 \text{ hours } (\$20.00 \text{ per hour} - \$21.00 \text{ per hour}) = -\$5{,}400 \text{ F}$$

In most companies, the rates paid to workers are quite predictable. Nevertheless, rate variances can arise through the way labour is used. Skilled workers with high hourly rates of pay may be given duties that require less skill and call for low hourly rates of pay. This will result in unfavourable labour rate variances, since the actual hourly rate of pay will exceed the standard rate specified for the particular task being performed. A reverse situation exists when unskilled or untrained workers are assigned to jobs that require higher levels of skill or training. The lower pay scale for these workers will result in favourable rate variances, although the workers may be less efficient. Finally, unfavourable rate variances can arise from overtime work paid at premium rates if any portion of the overtime premium is added to the direct labour account.

Who is responsible for controlling the labour rate variance? Since rate variances generally arise as a result of how labour is used, production supervisors bear responsibility for controlling them.

Labour Efficiency Variance—A Closer Look

The quantity variance for direct labour, more commonly called the **labour efficiency variance**, measures the productivity of labour time. No variance is more closely watched by management, since it is widely believed that increasing the productivity of direct labour time is vital to reducing costs. The formula for the labour efficiency variance is expressed as follows:

Labour efficiency variance A measure of the difference between the actual hours taken to complete a task and the standard hours allowed, multiplied by the standard hourly labour rate.

$$\text{Labour efficiency variance} = (AH \times SR) - (SH \times SR)$$

Actual	Standard	Standard Hours
Hours	Rate	Allowed for Actual Output

Factored into simpler terms, the formula is as follows:

$$\text{Labour efficiency variance} = SR(AH - SH)$$

Using the data from Exhibit 10–6 in the formula, we have the following:

$$\$21.00 \text{ per hour } (5{,}400 \text{ hours} - 5{,}000 \text{ hours*}) = \$8{,}400 \text{ U}$$

---

*2,000 units × 2.5 hours per unit = 5,000 hours.

Possible causes of an unfavourable labour efficiency variance include poorly trained or motivated workers; poor-quality materials, requiring more labour time for processing; faulty equipment, causing breakdowns and work interruptions; poor supervision of workers; and inaccurate standards. The managers in charge of production would generally be responsible for the labour efficiency variance. However, an unfavourable variance might be attributed to purchasing if the acquisition of lower quality materials resulted in excessive labour processing time.

EXHIBIT 10–14 An Overhead Performance Report with Only Spending or Budget Variances

HEIRLOOM PEWTER CORPORATION Overhead Performance Report For the Month Ended June 30				
Actual production (units) 2,000				
Actual direct labour-hours. 5,400				
Overhead Costs	**Cost Formula (per Direct Labour-Hour)**	**(1) Actual Costs 5,400 Direct Labour-Hours**	**(2) Budget Based on 5,400 Direct Labour-Hours***	**Spending (Budget) Variance (1) − (2)**
Variable overhead costs				
Indirect labour	$1.50	$ 7,830	$ 8,100	$ 270 F
Lubricants	1.00	5,022	5,400	378 F
Power.	0.50	2,538	2,700	162 F
Total variable overhead cost	$3.00	15,390	16,200	810 F
Fixed overhead costs				
Depreciation.		10,000	10,000	0
Supervisory salaries.		14,000	12,000	2,000 U
Insurance		3,500	3,000	500 U
Total fixed overhead cost.		27,500	25,000	2,500 U
Total overhead cost.		$42,890	$41,200	$1,690 U

*Budget amounts for variable overhead costs are determined by multiplying budgeted direct labour-hours by the cost formula amount (per direct labour-hour). For example, indirect labour costs of $8,100 for 5,400 hours = $1.50 × 5,400.

cause of the variance? Identifying which variances to target for investigation is an important part of the variance analysis cycle presented in Exhibit 10–1. In the next section, we examine how managers make these decisions.

IN BUSINESS

Particularly in small companies, the controller may be the only person who understands concepts such as overhead variances and overapplied and underapplied overhead. Furthermore, a small-company controller may be able to both authorize cash disbursements and account for them. Since small, closely held companies often do not hire external auditors, these circumstances create an ideal environment for fraud.

Such was the case in a small manufacturing company with 100 employees and $30 million in annual sales. The controller embezzled nearly $1 million from the company over three years by writing cheques to himself. The consultant who uncovered the fraud was tipped off by the unusually high overhead variances that resulted from the controller recording fictitious expenses in the overhead accounts to offset his fraudulent cash withdrawals. After the fraud was exposed, the company implemented various controls to reduce the risk of future problems. These controls included hiring an internal auditor and requiring periodic review of overhead variances to identify and explain significant discrepancies.

Source: Reproduced with permission of INSTITUTE OF MANAGEMENT ACCOUNTANTS, and John B. MacArthur, Bobby E. Waldrup, and Gary R. Fane, "Caution: Fraud Overhead," *Strategic Finance*, October 2004, pp. 28–32; permission conveyed through Copyright Clearance Center, Inc.

Variance Investigation Decisions

Variance analysis and performance reports are important elements of *management by exception*, which emphasizes focusing on those areas of responsibility where goals and expectations are not being met.

The budgets and standards discussed in this chapter and in the preceding chapter reflect management's plans. If all goes according to plan, there will be little difference between actual results and the budgets and standards. However, if actual results do not conform to the budget and to standards, the performance reporting system sends a signal to the manager that an "exception" has occurred. This signal is in the form of a variance from the budget or standards.

However, are all variances worth investigating? The answer is no. Differences between actual results and what was expected will almost always occur. If every variance was investigated, management would spend a great deal of time tracking down immaterial differences. Variances may occur for any of a variety of reasons—only some of which warrant management attention. For example, hotter-than-normal weather in the summer may result in higher-than-expected electricity bills for air conditioning. Because of unpredictable random factors, every cost category will produce a variance of some kind.

How should managers decide which variances are worth investigating? One indicator is the dollar amount of the variance. A variance of $5 is probably not big enough to warrant attention, whereas a variance of $5,000 might well be worth investigating. Another indicator is the size of the variance relative to the amount of spending involved. A variance that is only 0.1% of spending on an item is likely due to random factors, while a variance of 10% of spending is more indicative that something is wrong and should be investigated.

Another approach is to plot variance data on a statistical control chart, as illustrated in Exhibit 10–15. The basic idea underlying a statistical control chart is that some random fluctuations in variances from period to period are to be expected even when costs are under control. A variance should be investigated only when it is unusual relative to the normal level of random fluctuation. Typically, the standard deviation of the variances is used as the measure of the normal level of fluctuations. Often a simple decision rule is adopted such as "investigate all variances that are more than X standard deviations from zero." In the control chart in Exhibit 10–15, X is 1.0. That is, the decision rule in this company is to investigate all variances that are more than one standard deviation above (unfavourable) or below (favourable) zero. This means that the variances in weeks 7, 11, and 17 would have been investigated, but none of the others.

What value of X should be chosen? The greater the value of X, the wider the band of acceptable variances that would not be investigated. Thus, the greater the value of X, the less time will be spent tracking down variances, but the more likely it is that a real out-of-control situation would be overlooked. Ordinarily, if X is selected to be 1.0, roughly 30% of all variances will trigger an investigation even when there is no real problem. If X is set at 1.5, the figure drops to about 13%. If X is set at 2.0, the figure drops all the way to about 5%.

In addition to watching for unusually large variances, the pattern of the variances should be monitored. For example, a series of steadily increasing variances should trigger an investigation even if none of the variances is large enough by itself to warrant investigation.

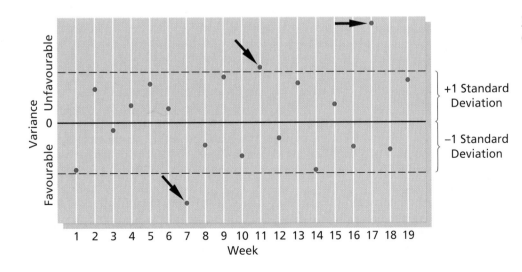

EXHIBIT 10–15   A Statistical Control Chart

Capacity Analysis

Capacity analysis allows managers to evaluate the financial impact of not fully utilizing available productive capacity, making it an important strategic tool for management. However, increasing the utilization of capacity by eliminating bottlenecks or increasing demand for products can take time. Similarly, reducing capacity because of insufficient long-term demand cannot be done overnight, so it is important that capacity analysis be conducted on an ongoing basis.

We use Heirloom Pewter Company to illustrate a basic approach to capacity analysis. Recall that the company has a budgeted production level of 20,000 pairs of bookends for the year. This denominator level of activity was used earlier in this chapter to determine a standard cost per pair of bookends of $87.00, based on 20,000 units or 50,000 direct labour-hours (see Exhibit 10–9). Assume now that the year has ended and 16,000 pairs of bookends have been sold.

Theoretical capacity
The volume of activity resulting from operations conducted 24 hours per day, 7 days per week, 365 days per year, with no downtime.

Practical capacity
The productive capacity possible after subtracting unavoidable downtime from theoretical capacity.

If all available production time was used and no waste occurred, Heirloom Pewter could reach a level of capacity known as **theoretical capacity**. This level of capacity would require operations to be conducted around the clock, 365 days per year, with no downtime, similar to the definition of an ideal standard presented earlier in this chapter. If the denominator level of 20,000 units or 50,000 direct labour-hours represented 50% of the theoretical capacity, then Heirloom Pewter could produce 40,000 units (20,000 ÷ 0.50) in 100,000 hours.

Practical capacity represents what could be produced if unavoidable downtime was subtracted from theoretical capacity. Maintenance, breakdowns, and setup times for new operations are considered to be unavoidable downtime. If the denominator level was 80% of practical capacity, then 25,000 units (20,000 ÷ 0.80) could be produced using 62,500 direct labour-hours.

Capacity analysis proceeds by first examining the overhead cost (variable + fixed) at each level of capacity.

		Total Overhead Costs
Theoretical...................	(100,000 DLH × $3.00) + $300,000 =	$600,000
Practical.....................	(62,500 DLH × $3.00) + $300,000 =	$487,500
Denominator	(50,000 DLH × $3.00) + $300,000 =	$450,000
Actual.......................	(40,000 DLH × $3.00) + $300,000 =	$420,000

If Heirloom Pewter can sell all that it can produce at $105 per unit, then an indication of the opportunity cost incurred of not operating at the various levels of capacity can be computed as follows:

	Contribution Margin*	Total Overhead	Operating Income
Theoretical.......	40,000 units × ($105.00 − $64.50) −	$600,000 =	$1,020,000
Practical.........	25,000 units × ($105.00 − $64.50) −	$487,500 =	$ 525,000
Denominator	20,000 units × ($105.00 − $64.50) −	$450,000 =	$ 360,000
Actual...........	16,000 units × ($105.00 − $64.50) −	$420,000 =	$ 228,000

*$64.50 variable costs exclude $7.50 per unit variable overhead because it is included in the total overhead amount.

Note that $64.50 is composed of the standard materials cost of $12 per unit and the standard direct labour cost of $52.50 per unit shown in Exhibit 10–9. The remaining variable production cost of $7.50 per unit for overhead is included in the overhead charges calculated above.

To calculate the opportunity cost of operating at 16,000 units (a profit of $228,000) we begin by looking at what additional profit would have been possible at the theoretical capacity: $1,020,000 − $228,000, or $792,000 in lost profits. By examining marketing strategies or product design changes necessary to sell an additional 24,000 units (40,000 − 16,000), management might be able to significantly improve its profit picture. Analysis would also have to be conducted to evaluate the potential impact of any additional unit sales on setup costs, maintenance, wastage, etc. However, before making a decision to increase productive capacity, managers should conduct the type of analysis discussed in Chapter 13, where we examine capital project decisions. Alternatively, if the long-term demand for bookends is expected to be only 16,000 units, management may consider reducing productive capacity, since only 64% ($16,000 \div 25,000$) of practical capacity is required to meet this level of demand. Reducing the fixed costs such as insurance, taxes, and maintenance associated with the unused capacity can lead to improvements in operating profits.

INTERNATIONAL USES OF STANDARD COSTS

Despite claims by some that standard costing systems are outdated, they continue to be used by companies worldwide. Survey evidence indicates that over 70% of companies in the United Kingdom use standard costs, while over 80% of companies in Japan use the approach.[6] Moreover, recent surveys of management accounting practices show that the use of standard costing is far-reaching, and that the approach is commonly used in New Zealand (73%), Malaysia (70%), and Dubai (United Arab Emirates) (77%).

Standard costs were first introduced in Japan after World War II. Nippon Electric Company (NEC) was one of the first Japanese companies to adopt standard costs for all of its products. Many other Japanese companies followed NEC's lead after the war and developed standard cost systems. Commonly cited reasons by companies for using standard costs include

- Cost control and performance evaluation.
- Product costing.
- Budgeting and forecasting.

According to managers who participated in the surveys reported above, the key variances used for control purposes, in order of importance are the fixed overhead budget variance, materials price variance, materials quantity variance, and direct labour efficiency variance. Overall, the evidence suggests that standard costing is far from obsolete and continues to play an important role in organizations worldwide.

EVALUATION OF CONTROLS BASED ON STANDARD COSTS

Advantages of Standard Costs

Standard cost systems have a number of advantages:

1. Standard costs are a key element in a management by exception approach. If costs remain within the standards, managers can focus on other issues. When costs fall significantly outside the standards, managers are alerted that problems may exist. This approach helps managers focus on important issues.
2. Standards that are viewed as reasonable by employees can promote efficiency. They provide benchmarks that individuals can use to judge their own performance.
3. Standard costs can greatly simplify bookkeeping. Instead of recording actual costs for each job, the standard costs for materials, labour, and overhead can be charged to jobs.
4. Standard costs fit naturally in an integrated system of "responsibility accounting." The standards establish what costs should be, who should be responsible for them, and whether actual costs are under control.

Potential Problems with the Use of Standard Costs

The use of standard costs can present a number of potential problems.

1. Standard cost variance reports are usually prepared on a monthly basis and often are released days or even weeks after the end of the month. As a consequence, the

information in the reports may be very outdated. Timely, frequent reports that are approximately correct are better than infrequent reports that are very precise but out of date by the time they are released. Some companies are now reporting variances and other key operating data daily or even more frequently.

2. If managers are insensitive and use variance reports to lay blame, morale may suffer. If variances are used to lay blame, subordinates may be tempted to cover up unfavourable variances or take actions that are not in the best interests of the company to make sure the variances are favourable. For example, workers may intensify their efforts to increase output at the end of the month to avoid an unfavourable labour efficiency variance. In the rush to increase output, quality may suffer.

3. Labour quantity standards and efficiency variances make two important assumptions. First, they assume that the production process is labour-paced: If labour works faster, output will go up. However, output in many companies is no longer determined by how fast labour works; rather, it is determined by the processing speed of machines. Second, the computations assume that labour is a variable cost. However, as discussed, direct labour may essentially be fixed in many companies. If labour is fixed, then an undue emphasis on labour efficiency variances creates pressure to build excess inventories.

4. In some cases, a "favourable" variance can be as bad or worse than an "unfavourable" variance. For example, Harvey's has a standard for the amount of hamburger meat that should be in a burger. If there is a "favourable" variance, it means that less meat was used than the standard specifies. The result is a substandard burger and possibly a dissatisfied customer.

5. There may be a tendency with standard cost reporting systems to emphasize meeting the standards to the exclusion of other important objectives, such as maintaining and improving quality, on-time delivery, and customer satisfaction. This tendency can be reduced by using supplemental performance measures that focus on these other objectives.

6. Just meeting standards may not be sufficient; continual improvement may be necessary to survive in the current competitive environment. For this reason, some companies focus on trends in standard cost variances—aiming for continual improvement rather than just meeting the standards. In other companies, engineered standards are being replaced either by a rolling average of actual costs, which is expected to decline, or by very challenging target costs.

In summary, managers should exercise considerable care in their use of a standard cost system. It is particularly important that managers go out of their way to focus on the positive, rather than just on the negative, and to be aware of possible unintended consequences.

IN BUSINESS

Significant increases in health care costs over the past several decades in Canada, the United States, and other countries worldwide has prompted calls for new measures directed at improving cost control. In a recent article, Thibadoux, Scheidt, and Luckey (2007) explored the possible development and use of the standard costing methodology in the U.S. health care system. Developing standard costs would involve the use of evidence-based best practices (EBBP), which are clinical guidelines for diagnosis and treatment that are derived from scientific research. EBBP prescribe a standard approach to be followed by physicians in treating patients, involving the use of published checklists for every major diagnostic-related group (DRG). An example of a DRG would be cardiac disease bypass surgery. By determining the cost of each "step" included in the EBBP checklist for a particular DRG, a standard cost could be developed for diagnosing and treating each patient. Actual costs could then be compared to the standard cost and variances investigated.

Interviews with several practising physicians about the possible use of standard costs in the health care system suggest that the disadvantages may outweigh the benefits. While some interviewees indicated that a standard costing approach could be useful in identifying possible causes of cost increases, most had serious concerns about the concept. For example, many noted that being held responsible for adhering to standard costs could lead to decisions aimed more at controlling costs than ensuring the well-being of their patients. Similarly, others indicated that interpreting variances from standard costs could also be problematic in that a favourable cost variance could mean poor care had been given to the patient. Finally, some respondents stated that unlike manufacturing companies where relatively precise standards can be developed for production, the approach used to treat a serious illness can vary considerably from one patient to the next. Therefore they questioned whether meaningful standards could even be developed.

Whether or not health care administrators adopt the standard costing methodology remains to be seen. However, it is interesting to note the similarities between the standard costing problems identified by physicians and those noted earlier in this chapter.

Source: With kind permission from Springer Science + Business Media: *Journal of Business Ethics,* "Accounting and Medicine: An Exploratory Investigation into Physicians' Attitudes toward the Use of Standard Cost-Accounting Methods in Medicine," *75,* 2007, pp. 137–149, Greg Thibadoux, Marsha Scheidt, and Elizabeth Luckey.

Summary

- A standard is a benchmark or "norm" for measuring performance. Standards are set for both the cost and the quantity of inputs needed to manufacture goods or to provide services. Quantity standards indicate how much of a cost element, such as labour time or raw materials, should be used in manufacturing a unit of product or in providing a unit of service. Cost standards indicate what the cost of the time or the materials should be. **[LO1]**
- Standards are normally practical in nature, meaning that they can be attained by reasonable, although highly efficient, efforts. Such standards are generally felt to have a favourable motivational impact on employees. Ideal standards are those attainable only under the best circumstances by the most skilled and efficient workers. While serving as a reminder that continuous improvement is needed, ideal standards can be discouraging. **[LO1]**
- The difference between actual cost and standard cost is referred to as a *variance.* Variances are computed for both the price and the quantity elements of materials, labour, and variable overhead. Price, rate, and spending variances for inputs are computed by taking the difference between the actual and standard prices of the inputs and multiplying the result by the amount of input purchased or used. Quantity and efficiency variances are computed by taking the difference between the actual amount of the input used and the amount of input that is allowed for the actual output, and then multiplying the result by the standard price of the input. **[LO2, LO3, LO4]**
- The denominator activity is the figure used to calculate the predetermined overhead rate for variable and fixed overhead. The overhead rate is used in determining the total standard cost per unit of a product by multiplying the rate by the quantity of the activity required to produce each unit. **[LO5]**
- Two variances exist for fixed overhead. The budget variance is simply the difference between the actual and budgeted amounts for total fixed overhead costs. The volume variance is the difference between the amount of fixed overhead cost applied to inventory and the total amount of fixed overhead that was originally budgeted for the period. **[LO6]**
- An overhead performance report provides details on each item that makes up total variable and fixed overhead. Both actual and budget figures are included in the report. Companies that use a standard cost system can prepare a performance report that includes both spending and efficiency variances for variable overhead and the budget variance for fixed overhead. Managers use the performance report to gain an understanding of which specific overhead items are contributing the most to the overall variances for variable and fixed overhead. **[LO7]**
- Only unusual or particularly *significant* variances should be investigated—otherwise, a great deal of time could be spent investigating unimportant matters. Variance investigation decisions can be based on the dollar amount of the variance, or the size of the variance relative to the amount of

spending. A statistical control approach can also be employed, whereby only variances that are a certain number of standard deviations above or below zero are investigated. **[LO7]**

- Capacity analysis is a useful strategic tool that allows managers to evaluate the financial impact of operating at less than full productive capacity. Different definitions of "full capacity" exist, including theoretical capacity and practical capacity. Theoretical capacity is the volume of activity that would result from conducting operations with no downtime, 365 days a year, 24 hours per day. Practical capacity is determined by deducting unavoidable downtime from theoretical capacity. **[LO7]**

Review Problem: Standard Costs

Fun Unlimited Corp. produces a toy called the Challenge. Overhead is applied to products on the basis of direct labour-hours. The company recently implemented a standard cost system to help control costs and has established the following standards for the Challenge toys:

Direct materials: 6 microns per toy at $0.50 per micron
Direct labour: 1.3 hours per toy at $15 per hour
Variable manufacturing overhead: 1.3 hours per toy at $4 per hour
Fixed manufacturing overhead: 1.3 hours per toy at $6 per hour

During July, the company produced 3,000 Challenge toys. The fixed overhead expense budget for July was $24,180 with 4,030 direct labour-hours as the denominator level of activity. Production data for the month on the toys follow:

Direct materials: 25,000 microns were purchased at a cost of $0.48 per micron; 5,000 of these microns were still in inventory at the end of the month.
Direct labour: 4,000 direct labour-hours were worked, at a cost of $64,000.
Variable overhead: Actual cost in July was $17,000.
Fixed overhead: Actual cost in July was $25,000.

Required:
1. Compute the materials, labour, variable manufacturing overhead, and fixed manufacturing overhead variances.
2. Calculate total overapplied or underapplied overhead for July.

Solution to Review Problem

1. **Materials Variances**

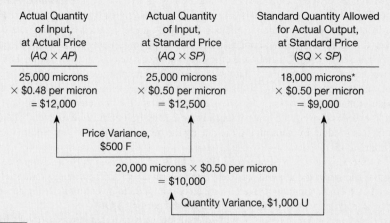

Actual Quantity of Input, at Actual Price (*AQ* × *AP*)	Actual Quantity of Input, at Standard Price (*AQ* × *SP*)	Standard Quantity Allowed for Actual Output, at Standard Price (*SQ* × *SP*)
25,000 microns × $0.48 per micron = $12,000	25,000 microns × $0.50 per micron = $12,500	18,000 microns* × $0.50 per micron = $9,000

Price Variance, $500 F

20,000 microns × $0.50 per micron = $10,000

Quantity Variance, $1,000 U

_____
*3,000 toys × 6 microns per toy = 18,000 microns

A total variance is not computed in this situation because the amount of materials purchased (25,000 microns) differs from the amount of materials used in production (20,000 microns).
Using the formulas in the chapter, the same variances would be computed as:

Materials price variance = $AQ(AP - SP)$
25,000 microns ($0.48 per micron − $0.50 per micron) = −$500 F

Materials quantity variance = $SP(AQ - SQ)$
$0.50 per micron (20,000 microns − 18,000 microns) = $1,000 U

Direct Labour Variances

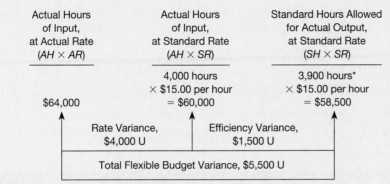

Actual Hours of Input, at Actual Rate ($AH \times AR$)	Actual Hours of Input, at Standard Rate ($AH \times SR$)	Standard Hours Allowed for Actual Output, at Standard Rate ($SH \times SR$)
	4,000 hours × $15.00 per hour = $60,000	3,900 hours* × $15.00 per hour = $58,500
$64,000		

Rate Variance, $4,000 U   Efficiency Variance, $1,500 U

Total Flexible Budget Variance, $5,500 U

*3,000 toys × 1.3 hours per toy = 3,900 hours

Using the formulas in the chapter, the same variances would be computed as

Labour rate variance = $AH(AR - SR)$
4,000 hours ($16.00 per hour* − $15.00 per hour) = $4,000 U

*$64,000 ÷ 4,000 hours = $16.00 per hour

Labour efficiency variance = $SR(AH - SH)$
$15.00 per hour (4,000 hours − 3,900 hours) = $1,500 U

Variable Manufacturing Overhead Variances

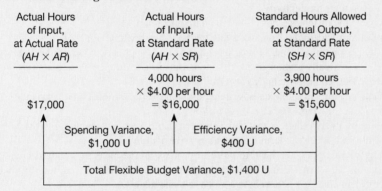

Actual Hours of Input, at Actual Rate ($AH \times AR$)	Actual Hours of Input, at Standard Rate ($AH \times SR$)	Standard Hours Allowed for Actual Output, at Standard Rate ($SH \times SR$)
	4,000 hours × $4.00 per hour = $16,000	3,900 hours × $4.00 per hour = $15,600
$17,000		

Spending Variance, $1,000 U   Efficiency Variance, $400 U

Total Flexible Budget Variance, $1,400 U

Using the formulas in the chapter, the same variances would be computed as:

Variable overhead spending variance = $AH(AR - SR)$
4,000 hours ($4.25 per hour* − $4.00 per hour) = $1,000 U

*$17,000 ÷ 4,000 hours = $4.25 per hour

Variable overhead efficiency variance = $SR(AH - SH)$
$4.00 per hour (4,000 hours − 3,900 hours) = $400 U

Fixed Manufacturing Overhead Variances

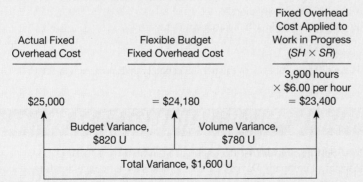

Actual Fixed Overhead Cost	Flexible Budget Fixed Overhead Cost	Fixed Overhead Cost Applied to Work in Progress ($SH \times SR$)
		3,900 hours × $6.00 per hour = $23,400
$25,000	= $24,180	

Budget Variance, $820 U   Volume Variance, $780 U

Total Variance, $1,600 U

Using the formula in the chapter, the volume variance would be computed as:

$6(4,030 − 3900) = $780 U

2. Actual overhead costs incurred:

Variable	$17,000
Fixed	25,000
Total	$42,000

Overhead costs applied:

Variable	$15,600
Fixed	23,400
Total	$39,000

Therefore, overhead is underapplied by $3,000 ($42,000 − $39,000).

Glossary

Review key terms and definitions on Connect.

Questions

10–1 What is a quantity standard? What is a price standard?

10–2 Distinguish between ideal and practical standards.

10–3 If employees are constantly unable to meet a standard, what effect would you expect this to have on their productivity?

10–4 What is the difference between a standard and a budget?

10–5 What is included in the standard rate per hour for direct labour?

10–6 Why are variances generally segregated in terms of a price variance and a quantity variance?

10–7 Who is generally responsible for the materials price variance? The materials quantity variance? The labour efficiency variance?

10–8 What are some possible causes of an unfavourable labour efficiency variance?

10–9 What does the term *standard hours allowed* mean?

10–10 What are the two factors that can cause a variable overhead spending variance?

10–11 What is meant by the term *denominator level of activity*?

10–12 Why do we apply overhead to work in process on the basis of standard hours allowed in Chapter 10, when we applied it on the basis of actual hours in Chapter 3? What is the difference in costing systems between the two chapters?

10–13 In a standard cost system, what two variances are computed for fixed manufacturing overhead?

10–14 What does the fixed overhead budget variance measure?

10–15 Under what circumstances would you expect the volume variance to be favourable? Unfavourable? Does the volume variance measure deviations in spending for fixed overhead items? Explain.

10–16 How might the volume variance be measured other than in dollars?

10–17 In Chapter 3, you became acquainted with the concept of under- or overapplied overhead. The under- or overapplied overhead can be broken down into what four variances?

10–18 "If factory overhead in total is underapplied, the overhead variances will be unfavourable." Do you agree? Why or why not?

10–19 How do managers decide which variances to investigate?

10–20 Why can undue emphasis on labour efficiency variances lead to excess work in process inventories?

10–21 What is the difference between theoretical capacity and practical capacity?

Exercises

EXERCISE 10–1 Setting Standards; Preparing a Standard Cost Card [LO1]
Swedish pharmaceutical company Davos Pharmacia makes an anticoagulant drug. The main ingredient in the drug is a raw material called Alpha SR40. Information concerning the purchase and use of Alpha SR40 follows:

Purchase of Alpha SR40: The raw material Alpha SR40 is purchased in 2-kilogram containers at a cost of 3,000 Kr per kilogram. (The Swedish currency is the krona, which is abbreviated as Kr.) A discount of 2% is offered by the supplier for payment within 10 days and Davos Pharmacia takes all discounts. Shipping costs, which Davos Pharmacia must pay, amount to 1,000 Kr for an average shipment of ten 2-kilogram containers.

Use of Alpha SR40: The bill of materials calls for 6 grams of Alpha SR40 per capsule of the anticoagulant drug. (A kilogram equals 1,000 grams.) About 4% of all Alpha SR40 purchased is rejected as unsuitable before being used to make the anticoagulant drug. Thus, on average the 6 grams of suitable Alpha SR40 required for each capsule represents 96% of the amount that initially goes into production.

Required:
1. Compute the standard purchase price for one gram of Alpha SR40.
2. Compute the standard quantity of Alpha SR40 (in grams) per capsule that passes final inspection. (Carry computations to two decimal places.)
3. Using the data from (1) and (2) above, prepare a standard cost card showing the standard cost of Alpha SR40 per capsule of the anticoagulant drug.

EXERCISE 10–2 Material Variances [LO2]

Fantastic Feeder Products, Inc., manufactures a number of bird feeders for general household and backyard use. One of these products, a rustic bird feeder, requires an expensive hardwood. During a recent month, the company manufactured 9,000 rustic bird feeders using 6,200 metres of hardwood. The hardwood cost the company $23,560.

The company's standards for one rustic bird feeder are 0.6 metres of hardwood, at a cost of $4.05 per metre.

Required:
1. What cost for wood should have been incurred to make 9,000 rustic bird feeders? How much greater or less is this than the cost that was incurred?
2. Break down the difference computed in (1) above into a materials price variance and a materials quantity variance.

EXERCISE 10–3 Direct Labour Variances [LO3]

SkyInc provides in-flight meals for a number of major airlines. One of the company's products is stuffed cannelloni with roasted pepper sauce, fresh baby corn, and spring salad. During the most recent week, the company prepared 6,000 of these meals, using 1,150 direct labour-hours. The company paid these direct labour workers a total of $11,500 for this work, or $10 per hour.

According to the standard cost card for this meal, it should require 0.20 direct labour-hours at a cost of $9.50 per hour.

Required:
1. What direct labour cost should have been incurred to prepare 6,000 meals? How much does this differ from the actual direct labour cost?
2. Break down the difference computed in (1) above into a labour rate variance and a labour efficiency variance.

EXERCISE 10–4 Variable Overhead Variances [LO4]

OrderUp Company provides customer help centre services for online merchants. The company maintains catalogues and service manuals for stock items carried by its online retail clients. When a client receives a product inquiry or service request from a customer, the request is forwarded to OrderUp, which responds to the customer inquiry on behalf of the online retail client. The company uses a predetermined variable overhead rate based on direct labour-hours.

In the most recent month, 35,000 inquiry requests were responded to and solutions provided to customers, using 5,700 direct labour-hours. The company incurred a total of $7,125 in variable overhead costs.

According to the company's standards, 0.15 direct labour-hours are required to fulfill a service request for one customer and the variable overhead rate is $1.30 per direct labour-hour.

Required:
1. What variable overhead cost should have been incurred to fill the service requests for the 35,000 items? How much does this differ from the actual variable overhead cost?
2. Break down the difference computed in (1) above into a variable overhead spending variance and a variable overhead efficiency variance.

EXERCISE 10–5 Fixed Overhead Variances [LO5, LO6]

Carlton Corporation uses a standard cost system that applies overhead to products based on the standard direct labour-hours allowed for the actual output of the period. Data concerning the most recent year appear below:

Total budgeted fixed overhead cost for the year............................	$400,000
Actual fixed overhead cost for the year....................................	$394,000
Budgeted standard direct labour-hours (denominator level of activity).........	50,000
Actual direct labour-hours..	51,000
Standard direct labour-hours allowed for the actual output	48,000

Required:
1. Compute the fixed portion of the predetermined overhead rate for the year.
2. Compute the fixed overhead budget and volume variances.

EXERCISE 10–6 Variable Overhead Performance Report [LO7]

Hastings Company bases its variable overhead performance report on the actual direct labour-hours of the period. Data concerning the most recent year that ended on December 31 are as follows:

Budgeted direct labour-hours	42,000
Actual direct labour-hours.....................	44,000
Standard direct labour-hours allowed............	45,000
Cost formula (per direct labour-hour):	
Indirect labour	$0.90
Supplies...................................	$0.15
Electricity.................................	$0.05
Actual costs incurred:	
Indirect labour	$42,000
Supplies...................................	$6,900
Electricity.................................	$1,800

Required:
Prepare a variable overhead performance report using the format in Exhibit 10–13. Compute both variable overhead spending and efficiency variances.

EXERCISE 10–7 Setting Standards [LO1]

Agnessa Premium Chocolate Ltd. produces specialty chocolate confections in England. The owner of the company is setting up a standard cost system; the following data is for one of the company's products, the Truffle Supreme, made with the finest white chocolate and various fillings. The data below pertain only to the white chocolate used in the product. (The currency in the United Kingdom is the British pound sterling, which is denoted by £.)

Material requirements, kilograms of white chocolate per dozen truffles.....	0.80 kilograms
Allowance for waste, kilograms of white chocolate per dozen truffles......	0.02 kilograms
Allowance for rejects, kilograms of white chocolate per dozen truffles	0.03 kilograms
Purchase price, finest-grade white chocolate.........................	£9.00 per kilogram
Purchase discount.......................................	5% of purchase price
Shipping cost from the supplier in Belgium	£0.20 per kilogram
Receiving and handling cost.......................................	£0.05 per kilogram

Required:
1. Determine the standard price of a kilogram of white chocolate.
2. Determine the standard quantity of white chocolate for a dozen truffles.
3. Determine the standard cost of the white chocolate in a dozen truffles.

EXERCISE 10–8 Material and Labour Variances [LO2, LO3]

Toy Mountain has developed a new toy called the Braingame The company has a standard cost system to help control costs and has established the following standards for the Braingame:

Direct materials: 8 diodes per toy at $0.30 per diode
Direct labour: 1.2 hours per toy at $7 per hour

During August, the company produced 5,000 Braingames. Production data on the toy for August follow:

Direct materials: 70,000 diodes were purchased at a cost of $0.28 per diode. 20,000 of these diodes were still in inventory at the end of the month. (There was no opening inventory.)
Direct labour: 6,400 direct labour-hours were worked at a cost of $48,000.

Required:
1. Compute the following variances for August:
   a.   Direct materials price and quantity variances.
   b.   Direct labour rate and efficiency variances.
2. Prepare a brief explanation of the possible causes of each variance.

EXERCISE 10–9 Material and Labour Variances [LO2, LO3]

The direct materials and direct labour standards for one bottle of Whisper perfume, a product of the Farante Company, are given below:

	Standard Quantity or Hours	Standard Price or Rate	Standard Cost
Direct materials	7.2 grams	$2.50 per gram	$18.00
Direct labour.	0.4 hours	$10.00 per hour	$4.00

During the most recent month, the following activity was recorded:
a.   Twenty thousand grams of material were purchased at a cost of $2.40 per gram.
b.   All of the material was used to produce 2,500 bottles of Whisper.
c.   Nine hundred hours of direct labour time were recorded at a total labour cost of $10,800.

Required:
1. Compute the direct materials price and quantity variances for the month.
2. Compute the direct labour rate and efficiency variances for the month.

EXERCISE 10–10 Material Variances [LO2]

Refer to the data in Exercise 10–9. Assume that instead of producing 2,500 bottles of Whisper during the month, the company produced only 2,000 bottles, using 16,000 grams of material. (The rest of the material purchased remained in raw materials inventory.)

Required:
Compute the direct materials price and quantity variances for the month.

EXERCISE 10–11 Labour and Variable Manufacturing Overhead Variances [LO3, LO4]

Affordable Electronics, Inc., manufactures medium-quality, reasonably priced DVD players. The company uses standards to control its costs. The labour standards that have been set for one disc are as follows:

Standard Hours	Standard Rate per Hour	Standard Cost
12 minutes	$15.00	$3.00

During July, 3,400 hours of direct labour time were recorded to make 16,000 units. The direct labour cost totalled $49,300 for the month.

Required:
1. What direct labour cost should have been incurred to make the 16,000 DVD players? By how much does this differ from the cost that was incurred?
2. Break down the difference in cost from (1) above into a labour rate variance and a labour efficiency variance.
3. The budgeted variable manufacturing overhead rate is $4.00 per direct labour-hour. During July, the company incurred $15,640 in variable manufacturing overhead cost. Compute the variable overhead spending and efficiency variances for the month.

EXERCISE 10–12 Working Backward from Labour Variances [LO3]
Worldwide Credit Card Inc. uses standards to control the labour time involved in opening mail from cardholders and recording the enclosed remittances. Incoming mail is gathered into batches, and a standard time is set for opening and recording each batch. The labour standards relating to one batch are as follows:

	Standard Hours	Standard Rate	Standard Cost
Per batch	2.5	$12.00	$30.00

The record showing the time spent last week in opening batches of mail has been misplaced. However, the batch supervisor recalls that 168 batches were received and opened during the week, and the controller recalls the following variance data relating to these batches:

Total labour variance	$660 U
Labour rate variance	$300 F

Required:
1. Determine the number of actual labour-hours spent opening batches during the week.
2. Determine the actual hourly rate paid to employees for opening batches last week.

(*Hint:* A useful way to proceed would be to work from known to unknown data, either by using the variance formulas or by using the columnar format shown in Exhibit 10–6.)

EXERCISE 10–13 Predetermined Overhead Rate; Overhead Variances [LO4, LO5, LO6]
The condensed form of Nordstrop Company's flexible budget for manufacturing overhead follows:

Overhead Costs	Cost Formula (per machine-hour)	Machine-Hours		
		8,000	9,000	10,000
Variable cost	$1.05	$ 8,400	$ 9,450	$10,500
Fixed cost		24,800	24,800	24,800
Total overhead cost.		$33,200	$34,250	$35,300

The following information is available for a recent period:
a. The denominator activity of 8,000 machine-hours was chosen to compute the predetermined overhead rate.
b. At the 8,000 standard machine-hours level of activity, the company should produce 3,200 units of product.
c. The company's actual operating results were as follows:

Number of units produced	3,500
Actual machine-hours	8,500
Actual variable overhead costs	$9,860
Actual fixed overhead costs	$25,100

Required:
1. Compute the predetermined overhead rate and break it down into variable and fixed cost elements.
2. What were the standard hours allowed for the year's actual output?
3. Compute the variable overhead spending and efficiency variances and the fixed overhead budget and volume variances.

EXERCISE 10–14 Using Fixed Overhead Variances [LO5, LO6]
The standard cost card for the single product manufactured by Princess Company is given below:

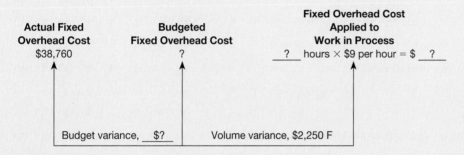

Standard Cost Card—Per Unit	
Direct materials, 2.1 metres at $6 per metre	$12.60
Direct labour, 0.6 direct labour-hours at $27 per direct labour-hour.	16.20
Variable overhead, 0.6 direct labour-hours at $3.75 per direct labour-hour	2.25
Fixed overhead, 0.6 direct labour-hours at $9 per direct labour-hour.	5.40
Total standard cost per unit.	$36.45

Last year, the company produced 7,500 units of product and worked 6,150 actual direct labour-hours. Manufacturing overhead cost is applied to production on the basis of direct labour-hours. Selected data relating to the company's fixed manufacturing overhead cost for the year are shown below.

Actual Fixed Overhead Cost	Budgeted Fixed Overhead Cost	Fixed Overhead Cost Applied to Work in Process
$38,760	?	__?__ hours × $9 per hour = $ __?__

Budget variance, __$?__   Volume variance, $2,250 F

Required:
1. What were the standard hours allowed for the year's production?
2. What was the amount of budgeted fixed overhead cost for the year?
3. What was the budget variance for the year?
4. What denominator activity level did the company use in setting the predetermined overhead rate for the year?

EXERCISE 10–15 Fixed Overhead Variances [LO5, LO6]
Selected operating information on three different companies for a recent period is given below:

	Company		
	X	Y	Z
Full-capacity direct labour-hours	20,000	9,000	10,000
Budgeted direct labour-hours*	19,000	8,500	8,000
Actual direct labour-hours	19,500	8,000	9,000
Standard direct labour-hours allowed for actual output	18,500	8,250	9,500

*Denominator activity for computing the predetermined overhead rate.

Required:
For each company, state whether the volume variance would be favourable or unfavourable; also, explain in each case *why* the volume variance would be favourable or unfavourable.

EXERCISE 10–16 Overhead Performance Report with Both Spending and Efficiency Variances [LO4, LO7]
The cheque-clearing office of Pay Loans Company is responsible for processing all cheques that come to the company for payment. Managers at the company believe that variable overhead costs are essentially proportional to the number of labour-hours worked in the office, so labour-hours are

used as the activity base when preparing variable overhead budgets and performance reports. Data for October, the most recent month, appear below:

Budgeted labour-hours	1,300
Actual labour-hours	1,290
Standard labour-hours allowed for the actual number of cheques processed	1,320

	Cost Formula (per labour-hour)	Actual Costs Incurred in October
Variable overhead costs:		
Office supplies	$0.30	$ 219
Staff coffee lounge.............	0.10	186
Indirect labour	3.90	3,348
Total variable overhead cost	$4.30	$3,753

Fixed overhead at Pay Loans Company consists entirely of supervisory salaries and is applied at the rate of $6 per direct labour-hour. Actual fixed overhead costs totalled $6,300 in October, while the flexible budget was $6,000 for the month.

Required:
Prepare an overhead performance report for October for the cheque-clearing office that includes both spending and efficiency variances for variable overhead and the budget variance for fixed overhead. Use Exhibit 10–13 as a guide in preparing the performance report.

EXERCISE 10–17 Capacity Analysis [LO7]
Johnson Company produces leather seats for racing bikes. The standard cost per seat is as follows:

Direct materials	$28
Direct labour.................................	12
Variable overhead (2 machine-hours at $3.00)*......	6
Fixed overhead (2 machine-hours at $12.00)*.......	24
Total standard cost per seat	$70

*Overhead rates are based on a denominator activity level of 50,000 machine-hours.

During 2011, Johnson Company produced and sold 22,000 seats. Management believes that the denominator level of activity represents 75% of theoretical capacity and 80% of practical capacity.

Required:
1. Calculate the total overhead costs at the following levels of activity: theoretical, practical, denominator, and actual (2011).
2. Assuming Johnson Company can sell all of the seats it can produce for $75 per unit, calculate the opportunity loss of producing 22,000 seats in 2011 compared to the following capacity utilization alternatives: theoretical, practical, and denominator.

Problems connect

PROBLEM 10–18 Comprehensive Variance Analysis [LO2, LO3, LO4]
London Company's Forest City Plant produces precast ingots for industrial use. Anne-Marie Gosnell, who was recently appointed general manager of the Forest City Plant, has just been handed the plant's income statement for October. The statement is shown on the next page.

Gosnell was shocked to see the poor results for the month, particularly since sales were exactly as budgeted. She stated, "I sure hope the plant has a standard cost system in operation. If it doesn't, I won't have the slightest idea of where to start looking for the problem."

	Budgeted	Actual
Sales (2,500 ingots)	$125,000	$125,000
Variable expenses:		
Variable cost of goods sold*.	40,000	45,455
Variable selling expenses	10,000	10,000
Total variable expenses	50,000	55,455
Contribution margin	75,000	69,545
Fixed expenses:		
Manufacturing overhead	30,000	29,500
Selling and administrative	37,500	37,500
Total fixed expenses	67,500	67,000
Operating income (loss)	$ 7,500	$ 2,545

*Contains direct materials, direct labour, and variable manufacturing
overhead.

The plant does use a standard cost system, with the standard variable cost per ingot details shown below.

	Standard Quantity or Hours	Standard Price or Rate	Standard Cost
Direct materials	2.0 kilograms	$1.25 per kilogram	$2.50
Direct labour	0.54 hours	$10.00 per hour	5.40
Variable manufacturing overhead . . .	0.27 hours*	$1.00 per hour	0.27
Total standard variable cost			$8.17

*Based on machine-hours.

Gosnell has determined that during October the plant produced 2,500 ingots and incurred the following costs:

a. Purchased 6,300 kilograms of materials at a cost of $1.50 per kilogram. There were no raw materials in inventory at the beginning of the month.

b. Used 4,900 kilograms of materials in production. (Finished goods and work in process inventories are insignificant and can be ignored.)

c. Worked 1,800 direct labour-hours at a cost of $9.50 per hour.

d. Incurred a total variable manufacturing overhead cost of $1,080 for the month. A total of 900 machine-hours was recorded. It is the company's policy to close all variances to cost of goods sold on a monthly basis.

Required:

1. Compute the following variances for October:
    a. Direct materials price and quantity variances.
    b. Direct labour rate and efficiency variances.
    c. Variable manufacturing overhead spending and efficiency variances.

2. Summarize the variances that you computed in (1) above by showing the net overall favourable or unfavourable variance for October. What impact did this figure have on the company's income statement?

3. Pick out the two most significant variances that you computed in (1) above. Explain to Gosnell possible causes of these variances.

PROBLEM 10–19 Comprehensive Variance Analysis in a Hospital [LO2, LO3, LO4, LO5, LO6]

eXcel

Marc Goudreau, administrator of Clearwater Hospital, was puzzled by the prior month's reports. "Every month, it's anyone's guess whether the lab will show a profit or a loss. Perhaps the only answer is to increase our lab fees again."

"We can't," replied Rhoda Groves, the controller. "There are still a lot of complaints about the last increase, particularly from the insurance companies and government health units. They're now paying only about 80% of what we bill. I'm beginning to think the problem is on the cost side."

To determine if the Clearwater lab costs are in line with those of other hospital labs, Goudreau has asked you to evaluate the costs for the past month. Groves has provided you with the following information:

a. Two basic types of tests are performed in the lab—smears and blood tests. During the past month, 2,700 smears and 900 blood tests were performed in the lab.

b. Small glass plates are used in both types of tests. During the past month, the hospital purchased 16,000 plates at a cost of $38,400. This cost is net of a 4% purchase discount. A total of 2,000 of these plates were unused at the end of the month; no plates were on hand at the beginning of the month.

c. During the past month, 1,800 hours of labour time were used in performing smears and blood tests. The cost of this labour time was $18,450.

d. The lab's variable overhead cost last month totalled $11,700.

e. Fixed overhead cost last month totalled $10,400.

Clearwater Hospital has never used standard costs. By searching industry literature, however, you have determined the following nationwide averages for hospital labs:

Plates: Three plates are required per lab test. These plates cost $2.50 each and are disposed of after the test is completed.

Labour: Each smear should require 0.3 hours to complete, and each blood test should require 0.6 hours to complete. The average cost of this lab time is $12 per hour.

Overhead: Overhead cost is based on direct labour-hours. The average rate of variable overhead is $6 per hour. The average rate of fixed overhead is $8 per hour. These rates are based on a denominator activity level of 1,250 hours per month.

Required:

1. Compute the materials price variance for the plates purchased last month, and compute a materials quantity variance for the plates used last month.

2. For labour cost in the lab:
    a. Compute a labour rate variance and a labour efficiency variance.
    b. In most hospitals, three-quarters of the workers in the lab are certified technicians and one-quarter are assistants. In an effort to reduce costs, Clearwater Hospital employs only one-half certified technicians and one-half assistants. Would you recommend that this policy be continued? Explain.

3. Compute the variable overhead spending and efficiency variances. Is there any relationship between the variable overhead efficiency variance and the labour efficiency variance? Explain.

4. Compute the fixed overhead budget and volume variances.

PROBLEM 10–20 Comprehensive Standard Cost Variances [LO2, LO3, LO4, LO5, LO6]
Clarissa McWhirter, vice-president of Cyprus Company, was pleased to see a small variance on the income statement after the trouble the company had been having in controlling manufacturing costs. She noted that the $12,250 overall manufacturing variance reported last period was well below the 3% limit that had been set for variances. The company produces and sells a single product. The standard cost card for the product follows:

Standard Cost Card—Per Unit	
Direct materials, 4 metres at $3.50 per metre	$14
Direct labour, 1.5 direct labour-hours at $12 per direct labour-hour.	18
Variable overhead, 1.5 direct labour-hours at $2 per direct labour-hour.	3
Fixed overhead, 1.5 direct-labour hours at $6 per direct labour-hour.	9
Standard cost per unit	$44

The following additional information is available for the year just completed:

a. The company manufactured 20,000 units of product during the year.

b. A total of 78,000 metres of material was purchased during the year at a cost of $3.75 per metre. All of this material was used to manufacture the 20,000 units. There were no beginning or ending inventories for the year.

c. The company worked 32,500 direct labour-hours during the year at a cost of $11.80 per hour.

d.   Overhead cost is applied to products on the basis of standard direct labour-hours. Data relating to manufacturing overhead costs follow:

Denominator activity level (direct labour-hours)................	25,000
Budgeted fixed overhead costs (from the flexible budget)......	$150,000
Actual fixed overhead costs..............................	$148,000
Actual variable overhead costs...........................	$68,250

Required:
1.   Compute the direct materials price and quantity variances for the year.
2.   Compute the direct labour rate and efficiency variances for the year.
3.   For manufacturing overhead, compute the following:
    a.   The variable overhead spending and efficiency variances for the year.
    b.   The fixed overhead budget and volume variances for the year.
4.   Total the variances you have computed, and compare the net amount with the $12,250 mentioned by the vice-president. Do you think that everyone should be congratulated for a job well done? Explain.

PROBLEM 10–21 Applying Overhead; Overhead Variances [LO4, LO5, LO6]

The Scottish firm of Cullen and MacNeil produces a single product and uses a standard cost system to help control costs. Manufacturing overhead is applied to production on the basis of standard machine-hours. The Scottish currency is the British pound. According to the company's flexible budget, the following overhead costs should be incurred at an activity level of 18,000 machine-hours (the denominator activity level chosen for the year):

Variable manufacturing overhead cost	£ 31,500
Fixed manufacturing overhead cost	72,000
Total manufacturing overhead cost.............	£103,500

During the year, the following operating results were recorded:

Actual machine-hours worked	15,000
Standard machine-hours allowed.........................	16,000
Actual variable manufacturing overhead cost incurred	£26,500
Actual fixed manufacturing overhead cost incurred.............	£70,000

At the end of the year, the company's manufacturing overhead account contained the following data:

Manufacturing Overhead

Actual costs	96,500	Applied costs	92,000
	4,500		

Management would like to determine the cause of the £4,500 underapplied overhead.

Required:
1.   Compute the predetermined overhead rate for the year. Break it down into variable and fixed cost elements.
2.   Show how the £92,000 "Applied costs" figure in the manufacturing overhead account was computed.
3.   Analyze the £4,500 underapplied overhead figure in terms of the variable overhead spending and efficiency variances and the fixed overhead budget and volume variances.
4.   Explain the meaning of each variance that you computed in (3) above.

PROBLEM 10–22 Basic Variance Analysis [LO2, LO3, LO4]

Organics, Inc., manufactures a product called Fruit-Aid. The company uses variable costing in conjunction with a standard cost system and has established the following standards for one unit of Fruit-Aid:

◇	B	C	D	E	F	G
34						
35		*Standard*		*Standard*		*Standard*
36		*Quantity or Hours*		*Price or Rate*		*Cost*
37	Direct materials	1.2	kg	$ 7.20	per kilogram	$ 8.64
38	Direct labour	0.5	hours	$14.50	per hour	7.25
39	Variable manufacturing overhead	0.5	hours	$ 3.00	per hour	1.50
40	Total standard variable cost					$17.39
41						
42						
43						

⌐◀ ◀ ▶ ▶⌐ **Sheet1** Sheet2 Sheet3

During June, the company recorded the following activity relative to production of Fruit-Aid:
a.   The company produced 3,000 units during June.
b.   A total of 7,000 kilograms of material were purchased at a cost of $48,300.
c.   There was no beginning inventory of materials; however, at the end of the month, 2,000 kilograms of material remained in ending inventory.
d.   The company employs 8 persons to work on the production of Fruit-Aid. During June, each worked an average of 150 hours at an average rate of $15.00 per hour.
e.   Variable manufacturing overhead is assigned to Fruit-Aid on the basis of direct labour-hours. Variable manufacturing overhead costs during June totalled $3,300.

The company's management is anxious to determine the efficiency of the Fruit-Aid production activities.

Required:
1.   For direct materials used in the production of Fruit-Aid:
   a.   Compute the price and quantity variances.
   b.   The materials were purchased from a new supplier who is anxious to enter into a long-term purchase contract. Would you recommend that the company sign the contract? Explain.
2.   For labour employed in the production of Fruit-Aid:
   a.   Compute the rate and efficiency variances.
   b.   In the past, the 8 people employed in the production of Fruit-Aid consisted of 3 senior workers and 5 assistants. During June, the company experimented with 4 senior workers and 4 assistants. Would you recommend that the new labour mix be continued? Explain.
3.   Compute the variable overhead spending and efficiency variances. What relationship can you see between this efficiency variance and the labour efficiency variance?

PROBLEM 10–23 Overhead Performance Report [LO7]
Asper Company has recently introduced budgeting as an integral part of its corporate planning process. An inexperienced member of the accounting staff was given the assignment of constructing a flexible budget for manufacturing overhead costs and prepared it in the format that follows:

Percentage of Capacity	80%	100%
Machine-hours	40,000	50,000
Utilities.	$ 41,000	$ 49,000
Supplies	4,000	5,000
Indirect labour	8,000	10,000
Maintenance	37,000	41,000
Supervision	10,000	10,000
Total manufacturing overhead cost	$100,000	$115,000

The company assigns manufacturing overhead costs to production on the basis of standard machine-hours. The cost formulas used to prepare the budgeted figures above are relevant over a range of 80% to 100% of capacity in a month. The managers who will be working under these budgets have control over both fixed and variable manufacturing overhead costs.

Required:
1. Use the high–low method (see Chapter 6) to separate fixed and variable costs.
2. Come up with a single cost formula for all overhead costs based on your analysis in (1) above. (*Hint*: Your cost formula should be of the form: $y = a + bx$.)
3. During May, the company operated at 86% of machine-hour capacity. Actual manufacturing overhead costs incurred during the month were as follows:

Utilities	$ 42,540
Supplies	6,450
Indirect labour	9,890
Maintenance	35,190
Supervision	10,000
Total actual manufacturing overhead cost	$104,070

Fixed costs had no budget variances. Prepare an overhead performance report for May. Include both fixed and variable costs in your report (in separate sections). Structure your report so that it shows only a spending variance for variable overhead. The company originally budgeted to work 40,000 machine-hours during the month; standard hours allowed for the month's production totalled 41,000 machine-hours. (Use Exhibit 10–14 as a guide.)
4. Explain possible causes of the spending variance for supplies.

PROBLEM 10–24 Setting Standards [LO1]
Quintessence, a small cosmetics company in the south of France, plans to introduce a new body oil, called Dynamique, for which it needs to develop a standard product cost. The following information is available on the production of Dynamique:
a. The Dynamique base is made by mixing high-grade lanolin and alcohol. Both the lanolin and the alcohol lose some volume during the mixing process. As a result, each 100-litre batch of Dynamique base requires 100 litres of lanolin and 8 litres of alcohol.
b. After the base has been prepared, a highly concentrated jasmine powder is added to impart a pleasing scent. Only 200 grams of the powder are added to each 100-litre batch. The addition of the jasmine powder does not significantly change the total liquid volume.
c. Both the lanolin and the jasmine powder are subject to some contamination from naturally occurring materials. For example, the jasmine powder often contains some traces of insects that are not detected and removed when the jasmine petals are processed. Occasionally such contaminants interact in ways that result in an unacceptable product with an unpleasant odour. About one 100-litre batch in twenty is rejected as unsuitable for sale for this reason and is thrown away.
d. It takes a worker two hours to process one 100-litre batch of Dynamique. Employees work an eight-hour day, including two hours per day for lunch, rest breaks, and cleanup.

Required:
1. Determine the standard quantity for each of the raw materials needed to produce an acceptable 100-litre batch of Dynamique.
2. Determine the standard labour time allowed to produce an acceptable 100-litre batch of Dynamique.
3. The standard prices for direct materials and direct labour in euros (€) appear below:

Lanolin.	€16 per litre
Alcohol	€2 per litre
Jasmine powder	€1 per gram
Direct labour cost	€12 per hour

Prepare a standard cost card for materials and labour for one acceptable 100-litre batch of Dynamique.

(CMA, adapted)

PROBLEM 10–25 Applying Overhead; Overhead Variances [LO4, LO5, LO6]
Ryder Company produces a single product that requires a large amount of labour time. Overhead
cost is applied on the basis of standard direct labour-hours. The company's condensed flexible budget for manufacturing overhead is given below:

Overhead Costs	Cost Formula (per DLH)	Direct Labour-Hours		
		12,000	15,000	18,000
Variable manufacturing overhead cost	$1	$12,000	$15,000	$18,000
Fixed manufacturing overhead cost		75,000	75,000	75,000
Total manufacturing overhead cost.		$87,000	$90,000	$93,000

The company's product requires 2 metres of direct material that has a standard cost of
$1.50 per metre. The product requires 1.5 hours of direct labour time. The standard labour rate is
$10 per hour.
During the year, the company had planned to operate at a denominator activity level of 15,000
direct labour-hours and to produce 10,000 units of product. Actual activity and costs for the year
were as follows:

Number of units produced	11,000
Actual direct labour-hours worked	17,500
Actual variable manufacturing overhead cost incurred. . . .	$15,750
Actual fixed manufacturing overhead cost incurred	$76,500

Required:
1. Compute the predetermined overhead rate for the year. Break the rate down into variable and
    fixed components.
2. *a.* Compute the standard direct labour-hours allowed for the year's production.
    b. Complete the following manufacturing overhead T-account for the year:

Manufacturing Overhead

?	?
?	?

3. Determine the reason for the underapplied or overapplied overhead from (2) above by comput-
    ing the variable overhead spending and efficiency variances and the fixed overhead budget and
    volume variances.
4. Suppose the company had chosen 18,000 direct labour-hours as the denominator activity
    rather than 15,000 hours. State which, if any, of the variances computed in (3) above would
    have changed, and explain how the variance(s) would have changed. No computations are
    necessary.

**PROBLEM 10–26 Flexible Budget and Overhead Performance Report [LO4, LO5, LO6,
LO7]**
Groschl Company has had great difficulty in controlling manufacturing overhead costs. At a
recent convention, the president heard about a control device for overhead costs known as a *flex-
ible budget*, and he has hired you to implement this budgeting program in Groschl Company.
After some effort, you have developed the following cost formulas for the company's Machining
Department. These costs are based on a normal operating range of 10,000 to 20,000 machine-
hours per month:

Overhead Cost	Cost Formula
Utilities	$0.70 per machine-hour
Lubricants.	$1.00 per machine-hour plus $8,000 per month
Machine setup	$0.20 per machine-hour
Indirect labour.	$0.60 per machine-hour plus $120,000 per month
Depreciation	$32,000 per month

During March, the first month after your preparation of the above data, the Machining Department worked 18,000 machine-hours and produced 9,000 units of product. The actual manufacturing overhead costs for March were as follows:

Utilities	$ 12,000
Lubricants	24,500
Machine setup	4,800
Indirect labour	132,500
Depreciation.	32,000
Total manufacturing overhead cost	$205,800

Fixed costs had no budget variances. The department had originally been budgeted to work 20,000 machine-hours during March.

Required:
1. Prepare an overhead performance report for the Machining Department for the month of March. Include both variable and fixed costs in the report (in separate sections). Show only a spending variance on the report. (Use Exhibit 10–14 as your guide.)
2. What additional information would you need to compute an overhead efficiency variance for the department?

PROBLEM 10–27 Evaluating an Overhead Performance Report [LO5, LO6, LO7]
Timothy Hawkins, superintendent of Kal-Tubing Company's Machining Department, is very happy with his performance report for the past month. The report follows:

◇	B	C	D	E	F	G
1						
2		Kal-Tubing Company				
3		Overhead Performance Report - Machining Department				
4						
5			*Actual*	*Budget*	*Variance*	
6	Machine-hours		15,000	17,500		
7	Variable manufacturing overhead:					
8	Indirect labour		$39,400	$42,000	$2,600 F	
9	Utilities		101,600	119,000	17,400 F	
10	Supplies		25,200	28,000	2,800 F	
11	Maintenance		49,800	56,000	6,200 F	
12	Total variable manufacturing overhead		216,000	245,000	29,000 F	
13	Fixed manufacturing overhead:					
14	Maintenance		78,000	78,000	0	
15	Supervision		165,000	165,000	0	
16	Depreciation		120,000	120,000	0	
17	Total fixed manufacturing overhead		363,000	363,000	0	
18	Total manufacturing overhead		$579,000	$608,000	$29,000 F	
19						
20						
21						
22						
23						

I◄ ◄ ► ►I   Sheet1   Sheet2   Sheet3

When he received a copy of this report, Wayne Lockhart, the production manager, commented, "I've been getting these reports for months now, and I still can't see how they help me assess efficiency and cost control in that department. I agree that the budget for the month was 17,500 machine-hours, but that represents 4,375 units of product, since it should take four hours to produce one unit. The department produced only 3,500 units during the month, and took 15,000 machine-hours to do it. Why do all the variances turn up favourable?"

Required:
1. In answer to Lockhart's question, why are all the variances favourable? Is the performance report useful? Explain.
2. Prepare a new overhead performance report that will help Lockhart assess efficiency and cost control in the Milling Department. (*Hint*: Exhibit 10–13 may be helpful in structuring your report.)

Goster: I seem to get more reports than I need, and I am never asked to comment on them until top management calls me onto the carpet about my department's shortcomings. Do you ever hear comments when your department shines?

Flores: I guess they don't have time to review the good news. One of my problems is that all the reports are in dollars and cents. I work with people, machines, and materials. I need information to help me solve *this* month's problems—not another report of the dollars expended *last* month or the month before.

Required:

1. Based on the conversation between José Flores and Adriana Goster, describe the likely motivation and behaviour of these two employees resulting from Newmarket Manufacturing Company's standard cost and variance reporting system.

2. When properly implemented, both employees and companies should benefit from a system involving standard costs and variances.

   a. Describe the benefits that can be realized from a standard cost system.

   b. Based on the situation presented above, recommend ways for Newmarket Manufacturing Company to improve its standard cost and variance reporting system so as to increase employee motivation.

(CMA, adapted)

CASE 10–36 Ethics and the Manager [LO7]

Lance Prating is the controller of the Colchester manufacturing facility of Tech Systems, Incorporated. Among the many reports that must be filed with corporate headquarters is the annual overhead performance report. The report covers the year that ends on December 31 and is due at corporate headquarters shortly after the beginning of the new year. Prating does not like putting work off until the last minute, so just before Christmas, he put together a preliminary draft of the overhead performance report. Some adjustments would later be required for the few transactions that occur between Christmas and New Year's Day. A copy of the preliminary draft report, which Prating completed on December 21, is shown on the next page.

Tab Kapp, the general manager at the Colchester facility, asked to see a copy of the preliminary draft report at 4:45 P.M. on December 23. Prating carried a copy of the report to Kapp's office, where the following discussion took place:

Kapp: Wow! Almost all of the variances on the report are unfavourable. The only thing that looks good at all are the favourable variances for supervisory salaries and for industrial engineering. How did we have an unfavourable variance for depreciation?

Prating: Do you remember that milling machine that broke down because the wrong lubricant was used by the machine operator?

Kapp: Only vaguely.

Prating: It turned out we couldn't fix it. We had to scrap the machine and buy a new one.

Kapp: This report doesn't look good. I was raked over the coals last year when we had just a few unfavourable variances.

Prating: I'm afraid the final report is going to look even worse.

Kapp: Oh?

Prating: The line item for industrial engineering on the report is for work we hired Klein Engineering to do for us on a contract basis. The original contract was for $160,000, but we asked them to do some additional work that was not in the contract. Under the terms of the contract, we have to reimburse Klein Engineering for the costs of the additional work. The $154,000 in actual costs that appear on the preliminary draft report reflects only their billings through December 21. The last bill they had sent us was on November 28, and they completed the project just last week. Yesterday I got a call from Maria over at Klein and she said they would be sending us a final bill for the project before the end of the year. The total bill, including the reimbursements for the additional work, is going to be. . . .

Kapp: I am not sure I want to hear this.

Prating: $176,000.

Kapp: Ouch!

Prating: The additional work we asked them to do added $16,000 to the cost of the project.

Kapp: No way can I turn in a performance report with an overall unfavourable variance. They'll really get on my back at corporate headquarters. Call Maria at Klein and ask her not to send the bill until after the first of the year. We have to have that $6,000 favourable variance for industrial engineering on the performance report.

COLCHESTER MANUFACTURING FACILITY
Overhead Performance Report
December 21 Preliminary Draft

Budgeted machine-hours 100,000
Actual machine-hours 90,000

Overhead Costs	Cost Formula (per Machine-hour)	Actual Costs for 90,000 Machine-Hours	Flexible Budget Based on 90,000 Machine-Hours	Spending or Budget Variance
Variable overhead costs:				
Power.	$0.03	$ 2,840	$ 2,700	$ 140 U
Supplies	0.86	79,060	77,400	1,660 U
Abrasives	0.34	32,580	30,600	1,980 U
	$1.23	114,480	110,700	3,780 U
Fixed overhead costs				
Depreciation.		228,300	226,500	1,800 U
Supervisory salaries.		187,300	189,000	1,700 F
Insurance		23,000	23,000	0
Industrial engineering.		154,000	160,000	6,000 F
Factory building lease		46,000	46,000	0
Total fixed overhead cost		638,600	644,500	5,900 F
Total overhead cost.		$753,080	$755,200	$2,120 F

Required:
What should Lance Prating do? Explain.

CASE 10–37 Working Backward from Variance Data [LO2, LO3, LO4, LO6]

You have recently graduated from university and have accepted a position with Sea-Jewels, Inc., the manufacturer of a popular consumer product. During your first week on the job, the vice-president has been favourably impressed with your work. She has been so impressed, in fact, that yesterday she called you into her office and asked you to attend the executive committee meeting this morning for the purpose of leading a discussion on the variances reported for last period. Anxious to favourably impress the executive committee, you took the variances and supporting data home last night on a memory stick to study.

Unfortunately, when you tried to open the files this morning some of them had become corrupted. All you could retrieve is shown below.

You recall that manufacturing overhead cost is applied to production on the basis of direct labour-hours and that all of the materials purchased during the period were used in production. Since the company uses JIT to control work flows, work in process inventories are insignificant and can be ignored.

Standard Cost Card

Direct materials, 9 kilograms at $3 per kilogram.	$27.00
Direct labour, 1.2 direct labour-hours at $15 per direct labour-hour	18.00
Variable manufacturing overhead, 1.2 direct labour-hours at $3 per direct labour-hour	3.60
Fixed manufacturing overhead, 1.2 direct labour-hours at $7 per direct labour-hour	8.40
Standard cost per unit.	$57.00

	Total Standard Cost*	Variances Reported			
		Price or Rate	Spending or Budget	Quantity or Efficiency	Volume
Direct materials	$202,500	$3,450 F		$4,500 U	
Direct labour	$135,000	$7,275 U		$10,500 U	
Variable manufacturing overhead . .	$27,000		$650 F	$?† U	
Fixed manufacturing overhead	$63,000		$250 F		$7,000 U

*Applied to work in process during the period.
†Data corrupted.

It is now 8:30 a.m. The executive committee meeting starts in just one hour; you realize that to avoid looking grossly incompetent, you must somehow generate the necessary "backup" data for the variances before the meeting begins. Without backup data, it will be impossible to lead the discussion or answer any questions.

Required:
1. How many units were produced last period? (Think hard about this one!)
2. How many kilograms of direct material were purchased and used in production?
3. What was the actual cost per kilogram of material?
4. How many actual direct labour-hours were worked during the period?
5. What was the actual rate paid per direct labour-hour?
6. How much actual variable manufacturing overhead cost was incurred during the period?
7. What is the total fixed manufacturing overhead cost in the company's flexible budget?
8. What were the denominator direct labour-hours for last period?

CASE 10–38 Full Variance Analysis: Variable Costing [LO3, LO4, LO5, LO6]
Anchorvale Electronics Limited manufactures and distributes transistors for electronics firms. In December 2010, Anchorvale required a bank loan and the bank manager insisted that Tracy Miller, Anchorvale's president, prepare a budget for 2011. In January 2012, Anchorvale needed an additional loan and Miller asked her accountant to prepare a budget for 2012 to show the bank manager. Miller was concerned because Anchorvale's profit for 2011 was considerably less than the 2011 budget figure given to the bank and she knew that the bank manager would want to know why. As a first step in analyzing the differences, Miller copied the 2011 actual figures onto the 2011 bank budget form shown below and prepared the standard cost details shown on the next page.

ANCHORVALE ELECTRONICS LIMITED 2011 Budget Prepared for Bank Loan			
	Dollars in (000s)		
	Static Budget	Actual	Variance
Sales—units.	110,000	105,000	5,000 U
Sales—dollars	$2,750	$2,520	$ 230 U
Cost of sales:			
Materials.	440	421	19 F
Labour	880	845	35 F
Overhead	220	205	15 F
Fixed factory overhead	300	303	3 U
	1,840	1,774	66 F
Gross profit	910	746	164 U
Selling expenses:			
Variable	220	209	11 F
Fixed	100	102	2 U
Administration—fixed	200	197	3 F
	520	508	12 F
Profit before income tax	390	238	152 U
Income tax (40% of profit before tax)	156	95	61 F
Net earnings	$ 234	$ 143	$ 91 U

Required:
1. Redraft the budget to show the 2011 static budget, flexible budget, actual, and variances from the flexible budget, with contribution margins separately identified. *Note:* See the standard cost details on the next page.
2. Prepare quantitative analysis to demonstrate to management the main causes for the variance from the flexible budget, as a basis both for taking corrective action and for explaining the variance from the static budget to the bank manager.
3. If expected 2012 operating results are similar to 2011, explain to the bank manager how much of the loan you would be able to repay from 2012 earnings. (Assume no changes in accounts receivable and accounts payable.)
4. If competition became intense in 2012 and Anchorvale was operating well below capacity at 85,000 units, explain with calculations the minimum bid you would make on an order for 10,000 units.
5. What changes to the management accounting and reporting system for Anchorvale Electronics would you propose?

(CGAC, Adapted)

Standard Costs on Which Budget Is Based	
	Standard per Unit
Sales price	$25
Variable costs:	
Direct Material	$ 4
Labour 1/2 hour at $16 per hour	8
Overhead 1/2 hour at $4 per hour	2
Fixed factory overhead:	
Depreciation $200,000	
Other. 100,000	
$300,000	
Standard output 100,000 units at 1/2 hour = 50,000 direct labour hours	
($300,000 ÷ 50,000) × 1/2 hour	3
Selling expenses:	
Variable.	2
Fixed $100,000 ÷ 100,000 units	1
Administration Fixed:	
$200,000 ÷ 100,000 units	2
	$22

Standard costs were used for preparing bids whereas the cost accounting system recorded actual costs.

Research and Application

R 10–39 Standard Costing in Practice [LO1]

Identify a company in your local area that is likely to use standards and conduct variance analysis, such as a manufacturer, a chain restaurant, a service department at an auto dealership, or a commercial bakery. Once you have determined that the company uses standards, set up a meeting with a manager in the financial reporting department.

Required:
At the meeting, get answers to the following questions:
1. Which types of variances are calculated (price, efficiency, etc.)?
2. How often are they calculated?
3. How do managers decide which variances to investigate?
4. Are favourable and unfavourable variances investigated?
5. What is the mechanism for reviewing the explanations provided for variances?
6. What are some examples of corrective actions taken as the result of a variance investigation?
7. How often are standards updated or revised?

R 10–40 Overhead Reporting and Control [LO7]

Identify a company in your local area that is likely to have significant manufacturing overhead costs. An example would be a manufacturing company that has automated at least some of its production activities.

    Once you have determined that the company uses standards, set up a meeting with a manager in the financial reporting department.

Required:
At the meeting, get answers to the following questions:
1. How are overhead costs controlled in the organization?
2. What types of performance reports are prepared for overhead?
3. How often are performance reports prepared for overhead?
4. Does the company distinguish between variable and fixed overhead in its reporting and control system?
5. How are overhead costs allocated to products or services?
6. What is the biggest challenge in managing overhead costs?

APPENDIX 10A: FURTHER ANALYSIS OF MATERIALS VARIANCES

LEARNING OBJECTIVE 8
Compute the mix and yield variances for materials and explain their significance.

Mix variance
The dollar effect on total materials cost of a difference between the actual mix of materials inputs and the standard mix of materials.

Yield variance
The dollar effect on total materials costs of the total quantity of inputs actually used generating a different output from what would have been achieved using standard quantities of inputs at the standard mix.

A survey of the cost accounting practices of the 1,000 largest U.S. industrial companies found that two other types of standard cost variances are frequently computed.[7] These are subcomponents of the materials quantity variance: a *materials mix* and *materials yield variance.* The extended model for calculating these variances is presented in Exhibit 10A–1.

The production of most goods generally requires more than one type of direct materials input. Chemical firms use varying proportions of interchangeable materials, and the same is true of food processing companies. For example, a company that produces flour with a mixture of red and white wheat may, on occasion, substitute one kind of wheat for another. When legally permitted, a manufacturer of canned fruit cocktail may substitute peaches for pears and a manufacturer of sausages may substitute beef for pork. The calculation of mix and yield variances is appropriate *only* if different types of materials can be substituted for one another. A **mix variance** results if the actual mix of materials inputs differs from the standard mix of materials. The standard mix reflects the proportional mix of materials that is expected to be used to produce a given product. A mix variance is calculated to determine the effects of a change in the materials mix on the total materials cost. The mix variance is favourable if the actual mix of materials inputs is cheaper than the standard mix. This means that a greater proportion of less-expensive materials was used in production. The mix variance is unfavourable if the actual mix of materials inputs is more expensive than the standard mix because a greater proportion of more-expensive materials was used. Where a manager has control over the composition of the mix, the mix variance can be a useful measure of the manager's performance.

A **yield variance** occurs when the total quantity of inputs actually used generates a different rate of output from what would have been achieved using standard quantities of inputs at the standard mix. To isolate the effects of the yield variance from the mix variance, the yield variance is calculated using the standard mix of materials inputs. By so doing, managers can calculate the dollar impact on total materials costs of the actual total quantity of inputs differing from the quantities that should have been used according to the standard cost system. A favourable yield variance means a lower total quantity of inputs was used than planned, while an unfavourable yield variance means more inputs were used in total than planned.

To illustrate the calculation of the mix and yield variances, assume that Cape Breton Chemical Company combines secret ingredients A and B to make a product known as Super-Cleaner Bjax. The standard mix calls for 2 kilograms of A and 3 kilograms of B to

EXHIBIT 10A–1 Extended Model for Variance Analysis— Materials

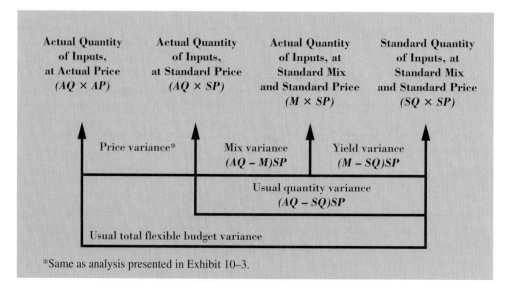

produce one unit of Bjax. The standard mix for A and B is therefore $^2/_5$ and $^3/_5$, respectively. Assume that 150 units were produced in July using 350 kilograms of A and 450 kilograms of B. Material A has a standard unit price of $1.50 and material B has a standard price of $2.50 per unit.

We begin by calculating the materials quantity variance for each type of material input and in total, using the formula presented earlier in the chapter: $SP(AQ - SQ)$.

> Material A: $1.50(350 − 300*) = $75 U
> Material B: $2.50(450 − 450*) = $ 0
> _____
> *Material A: 2 kilograms per unit × 150 units;
> Material B: 3 kilograms per unit × 150 units

Thus, the total quantity variance to be further analyzed into its mix and yield components is $75 unfavourable.

For each type of input, the mix variance can be calculated in two steps. First, multiply the budgeted mix percentage for that input by the actual *total* inputs of all types and subtract the result from the actual quantity of that input used in production for the period. This is the mix variance expressed in physical terms for each type of input. Second, multiply your answer from step one by the standard price of that input. The formula for the mix variance that is applied to *each* type of material input is shown below:

$$\frac{\text{Mix}}{\text{Variance}} = \left[\begin{array}{c} \text{Actual} \\ \text{quantity} \end{array} - \left(\begin{array}{c} \text{Budgeted} \\ \% \end{array} \times \begin{array}{c} \text{Total} \\ \text{input} \end{array} \right) \right] \times \begin{array}{c} \text{Standard} \\ \text{price} \end{array}$$

or for each input used in production:

$$\text{Mix variance} = (AQ_A - M_A)SP_A$$

where

AQ_A is the actual quantity used of material A.
M_A is the standard mix of material A given the total quantity of material actually used.
SP_A is the standard price of material A.

For material A, the mix variance in July would be

$$\left[350 - \frac{2}{5}(350 + 450) \right] \times \$1.50 = \$45 \text{ U}$$

Similarly, for material B, the mix variance in July would be:

$$\left[450 - \frac{3}{5}(350 + 450) \right] \times \$2.50 = \$75 \text{ F}$$

The result of multiplying the budgeted mix percentage for material A by the total quantity of inputs actually used in July is 320 kilograms [$^2/_5$(350 + 450)]. This is the amount of material A that would have been used if the budgeted mix had been adhered to. Since the amount of material actually used, 350 kilograms, exceeds the budgeted amount, the mix variance is unfavourable. If the budgeted mix had been adhered to for material B, 480 kilograms [$^3/_5$(350 + 450)] would have been used in July. Since the actual usage of material B was only 450 kilograms, the materials mix variance of material B is favourable. Note that the mix variances are calculated using the total quantity of materials inputs actually used (800 kilograms) and thus focus on the effects of the actual mix of inputs differing from the standard mix of inputs.

Overall, the mix variance is $30 favourable, which is the result of using a higher percentage of the less-expensive material A in July (350 ÷ 800 = 43.75%) than planned in the budget (2 ÷ 5 = 40%). If the opposite had been true and a higher percentage of the more-expensive material B had been used in July compared to the budgeted mix, the overall mix variance would have been unfavourable.

The yield variance is also calculated in two steps for each type of input. First, multiply the total quantity of all inputs used for the period by the standard mix percentage for that input and from this result, subtract the standard quantity of the input allowed for the output achieved. Note that this approach holds mix constant at the standard proportions, allowing the yield variance to be isolated from any differences between the actual and standard mix. Second, multiply the result of the first step by the standard price for that input. The formula for the yield variance that is applied to *each* type of material input is shown below:

Yield variance = [(Budgeted % × Total input) – Standard quantity] × Standard price

or for each input used in production:

$$\text{Yield variance} = (M_A - SQ_A)SP_A$$

where

SQ_A is the standard quantity of material A with the other items in the formula as defined above.

For material A, the yield variance in July would be

$$\left[\frac{2}{5}(350 + 450) - 2(150)\right] \$1.50 = \$30 \text{ U}$$

Similarly, for material B, the yield variance in July would be

$$\left[\frac{3}{5}(350 + 450) - 3(150)\right] \$2.50 = \$75 \text{ U}$$

Note that the yield variances are calculated using the standard mix of materials (40% A, 60% B) and thus focus on the effects of the actual quantity of inputs (at the standard mix) differing from the standard quantity of inputs. Overall, the yield variance for July is $105 unfavourable comprised of the individual amounts shown above. This indicates that, in total, more inputs were used for production than should have been according to the standards.

It is important to note how the sum of the mix and yield variances is equal to the total materials quantity variance calculated above:

Variance	Amount
Mix:	
Material A.	$ 45 U
Material B	75 F
Total mix variance	$ 30 F
Yield:	
Material A.	$ 30 U
Material B	75 U
Total yield variance	$105 U
Total mix and yield variances	$ 75 U

Collectively, the mix and yield variances explain why the total quantity variance occurred. In our example, using an actual mix of inputs that favoured the less-expensive material A resulted in a favourable mix variance. However this was offset by the fact that more inputs in total (particularly for material B) were required to produce the output for the period. Specifically, 800 kg of materials inputs were actually used (350 kg material A and 450 kg material B), while the standard amount allowed for the output achieved was 750 kg (300 kg material A and 450 kg material B). This resulted in a $105 unfavourable yield variance. It could be that the less-expensive material A was more easily damaged, was harder to work with, or had other characteristics that led to the unfavourable yield variance. Whatever the reason, the manager's decision to increase the proportion of material A used in July production led to an unfavourable yield variance and an unfavourable total materials quantity variance. By separately examining the mix and yield components of the total quantity variance, the effects of the trade-offs between mix and yield effects can be detected. Moreover, there may be implications for other variances that arise from using an actual mix of inputs that differs from the standard. In our example, if material A is harder to work with, this could lead to an unfavourable labour efficiency variance if employees need to spend more time working with substandard material. So, calculating the mix and yield variances may help managers understand the causes of other variances for the period.

Labour efficiency variances, described earlier in the chapter, can be analyzed in a similar manner if the composition of a work group is provided in the standard. The effects of departing from the standard mix of skilled and unskilled workers or experienced and less-experienced employees can be broken down into mix and yield components. As with our example above, this will allow managers to quantify the financial impact of changing the mix of labour inputs.

Appendix 10A Summary

- When the production of a good requires more than one type of direct materials input, the total materials quantity variance can be further analyzed into mix and yield components if those inputs are substitutes for each other. **[LO8]**
- A mix variance quantifies the dollar impact on materials costs of using an actual mix of inputs that differs from the standard mix. A yield variance quantifies the dollar impact of the actual total quantity of inputs differing from the standard quantity allowed for the output achieved. Because the yield variance is calculated using the standard mix of inputs, it permits the isolation of quantity differences (actual versus standard) from the mix differences (actual versus standard) calculated for the mix variance. **[LO8]**
- Calculating the mix and yield variances allows for a more complete evaluation of managers' decisions to change the mix of inputs in any given period. Because changing the mix of inputs can often impact the yield generated by those inputs, the dollar impact of this trade-off becomes clear after calculating the mix and yield variances. Changing the mix of inputs can also impact other variances such as labour efficiency and thus may be helpful in explaining outcomes on those variances. **[LO8]**
- Mix and yield variances can also be calculated when different types of labour inputs are required to produce a product or deliver a service and can be substituted for each other. **[LO8]**

connect Appendix 10A Exercises and Problems

EXERCISE 10A–1 Mix and Yield Variances [LO8]

The Groovy Gadget Company uses standard costs to account for its production of gadgets. The standard cost of a gadget is given as follows for materials and direct labour:

Material A..........	12 kilograms at 90 cents	$10.80
Material B..........	3 kilograms at $2.50	7.50
Direct labour........	4 hours at $14.00	56.00

Both material A and material B are added at the start of the process. Production data for June 2011 are as follows:

a. Beginning work process, 7,000 units, 30% complete.
b. Started during June, 26,000 units.
c. Ending work in process, 8,000 units, 60% complete.
d. No units were spoiled.
e. 325,000 kilograms of material A were issued to production.

f.   77,000 kilograms of material B were used during June.

g.   Direct labour worked: 111,000 hours at a cost of $1,576,200 for the month.

Required:

Determine all of the material and labour variances possible from the preceding data for the month of June.

EXERCISE 10A–2 Mix and Yield Variances [LO8]

Davis Division uses three secret materials—A, B, and C—to produce its product, called Corzon. The materials are mixed in the following standard proportions to yield 100 litres of Corzon:

Secret Material	Quantity (Litres)	Cost per Litre
A........................	80	$ 4.00
B........................	40	$ 8.00
C........................	30	$20.00

It requires 50 hours of direct labour at $20.00 per hour to produce 100 litres of Corzon.

On average, the division can produce and sell 200,000 litres of Corzon per month. In a recent month, the division used the following amounts of materials and labour to produce 175,000 litres of Corzon:

Secret Material	Quantity (Litres)	Total Actual Cost
A........................	159,000	$ 647,130
B........................	72,000	580,204
C........................	44,000	870,000
	275,000	$2,097,334
Direct labour...............	91,000 hours	$1,380,000

Required:

1.   Calculate the following materials variances for Corzon:
  a.   Price.
  b.   Quantity.
  c.   Mix.
  d.   Yield.

2.   The supervisor of the Corzon product line argued that the workers were operating at standard, if not better, despite a large unfavourable labour efficiency variance of $52,500. Is the supervisor correct? Why or why not?

(SMAC, Adapted)

PROBLEM 10A–3 Mix and Yield Variances [LO8]

Dundas Company manufactures and sells two special-purpose cleaning solvents, Brill and Daz. The two products emerge from the same production process, which requires three materials: C12, D24, and E48. The division developed standard costs for these two solvents as shown below.

Normal monthly volume is 22,000 kilograms of input materials processed or 20,000 kilograms of good output. Some variations of input quantities are permissible without affecting the quality of the finished products.

Joint Processing Costs		
Materials—C12	12 kilograms at $4.80 per kilogram	$ 57.60
—D24	8 kilograms at $8.40 per kilogram	67.20
—E48	2 kilograms at $10.30 per kilogram	20.60
Total materials input	22 kilograms	145.40
Labour (applied at $11.20 per kilogram × 22 kilograms)		246.40
Overhead—Variable (applied at $5.60 per kilogram × 22 kilograms)		123.20
—Fixed (applied at $10.00 per kilogram × 22 kilograms)		220.00
Joint costs to produce 20 kilograms of good output		$735.00

Costs Assigned to the Two Joint Products Using Market Value					
Product	**Good Output**	**Per Kilogram**	**Total**	**Joint* Costs**	**Standard Cost Per Kilogram**
Brill............	14 kilograms	$40	$560	$420.00	$30.00
Daz............	6 kilograms	70	420	315.00	52.50
	20 kilograms		$980	$735.00	

*Joint costs are allocated to the products on the basis of market value.

Materials are purchased from another division and are readily available; therefore, very little raw materials inventory is kept by Dundas Company. Materials prices are negotiated annually between the divisions. All production is finished daily; therefore, there are no work in process inventories.

Actual production of good output in July amounted to 22,800 kilograms. The production costs were calculated as follows:

Materials input—C12..............	15,000 kilograms at $4.80 per kilogram	$ 72,000
—D24..............	8,100 kilograms at $8.40 per kilogram	68,040
—E48..............	2,200 kilograms at $10.30 per kilogram	22,660
Total Input	25,300 kilograms	$162,700
Labour for 25,300 kilograms processed		$283,360

Good output: Brill 15,800 kilograms
             Daz 7,000 kilograms

Required:

Calculate the materials and labour cost variances in as much detail as the data permit for the Dundas Company for the month of July. Comment on the performance of the production function of the Dundas Company during July by explaining the significance of the variances you calculated.

(SMAC, Adapted)

APPENDIX 10B: GENERAL LEDGER ENTRIES TO RECORD VARIANCES

Although standard costs and variances can be computed and used by management without being formally entered into the accounting records, most organizations prefer to make formal entries. Formal entry tends to give variances a greater emphasis than informal, off-the-record computations. This emphasis gives a clear signal of management's desire to keep costs within the standards that have been set. In addition, formal use of standard costs considerably simplifies the bookkeeping process. Inventories and cost of goods sold can be valued at their standard costs—eliminating the need to keep track of the actual cost of each unit.

> **LEARNING OBJECTIVE 9**
> Prepare journal entries to record standard costs and variances.

Direct Materials Variances

To illustrate the general ledger entries needed to record standard cost variances, we will return to the data contained in the review problem at the end of the main body of the chapter. The entry to record the purchase of direct materials would be as follows:

Raw materials (25,000 microns at $0.50 per micron)	12,500	
Materials price variance (25,000 microns at $0.02 per micron F)............		500
Accounts payable (25,000 microns at $0.48 per micron)		12,000

Notice that the price variance is recognized when purchases are made, rather than when materials are actually used in production. This permits the price variance to be isolated early, and it also permits the materials to be carried in the inventory account at standard cost. As direct materials are later drawn from inventory and used in production, the quantity variance is isolated as follows:

Work in process (18,000 microns at $0.50 per micron)...................	9,000	
Materials quantity variance (2,000 microns U at $0.50 per micron)	1,000	
Raw materials (20,000 microns at $0.50 per micron)		10,000

Thus, direct materials enter into the work in process account at standard cost, in terms of both price and quantity. Notice that the favourable price variance is a credit and the unfavourable quantity variance is a debit.

The term *direct materials* is not the same as *raw materials*, even though they are often used interchangeably. Technically, *raw materials* refer to materials that are basic to the production process and usually no processing has been done that changes their nature. *Direct materials* refer to materials identified in the product as opposed to indirect supplies or materials that are not identified in the product. For example, oil is a direct material for the production of electricity and it is considered a raw material by most. Steel is a direct material in the production of automobiles. However, a car seat is a direct material, not a raw material. Because of the confusion, we will consider the two terms interchangeable unless an obvious distinction is necessary.

Direct Labour Variances

Referring again to the cost data in the review problem at the end of the chapter, the general ledger entry to record the incurrence of direct labour cost would be:

Work in process (3,900 hours at $15.00 per hour)	58,500	
Labour efficiency variance (100 hours U at $15.00 per hour)	1,500	
Labour rate variance (4,000 hours at $1.00 per hour U)	4,000	
Wages payable (4,000 hours at $16.00 per hour)		64,000

Thus, as with direct materials, direct labour costs enter into the work in process account at standard, both in terms of the rate and in terms of the hours allowed for the actual production of the period.

Variable and Fixed Manufacturing Overhead Variances

Referring to the cost data in the review problem at the end of the chapter, the entries to record actual overhead, the application of overhead, the overhead variances, and the disposition of underapplied overhead for July are shown below.

To record actual variable and fixed overhead for July:

Overhead costs ($17,000 + $25,000)	42,000	
Various credits such as accounts payable............		42,000

To record the application of variable overhead (3,900 × $4) and fixed overhead (3,900 × $6) in July:

Work in progress ($15,600 + $23,400)	39,000	
Overhead costs		39,000

To record the overhead variances and the disposition of underapplied overhead for July:

Variable overhead spending variance U................	1,000	
Variable overhead efficiency variance U	400	
Fixed overhead budget variance U	820	
Fixed overhead volume variance U	780	
Overhead costs		3,000

Cost Flows in a Standard Cost System

The flows of costs through the company's accounts are illustrated for direct materials and direct labour in Exhibit 10B–1. Note that entries into the various inventory accounts are made at standard cost—not actual cost. The differences between actual and standard costs

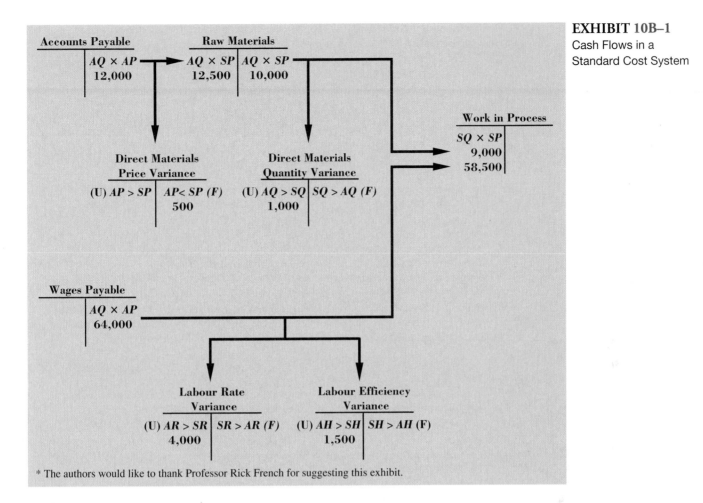

EXHIBIT 10B–1
Cash Flows in a
Standard Cost System

* The authors would like to thank Professor Rick French for suggesting this exhibit.

are entered into special accounts that accumulate the various standard cost variances. Ordinarily, these standard cost variance accounts are closed out to cost of goods sold at the end of the period. Unfavourable variances increase cost of goods sold, and favourable variances decrease cost of goods sold.

Appendix 10B Summary

- Entering standard costs and variances into the accounting records emphasizes management's desire to keep actual costs as close to standard as possible. It also simplifies the bookkeeping process because inventories and cost of goods sold can be valued at standard costs, negating the need to keep track of the actual costs of each unit. **[LO9]**
- Differences between the actual amounts paid for materials, labour, and overhead and standard costs are charged to accounts for price, rate, quantity, and efficiency variances. At the end of each reporting period, the variance accounts are closed out to cost of goods sold. Unfavourable variances increase cost of goods sold, while favourable variances decrease cost of goods sold. **[LO9]**

connect Appendix 10B Exercises and Problems

EXERCISE 10B–1 Recording Variances in the General Ledger [LO9]

Wannabe Corporation makes a product with the following standard costs for direct materials and direct labour:

Direct materials: 1.90 metres at $6.70 per metre	$12.73
Direct labour: 0.35 hours at $17.00 per hour	$5.95

During the most recent month, 10,000 units were produced. The costs associated with the month's production of this product were as follows:

> Materials purchased: 19,500 metres at $7.00 per metre $136,500
> Materials used in production: 17,400 metres . . . .   —
> Direct labour: 2,540 hours at $17.75 per hour $45,085

The standard cost variances for direct materials and direct labour are

> Materials price variance: 19,500 metres at $0.30 per metre U . . . . $5,850 U
> Materials quantity variance: 1,600 metres at $6.70 per metre F . . . . . . $10,720 F
> Labour rate variance: 2,540 hours at $0.75 per hour U . . . . $1,905 U
> Labour efficiency variance: 960 hours at $17.00 per hour F . . . . $16,320 F

Required:
1. Prepare the journal entry to record the purchase of materials on account for the month.
2. Prepare the journal entry to record the use of materials for the month.
3. Prepare the journal entry to record the incurrence of direct labour cost for the month.

EXERCISE 10B–2 Materials and Labour Variances; Journal Entries [LO2, LO3, LO9]
Marmot Products began production of a new product on April 1. The company uses a standard cost system and has established the following standards for one unit of the new product:

	Standard Quantity or Hours	Standard Price or Rate	Standard Cost
Direct materials	3.5 metres	$6 per metre	$21
Direct labour.	0.4 hours	$10 per hour	$4

During April, the following activity was recorded regarding the new product:
a. Purchased 7,000 metres of materials at a cost of $5.75 per metre.
b. Used 6,000 metres of materials to produce 1,500 units of the new product.
c. Worked 725 direct labour-hours on the new product at a cost of $8,120.

Required:
1. For direct materials:
    a. Compute the direct materials price and quantity variances.
    b. Prepare journal entries to record the purchase of materials and the use of materials in production.
2. For direct labour:
    a. Compute the direct labour rate and efficiency variances.
    b. Prepare journal entries to record the incurrence of direct labour cost for the month.
3. Post the entries you have prepared to the T-accounts below:

Raw Materials		Accounts Payable
?	?	
Bal. ?		

Materials Price Variance	Wages Payable

Materials Quantity Variance	Labour Rate Variance

Work in Process	Labour Efficiency Variance
Materials used ?	
Labour cost ? ?	

PROBLEM 10B–3 Comprehensive Variance Analysis; Journal Entries [LO2, LO3, LO4, LO5, LO6, LO9]

Haliburton Mills, Inc., is a large producer of men's and women's clothing. The company uses standard costs for all of its products. The standard costs and actual costs for a recent period are given below for one of the company's product lines (per unit of product):

	Standard Cost	Actual Cost
Direct materials:		
Standard: 4.0 metres at $3.60 per metre	$14.40	
Actual: 4.4 metres at $3.35 per metre		$14.74
Direct labour:		
Standard: 1.6 hours at $4.50 per hour	7.20	
Actual: 1.4 hours at $4.85 per hour		6.79
Variable manufacturing overhead:		
Standard: 1.6 hours at $1.80 per hour	2.88	
Actual: 1.4 hours at $2.15 per hour		3.01
Fixed manufacturing overhead:		
Standard: 1.6 hours at $3.00 per hour	4.80	
Actual: 1.4 hours at $3.05 per hour		4.27
Total cost per unit	$29.28	$28.81

Actual costs: 4,800 units at $28.81	$138,288
Standard costs: 4,800 units at $29.28	140,544
Difference in cost—favourable.	$ 2,256

During this period, the company produced 4,800 units of product. A comparison of standard and actual costs for the period on a total cost basis is also given above.

There was no inventory of materials on hand to start the period. During the period, 21,120 metres of materials were purchased and used in production. The denominator level of activity for the period was 6,860 hours.

Required:

1. For direct materials:
   a. Compute the price and quantity variances for the period.
   b. Prepare journal entries to record all activity relating to direct materials for the period.
2. For direct labour:
   a. Compute the rate and efficiency variances.
   b. Prepare a journal entry to record the incurrence of direct labour cost for the period.
3. Compute the variable manufacturing overhead spending and efficiency variances.
4. Compute the fixed overhead budget and volume variances.
5. On seeing the $2,256 total cost variance, the company's president stated, "It's obvious that our costs are well under control." Do you agree? Explain.
6. State possible causes of each variance that you have computed.

PROBLEM 10B–4 Comprehensive Variance Analysis with Incomplete Data; Journal Entries [LO2, LO3, LO4, LO5, LO6, LO9]

Topline Surf Boards manufactures a single product. The standard cost of one unit of this product is as follows:

Direct materials: 2 metres at $3 per metre	$ 6.00
Direct labour: 1 hour at $4.50 per hour	4.50
Variable manufacturing overhead: 1 hour at $3 per hour	3.00
Fixed manufacturing overhead: 1 hour at $5 per hour	5.00
Total standard variable cost per unit	$18.50

During October, 6,000 units were produced. Selected data relating to the month's production follow:

Materials purchased: 20,000 metres at $2.85 per metre........	$57,000
Materials used in production: 12,650 metres................	—
Direct labour: __?__ hours at $ __?__ per hour	$27,950
Variable manufacturing overhead cost incurred	$20,475
Variable manufacturing overhead efficiency variance	$1,500 U
Denominator level of activity for October	6,200 hours
Fixed manufacturing overhead budget variance	1,000 U

There was no beginning inventory of raw materials. The variable and fixed manufacturing overhead rates are based on direct labour-hours.

Required:

1. For direct materials:
   a. Compute the price and quantity variances for October.
   b. Prepare journal entries to record activity for October.
2. For direct labour:
   a. Compute the rate and efficiency variances for October.
   b. Prepare a journal entry to record labour activity for October.
3. For variable manufacturing overhead:
   a. Compute the spending variance for October, and verify the efficiency variance given above.
   b. If manufacturing overhead is applied to production on the basis of direct labour-hours, is it possible to have a favourable direct labour efficiency variance and an unfavourable variable overhead efficiency variance? Explain.
4. For fixed manufacturing overhead:
   a. Compute the volume variance for October.
   b. Compute actual costs for October.
5. State possible causes of each variance that you have computed.

APPENDIX 10C: PREDICTION OF LABOUR TIME—LEARNING CURVE

Appendix available on Connect.

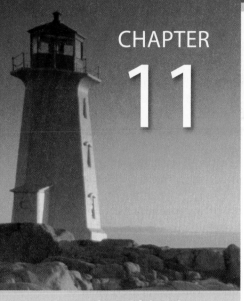

Learning Objectives

After studying Chapter 11, you should be able to

1. Prepare a segmented income statement using the contribution format, and explain the difference between traceable fixed costs and common fixed costs.

2. Differentiate among responsibility centres such as cost centres, profit centres, and investment centres, and explain how performance is measured in each.

3. Determine the range, if any, within which a negotiated transfer price should fall, and explain other approaches to setting the transfer price.

4. Analyze the return on investment (ROI).

5. Compute residual income and describe the strengths and weaknesses of this method of measuring performance.

6. Explain the use of balanced scorecards to assess performance.

7. Identify the four types of quality costs, explain their interaction, and prepare a quality cost report.

8. (Appendix 11A) Analyze variances from sales budgets.

9. (Appendix 11B) Analyze marketing expenses using cost drivers.

REPORTING FOR CONTROL

MANAGING PERFORMANCE: HOW WELL ARE WE DOING?

A survey of nearly 2,100 financial professionals at Canadian companies was conducted to find out how well Canadian companies are doing at managing their financial and operational performance. In light of the amount of attention given in the business press over the past 10 years to the development and use of more sophisticated performance measurement systems, some of the findings are surprising. For example, when asked to rate the overall performance of their organization (e.g., revenues, profits) almost one-third of respondents indicated that it is *below* target. Of those companies attempting to use more comprehensive performance measurement systems that incorporate both financial and non-financial metrics (e.g., number of customer complaints), almost half claimed they did not believe that it had helped their financial performance. Perhaps even more surprising is the finding that a large majority of the respondents indicated that they were in the very early stages of developing better performance measurement systems. Of these respondents, many claimed that they still use traditional reporting and control systems focused on financial performance measures and are just beginning to implement non-financial metrics.

These results suggest that despite the growing popularity of comprehensive performance measurement approaches such as the balanced scorecard (discussed in this chapter), many companies are struggling to put the pieces together. The survey responses provide some clues as to the nature of the obstacles. First, many companies are not doing a good job of linking their performance measures to the strategic objectives of the firm. The survey respondents who are having success in managing performance indicated that identifying the key drivers of strategic performance and measuring them is critically important. Second, the cost and difficulty of acquiring data for some performance measures (e.g., customer satisfaction) can be prohibitive. Many companies know what they want to measure, but gathering and analyzing the data is expensive. Finally, many companies fail to set specific targets for the metrics used at the departmental or individual level. While having organizational level targets for revenue growth or return on investment is important, it is essential to cascade these goals to the lower levels of the organization to ensure all employees understand their performance expectations.

In this chapter, we will examine the common financial and non-financial measures used by organizations today for management control purposes. In addition, we will attempt to better understand how strategic goals can drive the choice of performance measures allowing organizations to do a better job of measuring the "right" aspects of performance given their strategies.

Source: Robert Angel and Daryl-Lynn Carlson, "Why Don't They Just Do It," *CA Magazine*, August 2007, pp. 28–33. Article printed with permission from *CA Magazine*, published by the Canadian Institute of Chartered Accountants, Toronto.

Managers of organizations determine the direction they want the organization to take. *Strategic planning* is the term applied to this planning process. Budgeting is the financial expression of the plans. The short-term version of budgeting was presented in Chapter 9, while Chapter 13 describes long-term capital budgets. Planning, however, is only part of the management process. Through a combination of feedback of actual results, comparisons to budgets, comparisons to results of previous periods, and even comparisons to other organizations, managers attempt to ensure that the organization moves in the planned direction, termed *performance assessment* or *control*.

Managers control the organization using a variety of approaches. Accounting reports of financial results represent one important approach to controlling operations because such reports provide a means of obtaining comparisons to budgets, to previous results, and to the results of other organizations, as well as providing knowledge of actual financial results. Such financial comparisons also serve as a base for reward schemes or contracts used to motivate managers to work toward the achievement of planned goals and objectives.

These financial performance reports can be constructed in various ways so that they better serve the specific control functions that management desires. As this chapter illustrates, segment reporting, responsibility centre reporting, investment performance, and profitability analysis are four commonly used reporting structures that provide somewhat different types of information. Each presents information in a manner that permits a different view of the organization and a different aspect of organizational control. Understanding how the aspects change and why managers would want these changes will permit you to integrate the concepts of control with reports about standard cost variances, cost of production, and flexible budget analyses described in earlier chapters.

The modern manufacturing environment has promoted the need for flexibility in management to accompany flexibility in production. Flexibility in management requires timely and accurate decisions by members of the organization ranging from top management to the production worker. Accounting formats often represent approaches that are not well understood by production workers. Increasingly, companies are using non-financial indicators of performance such as scrap levels, rework efforts, market share, employee morale, pollutant discharges, and customer satisfaction. The process of collecting and presenting these data on a real-time basis is assisted by computer systems. Properly configured enterprise resource planning (ERP) systems (as discussed earlier in Chapter 3) enable the operational and financial data to be maintained consistently by using a common interactive database.

This chapter provides an explanation of common financial performance indicators as well as the non-financial indicators often included in balanced scorecards, a performance management framework that provides a useful way to organizing and presenting a variety of performance measures. More than ever, organizations are using a combination of financial and non-financial measures in their reporting and control systems. Integrating material on performance from previous chapters with discussions in this and later chapters will provide you with a foundation for understanding developments in performance reporting.

DECENTRALIZATION IN ORGANIZATIONS

Decentralized organization
An organization in which decision making is spread throughout the organization rather than being confined to a few top executives.

In a **decentralized organization**, decision making is spread throughout the organization, rather than being confined to a few top executives. All large organizations are decentralized to some extent, out of necessity. At one extreme, a strongly decentralized organization is one in which there are few, if any, constraints on the freedom of even the lowest-level managers and employees to make decisions. At the other extreme, in a strongly centralized organization, lower-level managers have little freedom to make decisions. Most organizations fall somewhere between these two extremes.

Decentralization and Segment Reporting

Effective decentralization requires *segment reporting* to permit an analysis and evaluation of the decisions made by the segment managers. In addition to the companywide income statement, reports are needed for individual segments of the organization. A *segment* is defined as a part or activity of an organization about which managers would like cost, revenue, or profit data. A company's operations can be segmented in many ways. For example, a grocery store chain like Loblaw or Sobeys can segment its business by geographic region, by individual store, by the nature of the merchandise (i.e., fresh foods, canned goods, paper goods), by brand name, and so on. As we will see, it is possible to classify segments according to managers' ability to control revenues, costs, and profits. Importantly, the tools used to evaluate segment managers' performance depend directly on what they have control over.

◼ SEGMENT REPORTING

To operate effectively, managers and decision makers must have a great deal more information available to them than the information provided by a single companywide income statement. Whether prepared on a variable costing or absorption basis, such statements usually provide only a summary of overall operations; as such, they typically do not contain enough detail to allow the manager or investor to detect problems that may exist in the organization. For example, some product lines may be profitable while others are unprofitable; some sales territories may have a poor sales mix or may be overlooking sales opportunities. Managers may want to analyze the results at a more detailed level to see if some salespeople are more effective than others, or to see if some producing divisions are effectively or ineffectively using their capacity and/or resources. To uncover such problems the manager may need not one but several income statements that focus on the segments of a company. The preparation of income statements of this type is known as *segmented reporting*.

An operating segment for financial accounting purposes is a component of an enterprise

- That engages in business activities from which it may earn revenues and incur expenses.
- Whose operating results are regularly reviewed by the enterprise's chief operating officer to make decisions about resources to be allocated to the segment and assess its performance.
- For which discrete financial information is available.

> **LEARNING OBJECTIVE 1**
> Prepare a segmented income statement using the contribution format and explain the difference between traceable fixed costs and common fixed costs.

Differing Levels of Segmented Statements

Segmented statements can be prepared for different levels of activity in an organization and in differing formats; Exhibit 11–1 illustrates three levels of segmented statements for Cassalatta Inc., presented in a widely used format. The contribution-format income statement for the entire company appears at the very top of the exhibit under the column labelled Total Company. Immediately to the right of this column are two columns—one for each of the two divisions. We can see that the Business Products Division's segment margin is $60,000 and the Consumer Products Division's is $40,000. These segment margins show the company's divisional managers how much each of their divisions is contributing to the company's profits.

Segmented income statements can be prepared for activities at many levels in a company. The divisions are segmented according to their major product lines. In the case of the Consumer Products Division, the product lines are animation and computer games. Going even further, each of the product lines is segmented according to how they are sold—in retail stores or by online sales. Notice that as we go from one segmented statement to another, we are looking at smaller and smaller pieces of the company. While not

EXHIBIT 11–1   Cassalatta Inc.—Segmented Income Statements in the Contribution Format

Segments Defined as Divisions

| | Total Company | Divisions | |
		Business Products Division	Consumer Products Division
Sales	$500,000	$300,000	$200,000
Variable expenses:			
Variable cost of goods sold	180,000	120,000	60,000
Other variable expenses	50,000	30,000	20,000
Total variable expenses	230,000	150,000	80,000
Contribution margin	270,000	150,000	120,000
Traceable fixed expenses	170,000	90,000	80,000*
Divisional segment margin	100,000	$ 60,000	$ 40,000
Common fixed expenses not traceable to individual divisions	85,000		
Operating income	$ 15,000		

Segments Defined as Product Lines of the Consumer Products Division

| | Consumer Products Division | Product Line | |
		Computer Animation	Computer Games
Sales	$200,000	$ 75,000	$125,000
Variable expenses:			
Variable cost of goods sold	60,000	20,000	40,000
Other variable expenses	20,000	5,000	15,000
Total variable expenses	80,000	25,000	55,000
Contribution margin	120,000	50,000	70,000
Traceable fixed expenses	70,000	30,000	40,000
Product line segment margin	50,000	$ 20,000	$ 30,000
Common fixed expenses not traceable to individual product lines	10,000		
Divisional segment margin	$ 40,000		

Segments Defined as Sales Territories for One Product Line—Computer Games—of the Consumer Products Division

| | Computer Games | Sales Territories | |
		Online Sales	Retail Stores
Sales	$125,000	$100,000	$ 25,000
Variable expenses:			
Variable cost of goods sold	40,000	32,000	8,000
Other variable expenses	15,000	5,000	10,000
Total variable expenses	55,000	37,000	18,000
Contribution margin	70,000	63,000	7,000
Traceable fixed expenses	25,000	15,000	10,000
Sales channel segment margin	45,000	$ 48,000	$ (3,000)
Common fixed expenses not traceable to individual sales channels	15,000		
Product line segment margin	$ 30,000		

*Notice that this $80,000 in traceable fixed expenses is divided into two parts when the Consumer Products Division is broken down into product lines—$70,000 traceable and $10,000 common. The reasons for this are discussed later in the section "Traceable Costs Can Become Common."

shown in Exhibit 11–1, segmented income statements could have also been prepared for the major product lines in the Business Products Division.

The benefits accruing to the manager from a series of statements such as those contained in Exhibit 11–1 are substantial. By carefully examining trends and results in each segment, the manager can gain considerable insight into the company as a whole, and perhaps discover opportunities and courses of action that would otherwise have remained hidden from view. Advanced computer-based information systems make it easier to construct such statements and to keep them continuously current.

One obvious question becomes evident from a careful review of Exhibit 11–1: Why break down results by divisions first, product lines next, and then sales territories? The order of breakdown depends on what information is desired. Certainly it might be advantageous to begin with each sales territory. Then it would be possible to examine product lines for each sales territory, and then divisions for each product line. This alternative would permit a product line comparison between divisions. What management wants to learn and the types of comparisons desired are factors used for deciding the order of breakdown. The order of the breakdown should not affect the numbers, but it can alter what appears on a given report and the ease of review.

Assigning Costs to Segments

Segmented statements for internal use are typically prepared in the contribution format as described in Chapter 6. The same costing guidelines are used in preparing these statements as are used in preparing a contribution statement generally, with one exception. This lies in the handling of fixed costs. Notice from Exhibit 11–1 that the fixed costs are divided into two parts on a segmented statement—one part labelled *traceable* and the other part labelled *common*. Only those fixed costs labelled *traceable* are charged to the various segments. If a fixed cost is not traceable directly to some segment, then it is treated as a common cost and kept separate from the segments themselves. Thus, under the contribution approach, a cost is never arbitrarily assigned to a segment of an organization.

In summary, two guidelines are followed in assigning costs to the various segments of a company under the contribution approach:

1. First, according to cost behaviour patterns (i.e., variable and fixed).
2. Second, according to whether the costs are directly traceable to the segments involved.

We now consider various aspects of Exhibit 11–1 in more depth.

Sales and Contribution Margin

To prepare segmented statements for management purposes, it is necessary to keep records of sales by individual segment, as well as in total for the organization. After deducting related variable expenses, a contribution margin figure can be computed for each segment, as illustrated in Exhibit 11–1.

Recall from our discussion of variable costing that the contribution margin (CM) is an extremely useful piece of data for the manager—particularly for determining the effect on net income of increases or decreases in sales volume. If sales volume goes up or down, the effect on operating income can easily be computed by simply multiplying the unit contribution margin by the change in units sold or by multiplying the change in sales dollars by the CM ratio. One assumption implicit here is that selling prices and variable costs do not change with changes in volume. Segmented statements give the manager the ability to make such computations on a product-by-product, division-by-division, or territory-by-territory basis, thereby providing the information needed to show up areas of weakness or to capitalize on areas of strength.

The contribution margin is basically a short-run planning tool. As such, it is especially valuable in decisions relating to temporary uses of capacity, to special orders, or to short-run product-line promotion. Decisions relative to the short run usually involve only variable costs and revenues, which of course are the very elements involved in contribution margin. By carefully monitoring segment contribution margin and segment contribution margin ratios, the manager is in a position to make those short-run decisions that maximize each segment's contribution to the overall profitability of the organization. Such decisions will be discussed in detail in Chapter 12.

The Importance of Fixed Costs

The emphasis we place on the usefulness of the contribution margin should not be taken as a suggestion that fixed costs are not important. Fixed costs are very important in any organization. What the contribution approach does imply is that *different costs are needed for different purposes*. For one purpose, variable costs and revenues alone may be adequate for a manager's needs; for another purpose, his or her needs may encompass the fixed costs as well.

The breaking apart of fixed and variable costs also emphasizes to management that the costs are controlled differently and that these differences must be kept clearly in mind for both short-run and long-run planning. Moreover, the grouping of fixed costs under the contribution approach highlights the fact that, after the fixed costs have been covered, operating income increases to the extent of the contribution margin generated on each additional unit sold. All of these concepts are useful to the manager *internally* for planning purposes.

Traceable and Common Fixed Costs

Traceable fixed costs
Fixed costs that can be identified with a particular segment and that arise because of the existence of the segment.

Traceable fixed costs can be defined as those fixed costs that can be identified with a particular segment and that arise because of the existence of the segment—if the segment had never existed, the fixed cost would not have been incurred, and/or if the segment were eliminated, the fixed cost would disappear. Only the traceable fixed costs are charged to particular segments. If a cost is not traceable to a segment, then it is not assigned to the segment. Examples of traceable fixed costs include the following:

- The salary of the Frito-Lay product manager at PepsiCo is a *traceable* fixed cost of the Frito-Lay business segment of PepsiCo.
- The maintenance cost for the building in which a Challenger jet is assembled is a *traceable* fixed cost of the Challenger business segment of Bombardier Ltd.

Common fixed cost
A fixed cost that supports the operations of more than one segment but is not traceable in whole or in part to any one segment.

A **common fixed cost** is a fixed cost that supports the operations of more than one segment but is not traceable in whole or in part to any one segment. Even if the segment was entirely eliminated, there would be no change in a true common fixed cost. Note the following:

- The salary of the CEO of General Motors Canada is a *common* fixed cost of the various divisions of General Motors Canada.
- The cost of the automatic bar-coding machine at Cassalatta is a *common* fixed cost of the Consumer Products Division and of the Business Products Division.
- The cost of the receptionist's salary at an office shared by a number of doctors is a *common* fixed cost of the doctors. The cost is traceable to the office, but not to any one of the doctors individually.

Common fixed costs are not allocated to segments—the total amount is deducted to arrive at the income for the company as a whole (see Exhibit 11–1). The managerial accountant may contend that nothing is added to the overall usefulness of a segmented statement by allocating the common costs among segments. The accountant would argue that such allocations tend to reduce the usefulness of segmented statements. The reason is that arbitrary allocations draw attention away from those costs that are traceable to a segment and that should form a basis for appraising performance.

It is argued that any attempt to allocate common fixed costs among segments may result in misleading data or may obscure important relationships between segment revenues and segment earnings. Arbitrary allocation of common fixed costs often results in a segment appearing to be unprofitable, whereas it may be contributing substantially above its own traceable costs toward the overall profitability of a firm. In such cases, the allocated costs may lead to the unwise elimination of a segment and to a decrease in profits for the company as a whole because common costs do not disappear if the segment is closed down.

A word of caution is necessary here. Management reaction to common costs may help control the growth of such costs. Managers may use common cost allocation as a form of cost price or as a signal about the benefits received from headquarters and thus modify their actions for the common good of the organization. Empirical investigations suggest firms often allocate common costs to segments for a number of reasons. Rigorous analysis of the treatment of uncontrollable costs and allocated common costs suggests there may be some benefit to charging managers with uncontrollable costs or allocating common costs to segments. Managerial behaviour is complex, and investigation of it often finds results that were previously thought to be fallacious but may not be so.

Identifying Traceable Fixed Costs

The distinction between traceable and common fixed costs is crucial in segmented reporting, because traceable fixed costs are charged to the segments, but common fixed costs are not. In an actual situation, it is sometimes hard to determine whether a cost should be classified as traceable or common.

The general guideline is to treat as traceable costs *only those costs that would disappear over time if the segment itself disappeared*. For example, if the Consumer Products Division in Exhibit 11–1 was sold or discontinued, it would no longer be necessary to pay the division manager's salary. Therefore the division manager's salary should be classified as a traceable fixed cost of the Consumer Products Division. On the other hand, the president of the company undoubtedly would continue to be paid even if the Consumer Products Division was dropped. In fact, he or she might even be paid more if dropping the division was a good idea. Therefore, the president's salary is common to both divisions and should not be charged to either division.

There will always be some costs that fall between the traceable and common categories, and considerable care and good judgment will be required for their proper classification. The important point is to resist the temptation to allocate costs (such as depreciation of corporate facilities) that are clearly common and that will continue regardless of whether the segment exists or not. *Any allocation of common costs to segments reduces the value of the segment margin as a guide to long-run segment profitability and segment performance.*

Breakdown of Traceable Fixed Costs

In preparing segmented income statements, some managers like to separate the traceable fixed costs into two classes—discretionary and committed. As discussed in Chapter 6, discretionary fixed costs are under the immediate control of the manager, whereas committed fixed costs are not. Therefore, a breakdown of the traceable fixed costs into these two classes allows a company to make a distinction between the performance of the segment manager and the performance of the segment as a long-term investment.

In some situations, this distinction in performance can be very important. A top-flight manager, for example, may be assigned to a division that has an antiquated plant or that is saddled with other committed fixed costs that are beyond the segment manager's control. Under these conditions, it would be unfair to judge the segment manager's performance simply on the basis of overall margin generated by the segment. Rather, in these circumstances, the discretionary fixed costs should be separated from the committed fixed costs and deducted as a separate group from the segment's contribution margin. The amount remaining after deducting the discretionary fixed costs, sometimes called a *segment performance margin*, should then be used as a basis for evaluating the segment manager's performance. This would be a valid measure of performance, as the amount involved would represent the margin generated by the segment after deducting all costs controllable by the segment manager. The committed fixed costs of a segment can be broken down in still other ways. However, the preceding discussion is adequate for our purposes.

Activity-Based Costing   Some costs are easy to identify as traceable costs. For example, the costs of advertising Crest toothpaste on television are clearly traceable to Crest. A more difficult situation arises when a building, machine, or other resource is shared by two or more segments. For example, assume that a multi-product company leases warehouse space that is used for storing the full range of its products. Would the lease cost of the warehouse be a traceable or a common cost of the products? Managers familiar with activity-based costing might argue that the lease is traceable and should be assigned to the products according to how much space the products use in the warehouse. In like manner, these managers would argue that order-processing costs, sales-support costs, and other selling, general, and administrative (SG&A) expenses should also be charged to segments according to the segments' consumption of SG&A resources.

To illustrate, consider the Holt Corporation, a company that manufactures concrete pipe for industrial uses. The company has three products—9-inch pipe, 12-inch pipe, and 18-inch pipe. Space is leased in a large warehouse on a yearly basis as needed. The lease cost of this space is $10 per square metre per year. The 9-inch pipe occupies 400 square metres of space, 12-inch pipe occupies 1,600 square metres, and 18-inch pipe occupies 2,000 square metres. The company also has an order-processing department that incurred $150,000 in order-processing costs last year. Management believes that order-processing costs are driven by the number of orders placed by customers in a year. Last year, 2,500 orders were placed, of which 1,200 were for 9-inch pipe, 800 were for 12-inch pipe, and 500 were for 18-inch pipe. Given these data, the following costs would be assigned to each product using the activity-based costing approach:

Warehouse space cost:
9-inch pipe: $10 × 400 square metres . . . . $ 4,000
12-inch pipe: $10 × 1,600 square metres 16,000
18-inch pipe: $10 × 2,000 square metres 20,000
Total cost assigned $40,000

Order-processing costs:
$150,000 ÷ 2,500 orders = $60 per order
9-inch pipe: $60 × 1,200 orders . . . . $ 72,000
12-inch pipe: $60 × 800 orders 48,000
18-inch pipe: $60 × 500 orders 30,000
Total cost assigned $150,000

This method of assigning costs combines the strength of activity-based costing with the power of the contribution approach and greatly enhances the manager's ability to measure the profitability and performance of segments. However, managers must still ask themselves if the costs would in fact disappear over time if the segment itself disappeared. In the case of Holt Corporation, it is clear that the $20,000 in warehousing costs for 18-inch pipe would be eliminated if 18-inch pipe was no longer being produced. The company would simply rent less warehouse space the following year. However, suppose the company owns the warehouse. Then it is not so clear that the $20,000 of the cost of the warehouse would really disappear if 18-inch pipe was discontinued as a product. The company warehouse might simply be empty while the costs of the warehouse continue to be incurred.

Traceable Costs Can Become Common

Fixed costs that are traceable to one segment may be common costs of another segment. This is because there are limits to how finely a cost can be separated without resorting to arbitrary allocation. The more finely segments are defined, the more costs there are that are common.

This concept can be seen in Exhibit 11–2. Notice that when segments are defined as divisions, the Consumer Products Division has $80,000 in traceable fixed expenses. Only $70,000 of this amount remains traceable, however, when we narrow our definition to that of the product lines. Notice that the other $10,000 then becomes a common cost of these product lines of the Consumer Products Division.

	Total Company	Segment	
		Business Products Division	Consumer Products Division
Contribution margin	$270,000	$150,000	$120,000
Traceable fixed expenses	170,000	90,000	80,000

	Consumer Products Division	Segment	
		Computer Animation	Computer Games
Contribution margin	$120,000	$ 50,000	$ 70,000
Traceable fixed expenses	70,000	30,000	40,000
Product line segment margin	50,000	$ 20,000	$ 30,000
Common fixed expenses	10,000		
Divisional segment margin	$ 40,000		

EXHIBIT 11–2
Reclassification of Traceable Fixed Expenses from Exhibit 11–1

Why would $10,000 of traceable fixed cost become a common cost when the division is divided into product lines? The $10,000 is the monthly salary of the manager of the Consumer Products Division. This salary is a traceable cost of the division as a whole, but is a common cost of the division's product lines. The manager's salary is a necessary cost of having the two product lines, but even if one of the product lines was discontinued entirely, the manager's salary would probably not be cut. Therefore, none of the manager's salary can really be traced to the individual products.

The $70,000 traceable fixed cost of the product lines consists of the cost of product-specific advertising. A total of $30,000 was spent on advertising animation software and $40,000 was spent on advertising computer games. These costs can clearly be traced to the individual product lines.

Segment Margin

Observe from Exhibit 11–1 that the **segment margin** is obtained by deducting a segment's traceable fixed costs from the segment's contribution margin. It represents the margin available after a segment has covered all of its own costs. The segment margin is the best gauge of the long-run profitability of a segment, because it includes only those costs that are caused by the segment. The term *long-run* is applied here because fixed costs could be altered if the segment was eliminated. If a segment cannot cover its own costs, that segment probably should be dropped (unless it is essential to sales of other segments). Notice from Exhibit 11–1, for example, that the Retail Stores sales channel has a negative segment margin. This means that the segment is not generating enough revenue to cover its own costs. In fact, it is detracting from profits in that its $3,000 loss must be covered by other segments. Retention or elimination of product lines and other segments is covered in more depth in Chapter 12.

From a decision-making point of view, the segment margin is most useful in major decisions that affect capacity, such as dropping a segment. By contrast, as noted earlier, the contribution margin is most useful in decisions relating to short-run changes, such as pricing of special orders that involve temporary use of existing capacity.

Segment margin
A segment margin is obtained by deducting a segment's traceable fixed costs from the segment's contribution margin.

Segment Reporting for Financial Accounting

Differences in segment profits reports for internal management decision making and those required for external reporting are minimized given Section 1701 of the *CICA Handbook* and *International Financial Reporting Standard (IFRS) 8—Operating Segments.* These standards require that segmented reports prepared for external users use the same methods and definitions used for internal segmented reports that are prepared to aid in making operating decisions. This is a very unusual requirement. Companies are not ordinarily required to report the same data to external users that are reported internally for decision-making purposes. This requirement has some serious drawbacks. First, segmented data are often highly sensitive and companies are reluctant to release such data to the public for the simple reason that their competitors will then have access to the data. Second, segmented statements prepared in accordance with GAAP do not distinguish between fixed and variable costs and between traceable and common costs. Indeed, the segmented income statements illustrated earlier in this chapter do not conform to GAAP for that reason. To avoid the complications of reconciling non-GAAP segment earnings with GAAP consolidated earnings, it is likely that at least some managers will choose to construct their segmented financial statements in a manner that conforms to GAAP. This will result in more occurrences of the problems discussed in the following section.

Hindrances to Proper Cost Assignment

Costs must be properly assigned to segments. All of the costs attributable to a segment—and only those costs—should be assigned to the segment. Unfortunately, companies often make mistakes when assigning costs to segments. They omit some costs, inappropriately assign traceable fixed costs, and arbitrarily allocate common fixed costs.

Omission of Costs   The costs assigned to a segment should include all costs attributable to that segment from the company's entire value chain, as discussed in Chapter 1. All of these functions, from research and development, through product design, manufacturing, marketing, distribution, and customer service, are required to bring a product or service to the customer and generate revenues.

However, as discussed in Chapters 2, 3, and 8, only manufacturing costs are included in product costs under absorption costing, which is widely regarded as required for financial reporting. To avoid having to maintain two costing systems and to provide consistency between internal and external reports, many companies also use absorption costing for their internal reports, such as segmented income statements. As a result, such companies omit from their profitability analysis part or all of the "upstream" costs in the value chain, which consist of research and development and product design, and the "downstream" costs, which consist of marketing, distribution, and customer service. Yet these non-manufacturing costs are just as essential as manufacturing costs in determining product profitability. These upstream and downstream costs, which are usually included in selling and administrative expenses on the income statement, can represent half or more of the total costs of an organization. If either the upstream or downstream costs are omitted in profitability analysis, then the product is undercosted and management may unwittingly develop and maintain products that result in losses in the long run.

Inappropriate Methods for Assigning Traceable Costs among Segments   In addition to omitting costs, many companies do not correctly handle traceable fixed expenses on segmented income statements. First, they may not trace fixed expenses to segments even when it is feasible to do so. Second, they may use inappropriate allocation bases to allocate traceable fixed expenses to segments.

Failure to Trace Costs Directly   Costs that can be traced directly to a specific company segment should be charged directly to that segment. Failure to trace these costs directly results in these costs being placed in a companywide overhead pool. While a portion of these costs would then be allocated to the segment generating the costs, the rest would be incorrectly allocated to other segments. For example, the rent for a branch office of an insurance company should be charged directly against the branch to which it relates rather than included in a companywide overhead pool and then spread throughout the company.

Inappropriate Allocation Base Some companies allocate costs to segments using arbitrary bases such as sales dollars or cost of goods sold. For example, under the sales dollars approach, costs are allocated to the various segments according to the percentage of company sales generated by each segment. Thus, if a segment generates 20% of the company's sales, it is allocated 20% of the company's selling, general, and administrative (SG&A) expenses as its "fair share." This same basic procedure is followed if costs of goods sold or some other measure is used as the allocation base.

Costs should be allocated to segments for internal decision-making purposes only when the allocation base actually drives the cost being allocated (or is very highly correlated with the real cost driver). For example, sales should be used to allocate selling and administrative expenses only if a 10% increase in sales will result in a 10% increase in selling and administrative expenses. To the extent that selling and administrative expenses are not driven by sales volume, these expenses will be improperly allocated—with a disproportionately high percentage of the selling and administrative expenses assigned to the segments with the largest sales.

Arbitrarily Dividing Common Costs among Segments Another business practice that leads to distorted segment costs is the practice of assigning non-traceable costs to segments. For example, some companies allocate the costs of the corporate headquarters building to products on segment reports. However, in a multi-product company, no single product is likely to be responsible for any significant amount of this cost. Even if a product was eliminated entirely, there would usually be no significant effect on any of the costs of the corporate headquarters building. In short, there is no cause-and-effect relationship between the cost of the corporate headquarters building and the existence of any one product. As a consequence, any allocation of the costs of the corporate headquarters building to the products must be arbitrary.

Common costs like the costs of the corporate headquarters building are necessary, of course, to have a functioning organization. The common practice of arbitrarily allocating these costs to segments is often justified on the grounds that "someone" has to "cover the common costs." While it is undeniably true that the common costs must be covered, arbitrarily allocating common costs to segments does not ensure that this will happen. In fact, adding a share of common costs to the real costs of a segment may make an otherwise profitable segment appear to be unprofitable. If a manager eliminates the apparently unprofitable segment, the real traceable costs of the segment will be saved, but its revenues will be lost. What happens to the common fixed costs that were allocated to the segment? They don't disappear; they are reallocated to the remaining segments of the company. That makes all of the remaining segments appear to be less profitable—possibly resulting in dropping other segments. The net effect will be to reduce the profits of the company as a whole and make it even more difficult to "cover the common costs."

Additionally, common fixed costs are not manageable by the manager to whom they are arbitrarily allocated; they are the responsibility of higher-level managers. Allocating common fixed costs to responsibility centres is counterproductive in a responsibility accounting system. When common fixed costs are allocated to managers, they are held responsible for those costs even though they cannot control them.

In summary, the way many companies handle segment reporting results in cost distortion. This distortion results from three practices—the failure to trace costs directly to a specific segment when it is feasible to do so, the use of inappropriate bases for allocating costs, and the allocation of common costs to segments. The examples of segment reporting provided in Exhibits 11–1 and 11–2 avoid many of the problems encountered by companies who do not use variable costing. Variable costing permits a clearer allocation of costs to segments because it avoids the distortions created by the allocation of fixed manufacturing overhead that would be present with the use of absorption costing. Thus, our suggestions are to use variable costing for segment reports and allocate fixed manufacturing overhead as a period expense based on the criterion of traceability; that is, *fixed costs that will disappear over time if the segment itself disappears.*

RESPONSIBILITY CENTRES

LEARNING OBJECTIVE 2
Differentiate among responsibility centres such as cost centres, profit centres, and investment centres, and explain how performance is measured in each.

Responsibility centre
Any business segment whose manager has control over cost or profit or the use of investment funds.

Cost centre
A business segment whose manager has control over cost but has no control over revenue or the use of investment funds.

Profit centre
A business segment whose manager has control over cost and revenue but has no control over the use of investment funds.

Investment centre
A business segment whose manager has control over cost and revenue and also has control over the use of investment funds.

A **responsibility centre** is broadly defined as any part of an organization whose manager has control over and is accountable for cost, profit, or investments. The three primary types of responsibility centres are cost centres, profit centres, and investment centres.[1] As discussed below, organizations categorize responsibility centres into one of these three types based on the manager's authority to control cost, revenue, and investment funds.

Cost Centre   A **cost centre** is a business segment whose manager has control over costs but not over revenue or investment funds. Service departments, such as accounting, finance, general administration, legal, personnel, and so on, are usually considered to be cost centres. In addition, manufacturing facilities are often considered to be cost centres. The managers of cost centres are expected to minimize cost while providing the level of services or the amount of product demanded by the other parts of the organization. For example, the manager of a production facility would be evaluated at least in part by comparing actual costs to how much the costs should have been for the actual number of units produced during the period. Standard cost variances and flexible budget variances discussed in Chapter 10 are often used to evaluate cost centre performance. However, managers should not be held accountable for controlling common costs arbitrarily allocated to their segment.

Profit Centre   In contrast to a cost centre, a **profit centre** is any business segment whose manager has control over both cost and revenue. Like a cost centre, however, a profit centre manager generally does not have control over investment funds. For example, the manager in charge of one of six resorts would be responsible for both the revenues and costs, and hence the profits, of the resort but might not have control over major investments in the resort. Profit centre managers are often evaluated by comparing actual profit to targeted or budgeted profit.

Investment Centre   An **investment centre** is any segment of an organization whose manager has control over cost, revenue, and investments in operating assets. For example, the president of General Motors Canada, a division of the General Motors Company, would have a great deal of discretion over investments in the division. The president of the division would be responsible for initiating investment proposals, such as funding research into more fuel-efficient engines for sport-utility vehicles. Once the proposal has been approved by GM's top-level executives and the board of directors, the president of General Motors Canada would then be responsible for making sure that the investment pays off. Investment centre managers are usually evaluated using return on investment or residual income measures, as discussed later in the chapter.

A partial organization chart for Universal Foods Corporation, a company in the snack food and beverage industry, appears in Exhibit 11–3. This partial organization chart indicates how the various business segments of the company are classified in terms of responsibility. Note that the cost centres are the departments and work centres that do not generate significant revenues by themselves. These are staff departments such as Finance, Legal, and Personnel, and operating units such as the bottling plant, warehouse, and beverage distribution centre. The profit centres are business segments that generate revenues and costs and include the Beverage, Salty Snacks, and Confections product segments. The vice-president of Operations oversees allocation of investment funds across the product segments and is also responsible for revenues and costs; therefore, Operations is treated as an investment centre. And finally, corporate headquarters is an investment centre, since it is responsible for all revenues, costs, and investments.

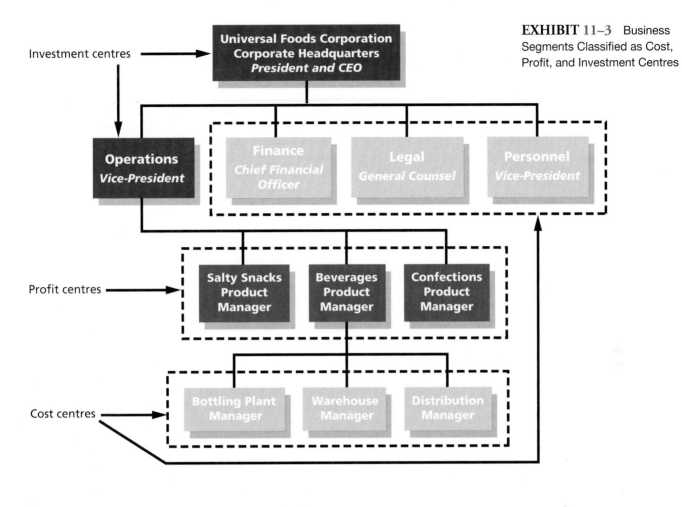

EXHIBIT 11–3 Business Segments Classified as Cost, Profit, and Investment Centres

TRANSFER PRICING

In the previous section, we discussed various issues related to responsibility centre reporting and profitability analysis. In this section, we discuss another key issue that arises when segments of the same company (often referred to as *divisions*) supply goods and services to each other. The issue is determining the transfer price of the goods or services being sold between segments. A **transfer price** is the price charged when one segment sells goods or services to another segment of the same company. Because the dollar amount of these transfers can be very large, the transfer price at which they occur can have a significant impact on the profits of both the buying and selling segment. As a result, managers are intensely interested in how transfer prices are set.

As an example of a transfer pricing scenario, most companies in the oil industry, such as Imperial, Shell, and Petro-Canada, have petroleum refining and retail sales divisions that are evaluated on the basis of return on investment (ROI) or residual income, two performance measures that will be discussed in detail later in this chapter. The petroleum refining division processes crude oil into gasoline, kerosene, lubricants, and other end products. The retail sales division takes gasoline and other products from the refining division and sells them through the company's chain of service stations. Each product has a price for transfers within the company. Suppose the transfer price for gasoline is $1.00 per litre. Then the refining division gets credit for $1.00 per litre of revenue on its segment report and the retailing division must deduct $1.00 per litre as an expense on its segment report. Clearly, the refining division would like the transfer price to be as high as possible, whereas the retailing division would like the transfer price to be as low as possible. However, the transaction has no direct effect on the entire company's reported profit because the revenue recorded for the transfer by the selling division is exactly offset by the cost recorded by the buying divisions.

LEARNING OBJECTIVE 3
Determine the range, if any, within which a negotiated transfer price should fall and explain other approaches to setting the transfer price.

Transfer price
The price charged when one division or segment provides goods or services to another division or segment of an organization.

Three common approaches are used to set transfer prices:

1. Allow the managers involved in the transfers to negotiate their own transfer prices.
2. Set transfer prices at cost, using either variable cost or full absorption cost.
3. Set transfer prices at the market price.

We consider each of these transfer pricing methods in turn, beginning with negotiated transfer prices. Throughout the discussion, keep in mind that *the fundamental objective in setting transfer prices is to motivate the managers to act in the best interests of the overall company.* In contrast, **suboptimization** occurs when managers do not act in the best interests of the overall company or even in the best interests of their own segment.

Negotiated Transfer Prices

A **negotiated transfer price** is a transfer price that is agreed on between the selling and purchasing segments or divisions. Negotiated transfer prices have several important advantages. First, this approach preserves the autonomy of the divisions and is consistent with the spirit of decentralization. Second, the managers of the divisions are likely to have much better information about the potential costs and benefits of the transfer than others in the company.

When negotiated transfer prices are used, the managers who are involved in a proposed transfer within the company meet to discuss the terms and conditions of the transfer. Perhaps most importantly, they must agree to a transfer price. Generally speaking, we cannot predict the exact transfer price to which they will agree. However, we can confidently predict two things: (1) The selling division will agree to the transfer only if the profits of the selling division increase as a result of the transfer, and (2) the purchasing division will agree to the transfer only if the profits of the purchasing division also increase as a result of the transfer. This may seem obvious, but it is an important point.

Clearly, if the transfer price is below the selling division's cost, a loss will occur on the transaction and the selling division will refuse to agree to the transfer. Likewise, if the transfer price is set too high, it will be impossible for the purchasing division to make any profit on the transferred item. For any given proposed transfer, the transfer price has both a lower limit (determined by the situation of the selling division) and an upper limit (determined by the situation of the purchasing division). The actual transfer price agreed to by the two division managers can fall anywhere between those two limits. These limits determine the **range of acceptable transfer prices**—the range of transfer prices within which the profits of both divisions participating in a transfer would increase.

In the Learning Aid at the top of the next page, we summarize the range of acceptable transfer prices that a divisional manager would consider under various conditions. We also consider the range of acceptable transfer prices that might be considered by the divisional managers of Harrison Ltd. to help illustrate the key points in the Learning Aid. Assume that Harrison Ltd. owns fast-food restaurants and snack food and beverage manufacturers in Atlantic Canada. One of the restaurants, Pizza Place, serves a variety of beverages along with pizzas. One of the beverages is ginger beer, which is served on tap. Harrison has just purchased a new division, Cumberland Beverages, that produces ginger beer. The managing director of Cumberland Beverages has approached the managing director of Pizza Place about purchasing Cumberland Beverages ginger beer for sale at Pizza Place restaurants rather than its usual brand of ginger beer. Managers at Pizza Place agree that the quality of Cumberland Beverages' ginger beer is comparable to the quality of their regular brand. It is just a question of price. The basic facts follow:

Suboptimization
An overall level of profitability that is less than a segment or a company is capable of earning.

Negotiated transfer price
A transfer price agreed on between buying and selling divisions.

Range of acceptable transfer prices
The range of transfer prices within which the profits of both the selling division and the purchasing division would increase as a result of a transfer.

Cumberland Beverages:	
Ginger beer production capacity per month	10,000 barrels
Variable cost per barrel of ginger beer.........................	$8 per barrel
Fixed costs per month..	$70,000
Selling price of Cumberland Beverages ginger beer on the outside market...................................	$20 per barrel
Pizza Place:	
Purchase price of regular brand of ginger beer..................	$18 per barrel
Monthly consumption of ginger beer..........................	2,000 barrels

RANGE OF NEGOTIATED TRANSFER PRICES

Minimum price selling division would accept	**Maximum price buying division would pay**
Selling division with idle capacity: Transfer price $\geq$ Variable cost per unit	Transfer price $\leq$ Cost of buying from outside supplier
Cumberland Beverages minimum transfer price: Transfer price $\geq \$8 + \dfrac{\$0}{2,000} = \$8$	Pizza Place maximum transfer price: Transfer price $\leq$ Cost of buying from outside supplier = \$18 If no outside supplier, transfer price $\leq$ expected net profit from sale to final customer.
Selling division with no idle capacity: Transfer price $\geq$ Variable cost per unit $+ \dfrac{\text{Total contribution margin on lost sales}}{\text{Number of units transferred}}$	Transfer price $\leq$ Cost of buying from outside supplier
Cumberland Beverages minimum transfer price: Transfer price $\geq \$8 + \dfrac{(\$20 - \$8) \times 2,000}{2,000} = \$8 + (\$20 - \$8) = \$20$	Pizza Place maximum transfer price: Transfer price $\leq$ Cost of buying from outside supplier = \$18 If no outside supplier, transfer price $\leq$ expected net profit from sale to final customer.

Selling division with some idle capacity:
   Transfer price $\geq$ Variable cost per unit $+ \dfrac{\text{Total contribution margin on lost sales}}{\text{Number of units transferred}}$
Cumberland Beverages minimum transfer price:
   Transfer price $\geq \$8 + \dfrac{(\$20 - \$8) \times 1,000}{2,000} = \$8 + \$6 = \$14$
	Transfer price $\leq$ Cost of buying from outside supplier
	Pizza Place maximum transfer price:
	Transfer price $\leq$ Cost of buying from outside supplier = \$18
	If no outside supplier, transfer price $\leq$ expected net profit from sale to final customer.

The Selling Division's Lowest Acceptable Transfer Price   The selling division, Cumberland Beverages, will be interested in a proposed transfer only if its profit increases. Clearly, the transfer price must not fall below the variable cost per barrel of $8. In addition, if Cumberland Beverages has insufficient capacity to fill the Pizza Place order, then it would have to give up some of its regular sales. Cumberland Beverages would expect to be compensated for the contribution margin on these lost sales. In summary, if the transfer has no effect on fixed costs, then from the selling division's standpoint, the transfer price must cover both the variable costs of producing the transferred units and any opportunity costs from lost sales.

Seller's perspective:

$$\text{Transfer price} \geq \frac{\text{Variable cost}}{\text{per unit}} + \frac{\text{Total contribution margin on lost sales}}{\text{Number of units transferred}}$$

The Purchasing Division's Highest Acceptable Transfer Price   The purchasing division, Pizza Place, will be interested in the proposal only if its profit increases. In cases like this where a purchasing division has an outside supplier, the purchasing division's decision is simple: Buy from the inside supplier if the price is less than the price offered by the outside supplier.

Purchaser's perspective:

$$\text{Transfer price} \leq \text{Cost of buying from outside supplier}$$

We will consider several different hypothetical situations and see what the range of acceptable transfer prices would be in each situation.

Selling Division with Idle Capacity   Suppose that Cumberland Beverages has sufficient idle capacity to satisfy the demand for ginger beer from Pizza Place without cutting into sales of ginger beer to its regular customers. To be specific, let's suppose that Cumberland Beverages is selling only 7,000 barrels of ginger beer per month on the outside market. That leaves unused capacity of 3,000 barrels per month—more than enough to satisfy Pizza Place's requirement of 2,000 barrels per month. What range of transfer prices, if any, would make both divisions better off with the transfer of 2,000 barrels per month?

1. The selling division, Cumberland Beverages, will be interested in the proposal only if

$$\text{Transfer price} \geq \frac{\text{Variable cost}}{\text{per unit}} + \frac{\text{Total contribution margin on lost sales}}{\text{Number of units transferred}}$$

Since Cumberland Beverages has ample idle capacity, there are no lost outside sales. And since the variable cost per unit is $8, the lowest acceptable transfer price as far as the selling division is concerned is also $8:

$$\text{Transfer price} \geq \$8 + \frac{\$0}{2,000} = \$8$$

2. The purchasing division, Pizza Place, can buy similar ginger beer from an outside vendor for $18 per barrel. Therefore, Pizza Place would be unwilling to pay more than $18 per barrel for Cumberland Beverages' ginger beer:

$$\text{Transfer price} \leq \text{Cost of buying from outside supplier} = \$18$$

3. Combining the requirements of both the selling division and the purchasing division, the acceptable range of transfer prices in this situation is

$$\$8 \leq \text{Transfer price} \leq \$18$$

Assuming that the managers understand their own businesses and that they are cooperative, they should be able to agree on a transfer price within this range.

Selling Division with No Idle Capacity   Suppose that Cumberland Beverages has *no* idle capacity; it is selling 10,000 barrels of ginger beer a month on the outside market at $20 per barrel. To fill the order from Pizza Place, Cumberland Beverages would have to divert 2,000 barrels from its regular customers. What range of transfer prices, if any, would make both divisions better off transferring the 2,000 barrels within the company?

1. The selling division, Cumberland Beverages, will be interested in the proposal only if

$$\text{Transfer price} \geq \frac{\text{Variable cost}}{\text{per unit}} + \frac{\text{Total contribution margin on lost sales}}{\text{Number of units transferred}}$$

Since Cumberland Beverages has no idle capacity, there *are* lost outside sales. The contribution margin per barrel on these outside sales is $12 ($20 − $8):

$$\text{Transfer price} \geq \$8 + \frac{(\$20 - \$8) \times 2,000}{2,000} = \$8 + (\$20 - \$8) = \$20$$

Thus, as far as the selling division is concerned, the transfer price must at least cover the revenue on the lost sales, which is $20 per barrel. This makes sense since the cost of producing the 2,000 barrels is the same whether they are sold on the inside market or on the outside. The only difference is that the selling division loses the revenue of $20 per barrel if it transfers the barrels to Pizza Place.

2. As before, the purchasing division, Pizza Place, would be unwilling to pay more than the $18 per barrel it is already paying for similar ginger beer from its regular supplier:

$$\text{Transfer price} \leq \text{Cost of buying from outside supplier} = \$18$$

3. Therefore, the selling division would insist on a transfer price of at least $20, but the purchasing division would refuse any transfer price above $18. It is impossible to satisfy both division managers simultaneously; there can be no agreement on a transfer price and no transfer will take place. Is this good? The answer is yes. From the standpoint of the entire company, the transfer does not make sense. Why give up sales of $20 to save $18?

Basically, the transfer price is a mechanism for dividing between the two divisions any profit the entire company earns as a result of the transfer. If the company loses money on the transfer, there will be no profit to divide up, and it will be impossible for the two divisions to come to an agreement. On the other hand, if the company makes money on the transfer, there will be a potential profit to share, and it will always be possible for the two divisions to find a mutually agreeable transfer price that increases the profits of both divisions. If the pie is bigger, it is always possible to divide it up in such a way that everyone has a bigger piece.

Selling Division with Some Idle Capacity   Suppose now that Cumberland Beverages is selling 9,000 barrels of ginger beer per month on the outside market. Pizza Place can sell only one kind of ginger beer on tap. It cannot buy 1,000 barrels from Cumberland Beverages and 1,000 barrels from its regular supplier; it must buy all of its ginger beer from one source.

To fill the entire 2,000-barrel per month order from Pizza Place, Cumberland Beverages would have to divert 1,000 barrels from its regular customers who are paying $20 per barrel. The other 1,000 barrels can be made using idle capacity. What range of transfer prices, if any, would make both divisions better off transferring the 2,000 barrels within the company?

1. As before, the selling division, Cumberland Beverages, will insist on a transfer price that at least covers its variable cost and opportunity cost:

$$\text{Transfer price} \geq \frac{\text{Variable cost}}{\text{per unit}} + \frac{\text{Total contribution margin on lost sales}}{\text{Number of units transferred}}$$

Since Cumberland Beverages does not have enough idle capacity to fill the entire order for 2,000 barrels, there *are* lost outside sales. The contribution margin per barrel on the 1,000 barrels of lost outside sales is $12 ($20 − $8):

$$\text{Transfer price} \geq \$8 + \frac{(\$20 - \$8) \times 1,000}{2,000} = \$8 + \$6 = \$14$$

Thus, as far as the selling division is concerned, the transfer price must cover the variable cost of $8 plus the average opportunity cost of lost sales of $6.

2. As before, the purchasing division, Pizza Place, would be unwilling to pay more than the $18 per barrel it pays its regular supplier:

$$\text{Transfer price} \leq \text{Cost of buying from outside suppliers} = \$18$$

3. Combining the requirements for both the selling and purchasing divisions, the range of acceptable transfer prices is

$$\$14 \leq \text{Transfer price} \leq \$18$$

Again, assuming that the managers understand their own businesses and that they are cooperative, they should be able to agree on a transfer price within this range.

No Outside Supplier   If Pizza Place has no outside supplier for the ginger beer, the highest price the purchasing division would be willing to pay depends on how much the purchasing division expects to make on the transferred units—excluding the transfer price. If, for example, Pizza Place expects to earn $30 per barrel of ginger beer after paying its own expenses, then it should be willing to pay up to $30 per barrel to Cumberland Beverages. Remember, however, that this assumes Pizza Place cannot buy ginger beer from other sources.

Evaluation of Negotiated Transfer Prices   As discussed earlier, if a transfer within the company would result in higher overall profits for the company, there is always a range of transfer prices within which both the selling and purchasing divisions would also have higher profits if they agree to the transfer. Therefore, if the managers understand their own businesses and are cooperative, then they should always be able to agree on a transfer price if it is in the best interests of the company that they do so.

Unfortunately, not all managers understand their own businesses and not all managers are cooperative. As a result, negotiations often break down even when it would be in the managers' own best interests to come to an agreement. Sometimes that is the fault of the way managers are evaluated. If managers are pitted against each other rather than against their own past performance or reasonable benchmarks, a non-cooperative atmosphere is almost guaranteed. Nevertheless, it must be admitted that even with the best performance evaluation system, some people by nature are not cooperative.

Given the potential problems of the negotiation process, most companies rely on some other means of setting transfer prices. Unfortunately, as we will see below, the alternatives to negotiated transfer prices have their own serious drawbacks.

Transfers to the Selling Division at Cost

Many companies set transfer prices at either the variable cost or full absorption cost incurred by the selling division. Although the cost approach to setting transfer prices is relatively simple to apply, it has some major defects.

First, the use of cost—particularly full cost—as a transfer price can lead to bad decisions and thus suboptimization. Return to the example involving the ginger beer. The full cost of ginger beer can never be less than $15 per barrel ($8 per barrel variable cost + $7 per barrel fixed cost at capacity). What if the cost of buying the ginger beer from an outside supplier is less than $15—for example, $14 per barrel? If the transfer price was bureaucratically set at full cost, then Pizza Place would never want to buy ginger beer from Cumberland Beverages, since it could buy its ginger beer from the outside supplier at less cost. However, from the standpoint of the company as a whole, ginger beer should be transferred from Cumberland Beverages to Pizza Place whenever Cumberland Beverages has more than 1,000 units of idle capacity. Why? Because when Cumberland Beverages has more than 1,000 units of idle capacity, the total transfer price (including the opportunity cost) will be less than the $14 per barrel to buy from outside suppliers.[2]

Second, if cost is used as the transfer price, the selling division will never show a profit on any internal transfer. The only division that shows a profit is the division that makes the final sale to an outside party.

A third problem with cost-based prices is that they do not provide incentives to control costs. If the costs of one division are simply passed on to the next, then there is little incentive for anyone to work to reduce costs. This problem can be overcome to some extent by using standard costs rather than actual costs for transfer prices.

Despite these shortcomings, cost-based transfer prices are commonly used in practice. Advocates argue that they are easily understood and convenient to use.

Transfers at Market Price

Market price
The price being charged for an item on the open (intermediate) market.

Intermediate market
A market in which a transferred product or service is sold in its present form to outside customers.

Some form of competitive **market price** (i.e., the price charged for an item on the open market) is often regarded as the best approach to the transfer pricing problem—particularly if transfer price negotiations routinely become bogged down.

The market price approach is designed for situations in which there is an *intermediate market* for the transferred product or service. By **intermediate market**, we mean a market in which the product or service is sold in its present form to outside customers. If the selling division has no idle capacity, the market price in the intermediate market is the perfect choice for the transfer price. The reason for this is that if the selling division can sell a transferred item on the outside market instead, then the real cost of the transfer as far as the company is concerned is the opportunity cost of the lost revenue on the outside sale.

Whether the item is transferred internally or sold on the outside intermediate market, the production costs are exactly the same. If the market price is used as the transfer price, the selling division manager will not lose anything by making the transfer, and the purchasing division manager will get the correct signal about how much it really costs the company for the transfer to take place.

While the market price works well when there is no idle capacity, difficulties occur when the selling division has idle capacity. Recalling once again the ginger beer example, the outside market price for the ginger beer produced by Cumberland Beverages is $20 per barrel. However, Pizza Place can purchase all of the ginger beer it wants from outside suppliers for $18 per barrel. Why would Pizza Place ever buy ginger beer from Cumberland Beverages if Pizza Place is forced to pay Cumberland Beverages' market price? In some market price-based transfer pricing schemes, the transfer price would be lowered to $18, the outside vendor's market price, and Pizza Place would be directed to buy from Cumberland Beverages, as long as Cumberland Beverages is willing to sell. This scheme can work reasonably well, but a drawback is that managers at Pizza Place will regard the cost of ginger beer as $18 rather than the $8, which is the real cost to the company when the selling division has sufficient idle capacity to fill the entire order. Consequently, the managers of Pizza Place will make pricing and other decisions based on an incorrect cost.

Unfortunately, none of the possible solutions to the transfer pricing problem are perfect—not even market-based transfer prices.

Divisional Autonomy and Suboptimization

The principles of decentralization suggest that companies should grant managers autonomy to set transfer prices and to decide whether to sell internally or externally. It may be very difficult for top managers to accept this principle when their subordinate managers are about to make a suboptimal decision. However, if top management intervenes, the purposes of decentralization are defeated. Furthermore, to impose the correct transfer price, top managers would have to know details about the buying and selling divisions' outside market, variable costs, and capacity utilization. The whole premise of decentralization is that local managers have access to better information for operational decisions than top managers at corporate headquarters.

Of course, if a division manager consistently makes suboptimal decisions, the performance of the division will suffer. The offending manager's compensation will be adversely affected and promotion will become less likely. However, if top managers wish to create a culture of autonomy and independent profit responsibility, they must allow their subordinate managers to control their own destiny—even to the extent of granting their managers the right to make mistakes.

International Aspects of Transfer Pricing

Transfer pricing is used worldwide to control the flow of goods and services among segments of an organization. However, the objectives of transfer pricing change when a multinational corporation (MNC) is involved and the goods and services being transferred must cross international borders. The objectives of international transfer pricing, as compared to domestic transfer pricing, are summarized below.

Transfer Pricing Objectives	
Domestic	**International**
Greater divisional autonomy	Lower taxes, duties, and tariffs
Greater motivation for managers	Fewer foreign exchange risks
Better performance evaluation	Better competitive position
Better goal congruence	Better governmental relationships

As shown in the table, the objectives of international transfer pricing focus on minimizing taxes, duties, and foreign exchange risks, along with enhancing a company's competitive position and improving its relationships with foreign governments. Although domestic objectives such as managerial motivation and divisional autonomy are always desirable in an organization, they usually become secondary when international transfers are involved. Companies will focus instead on charging a transfer price that will reduce its total tax bill or that will strengthen a foreign subsidiary.

For example, charging a low transfer price for parts shipped to a foreign subsidiary may reduce Customs duty payments as the parts cross international borders, or it may help the subsidiary to compete in foreign markets by keeping the subsidiary's costs low. On the other hand, charging a high transfer price may help an MNC draw profits out of a country that has stringent controls on foreign remittances, or it may allow an MNC to shift income from a country that has high income tax rates to a country that has low rates.

Transfer prices have a significant influence on a firm's duties and income taxes. Given that transfer prices are set by parties who are not independent of each other (non-arm's length), the opportunity exists to minimize taxes by shifting profit to low-tax jurisdictions or by minimizing duties paid. The Canada Revenue Agency (CRA) seeks Canada's fair share of tax revenue by adopting policies and practices based on the principle of arm's length pricing. In simple cases, management simply needs to show CRA that the transfer price is comparable to an appropriately arm's length market price. In other cases, complex cost–profit allocation processes have to be documented by the company, together with the reasons for adopting such processes for determining the transfer price. Severe penalties exist for violations of the arm's length market price rule of the Income Tax Act, Section 247, in foreign dealings with non-arm's length parties of an organization.

In summary, managers need to be sensitive to legal rules in establishing transfer prices. In particular, the strict practices demonstrated with foreign transfer prices by the CRA rules illustrate the potential issues associated with provincial sales taxes, foreign trade practices under NAFTA and GATT, and the income tax provisions dealing with artificial tax-based transactions used to manipulate income taxes.

EVALUATING INVESTMENT CENTRE PERFORMANCE— RETURN ON INVESTMENT

LEARNING OBJECTIVE 4
Analyze the return on investment (ROI).

So far in this chapter we have focused on how to assign costs properly to responsibility centres and how to set transfer prices on goods and services being transferred between segments within the same organization. These are important issues when evaluating cost and profit centres. However, evaluating an investment centre's performance requires more than accurate cost and segment margin reporting. In addition, an investment centre is responsible for earning an adequate return on investment. The next two sections of this chapter present two methods for evaluating this aspect of an investment centre's performance. The first method is called *return on investment (ROI)*. The second method is called *residual income*.

The Return on Investment (ROI) Formula

Return on investment (ROI)
Operating income divided by average operating assets. ROI also equals margin multiplied by turnover.

The **return on investment (ROI)** is defined as operating income divided by average operating assets:

$$\text{ROI} = \frac{\text{Operating income}}{\text{Average operating assets}}$$

The higher the return on investment of a business segment, the greater the profit generated per dollar invested in the segment's operating assets.

Operating Income and Operating Assets Defined

Operating income
Income before interest and income taxes have been deducted.

Note that *operating income*, rather than net income, is used in the ROI formula. **Operating income** is income before interest and taxes and is sometimes referred to as *EBIT* (earnings before interest and taxes). The reason for using operating income in the formula is that the income figure used should be consistent with the base to which it is applied. Notice that the base (i.e., denominator) consists of *operating assets*. Thus, to be consistent we use operating income in the numerator because no debt is included in the denominator, and interest expense is paid for by the profits from the operating assets and thus is a distribution of those profits rather than an expense.

Operating assets include cash, accounts receivable, inventory, plant and equipment, and all other assets held for productive use in the organization and/or the investment centre. Examples of assets that would not be included in the operating assets category (i.e., examples of non-operating assets) would include land held for future use, an investment in another company, or a factory building rented to someone else. The operating assets base used in the formula is typically computed as the average of the operating assets between the beginning and the end of the year.

Operating assets
Cash, accounts receivable, inventory, plant and equipment, and all other assets held for productive use in an organization.

A major issue in ROI computations is the dollar amount of plant and equipment that should be included in the operating assets base. To illustrate the problem involved, assume that a company reports the following amounts for plant and equipment on its balance sheet:

Plant and equipment	$3,000,000
Less accumulated depreciation	900,000
Net book value	$2,100,000

What dollar amount of plant and equipment should the company include with its operating assets in computing ROI? One widely used approach is to include only the plant and equipment's *net book value*—that is, the plant's original cost less accumulated depreciation ($2,100,000 in the example above). A second approach is to ignore depreciation and include the plant's entire *gross cost* in the operating assets base ($3,000,000 in the example above). Both of these approaches are used in actual practice, even though they will obviously yield very different operating asset, operating income, and ROI figures.

The following arguments can be raised for using net book value to measure operating assets and for using gross cost to measure operating assets in ROI computation.

Arguments for Using Net Book Value to Measure Operating Assets in ROI Computations:
1. The net book value method is consistent with how plant and equipment are reported on the balance sheet (i.e., cost less accumulated depreciation to date).
2. The net book value method is consistent with the computation of operating income, which includes depreciation as an operating expense.

Arguments for Using Gross Cost to Measure Operating Assets in ROI Computations:
1. The gross cost method eliminates both the age of equipment and the method of depreciation as factors in ROI computations. (Under the net book value method, ROI will tend to increase over time as net book value declines due to depreciation.)
2. The gross cost method does not discourage replacement of old, worn-out equipment. (Under the net book value method, replacing fully depreciated equipment with new equipment can have a dramatic adverse effect on ROI.)

Managers generally view consistency as the most important of the considerations above. As a result, a majority of companies use the net book value approach in ROI computations. In this text, we will also use the net book value approach unless a specific exercise or problem directs otherwise.

Understanding ROI

The equation for ROI, operating income divided by average operating assets, does not provide much help to managers interested in taking action to improve their ROI. It offers only two levers for improving performance—operating income and average operating assets. Fortunately, ROI can also be expressed as follows:

$$ROI = Margin \times Turnover$$

where

$$Margin = \frac{Operating\ income}{Sales}$$

and

$$Turnover = \frac{Sales}{Average\ operating\ assets}$$

Margin
Operating income divided by sales.

Turnover
The amount of sales generated in an investment centre for each dollar invested in operating assets. Sales divided by average operating assets.

The **margin** is a measure of management's ability to control operating expenses in relation to sales. The lower operating expenses are per dollar of sales, the higher the margin earned. **Turnover** is a measure of the sales that are generated for each dollar invested in operating assets. Note that the sales terms in the margin and turnover formulas cancel out when they are multiplied together, yielding the original formula for ROI stated in terms of operating income and average operating assets. So either formula for ROI will give the same answer. However, the margin and turnover formulation provides some additional insights.

From a manager's perspective, margin and turnover are very important concepts. Margin is ordinarily improved by increasing sales or reducing operating expenses, including cost of goods sold and selling and administrative expenses. Some managers tend to focus too much on margin and ignore turnover. However, turnover incorporates a crucial area of a manager's responsibility—the investment in operating assets. Excessive funds tied up in operating assets (e.g., cash, accounts receivable, inventories, plant and equipment, and other assets) depress turnover and lower ROI. In fact, inefficient use of operating assets can be just as much of a drag on profitability as excessive operating expenses, which depress margin.

E.I. du Pont de Nemours and Company (better known as DuPont) pioneered the use of ROI and recognized the importance of looking at both margin and turnover in assessing a manager's performance. ROI is now widely used as the key measure of investment centre performance. ROI reflects in a single figure many aspects of the manager's responsibilities. It can be compared to the returns of other investment centres in the organization, the returns of other companies in the industry, and to the past returns of the investment centre itself.

DuPont also developed the diagram that appears in the Learning Aid on the next page. This diagram helps managers understand how they can improve ROI. Any increase in ROI must involve at least one of the following:

1.   Increased sales
2.   Reduced operating expenses
3.   Reduced operating assets

Many actions involve combinations of changes in sales, expenses, and operating assets. For example, a manager may make an investment in (i.e., increase) operating assets to reduce operating expenses or increase sales. Whether the net effect is favourable or not is judged in terms of its overall impact on ROI.

To illustrate how ROI is impacted by various actions, we will use the Monthaven outlet of the Burger Grill chain as an example. Burger Grill is a small chain of upscale casual restaurants that has been rapidly adding outlets via franchising. The Monthaven franchise is owned by a group of local surgeons who have little time to devote to management and little expertise in business matters. Therefore, they delegate operating decisions—including decisions concerning investments in operating assets such as inventories—to a professional manager they have hired. The manager is evaluated largely based on the ROI the franchise generates.

ELEMENTS OF RETURN ON INVESTMENT (ROI)

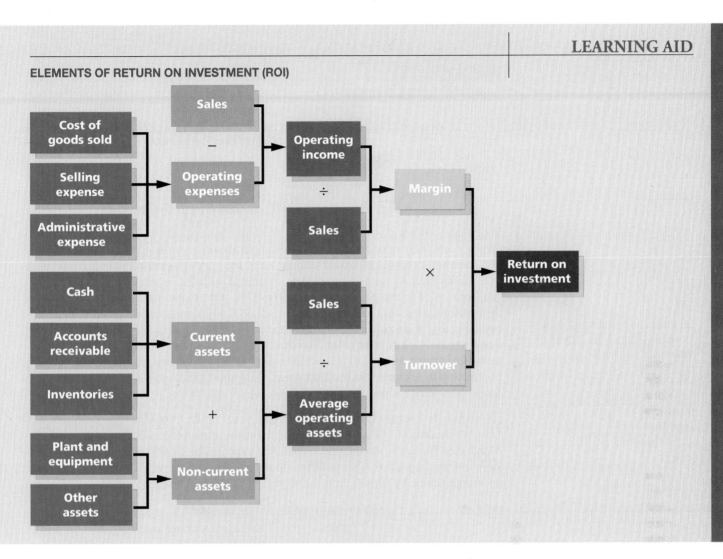

The following data represent the results of operations for the most recent month:

Sales	$100,000
Operating expenses	$90,000
Operating income	$10,000
Average operating assets	$50,000

The return on investment (ROI) for the month is computed as follows:

$$\text{ROI} = \frac{\text{Operating income}}{\text{Sales}} \times \frac{\text{Sales}}{\text{Average operating assets}}$$

$$= \frac{\$10,000}{\$100,000} \times \frac{\$100,000}{\$50,000}$$

$$= 10\% \times 2 = 20\%$$

Example 1: Increased Sales without Any Increase in Operating Assets   Assume that the manager of the Monthaven Burger Grill can increase sales by 10% without any increase in operating assets. The increase in sales will require additional operating expenses. However, operating expenses include some fixed expenses, which would probably not be affected by a 10% increase in sales. Therefore, the increase in operating expenses would probably be less than 10%; let's assume the increase is 7.8%. Under those assumptions, the new operating income would be $12,980, an increase of 29.8%, determined as follows:

Sales (1.10 × $100,000)	$110,000
Operating expenses (1.078 × $90,000)	97,020
Operating income	$ 12,980

In this case, the new ROI would be

$$\text{ROI} = \frac{\text{Operating income}}{\text{Sales}} \times \frac{\text{Sales}}{\text{Average operating assets}}$$

$$= \frac{\$12,980}{\$110,000} \times \frac{\$110,000}{\$50,000}$$

$$= 11.8\% \times 2.2 = 25.96\% \text{ (as compared to 20\% originally)}$$

When sales are increased *without* an increase in operating assets, both the margin and turnover are likely to be affected. In the example above, because sales increased by 10% and operating expenses increased by only 7.8%, the margin increased to 11.8% (up from 10%). This improvement in the margin combined with the increase in turnover to 2.2 (up from 2) led to the gain in ROI. Clearly, if the percentage increase in sales exceeds the percentage increase in operating expenses, ROI will always improve, if no additional operating assets are required to generate the new sales. However, it is worth pointing out that given the increase in turnover, the old ROI of 20% could have been maintained as long as the new margin did not fall below 9.09% (20% ÷ 2.2). If the new margin exceeds 9.09%, as it does in the example, ROI will increase. Using this type of analysis can help managers assess the extent to which operating expenses can increase before ROI begins to decrease.

Example 2: Decreased Operating Expenses with No Change in Sales or Operating Assets   Assume that by improving business processes, the manager of the Monthaven Burger Grill can reduce operating expenses by $1,000 without any effect on sales or operating assets. This reduction in operating expenses would result in increasing operating income by $1,000, from $10,000 to $11,000. The new ROI would be

$$\text{ROI} = \frac{\text{Operating income}}{\text{Sales}} \times \frac{\text{Sales}}{\text{Average operating assets}}$$

$$= \frac{\$11,000}{\$100,000} \times \frac{\$100,000}{\$50,000}$$

$$= 11\% \times 2 = 22\% \text{ (as compared to 20\% originally)}$$

When margins or profits are being squeezed, the first line of attack is often to cut costs. Discretionary fixed costs are particularly vulnerable to cuts. However, managers must be careful not to cut too much or in the wrong place. Inappropriate cost cutting can lead to decreased sales, increased costs elsewhere, and a drop in morale.

Example 3: Invest in Operating Assets to Increase Sales   Assume that the manager of the Monthaven Burger Grill invests $2,000 in a state-of-the-art soft-serve ice cream machine that can dispense a number of different flavours. This new machine will boost sales by $4,000, but will require additional operating expenses of $1,000. Thus, operating income will increase by $3,000, to $13,000. The new ROI will be

$$\text{ROI} = \frac{\text{Operating income}}{\text{Sales}} \times \frac{\text{Sales}}{\text{Average operating assets}}$$

$$= \frac{\$13,000}{\$104,000} \times \frac{\$104,000}{\$52,000}$$

$$= 12.5\% \times 2 = 25\% \text{ (as compared to 20\% originally)}$$

In this particular example, the investment had no effect on turnover, which remained at 2, so there had to be an increase in margin in order to improve the ROI.

As part of a proposal to persuade Ford Motor Company Limited to construct a $750 million assembly plant in St. Thomas, Ontario, the Canadian Auto Workers (CAW) union estimated that the return on investment (ROI) would be 18.3% per year over a seven-year period. The proposal calculated that a similar assembly plant built in the United States or Mexico would yield annual ROI of 4.9% and 9.2%, respectively. The superior ROI from the Canadian plant would stem, in part, from the CAW's suggestion to limit spending on operating assets by combining the new plant with an existing assembly plant in St. Thomas. Further, the proposal indicates that the operating margin would be strengthened by the CAW agreeing to initially set employees' wages at 75% of the levels earned at other assembly plant sites. The CAW proposal provides a good example of how both components of ROI, margin and turnover, can be managed to maximize potential profits in an organization.

Source: Tony Van Alphen, "CAW Makes Unusual Pitch to Ford: Wage Concessions Part of Proposed Assembly Plant for St. Thomas," *Toronto Star*, August 30, 2006, p. F1.

Criticisms of ROI

Although ROI is widely used in evaluating performance, it is not a perfect tool. The method is subject to the following criticisms:

1. Just telling managers to increase ROI may not be enough. Managers may not know how to increase ROI; they may increase ROI in a way that is inconsistent with the company's strategy; or they may take actions that increase ROI in the short run but harm the company in the long run (such as cutting back on research and development).
2. A manager who takes over a business segment typically inherits many committed costs over which the manager has no control. These committed costs may be relevant in assessing the performance of the business segment as an investment but make it difficult to fairly assess the performance of the manager relative to other managers.
3. As discussed in the next section, a manager who is evaluated based on ROI may reject profitable investment opportunities.

■ RESIDUAL INCOME

Another approach to measuring an investment centre's performance focuses on a concept known as *residual income*. **Residual income** is the operating income that an investment centre earns above the minimum required return on its operating assets. Thus, we use operating income as defined with ROI but reduce it by a special charge computed as a percentage of average operating assets. In equation form, residual income is calculated as follows:

$$\frac{\text{Residual}}{\text{income}} = \frac{\text{Operating}}{\text{income}} - \left(\frac{\text{Average operating}}{\text{assets}} \times \frac{\text{Minimum required}}{\text{rate of return}}\right)$$

Economic value added (EVA®) is a similar concept that differs in some details from residual income. EVA® has been popularized and trademarked by the consulting firm Stern, Stewart & Co. For example, under the economic value-added concept, funds used for research and development are treated as investments rather than as expenses. However, for our purposes, we will not draw any distinction between residual income and economic value added. We will illustrate residual income because the adjustments for EVA® are complex and would create more confusion than is appropriate for this introduction.

When residual income or EVA® is used to measure performance, the purpose is to maximize the total amount of residual income or EVA®, not to maximize overall ROI.

LEARNING OBJECTIVE 5
Compute residual income and describe the strengths and weaknesses of this method of measuring performance.

Residual income
The operating income that an investment centre earns above the required return on its operating assets.

Economic value added (EVA®)
A concept similar to residual income.

Organizations as diverse as Loblaw, Quaker Oats, and Domtar have embraced some version of residual income in recent years.

For purposes of illustration, consider the following data for an investment centre—the Whitehorse Division of Yukon Marine Services Corporation.

YUKON MARINE SERVICES CORPORATION
Whitehorse Division
Basic Data for Performance Evaluation

Average operating assets..........................	$100,000
Operating income................................	$ 20,000
Minimum required rate of return....................	15%

Yukon Marine Services Corporation has long had a policy of evaluating investment centre managers based on ROI, but is considering a switch to residual income. The controller of the company, who is in favour of the change to residual income, has provided the following table that shows how the performance of the division would be evaluated under each of the two methods:

YUKON MARINE SERVICES CORPORATION
Whitehorse Division
Alternative Performance Measures

	ROI	Residual Income
Average operating assets........................	$100,000 (a)	$100,000
Operating income...............................	$ 20,000 (b)	$ 20,000
ROI, (b) ÷ (a)	20%	
Minimum required return (15% × $100,000).........		15,000
Residual income................................		$ 5,000

The reasoning underlying the residual income calculation is straightforward. The company is able to earn a rate of return of at least 15% on its investments. Since the company has invested $100,000 in the Whitehorse Division in the form of operating assets, the company should be able to earn at least $15,000 (15% × $100,000) on this investment. Since the Whitehorse Division's operating income is $20,000, the residual income exceeds the minimum required return by $5,000. If residual income is adopted as the performance measure to replace ROI, then the manager of the Whitehorse Division would be evaluated based on the growth from year to year in residual income.

Motivation and Residual Income

One of the primary reasons why the controller of Yukon Marine Services Corporation would like to switch from ROI to residual income has to do with how managers view new investments under the two performance measurement schemes. The residual income approach encourages managers to make investments that are profitable for the entire company but that would be rejected by managers who are evaluated by the ROI formula.

To illustrate this problem, suppose that the manager of the Whitehorse Division is considering purchasing a computerized diagnostic machine to aid in servicing marine diesel engines. The machine would cost $25,000 and is expected to generate additional operating income of $4,500 a year. From the standpoint of the company, this would be a good investment since it promises a rate of return of 18% ($4,500 ÷ $25,000), which is in excess of the company's minimum required rate of return of 15%.

If the manager of the Whitehorse Division is evaluated based on residual income, she would be in favour of the investment in the diagnostic machine evaluated below:

YUKON MARINE SERVICES CORPORATION Whitehorse Division Performance Evaluated Using Residual Income	Present	New Project	Overall
Average operating assets........	$100,000	$25,000	$125,000
Operating income..............	$ 20,000	$ 4,500	$ 24,500
Minimum required return	15,000	3,750*	18,750
Residual income...............	$ 5,000	$ 750	$ 5,750

* $25,000 × 15% = $3,750.

Since the project would increase the residual income of the Whitehorse Division, the manager would want to invest in the new diagnostic machine.

Now suppose that the manager of the Whitehorse Division is evaluated based on ROI. The effect of the diagnostic machine on the division's ROI is computed below:

YUKON MARINE SERVICES CORPORATION Whitehorse Division Performance Evaluated Using ROI	Present	New Project	Overall
Average operating assets (a)	$100,000	$25,000	$125,000
Operating income (b)	$ 20,000	$ 4,500*	$ 24,500
ROI, (b) ÷ (a)	20%	18%	19.6%

* $25,000 × 18% = $4,500.

The new project reduces the division's ROI from 20% to 19.6%. This happens because the 18% rate of return on the new diagnostic machine, while above the company's 15% minimum rate of return, is below the division's present ROI of 20%. Therefore, the new diagnostic machine would reduce the division's ROI, even though it would be a good investment from the standpoint of the company as a whole. If the manager of the division is evaluated based on ROI, she will be reluctant to even propose such an investment.

Generally, a manager who is evaluated based on ROI will want to reject any project whose rate of return is below the division's current ROI even if the rate of return on the project is above the minimum required rate of return for the entire company. In contrast, any project whose rate of return is above the minimum required rate of return for the company will result in an increase in residual income and thus add value for the shareholders. Since it is in the best interests of the company as a whole to accept any project whose rate of return is above the minimum required rate of return, managers who are evaluated based on residual income will tend to make better decisions concerning investment projects than managers who are evaluated based on ROI.

Divisional Comparison and Residual Income

The residual income approach has one major disadvantage. It cannot be used to compare the performance of divisions of different sizes. You would expect larger divisions to have more residual income than smaller divisions, not necessarily because they are better managed but simply because they are bigger.

As an example, consider the following residual income computations for Division X and Division Y:

	Division	
	X	**Y**
Average operating assets (a)	$1,000,000	$250,000
Operating income.	$ 120,000	$ 40,000
Minimum required return: 10% × (a)	100,000	25,000
Residual income.	$ 20,000	$ 15,000

Observe that Division X has slightly more residual income than Division Y, but that Division X has $1,000,000 in operating assets as compared to only $250,000 in operating assets for Division Y. Thus, Division X's greater residual income is probably more a result of its size than the quality of its management. In fact, it appears that the smaller division is better managed, since it has been able to generate nearly as much residual income with only one-fourth as much in operating assets with which to work. This problem can be reduced to some degree by focusing on the percentage change in residual income from year to year rather than on the absolute amount of the residual income.

Criticisms of Residual Income

As shown above, compared to ROI, the use of residual income can lead managers to make decisions more consistent with shareholders' objectives. Further, some claim that residual income is more closely related to shareholder returns than other metrics such as sales growth, net income, or ROI. However the following criticisms of residual income are worth noting:

1. Residual income is based on historical accounting data, which means that in particular, the accounting values used for capital assets can suffer from being out of date when costs are rising. This can lead to inflated amounts for residual income.
2. The residual income approach does not indicate what earnings *should* be for a particular business unit. A means of comparison is needed, which could involve using external benchmarks based on key competitors or evaluating trends in residual income over time (e.g., tracking the percentage change over several periods).
3. Calculating residual income requires numerous adjustments to financial information recorded using generally accepted accounting principles that can increase the cost of preparing the information.
4. Residual income is a financial metric that does not incorporate important leading nonfinancial indicators of success, such as employee motivation or customer satisfaction.

◼ BALANCED SCORECARD

LEARNING OBJECTIVE 6
Explain the use of balanced scorecards to assess performance.

Balanced scorecard
An integrated set of performance measures that is derived from and supports the organization's strategy.

A **balanced scorecard** consists of an integrated set of performance measures that is derived from the company's strategy and that supports the company's strategy throughout the organization.[3, 4] A strategy is essentially a theory about how to achieve the organization's goals and deals with issues such as how to attract customers, what products or services to sell, what markets to enter, and how to compete with rivals. According to some experts, there are three potentially successful generic strategic approaches to outperforming competitors:[5]

1. **Cost leadership:** By maintaining low cost through efficiency relative to competitors, a company will be able to make superior profits at current industry prices. Alternatively, the company can become a price leader because other firms are unable to undercut its prices. Low costs may also serve as a barrier against potential new market entrants and thereby protect long-term profitability. However, technological change or imitation of low-cost techniques by rivals can threaten the success of this strategy.

2. **Differentiation:** For products or services that are perceived as unique, customers sometimes will pay premium prices, giving the company higher profit margins. This cushion of higher profits reduces the effect of supplier or buyer power. Brand loyalty, however, may fail if the cost differential between the firm and the cost leader in the industry becomes too wide.

3. **Focus or niche:** By serving a narrow, strategic target market more effectively than rivals who are competing more broadly, a firm may be able to achieve superior profitability. The risk of being overtaken by broad-target firms who have economies of scale is a constant threat to the success of this strategy.

Under the balanced scorecard approach, top management translates its strategy into performance measures that employees can understand and can do something about. For example, the length of time passengers have to wait in line to have their baggage checked might be a performance measure for the supervisor in charge of the Air Canada check-in counter at the Vancouver airport. This performance measure is easily understood by the supervisor, and can be improved by the supervisor's actions.

Common Characteristics of Balanced Scorecards

Performance measures used in the balanced scorecard approach tend to fall into the four groups illustrated in Exhibit 11–4: financial, customer, internal business processes, and learning and growth. Internal business processes are what the company does in an attempt to satisfy customers. For example, in a manufacturing company, assembling a product is an internal business process. For an airline, handling baggage is an internal business process. The basic idea is that learning is necessary to improve internal business processes, improving business processes is necessary to improve customer satisfaction, and improving customer satisfaction is necessary to improve financial results.

Note that the emphasis in Exhibit 11–4 is on *improvement*—not on just attaining some specific objective such as profits of $10 million. In the balanced scorecard approach, continual

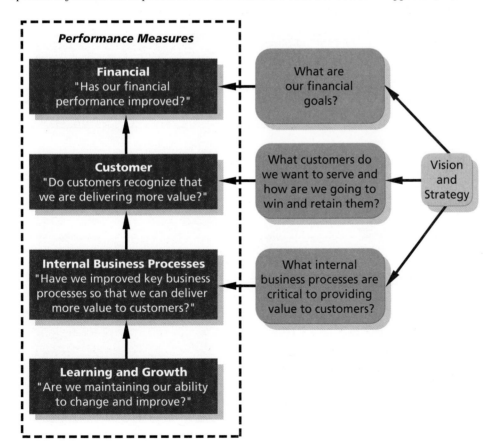

EXHIBIT 11–4   From Strategy to Performance Measures: The Balanced Scorecard

improvement is encouraged. In many industries, this is a matter of survival. If an organization does not continually improve, it will eventually lose out to competitors that do.

Financial performance measures appear at the top of Exhibit 11–4. Ultimately, most companies exist to provide financial rewards to owners. There are exceptions. Some companies—for example, The Body Shop—may have loftier goals, such as providing environmentally friendly products to consumers. However, even non-profit organizations must generate enough financial resources to stay in operation.

However, for several reasons, financial performance measures (even ROI or EVA®) are not sufficient in themselves—they should be integrated with non-financial measures in a well-designed balanced scorecard. First, financial measures are lag indicators that report on the results of past actions. In contrast, non-financial measures of key success drivers such as customer satisfaction are leading indicators of future financial performance. Second, top managers are ordinarily responsible for the financial performance measures—not lower-level managers. The supervisor in charge of checking in passengers can be held responsible for how long passengers have to wait in line. However, this supervisor cannot reasonably be held responsible for the entire company's profit. That is the responsibility of the airline's top managers.

Exhibit 11–5 lists some examples of performance measures that can be found in the customer, internal business process, and learning and growth categories of the balanced scorecards at many companies. However, few companies, if any, would use all of these performance measures, and almost all companies would add other performance measures. Managers should carefully select the performance measures for their company's balanced

EXHIBIT 11–5 Examples of Performance Measures for Balanced Scorecards

Customer Perspective

Performance Measure	Desired Change
Customer satisfaction as measured by survey results	+
Number of customer complaints	−
Market share	+
Product returns as a percentage of sales	−
Percentage of customers retained from last period	+
Number of new customers	+

Internal Business Processes Perspective

Performance Measure	Desired Change
Percentage of sales from new products	+
Defect-free units as a percentage of completed units	+
Delivery cycle time*	−
Throughput time*	−
Manufacturing cycle efficiency*	+
Quality costs*	−
Setup time	−

Learning and Growth Perspective

Performance Measure	Desired Change
New products under development	+
Break-even time to market for new products	+
Suggestions per employee	+
Employee satisfaction	+
Employee turnover	−
Hours of in-house training per employee	+

*Explained later in this chapter.

scorecard, keeping the following points in mind. First, the performance measures should be consistent with, and follow from, the company's strategy. If the performance measures are not consistent with the company's strategy, people will find themselves working at cross-purposes. Second, the scorecard should not have too many performance measures. This can lead to a lack of focus and confusion.

While the entire organization will have an overall balanced scorecard, each responsible individual may have his or her own personal scorecard as well. This scorecard should consist of items the individual can personally influence that relate directly to the performance measures on the overall balanced scorecard (e.g., hours spent in training courses). The performance measures on this personal scorecard should not be overly influenced by actions taken by others in the company or by events that are outside of the individual's control. Also, the personal scorecard measures should not lead an individual to take actions that are inconsistent with the organization's objectives.

With those broad principles in mind, we will now take a look at how a company's strategy affects its balanced scorecard.

A Company's Strategy and the Balanced Scorecard

Returning to the performance measurement categories in Exhibit 11–4, each company must decide which customers to target and what internal business processes are crucial to attracting and retaining those customers. Different companies, having different strategies, will target different customers with different kinds of products and services. Because of differences in emphasis, a one-size-fits-all approach to performance measurement will not work within this industry. Performance measures must be tailored to the specific strategy of each company.

Consider the strategy of a regional airline with the following strategy: to uniquely position ourselves by focusing on only short-haul, low-fare, high-frequency, point-to-point carrier in eastern North America. Exhibit 11–6 suggests how the airline might reflect this strategy in its balanced scorecard.

If the balanced scorecard is correctly constructed, the performance measures should be linked together on a cause-and-effect basis. Each link can then be read as a hypothesis in the form "If we improve this performance measure, then this other performance measure

Vision: Continue building on our unique position—the *only* short haul, low-fare, high-frequency, point-to-point carrier in America.

EXHIBIT 11–6   A Possible Strategy for a Regional Airline and the Balanced Scorecard

Simplified Strategy Map	Performance Measures	Targets	Initiatives
Financial Increase Profitability Lower costs Increase Revenue	• Market Value • Seat Revenue • Plane Lease Cost	• 25% per year • 20% per year • 5% per year	• Optimize routes • Standardize planes
Customer More Customers On-time flights Lowest Prices	• FAA On Time Arrival Rating • Customer Ranking • No. Customers	• First in industry • 98% Satisfaction • % change	• Quality management • Customer loyalty program
Internal Improve Turnaround Time	• On Ground Time • On-Time Departure	• <25 Minutes • 93%	• Cycle time optimization program
Learning Align Ground Crews	• % Ground crew shareholders • % Ground crew trained	• yr. 1 70% yr. 4 90% yr. 6 100%	• Stock ownership plan • Ground crew training

Developed from material by the Balanced Scorecard Collaborative and Harvard Business Review (Kaplan & Norton).

should also improve." Starting from the bottom of Exhibit 11–6, we can read the links between performance measures as follows: If ground crews acquire the skills to perform better and become shareholders, they will perform better and be motivated to increase turnaround times, ensuring more on-time flights. More on-time flights when accompanied by low prices should increase customer satisfaction and loyalty, leading to increased revenues and decreased costs, resulting in an increase in profits.

In essence, the balanced scorecard illustrates a theory of how the company can attain its desired outcomes (financial, in this case) by taking concrete actions. While the strategy laid out in Exhibit 11–6 seems plausible, it should be regarded as only a theory that should be discarded if it proves to be invalid. One of the advantages of the balanced scorecard is that it can be used to continually test the theories underlying management's strategy. If a strategy is not working, it should become evident when some of the predicted effects (i.e., more repeat customers) do not occur. Without this feedback, management may drift on indefinitely with an ineffective strategy based on faulty assumptions.

IN BUSINESS

Professors Christopher D. Ittner and David F. Larcker surveyed 157 companies and found that only 23% consistently verified the hypothesized cause-and-effect linkages embedded in their balanced scorecards. These companies earned a 5.14% higher return on common shareholders' equity than the 77% of companies that did not verify their cause-and-effect linkages.

The authors found that most companies do not verify cause-and-effect linkages because they erroneously believe that they are self-evident. For example, one fast-food chain chose employee turnover as a performance measure, believing that its positive effects on profits were obvious. However, the professors' research revealed that the fast-food chain's profitability was influenced only by turnover among its supervisors, not lower-level employees. A broad measure of employee turnover did not help explain differences in profitability across restaurants.

Source: Christopher D. Ittner and David F. Larcker, "Coming Up Short on Nonfinancial Performance Measurement," *Harvard Business Review,* November 2003, pp. 88–95.

Tying Compensation to the Balanced Scorecard

Incentive compensation for employees, such as bonuses, can, and probably should, be tied to balanced scorecard performance measures. However, this should be done only after the organization has been successfully managed with the scorecard for some time—perhaps a year or more. Managers must be confident that the performance measures are reliable, sensible, understood by those who are being evaluated, and not easily manipulated. As Robert Kaplan and David Norton, the promoters of the balanced scorecard concept point out, "compensation is such a powerful lever that you have to be pretty confident that you have the right measures and have good data for the measures before making the link."[6]

Advantages of Timely Feedback

Whatever performance measures are used, they should be reported on a frequent and timely basis. For example, data about defects should be reported to the responsible managers at least once a day so that action can be taken quickly if an unusual number of defects occur. In the most advanced companies, any defect is reported *immediately,* and its cause is tracked down before any more defects occur. Another common characteristic of the performance measures under the balanced scorecard approach is that managers focus on *trends* in the performance measures over time. The emphasis is on progress and *improvement* rather than on meeting any specific standard.

Sharp Corporation has created a first-of-its-kind integrated LCD panel manufacturing facility, called Green Front Sakai. The city of Sakai has been designated as an environmental model city by the Japanese government. With 19 suppliers and business partners under one roof operating integrated systems in a single virtual company, Green Front Sakai hopes to eliminate waste completely, accelerate manufacturing performance, and maximize operating efficiency.

Sharp uses an enterprise resource planning system to collect and analyze data of all types across the new facility. The wide variety of measures taken is then presented in a "performance dashboard," basically a balanced scorecard in graphical format. For the first time, across the entire production facility, inventory, sales, and accounting information can be viewed in real time, helping managers and production workers to maximize operating efficiency.

Source: Sharp, *Green Front Sakai*, www.sharp.co.jp/sakai/en/enter.html and http://www-01.ibm.com/software/lotus/category/dashboard.

Some Measures of Internal Business Process Performance

Internal business process performance measures included on a balanced scorecard provide feedback needed for improving these processes. This information is essential for making cost and quality improvements that lead to greater profitability and customer satisfaction.

Most of the performance measures listed in Exhibit 11–5 are self-explanatory. However, three are not—*delivery cycle time*, *throughput time*, and *manufacturing cycle efficiency (MCE)*. Because of their importance to organizations and their common use in balanced scorecards, they are discussed next.

Delivery Cycle Time   The amount of time from when an order is received from a customer to when the completed order is shipped is called **delivery cycle time**. This time is clearly a key concern to many customers, who would like the delivery cycle time to be as short as possible. Cutting the delivery cycle time may give a company a key competitive advantage—and may be necessary for survival—and therefore many companies would include this performance measure on their balanced scorecard.

> **Delivery cycle time**
> The amount of time required from receipt of an order from a customer to shipment of the completed goods.

Throughput (Manufacturing Cycle) Time   The amount of time required to turn raw materials into completed products is called **throughput time**, or *manufacturing cycle time*. The relationship between the delivery cycle time and the throughput time is illustrated in Exhibit 11–7.

> **Throughput time**
> The amount of time required to turn raw materials into completed products.

Note that, as shown in Exhibit 11–7, the throughput time, or manufacturing cycle time, is made up of process time, inspection time, move time, and queue time. *Process time* is the amount of time in which work is actually done on the product. *Inspection time* is the amount of time spent ensuring that the product is not defective. *Move time* is the time required to move materials or partially completed products from workstation to workstation. *Queue time* is the amount of time a product spends waiting to be worked on, to be moved, to be inspected, or in storage waiting to be shipped.

As shown at the bottom of Exhibit 11–7, the only one of these four activities that adds value to the product is process time. The other three activities—inspecting, moving, and queuing—add no value and should be eliminated as much as possible.

Manufacturing Cycle Efficiency (MCE)   Through concerted efforts to eliminate the *non-value-added* activities of inspecting, moving, and queuing, some companies have reduced their throughput time to only a fraction of previous levels. In turn, this has helped to reduce the delivery cycle time from months to only weeks or hours. The throughput time, which is considered to be a key measure in delivery performance, can be put into better perspective by computing the **manufacturing cycle efficiency (MCE)**.

> **Manufacturing cycle efficiency (MCE)**
> Process (value-added) time as a percentage of throughput time.

EXHIBIT 11–7   Delivery Cycle Time and Throughput (Manufacturing Cycle) Time

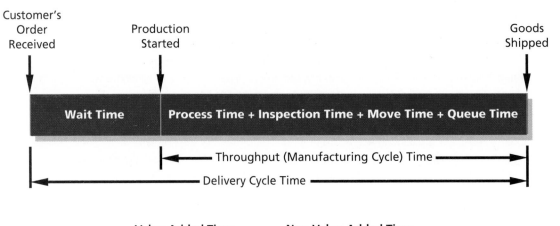

The MCE is computed by relating the value-added time to the throughput time. The formula is as follows:

$$\text{MCE} = \frac{\text{Value-added time}}{\text{Throughput (manufacturing cycle) time}}$$

If the MCE is less than 1, then non-value-added time is present in the production process. An MCE of 0.5, for example, would mean that half of the total production time consisted of inspection, moving, and similar non-value-added activities. In many manufacturing companies, the MCE is less than 0.1 (10%), which means that 90% of the time a unit is in process is spent on activities that do not add value to the product. By monitoring the MCE, companies are able to reduce non-value-added activities and thus get products into the hands of customers more quickly and at a lower cost.

To provide a numeric example of these measures, assume the following data for Novex Company:

Novex Company keeps careful track of the time relating to orders and their production. During the most recent quarter, the following average times were recorded for each unit or order:

	Days
Wait time	17.0
Inspection time	0.4
Process time	2.0
Move time	0.6
Queue time	5.0

Goods are shipped as soon as production is completed.

Based on this data, we can calculate the following:

1. Throughput time.
2. Manufacturing cycle efficiency (MCE).
3. Percentage of the production time spent in non-value-added activities.
4. Delivery cycle time.

The calculations are as follows:

1. Throughput time = Process time + Inspection time + Move time + Queue time

    = 2.0 days + 0.4 days + 0.6 days + 5.0 days

    = 8.0 days

2. Only process time represents value-added time; therefore, the computation of the MCE would be as follows:

$$\text{MCE} = \frac{\text{Value-added time, 2.0 days}}{\text{Throughput time, 8.0 days}}$$

$$= 0.25$$

Thus, once put into production, a typical unit is actually being worked on only 25% of the time.

3. Since the MCE is 25%, the complement of this figure, or 75% of the total production time, is spent in non-value-added activities.

4. Delivery cycle time = Wait time + Throughput time

    = 17.0 days + 8.0 days

    = 25.0 days

Some Final Observations Concerning the Balanced Scorecard   We would like to emphasize a few points concerning the balanced scorecard. First, the balanced scorecard should be tailored to the company's strategy; each company's balanced scorecard should be unique. The examples given in this chapter are just that—examples. They should not be interpreted as general templates to be fitted to each company. Second, the balanced scorecard reflects a particular strategy, or theory, about how a company can further its objectives by taking specific actions. The theory should be viewed as tentative and subject to change if the actions do not in fact lead to attaining the company's financial and other goals. If the theory (i.e., strategy) changes, then the performance measures on the balanced scorecard should also change. The balanced scorecard should be viewed as a dynamic system that evolves as the company's strategy evolves. Third, while the balanced scorecard is an important component of an organization's reporting and control system, it is not the only piece. Numerous supporting schedules and supplementary information will also be regularly prepared and used by managers to monitor and control the day-to-day activities under their responsibility. An example of the need for additional reporting beyond the summary information contained in a balanced scorecard is presented in the next section, where quality costs are discussed. A balanced scorecard does not replace the need for the regular preparation and use of detailed reports on key operating activities.

COST OF QUALITY

One of the internal business process measures shown in Exhibit 11–5 that many companies include on their balanced scorecard is quality costs. This is usually a summary metric made up of different types or categories of quality costs. Increasingly, managers at both manufacturing and service companies are emphasizing the importance of understanding the various kinds of quality costs and how they can be managed. In this section, we discuss the types of quality costs and their interaction as well as illustrate how some companies extend the reporting of these costs beyond the summary metrics included in the scorecard.

A company may have a product with a high-quality design that uses high-quality components, but if the product is poorly assembled or has other defects, the company will have high warranty repair costs and dissatisfied customers. People who are dissatisfied with a product are unlikely to buy the product again and may tell others about their bad experiences. This is the worst possible sort of advertising. To prevent such problems, companies have been expending a great deal of effort to reduce defects. The objective is to have high *quality of conformance.*

LEARNING OBJECTIVE 7
Identify the four types of quality costs, explain their interaction, and prepare a quality cost report.

IN BUSINESS

There was a time when Hyundai's product quality was the laughingstock of the automobile industry. However, in 2010, Hyundai's Genesis and Tucson models were both "top safety picks" of the Insurance Institute for Highway Safety and the 2010 Accent model was the highest ranked subcompact car in initial quality according to a study performed by J. D. Power and Associates, a well-known market research firm that regularly collects and reports customer satisfaction data.

Why the dramatic turnabout? In 2005, Hyundai expanded its quality department to 1,000 employees—a tenfold increase—and required the department to report directly to the company's chairman, Mong-Koo Chung. Employees were paid bonuses for sharing and implementing ideas for improvement. At Hyundai's Asian factory outside Seoul, workers have dropped 25,000 ideas into the suggestion box, of which 30% have been adopted. When test drives revealed a flaw in the Sonata's front door, engineers found a solution that cost 40 cents per car. Had the same problem occurred before this shift in quality focus, one manager at Hyundai commented that the company would probably not have fixed it unless customers eventually complained about the problem.

Sources: Joann Muller and Robyn Meredith, "Last Laugh," *Forbes*, April, 18, 2005, pp. 98–104; www.hyundaicanada.com; and http://www.jdpower.com/autos.

Quality of Conformance

Quality of conformance
The degree to which a product or service meets or exceeds its design specifications and is free of defects or other problems that mar its appearance or degrade its performance.

A product that meets or exceeds its design specifications and is free of defects that mar its appearance or degrade its performance is said to have high **quality of conformance**. Note that if an economy car is free of defects, it can have a quality of conformance that is just as high as a defect-free luxury car. The purchasers of economy cars cannot expect their cars to be as opulently equipped as luxury cars, but they can and do expect them to be free of defects.

Preventing, detecting, and dealing with defects cause costs that are called *quality costs* or the *cost of quality*. The use of the term *quality cost* is confusing to some people. It does not refer to costs such as using a higher grade of leather to make a wallet or using 14K gold instead of gold-plating in jewellery. Instead, the term **quality cost** refers to all of the costs that are incurred to prevent defects or that are incurred as a result of defects occurring.

Quality cost
Costs that are incurred to prevent defective products from reaching customers or that are incurred as a result of defective units.

Quality costs can be broken down into four broad groups. Two of these groups—known as *prevention costs* and *appraisal costs*—are incurred in an effort to keep defective products from reaching customers. The other two groups—known as *internal failure costs* and *external failure costs*—are incurred because defects are produced despite efforts to prevent them. Examples of specific costs involved in each of these four groups are given in Exhibit 11–8.

Several things should be noted about the quality costs shown in the exhibit. First, quality costs do not relate to just manufacturing; rather, they relate to all of the activities in a company from initial research and development (R&D) through customer service. Second, the number of costs associated with quality is very large; therefore, total quality cost can be quite high unless management gives this area special attention. Finally, the costs in the four groupings are quite different. We will now look at each of these groupings more closely.

Prevention Costs

Prevention costs
Costs incurred to keep defects from occurring.

Generally the most effective way to minimize quality costs while maintaining high-quality output is to avoid having quality problems arise in the first place. This is the purpose of **prevention costs**; such costs relate to any activity that reduces the number of defects in products or services. Companies have learned that it is much less costly to prevent a problem from ever happening than it is to find and correct the problem after it has occurred.

Prevention Costs	**Internal Failure Costs**
Systems development	Net cost of scrap
Quality engineering	Net cost of spoilage
Quality training	Rework labour and overhead
Quality circles	Reinspection of reworked products
Statistical process control activities	Retesting of reworked products
Supervision of prevention activities	Downtime caused by quality problems
Quality data gathering, analysis, and reporting	Disposal of defective products
Quality improvement projects	Analysis of the cause of defects in production
Technical support provided to suppliers	Re-entering data because of keying errors
Audits of the effectiveness of the quality system	Debugging software errors
	External Failure Costs
Appraisal Costs	Cost of field servicing and handling complaints
Test and inspection of incoming materials	Warranty repairs and replacements
Test and inspection of in-process goods	Repairs and replacements beyond the warranty period
Final product testing and inspection	Product recalls
Supplies used in testing and inspection	Liability arising from defective products
Supervision of testing and inspection activities	Returns and allowances arising from quality problems
Depreciation of test equipment	Lost sales arising from a reputation for poor quality
Maintenance of test equipment	
Plant utilities in the inspection area	
Field testing and appraisal at customer site	

EXHIBIT 11–8   Typical Quality Costs

Note from Exhibit 11–8 that prevention costs include activities relating to quality circles and statistical process control. **Quality circles** consist of small groups of employees who meet on a regular basis to discuss ways to improve the quality of output. Both management and workers are included in these circles. Quality circles are widely used in manufacturing companies, utilities, health care organizations, banks, and many other organizations.

Statistical process control is a technique used to detect whether a process is in or out of control. An out-of-control process results in defective units and may be caused by a miscalibrated machine or some other factor. In statistical process control, workers use charts to monitor the quality of units that pass through their workstations. Using these charts, workers can quickly spot processes that are out of control and that are creating defects. Problems can be corrected immediately and further defects prevented, rather than waiting for an inspector to catch the defects later.

Note also from the list of prevention costs in Exhibit 11–8 that some companies provide technical support to their suppliers as a way of preventing defects. Particularly in just-in-time (JIT) systems, such support to suppliers is vital. In a JIT system, parts are delivered from suppliers just in time and in just the correct quantity to fill customer orders.

If a defective part is received from a supplier, the part cannot be used and the order for the ultimate customer cannot be filled on time. Hence, every part received from a supplier must be free of defects. Consequently, companies that use JIT often require that their suppliers use sophisticated quality control programs such as statistical process control and that their suppliers certify that they will deliver parts and materials that are free of defects.

Quality circles
Small groups of employees who meet on a regular basis to discuss ways of improving quality.

Statistical process control
A charting technique used to monitor the quality of work being done at a workstation for the purpose of immediately correcting any problems.

Appraisal Costs

Any defective parts and products should be caught as early as possible. **Appraisal costs,** which are sometimes called *inspection costs*, are incurred to identify defective products *before* the products are shipped to customers. Unfortunately, performing appraisal activities doesn't keep defects from happening again, and most managers now realize that maintaining an army of inspectors is a costly (and ineffective) approach to quality control.

The late professor John K. Shank of Dartmouth College once stated, "The old-style approach was to say, 'We've got great quality. We have 40 quality control inspectors in the factory.' Then somebody realized that if you need 40 inspectors, it must be a lousy factory. So now the trick is to run a factory without any quality control inspectors; each employee is his or her own quality control person."[7]

Appraisal costs
Costs that are incurred to identify defective products before the products are shipped to customers.

Employees are increasingly being asked to be responsible for their own quality control. This approach, along with designing products to be easy to manufacture properly, allows quality to be built into products rather than relying on inspection to get the defects out.

Internal Failure Costs

Internal failure costs
Costs that are incurred as a result of identifying defective products before they are shipped to customers.

Failure costs are incurred when a product fails to conform to its design specifications. Failure costs can be either internal or external. **Internal failure costs** result from identification of defects during the appraisal process. Such costs include scrap, rejected products, reworking of defective units, and downtime caused by quality problems. It is crucial that defects be discovered before a product is shipped to customers. Of course, the more effective a company's appraisal activities, the greater the chance of catching defects internally and the greater the level of internal failure costs (as compared to external failure costs). Unfortunately, appraisal activities focus on symptoms rather than on causes and they do nothing to reduce the number of defective items. However, appraisal activities do bring defects to the attention of management, which may lead to efforts to increase prevention activities so that the defects do not happen.

External Failure Costs

External failure costs
Costs that are incurred when a product or service that is defective is delivered to a customer.

External failure costs result when a defective product is delivered to a customer. As shown in Exhibit 11–8, external failure costs include warranty repairs and replacements, product recalls, liability arising from legal action against a company, and lost sales arising from a reputation for poor quality. Such costs can significantly reduce profits.

In the past, some managers have taken the attitude, "Let's go ahead and ship everything to customers, and we'll take care of any problems under the warranty." This attitude generally results in high external failure costs, customer ill will, and declining market share and profits.

Distribution of Quality Costs

Studies show that quality costs for some Canadian and U.S. companies range between 10% and 20% of total sales, whereas experts say that these costs should be more in the 2% to 4% range. How does a company reduce its total quality cost? The answer lies in how the quality costs are distributed. Refer to the graph in Exhibit 11–9, which shows total quality costs as a function of the quality of conformance.

The graph shows that when the quality of conformance is low, total quality cost is high and that most of this cost consists of internal and external failure costs. A low quality of conformance means that a high percentage of units are defective and hence the company must incur high failure costs. However, as a company spends more and more on prevention and appraisal, the percentage of defective units drops. This results in lower costs of internal and external failure. Ordinarily, total quality cost drops rapidly as the quality of conformance increases. Thus, a company can reduce its total quality cost by focusing its efforts on prevention and appraisal. The cost savings from reduced defects usually exceed the costs of the additional prevention and appraisal efforts.

The graph in Exhibit 11–9 has been drawn so that the total quality cost is minimized when the quality of conformance is less than 100%. However, some experts contend that the total quality cost is not minimized until the quality of conformance is 100% and there are no defects. Indeed, many companies have found that the total quality costs seem to keep dropping even when the quality of conformance approaches 100% and defect rates are as low as one in a million units. Others argue that eventually total quality cost increases as the quality of conformance increases. However, in most companies, this does not seem to happen until the quality of conformance is very close to 100% and defect rates are very close to zero.

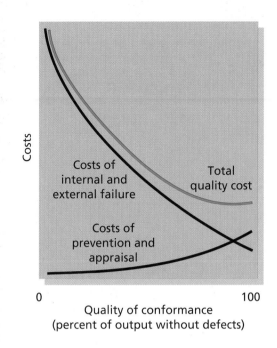

EXHIBIT 11–9   Effect of Quality Costs on Quality of Conformance

As a company's quality program becomes more refined and as its failure costs begin to fall, prevention activities usually become more effective than appraisal activities. Appraisal can only find defects, whereas prevention can eliminate them. The best way to prevent defects from happening is to design processes that reduce the likelihood of defects and to continually monitor processes using statistical process control methods.

Quality Cost Reports

As an initial step in quality improvement programs, companies often construct a *quality cost report* that provides an estimate of the financial consequences of the company's current level of defects. A **quality cost report** details the prevention costs, appraisal costs, and costs of internal and external failures that arise from the company's current level of defective products and services. A typical quality cost report is shown in Exhibit 11–10. For companies that use a balanced scorecard, this type of quality cost report would serve as a supplement to the summary information contained in the scorecard. For example, companies might choose to report only the total cost of quality in the balanced scorecard, or the total for each of the four quality cost categories. The quality cost report would then provide important details about the composition of the summary amounts.

Quality cost report
A report that details prevention costs, appraisal costs, and the costs of internal and external failures.

Several things should be noted from the data in Exhibit 11–10. First, Ventura Company's quality costs are poorly distributed in both years, with most of the costs being traceable to either internal failure or external failure. The external failure costs are particularly high in year 1 in comparison to other costs.

Second, the company increased its spending on prevention and appraisal activities in year 2. As a result, internal failure costs go up in that year (from $2 million in year 1 to $3 million in year 2), but external failure costs drop sharply (from $5.15 million in year 1 to only $2 million in year 2). Because of the increase in appraisal activity in year 2, more defects are being caught inside the company before goods are shipped to customers. This results in more cost for scrap, rework, and so forth, but saves huge amounts in warranty repairs, warranty replacements, and other external failure costs.

Third, as a result of greater emphasis on prevention and appraisal, *total* quality cost has decreased in year 2. As continued emphasis is placed on prevention and appraisal in future years, total quality cost should continue to decrease. Moreover, appraisal costs should also decrease as more effort is put into prevention.

EXHIBIT 11–10   Quality Cost Report

VENTURA COMPANY Quality Cost Report For Years 1 and 2				
	Year 1		Year 2	
	Amount	Percent*	Amount	Percent*
Prevention costs:				
Systems development	$ 270,000	0.54%	$ 400,000	0.80%
Quality training	130,000	0.26%	210,000	0.42%
Supervision of prevention activities	40,000	0.08%	70,000	0.14%
Quality improvement projects	210,000	0.42%	320,000	0.64%
Total prevention cost	650,000	1.30%	1,000,000	2.00%
Appraisal costs:				
Inspection	560,000	1.12%	600,000	1.20%
Reliability testing	420,000	0.84%	580,000	1.16%
Supervision of testing and inspection	80,000	0.16%	120,000	0.24%
Depreciation of test equipment	140,000	0.28%	200,000	0.40%
Total appraisal cost	1,200,000	2.40%	1,500,000	3.00%
Internal failure costs:				
Net cost of scrap	750,000	1.50%	900,000	1.80%
Rework labour and overhead	810,000	1.62%	1,430,000	2.86%
Downtime due to defects in quality	100,000	0.20%	170,000	0.34%
Disposal of defective products	340,000	0.68%	500,000	1.00%
Total internal failure cost	2,000,000	4.00%	3,000,000	6.00%
External failure costs:				
Warranty repairs	900,000	1.80%	400,000	0.80%
Warranty replacements	2,300,000	4.60%	870,000	1.74%
Allowances	630,000	1.26%	130,000	0.26%
Cost of field servicing	1,320,000	2.64%	600,000	1.20%
Total external failure cost	5,150,000	10.30%	2,000,000	4.00%
Total quality cost	$9,000,000	18.00%	$7,500,000	15.00%

*As a percentage of total sales. In each year sales totalled $50,000,000.

Quality Cost Reports in Graphic Form

As a supplement to the quality cost report shown in Exhibit 11–10, companies frequently prepare quality cost information in graphic form. Graphic presentations include pie charts, bar graphs, trend lines, etc. The data for Ventura Company from Exhibit 11–10 are presented in bar graph form in Exhibit 11–11.

The first bar graph in Exhibit 11–11 is scaled in terms of dollars of quality cost, and the second is scaled in terms of quality cost as a percentage of sales. In both graphs, appraisal costs are stacked on top of prevention costs, internal failure costs are stacked on top of the sum of prevention costs plus appraisal costs, and so forth. The percentage figures in the second graph show that total quality cost equals 18% of sales in year 1 and 15% of sales in year 2, the same as reported earlier in Exhibit 11–10.

Data in graphic form help managers to see trends more clearly and to see the magnitude of the various costs in relation to each other. Such graphs are easily prepared using computer graphics packages.

Uses of Quality Cost Information

The information provided by a quality cost report is used by managers in several ways. First, quality cost information helps managers see the financial significance of defects. Managers usually are not aware of the magnitude of their quality costs because they cut across departmental lines and are not normally tracked and accumulated by the cost system.

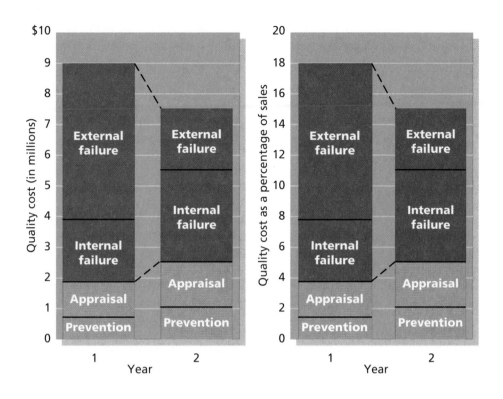

EXHIBIT 11–11   Quality
Costs in Graphic Form

Second, quality cost information helps managers identify the relative importance of the quality problems faced by the firm. For example, the quality cost report may show that scrap is a major quality problem or that the company is incurring significant warranty costs. With this information, managers have a better idea of where to focus efforts.

Third, quality cost information helps managers see whether their quality costs are poorly distributed. In general, quality costs should be distributed more toward prevention and appraisal activities and less toward failures.

Counterbalancing these uses, three limitations of quality cost information should be recognized. First, simply measuring and reporting quality costs will not solve quality problems. Problems can be solved only by taking action. Second, results usually lag behind quality improvement programs. Initially, total quality cost may even increase as quality control systems are designed and installed. Decreases in these costs may not begin to occur until the quality program has been in effect for a year or more. And third, the most important quality cost, lost sales arising from customer ill will, is usually omitted from the quality cost report because it is difficult to estimate.

Typically, during the initial years of a quality improvement program, the benefits of compiling a quality cost report outweigh the costs and limitations of the reports. As managers gain experience in balancing prevention and appraisal activities, the need for quality cost reports often diminishes.

International Aspects of Quality

Many of the tools used in quality management today were developed in Japan after World War II. In statistical process control, Japanese companies borrowed heavily from the work of W. Edwards Deming. However, Japanese companies are largely responsible for quality circles, JIT, the idea that quality is everyone's responsibility, and the emphasis on prevention rather than on inspection.

In the 1980s, quality re-emerged as a pivotal factor in the market. Many companies now find that it is impossible to effectively compete without a very strong quality program in place. This is particularly true of companies that want to compete in the European market.

The International Organization for Standardization (ISO), based in Geneva, Switzerland, has established quality control guidelines known as the **ISO 9000 standards**

ISO 9000 standards
Quality control requirements issued by the International Standards Organization.

(see www.iso.org/iso/home.htm). Many companies and organizations in Europe will buy only from ISO 9000 standard-certified suppliers. This means that the suppliers must demonstrate to a certifying agency that

1. A quality control system is in use, and the system clearly defines an expected level of quality.
2. The system is fully operational and is backed up with detailed documentation of quality control procedures.
3. The intended level of quality is being achieved on a sustained, consistent basis.

The key to receiving certification under the ISO 9000 standards is documentation. It is one thing for a company to say that it has a quality control system in operation, but it is quite different to be able to document the steps in that system. Under ISO 9000, this documentation must be so detailed and precise that if all of the employees in a company were suddenly replaced, the new employees could use the documentation to make the product exactly as it was made by the former employees. Even companies with good quality control systems find that it takes up to two years of painstaking work to develop this detailed documentation. But companies often find that compiling this documentation results in improvements in their quality systems.

The ISO 9000 standards have become an international measure of quality. Although the standards were widely developed to control the quality of goods sold in European countries, they have become widely accepted elsewhere as well. Companies in North America that export to Europe often expect their own suppliers to comply with the ISO 9000 standards, since these exporters must document the quality of the materials going into their products as part of their own ISO 9000 certification.

The ISO has also introduced international standards on other important issues including risk management (ISO 31000) and environmental management (ISO 14000), and is developing standards on social responsibility (ISO 26000). ISO 14000, a set of standards that detail the requirements for an environmental management system (EMS), provides organizations with a tool to identify and control the environmental impact of its activities, products or services; continually improve its environmental performance; and develop an approach to setting environmental performance objectives and goals. Although ISO 14000 does not identify specific levels of environmental performance (e.g., greenhouse gas emissions), it has established a common framework that can be used by organizations and their stakeholders when communicating about environmental issues. An increasing number of organizations are becoming ISO 14000 certified.

Summary

- Segment income statements provide information for evaluating the profitability and performance of divisions, product lines, sales territories, and other company segments. Under the contribution approach, variable costs and fixed costs are clearly distinguished from each other and only those costs that are traceable to a segment are assigned to the segment. **[LO1]**
- A responsibility centre is any segment of an organization whose manager has control over and is accountable for cost, profit, or investments. Responsibility centre managers are evaluated based on what they can control. **[LO2]**
- A cost centre is a business segment whose manager has control over costs only. A profit centre is a segment whose manager controls revenues and costs but not investments in operating assets. An investment centre manager controls profits and investments in operating assets. **[LO2]**
- When products or services are transferred from one division to another, a transfer price must be determined. Three approaches to setting transfer prices are possible: negotiation, cost-based prices, and market price. When negotiating a transfer price, the minimum acceptable price for the selling division should be variable costs plus any opportunity costs incurred on the transaction. The buying division should not be willing to pay the selling division more than the price being charged by an external supplier (i.e., the market price). **[LO3]**

- Return on investment (ROI), residual income, or economic value added (EVA®) can be used to evaluate investment centre performance. **[LO4, LO5]**
- The balanced scorecard consists of an integrated system of performance measures that are derived from and support the company's strategy. It has four main categories of performance measures: financial, customer, internal business processes, and learning and growth. Different companies will have different balanced scorecards because they have different strategies. **[LO6]**
- Examples of internal business process measures include delivery cycle time, manufacturing cycle time, manufacturing cycle efficiency, and quality costs. Quality costs are incurred to prevent defects and also arise when defects do occur. They can be classified into four broad groups: prevention costs, appraisal costs, internal failure costs, and external failure costs. **[LO7]**

Review Problem 1: Segmented Statements

The business staff of the law firm Frampton, Davis & Smythe has constructed the following report, which breaks down the firm's overall results for last month into two main business segments—family law and commercial law:

	Total	Family Law	Commercial Law
Revenues from clients	$1,000,000	$400,000	$600,000
Variable expenses	220,000	100,000	120,000
Contribution margin	780,000	300,000	480,000
Traceable fixed expenses.	670,000	280,000	390,000
Segment margin.	110,000	20,000	90,000
Common fixed expenses	60,000	24,000	36,000
Operating income.	$ 50,000	$ (4,000)	$ 54,000

However, this report is not quite correct. The common fixed expenses such as the managing partner's salary, general administrative expenses, and general firm advertising have been allocated to the two segments based on revenues from clients.

Required:
1. Redo the segment report, eliminating the allocation of common fixed expenses. Would the firm be better off financially if the family law segment was dropped? (*Note*: Many of the firm's commercial law clients also use the firm for their family law requirements, such as drawing up wills.)
2. The firm's advertising agency has proposed an ad campaign targeted at boosting the revenues of the family law segment. The ad campaign would cost $20,000, and the advertising agency claims that it would increase family law revenues by $100,000. The managing partner of Frampton, Davis & Smythe believes this increase in business could be accommodated without any increase in fixed expenses. What effect would this ad campaign have on the family law segment margin and on the firm's overall operating income?

Solution to Review Problem 1

1. The corrected segmented income statement appears below:

	Total	Family Law	Commercial Law
Revenues from clients	$1,000,000	$400,000	$600,000
Variable expenses	220,000	100,000	120,000
Contribution margin	780,000	300,000	480,000
Traceable fixed expenses.	670,000	280,000	390,000
Segment margin.	110,000	$ 20,000	$ 90,000
Common fixed expenses	60,000		
Operating income.	$ 50,000		

No, the firm would not be financially better off if the family law practice was dropped. The family law segment is covering all of its own costs and is contributing $20,000 per month to covering the common fixed expenses of the firm. While the segment margin for family law is much lower than for commercial law, it is still profitable. Moreover, family law may be a service that the firm must provide to its commercial clients in order to remain competitive.

2. The ad campaign would increase the family law segment margin by $55,000, as follows:

Increased revenues from clients	$100,000
Family law contribution margin ratio ($300,000 ÷ $400,000)	× 75%
Incremental contribution margin	$ 75,000
Less cost of the ad campaign	20,000
Increased segment margin.	$ 55,000

Since there would be no increase in fixed expenses (including common fixed expenses), the increase in overall operating income is also $55,000.

Review Problem 2: Transfer Pricing

Situation A

Collyer Products, Inc., has a Valve Division that manufactures and sells a standard valve as follows:

Capacity in units.	100,000
Selling price to outside customers on	
the intermediate market	$15
Variable costs per unit	8
Fixed costs per unit (based on capacity	5

The company has a Pump Division that could use this valve in the manufacture of one of its pumps. The Pump Division is currently purchasing 10,000 valves per year from an overseas supplier at a cost of $14 per valve.

Required:

1. Assume that the Valve Division has ample idle capacity to handle all of the Pump Division's needs. What is the acceptable range, if any, for the transfer price between the two divisions?
2. Assume that the Valve Division is selling all that it can produce to outside customers on the intermediate market. What is the acceptable range, if any, for the transfer price between the two divisions?
3. Assume again that the Valve Division is selling all that it can produce to outside customers on the intermediate market. Also assume that $2 in variable expenses can be avoided on transfers within the company, due to reduced selling costs. What is the acceptable range, if any, for the transfer price between the two divisions?

Solution to Situation A

1. Since the Valve Division has idle capacity, it does not have to give up any outside sales to take on the Pump Division's business. Applying the formula for the lowest acceptable transfer price from the viewpoint of the selling division, we get

$$\text{Transfer price} \geq \text{Variable cost per unit} + \frac{\text{Total contribution margin on lost sales}}{\text{Number of units transferred}}$$

$$\text{Transfer price} \geq \$8 + \frac{\$0}{10,000} = \$8$$

The Pump Division would be unwilling to pay more than $14, the price it is currently paying an outside supplier for its valves. Therefore, the transfer price must fall within the range:

$$\$8 \leq \text{Transfer price} \leq \$14$$

2. Since the Valve Division is selling all that it can produce on the intermediate market, it would have to give up some of these outside sales to take on the Pump Division's business. Thus, the Valve Division has an opportunity cost that is the total contribution margin on lost sales:

$$\text{Transfer price} \geq \text{Variable cost per unit} + \frac{\text{Total contribution margin on lost sales}}{\text{Number of units transferred}}$$

$$\text{Transfer price} \geq \$8 + \frac{(\$15 - \$8) \times 10{,}000}{10{,}000} = \$8 + \$7 = \$15$$

Since the Pump Division can purchase valves from an outside supplier at only $14 per unit, no transfers will be made between the two divisions.

3. Applying the formula for the lowest acceptable price from the viewpoint of the selling division, we get:

$$\text{Transfer price} \geq \text{Variable cost per unit} + \frac{\text{Total contribution margin on lost sales}}{\text{Number of units transferred}}$$

$$\text{Transfer price} \geq (\$8 - \$2) + \frac{(\$15 - \$8) \times 10{,}000}{10{,}000} = \$6 + \$7 = \$13$$

In this case, the transfer price must fall within the range:

$$\$13 \leq \text{Transfer price} \leq \$14$$

Situation B

Referring to the original data in situation A above, assume the Pump Division needs 20,000 special high-pressure valves per year. The Valve Division's variable costs to manufacture and ship the special valve would be $10 per unit. To produce these special valves, the Valve Division would have to reduce its production and sales of regular valves from 100,000 units per year to 70,000 units per year.

Required:
As far as the Valve Division is concerned, what is the lowest acceptable transfer price?

Solution to Situation B

To produce the 20,000 special valves, the Valve Division will have to give up sales to outside customers of 30,000 regular valves. Applying the formula for the lowest acceptable price from the viewpoint of the selling division, we get

$$\text{Transfer price} \geq \text{Variable cost per unit} + \frac{\text{Total contribution margin on lost sales}}{\text{Number of units transferred}}$$

$$\text{Transfer price} \geq \$10 + \frac{(\$15 - \$8) \times 30{,}000}{20{,}000} = \$10 + \$10.50 = \$20.50$$

Review Problem 3: Return on Investment (ROI) and Residual Income

Selected operating data for two divisions of Outback Brewing Ltd. are given below:

	Queensland	New South Wales
Sales.	$4,000,000	$7,000,000
Average total operating assets.	$2,000,000	$2,000,000
Operating income.	$360,000	$420,000
Property, plant, and equipment (net)	$950,000	$800,000

Required:
1. Compute the rate of return for each division using the return on investment (ROI) formula stated in terms of margin and turnover.
2. Compute residual income for each division assuming the required rate of return is 15%.

Solution to Review Problem 3

1. ROI computations:

    ROI = Margin × Turnover

    $$= \frac{\text{Operating income}}{\text{Sales}} \times \frac{\text{Sales}}{\text{Average operating assets}}$$

    Queensland Division:

    $$\text{ROI} = \frac{\$360,000}{\$4,000,000} \times \frac{\$4,000,000}{\$2,000,000}$$
    $$= 9\% \times 2 = 18\%$$

    New South Wales Division:

    $$\text{ROI} = \frac{\$420,000}{\$7,000,000} \times \frac{\$7,000,000}{\$2,000,000}$$
    $$= 6\% \times 3.5 = 21\%$$

2. Residual income for each division is calculated as follows:

    Queensland Division:
    $360,000 − ($2,000,000 × 15%) = $60,000

    New South Wales Division:
    $420,000 − ($2,000,000 × 15%) = $120,000

Glossary

Review key terms and definitions on Connect.

Questions

11–1   What is meant by the term *decentralization*?
11–2   What is a segment of an organization? Give several examples of segments.
11–3   What costs are assigned to a segment under the contribution approach?
11–4   Distinguish between a traceable cost and a common cost. Give several examples of each.
11–5   Explain how the segment margin differs from the contribution margin.
11–6   Why aren't common costs allocated to segments under the contribution approach?
11–7   How is it possible for a cost that is traceable to a segment to become a common cost if the segment is divided into further segments?
11–8   Identify three inappropriate methods for assigning traceable costs among segments.
11–9   Identify three types of responsibility centres and describe how performance is measured for each one.
11–10 From the standpoint of a selling division that has idle capacity, what is the minimum acceptable transfer price for an item?
11–11 What are the advantages and disadvantages of negotiated transfer prices?
11–12 If a market price for a product can be determined, why is it usually the best transfer price?
11–13 What is meant by the terms *margin* and *turnover*?
11–14 What are the three approaches to improving return on investment (ROI)?
11–15 What is meant by the term *residual income*?
11–16 In what way can the use of ROI for investment centres lead to bad decisions? How does the residual income approach overcome this problem?

11–17 Should residual income be used to compare divisions of different sizes? Why or why not?

11–18 What are the four groups of performance measures typically included in a balanced scorecard?

11–19 Why do the measures used in a balanced scorecard differ from company to company?

11–20 Why does the balanced scorecard include financial performance measures as well as measures of non-financial performance?

11–21 Quality cost reports typically break down types of quality costs into four broad groups. What are these four groups and how do they differ?

11–22 In their efforts to reduce the total cost of quality, should companies generally focus on decreasing prevention and appraisal costs?

connect Exercises

EXERCISE 11–1 Basic Segmented Income Statement [LO1]

Bastion Inc. produces and sells recordable CD and DVD packs. Revenue and cost information relating to the products follow:

	Product	
	CD	**DVD**
Selling price per pack.	$8.00	$20.00
Variable expenses per pack	$3.20	$10.50
Traceable fixed expenses per year.	$138,000	$45,000

Common fixed expenses in the company total $105,000 annually. Last year the company produced and sold 37,500 CD packs and 18,000 DVD packs.

Required:
Prepare a contribution-format income statement for the year, segmented by product lines.

EXERCISE 11–2 Segmented Income Statement [LO1]

Bovine Company, a wholesale distributor of umbrellas, has been experiencing losses for some time, as shown by its most recent monthly contribution format income statement below:

Sales	$2,000,000
Variable expenses.	792,000
Contribution margin	1,208,000
Fixed expenses	1,305,000
Operating loss.	$ (97,000)

In an effort to isolate the problem, the president has asked for an income statement segmented by geographic market. Accordingly, the Accounting Department has developed the following:

	Geographic Market		
	South	**Central**	**North**
Sales	$600,000	$800,000	$600,000
Variable expenses as a percentage			
of sales.	52%	30%	40%
Traceable fixed expenses	$320,000	$530,000	$300,000

Required:
1. Prepare a contribution-format income statement segmented by geographic market, as requested by the president.
2. The company's sales manager believes that sales in the Central geographic market could be increased by 15% if monthly advertising was increased by $25,000. Would you recommend the increased advertising? Show computations to support your answer.

EXERCISE 11–3 Working with a Segmented Income Statement [LO1]
Middleton Associates is a consulting firm that specializes in information systems for construction and landscaping companies. The firm has two offices—one in Toronto and one in Vancouver. The firm classifies the direct costs of consulting jobs as variable costs. A segmented contribution-format income statement for the company's most recent year is given below.

| | Total Company | | Office | | | |
			Toronto		Vancouver	
Sales	$750,000	100.0%	$150,000	100%	$600,000	100%
Variable expenses	405,000	54.0	45,000	30	360,000	60
Contribution margin...........	345,000	46.0	105,000	70	240,000	40
Traceable fixed expenses	168,000	22.4	78,000	52	90,000	15
Office segment margin	177,000	23.6	$ 27,000	18%	$150,000	25%
Common fixed expenses						
not traceable to offices	120,000	16.0				
Operating income	$ 57,000	7.6%				

Required:
1. By how much would the company's operating income increase if Vancouver increased its sales by $75,000 per year? Assume no change in cost behaviour patterns.
2. Refer to the original data. Assume that sales in Toronto increase by $50,000 next year and that sales in Vancouver remain unchanged. Assume no change in fixed costs.
   a. Prepare a new segmented income statement for the company using the above format. Show both amounts and percentages.
   b. Observe from the income statement you have prepared that the CM ratio for Toronto has remained unchanged at 70% (the same as in the above data) but that the segment margin ratio has changed. How do you explain the change in the segment margin ratio?

EXERCISE 11–4 Working with a Segmented Income Statement [LO1]
Refer to the data in Exercise 11–3. Assume that Vancouver's sales by major market are as follows:

| | Vancouver | | Market | | | |
			Construction Clients		Landscaping Clients	
Sales	$600,000	100.0%	$400,000	100%	$200,000	100%
Variable expenses	360,000	60	260,000	65	100,000	50
Contribution margin........	240,000	40	140,000	35	100,000	50
Traceable fixed expenses ...	72,000	12	20,000	5	52,000	26
Market segment margin.....	168,000	28	$120,000	30%	$ 48,000	24%
Common fixed expenses						
not traceable to offices ...	18,000	3				
Office segment margin	$150,000	25%				

The company would like to initiate an intensive advertising campaign in one of the two markets during the next month. The campaign would cost $8,000. Marketing studies indicate that such a campaign would increase sales in the construction market by $70,000 or increase sales in the landscaping market by $60,000.

Required:
1. In which of the markets would you recommend that the company focus its advertising campaign? Show computations to support your answer.
2. In Exercise 11–3, Vancouver shows $90,000 in traceable fixed expenses. What happened to the $90,000 in this exercise?

EXERCISE 11–5 Transfer Pricing Basics [LO3]
Gerbig Company's Electrical Division produces a high-quality transformer. Sales and cost data on
the transformer follow:

Selling price per unit on the outside market............	$40
Variable costs per unit	$21
Fixed costs per unit (based on capacity)	$9
Capacity in units.................................	60,000

Gerbig Company has a Motor Division that would like to begin purchasing this transformer from
the Electrical Division. The Motor Division is currently purchasing 10,000 transformers each year
from another company at a cost of $38 per transformer. Gerbig Company evaluates its division
managers on the basis of divisional profits.

Required:
1. Assume that the Electrical Division is now selling only 50,000 transformers each year to outside customers.
   a. From the standpoint of the Electrical Division, what is the lowest acceptable transfer price
      for transformers sold to the Motor Division?
   b. From the standpoint of the Motor Division, what is the highest acceptable transfer price for
      transformers acquired from the Electrical Division?
   c. If left free to negotiate without interference, would you expect the division managers to
      voluntarily agree to the transfer of 10,000 transformers from the Electrical Division to the
      Motor Division? Why or why not?
   d. From the standpoint of the entire company, should a transfer take place? Why or why not?
2. Assume that the Electrical Division is now selling to outside customers all of the transformers
   it can produce.
   a. From the standpoint of the Electrical Division, what is the lowest acceptable transfer price
      for transformers sold to the Motor Division?
   b. From the standpoint of the Motor Division, what is the highest acceptable transfer price for
      transformers acquired from the Electrical Division?
   c. If left free to negotiate without interference, would you expect the division managers to
      voluntarily agree to the transfer of 10,000 transformers from the Electrical Division to the
      Motor Division? Why or why not?
   d. From the standpoint of the entire company, should a transfer take place? Why or why not?

EXERCISE 11–6 Transfer Pricing Situations [LO3]
In each of the cases below, assume that Division X has a product that can be sold either to outside
customers or to Division Y of the same company for use in its production process. The managers of
the divisions are evaluated based on their divisional profits.

	Case	
	A	**B**
Division X:		
Capacity in units	100,000	100,000
Number of units being sold to outside customers.......	100,000	80,000
Selling price per unit to outside customers............	$50	$35
Variable costs per unit...........................	$30	$20
Fixed costs per unit (based on capacity).............	$8	$6
Division Y:		
Number of units needed for production	20,000	20,000
Purchase price per unit now being paid to an		
outside supplier	$47	$34

Required:
1. Refer to the data in Case A above. Assume that $2 per unit in variable selling costs can be
   avoided on intracompany sales. If the managers are free to negotiate and make decisions on
   their own, will a transfer take place? If so, within what range will the transfer price fall?
   Explain.

2. Refer to the data in Case B above. In this case there will be no reduction in variable selling costs on intracompany sales. If the managers are free to negotiate and make decisions on their own, will a transfer take place? If so, within what range will the transfer price fall? Explain.

EXERCISE 11–7 Transfer Pricing from the Viewpoint of the Entire Company [LO3]

Division A manufactures components for plasma TVs. The components can be sold either to Division B of the same company or to outside customers. Last year, the following activity was recorded in Division A:

Selling price per component.	$525
Variable cost per component	$390
Number of components:	
Produced during the year	20,000
Sold to outside customers	16,000
Sold to Division B	4,000

Sales to Division B were at the same price as sales to outside customers. The components purchased by Division B were used in a TV set manufactured by that division. Division B incurred $900 in additional variable cost per TV and then sold the TVs for $1,800 each.

Required:

1. Prepare income statements for last year for Division A, Division B, and the company as a whole.
2. Assume that Division A's manufacturing capacity is 20,000 components per year. Next year, Division B wants to purchase 5,000 components from Division A, rather than only 4,000 components as it did last year. (Components of this type are not available from outside sources.) From the standpoint of the company as a whole, should Division A sell the 1,000 additional components to Division B, or should it continue to sell them to outside customers? Explain.

EXERCISE 11–8 Compute the Return on Investment (ROI) [LO4]

Tamarind Services Company, a division of a major oil company, provides various services to the operators of an oil field in northern Alberta. Data concerning the most recent year are as follow:

Sales	$12,000,000
Operating income	$3,600,000
Average operating assets	$24,000,000

Required:

1. Compute the margin for Tamarind Services Company.
2. Compute the turnover for Tamarind Services Company.
3. Compute the return on investment (ROI) for Tamarind Services Company.

EXERCISE 11–9 Residual Income [LO5]

British firm Midlands Design Ltd. specializes in providing design services to residential developers. Last year the company had operating income of £600,000 on sales of £2,400,000. The company's average operating assets for the year were £4,400,000 and its minimum required rate of return was 9%.

Required:

Compute the company's residual income for the year.

EXERCISE 11–10 Computing and Interpreting Return on Investment (ROI) [LO4]

Selected operating data on the two divisions of Prism Company are given below:

	Division	
	Eastern	**Western**
Sales	$800,000	$1,850,000
Average operating assets	$300,000	$400,000
Operating income.	$70,000	$115,000
Property, plant, and equipment	$125,000	$200,000

Required:
1. Compute the rate of return for each division using the return on investment (ROI) formula stated in terms of margin and turnover.
2. Which divisional manager seems to be doing the better job? Why?

EXERCISE 11–11 Contrasting Return on Investment (ROI) and Residual Income [LO4, LO5]

Ferris Ltd. of Australia has two divisions, one in Perth and one in Darwin. Selected data on the two divisions follow:

	Division	
	Perth	Darwin
Sales	$9,000,000	$20,000,000
Operating income....................	$630,000	$1,800,000
Average operating assets	$3,000,000	$10,000,000

Required:
1. Compute the return on investment (ROI) for each division.
2. Assume that the company evaluates performance using residual income and that the minimum required rate of return for any division is 16%. Compute the residual income for each division.
3. Is the Darwin Division's greater residual income an indication that it is better managed? Explain.

EXERCISE 11–12 Return on Investment (ROI) and Residual Income Relationships [LO4, LO5]

A family friend has asked your help in analyzing the operations of three companies operating in the same service sector industry. Supply the missing data in the following table:

	Company		
	A	B	C
Sales	$400,000	$750,000	$600,000
Operating income	$?	$45,000	$?
Average operating assets	$160,000	?	$150,000
Return on investment (ROI)..........	20%	18%	?
Minimum required rate of return:			
Percentage	15%	?	12%
Dollar amount	$?	$50,000	$?
Residual income	$?	$?	$ 6,000

EXERCISE 11–13 Return on Investment (ROI) Relationships [LO4]

Provide the missing data in the following table:

	Division		
	Fab	Consulting	IT
Sales	$800,000	$?	$?
Operating income	$72,000	$?	$40,000
Average operating assets	$?	$130,000	$?
Margin	?	4%	8%
Turnover	?	5	?
Return on investment (ROI)..........	18%	?	20%

EXERCISE 11–14 Effects of Changes in Profits and Assets on Return on Investment (ROI) [LO4]

FitPlus is a regional chain of health clubs. Each club's manager has authority to make investments as needed and is evaluated based largely on return on investment (ROI). FitPlus Club 52 reported the following results for the past year:

Sales..................................	$500,000
Operating income......................	$15,000
Average operating assets................	$80,000

Required:

The following questions are to be considered independently. Carry out all computations to two decimal places.

1. Compute the club's return on investment (ROI).
2. Assume that the manager of the club is able to increase sales by $80,000 and that as a result operating income increases by $6,000. Further assume that this is possible without any increase in operating assets. What would be the club's return on investment (ROI)?
3. Assume that the manager of the club is able to reduce expenses by $3,200 without any change in sales or operating assets. What would be the club's return on investment (ROI)?
4. Assume that the manager of the club is able to reduce operating assets by $20,000 without any change in sales or operating income. What would be the club's return on investment (ROI)?

EXERCISE 11–15 Evaluating New Investments Using Return on Investment (ROI) and Residual Income [LO4, LO5]

Three divisions of Watcore Inc. report the following sales and operating data:

	Division A	Division B	Division C
Sales.	$6,000,000	$10,000,000	$8,000,000
Average operating assets	$1,500,000	$5,000,000	$2,000,000
Operating income	$300,000	$900,000	$180,000
Minimum required rate of return	15%	18%	12%

Required:

1. Compute the return on investment (ROI) for each division, using the formula stated in terms of margin and turnover.
2. Compute the residual income for each division.
3. Assume that each division is presented with an investment opportunity that would yield a rate of return of 17%.
    a. If performance is being measured by ROI, which division or divisions will probably accept the opportunity? Reject it? Why?
    b. If performance is being measured by residual income, which division or divisions will probably accept the opportunity? Reject it? Why?

EXERCISE 11–16 Classification of Quality Costs [LO7]

Below are listed a number of activities that are part of a company's quality control system:

a. Repairs of goods still under warranty.	i. Recalls of defective products.
b. Customer returns due to defects.	j. Training quality engineers.
c. Statistical process control.	k. Re-entering data due to typing errors.
d. Disposal of spoiled goods.	l. Inspecting materials received from suppliers.
e. Maintaining testing equipment.	m. Audits of the quality system.
f. Inspecting finished goods.	n. Supervision of testing personnel.
g. Downtime caused by quality problems.	o. Rework labour.
h. Debugging errors in software.	

Required:

1. Classify the costs associated with each of these activities into one of the following categories: prevention cost, appraisal cost, internal failure cost, or external failure cost.
2. Which of the four types of costs listed in (1) above are incurred to keep poor quality of conformance from occurring? Which of the four types of costs are incurred because poor quality of conformance has occurred?

EXERCISE 11–17 Measures of Internal Business Process Performance [LO6]

Welsh firm Cardiff Inc. is interested in cutting the amount of time between when a customer places an order and when the order is completed. For the first quarter of the year, the following data were reported:

Inspection time	0.3 days
Process time	3.2 days
Wait time	12.0 days
Queue time	1.0 days
Move time	0.5 days

Required:
1. Compute the throughput time.
2. Compute the manufacturing cycle efficiency (MCE) for the quarter.
3. What percentage of the throughput time was spent on non-value-added activities?
4. Compute the delivery cycle time.
5. If by using lean production all queue time can be eliminated in production, what will be the new MCE?

EXERCISE 11–18 Measures of Internal Business Process Performance [LO6]

MacIntyre Fabrications Ltd. recently started a continuous improvement campaign in conjunction with a move toward lean production. Management has developed new performance measures as part of this campaign. The following operating data have been gathered over the last four months:

	Month			
	1	2	3	4
Throughput time.	?	?	?	?
Manufacturing cycle efficiency.	?	?	?	?
Delivery cycle time	?	?	?	?
Percentage of on-time deliveries	72%	73%	78%	85%
Total sales (units)	10,620	10,570	10,450	10,390

Management would like to know the company's throughput time, manufacturing cycle efficiency, and delivery cycle time. The data to compute these measures have been gathered and appear below:

	Month			
	1	2	3	4
Move time per unit, in days.	0.5	0.5	0.6	0.5
Process time per unit, in days	0.4	0.5	0.5	0.6
Wait time per order before start of				
production, in days	8.6	7.7	6.3	5.7
Queue time per unit, in days.	3.6	3.6	2.6	1.7
Inspection time per unit, in days.	0.7	0.7	0.4	0.3

Required:
1. For each month, compute the following:
   a. The throughput time.
   b. The manufacturing cycle efficiency (MCE).
   c. The delivery cycle time.
2. Using the performance measures given in the problem and those you computed in (1) above, identify whether the trend over the four months is generally favourable, generally unfavourable, or mixed. What areas apparently require improvement and how might they be improved?
3. Refer to the move time, process time, and so forth, given above for month 4.
   a. Assume that in month 5 the move time, process time, and so forth are the same as for month 4, except that through the implementation of lean production, the company is able to completely eliminate the queue time during production. Compute the new throughput time and MCE.
   b. Assume that in month 6 the move time, process time, and so forth are the same as for month 4, except that the company is able to completely eliminate both the queue time during production and the inspection time. Compute the new throughput time and MCE.

connect Problems

PROBLEM 11–19 Restructuring a Segmented Income Statement [LO1]
Brabant NV of the Netherlands is a wholesale distributor of Dutch cheeses that it sells throughout the European Community. Unfortunately, the company's profits have been declining, which has caused considerable concern. To help understand the condition of the company, the managing director of

the company has requested that the monthly income statement be segmented by sales territory. Accordingly, the company's accounting department has prepared the following statement for March, the more recent month. (The Dutch currency is the euro, which is designated by €.)

	Sales Territory		
	Southern Europe	Middle Europe	Northern Europe
Sales.	€300,000	€800,000	€ 700,000
Territorial expenses (traceable):			
Cost of goods sold.	93,000	240,000	315,000
Salaries.	54,000	56,000	112,000
Insurance.	9,000	16,000	14,000
Advertising.	105,000	240,000	245,000
Depreciation.	21,000	32,000	28,000
Shipping.	15,000	32,000	42,000
Total territorial expenses.	297,000	616,000	756,000
Territorial income (loss) before			
corporate expenses.	3,000	184,000	(56,000)
Corporate expenses:			
Advertising (general).	15,000	40,000	35,000
General administrative.	20,000	20,000	20,000
Total corporate expenses.	35,000	60,000	55,000
Operating income (loss).	€ (32,000)	€124,000	€(111,000)

Cost of goods sold and shipping expenses are both variable; other costs are all fixed. Brabant NV purchases cheeses at auction and from farmers' cooperatives, and it distributes them in the three territories shown in the statement above. Each of the three sales territories has its own manager and sales staff. The cheeses vary widely in profitability; some have a high margin and some have a low margin. (Certain cheeses, after having been aged for long periods, are the most expensive and carry the highest margins.)

Required:
1. List any disadvantages or weaknesses of the statement format illustrated above.
2. Explain the basis that is apparently being used to allocate the corporate expenses to the territories. Do you agree with these allocations? Explain.
3. Prepare a new segmented contribution-format income statement for May. Show a Total column as well as data for each territory. Include percentages on your statement for all columns. Carry percentages to one decimal place.
4. Analyze the statement that you prepared in (3) above. What points that might help to improve the company's performance would you bring to management's attention?

PROBLEM 11–20 Segment Reporting and Decision Making [LO1]
Creaston Limited's most recent monthly contribution-format income statement is given below:

CREASTON LIMITED Income Statement for the Month Ended May 31		
Sales.	$900,000	100.0%
Variable expenses.	408,000	45.3
Contribution margin.	492,000	54.7
Fixed expenses.	465,000	51.7
Operating income.	$ 27,000	3.0%

Management is disappointed with the company's performance and is wondering what can be done to improve profits. By examining sales and cost records, you have determined the following:
a.   The company is divided into two sales territories—Central and Eastern. Central Territory recorded $400,000 in sales and $208,000 in variable expenses during May. The remaining

sales and variable expenses were recorded in Eastern Territory. Fixed expenses of $160,000 and $130,000 are traceable to Central and Eastern Territories, respectively. The rest of the fixed expenses are common to the two territories.

b. The company is the exclusive distributor for two products—Kiks and Dows. Sales of Kiks and Dows totalled $100,000 and $300,000, respectively, in Central Territory during May. Variable expenses are 25% of the selling price for Kiks and 61% for Dows. Cost records show that $60,000 of Central Territory's fixed expenses are traceable to Kiks and $54,000 to Dows, with the remainder common to the two products.

Required:
1. Prepare contribution-format segmented income statements, first showing the total company broken down between sales territories and then showing Central Territory broken down by product line. Show both Amount and Percentage columns for the company in total and for each segment. Round percentage computations to one decimal place.
2. Look at the statement you have prepared showing the total company segmented by sales territory. What points revealed by this statement should be brought to management's attention?
3. Look at the statement you have prepared showing Central Territory segmented by-product lines. What points revealed by this statement should be brought to management's attention?

PROBLEM 11–21 Basic Segmented Statement; Activity-Based Cost Assignment [LO1]

Vega Foods, Inc., recently purchased a small mill that it intends to operate as one of its subsidiaries. The newly acquired mill has three products that it offers for sale—wheat cereal, pancake mix, and flour. Each product sells for $10 per package. Materials, labour, and other variable production costs are $3.00 per bag of wheat cereal, $4.20 per bag of pancake mix, and $1.80 per bag of flour. Sales commissions are 10% of sales for any product. All other costs are fixed.

The mill's income statement for the most recent month is given below:

		Product Line		
	Total Company	Wheat Cereal	Pancake Mix	Flour
Sales	$600,000	$200,000	$300,000	$100,000
Expenses:				
Materials, labour, and other.	204,000	60,000	126,000	18,000
Sales commissions	60,000	20,000	30,000	10,000
Advertising	123,000	48,000	60,000	15,000
Salaries.	66,000	34,000	21,000	11,000
Equipment depreciation.	30,000	10,000	15,000	5,000
Warehouse rent	12,000	4,000	6,000	2,000
General administration.	90,000	30,000	30,000	30,000
Total expenses	585,000	206,000	288,000	91,000
Operating income (loss).	$ 15,000	$ (6,000)	$ 12,000	$ 9,000

The following additional information about the company is available:
a. The same equipment is used to mill and package all three products. In the above income statement, equipment depreciation has been allocated on the basis of sales dollars. An analysis of equipment usage indicates that it is used 40% of the time to make wheat cereal, 50% of the time to make pancake mix, and 10% of the time to make flour.
b. All three products are stored in the same warehouse. In the above income statement, the warehouse rent has been allocated on the basis of sales dollars. The warehouse contains 24,000 square metres of space, of which 8,000 square metres are used for wheat cereal, 14,000 square metres are used for pancake mix, and 2,000 square metres are used for flour. The warehouse space costs the company $0.50 per square metre to rent.
c. The general administration costs relate to the administration of the company as a whole. In the above income statement, these costs have been divided equally among the three product lines.
d. All other costs are traceable to the product lines.
Vega Foods' management is anxious to improve the mill's 2.5% margin on sales.

4.   Refer to Case 4. Assume that Division B wants Division A to provide it with 60,000 units of a *different* product from the one that Division A is now producing. The new product would require $25 per unit in variable costs and would require that Division A cut back production of its present product by 30,000 units annually. What is the lowest acceptable transfer price from Division A's perspective?

PROBLEM 11–24 Transfer Pricing with an Outside Market [LO3]

Wallen Products Inc. has just purchased a small company that specializes in the manufacture of electronic tuners that are used as a component part of TV sets. Wallen Products is a decentralized company, and it will treat the newly acquired company as an autonomous division with full profit responsibility. The new division, called the Tuner Division, has the following revenue and costs associated with each tuner that it manufactures and sells:

Selling price		$20
Expenses:		
Variable	$11	
Fixed (based on a capacity of		
100,000 tuners per year)	6	17
Operating income		$ 3

Wallen Products also has an Assembly Division that assembles TV sets. This division is currently purchasing 30,000 tuners per year from an overseas supplier at a cost of $20 per tuner, less a 10% purchase discount. The president of Wallen Products is anxious to have the Assembly Division begin purchasing its tuners from the newly acquired Tuner Division in order to "keep the profits within the corporate family."

Required:

For (1) and (2) below, assume that the Tuner Division can sell all of its output to outside TV manufacturers at the normal $20 price.

1.   Are the managers of the Tuner and Assembly Divisions likely to voluntarily agree to a transfer price for 30,000 tuners each year? Why or why not?
2.   If the Tuner Division meets the price that the Assembly Division is currently paying to its overseas supplier and sells 30,000 tuners to the Assembly Division each year, what will be the effect on the profits of the Tuner Division, the Assembly Division, and the company as a whole?

For (3) through (6) below, assume that the Tuner Division is currently selling only 60,000 tuners each year to outside TV manufacturers at the stated $20 price.

3.   Are the managers of the Tuner and Assembly Divisions likely to voluntarily agree to a transfer price for 30,000 tuners each year? Why or why not?
4.   Suppose that the Assembly Division's overseas supplier drops its price (net of the purchase discount) to only $16 per tuner. Should the Tuner Division meet this price? Explain. If the Tuner Division does *not* meet this price, what will be the effect on the profits of the company as a whole?
5.   Refer to (4) above. If the Tuner Division refuses to meet the $16 price, should the Assembly Division be required to purchase from the Tuner Division at a higher price for the good of the company as a whole? Explain.
6.   Refer to (4) above. Assume that due to inflexible management policies, the Assembly Division is required to purchase 30,000 tuners each year from the Tuner Division at $20 per tuner. What will be the effect on the profits of the company as a whole?

PROBLEM 11–25 Comparison of Performance Using Return on Investment (ROI) [LO4]

The following are comparative data submitted by three companies in the same industry:

	Company		
	A	**B**	**C**
Sales	$5,000,000	$1,500,000	$?
Operating income	$700,000	$210,000	$?
Average operating assets	$2,500,000	?	$3,000,000
Margin	?	?	3.5%
Turnover	?	?	2
Return on investment (ROI)	?	7%	?

Required:
1. What advantages are there to breaking down the ROI computation into two separate elements, margin and turnover?
2. Fill in the missing information above, and comment on the relative performance of the three companies in as much detail as the data permit. Make *specific recommendations* about how to improve the ROI.

(Adapted from National Association of Accountants, Research Report No. 35, p. 34)

PROBLEM 11–26 Return on Investment (ROI) and Residual Income [LO4, LO5]

Faced with headquarters' desire to add a new product line, Stefan Grenier, manager of Bilti Products' East Division, felt that he had to see the numbers before he made a move. His division's return on investment (ROI) had led the company for three years, and he don't want any letdown."

Bilti Products is a decentralized wholesaler with four autonomous divisions. The divisions are evaluated on the basis of ROI, with year-end bonuses given to divisional managers who have the highest ROI. Operating results for the company's East Division for last year are given below:

Sales..............................	$21,000,000
Variable expenses	13,400,000
Contribution margin	7,600,000
Fixed expenses....................	5,920,000
Operating income..................	$ 1,680,000
Divisional operating assets..........	$ 5,250,000

The company had an overall ROI of 18% last year (considering all divisions). The new product line that headquarters wants Grenier's East Division to add would require an investment of $3,000,000. The cost and revenue characteristics of the new product line per year would be as follows:

Sales..............................	$9,000,000
Variable expenses	65% of sales
Fixed expenses....................	$2,520,000

Required:
1. Compute the East Division's ROI for last year; also compute the ROI as it would appear if the new product line is added.
2. If you were in Grenier's position, would you accept or reject the new product line? Explain.
3. Why do you suppose headquarters is anxious for the East Division to add the new product line?
4. Suppose that the company's minimum required rate of return on operating assets is 15% and that performance is evaluated using residual income.
   a. Compute East Division's residual income for last year; also compute the residual income as it would appear if the new product line is added.
   b. Under these circumstances, if you were in Grenier's position, would you accept or reject the new product line? Explain.

PROBLEM 11–27 Return on Investment (ROI) and Residual Income [LO4, LO5]

Financial data for Bridger, Inc., for last year are as follows:

BRIDGER, INC. Balance Sheet		
	Ending Balance	Beginning Balance
Assets		
Cash.....................................	$ 150,000	$ 145,000
Accounts receivable........................	500,000	360,000
Inventory..................................	510,000	590,000
Plant and equipment, net....................	840,000	865,000
Investment in Brier Company................	450,000	420,000
Land (undeveloped)	270,000	270,000
Total assets	$2,720,000	$2,650,000
Liabilities and shareholders' equity		
Accounts payable..........................	$ 340,000	$ 380,000
Long-term debt	1,000,000	1,000,000
Shareholders' equity	1,380,000	1,270,000
Total liabilities and shareholders' equity	$2,720,000	$2,650,000

The costs, revenues, and operating income associated with the Consumer Products Division's HD-DVD player are given below:

Selling price per player		$580
Variable costs per player:		
Cost of the control board	$190	
Variable cost of other parts	230	
Total variable costs		420
Contribution margin		160
Fixed costs per player		85*
Operating income per player		$ 75

*Based on a capacity of 200,000 HD-DVD players per year.

The Consumer Products Division has an order from an overseas distributor for 5,000 HD-DVD players. The distributor wants to pay only $400 per DVD player.

Required:
1. Assume that the Consumer Products Division has enough idle capacity to fill the 5,000-unit order. Is the division likely to accept the $400 price or to reject it? Explain.
2. Assume that both the Board Division and the Consumer Products Division have idle capacity. Under these conditions, would rejecting the $400 price be advantageous for the company as a whole, or would it result in the loss of potential profits? Show computations to support your answer.
3. Assume that the Board Division is operating at capacity and could sell all of its control boards to outside manufacturers of HD-DVD players. Assume, however, that the Consumer Products Division has enough idle capacity to fill the 5,000-unit order. Under these conditions, compute the profit impact to the Consumer Products Division of accepting the order at the $400 price.
4. What conclusions do you draw concerning the use of market price as a transfer price in intra-company transactions?

PROBLEM 11–31 Transfer Pricing and Inefficiency [LO3]
Airflow Inc. produces ceiling fans for home and industrial use. The parts for the different styles of fans are produced and sold by the Parts Division to the Assembly Division of Airflow Inc. The cost to the Parts Division is $12 per fan. The Assembly Division assembles the purchased parts into finished fans at a cost of $6 per unit and sells the assembled product to an outside wholesaler for $25 per unit. Due to the proprietary technology used to make the Airflow fans to operate particularly quietly, the Parts Division is not allowed to sell the parts it produces to external customers. Both divisions have some idle capacity. The managers of both divisions are evaluated based on the profitability of their divisions.

Required:
1. What is the profit per unit of the two divisions if the transfer price is $15 per unit?
2. What is the profit per unit of the two divisions if the transfer price is $12 per unit?
3. If the Parts Division operates inefficiently, causing the cost of the parts to rise to $13 per unit and that cost is used as the transfer price, what is the profit of the two divisions?
4. Take on the role of the Assembly Division manager and evaluate the answer in (4) above. Would you agree or disagree with the $13 transfer price? Why?
5. Which transfer price is best from the point of view of the company as a whole? Why?

PROBLEM 11–32 Creating a Balanced Scorecard [LO6]
Mason Paper Company (MPC) manufactures commodity-grade papers for use in computer printers and photocopiers. MPC has reported operating losses for the last two years due to intense price pressure from much larger competitors. The MPC management team—including Kristen Townsend (CEO), Mike Martinez (vice-president of Manufacturing), Tom Andrews (vice-president of Marketing), and Wendy Chen (CFO)—is contemplating a change in strategy to save the company from impending bankruptcy. Excerpts from a recent management team meeting are shown below:

Townsend: As we all know, the commodity paper manufacturing business is all about economies of scale. The largest competitors with the lowest cost per unit win. The limited capacity of our older machines prohibits us from competing in the high-volume commodity paper grades. Furthermore, expanding our capacity by acquiring a new paper-making machine is out of the question given the extraordinarily high price tag. Therefore, I propose that we abandon cost reduction as a strategic goal and instead pursue manufacturing flexibility as the key to our future success.

Chen: Manufacturing flexibility? What does that mean?

Martinez: It means we have to abandon our "crank out as many tonnes of paper as possible" mentality. Instead, we need to pursue the low-volume business opportunities that exist in the non-standard, specialized paper grades. To succeed in this regard, we'll need to improve our flexibility in three ways. First, we must improve our ability to switch between paper grades. Right now, we require an average of four hours to change over to another paper grade. Timely customer deliveries are a function of changeover performance. Second, we need to expand the range of paper grades that we can manufacture. Currently, we can manufacture only three paper grades. Our customers must perceive that we are a "one-stop shop" that can meet all of their paper-grade needs. Third, we will need to improve our yields (e.g., tonnes of acceptable output relative to total tonnes processed) in the non-standard paper grades. Our percentage of waste within these grades will be unacceptably high unless we do something to improve our processes. Our variable costs will go through the roof if we cannot increase our yields!

Chen: Wait just a minute! These changes are going to destroy our equipment utilization numbers!

Andrews: You're right, Wendy; however, equipment utilization is not the name of the game when it comes to competing in terms of flexibility. Our customers don't care about our equipment utilization. Instead, as Mike just indicated, they want just-in-time delivery of smaller quantities of a full range of paper grades. If we can shrink the elapsed time from order placement to order delivery and expand our product offerings, it will increase sales from current customers and bring in new customers. Furthermore, we will be able to charge a premium price because of the limited competition within this niche from our cost-focused larger competitors. Our contribution margin per tonne should drastically improve!

Martinez: Of course, executing the change in strategy will not be easy. We'll need to make a substantial investment in training because ultimately it is our people who create our flexible manufacturing capabilities.

Chen: If we adopt this new strategy, it is definitely going to impact how we measure performance. We'll need to create measures that motivate our employees to make decisions that support our flexibility goals.

Townsend: Wendy, you hit the nail right on the head. For our next meeting, could you pull together some potential measures that support our new strategy?

Required:

1.   Contrast MPC's previous manufacturing strategy with its new manufacturing strategy.
2.   Generally speaking, why would a company that changes its strategic goals need to change its performance measurement system as well? What are some examples of measures that would have been appropriate for MPC prior to its change in strategy? Why would those measures fail to support MPC's new strategy?
3.   Using Exhibit 11–5 as a guide, construct a balanced scorecard that would support MPC's new manufacturing strategy. Use arrows to show the causal links between the performance measures and show whether the performance measure should increase or decrease over time. Feel free to create measures that may not be specifically mentioned in the chapter, but nonetheless make sense given the strategic goals of the company.
4.   What hypotheses are built into MPC's balanced scorecard? Which of these hypotheses do you believe are most questionable and why?

PROBLEM 11–33 Creating Balanced Scorecards That Support Different Strategies [LO6]

The Performance Enhancement Group (PEG) helps companies to build balanced scorecards. As part of its marketing efforts, PEG conducts an annual balanced scorecard workshop for prospective clients. As PEG's newest employee, your boss has asked you to participate in this year's workshop by explaining to attendees how a company's strategy determines the measures that are appropriate for its balanced scorecard. Your boss has provided you with the excerpts below from the annual reports of two current PEG clients. She has asked you to use these excerpts in your portion of the workshop.

Excerpt from Applied Pharmaceuticals' annual report:

   The keys to our business are consistent and timely new product introductions and manufacturing process integrity. The new-product introduction side of the equation is a function of research and development (R&D) yield (e.g., the number of marketable drug compounds created relative to the total number of potential compounds pursued). We seek to optimize our R&D yield and first-to-market capability by investing in state-of-the-art technology, hiring the highest possible percentage of the "best and the brightest" engineers, and providing world-class training to those engineers. Manufacturing process integrity is all about establishing world-class quality specifications and then relentlessly engaging in prevention and appraisal activities to minimize defect rates. Our customers must have an awareness of and respect for our brand image of being "first to market and first in quality." If we deliver on this pledge to our customers, then our financial goal of increasing our return on shareholders' equity should take care of itself.

Excerpt from Destination Resorts International's annual report:

Our business succeeds or fails based on the quality of the service that our front-line employees provide to customers. Therefore, it is imperative that we strive to maintain high employee morale and minimize employee turnover. In addition, it is critical that we train our employees to use technology to create one seamless worldwide experience for our repeat customers. Once an employee enters a customer preference (e.g., provide two extra pillows in the room, deliver fresh brewed coffee to the room at 8:00 A.M., etc.) into our database, our worldwide workforce strives to ensure that a customer will never need to repeat it at any of our destination resorts. If we properly train and retain a motivated workforce, we should see continuous improvement in our percentage of error-free repeat customer check-ins, the time taken to resolve customer complaints, and our independently assessed room cleanliness. This in turn should drive improvement in our customer retention, which is the key to meeting our revenue growth goals.

Required:
1. Based on the excerpts above, compare and contrast the strategies of Applied Pharmaceuticals and Destination Resorts International.
2. Select balanced scorecard measures for each company and link the scorecard measures using the framework from the Learning Aid on page 495. Use arrows to show the causal links between the performance measures and show whether the performance measure should increase or decrease over time. Feel free to create measures that may not be specifically mentioned in the chapter, but nonetheless make sense given the strategic goals of each company.
3. What hypotheses are built into each balanced scorecard? Why do the hypotheses differ between the two companies?

PROBLEM 11–34 Internal Business Process Performance Measures [LO6]
Dexeter Corporation has recently begun a continuous improvement campaign. As a consequence, there have been many changes in operating procedures. Progress has been slow, particularly in trying to develop new performance measures for the factory.

Management has been gathering the following data over the past four months:

	Month			
	1	**2**	**3**	**4**
Quality control measures:				
Customer complaints as a percentage of units sold	1.4%	1.3%	1.1%	1.0%
Warranty claims as a percentage of units sold	2.3%	2.1%	2.0%	1.8%
Defects as a percentage of units produced.	4.6%	4.2%	3.7%	3.4%
Material control measures:				
Scrap as a percentage of total cost.	3.2%	2.9%	3.0%	2.7%
Machine performance measures:				
Percentage of machine availability	80%	82%	81%	79%
Use as a percentage of availability	75%	73%	71%	70%
Average setup time (hours)	2.7	2.5	2.5	2.6
Delivery performance measures:				
Throughput time.	?	?	?	?
Manufacturing cycle efficiency	?	?	?	?
Delivery cycle time.	?	?	?	?
Percentage of on-time deliveries.	84%	87%	91%	95%

The president has attended conferences at which the importance of throughput time, manufacturing cycle efficiency, and delivery cycle time were stressed, but no one at the company is sure how they are computed. The data to compute these measures have been gathered and appear below:

	Month			
	1	**2**	**3**	**4**
Wait time per order before start of production, in days	16.7	15.2	12.3	9.6
Inspection time per unit, in days	0.2	0.6	1.2	1.6
Process time per unit, in days.............................	1.2	1.2	1.2	1.2
Queue time per unit, in days	5.6	5.7	5.6	5.7
Move time per unit, in days	2.8	2.6	2.6	2.8

Required:
1. For each month, compute the following operating performance measures:
    a. Throughput time.
    b. Manufacturing cycle efficiency (MCE).
    c. Delivery cycle time.
2. Using the performance measures given in the problem and those you computed in (1) above, do the following:
    a. Identify areas where the company seems to be improving.
    b. Identify areas where the company seems to be deteriorating or stagnating.
    c. Explain why you think some specific areas are improving while others are not.
3. Refer to the move time, process time, and so forth given above for month 4.
    a. Assume that in month 5 the move time, process time, and so forth are the same as for month 4, except that through the implementation of lean production, the company is able to completely eliminate the queue time during production. Compute the new throughput time and MCE.
    b. Assume that in month 6 the move time, process time, and so forth are the same as for month 4, except that the company is able to completely eliminate the queue time during production and reduce the move time to 1.0 day. Compute the new throughput time and MCE.

PROBLEM 11–35 Building a Balanced Scorecard [LO6]

Deer Creek Ski Resort was for many years a small, family-owned resort serving day skiers from nearby towns. Deer Creek was recently acquired by Mountain Associates, a major ski resort operator with several destination resorts in western Canada. The new owners have plans to upgrade the resort into a destination resort for vacationers staying for a week or more. As part of this plan, the new owners would like to make major improvements in the Lynx Lair Lodge, the resort's on-the-hill fast-food restaurant. The menu at the Lodge is very limited—hamburgers, hot dogs, chili, tuna fish sandwiches, French fries, and packaged snacks. The previous owners of the resort had felt no urgency to upgrade the food service at the Lodge since there is little competition. If skiers want lunch on the mountain, the only possibilities are the Lynx Lair Lodge or a lunch brought from home.

As part of the deal when acquiring Deer Creek, Mountain Associates agreed to retain all of the current employees of the resort. The manager of the Lodge, while hardworking and enthusiastic, has very little experience in the restaurant business. The manager is responsible for selecting the menu, finding and training employees, and overseeing daily operations. The kitchen staff prepares food and washes dishes. The dining room staff takes orders, serves as cashiers, and cleans the dining room area.

Shortly after taking over Deer Creek, management of Mountain Associates held a day-long meeting with all of the employees of the Lynx Lair Lodge to discuss the future of the ski resort and management's plans for the Lodge. At the end of this meeting, top management and Lodge employees created a balanced scorecard for the Lodge that would help guide operations for the coming ski season. Almost everyone who participated in the meeting seemed to be enthusiastic about the scorecard and management's plans for the Lodge.

The following performance measures were included on the balanced scorecard for the Lynx Lair Lodge:
- Customer satisfaction with service, as measured by customer surveys.
- Total Lynx Lair Lodge profit.
- Dining area cleanliness, as rated by a representative from Mountain Associates management.
- Average time to prepare an order.
- Customer satisfaction with menu choices, as measured by surveys.
- Average time to take an order.

- Percentage of kitchen staff completing institutional cooking course at the local community college.
- Sales.
- Percentage of dining room staff completing hospitality course at the local community college.
- Number of menu items.

Mountain Associates will pay for the costs of staff attending courses at the local community college.

Required:

1. Using the above performance measures, construct a balanced scorecard for the Lynx Lair Lodge. Use the Learning Aid on page 495 as a guide. Use arrows to show causal links and indicate with + or − whether the performance measure should increase or decrease.
2. What hypotheses are built into the balanced scorecard for the Lynx Lair Lodge? Which of these hypotheses do you believe are most questionable? Why?
3. How will management know if one of the hypotheses underlying the balanced scorecard is false?

PROBLEM 11–36 Quality Cost Report [LO7]

Yedder Enterprises was a pioneer in designing and producing precision surgical lasers. Yedder's product was brilliantly designed, but the manufacturing process was neglected by management; consequently, quality problems have been chronic. When customers complained about defective units, Yedder would simply send out a repair person or replace the defective unit with a new one. Recently, several competitors came out with similar products without Yedder's quality problems, and Yedder's sales consequently have declined.

To remedy the situation, Yedder embarked on an intensive campaign to strengthen its quality control at the beginning of the current year. These efforts met with some success—the downward slide in sales was reversed, and sales grew from $95 million last year to $100 million this year. To help monitor the company's progress, costs relating to quality and quality control were compiled for last year and for the first full year of the quality campaign this year. The costs, which do not include the lost sales due to a reputation for poor quality, appear below:

	Costs (in thousands)	
	Last Year	This Year
Product recalls	$3,500	$600
Systems development................	$120	$680
Inspection	$1,700	$2,770
Net cost of scrap...................	$800	$1,300
Supplies used in testing	$30	$40
Warranty repairs	$3,300	$2,800
Rework labour.....................	$1,400	$1,600
Statistical process control............	$0	$270
Customer returns of defective goods	$3,200	$200
Cost of testing equipment.............	$270	$390
Quality engineering	$1,080	$1,650
Downtime due to quality problems	$600	$1,100

Required:

1. Prepare a quality cost report for both this year and last year. Carry percentage computations to two decimal places.
2. Prepare a bar graph showing the distribution of the various quality costs by category.
3. Prepare a written evaluation to accompany the reports you have prepared in (1) and (2) above. This evaluation should discuss the distribution of quality costs in the company, changes in the distribution over the last year, and any other information you believe would be useful to management.

PROBLEM 11–37 Analyzing a Quality Cost Report [LO7]

Belanger Ltée. produces telephone equipment at its Quebec plant. In recent years, the company's market share has been eroded by stiff competition from Asian and European competitors. Price and product quality are the two key areas in which companies compete in this market.

Two years ago, Jean Houle, Belanger's president, decided to devote more resources to improving product quality after learning that his company's products had been ranked fourth in quality in a survey of telephone equipment users. He believed that Belanger could no longer afford to ignore the importance of product quality. Houle set up a task force that he headed to implement a formal quality improvement program. Included on this task force were representatives from engineering, sales, customer service, production, and accounting. This broad representation was needed because Houle believed that this was necessarily a companywide program, and that all employees should share the responsibility for its success.

After the first meeting of the task force, Pascale Richard, manager of sales, asked Guy Laflamme, production manager, what he thought of the proposed program. Laflamme replied, "I have reservations. Quality is too abstract to be attaching costs to it and then to be holding you and me responsible for cost improvements. I like to work with goals that I can see and count! I'm nervous about having my annual bonus based on a decrease in quality costs; there are too many variables that we have no control over."

Belanger's quality improvement program has now been in operation for two years. The company's most recent quality cost report is shown below.

BELANGER LTÉE. Quality Cost Report (in thousands)		
	Year 1	Year 2
Prevention costs:		
Machine maintenance	$ 215	$ 160
Training suppliers.	5	15
Design reviews.	20	95
Total prevention cost.	240	270
Appraisal costs:		
Incoming inspection.	45	22
Final testing	160	94
Total appraisal cost.	205	116
Internal failure costs:		
Rework.	120	62
Scrap	68	40
Total internal failure cost	188	102
External failure costs:		
Warranty repairs	69	23
Customer returns.	262	80
Total external failure cost	331	103
Total quality cost.	$ 964	$ 591
Total production cost	$4,120	$4,510

As they were reviewing the report, Richard asked Laflamme what he now thought of the quality improvement program. "The work is really moving through the production department," Laflamme replied. "We used to spend time helping the customer service department solve their problems, but they are leaving us alone these days. I have no complaints so far, and I'm relieved to see that the new quality improvement hasn't adversely affected our bonuses. I'm anxious to see if it increases our bonuses in the future."

Required:
1. By analyzing the company's quality cost report, determine if Belanger Ltée.'s quality improvement program has been successful. *List specific evidence to support your answer.* Show percentage figures in two ways: first, as a percentage of total production cost; and second, as a percentage of total quality cost. Carry all computations to one decimal place.
2. Discuss why Laflamme's current reaction to the quality improvement program is more favourable than his initial reaction.
3. Jean Houle believed that the quality improvement program was essential and that Belanger Ltée. could no longer afford to ignore the importance of product quality. Discuss how Belanger could measure the opportunity cost of not implementing the quality improvement program.

(CMA, adapted)

Connect Cases

CASE 11–38 Transfer Pricing; Divisional Performance [LO2, LO3]
Stanco, Inc., is a decentralized organization with five divisions. The company's Electronics Division produces a variety of electronics items, including an XL5 circuit board. The division (which is operating at capacity) sells the XL5 circuit board to regular customers for $12.50 each. The circuit boards have a variable production cost of $8.25 each.

The company's Clock Division has asked the Electronics Division to supply it with a large quantity of XL5 circuit boards for only $9 each. The Clock Division, which is operating at only 60% of capacity, will put the circuit boards into a timing device that it will produce and sell to a large oven manufacturer. The cost of the timing device being manufactured by the Clock Division follows:

XL5 circuit board (desired cost).	$ 9.00
Other purchased parts (from outside vendors)	30.00
Other variable costs.	20.75
Fixed overhead and administrative costs	10.00
Total cost per timing device.	$69.75

The manager of the Clock Division feels that she can't quote a price greater than $70 per timing device to the oven manufacturer if her division is to get the job. As shown above, in order to keep the price at $70 or less, she can't pay more than $9 per unit to the Electronics Division for the XL5 circuit boards. Although the $9 price for the XL5 circuit boards represents a substantial discount from the normal $12.50 price, she feels that the price concession is necessary for her division to get the oven manufacturer contract and thereby keep its core of highly trained people.

The company uses return on investment (ROI) to measure divisional performance.

Required:

1. Assume that you are the manager of the Electronics Division. Would you recommend that your division supply the XL5 circuit boards to the Clock Division for $9 each as requested? Why or why not? Show all computations.
2. Would it be profitable for the company as a whole for the Electronics Division to supply the Clock Division with the circuit boards for $9 each? Explain your answer.
3. In principle, should it be possible for the two managers to agree to a transfer price in this particular situation? If so, within what range would that transfer price lie?
4. Discuss the organizational and manager behaviour problems, if any, inherent in this situation. What would you advise the company's president to do in this situation?

(CMA, adapted)

CASE 11–39 Balanced Scorecard [LO6]

Donnally Department Store is located in the downtown area of a medium-sized city in western Canada. While the store had been profitable for many years, it is facing increasing competition from large national chains that have set up stores in the city's suburbs. Recently, the downtown area has been undergoing revitalization, and the owners of Donnally Department Store are somewhat optimistic that profitability can be restored.

In an attempt to accelerate the return to profitability, the management of Donnally Department Store is in the process of designing a balanced scorecard for the company. Management believes the company should focus on two key problems. First, customers are taking longer and longer to pay the bills they incur on the department store's charge card, and they have far more bad debts than are normal for the industry. If this problem was solved, the company would have more cash to make much needed renovations. Investigation has revealed that much of the problem with late payments and unpaid bills is apparently due to disputed bills that are the result of incorrect charges on the customer bills. These incorrect charges usually occur because salesclerks enter data incorrectly on the charge account slip. Second, the company has been incurring large losses on unsold seasonal apparel. Such items are ordinarily resold at a loss to discount stores that specialize in such distress items.

The meeting in which the balanced scorecard approach was discussed was disorganized and ineffectively led—possibly because no one other than you and one of the vice-presidents had read anything about how to put a balanced scorecard together. Nevertheless, a number of potential performance measures were suggested by various managers as follows.

Performance measures suggested by various managers:

- Total sales revenue.
- Percentage of salesclerks trained to correctly enter data on charge account slips.
- Customer satisfaction with accuracy of charge account bills from monthly customer survey.
- Sales per employee.
- Travel expenses for buyers for trips to fashion shows.

- Average age of accounts receivables.
- Courtesy shown by junior staff members to senior staff members based on surveys of senior staff.
- Unsold inventory at the end of the season as a percentage of total cost of sales.
- Sales per square metre of floor space.
- Percentage of suppliers making just-in-time deliveries.
- Quality of food in the staff cafeteria based on staff surveys.
- Written-off accounts receivables (bad debts) as a percentage of sales.
- Percentage of charge account bills containing errors.
- Percentage of employees who have attended the city's cultural diversity workshop.
- Total profit.
- Profit per employee.

Required:
1. As someone with more knowledge of the balanced scorecard than anyone else in the company, you have been asked to build an integrated balanced scorecard. In your scorecard, use only performance measures suggested by the managers above. You do not have to use all of the performance measures suggested by the managers, but you should build a balanced scorecard that reveals a strategy for dealing with the problems with accounts receivable and with unsold merchandise. Construct the balanced scorecard following the format used in the Learning Aid on page 495. Do not be particularly concerned about whether a specific performance measure falls within the learning and growth, internal business process, customer, or financial perspective. However, clearly show the causal links between the performance measures with arrows and whether the performance measures should show increases or decreases.
2. Assume that the company adopts your balanced scorecard. After operating for a year, there are improvements in some performance measures but not in others. What should management do next?
3. *a.* Suppose that customers express greater satisfaction with the accuracy of their charge account bills but the performance measures for the average age of accounts receivable and for bad debts do not improve. Explain why this might happen.
   b. Suppose that the performance measures for the average age of accounts receivable, bad debts, and unsold inventory improve, but total profits do not. Explain why this might happen. Assume in your answer that the explanation lies within the company.

CASE 11–40 Return on Investment (ROI) and Residual Income; Decentralization [LO4, LO5]

Kaiser Industries produces tool and die machinery for manufacturers. The company expanded vertically several years ago by acquiring Superior Steel Company, one of its suppliers of alloy steel plates. Kaiser decided to maintain Superior's separate identity and therefore established the Superior Steel Division as one of its investment centres.

Kaiser evaluates its divisions on the basis of ROI. Management bonuses are also based on ROI. All investments in operating assets are expected to earn a minimum required rate of return of 11%.

Superior's ROI has ranged from 14% to 17% since it was acquired by Kaiser. During the past year, Superior had an investment opportunity that would yield an estimated rate of return of 13%. Superior's management decided against the investment because it believed the investment would decrease the division's overall ROI.

Last year's absorption costing income statement for Superior Steel Division follows. The division's operating assets employed were $6,480,000 at the end of the year, which represents an 8% increase over the previous year-end balance.

SUPERIOR STEEL DIVISION Divisional Income Statement For the Year ended December 31		
Sales		$15,600,000
Cost of goods sold		8,250,000
Gross margin		7,350,000
Less operating expenses:		
Selling expenses	$2,810,000	
Administrative expenses	3,604,000	6,414,000
Operating income		$ 936,000

Required:

1. Compute the following performance measures for the Superior Steel Division:
   a. ROI. (Remember, ROI is based on the *average* operating assets, computed from the beginning-of-year and end-of-year balances.) State ROI in terms of margin and turnover.
   b. Residual income.
2. Would the management of Superior Steel Division have been more likely to accept the investment opportunity it had last year if residual income was used as a performance measure instead of ROI? Explain.
3. The Superior Steel Division is a separate investment centre within Kaiser Industries. Identify the items Superior must be free to control if it is to be evaluated fairly by either the ROI or residual income performance measures.

(CMA, adapted)

CASE 11–41 Service Organization; Segment Reporting [LO1]

The Canadian Association of Nutritionists, a fictional professional association for nutritional counsellors, has 10,000 members. The association operates from a central headquarters but has local chapters throughout North America. The association's monthly journal, *Good Nutrition Today*, features recent developments in the field. The association also publishes special reports and books, and it sponsors courses that qualify members for the continuing professional education credit required by certification boards. The association's statement of revenues and expenses for the current year is presented below:

CANADIAN ASSOCIATION OF NUTRITIONISTS Statement of Revenues and Expenses for the Year Ended December 31	
Revenues	$970,000
Expenses:	
Salaries	440,000
Occupancy costs	120,000
Distributions to local chapters	210,000
Printing	82,000
Mailing	24,000
Continuing education instructors' fees	60,000
General and administrative	27,000
Total expenses	963,000
Excess of revenues over expenses	$ 7,000

The board of directors of the association has requested that you construct a segmented income statement that shows the financial contribution of each of the association's four major programs—membership service, journal, books and reports, and continuing education. The following data have been gathered to aid you:

a. Membership dues are $60 per year, of which $15 covers a one-year subscription to the association's journal. The other $45 pays for general membership services.

b. One-year subscriptions to *Good Nutrition Today* are sold to non-members and libraries at $20 per subscription. A total of 1,000 of these subscriptions were sold last year. In addition to subscriptions, the journal generated $50,000 in advertising revenues. The costs per journal subscription, for members as well as non-members, were $4 for printing and $1 for mailing.

c. A variety of technical reports and professional books were sold for a total of $70,000 during the year. Printing costs for these materials totalled $25,000, and mailing costs totalled $8,000.

d. The association offers a number of continuing education courses. The courses generated revenues of $230,000 last year.

e. Salary costs and the cost of space occupied by each program and the central staff follow:

	Salaries	Space Occupied (square metres)
Membership services	$170,000	3,000
Journal	60,000	1,000
Books and reports	40,000	1,000
Continuing education	50,000	2,000
Central staff	120,000	3,000
Total	$440,000	10,000

f.   The $120,000 in occupancy costs incurred last year includes $20,000 in rental cost for a portion of the warehouse used by the Membership Services program for storage purposes. The association has a flexible rental agreement that allows it to pay rent only on the warehouse space it uses.

g.   Printing costs are for printing the journal, books and reports, and continuing education materials.

h.   Distributions to local chapters are for general membership services.

i.   General and administrative expenses include costs relating to overall administration of the association as a whole. The association's central staff does some mailing of materials for general administrative purposes.

j.   The expenses that can be traced or assigned to the central staff, as well as any other expenses that are not traceable to the programs, will be treated as common costs. It is not necessary to distinguish between variable and fixed costs.

Required:

1.   Prepare a contribution-format segmented income statement for the Canadian Association of Nutritionists for last year. This statement should show the segment margin for each program as well as results for the association as a whole.

2.   Give arguments for and against allocating all costs of the association to the four programs.

(CMA, adapted)

CASE 11–42 Performance Evaluation; ROI and Residual Income [LO4, LO5]

Convenient Food Markets (CFM) has a chain of more than 100 convenience stores The company has faced increasing competition over the past several years, mainly because department store chains have been adding grocery departments and gas stations have been adding full-service convenience stores to their locations. As a consequence, the company has lost market share recently to competitors. The company has set a target minimum rate of return for its stores of 22%.

John Nicholson is the district manager of the 17 CFM stores in Bailingham, Nicholson's district happens to include the "original" store, the first in the Convenient Food Markets chain, which opened more than 40 years ago. In fact, Nicholson's first summer job was as a "stock boy" at the original store in the year that it opened. After university, he returned to CFM as a store manager, has worked his way up to district manager, and plans to retire in about five year's time.

Convenient Food Markets leases store buildings, investing significantly in the interior design, display, and decoration. The original CFM, store remains profitable, in part because the fixtures and fittings are almost fully depreciated. While the company has invested in significant leasehold improvements in other newer stores, little has changed in the original store since opening day. While Nicholson has a sense of nostalgia for the original store, in reality, sales volumes have been falling and foot traffic has declined significantly in recent years. Fewer people are moving to the neighbourhood, as more and more people are moving to the suburbs.

All 17 stores in the district report to Nicholson, who is evaluated on the basis of average return on investment for the stores in his district. For purposes of this calculation, the net book value of investment in furnishings and fixtures represents the operating assets of each of the stores. Operating income after depreciation on leasehold improvements represents the numerator for this calculation.

Nicholson is considering a proposal from a developer to open a new store in a newly developed residential neighbourhood. The developer has completed about 60% of the new homes planned for this neighbourhood and will complete the other 40% within the next 18 months. Due to limited capital to invest, Nicholson realizes that opening the new store would mean closing down an old store, and the original store seems to be the best candidate. To aid in his decision, Nicholson has collected the following information:

	Original Store (prior year actual)	New Store (forecast)
Operating income less depreciation	$75,000	$145,000
Net book value of operating assets.	$195,000	$475,000

Required:

1.   Calculate the ROI and residual income for both the original store and the new store.

2.   Take on the role of an internal auditor at CFM. Assume that your task is to evaluate the effectiveness of the performance evaluation system for CFM district managers. In this capacity, write a short memo to the CFO of Convenience Food Markets to discuss your findings. In the memo, you should indicate whether you believe Nicholson will want to open the new store, whether your analysis indicates that Nicholson should open the new store, and discuss why or why not. You should also include your observations about the effect of the performance evaluation system on the decisions made by CFM district managers and what might be done to improve it.

Research and Application

APPENDIX 11A: PROFITABILITY ANALYSIS

LEARNING OBJECTIVE 8
Analyze variances from sales budgets.

A frequently overlooked way to analyze profitability is by customer. Although managers generally assume that a dollar of sales to one customer is just as profitable as a dollar of sales to any other customer, this assumption may not be correct. The reason is that customers have varying demands for resource-consuming activities, just as products, markets, and other segments of a company have varying demands. For example, some customers order in smaller lots and more frequently than other customers, requiring more paperwork and materials handling. Some customers order non-standard parts that require special engineering work, special machinery setups, and perhaps special packaging and handling. Other customers always seem to be in a hurry and want special expediting and delivery services. Customers who demand high levels of these resource-consuming activities should not be cross-subsidized by customers who demand little in the way of customized services, special packaging, and so forth. However, unless the activities that are provided for customer support are traced to the company's various customers, cross-subsidization almost certainly will occur.

After the various customer-support activities in a company have been identified, the costs of providing these activities should be charged to the customers who require them. Thus, a customer who requires special accounts receivable terms, many small orders and deliveries, the packing of goods in shop-ready containers, and specialized field service should be quoted a price that reflects these costly activities. This is why we stated in earlier chapters that suppliers who make deliveries to customers in a JIT environment frequently quote prices that are somewhat higher than prices charged by other suppliers. The higher prices are needed to compensate these suppliers for the special activities required on their part to support JIT customers.

Businesses that have analyzed customer profitability have been surprised to find that a fairly small number of customers are apparently responsible for most of their profits. It is also common to find that a small number of customers consume far more resources than are warranted by the revenue generated.

Sales Variance Analysis

Segment reporting, first discussed in Chapter 8 and continued in this chapter as part of our discussion of responsibility centres, represents an important tool for evaluating managers' performance. As pointed out, the metrics used to evaluate managers depend on what they have control over. Cost centre managers will be evaluated on the basis of how well they did in controlling costs, while investment centre managers can be evaluated using more comprehensive measures such as ROI or residual income. However, segmented profitability analysis can also be combined with the variance analysis discussed in Chapter 10 to generate a series of performance reports so that prices and volumes (quantities) can be compared to targets set by the budgeting process. The interaction of price and quantity represents important information for businesses to analyze to determine why the strategic goals and specific budgeted targets were not achieved. Managers want to know the effects of market volume changes, market penetration or share changes, sales mix changes, and price changes. Each of these elements can be isolated, but the true test of management is to reconstitute the combination needed for a new marketing strategy. Variances from previous results can provide a valuable start for this process.

The ability to have segment revenue data for analysis depends on the coding attached to the revenue information. Geographic market, product line, customer, and sales personnel are common classifications. Managers, with the assistance of the accountant, must decide what they wish to know and what classifications can be realistically structured, given the degree of substitutes and complements that exist, the number of products that exist, and the nature of meaningful groupings.

To illustrate the nature of variance reporting in the revenue area, consider the following example for Ace Video Company:

Budget sales in units:	
Deluxe video game..........	10,000
Standard video game........	5,000
Budget price:	
Deluxe	$60
Standard..................	$30
Market volume expected:	
Deluxe	70,000
Standard..................	90,000
Budget variable expense:	
Deluxe	$24
Standard..................	$15

The sales price for the deluxe video game was reduced to $54 from the anticipated $60. This resulted in a $48,000 increase in revenue. The standard video game price was increased by $3 per unit, resulting in a revenue decrease of $18,000. The reasoning behind the price and revenue changes is something marketing management should explain, so that a new pricing strategy can be considered.

Actual results for the period were

Unit sales:	
Deluxe	12,000
Standard..................	4,000
Sales prices:	
Deluxe	$54
Standard..................	$33
Market volume:	
Deluxe	75,000
Standard..................	85,000

Exhibit 11A–1 presents a summary of the relationships among budgeted and actual results. Analysis of revenue variances can proceed as follows:

$$\textbf{Sales price variance} = \left(\begin{array}{c} \text{Actual} \\ \text{sales price} \end{array} - \begin{array}{c} \text{Budgeted} \\ \text{sales price} \end{array} \right) \times \begin{array}{c} \text{Actual} \\ \text{sales volume} \end{array}$$

Deluxe	($54 − $60) × 12,000 units =	$72,000 U
Standard	($33 − $30) × 4,000 units =	12,000 F
	Total sales price variance =	$60,000 U

Note in Exhibit 11A–1 that the total $60,000 unfavourable **sales price variance** in contribution margin resulting from the change in sales price is calculated using actual sales volume in units times the difference in sales price (actual versus budget) because actual and budgeted variable costs per unit are the same.

Firms often want to know how well they are performing compared to the market for their product. If the total market demand changes, they want to evaluate the impact on

Sales price variance
Actual sales price minus budgeted sales price, multiplied by actual sales quantity.

EXHIBIT 11A–1   Actual and Budgeted Results: Ace Video Company

	Actual Results		Flexible Budget		Master Budget	
Revenue:						
Deluxe	(12,000 × $54)	$648,000	(12,000 × $60)	$720,000	(10,000 × $60)	$600,000
Standard	(4,000 × $33)	132,000	(4,000 × $30)	120,000	(5,000 × $30)	150,000
		780,000		840,000		750,000
Variable expenses:						
Deluxe	(12,000 × $24)	288,000	(12,000 × $24)	288,000	(10,000 × $24)	240,000
Standard	(4,000 × $15)	60,000	(4,000 × $15)	60,000	(5,000 × $15)	75,000
		348,000		348,000		315,000
Contribution margin		$432,000		$492,000		$435,000
			Sales Price Variance		Sales Volume Variance	
Total variances			$60,000 U		$57,000 F	

profits. Importantly, to avoid the problems associated with the arbitrary allocation of common costs discussed in Chapter 11, the variances that follow focus on the effects of volume, quantity, and mix changes on contribution margin. If these changes also impacted the segment's traceable fixed costs, managers would also want to analyze these effects, but this is beyond the scope of our discussion. *Market volume variances* and *market share variances* can provide a method of seeing the contribution margin effects of market volume changes or changes in the portion of the market, termed *market share* or *market penetration*, captured by the firm.

Market volume variance
Actual market volume minus budget market volume, times anticipated market share, multiplied by budgeted contribution margin.

We begin with the **market volume variance**, holding market share constant.

$$\begin{matrix} \textbf{Market} \\ \textbf{volume} \\ \textbf{variance} \end{matrix} = \begin{pmatrix} \text{Actual} & & \text{Budget} \\ \text{market} & - & \text{market} \\ \text{volume} & & \text{volume} \end{pmatrix} \times \begin{matrix} \text{Anticipated market} \\ \text{share percentage} \end{matrix} \times \begin{matrix} \text{Budgeted} \\ \text{contribution} \\ \text{margin per unit} \end{matrix}$$

Deluxe	(75,000 − 70,000) × (10,000/70,000) × ($60 − $24) =	$25,714 F
Standard	(85,000 − 90,000) × (5,000/90,000) × ($30 − $15) =	$ 4,167 U
Total		$21,547 F

The market volume variance represents the effect on contribution margin of the total market size (demand) differing from what was anticipated. Using Ace Video's budgeted market share percentages for each product, the analysis above indicates that the net effect of higher than anticipated total market demand for Deluxe video games and lower than anticipated total market demand for Standard video games is an increase in contribution margin of $21,547. This variance, although favourable, is not the result of any actions taken by Ace Video managers; instead it simply reflects the impact on contribution margin of the total market demand for video games differing from the estimates prepared by the company.

To calculate the impact on contribution margin of Ace Video's market share differing from budget, holding the effects of total market demand constant, we use the following **market share variance** approach:

Market share variance
Actual sales volume minus the anticipated portion of the actual market volume, multiplied by budgeted contribution margin per unit.

$$\begin{matrix} \textbf{Market} \\ \textbf{share} \\ \textbf{variance} \end{matrix} = \begin{matrix} \text{Actual} \\ \text{sales} \\ \text{quantity} \end{matrix} - \begin{pmatrix} \text{Actual} & & \text{Anticipated} \\ \text{market} & \times & \text{market share} \\ \text{volume} & & \text{percentage} \end{pmatrix} \times \begin{matrix} \text{Budgeted} \\ \text{contribution} \\ \text{margin per unit} \end{matrix}$$

Deluxe	{12,000 − [75,000 × (10,000/70,000)]} × ($60 − $24) =	$46,286 F
Standard	{4,000 − [85,000 × (5,000/90,000)]} × ($30 − $15) =	10,833 U
Total		$35,453 F

The favourable market share variance of $35,453 reflects the net effect of Ace Video enjoying a higher than budgeted market share for Deluxe video games (16% actual versus 14.3% budgeted) but a lower than budgeted market share for Standard video games (4.7% versus 5.6%).[8] The market share variance can be influenced by actions taken by managers. For example, the favourable market share variance for Deluxe video games is likely in part attributable to the $6 per unit price decrease. Another controllable factor that could influence the market share variance is a change to the company's marketing campaign.

Two aspects of the market volume variance and market share variance are worth emphasizing. First, each variance was calculated at the contribution margin level rather than individually analyzing revenues and variable expenses. This permits a direct evaluation of the profit effect of actual sales volumes differing from the master budget. Second, the use of the budgeted contribution margin per unit isolates the effects of volume variances from those of price (or cost) variances. The impact of actual selling prices differing from budget is captured by the sales price variance while the impact of actual variable costs per unit differing from budget was analyzed in Chapter 10.

The market volume variance and the market share variance help managers understand why actual sales quantities were 12,000 units for Deluxe and 4,000 units for Standard compared to budgeted unit sales of 10,000 and 5,000, respectively. In total, these volume differences resulted in the following contribution margin variances:

Deluxe	(12,000 − 10,000) × ($60 − $24) =	$72,000 F
Standard	(4,000 − 5,000) × ($30 − $15) =	15,000 U
Total		$57,000 F
Composition: Market volume		= $21,547 F
Market share		= 35,453 F
		$57,000 F

An alternative view of sales volume variances can be generated by examining **sales mix variance** and **sales quantity variance** in terms of their relationship to the budgeted contribution margin. For this approach to be meaningful, management must be in a position to control the mix of products it sells in the market. While alternative formulations are possible using gross margins, sales prices, or weighted average contribution margins, the straightforward use of contributions will be used in the illustration that follows, so that the principle can be understood.

Sales mix variance
Quantifies the effects on contribution margin of selling the two products in a mix that differs from the original budget.

Sales quantity variance
Quantifies the effects on contribution margin of unit sales differing from the budget, holding constant the sales mix at the budgeted proportions.

$$\textbf{Sales mix variance} = \left(\text{Actual sales quantity} - \text{Actual sales quantity at anticipated sales mix} \right) \times \text{Budgeted contribution margin per unit}$$

Deluxe	{[12,000 − 16,000* × (10/15)]} × ($60 − $24) =	$48,000 F
Standard	{[4,000 − 16,000 × (5/15)]} × ($30 − $15) =	20,000 U
Total sales mix variance		$28,000 F

*Note: 16,000 units = (12,000 + 4,000) and 10/15 is the anticipated proportion of Deluxe sales while 5/15 is the anticipated Standard mix proportion.

$$\textbf{Sales quantity variance} = \left\{ \left[\text{Actual sales quantity at anticipated sales mix} \right] - \text{Anticipated sales quantity} \right\} \times \text{Budgeted contribution margin per unit}$$

Deluxe	{[16,000 × (10/15)] − 10,000} × ($60 − $24) =	$24,000 F
Standard	{[16,000 × (5/15)] − 5,000} × ($30 − $15) =	$ 5,000 F
Total sales quantity variance		$29,000 F

The total sales volume variance is $57,000 favourable, composed of the following:

Sales mix	$28,000 F
Sales quantity	29,000 F
Total	$57,000 F

The sales mix variance quantifies the effects on contribution margin of selling the two products in a mix that differs from the original budget. As shown in the analysis above, Ace Video had a budgeted mix of 66.7% Deluxe games (10,000/15,000) and 33.3% Standard games (5,000/15,000). However, the actual mix turned out to be 75% Deluxe games (12,000/16,000) and 25% Standard games (4,000/16,000). Selling a higher proportion of Deluxe games generates a favourable total sales mix variance because Deluxe has a contribution margin of $36 per unit compared to $15 per unit for Standard. The sales quantity variance isolates the effects on contribution margin of unit sales differing from the budget, holding constant the sales mix at the budgeted proportions. Because total sales quantity was 16,000 units compared to the budget of 15,000 units, the total quantity variance is favourable.[9]

APPENDIX 11B: MARKETING EXPENSE

LEARNING OBJECTIVE 9
Analyze marketing expenses using cost drivers.

Knowledge of the nature and behaviour of marketing expenses provides managers with information about the costs of their marketing endeavours. Such information represents a significant aspect of marketing efforts, one that is needed to complement the pricing strategy previously discussed. Transport, warehousing, selling, advertising, and credit are some of the key factors that managers need to consider in their marketing strategies. Accurate cost behaviour and allocation by the accounting function can assist marketing decision makers.

Accountants typically decompose marketing expense into two general categories: order-getting and order-filling. Order-getting costs are the pure marketing costs such as advertising, selling commissions, and travel. Order-filling includes the costs of warehousing, transportation, packing, and credit. Order-getting costs tend to be somewhat more discretionary than order-filling because order-filling occurs after the sale rather than to obtain the sale. Nevertheless, marketing managers need to understand the cost behaviour associated with both sets of costs so that analysis can be conducted to decide what should be done and how. Consider the following data:

Driver analysis	Total for Period
Transport (kilometres to customer)	390 km
Jones Ltd.—30 km per shipment	
Smith Ltd.—60 km per shipment	
Selling (hours spent on customers per period)	150 hours
Jones Ltd.—50 hours	
Smith Ltd.—100 hours	
Advertising (cost of medium per period)	$4,000
Jones Ltd.—3 weight for mostly television (75% of total)	
Smith Ltd.—1 weight for mostly Internet (25% of total)	
Warehousing (space occupied)	5,880 m³
Product A—50 cubic metres per unit	
Product B—80 cubic metres per unit	
Credit/Collection (invoices per shipment—Jones requires more time to pay and line-item invoicing):	
Jones Ltd.—1 invoice per shipment, 10 units per invoice (4 of A, 6 of B)	5 shipments
Smith Ltd.—1 invoice per shipment, 10 units per invoice (6 of A, 4 of B)	4 shipments

continued

	Total Costs and Per Unit Amounts for Period		
	Total	Driver Level	Unit
Transport.........................	$ 1,950	390 km	$5 per km
Selling	7,500	150 hrs	$50 per hr
Advertising......................	4,000	—	—
Warehousing	6,500	5,880 m³*	$1.105 per m³
Credit/Collection	750	9 invoices†	$83.33 per invoice
Total..........................	$20,700		

*[(4 × 5) + (6 × 4) × 50m³] + [(6 × 5) + (4 × 4) × 80m³]
†(1 × 5) + (1 × 4)

When costs for a period are associated with their drivers and drivers can be associated with customers, marketing costs can be allocated to particular customers.

	Costs to Customer		
	Jones Ltd.	Smith Ltd.	Total
Transport:			
$5/km × 5 shipments × 30 km	$ 750		
$5/km × 4 shipments × 60 km		$ 1,200	$ 1,950
Selling:			
$50/hr × 50 hours	2,500		
$50/hr × 100 hours		5,000	7,500
Advertising:			
3/4 × $4000...........................	3,000		
1/4 × $4000...........................		1,000	4,000
Warehousing:			
$1.105 m³ × 5 × [(4 × 50) + (6 × 80)]	3,760*		
$1.105 m³ × 4 × [(6 × 50) + (4 × 80)]		2,740	6,500
Credit/Collection:			
$83.33/invoice × 1 × 5	417		
$83.33/invoice × 1 × 4		333	750
	$10,427	$10,273	$20,700

*Rounded up. 5 shipments × m³ per shipment.

	Costs to Products		
	Product A	Product B	Total
Transport—common	—	—	$ 1,950
Selling—common	—	—	7,500
Advertising—common.....................	—	—	4,000
Warehousing:			
$1.105 m³ × [(4 × 5) + (6 × 4)] × 50 m³..........	$2,431		
$1.105 m³ × [(6 × 5) + (6 × 4)] × 80 m³..........		$4,069*	$ 6,500
Credit/Collection—common	—	—	750
	$2,431	$4,069	$20,700

*Rounded up. Cost per m³ × units of product × space occupied per unit of A or B.

If the data are allocated to the two products, A and B, then the marketing expense can be broken down for the warehousing. However, the other costs cannot be broken down because transport, selling, and advertising are independent of the type of product, and are treated as common costs for the product breakdown above. Similarly, credit/collection are treated as common costs since invoicing and collection costs are not driven by product type. Only warehousing is a function of the product type and thus can be broken down by product type as well as by customer.

Marketing expense analysis uses the concepts of drivers to provide alternative views of the relationship of marketing costs to sales. The complexity of the analysis depends on the ability to define appropriate cost drivers for the marketing costs in a manner similar to the approach used with overhead costs, as explained in Chapter 5. To avoid arbitrary allocations, expenses that do not have suitable drivers should be treated as common costs that are not incremental for the particular categories of the analysis being conducted. Management may decide that further analysis of these common costs can result in refined driver definitions, which in turn will permit cause–effect allocations of common marketing costs.

Appendices 11A and 11B Summary

- Analysis of customer profitability by including drivers for marketing and administration can provide opportunities for important strategic decisions. [LO8, LO9]
- Knowledge of the profitability of customers or customer classes can facilitate selling decisions, surcharges for extra services, cross-selling opportunities, and changes in marketing approaches. Enterprise resource planning or similar computer systems can make the detailed analysis feasible and provide personnel with ratings of customer types so that the appropriate approach can be instituted for individual customers. With a wide variety of products and services, such analysis can be important, because all customers are not necessarily homogeneous and thus not equally profitable [LO8, LO9]
- Increases in sales value do not necessarily equate to increases in profitability because of the cost of providing the product services that customers demand. [LO9]

Appendices 11A and 11B Review Problem: Profitability Analysis

The Leo Company produces and sells two product lines with budgeted revenues and expenses as follows.

	Spars	Masts
Expected total industry sales	48,000 units	85,000 units
Expected Leo Company sales.........................	4,200 units	17,000 units
Expected selling price................................	$200 per unit	$300 per unit
Expected cost of manufacturing (40% fixed)	110 per unit	180 per unit
Expected selling and administration costs (70% fixed)......	60 per unit	70 per unit
Expected product profit margin........................	$30 per unit	$ 50 per unit
Actual results for 2010 included:		
Actual total industry sales	60,000 units	100,000 units
Actual Leo Company sales	6,000 units	18,000 units
Actual selling price..................................	$180 per unit	$300 per unit

All costs behaved exactly as expected.

W. Gallant, vice-president of marketing and sales, has requested that the employees of his department be paid a bonus for the year based on the fact that they have been able to increase sales by 2,800 units over budget level for the year, an increase of over 13%.

Required:
1. Calculate the changes in overall company profits caused by the following factors:
    a. Sales price
    b. Sales mix
    c. Sales quantity
    d. Market share
    e. Market volume

Solution to Appendices 11A and 11B Review Problem

1. **Budgeted Contribution Margin:**	**Spars**	**Masts**
Selling price	$200	$300
Variable costs:		
Manufacturing.	66	108
Selling & administration	18	21
Total variable costs	84	129
Budgeted contribution margin per unit	$116	$171

a. **Sales Price Variance:**

Spars ($180 − $200) × 6,000 =	$120,000	U
Masts ($300 − $300) × 18,000 =	−0−	
Total	$120,000	U

b. **Sales Mix Variance:**

Spars [6,000 − (4,200/21,200 × 24,000)] × $116 =	$144,453	F
Masts [18,000 − (17,000/21,200 × 24,000)] × $171 =	212,943	U
Total	$ 68,490	U

c. **Sales Quantity Variance:**

Spars [(4,200/21,200 × 24,000) − 4,200] × $116 =	$ 64,347	F
Masts [(17,000/21,200 × 24,000) − 17,000] × $171 =	383,943	F
Total	$448,290	F

d. **Sales Share Variance:**

Spars [6,000 − (4,200/48,000 × 60,000)] × $116 =	$ 87,000	F
Masts [18,000 − (17,000/85,000 × 100,000)] × $171 =	342,000	U
Total	$255,000	U

e. **Sales Volume Variance:**

Spars [(60,000 − 48,000) × (4,200/48,000)] × $116 =	$121,800	F
Masts [(100,000 − 85,000) × (17,000/85,000)] × $171 =	513,000	F
Total	$634,800	F

Appendices 11A and 11B Questions

11A–1   What is the advantage of examining a customer's profits over other segment analysis?

11A–2   What is the *market share variance* and is it controllable by managers?

11A–3   What is the *sales mix variance* and is it controllable by managers?

11B–1   What are the two categories of marketing expenses?

connect   Appendices 11A and 11B Exercise

EXERCISE 11A–1 Variance Analysis [LO8]

Johnston Company (JC) sells two types of bicycles with details as follows for 2011:

	Mountain	**Road**
Plan		
Expected total industry unit sales	96,000	170,000
Budgeted JC unit sales	8,400	34,000
Budgeted selling price per unit	$1,200	$1,600
Budgeted variable costs per unit	$968	$1,258
Actuals		
Actual total industry unit sales	120,000	200,000
Actual JC unit sales.	12,000	36,000
Actual selling price per unit	$1,240	$1,575
Actual variable costs per unit	$1,000	$1,275

Required:
1. Calculate the budgeted contribution margin for each model.
2. Calculate the following variances:
   a. Sales price   d. Sales mix
   b. Market volume   e. Sales quantity
   c. Market share

Appendices 11A and 11B Problems

PROBLEM 11A–2 Variance Analysis [LO8]

Rest Easy produces two types of mattresses: Regular and Heavenly. Budgeted and actual data for 2010 were as follows:

	Master Budget		Actual	
	Regular	Heavenly	Regular	Heavenly
Price per unit	$300	$800	$325	$700
Variable costs per unit.	$220	$590	$238	$583
Unit sales.	4,500	5,500	7,200	4,800

Market Data for 2011:

Expected total market unit sales of mattresses: Regular 300,000; Heavenly 200,000
Actual total market sales of beds: Regular 444,444; Heavenly 222,223

Required:
1. Calculate the following variances:
   a. Sales price   d. Sales mix
   b. Market volume   e. Sales quantity
   c. Market share
2. During 2011, Big Sleep, one of Rest Easy's key competitors introduced an aggressive new marketing campaign that included online advertising. Big Sleep also reduced prices on its mattress that competes directly with Rest Easy's Heavenly model. Management at Rest Easy decided to follow suit by reducing the price on the Heavenly model but decided against changing the marketing approach. Using any of the variances that you believe are relevant from (1) above, evaluate the decisions made by Rest Easy's managers regarding the Heavenly model.

PROBLEM 11B–1 Costing for Customers [LO9]

Clearview Manufacturing & Distributing Ltd. distributes preformed windows to two classes of customers: wholesalers and contractors. In an effort to analyze its marketing expenses by distribution channel, the following statistics were obtained:

	Wholesalers	Contractors
Units sold	6,000	7,500
Kilometres travelled	90,000	126,000
Orders.	3,600	4,500
Customers	114	480
Costs:		
Warehousing per unit	$10.00	$13.00
Transport.	$1.80 per kilometre	
Credit and collection.	$0.60 per order plus	
	$150 per customer	
Selling	$2.00 per order	
Advertising	$100.00 per customer	

Required:
1. Analyze the marketing costs by customer class.
2. Clearview is considering purchasing its own truck and hiring a driver for $48,000 per year. Determine how much it could afford to spend on a truck in year 1 (capital plus operating costs) to equal its current costs.

McGraw Hill connect™   Practise and learn online with Connect.

SHORT-TERM AND LONG-TERM DECISIONS
Chapters 12 and 13

Two time frames are commonly used to characterize the types of decision analysis covered in this final section. **Chapter 12** presents a framework for making short-term decisions where the analysis involves examining those revenues and costs that differ across the alternatives under consideration. Several commonly encountered decision situations are presented, along with the approach used to identify and use relevant costs and benefits. However, the situations examined in this chapter do not involve long-term capital expenditures for items such as plant and equipment, so the time value of money (cost of interest) does not need to be incorporated into the analysis.

Long-term decision analysis typically involves significant capital expenditures and requires explicit consideration of the time value of money. The approach presented in **Chapter 13** is commonly described as *capital budgeting*. The concept of using only relevant costs and benefits in the analysis still holds in this chapter. The chapter also introduces corporate income taxes into the analysis because of their effects on cash flows.

RELEVANT COSTS FOR DECISION MAKING

Learning Objectives

After studying Chapter 12, you should be able to

1. Distinguish between relevant and irrelevant costs in decision making.

2. Prepare analyses for various decision situations.

3. Determine the most profitable use of a constrained resource and the value of obtaining more of the constrained resource.

4. (Appendix 12A) Compute selling prices based on costs.

5. (Appendix 12A) Compute target costs based on selling prices.

REDUCING BRANDS TO CUT LOSSES AT GENERAL MOTORS

Companies that offer a variety of brands of a particular product type must regularly evaluate the profitability of each brand. From a financial perspective, a brand that is deemed to be unprofitable, with little prospect for improvement in the future, should be discontinued. A good example of this concept in practice was the decision by General Motors to discontinue its Pontiac, Saturn, and Hummer brands in the face of growing financial losses.

Discontinuing a brand can lead to improved profitability if the costs saved by no longer producing and selling that brand exceed the revenues lost. Companies such as GM that produce multiple brands of a particular product also hope that when a brand such as the Pontiac is discontinued, existing customers will switch to another more profitable brand, such as the Buick, when making their next automobile purchase. The possibility of getting consumers to substitute other more profitable brands for an unprofitable discontinued brand can have even greater beneficial effects on the financial health of a company.

There is also a human side to discontinuing brands that companies must consider. As a direct consequence of dropping the Pontiac brand, the last remaining GM manufacturing plant in Windsor, Ontario, was closed, resulting in 500 employees losing their jobs. For the first time in 91 years, GM no longer employs anyone in the city of Windsor. In addition to the hardship faced by the laid-off employees, the morale of those employees who retain their jobs with GM can be negatively affected. Some employees may interpret the layoffs as a sign that more bad news is coming and leave the company as soon as other employment opportunities arise. It may also be more difficult for GM to hire new employees when the need arises because of concerns about future layoffs. Although the financial effects of these human factors are very difficult, if not impossible, to determine, they are nonetheless important to consider as part of an overall decision to keep or discontinue a brand or product line.

Which revenues and costs are relevant when evaluating the financial effects of discontinuing a brand or product line? This and other related topics are considered in this chapter.

Sources: Nicholas Van Paret, "GM CEO Predicts Return to Profit This Year," *Financial Post*, January 5, 2010; and Grace Macaluso and Joseph Brean, "After 91 Years, GM Calls It Quits in Windsor," Postmedia Network and *National Post*, July 27, 2010.

ecision making is a critical aspect of managing an organization. Managers are constantly faced with having to decide which products or services to offer, which production methods to use, whether to make or buy component parts, what prices to charge, whether to accept special orders at special prices, how to allocate limited resources, and so on. In each case, the decision should lead to outcomes that contribute to achieving the performance goals identified as part of the organization's strategic objectives (e.g., grow revenues, reduce costs, improve return on investment, etc.). However, decision making is a complex process. Numerous alternatives may exist for each decision situation and large amounts of data must be analyzed, only some of which are relevant.

How can managers cope with these complexities in an effort to consistently make good decisions? The key is to identify and compare *only* the relevant costs and benefits for each alternative. **Relevant costs** are those that differ among the alternatives under consideration *and* that will be incurred in the future (i.e., the cost has not already been incurred). A key challenge for managers, and fundamental to good decision making, is differentiating between relevant and irrelevant costs. This is critical because consideration of irrelevant costs wastes managers' time and effort, and can lead to the wrong decisions. Further complicating matters is the fact that the relevance of specific costs and benefits depends on the decision situation. For example, a product supervisor's salary is typically irrelevant in deciding whether or not to accept a special order from a customer but can be relevant when deciding whether to keep or drop that product line. The purpose of this chapter is to provide a framework for distinguishing between relevant and irrelevant costs by illustrating their use in a wide range of decision-making situations.

We begin the chapter by developing a general framework for identifying relevant costs and benefits. We then apply this framework to a variety of non-recurring situations to illustrate how the relevance of a cost or benefit depends on the type of decision being made. Next we turn our attention to analyzing situations where managers must decide how to allocate a limited resource such as labour-hours. Finally, the relationship between relevant costs and pricing issues is further examined in the appendix.

Two aspects of the decision situations and the related analysis presented in this chapter are important to emphasize. First, none of the situations involve capital expenditures (e.g., replacing production equipment), where the time value of money can be an important factor in the analysis. This type of analysis, termed *capital budgeting*, is covered in Chapter 13. Second, the key criterion used in the various decision situations presented in this chapter is the maximization of operating income. However, in practice, managers may also consider qualitative factors when making decisions. For example, when deciding whether to keep or drop a product or segment, the effect on employee morale and the impact on the company's reputation with its customers may be important but very difficult or costly to quantify. The extent to which qualitative factors influence a decision will vary from situation to situation but they are often taken into account.

Relevant cost
A cost that differs among the alternatives in a particular decision and will be incurred in the future. In managerial accounting, this term is synonymous with *avoidable cost* and *differential cost.*

COST CONCEPTS FOR DECISION MAKING

Four cost terms discussed in Chapter 2 are particularly applicable to this chapter. These terms are *differential costs, incremental costs, opportunity costs,* and *sunk costs.* You may find it helpful to turn back to Chapter 2 and review the concepts before reading on.

LEARNING OBJECTIVE 1
Distinguish between relevant and irrelevant costs in decision making.

Identifying Relevant Costs and Benefits

Because it is fundamental to the proper analysis of the various decision situations covered in this chapter, we begin by identifying the nature of relevant costs and benefits. Only those costs and benefits that differ in total among alternatives and that will be incurred in the future are relevant in a decision. If a cost will be the same regardless of the alternative selected, then it can be ignored. For example, if you are trying to decide whether to go to a movie or to rent a DVD for the evening, the lease payments on your car are irrelevant. Whether you go to a movie or rent a DVD, the lease payments will be exactly the same and are therefore irrelevant in the decision. On the other hand, the cost of the movie ticket and the cost of renting the DVD would be relevant in the decision because they are *avoidable costs.*

Avoidable cost

Any cost that can be eliminated (in whole or in part) by choosing one alternative over another in a decision-making situation. In managerial accounting, this term is synonymous with *relevant cost* and *differential cost.*

An **avoidable cost** is a cost that can be eliminated in whole or in part by choosing one alternative over another. By choosing the alternative of going to the movie, the cost of renting the DVD can be avoided. By choosing the alternative of renting the DVD, the cost of the movie ticket can be avoided. Therefore, the cost of the movie ticket and the cost of renting the DVD are both avoidable costs. On the other hand, the lease payments on the car are not an avoidable cost because you would continue to lease your car under either alternative. Avoidable costs are relevant costs. Unavoidable costs are irrelevant costs.

Two broad categories of costs are never relevant in decisions. These irrelevant costs are

1. Sunk costs (e.g., previously owned DVD player).
2. Future costs that do not differ between the alternatives (e.g., car lease payments when making a "go to a movie versus renting the DVD" decision).

As we learned in Chapter 2, a *sunk cost* is a cost that has already been incurred and that cannot be avoided, regardless of what a manager decides to do. Sunk costs do not change, regardless of the alternatives being considered, and they are therefore always irrelevant and should be ignored. Similarly, future costs that are the same under each alternative being considered are also irrelevant since they will not affect the decision. The cost of the car lease next month is a future cost but will be the same whether you go to the move or rent the DVD. On the other hand, future costs that do differ between alternatives *are* relevant. For example, when deciding whether to go to a movie or rent a DVD, the cost of buying a movie ticket and the cost of renting a DVD have not yet been incurred. These are future costs that differ between alternatives when the decision is being made and therefore are relevant.

Along with sunk cost, the term *differential cost* was introduced in Chapter 2. In managerial accounting, the terms *avoidable cost, differential cost, incremental cost,* and *relevant cost* are often used interchangeably. To identify the costs and benefits that are relevant in a particular decision situation, these steps can be followed:

1. Eliminate costs and benefits that do not differ between alternatives. These irrelevant costs consist of (a) sunk costs and (b) future costs and benefits that do not differ between alternatives.
2. Use the remaining costs and benefits that do differ between alternatives in making the decision. The costs that remain are the differential, or avoidable, costs.

Different Costs for Different Purposes

It is important to recognize that costs that are relevant in one decision situation are not necessarily relevant in another. Simply put, this means that *the manager needs different costs for different purposes.* For one purpose, a particular group of costs may be relevant; for another purpose, an entirely different group of costs may be relevant. Thus, in *each* decision situation the manager must examine the data at hand and isolate the relevant costs. Otherwise, the manager runs the risk of being misled by irrelevant data.

The concept of "different costs for different purposes" is basic to managerial accounting; we will see its application frequently in the remainder of this chapter.

An Example of Identifying Relevant Costs and Benefits

Cynthia is currently a student in an MBA program in Halifax and would like to visit a friend in Moncton over the weekend. She is trying to decide whether to drive or take the train. Because she is on a tight budget, she wants to carefully consider the costs of the two alternatives. If one alternative is far less expensive than the other, that may determine her choice. By car, the distance between her apartment in Halifax and her friend's apartment in Moncton is 265 kilometres. Cynthia has compiled the list of items (shown in the table below) to consider.

	Automobile Costs		
Item		**Annual Cost of Fixed Items**	**Cost per km (based on 16,000 km per year)**
(a)	Annual straight-line depreciation on car [($24,000 original cost − $10,000 estimated resale value in 5 years)/5 years]	$2,800	$0.175
(b)	Cost of gasoline ($1.00 per litre ÷ 10 kilometres per litre)		0.100
(c)	Annual cost of auto insurance and licence	2,000	0.125
(d)	Maintenance and repairs		0.050
(e)	Parking fees at university ($45 per month × 8 months)	360	0.023
(f)	Tires ($600 to replace all 4 tires every 50,000 km kilometres)		0.012
(g)	Total average cost per kilometre		$0.485

	Additional Data	
Item		
(h)	Cost of round-trip VIA ticket	$125
(i)	Benefit of relaxing and being able to study during the train ride rather than having to drive	?
(j)	Cost of putting the cat in a kennel while gone	$40
(k)	Benefit of having a car available in Moncton	?
(l)	Hassle of parking the car in Moncton	?
(m)	Cost of parking the car in Moncton	$25 per day

Which costs and benefits are relevant in this decision? Remember, only those costs and benefits that differ between alternatives are relevant. Everything else is irrelevant and can be ignored. Starting at the top of the list, we consider the relevance of each item:

- Item (a): The original cost of the car is a sunk cost. This cost has already been incurred and therefore can never differ between alternatives. Consequently, it is irrelevant and can be ignored. The same is true of the accounting depreciation of $2,800 per year, which simply spreads the sunk cost across the useful life of the asset.
- Item (b): The cost of gasoline consumed by driving to Moncton would clearly be a relevant cost in this decision. If Cynthia takes the train, this cost would not be incurred. Hence, the cost differs between alternatives and is therefore relevant.
- Item (c): The annual cost of auto insurance and licence is not relevant. Whether Cynthia takes the train or drives on this particular trip, her annual auto insurance premium and her auto licence fee will remain the same.[1]
- Item (d): The cost of maintenance and repairs is relevant. While maintenance and repair costs have a large random component, over the long run they are typically proportional to the amount the car is driven. Thus, the average cost of $0.05 per kilometre is a reasonable estimate to use.
- Item (e): The monthly fee that Cynthia pays to park at her university during the academic year, would not be relevant in the decision of how to get to Moncton. Regardless of which alternative she selects—driving or taking the train—she will still need to pay for parking at school.
- Item (f): The cost of replacing all four tires ($600) every 50,000 kilometres is relevant. The more often Cynthia uses her car, the sooner she will have to replace the

tires. Therefore, the $0.012 per kilometre for tires is appropriate to use in deciding whether to drive or take the train.

- Item (g): Some elements of the total average cost of $0.485 per kilometre are relevant, but some are not relevant. Since it contains some irrelevant costs, it would be incorrect to estimate the cost of driving to Moncton and back by simply multiplying the $0.485 by 530 kilometres (265 kilometres each way × 2). This erroneous approach would yield a cost of driving of $257.05. Unfortunately, such mistakes are often made in both personal life and in business. Since the total cost is stated on a per kilometre basis, people are easily misled. Often people think that if the cost is stated as $0.485 per kilometre, the cost of driving 100 kilometres is $48.50. But it is not. Many of the costs included in the $0.485 cost per kilometre are sunk and/or fixed and will not increase if the car is driven another 100 kilometres. The $0.485 is an average cost, not an incremental cost. Study such unitized costs carefully (i.e., costs stated in terms of a dollar amount per unit, per kilometre, per direct labour-hour, per machine-hour, and so on)—they are often misleading.

- Item (h): The $125 cost of a round-trip ticket on VIA is clearly relevant in this decision. If Cynthia drives, she would not have to buy the ticket.

- Item (i): Although it is difficult to put a dollar value on relaxing and being able to study while on the train, this item is relevant to the decision. It is relevant because it is a benefit that is available only if she takes the train.

- Item (j): The cost of putting Cynthia's cat in the kennel while she is gone is clearly irrelevant to this decision. Whether she takes the train or drives to Moncton she will still need to put her cat in a kennel.

- Items (k) and (l): Like item (i), they are relevant to the decision even if it is difficult to measure their dollar impacts.

- Item (m): The cost of parking in Moncton is relevant to the decision since it will be incurred only if Cynthia takes her car.

Bringing together all of the relevant data, Cynthia would estimate the relative costs of driving and taking the train as follows:

Relevant financial cost of driving to Moncton:	
Gasoline (530 kilometres at $0.10 per kilometre)	$ 53.00
Maintenance and repairs (530 kilometres @ $0.05 per km)	26.50
Tires (530 kilometres @ $0.012 per km)	6.36
Cost of parking the car in Moncton (2 days @ $25 per day)	50.00
Total	$135.86
Relevant financial cost of taking the train to Moncton:	
Cost of round-trip VIA ticket from Halifax to Moncton	$125.00

What should Cynthia do? From a purely financial standpoint, it would be cheaper by $10.86 ($135.86 − $125.00) to take the train. Cynthia has to decide whether the benefit of having the car available in Moncton justifies the higher cost of driving.

In this example, we focused on identifying the relevant costs and benefits—everything else was ignored. In the next example, we will begin the analysis by including all of the costs and benefits—relevant or not. We will see that if we are very careful, we will still get the correct answer because the irrelevant costs and benefits will cancel out when we compare the alternatives.

Reconciling the Total and Differential Approaches

Oak Harbour Woodworks is considering a new labour-saving machine that rents for $3,000 per year. The machine will be used on the company's coat rack production line. Data concerning the company's annual sales and costs of coat racks with and without the new machine are shown in the following table.

	Current Situation	Situation with the New Machine
Units produced and sold..................	5,000	5,000
Selling price per unit	$ 40	$ 40
Direct materials cost per unit	14	14
Direct labour cost per unit.................	8	5
Variable overhead cost per unit.............	2	2
Fixed costs, other	62,000	62,000
Fixed costs, new machine..................	—	3,000

Given the annual sales and the price and cost data in this table, the operating income for the product under the two alternatives can be computed as shown in Exhibit 12–1.

Note that the operating income is higher by $12,000 with the new machine, so it is the better alternative. Note also that the $12,000 advantage for the new machine can be obtained in two different ways. It is the difference between the $30,000 operating income with the new machine and the $18,000 operating income for the current situation. It is also the sum of the differential costs and benefits as shown in the last column of Exhibit 12–1. A positive number in the Differential Costs and Benefits column indicates that the difference between the alternatives favours the new machine; a negative number indicates that the difference favours the current situation. A zero in that column simply means that the total amount for the item is exactly the same for both alternatives. So, since the difference in the operating incomes equals the sum of the differences for the individual items, any cost or benefit that is the same for both alternatives will have no impact on which alternative is preferred. This is why we stated earlier that costs and benefits that do not differ between alternatives are irrelevant and can be ignored. If we properly account for them, they will cancel out when we compare the alternatives.

We could have arrived at the same solution more quickly by ignoring the irrelevant costs and benefits:

- The selling price per unit and the number of units sold do not differ between the alternatives. Therefore, the total sales revenues are exactly the same for the two alternatives as shown in Exhibit 12–1. Since the sales revenues are exactly the same, they have no effect on the difference in operating income between the two alternatives. That is shown in the last column in Exhibit 12–1, which indicates a $0 differential benefit.

EXHIBIT 12–1   Total and Differential Costs

	Current Situation	Situation with New Machine	Differential Costs and Benefits
Sales (5,000 units @ $40 per unit)	$200,000	$200,000	$0
Less variable expenses:			
Direct materials (5,000 units @ $14 per unit)	70,000	70,000	0
Direct labour (5,000 units @ $8 and $5 per unit)	40,000	25,000	15,000
Variable overhead (5,000 units @ $2 per unit)	10,000	10,000	0
Total variable expenses	120,000	105,000	
Contribution margin	80,000	95,000	
Less fixed expenses:			
Other......................................	62,000	62,000	0
Rent of new machine	0	3,000	(3,000)
Total fixed expenses	62,000	65,000	
Operating income.............................	$ 18,000	$ 30,000	$12,000

- The direct materials cost per unit, the variable overhead cost per unit, and the number of units produced and sold do not differ between the alternatives. Consequently, the direct materials cost and the variable overhead cost will be the same for the two alternatives and can be ignored.
- The "other" fixed expenses do not differ between the alternatives, so they can be ignored as well.

Indeed, the only costs that do differ between the alternatives are direct labour costs and the fixed rental cost of the new machine. Hence, these are the only relevant costs. The two alternatives can be compared based on just these relevant costs:

Net advantage to renting the new machine:	
Decrease in direct labour costs (5,000 units at a cost savings of $3 per unit)	$15,000
Increase in fixed expenses (rent)	(3,000)
Net annual cost savings from renting the new machine	$12,000

If we focus on just the relevant costs and benefits, therefore, we get exactly the same answer that we got when we listed all of the costs and benefits—including those that do not differ between the alternatives and hence are irrelevant. We get the same answer because the only costs and benefits that matter in the final comparison of the operating incomes are those that differ between the two alternatives and therefore are not zero in the last column of Exhibit 12–1. Those two relevant costs are both listed in the above analysis showing the net advantage to renting the new machine.

Why Isolate Relevant Costs?

In the preceding example, we used two different approaches to analyze the alternatives. First, we considered only the relevant costs. Second, we considered all costs, both those that were relevant and those that were not. We obtained the same answer under both approaches. It would be natural to ask, "Why bother isolating relevant costs when total costs will do the job just as well?" Isolating relevant costs is desirable for at least two reasons.

First, only rarely will enough information be available to prepare a detailed income statement for both alternatives as we have done in the preceding examples. Assume, for example, that you are called on to make a decision relating to a *single product* of a multi-departmental, multi-product firm. Under these circumstances, it would be virtually impossible to prepare an income statement of any type. You would have to rely on your ability to recognize which costs are relevant and which are not in order to assemble the data necessary to make a decision.

Second, combining irrelevant costs with relevant costs may cause confusion and distract attention from the matters that are really critical. Furthermore, the danger always exists that an irrelevant piece of data may be used improperly, resulting in an incorrect decision. Indeed, research shows that managers will often attempt to use *all* information provided, relevant and irrelevant, when making a decision.[2] The best approach is to discard irrelevant data and base the decision entirely on the relevant data.

Relevant cost analysis, combined with the contribution approach to the income statement, provides a powerful tool for making decisions. We will investigate various uses of this tool in the remaining sections of this chapter.

A decision analysis can be flawed by incorrectly including irrelevant costs such as sunk costs and future costs that do not differ between alternatives. It can also be flawed by omitting future costs that do differ between alternatives. This is a problem particularly with environmental costs because they have dramatically increased in recent years and are often overlooked by managers.

Consider the environmental complications posed by a decision of whether to install a solvent-based or powder-based system for spray-painting parts. In a solvent painting system, parts are sprayed as they move along a conveyor. The paint that misses the part is swept away by a wall of water, called a *water curtain*. The excess paint accumulates in a pit as sludge that must be removed each month. Environmental regulations in some countries classify this sludge as hazardous waste. As a result, a permit must be obtained to produce the waste and meticulous records must be maintained of how the waste is transported, stored, and disposed of. The annual costs of complying with these regulations can easily exceed $140,000 in total for a painting facility that initially costs only $400,000 to build. The costs of complying with environmental regulations include the following:

- The waste sludge must be hauled to a special disposal site. The typical disposal fee is about $300 per barrel, or $55,000 per year for a modest solvent-based painting system.
- Workers must be specially trained to handle the paint sludge.
- The company must carry special insurance.
- The company must pay substantial fees to the government for releasing pollutants (i.e., the solvent) into the air.
- The water in the water curtain must be specially treated to remove contaminants. This can cost tens of thousands of dollars per year.

In contrast, a powder-based painting system avoids almost all of these environmental costs. Excess powder used in the painting process can be recovered and reused without creating hazardous waste. Additionally, the powder-based system does not release contaminants into the atmosphere. Therefore, even though the cost of building a powder-based system may be higher than the cost of building a solvent-based system, over the long run the costs of the powder-based system may be far lower due to the high environmental costs of a solvent-based system. Managers need to be aware of such environmental costs and take them fully into account when making decisions.

Source: Germain Böer, Margaret Curtin, and Louis Hoyt, "Environmental Cost Management," *Management Accounting, 80*: 3, 1998 pp. 28–38.

■ ANALYSIS OF VARIOUS DECISION SITUATIONS

Periodically, managers are faced with making non-routine or special decisions. Should a product line or segment be kept or dropped? Should a product component be made internally or purchased from an external supplier (outsourced)? Should special orders be accepted or rejected? Should a product be sold as is, or processed further? While on the surface these may appear to be very different decision situations, the approach to the analysis is similar in each case. For each situation, the relevant costs and benefits must be quantified, and the alternative with the most favourable impact on operating income selected. In some situations, the analysis will consist only of a comparison of relevant costs (make versus buy) while in others, both relevant benefits and relevant costs will be involved (keep or drop a product). As will be illustrated in the examples of each decision situation that follows, the challenge for managers is identifying and quantifying the relevant costs and benefits.

> **LEARNING OBJECTIVE 2**
> Prepare analyses for various decision situations.

Adding and Dropping Product Lines and Other Segments

Decisions relating to whether existing product lines or other segments of a company should be dropped and new ones added are among the most difficult that a manager has to make. In such decisions, many qualitative and quantitative factors must be considered. Ultimately, however, any final decision to drop an old segment or to add a new one is going to hinge primarily on the impact the decision will have on operating income. To assess this impact, it is necessary to prepare a careful analysis of the costs involved.

EXHIBIT 12–2   AFM
Electronics Product Lines

	Total	Product Line		
		Televisions	Stereos	Cameras
Sales..............................	$340,000	$187,500	$112,500	$40,000
Less variable expenses	136,500	75,000	37,500	24,000
Contribution margin	203,500	112,500	75,000	16,000
Less fixed expenses:				
Salaries..........................	69,400	44,250	18,750	6,400
Advertising	17,950	1,500	11,250	5,200
Utilities	2,300	750	750	800
Depreciation—fixtures	6,100	1,500	3,000	1,600
Rent	27,200	15,000	9,000	3,200
Insurance	4,150	3,000	750	400
General administrative	40,800	22,500	13,500	4,800
Total fixed expenses...............	167,900	88,500	57,000	22,400
Operating income (loss)	$ 35,600	$ 24,000	$ 18,000	$ (6,400)

Consider the three major product lines of AFM Electronics—televisions, stereos, and cameras. Sales and cost information for the preceding month for each separate product line and for the company in total are given in Exhibit 12–2.

What can be done to improve the company's overall performance? One product line—cameras—shows an operating loss for the month. Perhaps dropping this line would cause profits in the company as a whole to improve. In deciding whether the line should be dropped, management should employ the reasoning that follows.

If the camera line is dropped, then the company will lose $16,000 per month in contribution margin. By dropping the line, however, it may be possible to avoid some fixed costs by, for example, laying off certain employees or reducing advertising costs. If by dropping the camera line the company is able to avoid more in fixed costs than it loses in contribution margin, then it will be better off if the line is eliminated, because overall operating income should improve. On the other hand, if the company is not able to avoid as much in fixed costs as it loses in contribution margin, then the camera line should be retained. In short, the manager should ask, "What costs can I avoid if I drop this product line?"

As we have seen from our earlier discussion, not all costs are avoidable. For example, some of the costs associated with a product line may be sunk costs. Other costs may be allocated common costs that will not differ in total regardless of whether the product line is dropped or retained. As discussed in Chapter 5, an activity-based costing analysis may be used to help identify the relevant costs.

To show how the manager should proceed in a product-line analysis, suppose that the management of AFM Electronics has analyzed the costs being charged to the three product lines and has determined the following:

1. The salaries expense represents salaries paid to employees working directly in each product-line area. All of the employees working in camera-related activities would be laid off if the line is dropped.
2. The advertising expense represents direct advertising of each product line and is avoidable if the line is dropped.
3. The utilities expense represents utilities costs for the entire company. The amount charged to each product line is an allocation based on space occupied and is not avoidable if the product line is dropped.
4. The depreciation expense represents depreciation on fixtures used for display of the various product lines. Although the fixtures are nearly new, they are custom-built and will have little resale value if the camera line is dropped.
5. The rent expense represents rent on the entire building housing the company; it is allocated to the product lines on the basis of sales dollars. The monthly rent of $27,200 is fixed under a long-term lease agreement.

6. The insurance expense represents insurance carried on inventories within each of the three product-line areas.

7. The general administrative expense represents the costs of accounting, purchasing, and general management, which are allocated to the product lines on the basis of sales dollars. Total administrative costs will not change if the camera line is dropped.

With this information, management can identify costs that can and cannot be avoided if the product line is dropped (see the following).

	Total Cost	Not Avoidable*	Avoidable
Salaries	$ 6,400		$ 6,400
Advertising.	5,200		5,200
Utilities.	800	$ 800	
Depreciation—fixtures.	1,600	1,600	
Rent.	3,200	3,200	
Insurance.	400		400
General administrative.	4,800	4,800	
Total fixed expenses	$22,400	$10,400	$12,000

*These costs represent either (1) sunk costs or (2) future costs that will not change if the camera line is retained or discontinued.

To determine how dropping the line will affect the overall profits of the company, we can compare the contribution margin that will be lost to the costs that can be avoided if the line is dropped:

Contribution margin lost if the camera line is discontinued (see Exhibit 12–2).	$(16,000)
Less fixed costs that can be avoided if the camera line is discontinued (see above).	12,000
Decrease in overall company operating income	$ (4,000)

In this case, the fixed costs that can be avoided by dropping the product line are less than the contribution margin that will be lost. Therefore, based on the data given, the camera line should not be discontinued unless a more profitable use can be found for the floor and counter space that it is occupying.

A Comparative Format

Some managers prefer to approach decisions of this type by preparing comparative income statements showing the effects on the company as a whole of either keeping or dropping the product line in question. A comparative analysis of this type for AFM Electronics is shown in Exhibit 12–3.

As shown by column 3 in the exhibit, overall company operating income will decrease by $4,000 each period if the cameras line is dropped. This is the same answer, of course, as we obtained in our earlier analysis.

Beware of Allocated Fixed Costs

Our conclusion that the camera line should not be dropped seems to conflict with the data shown earlier in Exhibit 12–2. Recall from the exhibit that the camera line is showing a loss rather than a profit. Why keep a line that is showing a loss? The explanation for this apparent inconsistency lies at least in part with the common fixed costs that are being allocated to the product lines. As we observed in Chapter 11, one of the great dangers in

EXHIBIT 12–3
A Comparative Format for
Product-Line Analysis

	Keep Cameras	Drop Cameras	Difference: Operating Income Increase or (Decrease)
Sales.	$40,000	$0	$(40,000)
Less variable expenses	24,000	0	24,000
Contribution margin	16,000	0	(16,000)
Less fixed expenses:			
Salaries.	6,400	0	6,400
Advertising	5,200	0	5,200
Utilities	800	800	0
Depreciation—fixtures	1,600	1,600	0
Rent	3,200	3,200	0
Insurance	400	0	400
General administrative	4,800	4,800	0
Total fixed expenses.	22,400	10,400	12,000
Operating income (loss)	$ (6,400)	$(10,400)	$ (4,000)

allocating common fixed costs is that such allocations can make a product line (or other segment of a business) *look* less profitable than it really is. By allocating the common fixed costs among all product lines, the camera line has been made to *look* as if it was unprofitable, whereas, in fact, dropping the line would result in a decrease in overall company operating income. This point can be seen clearly if we recast the data in Exhibit 12–2 by eliminating the allocation of the common fixed costs. This recasting of data—using the segmented approach from Chapter 11—is shown in Exhibit 12–4.

Exhibit 12–4 gives us a much different perspective of the profitability of the camera line compared to Exhibit 12–2. As shown in Exhibit 12–4, the camera line is covering all of its own traceable fixed costs and is generating a $2,400 segment margin toward covering the common fixed costs of the company. Unless another product line can be found that will generate a greater segment margin than this, the company would be better off keeping

EXHIBIT 12–4   AFM
Electronics Produce Lines—
Recast in Contribution Format
(from Exhibit 12–2)

	Total	Product Line		
		Televisions	Stereos	Cameras
Sales.	$340,000	$187,500	$112,500	$40,000
Less variable expenses	136,500	75,000	37,500	24,000
Contribution margin	203,500	112,500	75,000	16,000
Less traceable fixed expenses:				
Salaries.	69,400	44,250	18,750	6,400
Advertising	17,950	1,500	11,250	5,200
Depreciation—fixtures	6,100	1,500	3,000	1,600
Insurance	4,150	3,000	750	400
Total fixed expenses.	97,600	50,250	33,750	13,600
Product-line segment margin.	105,900	$ 62,250	$ 41,250	$ 2,400*
Less common fixed expenses:				
Utilities	2,300			
Rent	27,200			
General administrative	40,800			
Total	70,300			
Operating income.	$ 35,600			

*If the cameras line is dropped, this $2,400 in segment margin will be lost to the company. In addition, we have seen that the $1,600 depreciation on the fixtures is a sunk cost that cannot be avoided. The sum of these two figures ($2,400 + $1,600 = $4,000) would be the decrease in the company's overall profits if the cameras line was discontinued.

the camera line. By keeping the line, the company's overall operating income will be higher than if the product line was dropped.[3]

Additionally, we should note that managers may choose to retain an unprofitable product line if the line is necessary to the sale of other products or if it serves as a "magnet" to attract customers. Bread, for example, is not an especially profitable line in food stores, but customers expect it to be available, and many would undoubtedly shift their buying elsewhere if a particular store decided to stop carrying that product. Accordingly, to the extent that dropping a product line or segment results in decreases (or increases) to sales of other products or segments, the related impact on contribution margin should be included in the keep versus drop analysis.

DECISION AID

KEEP OR DROP A PRODUCT/SEGMENT

Relevant Costs and Benefits
- Contribution margin (CM) lost if dropped
- Fixed costs avoided if dropped
- CM lost/gained on other products/segments

Irrelevant Costs
- Allocated common costs
- Sunk costs

Decision Rule:

Keep if   CM lost (all products/segments) > fixed costs avoided + CM gained (other products/segments)

Drop if   CM lost (all products/segments) < fixed costs avoided + CM gained (other products/segments)

The Make or Buy Decision

Many steps may be involved in getting a finished product into the hands of a consumer. First, raw materials may have to be obtained through mining, drilling, growing crops, raising animals, and so forth. Second, these raw materials may have to be processed to remove impurities and to extract the desirable and usable materials. Third, the usable materials may have to undergo some preliminary conversion so as to be usable in final products. For example, cotton must be made into thread and textiles before being made into clothing. Fourth, the actual manufacturing of the finished product must take place. And finally, the finished product must be distributed to the ultimate consumer. Each of these steps is part of the value chain discussed in Chapter 1.

Separate companies may carry out each of the steps in the value chain or a single company may carry out several of the steps. When a single company is involved in more than one of these steps in the value chain, it is following a policy of **vertical integration**. Vertical integration is very common. Some firms control *all* of the activities in the value chain from producing basic raw materials right up to the manufacture and final distribution of finished goods. Other firms integrate on a smaller scale by purchasing many of the parts and materials that go into their finished products.

A decision to produce internally, rather than to buy externally from a supplier, is called a **make or buy decision**. Indeed, any decision relating to vertical integration is a make or buy decision, since the company is deciding whether to meet its own needs internally or to buy externally.

Vertical integration
The involvement by a single company in more than one of the steps of the value chain from production of basic raw materials to the manufacture and distribution of a finished product.

Make or buy decision
A decision as to whether an item should be produced internally or purchased from an outside supplier.

Strategic Aspects of the Make or Buy Decision

Integration provides certain advantages. An integrated firm is less dependent on its suppliers and may be able to ensure a smoother flow of parts and materials for production than a non-integrated firm. For example, a strike against a major parts supplier can interrupt the operations of a non-integrated firm for many months, whereas an integrated firm that is producing its own parts might be able to continue operations. Also, many firms feel that they can control quality better by producing their own parts and materials, rather than by relying on the quality control standards of outside suppliers.

The positive aspects of integration are counterbalanced by some advantages of using external suppliers. By pooling demand from a number of firms, a supplier may be able to realize economies of scale in research and development and in manufacturing. These economies of scale can result in higher quality and lower unit costs than would be possible if the firm was to attempt to make the parts on its own. However, companies must be careful to retain control over activities that are essential to maintaining their competitive position. For example, in response to growing competition from Google and Apple, Research in Motion (RIM) recently purchased Cellmania, a company specializing in the development of mobile apps. This acquisition is intended to give RIM more control over the development of apps, which are so critical to the popularity of smartphones. Some analysts have suggested that acquisitions such as this by RIM are indicative of a more general recent trend toward vertical integration.

An Example of Make or Buy

To provide an illustration of a make or buy decision, consider OSN Cycles. The company is now producing the heavy-duty gear shifters used in its most popular line of mountain bikes. The company's Accounting Department reports the following costs of producing the shifter internally:

	Per Unit	8,000 Units
Direct materials	$ 6	$ 48,000
Direct labour	4	32,000
Variable overhead	1	8,000
Supervisor's salary	3	24,000
Depreciation of special equipment	2	16,000
Allocated general overhead	5	40,000
Total cost	$21	$168,000

An outside supplier has offered to sell OSN Cycles 8,000 shifters per year at a price of only $19 each. Should the company stop producing the shifters internally and start purchasing them from the outside supplier? To approach the decision from a financial point of view, the manager should again focus on the differential costs. As we have seen, the differential costs can be obtained by eliminating those costs that are not avoidable—that is, by eliminating (1) the sunk costs and (2) the future costs that will continue regardless of whether the shifters are produced internally or purchased outside. The costs that remain after making these eliminations are the costs that are avoidable to the company by purchasing outside. If these avoidable costs are less than the outside purchase price, then the company should continue to manufacture its own shifters and reject the outside supplier's offer. That is, the company should purchase outside only if the outside purchase price is less than the costs that can be avoided internally as a result of stopping production of the shifters.

Looking at the data above, note first that depreciation of special equipment is listed as one of the costs of producing the shifters internally. Since the equipment has already been purchased, this depreciation is a sunk cost and is therefore irrelevant. If the equipment could be sold, its salvage value would be relevant. Or if the machine could be used to make other products, this could be relevant as well. However, we will assume that the equipment has no salvage value and that it has no other use except in making the heavy-duty gear shifters.

Also note that the company is allocating a portion of its general overhead costs to the shifters. Any portion of this general overhead cost that would actually be eliminated if the gear shifters were purchased rather than made would be relevant in the analysis. However, it is likely that the general overhead costs allocated to the gear shifters are in fact common to all items produced in the factory and would continue unchanged even if the shifters are purchased from the outside. Such allocated common costs are not differential costs (because they do not differ between the make or buy alternatives) and should be eliminated from the analysis along with the sunk costs.

The variable costs of producing the shifters (materials, labour, and variable overhead) are differential costs, because they can be avoided by buying the shifters from the outside supplier. If the supervisor can be laid off and her salary avoided by buying the shifters, then it too will be a differential cost and relevant to the decision. Assuming that both the variable costs and the supervisor's salary can be avoided by buying from the outside supplier, the analysis takes the form shown in Exhibit 12–5.

Since it costs $5 less per unit to continue to make the shifters, OSN Cycles should reject the outside supplier's offer. However, there is one additional factor that the company may wish to consider before coming to a final decision. This factor is the opportunity cost of the space now being used to produce the shifters.

Opportunity Cost

If the space now being used to produce the shifters *would otherwise be idle,* then OSN Cycles should continue to produce its own shifters and the supplier's offer should be rejected, as stated above. Idle space that has no alternative use has an opportunity cost of zero.

But what if the space now being used to produce shifters could be used for some other purpose? In that case, the space would have an opportunity cost that would have to be considered in assessing the desirability of the supplier's offer. What would this opportunity cost be? It would be the segment margin that could be derived from the best alternative use of the space.

To illustrate, assume that the space now being used to produce shifters could be used to produce disc brakes that would generate a segment margin of $60,000 per year. Under

EXHIBIT 12–5   OSN Cycles Make or Buy Analysis

	Production "Cost" per Unit	Per Unit Differential Costs — Make	Per Unit Differential Costs — Buy	Total Differential Costs—8,000 Units — Make	Total Differential Costs—8,000 Units — Buy
Direct materials	$ 6	$ 6		$ 48,000	
Direct labour	4	4		32,000	
Variable overhead	1	1		8,000	
Supervisor's salary	3	3		24,000	
Depreciation of special equipment	2	—		—	
Allocated general overhead	5	—		—	
Outside purchase price			$19		$152,000
Total cost	$21	$14	$19	$112,000	$152,000
Difference in favour of continuing to make		$ 5		$40,000	

these conditions, OSN Cycles would be better off to accept the supplier's offer and to use the available space to produce the new product line:

	Make	Buy
Differential cost per unit (see Exhibit 12–5)	$ 14	$ 19
Number of units needed annually	× 8,000	× 8,000
Total annual cost	112,000	152,000
Opportunity cost—segment margin forgone on a potential new product line.	60,000	—
Total cost	$172,000	$152,000
Difference in favour of purchasing from the outside supplier		$ 20,000[4]

Opportunity costs are not recorded in the accounts of an organization because they do not represent actual dollar outlays. Rather, they represent economic benefits that are *forgone* as a result of pursuing a particular course of action. Because of this, opportunity costs are often erroneously ignored by managers when making decisions. The opportunity costs of OSN Cycles are sufficiently large in this case to make continued production of the shifters very costly from an economic point of view.

DECISION AID

MAKE OR BUY

Relevant Costs
- Incremental costs of making the product (variable and fixed)
- Opportunity cost of utilizing space to make the product
- Outside purchase price

Irrelevant Costs
- Allocated common costs
- Sunk costs

Total relevant costs of making = incremental costs + opportunity costs

Decision Rule:

Make if   total relevant costs of making < outside purchase price
Buy if   total relevant costs of making > outside purchase price

IN BUSINESS

Companies regularly review the outsourcing arrangements they have in place to meet their production needs in the short term and the long term. For financial or strategic reasons, production that had previously been outsourced may be "in-sourced," which means the use of an external supplier is discontinued and production is done internally. For example, if the cost of outsourcing becomes too high or it becomes more economically feasible to increase production capacity, companies may decide to increase the extent of vertical integration. Thus, "make or buy" decisions are not seen as permanent, but instead are monitored and managed on an ongoing basis to ensure that the company's objectives are being met.

A good example of the management of outsourcing arrangements is provided by the BMW decision to no longer use the services of Magna International Inc. (a Canadian-owned company) to produce BMW's X3, one of its sport utility vehicles. Magna had produced 113,000 X3s in 2006 at its plant in Austria. Citing the high cost of outsourcing, BMW announced that it would produce the X3 at its own plant in South Carolina. BMW officials also noted that moving production of the X3 to the United States, the biggest market for the vehicle, also protects the company against the possibility of further declines in the value of the U.S. dollar.

Source: Greg Keenan, "BMW Decision Costly for Magna's Austrian Operation," *The Globe and Mail*, May 16, 2007, p. B4.

Special Orders

Managers often must evaluate whether a *special order* should be accepted, and if the order is accepted, the price that should be charged. A **special order** is a one-time order that is not considered part of the company's normal ongoing business. The objective in setting a price for special orders is to achieve positive incremental operating income. To illustrate, OSN Cycles has just received a request from the police department of a large Canadian city to produce 100 specially modified mountain bikes at a price of $560 each. The bikes would be used to patrol some of the more densely populated residential sections of the city. OSN Cycles can easily modify its City Cruiser model to fit the specifications of the police department. The normal selling price of the City Cruiser bike is $700, and its unit product cost is $564 as shown below:

> **Special order**
> A one-time order that is not considered part of the company's normal ongoing business.

Direct materials	$372
Direct labour	90
Manufacturing overhead	102
Unit product cost	$564

The variable portion of the above manufacturing overhead is $12 per unit. The order would have no effect on the company's total fixed manufacturing overhead costs.

The modifications to the bikes consist of welded brackets to hold radios, nightsticks, and other gear. These modifications would require $34 in incremental variable costs per unit. In addition, the company would have to pay a graphics design studio $1,200 to design and cut stencils that would be used for spray painting the police department's logo and other identifying marks on the bikes.

This order should have no effect on the company's other sales. The production manager says that she can handle the special order without disrupting any of the regular scheduled production.

What effect would accepting this order have on the company's operating income?

Only the incremental costs and benefits are relevant. Since the existing fixed manufacturing overhead costs would not be affected by the order, they are not incremental costs and therefore are not relevant. The incremental operating income can be computed as follows:

	Per Unit	Total 100 Bikes
Incremental revenue	$560	$56,000
Incremental costs:		
Variable costs:		
Direct materials	372	37,200
Direct labour.	90	9,000
Variable manufacturing overhead.	12	1,200
Special modifications.	34	3,400
Total variable cost.	$508	50,800
Fixed cost:		
Purchase of stencils.		1,200
Total incremental cost.		52,000
Incremental operating income.		$ 4,000

Therefore, even though the price on the special order ($560) is below the normal unit product cost ($564) and the order would require incurring additional costs, it would result in an increase in operating income. In general, a special order is profitable as long as the incremental revenue from the special order exceeds the incremental costs of the order.

However, in performing the analysis it is important to make sure that there is indeed idle capacity and that the special order does not affect the company's ability to meet normal demand. For example, what if OSN Cycle is already operating at 100% of capacity and normally sells all the bikes it can produce for $700 each? What is the opportunity cost of accepting the order? Should the company accept the $560 price? If not, what is the minimum price it should accept? To answer these questions, the analysis can be conducted as follows:

	Per Unit
(a) Opportunity Costs:	
Normal selling price	$700
Less variable costs:	
Direct materials	372
Direct labour	90
Variable overhead	12
Total variable costs	474
Contribution margin forgone	$226*
(b) Total relevant costs:	
Incremental costs:	
Variable ($474 + $34)	$508
Fixed ($1,200/100)	12
	520
Opportunity costs	226
Total	$746

*If OSN Cycle is operating at 100% capacity, every bike it sells to the police department means forgoing the contribution margin of $226 the company would have earned on a sale to a regular customer. This is the per unit opportunity cost of accepting the special order.

Since the total relevant costs of $746 exceed the offer price of $560, OSN Cycle should decline the offer. Indeed, to be no worse off from a financial perspective, the minimum price that should be charged on the special order is $746 per bike. At this price, management should be indifferent between filling the special order and continuing to sell all it can produce to regular customers.

DECISION AID

ACCEPT OR REJECT A SPECIAL ORDER

Relevant Costs and Benefits
- Incremental costs of filling the order (variable and fixed)
- Opportunity cost of filling the order
- Incremental revenues from the order

Irrelevant Costs
- Allocated common costs
- Sunk costs

Total relevant costs = Incremental costs + Opportunity costs

Decision Rule:

Accept if incremental revenues > total relevant costs
Reject if incremental revenues < total relevant costs

Joint Product Costs and the Sell or Process Further Decision

In some industries, a number of end products are produced from a single raw material input. For example, in the petroleum refining industry a large number of products are extracted from crude oil, including gasoline, jet fuel, home heating oil, lubricants, asphalt, and various organic chemicals. Another example is provided by the St. Thomas Wool Cooperative. The company buys raw wool from local sheepherders, separates the wool into three grades—coarse, fine, and superfine—and then dyes the wool using traditional methods that rely on pigments from local materials. Exhibit 12–6 contains a diagram of the production process.

As mentioned above, the St. Thomas Wool Cooperative produces coarse wool, fine wool, and superfine wool from one input—raw wool. Two or more products that are produced from a common input are known as **joint products**. The term **joint product costs** is used to describe those manufacturing costs that are incurred in producing joint products up to the split-off point. The **split-off point** is the point in the manufacturing process at which the joint products can be recognized as separate products. This does not occur at the

Joint products
Two or more items that are produced from a common input.

Joint product costs
Costs that are incurred up to the split-off point in producing joint products.

Split-off point
That point in the manufacturing process where some or all of the joint products can be recognized as individual products.

EXHIBIT 12–6   Joint Products

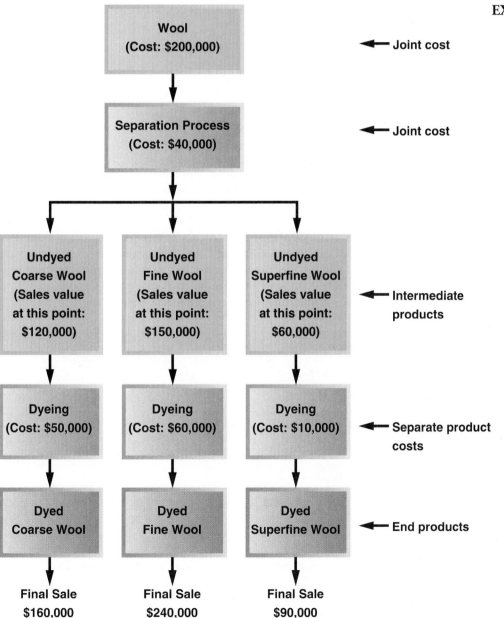

St. Thomas Wool Cooperative until the raw wool has gone through the separating process. At the Cooperative, the joint costs are the $200,000 cost of the raw wool and the $40,000 cost of separating the wool. The undyed wool is called an *intermediate product* because it is not finished at this point. Nevertheless, a market does exist for undyed wool—although at a significantly lower price than finished dyed wool.

The Pitfalls of Allocation

Joint product costs are really common costs incurred to simultaneously produce a variety of end products. Traditional cost accounting books cover various approaches to allocating these common costs among the different products at the split-off point. A typical approach is to allocate the joint product costs according to the relative sales value of the end products.

Although allocation of joint product costs is needed for some purposes, such as inventory valuation for financial reporting, allocations of this kind should be viewed with great caution *internally* in the decision making process. As will be discussed in the next section, because allocated joint product costs are sunk costs, they should never be used when making decisions about what to do with the joint products beyond the split-off point (i.e., sell immediately or process further).

Sell or Process Further Decisions

Sell or process further decision
A decision as to whether a joint product should be sold at the split-off point or processed further and sold at a later time in a different form.

Deciding what to do with a product from the split-off point forward is known as a **sell or process further decision**. Joint costs are irrelevant in these decisions because by the time the split-off point is reached, the joint product costs have already been incurred and therefore are sunk costs.

It will always be profitable to continue processing a joint product after the split-off point *as long as the incremental revenue from such processing exceeds the incremental processing cost incurred after the split-off point.* Joint product costs that have already been incurred up to the split-off point are sunk costs, which are irrelevant in decisions concerning what to do from the split-off point forward.

To provide a detailed example of the sell or process further decision, return to the data for the St. Thomas Wool Cooperative in Exhibit 12–6. We can answer several important questions using this data. First, is the company generating a profit if it runs the entire process from beginning to end? Assuming there are no costs other than those displayed in Exhibit 12–6, the company is indeed profitable, determined as follows:

Analysis of the profitability of the overall operation:		
Combined final sales value		
($160,000 + $240,000 + $90,000)		$490,000
Less costs of producing the end products:		
Cost of wool	$200,000	
Cost of separating wool	40,000	
Combined costs of dyeing		
($50,000 + $60,000 + $10,000)	120,000	360,000
Profit		$130,000

Note that the joint costs of buying the wool and separating the wool *are* relevant when considering the profitability of the entire operation. This is because these joint costs *could* be avoided if the entire operation were shut down. However, these joint costs are *not* relevant when considering the profitability of any one product. As long as the process is being run to make the other products, no additional joint costs are incurred to make the specific product in question.

Even though the company is making money overall, it may be losing money on one or more of the products. If the company buys wool and runs the separation process, it will get all three intermediate products. Nothing can be done about that. However, each of these products can be sold *as is* without further processing. It may be that the company would be better off selling one or more of the products prior to dyeing to avoid the dyeing costs. The appropriate way to make this choice is to compare the incremental revenues to the incremental costs from further processing, as done in Exhibit 12–7.

	Coarse Wool	Fine Wool	Superfine Wool
Final sales value after further processing	$160,000	$240,000	$90,000
Less sales value at the split-off point	120,000	150,000	60,000
Incremental revenue from further processing	40,000	90,000	30,000
Less cost of further processing (dyeing)	50,000	60,000	10,000
Profit (loss) from further processing	$(10,000)	$ 30,000	$20,000

EXHIBIT 12–7   Sell or Process Further Decision

As this analysis shows, the company would be better off selling the undyed coarse wool as is rather than processing it further. The other two products should be processed further and dyed before selling them.

Note that the joint costs of the wool ($200,000) and of the wool separation process ($40,000) play no role in the decision to sell or further process the intermediate products. These joint costs are relevant in a decision of whether to buy wool and to run the wool separation process, but they are not relevant in decisions about what to do with the intermediate products once they have been separated.

DECISION AID

SELL OR PROCESS FURTHER

Relevant Costs and Benefits
- Incremental costs of further processing
- Incremental revenues from further processing

Irrelevant Costs
- Allocated joint product costs

Decision Rule:

Process further if   incremental revenues > incremental costs of further processing
Sell at split-off if   incremental revenues < incremental costs of further processing

---

◼ UTILIZATION OF A CONSTRAINED RESOURCE

Another decision situation that managers often face is the problem of how to utilize a constrained resource. When a limited resource of some type restricts a company's ability to fully satisfy demand for its products or services, the company is said to have a **constraint**. A convenience store has limited shelf space so it must decide which products to sell. Manufacturing firms may have constraints on machine-hours, labour-hours, or the amount of raw materials available for production. The **theory of constraints (TOC)** maintains that effectively managing a constraint is important to the financial success of an organization. The challenge for managers is deciding how best to utilize the constrained resource in order to maximize the company's profits. As will be illustrated below, fixed costs are usually unaffected by the allocation of the constrained

> **LEARNING OBJECTIVE 3**
> Determine the most profitable use of a constrained resource and the value of obtaining more of the constrained resource.

Constraint
A limitation under which a company must operate (such as limited machine time available or limited raw materials available) that restricts the company's ability to satisfy demand for its products or services.

Theory of constraints (TOC)
A management approach that emphasizes the importance of managing constraints.

resource in the short run, so the focus will be on analyzing and maximizing contribution margin.

Contribution Margin in Relation to a Constrained Resource

To maximize total contribution margin, a firm should not necessarily promote those products that have the highest *unit* contribution margins. Rather, total contribution margin will be maximized by promoting those products or accepting those orders that provide the highest unit contribution margin *in relation to the constrained resource*. To illustrate, OSN Cycles makes a line of panniers—saddlebags for bicycles. There are two models of panniers—a touring model and a mountain model. Cost and revenue data for the two models of panniers are given below:

	Model	
	Mountain Pannier	**Touring Pannier**
Selling price per unit	$40	$50
Variable cost per unit	30	42
Contribution margin per unit	$10	$ 8
Contribution margin (CM) ratio	25%	16%

The mountain pannier appears to be much more profitable than the touring pannier. It has a $10 per unit contribution margin as compared to only $8 per unit for the touring model, and it has a 25% CM ratio as compared to only 16% for the touring model.

But now let us add one more piece of information—the plant that makes the panniers is operating at capacity. Ordinarily this does not mean that every machine and every person in the plant is working at the maximum possible rate. Because machines have different capacities, some machines will be operating at less than 100% of capacity. However, if the plant as a whole cannot produce any more units, some machine or process must be operating at capacity. The machine or process that is limiting overall output is called the *bottleneck*—it is the constraint.

At OSN Cycles, the bottleneck is a particular stitching machine. The mountain pannier requires four minutes of stitching time, and each unit of the touring pannier requires two minutes of stitching time. Since this stitching machine already has more work than it can handle, production will have to be cut back on one of the models. In this situation, which product is more profitable? To answer this question, the manager should look at the *contribution margin per unit of the constrained resource*, also known as the **profitability index**. This figure is computed by dividing the contribution margin by the quantity of the constrained resource required per unit. These calculations are carried out below for the mountain and touring panniers.

Profitability index =
Contribution margin per unit
÷ Quantity of constrained
resource required per unit

	Model	
	Mountain Pannier	**Touring Pannier**
Contribution margin per unit (a)	$10.00	$8.00
Time on the stitching machine required to produce one unit (b)	4 min.	2 min.
Contribution margin per unit of the constrained resource, (a) ÷ (b)	$2.50/min.	$4.00/min.

Using the profitability index, it is easy to decide which product is less profitable and should be de-emphasized. Each minute of processing time on the stitching machine that is devoted to the touring pannier results in an increase of $4 in contribution margin and profits. The comparable figure for the mountain pannier is only $2.50 per minute. Therefore, the touring model should be emphasized. Even though the mountain model has the larger per unit contribution margin and the larger CM ratio, the touring model provides the larger contribution margin in relation to the constrained resource.

To verify that the touring model is indeed the more profitable product when considering the constrained resource, suppose an hour of additional stitching time is available and that there are unfilled orders for both products. The additional hour on the stitching machine could be used to make either 15 mountain panniers (60 minutes ÷ 4 minutes) or 30 touring panniers (60 minutes ÷ 2 minutes), with the following consequences:

	Model	
	Mountain Pannier	Touring Pannier
Contribution margin per unit (a)	$ 10	$ 8
Additional units that can be processed in one hour	× 15	× 30
Additional contribution margin.	$150	$240

The analysis illustrated in this example generalizes well to situations where demand exceeds capacity and managers must allocate a constrained resource to three or more products. Demand should be fully satisfied for the product with the highest profitability index. Any capacity that remains should then be allocated to the product with the second-highest profitability index, and so on until all available capacity has been utilized. Simply looking at unit contribution margins alone is not enough when constraints exist; contribution margin per unit of the scarce resource must guide decision making.

Managing Constraints

Profits can be increased by effectively managing the organization's constraints. One aspect of managing constraints is to decide how to best utilize them. If the constraint is a bottleneck in the production process, the manager should select the product mix that maximizes the total contribution margin. In addition, the manager should take an active role in managing the constraint itself. Management should focus efforts on increasing the efficiency of the bottleneck operation (constraint) and on increasing its capacity. Such efforts directly increase the output of finished goods and will often pay off in an almost immediate increase in profits.

It is often possible for a manager to effectively increase the capacity of the bottleneck by what is called **relaxing** (or **elevating**) **the constraint**. For example, the stitching machine operator could be asked to work overtime. This would result in more available stitching time and hence more finished goods that can be sold. The benefits from relaxing the constraint in such a manner are often enormous and can easily be quantified. The manager should first ask, "What would I do with additional capacity at the bottleneck if it was available?" In the bicycle pannier example, the additional capacity was worth $4 ($2.50) per minute or $240 ($150) per hour because adding an hour of capacity would generate an additional $240 ($150) of contribution margin if it was used solely to process more touring (mountain) panniers. Based on the profitability indices, additional capacity should first be allocated to production of touring panniers, followed by mountain panniers if any capacity remains. Since overtime pay for the operator is likely to be much less than $240 (or $150 for that matter!), running the stitching machine on overtime would be an excellent way to increase the company's profits while satisfying its customers at the same time.

The implications are clear: Managers should focus much of their attention on managing bottlenecks. As we have discussed, managers should emphasize products that most profitably utilize the constrained resource. They should also make sure that products are processed smoothly through the bottlenecks, with minimal lost time due to breakdowns

Relaxing (or elevating) the constraint
An action that increases the capacity of a bottleneck.

and setups. And they should try to find ways to increase the capacity at the bottlenecks, which can be accomplished in a number of ways, including

- Working overtime on the bottleneck.
- Subcontracting some of the processing that would be done at the bottleneck.
- Shifting workers from processes that are not bottlenecks to the process that *is* a bottleneck.
- Focusing business process improvement efforts such as total quality management (TQM) and business process re-engineering on the bottleneck.
- Reducing defective units. Each defective unit that is processed through the bottleneck and subsequently scrapped takes the place of a good unit that could be sold.

The last three methods of increasing the capacity of the bottleneck are particularly attractive, because they are low-cost interventions and may even yield additional cost savings.

Bottlenecks, as the name implies, represent restrictions to the productive capacity of an organization. As the discussions about capacity in Chapter 10 suggested, numerous types of restrictions can exist, thus preventing the organization from producing at practical capacity. Chapter 10 provided a discussion of how management may try to analyze the implications of various forms of capacity restrictions. The implications of administrative decisions about work shift numbers or maintenance practices, as well as available backup capacity for breakdowns and other stoppages, can be analyzed to see what needs to be addressed by management to improve the economic performance of the organization.

The Problem of Multiple Constraints

What does a firm do if it has more than one potential constraint? For example, a firm may have limited raw materials, limited direct labour-hours available, limited floor space, and limited advertising dollars to spend on product promotion. How would it proceed to find the right combination of products to produce? The proper combination or "mix" of products can be found by use of a quantitative method known as *linear programming,* which is covered in quantitative methods and operations management courses.

Summary

- A framework was presented for distinguishing between relevant and irrelevant costs. Relevant costs and benefits are those that will be incurred in the future and that differ among the alternatives under consideration. As such, sunk costs are irrelevant (incurred in the past) while avoidable, differential, and opportunity costs are all relevant. [LO1]
- Application of relevant cost concepts was illustrated in several different decision situations often faced by managers: adding or dropping product lines/segments; making versus buying decisions; accepting or rejecting special orders; and selling versus processing joint products further. Aids were presented for each type of decision, identifying the relevant and irrelevant costs and the decision rule. [LO2]
- A simple approach was illustrated for allocating a constrained resource when demand exceeds production capacity because of a production bottleneck in the short run. The allocation approach is based on calculating the contribution margin per unit of the constrained resource, which is known as the *profitability index.* Demand should first be fully satisfied for the product with the highest profitability index, and then for the product with the next highest index, and so on, until all of the available capacity has been used. [LO3]

Review Problem: Relevant Costs

The St. Albert Cycle Company manufactures three types of bicycles—dirt bikes, mountain bikes, and racing bikes. Data on sales and expenses for the past quarter follow:

	Total	Dirt Bikes	Mountain Bikes	Racing Bikes
Sales	$300,000	$90,000	$150,000	$60,000
Less variable manufacturing				
and selling expenses	120,000	27,000	60,000	33,000
Contribution margin......................	180,000	63,000	90,000	27,000
Less fixed expenses:				
Advertising, traceable	30,000	10,000	14,000	6,000
Depreciation of special equipment	23,000	6,000	9,000	8,000
Salaries of product-line managers........	35,000	12,000	13,000	10,000
Allocated common fixed expenses*.......	60,000	18,000	30,000	12,000
Total fixed expenses	148,000	46,000	66,000	36,000
Operating income (loss)..................	$ 32,000	$17,000	$ 24,000	$ (9,000)

*Allocated on the basis of sales dollars.

Management is concerned about the continued losses shown by the racing bikes and wants a recommendation as to whether or not the line should be discontinued. The special equipment used to produce racing bikes has no resale value and does not wear out.

Required:
1. Should production and sale of the racing bikes be discontinued? Explain. Show computations to support your answer.
2. Recast the above data in a format that would be more usable to management in assessing the long-run profitability of the various product lines.

Solution to Review Problem

1. No, production and sale of the racing bikes should not be discontinued. If the racing bikes were discontinued, then the operating income for the company as a whole would decrease by $11,000 each quarter:

Lost contribution margin		$(27,000)
Fixed costs that can be avoided:		
Advertising, traceable	$ 6,000	
Salary of the product-line manager	10,000	16,000
Decrease in operating income for the company as a whole		$(11,000)

The depreciation of the special equipment is a sunk cost and is not relevant to the decision. The common costs are allocated and will continue regardless of whether or not the racing bikes are discontinued; thus, they are not relevant to the decision.

Alternative Solution:

	Current Total	Total If Racing Bikes Are Dropped	Difference: Operating Income Increase or (Decrease) If Dropped
Sales	$300,000	$240,000	$(60,000)
Less variable expenses......................	120,000	87,000	33,000
Contribution margin.........................	180,000	153,000	(27,000)
Less fixed expenses:			
Advertising, traceable	30,000	24,000	6,000
Depreciation on special equipment	23,000	23,000	0
Salaries of product managers	35,000	25,000	10,000
Common allocated costs....................	60,000	60,000	0
Total fixed expenses	148,000	132,000	16,000
Operating income	$ 32,000	$ 21,000	$(11,000)

2. The segmented report can be improved by eliminating the allocation of the common fixed expenses. Following the format introduced in Chapter 8 for a segmented income statement, a better report would be

	Total	Dirt Bikes	Mountain Bikes	Racing Bikes
Sales	$300,000	$90,000	$150,000	$60,000
Less variable manufacturing and selling expenses....................	120,000	27,000	60,000	33,000
Contribution margin....................	180,000	63,000	90,000	27,000
Less traceable fixed expenses:				
Advertising........................	30,000	10,000	14,000	6,000
Depreciation of special equipment	23,000	6,000	9,000	8,000
Salaries of the product-line managers....	35,000	12,000	13,000	10,000
Total traceable fixed expenses	88,000	28,000	36,000	24,000
Product line segment margin.............	92,000	$35,000	$ 54,000	$ 3,000
Less common fixed expenses............	60,000			
Operating income	$ 32,000			

Glossary

Review key terms and definitions on Connect.

Questions

12–1 What is a *relevant cost?*

12–2 Define the following terms: *incremental cost, opportunity cost,* and *sunk cost.*

12–3 Are avoidable costs always relevant costs? Explain.

12–4 Depreciation (as shown on the income statement) is an expense to a company, but this same expense is irrelevant in decision making. Explain why this is so.

12–5 "Sunk costs are easy to spot—they're simply the fixed costs associated with a decision." Do you agree? Explain.

12–6 Are variable costs always relevant in decision making? Explain.

12–7 "All future costs are relevant in decision making." Do you agree? Why?

12–8 Davis Company is considering dropping one of its product lines. What costs of the product line would be relevant to this decision? Irrelevant?

12–9 "If a product line is generating a loss, then that's pretty good evidence that the product line should be discontinued." Do you agree? Explain.

12–10 How does opportunity cost enter into the make or buy decision?

12–11 Which costs are relevant to special order decisions?

12–12 What is a constraint?

12–13 List four ways to increase capacity at bottlenecks.

12–14 How should the relative profitability of products be determined when trying to decide how to allocate a constrained resource such as machine-hours?

12–15 Define the following terms: *joint products, joint product costs,* and *split-off point.*

12–16 From a decision-making point of view, what pitfalls are there in allocating common costs among joint products?

12–17 What guideline can be used in determining whether a joint product should be sold at the split-off point or processed further?

12–18 Why should relevant costs be isolated when analyzing a decision situation?

Exercises

EXERCISE 12–1 Identifying Relevant Costs [LO1]

The management of Boehm & De Graaf A/S, a Danish furniture manufacturer, must determine whether certain costs are relevant in two different cases:

Case 1: The company chronically runs at capacity and the old Model A3000 machine is the company's constraint. Management is considering the purchase of a new Model B3800 machine to use in addition to the company's present Model A3000 machine. The old Model A3000 machine will continue to be used to capacity as before, with the new Model B3800 being used to expand production. The increase in volume will be large enough to require increases in fixed selling expenses and in general administrative overhead, but not in the general fixed manufacturing overhead.

Case 2: The old Model A3000 machine is not the company's constraint, but management is considering replacing it with a new Model B3800 machine because of the potential savings in direct materials cost with the new machine. The Model A3000 machine would be sold. This change will have no effect on production or sales, other than some savings in direct materials costs due to less waste.

Required:

Place an X in the appropriate column to indicate whether each item is relevant or not relevant to each of the two cases. Consider the two cases independently.

	Case 1		Case 2	
Item	**Relevant**	**Not Relevant**	**Relevant**	**Not Relevant**
a. Sales revenue............................				
b. Direct materials				
c. Direct labour...........................				
d. Variable manufacturing overhead				
e. Book value—Model A3000 machine				
f. Disposal value—Model A3000 machine				
g. Depreciation—Model A3000 machine.......				
h. Market value—Model B3800 machine (cost)..				
i. Fixed manufacturing overhead (general)				
j. Variable selling expense..................				
k. Fixed selling expense....................				
l. General administrative overhead...........				

EXERCISE 12–2 Dropping or Retaining a Segment [LO2]

Cumberland County Senior Services is a non-profit organization devoted to providing essential services to seniors who live in their own homes within the Cumberland County area. Three services are provided for seniors—home nursing, Meals on Wheels, and housekeeping. In the home nursing program, nurses visit seniors on a regular basis to check on their general health and to perform tests ordered by their physicians. The Meals on Wheels program delivers a hot meal once a day to each senior enrolled in the program. The housekeeping service provides weekly housecleaning and maintenance services. Data on revenue and expenses for the past year follow:

	Total	Home Nursing	Meals on Wheels	House-keeping
Revenues...........................	$900,000	$260,000	$400,000	$240,000
Variable expenses	490,000	120,000	210,000	160,000
Contribution margin...................	410,000	140,000	190,000	80,000
Fixed expenses:				
Depreciation......................	68,000	8,000	40,000	20,000
Liability insurance	42,000	20,000	7,000	15,000
Program administrators' salaries........	115,000	40,000	38,000	37,000
General administrative overhead*	180,000	52,000	80,000	48,000
Total fixed expenses	405,000	120,000	165,000	120,000
Operating income (loss)................	$ 5,000	$ 20,000	$ 25,000	$(40,000)

*Allocated on the basis of program revenues.

The head administrator of Cumberland County Senior Services, Judith Ewa is concerned about the organization's finances and considers the operating income of $5,000 last year to be razor-thin. (Last year's results were very similar to the results for previous years and are representative of what would be expected in the future.) She feels that the organization should be building its financial reserves at a more rapid rate in order to prepare for the next inevitable recession. After seeing the above report, Ewa asked for more information about the financial advisability of perhaps discontinuing the housekeeping program.

The depreciation in the housekeeping category is for a small van that is used to carry the housekeepers and their equipment from job to job. If the program was discontinued, the van would be donated to a charitable organization. Depreciation charges assume zero salvage value. None of the general administrative overhead would be avoided if the housekeeping program was dropped, but the liability insurance and the salary of the program administrator would be avoided.

Required:
1. Should the housekeeping program be discontinued? Explain. Show computations to support your answer.
2. Recast the above data in a format that would be more useful to management in assessing the long-run financial viability of the various services.

EXERCISE 12–3 Make or Buy a Component [LO2]

Current-Control, Inc., manufactures a variety of electrical switches. The company is currently manufacturing all of its own component parts. An outside supplier has offered to sell a switch to Current-Control for $32 per unit. To evaluate this offer, Current-Control, Inc., has gathered the following information relating to its own cost of producing the switch internally:

	Per Unit	12,000 Units per Year
Direct materials	$12	$144,000
Direct labour	10	120,000
Variable manufacturing overhead	3	36,000
Fixed manufacturing overhead, traceable	8*	96,000
Fixed manufacturing overhead, common, but allocated	16	192,000
Total cost	$49	$588,000

*25% supervisory salaries; 75% depreciation of special equipment (no resale value).

Required:
1. Assuming that the company has no alternative use for the facilities now being used to produce the switch, should the outside supplier's offer be accepted? Show all computations.
2. Suppose that if the switches were purchased, Current-Control, Inc., could use the freed capacity to launch a new product. The segment margin of the new product would be $78,000 per year. Should Current-Control, Inc., accept the offer to buy the switches from the outside supplier for $32 each? Show computations.

EXERCISE 12–4 Evaluating a Special Order [LO2]

Sato Jewellers has had a request for a special order for 10 gold bangles for the members of a wedding party. The normal selling price of a gold bangle is $389.95 and its unit product cost is $264.00, as shown below:

Direct materials	$143.00
Direct labour	86.00
Manufacturing overhead	35.00
Unit product cost	$264.00

Most of the manufacturing overhead is fixed and unaffected by variations in how much jewellery is produced in any given period. However, $7 of the overhead is variable, depending on the number of bangles produced. The customer would like special filigree applied to the bangles. This filigree would require additional materials costing $6 per bangle and would also require acquisition of a special tool costing $465 that would have no other use once the special order was completed. This order would have no effect on the company's regular sales, and the order could be filled using the company's existing capacity without affecting any other order.

Required:
What effect would accepting this order have on the company's operating income if a special price of $349.95 is offered per bangle for this order? Should the special order be accepted at this price?

EXERCISE 12–5 Utilization of a Constrained Resource [LO3]
The following are the selling price, variable costs, and contribution margin for one unit of each of
Banner Company's three products: A, B, and C:

	Product		
	A	B	C
Selling price..........................	$60	$90	$80
Variable costs:			
Direct materials.....................	27	14	40
Direct labour	12	32	16
Variable manufacturing overhead	3	8	4
Total variable cost....................	42	54	60
Contribution margin..................	$18	$36	$20
Contribution margin ratio	30%	40%	25%

Due to a strike in the plant of one of its competitors, demand for the company's products far exceeds
its capacity to produce. Management is trying to determine which product(s) to concentrate on next
week in filling its backlog of orders. The direct labour rate is $8 per hour, and only 3,000 hours of
labour time are available each week.

Required:
1. Compute the amount of contribution margin that will be obtained per hour of labour time spent
   on each product.
2. Which orders would you recommend that the company work on next week—the orders for
   product A, product B, or product C? Show computations.
3. By paying overtime wages, more than 3,000 hours of direct labour time can be made available
   next week. Up to how much should the company be willing to pay per hour in overtime wages
   as long as there is unfilled demand for the three products? Explain.

EXERCISE 12–6 Sell or Process Further [LO2]
In a joint processing operation, Nolen Company manufactures three products from a common input.
Joint processing costs up to the split-off point total $120,000 per year. The company allocates these
costs to the joint products on the basis of their total sales value at the split-off point. These sales
values are as follows: product X, $60,000; product Y, $108,000; and product Z, $72,000.

Each product may be sold at the split-off point or processed further. Additional processing
requires no special facilities. The additional processing costs and the sales value after further processing for each product (on an annual basis) are shown below:

Product	Additional Processing Costs	Sales Value
X............	$42,000	$ 96,000
Y............	$48,000	$180,000
Z............	$14,400	$ 90,000

Required:
Which product or products should be sold at the split-off point, and which product or products
should be processed further? Show computations.

EXERCISE 12–7 Identification of Relevant Costs [LO1]
Hart Company sells and delivers office furniture in the Maritime provinces.
The costs associated with the acquisition and annual operation of a delivery truck are given below:

Insurance....................................	$1,750
Licences	$ 250
Taxes (vehicle).............................	$ 150
Garage rent for parking (per truck).............	$1,350
Depreciation ($30,000 ÷ 5 years).............	$6,000
Gasoline, oil, tires, and repairs..............	$0.16/km

Required:

1. Assume that Hart Company owns one truck that has been driven 50,000 kilometres during the first year. Compute the average cost per kilometre of owning and operating the truck.
2. At the beginning of the second year, Hart Company is unsure whether to use the truck or leave it parked in the garage and have all hauling done commercially. (The government requires the payment of vehicle taxes even if the vehicle isn't used.) What costs from the previous list are relevant to this decision? Explain.
3. Assume that the company decides to use the truck during the second year. Near year-end, an order is received from a customer over 1,000 kilometres away. What costs from the previous list are relevant in a decision between using the truck to make the delivery and having the delivery done commercially? Explain.
4. Occasionally, the company could use two trucks at the same time. For this reason, some thought is being given to purchasing a second truck. The total kilometres driven would be the same as if only one truck was owned. What costs from the previous list are relevant to a decision about whether to purchase the second truck? Explain.

EXERCISE 12–8 Dropping or Retaining a Segment [LO2]

Anderson Document Services, a document creation and copying company, has two departments, Design and Copying. The company's most recent monthly contribution-format income statement follows:

		Department	
	Total	Design	Copying
Sales.	$1,000,000	$200,000	$800,000
Variable expenses	380,000	60,000	320,000
Contribution margin	620,000	140,000	480,000
Fixed expenses	540,000	180,000	360,000
Operating income (loss)	$ 80,000	$ (40,000)	$120,000

A study indicates that $74,000 of the fixed expenses being charged to the Design Department are sunk costs or allocated costs that will continue even if the Design Department is dropped. In addition, the elimination of the Design Department would result in a 5% decrease in the sales of the Copying Department.

Required:

If the Design Department is dropped, what will be the effect on the operating income of the company as a whole? Should the Design department be dropped?

EXERCISE 12–9 Make or Buy a Component [LO2]

For many years, Comstock Company has produced an electrical part that it uses in the production of diesel tractors. The company's unit product cost for the part, based on a production level of 60,000 parts per year, is as follows:

	Per Part	Total
Direct materials	$ 4.00	
Direct labour.	2.75	
Variable manufacturing overhead	0.50	
Fixed manufacturing overhead, traceable	3.00	$180,000
Fixed manufacturing overhead, common		
(allocated on the basis of labour-hours)	2.25	$135,000
Unit product cost	$12.50	

An outside supplier has offered to supply the electrical parts to Comstock Company for only $10.00 per part. One-third of the traceable fixed manufacturing cost is supervisory salaries and other costs that can be eliminated if the parts are purchased. The other two-thirds of the traceable fixed manufacturing costs consist of depreciation of special equipment that has no resale value. The decision to buy the parts from the outside supplier would have no effect on the common fixed costs of the company, and the space being used to produce the parts would otherwise be idle.

Required:

Prepare computations showing how much profits would increase or decrease as a result of purchasing the parts from the outside supplier rather than having the company make them.

EXERCISE 12–10 Special Order [LO2]

At the Kicher Company's current activity level of 8,000 units per month, the costs of producing and selling one unit of the company's only product are:

Direct materials	$2.50
Direct labour	$3.00
Variable manufacturing overhead	$0.50
Fixed manufacturing overhead	$4.25
Variable selling and administrative expenses	$1.50
Fixed selling and administrative expenses	$2.00

The normal selling price is $15 per unit. The company's capacity is 10,000 units per month. An order has been received from a potential customer overseas for 2,000 units at a price of $12.00 per unit. This order would not affect regular sales.

Required:

1. If the order is accepted, by how much will monthly profits increase or decrease? (The order would not change the company's total fixed costs.)
2. Assume the company has 500 units of this product left over from last year that are inferior to the current model. The units must be sold through regular channels at reduced prices. What unit cost is relevant for establishing a minimum selling price for these units? Explain.

EXERCISE 12–11 Utilization of a Constrained Resource [LO3]

Westburne Company produces three products: Alpha, Omega and Beta. Data (per unit) concerning the three products follow:

	Alpha	Omega	Beta
Selling price	$160	$112	$140
Less variable expenses:			
Direct materials	48	30	18
Labour and overhead	48	54	80
Total variable expenses	96	84	98
Contribution margin	$ 64	$ 28	$ 42
Contribution margin ratio	40%	25%	30%

Demand for the company's products is very strong, with far more orders each month than the company can produce with the available raw materials. The same material is used in each product. The material costs $6 per kilogram, with a maximum of 10,000 kilograms available each month.

Required:

Which orders would you advise the company to accept first, those for Alpha, Omega or Beta? Which orders second? Third?

EXERCISE 12–12 Sell or Process Further [LO2]

Senatory Limited produces several products from processing krypton, a rare mineral. Material and processing costs total $30,000 per tonne; one-third of the costs are allocated to the product castingard. The castingard produced from a tonne of krypton can either be sold at the split-off point, or processed further at a cost of $13,000 and then sold for $60,000. The sales value of castingard at the split-off point is $40,000.

Required:

Should castingard be processed further or sold at the split-off point?

EXERCISE 12–13 Volume Trade-Off Decision [LO3]

Car Art makes miniature reproductions of classic sports cars. The bottleneck in the production process is the requirement to apply several coats of paint to each car. This process requires the attention of the shop's most experienced craftsman. A total of 7,200 hours is available per year in this bottleneck operation. Data concerning the company's four products appear below:

	Corvette	Porsche	Ferrari	Jaguar
Unit contribution margin	$100	$64	$70	$144
Annual demand (units).	160	240	200	280
Hours required in the bottleneck operation per unit.	10	8	14	16

No fixed costs could be avoided by modifying how many units are produced of any product or even by dropping any one of the products.

Required:
1. Is there sufficient capacity in the bottleneck operation to satisfy demand for all products?
2. What is the optimal production plan for the year?
3. What would be the total contribution margin for the optimal production plan you have proposed?

EXERCISE 12–14 Identification of Relevant Costs [LO1]

Jason brought home eight ducks from his last hunting trip in northern Ontario. His friend Harry dislikes any type of hunting, and to discourage Jason from further hunting, Harry has presented him with the following cost estimates:

Camper and equipment:	
Cost, $16,000; usable for eight seasons; 10 hunting trips per season	$200
Travel expense (pickup truck):	
100 kilometres at $0.35 per kilometre (gas, oil, and tires—$0.25 per kilometre; depreciation and insurance—$0.10 per kilometre).	35
Shotgun shells (two boxes)	20
Boat:	
Cost, $4,000, usable for eight seasons; 10 hunting trips per season	50
Hunting licence:	
Cost, $30 for the season; 10 hunting trips per season	3
Money lost playing poker:	
Loss, $40 (Jason plays poker every weekend)	40
Coffee beans:	
Cost, $20	20
Total cost of the trip	$368
Cost per duck ($368 ÷ 8 ducks)	$ 46

Required:
1. Assuming that the duck hunting trip Jason has just completed is typical, what costs are relevant to a decision as to whether Jason should go duck hunting again this season?
2. Suppose that Jason gets lucky on his next hunting trip and shoots 10 ducks in the amount of time it took him to shoot 8 ducks on his last trip. How much would it have cost him to shoot the last two ducks? Explain.
3. Which costs are relevant in a decision of whether Jason should give up hunting? Explain.

EXERCISE 12–15 Dropping or Retaining a Segment [LO2]

Williams Products Inc. manufactures and sells a number of items, including school knapsacks. The company has been experiencing losses on the knapsacks for some time, as shown by the contribution-format income statement at the top of the next page.

Discontinuing the knapsacks would not affect sales of other product lines and would have no noticeable effect on the company's total general factory overhead or total purchasing department expenses.

WILLIAMS PRODUCTS INC. Income Statement—School Knapsacks For the Quarter Ended June 30		
Sales		$225,000
Variable expenses:		
Variable manufacturing expenses	$65,000	
Sales commissions	24,000	
Shipping	6,000	
Total variable expenses		95,000
Contribution margin		130,000
Fixed expenses:		
Salary of product-line manager	10,500	
General factory overhead	52,000*	
Depreciation of equipment (no resale value)	18,000	
Advertising—traceable	55,000	
Insurance on inventories	4,500	
Purchasing department	25,000†	
Total fixed expenses		165,000
Operating loss		$ (35,000)

*Allocated on the basis of machine-hours.
†Allocated on the basis of sales dollars.

Required:

Would you recommend that the company discontinue the manufacture and sale of school knapsacks? Support your answer with appropriate computations.

EXERCISE 12–16 Make or Buy a Component [LO2]

Royal Company manufactures 20,000 units of Part R-3 each year. At this level of activity, the cost per unit for Part R-3 follows:

Direct materials	$ 4.80
Direct labour	7.00
Variable manufacturing overhead	3.20
Fixed manufacturing overhead	10.00
Total cost per part	$25.00

An outside supplier has offered to sell 20,000 units of Part R-3 each year to Royal Company for $23.50 per part. If Royal Company accepts this offer, the facilities now being used to manufacture Part R-3 could be rented to another company at an annual rental of $150,000. However, Royal Company has determined that $6 of the fixed manufacturing overhead being applied to Part R-3 would continue even if the part was purchased from the outside supplier.

Required:

Prepare computations showing how much profits will increase or decrease if the outside supplier's offer is accepted.

connect Problems **eXcel**

PROBLEM 12–17 Dropping or Retaining a Tour [LO2]

A study has indicated that some of the bus tours operated by Clear Water Tours Inc. are not profitable. As a result, consideration is being given to dropping these unprofitable tours to improve the company's overall operating performance.

One such tour is a three-day Majestic Islands bus tour. Additional information and an income statement from a typical Majestic Islands tour are given at the top of the next page.

The following additional information is available about the tour:

a. Bus drivers are paid fixed annual salaries; tour guides are paid for each tour conducted.

b. The "Bus maintenance and preparation" cost in the statement is an allocation of the salaries of mechanics and other service personnel who are responsible for keeping the company's fleet of buses in good operating condition.

Ticket revenue (100 seat capacity × 40% occupancy ×		
$70 ticket price per person)	$2,800	100%
Variable expenses ($21.00 per person)	840	30
Contribution margin	1,960	70%
Tour expenses:		
Tour promotion	540	
Salary of bus driver	320	
Fee, tour guide	630	
Fuel for bus	110	
Depreciation of bus	410	
Liability insurance, bus	180	
Overnight parking fees, bus	50	
Room and meals, bus driver and tour guide	160	
Bus maintenance and preparation	270	
Total tour expenses	2,670	
Operating loss	$ (710)	

c. Depreciation of buses is due to obsolescence.

d. Liability insurance premiums are based on the number of buses in the company's fleet.

e. Dropping the Majestic Islands bus tour would not allow Clear Water Tours to reduce the number of buses in its fleet, the number of bus drivers on the payroll, or the size of the maintenance and preparation staff.

Required:

1. Prepare an analysis showing what the impact will be on the company's profits if this tour is discontinued.

2. The company's tour director has been criticized because only about 50% of the seats on Clear Water's tours are being filled, compared to an industry average of 60%. The tour director has explained that Clear Water's average seat occupancy could be improved considerably by eliminating about 10% of its tours, but that doing so would reduce profits. Explain how this could happen.

PROBLEM 12–18 Sell or Process Further [LO2]

Valley Meat Processing Corporation is a major processor of beef and other meat products. The company has a large number of T-bone steaks on hand, and it is trying to decide whether to sell the T-bone steaks as is or to process them further into filet mignon and New York-cut steaks.

Management believes that a kilogram of T-bone steak would yield the following profit:

Wholesale selling price ($16.00 per kilogram)	$16.00
Less joint costs incurred up to the split-off point where T-bone	
steak can be identified as a separate product	12.00
Profit per kilogram	$ 4.00

As mentioned above, instead of being sold as is, the T-bone steaks could be further processed into filet mignon and New York-cut steaks. Cutting one side of a T-bone steak provides the filet mignon, and cutting the other side provides the New York cut. One 480-gram T-bone steak cut in this way will yield one 181-gram filet mignon and one 241-gram New York cut; the remaining grams are waste. The cost of processing the T-bone steaks into these cuts is $1.40 per kilogram. The filet mignon can be sold retail for $26 per kilogram, and the New York-cut can be sold wholesale for $22 per kilogram.

Required:

1. Determine the profit for each 480-gram T-bone steak processed further into filet mignon and New York-cut steaks.

2. Would you recommend that the T-bone steaks be sold as is or processed further? Why?

(Prepared from a situation suggested by Professor John W. Hardy.)

PROBLEM 12–19 Close or Retain a Store [LO2]

The Tilots Corporation's segmented absorption costing income statement for the last quarter for its three metropolitan stores is given below.

Management is very concerned about the Downtown Store's inability to show a profit, and consideration is being given to closing the store. The company has asked you to make a recommendation as to what course of action should be taken. Additional information available on the store is provided after the statement.

	Total	Uptown Store	Downtown Store	Westpark Store
Sales	$2,500,000	$900,000	$600,000	$1,000,000
Cost of goods sold	1,450,000	513,000	372,000	565,000
Gross margin	1,050,000	387,000	228,000	435,000
Selling and administrative expenses:				
Selling expenses:				
Direct advertising	118,500	40,000	36,000	42,500
General advertising*	20,000	7,200	4,800	8,000
Sales salaries	157,000	52,000	45,000	60,000
Delivery salaries	30,000	10,000	10,000	10,000
Store rent	215,000	70,000	65,000	80,000
Depreciation of store fixtures	46,950	18,300	8,800	19,850
Depreciation of delivery				
equipment	27,000	9,000	9,000	9,000
Total selling expenses	614,450	206,500	178,600	229,350
Administrative expenses:				
Store management salaries	63,000	20,000	18,000	25,000
General office salaries*	50,000	18,000	12,000	20,000
Utilities	89,800	31,000	27,200	31,600
Insurance on fixtures and				
inventory	25,500	8,000	9,000	8,500
Employee benefits	36,000	12,000	10,200	13,800
General office				
expenses—other*	25,000	9,000	6,000	10,000
Total administrative expenses	289,300	98,000	82,400	108,900
Total operating expenses	903,750	304,500	261,000	338,250
Operating income (loss)	$ 146,250	$ 82,500	$ (33,000)	$ 96,750

*Allocated on the basis of sales dollars.

a. The manager of the store has been with the company for many years; he would be retained and transferred to another position in the company if the Downtown Store was closed. His salary is $6,000 per month, or $18,000 per quarter. If the store was not closed, a new employee would be hired to fill the other position at a salary of $5,000 per month.

b. The lease on the building housing the Downtown Store can be broken with no penalty.

c. The fixtures being used in the Downtown Store would be transferred to the other two stores if the Downtown Store was closed.

d. Employee benefits are 12% of salaries.

e. A single delivery crew serves all three stores. One delivery person could be discharged if the Downtown Store was closed; this person's salary amounts to $7,000 per quarter. The delivery equipment would be distributed to the other stores. The equipment does not wear out through use, but it does eventually become obsolete.

f. One-third of the Downtown Store's insurance relates to its fixtures.

g. The general office salaries and other expenses relate to the general management of the Tilots Corporation. The employee in the general office who is responsible for the Downtown Store would be discharged if the store was closed. This employee's compensation amounts to $8,000 per quarter.

Required:

1. Prepare a schedule showing the change in revenues and expenses and the impact on the overall company operating income that would result if the Downtown Store was closed.

2. Based on your computations in (1) above, what recommendation would you make to the management of the Tilots Corporation?

3. Assume that if the Downtown Store was closed, sales in the Uptown Store would increase by $200,000 per quarter due to loyal customers shifting their buying to the Uptown Store. The Uptown Store has ample capacity to handle the increased sales, and its gross margin is 43% of sales. What effect would these factors have on your recommendation concerning the Downtown Store? Show computations.

PROBLEM 12–20 Make or Buy Decision [LO2]

Bastion Company, a manufacturer of several types of ballpoint pens, has just received an offer from an outside supplier to provide the ink cartridge for the company's Zippo pen line, at a price of $0.48 per dozen cartridges. The company is interested in this offer, since its own production of cartridges is at capacity.

Bastion Company estimates that if the supplier's offer was accepted, the direct labour and variable manufacturing overhead costs of the Zippo pen line would be reduced by 10% and the direct materials cost would be reduced by 20%.

Under present operations, Bastion Company manufactures all of its own pens from start to finish. The Zippo pens are sold through wholesalers at $4 per box. Each box contains one dozen pens. Fixed manufacturing overhead costs charged to the Zippo pen line total $50,000 each year. (The same equipment and facilities are used to produce several pen lines.) The present cost of producing one dozen Zippo pens (one box) is given below:

Direct materials	$1.50
Direct labour	1.00
Manufacturing overhead	0.80*
Total cost	$3.30

*Includes both variable and fixed manufacturing overhead, based on production of 100,000 boxes of pens each year.

Required:

1. Should Bastion Company accept the outside supplier's offer? Show computations.
2. What is the maximum price that Bastion Company should be willing to pay the outside supplier per dozen cartridges? Explain.
3. Due to the bankruptcy of a competitor, Bastion Company expects to sell 150,000 boxes of Zippo pens next year. As stated above, the company presently has enough capacity to produce the cartridges for only 100,000 boxes of Zippo pens annually. By incurring $30,000 in added fixed cost each year, the company could expand its production of cartridges to satisfy the anticipated demand for Zippo pens. The variable cost per unit to produce the additional cartridges would be the same as at present. Under these circumstances, how many boxes of cartridges should be purchased from the outside supplier and how many should be made by Bastion? Show computations to support your answer.
4. What qualitative factors should Bastion Company consider in determining whether it should make or buy the ink cartridges?

(CMA, adapted)

PROBLEM 12–21 Relevant Cost Analysis in a Variety of Situations [LO2]

Ovation Company has a single product called a Bit. The company normally produces and sells 60,000 Bits each year at a selling price of $32 per unit. The company's unit costs at this level of activity are given below:

Direct materials	$10.00	
Direct labour.	4.50	
Variable manufacturing overhead	2.30	
Fixed manufacturing overhead	5.00	($300,000 total)
Variable selling expenses.	1.20	
Fixed selling expenses.	3.50	($210,000 total)
Total cost per unit	$26.50	

A number of questions relating to the production and sale of Bits follow. Each question is independent.

Required:

1. Assume that Ovation Company has sufficient capacity to produce 90,000 Bits each year without any increase in fixed manufacturing overhead costs. The company could increase its sales by 25% above the present 60,000 units each year if it was willing to increase the fixed selling expenses by $80,000. Would the increased fixed selling expenses be justified?

2.   Assume again that Ovation Company has sufficient capacity to produce 90,000 Bits each year. A customer in a foreign market wants to purchase 20,000 Bits. Import duties on the Bits would be $1.70 per unit, and costs for permits and licences would be $9,000. The only selling costs that would be associated with the order would be $3.20 per unit shipping cost. Compute the per unit break-even price on this order.

3.   The company has 1,000 Bits on hand that have some irregularities and are therefore considered to be "seconds." Due to the irregularities, it will be impossible to sell these units at the normal price through regular distribution channels. What unit cost figure is relevant for setting a minimum selling price? Explain.

4.   Due to a strike in its supplier's plant, Ovation Company is unable to purchase more material for the production of Bits. The strike is expected to last for two months. Ovation Company has enough material on hand to operate at 30% of normal levels for the two-month period. As an alternative, Ovation could close its plant down entirely for the two months. If the plant was closed, fixed manufacturing overhead costs would continue at 60% of their normal level during the two-month period and the fixed selling expenses would be reduced by 20%. What would be the impact on profits of closing the plant for the two-month period?

5.   An outside manufacturer has offered to produce Bits and ship them directly to Ovation's customers. If Ovation Company accepts this offer, the facilities that it uses to produce Bits would be idle; however, fixed manufacturing overhead costs would be reduced by 75%. Since the outside manufacturer would pay for all shipping costs, the variable selling expenses would be only two-thirds of their present amount. Compute the unit cost that is relevant for comparison to the price quoted by the outside manufacturer.

PROBLEM 12–22 Shutting Down or Continuing to Operate a Plant [LO2]

(Note: This type of decision is similar to dropping a product line.) Nicholas Company manufactures a fast-bonding glue, normally producing and selling 40,000 litres of the glue each month. This glue, which is known as MJ-7, is used in the wood industry to manufacture plywood. The selling price of MJ-7 is $35 per litre, variable costs are $21 per litre, fixed manufacturing overhead costs in the plant total $230,000 per month, and the fixed selling costs total $310,000 per month.

Strikes in the mills that purchase the bulk of the MJ-7 glue have caused Nicholas Company's sales to temporarily drop to only 11,000 litres per month. Nicholas Company's management estimates that the strikes will last for two months, after which sales of MJ-7 should return to normal. Due to the current low level of sales, Nicholas Company's management is thinking about closing down the plant during the strike.

If Nicholas Company does close down the plant, fixed manufacturing overhead costs can be reduced by $60,000 per month and fixed selling costs can be reduced by 10%. Start-up costs at the end of the shutdown period would total $14,000. Since Nicholas Company uses lean production methods, no inventories are on hand.

Required:

1.   Assuming that the strikes continue for two months, would you recommend that Nicholas Company close the plant? Explain. Show computations to support your answer.

2.   At what level of sales (in litres) for the two-month period should Nicholas Company be indifferent between closing the plant or keeping it open? Show computations. (*Hint:* This is a type of break-even analysis, except that the fixed cost portion of your break-even computation should include only those fixed costs that are relevant [i.e., avoidable] over the two-month period.)

PROBLEM 12–23 Make or Buy Analysis [LO2]

"That old equipment for producing carburetors is worn out," said Bill Seebach, president of Hondrich Company. "We need to make a decision quickly." The company is trying to decide whether it should rent new equipment and continue to make its carburetors internally or whether it should discontinue production of its carburetors and purchase them from an outside supplier. The alternatives follow:

Alternative 1: Rent new equipment for producing the carburetors for $120,000 per year.
Alternative 2: Purchase carburetors from an outside supplier for $16 each.

Hondrich Company's present costs per unit of producing the carburetors internally (with the old equipment) are given below. These costs are based on a current activity level of 40,000 units per year:

Direct materials.	$ 5.50
Direct labour.	8.00
Variable overhead	1.20
Fixed overhead ($1.50 supervision, $1.80 depreciation, and $4 general company overhead)	7.30
Total cost per unit.	$22.00

The new equipment would be more efficient and, according to the manufacturer, would reduce direct labour costs and variable overhead costs by 25%. Supervision cost ($60,000 per year) and direct materials cost per unit would not be affected by the new equipment. The new equipment's capacity would be 60,000 carburetors per year.

The total general company overhead would be unaffected by this decision.

Required:
1. The president is unsure what the company should do and would like an analysis showing the unit costs and total costs for each of the two alternatives given above. Assume that 40,000 carburetors are needed each year. Which course of action would you recommend to the president?
2. Would your recommendation in (1) above be the same if the company's needs were (*a*) 50,000 carburetors per year, or (*b*) 60,000 carburetors per year? Show computations in good form.
3. What other factors would you recommend that the company consider before making a decision?

eXcel

PROBLEM 12–24 Accept or Reject a Special Order [LO2]
Moore Company manufactures and sells a single product called a Lop. Operating at capacity, the company can produce and sell 30,000 Lops per year. Costs associated with this level of production and sales are given below:

	Unit	Total
Direct materials.	$15	$ 450,000
Direct labour	8	240,000
Variable manufacturing overhead.	3	90,000
Fixed manufacturing overhead	9	270,000
Variable selling expense	4	120,000
Fixed selling expense	6	180,000
Total cost	$45	$1,350,000

The Lops normally sell for $50 each. Fixed manufacturing overhead is constant at $270,000 per year within the range of 25,000 through 30,000 Lops per year.

Required:
1. Assume that due to a recession, Moore Company expects to sell only 25,000 Lops through regular channels next year. A large retail chain has offered to purchase 5,000 Lops if Moore is willing to accept a 16% discount off the regular price. There would be no sales commissions on this order; so variable selling expenses would be slashed by 75%. However, Moore Company would have to purchase a special machine to engrave the retail chain's name on the 5,000 units. This machine would cost $10,000. Moore Company has no assurance that the retail chain will purchase additional units in the future. Determine the impact on profits next year if this special order is accepted.
2. Refer to the original data. Assume again that Moore Company expects to sell only 25,000 Lops through regular channels next year. The provincial government would like to make a one-time-only purchase of 5,000 Lops. The government would pay a fixed fee of $1.80 per Lop, and it would reimburse Moore Company for all costs of production (variable and fixed) associated with the units. Since the government would pick up the Lops with its own trucks, there would be no variable selling expenses associated with this order. If Moore Company accepts the order, by how much will profits increase or decrease for the year?
3. Assume the same situation as that described in (2) above, except that the company expects to sell 30,000 Lops through regular channels next year, so accepting the government's order would require giving up regular sales of 5,000 Lops. If the government's order is accepted, by how much will profits increase or decrease from what they would be if the 5,000 Lops were sold through regular channels?

PROBLEM 12–25 Utilization of a Constrained Resource [LO3]

Demand for the dolls and doll dress sewing kits manufactured by RoseMarie Limited is increasing, and management requests assistance from you in determining the best sales and production mix for the coming year. The company has provided the following data:

	A	B	C	D	E	
1	Product	Demand Next Year (units)	Selling Price per Unit	Direct Materials	Direct Labour	
2	Marcy	26,000	$35.00	$3.50	$4.80	
3	Tina	42,000	$24.00	$2.30	$3.00	
4	Cari	40,000	$22.00	$4.50	$8.40	
5	Lenny	46,000	$18.00	$3.10	$6.00	
6	Sewing kit	450,000	$14.00	$1.50	$2.40	
7						

|◄ ◄ ► ►|\ **Sheet1** ⟨ Sheet2 ⟨ Sheet3 / |◄

The following additional information is available:

a.   The company's plant has a capacity of 150,000 direct labour-hours per year on a single-shift basis. The company's present employees and equipment can produce all five products.

b.   The direct labour rate of $12.00 per hour is expected to remain unchanged during the coming year.

c.   Fixed costs total $356,000 per year. Variable overhead costs are $4.00 per direct labour-hour.

d.   All of the company's non-manufacturing costs are fixed.

e.   The company's finished goods inventory is negligible and can be ignored.

Required:

1.   Determine the contribution margin per direct labour-hour expended on each product (the profitability index).

2.   Prepare a schedule showing the total direct labour-hours that will be required to produce the units estimated to be sold during the coming year.

3.   Examine the data you have computed in (1) and (2) above. How would you allocate the 150,000 direct labour-hours of capacity to RoseMarie's various products?

4.   What is the highest price, in terms of a rate per hour, that RoseMarie should be willing to pay for additional capacity (that is, for added direct labour time)?

5.   Identify ways in which the company might be able to obtain additional production capacity in the short run so that it would not have to leave some demand for its products unsatisfied.

(CMA, adapted)

PROBLEM 12–26 Sell or Process Further [LO2]

Clean and Shine Corporation produces several types of industrial and household cleaning compounds and solutions. While most of its products are processed independently, a few are related, such as the company's Clean 236 and its Sparkle silver polish.

Clean 236 is a coarse cleaning powder with many industrial uses. It costs $3.20 a kilogram to make, and it has a selling price of $4.00 a kilogram. A small portion of the annual production of Clean 236 is retained in the factory for further processing. It is combined with several other ingredients to form a paste that is marketed as Sparkle silver polish. The silver polish sells for $8.00 per jar.

This further processing requires one-half kilogram of Clean 236 per jar of silver polish. The additional direct costs involved in the processing of a jar of silver polish are

Other ingredients	$1.30
Direct labour	2.96
Total direct cost	$4.26

Overhead costs associated with the processing of the silver polish are

Variable manufacturing overhead cost	25% of direct labour cost
Fixed manufacturing overhead cost (per month):	
Production supervisor	$6,000
Depreciation of mixing equipment	$2,800

The production supervisor has no duties other than to oversee production of the silver polish. The mixing equipment, purchased two years ago, is special-purpose equipment acquired specifically to produce the silver polish. Its resale value is negligible and it does not wear out through use.

Direct labour is a variable cost at Clean and Shine Corporation.

Advertising costs for the silver polish total $8,000 per month. Variable selling costs associated with the silver polish are 7.5% of sales.

Due to a recent decline in the demand for silver polish, the company is wondering whether its continued production is advisable. The sales manager feels that it would be more profitable to sell all of the Clean 236 as a cleaning powder.

Required:
1. What is the incremental contribution margin per jar from further processing Clean 236 into silver polish?
2. What is the minimum number of jars of silver polish that must be sold each month to justify the continued processing of Clean 236 into silver polish? Explain. Show all computations in good form.

Cases [Mc Graw Hill] connect

CASE 12–27 Integrative Case: Relevant Costs; Pricing [LO1, LO2]
Double Duty, a combination fertilizer–weed killer, is Alanco's only product. It is sold nationwide through normal marketing channels to retail nurseries and garden stores.

Taylor Nursery plans to sell a similar fertilizer–weed killer compound through its regional nursery chain under its own private label. Taylor does not have manufacturing facilities of its own, so it has asked Alanco (and several other companies) to submit a bid for manufacturing and delivering a 25,000-kilogram order of the private brand compound to Taylor. While the chemical composition of the Taylor compound differs from that of Double Duty, the manufacturing processes are very similar.

The Taylor compound would be produced in 1,000-kilogram lots. Each lot would require 30 direct labour-hours and the following chemicals:

Chemicals	Quantity in Kilograms
CW–3	400
JX–6	300
MZ–8	200
BE–7	100

The first three chemicals (CW–3, JX–6, and MZ–8) are all used in the production of Double Duty. BE–7 was used in another compound that Alanco discontinued several months ago. The supply of BE–7 that Alanco had on hand when the other compound was discontinued was not discarded. Alanco could sell its supply of BE–7 at the prevailing market price less $0.10 per kilogram selling and handling expenses.

Alanco also has on hand a chemical called CN–5, which was manufactured for use in another product that is no longer produced. CN–5, which cannot be used in Double Duty, can be substituted for CW–3 on a one-for-one basis without affecting the quality of the Taylor compound. The CN–5 in inventory has a salvage value of $500.

Inventory and cost data for the chemicals that can be used to produce the Taylor compound are as shown below:

Raw Material	Kilograms in Inventory	Actual price per Kilogram When Purchased	Current Market Price per Kilogram
CW–3	22,000	$0.80	$0.90
JX–6	5,000	0.55	0.60
MZ–8	8,000	1.40	1.60
BE–7	4,000	0.60	0.65
CN–5	5,500	0.75	(Salvage)

The current direct labour rate is $14 per hour. The predetermined overhead rate is based on direct labour-hours (DLH). The predetermined overhead rate for the current year, based on a two-shift capacity of 400,000 total DLH with no overtime, is as follows:

Variable manufacturing overhead.............	$ 4.50 per DLH
Fixed manufacturing overhead...............	7.50 per DLH
Combined rate	$12.00 per DLH

Alanco's production manager reports that the present equipment and facilities are adequate to manufacture the Taylor compound. Therefore, the order would have no effect on total fixed manufacturing overhead costs. However, Alanco is within 400 hours of its two-shift capacity this month. Any additional hours beyond 400 hours must be done in overtime. If need be, the Taylor compound could be produced on regular time by shifting a portion of Double Duty production to overtime. Alanco's rate for overtime hours is 1½ times the regular pay rate, or $21 per hour. There is no allowance for any overtime premium in the predetermined overhead rate.

Required:
1.   Alanco has decided to submit a bid for a 25,000-kilogram order of Taylor Nursery's new compound. The order must be delivered by the end of the current month. Taylor Nursery has indicated that this is a one-time order that will not be repeated. Calculate the lowest price that Alanco could bid for the order without reducing its operating income.
2.   Refer to the original data. Assume that Taylor Nursery plans to place regular orders for 25,000-kilogram lots of the new compound during the coming year. Alanco expects the demand for Double Duty to remain strong. Therefore, the recurring orders from Taylor Nursery would put Alanco over its two-shift capacity. However, production could be scheduled so that 60% of each Taylor Nursery order could be completed during regular hours. As another option, some Double Duty production could be shifted temporarily to overtime so that the Taylor Nursery orders could be produced on regular time. Current market prices are the best available estimates of future market prices.

Alanco's standard markup policy for new products is 40% of the full manufacturing cost, including fixed manufacturing overhead. Calculate the price that Alanco would quote Taylor Nursery for each 25,000-kilogram lot of the new compound, assuming that it is to be treated as a new product and this pricing policy is followed.

CASE 12–28 Special Order and Constrained Resource [LO2]

East Coast Digital (ECD) produces high-quality audio and television equipment. One of the company's most popular products is a high-definition personal video recorder (PVR) for use with cable and satellite television systems. Demand has increased rapidly for the PVR over the past three years, given the appeal to customers of being able to easily record programs while they watch live television, watch recorded programs while they record a different program, and save dozens of programs for future viewing on the unit's large internal hard drive.

A complex production process is utilized for the PVR involving both laser and imaging equipment. ECD has a monthly production capacity of 4,000 hours on its laser machine and 1,000 hours on its image machine. However, given the recent increase in demand for the PVR, both machines are currently operating at 90% of capacity every month, based on existing orders from customers. Direct labour costs are $15 and $20 per hour to operate, respectively, the laser and image machines.

The revenue and costs on a per unit basis for the PVR are as follows:

Selling price		$320.00
Cost to manufacture:		
Direct materials......................	$50.00	
Direct labour—laser process.............	60.00	
Direct labour—image process...........	20.00	
Variable overhead	40.00	
Fixed overhead	50.00	
Variable selling costs	20.00	240.00
Operating profit......................		$ 80.00

On December 1, Dave Nance, vice-president of Sales and Marketing at ECD, received a special order request from a prospective customer, Jay Limited, which has offered to buy 250 PVRs at

$280 per unit if the product can be delivered by December 31. Jay Limited is a large retailer with outlets that specialize in audio and video equipment. This special order from Jay Limited is in addition to orders from existing customers that are utilizing 90% of the production capacity each month. Variable selling costs would not be incurred on this special order. Jay Limited is not willing to accept anything less than the 250 PVRs requested (i.e., ESD cannot partially fill the order).

Before responding to the customer, Dave Nance decided to meet with Dianne Davis, the product manager for the PVR, to discuss whether to accept the offer from Jay Limited. Excerpts from their conversation follow:

Dave: I'm not sure we should accept the offer. This customer is really playing hardball with its terms and conditions.

Dianne: Agreed, but it is a reputable company and I suspect this is the way it typically deals with its suppliers. Plus, this could be the beginning of a profitable relationship with Jay Limited since the company may be interested in some of our other product offerings in the future.

Dave: That may be true, but I'm not sure we should be willing to incur such a large opportunity cost just to get our foot in the door with this client.

Dianne: Have you calculated the opportunity cost?

Dave: Sure, that was simple. Jay Limited is offering $280 per unit and we sell to our regular customers at $320 per unit. Therefore, we're losing $40 per unit, which at 250 units is $10,000 in lost revenue. That's our opportunity cost and it's clearly relevant to the decision.

Dianne: I sort of follow your logic, but I think the fact that we're not currently operating at full capacity needs to be taken into consideration.

Dave: How so?

Dianne: Well, your approach to calculating the opportunity cost ignores the fact that we aren't currently selling all of the PVRs that we could produce. So, in that sense we aren't really losing $40 per unit on all 250 units required by Jay Limited.

Dave: I see your point but I'm not clear on how we should calculate the opportunity cost.

Dianne: This really isn't my area of expertise either, but it seems appropriate to start by trying to figure out how many of the 250 units required by Jay Limited we could produce without disrupting our ability to fill existing orders. Then we could determine how many units we would have to forgo selling to existing customers to make up the 250-unit order. That would then be our opportunity cost in terms of the number of physical units involved. Make sense?

Dave: I think so. So, to get the dollar amount of the opportunity cost of accepting the 250-unit order from Jay Limited we'd then simply multiply the number of units we'd have to forgo selling to existing customers by $40. Correct?

Dianne: I'm not so sure about the $40. I think we somehow need to factor in the incremental profit we typically earn by selling each PVR to existing customers to really get to the true opportunity cost.

Dave: Now I'm getting really getting confused. Can you work through the numbers and get back to me?

Dianne: I'll try.

Dave: Thanks. And by the way, Jay Limited is calling in an hour and wants our answer.

Required:
1. Is Dianne's general approach to calculating the opportunity cost in terms of the physical units involved correct? Explain.
2. Assuming productive capacity cannot be increased for either machine in December, how many PVRs would ECD have to forgo selling to existing customers to fill the special order from Jay Limited?
3. Calculate the opportunity cost of accepting the special order.
4. Calculate the net effect on profits of accepting the special order.
5. Now assume that ECD is operating at 75% of capacity in December. What is the minimum price ECD should be willing to accept on the special order?
6. What are some qualitative issues that should be considered when accepting special orders such as that proposed by Jay Limited?

CASE 12–29 Sell or Process Further Decision [LO2]
Turnberry Tomatoes has a plant that can process vineyard tomatoes, along with other ingredients, into various tomato sauces and salsas. The company can sell all of its unprocessed vineyard

tomatoes at a selling price of $6.15 per kilogram. In the past, the company has sold only part of its unprocessed vineyard tomatoes and has retained the rest for further processing into tomato sauces and salsas. The salsa has been selling for $8.75 per kilogram, but recently the price has become unstable and has dropped to $7.80 per kilogram. The costs and revenues associated with a kilogram of salsa follow:

		Per Kilogram of Salsa
Selling price		$7.80
Cost to manufacture:		
Raw materials:		
Extra salsa ingredients	$1.00	
Unprocessed tomatoes (1 kg).	5.90	6.90
Direct labour.		0.25
Manufacturing overhead		0.75
Manufacturing profit (loss)		$(0.10)

Because of the weak price for the company's processed sauces and salsas, the sales manager believes that the company should discontinue processing the salsas and instead simply sell the unprocessed vineyard tomatoes. Current cost and revenue data on the unprocessed vineyard tomatoes follow:

		Per Kilogram of Tomatoes
Selling price		$6.15
Cost to manufacture:		
Seeds, pesticides, and fertilizers	$4.90	
Direct labour	0.25	
Manufacturing overhead.	0.75	5.90
Manufacturing profit		$0.25

The sales manager argues that since the present $7.80 per kilogram price for the salsa results in a $0.10 per kilogram loss, the production of salsa should not be resumed until the price per kilogram rises above $7.90. The company assigns manufacturing overhead cost to the two products on the basis of labour-hours but virtually all manufacturing overhead costs are fixed. Materials and labour costs are variable. The company can sell all of the unprocessed vineyard tomatoes and salsa it can produce at the current market prices.

Required:
1. Do you agree with the sales manager that the company should discontinue the processing of salsa and use the entire labour capacity to grow, sort, and package tomatoes if the price of salsa remains at $7.80 per kilogram? Support your answer with computations and explanations.
2. What is the lowest price that the company should accept for a kilogram of salsa? Again support your answer with computations and explanations.

CASE 12–30 Plant Closing Decision [LO1, LO2]
Automotive Interiors (AI) manufactures seats for automobiles, vans, trucks, and boats. The company has a number of plants, including the Woodstock Cover Plant, which makes seat covers.

Bill Rice is the plant manager at the Woodstock Cover Plant but also serves as the regional production manager for the company. His budget as the regional manager is charged to the Woodstock plant.

Rice has just heard that AI has received a bid from an outside vendor to supply the equivalent of the entire annual output of the Woodstock Cover Plant for $42 million. Rice was astonished at the low outside bid because the budget for the plant's operating costs for the coming year was set at $48.6 million. If this bid is accepted, the Woodstock operation will be closed down.

The budget for the Woodstock Cover Plant's operating costs for the coming year is presented below.

Materials		$16,000,000
Labour:		
Direct	$13,400,000	
Supervision	800,000	
Indirect plant	3,800,000	18,000,000
Overhead:		
Depreciation—equipment	2,600,000	
Depreciation—building	4,200,000	
Pension expense	3,200,000	
Plant manager and staff*	1,200,000	
Corporate expenses†	3,400,000	14,600,000
Total budgeted costs		$48,600,000

*Expense for Rice and his regional staff.
†Fixed corporate expenses allocated to plants and other operating units based on total budgeted wage and salary costs.

The following are additional facts regarding the plant's operations:

a. Due to the plant's commitment to use high-quality fabrics in all of its products, the Purchasing Department was instructed to place blanket purchase orders with major suppliers to ensure the receipt of sufficient materials for the coming year. If these orders are cancelled as a consequence of the plant closing, termination charges would amount to 25% of the cost of direct materials.

b. Approximately 350 employees will lose their jobs if the plant is closed. This includes all of the direct labourers and supervisors, management and staff, and the plumbers, electricians, and other skilled workers classified as indirect plant workers. Some of these workers would have difficulty finding new jobs. Nearly all the production workers would have difficulty matching the plant's base pay of $12.50 per hour, which is the highest in the area. A clause in the plant's contract with the union may help some employees; the company must provide employment assistance and job training to its former employees for 12 months after a plant closing. The estimated cost to administer this service would be $1.6 million.

c. Some employees would probably choose early retirement because AI has an excellent pension plan. In fact, $1.4 million of the annual pension expenditures would continue whether the plant is open or not.

d. Rice and his regional staff would not be affected by the closing of the Woodstock plant. They would still be responsible for running three other area plants.

e. If the plant was closed, the company would realize about $4 million salvage value for the equipment in the plant. If the plant remains open, there are no plans to make any significant investments in new equipment or buildings. The old equipment is adequate for the job and should last indefinitely.

Required:
1. Without regard to costs, identify the advantages to AI of continuing to obtain covers from its own Woodstock Cover Plant.
2. AI plans to prepare a financial analysis that will be used in deciding whether or not to close the Woodstock Cover Plant. Management has asked you to identify
   a. The annual budgeted costs that are relevant to the decision regarding closing the plant (show the dollar amounts).
   b. The annual budgeted costs that are not relevant to the decision regarding closing the plant and explain why they are not relevant (again show the dollar amounts).
   c. Any non-recurring costs that would arise due to the closing of the plant and explain how they would affect the decision (again show any dollar amounts).
3. Looking at the data you prepared in (2) above, should the plant be closed? Show computations and explain your answer.
4. Identify any revenues or costs not specifically mentioned in the problem that AI should consider before making a decision.

(CMA, adapted)

CASE 12–31 Make or Buy; Utilization of a Constrained Resource [LO1, LO2, LO3]

Drums, bins, boxes, and other containers that are used in the petroleum industry are sold by Holden Inc. One of the company's products is a heavy-duty, environmentally friendly, corrosion-resistant metal drum, called the STR drum, used to store toxic wastes. Production is constrained by the capacity of an automated welding machine that is used to make precision welds. A total of 4,500 hours of welding time is available annually on the machine. Since each drum requires 0.6 hours of welding time, annual production is limited to 7,500 drums. At present, the welding machine is used exclusively to make the STR drums. The accounting department has provided the following financial data concerning the STR drums:

STR Drums		
Selling price per drum		$225.00
Cost per drum:		
Direct materials......................	$78.15	
Direct labour ($27 per hour)	5.40	
Manufacturing overhead..............	6.75	
Selling and administrative expense	44.70	135.00
Margin per drum......................		$ 90.00

Management believes that 9,000 STR drums could be sold each year if the company had sufficient manufacturing capacity. As an alternative to adding another welding machine, management has considered buying additional drums from an outside supplier of quality products, Anderson Industries, Inc. Anderson would be able to provide up to 6,000 STR-type drums per year at a price of $207 per drum, which Holden would relabel and sell to its customers at its normal selling price.

Candace Burke, Holden's production manager, has suggested that the company could make better use of the welding machine by manufacturing wrought iron park benches, which would require 0.75 hours of welding time per bench and yet sell for far more than the drums. Candace believes that Holden could sell up to 2,400 wrought iron park benches per year to municipalities and conservation areas at a price of $360 each. The Accounting Department has provided the following data concerning the proposed new product:

Wrought Iron Park Benches		
Selling price per bench..................		$360.00
Cost per bench:		
Direct materials......................	$149.10	
Direct labour ($27 per hour)	43.20	
Manufacturing overhead..............	54.00	
Selling and administrative expense	71.70	318.00
Margin per bench.....................		$ 42.00

The park benches could be produced with existing equipment and personnel. Manufacturing overhead is allocated to products on the basis of direct labour-hours. Most of the manufacturing overhead consists of fixed common costs such as rent on the factory building, but some of it is variable. The variable manufacturing overhead has been estimated at $2.00 per STR drum and $2.85 per park bench. The variable manufacturing overhead cost would not be incurred on drums acquired from the outside supplier.

Selling and administrative expenses are allocated to products on the basis of revenues. Almost all of the selling and administrative expenses are fixed common costs, but it has been estimated that variable selling and administrative expenses amount to $1.15 per STR drum whether made or purchased and would be $1.95 per park bench.

All of the company's employees—direct and indirect—are paid for full 40-hour workweeks and the company has a policy of laying off workers only in major recessions.

Required:

1. Should the financial analysis prepared by the company be used in deciding which product to sell? Why?
2. Compute the contribution margin per unit for
    a. Purchased STR drums.
    b. Manufactured STR drums.
    c. Manufactured park benches.

3. Determine the number of STR drums (if any) that should be purchased and the number of STR drums and/or park benches (if any) that should be manufactured. What is the increase in operating income that would result from this plan over current operations?

   As soon as your analysis was shown to the top management team at Holden, several managers got into an argument concerning how direct labour costs should be treated when making this decision. One manager argued that direct labour is always treated as a variable cost in textbooks and in practice and has always been considered a variable cost at Holden. After all, "direct" means you can directly trace the cost to products. "If direct labour is not a variable cost, what is?" Another manager argued just as strenuously that direct labour should be considered a fixed cost at Holden. No one had been laid off in over a decade, and for all practical purposes, everyone at the plant is on a monthly salary. Everyone classified as direct labour works a regular 40-hour workweek and overtime has not been necessary since the company adopted just-in-time techniques. Whether the welding machine is used to make drums or park benches, the total payroll would be exactly the same. There is enough slack, in the form of idle time, to accommodate any increase in total direct labour time that the park benches would require.

4. Redo requirements (2) and (3) above, making the opposite assumption about direct labour from the one you originally made. In other words, if you treated direct labour as a variable cost, redo the analysis treating it as a fixed cost. If you treated direct labour as a fixed cost, redo the analysis treating it as a variable cost.
5. What do you think is the correct way to treat direct labour cost in this situation—as variable or as fixed?

Research and Application

R 12–32 Dropping a Product or Service: Beyond the Numbers [LO2]
One of the decisions facing managers that is illustrated in this chapter is whether to keep or drop an existing product, service, or operating segment. The analysis presented indicates that if the costs avoided by dropping the product or segment exceed the contribution margin lost, then "drop" is the correct decision from a financial perspective. However, when companies such as **General Motors** or **Chrysler** decide to drop a major product, service, or operating segment, there may be non-financial consequences involving suppliers, creditors, employees, and customers.

Required:
Identify, using any examples you can find from the business press, some non-financial consequences that may occur when an organization decides to drop a major product, service, or operating segment.

APPENDIX 12A: PRICING PRODUCTS AND SERVICES

LEARNING OBJECTIVE 4
Compute selling prices based on costs.

Our consideration of special orders in the main body of this chapter focused on non-routine situations where companies receive an offer for a product or service at a specific price. By comparing to the offer price the relevant costs that would be incurred if the offer was accepted, managers can determine the incremental effect on operating income. In this appendix, we expand our discussion of the relationship between relevant costs and pricing issues to include two distinct pricing situations requiring ongoing analysis by managers. First, we examine situations where companies are faced with the problem of setting their own prices for products or services. In this setting, we present two approaches to setting prices based on costs. Second, we examine a setting where the company offers a product or service that competes with other similar products or services for which a market price already exists. In this setting, we introduce the concept of target costing. Importantly, in both settings managers must identify and use relevant cost information to make decisions that are in the best interests of the company. Setting prices is a critical decision for managers. If the price is set too high, customers will avoid purchasing the company's products. If the price is set too low, the company's costs may not be covered.

Cost-Plus Pricing

A common approach to pricing is to set prices based on a certain *markup* above cost.[5] A product's **markup** is the difference between its selling price and its cost. The markup is usually expressed as a percentage of cost. This approach is called **cost-plus pricing** because the predetermined markup percentage is applied to the cost base to determine a target selling price.

$$\text{Selling price} = \text{Cost} + (\text{Markup percentage} \times \text{Cost})$$

For example, if a company uses a markup of 50%, it adds 50% to the costs of its products to determine the selling price. If a product costs $10, then the company would charge $15 for the product.

There are two key issues when the cost-plus approach to pricing is used. First, what costs are relevant to the pricing decision? Second, how should the markup be determined? Several alternative approaches are considered in this appendix.

As discussed in Chapters 2 through 8 and Chapter 10, various definitions of *cost* exist, each of which could be used as the base for setting a selling price. To provide a coherent illustration of cost-plus pricing, absorption costing as described in Chapters 2, 3, 4, and 8 will be presented first. We will then present an example of cost-plus pricing using the total variable costing approach.

Setting a Target Selling Price Using the Absorption Costing Approach

To illustrate, let us assume that the management of Roper Company wants to set the selling price on a product that has just undergone some design modifications. The Accounting Department has provided cost estimates for the redesigned product as shown below:

	Per Unit	Total
Direct materials	$12	
Direct labour	8	
Variable manufacturing overhead	6	
Fixed manufacturing overhead	—	$140,000
Variable selling, general, and administrative expenses	4	
Fixed selling, general, and administrative expenses	—	120,000

The first step in the absorption costing approach to cost-plus pricing is to compute the unit product cost. For Roper Company, this amounts to $40 per unit at a volume of 10,000 units, as shown in the first part of Exhibit 12A–1.

Roper Company has a general policy of marking up unit product costs by 50%. A price quotation sheet for the company prepared using the absorption approach is also presented in Exhibit 12A–1. Note that selling, general, and administrative (SG&A) costs are not included in the cost base. Instead, the markup is set at a level that will cover these expenses.

Next we examine how some companies compute markup percentages.

Direct materials	$12
Direct labour	8
Variable manufacturing overhead	6
Fixed manufacturing overhead (based on 10,000 units)	14
Unit product cost	40
Markup to cover selling, general, and administrative expenses and desired profit—50% of unit manufacturing cost	20
Target selling price	$60

EXHIBIT 12A–1   Price Quotation Sheet—Absorption Basis (10,000 Units)

Determining the Markup Percentage

How did Roper Company arrive at its markup percentage of 50%? This figure could be based on industry norms or just a company tradition that seems to work. The markup percentage may also be the result of an explicit computation. As we have discussed, the markup over cost ideally should be largely determined by market conditions. However, a popular approach is to at least start with a markup based on cost and desired profit. The reasoning is as follows: The markup must be large enough to cover SG&A expenses and provide an adequate return on investment (ROI). Given the forecasted unit sales, the markup can be computed as follows:

$$\text{Markup percentage on absorption cost} = \frac{\left(\begin{array}{c}\text{Required ROI} \\ \times \text{ Investment}\end{array}\right) + \text{SG\&A expenses}}{\text{Unit sales} \times \text{Unit product cost}}$$

To show how the formula above is applied, assume Roper Company must invest $200,000 to produce and market 10,000 units of the product each year. The $200,000 investment covers the purchase of equipment and the funds needed for working capital items such as inventory and accounts receivable. If Roper Company requires a 20% ROI, then the markup for the product would be determined as follows:

$$\text{Markup percentage on absorption cost} = \frac{\left(\begin{array}{c}20\% \\ \times \$200,000\end{array}\right) + [(\$4 \times 10,000) + \$120,000]}{10,000 \times \$40}$$

$$\text{Markup percentage on absorption cost} = \frac{\$40,000 + \$160,000}{\$400,000} = 50\%$$

As shown earlier, this markup of 50% leads to a target selling price of $60 for the Roper Company product. As shown in Exhibit 12A–2, *if the company actually sells 10,000 units* of the product at this price, and actual costs are as expected, the company's ROI on this product will indeed be 20%. If it turns out that more than 10,000 units are sold at this price, the ROI will be greater than 20%. If fewer than 10,000 units are sold, the ROI will

EXHIBIT 12A–2 Income Statement and ROI Analysis— Roper Company Actual Unit Sales = 10,000 Units; Selling Price = $60

Direct materials	$12
Direct labour	8
Variable manufacturing overhead	6
Fixed manufacturing overhead ($140,000 ÷ 10,000 units)	14
Unit product cost	$40

ROPER COMPANY
Absorption Costing Income Statement

Sales ($60 × 10,000 units)	$600,000
Less cost of goods sold ($40 × 10,000 units)	400,000
Gross margin	200,000
Less selling, general, and administration expenses	
($4 × 10,000 units + $120,000)	160,000
Operating income	$ 40,000

ROI

$$\text{ROI} = \frac{\text{Operating income}}{\text{Average operating assets}}$$

$$= \frac{\$40,000}{\$200,000}$$

$$= 20\%$$

be less than 20%. *The required ROI will be attained only if the forecasted unit sales volume is attained or exceeded at the expected unit price (or higher),* and actual costs are equal to or less than expected costs for that level of sales activity.

Problems with the Absorption Costing Approach

Using the absorption costing approach, the pricing problem looks deceptively simple. All you have to do is compute your unit product cost, decide how much profit you want, and then set your price. It appears that you can ignore demand and arrive at a price that will safely yield whatever profit you want. However, as noted above, the absorption costing approach relies on a forecast of unit sales. Neither the markup nor the unit product cost can be computed without such a forecast.

The absorption costing approach essentially assumes that customers *need* the forecasted unit sales and will pay whatever price the company decides to charge. However, customers have a choice. If the price is too high, they can buy from a competitor or they may choose not to buy at all. Suppose, for example, that when Roper Company sets its price at $60, it sells only 7,000 units rather than the 10,000 units forecasted. As shown in Exhibit 12A–3, the company would then have a loss of $50,000 on the product instead of a profit of $40,000. Some managers believe that the absorption costing approach to pricing is safe. This is not necessarily so. The absorption costing approach is safe only as long as customers choose to buy at least as many units as managers forecasted they would buy and costs behave as predicted or come in at lower levels.

Setting a Target Selling Price Using the Variable Costing Approach

Some companies use a variable costing approach to determine the target selling price based either on variable manufacturing costs or total variable costs. The key advantages of the variable costing approach are (1) it is consistent with the cost–volume–profit analysis presented in Chapter 6, which allows managers to determine the profit effects of

EXHIBIT 12A–3   Income Statement and ROI Analysis— Roper Company Actual Unit Sales = 7,000 Units; Selling Price = $60

Direct materials	$12
Direct labour	8
Variable manufacturing overhead	6
Fixed manufacturing overhead ($140,000 ÷ 7,000 units)	20
Unit product cost	$46

ROPER COMPANY
Absorption Costing Income Statement

Sales ($60 × 7,000 units)	$420,000
Less cost of goods sold ($46 × 7,000 units)	322,000
Gross margin	98,000
Less selling, general, and administration expenses ($4 × 7,000 units + $120,000)	148,000
Operating income	$ (50,000)

ROI

$$\text{ROI} = \frac{\text{Operating income}}{\text{Average operating assets}}$$

$$= \frac{(\$50,000)}{\$200,000}$$

$$= -25\%$$

- Some companies develop and sell products or services for which an established market and price already exist. Target costing can be used in such situations. Desired profit is deducted from the estimated market price to determine the product's target cost. The product design and development team then has the responsibility of ensuring that the actual cost of the new product does not exceed the target cost. **[LO5]**

Appendix 12A Exercises   connect

EXERCISE 12A–1 Absorption Costing and Total Variable Costing Approaches to Setting a Selling Price [LO4]
Nolan Limited is considering the introduction of a new product. Management has gathered the following information:

Number of units to be produced and sold each year.	10,000
Unit product cost	$16
Projected annual selling and administrative expenses.	$40,000
Estimated investment required by the company	$400,000
Desired return on investment (ROI).	8%

Required:
1. Using the absorption costing approach to cost-plus pricing, compute the markup the company will have to use to achieve the desired ROI.
2. Assume that the $16 unit product cost includes $3 per unit for fixed manufacturing overhead based on producing and selling 10,000 units each year. Also assume that $26,000 of the total selling and administrative expenses of $40,000 is fixed. The remainder is variable. Use the total variable costing approach to calculate the markup the company will have to use to achieve the desired ROI.
3. Compute the target selling price per unit under each pricing approach from (1) and (2) above.

EXERCISE 12A–2 Target Costing [LO5]
Little River Cycles (LRC) produces and distributes carbon fibre road bikes. Management is eager to take advantage of the growing market for these bikes. To be competitive, LRC's sales manager estimates that the bike can't be priced at more than $2,000. At this price, management thinks the company can sell 1,000 bikes per year. Producing the bikes will require an initial investment of $2,000,000 and the company's target ROI is 25%.

Required:
Calculate the target cost of one carbon fibre road bike.

EXERCISE 12A–3 Time and Materials Pricing [LO4]
Ronnie's Repair Company provides repair services for small engines and uses time and materials pricing. The company has budgeted the following costs for next year:

Mechanics' wages and benefits.	$900,000
Other repair costs, except for parts-related costs	$450,000
Costs of ordering, handling, and storing parts.	40% of invoice cost

In total, the company expects to have 50,000 hours of billable repair time next year. According to competitive conditions, the company believes it should aim for a profit of $8 per hour of each mechanic's time. The competitive markup on parts is 40% of invoice cost.

Required:
1. Compute the time rate and the material loading charge that would be used to bill jobs.
2. One of the company's mechanics has just completed a repair job that required 12 hours of time and $100 in parts (invoice cost). Compute the amount that would be billed for the job.

PROBLEM 12A–4 Standard Costs; Absorption Costing and Total Variable Costing Approach to Setting Prices [LO4]

Gerber Clothing, Inc., has designed a rain suit for outdoor enthusiasts that is about to be introduced on the market.

	Standard Quantity or hours	Standard price or Rate	Standard Cost
Direct materials	2.5 metres	$10.00 per metre	$25.00
Direct labour	1.0 hours	28.00 per hour	28.00
Manufacturing overhead (⅙ variable)	1.0 hours	24.00 per hour	24.00
Total standard cost per suit.			$77.00

A standard cost card has been prepared for the new suit, as follows:

a.   The only variable selling, general, or administrative costs will be $4 per suit for shipping. Fixed selling, general, and administrative costs will be (per year)

Salaries.	$ 45,000
Advertising and other	200,000
Total	$245,000

b.   Since the company manufactures many products, it is felt that no more than 10,000 hours of labour time per year can be devoted to production of the new suits.

c.   An investment of $500,000 will be necessary to carry inventories and accounts receivable and to purchase some new equipment. The company wants a 20% return on investment (ROI) in new product lines.

d.   Manufacturing overhead costs are allocated to products on the basis of direct labour-hours.

Required:

1.   Assume that the company uses the absorption approach to cost-plus pricing.

    a.   Compute the markup that the company needs on the rain suits to achieve a 20% ROI if it sells all of the suits it can produce using 10,000 hours of labour time.

    b.   Using the markup you have computed, prepare a price quote sheet for a single rain suit.

    c.   Assume that the company is able to sell all of the rain suits that it can produce. Prepare an income statement for the first year of activity, and compute the company's ROI for the year on the suits, using the ROI formula from Chapter 11.

2.   Repeat requirements 1*a* and 1*b* above, assuming that the company uses the total variable costing approach to cost-plus pricing.

3.   After marketing the rain suits for several years, the company is experiencing a decrease in demand due to an economic recession. A large retail outlet will make a bulk purchase of suits if its company logo is affixed to each suit and if an acceptable price can be worked out. What is the minimum acceptable price per rain suit for this order?

PROBLEM 12A–5 Target Costing [LO5]

Free Riders Inc. is considering adding a scooter to its motorcycle line-up. Management will negotiate the price of the scooter with its manufacturer.

    Management of Free Riders believes the scooters can be sold to its customers for $4,000 each. At that price, annual sales of the scooters should be 200 units. If the scooters are added to Free Riders's product lines, the company will have to invest $200,000 in inventories and special warehouse fixtures. The variable cost of selling the scooters would be $1,000 per unit.

Required:

1.   If Free Riders requires a 20% return on investment (ROI), what is the maximum amount the company would be willing to pay the manufacturer for the scooters?

2.   After many hours of negotiations, management has concluded that the manufacturer is unwilling to sell the scooters at a low enough price for Free Riders to earn its 20% required ROI. Apart from simply giving up on the idea of adding the scooters to Free Riders' product lines, what could management do?

PROBLEM 12A–6 Time and Material Pricing [LO4]

Computer Repair Inc. uses time and materials pricing, and each year it reviews its rates in light of the actual costs incurred in the prior year. Actual costs incurred last year in connection with repair work and in connection with the company's parts inventory are shown below.

Customers were billed for 20,000 hours of repair work last year.

The company has a target profit of $10 per hour of repair service time and a target profit of 40% of the invoice cost of parts used. During the past year, the company billed repair service time at $50 per hour and added a material loading charge of 40% to parts. Management feels these rates may now be inadequate, since costs have risen somewhat over the last year.

	Repairs	Parts
Repair technicians—wages	$480,000	
Repair service manager—salary	56,000	
Parts manager—salary..............................		$60,000
Repairs and parts assistant—salary	28,800	7,500
Retirement benefits (20% of salaries and wages)	112,960	13,500
Health insurance (5% of salaries and wages)	28,240	3,375
Utilities	120,000	24,000
Truck operating costs	19,200	
Property taxes	9,280	5,400
Liability and fire insurance	6,720	3,000
Supplies	1,200	225
Rent—building	38,400	33,000
Depreciation—trucks and equipment	59,200	
Invoice cost of parts used		600,000
Total costs for the year	$960,000	$750,000

Required:

1. Using the above data, compute the following:
    a. The rate that would be charged per hour of repair service time using time and materials pricing.
    b. The materials loading charge that would be used in billing jobs. The materials loading charge should be expressed as a percentage of the invoice cost.
2. Assume that the company adopts the rates that you have computed in (1) above. What should be the total price charged on a repair job that requires 6 hours of service time and parts with an invoice cost of $500?
3. If the company adopts the rates that you have computed in (1) above, would you expect the company's profits to improve?

 Practise and learn online with Connect.

CAPITAL BUDGETING DECISIONS

Learning Objectives

After studying Chapter 13, you should be able to

1. Evaluate the acceptability of an investment project using the net present value method.

2. Evaluate the acceptability of an investment project using the internal rate of return method.

3. Evaluate an investment project that has uncertain cash flows.

4. Rank investment projects in order of preference.

5. Determine the payback period for an investment.

6. Calculate the simple rate of return for an investment.

7. (Appendix 13A) Explain present value concepts and become familiar with the use of present value tables.

8. (Appendix 13B) Incorporate income taxes into a capital budgeting analysis.

■ GOING FOR GOLD

Barrick Gold Corporation is the largest gold mining company in the world. Founded in the early 1980s, Barrick has its company headquarters in Toronto, Ontario, and has mining and exploration projects ongoing in numerous countries, including Canada, the United States, Australia, the Dominican Republic, Chile, South Africa, Russia, and Pakistan. The company had adjusted net income of (US)$1.8 billion in 2009 (up from $1.7 billion in 2008) on sales of (US)$8.1 billion (up from $7.6 billion in 2008).

To sustain growth in revenues and profits, Barrick must continually make significant capital investments to develop new projects, expand existing projects, and sustain operations. Barrick's 2009 annual report shows the following details for capital expenditures:

	$US Millions
Project capital expenditures	$ 965
Expansionary capital expenditures	60
Sustaining capital expenditures	784
Total	$1,809

Some of these expenditures were necessary in order to comply with safety and environmental regulations, while others were undertaken because they are expected to generate positive net cash inflows in the future. The challenge for capital-intensive companies such as Barrick is deciding from among many alternatives—which projects to invest in and when. For example, in any given year, Barrick has to decide whether to expand production capacity at existing locations, improve the efficiency of operations at existing locations, or develop new mines in new locations. Although these are not mutually exclusive alternatives, Barrick, as is the case with most companies, is constrained by the amount of funds available for annual capital expenditures and so must undertake a thorough analysis of the costs and benefits of each option. The stakes are high for this type of analysis, as making good capital budgeting decisions can have a considerable impact on the long-term financial health of a company.

How do companies make capital budgeting decisions and choose from among the alternatives when funds are limited? These are the key topics covered in this chapter.

Source: Barrick Gold Corporation, *2009 Annual Report.* Reprinted with permission.

Capital budgeting
The process of planning significant outlays on projects that have long-term implications, such as the purchase of new equipment or the introduction of a new product.

The term **capital budgeting** is used to describe how managers plan significant outlays on projects that have long-term implications, such as the purchase of new equipment and the introduction of new products. Most companies have many more potential projects than can actually be funded, so managers must carefully select those projects that promise the greatest future return. How well managers make these capital budgeting decisions can affect the long-run profitability of the company, given the magnitude of the spending involved. For example, in 2009, Bell Canada Enterprises (BCE) Inc. had capital expenditures of $2.8 billion.

Capital budgeting involves *investment*—a company must commit funds now in order to receive future returns. Investments are not limited to stocks and bonds. Purchasing manufacturing equipment, building new facilities, or acquiring other assets required to support some aspect of operations are also investments. For example, Tim Hortons makes an investment when it opens a new restaurant. McCain Foods makes an investment when it installs a new computer to handle customer billing. Chrysler Canada Inc. makes an investment when it redesigns a product such as the Jeep Eagle and must retool its production lines. All of these investments are characterized by a commitment of funds today in the expectation of receiving a return in the future in the form of additional cash inflows or reduced cash outflows.

◼ CAPITAL BUDGETING—PLANNING INVESTMENTS

Typical Capital Budgeting Decisions

Any decision that involves an outlay now in order to obtain some return (increase in revenue or reduction in costs) in the future is a capital budgeting decision. Typical capital budgeting decisions include:

1. *Cost-reduction decisions.* Should new equipment be purchased to reduce costs?
2. *Expansion decisions.* Should a new plant, warehouse, or other facility be acquired to increase capacity and production?
3. *Equipment selection decisions.* Which of several available machines should be purchased?
4. *Lease or buy decisions.* Should new equipment be leased or purchased?
5. *Equipment replacement decisions.* Should old equipment be replaced now or later?

Screening decision
A decision as to whether a proposed investment meets some pre-established profitability hurdle.

Capital budgeting decisions tend to fall into two broad categories—*screening decisions* and *preference decisions.* **Screening decisions** are those relating to whether a proposed project is acceptable—whether it passes a pre-established profitability hurdle. For example, a firm may have a policy of accepting projects only if they promise a return of at least 20% on the investment. The required rate of return is the minimum rate of return a project must yield to be acceptable.

Preference decision
A decision as to which of several competing acceptable investment proposals is best.

Preference decisions, by contrast, relate to selecting from among several acceptable alternatives. To illustrate, a firm may be considering several different machines to replace an existing machine on the assembly line. The choice of which machine to purchase is a *preference* decision.

In this chapter, we initially discuss screening decisions and then move on to preference decisions.

The Time Value of Money

Capital investments usually earn returns extending over fairly long periods of time. Therefore, when evaluating investment proposals, it is necessary to employ techniques that recognize the *time value of money.* A dollar today is worth more than a dollar a year from now. The same concept applies in choosing between investment alternatives. Projects that promise returns earlier in time are preferable to those that promise later returns.

The capital budgeting techniques that recognize the time value of money involve *discounted cash flows*. We will spend most of this chapter illustrating the use of discounted cash flow methods in making capital budgeting decisions. If you are not already familiar with discounting and the use of present value tables, you should read Appendix 13A, The Concept of Present Value, at the end of this chapter, before proceeding any further.

DISCOUNTED CASH FLOWS—THE NET PRESENT VALUE METHOD

Two approaches to making capital budgeting decisions use discounted cash flows. One is the *net present value method*, and the other is the *internal rate of return method*. The net present value method is discussed in this section; the internal rate of return method is discussed in the following section.

LEARNING OBJECTIVE 1
Evaluate the acceptability of an investment project using the net present value method.

The Net Present Value Method Illustrated

Under the net present value method, the present value of a project's cash inflows is compared to the present value of the project's cash outflows. The difference between the present value of these cash flows, called the **net present value**, determines whether the project is an acceptable investment. To illustrate, assume the following data outlined in Example A below.

Net present value
The difference between the present value of the cash inflows and the present value of the cash outflows associated with an investment project.

Example A

Harper Company is contemplating the purchase of a machine capable of performing certain operations that are now performed manually. The machine will cost $50,000, and it will last for five years. At the end of the five-year period, the machine will have a zero scrap value. Use of the machine will reduce labour costs by $18,000 per year. Harper Company requires a minimum return of 20% before taxes on all investment projects.[1]

Should the machine be purchased? Harper Company must determine whether a cash investment now of $50,000 can be justified if it will result in an $18,000 reduction in cost each year over the next five years. It may appear that the answer is obvious since the total cost savings are $90,000 ($18,000 per year $\times$ 5 years). However, the company can earn a

20% return by investing its money elsewhere. It is not enough that the cost reductions cover just the original cost of the machine; they must also yield at least a 20% return or the company would be better off investing the money elsewhere.

To determine whether the investment is desirable, the stream of annual $18,000 cost savings is discounted to its present value, which is then compared to the cost of the new machine. Since Harper Company requires a minimum return of 20% on all investment projects, this rate is used in the discounting process and is called the *discount rate*. Exhibit 13–1 shows how this analysis is done.

EXHIBIT 13–1   Net Present Value Analysis of a Proposed Project

Initial cost	$50,000
Life of the project (years)	5
Annual cost savings	$18,000
Salvage value	$0
Required rate of return	20%

Item	Year(s)	Amount of Cash Flow	20% Factor	Present Value of Cash Flows
Annual cost savings	1–5	$ 18,000	2.991*	$ 53,838
Initial investment	Now	(50,000)	1.000	(50,000)
Net present value				$ 3,838

*From Exhibit 13A–7 at the end of Appendix 13A at the end of this chapter.

According to the analysis, Harper Company should purchase the new machine. The present value of the cost savings is $53,838, compared to the present value of the required investment (cost of the machine) of only $50,000. Deducting the present value of the investment required from the present value of the cost savings gives a *net present value* of $3,838. Whenever the net present value is zero or greater, as in our example, an investment project is acceptable. Whenever the net present value is negative (the present value of the cash outflows exceeds the present value of the cash inflows), an investment project is not acceptable.

A full interpretation of the solution would be as follows: The new machine promises more than the required 20% rate of return. This is evident from the positive net present value of $3,838. Harper Company could spend up to $53,838 for the new machine and still obtain the minimum required 20% rate of return. The net present value of $3,838, therefore, shows the amount of "cushion" or "margin of error." One way to look at this is that the company could underestimate the cost of the new machine by up to $3,838, or overestimate the present value of the future cash savings by up to $3,838, and the project would still be financially attractive. If the present value of the cost savings was only $50,000 instead of $53,838, the project would still generate the required 20% return.

Emphasis on Cash Flows

In capital budgeting decisions, the focus is on cash flows and not on accounting income. Accounting income is based on accruals that ignore the timing of cash flows. From a capital budgeting standpoint, the timing of cash flows is critical, since a dollar received today is more valuable than a dollar received in the future. Therefore, instead of determining accounting income, when making capital budgeting decisions, the manager must concentrate on identifying the specific cash flows associated with an investment project.

Although the specific cash flows will vary from project to project, certain types of cash flows tend to recur, as explained in the following paragraphs.

Typical Cash Outflows   Most projects will have at least three types of cash outflows. First, they often require an immediate cash outflow in the form of an initial investment in equipment or other assets. Any salvage value realized from the sale of old equipment can be recognized as a cash inflow or as a reduction in the required investment. Second, some projects require that a company expand its working capital. **Working capital** is current assets (cash, accounts receivable, and inventory) less current liabilities. When a company takes on a new project, the balances in the current asset accounts will often increase. For example, opening a new Future Shop location would require additional cash in sales registers, increased accounts receivable for new customers, and more inventory to fill the shelves. These additional working capital needs should be treated as part of the initial investment in a project. Third, many projects require periodic outlays for repairs and maintenance and for additional operating costs. These should all be treated as cash outflows for capital budgeting purposes.

Working capital
The excess of current assets over current liabilities.

Typical Cash Inflows   Most projects will have at least three types of cash inflows. First, a project will normally increase revenues or reduce costs. Either way, the amount involved should be treated as a cash inflow for capital budgeting purposes. Notice that from a cash flow standpoint, a reduction in costs is equivalent to an increase in revenues. Second, cash inflows are also frequently realized from selling equipment for its salvage value when a project is terminated, although the company may actually have to pay for the cost of disposing of some low-value or hazardous items. Third, any working capital that was tied up in the project can be released for use elsewhere at the end of the project and should be treated as a cash inflow. Working capital is released, for example, when a company sells off its inventory or collects its receivables.

In summary, the following types of cash flows are common in business investment projects:

Cash outflows:

    Initial investment (including installation costs).

    Increased working capital needs.

    Repairs and maintenance.

    Incremental operating costs.

Cash inflows:

    Incremental revenues.

    Reduction in costs.

    Salvage value.

    Release of working capital.

Recovery of the Original Investment

When computing the present value of a project, depreciation is not deducted for two reasons. First, depreciation is not a current cash outflow.[2] As discussed previously, discounted cash flow methods of making capital budgeting decisions focus on *cash flows*. Although depreciation is used in computing net income for financial statements, it is not relevant in an analytical framework that focuses on cash flows.

A second reason for not deducting depreciation is that discounted cash flow methods *automatically* provide for return of the original investment, thereby making a deduction for depreciation unnecessary. To demonstrate this point, consider the information given in Example B.

Example B

Carver Dental Clinic is considering the purchase of an attachment for its X-ray machine that will cost $3,170. The attachment will be usable for four years, after which time it will have no salvage value. It will increase net cash inflows by $1,000 per year in the X-Ray Department. The clinic's board of directors has decided that no investments are to be made unless these investments have an annual return of at least 10%.

A present value analysis of the desirability of purchasing the X-ray attachment is presented in Exhibit 13–2. Notice that the attachment promises exactly a 10% return on the original investment, since the net present value is zero at a 10% discount rate.

EXHIBIT 13–2   Carver Dental Clinic—Net Present Value Analysis of X-Ray Attachment

Initial cost	$3,170
Life of the project (years)	4
Annual net cash inflow	$1,000
Salvage value	$0
Required rate of return	10%

Item	Year(s)	Amount of Cash Flow	10% Factor	Present Value of Cash Flows
Annual net cash inflow	1–4	$ 1,000	3.170*	$ 3,170
Initial investment	Now	(3,170)	1.000	(3,170)
Net present value				$ 0

*From Exhibit 13A–7 in Appendix 13A.

Each annual $1,000 cash inflow arising from use of the attachment is made up of two parts. One part represents a recovery of a portion of the original $3,170 paid for the attachment, and the other part represents a return on this investment. The breakdown of each year's $1,000 cash inflow between recovery *of* investment and return *on* investment is shown in Exhibit 13–3.

The first year's $1,000 cash inflow consists of a return *on* investment of $317 (a 10% return *on* the $3,170 original investment), plus a $683 return *of* that investment. Since the amount of the unrecovered investment decreases over the four years, the dollar amount of the return on investment also decreases each year. By the end of the fourth year, the entire $3,170 original investment has been recovered.

Simplifying Assumptions

Two simplifying assumptions are usually made in net present value analysis.

The first assumption is that all cash flows other than the initial investment occur at the end of periods. This is somewhat unrealistic in that cash flows typically occur *throughout* a period—rather than just at the end. The purpose of this assumption is to simplify computations and it does not significantly affect the accuracy of the analysis in most cases.

The second assumption is that all cash flows generated by an investment project are immediately reinvested at a rate of return equal to the discount rate. Unless these conditions are met, the return computed for the project will not be accurate. We used a discount rate of 10% for the Carver Dental Clinic in Exhibit 13–2. Unless the funds released each period are immediately reinvested at a 10% return, the net present value computed for the X-ray attachment will be misstated.

EXHIBIT 13–3   Carver Dental Clinic—Breakdown of Annual Cash Inflows

Year	(1) Investment Outstanding during the Year	(2) Cash Inflow	(3) Return on Investment (1) × 10%	(4) Recovery of Investment during the Year (2) − (3)	(5) Unrecovered Investment at the End of the Year (1) − (4)
1	$3,170	$1,000	$317	$ 683	$2,487
2	2,487	1,000	249	751	1,736
3	1,736	1,000	173	827	909
4	909	1,000	91	909	0
Total investment recovered				$3,170	

Choosing a Discount Rate

A positive net present value means that the project's return exceeds the discount rate. Therefore, if the company's minimum required rate of return is used as the discount rate, a project with a positive net present value has a return that exceeds the minimum required rate of return and is acceptable. Conversely, a project with a negative net present value has a return that is less than the minimum required rate of return and is unacceptable.

The firm's *cost of capital* is usually regarded as the most appropriate choice for the discount rate. The **cost of capital** is the average rate of return the company must pay to its long-term creditors and shareholders for the use of their funds. The cost of capital is the minimum required rate of return, because if a project's rate of return is less than the cost of capital, company earnings will not be enough to compensate its creditors and shareholders. Therefore, any rate of return less than the cost of capital should not be accepted. The cost of capital is known by various names. It is sometimes called the *hurdle rate*, the *cut-off rate*, or the *required rate of return*. Depending on the riskiness of the project under consideration, many companies may use a discount rate that differs from the cost of capital. For example, projects that are above an average level of risk will be analyzed using a discount rate that is higher than the cost of capital. The rationale for this approach is that riskier investments should generate higher returns. Decisions on the appropriate discount rate to use should be made on a project-by-project basis, taking the risk of the project's underlying cash flows into consideration. The mechanics involved in cost of capital computations are covered in finance texts and will not be considered here.

Cost of capital
The average rate of return companies must pay to long-term creditors and shareholders for the use of their funds.

An Extended Example of the Net Present Value Method

To continue our discussion of the net present value method, Example C presents an extended example of how this method is used in analyzing an investment proposal. This will help to tie together and to reinforce many of the ideas developed so far.

Example C

Under a special licensing arrangement, Swinyard Company has an opportunity to market a new product in western Canada for a five-year period. The product would be purchased from the manufacturer, with Swinyard Company responsible for all costs of promotion and distribution. The licensing arrangement could be renewed at the end of the five-year period at the option of the manufacturer. After careful study, Swinyard Company has estimated that the following costs and revenues would be associated with the new product:

Cost of equipment needed	$ 60,000
Working capital needed	100,000
Overhaul of the equipment in four years	5,000
Salvage value of the equipment in five years	10,000
Annual revenues and costs:	
Sales revenues	200,000
Cost of goods sold	125,000
Out-of-pocket operating costs (for salaries,	
advertising, and other direct costs)	35,000

At the end of the five-year period, the working capital would be released for investment elsewhere if the manufacturer decided not to renew the licensing arrangement. Swinyard Company's discount rate and cost of capital is 14%. Would you recommend that the new product be introduced?

This example involves a variety of cash inflows and cash outflows. The solution is given in Exhibit 13–4.

Notice how the working capital is handled in this exhibit. It is included as a cash outflow at the beginning of the project and as a cash inflow when it is released at the end of the project. Also notice how the sales revenues, cost of goods sold, and out-of-pocket costs are handled. **Out-of-pocket costs** are actual cash outlays for salaries, advertising, and

Out of pocket costs
Actual cash outlays for operating costs.

The project profitability index indicates that Project B is more desirable than Project A. This is in fact the case if the funds released from Project A at the end of one year can be reinvested at only 12% (the cost of capital). Although the computations will not be shown here, in order for Project A to be more desirable than Project B, the funds released from Project A would have to be reinvested at a rate of return *greater* than 14% for the remaining five years.

In short, the internal rate of return method of ranking tends to favour short-term, high-yield projects, whereas the net present value method of ranking (using the project profitability index) tends to favour longer-term projects.

The internal rate of return method is problematic. It assumes that funds can be reinvested at a particular project's yield. The problem becomes apparent in the context of MacInnis Company, which has projects in Cambridge, Guelph, and Waterloo that have internal rates of return of 20%, 15%, and 10%, respectively. It is meaningless to differentiate among the cash flows and assume that a dollar returned from the Waterloo project will earn less than a dollar returned from the Cambridge project. Obviously, a dollar is a dollar regardless of the project from which it comes. The net present value method does not suffer from this flaw but assumes that all funds can be reinvested at the firm's cost of capital. Because the net present value is conceptually superior, it should be used in ranking projects that are mutually exclusive.

Post-Audit of Investment Projects

Post-audit
Following up on a project that has been approved to see if expected results are being realized.

A *post-audit* should be conducted after an investment project has been approved and implemented. A **post-audit** involves checking whether expected results are actually realized. This is a key part of the capital budgeting process that helps keep managers committed to their investment proposals. Any tendency to inflate the benefits or understate the costs in a proposal should become evident after a few post-audits have been conducted. The post-audit also provides an opportunity to possibly expand successful projects or to cut losses on floundering projects.

The same capital budgeting method should be used in the post-audit that was used in the original approval process. That is, if a project was approved on the basis of a net present value analysis, then the same procedure should be used in performing the post-audit. However, the data used in the post-audit analysis should be the *actual results* rather than the estimates used in the original proposal. This gives management an opportunity to make a comparison to see how well the project has actually done relative to the original estimates. The accountability established by this approach also encourages managers to prepare realistic estimates when submitting capital budgets in the future, since they know that they will be compared to the actual results in the post-audit process.

The post-audit should be detailed enough to answer a variety of questions: Was the capital budgeting decision consistent with overall corporate strategy? Did the project meet the specifications that were set out in the original request? Were the financial estimates realistic versus excessively optimistic? Did unforeseen events occur that caused original estimates to vary from actual, such as an increase in installation costs? Have the estimated non-financial benefits (if any) such as improvements to quality been realized? Were any additional expenditures properly authorized?

Post-audits are not without their challenges. A proper review may be time-consuming, and it is often difficult to attribute incremental costs and revenues to a specific project. This is especially true if several projects were implemented around the same time and there is synergy among them.[5] Also, to ensure objectivity, the post-audit should be performed by an individual or team that has not been directly involved in developing or implementing the actual project. Importantly, the post-audit should not be aimed at placing blame; instead the objective should be to improve control over the capital budgeting process and to facilitate a learning process that will improve the estimates developed in support of future projects.

OTHER APPROACHES TO CAPITAL BUDGETING DECISIONS

Although conceptually inferior to the net present value or the internal rate of return methods, many companies employ other techniques to make capital budget decisions. In this section, we examine two of these methods, known as *payback* and *simple rate of return*. Neither involves the use of discounted cash flows but their popularity can be attributed to their simplicity and ease of understanding.

LEARNING OBJECTIVE 5
Determine the payback period for an investment.

The Payback Method

The payback method focuses on the *payback period*. The **payback period** is the length of time that it takes for a project to recover its initial cost from the net cash inflows that it generates. The basic premise of the payback method is that the more quickly the cost of an investment can be recovered, the more desirable the investment.

The payback period is usually expressed in years. *When the net annual cash inflow is the same every year*, the following formula can be used to compute the payback period:

$$\text{Payback period} = \frac{\text{Investment required}}{\text{Net annual cash inflow*}} \qquad (3)$$

_____

*If new equipment is replacing old equipment, this becomes incremental net annual cash inflow.

Payback period
The length of time that it takes for a project to recover its initial cost from the net cash inflows that it generates.

To illustrate the payback method, assume the data given in Example H.

Example H

York Company needs a new milling machine. The company is considering two machines: Machine A and Machine B. Machine A costs $15,000 and will reduce operating costs by $5,000 per year. Machine B costs only $12,000 but will also reduce operating costs by $5,000 per year.

Which machine should be purchased according to the payback method?

$$\text{Machine A payback period} = \frac{\$15,000}{\$5,000} = 3.0 \text{ years}$$

$$\text{Machine B payback period} = \frac{\$12,000}{\$5,000} = 2.4 \text{ years}$$

According to the payback calculations, York Company should purchase machine B, since it has a shorter payback period than machine A.

Evaluation of the Payback Method

The payback method is not a true measure of the profitability of an investment. Rather, it simply tells the manager how many years will be required to recover the original investment. Unfortunately, a shorter payback period does not always mean that one investment is more desirable than another.

To illustrate, refer to the example above. Since Machine B has a shorter payback period than Machine A, it *appears* that Machine B is more desirable than Machine A. But if we add one more piece of data, this illusion quickly disappears. Now assume that Machine A has a projected 10-year life, and Machine B has a projected 5-year life. It would take two purchases of Machine B, costing $24,000 in total (assuming no inflation or other changes to the price) to provide the same length of service as would be provided by a single purchase of Machine A for $15,000. Under these circumstances, Machine A would be a much better investment than Machine B, even though Machine B has a shorter payback period. Unfortunately, the payback method has no inherent mechanism for highlighting differences in useful lives between investments. Such differences can be very important, and relying on payback alone may result in incorrect decisions.

A further criticism of the payback method is that it does not adequately consider the time value of money. A cash inflow to be received several years in the future is weighed equally with a cash inflow to be received now. To illustrate, assume that for an investment of $8,000 you can purchase either of the two following streams of cash inflows:

Year	0	1	2	3	4	5	6	7	8
Stream 1		$0	$0	$0	($8,000)	$2,000	$2,000	$2,000	$2,000
Stream 2		$2,000	$2,000	$2,000	($8,000)	$8,000	$0	$0	$0

Which stream of cash inflows would you prefer to receive in return for your $8,000 investment? Each stream has a payback period of 4.0 years. Therefore, if payback alone was relied on in making the decision, you would be forced to say that the streams are equally desirable. However, from the point of view of the time value of money, Stream 2 is much more desirable than Stream 1 because the return occurs sooner. You can check this logic by calculating the net present value of the two projects using the method discussed earlier in the chapter. Using any discount rate you like, Project B will always have a higher net present value than Project A.

On the other hand, under certain conditions, the payback method can be very useful. For one thing, it can help identify which investment proposals are "in the ballpark." That is, the payback method can be used as an initial screening tool to help answer the question, "Should I consider this proposal further?" If a proposal doesn't provide a payback within some specified period, then there may be no need to consider it further. In addition, the payback period is often of great importance to firms that are "cash poor." When a firm is cash poor, a project with a short payback period but a low rate of return might be preferred over another project because the company may simply need a faster recovery of its cash investment. Finally, the payback method is sometimes used in industries where products become obsolete very rapidly—such as consumer electronics. Since products may last only a year or two, the payback period on investments must be very short.

IN BUSINESS

Investing in an energy solution can benefit hotels in many ways, ranging from conservation to guest satisfaction, according to research conducted by Direct Energy Business Services. Hotels that have invested in total energy management solutions have also reduced their operating costs by as much as 24% per annum. With larger hotels, this equates to approximately $1.5 million per year, or an average of $644 per room per year.

The research, conducted with hotel properties across Canada whose energy management projects varied widely, shows that paying close attention to this back-of-house strategy that encompasses how a property buys, converts, uses, and disposes of its energy, usually has a payback of three to five years and attractive ROI of up to 33%. For one hotel, whose solution had a price tag of more than $3.7 million and resulted in savings of more than $650,000 per annum when combined with incentives, the simple payback was 5.6 years. In particular, projects like lighting upgrades or automation can return investments in less than four years.

Source: Excerpted from "New Research Shows Managing Energy Benefits, ROI, Conservation and Guest Satisfaction," *Direct Energy Business Services*, Feb. 15, 2005.

An Extended Example of Payback

As shown by formula (3) on the previous page, the payback period is computed by dividing the investment in a project by the net annual cash inflows that the project will generate. If new equipment is replacing old equipment, then any salvage value to be received on disposal of the old equipment should be deducted from the cost of the new equipment, and only the *incremental* investment should be used in the payback computation. In addition, any depreciation deducted in arriving at the project's operating income must be added back to obtain the project's expected annual net cash inflow. To illustrate, consider the data in Example I.

Example I

Goodtime Fun Centres Inc. operates amusement parks. Some of the vending machines in one of its parks provide very little revenue, so the company is considering removing the machines and installing equipment to dispense soft ice cream. The equipment would cost $80,000 and have an eight-year useful life with no salvage value. Incremental annual revenues and costs associated with the sale of ice cream would be as follows:

Sales.	$150,000
Less cost of ingredients	90,000
Contribution margin	60,000
Less fixed expenses:	
Salaries	27,000
Maintenance	3,000
Depreciation	10,000
Total fixed expenses.	40,000
Operating income.	$ 20,000

The vending machines can be sold for a $5,000 scrap value. The company will not purchase equipment unless it has a payback period of three years or less. Does the ice cream dispenser pass this criterion?

Exhibit 13–11 shows the computation of the payback period for the ice cream dispenser. Several things should be noted. First, depreciation is added back to operating income to obtain the net annual cash inflow from the new equipment. Depreciation is not a cash outlay so it must be added back to adjust operating income to a cash basis. Second, the payback computation deducts the salvage value of the old machines from the cost of the new equipment so that only the incremental investment is used in computing the payback period.

EXHIBIT 13–11   Computation of the Payback Period

Step 1:   Compute the net annual cash inflow. Since the net annual cash inflow is not given, it must be computed before the payback period can be determined:

Operating income (given in Example I)	$20,000
Add: Non-cash deduction for depreciation	10,000
Net annual cash inflow	$30,000

Step 2:   Compute the payback period. Using the net annual cash inflow figure from above, the payback period can be determined as follows:

Cost of the new equipment	$80,000
Less salvage value of old equipment	(5,000)
Investment required	$75,000

$$\text{Payback period} = \frac{\text{Investment required}}{\text{Net annual cash inflow}}$$

$$= \frac{\$75,000}{\$30,000} = 2.5 \text{ years}$$

As Exhibit 13–11 shows, the proposed equipment has a payback period of less than three years, so the company's payback requirement has been met.

Payback and Uneven Cash Flows

When the cash flows associated with an investment project change from year to year, the simple payback formula provided earlier cannot be used. Consider the following data:

Year	Investment	Cash Inflow
1	$4,000	$1,000
2		0
3		2,000
4	2,000	1,000
5		500
6		3,000
7		2,000
8		2,000

What is the payback period on this investment? The answer is 5.5 years, but to obtain this figure it is necessary to track the unrecovered investment year by year. The steps involved in this process are shown in Exhibit 13–12. By the middle of the sixth year, sufficient cash inflows will have been realized to recover the entire investment of $6,000 ($4,000 + $2,000).

EXHIBIT 13–12   Payback Calculation and Uneven Cash Flows

Year	Investment (a)	Cash Inflow (b)	Unrecovered Investment* (c)
1	$4,000	$1,000	$3,000
2		0	$3,000
3		$2,000	$1,000
4	$2,000	$1,000	$2,000
5		$ 500	$1,500
6		$3,000	0
7		$2,000	0

*Year X unrecovered investment, column (c) = Year X − 1 unrecovered investment (column c) + Year X investment (column a) − Year X cash inflow (column b). For example, the unrecovered investment in year 4 is calculated as follows: $1,000 (year 3 unrecovered investment) + $2,000 (year 4 investment) − $1,000 (year 4 cash inflow) = $2,000.

◼ THE SIMPLE RATE OF RETURN METHOD

LEARNING OBJECTIVE 6
Calculate the simple rate of return for an investment

Simple rate of return
The rate of return computed by dividing a project's annual operating income by the initial investment required.

The **simple rate of return** method is another capital budgeting technique that does not involve discounted cash flows. The method is also known as the *accounting rate of return*, or *the unadjusted rate of return*.

Unlike the other capital budgeting methods that we have discussed, the simple rate of return method does not focus on cash flows. Rather, it focuses on accounting operating income. The approach is to estimate the revenues that will be generated by a proposed investment and then deduct from these revenues all of the projected operating expenses associated with the project. This operating income figure is then related to the initial investment in the project, as shown in the following formula:

$$\text{Simple rate of return} = \frac{\overset{\text{Incremental}}{\text{revenues}} - \overset{\text{Incremental expenses,}}{\text{including depreciation}} = \overset{\text{Incremental}}{\text{operating income}}}{\text{Initial investment*}} \quad (4)$$

*The investment should be reduced by any salvage from the sale of old equipment.

Or, if a cost reduction project is involved, the formula becomes

$$\text{Simple rate of return} = \frac{\text{Cost savings} - \text{Depreciation on new equipment}}{\text{Initial investment*}} \tag{5}$$

*The investment should be reduced by any salvage from
the sale of old equipment.

The logic of deducting depreciation on the investment in new equipment is subject to potential confusion, given how the initial investment was handled earlier in the chapter. However, deducting depreciation expense in formula 4 or 5 makes the calculation of the simple rate of return conceptually similar to the return on investment (ROI) performance metric illustrated in Chapter 11. Examples J and K demonstrate this.

Example J

Brigham Tea Company is a processor of a low-acid tea. The company is contemplating purchasing equipment for an additional processing line. The additional processing line would increase revenues by $90,000 per year. Incremental cash operating expenses would be $40,000 per year. The equipment would cost $180,000 and have a nine-year life. No salvage value is projected.

The simple rate of return for this example is calculated as follows:

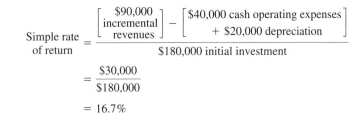

$$\text{Simple rate of return} = \frac{\left[\begin{array}{c}\$90,000\\ \text{incremental}\\ \text{revenues}\end{array}\right] - \left[\begin{array}{c}\$40,000 \text{ cash operating expenses}\\ + \$20,000 \text{ depreciation}\end{array}\right]}{\$180,000 \text{ initial investment}}$$

$$= \frac{\$30,000}{\$180,000}$$

$$= 16.7\%$$

Example K

Midwest Farms Limited hires people on a part-time basis to sort eggs. The cost of this hand-sorting process is $30,000 per year. The company is investigating the purchase of an egg-sorting machine that would cost $90,000 and have a 15-year useful life. The machine would have negligible salvage value, and it would cost $10,000 per year to operate and maintain. The egg-sorting equipment currently being used could be sold now for a scrap value of $2,500.

A cost-reduction project is involved in Example K. By applying the formula for the simple rate of return found in equation (5), we can compute the simple rate of return as follows:

$$\text{Simple rate of return} = \frac{\$20,000 \text{ cost savings*} - \$6,000 \text{ depreciation on new equipment**}}{\$90,000 - \$2,500}$$

$$= 16\%$$

*$30,000 − $10,000 = $20,000 cost savings per year.
**$90,000 ÷ 15 years = $6,000 depreciation per year.

Criticisms of the Simple Rate of Return

The most damaging criticism of the simple rate of return method is that it ignores the time value of money—it considers a dollar received 10 years from now just as valuable as a dollar received today. Thus, the simple rate of return can be misleading if the alternatives being considered have different cash flow patterns. Also, many projects do not have constant incremental revenues and expenses over their useful lives. As a result, the simple rate of return will fluctuate from year to year, with the possibility that a project may appear to be profitable in some years and unprofitable in others. In contrast, the net present value method provides a single number that summarizes all of the cash flows over the entire useful life of the project and explicitly incorporates the time value of money.

■ BEHAVIOURAL CONSIDERATIONS

So far, this chapter has emphasized the technical aspects of capital budgeting. The management accountant should also be cognizant of important behavioural considerations. An understanding of the functional and dysfunctional consequences of human behaviour can provide deeper insight into the capital budgeting process.

Capital budgeting requires creativity, judgment, and the ability to see ideas through to implementation. The entire capital budgeting process from idea generation to implementation can provide valuable training for managers. There may be non-financial reasons for accepting certain projects. Some marginal projects may be accepted because they provide good experience and training benefits.

Estimates of cash flows, discount rates, and salvage values may be affected by the attitudes of individual managers toward risk. Risk-averse managers tend to be more conservative in their estimates compared to managers who tend to seek risk and take on projects that have riskier cash flows.

The politics of organizations may also affect the capital budgeting process. Key managers may favour their own projects. Self-identification with projects may obscure management judgment of when to abandon a particular project, and obtaining accurate estimates may also become problematic. Internal politics may also influence preference decisions. With only limited funds available for capital investments, a division with several good investment proposals may be denied approval of some proposals in favour of less profitable projects of other divisions. Such allocations of resources (for non-financial reasons) may be deemed necessary to maintain harmony and to give the appearance of fairness.

The capital budgeting process may create additional pressure on top management. Top management may find it difficult to reject projects already approved by managers at lower levels. On the other hand, some projects that have been rejected at lower levels, and thus not considered by top management, may actually be beneficial because they help to diversify the firm's overall risk. Thus, the hierarchical nature of the project approval process may result in some projects never being considered by those senior members of the organization best able to evaluate the projects' contribution to risk management.

Some projects are approved even though they may not generate a positive net present value. For example, projects involving employee, consumer, or environmental safety, or that otherwise impact a firm's ability to operate in a socially responsible manner may have to be evaluated using non-financial criteria. Other projects that cannot be justified on financial grounds may have to be undertaken in order to conform to municipal, provincial or territorial, or federal laws.

In summary, the capital budgeting process involves more than just the analytical techniques presented in this chapter. A purely quantitative approach to capital budgeting is not representative of what actually happens in practice. Important qualitative factors imposed on the process by the political and social environment within the firm often strongly influence capital budgeting decisions.

IN BUSINESS

Not all capital expenditures incurred by companies are for projects expected to provide a positive net present value. Sometimes investments are made to improve environmental performance as part of a growing recognition by many companies that managing the "triple bottom line" of profits, people, and planet is essential. Suncor Energy Inc. provides a good example of a company undertaking significant capital expenditures in an effort to lessen the negative impact of its operations on the environment. Suncor is a Canadian energy company with headquarters in Calgary, Alberta. One of its key activities is the production of synthetic crude oil from the oil sands in Fort McMurray, Alberta.

One of the by-products of extracting oil from oil sands is liquid tailings, a toxic mix consisting of water, sand, clay, and residual hydrocarbons. The tailings are held in ponds that occupy a considerable area of land, and because of the nature of their composition, the tailings do not readily evaporate nor are they solid enough (the consistency is akin to yogurt) to use as landfill. Indeed, using existing technology for consolidating tailings, it takes several decades for them to become firm enough for land reclamation to begin. So, dealing with the tailings ponds presents an enormous environmental challenge for oil sands companies such as Suncor.

According to Rick George, Suncor's president and chief executive officer, the company's 2010 capital spending plan included a $450 million investment to begin the implementation of a new process ("tailings reduction operations") that will reduce the tailings reclamation timeline by up to two decades. Although there will be long-term economic benefits arising from Suncor's ability to reclaim land currently occupied by the tailings pond, this is not the primary motivation for undertaking the capital expenditures. The key reason for the expenditures, according to George, is to minimize the long-term environmental impact of oil sands development.

Source: Suncor Energy Inc., 2009 annual report and *Tailings Management*: www.suncor.com/en/responsible/3229.aspx. Reprinted with permission.

Summary

- Capital budgeting decisions fall into two categories: screening decisions and preference decisions. Screening decisions involve determining whether a proposed investment meets a predetermined standard of acceptability. Preference decisions involve selecting from among two or more acceptable investment proposals.
- Investment decisions should take into account the time value of money, since a dollar today is more valuable than a dollar received in the future. The net present value and internal rate of return methods both reflect this fact. In the net present value method, the difference between the present value of the cash inflows and the present value of the cash outflows is called the project's *net present value*. The discount rate used to calculate the net present value method is usually a minimum required rate of return, such as the company's cost of capital. [LO1]
- The internal rate of return is the rate of return that equates the present value of the cash inflows and the present value of cash outflows, resulting in a zero net present value. If the internal rate of return is less than the company's minimum required rate of return, the project is rejected. [LO2]
- Some projects have cash flows that are difficult to estimate. Intangible benefits that may result from upgrading production equipment such as improved quality or reliability can be difficult to quantify with any degree of certainty. However, management can cope with this uncertainty by estimating the dollar amount of intangible benefits that would be required in order to make a project attractive. If management believes the value of the intangible benefits will meet or exceed the required amount, the project should proceed. [LO3]
- After identifying projects that are estimated to provide an acceptable rate of return, managers can rank them using either the project profitability index or their internal rates of return. The project profitability index is conceptually superior to the internal rate of return approach and is computed by dividing the present value of the project's future net cash inflows by the required initial investment. [LO4]
- After a project has been approved, a post-audit should be performed to see whether expected results are actually being realized. This is a key part of the capital budgeting process, since it tends to improve the quality of the estimates going into future investment proposals and provides management with an opportunity to recognize any developing problems or opportunities with existing projects. [LO4]
- Some companies prefer to use the payback period as an approach for making capital budgeting decisions. The payback period is the number of periods (usually expressed in years) required to recover the cost of the initial investment from the net cash inflows generated by the project. The payback approach ignores the time value of money. [LO5]
- The simple rate of return is another approach to making capital budgeting decisions that also ignores the time value of money. It is determined by dividing a project's accounting income (incremental revenues and costs) by the initial investment in the project. [LO6]

Review Problem: Comparison of Capital Budgeting Methods

Dawson Company is considering making a capital expenditure for a project that would have a 10-year life and require a $1,800,000 investment in equipment. At the end of 10 years, the project would terminate and the equipment would have no salvage value. The project would provide operating income each year as follows:

Sales		$6,000,000
Variable expenses		3,600,000
Contribution margin		2,400,000
Fixed expenses:		
Advertising, salaries, and other		
fixed out-of-pocket costs	$1,999,000	
Depreciation	300,000	
Total fixed expenses		2,299,000
Operating income		$ 101,000

The company's discount rate is 8%.

Required:

1. Compute the net annual cash inflow from the project.
2. Compute the project's net present value. Is the project acceptable?
3. Find the project's internal rate of return to the nearest whole percentage point.
4. Compute the project's payback period.
5. Compute the project's simple rate of return.

Solution to Review Problem

1. The net annual cash inflow can be computed by deducting the cash expenses from sales:

Sales	$6,000,000
Variable expenses	3,600,000
Contribution margin	2,400,000
Advertising, salaries, and	
other fixed out-of-pocket costs	1,999,000
Net annual cash inflow	$ 401,000

Or the net annual cash inflow can be computed by adding depreciation back to operating income:

Operating income	$101,000
Add: Non-cash deduction for depreciation	300,000
Net annual cash inflow	$401,000

2. The net present value is computed as follows:

Item	Year(s)	Amount of Cash Flows	8% Factor	Present Value of Cash Flows
Cost of new equipment	Now	$(1,800,000)	1.000	$(2,400,000)
Net annual cash inflow	1–10	$ 401,000	6.710*	2,690,710
Net present value				$ 290,710

*Per Exhibit 13A–7, Appendix 13A.

Yes, the project is acceptable because it has a positive net present value.

3. The formula for computing the factor of the internal rate of return is

$$\text{Factor of the internal rate of return} = \frac{\text{Investment required}}{\text{Net annual cash inflow}}$$

$$= \frac{\$1,800,000}{\$401,000} = 4.49$$

Looking in Exhibit 13A–7 in Appendix 13A at the end of this chapter and scanning along the 10-period line, we find that a factor of 4.49 represents a rate of return of about 18%.

4. The formula for the payback period is:

$$\text{Payback period} = \frac{\text{Investment required}}{\text{Net annual cash inflow}}$$

$$= \frac{\$1,800,000}{\$401,000} = 4.49 \text{ years}$$

5. The formula for the simple rate of return is:

$$\text{Simple rate of return} = \frac{\text{Annual incremental operating income}}{\text{Initial investment}}$$

$$= \frac{\$101,000}{\$1,800,000}$$

$$= 5.6\%$$

Glossary

Review key terms and definitions on Connect.

McGraw Hill **connect**

Questions

13–1 "All of the proposals deemed to be acceptable by the capital budgeting screening process are typically implemented." Do you agree or disagree? Why?

13–2 What is meant by the term *time value of money?*

13–3 What is meant by the term *discounting?*

13–4 Why isn't depreciation on any equipment acquired as part of a project proposal used in the net present value and internal rate of return methods of making capital budgeting decisions?

13–5 Why are discounted cash flow methods of making capital budgeting decisions superior to other methods?

13–6 What is net present value? Can it ever be negative? Explain.

13–7 What is a post-audit? What are some benefits of conducting post-audits?

13–8 "If a company has to pay interest of 14% on long-term debt, then its cost of capital is 14%." Do you agree? Explain.

13–9 What is meant by an investment project's internal rate of return? How is the internal rate of return computed?

13–10 What are least-cost decisions? How are they evaluated?

13–11 "As the discount rate decreases, the present value of a given future cash flow also decreases." Do you agree? Explain.

13–12 Refer to Exhibit 13–4. Is the return on this investment proposal exactly 14%, more than 14%, or less than 14%? Explain.

13–13 How is the project profitability index computed, and what does it measure?

13–14 What is meant by the term *payback period?* How is the payback period determined? How can the payback method be useful?

13–15 What is the major criticism of the payback and simple rate of return methods of making capital budgeting decisions?

Exercises Mc Graw Hill **connect**

EXERCISE 13–1 Net Present Value Method [LO1]
The management of Oragami Company, a wholesale distributor of beachwear products, is considering the purchase of a $30,000 machine that would reduce operating costs in its warehouse by $5,000 per year. At the end of the machine's eight-year useful life, it will have no scrap value. The company's required rate of return is 11%.

Required:
(Ignore income taxes.)
1.   Determine the net present value of the investment in the machine.
2.   What is the difference between the total undiscounted cash inflows and cash outflows over the entire life of the machine?

EXERCISE 13–2 Internal Rate of Return [LO2]
Alberto's Pizza Parlour is investigating the purchase of a new $45,000 delivery truck that would contain specially designed warming racks. The new truck would have a six-year useful life. It would save $5,400 per year over the present method of delivering pizzas. In addition, it would result in the sale of 1,800 more pizzas each year. The company realizes a contribution margin of $2 per pizza.

Required:
(Ignore income taxes.)
1.   What would be the total annual cash inflows associated with the new truck for capital budgeting purposes?
2.   Find the internal rate of return promised by the new truck to the nearest whole percentage point.
3.   In addition to the data above, assume that due to the unique warming racks, the truck will have a $13,000 salvage value at the end of six years. Under these conditions, compute the internal rate of return to the nearest whole percentage point. (*Hint:* You may find it helpful to use the net present value approach; find the discount rate that will cause the net present value to be closest to zero. Use the format shown in Exhibit 13–1.)

EXERCISE 13–3 Uncertain Future Cash Flows [LO3]
Hanover Industries is investigating the purchase of automated equipment that would save $100,000 each year in direct labour and inventory carrying costs. This equipment costs $750,000 and is expected to have a 10-year useful life with no salvage value. The company requires a minimum 15% rate of return on all equipment purchases. This equipment would provide intangible benefits (such as greater flexibility and higher-quality output) that are difficult to estimate and yet are quite significant.

Required:
(Ignore income taxes.)
What dollar value per year would the intangible benefits have to be worth in order to make the equipment an acceptable investment?

EXERCISE 13–4 Preference Ranking [LO4]
Information on four investment proposals is given below:

	Investment Proposal			
	A	**B**	**C**	**D**
Investment required..............	$(85,000)	$(200,000)	$(90,000)	$(170,000)
Present value of cash inflows	119,000	250,000	135,000	221,000
Net present value.................	$ 34,000	$ 50,000	$ 45,000	$ 51,000
Life of the project...............	5 years	7 years	6 years	6 years

Required:
1.   Compute the project profitability index for each investment proposal.
2.   Rank the proposals in terms of preference.

EXERCISE 13–5 Payback Method [LO5]

The management of Deitrich Inc., a civil engineering design company, is considering an investment in a high-quality blueprint printer with the following cash flows:

Year	Investment	Cash Inflow
1	$28,000	$2,000
2	$ 4,000	$3,000
3		$6,000
4		$8,000
5		$9,000
6		$8,000
7		$6,000
8		$5,000
9		$4,000
10		$4,000

Required:
1. Determine the payback period of the investment.
2. Would the payback period be affected if the cash inflow in the last year was several times larger?

EXERCISE 13–6 Simple Rate of Return Method [LO6]

The management of Stillford MicroBrew is considering the purchase of an automated bottling machine for $80,000. The machine would replace an old piece of equipment that costs $33,000 per year to operate. The new machine would cost $10,000 per year to operate. The old machine currently in use could be sold now for a scrap value of $5,000. The new machine would have a useful life of 10 years with no salvage value.

Required:
Compute the simple rate of return on the new automated bottling machine.

EXERCISE 13–7 Comparison of Projects Using Net Present Value [LO1]

Sharp Company has $15,000 to invest. The company is trying to decide between two alternative uses of the funds shown below. Sharp Company uses a 16% discount rate.

	Invest in Project A	Invest in Project B
Investment required.........................	$15,000	$15,000
Annual cash inflows.........................	$4,000	$0
Single cash inflow at the end of 10 years		$60,000
Life of the project	10 years	10 years

Required:
(Ignore income taxes.) Which investment would you recommend that the company accept? Show all computations using net present value. Prepare separate computations for each investment.

EXERCISE 13–8 Basic Net Present Value Analysis [LO1]

Sean Laarner paid $18,000 for 900 common shares of Acme Company on January 2, four years ago. Laarner received an $0.80 per share dividend on the shares at the end of each year for four years. At the end of four years, he sold the shares for $22,500. Laarner's goal is to earn a minimum return of 12% on all of his investments.

Required:
(Ignore income taxes.) Did Laarner earn a 12% return on the shares? Use the net present value method and the general format shown in Exhibit 13–1. Round all computations to the nearest whole dollar.

EXERCISE 13–9 Internal Rate of Return and Net Present Value [LO1, LO2]

Scotia Family Health Team is investigating the purchase of an ultrasound machine for use in the patient clinic. The machine would cost $97,900, including invoice cost, freight, and the training of employees to operate it. Scotia has estimated that the new machine would increase the company's cash flows, net of expenses, by $17,000 per year. The machine would have a nine-year useful life with no expected salvage value.

Required:
(Ignore income taxes.)
1.   Compute the machine's internal rate of return to the nearest whole percentage point.
2.   Compute the machine's net present value. Use a discount rate of 10% and the format shown in Exhibit 13–1. Why do you have a zero net present value?
3.   Suppose that the new machine would increase the company's annual cash flows, net of expenses, by only $15,000 per year. Under these conditions, compute the internal rate of return to the nearest whole percentage point.

EXERCISE 13–10 Uncertain Future Life [LO3]
Willert Excavating Services has made an investment in certain equipment that cost the company $247,760. The equipment is expected to generate cash inflows of $40,000 each year.

Required:
How many years will the equipment have to be used in order to provide the company with a 12% return on its investment?

EXERCISE 13–11 Basic Payback Period and Simple Rate of Return Computations [LO5, LO6]
Colchester Company is considering the purchase of a new piece of equipment. Relevant information concerning the equipment follows:

Purchase cost.	$180,000
Annual cost savings that will be	
provided by the equipment.	$37,500
Life of the equipment	12 years

Required:
(Ignore income taxes.)
1.   Compute the payback period for the equipment. If the company rejects all proposals with a payback period of more than four years, would the equipment be purchased?
2.   Compute the simple rate of return on the equipment. Use straight-line depreciation based on the equipment's useful life, assuming $0 salvage value. Would the equipment be purchased if the company's required rate of return is 14%?

EXERCISE 13–12 Working with Net Present Value [LO1]
Piccadilly Hospital has purchased new lab equipment for $134,650. The equipment is expected to last for three years and to provide cash inflows as follows:

Year 1.	$45,000
Year 2.	$60,000
Year 3.	?

Required:
Assuming that the equipment will yield exactly a 16% rate of return, what is the expected cash inflow for year 3?

EXERCISE 13–13 Basic Net Present Value and Internal Rate of Return Analysis [LO1, LO2]
(Ignore income taxes.) Consider each case below independently.
1.   Slade Company's required rate of return is 15%. The company can purchase a new machine at a cost of $40,350. The new machine would generate cash inflows of $15,000 per year and have a four-year life with no salvage value. Compute the machine's net present value. (Use the format shown in Exhibit 13–1.) Is the machine an acceptable investment? Explain.
2.   Western Products, Inc., is investigating the purchase of a new grinding machine that has a projected life of 15 years. It is estimated that the machine will save $20,000 per year in cash operating costs. What is the machine's internal rate of return if it costs $111,500 new?
3.   Sunset Press has just purchased a new trimming machine that cost $14,125. The machine is expected to save $2,500 per year in cash operating costs and to have a 10-year life. Compute the machine's internal rate of return. If the company's required rate of return is 16%, did it make a wise investment? Explain.

EXERCISE 13–14 Net Present Value Analysis of Two Alternatives [LO1]

Over the Rainbow Company has $300,000 to invest. The company is trying to decide between two alternative uses of the funds. The alternatives are as follows:

	A	B
Cost of equipment required	$300,000	$0
Working capital investment required.	$0	$300,000
Annual cash inflows.	$80,000	$60,000
Salvage value of equipment in seven years	$20,000	$0
Life of the project	7 years	7 years

The working capital needed for Project B will be released for investment elsewhere at the end of seven years. Over the Rainbow Company uses a 20% discount rate.

Required:

(Ignore income taxes.) Which investment alternative (if either) would you recommend that the company accept? Show all computations using the net present value format. Prepare separate computations for each project.

EXERCISE 13–15 Payback Period and Simple Rate of Return [LO5, LO6]

The Family Paradise Campground would like to construct a new water park and playground area, which the campground management feels would be very popular. The water park and playground area would cost $340,000 to construct, and would have a $25,000 salvage value at the end of its five-year useful life. The company estimates that the following annual costs and revenues would be associated with the water park and playground area:

Ticket revenues		$190,000
Less operating expenses:		
Maintenance.	$30,000	
Salaries.	67,000	
Depreciation	21,000	
Insurance	22,000	
Total operating expenses.		140,000
Operating income		$ 50,000

Required:

(Ignore income taxes.)

1. Assume that the Family Paradise Campground will not construct the water park and playground unless they provide a payback period of five years or less. Does the proposal satisfy this requirement?

2. Compute the simple rate of return for the water park and playground. If Family Paradise Campground requires a simple rate of return of at least 10%, do the proposed water park and playground area meet this criterion?

connect Problems

PROBLEM 13–16 Basic Net Present Value Analysis [LO1]

Delorian Mines, Inc., owns a large tract of land, including the mining rights, in a mountainous area. The tract contains a mineral deposit that the company believes might be commercially attractive to mine and sell. An engineering and cost analysis has been made, and it is expected that the following cash flows would be associated with opening and operating a mine in the area:

Cost of equipment required.	$ 850,000
Net annual cash receipts	$ 230,000*
Working capital required	$ 100,000
Cost of road repairs in three years	$ 60,000
Salvage value of equipment in five years.	$ 200,000

*Receipts from sales of ore, less out-of-pocket costs for salaries, utilities, insurance, and so forth.

It is estimated that the mineral deposit would be exhausted after five years of mining. At that point, the working capital would be released for reinvestment elsewhere. The company's required rate of return is 14%.

Required:
(Ignore income taxes.) Determine the net present value of the proposed mining project. Should the project be accepted? Explain.

PROBLEM 13–17 Basic Net Present Value Analysis [LO1]
Sweetstuff Bakery would like to buy a special machine for icing and applying other toppings to pastries. These are now applied by hand. The machine that the bakery is considering costs $90,000 new. It would last the bakery for eight years but would require a $7,500 overhaul at the end of the fifth year. After eight years, the machine could be sold for $6,000.

The bakery estimates that it will cost $14,000 per year to operate the new machine. The present manual method of putting icing and other toppings on the pastries costs $35,000 per year. In addition to reducing operating costs, the new machine will allow the bakery to increase its production of pastries by 5,000 packages per year. The bakery realizes a contribution margin of $0.60 per package. The bakery requires a 16% return on all investments in equipment.

Required:
(Ignore income taxes.)
1. What are the net annual cash inflows that will be provided by the new machine?
2. Compute the new machine's net present value. Use the incremental cost approach, and round all dollar amounts to the nearest whole dollar.

PROBLEM 13–18 Net Present Value Analysis; Uncertain Cash Flows [LO1, LO3]
Stirling Windows, Inc., of Hong Kong is considering the purchase of an automated cutting machine for use in the production of its stained-glass windows. The machine would cost $675,000. (All currency amounts are in Hong Kong dollars.) An additional $487,500 would be required for installation costs and for software. Management believes that the automated machine would provide substantial annual reductions in costs, as shown below:

	Annual Reduction in Costs
Labour costs	$180,000
Material costs	$72,000

The new machine would require considerable maintenance work to keep it in proper adjustment. The company's engineers estimate that maintenance costs would increase by $3,200 per month if the machine was purchased. In addition, the machine would require a $67,500 overhaul at the end of the fifth year.

The new cutting machine would be usable for eight years, after which it would be sold for its scrap value of $157,500. It would replace an old cutting machine that can be sold now for its scrap value of $52,500. Stirling Windows requires a return of at least 16% on investments of this type.

Required:
(Ignore income taxes.)
1. Compute the net annual cost savings promised by the new cutting machine.
2. Using the data from (1) above and other data from the problem, compute the new machine's net present value. (Use the incremental-cost approach.) Would you recommend that the machine be purchased? Explain.
3. Assume that management can identify several intangible benefits associated with the new machine, including greater flexibility in shifting from one type of stained-glass window to another, improved quality of output, and faster delivery as a result of reduced throughput time. What dollar value per year would management have to attach to these intangible benefits in order to make the new cutting machine an acceptable investment?

PROBLEM 13–19 Preference Ranking of Investment Projects [LO4]
Information on four investment opportunity projects being investigated by Clenning Company is as follows:

	Project Number			
	1	2	3	4
Investment required...............	$(480,000)	$(360,000)	$(270,000)	$(450,000)
Present value of cash inflows at a 10% discount rate.............	567,270	433,400	336,140	522,970
Net present value................	$ 87,270	$ 73,400	$ 66,140	$ 72,970
Life of the project................	6 years	12 years	6 years	3 years
Internal rate of return.............	16%	14%	18%	19%

Since the company's required rate of return is 10%, a 10% discount rate has been used in the present value computations above. Limited funds are available for investment, so the company can't accept all of the available projects.

Required:
1. Compute the project profitability index for each investment project.
2. Rank the four projects according to preference, in terms of
   a. Net present value
   b. Project profitability index
   c. Internal rate of return
3. Which ranking do you prefer? Why?

PROBLEM 13–20 Simple Rate of Return; Payback [LO5, LO6]
The purchase of a large oven and related equipment for mixing and baking "crazy bread" is being considered by Perotti's Pizza. The oven and equipment would cost $120,000 delivered and installed. It would be usable for about 15 years, after which it would have a 10% scrap value. The following additional information is available:
a. Perotti, the owner, estimates that purchase of the oven and equipment would allow the pizza parlour to bake and sell 72,000 loaves of crazy bread each year. The bread sells for $1.25 per loaf.
b. The cost of the ingredients in a loaf of bread is 40% of the selling price. Perotti estimates that other costs each year associated with the bread would be the following: salaries, $18,000; utilities, $9,000; and insurance, $3,000.
c. The pizza parlour uses straight-line depreciation on all assets, deducting salvage value from original cost.
d. Perotti would like all projects to provide a return of at least 12%.

Required:
(Ignore income taxes.)
1. Prepare a contribution-format income statement showing the operating income each year from production and sale of the crazy bread.
2. Compute the simple rate of return for the new oven and equipment. Will this return be acceptable to Perotti. Explain.
3. Compute the payback period on the oven and equipment. If any of the equipment has less than a six-year payback, will Perotti purchase it?

PROBLEM 13–21 Net Present Value Analysis [LO1]

Frank White will retire in six years. He wants to open some type of small business operation that can be managed in the free time he has available now from his regular occupation, but that can be closed easily when he retires. He is considering several investment alternatives, one of which is to open a laundromat. After careful study, White has determined the following:
a. Washers, dryers, and other equipment needed to open the laundromat would cost $194,000. In addition, $6,000 in working capital would be required to purchase an inventory of soap, bleaches, and related items and to provide change for change machines. (The soap, bleaches, and related items would be sold to customers at cost.) After six years, the working capital would be released for investment elsewhere.
b. The laundromat would charge $1.50 per use for the washers and $0.75 per use for the dryers. White expects the laundromat to gross $1,800 each week from the washers and $1,125 each week from the dryers.
c. The only variable costs in the laundromat would be 7.5 cents per use for water and electricity for the washers and 9 cents per use for gas and electricity for the dryers.

d.   Fixed costs would be $3,000 per month for rent, $1,500 per month for cleaning, and $1,875 per month for maintenance, insurance, and other items.
e.   The equipment would have a 10% disposal value in six years.
White will not open a laundromat unless it provides at least a 12% return.

Required:
(Ignore income taxes.)
1.   Assuming that the laundromat would be open 52 weeks a year, compute the expected net annual cash receipts from its operation (gross cash receipts less cash disbursements). (Do not include the cost of the equipment, the working capital, or the salvage values in these computations.)
2.   Would you advise White to open the laundromat? Show computations, using the net present value method of investment analysis. Round all dollar amounts to the nearest whole dollar.

PROBLEM 13–22 Simple Rate of Return; Payback; Internal Rate of Return [LO2, LO5, LO6]
Europe's Selections is a family-owned fruit and vegetable farm located in the Burgundy region of France, and is headed by Donat Beauchamp. The harvesting season in early fall is the busiest part of the year for the farming operation, and many part-time workers are hired to help pick and process fruits and vegetables. Beauchamp is investigating the purchase of a harvesting machine that would significantly reduce the amount of labour required in the picking process. The harvesting machine is built to straddle fruit trees and bushes, which are laid out in low-lying rows. Two workers are carried on the machine just above ground level, one on each side of the tree. As the machine slowly crawls through the orchards, the workers cut bunches of fruit from the trees and bushes, which then fall into a hopper. The machine separates the fruit from the stems and other woody debris. The debris is then pulverized and spread behind the machine as a rich ground mulch. Beauchamp has gathered the following information relating to the decision of whether to purchase the machine:
a.   The farm would save €133,000 per year in labour costs with the new harvesting machine. In addition, the company would no longer have to purchase and spread ground mulch—at an annual savings of €7,000. (The French currency is the euro, which is denoted by the symbol €.)
b.   The harvesting machine would cost €336,000. It would have an estimated eight-year useful life and zero salvage value. The farm uses straight-line depreciation.
c.   Annual out-of-pocket costs associated with the harvesting machine would be insurance, €700; fuel, €6,300; and a maintenance contract, €8,000. In addition, two operators would be hired and trained for the machine, and they would be paid a total of €49,000 per year, including all benefits.
d.   Beauchamp feels that the investment in the harvesting machine should earn at least a 14% rate of return.

Required:
(Ignore income taxes.)
1.   Determine the annual net savings in cash operating costs that would be realized if the harvesting machine was purchased.
2.   Compute the simple rate of return expected from the harvesting machine.
3.   Compute the payback period on the harvesting machine. Beauchamp will not purchase equipment unless it has a payback period of five years or less. Under this criterion, should the harvesting machine be purchased?
4.   Compute (to the nearest whole percentage point) the internal rate of return promised by the harvesting machine. Based on this computation, does it appear that the simple rate of return is an accurate guide in investment decisions?

PROBLEM 13–23 Net Present Value; Uncertain Future Cash Flows; Post-Audit [LO1, LO3]
"If we can get that new robot to combine with our other automated equipment, we'll have a complete flexible manufacturing system (FMS) in place in our Northridge plant," said Hal Swain, production manager for Diller Products.
   "Let's just hope that reduced labour and inventory costs can justify its acquisition," replied Linda Wycoff, the controller. "Otherwise, we'll never get it. You know how the president feels about equipment paying for itself out of reduced costs."
   Selected data relating to the robot are provided below. Engineering studies suggest that use of the robot will result in a savings of 20,000 direct labour-hours each year. The labour rate is $16 per hour. Also, the smoother work flow made possible by the FMS will allow the company to reduce the amount of inventory on hand by $300,000. The released funds will be available for use elsewhere in the company. This inventory reduction will take place in the first year of operation. The company's required rate of return is 20%.

Cost of the robot	$1,600,000
Software and installation	$700,000
Annual savings in labour costs	?
Annual savings in inventory carrying costs	$190,000
Monthly increase in power and	
maintenance costs	$2,500
Salvage value in 12 years	$90,000
Useful life	12 years

Required:
(Ignore income taxes.)
1. Determine the net *annual* cost savings if the robot is purchased. (Do not include the $300,000 inventory reduction or the salvage value in this computation.)
2. Compute the net present value of the proposed investment in the robot. Based on these data, would you recommend that the robot be purchased? Explain.
3. Assume that the robot is purchased. At the end of the first year, Linda Wycoff has found that some items didn't work out as planned. Due to unforeseen problems, software and installation costs were $125,000 more than estimated, and direct labour has been reduced by only 17,500 hours per year, rather than by 20,000 hours. Assuming that all other cost data were accurate, does it appear that the company made a wise investment? Show computations, using the net present value format as in (2) above. (*Hint*: It might be helpful to place yourself back at the beginning of the first year, with the new data.)
4. On seeing your analysis in (3) above, the president stated, "That robot is the worst investment we've ever made and we'll be stuck with it for years."
    a. Explain to the president what benefits other than cost savings might accrue from using the new robot and FMS.
    b. Compute for the president the dollar amount of cash inflow that would be needed each year from the benefits in (*a*) above in order for the equipment to yield a 20% rate of return.

PROBLEM 13–24 Internal Rate of Return; Sensitivity Analysis [LO2]

Dr. Heidi Black is the managing partner of the Crestwood Dental Clinic. Black is trying to determine whether or not the clinic should move patient files and other items out of a spare room in the clinic and use the room for dental work. She has determined that it would require an investment of $142,950 for equipment and related costs of getting the room ready for use. Based on receipts being generated from other rooms in the clinic, Black estimates that the new room would generate a net cash inflow of $35,390 per year. The equipment purchased for the room would have a seven-year estimated useful life.

Required:
(Ignore income taxes.)
1. Compute the internal rate of return on the equipment for the new room to the nearest whole percentage point. Verify your answer by computing the net present value of the equipment using the internal rate of return you have computed as the discount rate.
2. Assume that Black will not purchase the new equipment unless it promises a return of at least 14%. Compute the amount of annual cash inflow that would provide this return on the $142,950 investment.
3. Although seven years is the average life for dental equipment, Black knows that due to changing technology, this life can vary substantially. Compute the internal rate of return to the nearest whole percentage point if the life of the equipment was (*a*) five years and (*b*) nine years, rather than seven years. Is there any information provided by these computations that you would be particularly anxious to show Black? Explain.
4. Black is unsure about the estimated $35,390 annual cash inflow from the room. She thinks that the actual cash inflow could be as much as 10% greater or less than this figure.
    a. Assume that the actual cash inflow each year is 10% greater than estimated. Recompute the internal rate of return to the nearest whole percentage point using the seven-year life.
    b. Assume that the actual cash inflow each year is 10% less than estimated. Recompute the internal rate of return to the nearest whole percentage point using the seven-year life.
5. Refer to the original data. Assume that the equipment is purchased and that the room is opened for dental use. However, due to an increasing number of dentists in the area, the clinic is able to generate only $30,000 per year in net cash receipts from the new room. At the end of five

years, the clinic closes the room and sells the equipment to a newly licensed dentist for a cash price of $61,375. Compute the internal rate of return to the nearest whole percentage point that the clinic earned on its investment over the five-year period. Round all dollar amounts to the nearest whole dollar. (*Hint*: A useful way to proceed is to find the discount rate that will cause the net present value of the investment to be equal to, or near, zero).

PROBLEM 13–25 Net Present Value Analysis of a Lease or Buy Decision [LO1]
Brinsley Transport wants to upgrade its fleet of highway transport trucks. The new trucks that the company wants to acquire can be either purchased or leased from the manufacturer. The company has made the following evaluation of the two alternatives:

Purchase alternative. If the new transport trucks are purchased, then the costs incurred by the company would be as follows:

Purchase cost of the trucks..................	$680,000
Annual cost of servicing, licences, and taxes	$7,200
Repairs:	
First four years, per year	$2,400
Fifth year...............................	$4,000
Sixth year	$8,000

The trucks would be sold after six years. Based on current resale values, the company would be able to sell them for about one-half of their original cost at the end of the six-year period.

Lease alternative. If the new transport trucks are leased, then the company would have to make an immediate deposit of $40,000 to cover any damage during use. The lease would run for six years, at the end of which time the deposit would be refunded. The lease would require an annual rental payment of $140,000 (the first payment is due at the end of year 1). As part of this lease cost, the manufacturer would provide all servicing and repairs, license the trucks, and pay all taxes. At the end of the six-year period, the trucks would revert to the manufacturer, as owner.
Brinsley Transport's required rate of return is 16%.

Required:
(Ignore income taxes.)
1. Use the total-cost approach to determine the present value of the cash flows associated with each alternative.
2. Which alternative would you recommend that the company accept? Why?

PROBLEM 13–26 Preference Ranking of Investment Projects [LO4]
Since limited funds are available for investment, Yancy & Company must ration the funds among four competing projects. Selected information on the four projects follows:

Project	Investment Required	Net Present Value	Life of the Project (years)	Internal Rate of Return
A.........	$800,000	$221,615	7	18%
B.........	$675,000	$210,000	12	16%
C.........	$500,000	$175,175	7	20%
D.........	$700,000	$152,544	3	22%

The net present values above have been computed using a 10% discount rate. The company wants your assistance in determining which project to accept first, which to accept second, and so forth. The company's investment funds are limited.

Required:
1. Compute the project profitability index for each project.
2. In order of preference, rank the four projects in terms of
   a. Net present value.
   b. Project profitability index.
   c. Internal rate of return.
3. Which ranking do you prefer? Why?

PROBLEM 13–27 Simple Rate of Return; Payback [LO5, LO6]

Nagoya Amusements Corporation places electronic games and other amusement devices in supermarkets and similar outlets throughout Japan. Nagoya Amusements is investigating the purchase of a new electronic game called Mystic Invaders. The manufacturer will sell 20 games to Nagoya Amusements for a total price of ¥180,000. (The Japanese currency is the yen, which is denoted by the symbol ¥.) Nagoya Amusements has determined the following additional information about the game:

a.   The game would have a five-year useful life and a negligible salvage value. The company uses straight-line depreciation.

b.   The game would replace other games that are unpopular and generating little revenue. These other games would be sold for a total of ¥30,000.

c.   Nagoya Amusements estimates that Mystic Invaders would generate annual incremental revenues of ¥200,000 (total for all 20 games). Annual incremental out-of-pocket costs would be (in total) maintenance, ¥50,000, and insurance, ¥10,000. In addition, Nagoya Amusements would have to pay a commission of 40% of total revenues to the supermarkets and other outlets in which the games were placed.

Required:
(Ignore income taxes.)

1.   Prepare a contribution-format income statement showing the operating income each year from Mystic Invaders.

2.   Compute the simple rate of return on Mystic Invaders. Will the game be purchased if Nagoya Amusements accepts any project with a simple rate of return greater than 14%?

3.   Compute the payback period on Mystic Invaders. If the company accepts any investment with a payback period of less than three years, will the game be purchased?

PROBLEM 13–28 Net Present Value Analysis of a New Product [LO1]

Clarion Company is considering an opportunity to produce and sell a revolutionary new smoke detector for homes. To determine whether this would be a profitable venture, the company has gathered the following data on probable costs and market potential:

a.   New equipment would have to be acquired to produce the smoke detector. The equipment would cost $100,000 and be usable for 12 years. After 12 years, it would have a salvage value equal to 10% of the original cost.

b.   Production and sales of the smoke detector would require a working capital investment of $40,000 to finance accounts receivable, inventories, and day-to-day cash needs. This working capital would be released for use elsewhere after 12 years.

c.   An extensive marketing study projects sales in units over the next 12 years as follows:

 e**X**cel

Year	Sales in Units
1............	4,000
2............	7,000
3............	10,000
4–12	12,000

d.   The smoke detectors would sell for $45 each; variable costs for production, administration, and sales would be $25 per unit.

e.   To gain entry into the market, the company would have to advertise heavily in the early years of sales. The advertising program follows:

Year	Amount of Advertising
1–2............	$70,000
3............	$50,000
4–12	$40,000

f.   Other fixed costs for salaries, insurance, maintenance, and straight-line depreciation on equipment would total $127,500 per year. (Depreciation is based on cost less salvage value.)

g.   The company's required rate of return is 20%.

Required:
(Ignore income taxes.)

1.   Compute the net cash inflow (cash receipts less yearly cash operating expenses) anticipated from sale of the smoke detectors for each year over the next 12 years.

2.   Using the data computed in (1) above and other data provided in the problem, determine the net present value of the proposed investment. Would you recommend that Clarion Company accept the smoke detector as a new product?

PROBLEM: 13–29 Net Present Value; Total-Cost and Incremental-Cost Approaches [LO1]
Eastbay Hospital has an auxiliary generator that is used when power failures occur. The generator is worn out and must be either overhauled or replaced with a new generator. The hospital has assembled the information presented below.

If the company keeps and overhauls its present generator, then the generator will be usable for eight more years. If a new generator is purchased, it will be used for eight years, after which it will be replaced. The new generator would be diesel-powered, resulting in a substantial reduction in annual operating costs, as shown below.

The hospital computes depreciation on a straight-line basis. All equipment purchases are evaluated using a 16% discount rate.

	Present Generator	New Generator
Purchase cost new.................	$16,000	$20,000
Remaining book value	$ 9,000	—
Overhaul needed now	$ 8,000	—
Annual cash operating costs	$12,500	$ 7,500
Salvage value now...................	$ 4,000	—
Salvage value eight years from now	$ 3,000	$ 6,000

Required:
(Ignore income taxes.)
1.   Should Eastbay Hospital keep the old generator or purchase the new one? Use the total-cost approach to net present value in making your decision.
2.   Redo (1) above, this time using the incremental-cost approach.

Cases

CASE 13–30 Capital Budget Reviews and the Role of the Post-Audit [LO1]
Stephen Scott recently joined the Finance and Planning Division of the Carrigan Bank (Bassillo) Limited as an assistant chief financial officer (CFO). Scott is a certified management accountant and had spent the previous four years working in the accounting department of a large Canadian manufacturing company. He took the job at the bank because it provided an opportunity to get some international business experience.

One of Scott's responsibilities is to perform an initial review of the capital budgeting proposals developed by the various divisions at the bank. Because the bank's divisions are very large and have a high degree of operating autonomy, each division has its own divisional controller who prepares the proposals with input from key managers in the division and other bank personnel. For 2012, the bank budgeted $500,000 for capital spending in each of the six major divisions for projects requiring less than $100,000 of expenditures. For projects of that size, the divisions are free to go ahead and spend the funds as they see fit, without the need for centralized review and approval. The bank budgeted a further $20 million in capital spending for 2012 to be allocated to the divisions on the basis of the project proposals submitted as part of the capital budget review process. These proposals are for individual projects requiring capital expenditures in excess of $100,000.

All project submissions are ranked from most to least profitable using the project profitability index: Present value of cash inflows ÷ Investment required. The final review of the proposals is conducted by the chief financial officer, the assistant CFO, and the vice-president of Finance. In addition to these three individuals, the review meeting is attended by the senior manager and controller of each division. Non-financial factors such as the importance of the expenditure for maintaining the bank's competitive position and its impact on customer retention and growth are considered as part of the review and approval process. However, these factors typically have a smaller impact on the final decision than the project profitability index, which senior management believes to be more objective and reliable.

As part of his initial review of the proposals, Scott was instructed by the CFO to evaluate the reasonableness of the assumptions, and to check the accuracy of the calculations. Where necessary, he was to follow up with the divisional controllers if he had any questions about the details. As Scott began his review, he was struck by the relatively high project profitability index on the vast majority of the projects. Indeed, most of the proposals (about 75%) had a project profitability index in excess of 1.30, while the remaining 25% had an index between 1.20 and 1.30. In several instances, the assumptions underlying the proposal seemed very optimistic, so he decided to follow up with the individual divisional controllers.

Almost without fail, the controllers matter of factly admitted to using highly optimistic cash inflows in order to make their proposals look as good as possible. The controllers also commented that the division managers viewed the capital budget review process as a game that they wanted to "win" by getting as many of their projects approved as possible. As one controller put it (but said he'd deny it if ever asked), "What's the harm in a little optimism as long as the estimates in all of the proposals are more or less equally overstated?" Scott also learned from the controllers that word had leaked out that last year only those projects with a project profitability index over 1.30 were funded, and that they had been instructed by their divisional managers to make sure the current year proposals met that threshold. The divisional controllers also suggested that it was pretty clear that senior management at the bank condoned the optimism included in their proposals since the use of post-audits had been discontinued several years ago after the CFO at the time (who has since been replaced) concluded that the cost of the audits exceeded their benefits.

As Scott sat in his office after a conversation with one of the divisional controllers, he wasn't sure what to do next. The divisional controllers told him he'd be wasting his time going to the CFO or the VP Finance, since they all knew how the capital budgeting game was being played. He was also concerned that rocking the boat would upset the divisional controllers, with whom he had to work closely on other aspects of his job. But he couldn't shake the feeling that this was an issue that deserved more attention.

Required:
1. What should Scott do?
2. Would the use of post-audits solve the problem of the overly optimistic project proposals being submitted at the bank? Why or why not?
3. Who should be involved in conducting the post-audit process?

CASE 13–31 Net Present Value Analysis of a Lease or Buy Decision [LO1]

High Street Stores operates a chain of superior-quality department stores. The company is going to open another store soon in a prosperous and growing suburban area. In discussing how the company can acquire the desired building and other facilities needed to open the new store, Jim Davis, the company's marketing vice-president, stated, "I know most of our competitors are starting to lease facilities, rather than buy, but I just can't see the economics of it. Our development people tell me that we can buy the building site, put a building on it, and get all the store fixtures we need for $14 million. They also say that property taxes, insurance, maintenance, and repairs would run $200,000 a year. When you figure that we plan to keep a site for 20 years, that's a total cost of $18 million. But then when you realize that the building and property will be worth at least $5 million in 20 years, that's a net cost to us of only $13 million. Leasing costs a lot more than that."

"I'm not so sure," replied Corinna Albrecht, the company's executive vice-president. "Guardian Insurance Company is willing to purchase the building site, construct a building, and install fixtures to our specifications, and then lease the facility to us for 20 years for an annual lease payment of only $1 million."

"That's just my point," said Davis. "At $1 million a year, it would cost us $20 million over the 20 years instead of just $13 million. What would we have left at the end? Nothing! The building would belong to the insurance company! I'll bet they would even want the first lease payment in advance."

"That's right," replied Albrecht. "We would have to make the first payment immediately and then one payment at the beginning of each of the following 19 years. However, you're overlooking a few things. For one thing, we would have to tie up a lot of our funds for 20 years under the purchase alternative. We would have to put $6 million down immediately if we buy the property, and then we would have to pay the other $8 million off over four years at $2 million a year."

"But that cost is nothing compared to $20 million for leasing," said Davis. "Also, if we lease, I understand we would have to put up a $400,000 security deposit that we wouldn't get back until the end. Besides that, we would still have to pay all of the repair and maintenance costs as if we owned the property. No wonder those insurance companies are so rich if they can swing deals like this."

"Well, I'll admit that I don't have all the figures sorted out yet," replied Albrecht. "But I do have the operating cost breakdown for the building, which includes $90,000 annually for property taxes, $60,000 for insurance, and $50,000 for repairs and maintenance. If we lease, Guardian will handle its own insurance costs and will pay the property taxes, but we'll have to pay for the repairs and maintenance. I need to put all this together and see if leasing makes any sense with our 12% before-tax required rate of return. The president wants a presentation and recommendation in the executive committee meeting tomorrow."

Required:

(Ignore income taxes.)

1.   Using the net present value approach, determine whether High Street Stores should lease or buy the new store. Assume that you will be making your presentation before the company's executive committee.

2.   How will you reply in the meeting if Jim Davis brings up the issue of the building's future sales value?

CASE 13–32 Comparison of Alternatives Using Net Present Value Analysis [LO1]

Hesselwood Company's market research division has projected a substantial increase in demand over the next several years for one of the company's products. To meet this demand, the company will need to produce units as follows:

Year	Production in Units
1.............	10,000
2.............	15,000
3.............	20,000
4–10	22,500

At present, the company is using a single Model 2360 machine to manufacture this product. To increase its productive capacity, the company is considering two alternatives:

Alternative 1. The company could purchase another Model 2360 machine that would operate along with the one it now owns. The following information is available on this alternative:

a.   The Model 2360 machine now in use was purchased for $82,500 four years ago. Its present book value is $49,500, and its present market value is $45,000.

b.   A new Model 2360 machine costs $90,000 now and will have a negligible salvage value at the end of 10 years. The old Model 2360 machine will have to be replaced in six years at a cost of $100,000. The replacement machine will have a market value of about $50,000 when it is four years old.

c.   The variable cost required to produce one unit of product using the Model 2360 machine is given in the "General information on the two alternatives" section below.

d.   Repairs and maintenance costs each year on a single Model 2360 machine total $1,500.

Alternative 2. The company could purchase a Model 4720 machine and use the old Model 2360 machine as standby equipment. The Model 4720 machine is a high-speed unit with double the capacity of the Model 2360 machine. The following information is available on this alternative:

a.   The cost of a new Model 4720 machine is $125,000.

b.   The variable cost required to produce one unit of product using the Model 4720 machine is given in the "General information on the two alternatives" section below.

c.   The Model 4720 machine is more costly to maintain than the Model 2360 machine. Repairs and maintenance on a Model 4720 machine and on a Model 2360 machine used as standby would total $2,300 per year.

General information on the two alternatives:

a.   Both the Model 2360 machine and the Model 4720 machine have a 10-year life from the time they are first used in production. Straight-line depreciation is used by the company.

b.   The two machine models are not equally efficient. Comparative variable costs per unit of product are as follows:

	Model 2360	Model 4720
Direct materials per unit.................	$0.54	$0.60
Direct labour per unit...................	0.75	0.33
Supplies and lubricants per unit	0.06	0.12
Total variable cost per unit..............	$1.35	$1.05

c.   No other factory costs would change as a result of the decision between the two machines.

d.   Hesselwood Company uses a 16% discount rate.

Required:

(Ignore income taxes.)

1.   Which alternative should the company choose? Use the net present value approach. (Round to the nearest whole dollar.)

2.   Suppose that the cost of direct materials increases by 50%. Would this make the Model 4720 machine more or less desirable? Explain. No computations are needed.

3.   Suppose that the cost of direct labour increases by 25%. Would this make the Model 4720 machine more or less desirable? Explain. No computations are needed.

Research and Application

R 13–33 Disclosure of Planned Capital Expenditures [LO1, LO2, LO3]

On page 15 of its 2009 annual report, Suncor Energy Inc. (**www.suncor.com**) discloses the details of significant planned capital expenditures for 2010 and thereafter. Given the capital-intensive nature of the energy industry, capital expenditures represent a significant ongoing use of financial resources and as such, the type of disclosures included in Suncor's annual report can be helpful to stakeholders.

Required:

1.   Which of the projects listed on page 15 of the annual report do you think could be classified as likely to generate a positive net present value and which ones would be classified as needing to be undertaken for other reasons?

2.   There is often uncertainty regarding the amount and timing of cash flows included in capital budget proposals. How does Suncor address this uncertainty in the planned capital expenditures disclosed in its annual report? Why would the company do this?

◼ APPENDIX 13A: THE CONCEPT OF PRESENT VALUE

The point was made in the main body of the chapter that a manager would rather receive a dollar today than a year from now. There are two reasons why this is true. First, a dollar received today is more valuable than a dollar received a year from now. The dollar received today can be invested immediately, and by the end of the year it will have earned some return, making the total amount in hand at the end of the year *greater* than the initial investment. The person receiving the dollar a year from now will simply have a dollar in hand at that time.

> **LEARNING OBJECTIVE 7**
> Explain present value concepts and become familiar with the use of present value tables.

Second, the future involves uncertainty. The longer people have to wait to receive a dollar, the more uncertain it becomes that they will actually get the dollar. As time passes, conditions change and future payment of the dollar might become impossible.

Since money has a time value, managers need a method of determining whether a cash outlay made now in an investment project can be justified in terms of the expected cash inflows from the project in future years. That is, the manager must have a means of expressing future receipts in present dollar terms so that the future receipts can be compared *on an equivalent basis* with whatever investment is required now in the project under consideration. The theory of interest provides managers with the means of making such a comparison.

The Theory of Interest

If a bank pays $102 one year from now in return for a deposit of $100 now, we would say that the bank is paying interest at an annual rate of 2%. The relationships involved in this notion can be expressed in mathematical terms by means of the following equation:

$$F_1 = P(1 + r) \tag{A1}$$

Present value
The value now of an amount that will be received in some future period.

where F_1 = the amount to be received in one year, P = the present outlay to be made, and r = the rate of interest involved. If the present outlay is $100 deposited in a bank savings account that is to earn interest at 2%, then P = $100 and r = 0.02. Under these conditions, F_1 = $102, the amount to be received in one year.

The $100 present outlay is called the **present value** of the $102 amount to be received in one year. It is also known as the *discounted value* of the future $102 receipt. The $100 figure represents the value in present terms of a receipt of $102 to be received a year from now when the interest rate is 2%.

Compound Interest   What if the investor leaves the money in the bank for a second year, and continues to earn 2% per year? In that case, by the end of the second year, the original $100 deposit will have grown to $104.04:

Original deposit	$100.00
Interest for the first year:	
$100 × 0.02	2.00
Amount at the end of the first year	102.00
Interest for the second year:	
$102 × 0.02	2.04
Amount at the end of the second year.	$104.04

Compound interest
The process of paying interest on interest in an investment.

Notice that the interest for the second year is $2.04, as compared to only $2 for the first year. The reason for the greater amount of interest earned during the second year is that during the second year, interest is being paid *on interest.* That is, the $2 interest earned during the first year has been left in the account and has been added to the original $100 deposit in computing interest for the second year. This concept is known as **compound interest**. The compounding we have done is on an annual basis. However, interest can be compounded on a semi-annual, quarterly, or even more frequent basis. Many financial institutions are now compounding interest on a daily basis. The more frequently compounding is done, the more rapidly the invested balance will grow.

How is the concept of compound interest expressed in equation form? It is expressed by taking equation (A1) and adjusting it to state the number of years, n, that a sum is going to be left deposited in the bank:

$$F_n = P(1 + r)^n \qquad\qquad (A2)$$

where n = *years.*

If n = 2 years, then our computation of the value of F two years hence will be as follows:

$$F_2 = \$100(1 + 0.02)^2$$
$$F_2 = \$104.04$$

Present Value and Future Value

Exhibit 13A–1 shows the relationship between present value and future value as expressed in the theory of interest equations. As shown in the exhibit, if $100 is deposited in a bank at 2% interest, it will grow to $110.40 by the end of five years if interest is compounded annually.

Exhibit 13A–1 illustrates that an investment can be viewed in two ways: either in terms of its future value or in terms of its present value. We have seen from our computations above that if we know the present value of a sum (such as our $100 deposit), it is a relatively simple task to compute the sum's future value in n years by using equation (A2). But what if the tables are reversed, and we know the *future* value of some amount but we do not know its present value?

For example, assume that you are to receive $200 two years from now. You know that the future value of this sum is $200, since this is the amount that you will be receiving in

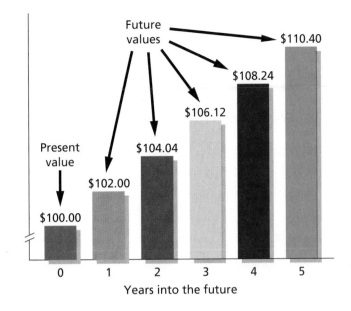

two years. But what is the sum's present value—what is it worth *right now?* The present value of any sum to be received in the future can be computed by rearranging equation (A2) and solving for *P*:

$$P = \frac{F_n}{(1 + r)^n} \tag{A3}$$

Suppose that in our example, $F = \$200$ (the amount to be received in the future), $r = 0.05$ (the rate of interest), and $n = 2$ (the number of years in the future that the amount is to be received):

$$P = \frac{\$200}{(1 + 0.05)^2}$$
$$P = \frac{\$200}{1.1025}$$
$$P = \$181.40$$

As shown by the computation above, the present value of $200 to be received two years from now is $181.40 if the interest rate is 5%. In effect, we are saying that $181.40 received *right now* is equivalent to $200 received two years from now if the rate of return is 5%. The $181.40 and the $200 are just two ways of looking at the same item at different points in time.

The process of finding the present value of a future cash flow, which we have just examined, is called **discounting**. We have *discounted* the $200 to its present value of $181.40. The 5% interest figure that we have used to find this present value is called the **discount rate**. As discussed in the body of the chapter, companies typically use the cost of capital as the discount rate, with adjustments to the rate possible depending on the riskiness of the particular project under consideration. Discounting of future sums to their present value is a common practice in business. Knowing the present value of a sum to be received in the future can be very useful to a manager, particularly in making capital budgeting decisions.

Some of the present value formulas we will be using are more complex and difficult to use. Fortunately, tables are available in which the calculations have already been done for you. For example, Exhibit 13A–6 shows the discounted present value of $1 to be received at various periods in the future at various interest rates. The table indicates that the present value of $1 to be received two periods from now at 5% is 0.907. Since in our example we want to know the present value of $200 rather than just $1, we simply multiply the factor in the table by $200:

$$\$200 \times 0.907 = \$181.40$$

Discounting
The process of finding the present value of a future cash flow.

Discount rate
The rate used to calculate the present value of future cash flows.

The answer we obtain is the same answer as we obtained earlier using the formula in equation (A3).

Example 1

A purchaser promises to pay $100,000 two years from now for a lot of land. This amount includes interest at an annual rate of 5%. What is the selling price of the land today?

As indicated in Exhibit 13A–6 (5% column, down two rows) the present value of $1 to be received two years from now is $0.907. Thus, the present value of $100,000 is $90,700 ($100,000 × 0.907). The answer can also be found as follows:

$$P = \$100,000(1 + 0.05)^{-2}$$
$$P = \$90,700$$

Example 2

A woman in Vancouver plans to take a vacation trip four years from now. She estimates that she will need $18,000 at that time. At an annual interest rate of 4%, compounded semi-annually, how much must be deposited into a bank account today to accumulate the required $18,000?

Because interest is compounded semi-annually in this example, the interest per period is 2% (the annual rate divided by two). As shown in Exhibit 13A–6, the present value of $1 to be received 8 periods in the future at 2% interest is $0.853. The present value of $18,000 is therefore $15,354 ($18,000 × 0.853). The formula solution is $18,000 × (1 + 0.02)^{-8,}$ which also equals $15,354.

Present Value of a Series of Cash Flows (Annuity)

Annuity
A series of equal cash payments or receipts.

The present value of an **annuity** is the present value of a series of equal payments or receipts discounted at compound interest and made at regular intervals. Stated differently, it is the total amount that allows the withdrawal of a series of equal amounts at regular intervals if the balance remaining after each withdrawal earns compound interest.

The present value of $1 to be received at the end of each of four periods at 4% interest per period is shown graphically in Exhibit 13A–2.

Two points are important in connection with Exhibit 13A–2. First, notice that the farther we go forward in time, the smaller is the present value of the $1 interest receipt. The present value of $1 received a year from now is $0.962 compared to only $0.855 for the $1 interest payment to be received four periods from now. This observation underscores the fact that money has a time value.

EXHIBIT 13A–2   Illustration of Present Value of Ordinary Annuity

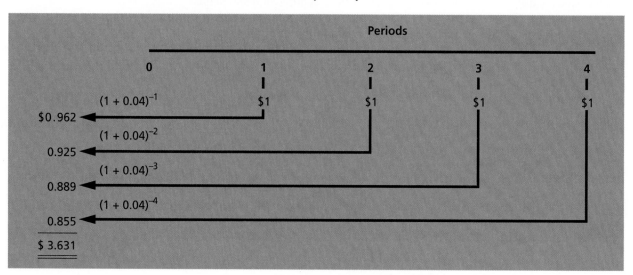

The second point is that even though the computations involved in Exhibit 13A–2 are accurate, they have involved unnecessary work. The same present value of $3.631 could have been obtained more easily by referring to Exhibit 13A–7 (4% column, Period 4). Exhibit 13A–7 contains the present value of $1 to be received each year over a *series* of years at various interest rates. Exhibit 13A–7 has been derived by summing the individual factors from Exhibit 13A–6.

The formula for the present value (P_n) of an annuity of $1 per period compounded at the rate of r for n periods is:

$$P_n = \frac{1 - (1 + r)^{-n}}{r} \quad \text{or} \quad \frac{1 - (1 + 0.04)^{-4}}{0.04} = \$3.631 \quad\quad \text{(A4)}$$

Example 3

What is the present value of receiving a series of six semi-annual payments of $2,000 at 4% interest compounded annually? Assume that it is now January 1, 2011, and the first payment is to be made on June 30, 2011.

The purpose of solving this problem could be to determine (1) the sum that will provide for six semi-annual withdrawals of $2,000 if invested at 2% per period (4% divided by two interest periods per year), and (2) the sum that is payable in settlement of a series of obligations of $2,000 that are due at six semi-annual intervals and discounted at 2% per period. Using Exhibit 13A–7 (2% column, in Period 6) the value 5.601 is found. This present value of an annuity of $1 factor is then multiplied by $2,000 to give $11,202. Alternatively, using the present value of an ordinary annuity (annuity in arrears) formula:

$$P_n = \frac{1 - (1 + 0.02)^{-6}}{0.02} \times \$2,000 = \$11,202$$

Example 4

How much money would a company be willing to invest in a project that would return $3,000 every three months for three years, and in addition, a lump sum of $20,000 at the end of the third year? The receipts begin three months from now. Interest is 8% per annum.

The $3,000 to be received at the end of each three-month period is an ordinary annuity. The number of interest periods is 12 (4 per year for three years) and the quarterly interest rate is 2% (8% ÷ 4 periods). Using Exhibit 13A–7 (2% column, Period 12) the value of 10.575 is found. The present value of this annuity is $31,725 (10.575 × $3,000). The present value factor for the single lump sum receipt is 0.788 (Exhibit 13A–6, 2% column, Period 12) so the present value of that amount is 0.788 × $20,000 = $15,760. The present value of the series of receipts and the single lump sum is $31,725 + $15,760, which totals $47,485. Note that the single amount is usually compounded at the same quarterly rate (2%) as the series of regular payments.

Present Value of an Annuity Due

An annuity due is one in which the payments or receipts occur at the *beginning* of each period. Exhibit 13A–3 compares the present value of an ordinary annuity of $1 for four periods with the present value of an annuity due for $1 for four periods. The interest rate is assumed to be 8%.

Note that part B of Exhibit 13A–3 can be interpreted as an ordinary annuity of $1 for three periods ($0.926 + $0.857 + $0.794) to which we add $1. We can calculate the present value of an annuity due by subtracting one period from n and calculating the present value of an ordinary annuity for $n - 1$ period. We then add $1 to this annuity factor, because the first payment is received immediately, which now gives the present value factor of an annuity due of $1.

Example 5

On February 1, 2011, Davis Company signed an 18-month lease with Kelly Leasing Company. The lease payments begin immediately. Calculate the present value of the lease, assuming that $2,000 is paid each quarter and that the annual interest rate is 8%.

EXHIBIT 13A–3   Present Value of an Ordinary Annuity and an Annuity Due

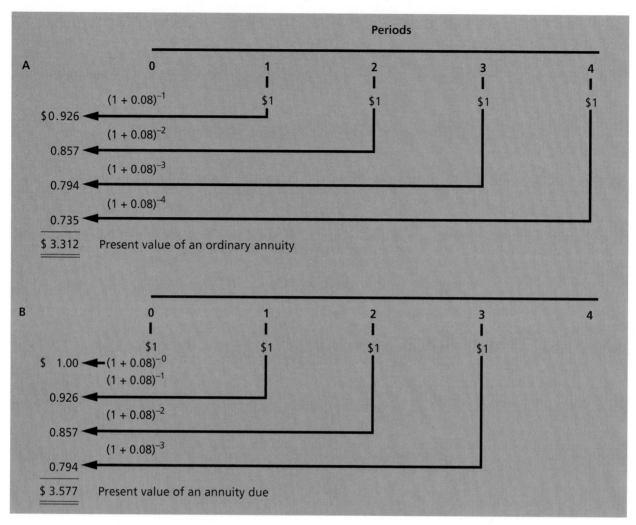

We can solve this problem by first determining the present value of an ordinary annuity for $n - 1$ periods, where n is equal to six periods (18 months = six quarters) as shown below:

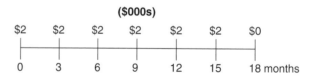

Using Exhibit 13A–7, the present value of an annuity factor for five periods ($n - 1$) is 4.713 (2% column, Period 5). To this factor we add 1, resulting in an interest factor of 5.713. Next, we multiply the $2,000 payments by 5.713 to arrive at $11,426, the present value of the lease payments. Using the formula approach, the present value of an annuity due is as follows:

$$PV \text{ (annuity due)} = \$2{,}000 \times \left[1 + \frac{1 - (1 + 0.02)^{-5}}{0.02} \right]$$

$$= \$2{,}000 \times (1 + 4.713)$$

$$= \$11{,}426$$

Deferred Annuities

A deferred annuity is one in which the first payment or receipt does not begin until more than one interest period has expired. This is common for capital expenditure decisions that may take several periods to become operational.

Example 6

What is the present value on January 1, 2011, of a series of five annual receipts of $1,000, the first of which is expected to be received on January 1, 2014? The interest rate is 5% per annum.

A graphical representation of the problem is as follows:

The most efficient way of solving this problem is by the following two-step procedure:

Step 1. Calculate the present value on January 1, 2013, of an ordinary annuity of a series of five receipts of $1,000 using an interest rate of 5%. This is $1,000 × 4.329, or $4,329.

Step 2. The problem is now translated into a simple present value problem, depicted as follows:

The present value on January 1, 2011, can now be computed by discounting the $4,329 back two interest periods (from January 1, 2013, to January 1, 2011):

$$PV \text{ (January 1, 2011)} = \$4,329(1 + 0.05)^{-2}$$
$$= \$3,926$$

This problem could have also been solved by adding fictitious receipts on January 1, 2013, and on January 1, 2012, and calculating the present value of an ordinary annuity on January 1, 2011, for seven periods and then subtracting the present value of the receipts that did not occur:

Step 1:

$$\$1,000 \times \left[\frac{1 - (1 + 0.05)^{-7}}{0.05} \right]$$
$$= \$5,786$$

Step 2:

$$\$5,786 - \left\{ \$1000 \times \frac{[1 - (1 + 0.05)^{-2}]}{0.05} \right\}$$
$$\$5,786 - \$1,860 = \$3,926$$

Future Value of an Annuity

Business transactions often involve a series of equal payments spaced evenly apart. As discussed earlier in this appendix, a series of equal payments at regular intervals is known as an *annuity*. The total that becomes due immediately after the last payment is the amount of an ordinary annuity or an annuity in arrears. If the payments are made or received at the beginning of the first interest period, the annuity is termed an *annuity due* or an *annuity in advance*.

The distinction between an ordinary annuity and an annuity due is presented graphically as follows:

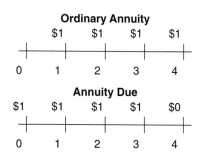

To illustrate how the future value of an ordinary annuity is determined, assume that $1 is deposited in a savings account at the end of each of four periods at 8% per period:

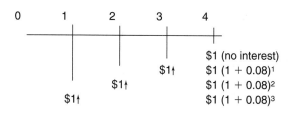

Thus, the value of an ordinary annuity of $1 due at the end of each period for four periods is

$$\$1 + \$1(1 + 0.08)^1 + \$1(1 + 0.08)^2 + \$1(1 + 0.08)^3$$
$$= \$1 + \$1.08 + \$1.1664 + \$1.2597$$
$$= \$4.5061$$

From the preceding illustration it can be seen that the $1 deposited at the end of the first year accumulates interest for a total of three periods, increasing to a value of $1.2597. The deposit at the end of the second year grows to $1.1664, and the $1 deposited at the end of the third period accumulates to $1.08. The $1 deposited at the end of the fourth period has not yet earned any interest. The series of four payments of $1 each period grows to $4.5061 at the end of the fourth period.

This problem can be solved quickly by using a mathematical expression based on a geometric progression. The future value of an annuity in arrears (F_n) compounded at an interest rate (r) for a given number of periods (n) is

$$F_n = \frac{(1 + r)^n - 1}{r} \tag{A5}$$

The value of a series of $1 deposits made at the end of each of four years compounded at 8% annually is

$$F_n = \$1 \times \frac{(1 + 0.08)^4 - 1}{0.08} = \$4.5061$$

The same calculation, rounded at three decimal places, can be determined by referring to Exhibit 13A–5 (on page 661: 8% column, Period 4) and multiplying this factor by the amount of each receipt ($1).

It should be apparent that Exhibits 13A–4 (page 660) and 13A–5 are related. We can treat each cash flow of the annuity separately and find the future value of each cash flow (Exhibit 13A–4) and sum them. Alternatively, it is much faster to find the sum of the annuity using Exhibit 13A–5.

To find the future value of an annuity of $1 per period for four periods if each payment is made at the *beginning* of each period (an annuity due), we can modify the formula as follows:

$$F_n \text{ (due)} = \frac{(1 + r)^n - 1}{r} \times (1 + r)$$

$$= \frac{(1 + 0.08)^4 - 1}{0.08} \times (1 + 0.08)$$

$$= \$4{,}867$$

The same result can be reached by looking up the interest factor in Exhibit 13A–5 for one additional interest period and then subtracting 1 from this factor (8% column, Period 5, deduct 1 from the factor 5.867 to give 4.867). This problem is illustrated by the following diagram:

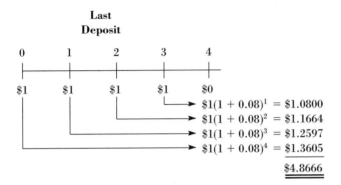

Using Microsoft Excel

You can also perform compound interest calculations using the following Microsoft Excel functions:

RATE(nper,pmt,pv,fv,type,guess)
NPER(rate,pmt,pv,fv,type)
PV(rate,nper,pmt,fv,type)
FV(rate,nper,pmt,pv,type)

where

- *rate* is the interest rate per period.
- *nper* is the total number of payment periods in an annuity.
- *pv* is the present value, the total amount that a series of future payments is worth now.
- *fv* is the future value, or a cash balance you want to attain after the last payment is made. If *fv* is omitted, it is assumed to be 0 (the future value of a loan, for example, is 0).
- *pmt* is the payment made each period and cannot change over the life of the annuity.
- *type* is the number 0 or 1 and indicates when payments are due. (0 or omitted, payment is at the end of the period; 1, it is at the beginning of the period).

Excel functions are particularly useful when you want to calculate compound interest when making regular payments, as for a mortgage or an annuity.

Appendix 13A Summary

- The concept of present value is based on the simple idea that a dollar received today is worth more than a dollar received in the future. This is so because a dollar received today can be invested immediately and will earn a positive return and because the future involves uncertainty. This uncertainty results in the possibility that the dollar will not be received in the future. **[LO7]**

- Several key concepts were covered in this appendix: *Present value* is the value now of an amount that will be received in some future period; an *annuity* is a stream of identical cash flows; *compound interest* is the process of paying interest on interest in an investment; and *discount rate* is the rate of return used to find the present value of future cash flows or the future value of amounts received now. **[LO7]**
- The factors used in the various present value and future value calculations can be determined by using the formulas presented throughout this appendix or the tables provided at the end of this appendix. Spreadsheet programs such as Excel can also calculate present and future value amounts, as can most financial calculators.

Appendix 13A Review Problem

Each of the following situations is independent. Work out your own solution to each situation, and then check it against the solution provided.

1. Greg plans to retire in 12 years. When he retires, he would like to take an extended vacation, which he expects will cost at least $40,000. What lump-sum amount must he invest now to have $40,000 at the end of 12 years if the rate of return is
   - *a.* 8%?
   - *b.* 12%?

2. The Morganthalers would like to send their daughter to a music camp at the end of each of the next five years. The camp costs $1,000 a year. What lump-sum amount would have to be invested now to have $1,000 at the end of each year if the rate of return is
   - *a.* 8%?
   - *b.* 12%?

3. You have just received an inheritance from a relative. You can either receive a $200,000 lump-sum amount at the end of 10 years or receive $14,000 at the end of each year for the next 10 years. If your discount rate is 12%, which alternative would you prefer?

Solution to Appendix 13A Review Problem

1. *a.* The amount that must be invested now would be the present value of the $40,000, using a discount rate of 8%. From Exhibit 13A–6, the factor for a discount rate of 8% for 12 periods is 0.397. Multiplying this discount factor by the $40,000 needed in 12 years will give the amount of the present investment required: $40,000 × 0.397 = $15,880.
    b. We will proceed as we did in (*a*) above, but this time we will use a discount rate of 12%. From Exhibit 13A–6, the factor for a discount rate of 12% for 12 periods is 0.257. Multiplying this discount factor by the $40,000 needed in 12 years will give the amount of the present investment required: $40,000 × 0.257 = $10,280.

    Notice that as the discount rate (desired rate of return) increases, the present value decreases.

2. This part differs from (1) above in that we are now dealing with an annuity rather than with a single future sum. The amount that must be invested now is the present value of the $1,000 needed at the end of each year for five years. Since we are dealing with an annuity, or a series of annual cash flows, we must refer to Exhibit 13A–7 for the appropriate discount factor.
    a. From Exhibit 13A–7, the discount factor for 8% for five periods is 3.993. Therefore, the amount that must be invested now to have $1,000 available at the end of each year for five years is $1,000 × 3.993 = $3,993.
    b. From Exhibit 13A–7, the discount factor for 12% for five periods is 3.605. Therefore, the amount that must be invested now to have $1,000 available at the end of each year for five years is $1,000 × 3.605 = $3,605.

    Again, notice that as the discount rate increases, the present value decreases. When the rate of return increases, less must be invested today to yield a given amount in the future.

3. For this part, we will need to refer to both Exhibits 13A–6 and 13A–7. From Exhibit 13A–6, we will need to find the discount factor for 12% for 10 periods and then apply it to the $200,000 lump sum to be received in 10 years. From Exhibit 13A–7, we will need to find the discount factor for 12% for 10 periods and then apply it to the series of $14,000 payments to be received

over the 10-year period. Whichever alternative has the higher present value is the one that should be selected.

$$\$200{,}000 \times 0.322 = \$64{,}400$$

$$\$14{,}000 \times 5.650 = \$79{,}100$$

Thus, you should prefer to receive the $14,000 per year for 10 years rather than the $200,000 lump sum. This means that you could invest the $14,000 received at the end of each year at 12% and have *more* than $200,000 at the end of 10 years.

---

connect **Appendix 13A Exercises**

EXERCISE 13A–1 Basic Present Value Concepts [LO7]
Each of the following parts is independent. (Ignore income taxes.)

1.   Express Delivery plans to build a new warehouse in four years to have more space for its products awaiting shipment. The warehouse will cost $500,000. What lump-sum amount should the company invest now to have the $500,000 available at the end of the four-year period? Assume that the company can invest money at
   a. 6%.
   b. 10%.
2.   Washington Products, Inc., can purchase a new electronic data storage server that will save $3,000 per year in paper storage and warehouse costs. The data server will last for five years and have no salvage value. What is the maximum purchase price that Washington Products would be willing to pay for the copier if the company's required rate of return is
   a. 9%
   b. 15%?
3.   Susan has just won the million-dollar Power Lottery jackpot at a gambling casino. The casino will pay her $50,000 per year for 20 years as the payoff. If Susan can invest money at 5% rate of return, what is the present value of her winnings? Did she really win a million dollars? Explain.

EXERCISE 13A–2 Basic Present Value Concepts [LO7]
Consider each of the following situations independently.

1.   Annual cash inflows from two competing investment opportunities are given below. Each investment opportunity will require the same initial investment. Compute the present value of the cash inflows for each investment using a 20% discount rate.

| | Investment | |
Year	X	Y
1	$ 1,000	$ 4,000
2	2,000	3,000
3	3,000	2,000
4	4,000	1,000
	$10,000	$10,000

2.   At the end of three years, when you graduate from college, your father has promised to give you a used car that will cost $12,000. What lump sum must he invest now to have the $12,000 at the end of three years if he can invest money at
   a. 6%?
   b. 10%?
3.   Mark has just won the grand prize on the *Hoot 'n' Holler* quiz show. He has a choice between (*a*) receiving $500,000 immediately and (*b*) receiving $60,000 per year for eight years plus a lump sum of $200,000 at the end of the eight-year period. If Mark can get a return of 10% on his investments, which option would you recommend that he accept? (Use present value analysis, and show all computations.)
4.   You have just learned that you are a beneficiary in the will of your late Aunt Susan. The executrix of her estate has given you three options as to how you may receive your inheritance:
   a. You may receive $50,000 immediately.
   b. You may receive $75,000 at the end of six years.
   c. You may receive $12,000 at the end of each year for six years (a total of $72,000).
   If you can invest money at a 12% return, which option would you prefer?

EXHIBIT 13A–4   Future Value of $1; $(1 + r)^n$

Periods	2%	4%	5%	6%	7%	8%	9%	10%	11%	12%	13%	14%	15%	16%	17%	18%	19%	20%
1	1.020	1.040	1.050	1.060	1.070	1.080	1.090	1.100	1.110	1.120	1.130	1.140	1.150	1.160	1.170	1.180	1.190	1.200
2	1.040	1.082	1.103	1.124	1.145	1.166	1.188	1.210	1.232	1.254	1.277	1.300	1.323	1.346	1.369	1.392	1.416	1.440
3	1.061	1.125	1.158	1.191	1.225	1.260	1.295	1.331	1.368	1.405	1.443	1.482	1.521	1.561	1.602	1.643	1.685	1.728
4	1.082	1.170	1.216	1.262	1.311	1.360	1.412	1.464	1.518	1.574	1.630	1.689	1.749	1.811	1.874	1.939	2.005	2.074
5	1.104	1.217	1.276	1.338	1.403	1.469	1.539	1.611	1.685	1.762	1.842	1.925	2.011	2.100	2.192	2.288	2.386	2.488
6	1.126	1.265	1.340	1.419	1.501	1.587	1.677	1.772	1.870	1.974	2.082	2.195	2.313	2.436	2.565	2.700	2.840	2.986
7	1.149	1.316	1.407	1.504	1.606	1.714	1.828	1.949	2.076	2.211	2.353	2.502	2.660	2.826	3.001	3.185	3.379	3.583
8	1.172	1.369	1.477	1.594	1.718	1.851	1.993	2.144	2.305	2.476	2.658	2.853	3.059	3.278	3.511	3.759	4.021	4.300
9	1.195	1.423	1.551	1.689	1.838	1.999	2.172	2.358	2.558	2.773	3.004	3.252	3.518	3.803	4.108	4.435	4.785	5.160
10	1.219	1.480	1.629	1.791	1.967	2.159	2.367	2.594	2.839	3.106	3.395	3.707	4.046	4.411	4.807	5.234	5.695	6.192
11	1.243	1.539	1.710	1.898	2.105	2.332	2.580	2.853	3.152	3.479	3.836	4.226	4.652	5.117	5.624	6.176	6.777	7.430
12	1.268	1.601	1.796	2.012	2.252	2.518	2.813	3.138	3.498	3.896	4.335	4.818	5.350	5.936	6.580	7.288	8.064	8.916
13	1.294	1.665	1.886	2.133	2.410	2.720	3.066	3.452	3.883	4.363	4.898	5.492	6.153	6.886	7.699	8.599	9.596	10.699
14	1.319	1.732	1.980	2.261	2.579	2.937	3.342	3.797	4.310	4.887	5.535	6.261	7.076	7.988	9.007	10.147	11.420	12.839
15	1.346	1.801	2.079	2.397	2.759	3.172	3.642	4.177	4.785	5.474	6.254	7.138	8.137	9.266	10.539	11.974	13.590	15.407
16	1.373	1.873	2.183	2.540	2.952	3.426	3.970	4.595	5.311	6.130	7.067	8.137	9.358	10.748	12.330	14.129	16.172	18.488
17	1.400	1.948	2.292	2.693	3.159	3.700	4.328	5.054	5.895	6.866	7.986	9.276	10.761	12.468	14.426	16.672	19.244	22.186
18	1.428	2.026	2.407	2.854	3.380	3.996	4.717	5.560	6.544	7.690	9.024	10.575	12.375	14.463	16.879	19.673	22.901	26.623
19	1.457	2.107	2.527	3.026	3.617	4.316	5.142	6.116	7.263	8.613	10.197	12.056	14.232	16.777	19.748	23.214	27.252	31.948
20	1.486	2.191	2.653	3.207	3.870	4.661	5.604	6.727	8.062	9.646	11.523	13.743	16.367	19.461	23.106	27.393	32.429	38.338
30	1.811	3.243	4.322	5.743	7.612	10.063	13.268	17.449	22.892	29.960	39.116	50.950	66.212	85.850	111.065	143.371	184.675	237.376

EXHIBIT 13A–5   Future Value of an Annuity of $1 in Arrears; $\dfrac{(1+r)^n - 1}{r}$

Periods	2%	4%	5%	6%	7%	8%	9%	10%	11%	12%	13%	14%	15%	16%	17%	18%	19%	20%
1	1.000	1.000	1.000	1.000	1.000	1.000	1.000	1.000	1.000	1.000	1.000	1.000	1.000	1.000	1.000	1.000	1.000	1.000
2	2.020	2.040	2.050	2.060	2.070	2.080	2.090	2.100	2.110	2.120	2.130	2.140	2.150	2.160	2.170	2.180	2.190	2.200
3	3.060	3.122	3.153	3.184	3.215	3.246	3.278	3.310	3.342	3.374	3.407	3.440	3.473	3.506	3.539	3.572	3.606	3.640
4	4.122	4.246	4.310	4.375	4.440	4.506	4.573	4.641	4.710	4.779	4.850	4.921	4.993	5.066	5.141	5.215	5.291	5.368
5	5.204	5.416	5.526	5.637	5.751	5.867	5.985	6.105	6.228	6.353	6.480	6.610	6.742	6.877	7.014	7.154	7.297	7.442
6	6.308	6.633	6.802	6.975	7.153	7.336	7.523	7.716	7.913	8.115	8.323	8.536	8.754	8.977	9.207	9.442	9.683	9.930
7	7.434	7.898	8.142	8.394	8.654	8.923	9.200	9.487	9.783	10.089	10.405	10.730	11.067	11.414	11.772	12.142	12.523	12.916
8	8.583	9.214	9.549	9.897	10.260	10.637	11.028	11.436	11.859	12.300	12.757	13.233	13.727	14.240	14.773	15.327	15.902	16.499
9	9.755	10.583	11.027	11.491	11.978	12.488	13.021	13.579	14.164	14.776	15.416	16.085	16.786	17.519	18.285	19.086	19.923	20.799
10	10.950	12.006	12.578	13.181	13.816	14.487	15.193	15.937	16.722	17.549	18.420	19.337	20.304	21.321	22.393	23.521	24.709	25.959
11	12.169	13.486	14.207	14.972	15.784	16.645	17.560	18.531	19.561	20.655	21.814	23.045	24.349	25.733	27.200	28.755	30.404	32.150
12	13.412	15.026	15.917	16.870	17.888	18.977	20.141	21.384	22.713	24.133	25.650	27.271	29.002	30.850	32.824	34.931	37.180	39.581
13	14.680	16.627	17.713	18.882	20.141	21.495	22.953	24.523	26.212	28.029	29.985	32.089	34.352	36.786	39.404	42.219	45.244	48.497
14	15.974	18.292	19.599	21.015	22.550	24.215	26.019	27.975	30.095	32.393	34.883	37.581	40.505	43.672	47.103	50.818	54.841	59.196
15	17.293	20.024	21.579	23.276	25.129	27.152	29.361	31.772	34.405	37.280	40.417	43.842	47.580	51.660	56.110	60.965	66.261	72.035
16	18.639	21.825	23.657	25.673	27.888	30.324	33.003	35.950	39.190	42.753	46.672	50.980	55.717	60.925	66.649	72.939	79.850	87.442
17	20.012	23.698	25.840	28.213	30.840	33.750	36.974	40.545	44.501	48.884	53.739	59.118	65.075	71.673	78.979	87.068	96.022	105.931
18	21.412	25.645	28.132	30.906	33.999	37.450	41.301	45.599	50.396	55.750	61.725	68.394	75.836	84.141	93.406	103.740	115.266	128.117
19	22.841	27.671	30.539	33.760	37.379	41.446	46.018	51.159	56.939	63.440	70.749	78.969	88.212	98.603	110.285	123.414	138.166	154.740
20	24.297	29.778	33.066	36.786	40.995	45.762	51.160	57.275	64.203	72.052	80.947	91.025	102.444	115.380	130.033	146.628	165.418	186.688
30	40.568	56.085	66.439	79.058	94.461	113.283	136.308	164.494	199.021	241.333	293.199	356.787	434.745	530.312	647.439	790.948	966.712	1181.882

EXHIBIT 13A–6 Present Value of $1; $\dfrac{1}{(1+r)^n}$ or $(1+r)^{-n}$

Periods	2%	4%	5%	6%	7%	8%	9%	10%	11%	12%	13%	14%	15%	16%	17%	18%	19%	20%
1	0.980	0.962	0.952	0.943	0.935	0.926	0.917	0.909	0.901	0.893	0.885	0.877	0.870	0.862	0.855	0.847	0.840	0.833
2	0.961	0.925	0.907	0.890	0.873	0.857	0.842	0.826	0.812	0.797	0.783	0.769	0.756	0.743	0.731	0.718	0.706	0.694
3	0.942	0.889	0.864	0.840	0.816	0.794	0.772	0.751	0.731	0.712	0.693	0.675	0.658	0.641	0.624	0.609	0.593	0.579
4	0.924	0.855	0.823	0.792	0.763	0.735	0.708	0.683	0.659	0.636	0.613	0.592	0.572	0.552	0.534	0.516	0.499	0.482
5	0.906	0.822	0.784	0.747	0.713	0.681	0.650	0.621	0.593	0.567	0.543	0.519	0.497	0.476	0.456	0.437	0.419	0.402
6	0.888	0.790	0.746	0.705	0.666	0.630	0.596	0.564	0.535	0.507	0.480	0.456	0.432	0.410	0.390	0.370	0.352	0.335
7	0.871	0.760	0.711	0.665	0.623	0.583	0.547	0.513	0.482	0.452	0.425	0.400	0.376	0.354	0.333	0.314	0.296	0.279
8	0.853	0.731	0.677	0.627	0.582	0.540	0.502	0.467	0.434	0.404	0.376	0.351	0.327	0.305	0.285	0.266	0.249	0.233
9	0.837	0.703	0.645	0.592	0.544	0.500	0.460	0.424	0.391	0.361	0.333	0.308	0.284	0.263	0.243	0.225	0.209	0.194
10	0.820	0.676	0.614	0.558	0.508	0.463	0.422	0.386	0.352	0.322	0.295	0.270	0.247	0.227	0.208	0.191	0.176	0.162
11	0.804	0.650	0.585	0.527	0.475	0.429	0.388	0.350	0.317	0.287	0.261	0.237	0.215	0.195	0.178	0.162	0.148	0.135
12	0.788	0.625	0.557	0.497	0.444	0.397	0.356	0.319	0.286	0.257	0.231	0.208	0.187	0.168	0.152	0.137	0.124	0.112
13	0.773	0.601	0.530	0.469	0.415	0.368	0.326	0.290	0.258	0.229	0.204	0.182	0.163	0.145	0.130	0.116	0.104	0.093
14	0.758	0.577	0.505	0.442	0.388	0.340	0.299	0.263	0.232	0.205	0.181	0.160	0.141	0.125	0.111	0.099	0.088	0.078
15	0.743	0.555	0.481	0.417	0.362	0.315	0.275	0.239	0.209	0.183	0.160	0.140	0.123	0.108	0.095	0.084	0.074	0.065
16	0.728	0.534	0.458	0.394	0.339	0.292	0.252	0.218	0.188	0.163	0.141	0.123	0.107	0.093	0.081	0.071	0.062	0.054
17	0.714	0.513	0.436	0.371	0.317	0.270	0.231	0.198	0.170	0.146	0.125	0.108	0.093	0.080	0.069	0.060	0.052	0.045
18	0.700	0.494	0.416	0.350	0.296	0.250	0.212	0.180	0.153	0.130	0.111	0.095	0.081	0.069	0.059	0.051	0.044	0.038
19	0.686	0.475	0.396	0.331	0.277	0.232	0.194	0.164	0.138	0.116	0.098	0.083	0.070	0.060	0.051	0.043	0.037	0.031
20	0.673	0.456	0.377	0.312	0.258	0.215	0.178	0.149	0.124	0.104	0.087	0.073	0.061	0.051	0.043	0.037	0.031	0.026
30	0.552	0.308	0.231	0.174	0.131	0.099	0.075	0.057	0.044	0.033	0.026	0.020	0.015	0.012	0.009	0.007	0.005	0.004

EXHIBIT 13A–7   Present Value of an Annuity of $1 in Arrears; $\dfrac{1}{r}\left[1-\dfrac{1}{(1+r)^n}\right]$ or $\dfrac{1-(1+r)^{-n}}{r}$

Periods	2%	4%	5%	6%	7%	8%	9%	10%	11%	12%	13%	14%	15%	16%	17%	18%	19%	20%
1	0.980	0.962	0.952	0.943	0.935	0.926	0.917	0.909	0.901	0.893	0.885	0.877	0.870	0.862	0.855	0.847	0.840	0.833
2	1.942	1.886	1.859	1.833	1.808	1.783	1.759	1.736	1.713	1.690	1.668	1.647	1.626	1.605	1.585	1.566	1.547	1.528
3	2.884	2.775	2.723	2.673	2.624	2.577	2.531	2.487	2.444	2.402	2.361	2.322	2.283	2.246	2.210	2.174	2.140	2.106
4	3.808	3.631	3.546	3.465	3.387	3.312	3.240	3.170	3.102	3.037	2.974	2.914	2.855	2.798	2.743	2.690	2.639	2.589
5	4.713	4.452	4.329	4.212	4.100	3.993	3.890	3.791	3.696	3.605	3.517	3.433	3.352	3.274	3.199	3.127	3.058	2.991
6	5.601	5.242	5.076	4.917	4.767	4.623	4.486	4.355	4.231	4.111	3.998	3.889	3.784	3.685	3.589	3.498	3.410	3.326
7	6.472	6.002	5.786	5.582	5.389	5.206	5.033	4.868	4.712	4.564	4.423	4.288	4.160	4.039	3.922	3.812	3.706	3.605
8	7.325	6.733	6.463	6.210	5.971	5.747	5.535	5.335	5.146	4.968	4.799	4.639	4.487	4.344	4.207	4.078	3.954	3.837
9	8.162	7.435	7.108	6.802	6.515	6.247	5.995	5.759	5.537	5.328	5.132	4.946	4.772	4.607	4.451	4.303	4.163	4.031
10	8.983	8.111	7.722	7.360	7.024	6.710	6.418	6.145	5.889	5.650	5.426	5.216	5.019	4.833	4.659	4.494	4.339	4.192
11	9.787	8.760	8.306	7.887	7.499	7.139	6.805	6.495	6.207	5.938	5.687	5.453	5.234	5.029	4.836	4.656	4.486	4.327
12	10.575	9.385	8.863	8.384	7.943	7.536	7.161	6.814	6.492	6.194	5.918	5.660	5.421	5.197	4.988	4.793	4.611	4.439
13	11.348	9.986	9.394	8.853	8.358	7.904	7.487	7.103	6.750	6.424	6.122	5.842	5.583	5.342	5.118	4.910	4.715	4.533
14	12.106	10.563	9.899	9.295	8.745	8.244	7.786	7.367	6.982	6.628	6.302	6.002	5.724	5.468	5.229	5.008	4.802	4.611
15	12.849	11.118	10.380	9.712	9.108	8.559	8.061	7.606	7.191	6.811	6.462	6.142	5.847	5.575	5.324	5.092	4.876	4.675
16	13.578	11.652	10.838	10.106	9.447	8.851	8.313	7.824	7.379	6.974	6.604	6.265	5.954	5.668	5.405	5.162	4.938	4.730
17	14.292	12.166	11.274	10.477	9.763	9.122	8.544	8.022	7.549	7.120	6.729	6.373	6.047	5.749	5.475	5.222	4.990	4.775
18	14.992	12.659	11.690	10.828	10.059	9.372	8.756	8.201	7.702	7.250	6.840	6.467	6.128	5.818	5.534	5.273	5.033	4.812
19	15.678	13.134	12.085	11.158	10.336	9.604	8.950	8.365	7.839	7.366	6.938	6.550	6.198	5.877	5.584	5.316	5.070	4.843
20	16.351	13.590	12.462	11.470	10.594	9.818	9.129	8.514	7.963	7.469	7.025	6.623	6.259	5.929	5.628	5.353	5.101	4.870
30	22.396	17.292	15.372	13.765	12.409	11.258	10.274	9.427	8.694	8.055	7.496	7.003	6.566	6.177	5.829	5.517	5.235	4.979

APPENDIX 13B: INCOME TAXES IN CAPITAL BUDGETING DECISIONS

LEARNING OBJECTIVE 8
Incorporate income taxes into a capital budgeting analysis.

In our discussion of capital budgeting, we ignored income taxes in the main body of the chapter for two reasons. First, some organizations do not pay income taxes. Not-for-profit organizations, such as hospitals and charitable foundations, and government agencies are exempt from income taxes. Second, capital budgeting is complex and is best covered in small steps. Now that we have a solid groundwork in the concepts of present value and discounting, we can explore the effects of income taxes on capital budgeting decisions.

Canadian income tax regulations are very complex, so we can cover only the basics in this appendix. To keep the material as easy to understand as possible, we have made many simplifying assumptions about the tax regulations throughout this section. Among the most important of these assumptions are (1) taxable income equals net income before income tax expense as computed for financial reports, and (2) the tax rate is a flat percentage of taxable income. The actual tax regulations are far more complex than this; however, the simplifications that we make throughout this appendix allow us to cover the most important implications of income taxes for capital budgeting without getting bogged down in too many details. It is also important to note that we focus on after-tax *cash* inflows and *cash* outflows in the discussion below. This is because capital project analysis, even on an after-tax basis, should be done using discounted cash inflows and outflows.

The Concept of After-Tax Cost

After-tax cost
The amount of a net cash outflow resulting from a tax-deductible cash expense after the income tax effects have been considered.

Businesses, like individuals, must pay income taxes. In the case of businesses, the amount of income tax that must be paid is determined by the company's net taxable income. Tax-deductible expenses (tax deductions) decrease the company's net taxable income and hence reduce the taxes the company must pay. For this reason, expenses are often stated on an *after-tax* basis. For example, if a company pays rent of $10 million per year but this expense results in a reduction in income taxes of $3 million (tax rate = 30%), the after-tax cost of the rent is said to be $7 million. The amount of an expenditure net of its tax effect is known as the **after-tax cost**.

To illustrate, assume that a company with a tax rate of 30% is contemplating a training program that costs $60,000. What impact will this have on the company's taxes? To keep matters simple, let's assume the training program has no immediate effect on sales. How much does the company actually pay for the training program after taking into account the impact of this expense on taxes? The answer is $42,000, as shown in Exhibit 13B–1. While the training program costs $60,000 before taxes, it would reduce the company's taxes by $18,000, so its *after-tax* cost would be only $42,000. This $18,000 reduction in taxes can also be calculated directly by simply multiplying $60,000 by the 30% tax rate.

EXHIBIT 13B–1   The Computation of After-Tax Cost

	Without Training Program	With Training Program
Sales	$850,000	$850,000
Less tax-deductible expenses:		
Salaries, insurance, and other	700,000	700,000
New training program		60,000
Total expenses	700,000	760,000
Taxable income	$150,000	$ 90,000
Income taxes (30%)	$ 45,000	$ 27,000
Cost of new training program	$60,000	
Less: Reduction in income taxes		
($45,000 − $27,000)		18,000
After-tax cost of the new training program	$42,000	

The after-tax cost of any tax-deductible cash expense can be determined using the following formula:[6]

$$\frac{\text{After-tax cost}}{\text{(net cash outflow)}} = (1 - \text{Tax rate}) \times \text{Tax-deductible cash expense} \quad \text{(B1)}$$

We can verify the accuracy of this formula by applying it to the $60,000 training program expenditure:

$$(1 - 0.30) \times \$60,000 = \$42,000 \text{ after-tax cost of the training program}$$

This formula is very useful since it provides the actual amount of cash a company must pay after taking into consideration tax effects. It is this actual after-tax cash outflow that should be used in capital budgeting decisions.

Similar reasoning applies to revenues and other *taxable* cash inflows. Since these cash receipts are taxable, the company must pay out a portion of them in taxes. The **after-tax benefit**, or net cash inflow, realized from a particular cash receipt can be obtained by applying a simple variation of the cash expenditure formula used above:

$$\text{After-tax benefit (net cash inflow)} = (1 - \text{Tax rate}) \times \text{Taxable cash receipt} \quad \text{(B2)}$$

> **After-tax benefit**
> The amount of net cash inflow realized from a taxable cash receipt after income tax effects have been considered.

We emphasize the term *taxable cash receipt* because not all cash inflows are taxable. For example, the release of working capital at the termination of a project would not be a taxable cash inflow. It is not counted as income for either financial accounting or income tax reporting purposes since it is simply a recovery of the initial investment.

Capital Cost Allowance (CCA) Tax Shield

Capital cost allowance (CCA) is the amount of depreciation expense allowed by the Canada Revenue Agency for tax purposes. Because CCA, like accounting depreciation, is not a cash outflow, it was ignored in this chapter in all discounted cash flow computations. However, CCA does affect the amount of taxes that must be paid and therefore has an indirect effect on the company's cash flows.

> **Capital cost allowance**
> The amount of depreciation expense allowed by the Canada Revenue Agency for tax purposes.

To illustrate the effect of CCA deductions on tax payments, consider a company with annual cash sales of $500,000 and cash operating expenses of $310,000. In addition, the company has a depreciable asset on which the CCA deduction is $90,000 per year. The tax rate is 30%. As shown in Exhibit 13B–2, the CCA deduction reduces the company's taxes by $27,000. In effect, the CCA deduction of $90,000 *shields* $90,000 in revenues from taxation and thereby *reduces* the amount of taxes that the company must pay. Because CCA deductions shield revenues from taxation, they are referred to as **capital cost allowance tax shields**.[7]

> **Capital cost allowance tax shield**
> The reduction in tax payments caused by CCA deductions.

	Without CCA Deduction	With CCA Deduction
Sales.	$500,000	$500,000
Cash operating expenses.	310,000	310,000
Cash flow from operations	190,000	190,000
Capital cost allowance	—	90,000
Taxable income	$190,000	$100,000
Income taxes (30%)	$ 57,000	$ 30,000
	$27,000 lower taxes with the CCA deduction	
Cash flow comparison:		
Cash flow from operations (above).	$190,000	$190,000
Income taxes (above)	57,000	30,000
Net cash flow	$133,000	$160,000
	$27,000 greater cash flow with the CCA deduction	

EXHIBIT 13B–2   The Effect of CCA Deductions on Tax Payments

The reduction in tax payments made possible by the CCA tax shield illustrated in Exhibit 13B–2 is equal to the amount of the CCA deduction, multiplied by the tax rate as follows:

$$\text{Tax savings from the CCA tax shield} = \text{Tax rate} \times \text{CCA deduction} \qquad \text{(B3)}$$

We can verify this formula by applying it to the $90,000 CCA deduction in our example:

$$0.30 \times \$90,000 = \$27,000 \text{ reduction in tax payments}$$

In this section, when we estimate after-tax cash flows for capital budgeting decisions, we will include the tax savings provided by the CCA tax shield.

Rules for CCA are complex and most companies take advantage of accelerated methods allowed under the tax regulations. These accelerated methods usually result in a reduction in current taxes because of higher CCA amounts and an offsetting increase in future taxes as CCA amounts fall. This shifting of part of the tax burden from the current year to future years is advantageous from a present value point of view, since tax savings received today are worth more than tax savings received in the future. A summary of the concepts we have introduced so far is given in Exhibit 13B–3.

Capital Cost Allowance Instead of Depreciation

As noted above, CCA is the Canada Revenue Agency's counterpart to depreciation. Depreciation is the allocation of the cost of an asset over its useful life. The amount deducted each period for financial statement reporting purposes is based on generally accepted accounting principles (GAAP). For income tax purposes, however, depreciation is not an allowable expense. Instead, a capital cost allowance is permitted by regulations that accompany the Canadian Income Tax Act. A CCA deduction is allowed for business-related capital property such as equipment and automobiles.

The income tax regulations group assets into classes and each class is then assigned a maximum CCA rate for tax purposes. Maximum capital cost allowance rates are prescribed by the regulations in the Income Tax Act for numerous classes or pools of assets. A company has the option of deducting capital cost allowance for each asset class for any amount ranging from zero to the maximum amount prescribed by the Act. The CCA rate applicable to each class is usually intended to reflect the economic life of the assets of that class.

These prescribed rates are subject to government change. Examples of these asset pools and maximum prescribed rates as per the 2010 Canadian Income Tax Act follow:

Asset	Class	Maximum Rate
Non-residential buildings.	1	4%
Automobiles	10	30%
Computer hardware and software	52	100%
Assets not included in other classes.	8	20%

EXHIBIT 13B–3 Tax Adjustments Required in a Capital Budgeting Analysis

Item	Treatment
Tax-deductible cash expense*.	Multiply by (1 − Tax rate) to get after-tax cost.
Taxable cash receipt*.	Multiply by (1 − Tax rate) to get after-tax cash inflow.
CCA deduction.	Multiply by the tax rate to get the tax savings from the CCA tax shield.

*Cash expenses can be deducted from the cash receipts and the difference multiplied by (1 − Tax rate). See the example at the top of Exhibit 13B–4 on page 669.

Capital cost allowance is calculated by applying the prescribed rate to a declining balance called the **undepreciated capital cost (UCC)**. The UCC of an asset class or pool of assets is the remaining book value that is available for tax-deductible depreciation (CCA). The maximum amount of CCA that may be deducted in a taxation year is the UCC multiplied by the CCA rate for that asset class. However, for net additions made to each asset class during the year, only one-half of the prescribed rate is permitted. Under this half-year rule, only half of the normal CCA for most assets is allowed as a tax-deductible expense in the year the asset is acquired.

Undepreciated capital cost (UCC)

The remaining book value of an asset class or pool of assets that is available for tax-deductible depreciation (capital cost allowance).

Example 1

Saskatoon Ltd. has obtained a $30,000 loan to acquire a truck (Class 10 for CCA purposes). Assuming that the company will have taxable income for the foreseeable future, calculate the present value of the capital cost allowance tax shield for the first three years if the cost of capital is 10% and the tax rate is 40%.

(1) Year	(2) Undepreciated Capital Cost	(3) CCA (2) × 30%	(4) Tax Savings (3) × 40%	(5) PV Factor at 10%†	(6) PV of Tax Savings (4) × (5)
1	$30,000	$4,500*	$1,800	0.909	$1,636
2	25,500	7,650	3,060	0.826	2,528
3	17,850	5,355	2,142	0.751	1,609

*$30,000 × 0.30 × (1/2) = $4,500.
†Per Exhibit 13A–6.

Because the capital cost allowance is calculated on the declining UCC balance of a pool of assets rather than on a single asset, a business is able to obtain tax savings from a project even after its disposition. As long as there are other assets in the pool and the proceeds from disposal are less than the UCC for the class, tax savings can be realized in perpetuity.

It can be shown mathematically that the present value of this perpetual stream of tax savings from a declining balance capital cost allowance is calculated by using the *CCA tax shield formula*:

$$PV = \frac{Cdt}{d+k} \times \frac{1+0.5k}{1+k} \qquad (B4)$$

where

C = The capital cost of the asset added to the asset pool.
d = CCA rate.
t = The firm's marginal income tax rate.
k = The cost of capital.

$\dfrac{1+0.5k}{1+k}$ = The correction factor to account for the provision that only one-half of the capital cost of an asset is included in UCC during the year of acquisition.

For the previous example, the present value of the CCA tax shield is

$$\frac{\$30,000 \times 0.3 \times 0.4}{0.3 + 0.10} \times \frac{1 + 0.5 \times 0.10}{1 + 0.10} = \$9,000 \times 0.95455 = \$8,591$$

Example 2

Using the data in the previous example, calculate the present value of the CCA tax shield, assuming that other assets remain in the pool and the asset is disposed of for $6,000 after five years' use.

The sale of the asset results in a cash inflow at the end of year 5. This disposal results in the asset pool balance (UCC) being reduced by the $6,000 proceeds. The present value of the CCA tax shield is also reduced, because from the end of year 5 onward, CCA will be applied to a smaller UCC balance than it otherwise would have been without the asset disposal. If S represents salvage value, the CCA tax shield formula must be adjusted by deducting:

$$\frac{Sdt}{d + k} \times (1 + k)^{-n}$$

where

$$\frac{Sdt}{d + k}$$

calculates the present value of the lost tax shield at the end of year 5 ($n = 5$). This lost tax shield is then discounted to time period zero by multiplying it by $(1 + k)^{-n}$ or by using Exhibit 13A–6. The present value of the tax shield lost is calculated as follows:

$$\frac{\$6,000 \times 0.3 \times 0.4}{0.3 + 0.1} \times (1 + 0.10)^{-5} = \$1,117.80$$

Therefore, the net present value of the CCA tax shields is $\$8,591 - \$1,117.80 = \$7,473.20$.

Example of Income Taxes and Capital Budgeting

Now that we have reviewed after-tax costs, after-tax benefits, and the CCA tax shield, we can examine a comprehensive example of income taxes and capital budgeting that incorporates all of these concepts.

Example 3

The mineral rights to land that has a deposit of ore are owned by the Englund Company. The company is uncertain whether it should purchase equipment and open a mine on the property. After careful study, the following data have been assembled by the company:

Cost of equipment needed	$300,000
Working capital needed.............................	75,000
Estimated annual cash receipts from sales of ore...........	250,000
Estimated annual cash expenses for salaries, insurance, utilities, and other cash expenses of mining the ore	170,000
Cost of road repairs needed in 6 years	40,000
Salvage value of the equipment in 10 years	100,000

The ore in the mine would be exhausted after 10 years of mining activity, at which time the mine would be closed. The equipment would then be sold for its salvage value. Englund Company uses a 20% rate, assuming no salvage value, to compute CCA deductions for tax purposes. The company's after-tax cost of capital is 12% and its tax rate is 30%. Should Englund Company purchase the equipment and open a mine on the property?

The solution to the problem is given in Exhibit 13B–4. We suggest that you go through this solution item by item and note the following points:

Cost of new equipment. The initial investment of $300,000 in the new equipment is included in full, with no reductions for taxes. This represents an *investment*, not an expense, so no tax adjustment is made. (Only revenues and expenses are adjusted for the effects of taxes.) However, this investment does affect taxes through the CCA deductions that are considered below.

Working capital. The working capital needed for the project is included in full, with no reductions for taxes. Like the cost of new equipment, working capital is an investment and not an expense so no tax adjustment is made. Also observe that no tax adjustment is made when the working capital is released at the end of the project's life. The release of working capital is not a taxable cash flow, since it merely represents a return of investment funds to the company.

Net annual cash receipts. The net annual cash receipts from sales of ore are adjusted for the effects of income taxes, as discussed earlier in this appendix. Note at the top of Exhibit 13B–4 that the annual cash expenses are deducted from the annual cash receipts to obtain the net cash receipts. This simplifies the computations.

Road repairs. Since the road repairs occur just once (in the sixth year), they are treated separately from other expenses. Road repairs would be a tax-deductible cash expense, and therefore they are adjusted for the effects of income taxes, as discussed earlier in this appendix.

Capital cost allowance deductions. The tax savings provided by CCA deductions are essentially an annuity that is included in the present value computations using the CCA tax shield formula.

Salvage value of equipment. The salvage value of $100,000 results in the present value inflow of $32,200. However, later in the analysis, note that the present value of the tax shield is reduced. The value of $18,750 is the present value at the end of year 10 of the lost CCA tax shield from the salvage. This amount therefore must be discounted to *now* by multiplying it by the present value factor of $1 at the end of 10 periods, $0.322 = (1 + 0.12)^{-10}$.

Since the net present value of the proposed mining project is positive, the equipment should be purchased and the mine opened. Study Exhibit 13B–4 thoroughly—*it is a key exhibit!*

EXHIBIT 13B–4 Example of Income Taxes and Capital Budgeting

	Per Year
Cash receipts from sales of ore	$250,000
Less payments for salaries, insurance, utilities, and other cash expenses.	170,000
Net cash receipts	$ 80,000

Items and Computations	Year(s)	(1) Amount	(2) Tax Effect*	After-Tax Cash Flows (1) × (2)	12% Factor	Present Value of Cash Flows
Cost of new equipment	Now	$(300,000)	—	$(300,000)	1.000	$(300,000)
Working capital needed	Now	(75,000)	—	(75,000)	1.000	(75,000)
Net annual cash receipts	1–10	80,000	1−0.30	56,000	5.650	316,400
Road repairs.	6	(40,000)	1−0.30	(28,000)	0.507	(14,196)
Salvage value of equipment.	10	100,000	—	100,000	0.322	32,200
Release of working capital	10	75,000	—	75,000	0.322	24,150
Subtotal						$ (16,446)

Present value of CCA tax shield:

$$PV = \left[\frac{Cdt}{d+k} \times \frac{1+0.5k}{1+k}\right] - \left[\frac{Sdt}{d+k} \times (1+k)^{-n}\right]$$

$$PV = \left[\frac{\$300,000 \times 0.2 \times 0.3}{0.2+0.12} \times \frac{1+0.06}{1+0.12}\right] - \left[\frac{\$100,000 \times 0.2 \times 0.3}{0.2+0.12} \times (1+0.12)^{-10}\right]$$

$$PV = [\$56,250 \times 0.9464] - [\$18,750 \times 0.322]$$

$$PV = \$53,235 - \$6,037$$

$PV = \$47,198$	47,198
Net present value.	$ 30,752

*Taxable cash receipts and tax-deductible cash expenses are multiplied by (1 − Tax rate) to determine the after-tax cash flow. CCA deductions are multiplied by the tax rate itself to determine the after-tax cash flow (i.e., tax savings from the CCA tax shield).

DECISION AID

NET PRESENT VALUE AND INTERNAL RATE OF RETURN METHODS (WITH TAXES)

Relevant cash inflows:
- Incremental revenues (after tax); reduction in costs (after tax); salvage value; release of working capital; CCA tax shield.

Relevant cash outflows:
- Initial investment; increased working capital needs; incremental operating costs (after tax); CCA tax shield lost upon disposal of asset.

Decision Rule (for determining project acceptability):

Acceptable if net present value ≥ $0; internal rate of return ≥ required rate of return.

Not acceptable if net present value < $0; internal rate of return < required rate of return.

Appendix 13B Summary

- Unless a company is a tax-exempt organization, such as a not-for-profit school or government unit, income taxes should be considered in making capital budgeting decisions. Tax-deductible cash expenditures and taxable cash receipts are placed on an after-tax basis by multiplying them by (1−Tax rate). Only after-tax amounts should be used in determining the desirability of an investment proposal. **[LO8]**
- Although CCA (depreciation for tax purposes) is not a cash outflow, it is a valid deduction for tax purposes and therefore affects income tax payments. The CCA tax shield—computed by multiplying the CCA deduction by the tax rate—also results in income tax savings. **[LO8]**
- When an asset is sold, the UCC is reduced by the amount of the proceeds from the sale. An adjustment must then also be made to the capital budgeting analysis to adjust for the present value of the CCA tax shields lost. **[LO8]**

Appendix 13B Review Problem: Capital Budgeting and Taxes

Ace Company is considering investing $70,000 in a passenger bus. The bus is expected to generate net annual cash inflows of $13,500 over an eight-year period. The bus will have a salvage value of $5,000 in eight years. The capital cost allowance is 30% and the income tax rate is 40%. Ace Company requires an after-tax return of 10% on all investments.

Required:
Compute the net present value of the investment. Should the investment be made?

Solution to Appendix 13B Review Problem

1. The net present value analysis would be

Items and Computations	Year(s)	(1) Amount	(2) Tax Effect	(1) × (2) After-Tax Cash Flows	10% Factor	Present Value of Cash Flows
Investment in passenger bus	Now	$(70,000)		$(70,000)	1.000	$(70,000)
Net annual cash receipts	1–8	13,500	1−0.40	8,100	5.335	43,214
CCA tax shield*	1–8					19,345
Salvage value of the bus	8	5,000		5,000	0.467	2,335
Net present value						$ (5,106)

$$PV = \left[\frac{Cdt}{d+k} \times \frac{1+0.5k}{1+k} \right] - \left[\frac{Sdt}{d+k} \times (1+k)^{-n} \right]$$

$$PV = \left[\frac{\$70,000 \times 0.3 \times 0.4}{0.3 + 0.10} \times \frac{1 + 0.05}{1 + 0.10} \right] - \left[\frac{\$5,000 \times 0.3 \times 0.4}{0.3 + 0.10} \times (1 + 0.10)^{-8} \right]$$

$$PV = [\$21,000 \times 0.9545] - [\$1,500 \times 0.467]$$

$$PV = \$19,345$$

2. No, the investment project should not be undertaken. It has a negative net present value when the company's cost of capital is used as the discount rate.

≡ connect™ Appendix 13B Exercises and Problems

EXERCISE 13B–1 After-Tax Costs [LO8]

Solve each of the following parts independently:

1. Stoffer Company has hired a management consulting firm to review and make recommendations concerning Stoffer's organizational structure. The consulting firm's fee will be $100,000. What will be the after-tax cost of the consulting firm's fee if Stoffer's tax rate is 30%?
2. The Green Hills Riding Club has redirected its advertising toward a different sector of the market. As a result of this change in advertising, the club's annual revenues have increased by $40,000. If the club's tax rate is 30%, what is the after-tax benefit from the increased revenues?
3. The Golden Eagles basketball team has just installed an electronic scoreboard in its playing arena at a cost of $210,000. Determine the yearly tax savings from the CCA tax shield for the next three years. Assume that the income tax rate is 30%, the CCA rate is 30%, and the cost of capital is 10%.

EXERCISE 13B–2 After-Tax Cash Flows in Net Present Value Analysis [LO8]

Draper Corporation is considering two investment projects, each of which would require a $60,000 initial investment. Cost and cash flow data concerning the two projects are given below:

	Project A	Project B
Investment in inventory scanning equipment	$60,000	
Investment in working capital		$60,000
Net annual cash inflows	$11,000	$11,000
Life of the project	10 years	10 years
CCA.	20%	

The inventory scanning equipment would have a salvage value of $6,000 in 10 years. The equipment would be depreciated over 10 years. At the end of 10 years, the investment in working capital would be released for use elsewhere. The company requires an after-tax return of 12% on all investments. The tax rate is 30%.

Required:
Compute the net present value of each investment project. (Round to the nearest whole dollar.)

EXERCISE 13B–3 Net Present Value Analysis Including Income Taxes [LO8]
Press Publishing Company hires students from the local university to collate pages on various print-ing jobs. This collating is all done by hand, at a cost of $60,000 per year. A collating machine has just come onto the market that could be used in place of the student help. The machine would cost $140,000 and have a 10-year useful life. It would require an operator at an annual cost of $18,000 and have annual maintenance costs of $7,000. New roller pads would be needed on the machine in five years at a total cost of $20,000. The salvage value of the machine in 10 years would be $40,000.

    The CCA rate is 30%. Management requires a 14% after-tax return on all equipment purchases. The company's tax rate is 30%.

Required:
1. Determine the before-tax net annual cost savings that the new collating machine will provide.
2. Using the data from (1) above and other data from the exercise, compute the collating machine's net present value. (Round all dollar amounts to the nearest whole dollar.) Would you recommend that the machine be purchased?

PROBLEM 13B–4 Basic Net Present Value Analysis Including Income Taxes [LO8]
Norris Property Management has been offered a six-year contract to provide grounds maintenance for various condominium corporations. To accept the contract, the company would have to purchase several pieces of equipment for both summer and winter grounds maintenance at a total cost of $280,000. Other data relating to the contract follow:

Net annual cash receipts (before taxes) from the contract.	$81,000
Cost of overhauling and rebuilding the mechanical equipment in four years	$33,000
Salvage value of the equipment at termination of the contract	$15,000

    If the contract was accepted, several old, fully depreciated pieces of equipment would be sold at a total price of $22,500. These funds would be used to help purchase the new equipment. For tax purposes, the company computes CCA deductions using the maximum rate of 20%. The company requires an 11% after-tax return on all equipment purchases. The tax rate is 30%.

Required:
Compute the net present value of this investment opportunity. Round all dollar amounts to the near-est whole dollar. Would you recommend that the contract be accepted?

PROBLEM: 13B–5 A Comparison of Investment Alternatives Including Income Taxes [LO8]
Kim Huang, an expert in architectural design and restoration of historic buildings, has just received a $160,000 after-tax bonus for the successful completion of a project on time and under budget. Business has been so good that she is planning to retire in 15 years, spending her time travelling, enjoying outdoor activities, and doing charitable work. Huang is considering two alternatives for investing her bonus.

    Alternative 1   Corporate bonds can be purchased that mature in 15 years and that bear interest at 10%. This interest would be paid semi-annually. (In discounting a cash flow that occurs semian-nually, the procedure is to halve the discount rate and double the number of periods. Use the same procedure for discounting the principal returned when the bonds reach maturity.)

    Alternative 2   A small discount perfume shop is available for sale at a nearby factory outlet centre. The business can be purchased from its current owner for $160,000. The following informa-tion relates to this alternative:
a. Of the purchase price, $64,000 would be for fixtures and other depreciable items. The remain-der would be for the company's working capital (inventory, accounts receivable, and cash). The fixtures and other depreciable items would have a remaining useful life of at least 15 years but would be depreciated for tax reporting purposes using a CCA of 20%. Salvage value is expected to be negligible at the end of 15 years but the working capital would be released for reinvestment elsewhere.
b. Store records indicate that sales have averaged $325,000 per year, and out-of-pocket costs have averaged $295,000 per year (before income taxes). These out-of-pocket costs include rent on the building, cost of goods sold, utilities, and wages and salaries for the sales staff and the store manager. Huang plans to entrust the day-to-day operations of the store to the manager.

c. Huang's tax rate is 40% and she wishes to use an after-tax discount rate of 10%, given the risk involved.

Required:

Advise Huang as to which alternative should be selected. Use the total-cost approach to discounted cash flow in your analysis and a discount rate of 10%. (Round all dollar amounts to the nearest whole dollar.)

PROBLEM: 13B–6 Net Present Value Analysis Including Income Taxes [LO8]

The Perth Mining Company owns the mining rights to several tracts of land on which metals have been found in the past. The amount of precious metals on some of the tracts is somewhat marginal, and the company is unsure whether it would be profitable to extract and sell the precious metals that these tracts contain. Tract 420 is one of these, and the following information about it has been gathered:

Investment in equipment needed for extraction work...............	$400,000
Working capital investment needed	$55,000
Annual cash receipts from sale of precious metals, net of related cash operating expenses (before taxes).................	$85,000
Cost of restoring land at completion of extraction work	$45,000

The natural gas in Tract 420 would be exhausted after eight years of extraction work. The equipment would have a useful life of 12 years, but it could be sold for only 20% of its original cost when extraction was completed. For tax purposes, the company would depreciate the equipment using a CCA rate of 20%. The tax rate is 30%, and the company's after-tax discount rate is 12%. The working capital would be released for use elsewhere at the completion of the project.

Required:

1. Compute the net present value of Tract 420. Round all dollar amounts to the nearest whole dollar.
2. Would you recommend that the investment project be undertaken?

Practise and learn online with Connect.

EXTERNAL REPORTING AND ANALYSIS
Chapter 14

Online Chapter 14 presents a basis for conducting financial statement analysis that will be of use to an organization's external stakeholders, such as shareholders and creditors, and to internal users, such as managers. Shareholders are concerned about future earnings and dividends; creditors are concerned about the organization's ability to repay existing or new debt. Financial statement analysis, although based on historical information, can provide useful signals about an organization's future prospects with respect to profitability and cash flow. Financial statement analysis can also highlight areas in need of managerial attention, such as inventory turnover, liquidity management, and capital structure. Where possible, an effective approach to financial statement analysis also incorporates comparative information related to industry trends and specific results for leading competitors.

Chapter 14 is available on the *Managerial Accounting*, Ninth Canadian Edition, Connect site.

Endnotes

Chapter 1

1. These three customer value propositions were defined by Michael Treacy and Fred Wiersema in "Customer Intimacy and Other Value Disciplines," *Harvard Business Review,* January/February 1993, pp. 84–93.
2. *The CICA's Guide to IFRS in Canada, 2009 Edition.* Chartered Accountants of Canada, Toronto, ON.
3. Web sites for these three groups contain background information. See **www.cga-canada.org**, **www.cica.ca**, and **www.cma-canada.org**.
4. Examples include the federal government sponsorship scandal and others involving businesses such as Enron, WorldCom, Global Crossing, Arthur Andersen, and many others. Currently, there are also class action suits outstanding against Nortel, alleging that it overstated revenues for the years 2000 and 2001.
5. James Surowiecki, "A Virtuous Cycle," *Forbes,* December 23, 2002, pp. 248–256.
6. The Web sites listed in endnote 3 for Canadian accounting associations provide details about the ethical standards of their members. Also, **www.ifac.org** presents ethical expectations for members of the International Federation of Accountants.
7. This definition of corporate governance was adapted from the 2004 report entitled *OECD Principles of Corporate Governance* published by the Organisation for Economic Co-operation and Development.
8. The insights presented in this paragraph and many of the examples in Exhibit 1–6 were drawn from Ronald W. Clement, "The Lessons from Stakeholder Theory for U.S. Business Leaders," *Business Horizons,* May/June 2005, pp. 255–264; and Terry Leap and Misty L. Loughry, "The Stakeholder-Friendly Firm," *Business Horizons*, March/April 2004, pp. 27–32.
9. The lean production literature uses the term *value stream* rather than *business process.*
10. Peter C. Brewer, "Six Sigma Helps a Company Create a Culture of Accountability," *Journal of Organizational Excellence,* Summer 2004, pp. 45–59.
11. *Enterprise systems* is a broad term that encompasses many enterprise-wide computer applications such as customer relationship management and supply chain management systems. Perhaps the most frequently mentioned type of enterprise system is an enterprise resource planning (ERP) system.
12. CanWest News Service, "Bauer Recalling 100,000 Children's Hockey Sticks after Lead Paint Discovered," *National Post,* March 19, 2010.

Chapter 2

1. J. Miller, A. DeMeyer, and J. Nakane, *Benchmarking Global Manufacturing*, Chapter 2 (Homewood, IL: Richard D. Irvin, 1992).

Chapter 3

1. Some firms prefer to make the allocation on the basis of the total cost of direct materials, direct labour, and applied manufacturing overhead in each of the accounts at the end of the period. This method is not as accurate as allocating the balance in the Manufacturing Overhead account on the basis of just the overhead applied in each of the accounts during the current period.

Chapter 5

1. Robin Cooper, "Cost Classification in Unit-Based and Activity-Based Manufacturing Cost Systems," *Journal of Cost Management,* Fall 1990, pp. 4–14.
2. Dan Swenson, "The Benefits of Activity-Based Cost Management to the Manufacturing Industry," *Journal of Management Accounting Research* 7, Fall 1995, pp. 165–180.
3. William T. Bonner, "Stormy Waters and the Canadian Coast Guard," *CMA Magazine*, February 1998, pp. 21–26; and Michael Senyshen, "ABC/M in the Federal Government," *CGA Magazine*, December 1997, p. 19.
4. Kambiz Foroohar, "Rx: Software," *Forbes*, April 7, 1997, p. 114.
5. Philip Beaulieu and Anila Lakra, "Coverage of the Criticism of Activity-Based Costing in Canadian Textbooks," *Canadian Accounting Perspectives, 4,* 2005, pp. 87–109. Provides relevant comments on the proper treatment of organization-sustaining activities and idle capacity based on earlier analysis in the literature.
6. The idea of using colours to code how easily costs can be adjusted was suggested to us at a seminar held by Boeing and by an article by Alfred King, "Green Dollars and Blue Dollars: The Paradox of

Cost Reduction," *Journal of Cost Management*, Fall 1993, pp. 44–52.

Appendix 6A

1. See calculus or statistics books for details concerning how these formulas are derived.
2. Newer versions of Microsoft Excel have a *Regression* function that will automatically calculate the intercept, slope, R^2, and other statistics for least-squares regression models without requiring the use of a separate formula for each. The regression function is available as part of the *Analysis Toolpak* add-in for Excel.

Chapter 7

1. In economics, incremental analysis is often termed *marginal analysis* because of the assumptions used in economics about the behaviour of revenues and costs. Accountants tend to use a more general term, *incremental*, so that less restrictive assumptions about the behaviour of revenues and costs can be made; for example, step-variable costs.
2. The shortcut version of the equation can be derived as follows:

   Profit = (Sales − Variable expenses) − Fixed expenses
   $$\$0 = (\$250Q - \$150Q) - \$35,000$$
   $$\$35,000 = \$100Q$$
   $$Q = \$35,000 \div \$100$$

   where Q = Number (quantity) of speakers sold.

Chapter 9

1. Stan Davis, Todd De Zoort, and Lori Kopp, "The Effect of Obedience Pressure and Perceived Responsibility on Management Accountants' Creation of Budgetary Slack," *Behavioural Research in Accounting, 18*, 2006, pp. 19–36.
2. Joseph Fisher, Sean Peffer, and Geoff Sprinkle, "Budget-Based Contracts, Budget Levels, and Group Performance," *Journal of Management Accounting Research, 15*, 2003, pp. 51–74.

3. This is a hypothetical example developed for illustrative purposes.
4. The algebraic solution is as follows, where LP = Loan principal to be repaid:
   $\$107,500 = [LP + (LP \times 0.0375)]$. Solving for LP yields $103,614, which we round to $103,500 to simplify the example.

Chapter 10

1. Soumitra Dutta and Jean-François Manzoni, *Process Reengineering, Organizational Change and Performance Improvement*, Chapter IV (New York: McGraw-Hill).
2. For further discussion, see Eliyahu M. Goldratt and Jeff Cox, *The Goal*, 2nd rev. ed. (Croton-on-Hudson, NY: North River Press, 1992).
3. Recall from Chapter 3 that using predetermined overhead application rates negates the need to track the actual quantity of variable overhead items used when assigning costs to products or services.
4. Normal cost systems are defined in Chapter 3.
5. If a company does employ monthly denominator activity levels and overhead application rates, then these would be used in the monthly fixed manufacturing overhead variance calculations.
6. Attiea Marie and Ananth Rao, "Is Standard Costing Still Relevant? Evidence from Dubai," *Management Accounting Quarterly*, Winter 2010, pp. 1–10.

Appendix 10A

7. Max Laudeman and F. W. Schaeberle, "The Cost Accounting Practices of Firms Using Standard Costs," *Cost and Management*, July–August 1985, pp. 21–25.

Chapter 11

1. Some companies classify business segments that are responsible mainly for generating revenue, such as an insurance sales office, as *revenue centres*. Other companies would consider this to be just

another type of profit centre, since costs of some kind (salaries, rent, utilities) are usually deducted from the revenues in the segment's income statement.
2. Recall that when Cumberland Beverages has 1,000 units of idle capacity, the minimum transfer price was calculated to be $14 ($8 + [($20 − $8) × 1,000/2,000]). Therefore if idle capacity is greater than 1,000 units, then the transfer price will always be less than the outside purchase price of $14 and the transfer should occur. For example if idle capacity is 1,200 units, then the transfer price would be $12.80 calculated as ($8 + [($20 − $8) × 800/2,000]).
3. The balanced scorecard concept was promoted by Robert Kaplan and David Norton. For further details, see their articles "The Balanced Scorecard—Measures That Drive Performance," *Harvard Business Review*, January/February 1992, pp. 71–79; "Using the Balanced Scorecard as a Strategic Management System," *Harvard Business Review*, January/February 1996, pp. 75–85; and "Why Does a Business Need a Balanced Scorecard?" *Journal of Cost Management*, May/June 1997, pp. 5–10; and their book *Translating Strategy into Action: The Balanced Scorecard* (Boston, MA: Harvard Business School Press, 1996).
4. In the 1960s, the French developed a concept similar to the balanced scorecard called *Tableau de Bord* or "dashboard." For details, see Michel Lebas, "Managerial Accounting in France: Overview of Past Tradition and Current Practice," *The European Accounting Review 3*:3, 1994, pp. 471–87; and Marc Epstein and Jean-François Manzoni, "The Balanced Scorecard and the Tableau de Bord: Translating Strategy into Action," *Management Accounting*, August 1997, pp. 28–36.
5. Michael E. Porter, *Competitive Strategy: Creating and Sustaining*

Superior Performance (New York, NY: Free Press, 1985).

6. Lori Calabro, "On Balance: A CFO Interview," *CFO,* February 2001, pp. 73–78.

7. Robert W. Casey, "The Changing World of the CEO," *PPM World* 24:2, 1990, p. 31.

Appendix 11A

8. Actual market shares for Deluxe and Standard video games are calculated as follows: Deluxe 16% = 12,000/75,000; Standard 4.7% = 4,000/85,000. Budgeted market shares for Deluxe and Standard video games are calculated as follows: Deluxe 14.3% = 10,000/70,000; Standard 5.6% = 5,000/90,000.

9. Because the sales quantity variance holds sales mix constant at the budgeted proportions, it can also be calculated using a weighted average contribution margin approach. The weighted average contribution margin, using the budgeted sales mix is $29 per unit: (10/15 × $36) + (5/15 × $15). The total sales quantity variance = (Actual total sales quantity − Budgeted total sales quantity) × Budgeted average contribution margin per unit. Using the data from our example: (16,000 − 15,000) × $29 = $29,000 F.

Chapter 12

1. If Cynthia has an accident while driving to Moncton or back, this might affect her insurance premium when the policy is renewed. If the expected cost of the increase in the insurance premium could be estimated, it would be a relevant cost of this particular trip, but the normal amount of the insurance premium is not relevant in any case.

2. K. Siegel-Jacobs and F. Yates, "Effects of Procedural and Outcome Accountability on Judgment Quality," *Organizational*

Behaviour and Human Decision Processes, 1996, *65*:1, pp. 7–17.

3. An alternative way of formulating the analysis is to start with the camera net loss of $(6,400) from Exhibit 12–2 and add back the non-avoidable (irrelevant) expenses of $10,400 to arrive at the relevant benefit (segment margin) of $4,000 that would be forgone if the product line was to be discontinued.

4. An alternative approach to the analysis is to add the incremental unit cost of continuing to make the shifters of $14 (see Exhibit 12–5) to the opportunity cost per unit of $7.50 ($60,000 opportunity cost ÷ 8,000 units), giving a total of $21.50. Since $21.50 is greater than the purchase price of $19 per unit, OSN Cycle should buy the shifter.

Appendix 12A

5. There are some legal restrictions on prices. Competition laws prohibit "predatory" pricing, which is generally interpreted by the courts to mean a price below average variable cost. "Price discrimination"—charging different prices to customers in the same market for the same product or service—is also prohibited by the law.

6. The variable manufacturing cost approach would exclude variable SG&A expenses from the cost base and instead include them in the numerator. Otherwise, it is the same as the total variable costing approach.

Chapter 13

1. For simplicity, we ignore inflation and taxes. The impact of income taxes on capital budgeting decisions is discussed in Appendix 13B.

2. Although depreciation itself is not a cash outflow, it does have an effect on cash outflows for income

taxes. We will take a look at this effect in when we discuss the impact of income taxes on capital budgeting in Appendix 13B.

3. The alternative with the highest net present value is not always the best choice, although it is the best choice in this case. For further discussion, see the section Preference Decisions—The Ranking of Investment Projects, later in this chapter.

4. Technically, the incremental-cost approach is misnamed, since it focuses on differential costs (that is, on both cost increases and decreases) rather than just on incremental costs. As used here, the term *incremental costs* should be interpreted broadly to include both cost increases and cost decreases.

5. Synergy occurs when the projects working together generate greater revenue than the sum of the revenues of all projects acting independently.

Appendix 13B

6. This formula assumes that a company is operating at a profit; if it is operating at a loss, the tax situation can be very complex. For simplicity, we assume in all examples, exercises, and problems that the company is operating at a profit.

7. The term *capital cost allowance (CCA) tax shield* may convey the impression that there is something underhanded about capital cost allowance deductions—that companies are getting some sort of a special tax break. However, to use the CCA deduction, a company must have already acquired a depreciable asset—which typically requires a cash outflow. Essentially, the tax regulations require companies to delay recognizing the cash outflow as an expense until CCA charges are recorded.

Photo Credits

Chapter 1, PhotoAlto/Veer; Chapter 2, Skip Nall/Getty Images; Chapter 3, Photo courtesy of IceJerseys.com; Chapter 4, Reprinted by permission of Girl Guides of Canada; Chapter 5, Andrew Simpson; Chapter 6, Digital Vision/Getty Images; Chapter 7, © Creatas/PunchStock; Chapter 8, © Tetra Images/Jupiter Images; Chapter 9, Rim Light/PhotoLink/Getty Images; Chapter 10, Steve Cole/Getty Images; Chapter 11, © CORBIS Images; Chapter 12, Bloomberg via Getty Images; Chapter 13, THE CANADIAN PRESS/Frank Gunn.

Company/Name Index

3M, 354*n*

A

AbitibiBowater, 131*n*
ABY Precision Machining, 72, 76, 78, 79
Ace Video Company, 545, 546, 546*e*, 547, 548
Acoustic Concepts, Inc., 270–278, 280, 282, 283, 285, 293
AFM Electronics, 562, 562*e*, 563, 564*e*, 605
Air Canada, 240
Airbus, 273*n*
Alcan, 129
American Institute of Certified Public Accountants, 12
Anderson, Stephen, 192*n*
Andreas STIHL, 326*n*
Apple, 566
Atlantic Superstore, 232

B

Bagranoff, Nancy A., 20*e*
Barrick Gold Corporation, 609
Bauer Hockey Corp., 21, 32
Bechtel Corporation, 71
Bell Canada Enterprises (BCE) Inc., 610
Black & Howell, 90, 91
BMW, 4, 31, 569*n*
Boeing, 273*n*
Boley Company, 316, 317, 318*e*
Bombardier Inc., 31, 71, 163, 478
Bombardier of Canada, 611*n*
Boyley Company, 316
Brentline Hospital, 241, 243
Brewer, Peter C., 20*e*
Bre-X, 15*n*
Brigham Tea Company, 631
Britvic, 20*n*

C

Canada Revenue Agency (CRA), 492
Canadian Auto Workers (CAW), 497*n*
Canadian Federation of Independent Business, 235*n*
Canadian Institute of Chartered Accountants, 12, 374*n*

Canadian National Railway (CN Rail), 4, 96*n*
Canadian Solar Inc., 269
Canadian Tire Corporation, 19, 232, 406
Cara, 71
Carver Dental Clinic, 613, 614, 614*e*
Cassalatta Inc., 475, 476e
Catalyst Paper Corporation, 403
CCM, 31
Cellmania, 566
Certified General Accountants Association of Canada, 12
Cervélo Cycles, 32, 229, 232, 404
Christie, 129
Chrysler Canada Inc., 329*n*, 604, 610
Chung, Mong-Koo, 508*n*
Cinar, 15*n*
Cisco Systems, 4
City of Burnaby, 3
Classic Brass, 175, 175*e*, 176, 177, 178*e*, 179, 181, 181*e*, 182, 184, 185, 186, 187, 188, 211, 215
CMA Canada, 12
CMA Ontario, 13
Coca-Cola Company, 71, 130*n*
Community Business Development Corporation, 7
Costco, 19
Crest, 480
Cumberland Beverages, 486, 487, 488, 489, 490, 491

D

Dare Foods Limited, 128
Dartmouth College, 509
Dell Computer Corporation, 4
Deming, W. Edwards, 513
Direct Energy Business Services, 628*n*
Domtar, 498
Double Diamond Skis, 133, 134*e*, 135, 136*e*, 137, 138, 139, 139*e*, 140, 140*e*, 155, 156*e*, 157, 158*e*
Dover Industries, 129
Drabinsky, Garth, 15*n*
DuPont, 494

E

E.I. du Pont de Nemours and Company, 494
Emerald Isle Knitters Ltd., 319, 320*e*, 319
Englund Company, 668
Enron, 15
Epicor, 96

F

Ford Canada, 232, 329*n*, 604, 611*n*
Ford Motor Company Limited, 497, 497*n*
Frito-Lay, 130, 478
Future Shop, 613

G

GATT, 492
General Electric, 20, 129, 354*n*
General Motors (GM), 329*n*, 484, 554
General Motors (GM) Canada, 478, 484
George, Rick, 633*n*
Girl Guides of Canada, 128
Glendale School District, 620, 621
Goodtime Fun Centres Inc., 629
Google, 566
Gottlieb, Myron, 15*n*
Graf Canada, 404
Graham Manufacturing, 36, 37, 38, 39, 39*e*
Grand River Hospital, 240
Green Front Sakai, 505*n*

H

Hallmark, 71
Hanlon, George, 407, 408, 409, 411, 416, 418, 420, 426, 428
Harper Company, 611, 612
Harrigan Freeze Inc., 356, 358*e*, 360, 361, 362, 363, 365, 367, 368, 369, 370, 370*e*, 371, 371*e*, 372*e*, 373*e*
Harris Ferry Company, 616, 617
Harvey's, 406
Heirloom Pewter Company, 407–411, 414–418, 420–423, 425–428, 429*e*, 430*e*, 432
Hewitt Associates, 17*n*

Hewlett-Packard, 129
Hollinger, 15*n*
Holt Corporation, 480
Honda, 329*n*
Hospital for Sick Children, 171
H&R Block, 236
Hyundai, 508*n*

I
IBM, 314
IceJerseys.com, 69
Imperial Oil, 129, 485
Industry Canada, 34*n*
Institute of Management Accountants, 12, 353*n*
Insurance Institute for Highway Safety, 508*n*
International Organization for Standardization (ISO), 513
Irving Shipbuilding, 32
Ittner, Christopher D., 504*n*

J
J.D. Power and Associates, 508*n*
J.M. Schneider Inc., 71
Job Bound, 237*n*

K
Kaplan, Robert, 192*n,* 504
Kimberly-Clark, 129
KPMG LLG, 17*n*

L
Larcker, David F., 504*n*
Levi Strauss, 71
Livent, 15*n*
Loblaws Companies Limited, 236, 475, 498
Luckey, Elizabeth, 434*n*

M
MacInnis Company, 626
Magna International Inc., 31, 569*n*
Majestic Ocean Kayaking, 233*n*
Manulife Insurance Company, 163
Maple Leaf Foods Inc., 71
Marconi, 191*n*
Maytag, 129
McCain Foods, 610
MDG Computers Canada, 404
MEGA Brands, 31
Metro Coffee, Inc., 3, 4, 5, 9, 10, 11, 11*e*
Michelin, 163
Midwest Farms Limited, 631
Moosehead Breweries, 46
Motorola, 20, 354*n*

N
NAFTA (North America Free Trade Agreement), 492
National Hockey League (NHL), 349
New Brunswick Power, 232
Nguyen, Kinh, 241
NHLHockeyJerseys.com, 69
Nippon Electric Company (NEC), 433
Norton, David, 504
Nova Bus Corporation, 44

O
Office Depot, 95
Open Standards Benchmarking Collabrative, 164
Oracle, 96
Ordre des comptables agréés, 12
OSN Cycles, 566, 567, 567*e,* 568, 569, 574

P
Panasonic, 31, 129
Parker Company, 625
Paron, Mario, 17*n*
PepsiCo, 478
Petro-Canada, 3, 71, 485
Pizza Hut, 240
Pizza Place, 486, 487, 488, 489, 490, 491
Public Sector Accounting Board (PSAB), 374*n*
Public Works and Government Services Canada, 97
Purolator Courier, 404

Q
Quaker Oats, 498
Quality Auto Shop, 603
Queen Elizabeth II (QEII) Hospital, 163, 164

R
Rand Company, 80, 81, 82, 83, 84, 85, 86, 87*e,* 88*e,* 89, 89*e,* 90, 91, 92, 93
Research in Motion (RIM), 4, 15, 40*n,* 236, 290, 404, 566
Reston Bookstore, 36, 37, 38, 38*e*
RIM (Research in Motion), 4, 15, 40*n,* 236, 290, 404, 566
Rogers Communications Inc., 544
Rogers Video, 45
Roots, 46
Roper Company, 599, 600, 600*e,* 601, 601*e,* 602
Royal Bank of Canada, 16

S
SABIAN Cymbals, 4
SAP AG, 96*n*
sap.com, 96*n*

Saskatchewan Clinic, 45
Saskatoon Ltd., 667
Saucony, 31
Scheidt, Marsha, 434*n*
Shank, John K., 509
Sharp Corporation, 505*n,* 604
Shaw Communications Inc., 544
Shell, 485
SIROPOLIS, 356*e*
Sobeys, 236, 475
Sony, 31, 129
Sport BUFF, 69
St. Mary's Cement, 71
St. Mary's University, 163
St. Thomas Wool Cooperative, 571, 571*e,* 572
Statistics Canada, 34*n*
Stern, Stewart & Co., 497
STIHL Inc., 326*n*
Suncor Energy Inc., 632*n*
Surowiecki, James, 12
Swinyard Company, 615

T
Tata Motors, 416*n*
Tesco, 20*n*
The Bay, 48
The Body Shop, 502
The Keg Steakhouse & Bar, 4
Thibadoux, Greg, 434*n*
Tim Hortons, 16, 232, 610
Toyota Motor Corporation, 18, 129, 329*n,* 604
TSN, 71
Turbo Crafters, 90, 91

U
Ultra Electronics Maritime Systems, 7*n*
Unilever Canada, 16
United Way, 3
University of Waterloo, 3

V
Val-Tek Company, 618
Ventura Company, 511, 512, 512*e*

W
Walmart, 4
Westjet, 4, 404
White Grizzly Adventures, 241*n,* 611*n*

X
Xi Agricultural Machine Company (XAMC), 176*n*

Y
Yukon Marine Services Corporation, 498, 499

Subject Index

A

ABC *see* activity-based costing (ABC)

absorption costing
  choice of, 325–329
  cost-plus pricing, 599
  and CVP analysis, 326–327
  defined, 70, 315
  external reports, 327
  fixed manufacturing overhead cost
      deferred in inventory, 317
  fixed manufacturing overhead
      cost released from inventory,
      322–323
  income effects, 322
  income statement, 317
  lean production, 329
  lean production, impact of, 329
  operating income, and production
      changes, 323–325,
      323–324e, 325e
  operating income, drivers of, 323
  overview, 315–317
  price quotation sheet, 599e
  problems with, 601
  reconciliation of, operating income
      data, 322e, 325e
  segment reporting *see* segment
      reporting
  standard cost card, 409
  standard cost record, 423e
  strategic uses of, 329
  unethical use of, 328
  unit cost computations, 316–317
  vs. variable costing, 316e
  vs. variable costing, extended
      comparison, 319–325,
      320–321e
  vs. variable costing, income
      comparison, 317–319, 318e
accountability, 374
account analysis, 240
accounting designations, 12
accounting rate of return, 630
  see also simple rate of return method
accrual concept, 34
action analysis report
  activity rates, 211

defined, 188
overhead costs, assignment of,
    211–214
activity, 173
activity base, 231–232
activity-based budgeting, 375
activity-based costing (ABC)
  ABC data, view of, 214–215
  action analysis report, 188,
      211–214
  activity, 173, 176–177
  activity cost pool, 173, 176–177,
      178–180, 180e
  activity measure, 173, 176–177
  activity rates, 180–182, 181e
  allocation bases, 173–174
  cost matrices, 213e
  cost objects, 182–184
  cost pools, 173–174, 176–177
  costs of idle capacity, 174
  customer margins, 184–186, 186e
  defined, 79, 172
  design of, 174–176
  duration driver, 173
  ease of adjustment codes, 214, 214e
  and external reports, 189–190
  first-stage allocation, 179, 180e
  implementation process, 176–186
  interpretation of results, 215
  limitations of, 191–193
  management reports, 184–185
  manufacturing costs, 173
  mechanics of, 178–182
  model, 175e, 181e
  modified form, for external reports,
      221–223
  non-manufacturing costs, 172
  overhead cost pools, 172
  overhead costs, 178–179, 178e,
      182–184, 183e, 184e,
      211–213
  process improvements, 186
  product margins, 184–186, 185e,
      187–188, 187e
  and relevant costs, 562
  second-stage allocation, 182–184
  traceable fixed costs, 480

vs. traditional product costs,
    186–191, 189e
transaction driver, 173
treatment of costs, 172–177
two-stage cost allocation
    process, 178e
activity-based management
    (ABM), 186
activity cost pool, 173, 176–177,
    178–180, 180e
activity measure, 173, 176–177
activity rates, 180–182, 181e
adjustment codes, ease of, 214, 214e
administrative costs, 33
administrative expense, 316–317
after-tax analysis, 284–285
after-tax benefit, 665
after-tax cost, 664–665, 664e
allocated fixed costs, 563–565
allocation base, 76, 78–79, 173–174
allocation of accounts, 91–92
allocation of costs *see* cost allocation
annuity
  annuity due, 653–654, 654e, 656
  annuity in advance, 656
  deferred annuities, 655
  defined, 652
  future value of, 655–657
  present value of, 652–653, 652e
annuity due, 653–654, 654e, 656
  see also future value
annuity in advance, 656
  see also future value
appraisal costs, 509–510
avoidable cost, 556

B

backflush costing, 94
balanced scorecard
  cause-and-effect linkages, 503–504
  characteristics of, 501–503,
      501e, 502e
  and company's strategy, 503–504,
      503e
  defined, 500
  examples of performance measures,
      501–503, 502e

balanced scorecard—*Cont.*
  feedback, advantages of, 504
  final observations, 507
  flowchart illustration, 501*e*
  improvement, emphasis on,
      501–502, 501*e*
  internal business process
      performance measures,
      501–503, 501*e,* 502e,
      505–507
  strategy and, 500–501
  test of theories, 504
  tying compensation to, 504
balance forward carried, 92–93
balance sheet
  budgeted balance sheet, 367–368
  described, 35–37
bar codes, 75, 95–96
basic equation for inventory
      accounts, 37
batch-level activities, 174
benchmarking, 186
beyond budgeting (BB) approach, 373
bill of materials, 72, 408
bottlenecks, 351, 575, 576
brand loyalty, 501
break-even analysis
  absorption costing, 327
  break-even computations, 281–283
  contribution margin (CM) method,
      282–283
  described, 281–283
  equation method, 281–282
  multiple-product break-even analysis,
      291–292, 291*e*, 292*e*
  and sales mix, 291–292
  variable expense ratio, 282
break-even point, 272
budget
  benefits of, 370
  budgeted balance sheet, 367–368
  budgeted income statement,
      366–367
  budget period, choice of, 351
  cash budget, 355, 364–366
  continuous budget, 351
  control, 350
  defined, 350
  direct labour budget, 360–361
  direct materials purchases budget,
      359–360
  dual role, 350
  ending finished goods inventory
      budget, 362–363
  expenditure basis budget, 374
  flexible budget, 369–370
  flexible budget variance, 371
  government budgets, 374

  as management tool, 368–369
  and managerial compensation, 354
  manufacturing overhead budget,
      361–362
  margin of safety, 285
  master budget, 350, 355–369, 356*e*
  one-year operating budget, 351
  participative budget, 352–353, 352*e*
  perpetual budget, 351
  planning, 350
  production budget, 357–358
  program basis budget, 374
  sales budget, 355, 357
  sales forecast, 355–356
  sales volume variance, 372
  selling and administrative expense
      budget, 363–364
  vs. standards, 410
  static budget, 369
  static budget variance, 371–372
  stretch budget, 354
  zero-base budget, 355
budgetary control, 350
budgetary slack, 352
budget committee, 353
budgeting
  activity-based budgeting, 375
  advantages of, 350–351
  basic framework, 350–355
  behavioural factors, 353–354
  beyond budgeting (BB)
      approach, 373
  capital budgeting *see* capital
      budgeting
  and hyperinflation, 375
  international aspects, 375
  key criticism, 368*n*
  not-for-profit entities, 374
  responsibility accounting, 351
budgets
  defined, 4
budget variance, 425
business plan
  defined, 6–7, 7*e*
business plan report, 7
business process, 17
business risks
  identification and control of, 22, 22*e*
business segments, 484, 485*e*

C
CA designation, 12
Calgary, AB, 632
Canada, 97, 434
capacity
  idle capacity, 488–489
  idle capacity, costs of, 174
  practical capacity, 432

  and predetermined overhead
      rate, 122–123
  theoretical capacity, 432
  unused capacity, cost of, 122–123
capacity analysis, 428–433
capacity costs
  see also fixed cost
capital budgeting
  approaches, 627–630
  behavioural considerations, 632
  cash flows, emphasis on, 612–613
  categories of decisions, 610
  cost of capital, 615, 621
  cost-reduction decisions, 610
  defined, 610
  discounted cash flows, 611–619,
      619–622, 620*e*
  equipment replacement
      decisions, 610
  equipment selection decisions, 610
  expansion decisions, 610
  income taxes, 664–670
  internal rate of return method,
      619–622, 620*e*
  lease or buy decisions, 610
  least-cost decisions, 618, 619*e*
  net present value method, 611–619
  and non-profit organizations, 664
  payback method, 627
  planning investments, 610–611
  post-audit of investment
      projects, 626
  preference decisions, 610
  real options, 622
  screening decisions, 610, 621, 621*e*
  screening tool, 621, 621*e*
  simple rate of return method,
      630–631
  tax adjustments, 666*e*
  typical capital budgeting
      decisions, 610
  uncertain cash flows, 623–624
capital cost allowance (CCA), 665
  see also depreciation
  depreciation, instead of, 666–668
capital cost allowance (CCA) tax
      shield, 665–666, 665*e,* 667
capital-intensive production
      system, 289
cash budget, 355, 364–366
cash flows
  in capital budgeting decisions,
      612–613
  cash inflows, 613, 614*e*
  cash outflows, 612–613
  discounted cash flows, 611–619
  salvage value, 620
  series of cash flows, 652–653

uncertain cash flows, 623–624
uneven, 630, 630*e*
cash inflows, 613, 614*e*
cash outflows, 612–613
cause-and-effect linkages, 503–504
cell, 19
certified management accountants
  (CMAs), 2
CGA designation, 12
chain of command, 10
chief executive officer (CEO), 10
chief financial officer (CFO), 11
CICA Handbook (Canadian Institute
  of Chartered Accountants),
  327, 482
classification of costs *see* cost
  classifications
clearing account, 83–84
CMA designation, 12
code of ethics, 12–15, 14*e*
committed fixed costs, 236, 238
common cost, 46
  see also joint product costs
common fixed costs, 478–479, 480–481
competency, 13
compound interest, 650, 652, 657
  see also present value
comprehensive performance
  report, 373*e*
computer technology *see* technology
confidentiality, 13
conformance, quality of, 508, 511*e*
constrained resource, 573–576
constraint
  defined, 573–574
  management of, 575–576
  multiple constraints, problem
    with, 576
continuous budget, 351
contract staff, 237
contribution approach, 247–248, 248*e*,
  327–329
contribution income statement,
  247–248, 248*e*
contribution margin (CM), 247–248,
  271–272, 477–478, 574–575
  importance of, 280–281
contribution margin (CM) approach,
  283–284
contribution margin (CM) method,
  282–283
contribution margin (CM) ratio,
  275–276
control
  approaches, 474
  and budgets, 350
  decentralization, 10, 474–475
  defined, 5, 350

evaluation of, based on standard
    costs, 433–434
  feedback, 5
  financial performance reports, 474
  negative connotations, 404
  profitability analysis, 544–548
  quality costs, 507–514
  responsibility centre, 484–485, 485*e*
  and standard costs, 405
  statistical control chart, 431*e*
  statistical process control, 509
control cycle, 5–6, 6*e*
controller, 5, 11–12, 430
controlling, 3, 5
conversion cost, 32, 135
corporate governance, 13–15
corporate social responsibility
    (CSR), 16, 16*e*
cost
  administrative costs, 33
  after-tax cost, 664–665, 664*e*
  appraisal costs, 509–510
  avoidable cost, 556
  committed fixed costs, 236
  common cost, 46
  computation and application of,
    137–140
  conversion cost, 32, 135
  cost flows *see* cost flows
  cost of capital, 615, 621
  cost of goods manufactured, 39,
    39*e*, 85–89
  cost of goods sold, 37, 38, 86
  cost of unused capacity, 122–123
  curvilinear cost, 234, 234*e*
  decremental costs, 47
  departmental costs, 130
  different costs for different
    purposes, 556
  differential cost, 46–47,
    558–560, 559*e*
  direct cost, 46
  direct labour cost, 73–75
  direct materials cost, 72–73
  discretionary fixed costs, 236, 238
  distribution costs, 423
  downstream costs, 482
  external failure costs, 510
  fixed cost *see* fixed cost
  future costs, 560
  gross cost, 493
  health care costs, 434–435
  of idle capacity, 174
  incremental cost, 47, 555, 569–570
  indirect cost, 46
  inspection costs, 509
  internal failure costs, 510
  inventoriable costs, 35, 42

labour costs, 32–33
manufacturing costs, 31–32, 39
manufacturing overhead *see*
    manufacturing overhead
marginal cost, 47
marketing costs, 33, 548–550
mixed costs *see* mixed costs
net book value, 493
non-manufacturing costs, 33–34,
    84–85, 172, 178–179, 178*e*
omission of, 482
opportunity cost, 48, 487, 489, 490
order-filling, 33, 548
order-getting, 33, 548
out-of-pocket costs, 615–616
overapplied overhead cost, 427–428
overhead costs *see* overhead costs
per equivalent unit, 137
period costs, 34–35
prevention costs, 508–509
prime cost, 32
product costs *see* product costs
quality costs, 507–514
vs. quantity, 430
relevant costs *see* relevant costs
selling costs, 33
standard costs *see* standard costs
step-variable costs, 232–233, 233*e*,
    238–239
sunk cost, 48, 560
terms, summary of, 36*e*
total manufacturing cost, 40–41
traceable fixed costs, 479–481
  as transfer price, 490
transferred-in costs, 131
true variable costs, 232–233,
    232*e*, 233*e*
underapplied overhead cost,
    427–428
unit costs, 79
upstream costs, 482
variable cost *see* variable cost
cost allocation
  allocation base, 76, 78–79, 164
  direct method, 164, 165*e*
  first-stage allocation, 179, 180*e*
  reciprocal method, 166
  second-stage allocation, 182–184
  service departments, 163
  step-down method, 165–166,
    165*e*, 166*e*
cost analysis *see* cost estimation
cost assignment
  hindrances to, 482–484
cost behaviour
  committed fixed costs, 236, 238
  contribution approach,
    247–248, 248*e*

financial statements—*Cont.*
   income statements *see* income
      statements
   manufacturing companies, 35–40
finished goods, 18, 36
first-stage allocation, 179, 180*e*
fixed cost
   allocated fixed costs, 563–565
   committed fixed costs, 236
   common fixed costs, 478–479
   defined, 45
   described, 44*e*, 45, 46*e*,
      234–235, 235*e*
   discretionary fixed costs, 236
   fixed manufacturing overhead cost
      deferred in inventory, 317
   fixed manufacturing overhead cost
      released from inventory,
      322–323
   illustration, 235*e*
   importance of, 478
   labour costs, 237
   mixed cost *see* mixed costs
   reclassification of traceable fixed
      cost, 481*e*
   relevant range, and, 238–239, 238*e*
   and sales price and sales volume,
      change in, 278–279
   and sales volume, change in, 277–278
   traceable fixed costs, 478, 479–480
   trend toward fixed costs, 236–237
   types of, 235–237
   vs. variable cost, 237
   and variable costs and sales volume,
      change in, 279
fixed manufacturing overhead cost
      deferred in inventory, 317
fixed manufacturing overhead cost
      released from inventory,
      322–323
fixed manufacturing overhead
      variances, 468
fixed overhead
   budget variance, 425, 430*e*
   cautions, in analysis, 427
   overhead application, 424–428,
      425*e*, 427*e*
   and overhead rates, 421–423
   volume variance, 425–426
fixed overhead variances, 424–428,
      425*e*, 427*e*
flexibility in management, 474
flexible budget
   vs. beyond budgeting (BB)
      approach, 373
   defined, 369
   described, 369–370
   flexible budget variance, 371

income statement, 370*e*
   and overhead rates, 422–423, 422*e*
   performance evaluation, 370–373
   performance report, 371*e*
   schedule, 422*e*
   standard cost system, 411
flexible budget variance, 371
flexible manufacturing system
      (FMS), 141
flow of costs *see* cost flows
focus, 501
foreign currency exchange rates, 375
foreseeable risks, 22
Fort McMurray, AB, 632
fraud, 430
full costing, 70
   see also absorption costing
future costs, 560
future value, 650–652, 651*e*, 655–657

G
GATT, 492
general ledger
   direct labour variances, 468
   direct materials variances, 467–468
   fixed manufacturing overhead
      variances, 468
   variable overhead variances, 468
   variances, recording, 467–468
generally accepted accounting principles
      (GAAP), 9, 190, 482
general model of product cost flows,
      93, 94*e*
Germany, 97, 237
global perspective *see* international
      perspective
government budgets, 374
graphic analysis, 426–427, 427*e*
gross cost, 493

H
health care costs, 434–435
highest acceptable transfer price, 487
high-low method, 244–247, 246*e*
HTML (Hypertext Markup Language), 95
hurdle rate, 621
   see also cost of capital
hyperinflation, 375

I
ideal standards, 406–407
identification of risks, 21–22, 22*e*
idle capacity, 174, 488–489
income data, extended comparison,
      319–325
income statements, 89*e*
   absorption costing approach, 317
   basic equation for inventory
      accounts, 37

budgeted income statement,
      366–367
comparative, 38*e*, 563, 564*e*
contribution approach,
      247–248, 248*e*
cost of goods sold in a
      manufacturing company, 38
cost of goods sold in a
      merchandising company, 38
described, 37–39, 38*e*
example, 175*e*
flexible budget, 370*e*
and ROI analysis, 600*e*, 601*e*
segment reporting, 475–477, 476*e*
variable costing approach, 317
Income Tax Act, 492
income taxes
   after-tax benefit, 665
   after-tax cost, 664–665, 664*e*
   and budgets, 368, 369
   in capital budgeting decisions,
      664–670, 669*e*
   capital cost allowance (CCA) tax
      shield, 665–666,
      665*e*, 667
   and external reporting, 327
   taxable cash receipt, 665
   and transfer prices, 492
   undepreciated capital cost
      (UCC), 667
incremental analysis, 278
incremental cost, 47, 555, 569–570
incremental-cost approach,
      617–618, 618*e*
independent variable, 242
indifference analysis, 289–290
indirect cost, 46
indirect labour, 32, 73
indirect manufacturing cost, 32
indirect materials, 32, 80–81
inflation rates, 375
informal relationships, 10
information technology, 95–96
input cost, 405
in-sourced, 568
inspection costs, 509
inspection time, 505
integrity, 13
interdepartmental services, 163
interest, 649–650
intermediate market, 490–491
internal business process performance
   delivery cycle time, 505, 506*e*
   manufacturing cycle efficiency
      (MCE), 505
   quality costs, 507–514
   throughput time, 505, 506*e*
internal failure costs, 510

internal rate of return method,
    619–622, 620e, 624
  vs. net present value method,
    621–622
*International Accounting Standard 2,
    Inventories,* 327
*International Financial Reporting
    Standards (IFRS),* 9
*International Financial Reporting
    Standards (IFRS) 8 Operating
    Segments,* 482
international job costing, 96–97
international perspective
  multinational company *see*
    multinational company
    (MNC)
  quality, 513–514
  standard costs, international uses
    of, 433
  transfer pricing, 491–492
*Interpretation Bulletin IT473R,
    Inventory Valuation,* 327
inventoriable costs, 35, 42
  see also product costs
inventory
  ending finished goods inventory
    budget, 362–363
  finished goods, 18, 36
  fixed manufacturing overhead cost
    deferred in inventory, 317
  fixed manufacturing overhead
    cost released from inventory,
    322–323
  merchandise purchases budget, 359
  raw materials, 18, 31
  work in process, 18, 36
inventory accounts, 37
inventory flow, 39e
investment centre
  defined, 484, 485e
  evaluation of performance, 492–497
  residual income, 497–500
  return on investment (ROI), 492–497
investment projects, post-audit, 626
ISO 9000 standards, 513–514
ISO 14000 standards, 514
ISO 26000 standards, 514
ISO 31000 standards, 514
isolation of variances, 414

J
Japan, 433, 505, 513
job cost sheet, 73, 74e, 77e
job-order costing system
  clearing account, 83–84
  cost flows, 71–72, 80–82, 80e, 82e
  cost of goods manufactured, 85–89
  defined, 71–72

direct labour cost, measurement
    of, 73–76
direct materials, issue of, 81
direct materials cost, measuring, 72
flow of documents, 79e
indirect materials, purchase and
    issue of, 80–81
information technology, use
    of, 95–96
international job costing, 96–97
job cost sheet, 73, 74e, 77e
labour cost, 81
manufacturing overhead,
    application, 82–84
manufacturing overhead
    costs, 81–82
non-manufacturing costs, 84–85
overhead application, 76–79,
    82–85
overhead application complications,
    89–95
overview, 72–76
  vs. process costing, 129–130, 130e
joint product costs, 571, 571e
joint products, 571, 571e
just-in-time (JIT) production, 19, 509

K
knowledge workers, 237

L
labour cost flows, 81–82, 82e
labour costs, 81, 133
  classification of, 32–33
  cost flows, 81–82, 82e
  direct labour budget, 360–361
  as fixed cost, 237
  job-order costing, 71–72, 80–82,
    80e, 82e
  overtime premium, 33
  process costing, 131–132, 132e, 133
  standard hours per unit, 409
  standard rate per hour, 408
  time component, 602–603
  as variable cost, 237
labour efficiency variance,
    417–418, 465
labour-intensive production (LIP)
    system, 289
labour rate variance, 411–412
lean production, 18, 329
lean thinking model, 18–19, 19e
lease or buy decisions, 610
least-cost decisions, 618, 619e
least-squares regression method,
    262–264, 263e
linear cost behaviour, 243
linearity assumption, 234
linear programming, 576

line positions, 11
lowest acceptable transfer price, 487

M
machine-hours (MH), 76
make or buy aid, 568
make or buy decision, 565–567, 567e
management
  activity-based management
    (ABM), 186
  flexibility in management, 474
  planning and control cycle, 5–6, 6e
  reports, 184–185
management accountants
  professional ethics, 12–15
  professional management
    accountants, 12
  role in organization, 10–12, 11e
management accounting guidelines, 12
management accounting practices, 12
management by exception, 405, 430
management performance
    evaluation, 327
managerial accounting
  defined, 3
  vs. financial accounting, 8–10, 8e
  future emphasis, 8–9
  and generally accepted accounting
    principles (GAAP), 9
  information needs of managers, 6
  non-mandatory nature of, 10
  and precision, 9
  relevance of data, 9
  segments of an organization, 9
managers
  and balanced scorecard, 504
  choice of costing method, impact
    on, 325–326
  compensation, and budget, 354
  and control cycle, 5–6, 6e
  controlling, 3, 5
  directing and motivating, 3, 5
  motivation, 491, 492, 498
  need for managerial accounting
    information, 3–7
  performance incentives, 490
  planning, 3, 5–6, 6e
  purchasing managers, 414
  results of activities, 5
  suboptimization, 486, 491
manufacturing cell, 19
manufacturing companies
  balance sheet, 35–37
  categories of, 31
  cost flows, 37–39, 39e, 41e, 42e,
    42–43
  financial statements, 35–40
  income statements, 37–39, 38e

manufacturing companies—*Cont.*
  production budget, 357–358
  standard cost systems, 406
manufacturing costs
  activity-based costing (ABC), 173
  direct labour, 32
  direct materials, 31
  indirect materials, 32
  labour costs, classifications
    of, 32–33
  manufacturing overhead, 32
manufacturing cycle efficiency
  (MCE), 505
manufacturing cycle time, 505, 506*e*
manufacturing overhead
  activity-based costing (ABC),
    178–179, 178*e*
  allocation base, 76, 78–79
  application of, 82–85
  budget, 361–362
  computation of unit costs, 79
  cost flow, in job-order costing,
    71–72, 80–82
  defined, 32
  denominator activity, 422
  disposition of under- or overapplied
    balances, 91–93
  document flows, summary of, 79, 79*e*
  fixed overhead, 421–428
  general model of product cost flows,
    93, 94*e*
  on job cost sheet, 73, 74*e*, 77*e*
  multiple predetermined overhead
    rates, 94
  vs. non-manufacturing costs, 84–85
  normal cost system, 78
  overapplied overhead, 89–91
  overapplied overhead cost, 427–428
  overhead application, 76–79, 89–95
  overhead application complications,
    89–95
  overhead cost pools, 172
  overhead performance reporting,
    428–433, 428*e*, 430*e*
  overhead rate, 421–423
  overhead spending variance, 411
  plantwide overhead rate, 94
  predetermined overhead rate, 76–79,
    82–84, 122–123, 421–423
  process costing, 131–133
  summary of overhead concepts, 93*e*
  underapplied overhead, 91–93
  underapplied overhead cost,
    427–428
  variable manufacturing overhead
    standards, 409
  variable manufacturing overhead
    variances, 418–421, 468

variable overhead efficiency
    variance, 419–421
variable overhead spending
    variance, 411, 419–420
  variations from the general model, 94
manufacturing overhead budget,
    361–362
manufacturing overhead costs,
    81–82
margin, 494
marginal cost, 47
marginal costing, 315
  see also variable costing
marginal revenue, 47
margin of safety, 285
marketing expenses, 33, 548–550
market price, 490–491
market share variance, 546–547
market volume variance, 546
markup, 599
markup percentage, 600–601
master budget
  budgeted balance sheet, 367–368
  budgeted income statement,
    366–367
  cash budget, 365, 364–366
  defined, 350
  direct labour budget, 360–361
  direct materials purchases budget,
    359–360
  ending finished goods inventory
    budget, 362–363
  interrelationships, 356*e*
  inventory purchases, 359
  as management tool, 368–369
  manufacturing company, 359
  manufacturing overhead budget,
    361–362
  merchandising companies, 359
  overview, 355–369, 356*e*
  preparation of, 356–357
  production budget, 357–358
  sales budget, 355, 357
  sales forecast, 355–356
  selling and administrative expense
    budget, 363–364
matching principle, 34
materials
  bill of materials, 72, 408
  cost-plus pricing, 603
  costs *see* materials costs
  direct materials *see* direct materials
  indirect materials, 32
  pricing, 603, 604*e*
  purchase and issue of, 80–81
  raw materials *see* raw materials
  variances *see* materials variances
materials component, 603

materials costs
    cost flows, 131–132, 132*e*
    cost-plus pricing, 603
    process costing, 131–132, 132*e*
materials loading charge, 603
materials price variance, 411,
    413–414
materials quantity variance, 415
materials requisition form,
    72, 73*e*
materials variances
    analysis of, 462–465
    direct materials variances, 411–415,
      467–468
    materials price variance, 411,
      413–414
    materials quantity variance, 415
    mix variance, 462
    variance analysis, 462*e*
    yield variance, 462
merchandise purchases budget, 359
merchandising company, 359
Microsoft Excel, 657
missions, 13
mixed costs
    account analysis, 240
    analysis of, 240–247
    as cost behaviour, 239–240, 239*e*
    defined, 45, 239–240
    engineering approach, 240–241
    equation, 240
    high-low method, 244–247, 246*e*
    illustration, 239*e*
    least-squares regression method,
      262–264, 263*e*
    multiple regression, 265
    scattergram method of cost analysis,
      241–243, 242*e*, 244*e*,
      245*e*, 264*e*
mix variance, 462
motivation
    and directing, 3, 5
    of managers, 491, 492, 498
    and residual income, 498–499
move time, 505
multinational company (MNC)
    see also international perspective
    budgeting, 375
    foreign currency exchange
      rates, 375
    hyperinflation, 375
    transfer pricing, 491–492
multiple constraints, 576
multiple predetermined overhead
    rates, 94
multiple-product break-even analysis,
    291–292, 291*e*, 292*e*
multiple regression, 265

N

NAFTA, 492
negotiated transfer price, 486
net book value, 493
net present value, 611
net present value method
    assumptions, simplified, 614
    cash flows, emphasis on, 612–613
    cost of capital, 615, 621
    discounted cash flows, 611–619
    discount rate, choice of, 615
    extended example, 615–616, 616e
    illustration of, 611–612, 612e
    incremental-cost approach,
        617–618, 618e
    vs. internal rate of return methods,
        621–622
    least-cost decisions, 618, 619e
    positive net present value, 615
    preference decisions, 624
    recovery of original investment,
        613–614, 614e
    total-cost approach, 616–617, 617e
niche, 501
non-government organizations
    (NGOs), 16
non-manufacturing costs
    activity-based costing (ABC), 172,
        178–179, 178e
    described, 33–34, 84–85
    job-order costing, 84–85
    vs. manufacturing overhead, 85
non-profit organizations *see* not-for-
    profit (NFP) entities
non-value-added activities, 21,
    505, 506e
normal cost system, 78
not-for-profit (NFP) entities
    accountability, 374
    budgeting, 374
    expenditure basis budget, 374
    program basis budget, 374
    standard cost systems, 406

O

objectivity, 13
Olympics 2010 (Vancouver), 48n
one-year operating budget, 351
Open Standards Benchmarking
    Collaborative, 164n
operating assets, 493
operating departments, 164, 165
operating income
    changes in production, 323–325,
        323–324e, 325e
    defined, 492–493
operating leverage, 287–288
operational excellence, 4

operation costing, 140–141
opportunity cost, 48, 487, 489, 490,
    567–568
order-filling costs, 33, 548
order-getting costs, 33, 548
ordinary annuity, 652e, 654e, 655, 656
organizational chart, 10, 11e
organizational structure
    controller, 11–12
    decentralization, 10, 474–475, 491
    described, 10–12
    line positions, 11
    organizational chart, 10, 11e
    staff positions, 11
organization-sustaining activities, 174
original investment, 613–614
out-of-control process, 509
out-of-pocket costs, 615–616
outside supplier, 489
outsourcing arrangements, 568
overapplied overhead, 89–91
overapplied overhead cost, 427–428
overhead application
    allocation base, choice of, 78–79
    clearing account, 83–84
    complications of, 89–95
    defined, 76
    disposition of under- or overapplied
        balance, 91–93
    document flows, 79, 79e
    fixed overhead variances, 424–428,
        425e, 427e
    flow of costs, 83e
    general model of product cost
        flows, 93, 94e
    multiple predetermined overhead
        rates, 94
    non-manufacturing costs, 84–85
    overapplied overhead, 89–91
    predetermined overhead rate, 76–79,
        82–84, 122–123
    standard cost system, 424–425, 424e
    summary of, 93e
    underapplied overhead, 89–91
    unit costs, computation of, 79
    variations from general model, 94
overhead cost pools, 172
overhead costs
    activity-based costing (ABC),
        178–179, 178e, 182–184,
        183e, 184e
    allocation base, choice of, 78–79
    assignment of, 211–213
    control of, 405
    cost flows, 133
    manufacturing overhead *see*
        manufacturing overhead
    in normal cost system, 424e

overhead efficiency variance,
    419–421
process costing, 133
in standard cost system, 424–425,
    424e
overhead performance reporting,
    428–433, 429e, 430e
overhead rates
    computation of, 423
    denominator activity, 422
    and fixed overhead analysis,
        421–423
    and flexible budgets, 422–423, 422e
overhead spending variance, 411,
    419–420
overhead variances
    fixed overhead *see* fixed overhead
    and overapplied overhead cost,
        427–428
    and underapplied overhead cost,
        427–428
    variable overhead *see* variable
        manufacturing overhead
overtime premiums, 33

P

parallels, 85
participative budget, 352–353, 352e
payback method
    described, 627
    evaluation of, 627–628
    extended example, 628–629
    payback period, 627, 629e
    uneven cash flows, 630, 630e
payback period, 627, 629e
per equivalent unit, 137
performance assessment, 474
performance evaluation *see*
    performance measurement
performance measurement
    balanced scorecard, 500–507, 502e
    delivery cycle time, 505, 506e
    described, 473
    financial performance measures,
        502, 502e
    financial performance reports, 474
    flexible budget, 370–373, 371e
    function of, 404
    internal business process, 505–507
    investment centre performance,
        492–497
    and management by exception,
        405, 430
    manufacturing cycle efficiency
        (MCE), 505
    negative connotations, 404
    overhead performance reporting,
        428–433, 429e, 430e

performance measurement—*Cont.*
 residual income, 497–500
 return on investment (ROI),
  492–497
 standard costs *see* standard costs
 throughput time, 505, 506*e*
 timely feedback, 504
performance report, 5, 428, 429*e*
 see also performance measurement
period costs
 defined, 35
 vs. product costs, 34–35
perpetual budget, 351
planning
 and budgets, 350
 defined, 3, 350
 described, 4–5
 negative connotations, 404
 strategic planning, 474
planning and control cycle, 5–6, 6*e*
plantwide overhead rate, 94
positive net present value, 615
post-audit, 626
postponement, 622
practical capacity, 432
practical standards, 407
predetermined overhead rate, 39*e*, 76–79,
  82–84, 122–123, 421–423
preference decisions, 610
 comparison of, 625–626
 defined, 610
 difficulty of, 624
 internal rate of return method, 624
 net present value method, 624
 profitability index, 625
 ranking of investment projects,
  624–626
prepaid insurance, 34
present value
 of annuity, 652–653, 652*e*
 annuity due, 653–654, 654*e*
 compound interest, 650
 concept of present value, 649–657
 deferred annuities, 655
 defined, 650
 discounting, 651
 discount rate, 651
 and future value, 650–652, 651*e*
 net present value *see* net
  present value
 net present value method *see* net
  present value method
 ordinary annuity, 652*e*, 654*e*,
  655, 656
 series of cash flows, 652–653
 theory of interest, 649–650
prevention costs, 508–509
price quotation sheet, 599*e*
price standards *see* cost standards

price variance
 described, 411
 favourable price variance,
  412–414, 468
 materials price variance, 411,
  413–414
 responsibility for, 414
pricing
 cost-plus pricing, 599
 products and services, 598–604
 target costing, 604–605
 time and materials pricing,
  602–603, 604*e*
*Prime Advantage Group Outlook (GO)
 Survey,* 75*n*
prime cost, 32
process cost flows, 130–133, 131*e*,
  132*e*, 134*e*
process costing
 application of costs, 137–140
 computation of costs, 137–140
 cost per equivalent unit, 137,
  155–157, 156*e*
 defined, 71, 130
 equivalent units of production,
  134–136, 136*e*,
  155–157, 156*e*
 FIFO method, 134–135, 154–159,
  156*e*, 158*e*
 flexible manufacturing system
  (FMS), 141
 formula, basic, 71
 vs. job-order costing, 129–130, 130*e*
 labour costs, 131–132, 132*e*, 133
 materials, labour, and overhead cost
  flows, 131–132, 132*e*
 materials costs, 132
 operation costing, 140–141
 overhead costs, 133
 process cost flows, 130–133, 131*e*,
  132*e*, 134*e*
 processing departments, 130, 131*e*,
  130–132, 131*e*, 132*e*
 production report, 129
 transferred-in costs, 131
 weighted-average method, 135–136,
  136*e*, 138–140, 139*e*,
  155–157, 156*e*
process costing system, 71, 130
processing departments, 130–132,
  131*e*, 132*e*
process management
 business process, 17
 enterprise risk management, 21–22
 enterprise systems, 21
 just-in-time (JIT) production, 19
 lean production, 18
 lean thinking model, 18–19, 19*e*
 manufacturing cell, 19

Six Sigma, 20–21, 20*e*
 supply chain management, 19
 value chain, 17, 17*e*
process time, 505, 506*e*
product cost flows
 model of, 93, 94*e*
 variations of, 94
product costs, 41–42
 cost flows, 41–42
 defined, 35
 general model of product cost
  flows, 93, 94*e*
 modified form of activity-based
  costing (ABC), 221–223
 vs. period costs, 34–35
 traditional *vs.* ABC, 186–190, 189*e*
production budget, 357–358
production order, 72
production report, 129, 157–159, 158*e*
productivity, and direct labour variance
  reporting, 417
product leadership, 4
product-level activities, 174
product line analysis, 561–563,
  562*e*, 564*e*
product margins, 184–186, 185*e*,
  187–188, 187*e*
professional accounting organizations, 12
professional ethics, 12–15
professional management
  accountants, 12
profitability analysis
 customer profitability analysis, 544
 decentralization and segment
  reporting, 475
 described, 544
 responsibility centres,
  484–485, 485*e*
 sales variance analysis, 544–548
profitability index, 574, 624–625
profit centre, 484, 485*e*
profit graph, 275*e*
profit stability, 285–287
program basis budget, 374
project profitability index, 624–625
*Public Sector Accounting
 Handbook,* 374
pull production, 18–19
push production, 18–19

Q
quality
 costs *see* quality costs
 international aspects, 513–514
 total quality management
  (TQM), 576
quality circles, 509
quality cost report, 511, 512,
  512*e*, 513*e*

quality costs
    appraisal costs, 509–510
    defined, 508
    described, 507
    distribution of, 510–511
    external failure costs, 510
    inspection costs, 509
    internal failure costs, 510
    prevention costs, 508–509
    quality of conformance, 508, 511*e*
    typical, 509*e*
    use of quality cost information, 512–513
quality of conformance, 508, 511*e*
quantity
    of inputs, 405
    materials quantity variance, 415
    vs. price, 410
    standard hours per unit, 409
    standard quantity allowed, 411
    standard quantity per unit, 407–408
    standards, 405
quantity variance
    favourable quantity variance, 412
    materials quantity variance, 415
    unfavourable quantity variance, 412–414, 468
queue time, 505

R
radio-frequency identification devices (RFID), 75
range of acceptable transfer prices, 486, 487
ranking decisions, 624
    see also preference decisions
ranking of investment projects, 624–626
rationing decisions, 624
    see also preference decisions
raw materials, 73
    see also direct materials
    cost flows, 80*e*
    defined, 18, 31
    vs. direct materials, 73
real option analysis, 622
recession, 288*n*
reciprocal method, 166
recovery of original investment, 613–614
regression errors, 262
regression line, 262, 263, 263*e*
relational database, 21
relaxing the constraint, 575–576
relevant benefits, 555–558
relevant costs
    and activity-based costing, 562
    benefits of, 555–556, 556–558
    defined, 555

different costs for different purposes, 556
differential approach, 558–560
examples of, 556–558
identification of, 555–556
isolation of relevant costs, 560
total approach, 558–560
relevant range
    curvilinear costs and, 234, 234*e*
    defined, 45
    fixed costs, 238–239, 238*e*
    linearity assumption, 234
    multiple relevant ranges, 244*e*
reports
    action analysis report, 188, 211–214
    external reports, 189–190, 221–223
    management reports, 184–185
    performance report, 5, 428, 429*e*
    quality cost report, 511, 512, 512*e*, 513*e*
required rate of return, 621
residual income
    calculation of, 497
    criticisms, 500
    defined, 497
    divisional comparison, 499–500
    vs. economic value added (EVA®), 497–498
    and motivation, 498–499
responsibility accounting, 351
responsibility centre, 484–485, 485*e*
return on investment (ROI)
    criticisms, 497
    defined, 492
    elements of, 495
    example computations, 495–496
    formula, 492
    income statement, 600*e*, 601*e*
    increase in, 495–496
    margin, 494
    plant and equipment, dollar amount of, 493
    turnover, 494
    understanding, 493–496
revenue, 46–47
revenue-producing department, 167
risk management, 21–22, 22*e*
Russia, 96

S
sales budget, 355, 357
sales commissions, 35, 36
sales division with some idle capacity, 489
sales forecast, 355–356
sales margin, 477–478
sales mix
    and break-even analysis, 291
    changes in, 290

defined, 290
    multiple-product break-even analysis, 291*e*, 292*e*
sales mix variance, 547–548
sales price
    and fixed costs and sales volume, change in, 278–279
    regular sales prices, change in, 280
sales price variance, 545, 546*e*
sales quantity variance, 547–548
sales variance analysis, 544–548
sales volume
    and fixed cost, change in, 277–278
    and fixed cost and sales price, change in, 278–279
    and fixed cost and variable cost, change in, 279
    and variable cost, change in, 278
sales volume variance, 372, 546*e*
salvage value, 620
Sarbanes-Oxley Act of 2002, 15
scattergram method, 241–243, 242*e*, 244*e*, 245*e*, 264*e*
schedule of cost of goods manufactured, 39*e*, 40–43
schedule of cost of goods sold, 89*e*
screening decisions, 610, 621, 621*e*
screening tool, 621, 621*e*
second-stage allocation, 182–184
segment, 9, 475, 561–563
segment margin, 481
segment reporting
    arbitrary division of common costs, 483–484
    assignment of costs to segments, 477
    common fixed costs, 478–479, 480–481
    contribution margin (CM), 477–478
    and decentralization, 474–475
    described, 475
    failure to trace costs directly, 482–483
    for financial accounting, 482
    fixed costs, importance of, 478
    hindrances to proper cost assignment, 482
    inappropriate allocation base, 483
    inappropriate cost assignment methods, 482
    omission of costs, 482
    sales margin, 477–478
    segment margin, 481
    traceable fixed costs, 478, 479–482
selling and administrative expense budget, 363–364
selling costs, 33
selling expense, 316
sell or process further decision, 571–573, 573*e*

semivariable cost *see* mixed costs
service department cost allocations
    direct method, 164, 165*e*
    interdepartmental services, 163
    reciprocal method, 166
    revenue-producing department, 167
    step-down method, 165–166,
        165*e*, 166*e*
service departments, 163, 164
simple rate of return, 630
simple rate of return method, 630–631
Six Sigma, 20–21, 20*e*
special order, 569–570
split-off point, 571, 572
staff positions, 11
stakeholders, 13, 14
standard cost card, 409
standard cost per unit, 409
standard cost record, 406, 423*e*
    variable production cost, 410*e*
standard costs
    see also standards
    advantages of, 433
    capacity analysis, 428–433
    and control, 405
    controls, evaluation of, 433–434
    cost flows, 468, 469*e*
    described, 405
    direct labour variances, 416–418
    direct materials variances, 411–415
    flexible budget, 411
    international uses of, 433
    management by exception, 405
    overhead application,
        424–425, 424*e*
    overhead performance reporting,
        428–433, 429*e*, 430*e*
    potential problems, 433–434
    setting standard costs, 406–411
    standard cost per unit, 409
    standard hours per unit, 409
    standard price per unit, 407
    standard quantity per unit,
        407–408
    standard rate per hour, 408
    use of, 406
    variable manufacturing overhead
        variances, 418–421
    variance analysis, 410–411, 410*e*
    variance analysis cycle, 405, 406*e*
standard hours allowed, 411
standard hours per unit, 409
standard price per unit, 407
standard quantity allowed, 411
standard quantity allowed for actual
    output, 411
standard quantity per unit, 407–408
standard rate per hour, 408

standards
    see also cost standards; standard costs
    vs. budgets, 410
    defined, 405
    direct labour standards, 408–409
    direct materials standards, 407–408
    ideal standards, 406–407
    ISO 9000 standards, 513–514
    ISO 14000 standards, 514
    ISO 26000 standards, 514
    ISO 31000 standards, 514
    practical standards, 407
    variable manufacturing overhead
        standards, 409
static budget, 369
static budget variance, 371–372
statistical control chart, 431*e*
statistical process control, 509
step-down method, 165–166, 165*e*, 166*e*
step-variable costs, 232–233, 233*e*,
    238–239
stewardship, 374
strategic planning, 474
strategy
    absorption costing, use of, 329
    and the balanced scorecard,
        500–501, 503–504, 503*e*
    committed *vs.* discretionary fixed
        costs, 236
    cost leadership, 500
    customer value propositions, 4
    defined, 3
    differentiation, 501
    focus, 501
    and make or buy decision,
        565–567, 567*e*
    niche, 501
stretch budget, 354
suboptimization, 486, 491
sunk cost, 48, 560
supply chain management, 19

T

T-account model of process costing
    flows, 131, 132*e*
tailings reduction operations, 633
target costing
    defined, 604
    example of, 605
    formula, 604
    use of, 604–605
target operating profit analysis,
    283–285
target selling price
    absorption costing approach, 599
    using time and materials
        pricing, 602
    variable costing approach, 601–602

taxable cash receipt, 665
tax-deductible depreciation, 677
taxes *see* income taxes
technology
    automation, from CVP
        perspective, 289
    enterprise systems, 21
    job-order costing, 95–96
theoretical capacity, 432
theory of constraints (TOC), 573–574
theory of interest, 649–650
throughput time, 505, 506*e*
throughput (manufacturing cycle) time,
    505, 506*e*
time and materials pricing, 602–603, 604*e*
time component, 602–603
time-driven activity-based costing
    (TDABC), 190–191
time ticket, 73
time value of money, 610–611
total-cost approach, 558–560, 559*e*,
    616–617, 617*e*
total manufacturing cost, 40–41
total quality management (TQM), 576
touch labour, 32
traceable fixed costs, 478
    activity-based costing, 480
    breakdown of, 479–480
    as common costs of another
        segment, 480–481
    defined, 478
    identification of, 479
    inappropriate cost assignment
        methods, 482
    reclassification of, 481*e*
    segment margin, 481
transaction drivers, 173
transfer price
    defined, 485–486
    divisional autonomy, 491
    highest acceptable transfer price, 487
    and idle capacity, 488–489
    international aspects, 491–492
    lowest acceptable transfer price, 487
    negotiated transfer price, 486, 490
    no outside supplier, 489
    range of acceptable transfer prices,
        486, 487
    suboptimization, 486
    transfers at cost, 490
    transfers at market price, 490–491
transferred-in costs, 131
transfers at cost, 490
transfers at market price, 490–491
triple bottom line, 632
true variable costs, 232–233, 232*e*, 233*e*
turnover, 494
two-stage cost allocation process, 178*e*

U

unadjusted rate of return, 630
    see also simple rate of return method
uncertain cash flows, 623–624
undepreciated capital cost (UCC), 667
underapplied overhead, 89–91
underapplied overhead cost, 427–428
uneven cash flows, 630, 630*e*
unfavourable quantity variance,
    412–414, 468
unit contribution margin *see*
    contribution margin (CM)
unit cost computations, 316–317
unit costs, 79
United States, 434
unit-level activities, 174
Universal Product Code, 75
upstream costs, 482
utilization of constrained resource,
    573–576

V

value chain, 17, 17*e*
variable cost, 70
    activity base, 231–232
    control, 231
    curvilinear cost, 234, 234*e*
    defined, 44
    described, 44–45, 44*e*, 46*e*, 230–233
    examples of, 232*e*
    extent of, 232
    vs. fixed cost, 237
    and fixed cost and sales volume,
        change in, 277–278
    illustration, 231*e*
    labour costs, 237
    linearity assumption, 234
    mixed cost *see* mixed costs
    and sales volume, change in, 278
    standard cost variances, 410
    step-variable costs, 232–233, 233*e*,
        238–239
    true variable costs, 232–233,
        232*e*, 233*e*
variable costing
    vs. absorption costing, 316*e*
    vs. absorption costing, extended
        comparison, 319–325,
        320–321*e*
    vs. absorption costing, income
        comparison, 317–319, 318*e*
    advantages of, 327–329
    choice of, 325–329
    cost-plus pricing, 601–602
    defined, 315
    income effects, 322
    income statement, 317
    lean production, impact of, 329

operating income, and production
    changes, 323–325,
    323–324*e*, 325*e*
operating income, drivers of, 323
overview, 315–317
reconciliation of, operating income
    data, 322*e*, 325*e*
segment reporting *see* segment
    reporting
target selling price, setting a, 601–602
unit cost computations, 316–317
variable expense ratio, 282
variable manufacturing overhead, 418*e*
    standards, 409
    variable overhead efficiency
        variance, 419–421
    variable overhead spending
        variance, 411, 419–420
    variances, 418–421
variable manufacturing overhead
    variances, 418–421, 468
variable overhead efficiency variance,
    419–421
variable overhead spending variance,
    411, 419–420
variable overhead variances
    general ledger entries, 468
    variable overhead efficiency
        variance, 419–421
    variable overhead spending
        variance, 411, 419–420
variable production cost, 410*e*
variables
    dependent variable, 242
    independent variable, 242
variance analysis
    cycle, 405, 406*e*
    described, 410–411
    direct labour, 416*e*
    direct materials, 412*e*, 413*e*
    extended model, 462*e*
    general model, 410–411, 410*e*
    and management by exception,
        405, 430
    materials variances, 462*e*
    sales variance analysis, 544–548
    variable manufacturing overhead, 418*e*
    variable production costs, 410*e*
variances
    analysis of *see* variance analysis
    budget variance, 425, 430*e*
    defined, 410
    direct labour variances, 416–418,
        416*e*, 468
    direct materials variances, 411–415,
        467–468
    favourable price variance,
        412–414, 468

fixed manufacturing overhead
    variances, 468
fixed overhead variances, 424–428,
    425*e*, 427*e*
flexible budget variance, 371
general ledger entries, 467–468
investigations of, 428–433, 430–431
isolation of, 414
labour efficiency variance,
    417–418, 465
labour rate variance, 411–412
market share variance, 546–547
market volume variance, 546
materials price variance, 411
materials quantity variance, 415
materials variances, 411–415,
    462–465, 467–468
mix variance, 462
overhead spending variance, 411
price variance, 411, 412–414, 468
quantity variance, 412–414, 415, 468
reasons for, 433
responsibility for, 414, 421
sales mix variance, 547–548
sales price variance, 545, 546*e*
sales quantity variance, 547–548
sales volume variance, 372, 546*e*
standard cost variances, 410
static budget variance, 371–372
unfavourable quantity variance,
    412–414, 468
variable manufacturing overhead
    variances, 418–421, 468
variable overhead efficiency
    variance, 419–421
variable overhead spending
    variance, 419–420
volume variance, 425–426
yield variance, 462
vertical integration, 565
volume variance, 425–426

W

weighted-average method, 135–136,
    136*e*, 138–140, 139*e*,
    155–157, 156*e*
working capital, 613
Work in Process, 83
work in process, 18, 36

X

XML (Extensible Markup Language),
    95–96

Y

yield variance, 462

Z

zero-base budget, 355
zero defects, 20